Your Office

Microsoft® Access® 2013
Comprehensive

Amy Kinser

HAMMERLE | KINSER | LENDING | NIGHTINGALE

PEARSON

Boston   Columbus   Indianapolis   New York   San Francisco   Upper Saddle River
Amsterdam   Cape Town   Dubai   London   Madrid   Milan   Munich   Paris   Montréal   Toronto
Delhi   Mexico City   São Paulo   Sydney   Hong Kong   Seoul   Singapore   Taipei   Tokyo

Editor in Chief: Michael Payne
Acquisitions Editor: Samantha McAfee Lewis
Product Development Manager: Laura Burgess
Editorial Project Manager: Anne Garcia
Development Editor: Vonda Keator
Editorial Assistant: Laura Karahalis
VP Director of Digital Strategy: Paul Gentile
Director of Digital Development: Taylor Ragan
Digital Media Editor: Eric Hakanson
Digital Content Producer: Jaimie Noy
Digital Project Manager: Zach Alexander
Production Media Project Manager: John Cassar
Director of Marketing: Maggie Moylan Leen

Marketing Manager: Brad Forrester
Marketing Coordinator: Susan Osterlitz
Marketing Assistant: Darshika Vyas
Managing Editor: Camille Trentacoste
Sr. Production Project Manager/IT Procurement Lead:
Natacha Moore
Senior Art Director: Jonathan Boylan
Manager, Cover Visual Research & Permissions:
Karen Sanatar
Manager of Rights & Permissions: Michelle McKenna
Cover and Interior Design: Jonathan Boylan
Composition: GEX Publishing Services
Full-Service Project Management: GEX Publishing Services

Credits and acknowledgments borrowed from other sources and reproduced, with permission, in this textbook appear on appropriate page within text.

Microsoft and/or its respective suppliers make no representations about the suitability of the information contained in the documents and related graphics published as part of the services for any purpose. All such documents and related graphics are provided "as is" without warranty of any kind. Microsoft and/or its respective suppliers hereby disclaim all warranties and conditions with regard to this information, including all warranties and conditions of merchantability, whether express, implied or statutory, fitness for a particular purpose, title and non-infringement. In no event shall Microsoft and/or its respective suppliers be liable for any special, indirect or consequential damages or any damages whatsoever resulting from loss of use, data or profits, whether in an action of contract, negligence or other tortious action, arising out of or in connection with the use or performance of information available from the services.

The documents and related graphics contained herein could include technical inaccuracies or typographical errors. Changes are periodically added to the information herein. Microsoft and/or its respective suppliers may make improvements and/or changes in the product(s) and/or the program(s) described herein at any time.

Microsoft® and Windows® are registered trademarks of the Microsoft Corporation in the U.S.A. and other countries. This book is not sponsored or endorsed by or affiliated with the Microsoft Corporation.

Copyright © 2014 by Pearson Education, Inc., Upper Saddle River, New Jersey, 07458. Pearson Prentice Hall. All rights reserved. Printed in the United States of America. This publication is protected by Copyright and permission should be obtained from the publisher prior to any prohibited reproduction, storage in a retrieval system, or transmission in any form or by any means, electronic, mechanical, photocopying, recording, or likewise. For information regarding permission(s), write to: Rights and Permissions Department.

Pearson Prentice Hall™ is a trademark of Pearson Education, Inc.
Pearson® is a registered trademark of Pearson plc
Prentice Hall® is a registered trademark of Pearson Education, Inc.
Pearson Education Ltd., London
Pearson Education Singapore, Pte. Ltd
Pearson Education, Canada, Inc.
Pearson Education–Japan
Pearson Education Australia PTY, Limited
Pearson Education North Asia Ltd., Hong Kong
Pearson Educación de Mexico, S.A. de C.V.
Pearson Education Malaysia, Pte. Ltd.
Pearson Education, Upper Saddle River, New Jersey

Library of Congress Cataloging-in-Publication Data available upon request

10 9 8 7 6 5 4 3 2 1
ISBN-13: 978-0-13-314303-4
ISBN-10: 0-13-314303-1

Dedications

I dedicate this series to my Kinser Boyz for their unwavering love, support, and patience; to my family; to my students for inspiring me; to Sam for believing in me; and to the instructors
I hope this series will inspire!

Amy Kinser

I dedicate this book to my husband, John, and my two boys, Matthew and Adam. They provide me with all the support, love, and patience I could ever ask for—thank you boys!

Patti Hammerle

For my wife, Amy, and our two boys Matt and Aidan. I cannot thank them enough for their support, love, and endless inspiration.

J. Eric Kinser

I dedicate this book to my mother, Dagmar, for inspiring my love of books. And to Art, for keeping life going while I work too much and for making life so much fun when I'm not working.

Diane Lending

To my parents, who always believed in and encouraged me. To my husband and best friend, who gave me support, patience, and love. To my brother and my hero—may you be watching from Heaven with joy in your heart.

Jennifer Nightingale

About the Authors

Amy S. Kinser, Esq., Series Editor

Amy holds a B.A. degree in Chemistry with a Business minor from Indiana University, and a J.D. from the Maurer School of Law, also at Indiana University. After working as an environmental chemist, starting her own technology consulting company, and practicing intellectual property law, she has spent the past 12 years teaching technology at the Kelley School of Business in Bloomington, Indiana—#1 ranked school for undergraduate program performance in the specialty of Information Systems according to 2012 Bloomberg Businessweek. Currently, she serves as the Director of Computer Skills and Senior Lecturer at the Kelley School of Business at Indiana University. She also loves spending time with her two sons, Aidan and J. Matthew, and her husband J. Eric.

Patti Hammerle

Patti holds a bachelor's degree in Finance and a master's degree in Business from Indiana University Kelley School of Business. She is an adjunct professor at the Kelley School of Business in Indianapolis where she teaches The Computer in Business. In addition to teaching, she owns U-Can Computer Manuals, a company that writes and publishes computer manuals primarily for libraries to teach from. She has also written and edited other computer application textbooks.

When not teaching or writing, she enjoys spending time with family, reading, and running.

J. Eric Kinser

Eric Kinser received his B.S. degree in Biology from Indiana University and his M.S. in Counseling and Education from the Indiana School of Education. He has worked in the medical field and in higher education as a technology and decision support specialist. He is currently a lecturer in the Operations and Decision Technology department at the Kelley School of Business at Indiana University.

When not teaching he enjoys experimenting with new technologies, traveling, and hiking with his family.

Dr. Diane Lending

Diane Lending is a Professor at James Madison University where she has taught Computer Information Systems since 2000. She received a Ph.D. in Management Information Systems from the University of Minnesota and a B.A. degree in Mathematics from the University of Virginia. Her research interests are in adoption of information technology and information systems education. She enjoys traveling; playing card and board games; and living in the country with her husband, daughter, and numerous pets.

Dr. Jennifer Paige Nightingale

Jennifer Nightingale, assistant professor at Duquesne University, has taught Information Systems Management since 2000. Before joining Duquesne University, she spent 15 years in industry with a focus in management and training. Her research expertise is in instructional technology, using technology as a teaching tool, and the impact of instructional technologies on student learning. She has earned numerous teaching and research honors and awards, holds an Ed.D. (instructional technology) and two M.S. degrees (information systems management and education) from Duquesne University, and a B.A. from the University of Pittsburgh.

Brief Contents

Contents

ACCESS MODULE 4

Contents   xi

Acknowledgments

The *Your Office* team would like to thank the following reviewers who have invested time and energy to help shape this series from the very beginning, providing us with invaluable feedback through their comments, suggestions, and constructive criticism.

We'd like to especially thank our Focus Group attendees and User Diary Reviewers:

Heather Albinger
Waukesha County Technical College

Melody Alexander
Ball State University

Mazhar Anik
Owens Community College

David Antol
Hartford Community College

Cheryl Brown
Delgado Community College

Janet Campbell
Dixie State College

Kuan Chen
Purdue Calumet

Jennifer Day
Sinclair Community College

Joseph F. Domagala
Duquesne University

Christa Fairman
Arizona Western University

Denise Farley
Sussex County Community College

Drew Foster
Miami University of Ohio

Lorie Goodgine
Tennessee Technology Center in Paris

Jane L. Hammer
Valley City State University

Kay Johnson
Community College of Rhode Island

Susumu Kasai
Salt Lake Community College

Linda Kavanaugh
Robert Morris University

Jennifer Krou
Texas State University, San Marcos

Michelle Mallon
Ohio State University

Sandra McCormack
Monroe Community College

Melissa Nemeth
Indiana University – Purdue University Indianapolis

Janet Olfert
North Dakota State University

Patsy Ann Parker
Southwestern Oklahoma State University

Cheryl Reindl-Johnson
Sinclair Community College

Jennifer Robinson
Trident Technical College

Tony Rose
Miami University of Ohio

Cindi Smatt
North Georgia College & State University

Jenny Lee Svelund
University of Utah

William VanderClock
Bentley University

Jill Weiss
Florida International University

Lin Zhao
Purdue Calumet

We'd like to thank all of our conscientious reviewers, including those who contributed to our previous editions:

Sven Aelterman
Troy University

Nitin Aggarwal
San Jose State University

Angel Alexander
Piedmont Technical College

Melody Alexander
Ball State University

Karen Allen
Community College of Rhode Island

Maureen Allen
Elon University

Wilma Andrews
Virginia Commonwealth University

Mazhar Anik
Owens Community College

David Antol
Harford Community College

Kirk Atkinson
Western Kentucky University

Barbara Baker
Indiana Wesleyan University

Kristi Berg
Minot State University

Kavuri Bharath
Old Dominion University

Ann Blackman
Parkland College

Jeanann Boyce
Montgomery College

Lynn Brooks
Tyler Junior College

Cheryl Brown
Delgado Community College West Bank Campus

Bonnie Buchanan
Central Ohio Technical College

Peggy Burrus
Red Rocks Community College

Richard Cacace
Pensacola State College

Margo Chaney
Carroll Community College

Shanan Chappell
College of the Albemarle, North Carolina

Kuan Chen
Purdue Calumet

David Childress
Ashland Community and
Technical College

Keh-Wen Chuang
Purdue University, North Central

Suzanne Clayton
Drake University

Amy Clubb
Portland Community College

Bruce Collins
Davenport University

Margaret Cooksey
Tallahassee Community College

Charmayne Cullom
University of Northern Colorado

Christy Culver
Marion Technical College

Juliana Cypert
Tarrant County College

Harold Davis
Southeastern Louisiana University

Jeff Davis
Jamestown Community College

Jennifer Day
Sinclair Community College

Anna Degtyareva
Mt. San Antonio College

Beth Deinert
Southeast Community College

Kathleen DeNisco
Erie Community College

Donald Dershem
Mountain View College

Bambi Edwards
Craven Community College

Elaine Emanuel
Mt. San Antonio College

Diane Endres
Ancilla College

Nancy Evans
Indiana University – Purdue University,
Indianapolis

Christa Fairman
Arizona Western College

Marni Ferner
University of North Carolina, Wilmington

Paula Fisher
Central New Mexico Community College

Linda Fried
University of Colorado, Denver

Diana Friedman
Riverside Community College

Susan Fry
Boise State University

Virginia Fullwood
Texas A&M University, Commerce

Janos Fustos
Metropolitan State College of Denver

John Fyfe
University of Illinois at Chicago

Saiid Ganjalizadeh
The Catholic University of America

Randolph Garvin
Tyler Junior College

Diane Glowacki
Tarrant County College

Jerome Gonnella
Northern Kentucky University

Connie Grimes
Morehead State University

Debbie Gross
Ohio State University

Babita Gupta
California State University, Monterey Bay

Lewis Hall
Riverside City College

Jane Hammer
Valley City State University

Marie Hartlein
Montgomery County Community College

Darren Hayes
Pace University

Paul Hayes
Eastern New Mexico University

Mary Hedberg
Johnson County Community College

Lynda Henrie
LDS Business College

Deedee Herrera
Dodge City Community College

Marilyn Hibbert
Salt Lake Community College

Jan Hime
University of Nebraska, Lincoln

Cheryl Hinds
Norfolk State University

Mary Kay Hinkson
Fox Valley Technical College

Margaret Hohly
Cerritos College

Brian Holbert
Spring Hill College

Susan Holland
Southeast Community College

Anita Hollander
University of Tennessee, Knoxville

Emily Holliday
Campbell University

Stacy Hollins
St. Louis Community College Florissant Valley

Mike Horn
State University of New York, Geneseo

Christie Hovey
Lincoln Land Community College

Margaret Hvatum
St. Louis Community College Meramec

Jean Insinga
Middlesex Community College

Jon (Sean) Jasperson
Texas A&M University

Glen Jenewein
Kaplan University

Gina Jerry
Santa Monica College

Dana Johnson
North Dakota State University

Mary Johnson
Mt. San Antonio College

Linda Johnsonius
Murray State University

Carla Jones
Middle Tennessee State University

Susan Jones
Utah State University

Nenad Jukic
Loyola University, Chicago

Sali Kaceli
Philadelphia Biblical University

Sue Kanda
Baker College of Auburn Hills

Robert Kansa
Macomb Community College

Susumu Kasai
Salt Lake Community College

Linda Kavanaugh
Robert Morris University

Debby Keen
University of Kentucky

Mike Kelly
Community College of Rhode Island

Melody Kiang
California State University, Long Beach

Lori Kielty
College of Central Florida

Richard Kirk
Pensacola State College

Dawn Konicek
Blackhawk Tech

John Kucharczuk
Centennial College

David Largent
Ball State University

Frank Lee
Fairmont State University

Luis Leon
The University of Tennessee at Chattanooga

Freda Leonard
Delgado Community College

Julie Lewis
Baker College, Allen Park

Suhong Li
Bryant Unversity

Renee Lightner
Florida State College

John Lombardi
South University

Rhonda Lucas
Spring Hill College

Adriana Lumpkin
Midland College

Lynne Lyon
Durham College

Nicole Lytle
California State University,
San Bernardino

Donna Madsen
Kirkwood Community College

Susan Maggio
Community College of Baltimore County

Kim Manning
Tallahassee Community College

Paul Martin
Harrisburg Area Community College

Cheryl Martucci
Diablo Valley College

Sebena Masline
Florida State College of Jacksonville

Sherry Massoni
Harford Community College

Lee McClain
Western Washington University

Sandra McCormack
Monroe Community College

Sue McCrory
Missouri State University

Barbara Miller
University of Notre Dame

Michael O. Moorman
Saint Leo University

Kathleen Morris
University of Alabama

Alysse Morton
Westminster College

Elobaid Muna
University of Maryland Eastern Shore

Jackie Myers
Sinclair Community College

Russell Myers
El Paso Community College

Bernie Negrete
Cerritos College

Melissa Nemeth
Indiana University – Purdue University
Indianapolis

Jennifer Nightingale
Duquesne University

Kathie O'Brien
North Idaho College

Michael Ogawa
University of Hawaii

Rene Pack
Arizona Western College

Patsy Parker
Southwest Oklahoma State Unversity

Laurie Patterson
University of North Carolina, Wilmington

Alicia Pearlman
Baker College

Diane Perreault
Sierra College and California State University,
Sacramento

Theresa Phinney
Texas A&M University

Vickie Pickett
Midland College

Marcia Polanis
Forsyth Technical Community College

Rose Pollard
Southeast Community College

Stephen Pomeroy
Norwich University

Leonard Presby
William Paterson University

Donna Reavis
Delta Career Education

Eris Reddoch
Pensacola State College

James Reddoch
Pensacola State College

Michael Redmond
La Salle University

Terri Rentfro
John A. Logan College

Vicki Robertson
Southwest Tennessee Community College

Dianne Ross
University of Louisiana at Lafayette

Ann Rowlette
Liberty University

Amy Rutledge
Oakland University

Candace Ryder
Colorado State University

Joann Segovia
Winona State University

Eileen Shifflett
James Madison University

Sandeep Shiva
Old Dominion University

Robert Sindt
Johnson County Community College

Cindi Smatt
Texas A&M University

Edward Souza
Hawaii Pacific University

Nora Spencer
Fullerton College

Alicia Stonesifer
La Salle University

Cheryl Sypniewski
Macomb Community College

Arta Szathmary
Bucks County Community College

Nasser Tadayon
Southern Utah University

Asela Thomason
California State University Long Beach

Nicole Thompson
Carteret Community College

Terri Tiedema
Southeast Community College, Nebraska

Lewis Todd
Belhaven University

Barb Tollinger
Sinclair Community College

Allen Truell
Ball State University

Erhan Uskup
Houston Community College

Lucia Vanderpool
Baptist College of Health Sciences

Michelle Vlaich-Lee
Greenville Technical College

Barry Walker
Monroe Community College

Rosalyn Warren
Enterprise State Community College

Sonia Washington
Prince George's Community College

Eric Weinstein
Suffolk County Community College

Jill Weiss
Florida International University

Lorna Wells
Salt Lake Community College

Rosalie Westerberg
Clover Park Technical College

Clemetee Whaley
Southwest Tennessee Community College

Kenneth Whitten
Florida State College of Jacksonville

MaryLou Wilson
Piedmont Technical College

John Windsor
University of North Texas

Kathy Winters
University of Tennessee, Chattanooga

Nancy Woolridge
Fullerton College

Jensen Zhao
Ball State University

Molly Zimmer
University of Evansville

Mary Anne Zlotow
College of DuPage

Matthew Zullo
Wake Technical Community College

Additionally, we'd like to thank our MyITLab team for their review and collaboration with our text authors:

LeeAnn Bates

Jennifer Hurley

Ralph Moore

Jerri Williams

Jaimie Noy
Media Producer

Preface

The *Your Office* series focuses first and foremost on preparing students to use both technical and soft skills in the real world. Our goal is to provide this to both instructors and students through a modern approach to teaching and learning Microsoft Office applications, an approach that weaves in the technical content using a realistic business scenario and focuses on using Office as a decision-making tool.

The process of developing this unique series for you, the modern student or instructor, requires innovative ideas regarding the pedagogy and organization of the text. You learn best when doing—so you will be active from Page 1. Your learning goes to the next level when you are challenged to do more with less—your hand will be held at first, but progressively, the case exercises require more from you. Since you care about how things work in the real world—in your classes, your future jobs, your personal life—Real World Advice, Videos, and Success Stories are woven throughout the text. These innovative features will help you progress from a basic understanding of Office to mastery of each application, empowering you to perform with confidence in Windows 8, Word, Excel, Access, and PowerPoint, including on mobile devices.

No matter what career you may choose to pursue in life, this series will give you the foundation to succeed. *Your Office* uses cases that will enable you to be immersed in a realistic business as you learn Office in the context of a running business scenario—the Painted Paradise Resort and Spa. You will immediately delve into the many interesting, smaller businesses in this resort (golf course, spa, restaurants, hotel, etc.) to learn how a larger organization actually uses Office. You will learn how to make Office work for you now, as a student, and in your future career.

Today, the experience of working with Office is not isolated to working in a job in a cubicle. Your physical office is wherever you are with a laptop or a mobile device. Office has changed. It's modern. It's mobile. It's personal. And when you learn these valuable skills and master Office, you are able to make Office your own. The title of this series is a promise to you, the student: Our goal is to make Microsoft Office *Your Office*.

Key Features

- **Starting and Ending Files:** These appear before every case in the text. Starting Files identify exactly which Student Data Files are needed to complete each case. Ending Files are provided to show students the naming conventions they should use when saving their files. Each file icon is color coded by application.

- **Workshop Objectives List:** The learning objectives to be achieved as students work through the workshop. Page numbers are included for easy reference. These are revisited in the Concept Check at the end of the workshop.

- **Real World Success:** A boxed feature in the workshop opener that shares an anecdote from a real former student, describing how knowledge of Office has helped him or her to get ahead or be successful in his or her life.

- **Active Text Box:** Represents the active portion of the workshop and is easily distinguishable from explanatory text by the blue shaded background. Active Text helps students quickly identify what steps they need to follow to complete the workshop Prepare Case.

- **Quick Reference Box:** A boxed feature in the workshop, summarizing generic or alternative instructions on how to accomplish a task. This feature enables students to quickly find important skills.

- **Real World Advice Box:** A boxed feature in the workshop, offering advice and best practices for general use of important Office skills. The goal is to advise students as a manager might in a future job.

- **Side Note:** A brief tip or piece of information aligned visually with a step in the workshop, quickly providing key information to students completing that particular step.

- **Consider This:** In-text critical thinking questions and topics for discussion, set apart as a boxed feature, allowing students to step back from the project and think about the application of what they are learning and how these concepts might be used in the future.

- **Concept Check:** Review questions appearing at the end of the workshop, which require students to demonstrate their understanding of the objectives in that workshop.

- **Visual Summary:** A visual review of the objectives learned in the workshop using images from the completed solution file, mapped to the workshop objectives using callouts and page references so students can easily find the section of text to refer to for a refresher.

- **Business Application Icons:** Appear with every case in the text and clearly identify which business application students are being exposed to, i.e., Finance, Marketing, Operations, etc.

- **MyITLab™ Icons:** Identify which cases from the book match those in MyITLab™.

- **Real World Interview Video Icon:** This icon appears with the Real World Success Story in the workshop opener and features an interview of a real business person discussing how he or she actually uses the skills in the workshop on a day-to-day basis.

- **Blue Box Video Icons:** These icons appear with each Active Text box and identify the brief video demonstrating how students should complete that portion of the Prepare Case.

- **Soft Skills Icons:** These appear with other boxed features and identify specific places where students are being exposed to lessons on soft skills.

Business Application Icons

 Customer Service

 Finance & Accounting

 General Business

 Human Resources

 Information Technology

 Production & Operations

 Sales & Marketing

 Research & Development

MyITLab Icons

Video Icons

 Real World Interview Videos

 Workshop Videos

 Soft Skills

Instructor Resources

The Instructor's Resource Center, available at **www.pearsonhighered.com**, includes the following:

- AACSB mapping that identifies which cases and exercises in the text prepare for AACSB certification.
- Business application mapping, which provides an easy-to-filter way of finding the cases and examples to help highlight whichever business application is of most interest.
- Annotated Solution Files with Scorecards assist with grading the Prepare, Practice, Problem Solve, and Perform Cases.
- Data and Solution Files
- Rubrics for Perform Cases in Microsoft Word format enable instructors to easily grade open-ended assignments with no definite solution.
- PowerPoint Presentations with notes for each chapter
- Audio PowerPoints which serve as great refreshers for students
- Instructor's Manual that provides detailed blueprints to achieve workshop learning objectives and outcomes and best use the unique structure of the modules.
- Complete Test Bank, also available in TestGen format
- Syllabus templates for 8-week, 12-week, and 16-week courses
- Additional Practice, Problem Solve, and Perform Cases to provide you with variety and choice in exercises both on the workshop and module levels.
- Scripted Lectures provide instructors with a lecture outline that mirrors the Workshop Prepare Case.
- Flexible, robust, and customizable content is available for all major online course platforms that include everything instructors need in one place. Please contact your sales representative for information on accessing course cartridges for WebCT or Blackboard.

Student Resources

- Student Data Files
- Blue Box videos walk students through each Blue Active Text box in the Workshop, showing and explaining the concepts and how to achieve the skills in the workshop. There is one video per Active Text box.
- Real World Interview videos introduce students to real professionals talking about how they use Microsoft Office on a daily basis in their work. These videos provide the relevance students seek while learning this material. There is one video per workshop.
- Soft Skills videos introduce students to important non-technical skills such as etiquette, managing priorities, proper interview preparation, etc.

Pearson's Companion Website

www.pearsonhighered.com/youroffice offers expanded IT resources and downloadable supplements. Students can find the following self-study tools for each workshop:

- Online Workshop Review
- Workshop Objectives
- Additional Cases
- Glossary
- MOS Certification Mapping

- Student Data Files
- Blue Box videos*
- Real World Interview videos*
- Soft Skills videos*

*Access code required for these premium resources

MyITLab for Office 2013 is a solution designed by professors for professors that allows easy delivery of Office courses with defensible assessment and outcomes-based training. The new **Your Office 2013** system will seamlessly integrate online assessment, training, and projects with My**IT**Lab for Microsoft Office 2013!

My**IT**Lab for Office 2013 features…

- **Assessment and training built to match Your Office 2013** instructional content so that My**IT**Lab works with Your Office to help students make Office their own.

- **Both project-based and skill-based assessment and training** allow instructors to test and train students on complete exercises or individual Office application skills.

Dear Students,

If you want an edge over the competition, make it personal. Whether you love sports, travel, the stock market, or ballet, your passion is personal to you. Capitalizing on your passion leads to success. You live in a global marketplace, and your competition is global. The honors students in China exceed the total number of students in North America. Skills can help set you apart, but passion will make you stand above. *Your Office* is the tool to harness your passion's true potential.

In prior generations, personalization in a professional setting was discouraged. You had a "work" life and a "home" life. As the Series Editor, I write to you about the vision for *Your Office* from my laptop, on my couch, in the middle of the night when inspiration strikes me. My classroom and living room are my office. Life has changed from generations before us.

So, let's get personal. My degrees are not in technology, but chemistry and law. I helped put myself through school by working full time in various jobs, including a successful technology consulting business that continues today. My generation did not grow up with computers, but I did. My father was a network administrator for the military. So, I was learning to program in Basic before anyone had played Nintendo's Duck Hunt or Tetris. Technology has always been one of my passions from a young age. In fact, I now tell my husband: don't buy me jewelry for my birthday, buy me the latest gadget on the market!

In my first law position, I was known as the Office guru to the extent that no one gave me a law assignment for the first two months. Once I submitted the assignment, my supervisor remarked, "Wow, you don't just know how to leverage technology, but you really know the law too." I can tell you novel-sized stories from countless prior students in countless industries who gained an edge from using Office as a tool. Bringing technology to your passion makes you well-rounded and a cut above the rest, no matter the industry or position.

I am most passionate about teaching, in particular teaching technology. I come from many generations of teachers, including my mother who is a kindergarten teacher. For over 12 years, I have found my dream job passing on my passion for teaching, technology, law, science, music, and life in general at the Kelley School of Business at Indiana University. I have tried to pass on the key to engaging passion to my students. I have helped them see what differentiates them from all the other bright students vying for the same jobs.

Microsoft Office is a tool. All of your competition will have learned Microsoft Office to some degree or another. Some will have learned it to an advanced level. Knowing Microsoft Office is important, but it is also fundamental. Without it, you will not be considered for a position.

Today, you step into your first of many future roles bringing Microsoft Office to your dream job working for Painted Paradise Resort and Spa. You will delve into the business side of the resort and learn how to use *Your Office* to maximum benefit.

Don't let the context of a business fool you. If you don't think of yourself as a business person, you have no need to worry. Whether you realize it or not, everything is business. If you want to be a nurse, you are entering the health care industry. If you want to be a football player in the NFL, you are entering the business of sports as entertainment. In fact, if you want to be a stay-at-home parent, you are entering the business of a family household where *Your Office* still gives you an advantage. For example, you will be able to prepare a budget in Excel and analyze what you need to do to afford a trip to Disney World!

At Painted Paradise Resort and Spa, you will learn how to make Office yours through four learning levels designed to maximize your understanding. You will Prepare, Practice, and Problem Solve your tasks. Then, you will astound when you Perform your new talents. You will be challenged through Consider This questions and gain insight through Real World Advice.

There is something more. You want success in what you are passionate about in your life. It is personal for you. In this position at Painted Paradise Resort and Spa, you will gain your personal competitive advantage that will stay with you for the rest of your life—*Your Office*.

Sincerely,

Amy Kinser

Series Editor

Welcome to the Team!

Welcome to your new office at Painted Paradise Resort and Spa, where we specialize in painting perfect getaways. As the Chief Technology Officer, I am excited to have staff dedicated to the Microsoft Office integration between all the areas of the resort. Our team is passionate about our paradise, and I hope you find this to be your dream position here!

Painted Paradise is a resort and spa in New Mexico catering to business people, romantics, families, and anyone who just needs to get away. Inside our resort are many distinct areas. Many of these areas operate as businesses in their own right but must integrate with the other areas of the resort. The main areas of the resort are as follows.

- The **Hotel** is overseen by our Chief Executive Officer, William Mattingly, and is at the core of our business. The hotel offers a variety of accommodations, ranging from individual rooms to a grand villa suite. Further, the hotel offers packages including spa, golf, and special events.

    Room rates vary according to size, season, demand, and discount. The hotel has discounts for typical groups, such as AARP. The hotel also has a loyalty program where guests can earn free nights based on frequency of visits. Guests may charge anything from the resort to the room.

- **Red Bluff Golf Course** is a private world-class golf course and pro shop. The golf course has services such as golf lessons from the famous golf pro John Schilling and playing packages. Also, the golf course attracts local residents. This requires variety in pricing schemes to accommodate both local and hotel guests. The pro shop sells many retail items online.

    The golf course can also be reserved for special events and tournaments. These special events can be in conjunction with a wedding, conference, meetings, or other event covered by the event planning and catering area of the resort.

- **Turquoise Oasis Spa** is a full-service spa. Spa services include haircuts, pedicures, massages, facials, body wraps, waxing, and various other spa services—typical to exotic. Further, the spa offers private consultation, weight training (in the fitness center), a water bar, meditation areas, and steam rooms. Spa services are offered both in the spa and in the resort guest's room.

    Turquoise Oasis Spa uses top-of-the-line products and some house-brand products. The retail side offers products ranging from candles to age-defying home treatments. These products can also be purchased online. Many of the hotel guests who fall in love with the house-brand soaps, lotions, candles, and other items appreciate being able to buy more at any time.

    The spa offers a multitude of packages including special hotel room packages that include spa treatments. Local residents also use the spa. So, the spa guests are not limited to hotel guests. Thus, the packages also include pricing attractive to the local community.

- **Painted Treasures Gift Shop** has an array of items available for purchase, from toiletries to clothes to presents for loved ones back home including a healthy section of kids' toys for traveling business people. The gift shop sells a small sampling from the spa, golf course pro shop, and local New Mexico culture. The gift shop also has a small section of snacks and drinks. The gift shop has numerous part-time employees including students from the local college.

3355 Hemmingway Circle • Santa Fe, New Mexico 89566

- **The Event Planning & Catering** area is central to attracting customers to the resort. From weddings to conferences, the resort is a popular destination. The resort has a substantial number of staff dedicated to planning, coordinating, setting up, catering, and maintaining these events. The resort has several facilities that can accommodate large groups. Packages and prices vary by size, room, and other services such as catering. Further, the Event Planning & Catering team works closely with local vendors for floral decorations, photography, and other event or wedding typical needs. However, all catering must go through the resort (no outside catering permitted). Lastly, the resort stocks several choices of decorations, table arrangements, and centerpieces. These range from professional, simple, themed, and luxurious.

- **Indigo5** and the **Silver Moon Lounge**, a world-class restaurant and lounge that is overseen by the well-known Chef Robin Sanchez. The cuisine is balanced and modern. From steaks to pasta to local southwestern meals, Indigo5 attracts local patrons in addition to resort guests. While the catering function is separate from the restaurant—though menu items may be shared—the restaurant does support all room service for the resort. The resort also has smaller food venues onsite such as the Terra Cotta Brew coffee shop in the lobby.

Currently, these areas are using Office to various degrees. In some areas, paper and pencil are still used for most business functions. Others have been lucky enough to have some technology savvy team members start Microsoft Office Solutions.

Using your skills, I am confident that you can help us integrate and use Microsoft Office on a whole new level! I hope you are excited to call Painted Paradise Resort and Spa *Your Office*.

Looking forward to working with you more closely!

Aidan Matthews

Aidan Matthews
Chief Technology Officer

Common Features of Microsoft Office 2013
Understanding the Common Features of Microsoft Office

WORKSHOP 1 | THE COMMON FEATURES OF MICROSOFT OFFICE

OBJECTIVES

1. Understand Office applications and accounts   p. 4
2. Start Office programs and manipulate windows   p. 7
3. Use the Office Ribbon, contextual tools, and other menus   p. 14
4. Manage files in Office   p. 24
5. Get help   p. 30
6. Print and share files   p. 33
7. Use Windows SkyDrive   p. 35
8. Use touch mode, gestures, and Reading Mode   p. 38

Prepare Case

Painted Paradise Resort and Spa Employee Training Preparation

Sales & Marketing

The gift shop at the Painted Paradise Resort and Spa has an array of items available for purchase from toiletries to clothes to souvenirs for loved ones back home. There are numerous part-time employees including students from the local college. Frequently, the gift shop holds training luncheons for new employees. Your first assignment will be to start two documents for a meeting with your manager, Susan Brock—the beginning of meeting minutes and an Excel budget. To complete this task, you need to understand and work with the common features within the Microsoft Office Suite.

DOC RABE Media / Fotolia

REAL WORLD SUCCESS

"I am a returning student and the thought of having to use a computer for anything other than e-mail and social networking scared me. It was not as bad as I anticipated by taking it one step at a time. Now, I feel comfortable typing a research paper and creating a budget on a spreadsheet. It is a welcoming feeling that all the Microsoft applications share the same look! Knowing the common elements gave me a jump-start for learning each additional Microsoft application."

- Esther, current student

Student data files needed for this workshop:

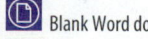 Blank Word document

 Blank Excel workbook

 Blank Word document in SkyDrive

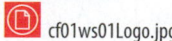 cf01ws01Logo.jpg

You will save your files as:

 cf01ws01Minutes_LastFirst.docx

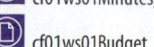 cf01ws01Budget_LastFirst.docx

 cf01ws01Minutes_LastFirst.pdf

 cf01ws01SkyDrive_LastFirst.docx

Working with the Office Interface

When you walk into a grocery store, you usually know what you are going to find and that items will be in approximately the same location, regardless of which store you are visiting. The first items you usually see are the fresh fruit and vegetables while the frozen foods are near the end of the store. This similarity among stores creates a comfortable and welcoming experience for the shopper—even if the shopper has never been in that particular store. The brands may be different, but the food types are the same. That is, canned corn is canned corn.

Microsoft Office 2013 creates that same level of welcoming feeling and comfort with its Ribbons, features, and functions. Each application has a similar appearance or user interface. The interface for Microsoft Office 2013 is called Modern because of its sleek appearance. The new look is minimalist, mimicking the tiles on the Windows 8 Start screen. There is now a more two-dimensional appearance. There is no more shading or shadows and if you choose a background, there is only a hint of a watermark. In this section, you will learn to navigate and use the Microsoft Office interface.

Understand Office Applications and Accounts

Microsoft Word is a word-processing program. This application can be used to create, edit, and format **documents** such as letters, memos, reports, brochures, resumes, and flyers. Word also provides tools for creating **tables**, which organize information into rows and columns. Using Word, you can add **graphics**, which consist of pictures, online pictures, SmartArt, shapes, and charts that can enhance the look of your documents.

Microsoft Excel is a spreadsheet program. Excel is a two-dimensional grid that can be used to model quantitative data and perform accurate and rapid calculations with results ranging from simple budgets to financial and statistical analyses. Data entered into Excel can be used to generate a variety of charts such as pie charts, bar charts, line charts, or scatter charts, to name a few, to enhance spreadsheet data. Excel files are known as **workbooks**, which contain one or more worksheets. Excel makes it possible to analyze, manage, and share information, which can also help you make better and smarter decisions. New analysis and visualization tools help you track and highlight important data trends.

Microsoft PowerPoint is a presentation and slide program. This application can be used to create slide shows for a presentation, as part of a website, or as a stand-alone application on a computer kiosk. These presentations can also be printed as handouts.

Microsoft OneNote is a planner and note-taking program. OneNote can be used to collect information in one easy-to-find place. With OneNote, you can capture text and images, as well as video and audio. By sharing your notebooks, you can simultaneously take and edit notes with other people in other locations, or just keep everyone in sync and up to date. You can also take your OneNote notebooks with you and then view and edit your notes from virtually any computer with an Internet connection or your Windows 8 phone device.

Microsoft Outlook is an e-mail, contact, and information management program. Outlook allows you to stay connected to the world with the most up-to-date e-mail and calendaring tools. You can manage and print schedules, task lists, phone directories, and other documents. Outlook's ability to manage scheduled events and contact information is why Outlook is sometimes referred to as an **information management program**.

Microsoft Access is a relational database management program. Access is a three-dimensional database program that allows you to make the most of your data. Access is known as **relational database** software—or three-dimensional database software—because it is able to connect data in separate tables. Access connects the data through relationships formed from common fields that exist in both tables. For example, a business might have one table that lists all the employees—their employee ID, first name, last name, address, hire date, and job title. Another table might track data for each shift they are working—their employee ID, date, start time, and end time. Since the common field of employee ID is in both database tables, you could create a report of which employees are working on Thursday at noon along with their name and job title. Thus, Access is used primarily to compile, store, query, and report data. Best practice is to use Access to store data and Excel to model and analyze data by creating charts.

Microsoft Publisher is a desktop publishing program that offers professional tools and templates to help easily communicate a message in a variety of publication types, saving time and money while creating a more polished and finished look. Whether you are designing brochures, newsletters, postcards, greeting cards, or e-mail newsletters, Publisher aids in delivering high-quality results without the user having graphic design experience. Publisher helps you to create, personalize, and share a wide range of professional-quality publications and marketing materials with ease.

Microsoft Lync is a unified communication platform. With Lync, which is able to be fully integrated with Microsoft Office, users can keep track of their contacts' availability; send an instant message; start or join an audio, video, or web conference; or make a phone call—all through a consistent, familiar interface.

InfoPath is used to design sophisticated electronic forms, which enables you to gather information quickly and easily.

Understanding Versions of Microsoft Office 2013

Microsoft Office 2013 is a suite of productivity applications or programs. You can purchase the each application separately or as a package. The exact applications available depends on the package installed. Office 2013 is available in greater variety and flexibility than ever before.

People use different devices for different purposes. You may use your tablet for information consumption and entertainment. Likewise, you may prefer your desktop computer to write a paper. Office 2013 has embraced the concept of every device has its purpose with more flexible versions for platforms such as **Windows Phone** and **Windows Run Time (RT)** and a revised interface to better make use of a touch interface and ARM chip devices. Advanced RISC Machine (ARM) chips are designed for low energy embedded systems, such as in an iPad. The Windows Phone and Windows RT versions of Office 2013 contain substantively similar functionality for Word, PowerPoint, Excel, and OneNote as the Windows version of Office 2013. Visually, Windows RT even looks the same as the full Office 2013 for Windows. However, applications that run on Windows Phone and RT do not support some of the more sophisticated Office features or back-end Visual Basic programming. The advantage is that these versions are optimized for phones and tablets—Office for every device or purpose. This text is written to the full version of Office 2013 for Windows, not Windows Phone or RT.

Office 2013 will be available in two different ways. You can purchase Office 2013 the traditional way from a retailer for a one-time fee that can be installed on exactly one computer. In addition, Office 2013 can also be purchased on a subscription, cloud basis called Office 365. The **Office 365** version is the same product that comes with more frequent updates, the ability to install on more than one computer, more SkyDrive storage space, tight integration with SkyDrive, and several other additional perks. However, the subscription version requires a yearly fee instead of a one-time fee. At the time of this writing, the Office 365 version is competitively priced to be cheaper for many people despite the yearly fee. Furthermore, many different packages for Office 2013 exist from Home to Enterprise for both the traditional and Office 365 versions. Each package contains a different combination of the applications and options available in Office 2013. Ultimately, the decision on which version to purchase depends on your needs and personal situation. For the latest in pricing and options, you can visit **http://office.microsoft.com**.

Using Office 2013 on a Mac

Traditionally, Office is available in different suites for Macs and also came later in time than the PC version. For example, Office 2010 (PC version) was followed by Office 2011 (Mac version). Typically, Access has not been supported on Mac versions of Office. According to the Microsoft website at the time of writing this text, Microsoft stated that the Office 365 Home Premium version of Office will support a Mac installation when the full version is available. Importantly, the Office 365 Home Premium includes Access.

Two other popular options exist for using Office 2013 on a Mac—virtualization and dual boot. Virtualization of Office on a Mac is software that mimics Windows. Many different applications provide virtualization. In any major search engine, search for "PC virtualization on Mac" and you will find many software options for emulating a PC on a Mac. While many virtualization programs promise to mimic entirely, there can be some—usually minor—differences.

Dual boot is the ability to choose the operating system on startup. **Bootcamp** is the Mac software that allows the user to decide which operating system to launch on Intel chip-based Macs. The computer has both the Mac operating system and Windows installed. When the computer is turned on, the user is given the choice of operating system. Thus, the user can be running Windows. If Office is installed on the Windows partition, then Office can run the same as it does on any PC.

You should consult your instructor about the policy in your course. Policies on the usage of the Mac operating system and the Mac versions of Office vary greatly from course to course and school to school. Your instructor will be best able to advise you on what is acceptable for you.

Obtaining a Microsoft Account

Before you get started, Office 2013 requires users to sign in with a Microsoft account that comes with a free SkyDrive account, as shown in Figure 1. This typically will be an account for either the Microsoft Hotmail or Live domain. The Microsoft account gives you free e-mail and tracks your licenses for Microsoft applications. If you have used

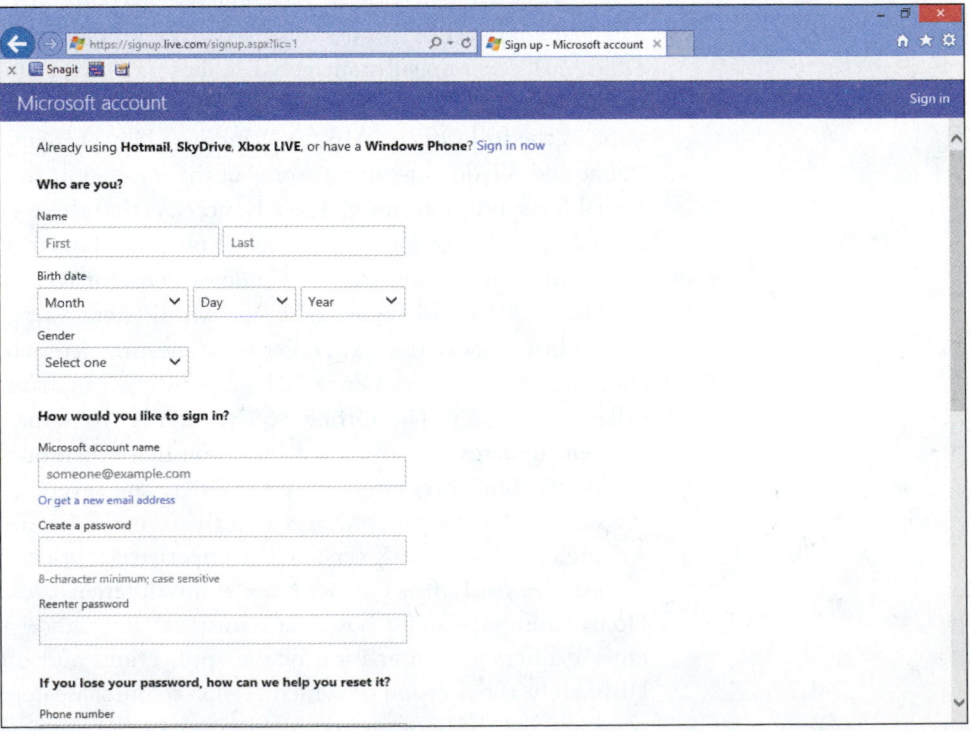

Figure 1   Microsoft account sign up page

Hotmail, SkyDrive, Xbox Live, or Windows phone in the past, you may already have a Microsoft account. The SkyDrive portion of the account is an online storage and collaboration cloud space. As of this writing, you are provided with 7+ GB of online cloud file storage on SkyDrive, additional storage is available for purchase. Microsoft has designed Office 2013 and SkyDrive to complement one another and is discussed in more detail later in this workshop.

If you are working in a computer lab or enterprise version of Windows 8, you may not need to sign into a Microsoft account to run Office or Windows 8. If you are running it on a personal computer, you will need to have a Microsoft account. You can create the account when you install Windows 8. If you install Office 2013 on an earlier version of Windows, you may need to sign up for an account. To sign up for an account, go to **https://signup.live.com** and follow the on-screen instructions. Your first name, last name, and profile image for your Microsoft account will appear in various screens of Windows and Microsoft Office.

Start Office Programs and Manipulate Windows

Office programs can start from the Windows 8 Start screen, as shown in Figure 2, or from search results. Windows 8 contains robust searching capabilities from the Search charm. The **Windows Start screen** is the main interface to launch applications, and it replaces the Windows 7 start button. The Windows **charms** are a specific and consistent set of buttons to users in every application: search, share, connect, settings, and start. Additionally, the procedure for opening an application via searching is the same no matter the configuration of the computer you are using. If you launch the application from the Windows 8 Start screen, the location of the application tile is dependent on the other applications installed on the computer and the applications pinned to the Start screen. On a personal computer you may prefer to use the Windows Start screen, but in a computer lab or unfamiliar computer the search method may be preferable.

Figure 2   Windows Start screen

In addition to the Windows Start screen, each application has its own specific application Start screen, as shown in Figure 3. From the **Application Start screen**, you can select a blank document, workbook, presentation, database, or one of many application specific templates. Files that have already been created can also be opened from this screen. When existing files are double-clicked from a File Explorer window, the Start screen is not needed and does not open.

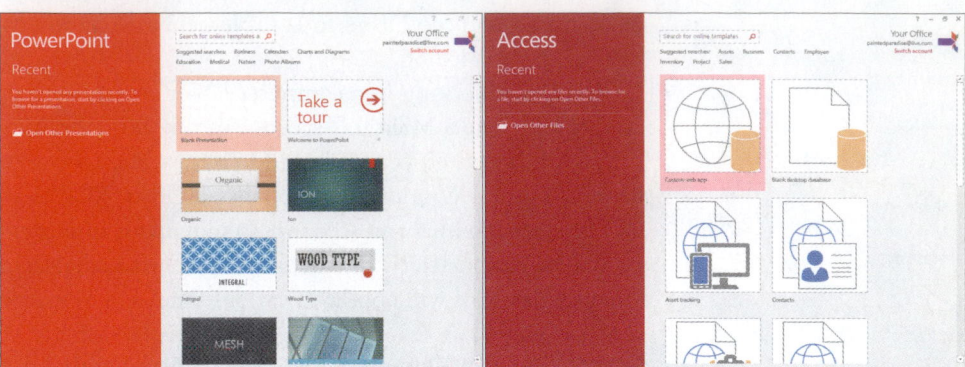

Figure 3   Application Start screens—PowerPoint and Access

Opening the Microsoft Word Start Screen

In the next exercise, you will use the search method to open the Word Start screen and start a new Word document. You will use this new document to start a template for meeting minutes with Susan Brock, the gift shop manager.

CF01.01

 To Open the Word Start Screen and Start a New Document

a. Click the **Start screen** or desktop, point to the **bottom-right corner** of the screen. The charms will be displayed on the right side of the screen.

b. Note the labels underneath each of the charms. Click the **Search** charm.

MyITLab®
Workshop 1 Training

SIDE NOTE
Opening the Charms
Particularly useful when not using a touch screen, you can also open Windows Charms by pressing + C.

SIDE NOTE
Alternate Method
Clicking a tile on the Windows Start screen will also open the application. Whereas, searching also finds unpinned applications.

Figure 4   Windows Start screen with Charms

c. Click the **Search** box at the top of the page. Type **Word**.

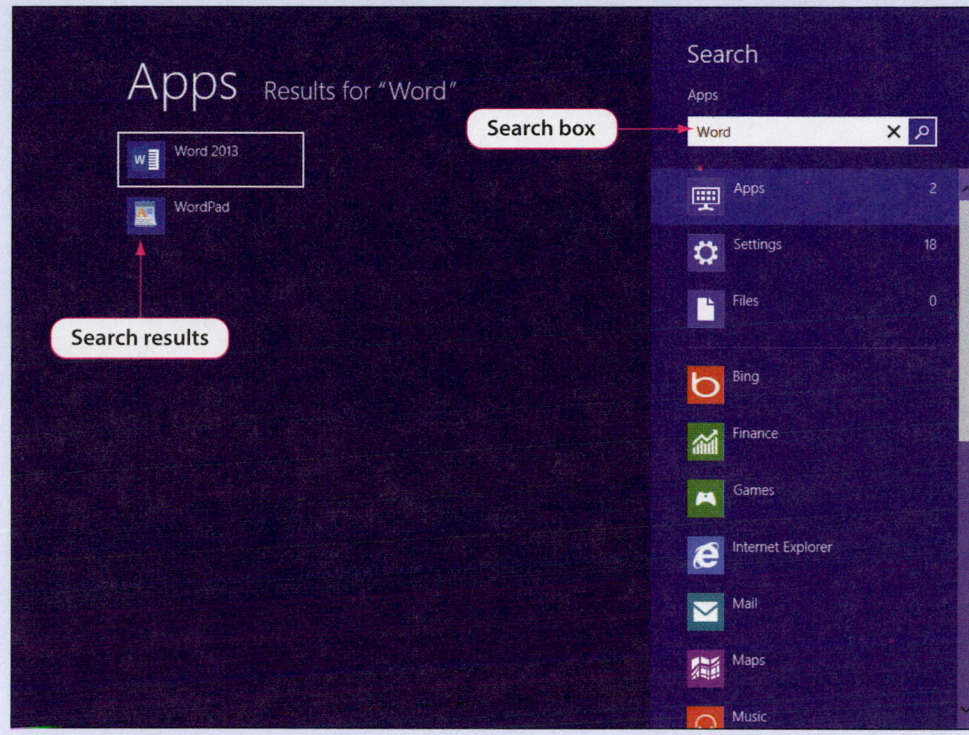

Figure 5   Windows Search screen

d. Click **Word 2013** in the search results. The Word Start screen is displayed when Word is launched.

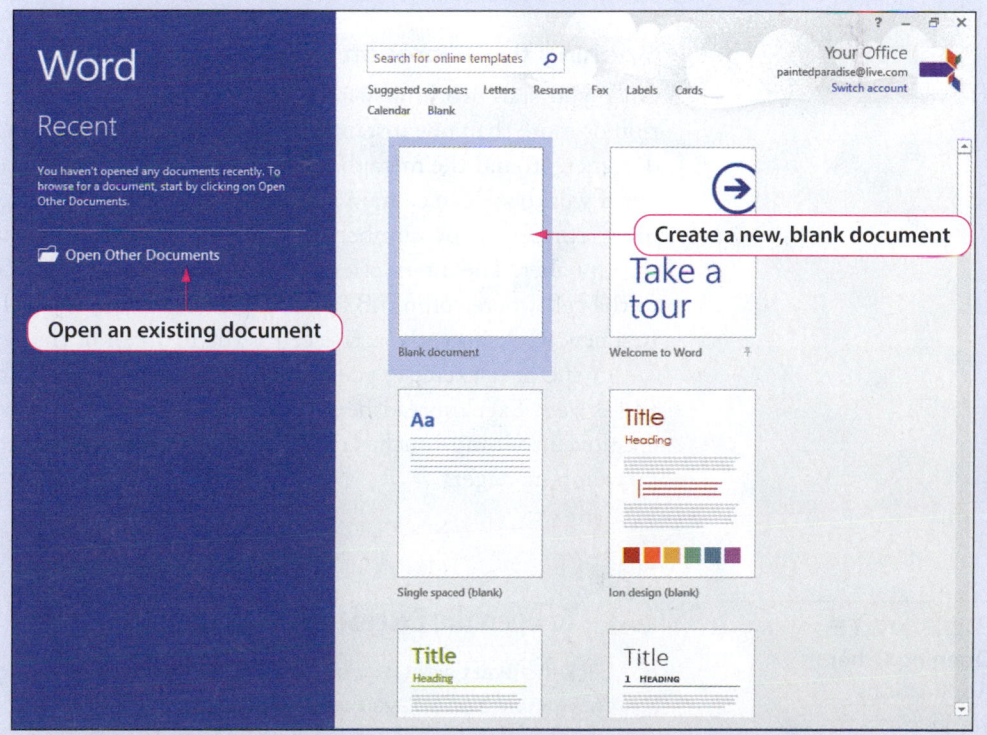

Figure 6   Word Start screen

e. Click **Blank document**.

Notice this opens a blank document—a blank piece of paper. The insertion point is at the first character of the first line.

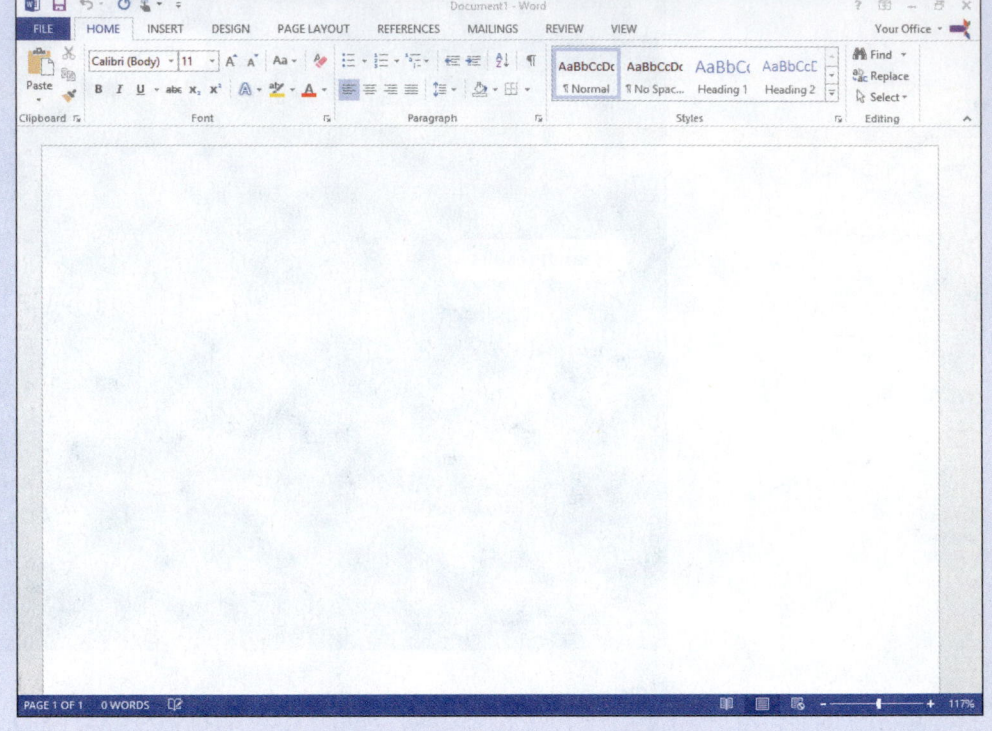

Figure 7   Blank Word document

Opening the Microsoft Excel Start Screen

Once you start working with these applications, you can have more than one application or more than one instance of the same application open at a time. Microsoft Excel is designed around the metaphor of a book. An Excel file is referred to as a workbook. Each Excel workbook can contain many different worksheets—pages in a book. Each sheet has rows represented by numbers. Further, each sheet has columns represented by letters of the alphabet. The intersection of any row and column is a cell. For example, cell B2 refers to the cell where column B and row 2 cross. The active cell is the currently selected cell. In a new worksheet, the active cell is the first cell of the first row, cell A1.

In the next exercise, you will use the search method to open the Excel Start screen and a new Excel spreadsheet. You will use this new document to start a budget for employee training lunches that you will finish in your meeting with Susan Brock, the gift shop manager.

CF01.02

 To Open the Excel Start Screen and Start a New Spreadsheet

a. Click the **Start screen** or desktop, point to the **bottom-right corner** of the screen. The charms will be displayed on the right side of the screen.

b. Point your mouse over the **charms** and note the labels that appear. Click the **Search** charm.

c. Click the **Search** box at the top of the page. Type **Excel**.

SIDE NOTE
Opening Other Applications
In Windows 8, you can open any of the other Office 2013 application with this search method.

d. Click **Excel 2013** in the search results.

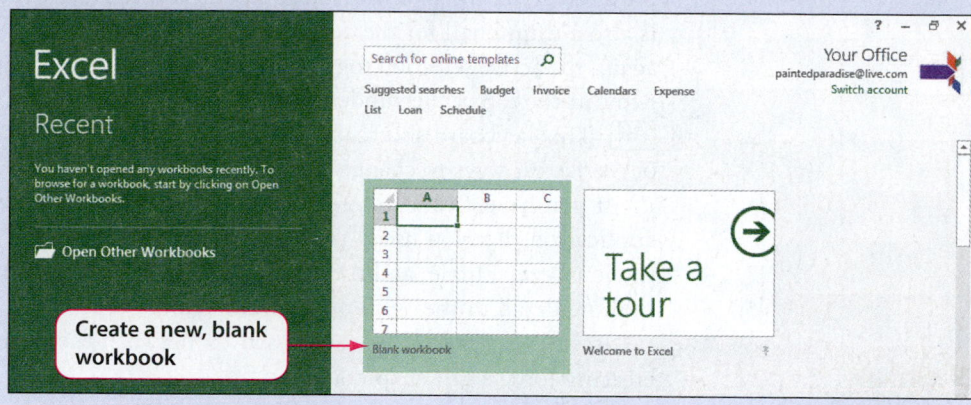

Figure 8 Excel Start screen

e. Click **Blank workbook**.

Notice this opens a blank workbook with one worksheet named Sheet1. The active cell is A1.

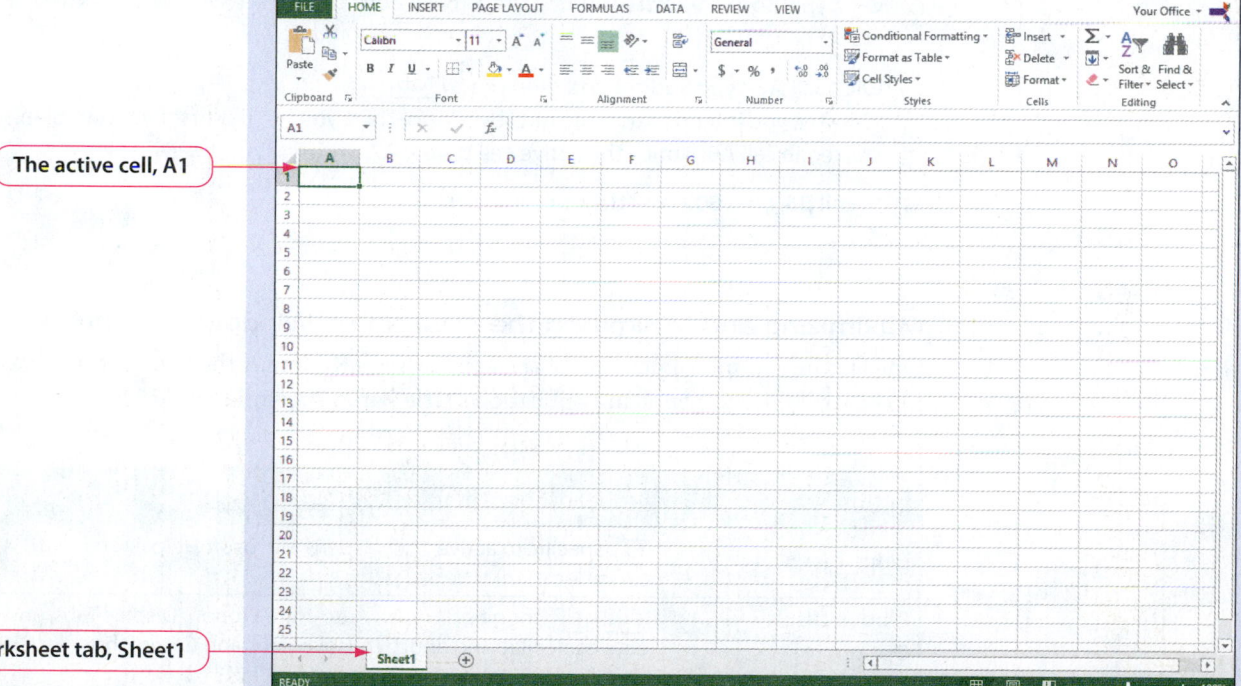

Figure 9 Blank Excel workbook

Switching Between Open Programs and Files

When two or more programs are running at the same time, you can also access them through the taskbar buttons. When moving your mouse pointer over a taskbar icon for an open program, a **thumbnail** or small picture of the open application file is displayed. This is a useful feature when two or more files are open for the same application. A thumbnail of each open file for that application is displayed, and you simply click the file thumbnail that you want to make the active application.

As an alternative to using the thumbnails, you can use the keyboard shortcut to move between applications by holding down Alt and pressing Tab. A small window appears in the center of the screen with thumbnails representing each of the open programs. There is also a thumbnail for the desktop. If you keep Alt pressed down, and then press Tab again, the active selection toggles and previews the selected open application. The program name at the top of the window indicates the program that will be active when you release Alt. This keyboard shortcut is particularly useful when giving presentations as it is one of the fastest ways to change the active application.

If you have a touch screen, you can also use a left bezel swipe to switch to the last application that you used. You can also show all open applications by swiping out from the left bezel a little, and then swipe back to the left bezel. Touch gestures are explained in more detail in the Windows 8 workshop.

In the next exercise, you will switch between the document and spreadsheet you are creating for the gift shop manager.

CF01.03

 To Switch Between Open Programs and Files

a. Press Alt + Tab at the same time. Notice the active application changes to Word.

b. On the taskbar, point to **Excel** 📗, and then observe the thumbnail of the Excel file.

c. Click the **Book1 - Excel** thumbnail to make sure the Book1 workbook is the current active program.

d. Click cell **A6**, type Budget and then press Tab.

   Later, you intend to add the gift shop logo. Thus, you left the first five rows blank and started in cell A6. Notice the active cell is now A7.

e. In cell **B6**, type 500, and then press Enter.

Maximizing and Minimizing the Application Window

One feature common among all of the application's Ribbon is the five buttons that appear in the top-right corner of an application's title bar as shown in Table 1.

Button	Keyboard Shortcut	Action
Help ?	F1 (specific to active cursor location)	Opens Microsoft Help
Ribbon Display Options 🗗	Ctrl+F1 (toggles between collapsing and showing the Ribbon)	Auto-Hide Ribbon, Display Tabs, and Display Tabs and Commands
Minimize ▬	Alt+Spacebar	Hides a window so it is only visible on the taskbar
Restore Down 🗗 and Maximize ☐	Alt+Spacebar	When the window is at its maximum size, the button will restore the window to a previous, smaller size. When a window is in the Restore Down mode, the button expands the window to its full size.
Close ✖	Alt+F4	Closes a file. Closes all files and **exits** the program if no other files are open for that program.

Table 1 Top-right Ribbon buttons

These buttons offer you the flexibility to size and arrange the windows to suit your purpose or to minimize a window and remove it from view. The largest workspace is when the window is maximized. If several applications are opened, the windows can be arranged using the Restore Down button so several windows can be viewed at the same time. If you are not working on an application and want to have it remain open, the Minimize button will hide the application on the taskbar.

In the next exercise, you will manipulate the sizing of the document and spreadsheet you are creating for the gift shop manager.

CF01.04

To Minimize, Maximize, and Restore Down the Windows

a. On the **Excel** title bar, click **Minimize** ▬ to reduce the program window to an icon on the taskbar. The Word window will now be the active window in view.

b. On the **Word** title bar, click the **Restore Down** ⧉ button. Notice the window becomes smaller and can be resized by clicking and dragging at the corners.

c. Click **Maximize** ▢ to expand the Word program window to fill the screen.

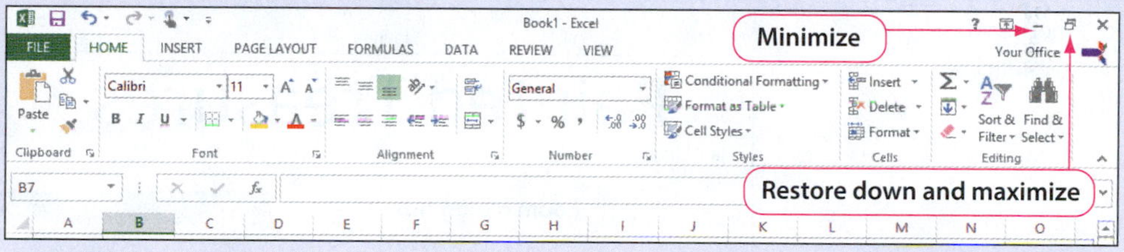

Figure 10   Minimize, Maximize, and Restore Down buttons

d. Click **Excel** on the taskbar to make Excel the active program. Notice the workbook is maximized.

Zooming and Scrolling

To get a closer look at the content within the program, you can zoom in. Alternatively, if you would like to see more of the contents, you can zoom out. Keep in mind that the Zoom level only affects your view of the document on the monitor and does not affect the printed output of the document, similarly to using a magnifying glass to see something bigger—the print on the page is still the same size. Therefore, the zoom level should not be confused with how big the text will print—it only affects your view of the document on the screen.

On the right side of the status bar is a slide control that permits zooming in Word from 10% to 500%. The plus and minus propose an easy method, or you can drag the Zoom Slider ▭▬▬▬▬|▬▬▬+. In Excel and PowerPoint the zoom range is from 10% to 400%. When using zoom, sometimes text is shifted off the viewing screen. Depending on the program and the Zoom level, you might see the vertical or horizontal scroll bars, or both scroll bars, which can be used to adjust what is displayed in the window. The scroll bars have arrows that can be clicked to shift the workspace in small increments in a specific direction and a scroll box that can be dragged to move a workspace in larger increments. Lastly, touch screens allow you to zoom in and out using pinch and stretch gestures.

In the next exercise, you will zoom in and out on the document you are creating for the gift shop manager.

CF01.05

▶ To Zoom and Scroll in Office Applications

a. On the taskbar, click **Word** ⬜. On the Word title bar, if necessary, click **Maximize** ⬜ to expand the Word program window to fill the screen.

b. The insertion point should be at the beginning of the blank document and the cursor should be blinking. Type **Painted Treasures**.

> **Troubleshooting**
>
> If you made any typing errors, you can press Backspace to remove the typing errors and then retype the text.

SIDE NOTE

Methods for Zooming

Several ways exist to zoom Office applications: Zoom Slider, View tab in the Zoom group, Ctrl and a mouse wheel, and touch gestures.

c. On the Word status bar, drag the **Zoom Slider** ▭────┃────+ to the right until it reaches 500%. The document is enlarged to its largest size. This makes the text appear larger. Scroll to see the words **Painted Treasures**, if necessary.

d. On the Word status bar, click **500%**. Notice, this percentage is the Zoom level button that opens the Zoom dialog box. This dialog box provides options for custom and preset settings.

Painted Treasures

Zoom dialog box

| Zoom |
| Zoom to |
| ○ 200%   ○ Page width   ○ Many pages: |
| ○ 100%   ○ Text width |
| ○ 75%   ○ Whole page |
| Percent: 500% |
| Preview |

AaB

Zoom level button

View icons   Zoom slider

PAGE 1 OF 1   2 WORDS   500%

Figure 11   Zoom controls and dialog box

e. Click **Page width**, and then click **OK**.

The Word document zooms to its page width. Notice that this zoom level will give you the maximum size without creating a horizontal scroll bar.

Use the Office Ribbon, Contextual Tools, and Other Menus

Office has a consistent design and layout that helps make it welcoming and comfortable to the user. Once you learn to use one Office 2013 program, you can use many of those skills when working with other Office programs. The **Ribbon** is the row of tabs with buttons across the top of the application. The Ribbon may be open as shown in Figure 12 or hidden. Your Ribbon may look different than as shown in Figure 12. The Ribbon will change based on the screen resolution of your monitor. This text shows all figures with a 1024×768 screen resolution.

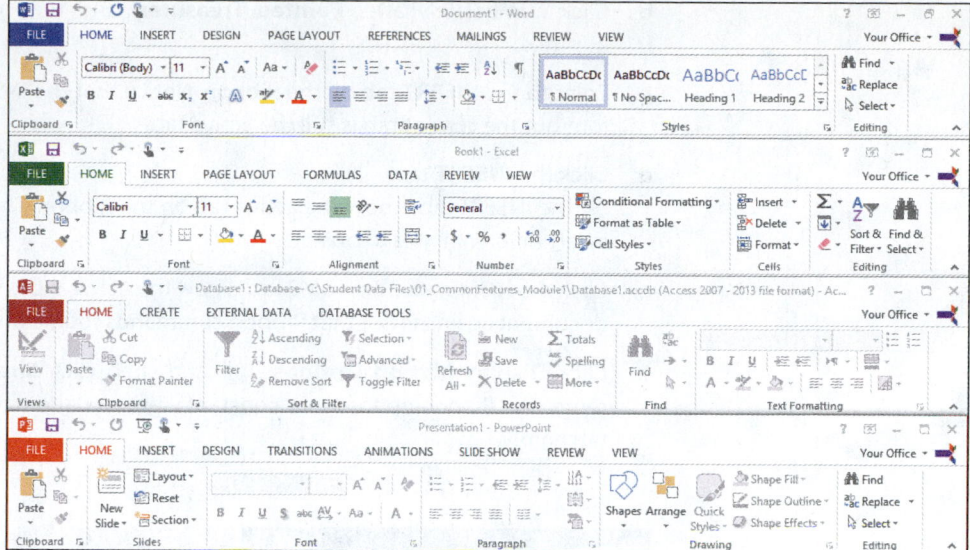

Figure 12 Ribbons of Word, Excel, Access, and PowerPoint

Each Office application's Ribbon has two tabs in common: the File tab and the Home tab. The File tab is the first tab on the Ribbon and is used for file management needs. When clicked, it opens a menu that provides access to the file-level features, such as saving a file, creating a new file, opening an existing file, printing a file, and closing a file, as well as program options. The Home tab is the second tab and contains the commands for the most frequently performed activities, including copying, cutting, and pasting; changing fonts and styles; and other various editing and formatting tools. The commands on these tabs may differ from program to program. Other tabs are program specific, such as the Formulas tab in Excel, the Design tab in PowerPoint, and the Database Tools tab in Access.

Using the Ribbon Tabs

You can enlarge your workspace by collapsing the Ribbon. The Ribbon Display Options button is located in the top-right corner of the window. In the next exercise, you will change the Ribbon display options and format the meeting minutes document using the Home tab.

CF01.06

To Change Ribbon Display Options

a. In Word, click the **Ribbon Display Options** button 🔳 , and then click **Show Tabs**. Notice that the Ribbon collapses, but the tabs are still visible.

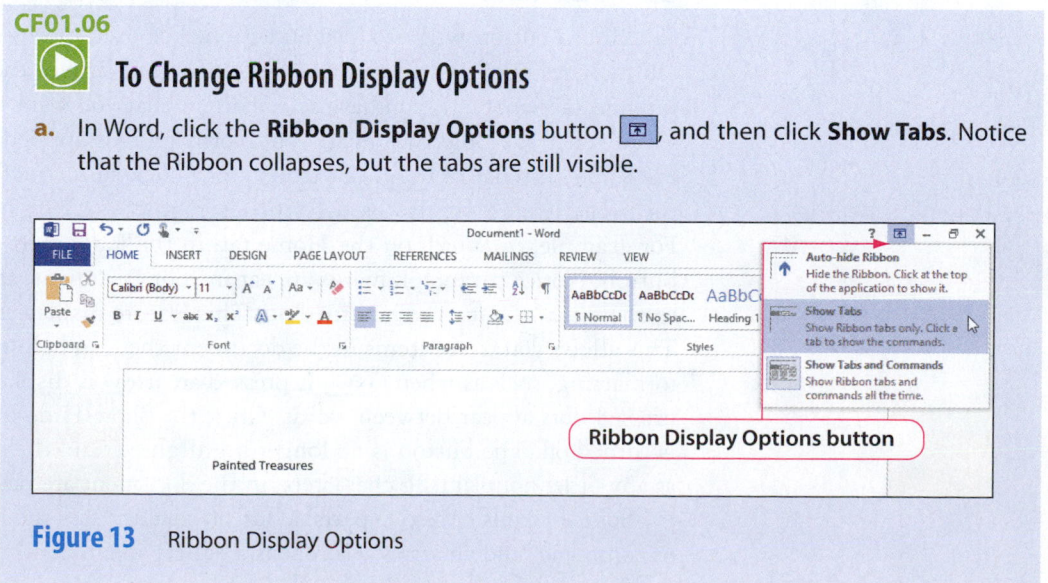

Figure 13 Ribbon Display Options

b. Click immediately after **Painted Treasures**, and then press Enter. Type **Meeting Minutes**.

c. Point to the **INSERT** tab on the Ribbon. Notice that the INSERT tab is in a different color font but the current tab is still the active tab.

d. Click the **INSERT** tab.

   The INSERT tab is now the active tab on the Ribbon. This tab provides easy access to insert different types of objects.

e. Click the **HOME** tab. The HOME tab is now the active tab on the Ribbon. If you click in the document again, notice that Ribbon commands toggle out of view again.

f. Click **Display Ribbon Options** 🖾, and then click **Show Tabs and Commands** to return the Ribbon options into constant view—or alternatively, double-click any of the tab names.

REAL WORLD ADVICE | **How Buttons and Groups Appear on the Ribbon**

If you noticed that your Ribbon appears differently from one computer to the next—the buttons and groups might seem condensed in size—there could be a few factors at play. The most common causes could be monitor size, lower screen resolution, or a reduced program window. Since the Ribbon changes to accommodate the size of the window or screen, buttons can appear as icons without labels and a group can be condensed into a button that must be clicked to display the group options. So, do not worry! All of the same features are on the Ribbon and in the same general area.

CONSIDER THIS | **Advantages of a Common Interface**

The Ribbon provides a common user interface. This common interface can help you learn additional applications quickly. What elements have you noticed that are common? What elements have you noticed that are different? Of the elements that are different, how are they still presented in a common way?

Using Buttons

Clicking a button will produce an action. For example, the Font group on the Home tab includes buttons for bold and italic. Clicking any of these buttons will produce an intended action. So, if you have selected text that you want to apply bold formatting to, simply click the Bold button and bold formatting is applied to the selected text.

Some buttons are **toggle buttons**—one click turns the feature on and a second click turns the feature off. When a feature is toggled on, the button remains highlighted. For example, in Word, on the Home tab in the Paragraph group, click the Show/Hide button. Notice paragraph marks appear in your document, and the button is highlighted to show that the feature is turned on. This feature displays characters that do not print. This allows you to see items in the document that can help to troubleshoot a document's formatting, such as when Tab is pressed an arrow is displayed, or when Spacebar is pressed dots appear between words. Click the Show/Hide button again, and the feature is turned off. The button is no longer highlighted, and the paragraph characters, as well as any other nonprinting characters, in the document are no longer displayed.

Some buttons have two parts: a button that accesses the most commonly used setting or command, and an arrow that opens a gallery menu of all related commands or options for that particular task or button. For example, on the Home tab in the Font group, the Font Color button 🅰 includes the different colors that are available for fonts. If you click the button, the default is to apply the last color used. Notice the last used color is also displayed on the icon. To access the gallery menu for other color options, click the arrow next to the Font Color button. Whenever you see an arrow next to a button, this is an indicator that more options are available.

The two buttons on your mouse operate in a similar fashion. The left mouse click performs an action. The right-click—or right mouse button—will never perform an action, but rather provides more options. The options that appear on the shortcut menu when you right-click change depending on the location of the mouse pointer.

In the next exercise, you will format the gift shop meeting minutes using bold and font color.

CF01.07

 To Use Buttons

a. In Word, click immediately before **Meeting Minutes** to position the insertion point to the left of the word **Meeting**, and then press and hold the left mouse button and drag to the right to select the words **Meeting Minutes**.

b. On the HOME tab, in the Font group, click **Bold** B . This will toggle on the Bold command. Notice that the bold button is now highlighted and the selected text is displayed in bold format.

SIDE NOTE
Text Selection

To select a single word, you can double-click the word to select it or triple-click for the entire paragraph. You can also use Shift and arrow keys to select text.

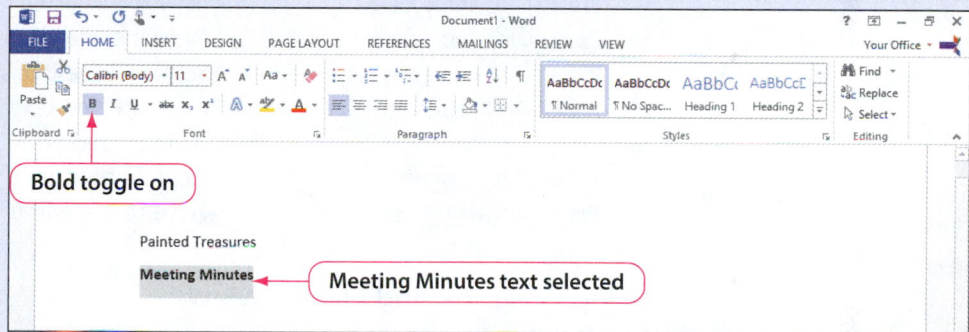

Figure 14   Bold toggled on with text highlighted

c. With the text selected, on the HOME tab, in the Font group, click the **Font Color** arrow A ▾ . Under Standard Colors, point to, but do not click, **Dark Red**—under standard colors it is the first one. Notice the Live Preview feature that shows how the selected document text will change color. As the mouse pointer hovers over a color, a ScreenTip appears to show the color name.

SIDE NOTE
Live Preview

Live Preview shows how formatting looks before you apply it. This feature is available for many of the gallery libraries.

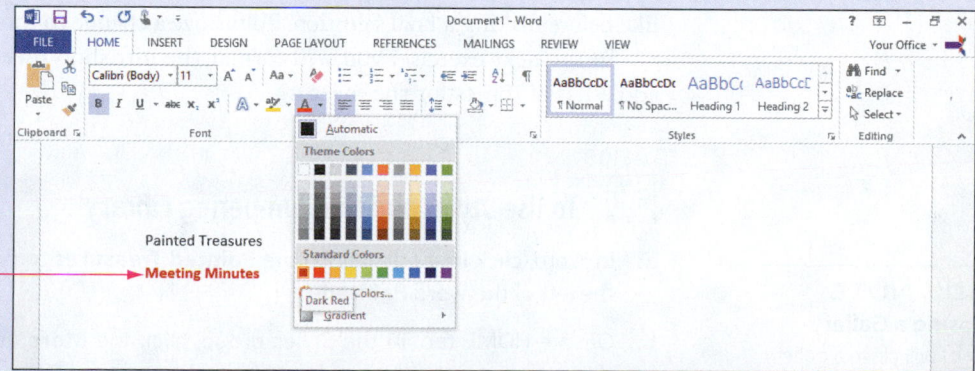

Figure 15   Live Preview of font color

d. Click **Dark Red**. The selected text should now be bold and dark red.

e. Click after **Meeting Minutes** to place your cursor after the end of the word **Minutes**. Notice that the Bold button is still highlighted and the Font Color button is shows Dark Red. Thus, any text you type right now will be bold and dark red.

f. In the Font group, click **Bold** B to toggle Bold off. Then, click the **Font Color** arrow A ▾, and then select **Automatic**.

g. Press Enter . Type your first name and last name.

REAL WORLD ADVICE | Using Keyboard Shortcuts and Key Tips

Keyboard shortcuts are extremely useful, and some are universal to all Windows programs. They keep your hands on the keyboard instead of reaching for the mouse —increasing efficiency and saving time.

Pressing Alt will toggle the display of **key tips**—or **keyboard shortcuts**—for items on the Ribbon and Quick Access Toolbar. After displaying the key tips, you can press the letter or number corresponding to request the action from the keyboard.

For multiple key shortcuts, you hold down the first key listed and press the second key once. Some common keyboard shortcuts are listed below.

Press Ctrl and type **C**	Copy the selected item
Press Ctrl and type **V**	Paste a copied item
Press Ctrl and type **A**	Select all the items in a document or window
Press Ctrl and type **B**	Bold selected text
Press Ctrl and type **Z**	Undo an action
Press Ctrl + Home	Move to the top of the document
Press Ctrl + End	Move to the end of the document

Using Galleries and Live Preview

Live Preview lets you see the effects of menu selections on your document file or selected item before making a commitment to a particular menu choice. A **gallery** is a set of menu options that appear when you click the arrow next to a button which, in some cases, may be referred to as a More arrow ▾. The menu or grid shows samples of the available options.

When you point to an option in a gallery, Live Preview shows the results that would occur in your file if you were to click that particular option. Using Live Preview, you can experiment with settings before making a final choice. When you point to a text style in the Styles gallery, the selected text or the paragraph in which the insertion point is located appears with that text style. Moving the pointer from option to option results in quickly seeing what your text will look like before making a final selection. To finalize a change to the selected option, click the style.

In the next exercise, you will format the gift shop meeting minutes using styles and add a list of topics for the meeting.

CF01.08

▶ To Use Styles and the Numbering Library

a. In Word, click immediately before **Painted Treasures** to position the insertion point to the left of the word **Painted**.

b. On the HOME tab, in the Styles group, click the **More** arrow ▾. This will show all of the options for different styles. Point your mouse to **Title** to see the Live Preview. Then, select **Title** to change the words "Painted Treasures" to Title style. Notice that the style changed the whole line even though you did not select the text.

SIDE NOTE
Closing a Gallery
Esc will close a gallery without making a selection. Alternatively, you can click outside the gallery menu.

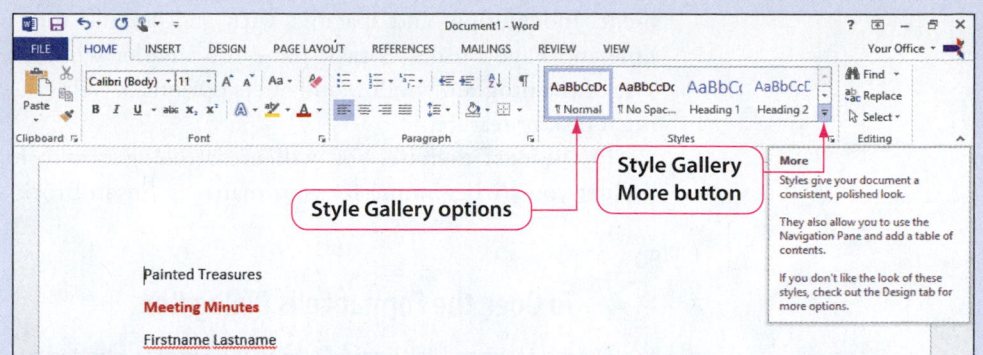

Figure 16 Styles gallery

c. Click immediately after your **last name**, press Enter twice, type Topics, and then press Enter one time.

d. On the HOME tab, in the Paragraph group, click the **Numbering** arrow ⌄. The Numbering Library gallery opens. Point to, but do not click, the **third option** in the first row, the number one followed by a closing parenthesis.

e. Select the **Number Alignment: Left** style with **1)**—the third button in the first row.

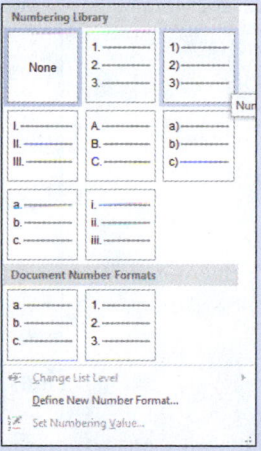

Figure 17 Numbering Library

f. Type Training Lunch Budget - and then press Enter. After the meeting, you intend to type the notes after the dash.

g. Type New Products - and then press Enter twice to end the numbered list.

Opening Dialog Boxes and Task Panes

Some Ribbon groups include a diagonal arrow in the bottom-right corner of the group section, called a **Dialog Box Launcher** ⌸ that opens a corresponding dialog box or task pane. Hovering the mouse pointer over the Dialog Box Launcher will display a ScreenTip to indicate more information. Click the Dialog Box Launcher to open a **dialog box**, which is a window that provides more options or settings beyond those provided on the Ribbon. It often provides access to more precise or less frequently used commands along with the commands offered on the Ribbon; thus using a dialog box offers the ability to apply many related options at the same time and located in one place. As shown in Figure 18, many dialog boxes organize related information into tabs. In the Paragraph dialog box shown in the figure, the active Indents and Spacing tab shows options to change alignment, indentation, and spacing, with another tab that offers options and settings for Line and Page Breaks. A **task pane** is a smaller window pane that often appears to the side of the program window and offers options or helps you to navigate through completing a task or feature.

In the next exercise, you will use a dialog box to format some of the cells in the budget you are beginning for your manager, Susan Brock.

CF01.09

▶ To Open the Format Cells Dialog Box

a. On the taskbar, click **Excel** 📊 to make Excel the active program.

b. Click cell **B6**, the second cell in the sixth row.

c. On the HOME tab, in the Number group, click the **Number Dialog Box Launcher** 🔲. The Format Cells dialog box opens with the Number tab displayed.

d. On the Number tab under Category, click **Currency**. Click in the **Decimal places** box, delete the 2, and then type **0**.

SIDE NOTE

Check Box and Radio Options

Check boxes allow you to select more than one option in the group. Radio options only allow you to select one.

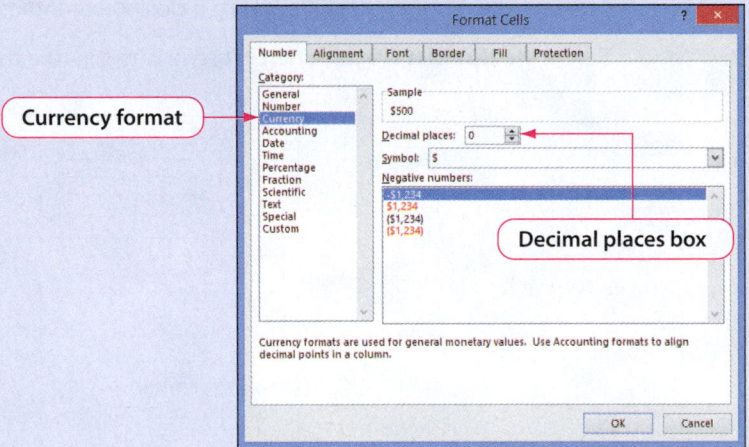

Figure 18   Format Cells Dialog Box

e. Click the **Alignment** tab, click the **Font** tab, and then click the **Border** tab to explore the available options.

f. Click the **Fill** tab. In the second row of colors, click the last **Light Green** color. The light green color will be shown in the Sample box.

g. Click **OK**. The format changes are made to the number, and the fill color is applied.

Inserting Images and Using Contextual Tools

In Word, Excel, PowerPoint, and Publisher, you can insert pictures from a file, a screen shot, or various online sources. The online options include inserting images within the Office Online Pictures collection, via a Bing search, or from your own SkyDrive. The Insert tab contains all of the options for using images in Word, PowerPoint, and Excel.

The term **contextual tools** refers to tools that only appear when needed for specific tasks. Some tabs, toolbars, and menus are displayed as you work and only appear if a particular object is selected. Because these tools become available only as you need them, the workspace remains less cluttered.

A **contextual tab** is a Ribbon tab that contains commands related to selected objects so you can manipulate, edit, and format the objects. Examples of objects that can be selected to produce contextual tabs include a table, a picture, a shape, or a chart. A contextual tab appears to the right of the standard Ribbon tabs. The contextual tab disappears when you click outside the target object—in the file—to deselect the object. In some instances, contextual tabs can also appear as you switch views.

In the next exercise, you will insert a Painted Treasures Gift Shop logo into the budget you are beginning for your manager, Susan Brock. This budget will become a part of Susan's larger budget that she must present to the CEO of Painted Paradise in an internal memo once a year. Logos are an excellent way to brand both internal and external communications.

CF01.10

 To Insert an Image

a. In **Excel**, click cell **A1**.

b. Click the **INSERT** tab, and then in the Illustrations group, click **Pictures**. The Insert Picture dialog box opens.

c. Navigate to your student data files, and then click **cf01ws01Logo**. Click the **Insert** button. The Painted Treasures Gift Shop logo is inserted on the worksheet and actively selected. Notice the logo is too large and covers the cells you created in row 6. Also, notice that the FORMAT contextual tab in the PICTURE TOOLS contextual tab group is now the active tab.

d. On the **FORMAT** tab, in the Size group, click in the **Shape Height** box. Delete **2.19**, type **1**, and then press Enter. Notice the width automatically adjusts to keep the original image proportions.

The FORMAT contextual tab in the PICTURE TOOLS tab group

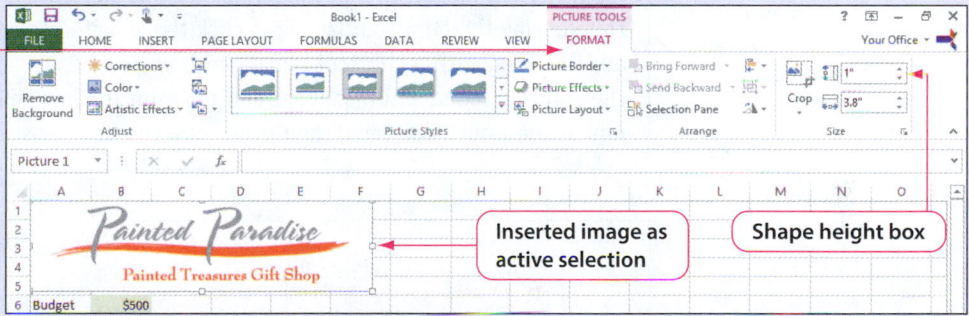

Figure 19 Picture Tools Format contextual tab and shape height

> **Troubleshooting**
> To see a contextual tab, the object relating to the tab must be selected. If you do not see it, click the image to reselect the image.

e. Click cell **A7**. Notice that the contextual tab disappears.

Accessing the Mini Toolbar

The **Mini toolbar** appears after text is selected and contains buttons for the most commonly used formatting commands, such as font, font size, font color, center alignment, bold, and italic. The Mini toolbar button commands vary for each Office program. The toolbar disappears if you move the pointer away from the toolbar, press a key, or click the workspace. All the commands on the Mini toolbar are available on the Ribbon; however, the Mini toolbar offers quicker access to common commands since you do not have to move the mouse pointer far away from the selected text for these commands.

In the next exercise, you will add some additional information to the budget you are beginning for your manager. You will also edit some of the cells with the Mini toolbar.

CF01.11

To Access the Mini Toolbar

a. Click cell **A8**, the first cell in the eighth row of the worksheet. Type **Expenses** and then press Enter.

b. In cell **A9**, type **Food** and then press Enter.

c. In cell **A10**, type **Drinks** and then press Enter.

d. Click cell **B9**, type **450** and then press Enter. In cell **B10**, type **50**.

e. Double-click cell **A8** to place the insertion point in the cell. Double-clicking a cell enables you to enter edit mode for the cell text.

f. Double-click cell **A8** again to select the text. The Mini toolbar appears and comes into view directly above the selected text. If you were to move the pointer off the cell, the Mini toolbar becomes transparent or disappears entirely. When you move the pointer back over the Mini toolbar it may become visible again or you may need to repeat the text selection.

> **Troubleshooting**
>
> If you are having a problem with the Mini toolbar disappearing, you may have inadvertently moved the mouse pointer to another part of the document. If you need to redisplay the Mini toolbar, right-click the selected text and the Mini toolbar will appear along with a shortcut menu. Once you select an option on the Mini toolbar, the shortcut menu will disappear and the Mini toolbar will remain while in use—or repeat the prior two steps, then make sure the pointer stays over the toolbar.

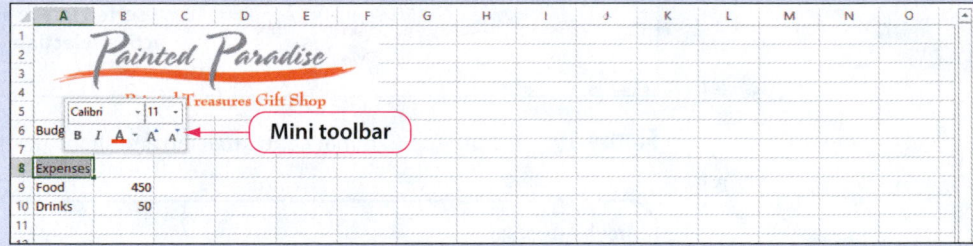

Figure 20 Mini toolbar

g. On the Mini toolbar, click **Italic** I.

h. Press Enter. Cell A9 is now selected.

The Mini toolbar is particularly helpful with the touch interface. When Office recognizes that you are using touch instead of a mouse or digitizer pen, it creates Mini toolbars that are larger and designed to work with fingers more easily. An example of a touch Mini toolbar in Excel touch mode is shown in Figure 21.

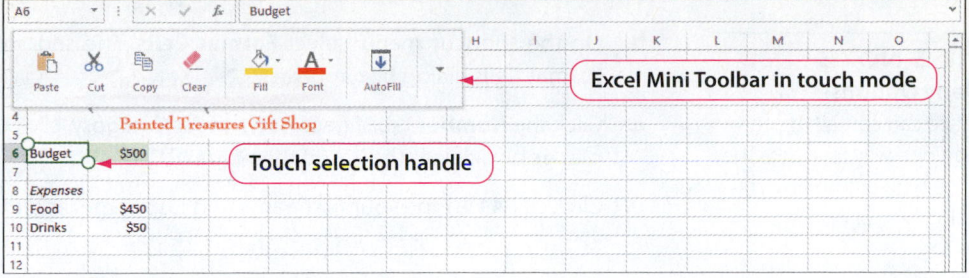

Figure 21   Excel Mini toolbar in touch mode

Using Shortcut Menus

Shortcut menus are also context sensitive and enable you to quickly access commands that are most likely needed in the context of the task being performed. A **shortcut menu** is a list of commands related to a selection that appears when you right-click—click the right mouse button. This means you can access popular commands without using the Ribbon. Included are commands that perform actions, commands that open dialog boxes, and galleries of options that provide Live Preview. As noted previously, the Mini toolbar opens when you click the right mouse button. If you click a button on the Mini toolbar, the shortcut menu closes, and the Mini toolbar remains open allowing you to continue formatting your selection.

In the next exercise, you will add some additional information to the budget you are beginning for your manager. You will also edit some of the cells with a shortcut menu.

CF01.12

To Use the Shortcut Menu to Add Currency Formatting

a. Click cell **B9**, hold down your left mouse button, and then drag down to cell **B10** to select both B9 and B10. Right-click the selected range, **B9:B10**. A shortcut menu opens with commands related to common tasks you can perform in a cell, along with the Mini toolbar.

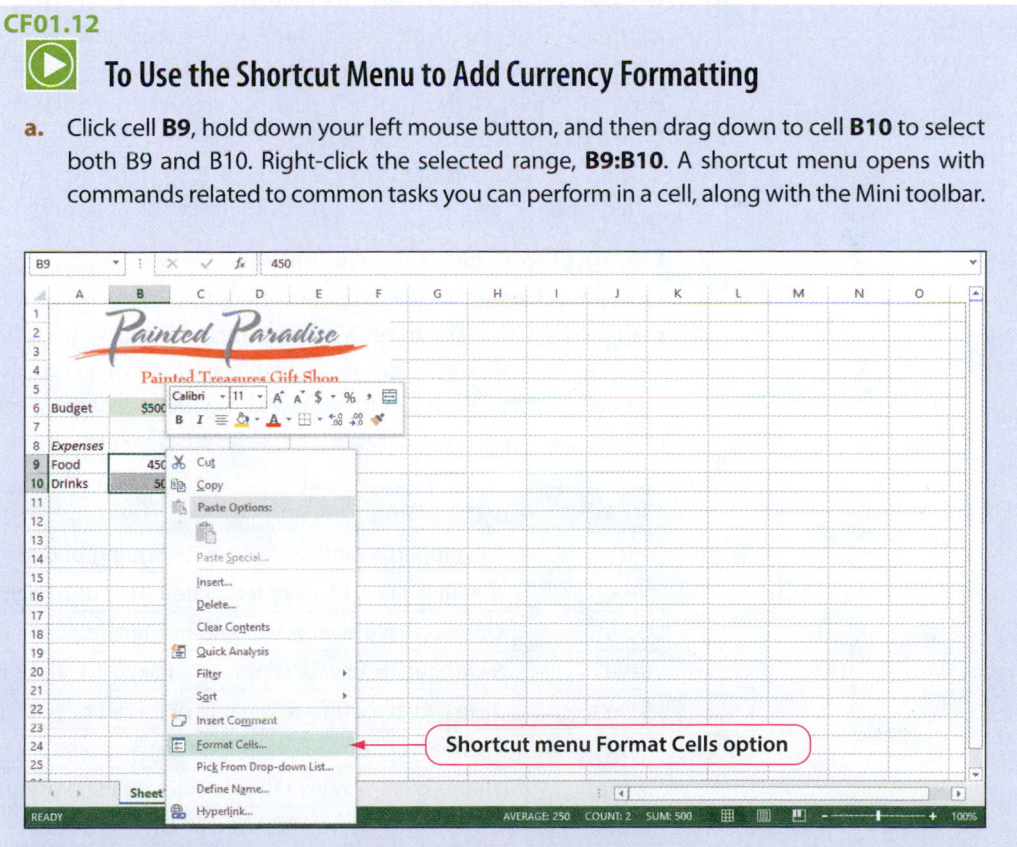

Figure 22   Shortcut menu with Mini toolbar

b. On the shortcut menu, select **Format Cells**. The shortcut menu closes, and then the Format Cells dialog box appears.

c. Click the **Number** tab, if necessary. Under Category, click **Currency**. Click in the **Decimal places** box, delete the 2, and then type **0**. Click **OK**.

d. Click cell **A13**, type your first name and last name, and then press Enter.

Manipulating Files and Finding Help in Office

Creating, opening, saving, closing, troubleshooting, and printing files are common everyday tasks performed in any Office program. Most of these tasks can all be accessed from the File tab. These processes are basically the same for all the Office programs. When you start a program, you either have to create a new file or open an existing one. Since Office has a common interface, learning a new Office application is easy as long as you can find help when needed. In this section, you will use Office Help, making it easy to learn more.

Manage Files in Office

While working on an Office file, whether creating a new file or modifying an existing file, your work is stored in the temporary memory on your computer, not on the hard drive or your USB flash drive. Any work done will be lost if you were to exit the program, turn off the computer, or experience a power failure without saving your work or the program automatically saving your work. To prevent losing your work, you need to save your work and remember to save frequently—at least every 10 minutes or after adding several changes. That saves you from having to re-create any work you did prior to the last save.

You can save files to the hard drive, which is located inside the computer; to an external drive, such as a USB flash drive; to a network storage device; or to SkyDrive. Office has an **AutoRecovery** feature—previously called AutoSave—that will attempt to recover any changes made to a document if something goes wrong, but this should not be relied upon as a substitute for saving your work manually.

Using Office Backstage View

Office Backstage View has many options for managing your files in Office and is accessed via the File tab. Office Backstage View now includes a new area called Account. This enables you to log in to your Microsoft account or switch accounts. You can also see a list of connected services and add services, such as LinkedIn and SkyDrive. Save & Send has been replaced by Export and has been downsized. Table 2 lists the areas you can modify in Office Backstage View.

Area	Description
Info	File properties and protecting, inspecting, and managing versions of the file
New	Creating a new blank or template-based document
Open	Opening a file from your computer, recent documents list, or SkyDrive account
Save	Save your file to your computer or SkyDrive account
Save As	Save your file with a new name or format to your computer or SkyDrive account
Print	Preview your document for printing and print
Share	Share your file by invitation, e-mail, online presentation, or blog post
Export	Change the file type or create a PDF/XPS document
Close	Close the file
Account	User and Production information including connected services
Options	Launches the Application Options dialog box with many options including advanced options

Table 2 Office Backstage View

Saving a File

In addition to Office Backstage View, Office provides several ways to save a file. To quickly save a file, simply click Save ⊞ on the Quick Access Toolbar or use the keyboard shortcut of pressing Ctrl and then pressing S. The **Quick Access Toolbar** is the series of small icons in the top-left corner that can be customized to offer commonly used buttons. There are two different Save icons to show whether you are saving to your computer or to SkyDrive. When saving to SkyDrive, the Save icon looks more like a syncing icon.

The first time you save a new file, it behaves the same as the Save As command where the Save As dialog box opens. This allows you to specify the save options. In the Save As dialog box, you can name the file and specify the location to save it, similar to the first time you save a file. Once you save a file, the simple shortcut methods to save any changes to the file work fine to update the existing file. No dialog box will open to save after the first time—as long as you do not need to change the file name or location as with the Save As command.

A file name includes the name you specify and a **file extension** assigned by the Office program to indicate the file type. The file extension may or may not be visible depending on your computer settings. You can check your computer's setting in the File Explorer window under the View tab in the Show/hide group. The check box for File name extensions should be checked to see file extension as shown in Figure 23. Each Office program adds a period and a file extension after the file name to identify the program in which that file was created. Table 3 shows the common default file extensions for Office 2013.

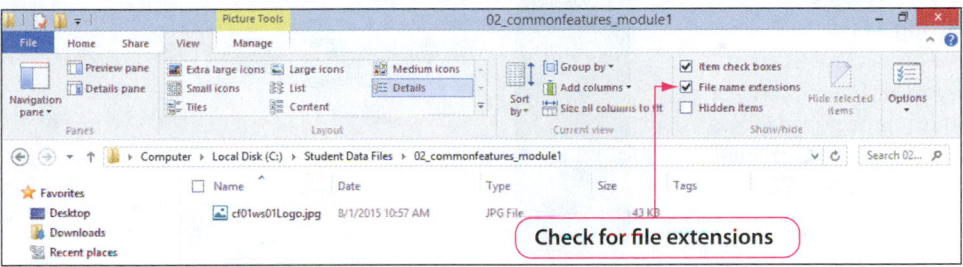

Check for file extensions

Figure 23   File Explorer file extension setting

Application	Extension
Word 2013	.docx
Excel 2013	.xlsx
PowerPoint 2013	.pptx
Access 2013	.accdb

Table 3   Office 2013 default file extensions

REAL WORLD ADVICE   Sharing Files Between Office Versions

Different Office versions are not always compatible. The general rule is that files created in an older version can always be opened in a newer version, but not the other way around—a 2013 Office file is not easily opened in versions of Office prior to Office 2007. Sharing files with Office 2003 users is a concern because different file extensions were used. For example, .doc was used for Word files instead of docx, .xls instead of .xlsx for Excel, and so on.

It is still possible to save the Office 2013 files in a previous format version. To save in one of these formats, use the Save As command, and click the 97-2003 format option. If the file is already in the previous format, it will open in Office 2013 and be saved with the same format in which it was created. If a file is saved with a previous version's extension, it may not save all the new formatting features.

Name your file with a descriptive name that accurately reflects the content of the document, workbook, presentation, or database, such as "January 2014 Budget" or "012014 Minutes". The descriptive name can include uppercase and lowercase letters, numbers, hyphens, spaces, and some special characters—excluding ? " / | < > * :—in any combination. File names can include a maximum of 255 characters including the extension—this includes the number of characters for the folder names to get to the file location known as the file path. Even though Windows 8 can handle a long file name, some systems cannot. Thus, shorter names can prevent complications when transferring files between different systems.

In the next exercise, you will name and save the files you have been creating for your meeting with your manager.

CF01.13

To Save a File

a. In Excel, click the **FILE** tab. Office Backstage View opens with command options and tabs for managing files, opening existing files, saving, printing, and exiting. Click **Save As**.

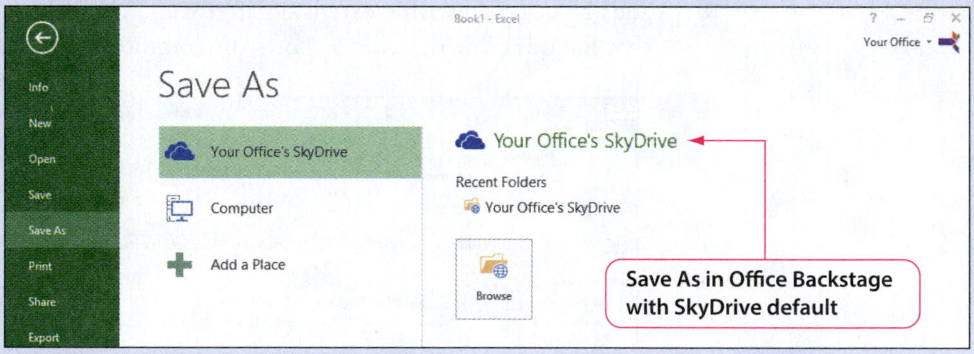

SIDE NOTE
Saving a File
The default save location is your SkyDrive account—you must be signed in. You can also save to Computer or Add a Place.

Figure 24   Save As with SkyDrive as default

b. Click **Computer**. Click **Browse**.
This will enable you to select the location on your computer where you are saving your files. The Save As dialog box opens. This provides the opportunity to enter a file-name and a storage location. The default storage location is the Documents folder and the suggested file name is the first few words of the first line of the document.

c. Click the **location** in the left pane, and then navigate through the folder structure to where your student data files are located. Click in the **File name** box, and then select the current suggested file name, if necessary. Navigate to where you are storing your files, and then type **cf01ws01Budget_LastFirst** using your last and first name in the File name box. Change the Save as type to **Excel Workbook**, if necessary.
This file name describes both the content of the file and the portion of this book that the file is associated. The "Budget" part describes the content. The "cf01ws01" describes Common Features workshop 1.

d. Click the **Save** button. The Save As dialog box closes, Excel returns to the HOME tab, and the name of your file appears in the Excel window title bar.

e. On the taskbar, click **Word** to make Word the active program. Repeat Steps b through d, and then save the file as **cf01ws01Minutes_LastFirst** using your last and first name.

Modifying Saved Files

Saved files only contain what was in the file the last time it was saved. Any changes made after the file was saved are only stored in the computer's memory and are not saved with the file. It is important to remember to save often—after making changes—so the file is updated to reflect its current contents. One of the most useful shortcuts is the keyboard shortcut for saving, which can be utilized by pressing Ctrl, and then pressing S.

Remember that it is not necessary to use the Save As dialog box once the file has been saved unless you want to save a copy of the file with a different name or you want to store it in a different location.

In the next exercise, you will modify and save the files that you have been creating for your meeting with your manager. You will save them to the same location you saved them to in the last exercise.

CF01.14

 To Modify and Save a File to the Previously Saved Location

a. In Word, click below the numbered list to make sure the insertion point is on the last line. Type **today's date** and then press Enter.

b. Press Ctrl+S. The changes you made to the document have just been saved to the file stored in the location you selected earlier. Recall that no dialog boxes will open for the Save after the first time the document has been saved.

SIDE NOTE
Customize Quick Access
You can customize the Quick Access Toolbar for favorite or common commands such as Print, Spelling & Grammar, or New.

REAL WORLD ADVICE | **Saving Files**

Most programs have an added safeguard or warning dialog box to remind you to save if you attempt to close a file without saving your changes first. Despite that warning, best practice dictates you save files before closing them or exiting a program. If you press the wrong answer on the warning by accident, you will lose work. Remembering to save before you close prevents this kind of accident.

Best practice also dictates saving often. The more often you save the less work you can lose in the event of an unexpected closing of the application. Pressing Ctrl and S only takes a few seconds. Train yourself now to use this keyboard shortcut regularly and often. If you do, it will become second nature and save you from losing work in the future!

Closing a File and Exiting an Application

When you are ready to close a file, you can click the Close command in Office Backstage View. If the file you close is the only file open for that particular program, the program window remains open with no file in the window. You can also close a file by using the Close button ✖ in the top-right corner of the window. However, if that is the only file open, the file and program will close when using that method of closing. If you exit the window, it will close both the file and the program. Exiting programs when you are finished with them helps save system resources and keeps your Windows desktop and taskbar uncluttered, as well as prevents data from being accidentally lost.

In the next exercise, you will modify, save, and close the Meeting Minutes document that you have been creating for your meeting with your manager. You are also finished with Excel. Thus, you will save and exit the budget you prepared.

SIDE NOTE

Best Practice

Best practice is to save the file before closing instead of allowing the warning dialog box to prompt for the save.

CF01.15

 To Modify and Close a Document

a. In Word, with the insertion point on the line under the date, type your **course number** and **section** and then press Enter. The text you typed should appear below the date.

b. Click the **FILE** tab, and then click **Close**. A warning dialog box opens, asking if you want to save the changes made to the document.

c. Click **Save**.

   The document closes after saving changes, but the Word program window remains open. You are able to create new files or open previously saved files. If multiple Word documents are open, the document window of the file you just closed will remain open with the other documents that are currently still open in the window.

d. On the taskbar, click **Excel** to make Excel the active program.

e. Press Ctrl + S to save the file to the previous location. Click **Close** X in the top-right corner. Notice that the file closes and you exit the Excel application.

Opening a File from the Recent Documents List

You create a new file when you open a blank document, workbook, presentation, or database. If you want to work on a previously created file, you must first open it. When you open a file, it copies the file from the file's storage location to the computer's temporary memory and displays it on the monitor's screen. When you save a file, it updates the storage location with the changes. Until then, the file only exists in your computer's memory. If you want to open a second file, while one is open, the keyboard shortcut of pressing Ctrl and then pressing O will open the Open tab of Office Backstage View. If you use the keyboard shortcut of Ctrl + F12 you will launch the Open dialog window without taking you to Office Backstage View.

In Office Backstage View, Office keeps a list of your most recently modified files—**Most Recently Used list**. As the list grows, older files are removed to make room for more recently modified files. You can also pin a frequently used file to always remain at the top of the list. To clear the recent files, right-click any file in the recent files list and select the option to clear unpinned files.

When opening files downloaded from the Internet, accessed from a shared network, or received as an attachment in e-mail, the file usually opens in a read-only format called **Protected View** in Reading Mode, as shown in Figure 25. In Protected View, the file contents can be seen and read, but you are not able to edit, save, or print the contents until you enable editing. If you see the information bar shown in Figure 25, and you trust the source of the file, simply click the Enable Editing button on the information bar.

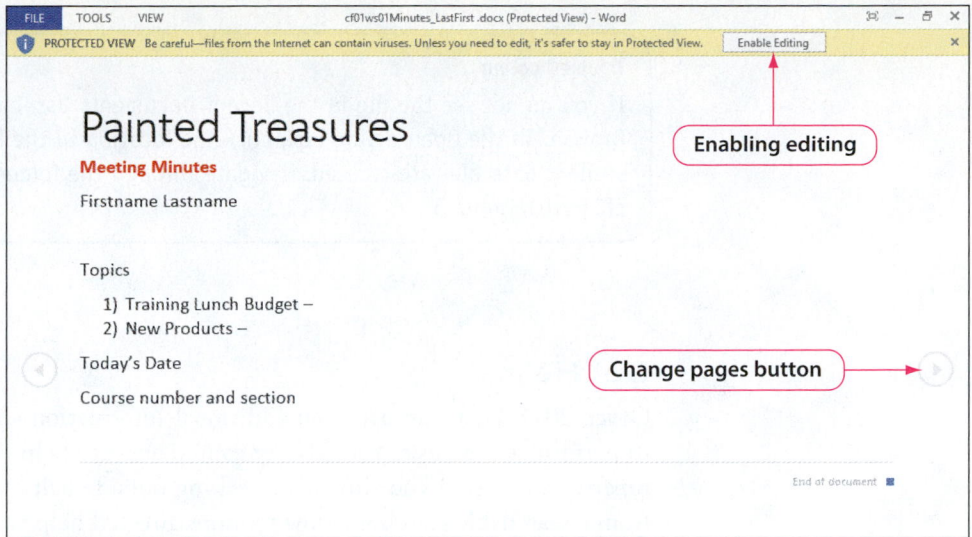

Figure 25   File opened in Protected View

CF01.16

▶ To Reopen a Document from the Recent Documents List

a.   In Word, click the **FILE** tab. Notice the Recent Documents list.

b.   Point to **cf01ws01Minutes_LastFirst**. Notice the Pin icon ⊷ . If you want the document to always remain at the top of this list, you would click the Pin icon.

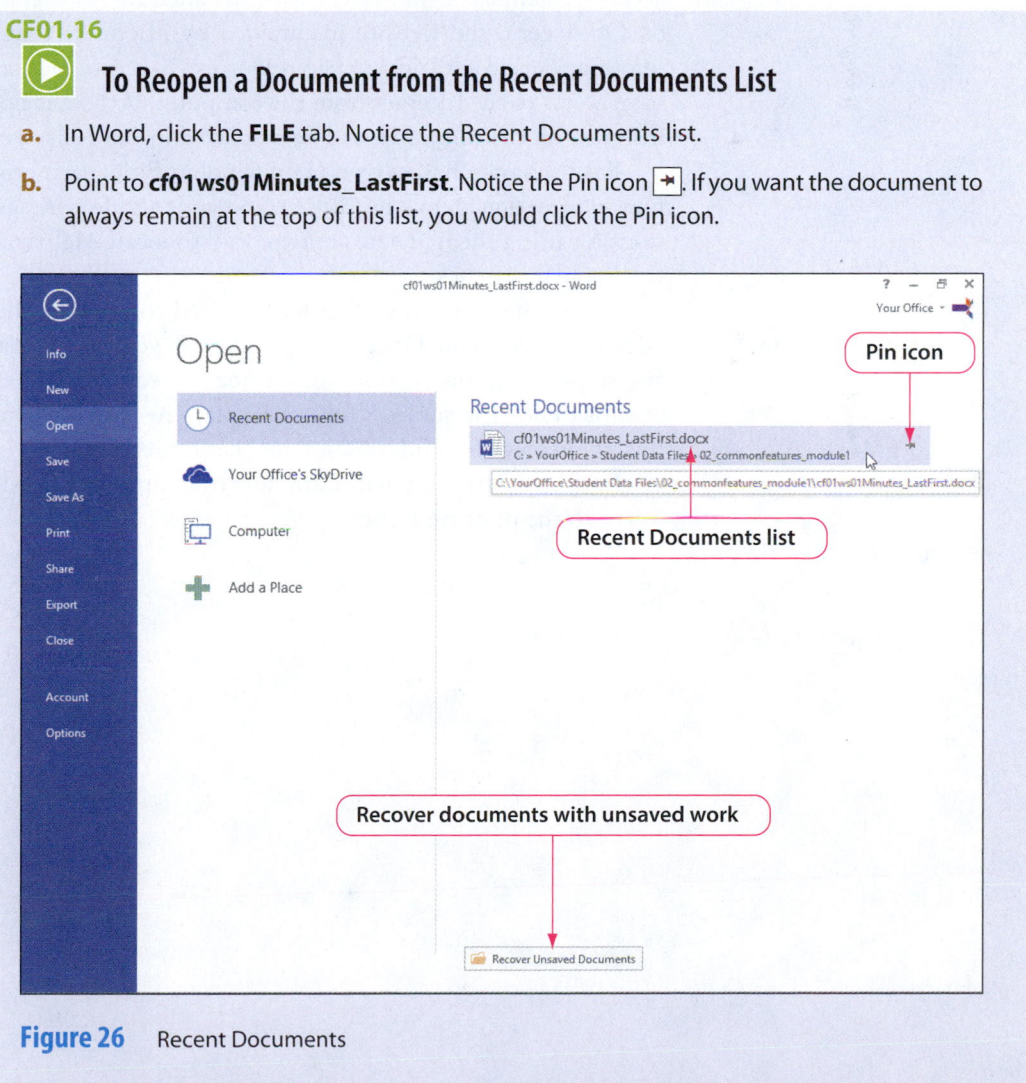

Figure 26   Recent Documents

c.   Click **cf01ws01Minutes_LastFirst**. Word opens the file and exits Office Backstage View.

> **Troubleshooting**
>
> If you do not see the file in the Recent Documents list, click Computer and then Browse. In the Open dialog box, click the location in the left pane where your student data files are located. Navigate through the folder structure, and then click cf01ws01Minutes.

Get Help

Office 2013 Help can give you additional information about a feature or steps for how to perform a new task. Your ability to find and use help can greatly increase your Office repertoire and save you time from seeking outside help. Office has several levels of help from a searchable search window to more directed help such as ScreenTips.

Using the Help Window

The **Help** window provides detailed information on a multitude of topics, as well as access to templates, training videos installed on your computer, and content available on Office.com, the website maintained by Microsoft that provides access to the latest information and additional Help resources. To access the contents at Office.com you must have access to the Internet from the computer. If there is no Internet access, only the files installed on the computer will be displayed in the Help window.

Each program has its own Help window. From each program's Help window you can find information about the Office commands and features as well as step-by-step instructions for using them. There are two ways to locate Help topics—the search function and the Popular searches categories.

To search the Help system on a desired topic, type the topic in the search box and click the Search icon. Once a topic is located, you can click a link to open it. Explanations and step-by-step instructions for specific procedures will be presented. To access a subject or topic, click the subject links to display the subtopic links, and then click a subtopic link to display Help information for that topic.

In this exercise, you will learn how to insert a footer using Word help and then add a footer to the meeting minutes.

To Search Help for Information about the Ribbon in Word

a. On the Word title bar, click **Microsoft Word Help** ⁇ . The Word Help window opens.

SIDE NOTE

Help Shortcut

For those who prefer keyboard shortcuts, pressing F1 is the shortcut to access Help.

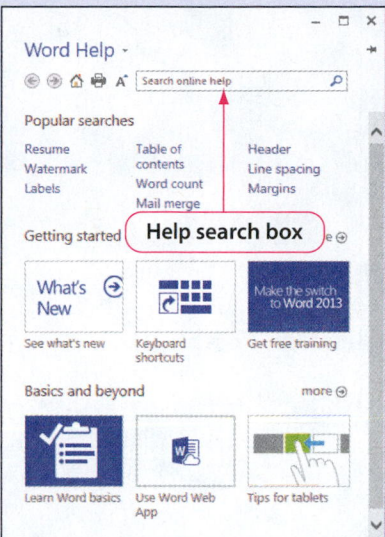

Figure 27   Word Help window

b. Click in the **Search** box or if you are online, the box will display **Search online help**. Type *add a footer* and then press Enter.

c. The Help window displays a list of the topics related to the keyword "footer". Scroll through the list to review the Help topics. Click the **Add a header or footer** from the list of results, and then read the information.

d. On the Help window title bar, click **Close** ✕ to close the window. Now that you know how to add a footer, you will add a footer to your Word document.

e. Click the **INSERT** tab, and then in the Header & Footer group, click **Footer**. Click **Blank**. Notice a footer is added at the bottom of your document.

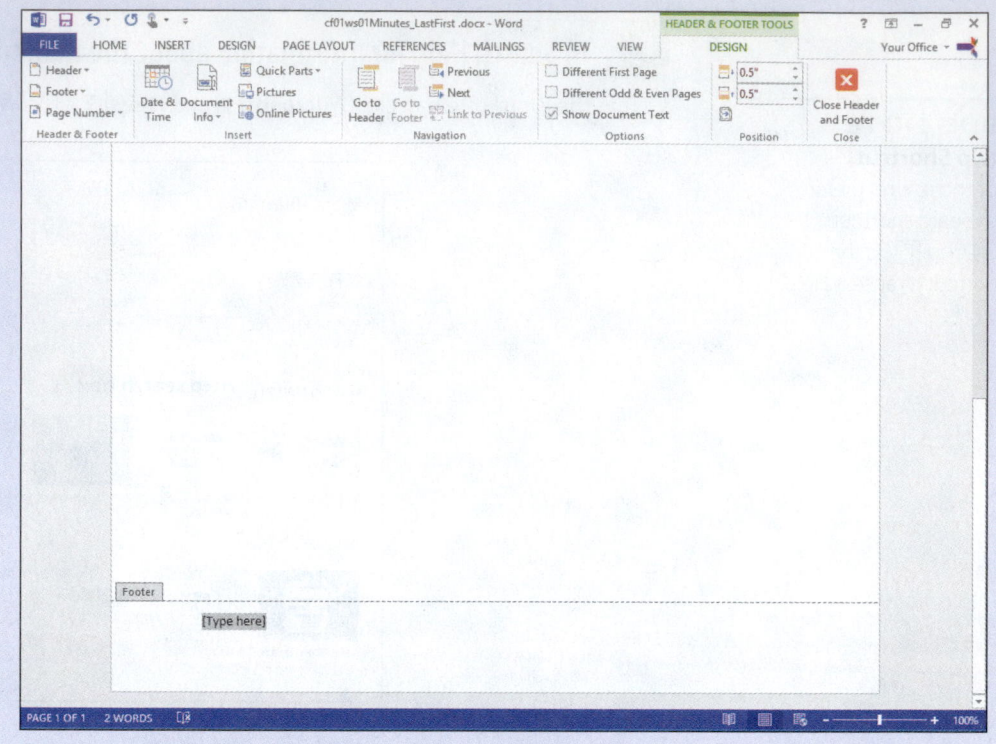

Figure 28 Document with blank footer inserted

f. On the HEADER & FOOTER TOOLS DESIGN tab, in the Insert group, click the **Document Info** button, and then select **File Name**. Notice Word inserts the name of the file.

g. On the HEADER & FOOTER DESIGN tab, in the Close group, click **Close Header and Footer**.

Using ScreenTips

ScreenTips are small windows that display descriptive text when you rest the mouse pointer over an object or button. You can point to a button or object in one of the Office applications to display its ScreenTip. In addition to the button's name, a ScreenTip might include the keyboard shortcut if one is available, a description of the command's function, and possibly more information.

In this exercise, you will use a ScreenTip to center the title of the meeting minutes.

CF01.18

 **To Open ScreenTips and Topic-Specific Help**

a. Press `Ctrl` + `Home` to place the insertion point right before **Painted Treasures**.

b. On the HOME tab, in the Paragraph group, hover the mouse over the **Center** button ≡. The ScreenTip is displayed with the button's name, its keyboard shortcut, and a brief description.

SIDE NOTE
ScreenTip and `F1`
If a topic for a ScreenTip does not exist in Help, the window will open to the starting search page.

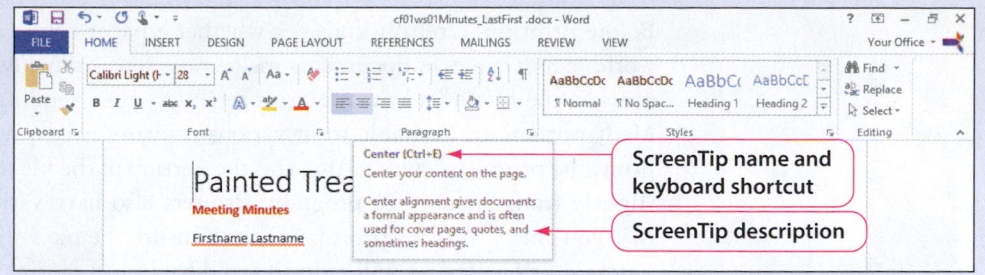

Figure 29   Center button Screen tip

c.   Click the **Center** button ☰ to center the Painted Treasures title.

d.   On the HOME tab, in the Clipboard group, point to the **Format Painter** 💅 to display the ScreenTip. With the mouse pointer still over the **Format Painter** 💅 and the ScreenTip showing, press F1 and notice that the Help window opens with information on how to use the Format Painter. Scroll down and read through the information.

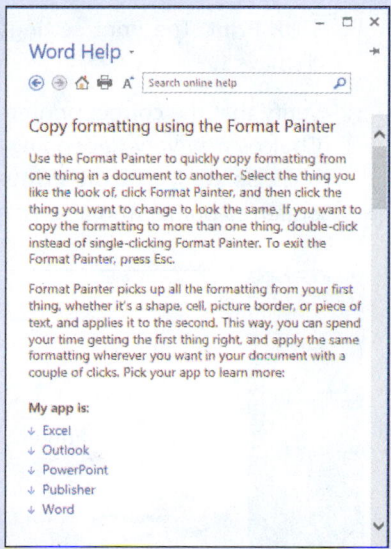

Figure 30   Format Painter Word Help

e.   When you are finished reading, click the **Close** ☒ button in the top-right corner of the Word Help window. You do not need to use the Format Painter at this time.

f.   Press Ctrl+S to save the document.

Print and Share Files

In Office 2013, many ways exist for sharing files. There are times you will need a paper copy, also known as a hard copy, of an Office document, spreadsheet, or presentation. When a printed version is not needed, a digital copy will save paper and costs. Office 2013 provides many ways to share your document. You can use traditional ways of sharing by printing or exporting a PDF. You can also save it to SkyDrive, invite others to share the document, and specify whether others are allowed to edit the document. From inside of Office Backstage View, the document can be e-mailed to others, transformed into an online, browser-not-required presentation, or posted to a blog.

Printing a File

Before printing, carefully consider whether a paper copy is necessary. Even in the digital world, paper copies of documents make more sense in many situations. Always review and preview the file and adjust the print settings before sending the document to the printer. Many options are available to fit various printing needs, such as the number of copies to print, the printing device to use, and the portion of the file to print. The print settings vary slightly from program to program. Printers also have varied capabilities. It is advisable that you check the file's print preview to ensure the file will print as you intended. Doing a simple print preview will help to avoid having to reprint your document, workbook, or presentation, which requires additional paper, ink, and energy resources.

In this exercise, you will print the start of the meeting minutes document to hand-write notes on during the meeting.

CF01.19

 To Print a File

a.   In Word, click the **FILE** tab to open Office Backstage View.

b.   Click **Print**. The Print settings and Print Preview appear. Verify that the Copies box displays **1**.

c.   Verify that the correct printer—as directed by your instructor—appears as the Printer. Choices may vary depending on the computer you are using. If the correct printer is not displayed, click the **Printer** button arrow, and then click to choose the correct or preferred printer from the list of available printers.

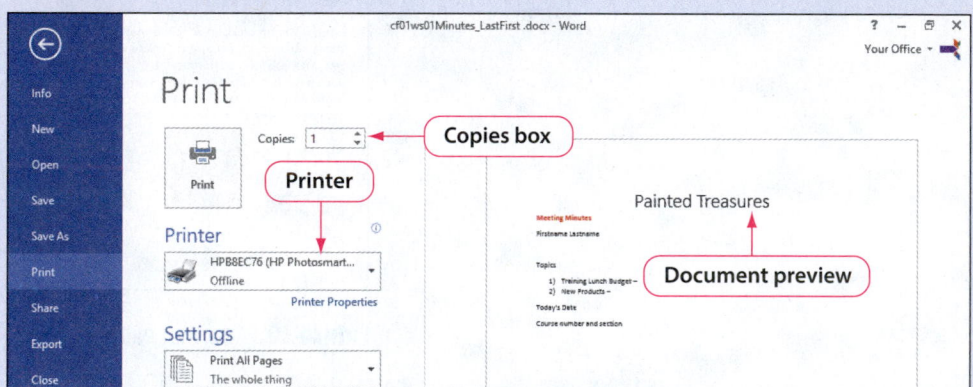

Figure 31   Printing settings

d.   If your instructor asks you to print the document, click **Print**.

Exporting a PDF

When you want to give someone else a document, consider whether an electronic version of the file is better than a printed copy. A **portable document format—PDF—** is a type of document that ensures the document will look the same on someone else's computer. For example, different computers may have different fonts installed. A PDF maintains the font. Even if the computer viewing the file does not have the same fonts as the computer used to create the file, the viewer will see the correct font. Further, PDFs are a common file format used in business to share documents because of the readily available free readers.

In this exercise, you will export a PDF of the meeting minutes and e-mail a copy to a colleague who is also attending the meeting.

CF01.20

 To Export a PDF

a. Click the **FILE** tab to open Office Backstage View.

b. Click **Export**, and then click **Create PDF/XPS**.

c. Navigate to the location where your student files are stored. Verify the file name selected is **cf01ws01Minutes_LastFirst**. Notice settings in the Publish as PDF or XPS dialog box for optimizing for online verses printing publishing. Since your colleague will print this document, the default setting of Standard is appropriate.

d. Click **Publish**. Close the **PDF** file.

CONSIDER THIS | **Sending Files Electronically**

Sending an electronic file can be easier and cheaper than sending a printed copy to someone. What should you consider when deciding the type of file to send? When you send an application specific file, such as Word or Excel, what happens if the recipient does not have the application installed? When you send a PDF, how easy is it for a recipient to edit a document? How does the file type affect the quality of a recipient's printout?

Understanding the Cloud and Touch Integration

Over the past few years, cloud networks and touch screens started to proliferate the market. Thus, Office 2013 made many changes to allow Office to work better with these technologies. If you have never used any cloud technology, Office 2013 makes SkyDrive easy to use and provides some free storage space. If you do not have a touch screen, you can still take advantage of touch technology with a Windows 8 mouse that accepts touch gestures. Over the next several years, these technologies will become standard for most computers and devices. In this next section, you will learn about using SkyDrive and touch features.

Use Windows SkyDrive

When you use computing resources—either hardware or software—of another computer over a network, you are using **cloud computing**. The cloud uses economies of scale by combining the power of many computers. One example of cloud computing is online file storage and syncing—services such as SkyDrive, DropBox, or Box. Some services, such as SkyDrive, also allow you to edit the document online through a browser or to collaborate with simultaneous document editing. Specifically, **SkyDrive** is an online cloud computing technology that offers a certain amount of collaborative storage space free that is integrated with Office 2013.

Traditionally for file storage, files are saved locally on a hard drive or external storage device like a USB drive. A **USB drive** is a small and portable storage device—popular for moving files back and forth between a lab, office, and/or home computer. However, USBs are also easily lost. Further, file versions and backups are usually manually maintained causing versioning problems.

File storage cloud technologies are made possible through Apps that sync all the files for all of your devices. When you edit a file, your computer or device automatically updates the file in the online storage location. All of the other computers and devices check the online storage for changes and update as needed. Thus, when saving your file, you automatically place a copy online and in all of your synced computers. This creates an online backup if your computer crashes. Additionally, there is no USB drive to lose. File-versioning problems are also minimized. Once all applications are properly set up, you have your files everywhere you want them and shared with exactly who needs them without having copies of files around or e-mailing attachments.

REAL WORLD ADVICE	Backing Up the Cloud

Best practice still dictates bringing files to important meetings on a physical drive such as a USB drive as backup. Cloud technologies are dependent on an Internet connection. Nothing is worse than showing up for a presentation and you cannot get to your files because of a poor Internet connection.

The Save As option in Office Backstage View gives you direct access to SkyDrive, which you can access with the same Microsoft account discussed earlier in the workshop—except Access, which requires you to save locally. With SkyDrive Apps or SkyDrive Pro, you have a local folder directly accessible from the File Explorer that automatically syncs with SkyDrive. Thus, you can sync Access files in the local syncing SkyDrive folder.

Microsoft has designed Office 2013 and SkyDrive to complement one another. When Office 2013 is not available on the computer you are using, you can even view, download, upload, and perform some limited revision via a browser at SkyDrive.com.

Creating a Document on SkyDrive

To use SkyDrive, you need your Microsoft account. After you sign in, you can create new folders and save files into the folders. You will need to have Internet access to complete this exercise.

CF01.21

 To Create a New Document at SkyDrive

a. On the taskbar, click **Internet Explorer** to open Internet Explorer; or alternatively, from the search screen, search for Internet Explorer to open the program.

b. In the address bar type skydrive.live.com.

c. If prompted, log in with your Microsoft account created earlier in the workshop.

d. Click **Create**, and then click **Word document** to create a new document.

e. Type cf01ws01SkyDrive_LastFirst using your last and first name, and then click **Create**.

f. Type your first name and last name, and then press Enter.

g. Type List of New Gift Shop Products. You intend to edit the list and share it will all employees after the meeting.

h. Click the **FILE** tab, and then click **Save**.

i. To return to your SkyDrive folders, click **Exit** [x] in the top-right corner of the document.

j. Explore the SkyDrive browser interface. To add a file you previously saved, click **Upload**. To delete a file from the folder, select the check box in the top-right corner of the file's tile, click **Manage** from the menu across the top, and then click **Delete**. To share a file, select the check box in the top-right corner of the file's tile, and then click **Share**. Follow the prompts for sharing.

k. Click your **name or picture**—located in the top-right corner—and then click **Sign Out** to exit SkyDrive. Close Internet Explorer.

Roaming Settings

Office 2013's **roaming settings** are a group of settings that offer easy remotely synced user-specific data that affects the Office experience. Across logins these settings remain the same. When signing into Office 2013, the user will experience Office the same way, no matter whether they are on a desktop, a laptop, or a mobile device.

Office 2013 includes the following roaming settings: Most Recently Used List (MRU) Documents and Places, MRU Templates, Office Personalization, Custom Dictionary, List of Connected Services, Word Resume Reading Position, OneNote—custom name a notebook view, and in PowerPoint the Last Viewed Slide.

Word Resume reading appears when you reopen a document. You are given a choice to keep reading where you left off. Word remembers where you were—even when you reopen an online document from a different computer.

Inserting Apps for Office

To enhance the features of Office, Office 2013 is the first version of Office to allow you to install apps from Microsoft's Office Store—**Apps for Office**, as shown in Figures 32 and 33. These apps run in the side pane to provide extra features like web search, dictionary, and maps. You will have to create an account to take advantage of them. You must be running Office 2013, and you must be signed into Office with your Microsoft Account.

1. Open up any Office applications in which you want to use apps.
2. Go to the Insert tab, and then select Apps for Office. Select See All from the menu.
3. The Apps for Office window appears showing all the apps you have installed to your Microsoft account under My Apps. If you see the app you want, select the app, and then click Insert.
4. If you do not see the app you want, click the Find more apps at the Office Store link.
5. Search for the app you want, and then follow the steps online to install the app to your account. You may have to sign into your Microsoft account.
6. Once installed, return to the Office application and repeat steps 2 and 3.

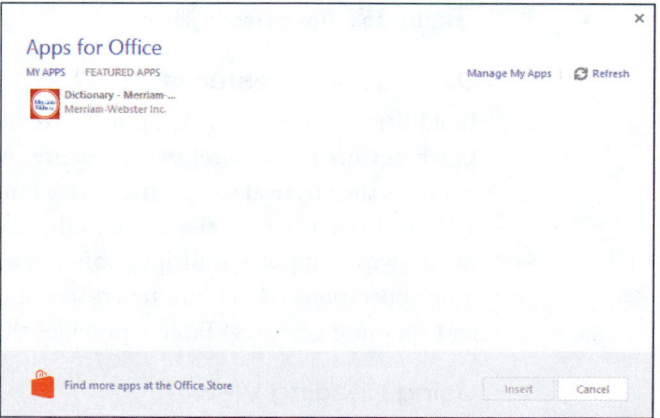

Figure 32   Apps for Office window with one app installed

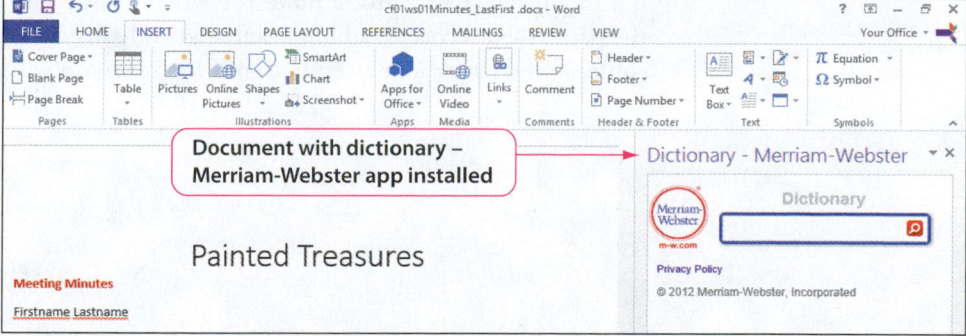

Figure 33   Dictionary - Merriam-Webster app

Use Touch Mode, Gestures, and Reading Mode

Office touch integration is based on the gestures underlying Windows 8 **touch gestures**. Microsoft provides an Office Touch Guide on the website and in Help by searching for Gesture Guide. The main gestures used are: tap, pinch, stretch, slide, and swipe. On a desktop with a touch-screen monitor, you can change this behavior back to the more traditional page navigation mode if you wish.

Using Touch Mode

Touch mode switches Office into a version that makes a touch screen easy to use. Click the Touch Mode button 👆 on the Quick Access Toolbar, and the Ribbon toolbar spreads its icons further apart for easier access to fingers. When you toggle this display mode, the on-screen controls space out a bit from each other to make them more accessible to users via touch. Figure 34 displays the normal Word 2013 Ribbon. Figure 35 displays the Ribbon in touch mode.

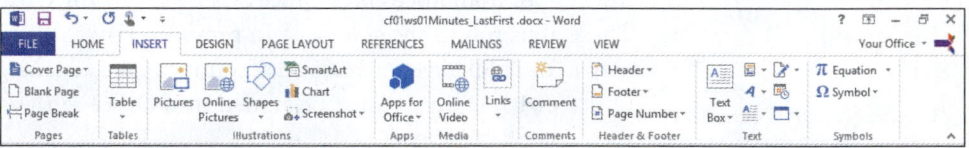

Figure 34   Normal Ribbon

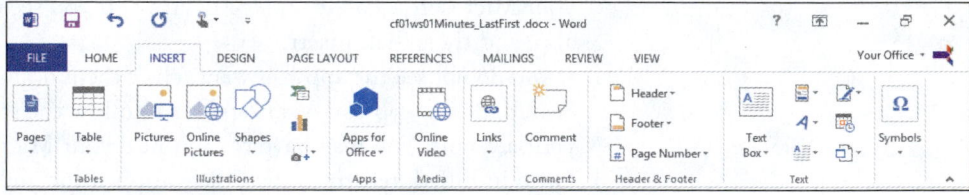

Figure 35   Touch mode Ribbon

Using Touch Gestures

In addition to the main tap, pinch, stretch, slide, and swipe gestures, another common touch gesture is the bezel swipe gesture. A **bezel swipe gesture** is started on the bezel, which is the physical touch-insensitive frame that surrounds the display. The user swipes a finger from a part of the display edge into the display. Depending upon the device, a bezel swipe supports multiple object selection such as cutting, copying, pasting, and other operations on mobile touch-screen devices without conflicting with the panning and zooming gestures. Table 4 provides the Microsoft touch gestures guide.

Using Reading View

The new Reading View in Word 2013 is optimized for touch screens. By swiping your finger horizontally, you can navigate through the document. If you are reading, not writing or editing, **Read Mode** hides the writing tools and menus to leave more room for the pages themselves. Read Mode automatically fits the page layout to your device, using columns and larger font sizes, both of which you can adjust.

To	Gestures Steps
Enter full screen	1. Tap the Ribbon Display Options button in the top-right corner. 2. Tap Auto-hide Ribbon.
Enter standard view	1. Tap the Ribbon Display Options button. 2. Tap Show Tabs and Commands.
Show or hide touch keyboard	1. Tap the Touch Keyboard button to show. 2. Tap the Close button on the Touch keyboard to hide.
Scroll	1. Touch the document. 2. Move finger up and down while maintaining contact.
Zoom in and out	1. Stretch two fingers to zoom in. 2. Pinch two fingers to zoom out.
Place the cursor insertion point	1. Tap the location for the cursor.
Select and format text	1. Tap. 2. Drag the selection handle to desired selection. 3. Tap the selection to show and use the Mini toolbar.
Edit an Excel cell	1. Double-tap.
Change PowerPoint slides in Normal view	1. Make a quick vertical flick.

Table 4 Microsoft's Touch Gestures Guide

CF01.22

To Use and Close Read Mode

a. Click the **VIEW** tab, and then in the Views group, click **Read Mode**. Notice this is the same view that protected documents are in when opened.

SIDE NOTE
Alternative Method
On the status bar, click the Read Mode icon. Click Print Layout View to exit Read Mode.

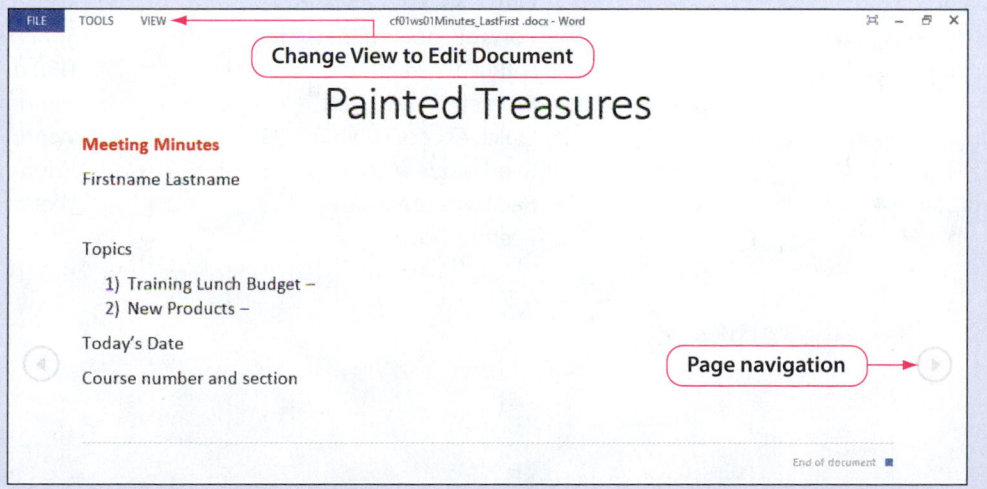

Figure 36 Meeting Minutes in Read Mode

b. Click the **VIEW** menu, and then select **Edit Document** to exit reading mode.

c. Press Ctrl+S. Then, click **Close** ✕ in the top-right corner. Notice that the file closes and you exit the Word application.

Concept Check

1. What kind of Microsoft account and program do you need to create a budget? p. 4–6

2. What is the difference between the Windows and Word Start screens? p. 7–8

3. Which tab on the Ribbon would you use to change the margins in a Word document? p. 15

4. Explain the main purpose of Office Backstage View. p. 24

5. Describe ways to obtain help in Office 2013. p. 30–33

6. How could you share a newsletter with all the members of your business fraternity without printing? p. 33–35

7. What are the advantages of using SkyDrive instead of a USB flash drive? p. 35–36

8. What features in Office 2013 make using a touch screen easier? p. 38

Key Terms

Application Start screen   7
Apps for Office   37
AutoRecovery   24
Bezel swipe gesture   38
Bootcamp   6
Charms   7
Close   12
Cloud computing   35
Contextual tab   20
Contextual tools   20
Dialog box   19
Dialog Box Launcher   19
Document   4
Exit   12
File extension   25
Gallery   18
Graphic   4
Help   30

Information management
   program   4
Key tip   18
Keyboard shortcut   18
Live Preview   18
Maximize   12
Mini toolbar   21
Minimize   12
Most Recently Used list   28
Office 365   5
Office Backstage View   24
Portable document format
   (PDF)   34
Protected View   28
Quick Access Toolbar   25
Read Mode   38
Relational database   4
Restore Down   12

Ribbon   14
Ribbon display options   12
Roaming settings   37
ScreenTip   32
Shortcut menu   23
SkyDrive   35
Table   4
Task pane   20
Thumbnail   11
Toggle buttons   16
Touch gestures   38
Touch mode   38
USB drive   35
Windows Phone   5
Windows Run Time (RT)   5
Windows Start screen   7
Workbook   4

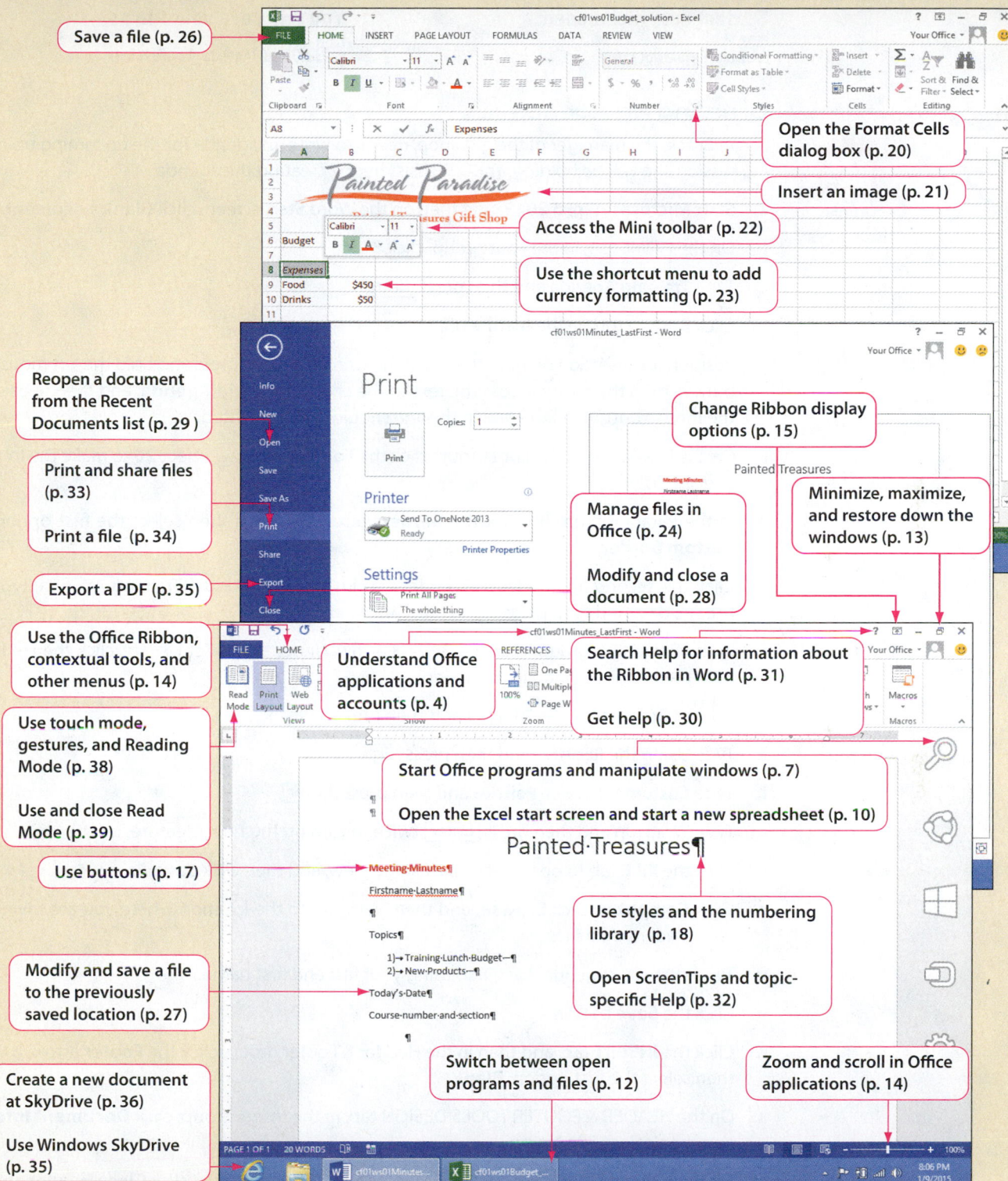

Save a file (p. 26)

Open the Format Cells dialog box (p. 20)

Insert an image (p. 21)

Access the Mini toolbar (p. 22)

Use the shortcut menu to add currency formatting (p. 23)

Reopen a document from the Recent Documents list (p. 29)

Print and share files (p. 33)

Print a file (p. 34)

Export a PDF (p. 35)

Use the Office Ribbon, contextual tools, and other menus (p. 14)

Use touch mode, gestures, and Reading Mode (p. 38)

Use and close Read Mode (p. 39)

Use buttons (p. 17)

Modify and save a file to the previously saved location (p. 27)

Create a new document at SkyDrive (p. 36)

Use Windows SkyDrive (p. 35)

Change Ribbon display options (p. 15)

Minimize, maximize, and restore down the windows (p. 13)

Manage files in Office (p. 24)

Modify and close a document (p. 28)

Search Help for information about the Ribbon in Word (p. 31)

Get help (p. 30)

Understand Office applications and accounts (p. 4)

Start Office programs and manipulate windows (p. 7)

Open the Excel start screen and start a new spreadsheet (p. 10)

Use styles and the numbering library (p. 18)

Open ScreenTips and topic-specific Help (p. 32)

Switch between open programs and files (p. 12)

Zoom and scroll in Office applications (p. 14)

Figure 37 Painted Paradise Resort and Spa Employee Training Preparation Complete

Student data file needed:
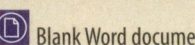 Blank Word document

You will save your file as:
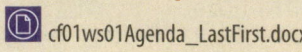 cf01ws01Agenda_LastFirst.docx

Creating an Agenda

Human Resources

Susan Brock, the manager of the gift shop, needs to write an agenda for the upcoming training session she will be holding. You will assist her by creating the agenda.

a. Start **Microsoft Word 2013**, and then on the Word Start screen, click **Blank document**.

b. On the HOME tab, in the Font group, click **Bold**.

c. Type Training Agenda and then press Enter.

d. Click **Bold** to toggle the feature off.

e. Position the insertion point to the left of the word **Training**, press and hold the left mouse button, drag the cursor across the text to the end of the word **Agenda**, and then release the mouse button. All the text in the line should be highlighted.

f. On the HOME tab, in the Font group, click the **Font Size** arrow. Select **20** to make the font size larger.

g. In the Paragraph group, click the **Borders** arrow ⊞▾, and then select the first option, **Bottom Border**.

h. Click the second line under the border you just inserted. Under Training Agenda, type today's date and then press Enter twice.

i. In the Paragraph group, click the **Bullets** arrow. Under the Bullet Library, click the **circle** bullet—the third option in the gallery.

j. Type Welcome trainees 2:00 pm and then press Enter.

k. Type Using the Register and then press Enter.

l. Type Customer Service Policies and then press Enter.

m. Type Wrap-Up and then press Enter twice to turn off the bullet feature.

n. Click the **FILE** tab to open Office Backstage View, and then click **Save As**.

o. Click **Computer**, click **Browse**, and then Navigate to the location where you are saving your student data files.

p. Type cf01ws01Agenda_LastFirst, using your last and first name.

q. Click the **Save** button.

r. Click the **INSERT** tab, and then in the Header & Footer group, click the **Footer** arrow, and then select the first option, **Blank**.

s. On the HEADER & FOOTER TOOLS DESIGN tab, in the Insert group, click **Document Info**, and then select **File Name**.

t. On the HEADER & FOOTER TOOLS DESIGN tab, in the Close group, click **Close Header and Footer** to exit the footer.

u. Press Ctrl + S to save your changes.

v. Close the cf01ws01Agenda_LastFirst document, and then exit Word.

w. Submit your file as directed by your instructor.

Problem Solve 1

MyITLab® Grader
Homework 1

Student data files needed:

 cf01ps1Expense.xlsx

 cf01ps1Cookies.jpg

You will save your file as:

 cf01ps1Expense_LastFirst.xlsx

Finance & Accounting

Formatting an Expense Report

Recently, you opened a business with a few partners called Midnight Sweetness. With the slogan "No more starving late-night studies," the business specializes in delivering freshly baked cookies, brownies, and other sweet treats to local college students. Midnight Sweetness has been a huge success. Currently, you rent a small building that includes major kitchen appliances. Now, you and your partners are looking for a bank loan to expand your business. You are responsible for putting together an expense report from last month to include in the bank application.

a. Open the **cf01ps1Expense** workbook. Save it as cf01ps1Expense_LastFirst. Click **Enable Content** if necessary.

b. Click cell **A1**, and then change the font to **bold**, **20** point, and the standard color **Blue**.

c. Click cell **A2**, and then change the font to **bold**.

d. Click cell **B3**, and then type your first and last name.

e. Click cell **A5**, and then right-align the text.

f. Click cell **A6**, and then right-align the text.

g. Click cell **A16**, and then right-align the text.

h. Click cell **A8**, and then change the font to italic.

i. Select the range **B9:B16**, and then format the cells as **Currency** with **0** decimals.

j. Click cell **B15**, and then add a **double bottom border**.

k. Click cell **D1**, insert the image **cf01ps1Cookies**, and then set the image height to **3.5**.

l. Save and close the cf01ps1Expense_LastFirst workbook, and then exit Excel.

m. Submit your file as directed by your instructor.

Perform 1: Perform in Your Career

Student data file needed:

 Blank Excel workbook

You will save your file as:

 cf01pf1OfficeTraining_LastFirst.xlsx

Information Technology

Creating a Training Schedule

One of the managers you work for at a local real estate company—Hope Properties—has asked you to create a training schedule in Excel for several of the trainings he is planning to schedule. The trainings include Windows 8, Word 2013, Excel 2013, and PowerPoint 2013. The trainings will be offered on Mondays: January 13, January 27, February 10, and February 24, 2014. Each training is three hours in length with one hour between sessions. The first session starts at 9:00 am. There are two trainings per day. You will create an attractive schedule using features you worked with in this workshop.

a. Start **Excel**. Using the features of Excel, create a training spreadsheet that is attractive and easy to read. Some suggestions include the following.

- Create column headings for the application and date of training.
- Enter the session times in the cells where the application and date meet.
- Format the date as a long date.
- Format the column headings.
- Format a title for the workbook.
- Use bold, italics, and colors.

b. Save and Close the cf01pf1OfficeTraining_LastFirst workbook, and then exit Excel.

c. Submit your file as directed by your instructor.

Perform 2: Perform in Your Life

Student data files needed:

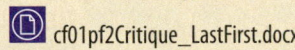 Blank Word document

cf01pf2Vintage.docx

cf01pf2Dinner.xlsx

You will save your file as:

cf01pf2Critique_LastFirst.docx

Improving the Appearance of Files

Finance & Accounting

Human Resources

Your boss at a local vintage clothing store has asked you to review a spreadsheet and a document—made by a prior employee—and make suggestions on what to do to improve the appearance of the document and spreadsheet. Examine the two files cf01pf2Vintage and cf01pf2Dinner. Answer the questions below.

a. Open a new blank document in Word, and then save the file as cf01pf2Critique_LastFirst.

b. List five items you would change in the document and why?

c. List five items you would change in the spreadsheet and why?

d. Exit Word, and then submit your file as directed by your instructor.

Additional Cases

Additional Workshop Cases are available on the companion website and in the instructor resources.

WORKSHOP 1 | THE FOUR MAIN DATABASE OBJECTS

Prepare Case

Red Bluff Golf Club Putts for Paws Charity Tournament

The Red Bluff Golf Club is sponsoring a charity tournament, Putts for Paws, to raise money for the Santa Fe Animal Center. An intern created a database to help run the tournament but did not finish it before leaving. You have been asked to finish the database to track the participants who enter the tournament, the orders they have placed, and the items they have purchased.

Production & Operations

Kati Molin / Shutterstock

REAL WORLD SUCCESS

"I used Access to create *ad hoc* reports for managers. My ability to quickly provide data has made me their 'go to' person."

 - Art, alumnus, materials analyst

Student data files needed for this workshop:

 a01ws01Putts.accdb

 a01ws01Participant.accdb

You will save your file as:

 a01ws01Putts_LastFirst.accdb

Understanding Database Basics and Tables

Businesses keep records about everything they do. If a business sells products, it keeps records about its products. It keeps records of its customers, the products it sells to each customer, and each sale. It keeps records about its employees, the hours they work, and their benefits. These records are collected and used for decision making, for sales and marketing, and for reporting purposes. A **database** is a collection of these records. The purpose of a database is to store, manage, and provide access to these business records.

In the past, many databases were paper based. Paper records were stored in files in file cabinets. Each file would be labeled and put in a drawer in a file cabinet. Elaborate filing schemes were developed so that one record could be located quickly. This was highly labor intensive and error-prone. Today, while most businesses use automated databases to store their records, you still see the occasional paper-based system. For example, your doctor's office may still use paper files for patient records.

Data are facts about people, events, things, or ideas, and they are an important asset to any organization as data allows companies to make better business decisions after converting it into useful information. **Information** is data that has been manipulated and processed to make it meaningful. For example, if you saw the number 2,000 out of context, the number has no meaning. If you are told that 2,000 represents the amount of an order in dollars, that piece of data becomes meaningful information. Businesses can leverage meaningful information to gain a competitive advantage, such as by providing discounts to those who order more expensive items. An automated database management system, such as Microsoft Access 2013, makes that possible.

Databases are used for two major purposes: for operational processing and for analytical purposes. In operational or transaction-based databases, each sale or transaction that a business makes is tracked. The information is used to keep the business running. Analytical databases are used for extracting data for decision making. The data in these databases are summarized and classified to make information available to the decision makers in the firms.

Automated databases provide many advantages over paper databases. The information in the databases is much easier to find in automated form. The information can be manipulated and processed more rapidly. Automated databases can be used to enforce accuracy and other quality standards. In today's fast-paced world, a business needs to manipulate information quickly and accurately to make decisions. Without today's automated databases, a business cannot compete. In this section, you will learn what Access is and learn about the four main object types in an Access database.

Understand What Access Is

Access is a relational **database management system (DBMS)** program created by Microsoft. It provides a tool for you to organize, store, and manipulate data, as well as to select and report on data.

Access stores data in tables. Similar data are stored in the same table. For example, if you are storing data about participants in an event, you would include all the participants' names, addresses, and telephone numbers in one table.

The power of a database system comes with the ability to link tables together. A separate table of purchases for the tournament can be linked with the participant table. This allows users to easily combine the two tables; for example, the tournament manager would be able to print out the participants with a record of their tournament purchases.

REAL WORLD ADVICE | What Advantage Does Using Access Give You?

There are many database management system (DBMS) software packages available. Why should you use Access?

- Access is an easily available DBMS. It is included with many Microsoft Office suites, which makes Access very attractive to businesses.

- Access is a relational DBMS. What you learn about Access is transferable to other relational DBMSs.

- Access allows for easy interaction with other products in the Office suite. You can export data and reports into Word, PowerPoint, or Excel. You can also import from Excel and Word into Access.

- Access is often used as a stand-alone DBMS, meaning a DBMS used by a single user. Even if a company uses another DBMS for many users, you can easily link to that database with Access. You can use Access queries to output the data you need to interact with other Office applications to perform tasks such as mail merges.

- Access allows you to create an app database and either give it to others or put it on the Windows App Store.

Understanding the Four Main Objects in a Database

Access has four main database **objects**: tables, queries, forms, and reports. A **table** is the database object that stores data organized in an arrangement of columns and rows. A **query** object retrieves specific data from other database objects and then displays only the data that you specify. Queries allow you to ask questions about the data in your tables. You can use a **form** object to enter new records into a table, edit or delete existing records in a table, or display existing records. The **report** object summarizes the fields and records from a table or query in an easy-to-read format suitable for printing.

QUICK REFERENCE | Access Object Types

There are four main database object types:

1. Table objects store data. Each row is a person, place, or thing. Each column is a field.

2. Query objects allow you to ask questions about your data. You can select, summarize, and sort data in a query.

3. Form objects give you a formatted way to add, modify, or delete data in your tables. They can also be used to display data.

4. Report objects provide an easy-to-read view of your data that is suitable for business purposes. Data in reports can be grouped, sorted, and totaled.

Access objects have several views. Each **view** gives you a different perspective on the objects and different capabilities. For example, the **Datasheet view** of a table shows the data contents within a table. Figure 1 shows Datasheet view of a participant table. **Design view** shows how fields are defined. Depending on the object, other views may exist. Figure 1 shows a toggle button you can use to switch between Datasheet view and Design view. Figure 2 shows how a participant table would appear in Design view.

In Datasheet view, you see the actual participants and their related information. In Design view, you see how the information is defined and structured. Figure 1 shows the charity event participant table. Each row contains corresponding pieces of data about the participant listed in that row. Each row in Access is called a **record**. A record is all of the data pertaining to one person, place, thing, or event. There are 17 participant records in the table. The second participant is John Trujillo.

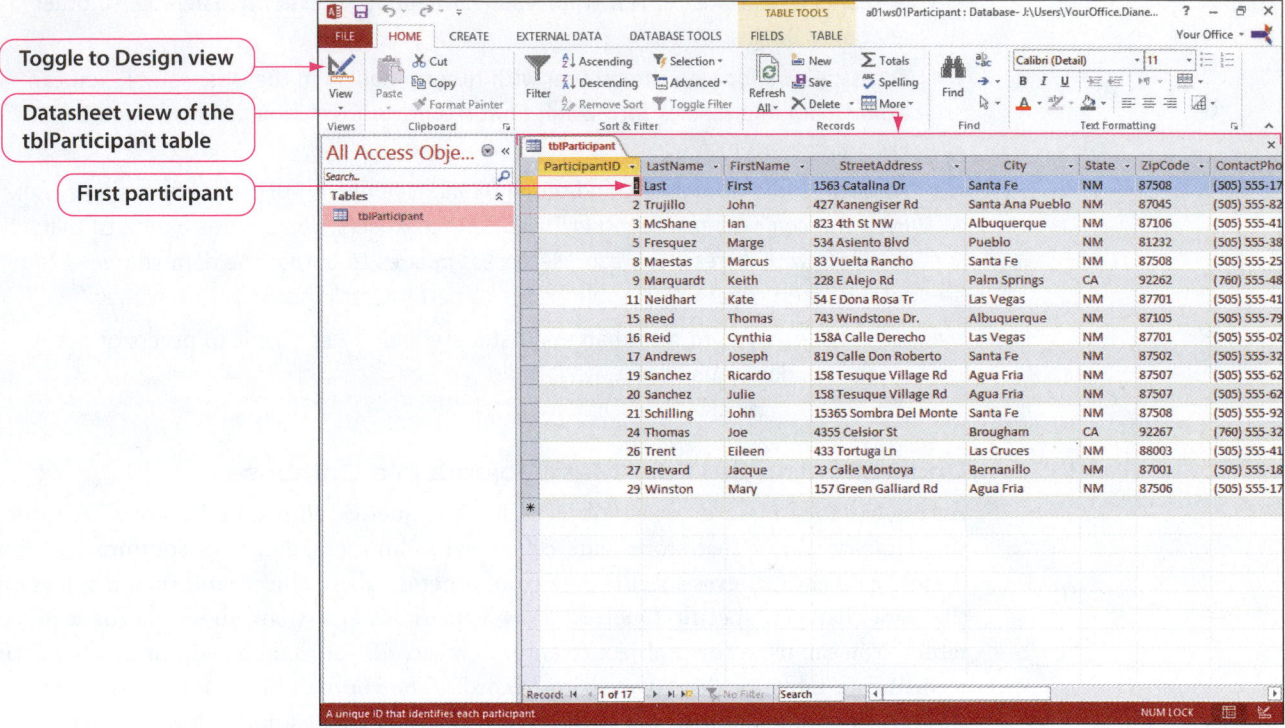

Figure 1 Datasheet view of the tblParticipant table

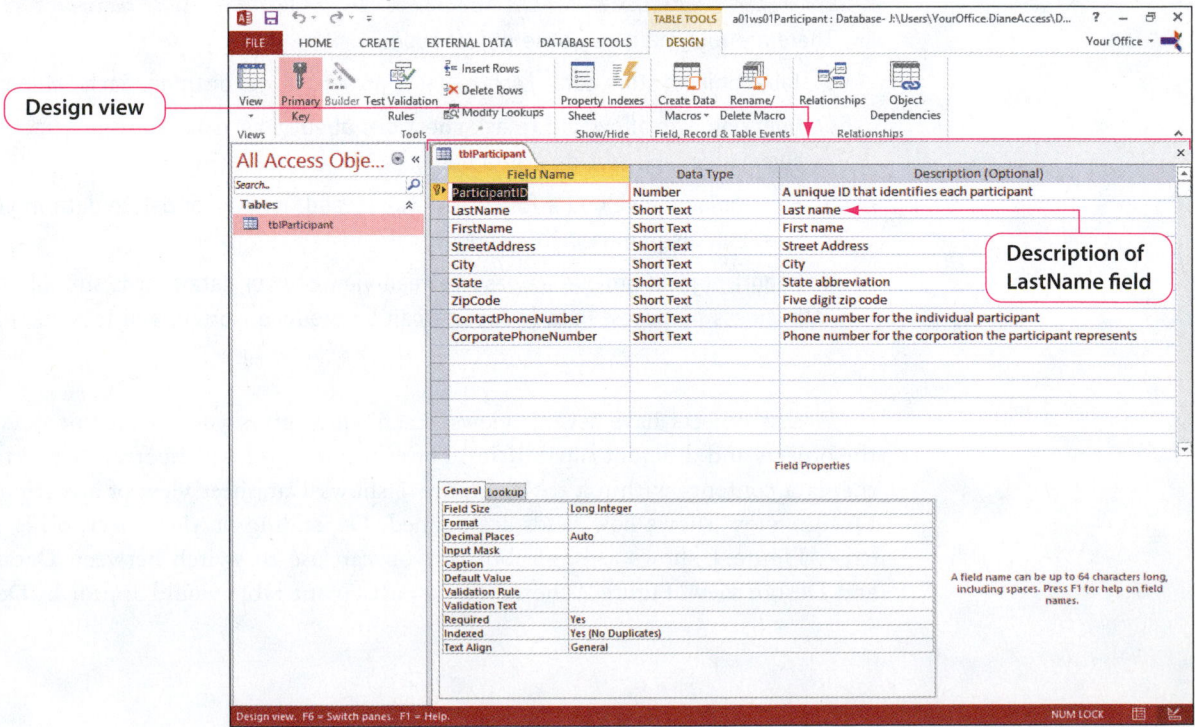

Figure 2 Design view of the tblParticipant table

Each column in Access is called a **field**. A field is a specific piece of information that is stored in every record. LastName is a field that shows the participant's last name. As you go across the table rows, you will see fields that represent the participant's first name and address.

Creating a New Database and Templates

When you create a new database, you can design it yourself starting with an empty database. If you take this approach, you develop the tables, fields, and the relationships—or links—between the tables. This requires you to decide what information you want to keep in your database, how this information should be grouped into tables, what relationships you need, and what queries and reports you need.

The other option in creating a new database is to start with a prebuilt template. A **template** is a structure of a database with tables, fields, forms, queries, and reports. Templates are professionally designed databases that you can either use as is or adapt to suit your needs. You can download a wide variety of templates from Microsoft's website Office.com. Microsoft provides sample database templates used for managing assets, contacts, issues, projects, and tasks.

Templates are created by Microsoft employees or other users. Microsoft then allows users to rate the template so you can see what others have found useful. You can also download sample databases to experiment with. The difference between a template and a sample database is that a sample database has presupplied data, whereas a template is empty except for the structure and definitions. One of the popular sample databases among Access users is Microsoft's Northwind database, which has sales, customer, and employee data for a fictitious company named Northwind Traders.

For the tournament, the intern created a new database and defined tables specifically for Putts for Paws. You will work with the database that has already been created. You need to start Access and open the database to get started.

SIDE NOTE

Do Not Confuse a DBMS with a Database

Access is DBMS software while a database is a collection of data. You could use paper files to manage your database, but you choose to use Access DBMS software instead.

A01.00

 To Start Access and Open a Database

a. From the Windows Start screen or desktop, point to the **bottom-right corner** of the screen. The Charms will be displayed on the right side of the screen.

b. Note the labels underneath each of the charms. Click the **Search** charm.

c. Click inside the **search** box at the top of the page. Type Access.

d. Click **Microsoft Access 2013** in the search results.

e. Click **Open Other Files** on the Access Start Screen, and then click **Computer**. Navigate to your student data files, click **a01ws01Putts**, and then click the **Open** button.

f. Click the **FILE** tab, and then click **Save As**. Under **File Types**, make sure **Save Database As** is selected. Under **Save Database As**, make sure **Access Database** is selected. Click **Save As**, and then navigate to the location where you are saving your files. In the **File name** box, type a01ws01Putts_LastFirst, using your last and first name. Click **Save**.

g. If the Security Warning message appears, click the **Enable Content** button.

REAL WORLD ADVICE | **Why Does Access Give You a Security Warning About Your Database?**

Access databases can contain dangerous code that can infect your computer with a virus. Therefore, Access displays a security warning asking you whether you trust the content of the database. Until you tell Access that you trust this content, Access disables features that might allow the virus to infect your computer.

- Make sure you run a virus scan on any file before you say it should be trusted. You do not want to trust content that you are unsure about.

- You can trust the content for a single use. Click Enable Content to say that you trust the file.

- To trust a database permanently, you can store it in a trusted location. Depending on your computer and operating system, certain locations are predefined as trusted. Click the File tab, click Options, and then select Trust Center for the Access Trust Center, where you can add other locations to the trusted locations.

Maneuver in the Navigation Pane

When you open a database, Access displays the **Navigation Pane** on the left side as shown in Figure 3. This pane allows you to view the objects in the database. The standard view in the Navigation Pane shows all objects in the database organized by object type. You can see that the database has three tables: tblItem, tblOrder, and tblOrderLine. There is one query, one form, and one report.

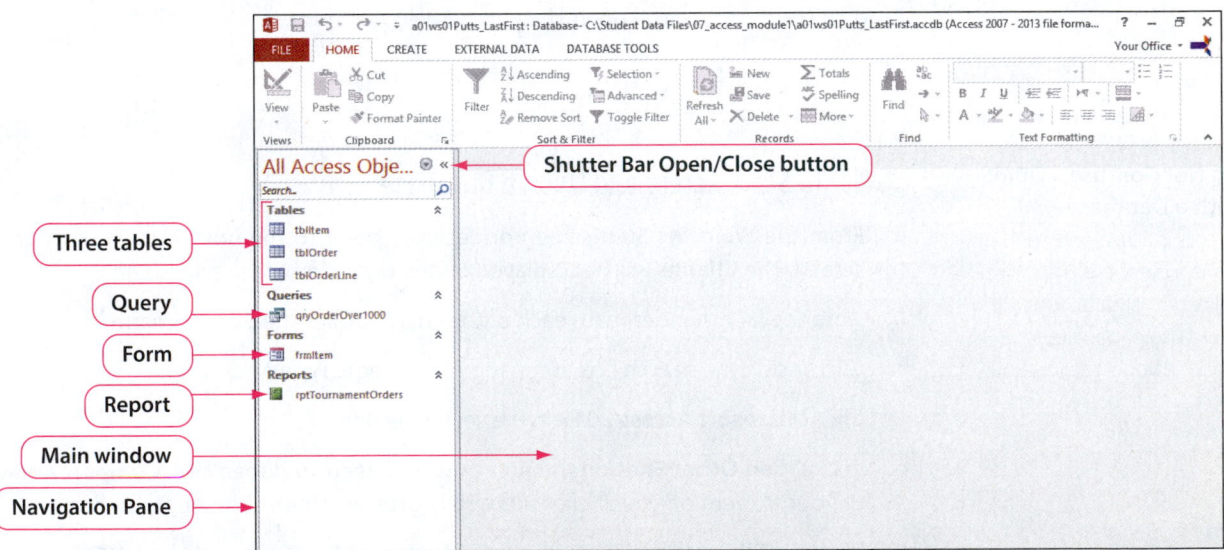

Figure 3 Opening screen for a01ws01Putts_LastFirst

Opening and Closing the Shutter Bar

You can work in Access with the Navigation Pane open or closed. The Shutter Bar Open/Close button at the top of the pane opens and closes the pane.

A01.01

▶ **To Open and Close the Navigation Pane**

a. Click the **Shutter Bar Close** button ⟨«⟩ to close the Navigation Pane. Access closes the pane, allowing for a larger workspace in the database, but it leaves the Navigation Pane on the side of the window for when you need it.

b. Click the **Shutter Bar Open** button ⟨»⟩ to open the pane again.

Customizing the Navigation Pane

While the default view of the Navigation Pane shows all objects such as tables, queries, forms, and reports, organized by object type, you have several choices of views.

A01.02

▶ **To Customize the Navigation Pane**

a. Click the **Navigation Pane** arrow ⊙ to display the Navigation Pane view options. The default view is displayed, which is Object Type and All Access Objects.

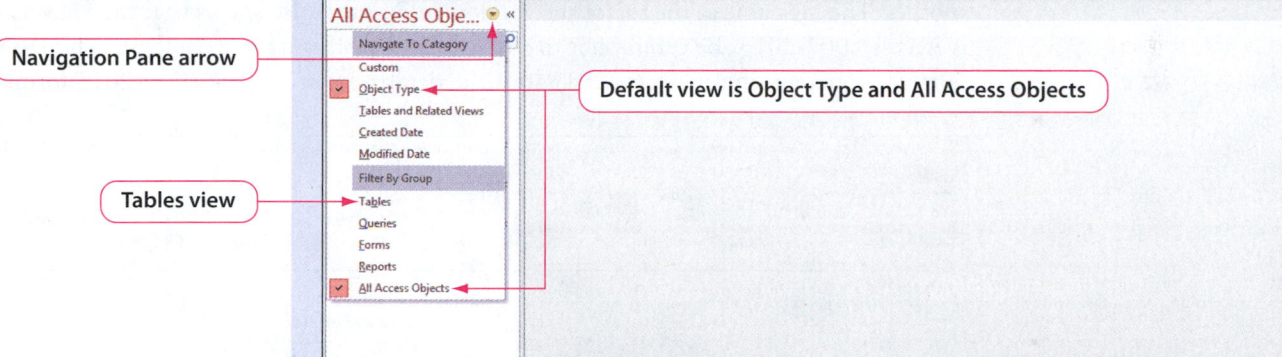

Figure 4 Navigation Pane options—default view

b. Click **Tables**.

Only the three tables are displayed in the Navigation Pane. When you have many objects in a database, it helps to restrict objects that are shown in the Navigation Pane.

c. Click the **Navigation Pane** arrow ⊙ again, and then click **Tables and Related Views**. The objects are organized by tables. Any query, report, or form related to a table is listed with that table.

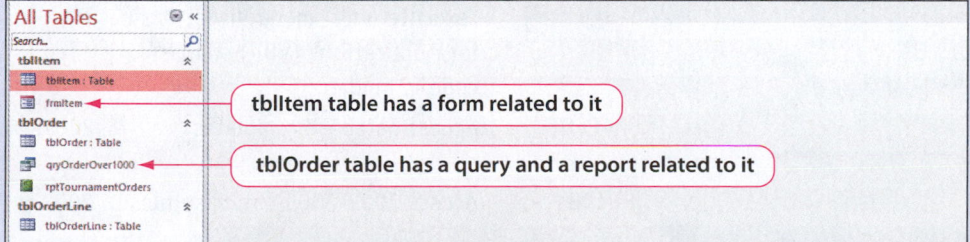

Figure 5 Tables and related views in Navigation Pane

Using the Search Box

Currently, there are only a few objects in your database. However, as you work with a database, more objects may be added as you develop reports and queries. As a result, to help you find objects, Access provides a Search box.

A01.03

⏵ To Search for an Object

a. In the **Search** box at the top of the **Navigation Pane**, type Order. Access searches for and displays all objects with the word **Order** in their name.

b. Click the **Clear Search String** button 🗙 to see all objects again.

c. Click the **Navigation Pane** arrow ⏷, click **Object Type**, click the **Navigation Pane** arrow ⏷ again, and then select **All Access Objects**. This returns you to the default view, which is what will be used throughout this text.

Understanding File Extensions in Access

A **file extension** is the suffix on all file names that helps Windows understand what information is in a file and what program should open the file. However, Windows automatically hides these extensions so you often do not notice them. The file name in Figure 6 shows the file name and location followed by its extension ".accdb". Access 2013 uses the same file extension that was used in Access 2010 and Access 2007. This ".accdb" extension indicates that databases created in the three versions are compatible with one another. The file name at the top of the window in Figure 6 also shows that the file version is Access 2007-2013. Be careful not to confuse the DBMS with the database. The DBMS software you are using is Access 2013, but the database is in Access 2007-2013 format.

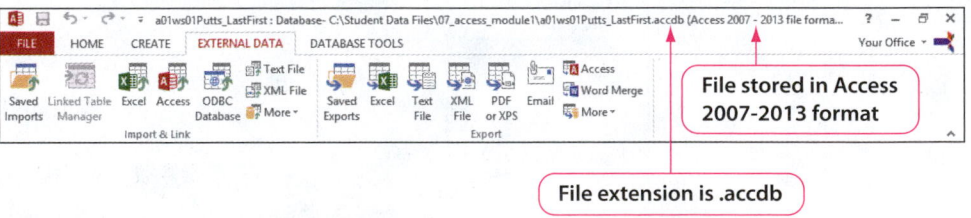

File stored in Access 2007-2013 format

File extension is .accdb

Figure 6 Title bar showing file extension

QUICK REFERENCE	Access File Extensions		
Extension	**Description**	**Version of Access**	**Compatibility**
ACCDB	Access database files	2007-2013	Cannot be opened in Access 2002-2003
ACCDE	Access database files that are in "execute only" mode Visual Basic for Applications (VBA) source code is hidden.	2007-2013	Cannot be opened in Access 2002-2003
ACCDT	Access database templates	2007-2013	Cannot be opened in Access 2002-2003
MDB	Access 2002-2003 database files	2002-2003	Can be opened in Access 2007-2013 Access 2007-2013 can save files in this format.
MDE	Access database files that are in "execute only" mode Visual Basic for Applications (VBA) source code is hidden.	2002-2003	Can be opened in Access 2007-2013 Access 2007-2013 can save files in this format.

Understand What a Table Is

Tables store data organized in an arrangement of columns and rows. For illustration, think about the charity event, Putts for Paws. There are many ways participants and companies can participate in the event and help the charity. For example, a participant can play in the event, a company can pay for a foursome to play in the event, or the company can sponsor various items such as a cart, hole, or flag. As a result, Painted Paradise needs to keep a record of the available options and what corporations or participants have purchased, as shown in Table 1.

Item ID	Item Description	Quantity Available	Amount To Be Charged	Notes
G1	Golfer—one	100	$200.00	
TEAM	Golfers—team of four	10	$550.00	
CTEAM	Golfers—corporate team of four	10	$850.00	Includes hole sponsorship
CART	Cart sponsor	40	$2,000.00	Logo or brand displayed on cart
HOLE	Hole sponsor	18	$500.00	Logo or brand displayed on hole
FLAG	Flag sponsor	18	$500.00	Logo or brand displayed on flagstick

Table 1 Data in the tblItem table

As mentioned previously, the power of a **relational database** comes when you link tables. A relational database is a database where data is stored in tables with relationships between the tables. The tblItem table shown in Table 1 contains information about items that a participant or corporation can buy to support the charity, including the items available, a description, the quantity available to be sold, the amount that will be charged for the item, and notes about the item. However, you cannot see who has ordered these items. That additional information becomes available when you use relationships to look at other tables.

Importing a Table

Recently, a colleague compiled a list of participants in the charity event in an Access table in another database. You will begin your work for Putts for Paws by importing this participant table from the Participant database into your database. **Importing** is the process of copying data from another file, such as a Word file or Excel workbook, into a separate file, such as an Access database.

A01.04

 To Import an Access Object

a. Click the **EXTERNAL DATA** tab, and then in the Import & Link group, click **Access**. The Get External Data - Access Database dialog box is displayed.

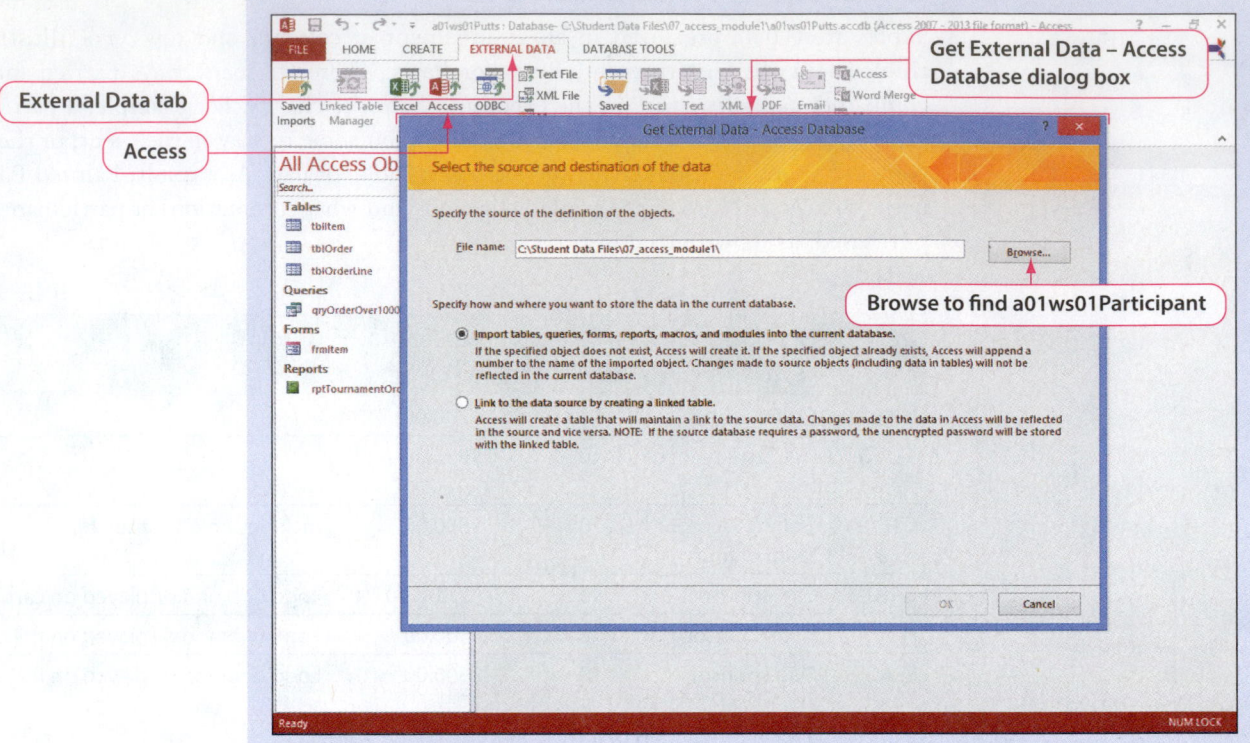

External Data tab

Access

Get External Data – Access Database dialog box

Browse to find a01ws01Participant

Figure 7   Get External Data – Access Database dialog box

b. Click **Browse**, navigate to your student data folder, and then select the **a01ws01Participant** database. Click **Open**, and then click **OK**. Access opens the Import Objects dialog box.

> **Troubleshooting**
>
> If you do not see the Import Objects dialog box, you may have chosen Access from the Export group on the Ribbon rather than from the Import & Link group.

c. If necessary, click the **Tables** tab. Click **tblParticipant**, and then click **OK**. Access displays the message: All objects were imported successfully.

d. Click **Close** at the bottom of the dialog box.

e. Double-click **tblParticipant** in the Navigation Pane.

Access opens the table. You may not see exactly the same number of columns and rows in your table because how much of the table is visible is dependent on how large your Access window is. You can change the size of the Access window by using your mouse to resize it or by clicking the Maximize button □ to maximize the Access window.

tblParticipant table

Highlighted ID shows the active record

Maximize Access window

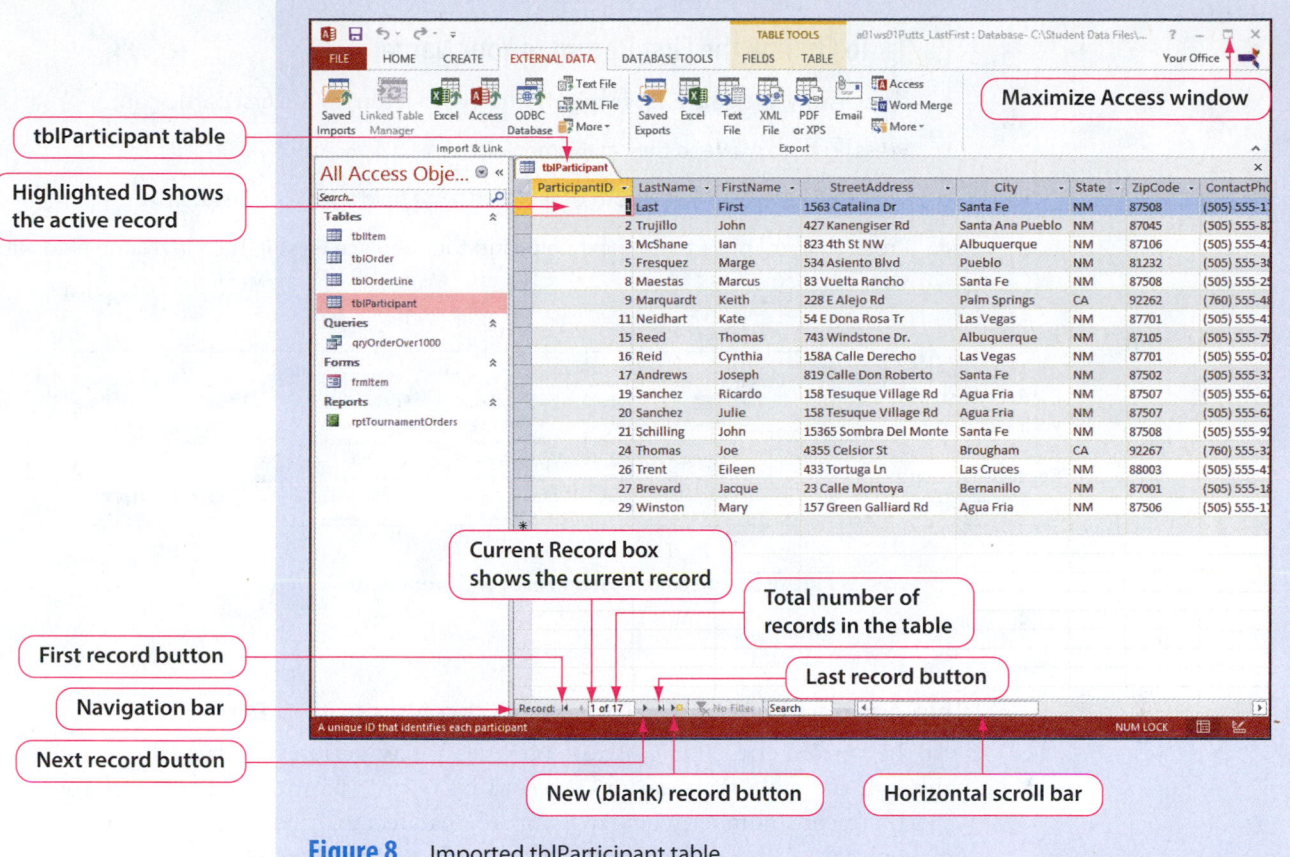

Current Record box shows the current record

Total number of records in the table

First record button

Last record button

Navigation bar

Next record button

New (blank) record button

Horizontal scroll bar

Figure 8 Imported tblParticipant table

REAL WORLD ADVICE | **What Should You Name Your Tables?**

If other people use the database and cannot find the right table, how useful is your database? Thus, you want to use names that are easy to understand. While Access allows you to give any name you want to a table, the name "tblParticipant" follows a standard naming convention:

- Use a name that starts with "tbl". That allows you to distinguish tables from queries at a glance.
- Follow with a name that is descriptive. You want it to be easy to remember what is in the table.
- Make the name short enough that it is easy to see in the Navigation Pane.
- You can use spaces in table names (e.g., tbl Participant), but avid Access users avoid them because it makes advanced tasks more difficult.
- You can use special characters in names. Some people use underscores where a space would otherwise be, such as tbl_Participant.

Navigating Through a Table

Carefully examine the tblParticipant table. Each row of data contains information about the participant listed in the LastName field. There are 17 participant records in the table, with the second record being John Trujillo. You will change the name in the record for the first participant to your name.

A01.05

To Change the First Record to Your Name

a. If necessary, click the **First record** button ⏮ to return to the first participant.

b. Press ⎚Tab⎚ to move to the LastName field.

c. Replace **Last** in the first record of the LastName field with your last name.

d. Press ⎚Tab⎚ to move to the next field, and then replace **First** in the FirstName field with your first name.

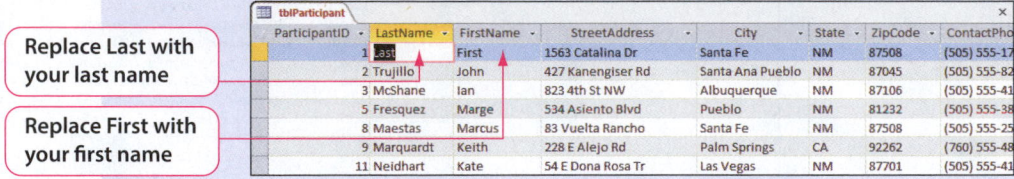

Replace Last with your last name

Replace First with your first name

Figure 9   Replace Last and First with your name

Navigating Through a Table with the Navigation Bar

At the bottom of the table, Access provides a **Navigation bar** that allows you to move through the table. You can move record by record, skip to the end, or if you know a specific record number, you can jump to that record. The highlighted ID shows the active record. When you open the table, the first record is active.

Examine the various parts of the Navigation bar as shown in Figure 8. The Current Record box shows which record is active and how many records are in the table. There are four arrow buttons in the Navigation bar that you can use to move between records.

 A01.06

To Navigate Through the Table Using the Navigation Bar

a. Click the **Next record** button ▶ to move to the second record. The **Current Record** box changes to show **2 of 17**. Access highlights the first name of participant John Trujillo.

b. Click the **Next record** button ▶ again to move to the third participant. The **Current Record** box changes to show **3 of 17**.

c. Click the **First record** button ⏮ to return to the first participant.

d. Click the **New (blank) record button** ⏭ to go to the first blank row. Alternatively, you could click in the ParticipantID field of the first blank row.

The first blank row at the end of the table is the **append row**. This row allows you to enter new records to the table. Notice that Access displays an asterisk in the **record selector** box—it is the small box at the left of the record—to indicate that it is the append row. When you type information here, you create a new participant record. Whenever you add a participant, you want to make sure you are in the append row so you are not changing the information for an existing participant. You will add a participant to this empty row.

Append row

Asterisk in the record selector box

Figure 10 Append a new record

e. Make sure that the append row (blank row) is selected and that the record selector box contains an asterisk. In the ParticipantID field, type **30**. Press [Tab] to move to the next field, and then in the **LastName** column, type **Fox**.

Alternatively, you can press [Enter] after typing text in a field to move to the next field. Also, notice that when you start typing, the record indicator changed from an asterisk to a pencil [✏]. The pencil means that you are in edit mode. The record after Fox now becomes the new append row. Press [Enter], and then in the FirstName column, type **Jeff**.

Record indicator is now a pencil

Enter Fox as LastName and Jeff as FirstName

Figure 11 Enter participant Jeff Fox into the append row

f. Continue entering the data for Jeff Fox using the following information:

StreetAddress	1509 Las Cruces Drive
City	Las Cruces
State	NM
ZipCode	88003
ContactPhoneNumber	(505) 555–8786
CorporatePhoneNumber	(leave blank)

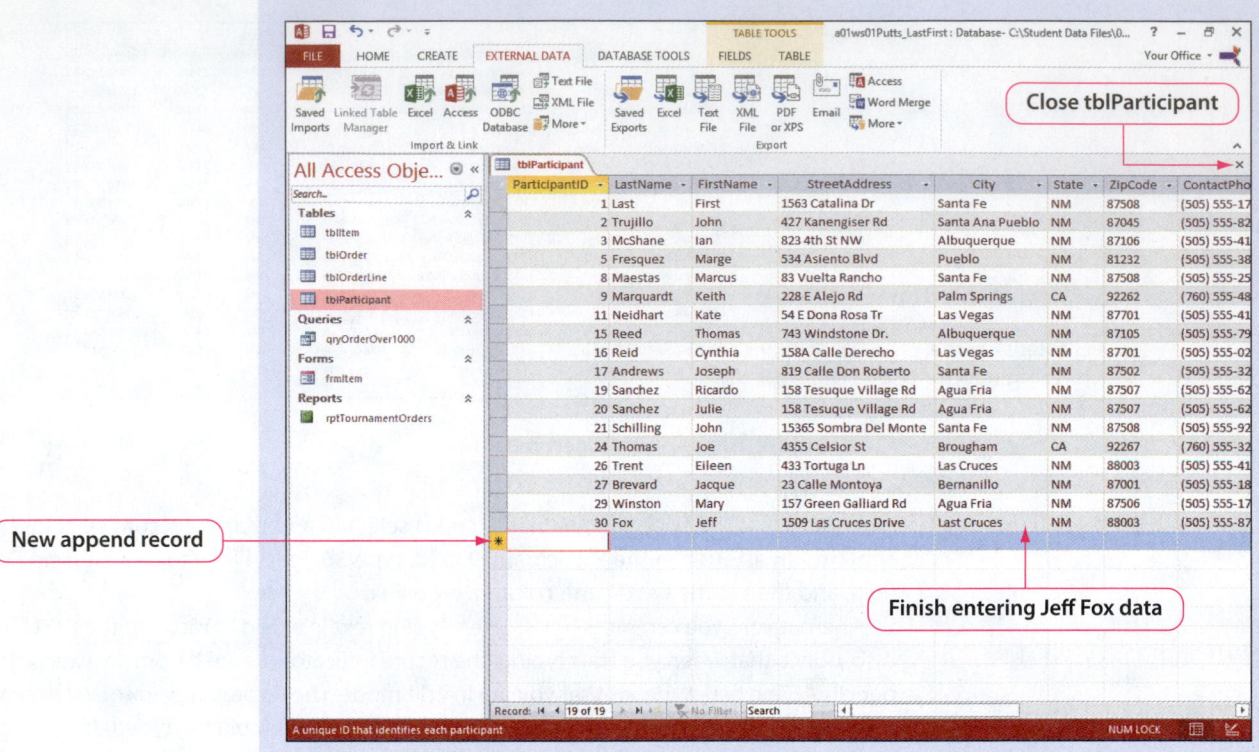

Figure 12 Finish entering the record for Jeff Fox

g. Click **Close** ✕ to close the tblParticipant table. Keep Access and the database open.
Notice that Access did not ask you if you want to save the table. Access is not like Word or the other Office applications where you must choose an option to save the file. Access automatically saves the data you enter as you type it.

Understanding Differences Between Access and Excel

An Access table looks similar to an Excel worksheet. Both have numbered rows of data and columns with labels. In addition, both applications allow you to manage data, perform calculations, and report on the data. The major difference between the two applications is that Access allows multiple tables with relationships between the tables, thus the term "relational database". For example, if you are keeping track of participants and the items that they order, you create a table of participants and another table of orders. Excel 2013 has some of these features so it now blurs the distinction between spreadsheets and relational databases.

When you look at Access, you notice that several tables are used for an order. Why use multiple tables for a single order? Figure 13 shows how an order would look in Access and in Excel. The Excel version has to repeat the participant's information on multiple lines. This leads to problems:

- Data redundancy—With repetition, you create redundant information. John Trujillo bought a cart and a team, so in Excel you have two rows. You would have to repeat the address information on both records. It is not efficient to enter the address information twice.

- Errors—Redundant information leads to errors. If the address needs to be changed, you have to look for all records with that information to make sure it is fixed everywhere.

- Loss of data—Suppose that John Trujillo orders just one item. If you deleted the ordered item, it would mean deleting all the information about him as well as the order.

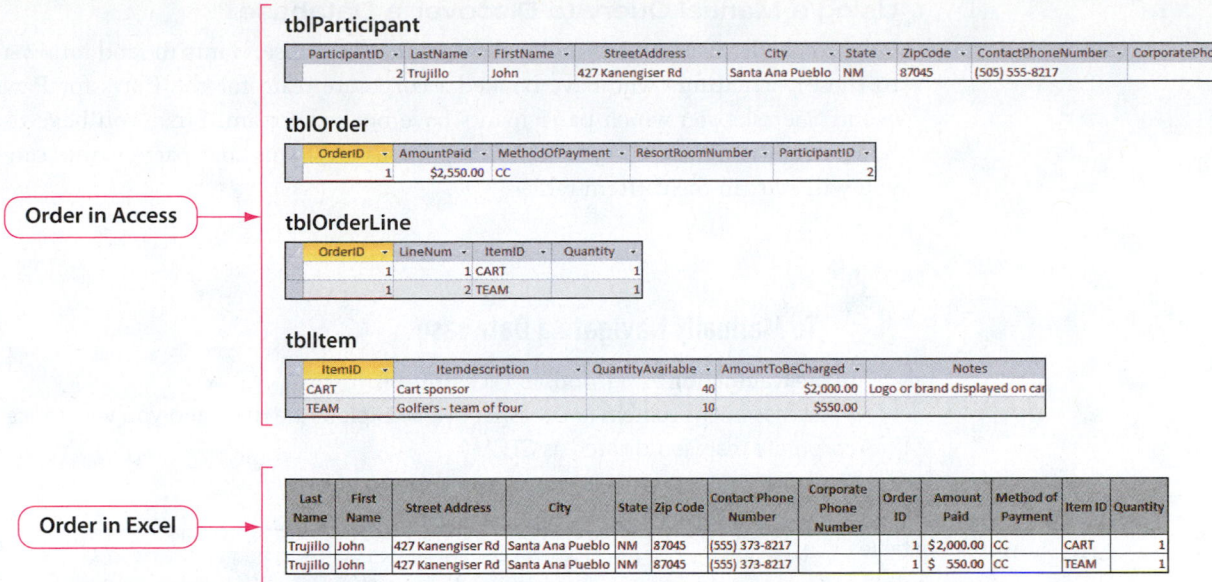

Order in Access

Order in Excel

Figure 13   John Trujillo's order in Access and in Excel

Because Access and Excel have so many common functionalities, many people use the tool that they are more confident using. If you prefer to use both, however, you can easily switch by exporting your data from Access to Excel or from Excel into Access. You can also use one tool for most uses and import your data into the other when you need to.

REAL WORLD ADVICE   When Do You Use Access Instead of Excel?

Generally, Access is designed to store data, and Excel is designed to analyze data and model situations. Fortunately, you can easily store data in Access and export a query to Excel for analysis.

Use Access for the following:

- You need to store data in multiple tables.
- You have a very large amount of data, as in thousands of records.
- You have large amounts of nonnumeric data.
- You want to run many different queries and reports from your data.
- You have multiple users accessing your data.

Use Excel for the following:

- Your data fits well into one table.
- You want to primarily do calculations, summaries, or comparisons of your data.
- You are using a report that you create just one time or in just one format.

Manually Navigate a Database

Before you explore the database using Access queries, you will explore the database manually. This will give you an understanding of what Access can do. Additionally, before you write queries and reports, you should examine your tables and fields so that you understand the database.

Using a Manual Query to Discover a Database

Patti Rochelle, the events coordinator at Painted Paradise, wants to send follow-up letters to those participants who have booked a corporate team for the Putts for Paws charity event. She asks you which participants have booked a team. First, you have to discover how a team is indicated in the database. Teams are items that participants can order, so you will start in the tblItem table.

A01.07

 To Manually Navigate a Database

a. In the **Navigation Pane**, double-click **tblItem**.

Access opens tblItem in Datasheet view. Explore the data, and you will notice that a corporate team is indicated as CTEAM.

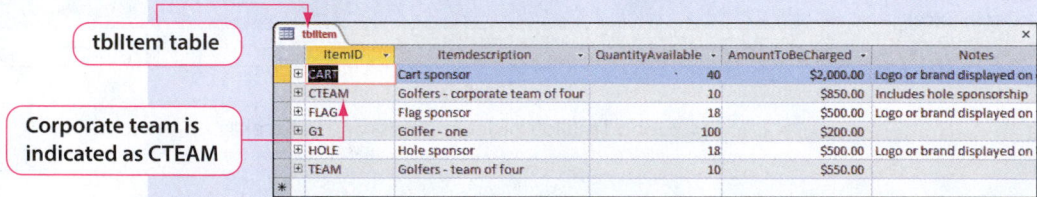

Figure 14   tblItem table

b. **Close** ☒ the tblItem table.

Next you need to determine which orders include CTEAM. Orders are composed of data from tblOrderLine and tblOrder.

c. Double-click **tblOrderLine** to open the table.

Scan for orders that include CTEAM. There are two, OrderID 4 and OrderID 11.

d. **Close** ☒ the tblOrderLine table.

e. Double-click **tblOrder** to open the table, and then find OrderID **4** and **11**.

You need to find which participants placed these orders. Access uses common fields to relate tables. tblParticipant and tblOrder have ParticipantID in common. You find that the ParticipantID for OrderID 4 is 5, and for OrderID 11 the ParticipantID is 19.

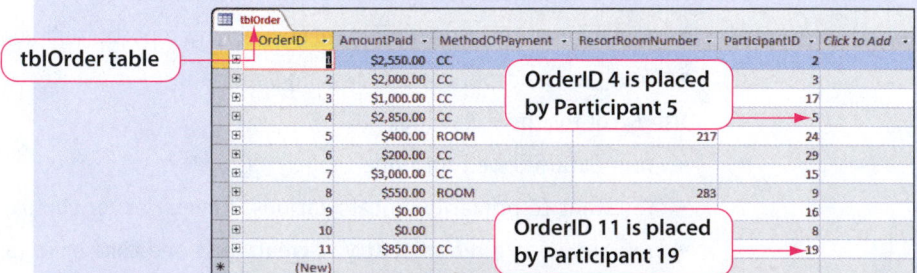

Figure 15   tblOrder table

f. **Close** ☒ the tblOrder table.

g. Double-click **tblParticipant** to open the table.

Scan for the participants that match the two ParticipantIDs you identified earlier, 5 and 19. You find that OrderID 4 was placed by ParticipantID 5, Marge Fresquez. In addition, OrderID 11 was placed by ParticipantID 19, Ricardo Sanchez.

tblParticipant table

Participant 5 is Marge Fresquez

Participant 19 is Ricardo Sanchez

ParticipantID	LastName	FirstName	StreetAddress	City	State	ZipCode	ContactPho
1	Last	First	1563 Catalina Dr	Santa Fe	NM	87508	(505) 555-17
2	Trujillo	John	427 Kanengiser Rd	Santa Ana Pueblo	NM	87045	(505) 555-82
3	McShane	Ian	823 4th St NW	Albuquerque	NM	87106	(505) 555-41
5	Fresquez	Marge	534 Asiento Blvd	Pueblo	NM	81232	(505) 555-38
8	Maestas	Marcus	83 Vuelta Rancho	Santa Fe	NM	87508	(505) 555-25
9	Marquardt	Keith	228 E Alejo Rd	Palm Springs	CA	92262	(760) 555-48
11	Neidhart	Kate	54 E Dona Rosa Tr	Las Vegas	NM	87701	(505) 555-41
15	Reed	Thomas	743 Windstone Dr.	Albuquerque	NM	87105	(505) 555-79
16	Reid	Cynthia	158A Calle Derecho	Las Vegas	NM	87701	(505) 555-02
17	Andrews	Joseph	819 Calle Don Roberto	Santa Fe	NM	87502	(505) 555-32
19	Sanchez	Ricardo	158 Tesuque Village Rd	Agua Fria	NM	87507	(505) 555-62
20	Sanchez	Julie	158 Tesuque Village Rd	Agua Fria	NM	87507	(505) 555-62
21	Schilling	John	15365 Sombra Del Monte	Santa Fe	NM	87508	(505) 555-92
24	Thomas	Joe	4355 Celsior St	Brougham	CA	92267	(760) 555-32
26	Trent	Eileen	433 Tortuga Ln	Las Cruces	NM	88003	(505) 555-41
27	Brevard	Jacque	23 Calle Montoya	Bernanillo	NM	87001	(505) 555-18
29	Winston	Mary	157 Green Galliard Rd	Agua Fria	NM	87506	(505) 555-17
30	Fox	Jeff	1509 Las Cruces Drive	Last Cruces	NM	88003	(505) 555-87

Figure 16   tblParticipant table

h. Close ☒ the tblParticipant table.

You now can tell Ms. Rochelle which participants have booked corporate teams and the address that the follow-up should be sent to. However, it may seem like a lot of work to find out who booked the corporate teams. Access queries make this task easier. It is important to know what data is in your database. While Access will do the hard part of matching tables on common fields and finding the results, you still need to tell it what fields you want and where the fields are located.

REAL WORLD ADVICE | **Closing Tables**

While Access allows you to leave several tables open at the same time, it is a good idea to get into the habit of closing a table when you are done with it.

- First, there are many Access functions that use a table that cannot be completed while the table is open. If you close the table, you no longer risk running into this problem.

- Second, closing tables makes it less likely that you will accidently change the wrong table.

- Third, each open table requires more memory for Access. With larger tables, Access could be slowed down by having multiple tables open.

Understanding Queries, Forms, and Reports

You have explored tables, the first of the four main object types in Access. As mentioned previously, the other three object types are queries, forms, and reports. Each object provides a different way to work with data stored in tables. A query is used to ask questions about your data. A form is primarily used to enter data into your database or display data in your database. Reports are used to provide professional looking displays of your tables that are suitable for printing. In this section, you will work with queries, forms, and reports within your database.

Understand What a Query Is

A query is a way to ask questions about your data. For your charity golf tournament, you can use queries to get answers to questions, such as "What is Ian McShane's phone number?", "What has John Trujillo ordered?", and "What orders are over $1,000?"

You can also conduct more complex queries such as calculating a score given a player's strokes and their handicap.

One of the strengths of Access is the ability to ask such questions and get answers quickly. You traced who ordered corporate teams earlier in the workshop. That was difficult because you had to keep track of fields such as ParticipantID in one table and then look them up in another table. By using queries, Access will match common fields in the tables and trace the order for you.

You will look at two different views of queries in this workshop:

- Datasheet view shows the results of your query.
- Design view shows how the query is constructed. It shows the tables, fields, and selection criterion for the query.

Creating a Query Using a Wizard

Access provides wizards to help you with tasks. A **wizard** is a step-by-step guide that walks you through tasks by asking you questions to help you decide what you want to do. Once you have some experience, you can also do the task yourself without a guide. You would like to know which participants are from Santa Fe, New Mexico. You will use the Query Wizard to create the query getting all participants, and then you will modify the query design to select those from Santa Fe.

REAL WORLD ADVICE | **Using Wizards in Access**

Wizards can sometimes save you time! Access wizards are shortcuts to building objects such as queries, reports, and forms. They select fields, format the data, and perform calculations. After the wizard does the initial formatting, you can always modify the resulting query, report, or form to get exactly what you want.

However, anything that can be done with a wizard could also be done without a wizard. A wizard may limit your choices. On the other hand, starting in design view requires you to make choices without guidance. Whether you start with a wizard or with design view is usually personal choice. As you become more comfortable with Access, pick the method that you prefer. The results will be the same.

A01.08

▶ **To Create a Query with a Wizard**

a. Click the **CREATE** tab, and then in the Queries group, click **Query Wizard**.

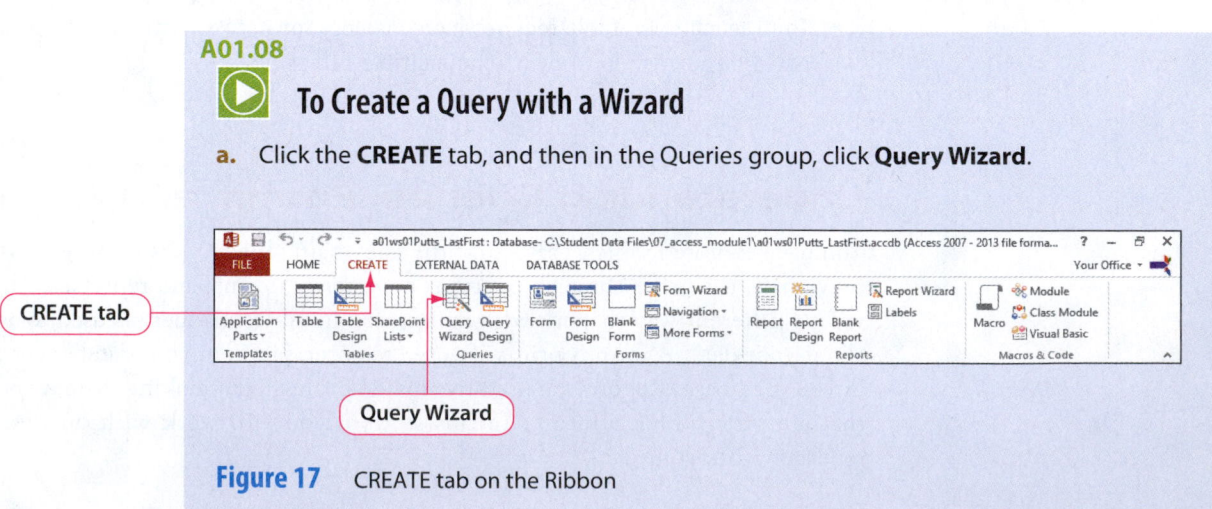

CREATE tab

Query Wizard

Figure 17 CREATE tab on the Ribbon

Access displays the New Query dialog box and asks you what kind of query you want.

Troubleshooting

If this is the first time that you have used an Access wizard, Access will need to set up the wizards. You will get a message "Setting up wizard" and will need to wait while the wizards are installed.

b. If necessary, click **Simple Query Wizard**, and then click **OK**.

Access asks you which fields you want to include in the query. You have choices of tables or queries as the source for your fields. Your database has four tables to select as a source. You will choose only one table. You could choose fields from multiple tables, but that is not necessary in this query.

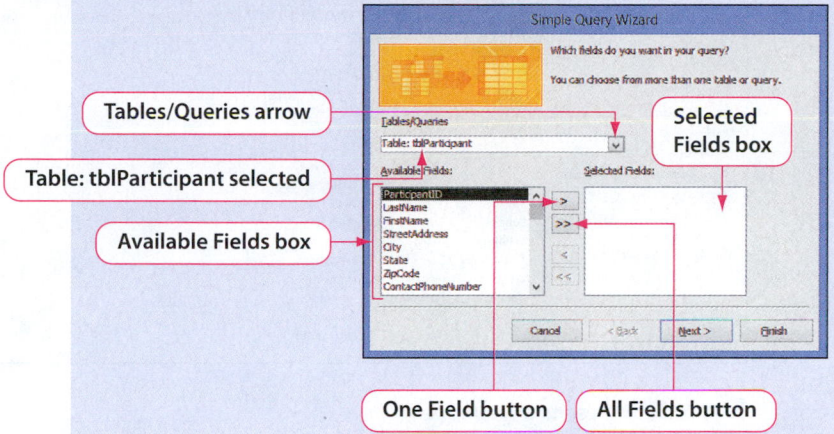

Tables/Queries arrow

Selected Fields box

Table: tblParticipant selected

Available Fields box

One Field button All Fields button

Figure 18 Select tblParticipant

c. Click the **Tables/Queries** arrow to see available field sources, and then select **Table: tblParticipant** as the source of your fields.

The dialog box has two lists. The box on the left shows you all available fields from the selected table or query. The box on the right shows you all the fields that you have selected for this query. You use the buttons between the two lists to move fields from one box to the other. Selecting a field and clicking the One Field button ▶ moves that field from the Available Fields box to the Selected Fields box. Clicking the All Fields button ▶▶ moves all fields.

d. Under Available Fields, click **LastName**, and then click the **One Field** button ▶ . Access moves the LastName field to the Selected Fields box.

e. Click **FirstName**, and then click the **One Field** button ▶ .

f. Click **City**, and then click the **One Field** button ▶ .

Your field list in the right box should display fields in the following order: LastName, FirstName, and City.

Troubleshooting

If you accidently add the wrong field to the Selected Fields box, select the field and use the One Field Back button ◀ to place it back in the Available Fields box.

If you select the fields in the wrong order, Access does not have a way to reorder the fields. It is best to place them all back in the Available Fields box using the All Fields Back button ◀◀ and then select them again in the right order.

g. Click **Next** to continue to the next page of the wizard. In the **What title do you want for your query?** box type **qryParticipantSantaFe_initialLastname** using your first initial and last name.

h. Click **Open the query to view information**, and then click **Finish**.

Access shows you the results of your query. Once you have created this query, the query name is displayed under All Access objects in the Navigation Pane.

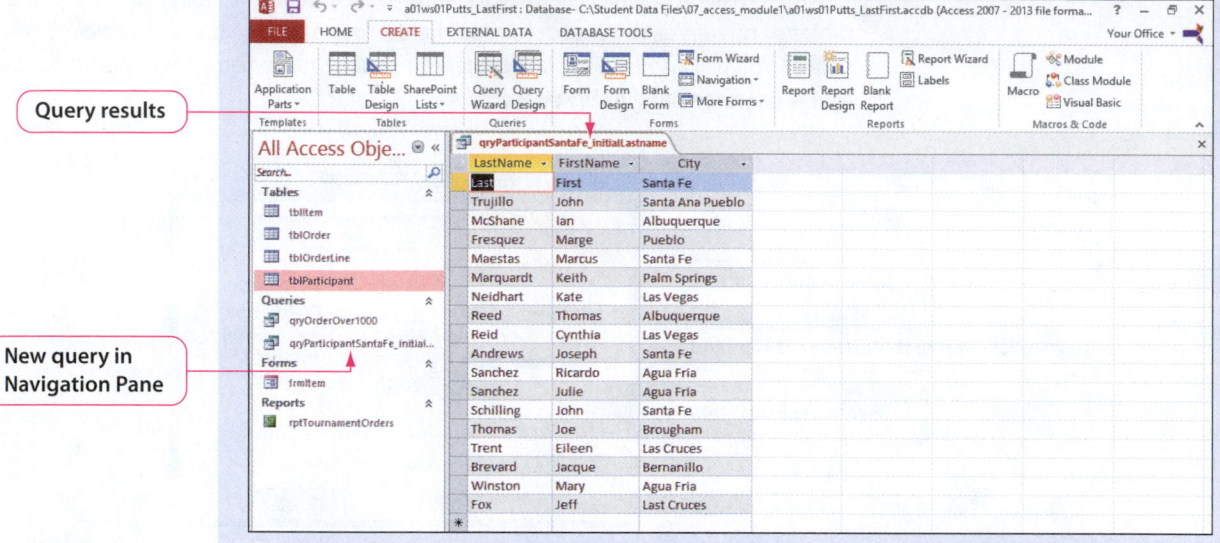

Figure 19 Results of your query

SIDE NOTE

Saving Design Changes

While Access automatically saves data changes, you need to tell it to save design changes. A new query is a design change.

i. Click **Save** 🖫 to save the query, and then **close** ✖ the query.

Query results are a recordset that provide an answer to a question posed in a query. The query results show records and fields created at **run time**, which means that the results are created each time you run the query. This run time table is referred to as a **recordset**. The method to create the query is saved but not the actual results. That means that if you add a participant who meets the query criteria to the participant table, the next time you run this query, that participant will appear in the results of this query.

REAL WORLD ADVICE | Naming Your Queries

Similar to tables, Access will allow you to give your query any name you want. There are two important considerations:

- You want to remember what a query does, so make the name as descriptive as possible. A query named "tblParticipant Query" will probably have no meaning for you in a few days. It will be easier to remember that "qryParticipantSantaFe" shows participants from Santa Fe.

- When you are looking at field sources, you often have a choice between tables and queries. Starting all your tables with "tbl" and all your queries with "qry" makes it easy to distinguish what you are choosing.

Selecting a Value Using Design View

The Query Wizard uses a question-and-answer dialog box to create a query. The other method of creating a query is to use Design view. Design view goes behind the scenes of the data and shows you the detailed structure of an Access object. You can also use Design view to modify an existing query.

A01.09

 To Switch to Design View of a Query

a. Right-click **qryParticipantSantaFe_initialLastname** in the Navigation Pane.

b. Select **Design View** from the shortcut menu.

Access opens the Design view of your query. The DESIGN tab is open on the Ribbon. The left side of the screen shows the Navigation Pane. The top half of the screen shows the **query workspace**, which is the source for data in the query. In this case, the source is the table tblParticipant. The bottom half is called the **query design grid**. It shows which fields are selected in this query: LastName, FirstName, and City.

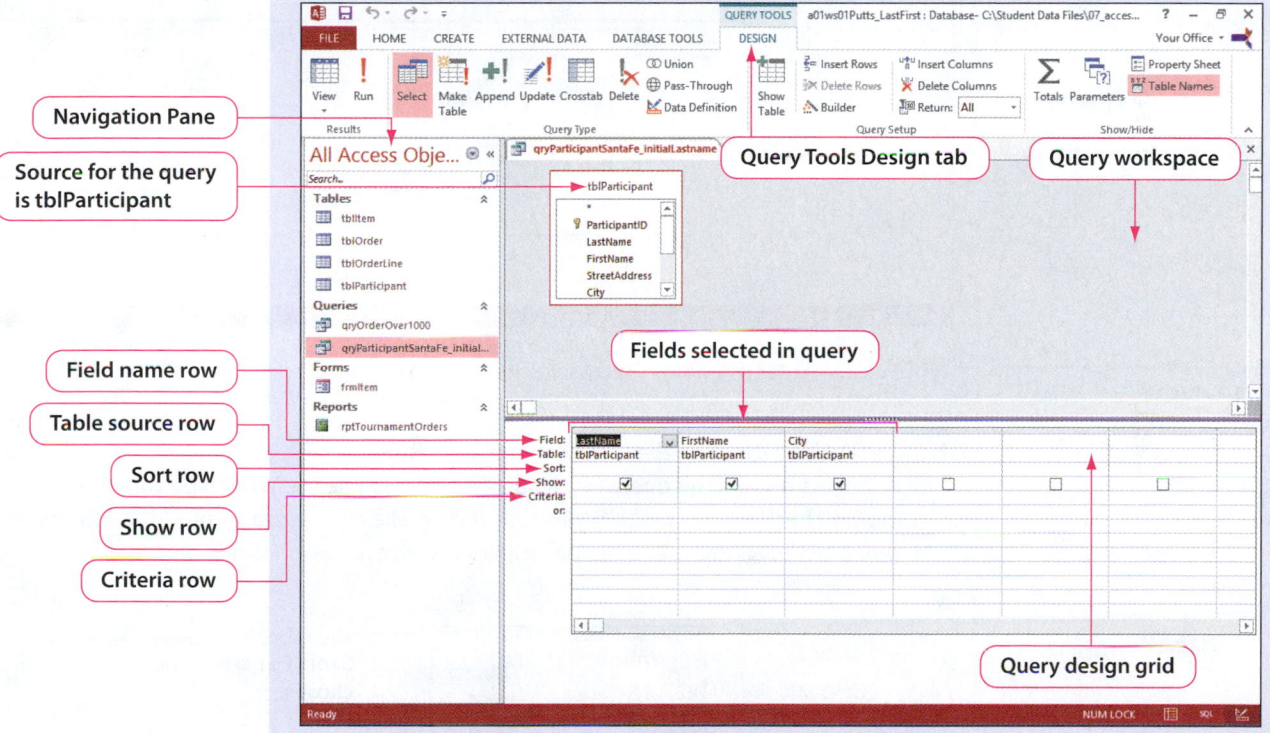

Figure 20   Design view for qryParticipantSantaFe_initialLastname

Selecting Values in a Query

Each row in the design grid shows information about the field. The top row is Field name. The next row shows the table or source for this field. The Sort row allows you to specify the order of records shown in your query results by setting one or more sort fields. The Show row is a check box that specifies whether the field is shown in the table of query results. The Criteria rows allow you to select certain records by setting conditions for the field contents. You are going to change this query to see which participants are from Santa Fe. You will do that by adding selection criteria.

A01.10

 To Select a Value in a Query

a. Click the **Criteria** cell in the City column.

b. Type **Santa Fe**.

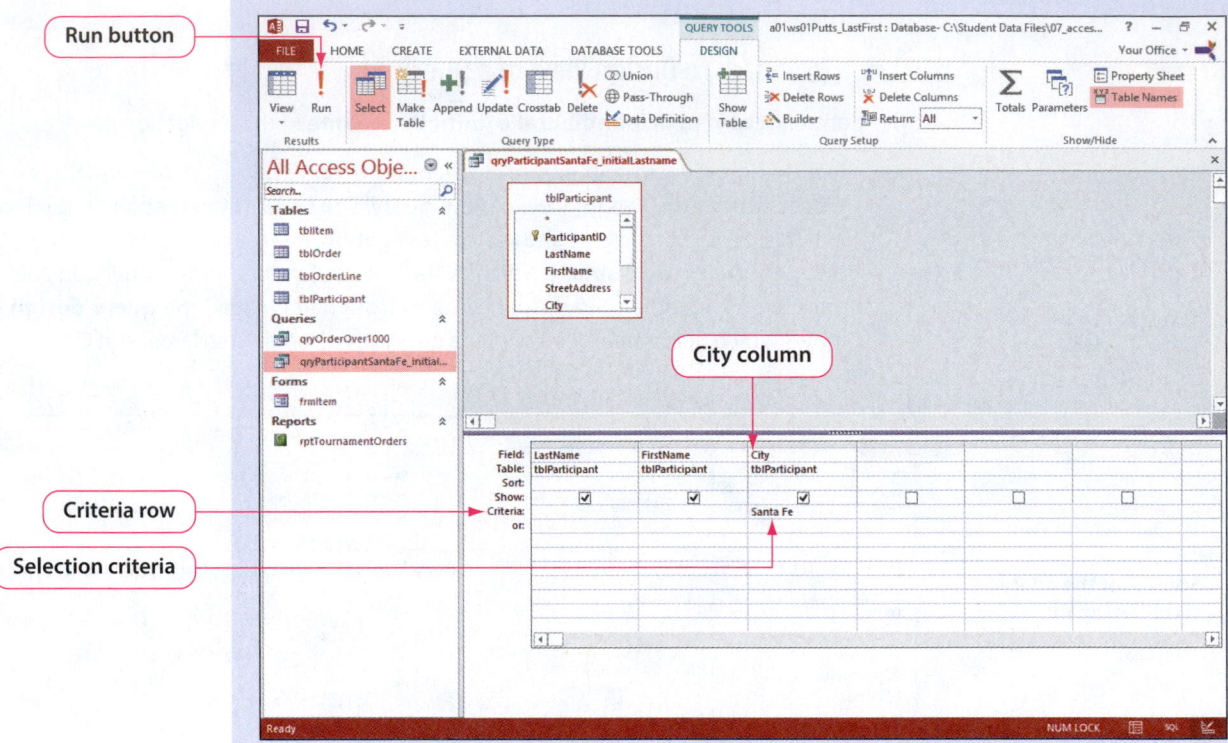

Figure 21   Enter criteria in a query selection

Run button

City column

Criteria row

Selection criteria

SIDE NOTE
Query Criteria
Because "City" is a text field, the criteria is treated as text, and Access adds quotation marks. You can also type the quotation marks.

c. On the DESIGN tab, in the Results group, click **Run**.

Access returns the query results as shown in Figure 22. When you run a query, you should check the results to make sure they make sense. You wanted the participants with a city of Santa Fe, and the participants shown are only from Santa Fe.

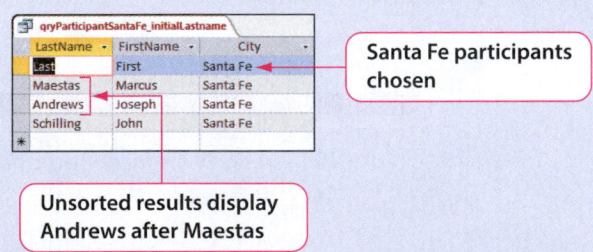

Santa Fe participants chosen

Unsorted results display Andrews after Maestas

Figure 22   Unsorted query results showing participants from Santa Fe

Troubleshooting

If your query results are not what you expect (compare to Figure 22), you made an error in entering your selection criteria. Click the View button on the Home tab to switch back to Design view. Compare your criteria with Figure 21. Make sure that you spelled "Santa Fe" correctly and that it is in the City column.

QUICK REFERENCE	Selecting in a Query

When you typed Santa Fe in the criteria, you asked Access to select those participants who had a city equal to "Santa Fe". The equals sign is implied, though you can enter it if you wish. Other operators that can be entered in the selection criteria follow:

Operator	Meaning	Description
=	Equal to	Selects the records where the field value is equal to the value provided. If no operator is used, equal to is assumed.
<	Less than	Selects the records where the field value is less than the value provided.
>	Greater than	Selects the records where the field value is greater than the value provided.
< =	Less than or equal to	Selects the records where the field value is less than or equal to the value provided.
> =	Greater than or equal to	Selects the records where the field value is greater than or equal to the value provided.
< >	Not equal	Selects the records where the field value is not equal to the value provided.
Between	Between	Selects the records where the field values listed are within the two values. For example, between 1 and 7 is true for any value between 1 and 7—this includes the value of 1 and the value of 7.

Sorting Query Results

When Access runs a query, it puts the results in a default order based on how the table is defined. As shown in Figure 22, the order of the participants does not make much sense with Joseph Andrews after Marcus Maestas. In addition, if the query result shows many records, it will be difficult to find a specific record. Usually you will want to change the sort order so that the order of the results makes sense. In this query, you will choose to put the participants in alphabetical order.

A01.11

▶ **To Sort Query Results**

a. In the Views group, click the **View** arrow, and then select **Design View**.

b. Click the **Sort cell** in the LastName column, click the **Selection** arrow ⌄, and then select **Ascending**.

c. Click the **Sort cell** in the FirstName column, click the **Selection** arrow ⌄, and then select **Ascending**.

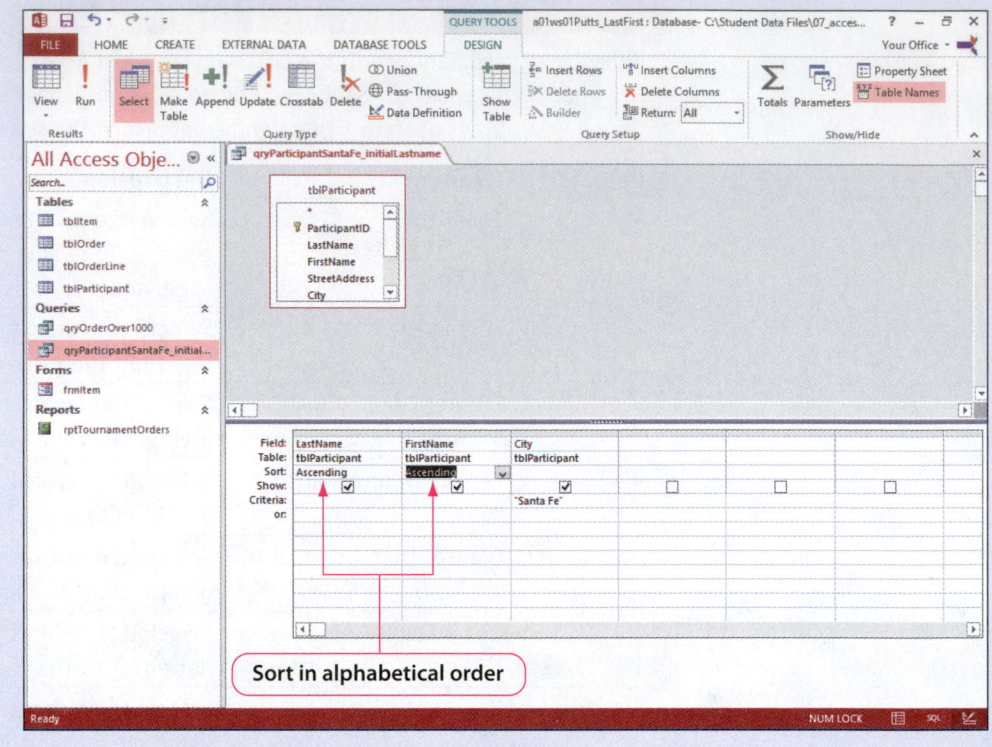

Figure 23 Sorting results of a query

d. On the DESIGN tab, in the Results group, click **Run**.

Access puts the participants in alphabetical order by Last name. If there were two participants with the same Last name, they would be sorted alphabetically by First name.

Printing Query Results

If you want to print your query results, you can do this on the File tab. Printing tables is done the same way.

A01.12

 To Print a Query

a. Click the **FILE** tab to display Backstage view.

b. Click **Print**, and then click **Print Preview** to see what the results would look like if printed.

c. If your instructor asks you to print your results, on the PRINT PREVIEW tab, click **Print**. In the Print dialog box, select the correct printer, and then click **OK**.

d. On the PRINT PREVIEW tab, click **Close Print Preview**.

e. Click **Save** 💾.

f. **Close** ✖ the qryParticipantSantaFe_initialLastname query.

> **Troubleshooting**
>
> If you accidently closed Access instead of just the query, open Access the same way you did at the beginning of the workshop. In the Recent databases, click the name a01ws01Putts_LastFirst to open the database again.

REAL WORLD ADVICE   Do You Need to Print?

Before you decide to print the results of a query, you may want to consider whether you really need a printed version. If you want to share the results with someone else, often you can share them via e-mail. Access provides an export-to-PDF feature for a query or table that allows you to save the results in PDF format. Right-click the object in the Navigation Pane, point to Export, and then select PDF or XPS. You can then publish your object as a PDF file, which you can e-mail to someone. Alternatively, you can use the External Data tab to export to a PDF format.

Understand What a Form Is

A form provides another interface to a table or query beyond the table in Datasheet view. In corporate databases, end users of a database computer system often use forms to enter and change data. You can also use forms to limit the amount of data you see from a table. In a personal database, you can create forms for entering data if you wish.

Forms have three views:

- **Form view** shows the data in the form. This is the view you use to enter or change data. You cannot change the form design in this view.

- **Layout view** shows the form and the data. Some of the form design such as field lengths and fonts can be changed in this view. The data cannot be changed.

- Design view shows the form design but not the data. Any aspect of the form design can be changed. The data cannot be changed.

REAL WORLD ADVICE   Layout View vs. Design View

Both Layout view and Design view allow you to change the design of forms. Which view is best for changing design? Part of this is personal preference, but some features are only able to be changed in Design view. Some considerations:

- Layout view shows both the form and the data. When changing column widths or field lengths, it is often easier if you see both. You can adjust the sizes while seeing the data and make sure you pick a size that is appropriate.

- Many features can only be changed in Design view. How do you remember which ones? If you prefer Layout view, try it in that view first, and switch to Design view whenever you have trouble changing something.

Creating a Form

You want to create a form to make it easier to enter participants. There are different types of forms that can be created. The default form shows one participant at a time and has each field clearly labeled.

A01.13

 To Create a Form

a. Click **tblParticipant** in the Navigation Pane. Click the **CREATE** tab, and then in the Forms group, click **Form**.

b. Click **Save** 🖫 to save the form. In the Save As dialog box, type frmParticipant_initialLastname using your first initial and last name, and then click **OK**.

Access creates a form. Notice that the form displays the same Navigation bar that you had in the table. That is because a form is a data entry or display tool for the table. You can use it to navigate through your table. The form is created in Layout view, which allows you make minor changes to the design.

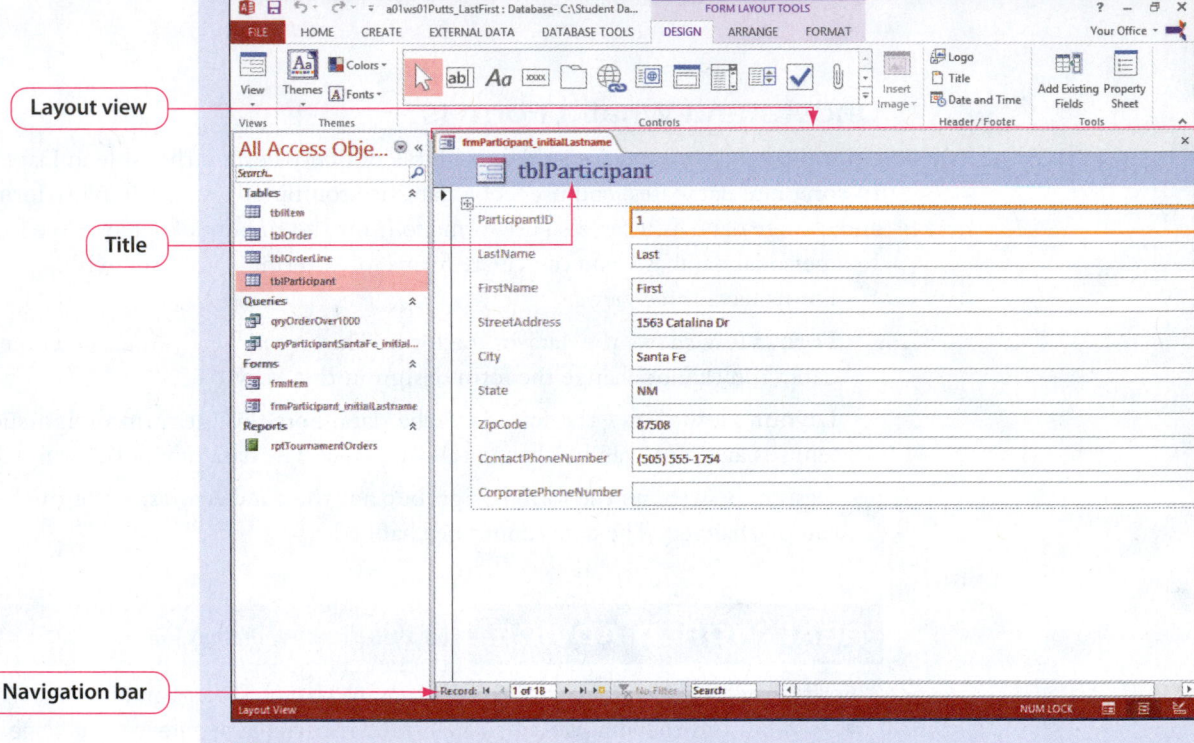

Figure 24   Form in Layout view

c. Click the **title** of the form, and then click again to select the **title**. Replace the current title with Participant form by initial Lastname using your first initial and last name.

d. Press Enter, and then click **Save** 🖫 to save your form.

Entering Data via a Form

Jackie Silva has asked to register for the tournament. You will use your newly created form to add her to the participant table. It is very important that you navigate to the append row so you enter her information into a blank form. If you see data about a participant in the form, you will be replacing that participant with Jackie Silva instead of adding a new participant.

A01.14

▶ **To Enter Data Using a Form**

a. Click the **DESIGN** tab, in the Views group, click the **View** arrow, and then click **Form View**. This view allows you to use the form to enter data into the table.

b. Click the **New (blank) record button** ▶▦ on the Navigation bar. If you see a participant's name in the form, try again. This will be record 19 of 19 in the Navigation bar.

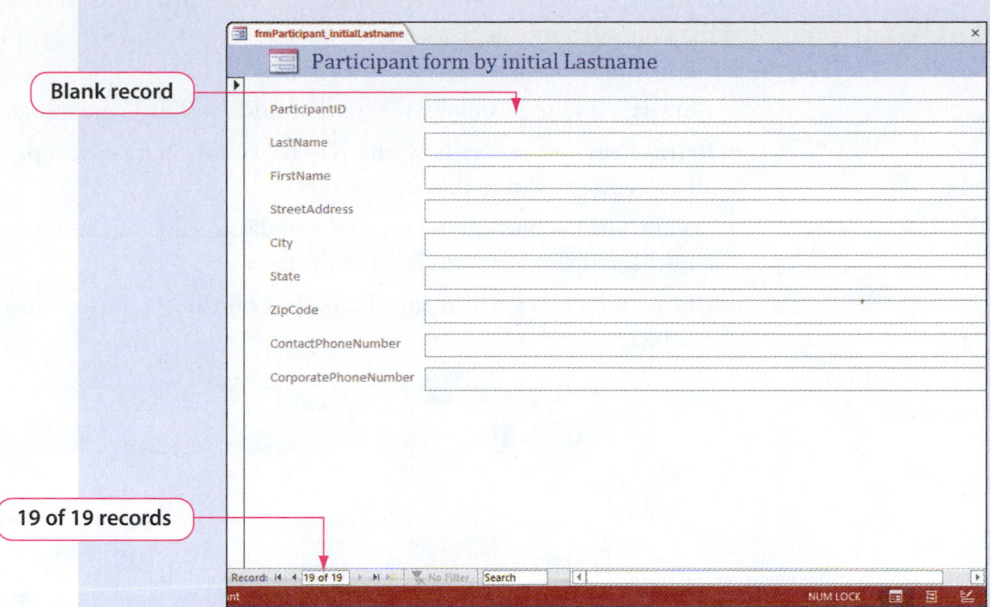

Blank record

19 of 19 records

Figure 25 Blank append record

SIDE NOTE
Saving in Access
Unlike Word, Access saves your data as it is entered. Typing over the data in another record means that you lose the data that was there.

c. Type the following information into the form. Press [Enter] or [Tab] to move to each field.

ParticipantID	31
LastName	Silva
FirstName	Jackie
StreetAddress	1509 Main Street
City	Santa Ana Pueblo
State	NM
ZipCode	87044
ContactPhoneNumber	(505) 555–3355
CorporatePhoneNumber	(leave blank)

d. **Close** ☒ the form. The participant data you entered in the form is saved to the table.

e. On the Navigation Pane, under Tables, double-click **tblParticipant**.

f. Click the **Last Record button** ▶⏐ on the Navigation bar. Verify that Jackie Silva has been added to your table.

g. **Close** ☒ the table.

CONSIDER THIS | **Adding Data Directly into a Table vs. Adding Data via a Form**

You have added two participants to your table. Earlier, you added a row to the table and added Jeff Fox. Now, you have added Jackie Silva via a form. Which was easier for you? Why would most companies use forms to enter data?

Understand What a Report Is

A report provides an easy-to-read format suitable for printing. A sample report is shown in Figure 26. As you can see, the report has page headers—the column headings— and a footer. You can easily provide column totals as needed. When printing data for management presentations, you usually use a report rather than a query. The source of the data for a report can be a table or query.

Reports have four views:

- **Report view** shows how the report would look in a continuous page layout.

- **Print Preview** shows how the report would look on the printed page. This view allows you to change the page layout.

- Layout view shows the report and the data. Some of the report design such as field lengths and fonts can be changed in this view.

- Design view shows the report design but not the data. Any aspect of the report design can be changed.

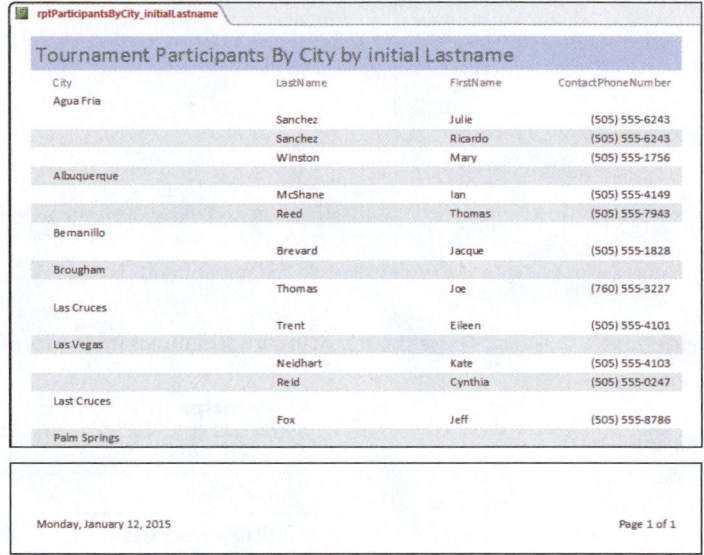

Figure 26 An Access report

Creating a Report Using a Wizard

The report feature in Access allows you to easily design reports that can serve management purposes and look professional. You will create a report listing the participants in the database. You will use the Report Wizard to create the report.

The Report Wizard starts similarly to the Query Wizard in selecting fields for the report. After that the wizard asks questions about report formatting that were not part of the Query Wizard.

You want to create a list of participants entered in the tournament with their contact phone numbers. You will group all the participants in a single city into a single group. You will print the participants in alphabetic order within each group.

A01.15

 To Create a Report Using a Wizard

a. Click the **CREATE** tab, and then in the Reports group, click **Report Wizard**. Click the **Tables/Queries** arrow, and then click **Table: tblParticipant**.

b. Using the One Field button ⟩ , move these fields to the Selected Fields box: **LastName**, **FirstName**, **City**, and **ContactPhoneNumber**.

c. Click **Next**. The wizard asks if you want to add grouping levels.

d. Click to select **City**, and then click the **One Field** button ⟩ to group by City. When you make this selection, the box on the right of the dialog box shows a preview of what the report grouping will look like.

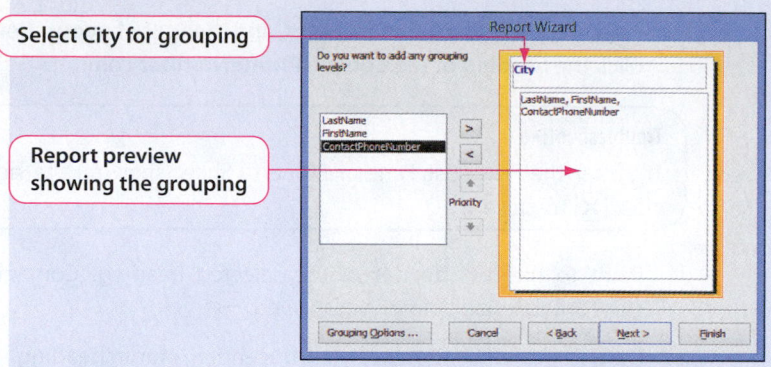

Select City for grouping

Report preview showing the grouping

Figure 27 Add grouping levels

e. Click **Next**.

The wizard asks what sort order you want. You always want to put your report in some order that makes it easy to read and understand. Otherwise, a report with a lot of information is difficult to understand. In this report, you will list participants alphabetically.

f. In the **1** box, click the **arrow**, and then select **LastName**. If necessary, make sure that the sort order is **Ascending**, meaning in alphabetical order from A to Z.

g. In the **2** box, click the **arrow**, and then select **FirstName**.

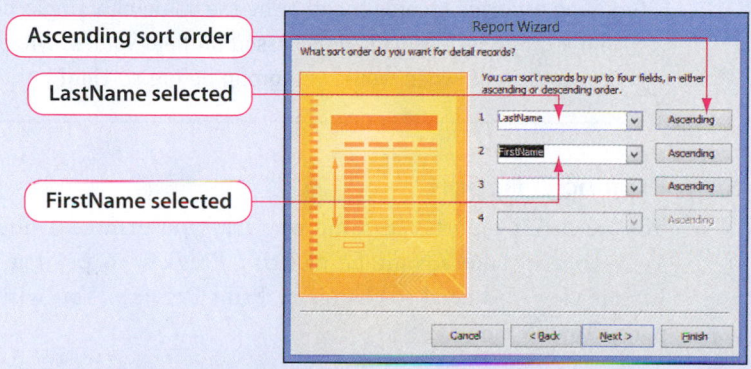

Ascending sort order

LastName selected

FirstName selected

Figure 28 Add sorting

h. Click **Next**. If necessary, change the layout to **Stepped** and the orientation to **Portrait**.

i. Click **Next**. In the **What title do you want for your report?** box, type **rptParticipantsByCity_initialLastname** using your first initial and last name.

j. Click **Finish**.

Access displays the report in Print Preview. You notice that the ContactPhoneNumber heading is not fully shown. You can fix that easily in Layout view.

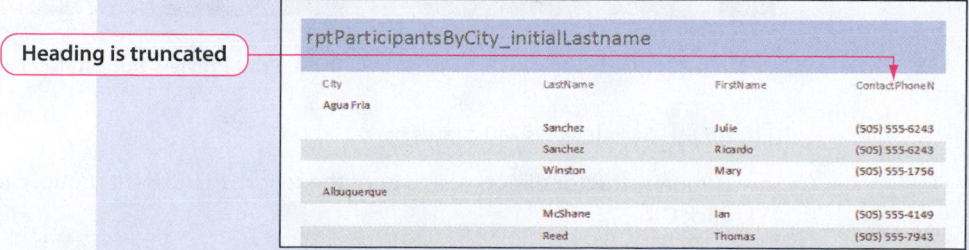

Heading is truncated

Figure 29 Report in Print Preview

k. Right-click anywhere on the report, and then click **Layout View** from the shortcut menu. Click the heading of the **ContactPhoneNumber** column.

> **Troubleshooting**
>
> If either the Field List Pane or Property Sheet show on the right side of the field, click ⊠ to close it.

l. Point to the **left border** of the selected heading (ContactPhoneNumber) until the Horizontal Resize pointer is displayed ↔.

m. Drag to the left until you can see the entire column heading.

n. Double-click the **title** of the report, and then change the report title to Tournament Participants By City by initial Lastname using your first initial and last name. Your report should look like Figure 26.

o. Click **Save** 🖫 to save the report.

Notice that the City data is a line above the data in the other columns. That is because the participants are grouped by city. Within a city, participants are sorted alphabetically.

CONSIDER THIS | **Grouping vs. Sorting**

Grouping arranges records together by the value of a single field. Sorting puts the records within a group in a specific order based on field values. When would you choose to sort your records, and when would you group before sorting?

Printing a Report

You can print reports the same way that you printed a query earlier using the File tab. You can also take advantage of Print Preview to print a report. You are currently in Layout view and need to change to Print Preview. You will use the button on the status bar to switch views.

A01.16

▶ To Print a Report

a. Click **Print Preview** 🔍 to change to Print Preview. Alternatively, you could change to Print Preview using the button on the Ribbon as you have done before.

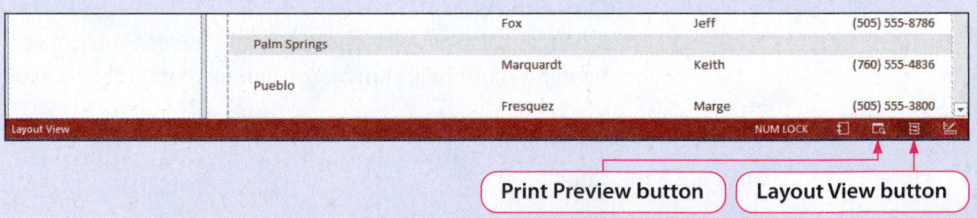

Figure 30 Switch views with status bar

b. If your instructor directs you to print the report, in the Print group, click **Print**, and then click **OK**.

c. In the Close Preview group, click **Close Print Preview**, and then **close** ⊠ the report.

REAL WORLD ADVICE | When Do You Use a Report vs. a Query?

Both reports and queries can be used to report on your data. A report provides a more formal presentation of your data and is designed for printing. A query has more selection capabilities, but the formatting is not as attractive. You can combine the two capabilities by first creating the query object and then creating a report using the query as your source.

Back Up a Database

A **backup database** is an extra copy of your database that you can use to protect yourself from the accidental loss of your database. Backups can help in cases of accidental deletion of data. You can return to the backup copy if you accidently delete the real database. The backup copy may not be as current as your real database, but it may save you from having to recreate the whole database. If you store the backup on another storage medium, it can also help in cases of hardware failure such as a hard drive crash.

Creating a Backup

In Access, you make backups by using the Back Up Database command, which is available on **Backstage view** under Save As. If you make multiple backup copies, you will want to give them different names. The backup feature appends the current date to the suggested file name. That allows you to easily distinguish between various versions of the backups. You can be sure that you are getting the most recent one.

If you ever need a backup, simply return to the most recent copy that you have and start working with that file. You can save it as the name of the file you want to work with.

A01.17

 To Back Up a Database

a. Click the **FILE** tab, and then click **Save As**. Make sure that **Save Database As** is selected under File Types. Access displays Save Database As options in the right pane.

b. Under **Advanced**, click **Back Up Database**, and then click the **Save As** button. The Save As dialog box appears with a suggested file name that has the date appended.

c. Navigate to the drive and folder where you want to store your backup. Change the file name if necessary, and then click **Save**.

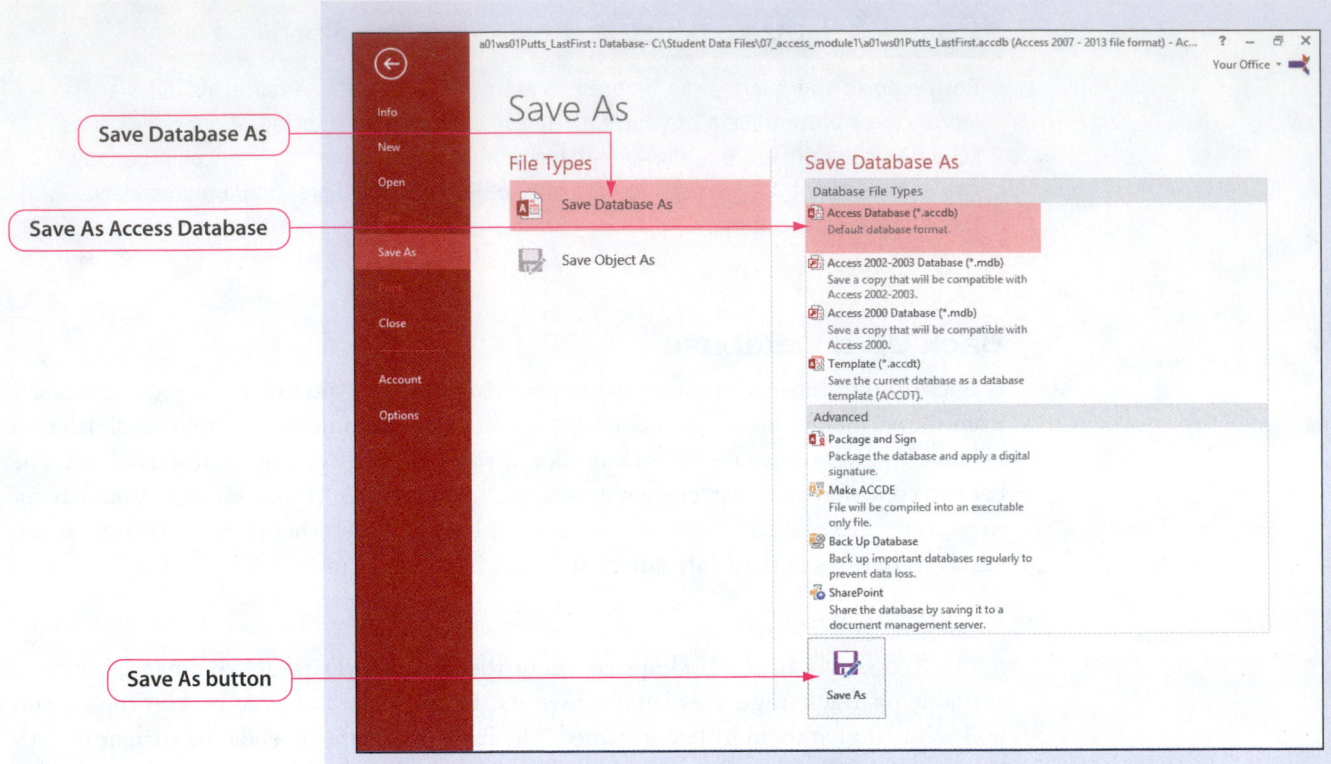

Figure 31 Make a backup copy of your database

CONSIDER THIS | **Backups**

What would you lose if your PC's hard drive crashed? Do you have copies of school work, photographs, or music? You may never need to retrieve the backup, but which would be worse: making unnecessary backups or losing all your files?

Compact a Database

While you work on an Access database, the size of the database file increases. When you delete a record or object, or if you make changes to an object, Access does not reuse the original space. Access provides a compacting feature that makes more efficient use of disk space. **Compacting** rearranges objects to use disk space more efficiently, thus releasing the now unused space to be used again. If you do not compact your database, its size can get very large quickly. The compact option also looks for damaged data and tries to repair it.

Compacting Your Database

You have two options for compacting: (1) You can perform a single Compact and Repair Database action at any time, or (2) You can select Compact on Close. If you select Compact on Close, Access automatically compacts your database anytime you close it. Both options are available on Backstage view.

A01.18

 To Compact a Database

a. Click the **FILE** tab.

b. Click **Compact & Repair Database**.

Access compacts your database, fixes it if necessary, and returns you to the HOME tab. On a small database such as Putts for Paws, this action is very fast. On a larger database with many changes made, there may be a noticeable delay.

c. Click the **FILE** tab, and then click **Options**.

d. Click **Current Database** in the left pane, and then under Application Options, click the **Compact on Close** check box.

By default, Compact on Close is turned off. Many professionals like to turn on Compact on Close so they do not need to remember to compact the database themselves.

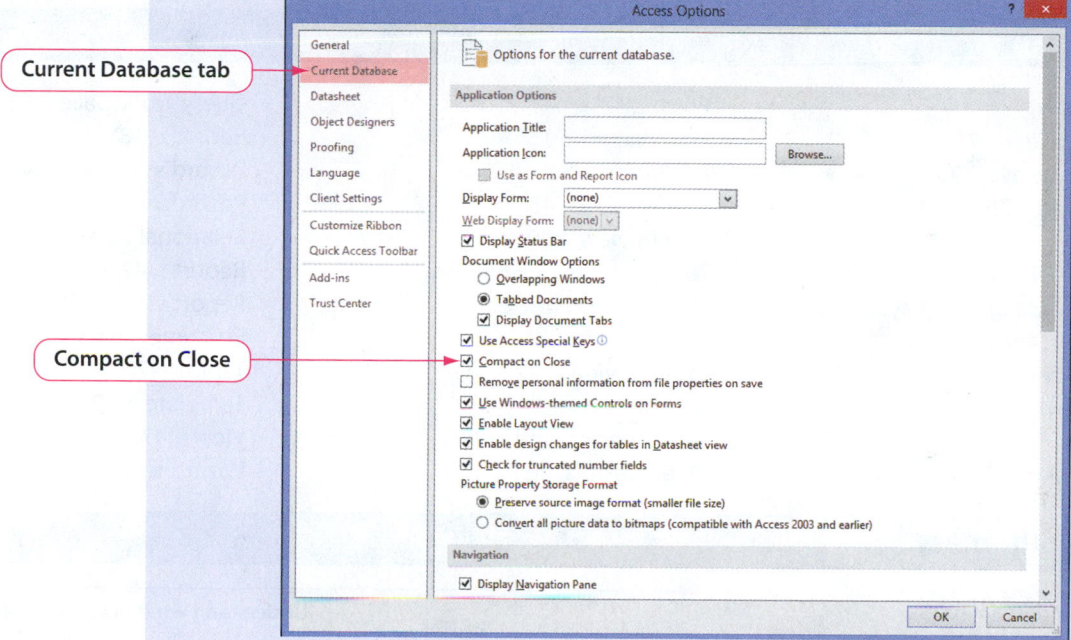

Figure 32 Select Compact on Close

e. Click **OK** to turn this option on. Access warns you that the option will not take effect until you close and reopen the database.

f. Click **OK**, and then **close** ❎ Access.

MODULE 1

Understanding Queries, Forms, and Reports   77

Concept Check

1. What is Access? When would you use Access instead of Excel? p. 46, 56

2. What is the Navigation Pane? Where do you find it? p. 50

3. What is a record? What is a field? How are they represented in Access? p. 55–58

4. How do you manually navigate a database? p. 59–61

5. How is a query used? What is the difference between Datasheet view and Design view of a query? p. 61–62

6. How is a form used? p. 69

7. How is a report used? What is Report Layout view? p. 71–72

8. What is a database backup, and how is it used? p. 75

9. What does it mean to compact and repair your database? What is the difference between a single compact and a compact on close? p. 76

Key Terms

Append row   56
Backstage view   75
Backup database   75
Compacting   76
Data   46
Database   46
Database management system (DBMS)   46
Datasheet view   47
Design view   47
Field   49
File extension   52

Form   47
Form view   69
Importing   53
Information   46
Layout view   69
Navigation bar   56
Navigation Pane   50
Object   47
Print Preview   72
Query   47
Query design grid   65
Query results   64

Query workspace   65
Record   48
Record selector   56
Recordset   64
Relational database   53
Report   47
Report view   72
Run time   64
Table   47
Template   49
View   47
Wizard   62

Visual Summary

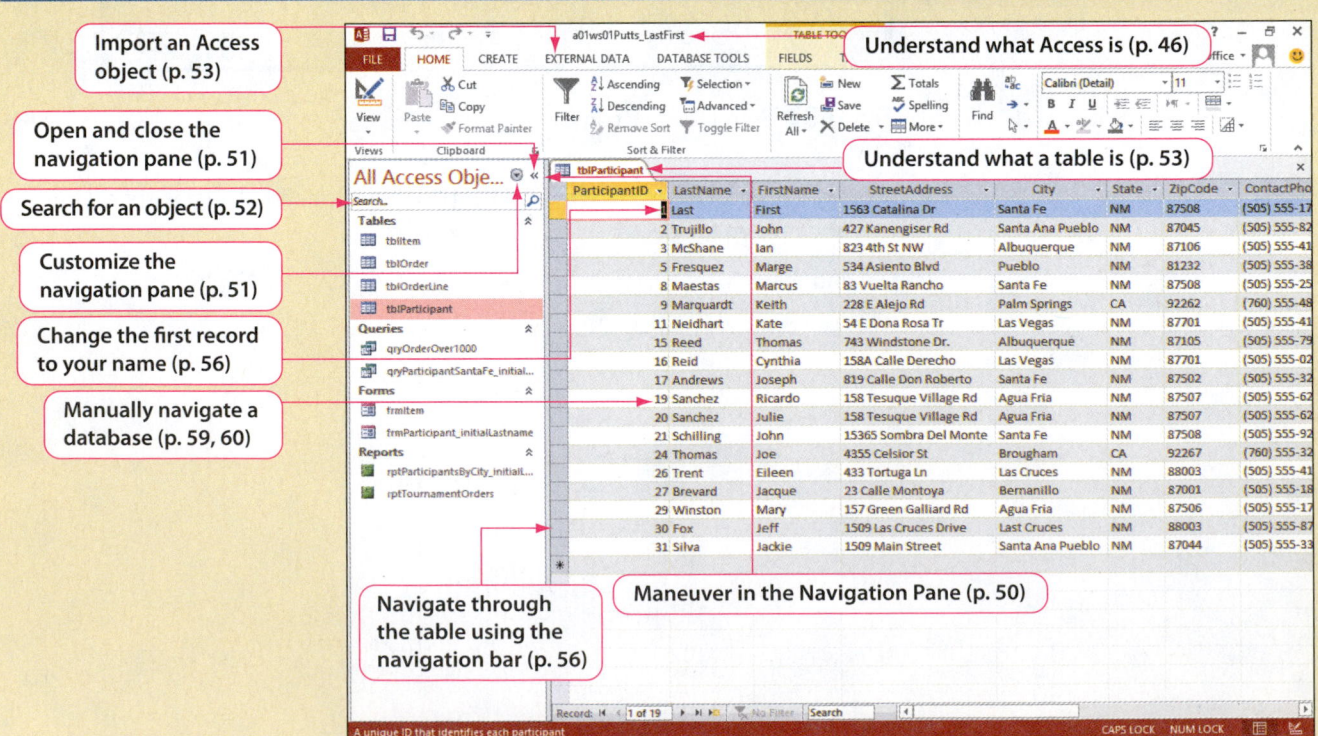

Import an Access object (p. 53)

Open and close the navigation pane (p. 51)

Search for an object (p. 52)

Customize the navigation pane (p. 51)

Change the first record to your name (p. 56)

Manually navigate a database (p. 59, 60)

Understand what Access is (p. 46)

Understand what a table is (p. 53)

Navigate through the table using the navigation bar (p. 56)

Maneuver in the Navigation Pane (p. 50)

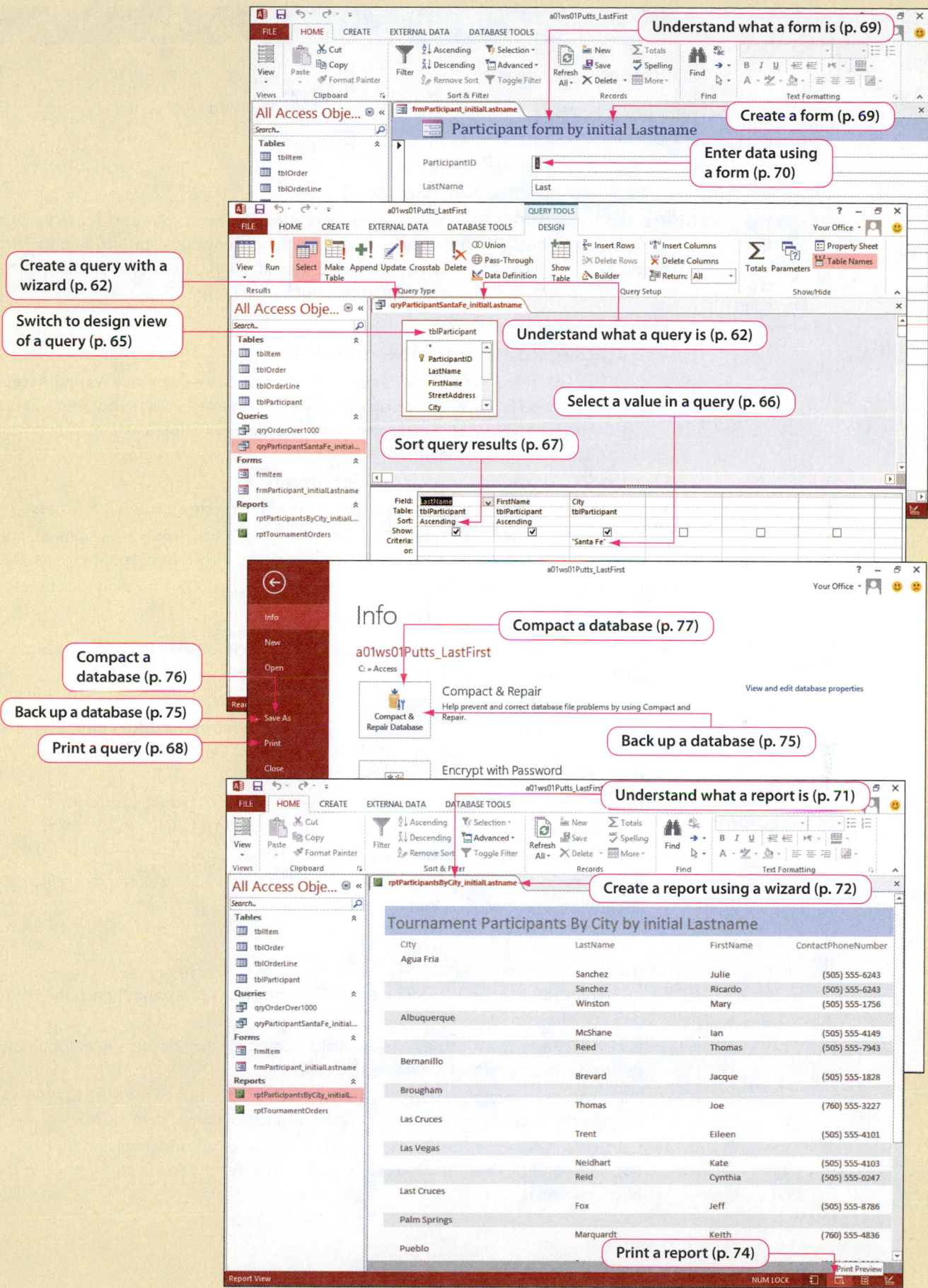

Figure 33 Putts for Paws Charity Tournament Participants Final Database

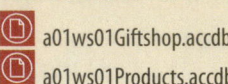 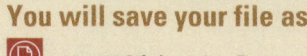
Student data files needed:

a01ws01Giftshop.accdb

a01ws01Products.accdb

You will save your file as:

a01ws01Giftshop_LastFirst.accdb

Painted Treasures Gift Shop

Sales & Marketing

The Painted Treasures Gift Shop sells many products for the resort patrons. These include jewelry from local artists, Painted Paradise linens, products from the resort's restaurant, and spa products. You will create a database that stores the gift shop's products. You will create a form to enter products and create an inventory report.

a. Create your database.

- Start **Access**, and then open **a01ws01Giftshop**.
- Click the **FILE** tab, and then click **Save As**. Make sure **Save Database As** and **Access Database** are selected, and then click **Save As**. In the Save As dialog box, navigate to where you are saving your files, and then type a01ws01Giftshop_LastFirst, using your last and first name. Click **Save**.
- In the SECURITY WARNING, click **Enable Content**.
- Click the **EXTERNAL DATA** tab, and then in the Import & Link group, click **Access**.
- In the Get External Data - Access Database dialog box, click **Browse**, navigate to your student data files, and then select **a01ws01Products**. Click **Open**, and then click **OK**.
- In the **Import Objects** dialog box, select **tblProduct**, click **OK**, and then click **Close**.

b. Create a query to find the clothing products.

- Click the **CREATE** tab, and then in the Queries group, click **Query Wizard**. Click **Simple Query Wizard**, and then click **OK**.
- Select **Table: tblProduct** as the source of your fields.
- In this order, select the **ProductID**, **Category**, **ProductDescription**, **Color**, **Size**, and **Price** fields and move them to the Selected Fields box. Click **Next**, click **Detail (shows every field of every record)**, and then click **Next**.
- Under **What title do you want for your query?**, type qryProductsClothingType_initialLastname using your first initial and last name.
- Click **Modify the query design**, and then click **Finish**.
- In the Category Criteria cell, type Clothing, in the ProductDescription Sort cell, select **Ascending**, and then click **Run** in the Results group.
- Save and close the query.

c. Create a form to enter new products.

- Click **tblProduct** in the Navigation Pane. Click the **CREATE** tab, and then in the Forms group, click **Form**.
- Click **Save**, and then in the Save As dialog box, type frmProduct_initialLastname using your first initial and last name. Click **OK**.
- In Layout view, select the **form title**, and then change the title of the form to Products Form by initial Lastname using your first initial and last name. Save the form.
- On the DESIGN tab, in the Views group, click the **View** button arrow, and then select **Form View**. Click **New (blank) record**, and then enter the following product in the blank append record.

ProductID	42
ProductDescription	Polo Shirt
Category	Clothing
QuantityInStock	35
Price	30.00
Size	L
Color	Blue

- Close the form.

d. Create an inventory report.

- Click the **CREATE** tab, and then in the Reports group, click **Report Wizard**.
- Click the **Tables/Queries** arrow, and then click **Table: tblProduct**.
- Select the fields in the following order: **Category**, **ProductDescription**, **Color**, **Size**, and **QuantityInStock**, and then click **Next**.
- Under **Do you want to add any grouping levels?**, double-click **Category** and **ProductDescription**, and then click **Next**.
- In the **1** box, click the **arrow**, and then select **Color**. In the **2** box, click the **arrow**, select **Size**, and then Click **Next**.
- Change the Layout to **Stepped**, the Orientation to **Landscape**, and then click **Next**.
- Type rptInventory_initialLastname, using your first initial and last name, as the title for your report, and then click **Finish**.
- Switch to **Layout** view, and then change the report title to Inventory Report by initial Lastname using your first initial and last name.
- Save and close the report, and then close the database. Submit your file as directed by your instructor.

Problem Solve 1

MyITLab® Grader
Homework 1

Production & Operations

Student data files needed:

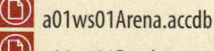 a01ws01Arena.accdb

a01ws01Employee.accdb

You will save your file as:

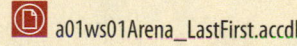 a01ws01Arena_LastFirst.accdb

Sunshine Event Arena

The Sunshine Event Arena (SEA) is an arena that hosts such local events as banquets, concerts, and sporting events. The database contains tables that track events, ticket sales, and patrons of the arena.

You will expand the database by importing an employee table and creating a form, a report, and a query.

a. Start **Access**, and then open **a01ws01Arena**.

b. Click the **FILE** tab, and then click **Save As**. Make sure **Save Database As** and **Access Database** are selected, and then click **Save As**. Browse to where you are storing your files, name your database a01ws01Arena_LastFirst, using your last and first name, and then click **Save**. Click **Enable Content** in the SECURITY WARNING.

c. Import tables from the Access database **a01ws01Employee**, selecting the **tblEmployee** table. Do not save the import steps.

d. Create a form for **tblEmployee**, and then save the form as frmEmployee_initialLastname.

e. Change the title of the form to Employee Form by initial Lastname using your first initial and last name.

f. Switch to Form view. Use the navigation bar at the bottom of the screen to navigate to the **New (blank) record** for tblEmployee. Make sure the employee fields are blank, and enter the following information for a new employee:

Employee ID	(Access will fill)
First Name	Your actual first name
Last Name	Your actual last name
Address	1020 Range Drive
City	Pueblo
State	NM
Phone	(505) 555–1222

g. A patron named Elaine called, and you want to call her back but need her number. Use the Query Wizard to create a query listing **FirstName**, **LastName**, and **Phone** from tblPatrons. Save your query as qryPatronNamedElaine_initialLastname.

h. In **Design** view for **qryPatronNamedElaine_initialLastname**, select the patrons with a FirstName of Elaine. Sort the results by **LastName**, and then run the query.

i. Create a report on events showing **EventDate**, **EventName**, **EventType**, **TicketsAvailable**, and **TicketPrice** from tblEvents. Group by **EventType**, sort by **EventDate**, and then change to **Landscape** orientation. Name your report rptEvents_initialLastname. In Layout view, change the report title to read Event Report by initial Lastname.

j. Close the database. Submit your file as directed by your instructor.

Perform 1: Perform in Your Career

Student data file needed:

 a01ws01Roadhouse.accdb

You will save your file as:

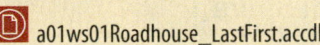 a01ws01Roadhouse_LastFirst.accdb

Beverage Database at The Roadhouse Bar and Grill

Production & Operations

You are the bar manager at The Roadhouse Bar and Grill, a local restaurant that specializes in home-cooked meals for breakfast, lunch, and dinner. You have a database that you use for managing the inventory of beverage items.

You will expand the database by creating a form, reports, and queries.

a. Start **Access**, open the student data file **a01ws01Roadhouse**, and then save it as a01ws01Roadhouse_LastFirst, using your first and last name. Manually navigate the tables in the database to explore the types of data in the database.

b. Create a form for **tblSuppliers** and name it frmSuppliers_initialLastname. Use your form to change the name of the first supplier to your full name.

c. Create a report showing suppliers and name it rptSuppliers_initialLastname.

d. Create a query that shows what types of beverages you have that are in a can and name it qryCannedBeverage_initialLastname.

e. Create another report that you would find useful in your job.

f. Create another query that you would find useful in your job.

g. If your instructor asks you to print your results, print all reports and queries.

h. Close your database. Submit your file as directed by your instructor.

Additional Cases

Additional Workshop Cases are available on the companion website and in the instructor resources.

WORKSHOP 2 | TABLES, KEYS, AND RELATIONSHIPS

Prepare Case

Red Bluff Golf Club Putts for Paws Charity Tournament Database

Production & Operations

The Red Bluff Golf Club is sponsoring a charity tournament, Putts for Paws, to raise money for the local pet shelter. You are modifying a database for the tournament that tracks money being raised from the event. The scope of this database is limited to tracking monies. Thus, in this instance, you are not tracking whether a participant is a golfer, volunteer, or other role. Anyone can donate money in the form of hole

Nico Traut / Shutterstock

sponsorship or other donation item. You will want to track monies derived from corporate sponsorship. You will bring in data for the event from various sources including Excel worksheets and text files.

REAL WORLD SUCCESS

"Reports on open issues were very important to my project manager. I set up a database with a main table of open issues. I used foreign keys to link it to employee tables and to a table of priorities. That way I could give a report on the issue and who reported it with how important it was."

- Joseph P., IT intern

Student data files needed for this workshop:

 a01ws02Putts.accdb   a01ws02PuttsGolf.xlsx    a01ws02PuttsCont.xlsx

 a01ws02PuttsVol.xlsx   a01ws02PuttsDon.txt

You will save your files as:

 a01ws02Putts_LastFirst.accdb

 a01ws02PuttsDon_LastFirst.txt

Inserting Data into a Database

In designing a database, you will develop the tables, fields, and relationships of the tables. To manage the golf tournament, you will need to keep track of participants, the corporations that participate, the tee times, and the items each of the participants purchase. Each of these will be a table in your database. In this section, you will load tables from already existing databases and from Excel worksheets, in addition to creating two new tables.

Understand Database Design

Database design can be thought of as a three-step process:

1. Identify your entities—they become the tables.
2. Identify the attributes—they become the fields.
3. Specify the relationships between the tables.

An **entity** is a person, place, item, or event that you want to keep data about. You decide that you need to keep track of participants including golfers, donors, and corporate representatives. You need a participant table to track these people. A single participant is an instance of the participant entity and will become a record in the participant table.

An **attribute** is information about the entity. For example, for each participant you will want to keep information, such as name and address. These attributes will become the fields in your table.

A **relationship** is an association between tables based on common fields. You can see the power of Access when you relate tables together. For example, you can relate participants to orders that the participants place.

Later in the workshop, you will look more closely at designing a database. While you explore the database tables and data, think about these general principles or steps to follow.

1. Brainstorm a list of all the types of data you will need.
2. Rearrange data items into groups that represent a single entity. These groups will become your tables.
3. If one item can have several attributes, such as a credit card number, expiration date, name on a card, and security code, then put it into one group that will later become a table of its own. In this example, it would be a group named "credit card".
4. Break each attribute into the smallest attributes; they will become the fields. Give each attribute a descriptive name. For example, split addresses into street, city, state, and zip code.
5. Do not include totals, but do include all of the data needed so the calculation can be done in a query. For example, include the price of an item and the quantity ordered so the total cost can be calculated.
6. Remove any redundant data that exists in multiple groupings. For example, do not repeat customer names in both the customer grouping and the sales grouping.
7. Ensure common fields connect the groupings. For example, make sure that there is a common field between the customer grouping and the sales grouping so they can be connected. Later in this workshop, you will learn more about common fields.

You start with the participant entity, which is the tblParticipant table. You notice that it contains the fields shown in Table 1 to track the participants in the tournament.

Field Name	Data Type	Description	Field Size
ParticipantID	Number—Long Integer	A unique ID that identifies each participant	
LastName	Short Text	Last name	25
FirstName	Short Text	First name	20
StreetAddress	Short Text	Street address	35
City	Short Text	City	25
State	Short Text	State abbreviation	2
ZipCode	Short Text	Five digit zip code	5
ContactPhoneNumber	Short Text	Phone number for the individual participant	14
CorporatePhoneNumber	Short Text	Phone number for the corporation the participant represents	14

Table 1 Fields for tblParticipant

REAL WORLD ADVICE | Break Compound Fields into Their Parts

You might wonder why the name field and address fields are divided into multiple fields. Would it not be easier to have a single field for Name and a single field for Address? It might be easier for data entry, but it is much more difficult for reporting.

- Break names into first name and last name fields. That means you can sort on people alphabetically by last name, and if two people have the same last name, by first name.

- Break addresses into fields such as StreetAddress, City, State, and ZipCode. This allows reporting by state, city, or other fields.

- For other fields, consider whether you might want to report on smaller parts of the field. For example, for PhoneNumber in some applications, you might want to report on AreaCode. However, that would be rare, and so you usually use just one field.

Illustrating some of the basic principles of database design, notice that the participant's name is split into two fields and the address is split into four fields. Why should you do this? When you have fields such as name or address that are composed of several smaller fields, you should split them into their component parts. This allows for more flexibility for reporting. For example, often a report is needed in alphabetic order by last or first name. You could not do this if you had stored the first and last name combined in the same field. Further, a field named "Name" is confusing, leading to inconsistent data such as nicknames and incomplete names. This also allows you to report or query on just part of the field such as which participants are from a particular state.

CONSIDER THIS | Street Address Components

Street addresses contain two parts, the number and street name. While some databases split these apart, this is not necessary for most business uses. What are some businesses that would benefit from separating these?

| REAL WORLD ADVICE | First and Last Names |

Painted Paradise is a U.S. company with guests who primarily use a first name followed by a last name. However, not all cultures around the world break names into first and last. For example, Korean names are designated as family name followed by given name. Designing database fields to accommodate all of the different cultures in the world is challenging. Always keep in mind the typical name for the database, but try to design it in such a way that other naming practices can fit into the database. Because businesses today are global, designing a database sensitive to all global cultures is difficult but important.

Opening the Starting File

For the golf tournament, you will need to keep track of participants, the corporations that participate, and the items each of the participants purchase. There are several files that tournament organizers have been keeping about the tournament. You will import all the files into your Access database.

A02.00

 To Open the a01ws02Putts Database

a. Start **Access**, and then open the student data file named **a01ws02Putts** in the folder location designated by your instructor.

b. Click the **FILE** tab, click **Save As,** click **Save Database As**, click **Save As** and then locate the folder or location designated by your instructor. Save the file as an Access Database in the location where you save your files with the name **a01ws02Putts_LastFirst** using your last and first name. If necessary, enable the content.

Understanding Data and Design Views of Tables

Tables have two views: Datasheet view and Design view. Datasheet view shows the values of the data within the table. The Design view shows the structure of the table with the fields and their definitions.

A02.01

MyITLab®

Workshop 2 Training

 To View Table Design View

a. Double-click the **tblParticipant** table to open it.
   When you open the tblParticipant table, it opens in Datasheet view. In Datasheet view, you can see the information about the participants.

b. If necessary, click the **First record** button ⏮ in the Navigation bar to return to the first participant.

c. Press [Tab] to move to the **LastName** column.

d. Replace **Last** in the first record of the LastName column with your last name, press [Tab] to move to the next column, and then replace **First** in the FirstName column with your first name.

Replace Last and First with your last and first name

ParticipantID	LastName	FirstName	StreetAddress	City	State	ZipCode	ContactPho
1	Last	First	1563 Catalina Dr	Santa Fe	NM	87508	(505) 555-17
2	Trujillo	John	427 Kanengiser Rd	Santa Ana Pueblo	NM	87045	(505) 555-82
3	McShane	Ian	823 4th St NW	Albuquerque	NM	87106	(505) 555-41
5	Fresquez	Marge	534 Asiento Blvd	Pueblo	NM	81232	(505) 555-38
8	Maestas	Marcus	83 Vuelta Rancho	Santa Fe	NM	87508	(505) 555-25

Figure 1 Datasheet view of tblParticipant

e. Click the **HOME** tab, and then in the Views group, click the **View** arrow, and then select **Design View**. When you switch to Design view, you see the structure of the fields and the field properties.

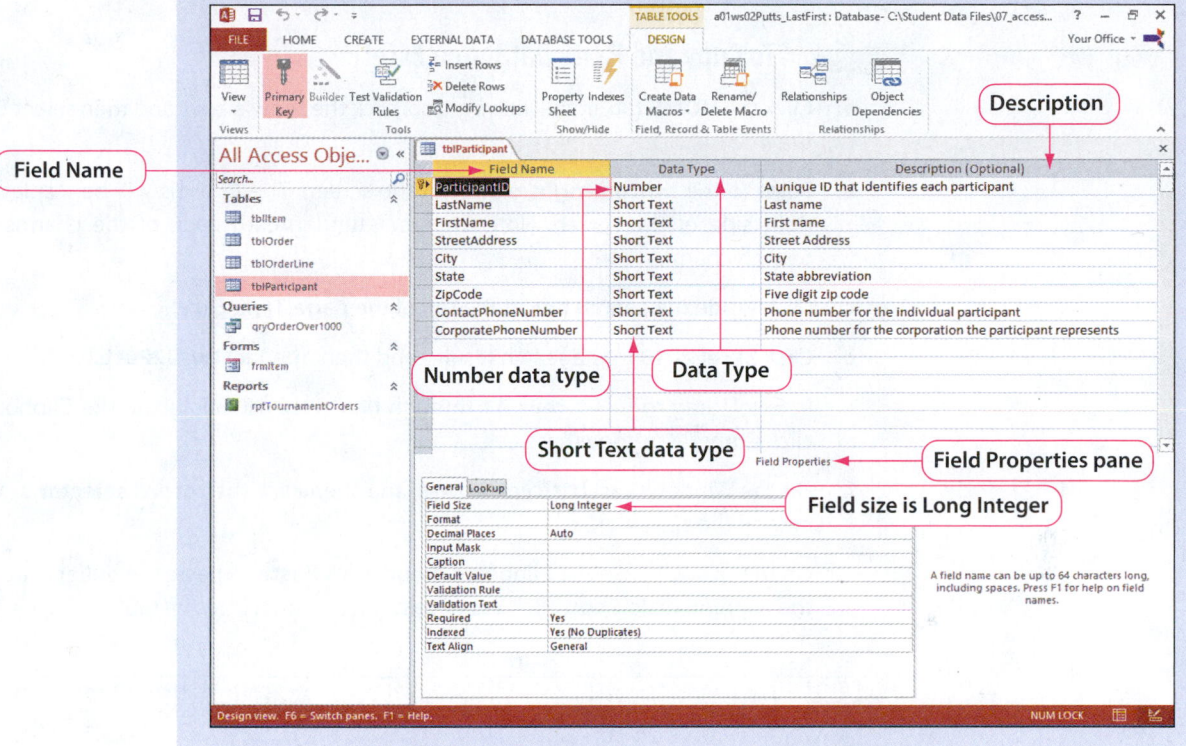

Figure 2 Design view of tblParticipant

The upper pane of Design view has three columns: Field Name, Data Type, and Description. The Field Name is the column label in Datasheet view. **Data types** define the kind of data that can be entered into a field, such as numbers, text, or dates. The data type tells Access how to store and display the field. Number and Short Text are the two most common data types. In this table, you can see that one field is stored as a **Number data type**. That means that the data can only contain numeric characters. The Short **Text data type** allows any text and numeric characters to be stored. Street Address is the Short Text data type, so a street address in this database can contain numbers, letters, and special characters. The third column, Description, helps the user discern the meaning of the field.

The Field Properties pane in Design view gives more information on how the data is stored, entered, and processed. If the ParticipantID field is selected, you can see that its Field Size is Long Integer.

Import Data from Other Sources

Painted Paradise has had different employees collecting data in different ways. Luckily, the applications within the Microsoft Office suite work together. This allows you to import—move data—easily between Excel and Access. You will import the files from Excel, Access, and Notepad. After importing the data, you will be able to further analyze and refine the table structure for the database. Even though other employees have kept track of the roles that each participant plays, remember that the scope of this database does not include tracking the participants' roles in the event. You are only tracking corporate involvement.

Copying and Pasting

Only a few golfer participants were entered into the tblParticipant table. Some others were put in an Excel worksheet. You will copy and paste them from Excel into your Access table.

A02.02

To Copy and Paste Data from Excel

a. Click the **HOME** tab, in the Views group, click the **View** arrow, and then select **Datasheet View**.

b. Point to the **bottom-right corner** of the screen. The Charms will be displayed on the right side of the screen. Note the labels underneath each of the charms. Click the **Search** charm.

c. Click inside the **search box** at the top of the page. Type Excel.

d. Click **Excel 2013** in the search results, and then open **a01ws02PuttsGolf**.

e. In Excel, drag to select **cells A1** through **I9**. On the HOME tab, in the Clipboard group, click **Copy** to copy these cells.

f. On the Windows taskbar, click **Access**, and then click the **record selector** at the beginning of the append row.

g. On the HOME tab, in the Clipboard group, click **Paste** to paste the golfers into Access. In the warning dialog box, click **Yes** to paste the records into the table.

New golfers added to table

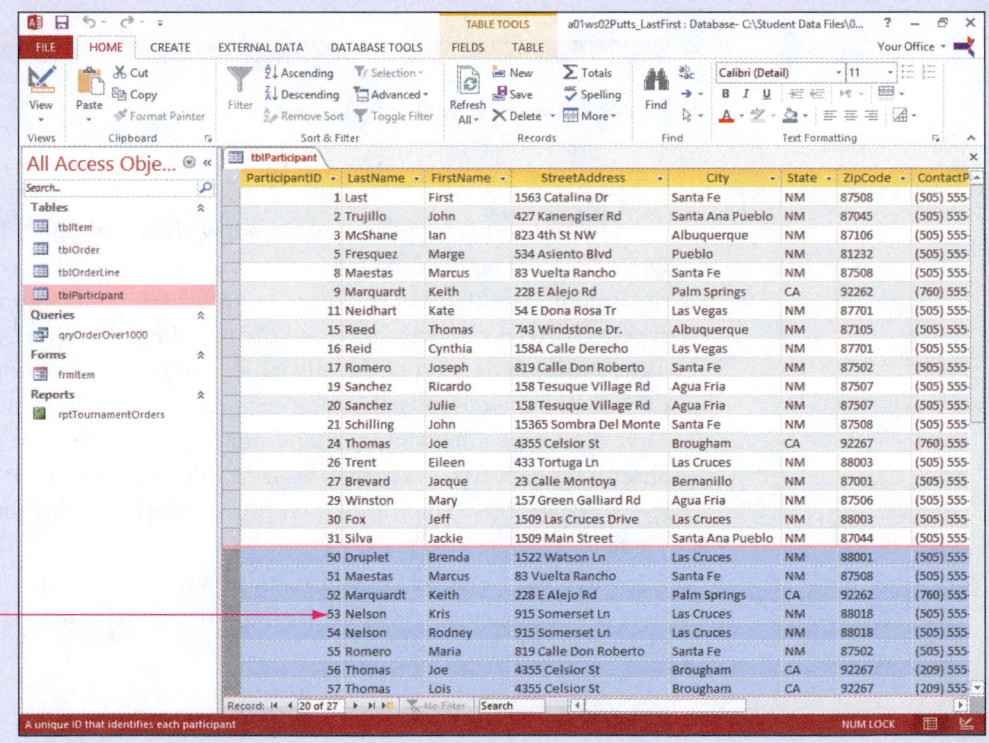

Figure 3 New golfers at the end of the tblParticipant table

Troubleshooting

If you accidently click in a single cell of the append row and try to paste there, you get the error message "The text is too long to be edited." It appears that you are trying to paste all the data into one cell, and Access will not let you continue. If this happens, click OK, indicating that you do not want to put all the text into the one cell.

After that it may be difficult to exit that row and click in the record selector column. It appears you are trying to paste an invalid row, and Access will not let you continue. You will get an error message saying "Index or primary key cannot contain a Null value." When you click OK and try to recover, the message will reappear. If this happens, press Esc indicating that you do not want to keep that record.

h. **Close** ☒ the tblParticipant table.

REAL WORLD ADVICE | **Copying and Pasting from Excel into Access**

Copying and pasting requires that the columns be exactly the same in Excel and Access. There cannot be missing columns or columns in different orders. You cannot paste fields that are nonnumeric into numeric fields. If you have any doubt about the data being compatible, use the Import feature to append the data to the table.

Use Copy and Paste when:

- You started in Access and exported the data to Excel, made additions, and now want to import it into Access. That way you know that the columns are the same.

- You are copying and pasting the contents of a single field from Excel into Access, such as a street address.

Importing a Worksheet

Access allows you to import an entire worksheet or a smaller portion of a worksheet into a table. This is quite useful as Excel is so frequently used in organizations. Excel column headings are frequently imported as field names.

The golf club has been keeping corporate contacts for the event in an Excel worksheet. You will import this Excel worksheet into your tblParticipant table.

A02.03

 To Import an Excel Spreadsheet

a. On the Windows taskbar, click **Excel**, click the **FILE** tab, and then click **Close**.

b. Click the **FILE** tab, and then click **Open**. Navigate to your student data files, click **a01ws02PuttsCont**, and then click **Open**.

Notice that the contacts data looks like the tblParticipant table in many ways. However, the corporate phone number immediately follows the participant's name rather than being at the end of the record as it is in the Access table. An import from Excel into an existing Access table is ideal for this type of import because as long as the columns have the same name, Access will match up the columns, skipping any missing column. You cannot copy and paste the way you did earlier because the columns are not arranged in the same order.

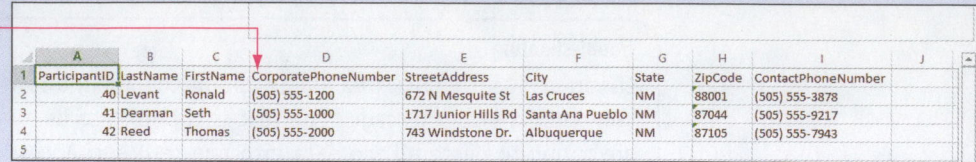

CorporatePhoneNumber immediately follows FirstName

	A	B	C	D	E	F	G	H	I	J
1	ParticipantID	LastName	FirstName	CorporatePhoneNumber	StreetAddress	City	State	ZipCode	ContactPhoneNumber	
2	40	Levant	Ronald	(505) 555-1200	672 N Mesquite St	Las Cruces	NM	88001	(505) 555-3878	
3	41	Dearman	Seth	(505) 555-1000	1717 Junior Hills Rd	Santa Ana Pueblo	NM	87044	(505) 555-9217	
4	42	Reed	Thomas	(505) 555-2000	743 Windstone Dr.	Albuquerque	NM	87105	(505) 555-7943	
5										

Figure 4 Contact data in Excel

c. **Close** ☒ Excel.

d. In Access, click the **EXTERNAL DATA** tab, and then in the Import & Link group, click **Excel**. The Get External Data - Excel Spreadsheet dialog box appears.

e. Click **Browse**, navigate to your student data files, click **a01ws02PuttsCont**, and then click **Open**. Select **Append a copy of the records to the table**, click the **arrow**, select **tblParticipant**, and then click **OK**.

   The Import Spreadsheet Wizard opens, which displays worksheets and named ranges in the Excel workbook.

f. Make sure **Show Worksheets** is selected and the **Corporate contacts** worksheet is highlighted, and then click **Next**.

   Access displays the next page of the wizard. This shows that Access found the column headings in Excel and matched them to the field names in Access.

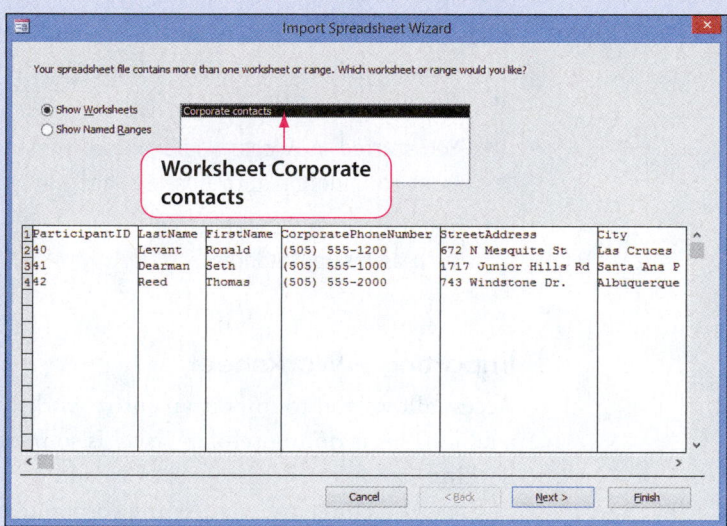

Worksheet Corporate contacts

Figure 5 Worksheet to be imported

SIDE NOTE
Tables Are Ordered by Primary Key

When you added the contacts, they were added in the middle of the table because Access orders tables by primary key.

g. Click **Next**, click **Finish**, and then click **Close**.

h. In the Navigation Pane, double-click the **tblParticipant table** to open the table.

   Your table has the three corporate contacts added. The contacts were imported and because the field names in Access matched the Excel column headings, the fields were rearranged to match the Access table order.

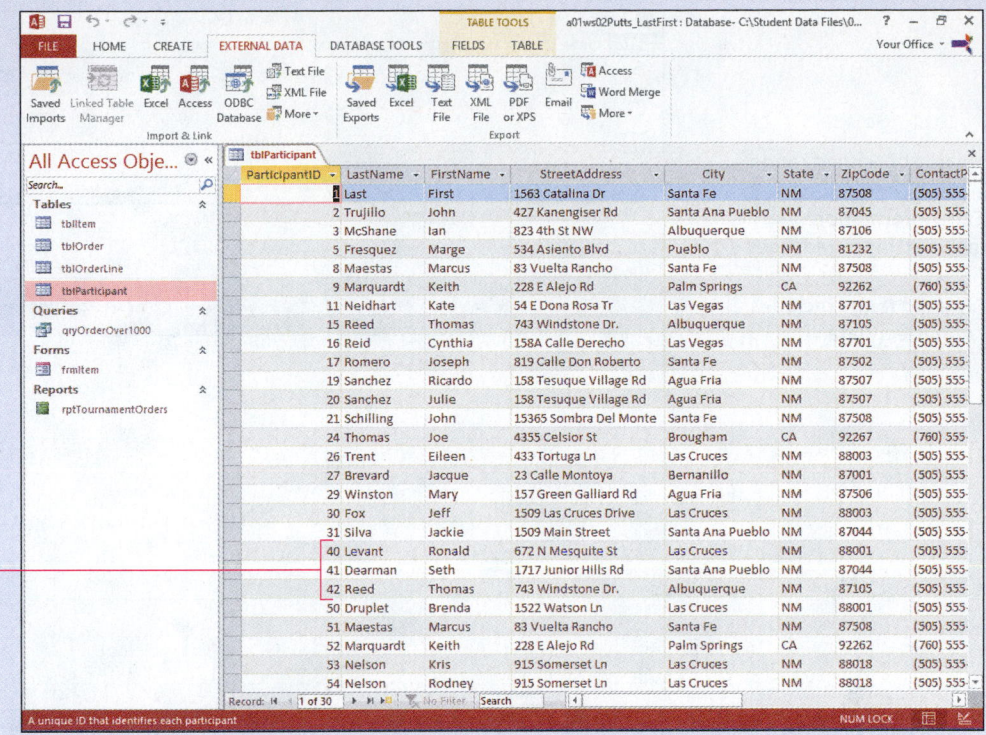

Contacts imported

Figure 6 Corporate contacts imported into tblParticipant table

i. Close ☒ the tblParticipant table.

Importing from a Named Range

Access allows you to import a smaller portion of a worksheet, known as a named range, into a table. A named range is a group of cells that have been given a name that can then be used within a formula or function. This part of the worksheet can then be referenced in formulas or charts by name rather than by cell address or range address.

The golf club has been keeping information about the volunteers for the event in an Excel worksheet. This worksheet contains other information about volunteering that you will not need. The range containing the contact information for the volunteers has been named VolunteerNamesAddress.

A02.04

 To Import a Named Range

a. Start **Excel 2013**, and then open **a01ws02PuttsVol**.

Notice the Volunteers worksheet contains the volunteer information as well as other data.

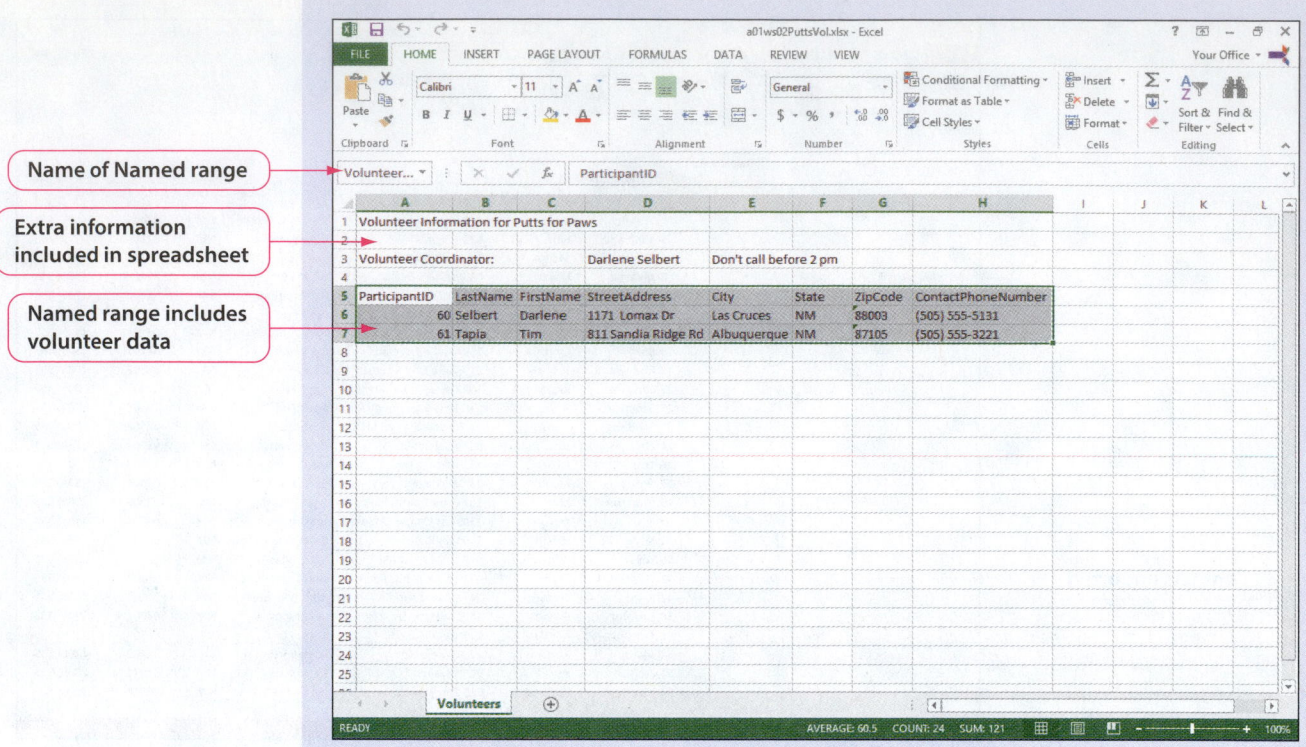

Name of Named range

Extra information included in spreadsheet

Named range includes volunteer data

Figure 7 Volunteers worksheet with extra information

b. **Close** ☒ Excel.

c. In Access, click the **EXTERNAL DATA** tab, and then in the Import & Link group, click **Excel**. The Get External Data - Excel Spreadsheet dialog box appears.

d. Click **Browse**, navigate to your student data files, click **a01ws02PuttsVol**, and then click **Open**.

e. Select **Append a copy of the records to the table**, click the **arrow**, and then select **tblParticipant**.

f. Click **OK**, and then click **Show Named Ranges**.

One named range, VolunteerNamesAddress, is displayed and highlighted in the list box.

g. Click **Next**. Access tells you that it found your column headings in Excel and matched them to the field names in Access. Click **Next**.

h. Click **Finish**, and then click **Close**.

i. In the Navigation Pane, double-click the **tblParticipant table** to open the table. Your table has the two volunteers added.

j. **Close** ☒ the tblParticipant table.

Importing from a Text File

Access enables you to import data from text and Word files. Typically these files would have data organized in tables. In Word, these tables will have actual rows and columns. In text files, the tables are implied by the separation of the columns. This separation is done by delimiter characters. A **delimiter** is a character such as a tab or comma that separates the fields. The rows in the text tables will be imported as records into your Access table.

The golf course has been keeping information about the donors for the event in a text file. You want to import that data into your Access database.

A02.05

 To Import from a Text File

a. Point to the **bottom-right corner** of the screen. The Charms will be displayed on the right side of the screen. Click the **Search** charm.

b. Click inside the **search box** at the top of the page, type Notepad and then click **Notepad** in the search results.

c. Click **File**, click **Open**, and in the Open dialog box in the left pane, navigate to your student data files, click **a01ws02PuttsDon**, and then click **Open**.

   Notice that there are three donors in this file. The fields are separated by unseen tabs.

d. **Close** ☒ Notepad.

> **Troubleshooting**
>
> Your columns may not line up the way that Figure 8 shows them lining up. This happens because Notepad does not save font formatting. Notepad does save tabs so you do not need to worry about any display differences.

File menu →

Three donors in text file →

```
a01ws02PuttsDon.txt - Notepad
File  Edit  Format  View  Help
ParticipantID  LastName        FirstName    StreetAddress      City      State   ZipCode  ContactPhoneNumber
30      Ortiz     Luis     1801 Brilliant Sky Dr   Santa Fe   NM      87508    (505) 555-1722
33      Ramirez   Alice    124 Nana Lou St.        Avondale   CO      81022    (719) 555-9247
34      Victor    Lisa     988 Elguitarra Rd       Santa Fe   NM      87507    (505) 555-2757
```

Figure 8 Donor text file in Notepad

e. In Access, click the **EXTERNAL DATA** tab, and then in the Import & Link group, click **Text File**. The Get External Data - Text File dialog box appears.

f. Click **Browse**, navigate to your student data files, click **a01ws02PuttsDon**, and then click **Open**.

g. Click **Append a copy of the records to the table**, click the **arrow** to select **tblParticipant**, and then click **OK**. Access recognizes that this data has columns that are delimited—separated by tabs or commas.

h. Click **Next**, select the **Tab** delimiter, and then click to select the **First Row Contains Field Names** check box.

i. Click **Next**, and then click **Finish**.

   An error message appears saying that Access is unable to append all the data to the table and that one record was lost because of key violations. The first field in your table is a primary key that must be unique. Apparently one of the donors has a ParticipantID that was already used in the Access table.

j. Click **No**, click **OK**, click **OK**, and then click **Cancel**.

k. Double-click **tblParticipant** to open the table in Datasheet view.

l. Open **Notepad**, click **File,** select **Open...**, navigate to your student data files, click **a01ws02PuttsDon**, and then click **Open**. There are three donors in the file that have ParticipantIDs of 30, 33, and 34 as shown in Figure 8.

m. Compare the donor data in the text file to the records in the tblParticipant table. Notice ParticipantID 30 has been used twice, once for Jeff Fox in the Access table and once for Luis Ortiz in the Notepad file. You talk to the person keeping records of donors and discover she meant to type "32" for Luis Ortiz.

n. In Notepad, click **File**, and then click **Save As**. In the Save As dialog box, navigate to the location where you are saving your files. In the **File** name box, type **a01ws02PuttsDon_LastFirst** using your last and first name. Click **Save**.

> **Troubleshooting**
>
> If your Save As dialog box does not show folders, click Browse Folders at the bottom of the dialog box.

o. In Notepad, select the text **30**, and then type **32**.

ParticipantID 30 changed to 32

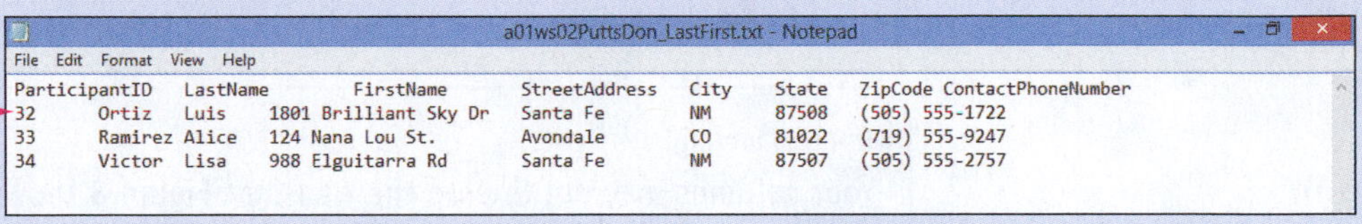

ParticipantID	LastName	FirstName	StreetAddress	City	State	ZipCode	ContactPhoneNumber
32	Ortiz	Luis	1801 Brilliant Sky Dr	Santa Fe	NM	87508	(505) 555-1722
33	Ramirez	Alice	124 Nana Lou St.	Avondale	CO	81022	(719) 555-9247
34	Victor	Lisa	988 Elguitarra Rd	Santa Fe	NM	87507	(505) 555-2757

Figure 9 Change ParticipantID from 30 to 32

p. **Close** ❌ Notepad, and then save the file.

q. In Access, **close** ❌ the tblParticipant table. On the EXTERNAL DATA tab, in the Import & Link group, click **Text File**. The Get External Data - Text File dialog box appears.

r. Click **Browse**, navigate to where you are storing your solution files, click **a01ws02PuttsDon_LastFirst**, and then click **Open**.

s. Repeat the import Steps g–i. This time Access successfully imports the donors.

t. Click **Close**. Double-click **tblParticipant** to open the table and verify that the records for Luis Ortiz, Alice Ramirez, and Lisa Victor were imported.

u. **Close** ❌ the tblParticipant table.

REAL WORLD ADVICE | **Importing an Excel Worksheet into a New Table**

In all the previous examples of importing, you imported into an already existing table. You can also import into a new table. Access creates a table using the column headings for field names. Access defines fields with default definitions. After performing the import, open the table in Design view and adjust fields and properties as necessary. Some things that you should consider in these adjustments are the following:

- What field did Access assign as the primary key for the table? Access defaults to creating a new field called ID for the primary key. Later in the workshop, you will learn what field might work better as a primary key.

- The default length for all short text fields is 255 characters. Adjust the field size properties to sizes that are appropriate for your fields. Check all field definitions for errors.

- Are the field names descriptive? The column headings from Excel might not be appropriate as field names in Access.

Enter Data Manually

If the data does not already exist in another form, you can type the data directly into Access. There are two methods: entering data directly into the table or entering the data in a form.

Entering Data Using Datasheet View

When you open a table in Datasheet view, you can type data directly into the table. You want to enter a new order. You will need to enter data into tblOrder and the details of the order in tblOrderLine. The order to enter is your own; you are entering the tournament as a golfer.

A02.06

To Enter Data in Datasheet View

a. In the Navigation Pane, double-click **tblOrder**, click in the **AmountPaid** column of the append row, and then type **200**.

As you type the "200", a pencil icon ✎ appears in the record selector on the left. The pencil icon means that this record is actively being modified. Additionally, the OrderID was filled in with "12". This happens because the field has a data type of AutoNumber, which means that Access assigns the next highest number.

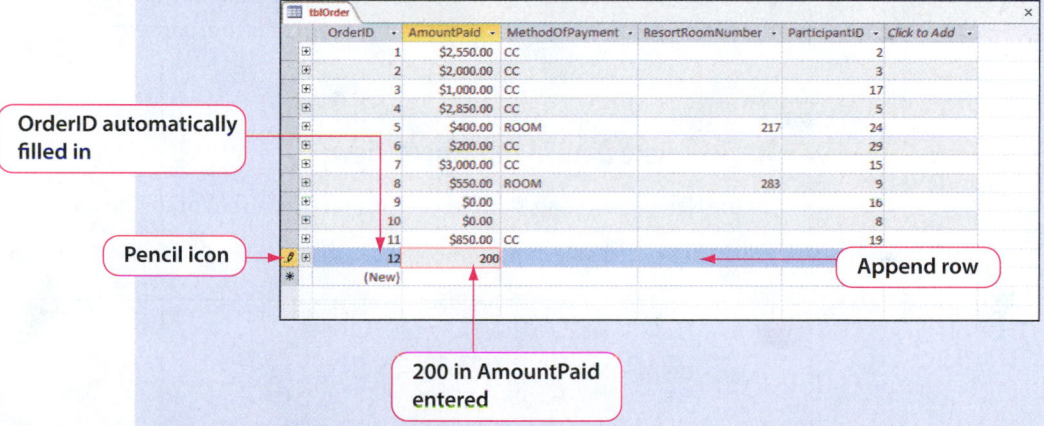

OrderID automatically filled in

Pencil icon

Append row

200 in AmountPaid entered

Figure 10 Type 200 in AmountPaid

b. Press [Tab] to continue filling in the record with a MethodOfPayment of **CC**, leave the ResortRoomNumber empty, and then type **1** in ParticipantID.

c. Press [Tab] to go to the next record. The pencil icon disappears. Unlike Word and Excel, Access immediately saves the data change.

d. **Close** ☒ the tblOrder table.

e. In the Navigation Pane, double-click **tblOrderLine**, click in **OrderID** of the append row, and then type **12**.

f. Press [Tab] to continue filling in the record with LineNum **1**, ItemID **G1**, and Quantity **1**.

g. **Close** ☒ the tblOrderLine table.

REAL WORLD ADVICE | Undoing in Access

Access immediately saves the changes you make to data. There is very limited undo/redo functionality in Access. If the Undo button 🔄 is dimmed, you cannot undo the change you made.

- Typically you can undo a single typing change even if you have gone on to the next record. However, if you made several changes to different records, you cannot undo more than the changes to the last record.

- If you have made changes to several fields in a single record, you can click Undo to undo each of them.

- You can also press Esc to stop editing a record and revert to the record data as it appeared before you started changing the record.

- If you make an error, you can press Esc to get out of the error.

  Because of the limited undo features in Access, do not count on undoing your changes. You will often find that you cannot undo. For example, when you delete a record or records, you cannot undo the deletion.

  Design changes are not saved until you save the object you changed. Thus, you can undo design changes until you save.

Removing Data

You can delete records from a table. These are permanent deletions and cannot be undone. Golfer Kate Neidhart needs to withdraw from the tournament.

A02.07

▶ To Delete Data in Datasheet View

a. In the Navigation Pane, double-click **tblParticipant** to open the table in Datasheet view.

b. Click the **record selector** for record 7, Kate Neidhart, ParticipantID 11, to select the row.

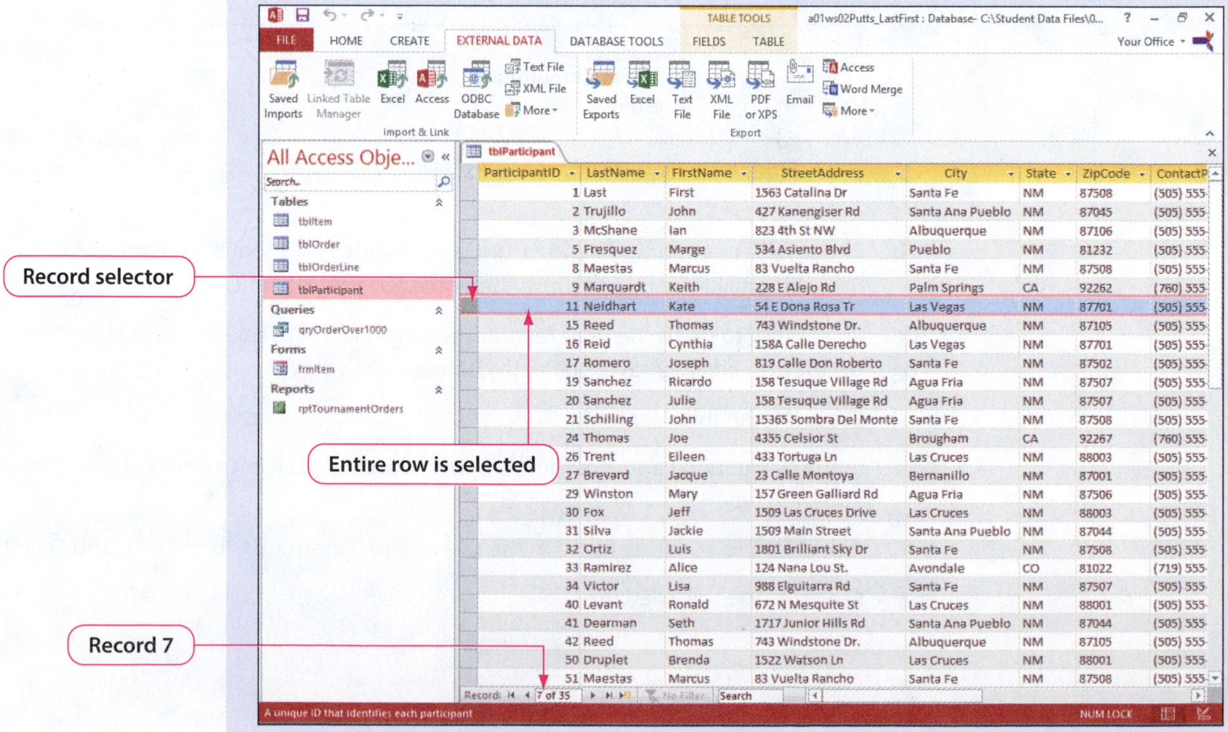

Figure 11 Delete Kate Neidhart record

c. Right-click the **row**, and then select **Delete Record**. Because you cannot undo a delete, Access asks if you are sure you want to delete this record.

d. Click **Yes**. The record is deleted.

> **Troubleshooting**
>
> If you do not get the Access confirmation message asking if you are sure you want the deletion to occur, the confirmation message setting may be turned off. If you would like to turn it back on, on the File tab, click Options, and then click Client Settings. Scroll down to find the Confirm section under Editing, click the Document deletions check box, and click OK.

You can also delete individual fields from a table. These are also permanent deletions and cannot be undone. You decide that you will create a table for corporations involved with the tournament, tblCorporate, and that the CorporatePhoneNumber will be a part of that table. Thus, you will not need CorporatePhoneNumber for each tblParticipant record, and you will delete that field. You can delete a field in either Design view or Datasheet view. In Datasheet view, you can see the contents of the field that you are deleting, which gives you an extra check on whether you really want to delete the field.

A02.08

 To Delete a Field in Datasheet View

a. Scroll to the right to find the **CorporatePhoneNumber** column. Point to the **column heading** until it changes to a black down arrow, and then click so the entire column is highlighted. Make sure that you selected **CorporatePhoneNumber** and not **ContactPhoneNumber**.

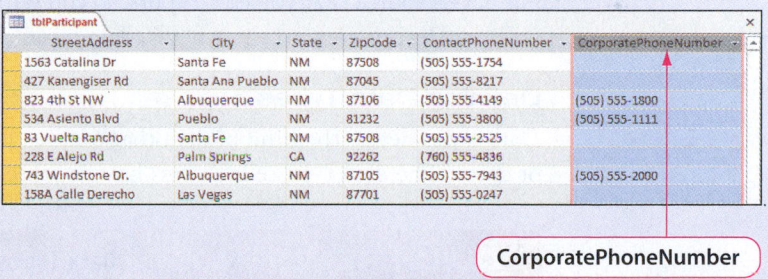

CorporatePhoneNumber

Figure 12   Select the CorporatePhoneNumber column

b. Click the **HOME** tab, and then in the Records group, click **Delete**.
    Because you cannot undo a delete, Access asks, "Do you want to permanently delete the selected field(s) and all the data in the field(s)? To permanently delete the field(s), click Yes." Because you are in Datasheet view, you can glance at it and make sure this is the data you want to delete.

c. Click **Yes**. The column is deleted.

d. **Close** ☒ the tblParticipant table.

> **Troubleshooting**
>
> If when you clicked in the column heading you accidently double-clicked and then clicked Delete, Access blanked out the field name rather than deleting the column. This put you in edit mode, ready to rename the field. Press ‾Esc‾ to cancel edit mode and try again.

Understanding Tables and Keys

Now that you have imported data into the tblParticipant table, you need to further examine and evaluate how the tables have been set up. Tables represent entities—or people, places, things, or events that you want to track. Each row represents a single person, place, and so on. To identify that entity, you use a primary key field. A **primary key** field is a field that uniquely identifies the record; it can be any data type, but it should be a field that will not change. For example, a person's name is not a good primary key for two reasons. First of all, it is not unique—several people may have the same name, and second, a person's name could change. If you define a primary key for a table, the field cannot be blank.

In this section, you will create a table from scratch, minimize file size, facilitate quick data entry, minimize errors, and encourage data consistency as shown in Table 2.

Goal	Example
Minimize file size	If a field is an integer that is always less than 32,767, use Integer rather than Long Integer to define the field.
Facilitate quick data entry, including removing redundant data	Store a state abbreviation rather than the state name spelled out.
Minimize errors	Use the Date/Time data type for dates and not a Text data type. Access will then only accept valid dates, and not 2/31/2013, which is invalid.
Encourage data consistency	Use a Yes/No check box rather than having the word Yes or No typed into a text field where misspellings could occur.

Table 2 Table design goals

Create a Table in Design View

You want to keep track of corporations who are involved with the tournament. You do not have a source that you can import, so you will need to design and create the table. You will use Design view to enter fields, data types, and descriptions.

Defining Data Types

Data types define the kind of data that can be entered into a field, such as numbers, text, or dates. The data type tells Access how to store and display the field.

QUICK REFERENCE	Data Types	
Data Type	**Description**	**Examples**
Short Text	Used to store textual or character information. Any character or number can be entered into this type of field. You should store any data that will never be used in calculations, such as a Social Security number, as text, not a number. There is an upper limit of 255 characters that can be stored in a Short Text field.	Names, addresses
Long Text	Used to capture large amounts of text. Can store up to 1 gigabyte of characters, of which you can display 65,535 characters in a control on a form or report. This is a good data type to use if you need more than 255 characters in one field.	Comments
Number	Used for numeric data.	Quantity

Data Type	Description	Examples
Date/Time	Used to store a date and/or time.	Start time
Currency	A numeric value that is used for units of currency. It follows the regional settings preset in Windows to determine what the default currency should be. In the United States, the data is displayed with a dollar sign and two decimal places.	Salary
AutoNumber	Used for keys. Access generates the value by automatically incrementing the value for each new record to produce unique keys. For example, it would set the value as 1 for the first record, 2 for the next, and 3 for the third.	ProductID
Yes/No	A checked box where an empty box is no, and a checked box is yes.	EntryPaid
OLE Object	Use to attach an OLE object, such as a Microsoft Office Excel worksheet, to a record. An OLE object means that when you open the object, you open it in its original application such as Excel. It allows cross-application editing.	SalarySpreadsheet
Hyperlink	Text or combinations of text and numbers stored as text and used as a hyperlink address.	CompanyWebsite
Attachment	Images, worksheet files, documents, charts, and other types of supported files that are attached to the records in your database, similar to attaching files to e-mail messages.	EmployeePhoto
Calculated	A field calculated from other fields in the table. A calculated field may not be edited as it performs a calculation on other data that is entered.	GrossPay, which is calculated based upon HoursWorked and HourlySalary
Lookup Wizard	Lists either values retrieved from a table or query, or a set of values that you specified when you created the field.	ProductType, which gives a list of valid types

REAL WORLD ADVICE   **Number or Text?**

Any character can be used in a text field. However, if you expect a field to contain only numbers, you should only store the data in a text field if the numbers will never be used in a calculation. If you store numbers as text, you cannot use them in calculations. Conversely, if you improperly store numeric text as a number, Access will remove any leading zeros. For example, you would not use zip codes in calculations, so a zip code should be stored as text. A person living in Boston might have a zip code of 02108. If you stored the zip code as a number, Access would convert this to 2108.

Determining Field Size

Field size indicates the maximum length of a data field. Whenever you use a Text data type, you should determine the maximum number of text characters that can exist in the data to be stored. That number would then be the field size. For example, a state abbreviation can only be two characters long, so the size for this field should be 2. If you allow more than two characters, you are likely to get a mix of abbreviations and spelled-out state names. Limiting the size will limit errors in the data. There is an upper limit of 255 characters for a Short Text field. If you need more than 255 characters, use a Long Text data type.

For numeric fields, the type defines the maximum length or range of values. You should use the number size that best suits your needs. For example, if a value in a field is always going to be a whole number and is never going to be above 32,768 then Integer is the best field size. If the number is currency, you should use the Currency data type instead of Number.

QUICK REFERENCE	Number Field Sizes
Field Size	**Description**
Byte	For integers that range from 0 to 255. These numbers can be stored in a single byte.
Integer	For integers that range from −32,768 to +32,767. Must be whole numbers. Integers cannot have decimal places.
Long Integer	For integers that range from −2,147,483,648 to +2,147,483,647. Long Integers cannot have decimal places. (AutoNumber is a long integer.)
Single	For large numbers with up to seven significant digits. Can contain decimal places. Numbers can be negative or positive. For numeric floating point values that range from -3.4×10^{38} to $+3.4 \times 10^{38}$.
Double	For very large numbers with up to 15 significant digits. Can contain decimal places. Numbers can be negative or positive. For numeric floating point values that range from -1.797×10^{308} to $+1.797 \times 10^{308}$.
Decimal	For numeric values that contain decimal places. Numbers can be negative or positive. For numeric values that range from $-9.999\ldots \times 10^{27}$ to $+9.999\ldots \times 10^{27}$.

You determine that your corporation table, tblCorporate, should contain the company name, address, and phone number.

A02.09

 To Create a Table in Design View

a. Click the **CREATE** tab, and then in the Tables group, click **Table Design**.
    Access opens a blank table in Design view. You will enter each field in the appropriate row.

b. Type CompanyName for the Field Name, and then press [Tab] to move to the Data Type column.
    Notice that Short Text is the default data type, so you do not need to make a selection to keep Short Text for this field. For other data types, click the arrow and select the data type.

c. Press [Tab] to move to the Description column, and then type Company name.

d. In the Field Properties pane, type 50 in the Field Size box.

SIDE NOTE
Select Data Type
Alternatively, you can type the first letter of the data type, and it will appear, such as "N" for Number.

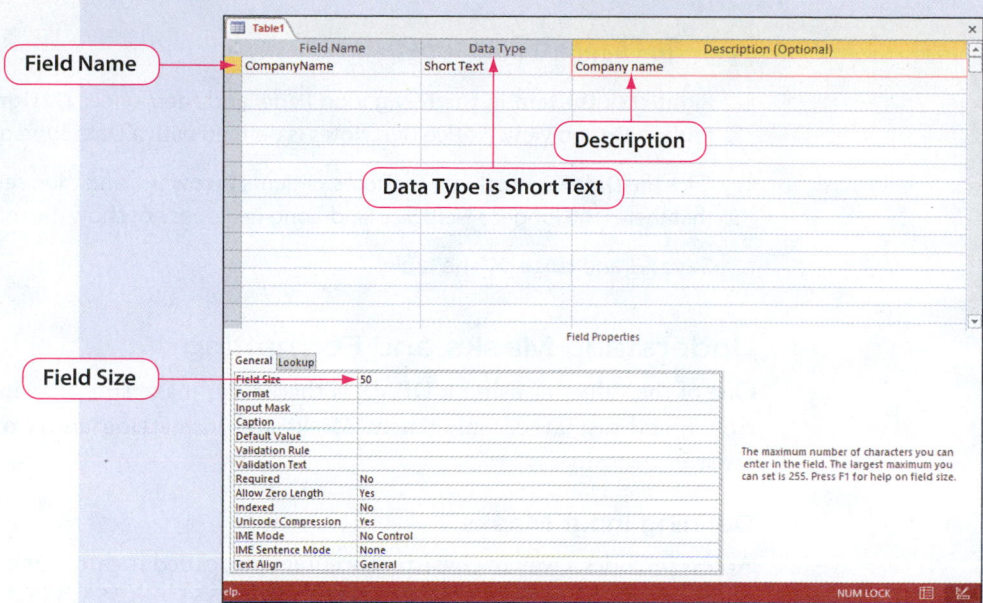

Field Name
Data Type is Short Text
Description
Field Size

Figure 13 First field in the tblCorporate table

e. Continue defining the table with the following information, being sure to enter maximum length in the Field Size box.

Field Name	Data Type	Description	Field Size
StreetAddress	Short Text	Company's street address	40
City	Short Text	Company's city	40
State	Short Text	State abbreviation	2
ZipCode	Short Text	Zip code either 5- or 9-character format	10
PhoneNumber	Short Text	Phone number with area code	14

f. **Save** 🖫 the table, and name it **tblCorporate** and then click **OK**. In the warning message that asks if you want to create a primary key, click **No**. You will define a key later.

g. **Close** ☒ the tblCorporate table.

Changing Data Type

In Design view, you can change the size of a field. If you decide that a field length needs to be longer, you can change the field without concern. If you make a field length shorter and there were data that needed the longer length, you may truncate those values. For that reason, Access will always warn you that data may be lost if you change the length to a smaller size.

The tblItem table has a Notes field that has a data type of Short Text. The tournament director asks you to change that to have a data type of Long Text so that full comments can be added for items.

A02.10

To Change a Data Type

a. Right-click **tblItem** in the Navigation Pane, and then select **Design View** to open the table in Design view. Notice that Notes is defined with a Data Type of Short Text.

b. Click the **Data Type** column for Notes, click the **arrow**, and then select **Long Text**. Note that there is no longer a Field Size field. Long Text does not show the maximum field length.

c. **Save** and **close** the table.

Understand Masks and Formatting

One of the values of using a DBMS is that it can make sure that information is entered, stored, and displayed consistently. Masks and formatting are two of the methods that assist in that process.

Defining Input Masks

Access provides a way to consistently enter data, called **input masks**. For example, phone numbers can be typed (555) 555-5555, 555-5555, or 555-555-5555. An input mask defines a consistent template and provides the punctuation, so you do not have to type it. Access also has a wizard that creates automatic masks for Social Security numbers, zip codes, passwords, extensions, dates, and times. You can also create your own custom masks. Input masks can affect how data is stored.

A02.11

To Create an Input Mask

a. Right-click **tblCorporate** in the Navigation Pane, and then select **Design View** to open the table in Design view.

b. Click the **PhoneNumber** Field Name to select the PhoneNumber field. In the Field Properties pane, click in the **Input Mask** box.

c. Click the **Build** button to start the Input Mask Wizard. If necessary, select **Phone Number**.

d. Click **Next** to start the phone number Input Mask Wizard.

Access suggests the format !(999) 000-0000. This means that the area code is optional and will be enclosed in parentheses. The rest of the phone number is required and will have a dash between the two parts. The exclamation mark specifies that characters should be typed from left to right.

e. Click **Next** to accept the format.

f. Access asks if you want to store the symbols with the data. Select **With the symbols in the mask, like this**.

g. Click **Next**, and then click **Finish**.

SIDE NOTE
Semicolons in Mask
The semicolons indicate that there are three sections of the mask. The dash in the last section shows the placeholder.

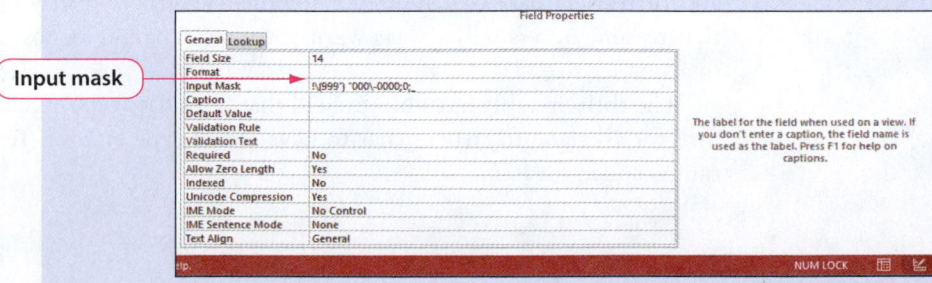

Figure 14 Finished input mask

h. **Save** 💾 the table design. On the DESIGN tab, in the Views group, click the **View** arrow, and then select **Datasheet View**.

i. Notice that the columns are not wide enough for the entire heading text to show. Move your mouse pointer to the border between **CompanyName** and **StreetAddress** until it becomes the Horizontal resize pointer ⊹, and then double-click the **border** to widen the column.

j. Double-click the **border** after the **StreetAddress** and **PhoneNumber** headings to widen the columns.

k. Click in the **append row** for **CompanyName**, and then type Tesuque Mirage Market. Press ⎋Tab to move to **StreetAddress**.

l. Continue entering the records as follows.

SIDE NOTE
Masks Save Keystrokes
Notice that the phone number mask that you entered means that you do not need to type the parentheses and dashes in the phone number.

CompanyName	StreetAddress	City	State	ZipCode	PhoneNumber
Tesuque Mirage Market	8 Tesuque Mirage Rd	Santa Fe	NM	87506	(505) 555-1111
Hotel Playa Real	125 Madison Avenue	Santa Fe	NM	87508	(505) 555-1800
Bouzouki Museum	716 Camino Cercano	Santa Fe	NM	87505	(505) 555-1200
McDoakes Restaurant	2017 High St	Santa Fe	NM	87501	(505) 555-1000
Benson & Diaz	1953 A Piazza Pl, Suite 101	Santo Domingo	NM	87052	(505) 555-2000

m. **Close** ✖ the tblCorporate table, and then in the Microsoft Access dialog box click **Yes** to save the layout.

Formatting

In a table design, you can define a Format field property that customizes how data is displayed and printed in tables, queries, reports, and forms. The **Format** property tells Access how data is to be displayed. It does not affect the way the data is stored. For example, you can specify that currency fields are displayed in dollars, such as $1,234.56 in American databases, or in euros, such as €1.234,56 in European databases. Formats are available for Date/Time, Number, Currency, and Yes/No data types. You can also define your own custom formats for Short Text and Long Text fields.

Data Type	Format	Example
Date/Time	General Date	11/9/2015 10:10:10 PM
	Long Date	Wednesday, November 9, 2015
	Medium Date	9-Nov-15
	Short Date	11/9/2015
	Long Time	10:10:10 PM
	Medium Time	10:10 PM
	Short Time	22:10
Number and Currency	General Number	Display the number as entered
	Currency	Follows the regional settings preset in Windows. In the United States: $1,234.56. In much of Europe, €1.234,56.
	Euro	Uses the euro symbol regardless of the Windows setting.
	Fixed	Displays at least one digit after the decimal point. In the Decimal Places property, you choose how many fixed digits to show after the decimal point.
	Standard	Use the regional settings preset in Windows for the thousands divider. 1,234 in the United States; 1.234 in much of Europe.
	Percent	Multiply the value by 100 and follow with %.
	Scientific	Use standard scientific notation, for example, 4.5E + 13.
Yes/No	Yes/No	Yes or No display options.
	True/False	True or False display options.
	On/Off	On or Off display options.

A02.12

To Define a Date Field

a. In the Navigation Pane, right-click **tblOrder**, and then select **Design View**.

b. In the first **blank row**, in the Field Name column, type OrderDate. Select a Data Type of **Date/Time**, and then enter a Description of Date order was placed.

c. Click in the **Format** box in the Field Properties pane.

d. Click the **Format** arrow, and then select **Short Date**.
Notice that the Property Update Options button ⚡ appears. Clicking it would display an option to change the format of OrderDate wherever else it appears. Because it does not appear anywhere else yet, you do not need to click the button.

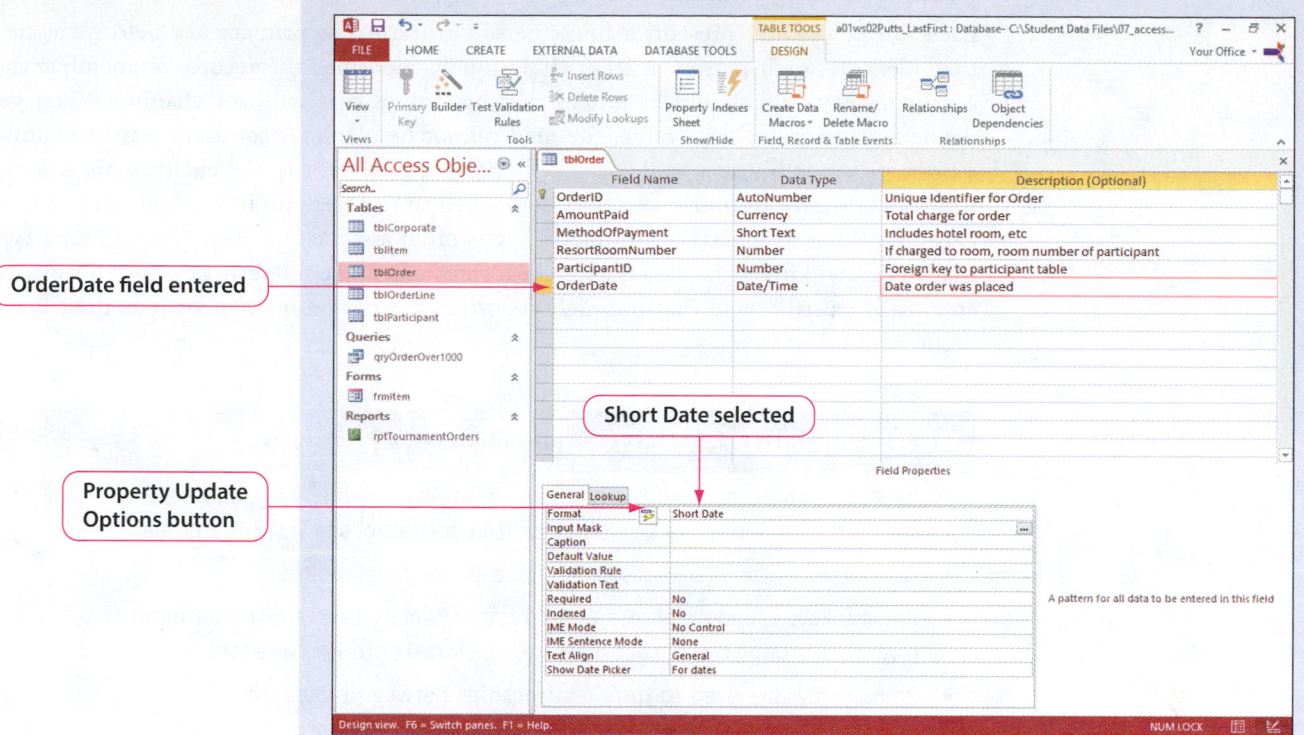

OrderDate field entered

Property Update Options button

Short Date selected

Figure 15 Adding a Short Date field

e. **Save** 🖫 the table design, and then in the Views group, click the **View** button to switch to Datasheet view.

The orders were placed on May 4, 2015, but no date was entered.

f. For the first order, in the OrderDate field type **May 4, 2015**. Press ⬇ to move to the next record. Notice the display changes to **5/4/2015**, the short date format.

g. For the second order, type **05/04/2015** and then press ⬇ to move to the next record. Again, the display changes to the new format.

h. For the next order, type **May 4 15** and then press ⬇ to move to the next record. Once again, the display changes to 5/4/2015.

i. Continue typing **May 4 15** for all the orders.

j. **Close** ❌ the table.

CONSIDER THIS | **Database Design Principles**

Some principles for database design are shown in Table 2. How do field sizes, formatting, and input masks facilitate these principles? When would you use a format? When would you use an input mask?

Understand and Designate Keys

Each table should have a field that uniquely identifies each of the records in the table. This field is called the primary key. If you know the primary key, you know exactly what record you want. Another type of key is a **foreign key**. A foreign key is a value in a table that is the primary key of another table. The primary and foreign keys form the common field between tables that allow you to form a relationship between the two tables.

Understanding Primary Keys

Each row of a table represents a single person or item. The primary key field is the field that identifies each person or item. It uniquely identifies the record. Remember that a primary key field should be a field that has values that will not change. When you define a primary key for a table, the field cannot be blank. A common way of defining a primary key is to use a field specifically designed to identify the entity. This is sometimes an arbitrary **numeric key** that is assigned to represent an individual item, such as CustomerID or ProductID. A numeric key is often assigned an AutoNumber data type that Access will fill as the data is entered. Instead of using a numeric key, you can also use an already existing field that uniquely identifies the person or item such as their Social Security number.

REAL WORLD ADVICE | **Do You Need a Primary Key?**

While Access does not require a primary key for every table, you almost always want to give the table a primary key. What are the advantages of having a primary key?

- It helps organize your data. Each record is uniquely identified.

- Primary keys speed up access to your data. Primary keys provide an index to a record. In a large table, that makes it much faster to find a record.

- Primary keys are used to form relationships between tables.

Understanding Foreign Keys

A foreign key is a field in a table that stores a value that is the primary key in another table. It is called foreign because it does not identify a record in this table; it identifies a record in another—foreign—table. For example, you have two tables, tblParticipant and tblOrder, in your database. You want to know which participants have placed certain orders. The primary key for your Participant table is ParticipantID. You can add a field called ParticipantID to the Order table that indicates which participant placed the order. ParticipantID is the foreign key in the tblOrder table; it identifies the participant in the tblParticipant table. Figure 16 illustrates this relationship. Foreign keys do not need to be unique in the table. Participants can place several orders.

You will use the ParticipantID to form a relationship between the two tables later in this workshop.

Figure 16 Relationship between tblParticipant and tblOrder tables

Continued

Continued

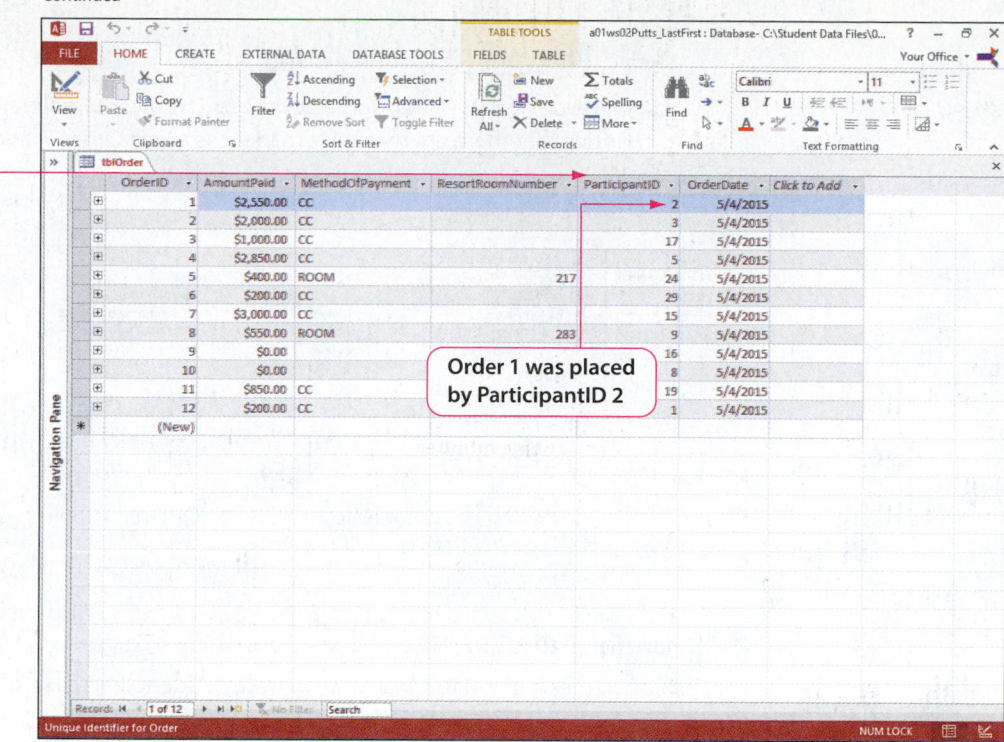

ParticipantID is the foreign key in the tblOrder table

Order 1 was placed by ParticipantID 2

Figure 16 Relationship between tblParticipant and tblOrder tables

Composite Keys

Sometimes, two fields are needed to uniquely identify a record. In that case, both fields are used to create the key and are called a **composite key**. For example, a university might identify a class by subject area and course number. The university could have classes Math 101, Math 102, and MIS 101. It takes both subject and course number to identify a single course. The combination of the two fields is called a composite key.

A typical use of a composite key is on an order form. Figure 17 shows a paper form that the golf tournament organizers used before they used Access. To uniquely identify the items that have been ordered, a composite key can be made combining the order number with the line number of the order form. You notice that this composite key is used for orders in the golf tournament database.

Order number

Line number

		Putts for Paws				
		Order: 100				
LINE NUMBER	ITEM ORDERED	TYPE OF ITEM	COST PER ITEM	QUANTITY ORDERED	TOTAL COST	
1	CTEAM	Corporate Team of 4	$ 850.00	1	$ 850.00	
2	CART	Cart Sponsor	$2000.00	1	$ 2000.00	
					BALANCE DUE:	$ 2850.00

Figure 17 Composite key on a paper order form

A02.13

To Identify a Composite Key

a. In the Navigation Pane, right-click the **tblOrderLine** table, and then select **Design View**. Notice that there are two fields marked as a key: OrderID and LineNum.

b. **Close** ☒ the tblOrderLine table.

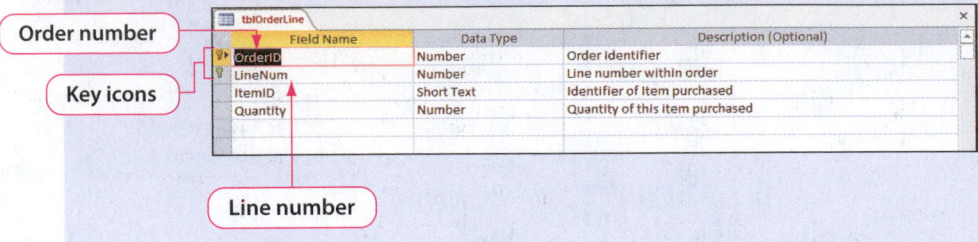

Figure 18 Composite key in the tblOrderLine table

Understanding Natural vs. Numeric Keys

Sometimes your data will have a unique identifier that is a natural part of your data. When that is true, you can use the field as a **natural primary key**. If you already identify orders by order number, that would make a good primary key.

The important point is that the natural primary key is a value that will not change. You might start by thinking that telephone number is a natural way to identify a customer. But people change their telephone numbers. When the natural key might change, it is better to use an arbitrary unique number to identify the customer. When natural keys do exist, they are favored over numeric keys.

You can use the data type AutoNumber for the primary key. In that case, Access will automatically assign a unique value for every record. You can also define a key as numeric, and fill the key values yourself.

You decide that you need to create a numeric primary key for your tblCorporate table named CorporateID. You will let Access automatically create the key by using an AutoNumber data type.

CONSIDER THIS | Social Security Number as a Primary Key

While a Social Security number seems like the perfect primary key, it is seldom used. What privacy concerns might arise in using Social Security numbers? Are there other issues that might arise with using Social Security numbers?

A02.14

To Define a Primary Key

a. In the Navigation Pane, right-click **tblCorporate**, and then select **Design View**.

b. On the DESIGN tab, in the Tools group, click **Insert Rows**. Because CompanyName was the active field, a blank row is added above **CompanyName**.

c. Type CorporateID in the Field Name column.

d. Select **AutoNumber** as the Data Type. The field size is set to Long Integer.

e. Type Unique corporate identifier in the Description column.

f. With the CorporateID row still selected, on the DESIGN tab, in the Tools group, click **Primary Key** to make "CorporateID" the primary key. A key icon is displayed in the record selector bar.

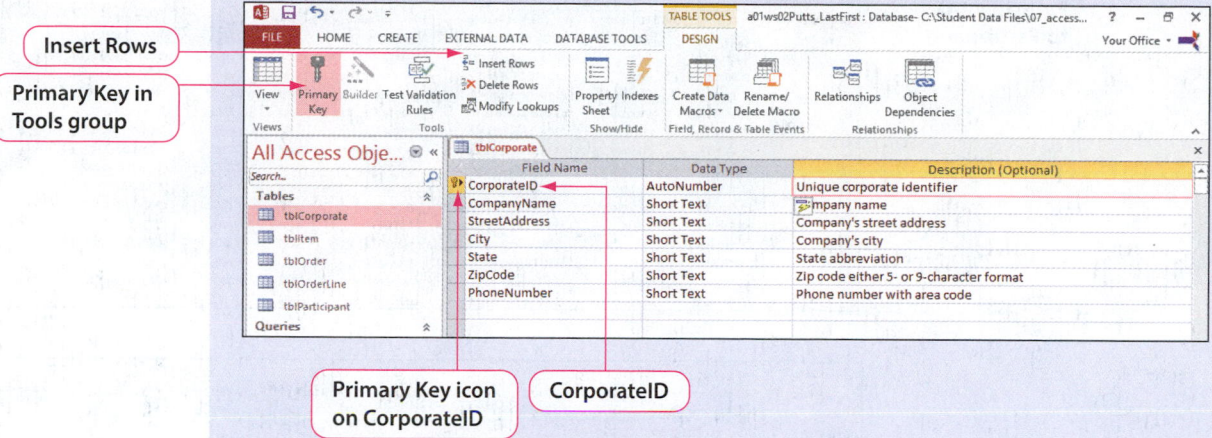

Figure 19 Defining a primary key

g. **Save** 🖫 your table design. Click the **HOME** tab, and then in the Views group, click **View**. Notice that Access has populated the CorporateID field with automatic numbers starting at 1 and going through 5.

h. **Close** ☒ the tblCorporate table.

REAL WORLD ADVICE **Read Your Error Messages**

The error message "Index or primary key cannot contain a Null value" is one example of an error message that Access displays when you make changes to an Access database that would break the rules you set up in your table design. You should read the error message carefully to understand what it is telling you.

If you get the error message "Index or primary key cannot contain a Null value," that means that one of your records has no entry in the primary key field. Enter the primary key. Often the issue is that you accidently entered data in the append record. If you do not want that record to be created, press [Esc] to cancel the addition of the record.

Understanding Relational Databases

One of the benefits of using Access is the ability to add relationships to the tables. This allows you to work with two or more tables in the same query, report, or form. For the tournament database, when you relate tables together, you can ask such questions as "What golfers are playing for the Tesuque Mirage Market?", "Did the market agree to purchase any other items?", and "Have they paid for those items yet?"

Relationships in a relational database are created by joining the tables together. A **join** is created by creating a relationship between two tables based upon a common field in the two tables, as shown in Figure 20. The tblParticipant table has a field—column—named ParticipantID. tblOrder also has a field named ParticipantID. When you create the relationship, Access will match the ParticipantIDs between the two tables to find those participants that placed an order. Looking at the table, you can mentally join the two tables to see that John Trujillo has placed an order for $2,550. When Access runs a query, it uses an existing join to find the results. In this section, you will form relationships between tables, create a report, and check to make sure the relationships you are creating between tables make sense.

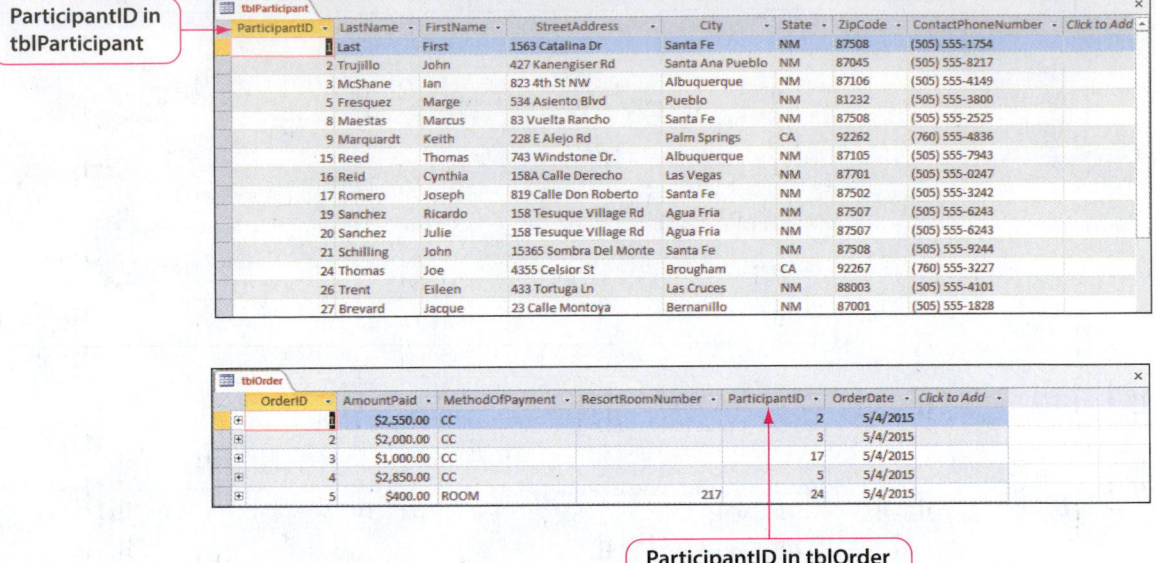

Figure 20 Tables joined between primary and foreign keys

Understand Basic Principles of Normalization

When you work with tables in Access, you want each table to represent a single entity and have data only about that entity. For example, you want a tblParticipant table to have data about participants and nothing else. You do not want to have data about the corporation they represent or the order they placed. You want the data about the participant to be in the participant table and no data about any other entity in the tblParticipant table as shown in Figure 20. There is no data that is about any other entity in the tblParticipant table. This is why you deleted the CorporatePhoneNumber field earlier in the exercise.

Representing Entities and Attributes

Recall that an entity is a person, place, or item that you want to keep data about. The data you keep about an entity are called attributes. An entity is generally stored in a single table in a relational database. The attributes form the fields or columns of the table. **Normalization** is the process of minimizing the duplication of information in a relational database through effective database design. If you know the primary key of an entity in a normalized database, each of the attributes will have just one value. When you normalize a database, you will have multiple smaller tables, each representing a different thing. There will be no redundant data in the tables. A complete discussion of normalization is beyond the scope of this workshop, but the following sections will give you an idea of why you normalize your tables.

Table 3 shows a nonnormalized view of tblParticipant. Suppose John Trujillo places two orders, Order 1 for $2,550 and Order 2 for $500. You can easily fill in his name and address. However, when you get to the order fields, you cannot fill in the attributes with just one value. You want to enter Order 1 for Order ID and Order 2 for Order ID. You want to enter $2,550 for AmountPaid and $500 for AmountPaid. But you only have one field for each.

Participant ID	Last Name	First Name	Street Address	Other Address Fields	Order ID	Amount Paid
2	Trujillo	John	427 Kanengiser Rd		??????	????

Table 3   Nonnormalized tblParticipant table

For each record's ParticipantID, you do not have a single value for OrderID and AmountPaid because each participant may make several orders. You could have a column for OrderID1 and OrderID2. But, how many columns would you make? What if this was for a grocery store where one transaction might contain hundreds of items? Any time you do not know how many columns to repeat, the table is not normalized and you need another table. Thus, this table does not fit the principles of normalization. It has two entities in the table: participants and orders.

> **CONSIDER THIS** | **Why Is a Nonnormalized Table Undesirable?**
>
> If you have a table as shown in Table 3, you could simply enter a record for each item. So, if you had five items, you would enter five records in the table. What kind of redundancy does that create? If you used this method, is there a primary key?

Minimizing Redundancy

Table 4 shows a nonnormalized view of the tblOrder table. In this case, when you know the OrderID, you do know the value of each field.

OrderID	Amount Paid	Method of Payment	Last Name	First Name	Address	Other Address Fields
1	$2,550.00	CC	Trujillo	John	427 Kanengiser Rd	
12	$500.00	CC	Trujillo	John	427 Kanengiser Rd	

Table 4   Nonnormalized tblOrder table

However, the table has redundant data. **Redundancy** occurs when data is repeated several times in a database. All of the data about John Trujillo is repeated for each order he makes. That means that the data will need to be entered multiple times. Beyond that, if the data changes, it has to be changed in multiple places. If his address or phone number changes, it will need to be changed on all his order records. Forgetting to change it in one place will lead to inconsistent data and confusion. Again, this table is not normalized because it contains data about two different entities: participant and orders.

In a normalized database, redundancy is minimized. The foreign keys are redundant, but no other data about the entity is repeated.

Understand Relationships Between Tables

To normalize the database, you need to have two tables: one for participants and one for orders. How then do you form a relationship between them? A table represents an entity—or the nouns—in the database. The relationship represents the verb that connects the two nouns. In the example, the two nouns are "participant" and "order." Is there a relationship between these two nouns? Yes. You can say that a participant places an order.

Once you determine that there is a relationship between the entities, you need to describe the relationship. You do that by asking yourself two questions starting with each entity in the relationship:

- Question 1, starting with the Participant entity: If you have one participant, what is the maximum number of orders that one participant can place? The only two answers to consider are one or many. In this case, the participant can place many orders.
- Question 2, starting with the Order entity: If you have one order, what is the maximum number of participants that can place that order? Again, the only answers to consider are one or many. An order is placed by just one participant.

The type of relationship where one question is answered "one" and the other is answered "many" is called a one-to-many relationship. A **one-to-many relationship** is a relationship between two tables where one record in the first table corresponds to many records in the second table. One-to-many is called the cardinality of the relationship. **Cardinality** indicates the number of instances of one entity that relates to one instance of another entity.

Using the Relationships Window

Access stores relationship information in the Relationships window as shown in Figure 21.

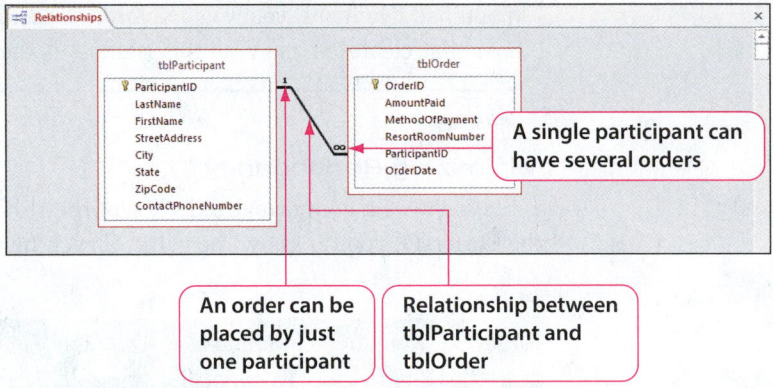

Figure 21 Relationships window

The Relationships window shows tables and the relationships between those tables. Notice the join line between tblParticipant and tblOrder. There is an infinity symbol on the line next to tblOrder. The infinity symbol indicates that a single participant can have several orders. There is a "1" on the line next to tblParticipant. The "1" indicates that an order can be placed by just one participant. Access indicates a one-to-many relationship in this way, putting a "1" on the one side of the join line and an infinity symbol on the many side.

REAL WORLD ADVICE	Other Uses for the Relationships Window

The Relationships window gives you an overview of all your tables and the relationships between them. It also shows all the fields in all the tables. It is often helpful to return to the Relationships window when developing queries and reports.

A02.15

 To Open the Relationships Window

a. Click the **DATABASE TOOLS** tab, and then in the Relationships group, click **Relationships**. The Relationships window opens. The window shows tables and the relationships between those tables.

Determining Relationship Types

The relationship between tblParticipant and tblOrder is a one-to-many relationship. There are other types of relationships. Consider the relationship between tblOrder and tblItem. There is a relationship: an item can be on an order. What is the cardinality? You need to ask yourself the two questions to determine the cardinality:

- Question 1, starting with the Order entity: If you have one order, what is the maximum number of items that can be part of that order? You care only about two answers: one or many. In this case, the order can contain many items. For example, a golfer could buy an entry into the tournament and a T-shirt.

- Question 2, starting with the Item entity: If you have one item, what is the maximum number of orders that that item can be part of? Again, the only answers to consider are one or many. Obviously you want more than one person to be able to order an entry to the tournament. Therefore, you say that an item can be on many orders.

With both answers being many, this is a many-to-many relationship. A **many-to-many relationship** is a relationship between tables in which one record in one table has many matching records in a second table, and one record in the related table has many matching records in the first table. Because these two tables in the charity database do not have a common field, in Access this kind of many-to-many relationship must have an additional table in between these two. This intermediate table is referred to by several synonymous terms: "intersection," "junction," or "link table." You will look at this later in the workshop.

A one-to-one relationship occurs when each question is answered with a maximum of one. A **one-to-one relationship** is a relationship between tables where a record in one table has only one matching record in the second table. In a small business, a department might be managed by no more than one manager, and each manager manages no more than one department. That relationship in that business is a one-to-one relationship.

There are three types of relationships: one-to-many, many-to-many, and one-to-one. The relationship type is based upon the rules of the business. In the charity golf tournament, the relationship between the order and the item is many-to-many, but in another business it might not be. For example, consider a business that sells custom-made jewelry where each item is one of a kind. In this case, an item can appear on just one order. Thus, the relationship between order and item in that business would be one-to-many.

REAL WORLD ADVICE   **Use of One-to-One Relationships**

When you have a one-to-one relationship, you could combine the two tables into a single table. A single table is simpler than two tables with a one-to-one relationship between them.

- You could keep the two tables separate when the two tables are obviously two different things like manager and department. You might want to keep private information about the manager in the manager table. Additionally, this would be easier to change if business rules change and multiple managers might manage the same department.

- You should combine the two tables when there are just a few attributes on one of the tables. For example, suppose you only wanted to keep the manager's name in the manager table with no other information about the manager. Then you might consider the manager's name to be an attribute of the department.

Create a One-to-Many Relationship

Consider the relationship between tblParticipant and tblOrder. This is a one-to-many relationship. To form a relationship between two tables, you need the tables to have a field in common. The easiest way to accomplish this is to put the primary key from the table on the one side in the table on the many side. In this case, this means that you use the ParticipantID from the one side table and add it as a field to the tblOrder table. The field that you add to the many side is called a foreign key because it is a key to another, or foreign, table. ParticipantID is already a field on the many side table, so you can use it to form the relationship.

QUICK REFERENCE	Creating a One-to-Many Relationship in Access

Creating a one-to-many relationship in Access takes three steps:

1. Make sure the two tables have a field in common. Use the primary key from the one side, and add it as a foreign key in the many side table.

2. Form the relationship in the Relationships window. This is done by connecting the primary key of the one side table to the foreign key in the many side table.

3. Populate the foreign key by adding data to the foreign key in the many side table.

Forming the Relationship

Because the tblParticipant and tblOrder tables already have a field in common, you can form the relationship. You will connect the primary key of the one side table to the foreign key on the many side table.

A02.16

▶ To Form a Relationship

SIDE NOTE

Adding Tables to the Relationships Window

You can also add tables to the Relationships window by clicking on a table in the Navigation Pane and dragging it to the window.

a. On the DATABASE TOOLS tab, in the Relationships group, click **Show Table**, click **tblParticipant**, and then click **Add**.

b. Click **Close** to close the Show Table dialog box, and then drag the **tblParticipant** table to appear below tblOrder in the Relationships window.

c. Use your pointer to resize **tblParticipant** by dragging the corner of the field list so all fields show. Drag **tblOrder** to the right.

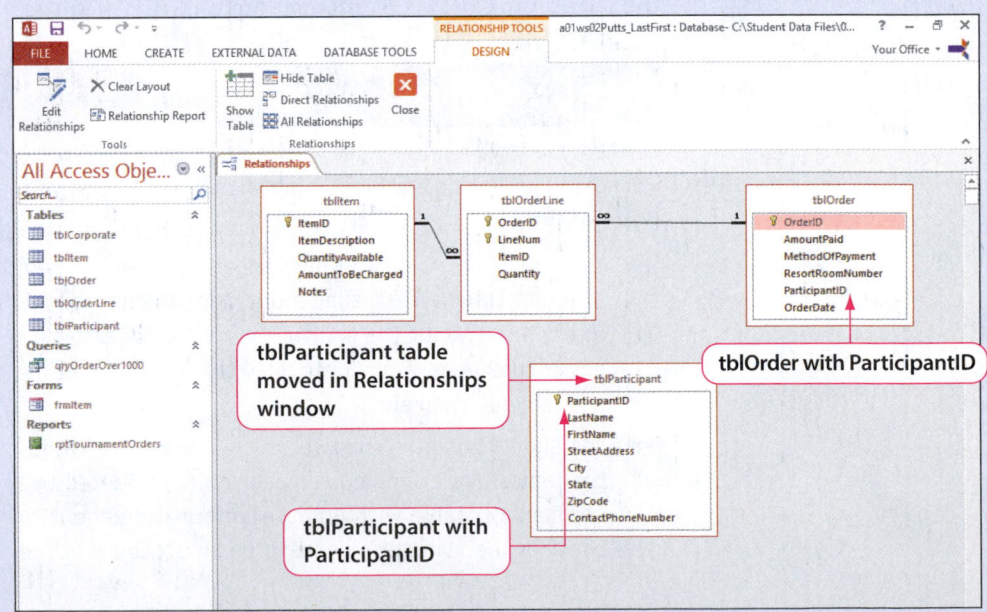

Figure 22 Move the table in the Relationships window

SIDE NOTE

Tables in the Relationships Window

Do not add a table twice to Relationships. If you do, close the window without saving and start over. A hidden table is still there.

d. Drag the primary key, **ParticipantID**, from tblParticipant to **ParticipantID** in tblOrder. Alternatively, you could drag from ParticipantID in tblOrder to ParticipantID in tblParticipant.

The Edit Relationships dialog box is displayed. Check that the fields shown in the box are both ParticipantID.

> **Troubleshooting**
>
> If you do not see two fields named ParticipantID in the Edit Relationships dialog box, click Cancel and retry Step d.

Notice that Access calls the relationship a one-to-many relationship. This is because the relationship is between a primary key and a foreign key.

e. Click **Enforce Referential Integrity** to select it, and then click **Create**. Later in the workshop you will look further at what referential integrity accomplishes.

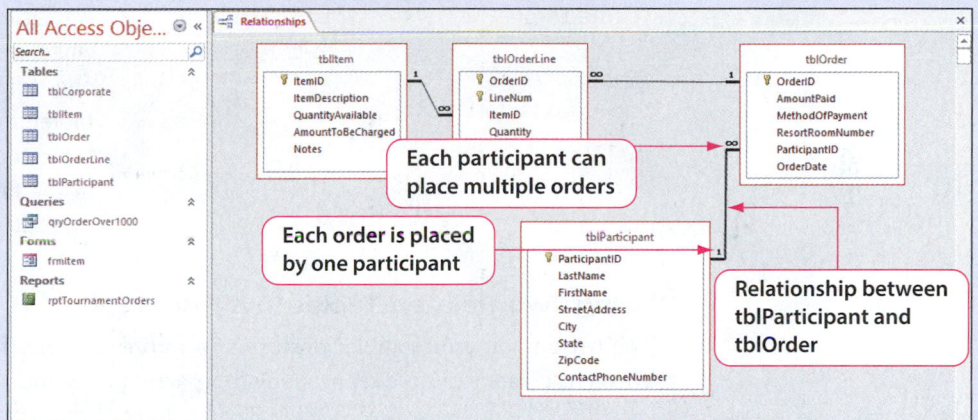

Figure 23 tblParticipant and tblOrder relationship

f. **Save** 💾 your relationships, and then **close** ✖ the Relationships window.

> **Troubleshooting**
>
> If you get the error message "The database engine could not lock table 'tblParticipant' because it is already in use by another person or process," this means that the tblParticipant table is still open. Close the table, and try again to form the relationship. You should get in the habit of closing tables when you are done with them.
>
> If you get the error message "Relationship must be on the same number of fields with the same data type," this means that the data types for the primary key and the foreign key are different. For example, they must be both Numeric and Long Integer or both Text. Make sure that you are creating the relationship between the correct fields. If you are, check the table designs, and fix the field with the wrong data type.
>
> If you add a relationship that you do not want, right-click the join line and click Delete. If you want to edit a relationship, right-click the join line and click Edit Relationship.

Type of Relationship	Alternate Notations	Meaning
One-to-many	1:N or 1:M 1-to-N	A relationship between two tables where one record in the first table corresponds to many records in the second table; however, each record in the second table corresponds to just one record in the first table.
Many-to-many	M:N M-to-N	A relationship between two tables where one record in the first table corresponds to many records in the second table; and, each record in the second table corresponds to many records in the first table.
One-to-one	1:1 1-to-1	A relationship between two tables where a record in one table has only one matching record in the second table; and, each record in the second table corresponds to just one record in the first table.

Using Two Related Tables in a Report

The reason you create a relationship is to join two tables for queries, reports, and forms. You will create a simple report showing participants and their orders.

A02.17

▶ To Create a Report from Two Tables

a. Click the **CREATE** tab, and then in the Reports group, click **Report Wizard**.

b. In the Report Wizard dialog box, click the **Tables/Queries** arrow, and then select **Table: tblParticipant**. Select the **LastName** field, and then click **One Field** . Select the **FirstName** field, and then click **One Field** >.

c. Click the **Tables/Queries** arrow, and then select **Table: tblOrder**. Select the **OrderID** field, and then click **One Field** >. Select the **AmountPaid** field, and then click **One Field** >.

> **Troubleshooting**
>
> If you clicked Next instead of selecting the tblOrder fields, you can go back a step in the wizard by clicking Back.

d. Click **Next**.

   You can see a preview of how your report will look if you group the participants by tblParticipant. Access uses the "one" side of a one-to-many relationship as the default for the grouping. This is the grouping you want.

e. Click **Next**. The wizard asks if you want more grouping levels; however, you do not want any other grouping levels.

f. Click **Next**.

g. Use the arrow to select **OrderID**. Ascending sort order is already selected. Click **Next**.

The wizard asks you to choose a layout and orientation for your report. You will accept the default layout and orientation.

h. Click **Next**.

i. Title your report rptParticipantOrders_initialLastname using your first initial and last name. Click **Finish**.

Access connects the participants and orders in a report.

j. Right-click anywhere on the report, and then select **Layout View** from the shortcut menu.

> **Troubleshooting**
>
> If the Field List shows on the right side of the Access window, close it so you can see the entire report layout.

k. Double-click the **title** of the report. Change the report title to Participant and Orders by initial Lastname using your first initial and last name and press ⌷Enter⌷. **Save** 🖫 your report.

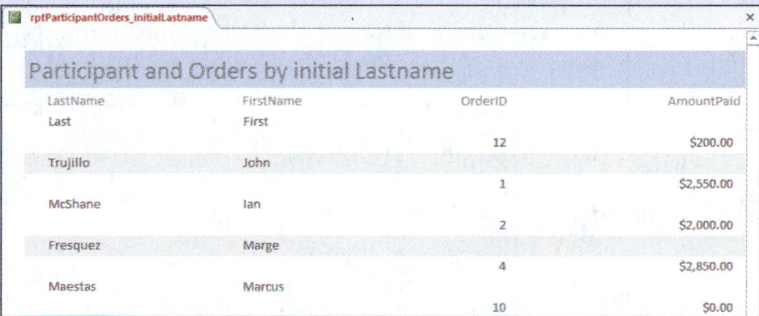

Figure 24 Complete report

l. If your instructor directs you to print the report, right-click anywhere on the report, switch to **Print Preview**, click **Print** in the Print group, and then click **OK**.

m. **Close** ⌧ your report.

Create a Many-to-Many Relationship

Unless you are connecting a common field such as a foreign key to the same foreign key in a different table, Access cannot form a many-to-many relationship with a single relationship. Instead you need to make two one-to-many relationships to represent the many-to-many relationship. As stated before, tblOrder and tblItem have a many-to-many relationship. An order can have many items on it. Each item can be on many orders. To form this relationship, a new table, tblOrderLine needs to be added. Both tblOrder and tblItem are related to the new table. The third table is called a junction table. A **junction table** breaks down the many-to-many relationship into two one-to-many relationships.

Look at the relationship between tblOrder and tblOrderLine in Figure 25. It is a one-to-many relationship with orders having many order lines but each order line on just one order. There is also a relationship between tblOrderLine and tblItem. It also is a one-to-many relationship with each order line having just one item but an item able to be on many order lines as shown in Figure 25.

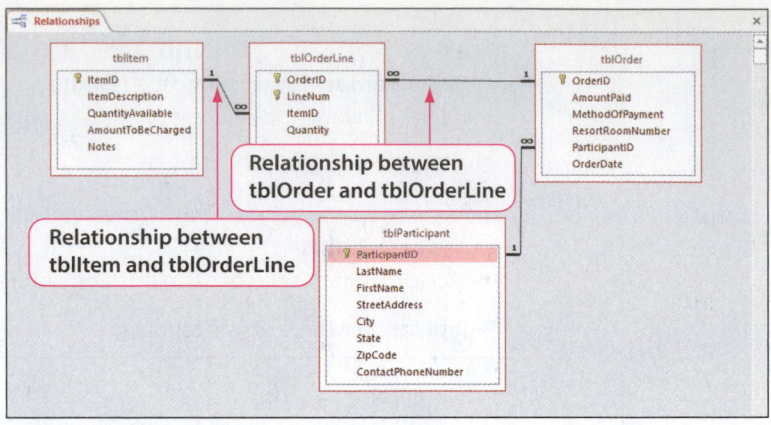

Figure 25 Relationship between tblOrder and tblItem with tblOrderLine

As shown in Figure 26, OrderID 4 has two order lines: one with an item of a corporate team and one with a cart. By traveling left to right across the three tables, you see that OrderID 4 has many items on it. OrderID 6 has one line: an entry to the tournament. By traveling from right to left across the three tables, you see that an entry to the tournament can be on many orders. Hence the junction table tblOrderLine forms a many-to-many relationship between tblOrder and tblItem.

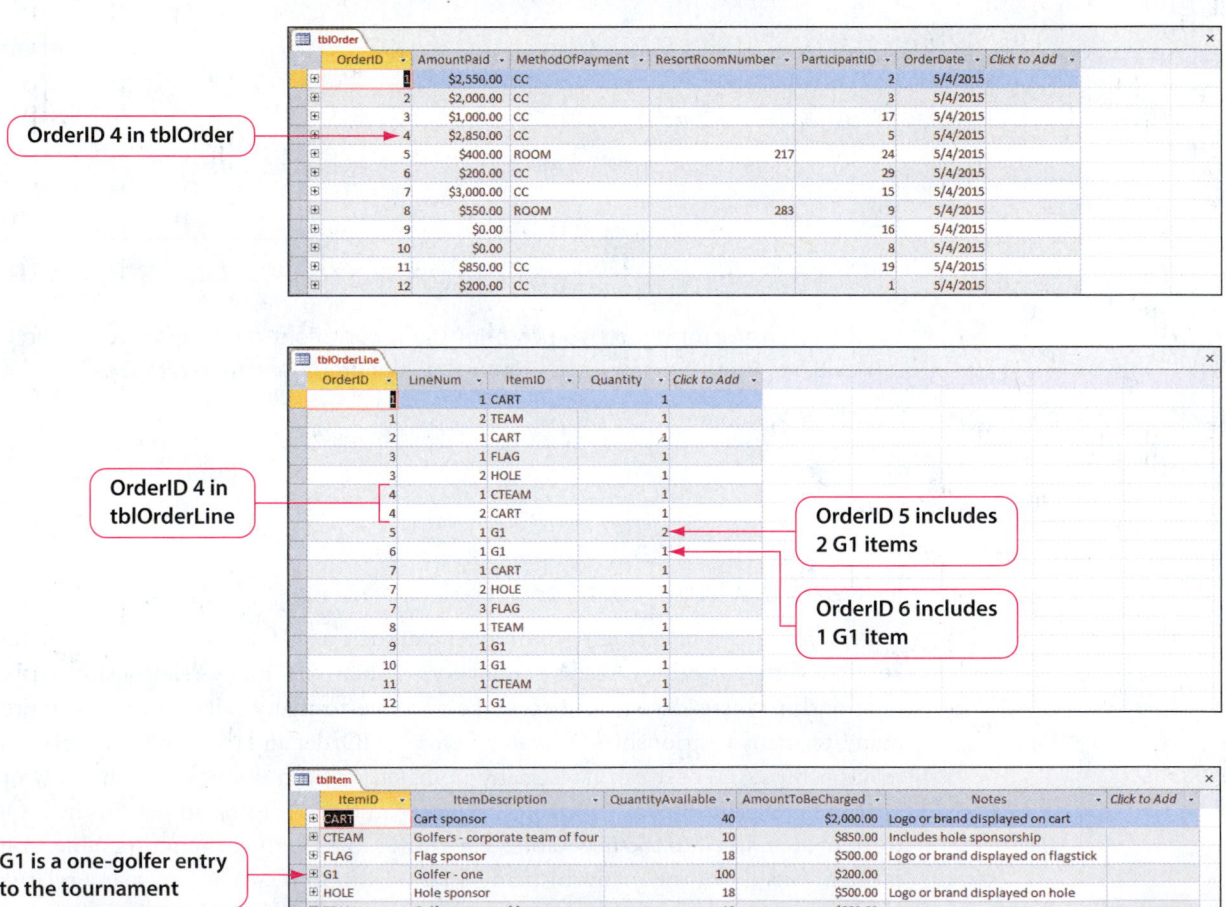

Figure 26 Data in tblOrder, tblOrderLine, and tblItem

tblOrderLine has foreign keys to tblOrder and tblItem. This allows the relationships to be formed. Notice that the relationship between tblOrder and tblOrderLine is formed with OrderID in tblOrder joined to OrderID in tblOrderLine. Similarly the relationship between tblItem and tblOrderLine is formed from ItemID in tblItem to ItemID in tblOrderLine.

The junction table, tblOrderLine, has one field beyond the key fields: Quantity. This indicates the quantity of each item on the order. As shown in Figure 26, OrderID 5 included two entries to the tournament.

Forming a New Many-to-Many Relationship

Consider the relationship between your new table, tblCorporate, and tblParticipant. There is a relationship: a participant can represent a corporation. A participant can be a golfer for a corporation, the corporate representative, or a donor. What is the cardinality? You need to ask yourself the two questions to determine the cardinality:

- Question 1, starting with the Corporate entity: If you have one corporation, what is the maximum number of participants that can represent that corporation? You care only about two answers: one or many. In this case, the corporation could be represented by many participants. A corporate team might have four golfer participants.

- Question 2, starting with the Participant entity: If you have one Participant, what is the maximum number of roles that Participant can represent for the corporation? Again, the only answers to consider are one or many. A Participant could be a golfer representing the corporation and also be a corporate representative.

QUICK REFERENCE	Creating a Many-to-Many Relationship in Access

Creating a many-to-many relationship in Access takes four steps:

1. Create a junction table. Create a primary key that will be a unique field for the junction table, and add two foreign keys, one to each of the many-to-many tables. Alternatively you can create a composite key made up of the two foreign keys.

2. Determine if there are any fields that you want to add to the junction table beyond the keys.

3. Form two relationships in the Relationships window. This is done by connecting the primary key of one of the original tables to the appropriate foreign key of the junction table. Repeat for the second of the original tables. The junction table is on the many side of both relationships.

4. Populate the junction table.

Creating a Junction Table

Because the relationship between tblCorporate and tblParticipant is many-to-many, you need a junction table. Recall that the junction table breaks down the many-to-many relationship into two one-to-many relationships. In this case, the junction table will indicate the role that the participant has for the corporation. The primary key for the junction table will be ParticipantRoleID, an AutoNumber field. You will have two foreign keys, the CorporateID field and the ParticipantID field. You will also add a field named Role that describes the role of the participant. Because the table represents roles, you will call the table tblParticipantRole.

To Create a Junction Table in Table Design View

a. Click the **CREATE** tab, and then in the Tables group, click **Table Design**.
   Access opens a blank table in Design view. You will enter each field in the appropriate row.

b. In the Field Name column, type ParticipantRoleID. Press [Tab] to move to the Data Type column, click the **arrow**, and then select the **AutoNumber** data type.
   Alternatively, you can type the "A," and "AutoNumber" will appear.

c. Notice that Field Size in the Field Properties pane defaults to Long Integer. Press [Tab] to move to the Description column, and then type Primary key for tblParticipantRole.

d. On the DESIGN tab, in the Tools group, click **Primary Key** to make the ParticipantRoleID field the primary key.

e. Press [Tab] to move to the next field. Continue filling in the table with the following information, being sure to enter the field size in the Field Properties pane.

Field Name	Data Type	Description	Field Size
CorporateID	Number	Foreign key to tblCorporate	Long Integer
ParticipantID	Number	Foreign key to tblParticipant	Long Integer
Role	Short Text	Role that this participant fills for the corporation	40

f. **Close** [X] the table, and then in the Microsoft Access dialog box click **Yes**. Name the table tblParticipantRole and then click **OK**.

Creating Two One-to-Many Relationships

The many-to-many relationship will turn into two one-to-many relationships between each of the original tables and the junction table. The rule is that the junction table is on the many side of the two relationships. But you can ask yourself the two questions to determine the cardinality:

- Question 1, starting with the Corporate entity: If you have one corporation, what is the maximum number of participant roles that can represent that corporation? You care only about two answers: one or many. In this case, the corporation could be represented by many participant roles. A corporation could have golfers and corporate contacts.

- Question 2, starting with the ParticipantRole entity: If you have one ParticipantRole, what is the maximum number of corporations that the participant can represent? Again, the only answers to consider are one or many. A ParticipantRole is for a single participant.

Thus tblCorporate to tblParticipantRole is a one-to-many relationship with Corporate on the "one" side.

You can ask the same questions between tblParticipant and tblParticipantRole.

A02.19

 To Form Two Relationships to the Junction Table

a. Click the **DATABASE TOOLS** tab, and then in the Relationships group, click **Relationships**.

b. On the DESIGN tab, in the Relationships group, click **Show Table**. Select **tblCorporate**, click **Add**, select **tblParticipantRole**, and then click **Add**.

c. **Close** the Show Table dialog box, and then drag the **tables** in the Relationships window, so there is some space between the tables to form the relationships.

d. Drag the primary key **ParticipantID** from tblParticipant to **ParticipantID** in tblParticipantRole. Alternatively, you could drag from ParticipantID in tblParticipantRole to ParticipantID in tblParticipant.

e. Access displays the Edit Relationships dialog box. Click **Enforce Referential Integrity** to select it, and then click **Create**.

f. Drag the primary key **CorporateID** from tblCorporate to **CorporateID** in tblParticipantRole.

g. Access displays the Edit Relationships dialog box. Click **Enforce Referential Integrity** to select it, and then click **Create**.

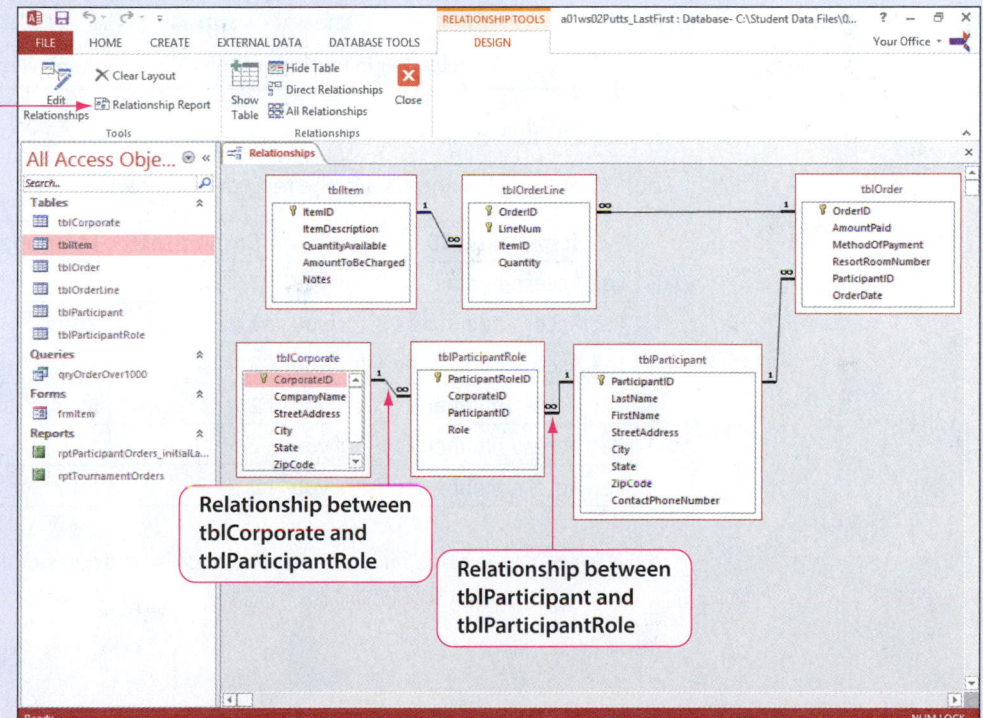

Figure 27 Completed Relationships window

h. On the DESIGN tab, in the Tools group, click **Relationship Report** to create a report for your relationships. **Save** 🖫 the report, accepting the report name **Relationships for a01ws02Putts_LastFirst**, and then click **OK**.

i. If your instructor asks you to print your report, on the PRINT PREVIEW tab, in the Print group, click **Print** to print the report. **Close** ✖ the Relationships report.

j. **Close** ✖ the Relationships window.

Populating the Junction Table

To complete the many-to-many relationship, you need to populate the junction table.

A02.20

 To Populate the Junction Table

a. Double-click **tblParticipantRole** to open the table in Datasheet view.

b. Click in the **CorporateID append row**. Enter a CorporateID of **1**, a ParticipantID of **5** and a Role of **Corporate Contact**. Access automatically numbers ParticipantRoleID as "1".

c. Because the last field is not totally visible, place your pointer in the **border** on the right of the **Role** column heading. When your pointer is a double-headed arrow ⊞, double-click the **border** to resize the column. This resizing is called AutoFitting. Repeat for each field.

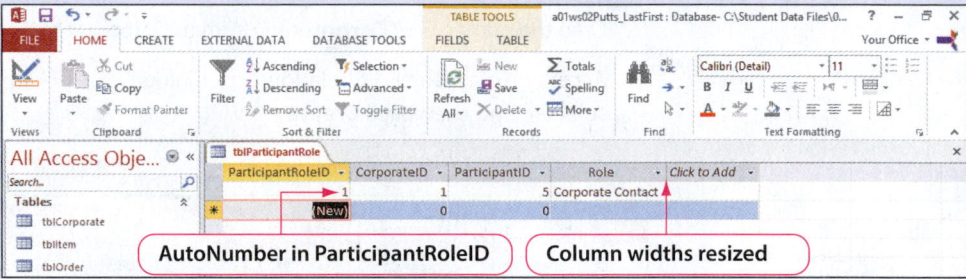

Figure 28 tblParticipantRole columns resized

d. Enter the following data in the records as follows.

ParticipantRoleID	CorporateID	ParticipantID	Role
Let Access number as 2 for you	1	5	Golfer
Let Access number as 3 for you	1	26	Golfer
Let Access number as 4 for you	2	1	Golfer
Let Access number as 5 for you	2	3	Golfer
Let Access number as 6 for you	2	54	Corporate Contact
Let Access number as 7 for you	2	54	Golfer

e. **Close** ✕ the table, and then in the Microsoft Access dialog box click **Yes** to save the changes to the table layout.

Defining One-to-One Relationships

One-to-one relationships in Access are formed very similarly to one-to-many relationships. You can put a foreign key in either table and establish the relationship by dragging with the primary key in one table joined to the foreign key. You can also make both tables have the same primary key.

Understand Referential Integrity

Referential integrity is a database concept that ensures that relationships between tables remain consistent. When one table has a foreign key to another table, the concept of referential integrity states that you may not add a record to the table that contains the foreign key unless there is a corresponding record in the linked table. Recall that when you created the relationship between tblParticipant and tblOrder, you told Access to enforce referential integrity.

Enforcing Referential Integrity

Enforcing referential integrity ensures that the following rules will be applied when you define the fields in Design view:

- The values in the field on the one side of the relationship is unique in the table. You must either use the primary key of the one side in the relationship or a field that you have set as unique in the table.

- You cannot add a foreign key value in the many side that does not have a matching primary key value on the one side.

- The matching fields on both sides of the relationship are defined with the same data types. For example, if the primary key is numeric and Long Integer, the foreign key must be numeric and Long Integer too. (For purposes of relationships, an AutoNumber primary key is considered Long Integer.)

If these rules are violated, when you try to form the relationship, you will get the following error message: "Relationship must be on the same number of fields with the same data type."

Double-check how you defined the relationship between tblParticipant and tblOrder.

A02.21

 To Check and Test Referential Integrity

a. Click the **DATABASE TOOLS** tab, and then in the Relationships group, click **Relationships**. The Relationships window is displayed. Notice the relationship that was formed between ParticipantID in tblParticipant and ParticipantID in tblOrder.

b. **Close** ⊠ the Relationships window.

c. Right-click **tblParticipant**, and then select **Design View**. Notice that ParticipantID is defined as Number and Long Integer. **Close** ⊠ tblParticipant, right-click **tblOrder**, select **Design View**, and then click the **ParticipantID** field. Notice that ParticipantID is also defined as Number and Long Integer in the tblOrder table.

Referential integrity means that Access will also enforce rules when you work with the data in the tables. You cannot enter a value in the foreign key field on the "many" side table that is not a primary key value on the "one" side table. For example, you cannot add a participant that does not exist in tblParticipant to a team. However, you can leave the foreign key unfilled, indicating that this participant is not part of a team.

d. Click the **HOME** tab, and then in the Views group, click the **View** button to switch to Datasheet View for tblOrder.

e. In the ParticipantID for the last record in the table, type **70** and then press ⎡Enter⎤ twice. Access responds with the error message "You cannot add or change a record because a related record is required in table tblParticipant." That is, you cannot add an order to participant 70 because there is no participant 70.

f. Click **OK**, and then change the ParticipantID for the last order back to **1**. Press ⎡Enter⎤ twice. ParticipantID 1 is a valid participant so you can make that change.

g. **Close** ⊠ the tblOrder table.

CONSIDER THIS | **Why Enforce Referential Integrity?**

You can decline to enforce referential integrity on a relationship. What are the pros and cons of enforcing referential integrity? What are the pros and cons of not enforcing referential integrity?

If you enforce referential integrity, you cannot delete a record from the "one" side table if matching records exist in the "many" side table. If you want to delete the record, you must delete the matching records or use Cascade Delete as explained later.

A02.22

 To Understand Relationships Between the One and Many Side Tables

a. In the Navigation Pane, double-click **tblParticipant** to open it in Datasheet view.

b. Click the **record selector** of the second row, John Trujillo.

c. Click the **HOME** tab, and then in the Records group, click **Delete**.
   Access responds that "The record cannot be deleted or changed because table 'tblOrder' includes related records." That means John Trujillo has placed an order.

d. Click **OK**.

e. **Close** ☒ the tblParticipant table.

f. **Close** ☒ the database and Access.

You also cannot change the primary key value in the "one" side table if that record has related records.

QUICK REFERENCE	Referential Integrity

Access enforces the following rules on defining a relationship with referential integrity:

1. The primary key field values on the one side of the relationship must be unique in the table.

2. The foreign key values on the many side of the relationship must exist as the primary key field for a record on the one side of the relationship.

3. The matching fields on both sides of the relationship are defined with the same data types.

The following rules are applied to data changes when referential integrity is enforced:

1. You cannot enter a value in the foreign key field on the "many" side table that is not a primary key on the "one" side table. However, you can leave the foreign key unfilled, indicating that this record is not in the relationship. It is not good practice to do this however.

2. You cannot delete a record from the "one" side table if matching records exist in a "many" side table, unless Cascade Delete has been selected for the relationship, in which case all the matching records on the many side are deleted.

3. You cannot change a primary key value in the "one" side table if that record has related records in the "many" side, unless Cascade Update has been selected for the relationship, in which case all the matching records on the many side have their foreign key updated.

Selecting Cascade Update

When you ask Access to enforce referential integrity, you can also select whether you want Access to automatically cascade update related fields or cascade delete related records. These options allow some deletions and updates that would usually be prevented by referential integrity. However, Access makes these changes and replicates or cascades the changes through all related tables so referential integrity is preserved.

If you select Cascade Update Related Fields when you define a relationship, then when the primary key of a record in the one side table changes, Access automatically changes the foreign keys in all related records. For example, if you change the ItemID in the tblItem table, Access automatically changes the ItemID on all order lines that include that item. Access makes these changes without displaying an error message.

If the primary key in the "one" side table was defined as AutoNumber, selecting Cascade Update Related Fields has no effect, because you cannot change the value in an AutoNumber field.

Selecting Cascade Delete

If you select Cascade Delete Related Records when you define a relationship, any time that you delete records from the one side table, the related records in the many side table are also deleted. For example, if you deleted a tblParticipant record, all the orders made by that participant are automatically deleted from the tblOrder table. Before you make the deletion, Access warns you that related records may also be deleted.

CONSIDER THIS | **Should You Cascade Delete Related Records?**

Should you cascade delete related records? Consider a customer who has made many orders. If the customer asks to be removed from your database, do you want to remove his or her past orders? How do you think the accountants would feel?

---

1. What is an entity? What is an attribute? What is a relationship? p. 84

2. If you have data in an Excel worksheet, what methods could you use to move the data in Excel to Access? How would you decide between the methods? p. 87–94

3. Why is it important to type a new record in the blank (append) row rather than on top of another record? p. 96

4. What data types would you use for the following fields: price, phone number, street address, ZIP code, and notes about product usage? p. 98–99

5. What is a mask used for? What is a format used for? Which can affect the way that data is stored? p. 102–105

6. What is the purpose of a primary key? p. 105–106

7. Why is redundancy of data undesirable? p. 110–111

8. What does it mean to say that there is a relationship between two tables? p. 111–113

9. How do you create a one-to-many relationship in Access? p. 113–115

10. How do you create a many-to-many relationship in Access? p. 117–119

11. What does it mean for a relationship to have referential integrity enforced? p. 122–124

Key Terms

Attribute 84
Cardinality 112
Composite key 107
Data type 87
Delimiter 92
Entity 84
Field size 99
Foreign key 105

Format 103
Input mask 102
Join 109
Junction table 117
Many-to-many relationship 113
Natural primary key 108
Normalization 110
Number data type 87

Numeric key 106
One-to-many relationship 112
One-to-one relationship 113
Primary key 98
Redundancy 111
Relationship 84
Text data type 87

Visual Summary

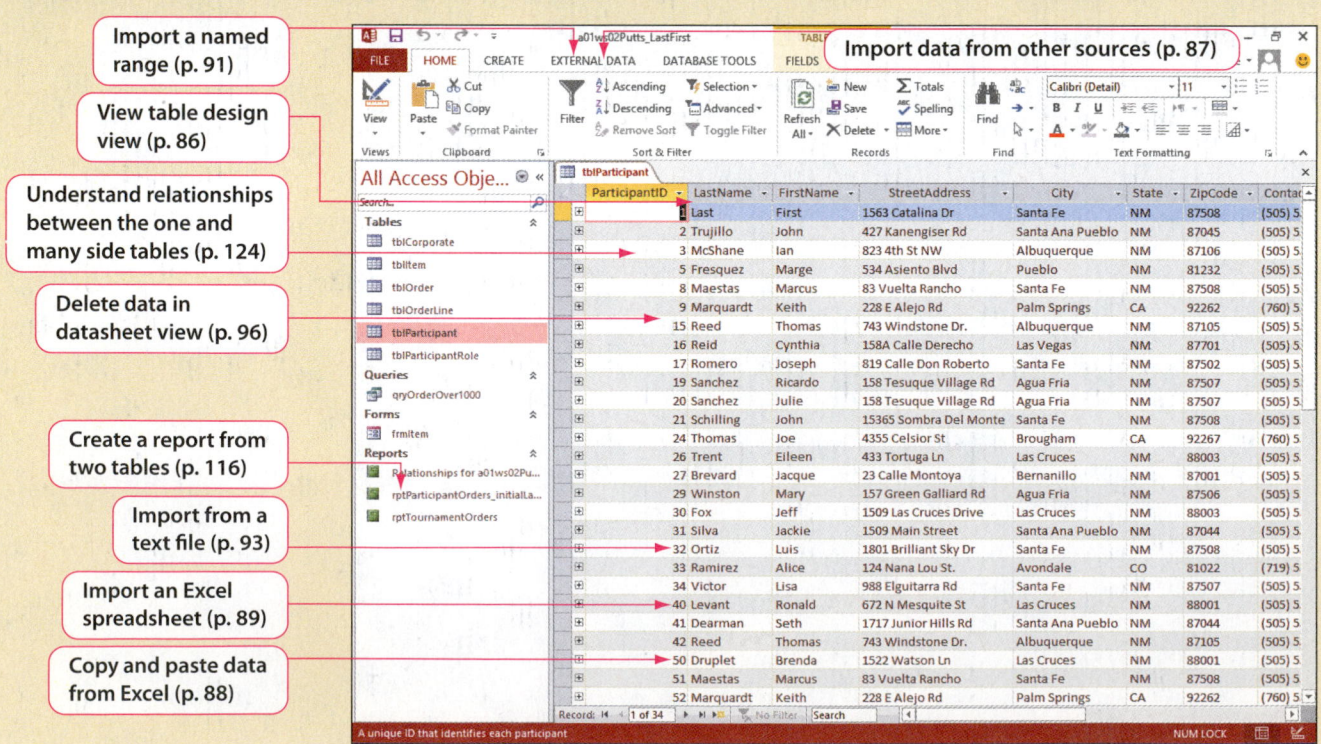

Import a named range (p. 91)

View table design view (p. 86)

Understand relationships between the one and many side tables (p. 124)

Delete data in datasheet view (p. 96)

Create a report from two tables (p. 116)

Import from a text file (p. 93)

Import an Excel spreadsheet (p. 89)

Copy and paste data from Excel (p. 88)

Import data from other sources (p. 87)

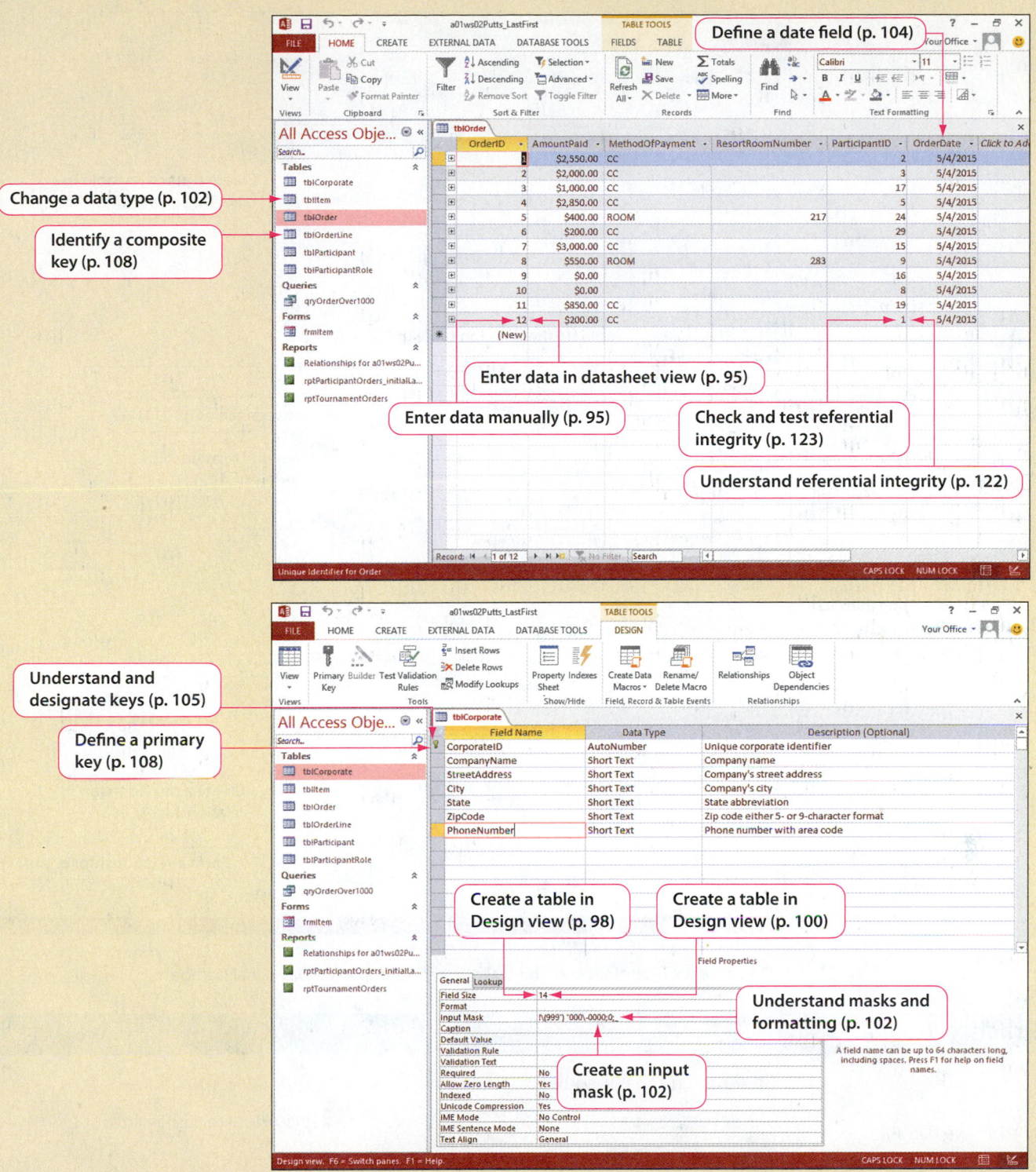

Change a data type (p. 102)

Identify a composite key (p. 108)

Define a date field (p. 104)

Enter data in datasheet view (p. 95)

Enter data manually (p. 95)

Check and test referential integrity (p. 123)

Understand referential integrity (p. 122)

Understand and designate keys (p. 105)

Define a primary key (p. 108)

Create a table in Design view (p. 98)

Create a table in Design view (p. 100)

Understand masks and formatting (p. 102)

Create an input mask (p. 102)

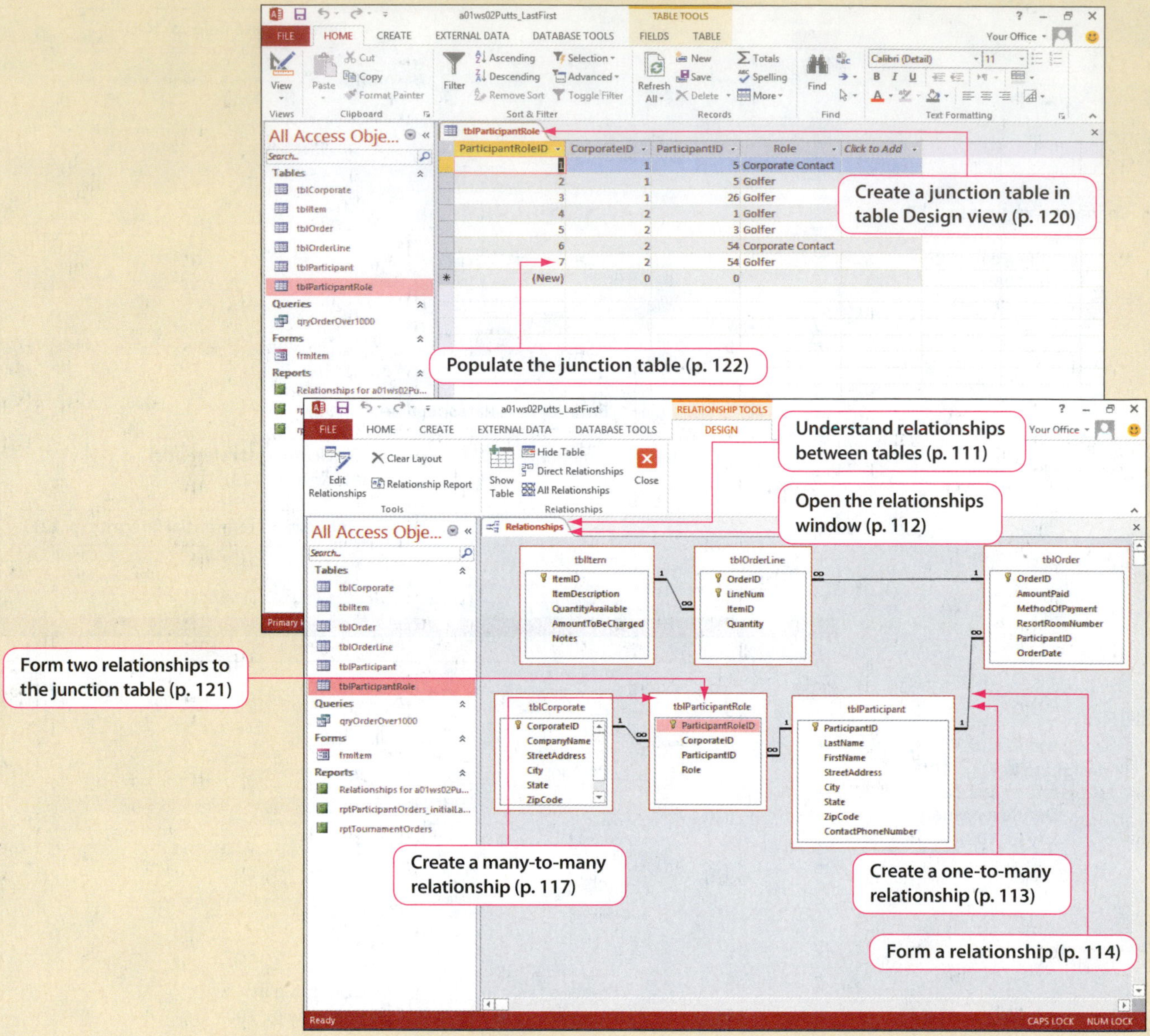

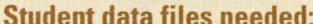

Figure 29 Putts for Paws Charity Tournament Imported Data Final Database

---

Practice 1

Student data files needed:

a01ws02Giftshop.accdb

a01ws02Products.xlsx

a01ws02Customers.xlsx

You will save your file as:

a01ws02Giftshop_LastFirst.accdb

Painted Treasures Gift Shop

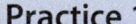

Sales &
Marketing

The Painted Treasures Gift Shop sells many products for the resort patrons including jewelry, clothing, and spa products. You will create a database of customers and their purchases. The three tables that you need are customers, purchases, and products. What are the relationships between these three tables? You will need to add a junction table between the two tables with a many-to-many relationship.

a. You will import the tblProduct table from Excel. When you import a new table from Excel, you need to change the field definitions in Access.

  • Start **Access**, and then open **a01ws02Giftshop**.

- Click the **FILE** tab, and save the file as an Access database in the location where you are saving your files with the name a01ws02Giftshop_LastFirst using your last and first name. If necessary, enable the content.

- Click the **EXTERNAL DATA** tab, and then in the Import & Link group, click **Excel**.

- Click **Browse.** Navigate to your student data files, select **a01ws02Products**, and then click **Open**. Make sure **Import the source data into a new table in the current database** is selected, and then click **OK**.

- In the Import Spreadsheet Wizard, note that **tblProduct** is selected, and then click **Next**.

- Be sure that the **First Row Contains Column Headings** check box is selected, click **Next**, and then click **Next** again.

- Select **Choose my own primary key**, click the **Primary Key** arrow, select **ProductID**, and then click **Next**.

- In the **Import to Table** box, keep the entry **tblProduct**, click **Finish**, and then click **Close**.

- Right-click **tblProduct**, and then select **Design View**.

- Change the data types as shown in the following table. Enter descriptions and change field sizes as noted.

Field Name	Data Type	Description	Field Size/Format
ProductID	Number	Unique identifier for product	Change Field Size to Long Integer
ProductDescription	Short Text	Description of product	Change Field Size to 40
Category	Short Text	Product category	Change Field Size to 15
QuantityInStock	Number	Quantity of product in stock	Change Field Size to Integer
Price	Change to Currency	Price to charge customer	Change format to Currency
Size	Short Text	Size of product	Change Field Size to 10
Color	Short Text	Color of product	Change Field Size to 15

- Save the table. Access tells you that some data might be lost because you are making fields shorter in length. Accept this by clicking **Yes**, and then close the table.

b. You will create a table named tblCustomer in Design view and import data to populate it.

- Click the **CREATE** tab, and then click **Table Design**. Access opens a blank table in Design view.

- Fill in the fields and change field sizes as noted.

Field Name	Data Type	Description	Field Size
CustomerID	AutoNumber	A unique ID that identifies each customer	Long Integer
LastName	Short Text	The customer's last name	25
FirstName	Short Text	The customer's first name	20
StreetAddress	Short Text	Street address	40
City	Short Text	City address	25
State	Short Text	State abbreviation	2
ZipCode	Short Text	Five-digit zip code	5
ResortHotelRoom	Short Text	Leave blank if not guest	6

- Highlight the **CustomerID** row by clicking the record selector to the left of the field, and then in the Tools group, click **Primary Key** to make CustomerID the primary key.

- Save your table design, naming it tblCustomer, click **OK**, and then close your table.

- Click the **EXTERNAL DATA** tab, and then in the Import & Link group, click **Excel**.

- Click **Browse**. Navigate to your student data files, click **a01ws02Customers**, and then click **Open**.

- Click **Append a copy of the records to the table** if necessary, click the arrow to select **tblCustomer**, and then click **OK**.

- Click **Next** twice, and then in the Import Spreadsheet Wizard dialog box, under Import to Table, in the Import to Table box accept the name **tblCustomer**. Click **Finish**, and then click **Close**. Double-click **tblCustomer** to open it in Datasheet view.

- In the first record in the table, change the **LastName** and **FirstName** fields to your last name and first name. Close the table.

c. Create relationships between your tables.

- Click the **DATABASE TOOLS** tab, and then in the Relationships group, click **Relationships**, and then click **Show Table**, if necessary.

- Add all four tables in the order **tblCustomer**, **tblPurchase**, **tblPurchaseLine**, and **tblProduct** to the Relationships window, and then close the Show Table dialog box.

- Drag the primary key **CustomerID** from tblCustomer to **CustomerID** in tblPurchase.

- Click **Enforce Referential Integrity**, and then click **Create**.

- Drag the primary key **PurchaseID** from tblPurchase to **PurchaseID** in tblPurchaseLine. Click **Enforce Referential Integrity**, and then click **Create**.

- Drag the primary key **ProductID** from tblProduct to **ProductID** in tblPurchaseLine. Click **Enforce Referential Integrity**, and then click **Create**.

- Click **Relationship Report**, and then save the report, accepting the name **Relationships for a01ws02Giftshop_LastFirst**. If your instructor directs you to print your results, print the report.

- Close the report, and then close the Relationships window.

d. Create a report of the customers, purchases, and products.

- Click the **CREATE** tab, and then in the Reports group, click **Report Wizard**.

- In the Report Wizard dialog box, click the **Tables/Queries** arrow, and then select **Table: tblCustomer**. Select the **LastName** and **FirstName** fields.

- Click the **Tables/Queries** arrow, click **Table: tblPurchase**, and then select **PurchaseDate**.

- Click the **Tables/Queries** arrow, click **Table: tblPurchaseLine**, and then select **Quantity**.

- Click the **Tables/Queries** arrow, click **Table: tblProduct**, select **ProductDescription**, and then click **Next**.

- Accept grouping by **tblCustomer** and then by **PurchaseDate** by clicking **Next**.

- You do not want any other grouping levels, click **Next**.

- Click the **arrow** to sort your report by ascending **ProductDescription**, and then click **Next**.

- Change the Orientation to **Landscape**, and then click **Next**.

- Title your report rptCustomerPurchases_initialLastname using your first initial and last name, and then click **Finish**.

- Switch to Layout view.

- Change the title of your report to **Customer and Purchases by initial Lastname** using your first initial and last name.

- Click the **column heading** for Quantity, press [Shift], and then click the **first value** for Quantity so both the column heading and values are selected. With your pointer, move the right border to the left of the dotted blue line. Save your report.

- If your instructor directs you to print your results, print the report.

- Close the report, and then exit Access. Submit your file as directed by your instructor.

Problem Solve 1

Student data files needed:

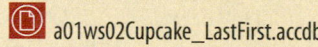 a01ws02Cupcake.accdb

a01ws02CupcakeSes.xlsx

You will save your file as:

a01ws02Cupcake_LastFirst.accdb

Managing Employees at Jellybean's Cupcakes

Production & Operations

You are the manager of the Human Resources Department of Jellybean's Cupcakes, a bakery franchise specializing in traditional and trendy cupcakes. You need to create a database that will help you track current employees along with training efforts for all of the bakeries' employees. You have a database with employee data. You will add the training sessions from an Excel spreadsheet. You will have to create a relationship between employees and training sessions. Each employee can take many training sessions, and each training session can be attended by many employees, so you will need to create a junction table.

a. Start **Access**, and then open **a01ws02Cupcake**. Click the **FILE** tab, and then save the file as **a01ws02Cupcake_LastFirst** using your last and first name. If necessary, enable the content.

b. Open the **tblEmployee** table, and then change the name in record 25 to your name.

c. Switch to Design view, and then add two new fields to tblEmployee.

Field Name	Data Type	Description	Field Size/Format
MobilePhone	Short Text	The employee's cell phone number	14
DOB	Date/Time	The employee's date of birth	Short Date

d. Add an input mask for MobilePhone. Use a mask that will show phone numbers as **(555) 555-5555** with a place holder "-" and then save with the symbols in the mask.

e. Import a new table, **tblSessions**, from the Excel workbook **a01ws02CupcakeSes**. Do not set a primary key during the import. Make the following changes to the table in Design view.

- Add a new field **SessionID** and then assign a data type of **AutoNumber**. Make this field a primary key.

- Make the changes shown to Data Type, Description, and Field Size/Format.

Field Name	Data Type	Description	Field Size/Format
SessionID		The key that identifies each training session	
SessionName		The name of the training session	50
Description	Long Text	The description of the training session	
SessionDate		The date this session was held	Short Date

f. Create a new table in Design view. This table will serve as the junction table. Add the following fields, data types, and descriptions.

Field Name	Data Type	Description	Field Size
EmpTrnID	AutoNumber	The key that identifies each training session and employee	
SessionID	Number	The foreign key to tblSessions	Long Integer
EmployeeID	Number	The foreign key to tblEmployee	Long Integer

Assign **EmpTrnID** as the primary key, and then save the table as tblEmployeeTraining.

g. Open the **Relationships** window, and then create a one-to-many relationship between **EmployeeID** in tblEmployee and **EmployeeID** in tblEmployeeTraining. Enforce referential integrity.

h. Create a one-to-many relationship between **SessionID** in tblSessions and **SessionID** in tblEmployeeTraining, and then enforce referential integrity. Do not cascade update or cascade delete.

i. Create a relationship report, accepting the default report name.

j. Enter the following data into **tblEmployeeTraining**.

EmpTrnID	SessionID	EmployeeID
Let Access autonumber as 1	1	13
Let Access autonumber as 2	1	21
Let Access autonumber as 3	1	18
Let Access autonumber as 4	2	5
Let Access autonumber as 5	2	25
Let Access autonumber as 6	10	3
Let Access autonumber as 7	10	5
Let Access autonumber as 8	10	25
Let Access autonumber as 9	10	21
Let Access autonumber as 10	10	4

k. Create a query named qryChocolate101_initialLastname that selects **LastName**, **FirstName**, **HomePhone**, and **SessionName**. Select those employees that signed up for **Chocolate 101**, and then sort by **LastName** and **FirstName**.

l. Close your database. Submit your file as directed by your instructor.

Perform 1: Perform in Your Career

Student data files needed:

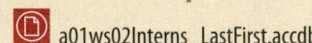 a01ws02Interns.accdb

a01ws02InternsCo.xlsx

You will save your file as:

a01ws02Interns_LastFirst.accdb

Internship Coordinator

Production & Operations

You take a job with an organization that matches students from Indiana schools to internship opportunities. You have a database with a table of information about interns and an Excel spreadsheet with companies that offer internships. You want to create a record of each intern's interviews. An intern can have many interviews, but an interview is with just one intern. A company can schedule many interviews, but an interview is with just one company.

a. Start **Access** and then open **a01ws02Interns**. Click the **FILE** tab, and save the file as an Access Database in the location where you save your files with the name a01ws02Interns_LastFirst.

b. Open **tblIntern**, familiarize yourself with the fields, add yourself as a new intern, and then close the table.

c. Start **Excel**, and then open **a01ws02InternsCo**. Familiarize yourself with the fields, and then close the workbook.

d. Import the companies from Excel into Access, creating a new table for companies called tblCompany. Fix data types and field sizes as appropriate. Add descriptions, and then set the **CompanyID** field as primary key.

e. Add a contact phone number field to the table formatted appropriately. Populate the phone number with the following information:

Company Name	Contact Phone Number
FreeMarkets	(408) 555-2049
BNY Mellon	(202) 555-8000
Adobe Systems, Incorporated	(408) 555-6799
Kraft Foods, Incorporated	(847) 555-9100
Oracle Corporation	(650) 555-3200

f. Design a table for interviews that will have the date of the interview and whatever primary keys and foreign keys you need. Create this table naming it tblInterview.

g. Form the relationships you need, and then create a relationship report accepting the default name.

h. Populate the interview table with the following information:

- Gloria Perry has an interview with BNY Mellon on 2/16/2015.
- You have an interview with Oracle Corporation on 2/13/2015.
- Thomas Jackson has an interview with Oracle Corporation on 2/13/2015.
- You have an interview with Adobe Systems, Incorporated, on 2/20/2015.
- Gloria Perry has an interview with FreeMarkets on 3/2/2015.

i. Create a report showing all companies and the interviews that are scheduled. Save the report as rptCompanyInterviews_initialLastname. Fix the columns as necessary to show them all.

j. Submit your file as directed by your instructor.

Additional Cases

Additional Workshop Cases are available on the companion website and in the instructor resources.

MODULE CAPSTONE

More Practice 1

Student data files needed:

a01mpRecipe.accdb

a01mpRecipePrep.xlsx

a01mpRecipeIng.xlsx

a01mpRecipeJunc.csv

You will save your file as:

a01mpRecipe_LastFirst.accdb

Indigo5 Restaurant

Production &
Operations

Robin Sanchez, the chef of the resort's restaurant, Indigo5, wants to keep track of recipes and the ingredients that they include in an Access database. This will allow her to plan menus and get reports and queries on the ingredients that are needed. Ingredients have already been stored in Excel worksheets and can be imported from Excel into Access. The dish preparation instructions can be copied from Excel and pasted into Access. Other data will need to be entered. Complete the following tasks:

a. Start **Access**, and then open the student data file **a01mpRecipe**. Click the **FILE** tab, and then save the file as an Access database in the location designated by your instructor with the name **a01mpRecipe_LastFirst** using your last and first name. If necessary, enable the content.

b. Create a new table in **Design** view. This table will store specific recipe items.

   • Add the following fields, data types, and descriptions. Change field sizes as noted.

Field Name	Data Type	Description	Field Size
RecipeID	Short Text	The recipe ID assigned to each menu item (primary key)	6
RecipeName	Short Text	The recipe name	30
FoodCategory	Short Text	The food category	15
TimeToPrepare	Number	Preparation time in minutes	Integer
Servings	Number	The number of servings this recipe makes	Integer
Instructions	Long Text	Cooking instructions	

   • Designate **RecipeID** as the primary key. Save the new table as **tblRecipes** and then close the table.

c. Create a form to enter recipes. Select **tblRecipes**, click the **CREATE** tab, and then in the Forms group, click **Form**. Save the form as **frmRecipes_initialLastname** using your first initial and last name.

   • Enter the following data into frmRecipes_initialLastname in Form view.

RecipeID	RecipeName	FoodCategory	TimeToPrepare	Servings
REC001	Chicken Soup	Soup	45	8
REC002	Black Beans	Beans	90	6

d. Start Excel, and then open **a01mpRecipePrep**. For each recipe, copy the **Cooking Instructions** from the Excel worksheet and paste the recipe instructions into the Access field **Instructions**. Close the form, and then close Excel.

e. Import Excel file **a01mpRecipeIng**, appending it to **tblIngredients**. Use the **Ingredients** worksheet. There are headers in the first row of this worksheet. Do not save the import steps.

f. Create a new table in **Design** view. This table will serve as the junction table between the tblIngredients and tblRecipes tables.

   - Add the following fields, data types, and descriptions, in this order. Change field sizes as noted.

Field Name	Data Type	Description	Field Size
RecipeIngredientID	AutoNumber	The recipe ingredient ID automatically assigned to each recipe ingredient (primary key)	
RecipeID	Short Text	The recipe ID from tblRecipes (foreign key)	6
IngredientID	Number	The ingredient ID from tblIngredients (foreign key)	Long Integer
Quantity	Number	The quantity of the ingredient required in the recipe	Double

   - Assign **RecipeIngredientID** as the primary key.
   - Save the new table as tblRecipeIngredients.
   - Close the table.

g. Open the **Relationships** window and add all three tables to the window.

   - Create a one-to-many relationship between **RecipeID** in tblRecipes and **RecipeID** in tblRecipeIngredients. Enforce referential integrity. Do not cascade update or cascade delete.
   - Create a one-to-many relationship between **IngredientID** in tblIngredients and **IngredientID** in tblRecipeIngredients. Enforce referential integrity. Do not cascade update or cascade delete.
   - Create a relationships report accepting the default name.
   - Save the relationships, and then close the Relationships window.

h. The Recipe Ingredients junction data were stored in a comma-separated values file or csv file. This is a comma-delimited format that can be read by Excel. Access treats a csv file as a text file. Import **a01mpRecipeJunc** as **Text** appending it to **tblRecipeIngredients**. Select **Delimited**, **Comma**, and **First Row Contains Field Names**. Do not save the import steps.

i. Use the Simple Query Wizard and the data in tblRecipes, tblRecipeIngredients, and tblIngredients to create a query that displays the ingredients for each dish. The query results should list **RecipeName**, **Quantity**, **Ingredient**, and **Units**. This will be a **Detail** query. Run your query. Adjust the width of the query columns as necessary. Save your query as qryRecipeIngredients_initialLastname.

j. Create a report with the source **qryRecipeIngredients_initialLastname** using the Report Wizard. Select all fields, group by **RecipeName**, and then sort by **Ingredient**. Accept all other defaults. Name your report rptRecipeIngredients_initialLastname and then modify the report title to be your Recipe Ingredients Report by initial Lastname. Adjust the report columns as necessary.

k. Close the database. Submit the file as directed by your instructor.

MyITLab®
Grader
Homework 1

Student data files needed:

a01ps1Hotel.accdb

a01ps1HotelGuest.accdb

a01ps1HotelRes.xlsx

a01ps1HotelRooms.csv

You will save your file as:

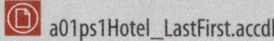

a01ps1Hotel_LastFirst.accdb

Hotel Reservations

Production & Operations

The main portion of the resort is the hotel. The hotel wants to store information about hotel guests, reservations, and rooms. You will design tables, import data from Access and Excel, and create relationships. Then you will be able to create queries and reports from the data. Complete the following tasks:

a. Start **Access**, and then open **a01ps1Hotel**. Click the **FILE** tab, and save the file as an Access database with the name **a01ps1Hotel_LastFirst** using your last and first name. If necessary, enable the content.

b. Import a table from the Access database **a01ps1HotelGuest**, selecting the **tblGuests** table. Do not save the import steps.

c. Open **tblGuests**, and then change the guest name in record **25** to your first and last name. Close the table.

d. Create a new table in **Design** view. This table will store reservations.
  • Add the following fields, data types, and descriptions, in this order. Change field sizes as noted.

Field Name	Data Type	Description	Field Size/Format
ReservationID	AutoNumber	A unique identifier for the reservation (primary key)	Long Integer
GuestID	Number	The guest ID from tblGuests (foreign key)	Long Integer
RoomNumber	Short Text	The room number from tblRooms (foreign key)	30
CheckInDate	Date/Time	The date the guest will check in	Short Date
NightsStay	Number	How many nights the guest will stay	Integer
NumberOfGuests	Number	The number of guests on this reservation	Integer

  • Assign **ReservationID** as the primary key.
  • Save the new table as **tblReservations**.

e. Import **a01ps1HotelRes** from Excel, appending it to **tblReservations**. The Excel column headers match the Access field names.

f. Select **tblReservations**, click the **CREATE** tab, and then in the Forms group, click **Form** to create a form to enter reservations. Save it as **frmReservations_initialLastname**, using your first initial and last name.
  • Enter the following data in the new (blank) record in frmReservations_initialLastname.

ReservationID	GuestID	RoomNumber	CheckInDate	NightsStay	NumberOfGuests
AutoNumber	25	105	4/20/2015	8	1

g. Create a new table in **Design** view. This table will store information about the hotel rooms.

- Add the following fields, data types, and descriptions, in this order. Change field sizes as noted.

Field Name	Data Type	Description	Field Size
RoomNumber	Short Text	The resort's room number or name (primary key)	30
RoomType	Short Text	The type of room this is	20

- Assign **RoomNumber** as the primary key.
- Save the new table as tblRooms.

h. The Hotel Rooms data was stored in a comma-separated values file or csv file. This is a comma-delimited format that can be read by Excel. Access treats a csv file as a text file. Import **a01ps1HotelRooms** as text, appending it to **tblRooms**. Select **Delimited**, **Comma**, and **First Row Contains Field Names**. Do not save the import steps.

i. Open the **Relationships** window, add **tblGuests**, **tblReservations**, and **tblRooms**. Create a one-to-many relationship between **GuestID** in tblGuests and **GuestID** in tblReservations. Enforce referential integrity. Do not cascade update or cascade delete.

j. Create a one-to-many relationship between **RoomNumber** in tblRooms and **RoomNumber** in tblReservations. Enforce referential integrity. Do not cascade update or cascade delete. Create a relationships report accepting the default name.

k. Use the Simple Query Wizard to create a query. The query results should list **GuestID**, **GuestFirstName**, **GuestMiddleInitial**, **GuestLastName**, **CheckInDate**, **NightsStay**, and **RoomType**. This query should show every field of every record.

l. Save your query as qryMyReservations_initialLastname. Run the query.

m. In Design view for **qryMyReservations_initialLastname**, select the guest with **GuestID** = 25. Sort by **CheckInDate**. Run the query.

n. Use the Report Wizard to create a report showing **ReservationID**, **CheckInDate**, **NightsStay**, and **RoomType**. View by **tblRooms** and sort by **CheckInDate** and **ReservationID**. Name your report rptReservations_initialLastname. Change the title to Reservations Report by initial Lastname. Adjust the report columns as necessary.

o. Close the database. Submit the file as directed by your instructor.

Problem Solve 2

MyITLab® Grader

Homework 2

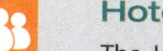

Human Resources

Student data files needed:

a01ps2HotelStaff.accdb

a01ps2HotelEmp.xlsx

a01ps2HotelAreas.accdb

You will save your file as:

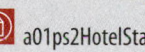

a01ps2HotelStaff_LastFirst.accdb

Hotel Reservations

The Hotel general manager needs a human resource database to store information on employees, the areas they work in, and the hours they are scheduled to work. The database will have three new tables: tblHotelAreas, tblEmployee, and tblSchedule.

Complete the following tasks:

a. Start **Access**, and then open the student data file **a01ps2HotelStaff**. Click the **FILE** tab, and save the file as an Access Database in the location designated by your instructor with the name a01ps2HotelStaff_LastFirst using your first and last name. If necessary, enable the content.

b. Create a new table in **Design** view. This table will store employees.

- Add the following fields, in this order. Where necessary, you decide upon data types and field sizes.

Field Name	Data Type	Description	Field Size
EmployeeID	AutoNumber	A unique identifier for the employee (primary key)	
AreaID	Number	The area ID from tblHotelAreas (foreign key)	Long Integer
FirstName	Pick appropriate type	The employee's first name	30
LastName	Pick appropriate type	The employee's last name	30
StreetAddress	Pick appropriate type	Home street address	40
City	Pick appropriate type	City	30
State	Pick appropriate type	State abbreviation	Pick appropriate size
ZipCode	Pick appropriate type	Zip code (5 digit)	Pick appropriate size
Phone	Pick appropriate type	Home phone number	14
HireDate	Pick appropriate type	Date employee was hired	Short Date
JobTitle	Pick appropriate type	Employee job title	30

- Make sure you have assigned the most appropriate field to be the primary key.
- Save the new table as tblEmployee.
- Define an input mask for the phone number. Use a mask that will show phone numbers as **(555) 555-5555** with a place holder of "-" and save with the symbols in the mask.

c. Import **a01ps2HotelEmp** from Excel, using the **Employee** worksheet and appending it to **tblEmployee**. Change the name and street address of the last employee to your name and address.

d. Import the **tblHotelAreas** table from the **a01ps2HotelAreas** Access database and create a new table.

e. Import **a01ps2HotelEmp** from Excel, using the **Area** worksheet and appending it to **tblHotelAreas**.

f. Create a new table in **Design** view. This table will store information about an employee's schedule.

- Add the following fields, data types, and descriptions, in this order.

Field Name	Data Type	Description	Field Size
ScheduleID	AutoNumber	A unique identifier for the schedule (primary key)	Long Integer
ScheduleDay	Date/Time	The day the schedule applies to	ShortDate
StartTime	Date/Time	Starting time for the shift	MediumTime
HoursScheduled	Number	Number of hours on shift	Integer
EmployeeID	Number	The person being scheduled	Long Integer

- Make sure you have assigned the most appropriate primary key.
- Save the new table as tblSchedule.

g. Import **a01ps2HotelEmployees** from Excel, using the **Schedule** worksheet, and appending it to **tblSchedule**.

h. Open the **Relationships** window, add the tables **tblSchedule**, **tblEmployee**, and **tblHotelAreas**. Create a one-to-many relationship between **EmployeeID** in tblEmployee and **EmployeeID** in tblSchedule. Enforce referential integrity. Do not cascade update or cascade delete.

i. Create a one-to-many relationship between **AreaID** in tblHotelAreas and **AreaID** in tblEmployee. Enforce referential integrity. Do not cascade update or cascade delete. Create a relationships report accepting the default name.

j. Create a form for **tblEmployee**. Notice that Access automatically includes the related records from tblSchedule at the bottom of the form. Save the form as frmEmployeeSchedule_initialLastname.

k. Using **frmEmployeeSchedule_initialLastname**, add a new schedule for yourself to work on January 3, 2015, starting at 8 am and working for 8 hours.

l. Use data in **tblHotelAreas**, **tblEmployee**, and **tblSchedule** to create a schedule query. The query results should list **AreaID**, **AreaName**, **FirstName**, **LastName**, **ScheduleDay**, **StartTime**, and **HoursScheduled**. Save your query as qryCoffeeShopSchedule_initialLastname.

m. In Design view for **qryCoffeeShopSchedule_initialLastname**, select only the data from **AreaID 4**. Run the query.

n. Create a report from **qryCoffeeShopSchedule_initialLastname**. Select these fields: **FirstName**, **LastName**, **ScheduleDay**, **StartTime**, and **HoursScheduled**. View by **tblSchedule**. Sort by **ScheduleDay**, **StartTime** and **LastName**, and then change to **Landscape** orientation. Name your report rptCoffeeShopSchedule_initialLastname. Modify the report title to be Coffee Shop Schedule by initial Lastname.

o. Close the database. Submit the file as directed by your instructor.

Student data file needed:

 Blank Access database

You will save your file as:

 a01pf1Club_LastFirst.accdb

Track Events for Your Organization

Research & Development

Pick an organization that you belong to. You want to track the members of the organization, events, and member attendance at the events. Because a member can attend many events and an event can be attended by many members, you will need a junction table. You will start by creating three tables, the relationships between the tables, and reports on attendance. Next, you will decide on one other table that makes sense for your organization, define that table, and relate it to one of the already existing tables.

a. Start **Access**, and then click **Blank desktop database**. Browse to where you are storing your data files, and name your database a01pf1Club_LastFirst.

b. Design a table to store members. Choose appropriate fields that would describe the members of your organization.

- Assign a field to be primary key, and then make it **AutoNumber**. For all fields, enter appropriate data types, descriptions, field sizes, and masks. Save your table as tblMember.

c. Enter yourself and a friend into the table. Enter as many other members as you wish.

d. Design a table to store events. Use the following fields: EventID, EventName, EventDate, and PlaceName. You may add other fields as appropriate.

- Assign EventID to be primary key, and then make it an AutoNumber. Enter appropriate data types, descriptions, and field sizes. Save your table as tblEvent.

e. Enter two events that you attended into the table. Enter as many other events as you wish.

f. Design a junction table to relate members and attendance at events. Use the following fields: EventID and the primary key of your member table.

- EventID is a foreign key and should be Number, Long Integer. Enter an appropriate description.
- Use the primary key of your member table as a foreign key in this table. Enter an appropriate type and description.
- Create a composite primary key using both EventID and the primary key from your member table.
- Save your table as tblAttendance.

g. Create relationships as appropriate for the tblMember, tblAttendance, and tblEvent tables.

h. Enter the following data into tblAttendance.

EventID	MemberID
Use the EventID for the first event	Your primary key in the member table
Use the EventID for the first event	Your friend's primary key in the member table
Use the EventID for the second event	Your primary key in the member table

i. Create a report on Events using **EventName**, **EventDate**, and **PlaceName**. Sort by EventDate. Name your report rptEventReport_initialLastname and then modify the report title to be Event Report by initial Lastname.

j. Create a query on Events including **EventName**, **EventDate**, and **PlaceName**. Save the query as qryEventName_initialLastname and then modify the query design to select the EventName for the first event. Run the query.

k. Create a report on event attendance. Use **EventName** and **EventDate** from tblEvent and the member's name. Group the report by **Event**. Sort the report by **LastName** and **FirstName**. Name your report rptEventAttendance_initialLastname and then modify the report title to be Event Attendance by initial Lastname.

l. Determine one additional table that would make sense for your organization to keep data in.

m. Design this table and the appropriate fields. Make sure to assign a primary key.

n. Enter data into the new table. Create relationships between this new table and your existing tables as appropriate. Ask yourself the two questions to determine the relationships. Create a relationships report accepting the default name.

o. Create a report showing data from your new table and data from another table that it is related to.

p. Submit the file as directed by your instructor.

Perform 2: Perform in Your Career

Student data file needed:

 Blank Access database

You will save your file as:

 a01pf2PetStore_LastFirst.accdb

Pet Store

Sales & Marketing

A pet store owner wants to create a database for the store. The database needs to include information about animals and the breeds of the animals. An animal is of one breed. The pet store can have many animals of each breed. The pet owner will want to keep records of the purchases and the customers that bought each animal. You will need to decide what tables you need to record purchases and customers. You will also need to decide what relationships you want to create.

a. Start **Access**, and then click **Blank desktop database**. Browse to where you are storing your data files, and name your database a01pf2PetStore_LastFirst.

b. Design a table to store breeds. Use the following fields: BreedID, AnimalType, BreedName, MaximumSize (in pounds), LengthOfLife (in years).

    • Assign **BreedID** to be primary key with the AutoNumber data type.

    • For all fields, enter appropriate data types, descriptions, and field sizes. Save your table as tblBreed.

c. Enter the following data into the table, in this order.

BreedID	AnimalType	BreedName	MaximumSize	LengthOfLife
1	Dog	Akita	110	12
2	Dog	Papillon	9	15
3	Cat	Devon	7	18
4	Cat	Birman	10	19
5	Chinchilla	Silver Mosaic	1	15

d. After entering those five breeds, pick another breed and add it to the table.

e. Design a table to store animals. Use the following fields: AnimalID, DateOfBirth, Price, Weight, Color, Sex, and BreedID.

- Assign **AnimalID** to be primary key with the AutoNumber data type.
- BreedID is the foreign key to tblBreed.
- For all fields, enter appropriate data types, descriptions, and field sizes.
- Save your table as tblAnimal.

f. Enter the following data into tblAnimal, in this order.

AnimalID	DateOfBirth	Price	Weight	Color	Sex	BreedID
1	6/17/2014	$125.00	28	White	M	1
2	6/17/2014	$125.00	30	White	M	1
3	7/25/2014	$610.00	4	Tan	F	2
4	8/7/2014	$610.00	3	White	F	2
5	8/7/2014	$550.00	3	White	M	2
6	5/10/2014	$225.00	2	Blue	F	3
7	5/10/2014	$225.00	2	Gray	M	3
8	6/26/2014	$150.00	2	White	F	4
9	7/17/2014	$125.00	2	Gray	M	4
10	8/18/2014	$ 30.00	1	Silver	F	5

g. After adding the 10 animals, add another animal which is of the breed you entered for the prior table.

h. Open the Relationships window. Create a one-to-many relationship between BreedID in tblBreed and BreedID in tblAnimal. Enforce referential integrity. Do not cascade update or cascade delete.

i. Determine the tables that the store owner would need to keep store customers and their purchases.

- Design these tables and the appropriate fields. Make sure to assign primary keys.
- Create relationships between these new tables and your existing tables as appropriate. Ask yourself the two questions to determine the relationships. Add foreign keys as appropriate. Create a relationships report accepting the default name.

j. Enter the appropriate customer and purchase data to capture the following events.

- You bought the chinchilla with AnimalID = 10 yesterday.
- A friend bought the Birman cat with AnimalID = 9 and the Akita with Animal ID = 1 today.

k. Create a report showing animals by breed. Show **AnimalType**, **BreedName**, **AnimalID**, **DateOfBirth**, and **Price**. Select correct groupings and sort orders.

l. Create a query to find out who purchased AnimalID = 10. Show **Customer name** (FirstName and LastName), **AnimalID**, **AnimalType**, and **BreedName**.

m. Create a report showing the animals purchased on all dates. Group and sort appropriately.

n. Submit the file as directed by your instructor.

Perform 3: Perform in Your Team

Student data files needed:

 Blank Access database

 Blank Word document

You will save your files as:

 a01pf3Music_TeamName.accdb

 a01pf3MusicPlan_TeamName.docx

Independent Music Label

Production & Operations

The owner of an independent music label needs to keep track of the groups, musicians, and their music. You have been asked to create a database for the label.

The label owner would like to be able to get a list of groups with all musicians, get a list of groups with albums, select an album and see all songs in the album, and select a group and see their albums with all songs in the album. You will need to design tables, fields, relationships, queries, and reports for the label.

Because databases can only be opened and edited by one person at a time, it is a good idea to plan ahead by designing your tables in advance. You will use a Word document to plan your database and to plan which team member will do what. You will use SkyDrive to store your Word document and Access database.

a. Select one team member to set up the Word document and Access database by completing Steps b–e.

b. Open your browser and navigate to **https://www.skydrive.live.com**, create a new folder, and name it a01pf3MusicFolder_TeamName. Replace TeamName with the name assigned to your team by your instructor.

c. Start **Access**, and then click **Blank desktop database**. Create a blank database, and then name it a01pf3Music_TeamName. Replace TeamName with the name assigned to your team by your instructor. Click the **Create** button to create the database.

d. Upload the **a01pf3Music_TeamName** database to the **a01pf3MusicFolder_TeamName** folder, and then share the folder with the other members of your team. Verify that the other team members have permission to edit the contents of the shared folder and that they are required to log in to SkyDrive to access it.

e. Create a new Word document in the assignment folder in SkyDrive, and then name it a01pf3MusicPlan_TeamName. Replace TeamName with the name assigned to your team by your instructor.

f. In the Word document, each team member must list his or her first and last name as well as a summary of their planned contributions. As work is completed on the database, this document should be updated with the specifics of each team member's contributions.

g. Use the Word document to list the fields you need in each table, the primary keys for each table, and the foreign keys.

h. In Access, your team members will need to complete the following steps.
- Design your tables.
- Enter data for three music groups into your tables.

Groups	Group Members	Albums	Songs
Clean Green, an Enviro-Punk band	Jon Smith (vocalist and guitar) Lee Smith percussion and keyboard)	Clean Green	Esperando Verde Precious Drops Recycle Mania Don't Tread on Me
		Be Kind to Animals	It's Our Planet Too Animal Rag Where Will We Live?
Spanish Moss, a Spanish Jazz band	Hector Caurendo (guitar) Pasquale Rodriguez (percussion) Perry Trent (vocalist) Meredith Selmer (bass)	Latin Latitude	Attitude Latitude Flying South Latin Guitarra Cancion Cancion
Your band	Your team members	You decide	You decide

- Create your relationships. Create a relationships report.
- Create a report showing all groups with all musicians.
- Create a report showing all groups, the group type, and their albums.
- Create a query to select an album from your band and see all songs in the album.
- Create a query to select your band and see all your albums with all songs in the albums.

i. Once the assignment is complete, share the **a01pf3MusicFolder_TeamName** folder with your instructor. Make sure that your instructor has permission to edit the contents of the folder.

Perform 4: How Others Perform

Student data file needed:

a01pf4Textbook.accdb

You will save your files as:

a01pf4Textbook_LastFirst.accdb

a01pf4Textbook_LastFirst.docx

College Bookstore

Production & Operations

A colleague has created a database for your college bookstore. He is having problems creating the relationships in the database and has come to you for your help. What problems do you see in his database design? He has three tables in his database: one for sections of courses, one for instructors, and one for textbooks, as shown in Figures 1, 2, and 3.

a. Start **Access**, and then open the student data file **a01pf4Textbook**. Save the file as a01pf4Textbook_LastFirst. You do not need to make changes to this database, but you will want to look at the database in more detail than is shown in the figures.

b. Create a Word document named a01pf4Textbook_LastFirst where you will answer the remaining questions.

c. Are there any errors in the way that fields are defined or named in the tables? In your a01pf4TextbookAnswers_LastFirst Word document, list your errors by table.

d. Are there any errors in the way that tables are named or defined? In your a01pf4TextbookAnswers_LastFirst Word document, list your errors by table.

e. He wants to define these relationships. How would you want to define the relationships?

- An instructor can teach many sections; a section is taught by just one instructor.
- A section can have many textbooks; a textbook can be used in many sections.

f. In your a01pf4TextbookAnswers_LastFirst Word document, describe how you would define the relationships.

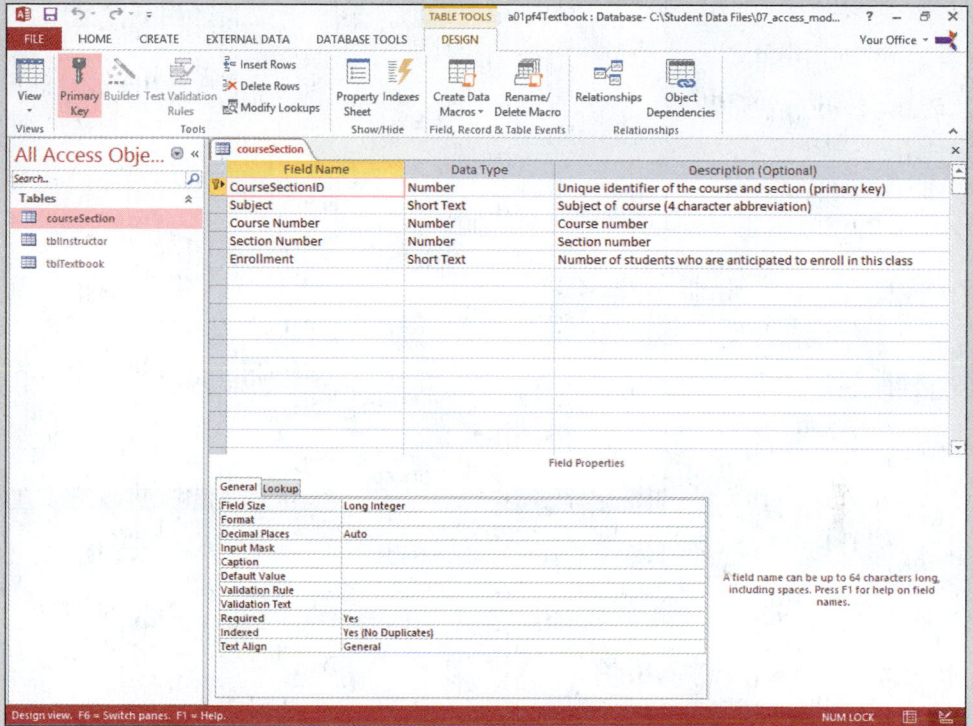

Figure 1 Table design for courseSection

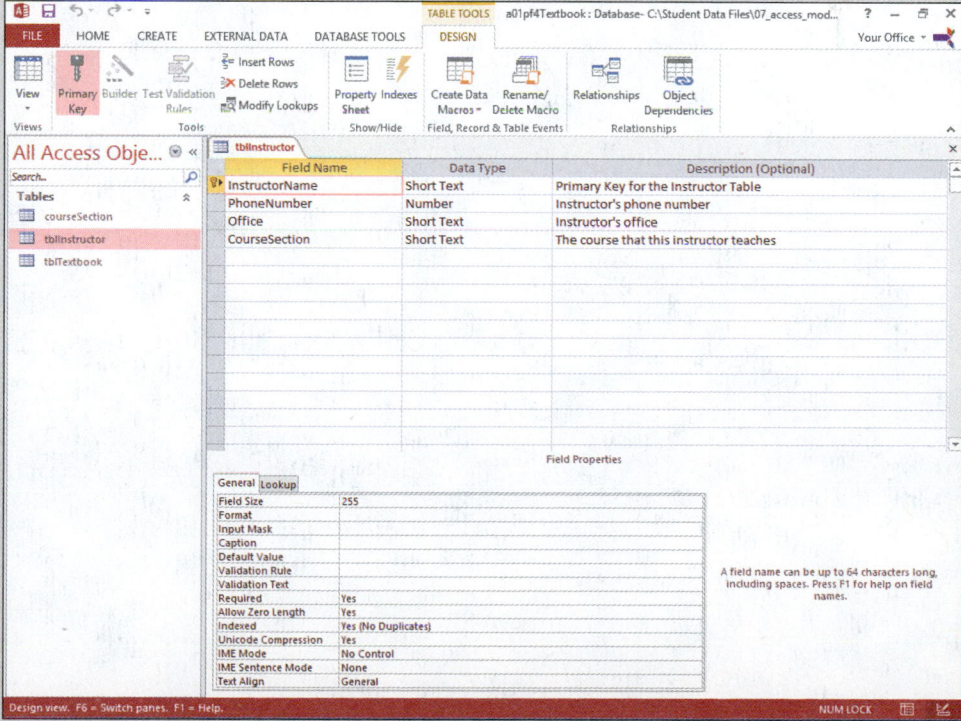

Figure 2 Table design for tblInstructor

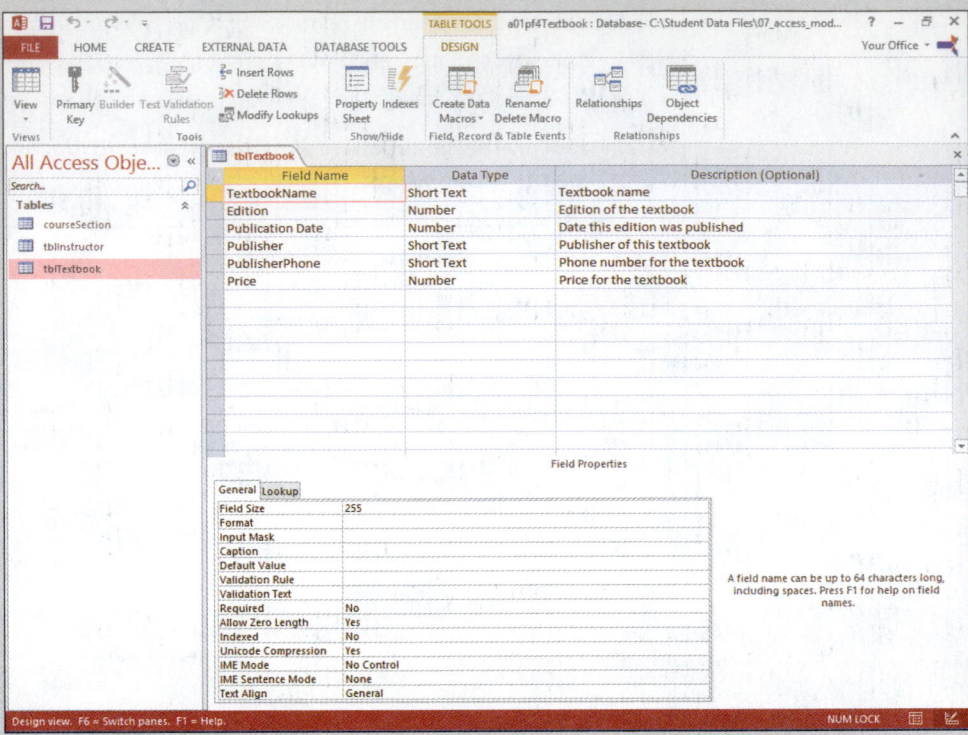

Figure 3 Table design for tblTextbook

g. Submit the files as directed by your instructor.

WORKSHOP 3 | QUERIES AND DATA ACCESS

OBJECTIVES

1. Find and replace records in the datasheet   p. 148

2. Modify datasheet appearance   p. 153

3. Run query wizards   p. 155

4. Create queries in Design view   p. 157

5. Sort query results   p. 164

6. Define selection criteria for queries   p. 166

7. Create aggregate functions   p. 181

8. Create calculated fields   p. 187

Prepare Case

Production & Operations

Turquoise Oasis Spa Data Management

The Turquoise Oasis Spa has been popular with resort clients. The owners have spent several months putting spa data into an Access database so they can better manage the data. You have been asked to help show the staff how best to use the database to find information about products, services, and customers. For training purposes, not all the spa records have been added yet. Once the staff is trained, the remaining records will be entered into the database.

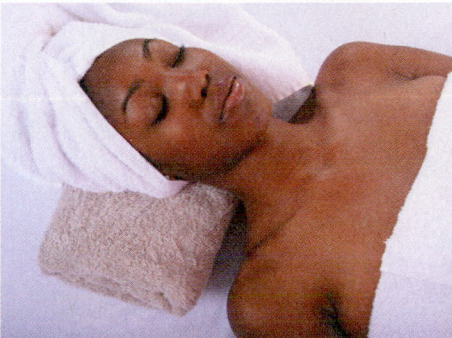

Dewayne Flowers / Shutterstock.com

REAL WORLD SUCCESS

"My company sells luxury appliances. Sometimes, we run out of products and don't have time to wait for the supplier. In the past, I'd have to get on the phone and call all our other locations in the region to see if they had extra that they could spare. Now, I run a query and in less than a minute I know who has it and when they need it. The queries are so popular that I've shared them with all of the managers."

\- David, alumnus and procurement specialist

Student data file needed for this workshop:

 a02ws03Spa.accdb

You will save your file as:

 a02ws03Spa_LastFirst.accdb

Working with Datasheets

Datasheets are used to view all records in a table at one time. Each record is viewed as a row in the table. Records can be entered, edited, and deleted directly in a datasheet. When a table becomes so large that all the records and fields are no longer visible in the datasheet window without scrolling, the Find command can be used to quickly find specific values in a record. In this section, you will find records in a datasheet as well as modify the appearance of a datasheet.

Find and Replace Records in the Datasheet

The Navigation bar allows you to move to the top and bottom of a table or scroll to a specific record; however, this can be inefficient if your table is large. To manage larger tables, Access provides ways for you to quickly locate information within the datasheet. Once that information is found, it can then be easily replaced with another value using the **Replace command**.

If you do not know the exact value you are looking for because you do not know how it is spelled or how someone entered it, you can use a wildcard character. A **wildcard character** is used as a placeholder for an unknown part of a value or to match a certain pattern in a value. For example, if you know the value you are looking for contains the word "market" you can use a wildcard character at the beginning and end such as *market*.

Opening the Starting File

The owners of the spa have spent several months entering spa data into an Access database so they can better manage the data. You have been asked to help show the staff how best to use the database to find information about products, services, and customers. For training purposes, not all the spa records have been added yet.

A03.00

 To Open the a02ws03Spa Database

a. Start **Access**, and then open the student data file **a02ws03Spa**.

b. On the **FILE** tab, save the file as an **Access Database** in the location designated by your instructor with the name a02ws03Spa_LastFirst using your first and last name. If necessary, enable the content.

Finding Records in a Table

In Datasheet view, you can use the **Find command** to quickly locate specific records using all or part of a field value. For this project, a staff member found a book left by one of the guests. A first name was printed on the inside of the book cover. The staff member remembers helping a gentleman named Guy who said he was from North Carolina, but is not certain of his last name. You will show the staff how to use the Find command to quickly navigate through the table to search for this guest.

MyITLab®

Workshop 3 Training

A03.01

 To Find Records in the Datasheet

a. In the Navigation Pane, double-click **tblCustomer** to open the table.

b. Add a record at the end of the table with your first name, last name, address, city, state, phone and e-mail address. Press Tab until the record selector is on the next row and your record has been added to the table.

SIDE NOTE
Find Shortcut
`Ctrl`+`F` is the keyboard shortcut for Find.

SIDE NOTE
Spelling Counts
Spelling counts in Access, so if you enter a search item and Access cannot find it, your search value may be spelled wrong.

c. On the Navigation bar, click **First Record** ⏮ to go to the first record in the table. On the HOME tab, in the Find group, click **Find** to open the Find and Replace dialog box.

d. Replace the text in the Find What box with **Guy**. Click the **Look In** arrow, and then select **Current document**.

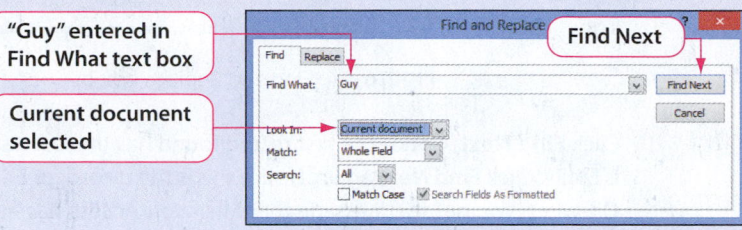

Figure 1 Find and Replace dialog box to find all records for "Guy"

e. Click **Find Next**. Access highlights the first record found for Guy Bowers from Derby, North Carolina (NC). This is a possibility, but there might be a second Guy.

f. Click **Find Next** again to check for more records with Guy. Guy Blake from Suffolk, Wisconsin, is found.

g. Click **Find Next** again to check for more records with Guy. When Access is done searching and cannot find any more matches, you will see the message "Microsoft Access finished searching the records. The search item was not found."

h. Click **OK**, and then click **Cancel** to close the Find and Replace dialog box.

> **Troubleshooting**
>
> If you did not get the results shown above, go back and carefully check the settings in the Find and Replace dialog box. Make sure Match Case is not checked. When Match Case is checked, the search will be case sensitive. Also check to make sure the Look In box shows Current document. If the Look In box shows Current field, Access will only look in the field selected.

Finding and Replacing Data in a Datasheet

Not only can you find records using the Find command, but you can also replace records once you find them with the Replace command. In a large table, it is helpful to locate a record using the Find command, and then replace the data using the Replace command.

For this project, the receptionist receives a notice from Erica Rocha about her upcoming marriage. The receptionist wants to go through the database and find any records related to Erica and change her last name to her married name, Muer. You will show the receptionist how to find Erica in the database and replace her last name of Rocha with Muer.

A03.02

 To Find and Replace Records

a. On the HOME tab, in the Find group, click **Find** to open the Find and Replace dialog box.

b. In the Find and Replace dialog box, click the **Replace** tab. In the Find What box, type **Rocha** and then in the Replace With box, type **Muer**.

c. Verify that Look in: Current document is selected. Leave all other options as they are.

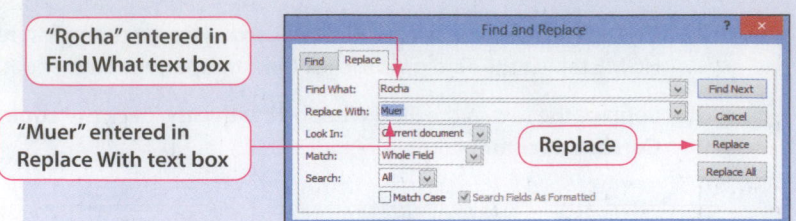

SIDE NOTE

Data Is Automatically Saved

Access automatically saves data changes when you close the table without prompting you to save it.

"Rocha" entered in Find What text box

"Muer" entered in Replace With text box

Replace

Figure 2   Find and Replace box options

d. Click **Find Next**. Notice the first record found has the last name Rocha, but the first name is Emily. Click **Find Next** again. Notice this is the record for Erica Rocha. Click **Replace**. Click **OK** when you get the message that Microsoft Access has finished searching the records. The Last Name should now be Muer instead of Rocha. Click **Cancel** to close the Find and Replace dialog box.

e. **Close** ☒ the table.

Using a Wildcard Character

A wildcard character, as shown in Table 1, is used as a placeholder for an unknown part of a value or to match a certain pattern in a value. A wildcard character can replace a single character or multiple characters and both text and numbers.

Wildcard Character	Example
*	To match any number of characters; to search for a word that starts with "ar" you would enter **ar***.
#	To match any single numeric character; to search for a three-digit number that starts with "75" you would enter **75#**.
?	To match any single character; to search for a three-letter word that starts with "t" and ends with "p" you would enter **t?p**.
[]	To match any single character within the brackets; to search for a word that starts with "e," contains any of the letters "a" or "r," and ends with "r," you would enter **e[ar]r** and get "ear" or "err" as a result.
!	To match any single character NOT within the brackets; to search for a word that starts with "e," contains any letter other than "a" or "r," and ends with "r," you would enter **e[!ar]r** to get anything except "err" or "ear".
-	To match any range of characters in ascending order—"a" to "z"; to search for a word beginning with "a" and ending in "e" with any letter between "b" and "t" in between, you would enter **a[b-t]e**.

Table 1   Wildcard characters

For this project, the staff is looking for products with the word "butter" in the name so they can put together a weekly promotion for all these products. You will show them how to use a wildcard character to find the products.

A03.03

 To Use a Wildcard Character to Find a Record

a. Double-click **tblProduct** to open the table.

b. In the first record, click the **ProductDescription** field. In the Find group, click **Find** to open the Find and Replace dialog box. Replace the text in the Find What box with *butter*. Click the **Look In** arrow, and then click **Current field**.

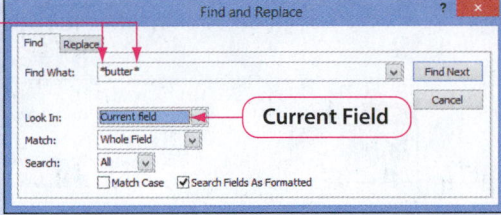

> **Wildcard character at beginning and end of text**

> **Current Field**

Figure 3   Find records with "butter" in the ProductDescription field

c. Click **Find Next**. The first record found is for ProductID P018 Cocoa Body Butter. Click **Find Next** again to find the record for ProductID P021 Lemon Body Butter.

d. Click **Find Next** again until Access has finished searching the records. When Access is done searching and cannot find any more matches, you will see the message "Microsoft Access finished searching the records. The search item was not found." Click **OK**, and then click **Cancel** to close the Find and Replace dialog box.

> **Troubleshooting**
>
> If Access highlights a record in the table and you cannot see it, drag the Find and Replace dialog box to another area of the screen.

e. **Close** ☒ the table.

Applying a Filter to a Datasheet

A **filter** is a condition you apply temporarily to a table or query. All records that do not match the filter criteria are hidden until the filter is removed or the table is closed and reopened. A filter is a simple technique to quickly reduce a large amount of data to a much smaller subset of data. You can choose to save a table with the filter applied so when you open the table later the filter is still available.

You can filter a datasheet by selecting a value in a record and telling Access to filter records that contain some variation of the record you choose, or you can create a custom filter to select all or part of a field value.

Filtering by Selection

When you **filter by selection**, you select a value in a record and Access filters the records that contain only the values that match what you have selected. For this exercise, a customer came into the spa and stated that she was from Minnesota and had previously been a spa customer but was just browsing today. She left her glasses on the counter, and the staff wants to return them to her. You will help the staff members find all customers from Minnesota to see if they recognize the customer's name.

To Select Specific Records Using a Selection Filter

SIDE NOTE
How to Clear Filters
To delete filters from the table, click Advanced in the Sort & Filter group, and select Clear All Filters.

a. Double-click **tblCustomer** to open the table, locate the first record with an address in the state of Minnesota (MN), and then click the **State** field. In the Sort & Filter group, click **Selection**, and then click the **Equals "MN"** option.

Access displays three records where all states are MN for Minnesota. The Toggle Filter in the Sort & Filter group allows you to go back and forth between viewing the filtered records and all the records in the table. To remove the filter, click Toggle Filter in the Sort & Filter group. To show the filter again, click Toggle Filter in the Sort & Filter group.

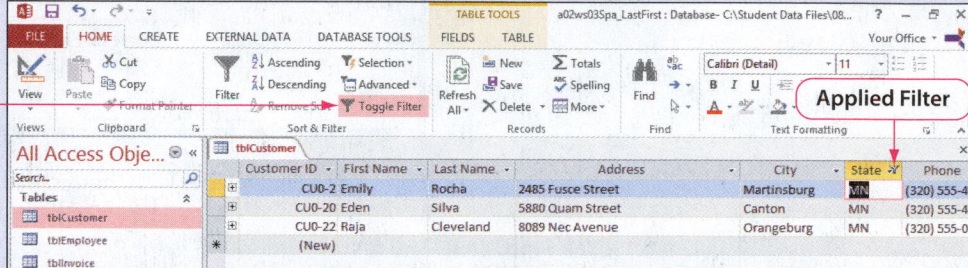

Figure 4   Filtered table for all records containing a state of MN

b. The filter is temporary unless you choose to save it with the table or query. If you do save it, the next time you open the table or query, you only have to click Toggle Filter to see the records from the state of Minnesota. Click **Save** 🔲 on the Quick Access Toolbar. This saves the table with the filter. Close 🗙 the table.

c. Double-click **tblCustomer** to open the table. On the HOME tab, in the Sort & Filter group, click **Toggle Filter** to see the filtered records. **Close** 🗙 the table.

CONSIDER THIS | **Finding Records**

You have now found records using Find and Replace and using a selection filter. What are the advantages of each method? When would you use each?

Using a Text Filter

Text filters allow you to create a custom filter to match all or part of the text in a field that you specify. For this exercise, the staff wants to create a mailing of sample products but cannot send the products to customers with a post office box. You will help the staff find all customers who have "P.O. Box" as part of their address.

To Select Specific Records Using a Text Filter

a. Double-click **tblCustomer** to open the table. Select the entire **Address** column by clicking the column name. In the column heading, click the **filter** arrow in the column heading, point to **Text Filters**, and then click **Begins With**.

b. In the Custom Filter dialog box, type **P** and then click **OK**.

Access retrieves the nine records where the addresses contain a P.O. box number. Notice that Toggle Filter in the Sort & Filter group is selected and the Filtered indicator in the Navigation bar is highlighted. You can toggle between the filtered table and the whole table by clicking on either Toggle Filter or the Filtered indicator. The filter indicator in the column heading indicates whether a filter is currently applied.

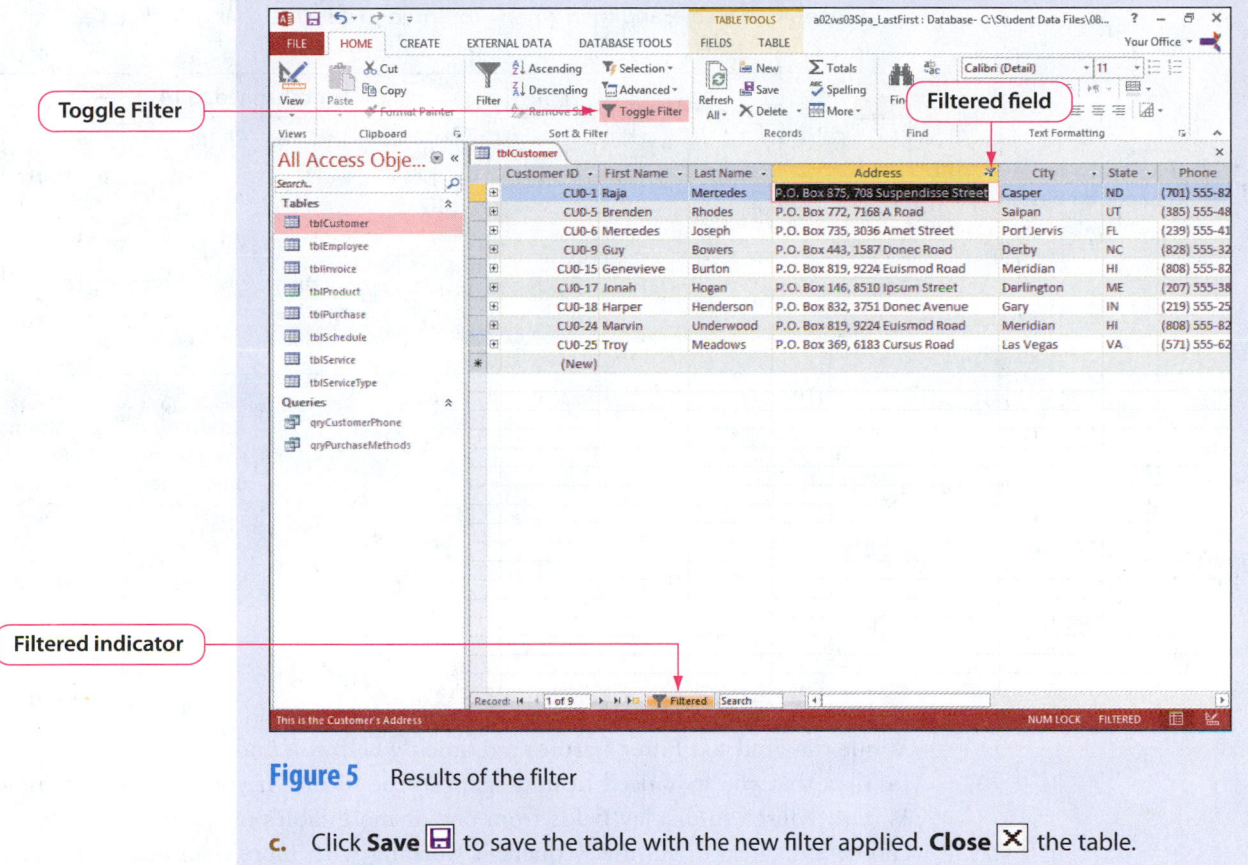

Figure 5   Results of the filter

c. Click **Save** 💾 to save the table with the new filter applied. **Close** ❎ the table.

Modify Datasheet Appearance

You can change the appearance of your datasheet by changing the font type, font size, column widths, and background colors to make it more readable. **AutoFit** is a feature that can change the column width of the data to match the widest data entered in that field. That allows you to see all the data in a particular field.

Changing the Look of a Datasheet

For this exercise, the manager is upset because the font is too small and she cannot see all the field headings in the invoice table. You will show her how to make the text larger and the columns wider.

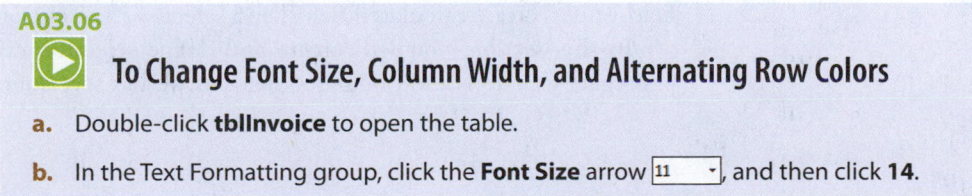

A03.06

▶ To Change Font Size, Column Width, and Alternating Row Colors

a. Double-click **tblInvoice** to open the table.

b. In the Text Formatting group, click the **Font Size** arrow ⌗ , and then click **14**.

SIDE NOTE

Alternate Method for Changing Column Width

You can also drag a column border to make the column wider.

c. Point to the **right border** of the first field name and double-click. The AutoFit feature resizes the column to best fit the data. Repeat this action for all the columns.

d. In the Text Formatting group, click the **Alternate Row Color** arrow 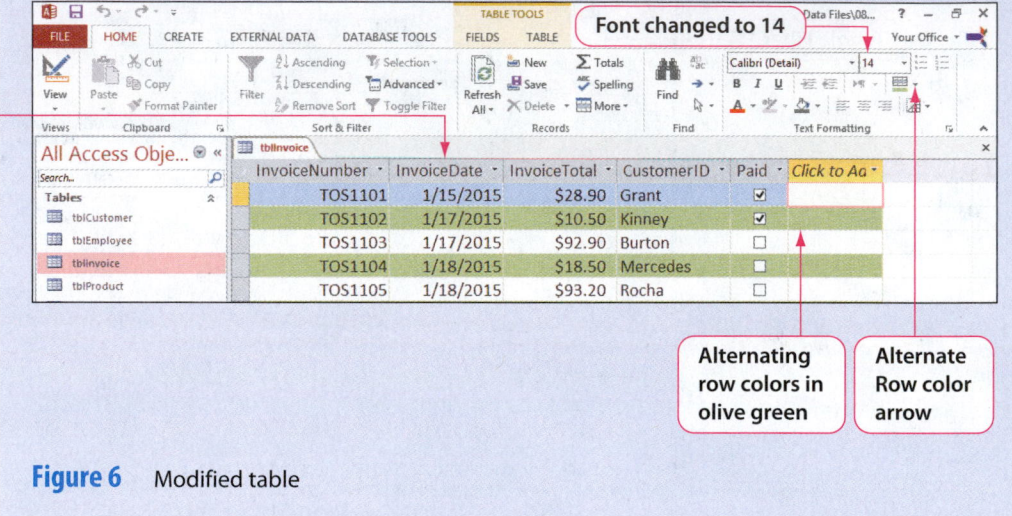, and then under Theme Colors select **Olive Green, Accent 3, Lighter 40%**. This is the seventh column and the fourth row under Theme Colors. The rows will still be alternating colors, but they will be changed to olive green.

e. **Close** the table, and then when prompted to save the changes, click **Yes**.

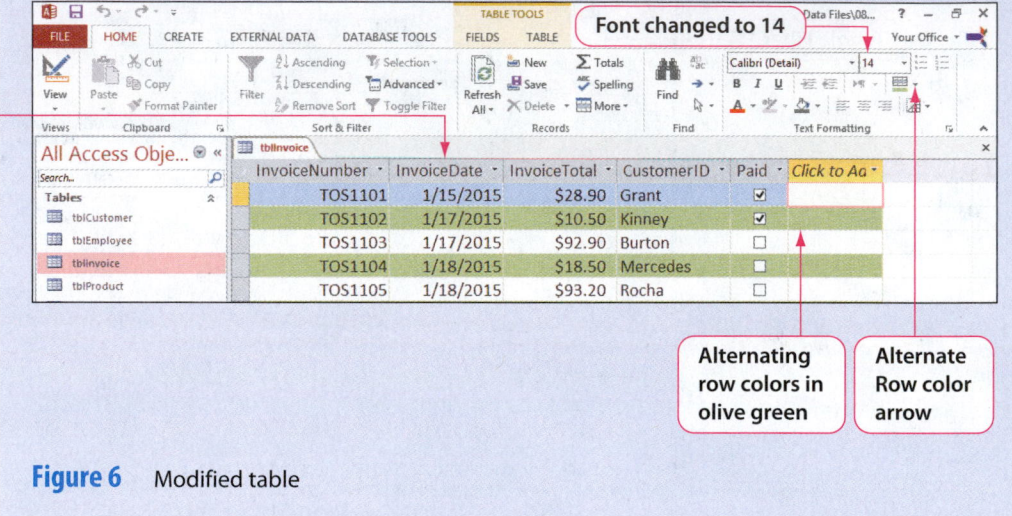

Figure 6   Modified table

Querying the Database

While the Find and Filter features can quickly help you find data, a query can be created for data that you may need to find again in the future. If you recall, the Simple Query Wizard is used to display fields from one or more tables or queries with the option to choose a detailed or summary query if working with more than one table. The Simple Query Wizard does not provide the opportunity to select data criteria.

In addition to the Simple Query Wizard, there are three additional query wizards available to make quick, step-by-step queries.

1. **Crosstab**: Used when you want to describe one field in terms of two or more fields in the table. Example: summarizing information or calculating statistics on the fields in the table.
2. **Find Duplicates**: Used when you want to find records with the same specific value. Example: duplicate e-mail addresses in a customer database.
3. **Find Unmatched**: Used when you want to find the rows in one table that do not have a match in the other table. Example: identifying customers who currently have no open orders.

Queries can also be created in Query Design view, which not only allows you to choose the tables and fields to include in the query, but also allows you to select criteria for the field values, create calculated fields, and select sorting options.

In this section, you will create and define selection criteria for queries and create aggregate functions and calculated fields as well as sort query results.

Run Query Wizards

Two other query wizards, the Find Duplicates Query Wizard and the Find Unmatched Query Wizard, allow you to find duplicate records or identify orphans by selecting criteria as part of the wizard steps. An **orphan** is a foreign key in one table that does not have a matching value in the primary key field of a related table.

Creating a Find Duplicates Query

The **Find Duplicates Query Wizard** finds duplicate records in a table or a query. You select the fields that you think may include duplicate information, and the wizard creates the query to find records matching your criteria.

For this exercise, the spa receptionist sends out mailings and reminders to spa customers throughout the year. She wants to be able to prevent multiple mailings to the same address to help reduce costs. You will show her how she can use a Find Duplicates query to check for duplicate addresses.

A03.07

 To Find Duplicate Customer Information

a. Click the **CREATE** tab, and then in the Queries group, click **Query Wizard**. Access displays the New Query dialog box and lists the different queries you can select.

b. Select **Find Duplicates Query Wizard**, and then click **OK**.

c. Select **Table: tblCustomer** as the table to search for duplicate field values, and then click **Next**.

> **Troubleshooting**
> If you get a Security Notice, click Open.

d. Under Available fields, click **CustAddress**, and then click the **One Field** button $\boxed{>}$. Access moves the CustAddress field to the Duplicate-value fields list. This is the field you think may have duplicate data.

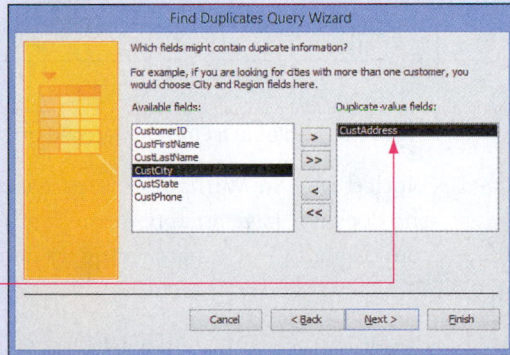

CustAddress moved to Duplicate-value fields list

Figure 7   Select the field that may have duplicate data

e. Click **Next**. Click the **All Fields** button $\boxed{>>}$ to move all available fields to the Additional query fields list to display all the fields in the query results. Click **Next**.

f. Under "What do you want to name your query?", type **qryDuplicateCustomers_initialLastname**, using your first initial and last name, and then click **Finish**. The result of the query should have two records with the same address.

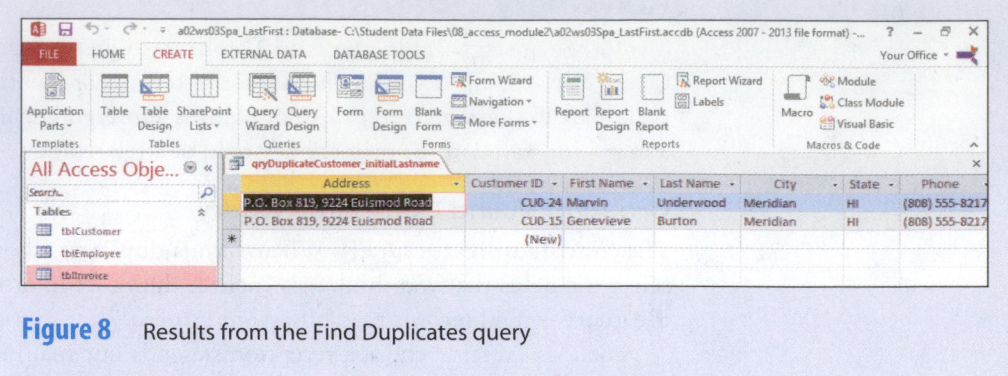

Figure 8   Results from the Find Duplicates query

g. **Close** ☒ the query.

Creating a Find Unmatched Query

The **Find Unmatched Query Wizard** is designed to find records in a table or query that have no related records in a second table or query. This can be very helpful if you wantto contact inactive customers or mail a notice to past clients who are still listed in the database. The wizard uses the primary key from the first table and matches it with the foreign key in the second table in order to determine if there are unmatched records. If a one-to-many relationship exists between the two tables, then the wizard will join the two correct fields automatically.

The wizard will try to match the primary key field and the foreign key field if there is a one-to-many relationship between the two tables. If there is not a one-to-many relationship, you can select the fields to be matched manually.

For this project, spa management would like to identify customers who have used the spa's services in the past but do not have a current appointment. This means a record for the customer would be listed in the customer table but not in the schedule table as shown in Figure 9.

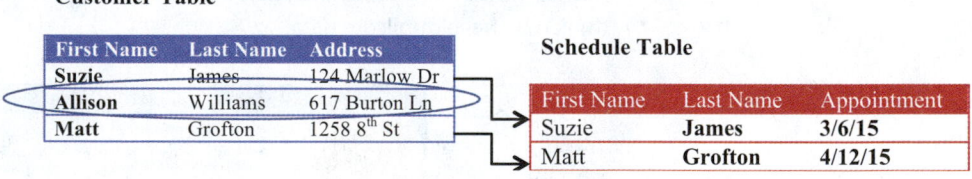

Figure 9   Tables in a Find Unmatched query

Notice Allison Williams is a past customer so she is listed in the customer table, but she does not have an appointment scheduled in the schedule table. Her record would be found in a Find Unmatched query comparing the customer and schedule tables.

A03.08

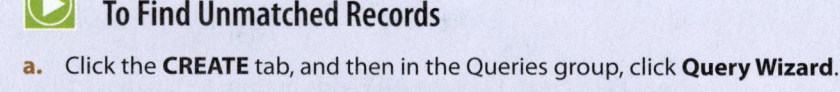 **To Find Unmatched Records**

a. Click the **CREATE** tab, and then in the Queries group, click **Query Wizard**.

b. Select **Find Unmatched Query Wizard**, and then click **OK**.

c. Select **Table: tblCustomer**, and then click **Next**. This is the table you think has past customers with no upcoming appointments.

d. Select **Table: tblSchedule**, and then click **Next**. This is the table that has customers with upcoming appointments you want to compare to the main tblCustomer table.

e. Under Fields in 'tblCustomer', verify **CustomerID** is selected, and then under Fields in 'tblSchedule', verify **Customer** is selected. This is the common field that the wizard will use to compare the tables.

SIDE NOTE
Manually Select Fields to Match
If your tables are not in a one-to-many relationship, select the fields manually and use the button to move them to the Matching fields box.

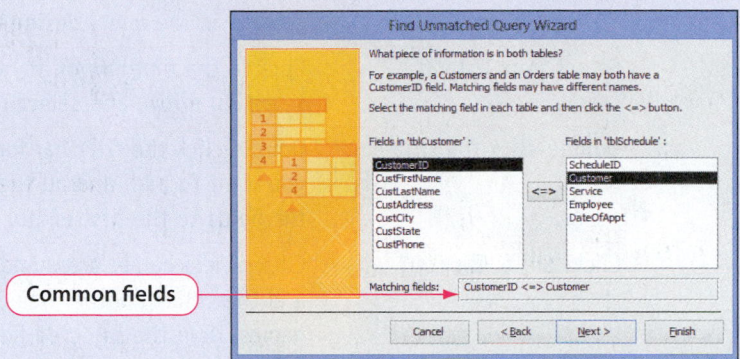

Figure 10 Compare the two tables using their common field

f. Click **Next**, click the **All Fields** button >> to add all the fields to the Selected fields list, and then click **Next**.

g. Under "What would you like to name your query?", type **qryCustomersWithout Appointments_initialLastname**, using your first initial and last name, and then click **Finish**. You should see the names and e-mails of three customers who do not currently have appointments at the spa including yourself. **Close** ✕ the query.

Create Queries in Design View

The query wizards work by prompting you to answer a series of questions about the tables and fields to display and then creating the query based upon your responses. Alternatively, you can use Design view to manually create queries. The query window in Design view allows you to specify the data you want to see by building a **query by example**. A query by example provides a sample of the data you want to see in the results. Access takes that sample of data and finds records in the tables you specify that match the example. In the query window, you can include specific fields, define criteria, sort records, and perform calculations. When you use the query window, you have more control and more options available to manage the details of the query design than with the Simple Query Wizard.

When you open Design view, by default, the Show Table dialog box opens with a list of available tables and queries to add. You can either select a table name and click Add, or you can double-click the table name. Either way the table will be added to the query window. If the Show Table dialog box is closed, you can drag a table or query from the Navigation Pane to the query window to add it to the query.

The next step in building your query is to add the fields you want to include from the various tables selected to the query design grid. There are a number of ways to add fields to the query design grid.

QUICK REFERENCE	Methods to Add Fields to a Query Design Grid
Action	**Description**
Drag	Once you click the field name, drag it to any empty column in the query design grid.
Double-click field name	Double-click the field name to add it to the first empty column in the query design grid.
Select from list	Click in the first row of any empty column, click the selection arrow, and select the field name from the list.
Double-click the title bar	Double-click the title bar for the table with the fields you want to add, and all the fields will be selected. Drag the fields to the first empty column.
Click, Shift, Click	Click a field name, press and hold down the [Shift] key, and then click another name to select a range of field names. Drag the selected fields to the query design grid.

If you add a field to the wrong column in the query design grid, you can delete the column and add it again, or you can drag it to another position in the grid.

All fields that have values you want included in a query—either for the criteria or to show in the results—must be added to the query design grid. For example, you may want to find all customers from New Mexico, but not necessarily show the state field in the query results. You can use the Show check box to indicate which fields to show in the results and which fields not to show.

REAL WORLD ADVICE | Increasing Privacy Concerns

There are many instances where the person running the query does not have the right to see confidential information in the database. An example of this is Social Security numbers. Although companies are doing away with this practice, many existing databases still use Social Security numbers as a unique identifier. You can include a Social Security number in query criteria, but uncheck the Show box so the actual value does not show in the query results.

Creating a Single-Table Query

A single-table query is a query that is based on only one table in your database.

For this exercise, the manager of the spa needs your help to print out a price list for all the products. She wants to see the product description, size, and price for each product, and she wants to see all the records. You will show her how to add only the fields she wants to the query.

A03.09

To Create a Single-Table Query

a. Click the **CREATE** tab, and then in the Queries group, click **Query Design** to open the query window with the Show Table dialog box.

b. In the Show Table dialog box, select **tblProduct**, and then click **Add**. Click **Close** to close the Show Table dialog box.

Troubleshooting

If you cannot see the query design grid at the bottom of the query design window, use the pointer ⊞ to drag the top border of the grid up.

SIDE NOTE
Seeing All Fields in a Table
Alternatively, you can scroll down to see all the fields.

c. Use your pointer to drag the lower border of **tblProduct** down to see all the fields.

d. Double-click **ProductDescription** to add it to the first column of the query design grid. Repeat for **Price** and **Size**.

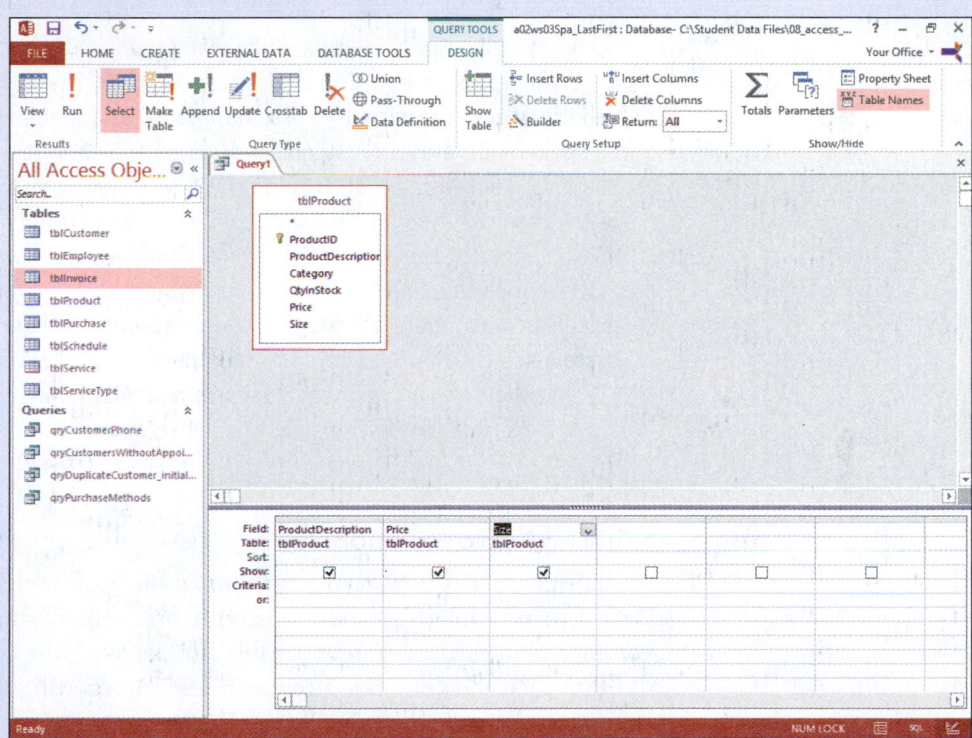

Figure 11 Fields from tblProduct added to the query design grid

e. In the Results group, click **Run** to run the query. You should have 25 records showing the ProductDescription, Price, and Size (ounces) fields.

f. In the Views group, click the **View** arrow, and then click **Design View**. To move the Size field to the left of the ProductDescription field, click the **top border** of the **Size** field to select the column. Again pointing to the top border of the field, drag the **Size field** to the left of the **ProductDescription** field. In the Results group, click **Run** to run the query again. The query will still have 25 records, but the field order will be Size, ProductDescription, and Price.

g. Click **Save** 🖫 on the Quick Access Toolbar. In the Save As dialog box, type **qryProductPriceList_initialLastname**, using your first initial and last name, and then click **OK**. **Close** ✕ the query.

QUICK REFERENCE | **Opening or Switching Views**

Access gives you several methods to open objects in different views or to switch views.

1. To open an object in default view, double-click it in the Navigation Pane.

2. To open an object in design view, right-click it in the Navigation Pane, and select Design View.

3. To switch views for an already open object, on the Home tab, in the Views group, click the View arrow, and then select your preferred view.

4. To switch views for an already open object, right-click the object tab, and then select the preferred view.

5. To switch views for an already open object, the right side of the status bar has small icons for each available view. Hover over the icon to see the ScreenTip. Click the icon to switch to the preferred view.

REAL WORLD ADVICE | **The Importance of Knowing Your Data**

Many times databases are shared by many users. Different people may enter data differently causing errors or inconsistency. Inconsistent data entry can affect the validity of query results. By misspelling a value or abbreviating a value that should be spelled out, a query may not find the record when it searches using criteria. You must know what your data looks like when you create queries. A quick scan of the records, or using Find with a wildcard for certain values, may help you find misspellings or other data entry errors before you run your query.

Having some idea of what the query results should look like will also help make sure your query has found the right record set. For example, if you query all customers from New Mexico and think there should be a dozen, but your query shows 75, you should check your table records and your query criteria to see why there might be such a big discrepancy from what you expected.

Viewing Table Relationships

A multiple-table query retrieves information from more than one table or query. For Access to perform this type of query, it uses relationships between the tables, or the common field that exists in both tables to "connect" the tables.

If two tables do not have a common field, Access will join the two tables by combining the records, regardless of whether they have a matching field. This is called the **multiplier effect**. For example, if one table has 10,000 records and another table also has 10,000 records, and if these two tables do not have a common field, all records in the first table will be matched with all records in the second table for a total of 100,000,000 records! Depending on the processing power and memory on the computer, Access could take a long time to run the query or even become nonresponsive.

You can view how your tables are related in the Relationships window. **Join lines** are the lines connecting the tables that represent relationships. The field that the line is pointing to in each table represents the common field between the tables. It is helpful to understand how tables are related before you try and create a multiple table query.

A03.10

 To View Table Relationships

a. On the **DATABASE TOOLS** tab, in the Relationships group, click **Relationships**. Click the **Shutter Bar Open/Close button** « to hide the Navigation Pane and display the whole Relationships window. Take a moment to study the table relationships.

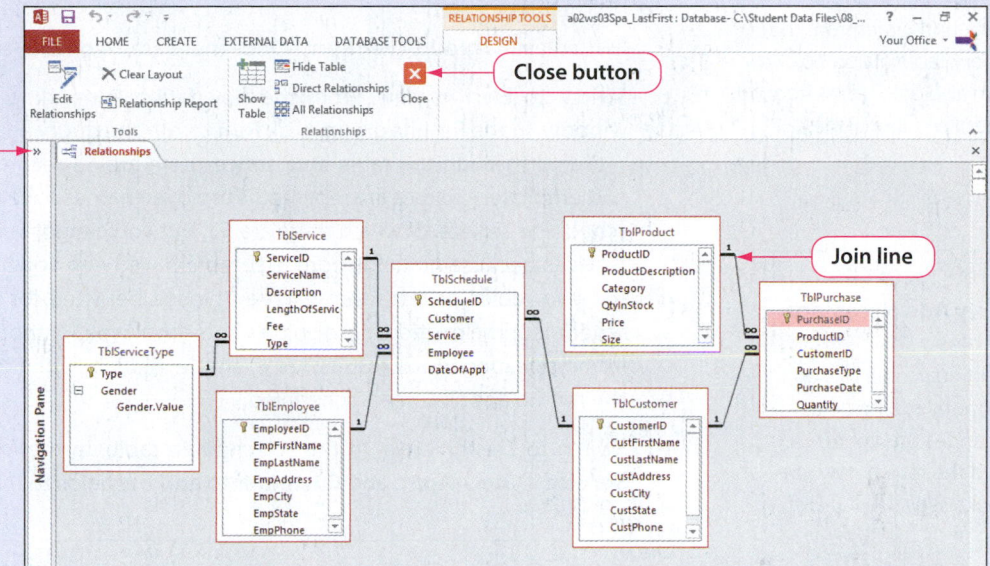

Figure 12 Spa Database table relationships

b. Click the **DATABASE TOOLS** tab, and then in the Relationships group, click **Close** to close the Relationships window. Click the **Shutter Bar Open/Close button** » to show the Navigation Pane again.

REAL WORLD ADVICE | **Which Tables to Choose?**

You should only select the tables you need when creating a query in the query window. Access treats all the tables selected as part of the query when it executes the query, which means unnecessary tables added to the query may cause performance problems or incorrect results. Best practice is to do the following:

- Understand the table structure and relationships before you construct your query—refer to the Relationships window often.

- Choose only those tables from which you need data.

- If no data from a table is needed, do not add the table. The exception to this rule is if a table is required to link the many-to-many relationship together. In other words, no table will be left unconnected and tables can be added to create that connection.

Creating a Query from Multiple Tables

All tables added to a query should be connected by relationships and have a common field. For this project, the staff would like to see one recordset that includes the services scheduled for each employee. tblEmployee includes the employee names, and tblSchedule lists the services scheduled for each employee. You will create a query that combines the two tables into one query.

A03.11

 To Create a Query from Multiple Tables

SIDE NOTE

Adding Tables from the Navigation Pane

Remember, in addition to selecting tables from the Show Table dialog box, you can also drag tables from the Navigation Pane.

a. Click the **CREATE** tab, and then in the Queries group, click **Query Design**, click **tblEmployee**, and then click **Add**. Close the Show Table dialog box.

b. Double-click **EmpFirstName** and **EmpLastName** in that order to add the fields to the query design grid.

c. In the Results group, click **Run**. Notice there are 14 employee records.

d. Switch to **Design** view. From the Navigation Pane, drag **tblSchedule** to the query window. In the Results group, click **Run** to run the query again.

Scroll through the table and notice there are 53 records in the query results now and employees names are repeated. Employee names have been matched up with each scheduled service, of which there are 53, but you cannot see any information about the services because no fields from that table have been added. The relationship between the two tables dictates that each employee be listed for each service he or she has scheduled. The relationship also prevents employees without a scheduled appointment from appearing in the results. For example, Mariah Paul does not appear here because she has no appointments scheduled.

SIDE NOTE

Only Add Necessary Tables

Adding a table to a query without adding fields changes the query results, and the results may not make sense.

e. Switch to **Design** view. In the tblSchedule table, in the following order, double-click **Service**, **DateOfAppt**, and **Customer** to add the fields to the query design grid.

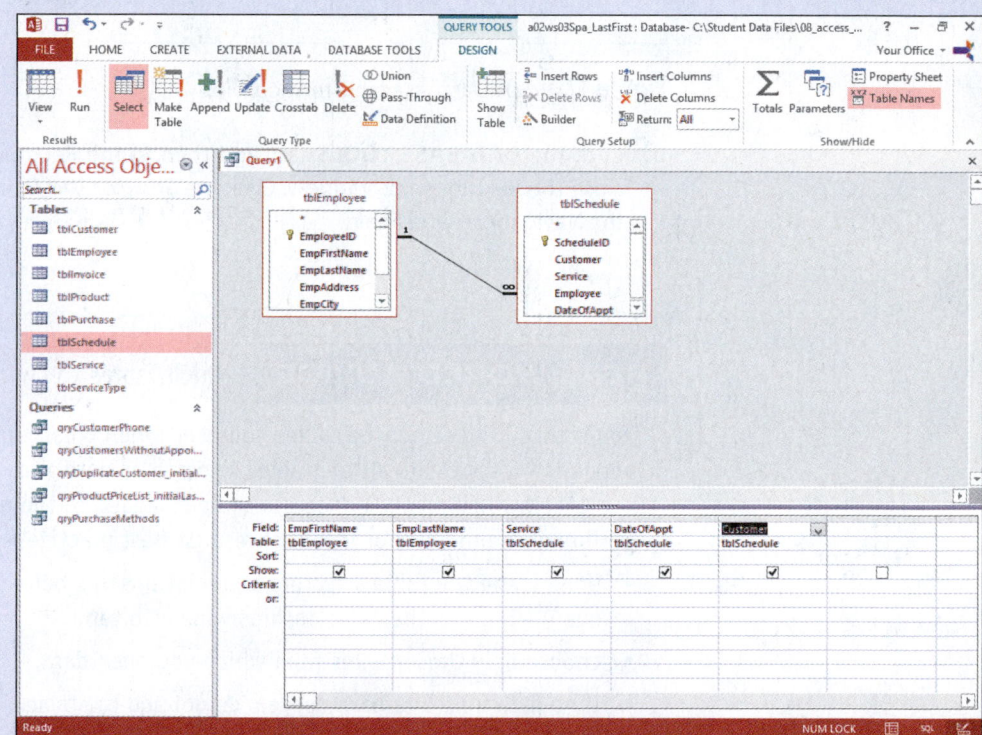

Figure 13   Query window for multiple-table query

f. In the Results group, click **Run** to run the query.

Notice there are 53 records again for each service scheduled, but now the detail for those services are included in the query because you added the fields to the query design grid.

g. Click **Save** 💾 on the Quick Access Toolbar, under Query Name type **qryEmployeeSchedule_initialLastname** using your first initial and last name, and then click **OK**. **Close** ✖ the query.

Removing a Table from a Query to Fix an Undesirable Multiplier Effect

When two tables without a common field are used in a query, you will see the multiplier effect. Recall that the multiplier effect occurs when each record in the first table is matched to each record in the second table.

For this exercise, someone in the spa wanted to find the phone number for each customer, but they created a multiple table query using two tables without a common field. One table has 25 records and the other has 26, so the multiplier effect caused the query result to have 650 records! You will run their query, and then fix it by removing the second table from the query.

A03.12

To Remove a Table from a Query

a. Double-click **qryCustomerPhone** to run the query.

Notice there are 650 records because every customer name is matched with every product. Since there are 25 products, each of the 26 customers is matched with every product for 25 times 26 = 650 records.

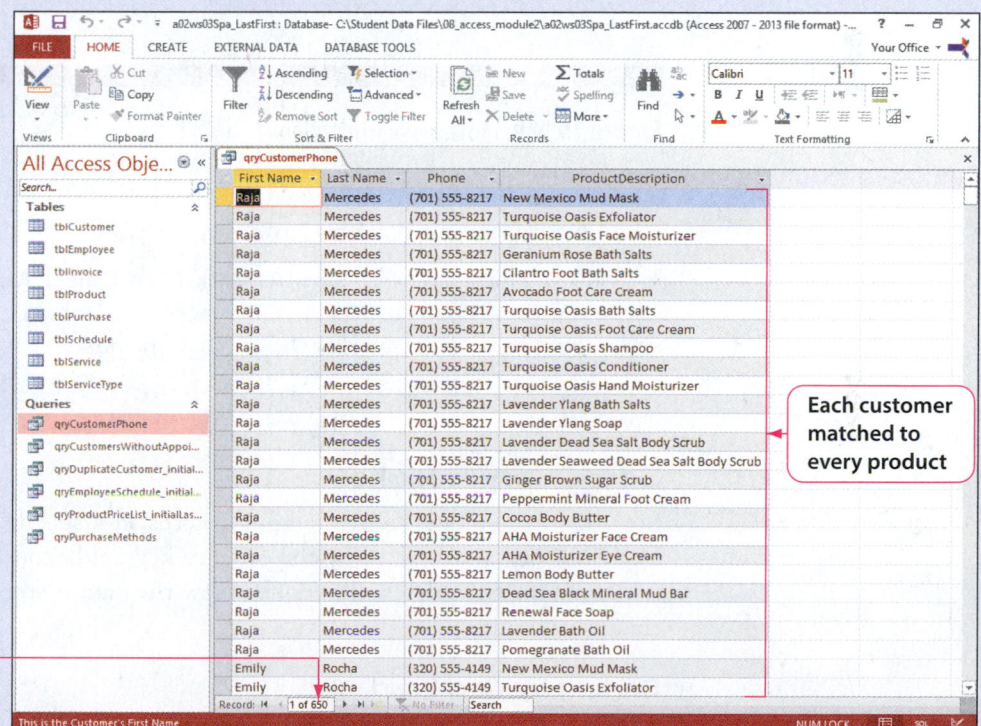

Figure 14 Query with multiplier effect

b. Switch to **Design** view. Notice there is no relationship between tblProduct and tblCustomer, which caused the multiplier effect. You will remove tblProduct from the query.

c. Right-click **tblProduct** in the query window, and then select **Remove Table**. The table is removed from the query window, and the ProductDescription is removed from the fields.

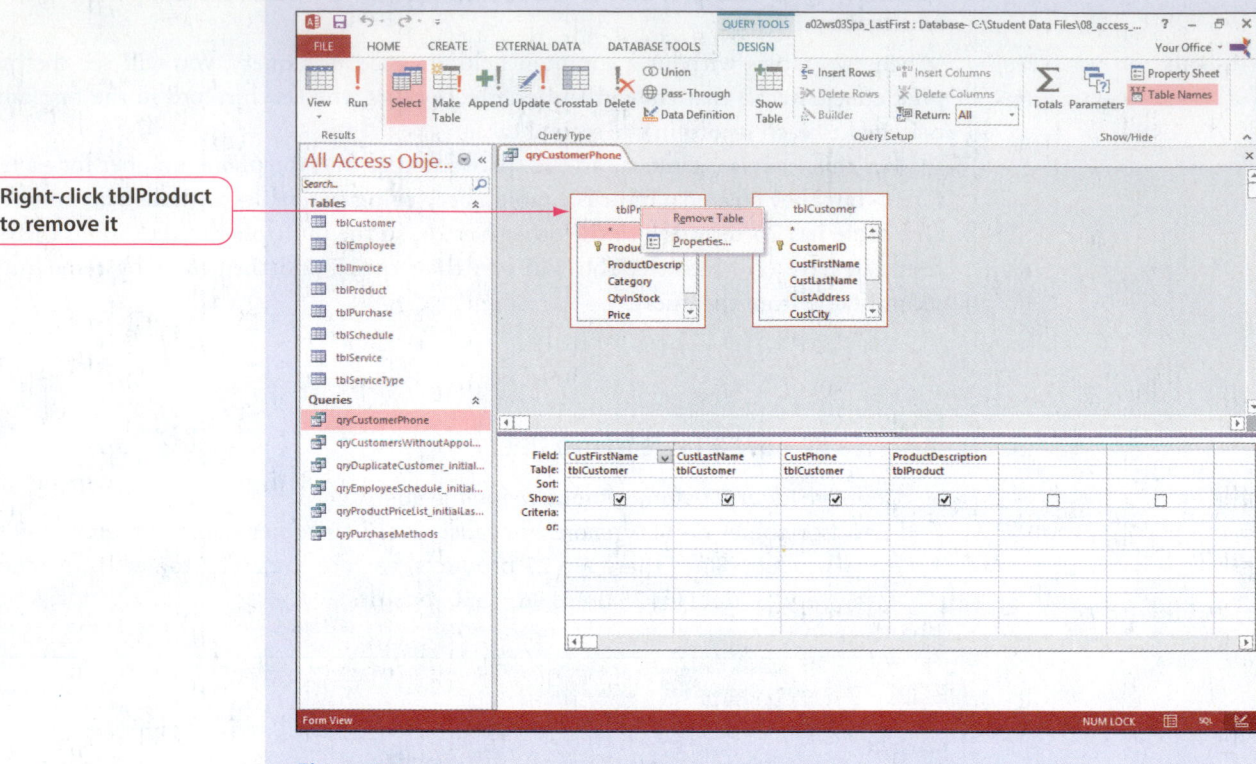

Right-click tblProduct to remove it

Figure 15 Remove table from query

d. Click **Run** to run the query.
   Notice there are now only 26 records.

e. On the **FILE** tab, select **Save As**, click **Save Object As**, click **Save As**, under Save 'qryCustomerPhone' to, type qryCustomerPhone_initialLastname using your first initial and last name, and then click **OK**. Close ☒ the query.

Sort Query Results

Sorting is the process of rearranging records in a specific order. By default, records in a table or query are sorted by the primary key field. You can change the sort order of a table in a query, which will not affect how the data is stored, only how it will appear in the query results.

Sorting by One Field

To sort records, you have to select a **sort field**, or a field used to determine the order of the records. The sort field can be a Short Text, Long Text, Number, Date/Time, Currency, AutoNumber, Yes/No, or Lookup Wizard field as shown in Table 2. A field may be sorted either in ascending order or descending order.

Type of Data	Sorting Options
Short and Long Text	Ascending (A to Z); Descending (Z to A)
Numbers (including Currency & AutoNumber)	Ascending (lowest to highest); Descending (highest to lowest)
Date/Time	Ascending (oldest to newest); Descending (newest to oldest)
Yes/No	Ascending (yes, then no values); Descending (no, then yes values)

Table 2 Methods for sorting data

If you have numbers that are stored as text—phone numbers, Social Security numbers, zip codes—then the characters 1 to 9 come before A to Z in the appropriate order sorted as alphanumeric text.

A table may be sorted by a single field in Datasheet view. When a table is sorted using a single field, a sort arrow will appear in the field name so you can see that it is sorted. For this project, you will show the spa manager how to sort the tblProduct table by category.

MODULE 2

SIDE NOTE
Alternative Method to Sorting Fields
Alternatively, you can select the field to be sorted and click Ascending or Descending on the Home tab in the Sort & Filter group.

A03.13

 To Sort a Table by a Single Field

a. Double-click **tblProduct** to open the table.

b. Click the Category column heading arrow, and then click **Sort A to Z**. This will sort the records by the Category field in ascending order.

c. **Close** [X] the table, and then click **Yes** when prompted to save the changes.

Sorting by More than One Field

You can also sort by multiple fields in Access. The first field you choose to sort by is called the **primary sort field**. The second and subsequent fields are called **secondary sort fields**.

In datasheet view, you can sort multiple fields by selecting all the fields at one time and using the Sort & Filter group sorts, but there are some restrictions. First, the fields in datasheet view must be next to each other and the sort is executed left to right; that is, the far-left field is the primary sort field, the next field is a secondary sort field, and so on. Secondly, you can only sort in ascending or descending order for all fields, you cannot have one field sorted in ascending order and another in descending order. These two restrictions do not exist if sorting is set in Design view. Thus, it is more efficient to create a query and sort by multiple fields using Design view.

Using Design view to sort records allows you to sequence the fields from left to right in an order that makes sense for your desired sort results and allows you to combine ascending and descending sorts. You can also sort in an order different than left to right by adding a field multiple times and clearing the Show check box. For this exercise, you will show the staff how to sort the tblSchedule table by Employee, then Date, and then Service by creating a query from the table and setting up the sort options.

A03.14

 To Sort a Query by More than One Field

a. Click the **CREATE** tab, and then in the Queries group, click **Query Design**. Double-click **tblEmployee** and **tblSchedule** to add the tables to the query. Click **Close** to close the Show Table dialog box.

b. Double-click **EmpLastName**, **EmpFirstName**, and **EmpPhone** from tblEmployee to add those fields to the query design grid. Double-click **DateOfAppt**, **Service**, and **Customer** from tblSchedule to add those fields to the query design grid.

c. Click the **Sort** row for **EmpLastName**, click the **selection** arrow, and then click **Ascending**. Click **Ascending** for the **EmpFirstName**, **DateOfAppt**, and **Service** fields.
   Notice that unlike sorting in Datasheet view, your sorting fields do not need to be next to each other to be sorted in a query.

SIDE NOTE
How Many Fields Is Too Many?
You may choose up to 10 fields to sort by in Design view.

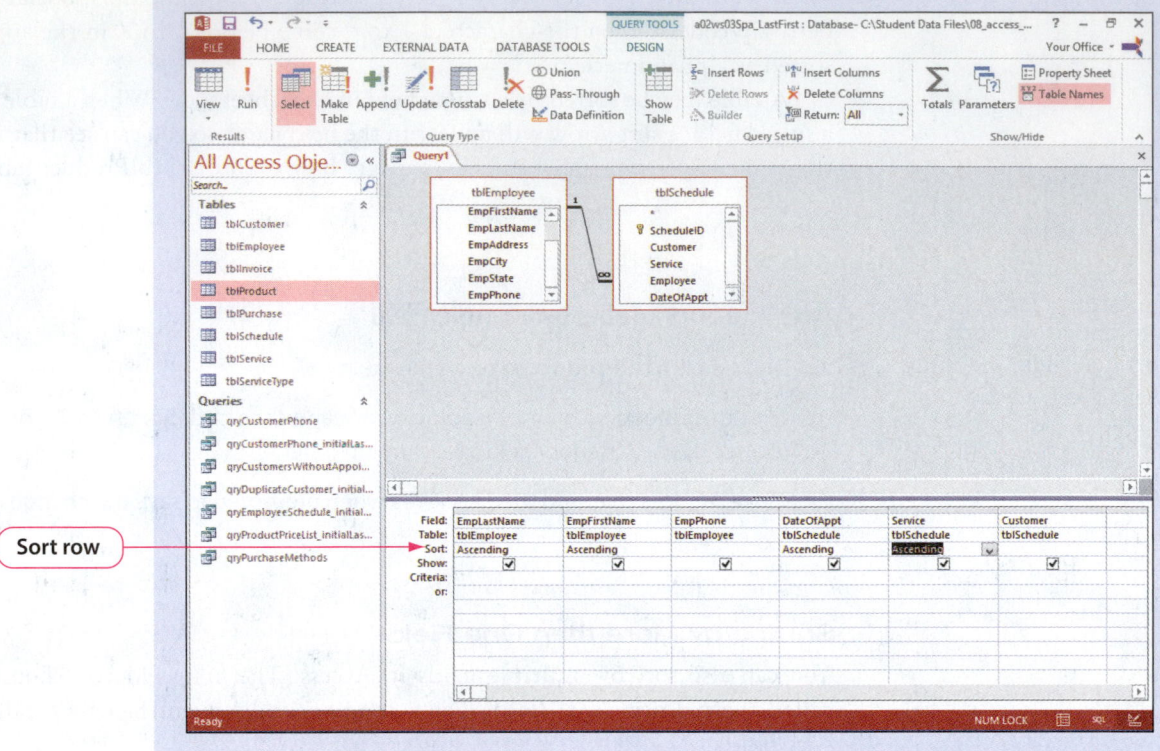

Figure 16 Sort options selected

d. Click **Run** to run the query. The table should be sorted by Employee, then Date, then Service.

e. Click **Save** 🖫 on the Quick Access Toolbar, name the query **qryEmployeeAppointments_initialLastname** using your first initial and last name, and then click **OK**. **Close** ✖ the query.

Define Selection Criteria for Queries

Databases, including Access, provide a robust set of selection criteria that you can use to make your queries well focused. You can use the different kinds of operators described below to choose criteria for one or more fields in one or more tables.

Using a Comparison Operator

Comparison operators compare the values in a table or another query to the criteria value you set up in a query. The different comparison operators, descriptions, and examples are shown in Table 3. Comparison operators are generally used with numbers and dates to find a range or a specific value. Equal to and not equal to can also be used with text to find an exact match to criteria. For example, to find all states that are not NY you could enter < >"NY" for the state criteria.

In query criteria, text is identified by quotation marks around it and dates with # in front of and at the end of the date. For example, 1/1/16 would appear as #1/1/16#. Access adds the necessary quotation marks and pound signs, but it is a good idea to double-check.

Operator	Description
=	Equal to
< =	Less than or equal to
<	Less than
>	Greater than
> =	Greater than or equal to
< >	Not equal to

Table 3 Comparison operators

For this project, the manager of the spa wants to see all products $10 and under so she can plan an upcoming special on the spa's lower-priced products. You will show her how to use a comparison operator in a query to find those products.

A03.15

 To Use a Comparison Operator in a Query

a. Click the **CREATE** tab, and then in the Queries group, click **Query Design**, click **tblProduct**, and then click **Add**. Click **Close** to close the Show Table dialog box.

b. In the following order, double-click **ProductID**, **ProductDescription**, **Size**, **Category**, **QtyInStock**, and **Price** to add the fields to the query design grid.

c. Click in the **Criteria** row for the **Price** field, and then type **<=10**.

d. Click **Run** to run the query. The results should show six records all with prices $10 or less.

e. Click **Save** 💾 on the Quick Access Toolbar, under Query Name type **qryLowPriceProducts_initialLastname** using your first initial and last name, and then click **OK**. **Close** ⊠ the query.

Hiding Fields That Are Used in a Query

For a field to be used in a query, it must be added to the query grid. If you just want to use the field to define criteria but do not want to see the results of that field in the query, it cannot be removed from the query grid, but it can be hidden from the results.

For this project, the manager is happy with the results of the low-price products query you created above, but she would like to post a list of the products without the prices so she can advertise the list as all under $10. You tell her that is possible by using the Show check box in the query design grid.

A03.16

To Use a Field Value in a Query but Not Show the Field in the Results

a. Open **qryLowPriceProduct_initialLastname** in Design view.

b. In the Price field, click the **Show** check box to clear the check mark.

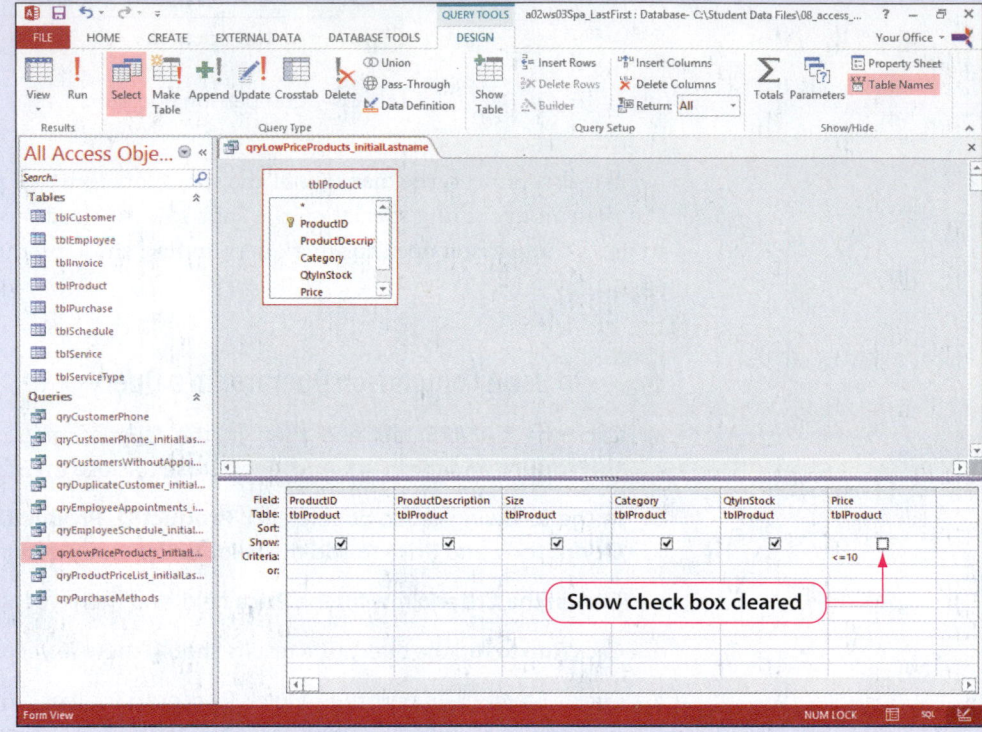

Figure 17   Clearing the Show check box

c. In the Results group, click **Run** to run the query. The results should show the same six records you found in the previous query, but without the price field showing.

d. On the **FILE** tab, select **Save As**, select **Save Object As**, and then click **Save As**. In Save 'qryLowPriceProducts_initialLa...' to: type qryTenAndUnder_initialLastname using your first initial and last name, and then click **OK**. **Close** ☒ the query.

Sorting on a Field That You Do Not Show

The manager liked the employee schedule query you created, but she would like it to show employee first name first in the query results. If you put first name first in the grid and then last name, Access will sort by first name first. You will show her how to add a field multiple times to the query design grid to sort fields one way but display them another way.

To Sort a Query by Multiple Fields in a Different Sort Order

a. Click the **CREATE** tab, and then in the Queries group, click **Query Design**. Double-click **tblEmployee** and **tblSchedule** to add the tables to the query. Click **Close** to close the Show Table dialog box.

b. Double-click **EmpFirstName** and **EmpLastName** from tblEmployee to add those fields to the query design grid. Double-click **DateOfAppt**, **Service**, and **Customer** from tblSchedule to add those fields to the query design grid.

c. Click the **Sort** row for **EmpFirstName**, click the **selection** arrow, and then click **Ascending**. Click **Ascending** for the **EmpLastName**, **DateOfAppt**, and **Service** fields.

d. In the Results group, click **Run** to run the query.

   Notice that the results are sorted by first name and not last name, for example, Alex Weaver is shown before Amanda Johnson. You will need to add another first name field to fix the sort order.

e. Switch to **Design** view. Double-click **EmpFirstName** in tblEmployee to add it to the query design grid. Click at the top of the second **EmpFirstName** field to select it, and then drag it to the right of EmpLastName.

f. Click the **Sort** row for the first **EmpFirstName**, and then change it to **(not sorted)**. Click the **Sort** row for the second **EmpFirstName**, and then change it to **Ascending**. Click the **Show** check box under the second EmpFirstName field in the third column to clear it.

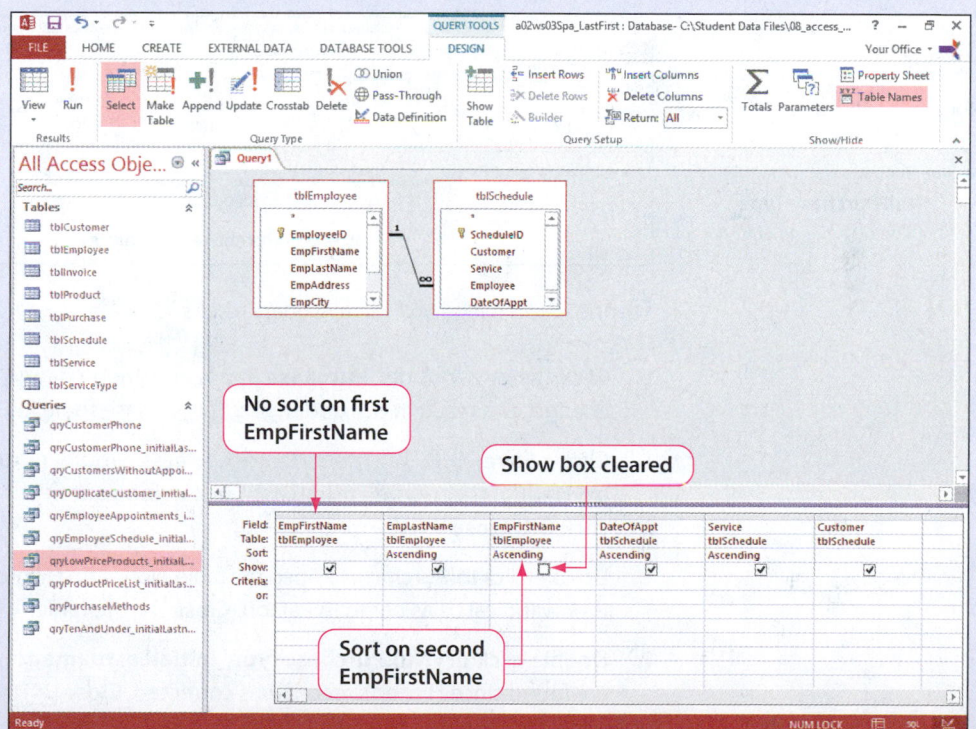

Figure 18   Sort options selected and EmpFirstName Show check box cleared

g. Click **Run** to run the query. The results should show 53 records sorted by employee last name, first name, date, and service. Notice that the main sort is by last name but Alex Weaver comes before Joseph Weaver.

h. Click **Save** 🖫 on the Quick Access Toolbar, name the query **qryEmployeeSort_initialLastname** using your first initial and last name, and then click **OK**. **Close** ☒ the query.

Using Is Null Criteria

You practiced entering a criteria value to get all records that meet the criteria. You can also select any records that have no value in a field using the Is Null criteria. Null is the absence of any value and is different from blank or zero.

For this exercise, one of the spa workers has created a purchase record without specifying that the order was placed in person. You will show the manager how to locate a record that is missing a value. You will also show her how to change the value in the query and have it changed in the table.

A03.18

To Use Is Null Criteria

a. Click the **CREATE** tab, and then in the Queries group, click **Query Design**. Double-click **tblPurchase**, and **tblCustomer** to add the tables to the query window. Click **Close** to close the Show Table dialog box.

b. In the following order, double-click **PurchaseType** and **PurchaseDate** from tblPurchase, and **CustFirstName** and **CustLastName** from tblCustomer to add them to the query design grid.

c. Click in the **Criteria** row for the PurchaseType field, and then type Is Null.

d. Click **Run** to run the query. The results show one record that was the purchase by Omar Hinton on 1/18/2015. That is the one that the employee forgot to enter.

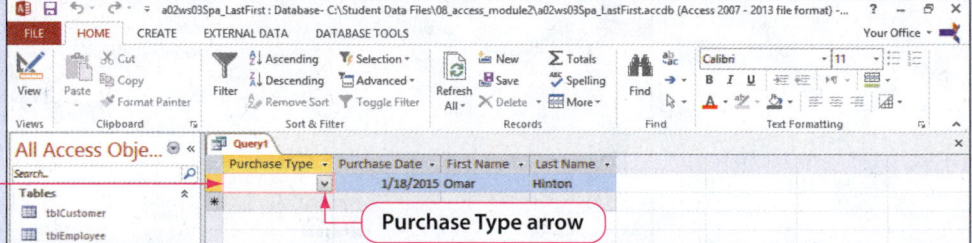

Figure 19   Change null value in query results

e. Click the arrow under **Purchase Type**, and then change the value to **In Person**. This changes the result in the underlying tblPurchase to be In Person.

f. Click **Save** 💾 on the Quick Access Toolbar, under **Query Name** type qryNullPurchaseType_initialLastname using your first initial and last name, and then click **OK**. **Close** ☒ the query.

g. Double-click **tblPurchase** to open the table. Notice that Hinton's purchase (PurchaseID = 25) is now indicated as being In Person. **Close** ☒ the table.

h. Double-click **qryNullPurchaseType_initialLastname** to run it. Notice that no records are found since Hinton's record was corrected. **Close** ☒ the query.

Using the AND Logical Operator

When you create a query, you can select criteria for one field or for multiple fields. If you use multiple criteria, then you must also use **logical operators** to combine these criteria. Logical operators are operators that allow you to combine two or more criteria, as shown in Table 4. For example, if you want a record selected when both criteria are met, then you would use the AND logical operator, but if you want a record selected if only one of the criteria is met, then you would use the OR logical operator. For an even more advanced query, you can combine the AND and the OR logical operators.

Operator	Description
AND	Returns records that meet both criteria
OR	Returns records that meet one or more criteria
NOT	Returns records that do not meet the criteria

Table 4 Logical operators

When you want to specify multiple criteria, and all criteria must be true for a record to be included in the results, then the AND logical operator is used, and the criteria must be in the same Criteria row in the query design grid. Access will look at the first field in the query design grid for criteria and continue moving from left to right looking for criteria. When criteria are in the same row, all criteria must match for the record to be included in the query results. For this project, you want to help the manager narrow down a sales strategy. She is trying to determine which customers place phone orders for products over $10.

A03.19

▶ To Use the AND Logical Operator

a. Click the **CREATE** tab, and then in the Queries group, click **Query Design**. Double-click **tblProduct**, **tblPurchase**, and **tblCustomer** to add the tables to the query window. Click **Close** to close the Show Table dialog box.

b. In the following order, double-click **PurchaseType** from tblPurchase, **ProductDescription** and **Price** from tblProduct, and **CustFirstName** and **CustLastName** from tblCustomer to add them to the query design grid.

c. Click in the **Criteria** row for the PurchaseType field, type **Phone**, and then for the Price field type **>10**.

d. Click in the **Sort** row for the **ProductDescription** field, and then select **Ascending**.

SIDE NOTE
Looks Do Not Matter
How the tables are laid out in the query window does not affect the results. You can move the tables by dragging them to a new location.

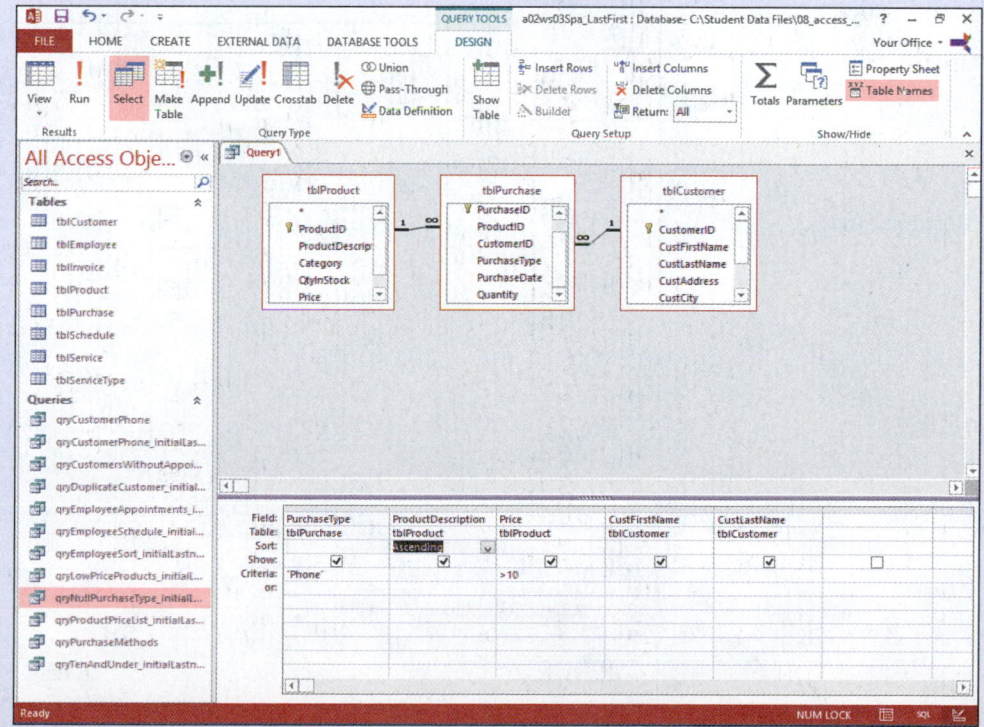

Figure 20 Criteria added for PurchaseType and Price fields

e. Click **Run** to run the query. The results show five records, with Phone as the purchase type and a price greater than $10. The results are sorted by ProductDescription.

f. Click **Save** 🖫 on the Quick Access Toolbar, under Query Name type **qryPhoneAndTen_initialLastname** using your first initial and last name, and then click **OK**. **Close** ✕ the query.

Using the OR Logical Operator

When you want to specify criteria in multiple fields, and at least one of the criteria must be true for a record to be included in the results, then the OR logical operator is used, and the criteria must be in different Criteria rows in the query design grid. Access will look at the first field in the first Criteria row for criteria and continue moving from left to right. Then it will start at the left again on the next criteria row that is labeled "or". For this exercise, you want to help the manager find all customers who make purchases either by phone or online.

A03.20

▶ To Use the OR Logical Operator

a. Click the **CREATE** tab, and then in the Queries group, click **Query Design**. Double-click **tblProduct**, **tblPurchase**, and **tblCustomer** to add the tables to the query. Click **Close** to close the Show Table dialog box.

b. Double-click **PurchaseType** from tblPurchase, double-click **ProductDescription** from tblProduct, and then double-click **CustFirstName** and **CustLastName** from tblCustomer in that order to add them to the query design grid.

c. Click in the **Criteria** row for the PurchaseType field, type **Phone**. In the **or** row just below the Criteria line in the PurchaseType field, type **Online**.

d. Click in the **Sort** row, and then select **Ascending** for the **PurchaseType** and **ProductDescription** fields.

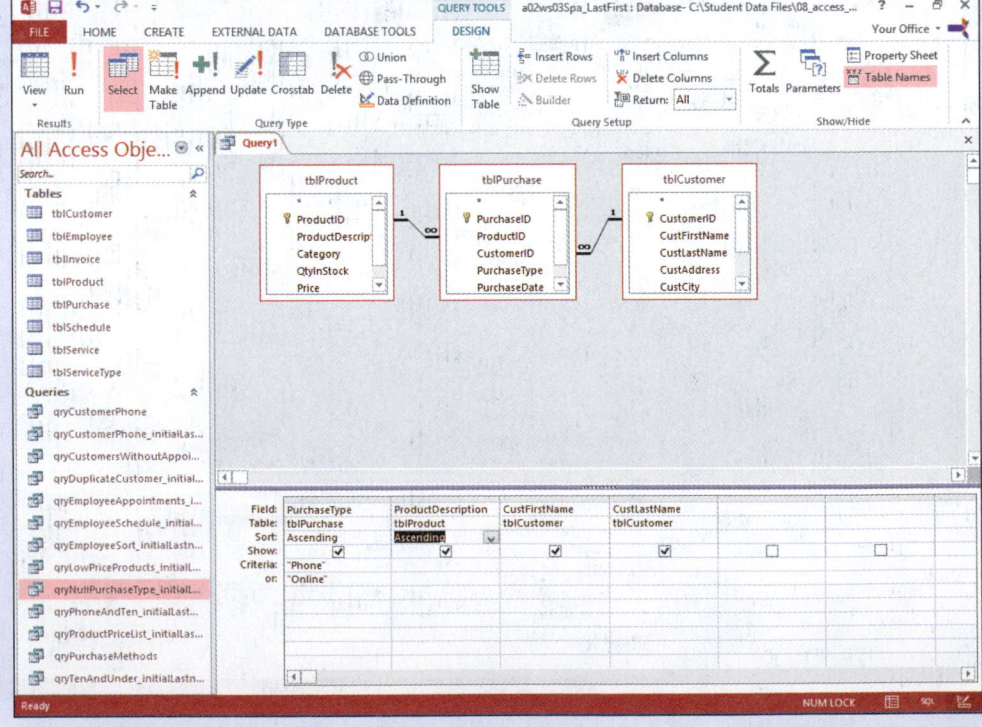

Figure 21   Or criteria for PurchaseType

e. In the Results group, click **Run** to run the query. The results should show 12 records, all with Phone or Online as the purchase type sorted by purchase type and product description.

f. Click **Save** 💾 on the Quick Access Toolbar, name the query **qryPhoneOrOnline_initialLastname** using your first initial and last name, and then click **OK**. **Close** ✖ the query.

Combining the AND and OR Logical Operators

There may be times when you want to use two logical operators, AND and OR, at the same time. Depending on the desired results, you may have to use one or both Criteria rows. If you use both Criteria rows for criteria for two fields, then Access treats it like two AND logical operators with one OR logical operator.

For this project, the manager wants you to find all phone purchase types for products over $20 as well as all online purchase types for products over $15. Phone and greater than 20 are one AND criteria. Online and greater than $15 are the other AND criteria. You want all purchases that are one OR the other of the two AND combinations. Access moves left to right on the first criteria so it will treat "Phone" and >20 as AND criteria and then move to the next row, which it will consider OR criteria. To see how this works, you will step through the query one criteria at a time.

A03.21

To Combine the AND and the OR Logical Operator

a. Click the **CREATE** tab, and then in the Queries group, click **Query Design**, and then double-click **tblProduct**, **tblPurchase**, and **tblCustomer** to add the tables to the query. Click **Close** to close the Show Table dialog box.

b. Double-click **PurchaseType** from tblPurchase, double-click **ProductDescription** and **Price** from tblProduct, and then double-click **CustFirstName** and **CustLastName** from tblCustomer in that order to add them to the query design grid.

c. Click in the **Sort** row, and then select **Ascending** for the **PurchaseType** and **Price** fields.

d. Click in the **Criteria** row for the PurchaseType field, and then type **Phone**. Click **Run** to run the query.

Notice that five orders are shown. Why do you see these orders? Access has found all records that are Phone orders.

e. Switch to **Design** view. In the same Criteria row for the Price field, type **>20**. Click **Run** to run the query.

Notice that two orders are shown. Why do you see these orders? They are both phone orders and both have prices of over $20. Access has found all records that are Phone AND >20.

f. Switch to **Design** view. In the **or** row below the Criteria row, type **Online** for the **PurchaseType** field. Click **Run** to run the query.

Notice that nine orders are shown. Why do you see those orders? You still see the two phone orders with prices of over $20. You also see all online orders. Access has found all records that are Phone AND >20 OR orders that are Online.

g. Switch to **Design** view. In the same **or** row as Online, type **>15** for the Price field.

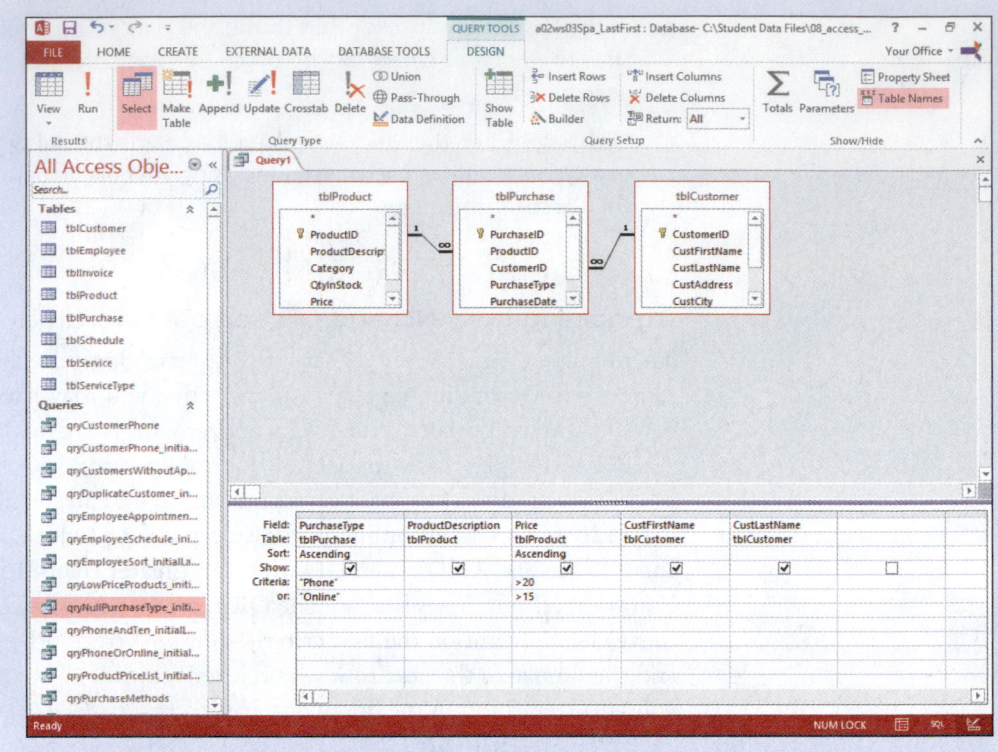

Figure 22 Two criteria rows added for PurchaseType and Price

h. Click **Run** to run the query.

Notice that six orders are shown. Why these six orders? You still see the two phone orders with prices of over $20. You also see four online orders with prices of over $15. Access has found all records that are Phone AND >20 OR orders that are Online AND >15.

Access moved left to right on the first criteria so it will treat "Phone" and >20 as AND criteria and then move to the next row, where it will consider "Online" and >15 as OR criteria.

i. Click **Save** on the Quick Access Toolbar, name the query **qryPhoneAndOnline_initialLastname** using your first initial and last name, and then click **OK**. **Close** ✖ the query.

Combining Multiple AND and OR Logical Operators

You cannot always use two rows for the OR criteria when you combine both logical operators. In cases like this, the word "or" can be used for two criteria used in the same field and the same Criteria row. For this project, the manager of the spa wants you to find all phone and online purchase types for products over $10. If you put the purchase type criteria on two rows and the price of >10 in one row, your results will show all records with phone purchase types over $10 or Online purchase types of any amount. Remember, Access moved left to right on the first criteria so it will treat "Phone" and >10 as AND criteria and then move to the next row, which it will consider OR criteria.

A03.22

 To Combine Multiple AND and OR Logical Operators

a. Click the **CREATE** tab, and then in the Queries group, click **Query Design**. Double-click **tblProduct**, **tblPurchase**, and **tblCustomer** to add the tables to the query. Click **Close** to close the Show Table dialog box.

b. In the following order, double-click **PurchaseType** from tblPurchase, **ProductDescription** and **Price** from tblProduct, and **CustFirstName** and **CustLastName** from tblCustomer to add them to the query design grid.

c. Click in the **Criteria** row for the PurchaseType field, type Phone, and then in the **Criteria** row for the Price field, type >10. In the **or** row for the PurchaseType field, type Online.

d. Click in the **Sort** row, and then select **Ascending** for the **PurchaseType** and **Price** fields.

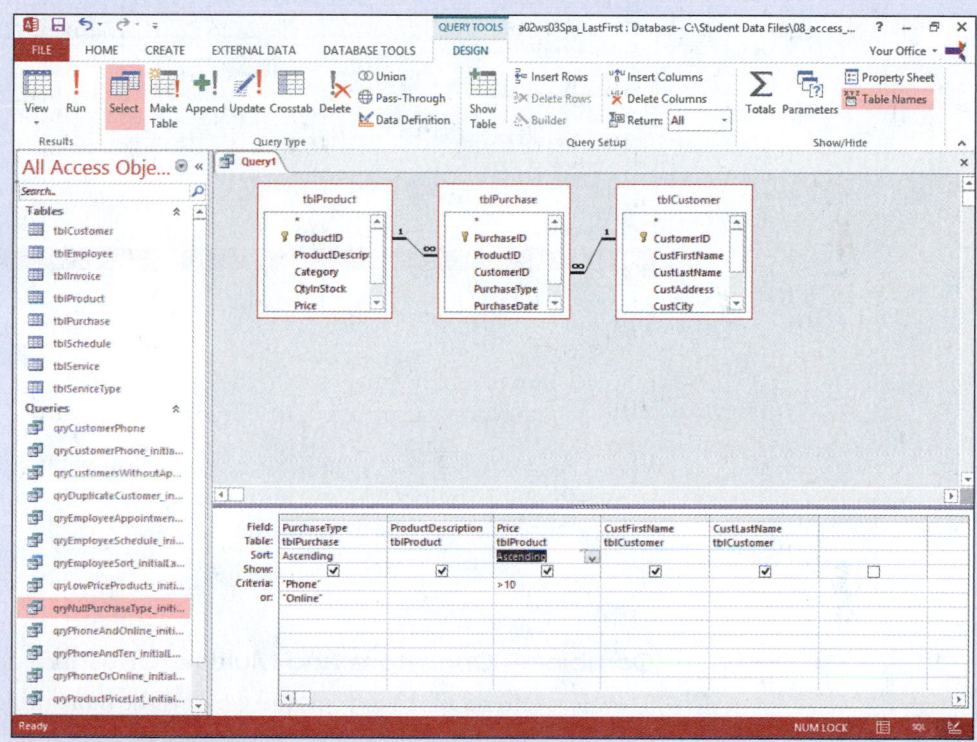

Figure 23　AND and OR criteria added to the query design grid

e. Click **Run** to run the query.

　　Notice the results are all Phone purchase types with prices over $10 or all Online purchase types, regardless of the price. The manager wants to see Phone or Online purchase types over $10, so this is not correct.

f. Switch to **Design** view. In the **or** row for the PurchaseType field, delete "Online." Click in the **Criteria** row for the PurchaseType field, and then change the criteria to Phone or Online.

SIDE NOTE

Access Puts in Quotes

You can leave the quotation marks around "Phone" or remove them. Access will add them for Short Text fields.

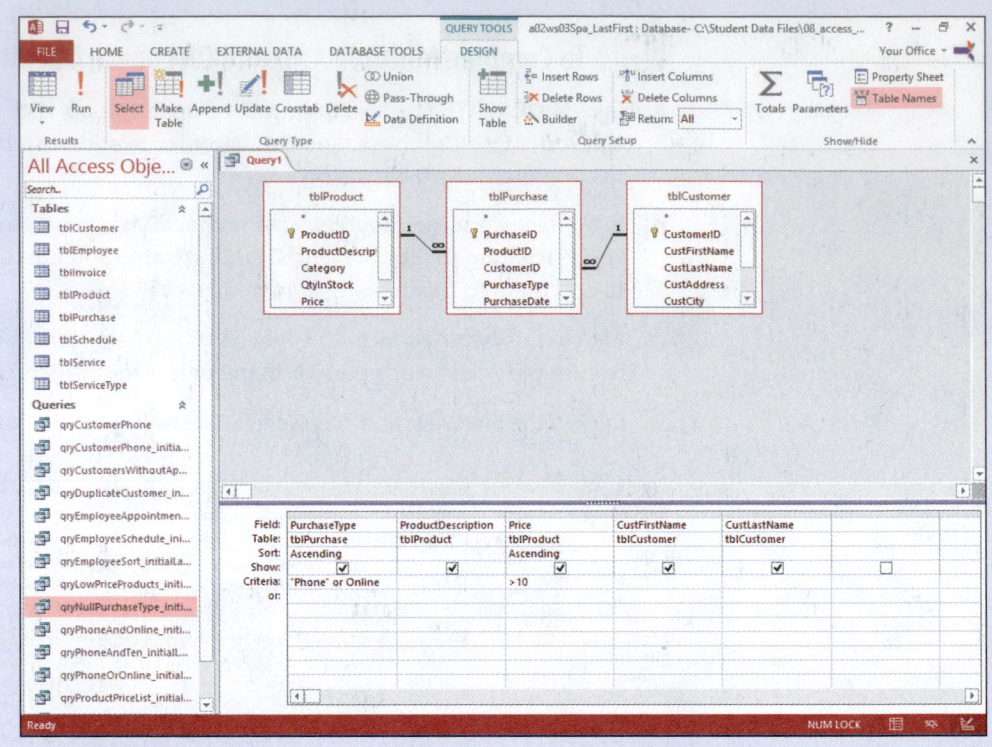

Figure 24   OR criteria in one row with AND criteria

g. Click **Run** to run the query again. The results should now show the 10 Phone or Online purchase types that are over $10.

h. Click **Save** 🖫 on the Quick Access Toolbar, under Query Name type qryPhoneOrOnlineOverTen_initialLastname using your first initial and last name, and then click **OK**. **Close** ✕ the query.

Combining Operators and Multiple Criteria

The more criteria added to your query means the more difficult it will be to see if you have the correct results. With multiple criteria, it is good practice to add one criteria, run the query to make sure you are getting the correct results, and then continue adding criteria one at a time.

For this project, the spa manager would like to see all of her high-end services listed by price and then service type, and she would like to break down the criteria as follows: Hands & Feet or Body Massage services $50 or more, Facial or Microdermabrasion services over $55, Beauty or Waxing services over $45, and all Botanical Hair & Scalp Therapy services.

A03.23

To Combine Operators and Multiple Criteria

a. Click the **CREATE** tab, and then in the Queries group, click **Query Design**, and double-click **tblService** to add the table to the query window. Click **Close** to close the Show Table dialog box.

b. In the following order, double-click **Fee**, **Type**, and **ServiceName** to add the fields to the query design grid.

c. Click in the **Criteria** row for the Fee field, type **>55**, and then in the **Criteria** row for the Type field type **Facial or Microdermabrasion**.

d. Click in the **Sort** row, and then select **Ascending** for the **Fee**, **Type**, and **ServiceName** fields.

e. Click **Run** to run the query. The results should show six records with Facial or Microdermabrasion for the Type field, and all values in the Fee field should be greater than $55.

f. Switch to **Design** view. In the **or** row for the Fee field, type **>=50**, and for the **or** row for the Type field type **"Hands & Feet" or Body Massage**. Click **Run** to run the query again.

   The query results should show 19 records with types Facial or Microdermabrasion that have fees greater than $55, and records with types Hands & Feet or Body Massage that have fees greater than or equal to $50.

> **Troubleshooting**
>
> If you only get 16 records in the results, you did not put the quotation marks around "Hands & Feet". Access will add those quotation marks for you. In this case, Access evaluates the ampersand character (&) as separating two values, so it will put the quotation marks around the word "Hands" and around the word "Feet" so it will look like "Hands" & "Feet". This is different than having the quotations around the whole phrase, which is what you want it to look like. In this case you should put the quotation marks around the phrase in order for it to appear as "Hands & Feet".

g. Switch to **Design** view. Click in the **second or** row for the Fee field, type **>45**, and then in the **Criteria** row for the Type field, type **Beauty or Waxing**. Click **Run** to run the query again.

   The results should show 23 records with types Facial or Microdermabrasion that have fees greater than $55, and records with types Hands & Feet or Body Massage that have fees greater than or equal to $50, and records with types Beauty or Waxing that have fees greater than $45.

h. Switch to **Design** view. Click in the **third or** row for the Type field, and then type **"Botanical Hair & Scalp Therapy"**.

SIDE NOTE

Wider Columns
You can widen the columns in the query design grid by double-clicking the right border of the column selector bar.

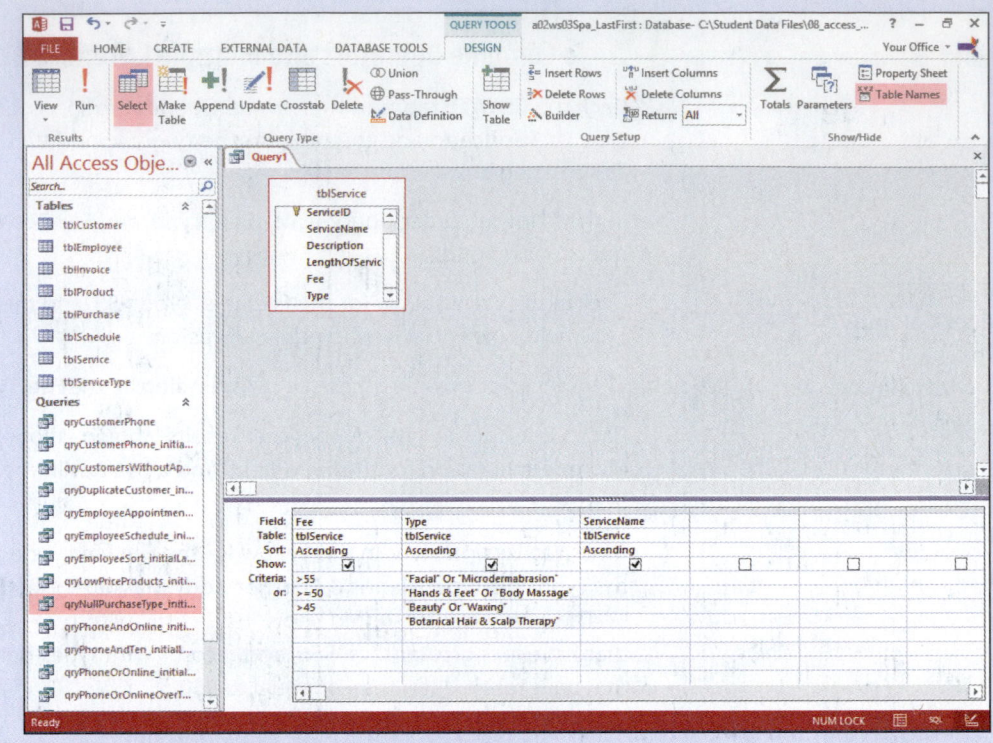

Figure 25 All criteria added to query design grid

i.   Click **Run** to run the query again.

   The results should show 25 records with types Facial or Microdermabrasion that have fees greater than $55, records with types Hands & Feet or Body Massage that have fees greater than or equal to $50, records with types Beauty or Waxing that have fees greater than $45, and all Botanical Hair & Scalp Therapy types.

> **Troubleshooting**
>
> If you still see 23 records, check to see that you put the quotation marks around "Botanical Hair & Scalp Therapy" and that you spelled the type correctly.

j.   Click **Save** 🖫 on the Quick Access Toolbar, name the query **qryHighEndServices_initialLastname** using your first initial and last name, and then click **OK**. **Close** ✕ the query.

Using Special Operators and Date Criteria

Special operators, as shown in Table 5, are used to compare text values using wildcards (LIKE), to determine whether values are between a range of values (BETWEEN), or in a set of values (IN).

Operator	Description
LIKE	Matches text values by using wildcards. These are the same wildcards that are shown in Table 1.
BETWEEN	Determines if a number or date is within a range.
IN	Determines if a value is found within a set of values.

Table 5 Special operators

For this project, the manager of the spa would like you to find all services scheduled for February 2015, along with the customer who is scheduled for those services. The Between special operator will return results that include and fall between the criteria you enter. If you recall, when working with dates as criteria, a # in front of and at the end of each date are required to identify the numbers as dates and not a string of text. You will use the Between special operator.

A03.24

To Use the Between Special Operator with a Date Criteria

a. Click the **CREATE** tab, and then in the Queries group, click **Query Design**. Double-click **tblSchedule** and **tblCustomer** to add the tables to the query. Click **Close** to close the Show Table dialog box.

b. Double-click **DateOfAppt**, **Service**, and **Employee**, from tblSchedule, and then double-click **CustFirstName** and **CustLastName** from tblCustomer in that order to add them to the query design grid.

c. Click in the **Sort** row, and then select **Ascending** for the **DateOfAppt**, **Service**, and **Employee** fields.

d. Click in the **Criteria** row for the DateOfAppt field, and then type **Between 2/1/15 and 2/29/15**.

e. Click **Run** to run the query.

Notice that the results do not show services in February. They show services in January. Access is misinterpreting your query criteria.

f. Switch to **Design** view to check the criteria. Move your pointer to the **border** between DateOfAppt and Service until it becomes ↔. Double-click to see the full criteria.

Notice that since there is no leap day in 2015, Access interpreted the 2/29/15 as 2/29/2012, the last leap day that occurred, and the /15 as a division. This is not what you wanted. This example shows why it is so important to check your results to see if they make sense.

SIDE NOTE
Formatting Criteria
Access will add pound signs around dates and quotation marks around text. However, if the criteria are ambiguous, you should put them in.

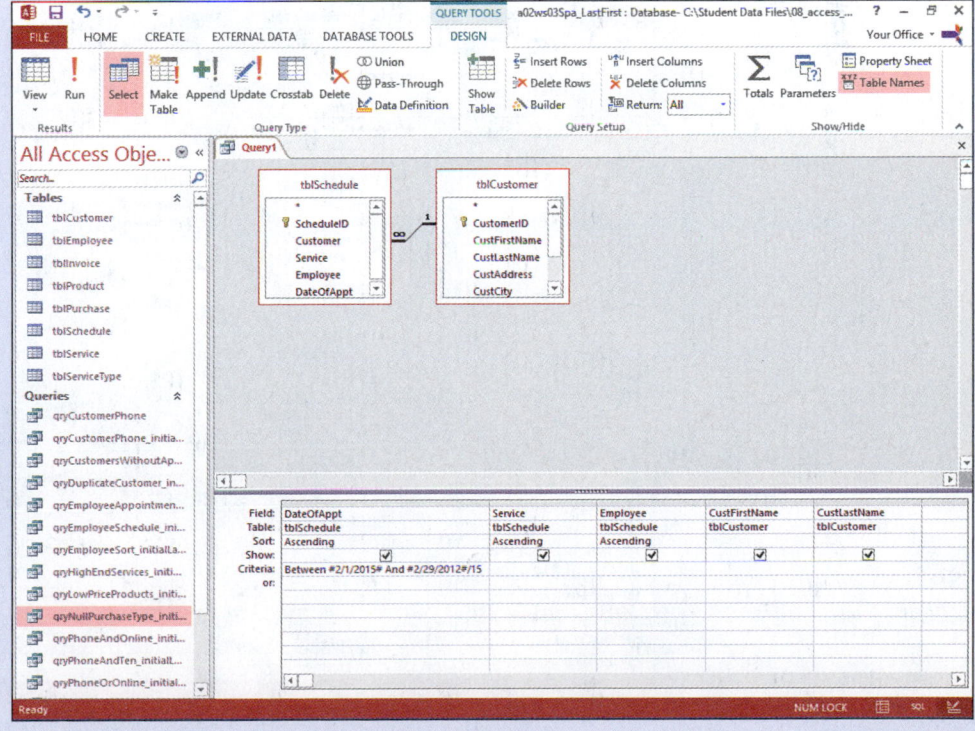

Figure 26   Misinterpreted criteria for DateOfAppt

g. Change the criteria to **Between 2/1/15 and 2/28/15**. Click **Run** to run the query. This time the results are as expected and show 47 appointments in February.

h. Click **Save** on the Quick Access Toolbar, under Query Name type **qryFebruaryServices_initialLastname** using your first initial and last name, and then click **OK**. **Close** [X] the query.

Combining Special Operators and Logical Operators

Special operators can be combined with logical operators. As your criteria get more complex, you need to carefully check how Access interprets your criteria and your results.

For this project, the manager of the spa would like you to find all services scheduled for months other than February 2015, along with the customer who is scheduled for that service. You will use the LIKE special operator and combine it with the NOT logical operator. This query is very similar to the one you just created so you will open that query and modify it.

A03.25

To Use Combine Logical and Special Operators

a. Right-click **qryFebruaryServices_initialLastname**, and then select **Copy**. Right-click the **Navigation Pane**, and then select **Paste**. In the Query Name box type **qryNotFebruaryServices_initialLastname**. Click **OK**.

b. Double-click **qryNotFebruaryServices_initialLastname** to open it.

c. Switch to **Design** view. Click in the **Criteria** row for the DateOfAppt field, and then replace the current criteria with **Like 2/*/2015**. Remember that the asterisk (*) is a wildcard that will select all dates that have a month of 2 and a year of 2015.

d. Click **Run** to run the query. Notice that the results show 47 February service appointments.

e. Switch to **Design** view. Type **Not** before the current criteria so it reads **Not Like "2/*/2015"**.

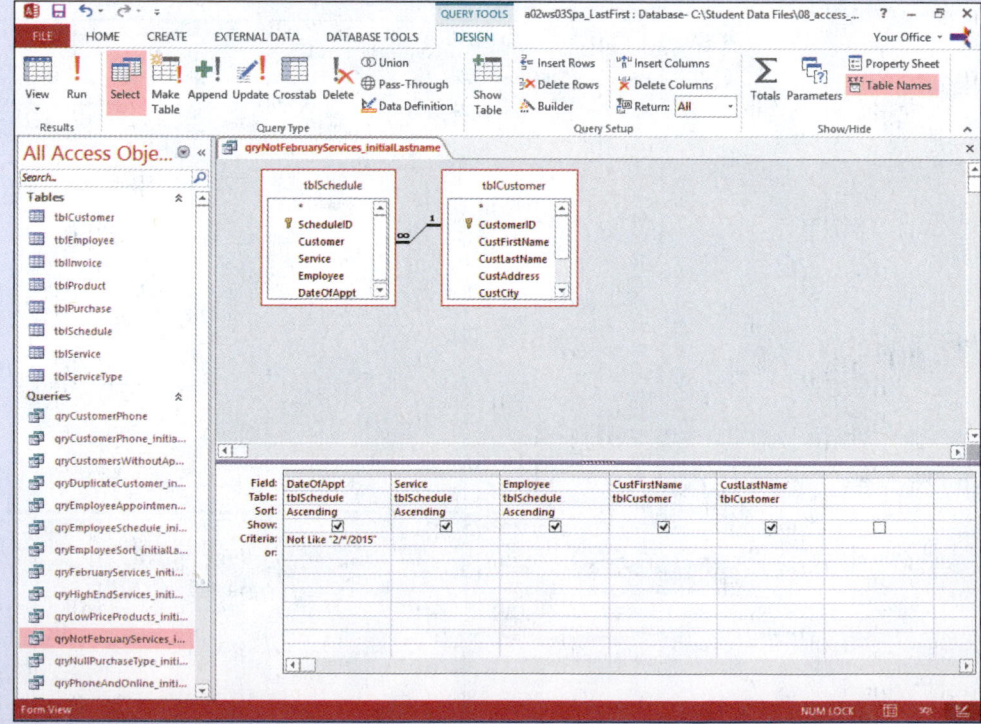

Figure 27 Combined Not and Like operators

f. Click **Run** to run the query. Notice that the results now show the six service appointments not in February.

g. **Save** and **close** ✕ your query.

Create Aggregate Functions

Aggregate functions perform arithmetic operations, such as calculating averages and totals, on records displayed in a table or query. An aggregate function can be used in Datasheet view by adding a total row to a table, or it can be used in a query on records that meet certain criteria.

QUICK REFERENCE	Commonly Used Aggregate Functions

There are a number of different aggregate functions that can be used depending on the type of calculation you want to perform.

1. **Sum**—Calculates the total value for selected records

2. **Average**—Calculates the average value for selected records

3. **Count**—Displays the number of records retrieved

4. **Minimum**—Displays the smallest value from the selected records

5. **Maximum**—Displays the largest value from the selected records

Adding a Total Row

If you need to see a quick snapshot of statistics for a table or query, you can use the **total row**. The total row is a special row that appears at the end of a datasheet that enables you to show aggregate functions for one or more fields. For this project, you will help the manager quickly find a total for all unpaid invoices listed in the invoices table and a count of the number of invoices in the table. The invoice table has a Yes/No field, so you will show her how to define criteria for Yes/No.

A03.26

▶ To Add a Total Row to a Query That Uses Yes/No Criteria

a. Double-click **tblInvoice** to open it. Notice that the Paid field is a check box. Switch to **Design** view and see that the Data Type is Yes/No. Click the **Data Type** and see that the Format is Yes/No. **Close** ✕ the table.

b. Click the **CREATE** tab, and then in the Queries group, click **Query Design**. Double-click **tblInvoice** and **tblCustomer** to add the tables to the query. Click **Close** to close the Show Table dialog box.

c. Double-click **InvoiceDate**, **InvoiceTotal**, and **Paid** from tblInvoice, and then double-click **CustFirstName** and **CustLastName** from tblCustomer in that order to add them to the query design grid.

d. Click in the **Sort** row, and then select **Ascending** for **InvoiceDate**.

e. Click in the **Criteria** row for the **Paid** field, and then type **No**.

f. Click **Run** to run the query. The six unpaid invoices are shown.

SIDE NOTE

Removing Totals
To remove the total row, on the Home tab, click Totals.

g. In the Records group, click **Totals** so that the Total row shows.

h. Click in the **Total row** under the InvoiceTotal field, click the arrow, and then select **Sum**. Click in the **Total row** under the First Name field, click the arrow, and then select **Count**.

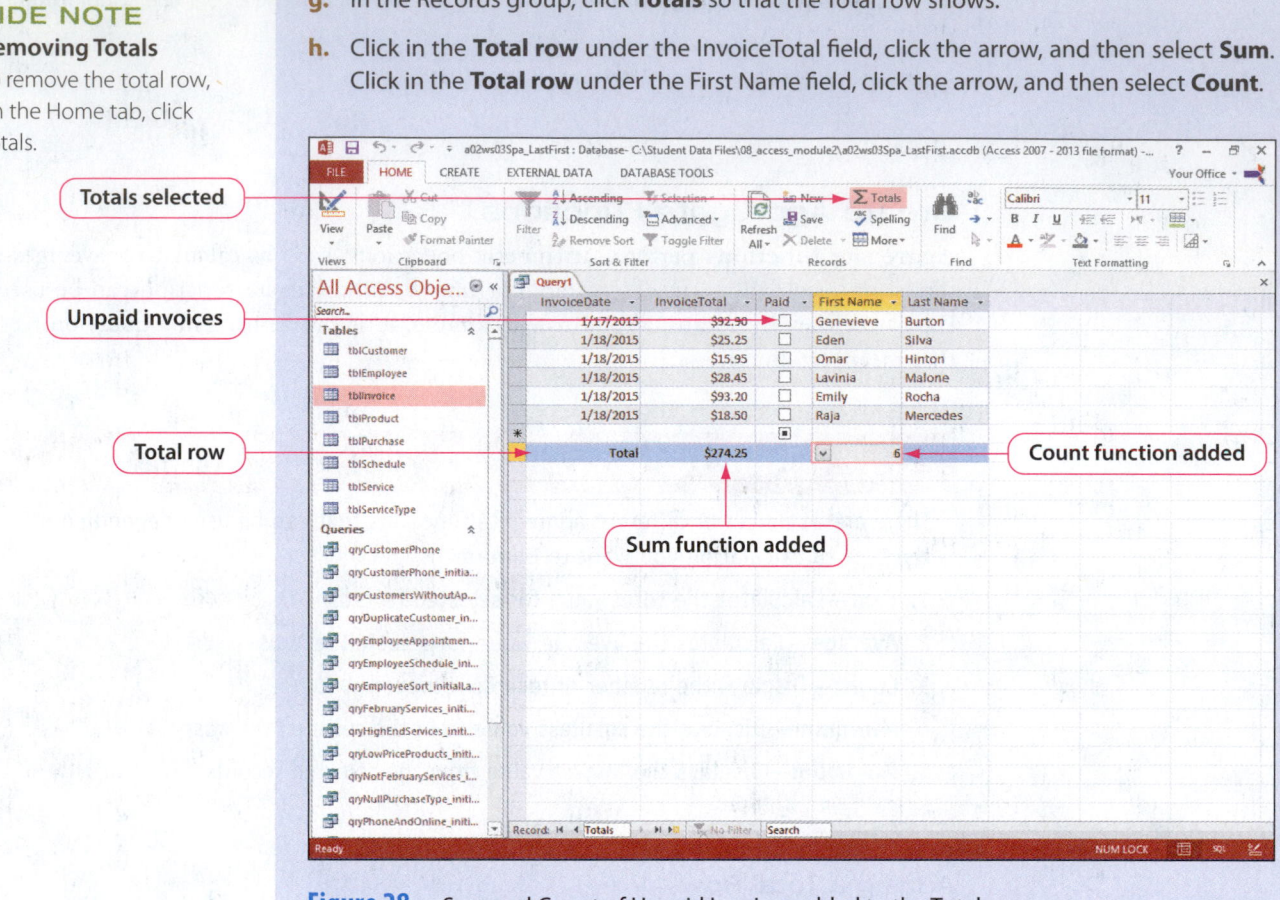

Figure 28 Sum and Count of Unpaid Invoices added to the Total row

i. Click **Save** 💾 on the Quick Access Toolbar, under **Query Name** type **qryUnpaidInvoices_initialLastname** using your first initial and last name, and then click **OK**. **Close** ✖ the query.

Using Aggregate Functions in a Query

Aggregate functions can be used in queries to perform calculations on selected fields and records. One advantage to using aggregate functions in queries, rather than just a total row, is that you can group criteria and then calculate the aggregate functions for a group of records. By default, the query design grid does not have a place to enter aggregate functions, so the total row must be added from the Query Tools Design tab. Each column or field can calculate only one aggregate function, so to calculate multiple functions on the same field, the field must be added to the grid multiple times.

For this project, you have been asked to provide a statistical summary of the spa's product prices. The manager would like to see how many products are offered, what the average product price is, and the minimum and maximum product prices.

A03.27

To Use Aggregate Functions in a Query

a. Click the **CREATE** tab, and then in the Queries group, click **Query Design**. Double-click **tblProduct** to add the table to the query. Click **Close** to close the Show Table dialog box.

b. Double-click **Price** four times to add the field four times to the query design grid.

c. In the Show/Hide group, click **Totals** to add a total row to the query design grid.

d. In the first Price column, click in the **Total** row, click the arrow, and then select **Count**. In the second Price column, click in the **Total** row, click the arrow, and then select **Avg**. Repeat for the next two **Price** columns selecting **Min** for the third column and **Max** for the last column.

SIDE NOTE
Pull Down Arrow
Alternatively, you can click the right side of the Total row and the pull down menu appears.

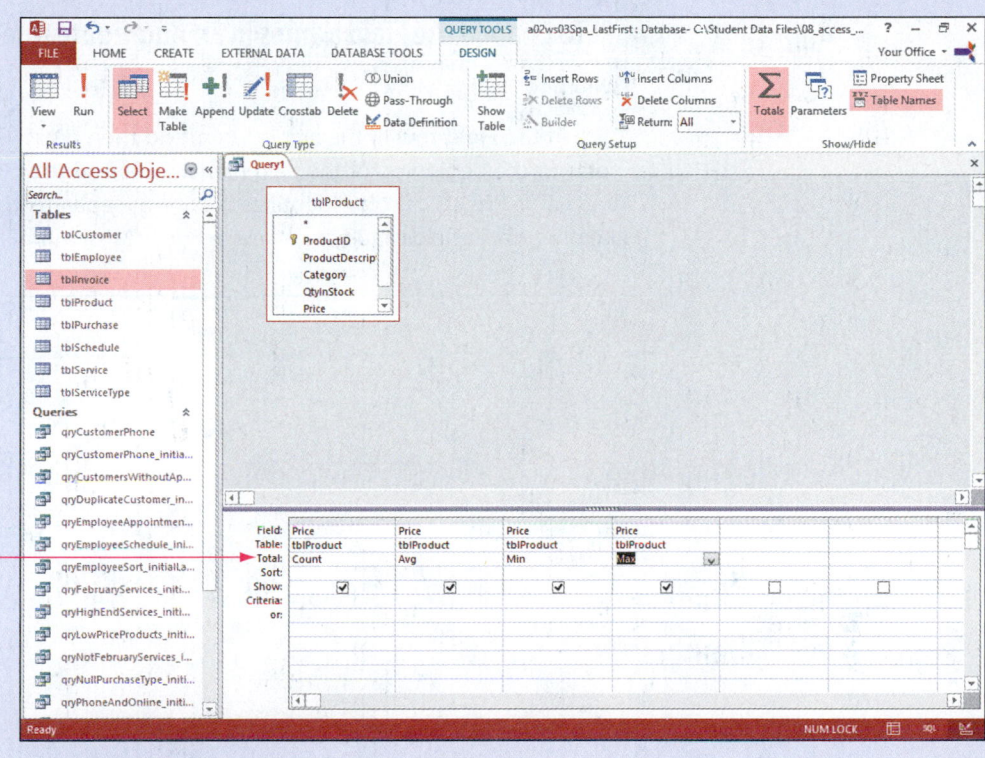

Total row added to query design grid

Figure 29 Aggregate functions selected for each column

e. Click **Run** to run the query. Because this is an aggregate query and you are calculating one statistic per column, there will only be one record in the results.

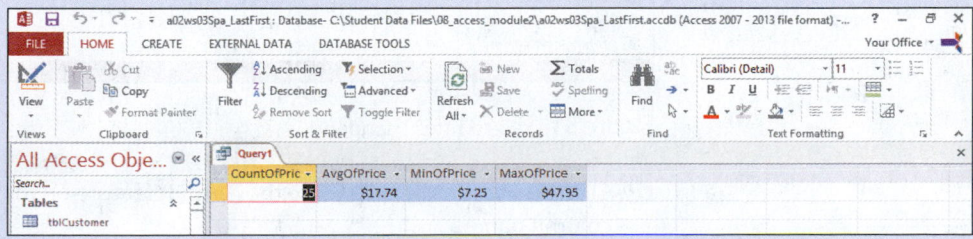

CountOfPric	AvgOfPrice	MinOfPrice	MaxOfPrice
25	$17.74	$7.25	$47.95

Figure 30 Aggregate query results

Changing Field Names

Field names in aggregate queries are a composite of the selected aggregate function and the table field name. For example, the Count function for Price is named CountOfPrice as shown in Figure 30. This is not particularly descriptive in what it actually shows is the number of products that have a price. The other functions are more descriptively named but still could have more useful names.

The field names assigned in an aggregate query can easily be changed either before or after the query is run. However, you must keep the original field name in the query design grid so Access knows what field to perform the calculation on. For this project, you will change the names of the fields in the aggregate query you just created.

A03.28

To Change the Field Names in an Aggregate Query

a. Switch to **Design** view.

b. Click in the **Field** row of the first column, and then press ⌞Home⌟ to move the insertion point to the beginning of the field name. Type **Count of Products:**. Do not delete the field name **Price**. The colon identifies the title as separate from the field name. Repeat for the other three fields and type **Average Price:**, **Minimum Price:**, and **Maximum Price:**.

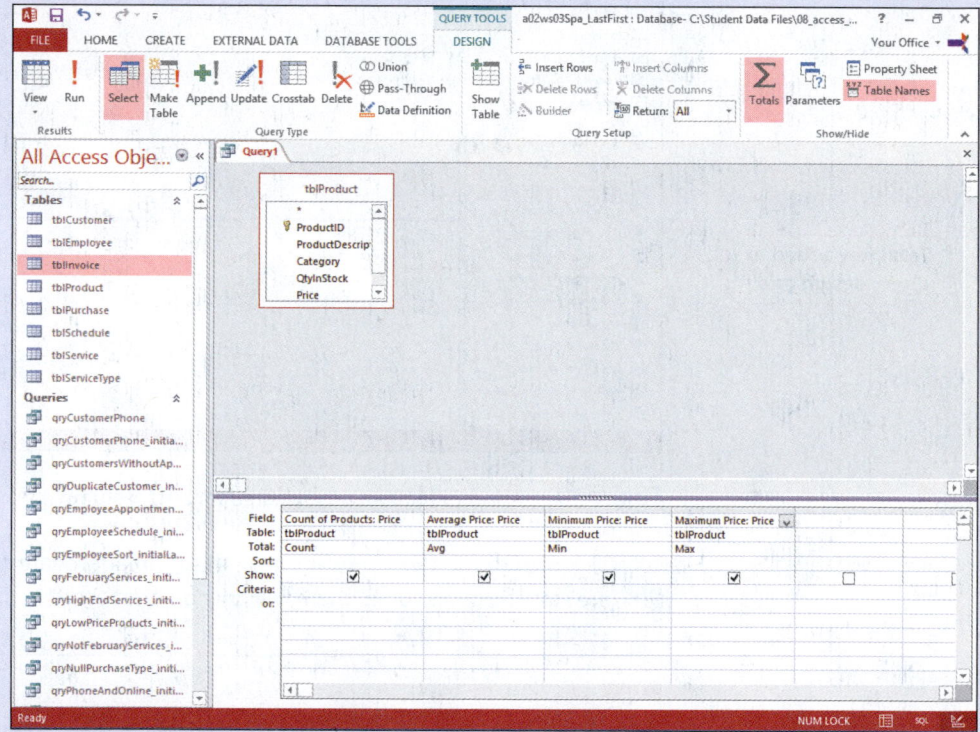

Figure 31   Field titles changed

c. Click **Run** to run the query. Use the **AutoFit** feature on the columns to see the complete column names.

d. Click **Save** 💾 on the Quick Access Toolbar, under Query name type **qryProductStatistics_initialLastname** using your first initial and last name, and then click **OK**. **Close** ✕ the query.

Creating Calculations for Groups of Records

Not only can you find statistical information on selected records using aggregate functions in a query, or for all records using the total row, you can also calculate statistics for groups of records. Creating a group to calculate statistics works the same way as an aggregate query but must include the field to group by. The additional field will not have a statistic selected for the total row, but instead it will have the default Group By entered in the total row.

For this exercise, you will help the spa manager find the same product price statistics you calculated above but this time grouped by product category.

A03.29

To Create a Group Calculation

a. Click the **CREATE** tab, and then in the Queries group, click **Query Design**, and then double-click **tblProduct** to add the table to the query. Click **Close** to close the Show Table dialog box.

b. Double-click **Category** to add it to the query design grid, and then double-click **Price** four times to add the field four times to the query design grid.

c. On the DESIGN tab, in the Show/Hide group, click **Totals** to add a total row to the query design grid.

d. In the first Price column, click in the **Total** row, click the **arrow**, and then select **Count**. In the second Price column, click in the **Total** row, click the **arrow**, and then select **Avg**. Repeat for the next two **Price** columns selecting **Min** for the third column and **Max** for the last column. Notice that the Category Total row displays Group By so the statistics will be grouped by each category type.

e. Click **Run** to run the query. Notice that there are five total lines, one for each category of product.

f. Switch to **Design** view.

g. Change the titles for the Price fields to the following: Number of Products, Average Price, Minimum Price, and Maximum Price remembering to put a colon between the name and the Price field name. **Run** the query again. Use the **AutoFit** feature on the columns to best fit the data.

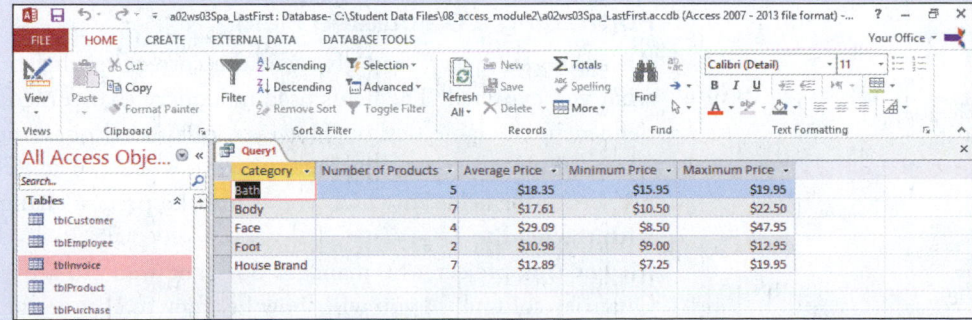

Figure 32   Query results with field titles changed

h. Click **Save** on the Quick Access Toolbar, under Query Name type qryPriceStatisticsByCategory_initialLastname using your first initial and last name, and then click **OK**. **Close** the query.

Troubleshooting an Aggregate Query

Caution should be used when using aggregate functions. Forgetting to add a function in the total row can cause a large number of records to be retrieved from the database, or a combination of records that do not make any sense. You must carefully select which field should have the Group By operator in the total row; many times only one field will use Group By. Combining search criteria and aggregate functions in a single query can make the query complex. It also makes troubleshooting more difficult if the query does not work. When in doubt, set all your criteria in one query and then use the aggregate functions in another query based on the query with the criteria. This way, you can first verify that your criteria worked and then concentrate on the aggregate function results.

For this exercise, the manager tried to create an aggregate query to calculate the total number of items and average number of items purchased by different methods—phone, online, and in person. The results made no sense, and she has asked you to help her figure out why.

A03.30

 To Troubleshoot an Aggregate Query

a. Double-click **qryPurchaseMethods** to open the query. Notice the results in the second and third columns are exactly the same, when the intent was to have one column contain a total and the other column contain an average.

b. Switch to **Design** view. Look at the second column, **Quantity**, and notice the Total row shows the Group By operator instead of a function. Change this to **Sum**.

c. Rename the second and third column field titles to Total Quantity and Average Quantity, remembering to put a colon between the name and the Quantity field name.

d. Click **Run** to run the query. Use the **AutoFit** feature on the columns to best fit the data.

e. Click the **FILE** tab, select **Save As**, click **Save Object As**, and then click **Save As**. Under Save 'qryPurchaseMethods' to: type qryPurchaseMethods_initialLastname, using your first initial and last name, and then click **OK**.

Formatting a Calculated Field

An aggregate query may give you the correct results, but the formatting may not be what you expected. The fields used in a query that come from a table use the formatting defined in the table design. However, calculated query fields must be formatted in the query design grid using the Field properties sheet. The **Property Sheet** contains a list of properties for fields in which you can make precise changes to each property associated with the field.

For this project, the manager does not want to see decimal places for the Average Quantity column, so you will show her how to change the formatting of that field.

A03.31

 To Change the Formatting of a Calculated Field

a. Switch to **Design** view.

b. Click the **Average Quantity: Quantity** column. On the DESIGN tab, in the Show/Hide group, click **Property Sheet**.

c. In the Property Sheet pane, on the General tab, click the **Format** box, click the **arrow**, and then select **Fixed**. Click the **Decimal Places** box, and then type **0**.

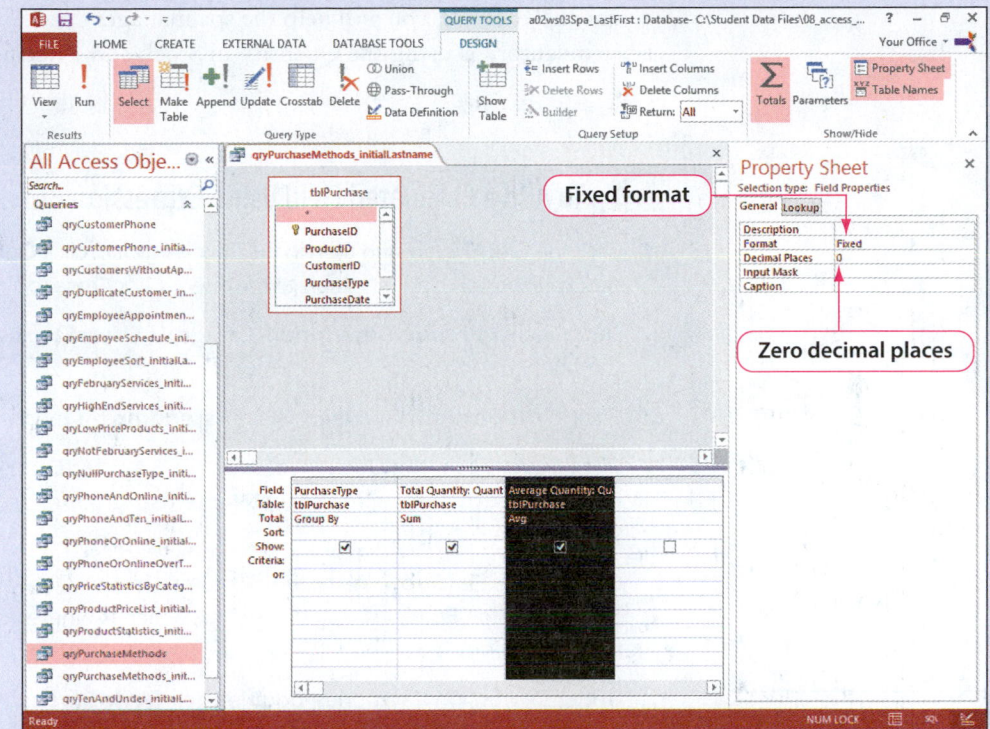

Figure 33 Property sheet open with changes

d. **Close** ☒ the Property Sheet pane, and then **run** the query again. The results should be formatted with no decimal places.

e. **Save** 🖫 and **close** ☒ the query.

 CONSIDER THIS | **How Many Decimal Places?**

Would having many decimal places for an average field give you a more accurate average? Why would you choose to show no decimal places on an average quantity field?

Create Calculated Fields

In addition to statistical calculations using aggregate functions, you can also perform an arithmetic calculation within a row of a query to create a new field. The result of the calculated field is displayed each time you run the query. However, this new field is not part of any other table.

A calculated field can be added to a query using the fields in the query or even fields in another table or query in the database. The calculation can use a combination of numbers and field values, which allows you flexibility in how you perform the calculation. For example, you can multiply a product price stored in the table by a sales tax rate that you enter into the calculation.

Building a Calculated Field Using Expression Builder

Expression Builder is a tool in Access that can help you format your calculated fields correctly. The Builder provides a list of expression elements, operators, and built-in functions. The capabilities of Expression Builder range from simple to complex.

For this exercise, you will help the spa manager create a query to show what the value of her inventory is using the Quantity in Stock and Price fields for each product.

A03.32

 To Add a Calculated Field Using Expression Builder

a. Click the **CREATE** tab, and then in the Queries group, click **Query Design**, and then double-click **tblProduct** to add the table to the query. Click **Close** to close the Show Table dialog box.

b. Double-click **ProductDescription**, **Category**, **QtyInStock**, and **Price** to add the fields to the query design grid.

c. Click in the **Sort** row, and then select **Ascending** for the **ProductDescription** field.

d. Click **Save** 🖫 on the Quick Access Toolbar, under **Query Name**, type **qryProductInventory_initialLastName** using your first initial and last name, and then click **OK**.

e. Click in the **Field** row in the fifth column, in the Query Setup group, click **Builder**. The Expression Builder dialog box opens, which is where you will build your formula for the calculation.

f. Under Expression Categories, double-click **QtyInStock** to add the field to the expression box, type * for multiplication, and then under Expression Categories double-click **Price**. Move the insertion point to the beginning of the expression, and then type **Total Inventory:**.

> **Troubleshooting**
>
> When you click Expression Builder to create a calculated field, and you do not see your field names listed in the Expression Categories box in the middle of the dialog box, it may be that the query has not been saved yet. If the query is not saved, then the field names will not appear and you will have to type them in the Expression Builder manually instead of clicking them to select them. It is good practice to save your query first, and then open the Expression Builder to create a calculated field.

SIDE NOTE
Expression Box

When you use multiple tables in Expression Builder, the table name is put in front of the field name with an exclamation mark.

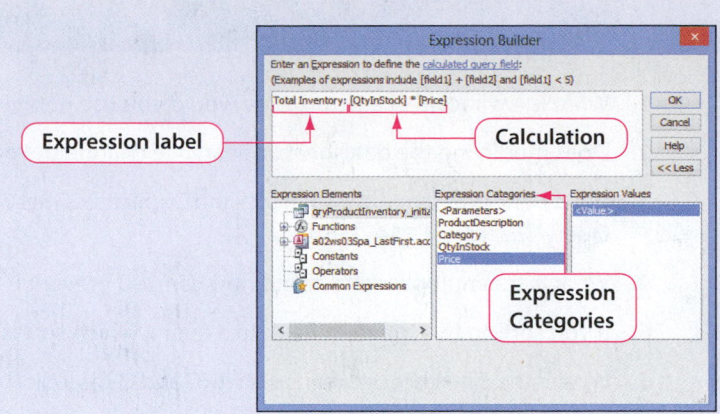

Figure 34 Expression Builder

g. Click **OK** to save the expression and add it to the query design grid. Use the **AutoFit** feature on all columns.

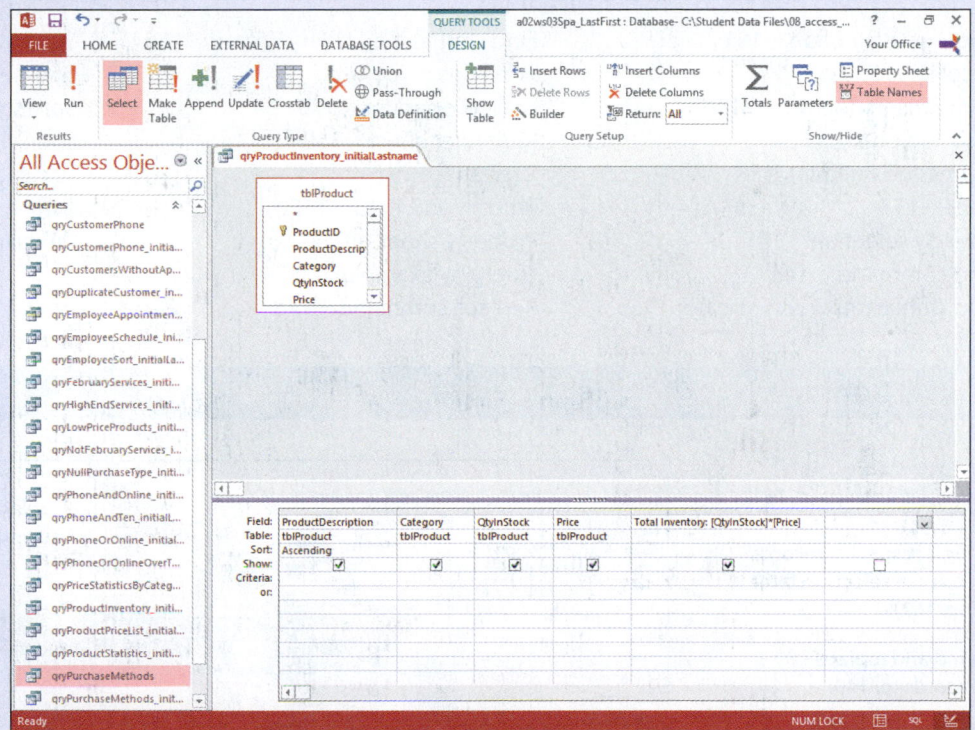

Figure 35 Design grid with calculated expression added

h. Click **Run** to run the query. Use the **AutoFit** feature on the Total Inventory column to best fit the data. The results should show 25 records with a new column titled **Total Inventory** that multiplies the QtyInStock and the Price fields.

i. **Close** ☒ the query, and then click **Yes** when prompted to save changes. **Close** Access.

Concept Check

1. What is a wildcard character? How would you use it to find a record? p. 150–151

2. Does modifying the datasheet appearance change the data in your database? p. 153

3. What is the difference between the Find Duplicates Query Wizard and the Find Unmatched Query Wizard? p. 154–156

4. What is the multiplier effect, and how can you prevent it from happening? p. 160, 163

5. If you sort on two different fields in a query, which sort is done first? p. 165

6. What is the difference between using AND and OR as logical operators in a query? p. 170–172

7. What is an aggregate query? Why would you add the same field multiple times to an aggregate query? p. 181–182

8. How does a calculated field differ from an aggregate function? p. 187–188

Key Terms

Aggregate function   181
AutoFit   153
Comparison operator   166
Crosstab query   154
Expression Builder   188
Filter   151
Filter by selection   151
Find command   148
Find Duplicates Query Wizard   155

Find Unmatched Query Wizard   156
Join lines   160
Logical operator   170
Multiplier effect   160
Orphan   155
Primary sort field   165
Property sheet   186
Query by example   157
Replace command   148

Secondary sort field   165
Sort field   164
Sorting   164
Special operator   178
Text filter   152
Total row   181
Wildcard character   148

Visual Summary

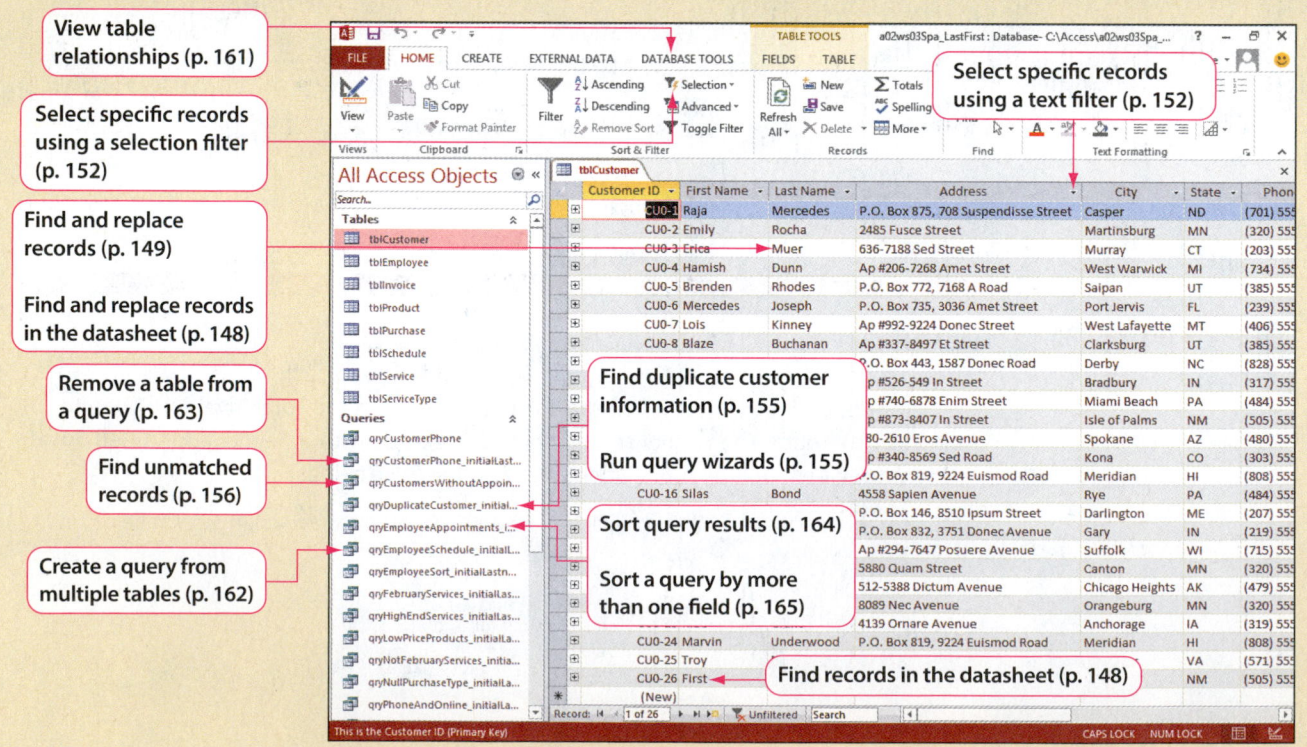

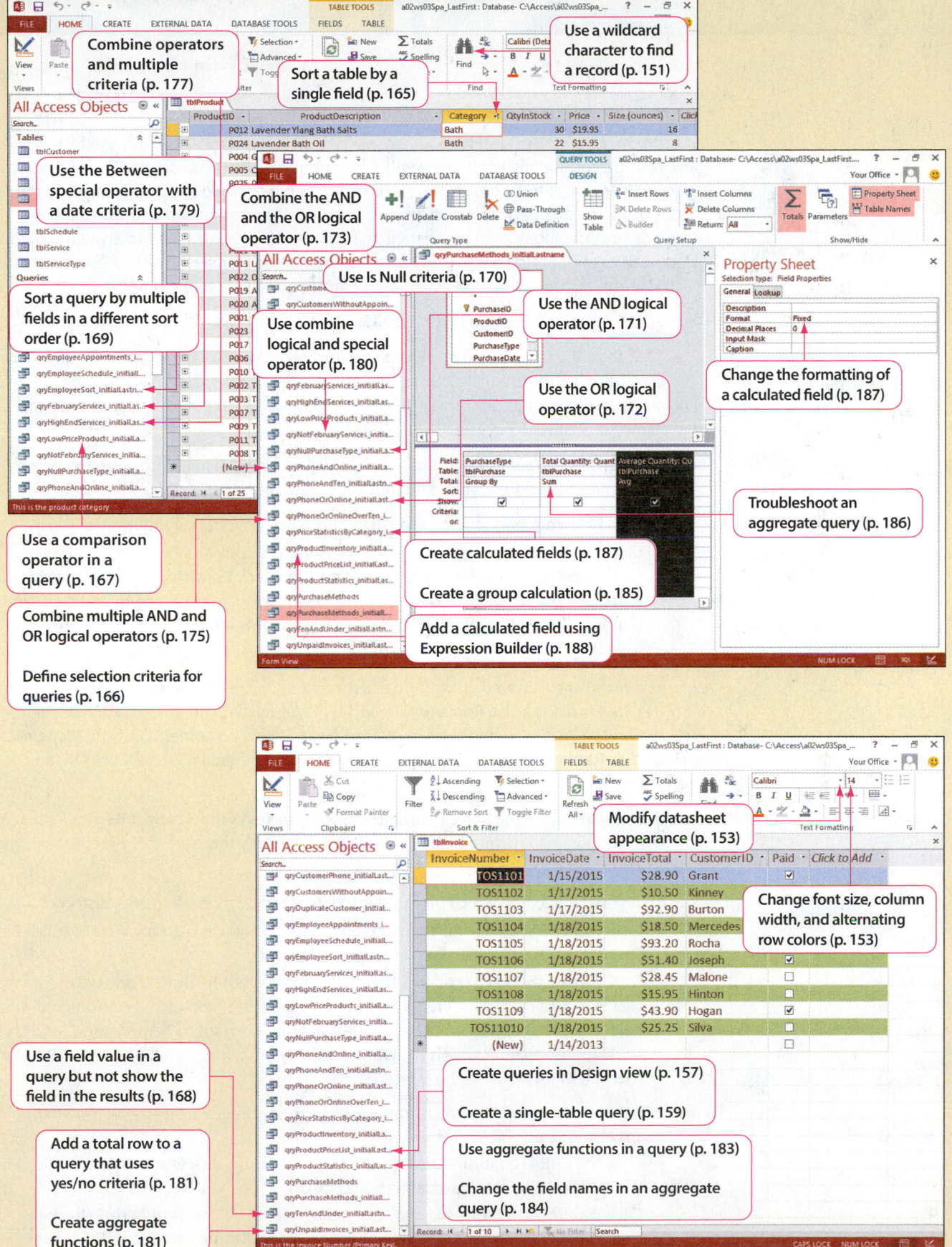

Figure 36 Turquoise Oasis Spa Data Management Final

The callouts in the figure read:

- Combine operators and multiple criteria (p. 177)
- Sort a table by a single field (p. 165)
- Use a wildcard character to find a record (p. 151)
- Use the Between special operator with a date criteria (p. 179)
- Combine the AND and the OR logical operator (p. 173)
- Use Is Null criteria (p. 170)
- Use the AND logical operator (p. 171)
- Change the formatting of a calculated field (p. 187)
- Sort a query by multiple fields in a different sort order (p. 169)
- Use combine logical and special operator (p. 180)
- Use the OR logical operator (p. 172)
- Troubleshoot an aggregate query (p. 186)
- Use a comparison operator in a query (p. 167)
- Create calculated fields (p. 187)
- Create a group calculation (p. 185)
- Combine multiple AND and OR logical operators (p. 175)
- Define selection criteria for queries (p. 166)
- Add a calculated field using Expression Builder (p. 188)
- Modify datasheet appearance (p. 153)
- Change font size, column width, and alternating row colors (p. 153)
- Use a field value in a query but not show the field in the results (p. 168)
- Create queries in Design view (p. 157)
- Create a single-table query (p. 159)
- Add a total row to a query that uses yes/no criteria (p. 181)
- Use aggregate functions in a query (p. 183)
- Create aggregate functions (p. 181)
- Change the field names in an aggregate query (p. 184)

Student data file needed:
a02ws03Spa2.accdb

You will save your file as:
a02ws03Spa2_LastFirst.accdb

Turquoise Oasis Spa

Sales & Marketing

The resort is considering hosting a large convention and is trying to sign a multiple-year contract with an out-of-town group. The spa is being asked to provide information about the services, products, and packages it offers. All the information can be found in the database, but it needs to come together in a coherent fashion. You have been asked to answer a number of questions about the spa and provide information to help answer those questions. You will also look for discrepancies or mistakes in the data, and correct them as necessary.

a. Start **Access**, and then open **a02ws03Spa2**.

b. Click the **FILE** tab, and then select **Save As**. Make sure **Save Database As** and **Access Database** are selected. Click **Save As**. In the Save As dialog box, navigate to where you are saving your files, and then type **a02ws03Spa2_LastFirst**, using your first and last name. Click **Save**. If necessary, click **Enable Content**.

c. Double-click **tblCustomer** to open the table. Add a new record with your first name and last name, your address, your city, your state, your phone, and your e-mail address.

d. Use the **Find** command to find spa customers who come from as far away as Alaska.

- Click in the **State** column for the first record. On the HOME tab, in the Find group, click **Find**. Type **AK** in the Find What box, and then click **Find Next** until Access finishes searching the table. Click **OK**, and then click **Cancel** to close the dialog box. Notice that the Alaska address selected is really a city in Hawaii.

e. Use the Replace command to replace **AK** with **HI** in the table.

- Click in the **State** column for the first record. On the HOME tab, in the Find group, click **Find**. Click the **Replace** tab, and type **AK** in the Find What box. Type **HI** in the Replace With box, and then click **Find Next**. When Customer ID CU0-21 is selected, click **Replace**. Click **Find Next** to check for any more similar errors. Click **OK**, and then click **Cancel** to close the dialog box.

f. Click the **arrow** on the **State** field column, point to **Text Filters**, select **Begins With**, type **H** in the State begins with box, and then click **OK**. Verify there are three records selected. Save and close the table.

g. Create a query to find which products are purchased by more than one customer.

- Click the **CREATE** tab, and then in the Queries group, click **Query Wizard**. Click **Find Duplicates Query Wizard**, and then click **OK**.
- Click **Table: tblPurchase**, and then click **Next**. Double-click **ProductID**, and then click **Next**. Click the **All Fields** button to add all the fields to the Additional query fields box, and then click **Next**. Under "What do you want to name your query?" type **qryDuplicateProducts_initialLastname** using your first initial and last name, and then click **Finish**. Close the query.

h. Create a query to find out which employees currently do not have any customer appointments at the spa.

- Click the **CREATE** tab, and then in the Queries group, click **Query Wizard**. Click **Find Unmatched Query Wizard**, and then click **OK**.
- Click **Table: tblEmployee**, and then click **Next**. Select **Table: tblSchedule**, and then click **Next**. Verify that Matching fields shows **EmployeeID <=> Employee**, and then click **Next**. Click the **All Fields** button to add all the fields to the Selected fields column, and then click **Next**.

- Name the query **qryEmployeesWithoutAppointments_initialLastname**, using your first initial and last name, and then click **Finish**.
- Switch to **Design** view. Click the **Sort** row for the EmpLastName field, click the **sort** arrow, and then click **Ascending** to sort the query in ascending order by Last Name. On the DESIGN tab, in the Results group, click **Run** to run the query. Close the query, and then click **Yes** when prompted to save the changes.

i. Create a query to list any customers who are not from New Mexico who have purchased bath products.

- Click the **CREATE** tab, and then in the Queries group, click **Query Design**. Double-click **tblCustomer**, **tblPurchase**, and **tblProduct** to add the tables to the query window. Click **Close** to close the Show Table dialog box.
- In the following order, from tblCustomer double-click **CustLastName**, **CustFirstName**, **CustState**; from tblPurchase double-click **PurchaseDate**; from tblProduct, double-click **ProductDescription**; and from tblPurchase, double-click **Quantity** to add the fields to the query design grid. Click the **Sort** row for the CustLastName and CustFirstName fields, and then select **Ascending**.
- In the **Criteria** row for **CustState**, type **Not NM**. In the same Criteria row for **ProductDescription**, type **Like *Bath***.
- On the DESIGN tab, in the Results group, click **Run** to run the query.
- Click **Save** on the Quick Access Toolbar, name the query **qryBathProductsNotNM_initialLastname** using your first initial and last name, and then close the query.

j. Create a query to list the spa's services by Type, Name, LengthOfService, and Fee.

- On the **CREATE** tab, in the Queries group, click **Query Design**. Double-click **tblService** and **tblServiceType** to add the tables to the query window. Click **Close** to close the Show Table dialog box.
- In the following order, from tblServiceType double-click **Type**, and from tblService double-click **ServiceName**, **LengthOfService**, and **Fee** to add the fields to the query design grid. Click the **Sort** row for the Type field, select **Ascending**, and then for the Fee field, select **Descending**. On the DESIGN tab, in the Results group, click **Run** to run the query.
- Use the **AutoFit** feature on all columns. Click **Save** on the Quick Access Toolbar, name the query **qryServicesAndFees_initialLastname** using your first initial and last name, and then close the query.

k. Create a query to find how much each customer spent on their product purchase, including 8% sales tax, but only if the purchase was a quantity greater than 1.

- Click the **CREATE** tab, and then in the Queries group, click **Query Design**. Add **tblProduct**, **tblPurchase**, and **tblCustomer** to the query window. Click **Close** to close the Show Table dialog box. From tblProduct, double-click **ProductDescription** and **Price**; from tblPurchase, double-click **Quantity**; and from tblCustomer, double-click **CustFirstName** and **CustLastName** in that order to add the fields to the query design grid.
- Click in the **Criteria** row for Quantity, and then type **>1**. Click **Save** on the Quick Access Toolbar, name the query **qryTotalPurchase_initialLastname** using your first initial and last name, and then click **OK**.
- In the sixth column, click in the **Field** row, and then on the DESIGN tab, in the Query Setup group, click **Builder**. Double-click **Price** to add it to the expression, type *****, double-click **Quantity** to add it to the expression, type *****, and then type **1.08**. Click at the beginning of the expression, type **Total Purchase with tax:**, and then click **OK**.
- Click the **Sort** row for the Quantity field, click the **arrow**, and then click **Ascending**. In the Results group, click **Run** to run the query.
- Switch to **Design** view. Click the **Total Purchase with tax** field, on the DESIGN tab, in the Show/Hide group, click **Property Sheet**. On the Property Sheet's General tab, click the **Format** arrow, and then select **Currency**. Click the **Decimal Places**

arrow, and then select **2**. Close the Property Sheet, and then on the DESIGN tab, in the Results group, click **Run** to run the query. The Total Purchase with tax field should be formatted with currency and two decimal places.

- Use the **AutoFit** feature on all the columns.
- Close the query, and then click **Yes** when prompted to save the changes.

l. Create an aggregate query to find the average, minimum, and maximum fee for each type of service the spa offers.

- Click the **CREATE** tab, and then in the Queries group, click **Query Design**. Add **tblService** to the query window. Click **Close** to close the Show Table dialog box. Double-click **Type** one time, and then double-click **Fee** three times in that order to add the fields to the query design grid. In the Show/Hide group, click **Totals** to add the Total row to the query design grid.
- Click in the **Total** row, for the first Fee column, click the **arrow**, and then click **Avg**. For the second Fee column select **Min**, and for the third Fee column select **Max**. Click in the **Sort** row in the Type field, click the **arrow**, and then select **Ascending**. In the Results group, click **Run** to run the query.
- Switch to **Design** view. Change the names of the three Fee columns to Average Fee, Minimum Fee, and Maximum Fee in that order, remembering to put a colon before the Fee field name. In the **Results** group, click **Run** to run the query.
- Use the **AutoFit** feature on all the columns.
- Click **Save** on the Quick Access Toolbar, name the query qryFeeStatistics_initialLastname using your first initial and last name, and then click **OK**. Close the query.

m. Close Access. Submit your file as directed by your instructor.

Problem Solve 1

Homework 1

Student data file needed: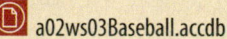

a02ws03Baseball.accdb

You will save your file as: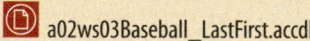

a02ws03Baseball_LastFirst.accdb

Production & Operations

Baseball Academy

Matt Davis is a retired baseball player who runs the Baseball Academy, an indoor baseball facility for middle school, high school, and college players. He offers lessons as well as practice times for individuals and teams. Due to his growing clientele and increased record keeping needs, Matt wants all his records in a database. While he has already set up a database, he now needs to take the database to the next level of performance by improving his ability to get specific data from the database. He has hired you to create the queries he will need to get this information.

a. Start **Access**, and then open **a02ws03Baseball**. Click the **FILE** tab, and save the file as an **Access Database** in the location where you store your files with the name a02ws03Baseball_LastFirst using your first and last name. If necessary, enable the content.

b. Open **tblMember**, and then add a new record with your first name, last name, address, city, state, zip code of 87594, and phone. Create a filter to show only those members who have a zip code of **87594**. Save and close the table.

c. Modify **tblPayments** so the font type is **Arial** and the font size is **14**. Adjust the column widths appropriately. Save and close the table.

d. Create a Find Duplicates Query that will show members who have the same address. Show all the fields in the query results. Name the query qryDupAddresses_initialLastname and then close the query.

e. Create an Unmatched Query that will return the last name, first name, address, city, state, zip code, and phone of anyone who is listed as a member in **tblMember** but has not made a payment matching on MemberID. Name the query **qryNonPayment_initialLastname**. Sort by last name and first name, and then save and close the query.

f. Create a query that will return the **member last name**, **first name**, **amount**, and **payment date**. Sort the query in ascending order first by last name then by first name. Name the query **qryPayments_initialLastname**.

   • Add a total row to show the sum of total payments made. Save and close the query.

g. Create a query that returns all the employees that have **Instructor** in their position. Include employee **first name**, **last name**, and **position**. Sort them by salary—highest to lowest but do not show the salary in the result. Name the query **qryInstructors_initialLastname**. Save and close the query.

h. Create a query to calculate employee salaries with a 3% raise. Include the employee's **last name**, **first name**, and **salary**. Name the query **qryRaises_initialLastname**.

   • The new calculated field is salary * 1.03 and should be called **SalaryWithRaise**. Format the new field as **Currency** with **Auto** decimal places, and then sort the results by SalaryWithRaise from highest salary to lowest.

   • Adjust the column widths as necessary. Include total payroll before and after the raises at the bottom of the datasheet. Save and close the query.

i. Create a query that returns the sum, average, minimum, and maximum of all the employee salaries. Name the fields Total Salary, Average Salary, Minimum Salary, and Maximum Salary. Adjust the column widths to fit. Name the query **qrySalaryStats_initialLastname**. Save and close the query.

j. Create a query that includes the member's **last name**, **first name**, **scheduled date**, and **fee** for any lesson between June 1 and June 30, 2015, which is greater than or equal to $250. Sort by last name and first name. Name the query **qryBigJuneFees_initialLastname**. Save and close the query.

k. Save and close the database. Submit your file as directed by your instructor.

Perform 1: Perform in Your Career

Student data file needed:

 a02ws03Roadhouse.accdb

You will save your file as:

 a02ws03Roadhouse_LastFirst.accdb

Production & Operations

Beverage Database at The Roadhouse Bar and Grill

You are the bar manager at The Roadhouse Bar and Grill, a local restaurant that specializes in home-cooked meals for breakfast, lunch, and dinner. You have developed a database for managing the inventory of beverage items.

You will expand the database by creating queries to help you manage the database. You have loaded a few sample transactions to help you develop these queries. For each query, choose which fields you need and which sort order makes sense.

a. Start **Access**, open **a02ws03Roadhouse**, and then save it as a02ws03Roadhouse_LastFirst.

b. Open **tblSuppliers**, and then change the name of the first supplier to your full name.

c. Open each table and familiarize yourself with the fields. Open the relationships window and note how the tables are related.

d. Change **tblSales** to have a larger font and alternating row colors.

e. Create a query that shows sales of beverages from suppliers in Maryland. Show the **Supplier Name** and **State**, the **Sales Date**, and beverage fields that make sense. Sort by fields that make sense. Save the query as qryMarylandSupplierSales_initialLastname.

f. Create a query to see if there are any Suppliers that are not supplying you with any beverages. Hint: this is a Find Unmatched Query. Save the query as qrySuppliersWithoutBeverages_initialLastname.

g. Create a query that shows beverages that have soda in their name, their size, the container type, and the suppliers that supply them. Sort by fields that make sense. Save the query as qrySodaSuppliers_initialLastname.

h. Create a query that shows all juices that were sold in February 2015. Sort by fields that make sense. Save the query as qryFebruaryJuiceSales_initialLastname.

i. Create a query that shows all root beer or cola sold in a bottle with the sale date. Sort by fields that make sense. Save the query as qryBottleSales_initialLastname.

j. Create an aggregate query that shows the average price, minimum price, and maximum price for each beverage serving. Hint: Group by beverage. Sort by fields that make sense. Save the query as qryBeveragePriceStatistics_initialLastname.

k. Create a query that calculates for each beverage the number of servings per container— container size divided by serving size. Sort by fields that make sense. Save the query as qryBeverageServings_initialLastname.

l. Create another query that you would find useful in your job.

m. Submit your file as directed by your instructor.

Additional
Cases

Additional Workshop Cases are available on the companion website and in the instructor resources.

ORKSHOP 4 | ACCESS INFORMATION FROM AN ACCESS DATABASE

OBJECTIVES

1. Navigate in datasheets and forms   p. 198
2. Update table records using forms   p. 206
3. Create a form using the Form Wizard   p. 209
4. Modify a form's design   p. 214
5. Create a report using the Report Wizard   p. 220
6. Customize a report   p. 228
7. Save a report as a PDF file   p. 235

Prepare Case

Turquoise Oasis Spa's New Database

The Turquoise Oasis Spa has a database with customer, employee, product, and service information for easier scheduling and access. An intern created the database, and the manager and staff members are struggling to use the database to its fullest capacity. You have recently been hired to work in the office of the spa and you have knowledge of Access, so the manager has asked for your help in maintaining the records and creating forms and reports to help better use the data in the database.

Production & Operations

Subbotina Anna / Fotolia

REAL WORLD SUCCESS

"After I started using Access for entering my data and running reports, my supervisor asked if I could set up a database for my coworker to use for her job. She didn't know Access so I created forms for her data entry. She just enters today's data and runs her daily reports."

- Elaine, marketing analyst and alumnus

Student data files needed for this workshop:

 a02ws04Spa.accdb    a02ws04Spa.thmx

a02ws04Spa.jpg

You will save your files as:

 a02ws04Spa_LastFirst.accdb

 a02ws04SpaEmployeeSchedule_LastFirst.pdf

Creating Customized Forms

Recall that forms are the objects in Access that are used to enter, edit, or view records in a table. Data can be entered, edited, or viewed directly in the table or in a form. Each option offers advantages and disadvantages.

In Datasheet view, data may be updated directly in the table where it is stored. When updating data in a table, you will be in Datasheet view. Datasheet view shows all the fields and records at one time, which provides all the information you need to update your data, unlike in a form or query, where some of the fields or records may not be in view. This section starts by describing how to navigate in datasheets and forms, continues to editing data in a table, and then finishes by discussing how to edit data in a form.

Navigate in Datasheets and Forms

As you may recall, you can navigate from record to record or field to field in a database using the Navigation bar, or in Navigation mode by using Tab, Enter, Home, End, ↑, ↓, ←, and →. **Navigation mode** allows you to move from record to record and field to field using keystrokes. To update data in a table, you must be in Edit mode. **Edit mode** allows you to edit, or change, the contents of a field. To switch between Navigation mode and Edit mode, press F2.

If you can see the blinking insertion point in a field, you are in Edit mode. When the text of a field is selected and highlighted, you are in Navigation mode.

QUICK REFERENCE	Keystrokes Used in Navigation Mode and Edit Mode	
Keystroke	**Navigation Mode**	**Edit Mode**
→ and ←	Move from field to field	Move from character to character
↑ and ↓	Move from record to record	Switch to Navigation mode and move from record to record
Home	Moves to the first field in the record	Moves to the first character in the field
End	Moves to the last field in the record	Moves to the last character in the field
Tab and Enter	Move one field at a time	Switch to Navigation mode and move from field to field
Ctrl + Home	Moves to the first field of the first record	Moves to the first character in the field, same as Home
Ctrl + End	Moves to the last field of the last record	Moves to the last character in the field, same as End

Opening the Starting File

The spa collects data about customers, employees, products, and services and uses them for scheduling. You will open the spa database to get started.

A04.00

To Open the a02ws04Spa Database

a. Start **Access**, and then open the student data file **a02ws04Spa**.

b. On the **FILE** tab, save the file as an **Access Database** in the location designated by your instructor with the name **a02ws04Spa_LastFirst** using your first and last name. If necessary, enable the content.

Editing a Table in Datasheet View

Datasheet view shows all the records and fields at one time, which is one advantage to using it to update your records. Another advantage is the ability to see all the records in the table, which gives you a perspective on the data you are entering. For this exercise, the staff has received a note from a customer who has changed his phone number. You will show the spa staff how to change that customer's record in the Customer table.

A04.01

To Edit a Record in a Table in Datasheet View

MyITLab®

Workshop 4 Training

a. In the Navigation Pane, double-click **tblCustomer** to open the table.

b. Locate the customer with the Customer ID **CU0-12** and the last name **Hinton**.

c. Click in the **CustomerID** field, and then press ⎡Tab⎤. You are now in Navigation mode, and the First Name field should be highlighted.

SIDE NOTE

Prefix for Key

When you click CustomerID, the "CU0" disappears. The key is defined as numeric but has a prefix identifying the table it is key to.

First Name highlighted in navigation mode

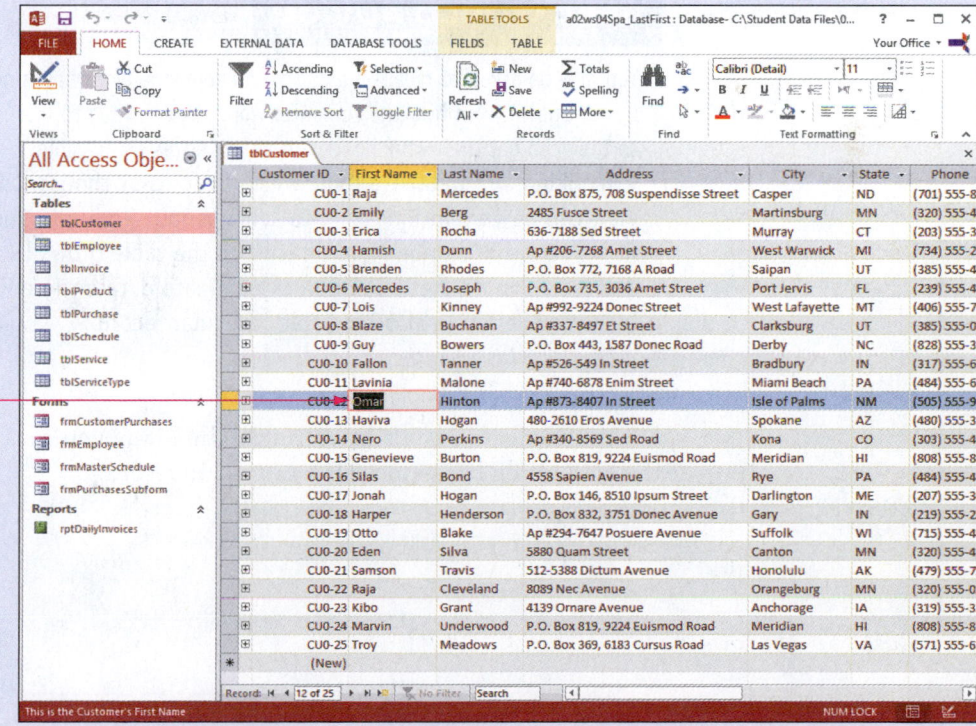

Figure 1   Table in navigation mode

d. Continue pressing Tab until the **Phone** field is highlighted. Press F2 to switch from Navigation mode to Edit mode. Notice the insertion point is at the beginning of the Phone field and the first character is highlighted. Type **5055552923** to enter the new phone number. Because the field is already formatted as a phone number, it is not necessary to enter parentheses or dashes.

e. Press Tab to switch to Navigation mode and move to the next field.

f. **Close** X the table.

SS | **CONSIDER THIS** | **Why Put a Prefix Before a Primary Key?**

CustomerID, the primary key for tblCustomer, is defined as AutoNumber but formatted to have the prefix "CU0-" (0 is a zero) before the number field. Similarly, EmployeeID, the key for tblEmployee, is formatted to have "EMP-" as a prefix before the number field. What is the advantage of putting a prefix before the primary key to a table? Are there disadvantages? Why were these two prefixes chosen?

Navigating Forms and Subforms

A form is an object in Access that you can use to enter, edit, or view records in a table. A simple form allows you to see records one at a time rather than as a group in Datasheet view.

REAL WORLD ADVICE | **Data Overload!**

You may be asked to create a database for someone else that is not familiar with how a database works or even how the computer works. Your role is to make their job as easy as possible so they can get their work done with as few errors as possible.

Looking at a database table with hundreds or thousands of records in Datasheet view can be very intimidating to some people. Trying to keep track of the record or field you are in can be more difficult as the table grows larger and larger. Often seeing one record at a time in a form can eliminate data entry errors and allow the user to focus on the information for that particular record.

You navigate records in a form the same way you navigate a table, using buttons on the Navigation bar to move from record to record.

QUICK REFERENCE	Navigation Buttons on the Navigation Bar
Button / **Description**	**What it does**

Button	Description	What it does
◄	First record	Moves to the first record in the table
►|	Last record	Moves to the last record in the table
◄	Previous record	Moves to the record just before the current record
►	Next record	Moves to the record just after the current record
►*	New (blank) record	Moves to a new row to enter a new record

When you create a form from two tables that have a one-to-many relationship, the first table selected becomes the **main form** and the second table you select becomes the **subform**. A form with a subform allows you to see one record at a time from the main form and multiple records in Datasheet view from the other related table. Because you only see one record at a time or one record and a datasheet, navigation tools become important when you are working with forms as you cannot see all the records at one time.

Navigating a Main Form

Within each record, you can use a combination of [Tab], [Home], [Enter], and [End], as well as [↓], [↑], [←], [→], to move from field to field as shown in the Quick Reference Box.

QUICK REFERENCE	Navigating Forms

Navigating a main form

Keystroke	What it does
[Tab]	Moves from field to field within a record; at the last field in a record, it moves you to the first field in the next record.
[Home]	Moves to the first field of the current record.
[Ctrl] + [Home]	Moves to the first field of the first record of the table.
[End]	Moves to the last field of the current record.
[Ctrl] + [End]	Moves to the last field of the last record of the table.
[↓], [↑], [←], [→]	Move up or down a field of the current record.

(Continued)

Navigating a form with a subform

Keystroke	What it does
Tab	Moves from field to field within a main record. At the last field in a record, it moves to the first field in the subform. At the last record in the subform, it moves to the first field in the next record of the main form.
Home	From the main form, moves to the first field of the current record. From the subform, moves to the first field of the current record in the subform.
Ctrl + Home	From the main form, moves to the first field of the first record. From the subform, moves to the first field of the first record in the subform.
End	From the main form, moves to the last field of the current record in the subform. From the subform, moves to the last field of the current record in the subform.
Ctrl + End	From the main form, moves to the last field of the last record of the subform. From the subform, moves to the last field of the current record of the subform.
↓, ↑, ←, →	Move up or down a field in the current record in either the form or subform.

For this exercise, you will show the spa staff how to navigate the form frmEmployee, which is a list of all employees, one record at a time.

A04.02

To Navigate a Single-Table Form

a. On the Navigation Pane, double-click **frmEmployee** to open the form.

b. Click **Last record** ▶| to go to the last record of the table.

c. Click **First record** |◀ to return to the first record in the table.

d. Click **Next record** ▶ to go to the next record in the table.

e. Click **Previous record** ◀ to go back to the previous record in the table.

f. **Close** ✕ the form.

Navigating a Form with a Subform

When navigating forms with a subform, the Navigation bar buttons at the bottom of the main window are used to navigate the records in the main form, and a second Navigation bar at the bottom of the subform datasheet is used to navigate the records in the subform.

The same navigation keystrokes are used; however, they work a little differently when a subform is included.

For this exercise, you will show the spa staff members how to navigate the form frmCustomerPurchases, which shows one customer at a time with all their recent product purchases.

A04.03

 To Navigate a Multiple-Table Form with a Subform

a. On the Navigation Pane, double-click **frmCustomerPurchases** to open the form.

Notice that the form has two parts. At the top is the main form that shows information about the customer. The lower part is the subform that shows all the purchases made by the customer. There are also two navigation bars, one for the main form and one for the subform.

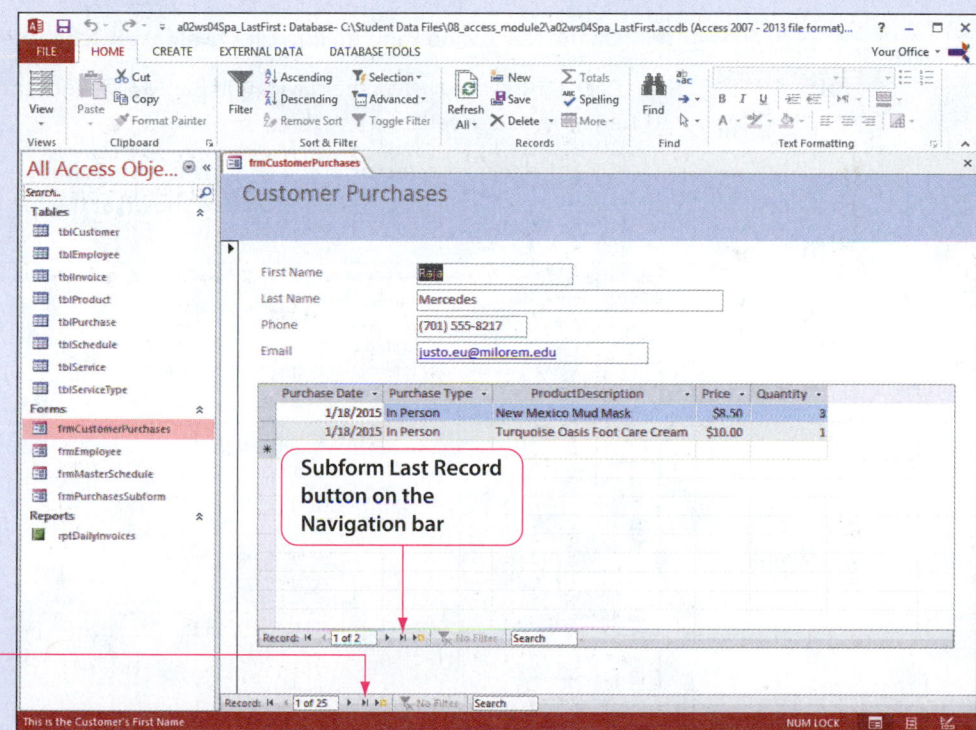

Main form Last Record button on the Navigation bar

Subform Last Record button on the Navigation bar

Figure 2 Form with a subform in Datasheet view

b. Click **Last record** ▶| on the subform Navigation bar to highlight the last record in the subform.

c. Click **Last record** ▶| on the main form Navigation bar to go to the last record in the table.

d. Click **Previous record** ◀ repeatedly to go to record 20 with the customer name Eden Silva.

e. Click **Next record** ▶ in the subform to go to the next record in the subform.

f. **Close** ✕ the form.

Navigating a Split Form

A **split form** is a form created from one table, but it has a Form view and a Datasheet view in the same window. You can view one record at a time at the top of the window, and see the whole table in Datasheet view at the bottom of the window. This kind of form is helpful when you want to work with one record at a time and still see the big picture in the main table. In a split form, there are buttons on the Navigation bar to move only from record to record, and each record shown at the top is the record highlighted in the datasheet at the same time. You cannot highlight a different record in the form part and the datasheet part at the same time.

For this exercise, you will show the spa staff how to navigate the form frmMasterSchedule, which shows the schedule as a form and a datasheet in the same window.

A04.04

 To Navigate a Split Form

a. On the Navigation Pane, double-click **frmMasterSchedule** to open the form.

b. Click **Last record** ⏭ on the Navigation bar to highlight the last record in both the form and the datasheet.

c. Click the **record selector** in the datasheet with **Schedule ID S046**. The record will be highlighted in the datasheet and also be shown at the top in Form view.

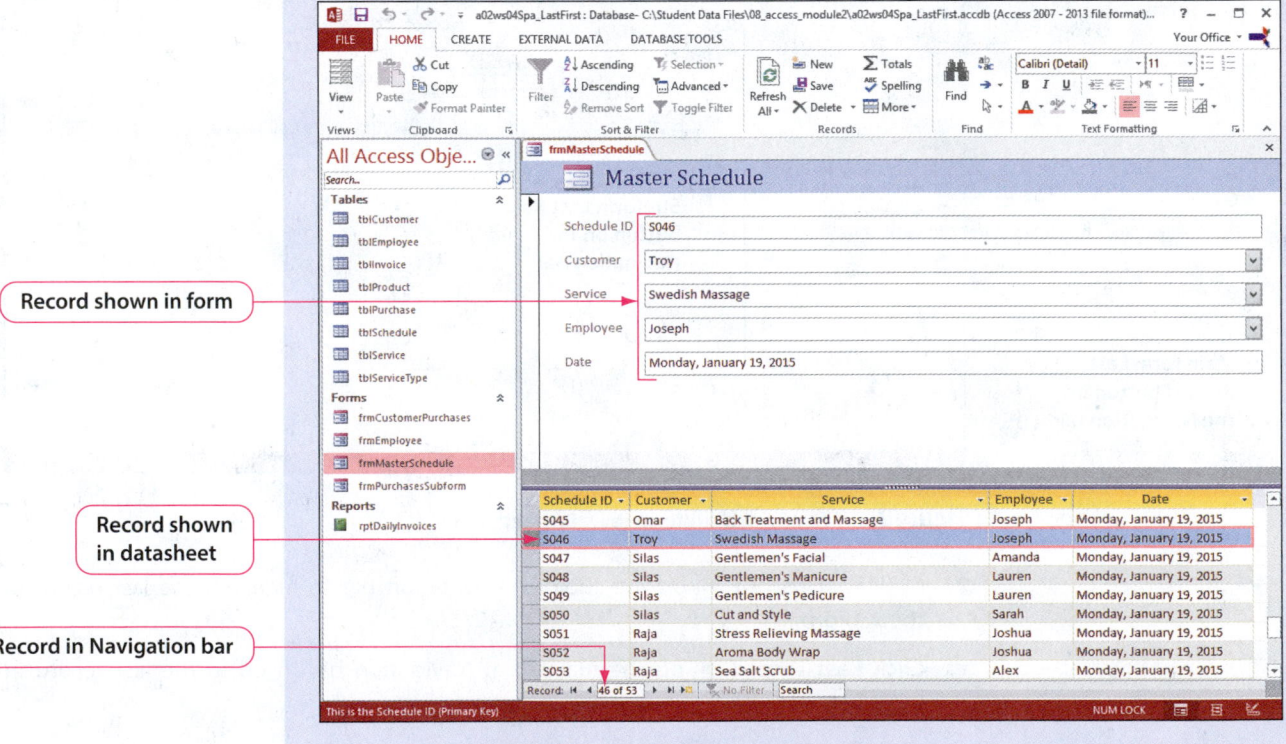

Figure 3 Navigating a split form

d. Close ✕ the form.

REAL WORLD ADVICE   Using Tabs

People have become accustomed to using tabs in browsers, and they tend to have many tabs open at one time. In fact, it makes work more efficient because you do not have to keep opening and closing those windows. Unfortunately, Access does not work the same way. Every time you open an object in Access it opens in a new window with a tab. Those tabs, however, do not work the same way as tabs in your browser. While websites can be updated when they are open in a tab on your desktop, Access objects cannot be updated when they are open. It is therefore a good idea to close an object when you are done working with it, and then reopen it again later when you need it.

Using the Find Command in a Form

Finding data in a form is similar to finding data in a datasheet—you use the Find command. Because you only see one record at a time with a form, using Find can be a quick way to find a record with a specific value in a field and prevents you from having to scroll through all the records in the table one at a time in Form view.

When you are looking for a specific value in a field, you are looking for an exact match. For this exercise, a staff member has asked you to search the employee table to find any employees who may live in Las Vegas so they can try to set up a carpool with them. You will show the staff member how to use a form to look for that information.

A04.05

 To Use the Find Command in a Form

a. On the Navigation Pane, double-click **frmEmployee** to open the form. Press Tab to move to the **City** field in the first record.

b. On the HOME tab, in the Find group, click **Find** to open the Find and Replace dialog box.

c. In the **Find What** box, type **Las Vegas**. Verify that the Look In text box is Current field, and then click **Find Next**.

Move the Find and Replace dialog box to see all the fields for the current record. The first record with Las Vegas as a value in the City field will be shown.

> **Troubleshooting**
>
> If you get the message that the search item was not found, make sure that you spelled "Las Vegas" correctly.

Las Vegas entered in box

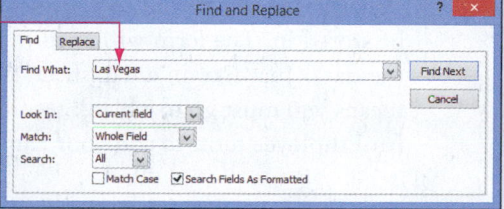

Figure 4   Find and Replace dialog box

d. Continue to click **Find Next** until Access gives you the message "Microsoft Access finished searching the records. The search item was not found." Click **OK**, and then click **Cancel** to close the Find and Replace dialog box.

Update Table Records Using Forms

Just as you can update data in a datasheet, you can also update data in a form. Remember, a form is just another way to view the data in the table, so when you see a record, you are seeing the record that is actually stored in the table. Nothing is actually stored in the form.

To make changes to data in a form, you must be viewing the form in Form view. You can also add a record to a table using the form. Using the Navigation bar, you can go directly to a new record.

QUICK REFERENCE	Updating Tables

Data can be edited in tables, queries, or forms. There are advantages and disadvantages to each method. The table below will help you decide the most appropriate place to edit data.

Method	Advantages	Disadvantages	Typical Situation to Use
Tables	All the records and fields are visible in the datasheet.	The number of records and/or fields in the datasheet can be overwhelming.	A user familiar with Access needs to add a record quickly to a smaller table.
Queries	There may be fewer records and/or fields in the datasheet making the data more manageable. A form can be based on a query rather than a table.	Not being able to see all the records and/or fields, you may inadvertently change related data in the fields you can see. Not all queries are editable, such as aggregate queries.	A user familiar with Access needs to see and modify appointments booked for a particular day.
Forms	Being able to view one record at a time can make the data seem more manageable.	Not all fields may be included in a form. If fields are missing, some data may mistakenly be left out of a record. Provides view of only one record at a time.	A user unfamiliar with Access needs to add data to a large table with many records.

Adding Records

When you add a record to a form, you are actually adding the record to the table it will be stored in. The form will open in Form view, which is the view that allows you to edit the data. Just like in a datasheet, new records are added at the end of the table, which means you must go to a blank record to enter new data. For this exercise, you will use the frmEmployee form to add your name to the list of employees in the tblEmployee table.

A04.06

To Add a New Record in a Form

a. On the Navigation bar, click **New (blank) record** 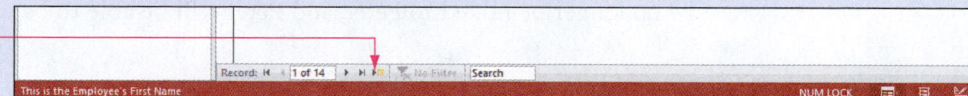.

New (blank)
record button

Record: ◄ ◄ 1 of 14 ► ►I ►⋇   No Filter   Search

This is the Employee's First Name   NUM LOCK

Figure 5   frmEmployee Navigation bar

b. Type your first name, last name, address, city, state, and phone in the new record.
Close ✕ the form.

c. On the Navigation Pane, double-click **tblEmployee** to open the table, and then click
Last record ►I to see that your record was added. **Close** ✕ the table.

Editing Records

When you edit a record in a form, you are actually editing the record in the table it is
stored in. Changes to data are saved automatically but can be undone while the table or
form is open by using the Undo button ↩ or by pressing Esc just after the change is
made while still in Edit mode.

For this exercise, you are asked to update the tblEmployee table with recent changes.
Mary Murphy has recently changed her phone number, but it has not been changed in
the table yet. You will show the staff how to find her record using a form and update her
phone number.

A04.07

To Edit Records Using a Form

a. On the Navigation Pane, double-click **frmEmployee** to open the form. Press Tab to
move to the **Last Name** field. On the HOME tab, in the Find group, click **Find** and then in
the **Find What** box, type Murphy. Click **Find Next**.

b. When the record for Mary Murphy is displayed, click **Cancel** to close the Find and Replace
dialog box, and then press Tab to move to the **Phone** field. Change Mary's phone number to 5055551289.

c. **Close** ✕ the form.

Deleting Records

Records can be deleted from a single table without additional steps if the table is not
part of a relationship. If the table is part of a relationship, referential integrity has been
enforced, and the cascade delete option has not been chosen, a record cannot be deleted
if there are related records in another table until those records have also been deleted.
For example, if you want to delete a customer from tblCustomer, and that customer has
appointments in tblSchedule, then the appointments for the customer have to be deleted
from the tblSchedule before the customer can be deleted from the tblCustomer. This
prevents leaving a customer scheduled in one table without the corresponding customer
information in another table.

For this exercise, the spa manager would like you to remove Peter Klein from tblEmployee because he has taken a new job and is leaving the spa. You explain to her that if he has any appointments scheduled in tblSchedule that those will have to be removed first. She tells you that rather than removing those records she would like to give those appointments to Alex instead. By changing the name to Alex, those appointments will no longer be linked to Peter, and Peter will be able to be deleted from tblEmployee.

 CONSIDER THIS | **Delete with Caution**

Deleting records in a table is permanent. Once you confirm a deletion, you cannot use the Undo button. This is very different than programs like Excel or Word. Can you think of ways you could safeguard your data from accidental deletion?

A04.08

 To Delete a Record with a Form

a. On the Navigation Pane, double-click **frmEmployee** to open the form. In the **Find** group, click **Find**, and then in the Find What box type Peter. Click **Find Next**, and then click **Cancel** to close the Find and Replace dialog box.

b. On the HOME tab, in the Records group, click the **Delete** arrow, and then click **Delete Record**. Access displays a message saying, "The record cannot be deleted or changed because table 'tblSchedule' included related records." Click **OK**.

> **Troubleshooting**
>
> If Access blanks out the First Name field, you chose Delete rather than Delete Record. Press Esc to undo the deletion, and then choose Delete Record.

c. On the Navigation Pane, double-click **tblSchedule** to open the table. Press Tab to move to the Employee field for the first record. Click the arrow next to **Peter**, and then click **Alex**.

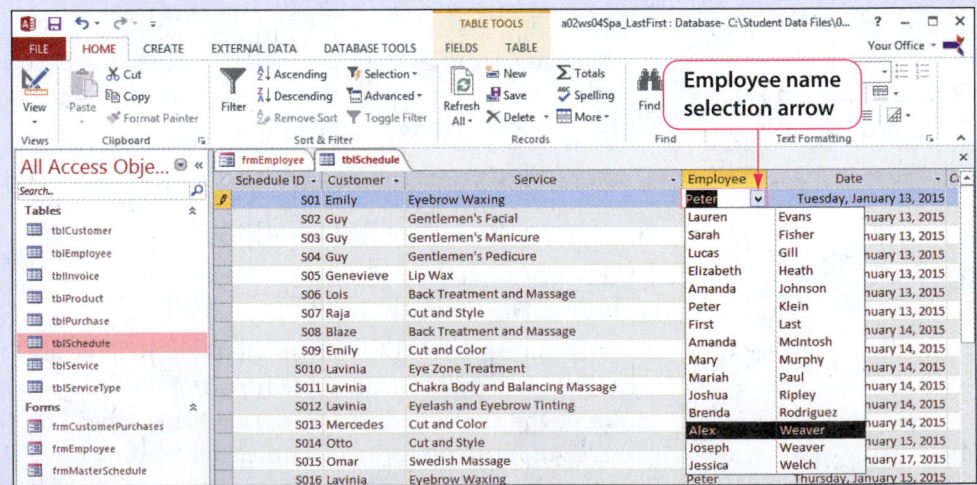

Figure 6 Replacing employee name using the selection arrow

d. On the HOME tab, in the Find group, click **Find**, and then in the **Find What** box, type Peter. Click **Find Next**. Click the **arrow** next to the name, and then click **Alex**. Click **Find Next**, and then repeat for all three records that have **Peter** listed as the Employee. Click **Cancel** to close the Find and Replace box.

e. **Close** ☒ the table. On the form, make sure the record showing is for **Peter**. On the HOME tab, in the Records group, click the **Delete** arrow, and then select **Delete Record**. Click **Yes** to confirm the deletion.

f. **Close** ☒ the form.

Create a Form Using the Form Wizard

Recall that the Query Wizard walks you through the steps in order to create a query, asking you questions and using your answers to build a query that you can then make changes to if necessary. The Form Wizard works in a similar fashion, walking you through step-by-step to create a form from one or more tables in your database.

Unlike creating a simple form using the Form button on the Create tab, when you create a form using the wizard, it opens automatically in Form view ready for you to enter or edit your records. To make changes to the form, you have to switch to either Layout view or Design view.

Exploring Form Views

Form view is only for viewing and changing data, so to make any changes to the form you need to switch to either Layout view or Design view. Layout view allows you to make changes to the form while viewing the data at the same time. The effects of your changes can be viewed right away. Design view is a more advanced view that allows you to change the properties or structure of the form. Data is not shown while you are in Design view.

Both Layout view and Design view work with controls, as shown in Figure 7. A **control** is a part of a form or report that you use to enter, edit, or display data. There are three major kinds of controls: bound, unbound, and calculated. A **bound control** is a control whose data source is a field in the table such as the customer name. An **unbound control** is a control that does not have a source of data such as the title of the form. A **calculated control** is a control whose data source is a calculated expression that you create. Every field from the table is made up of two controls: a label and a text box. A **label control** may be the name of the field or some other text you manually enter and is an unbound control. A **text box control** represents the actual value of a field and is a bound control. When you add a text box to a form, the label is automatically added as well. However, a label can be added independently from a text box.

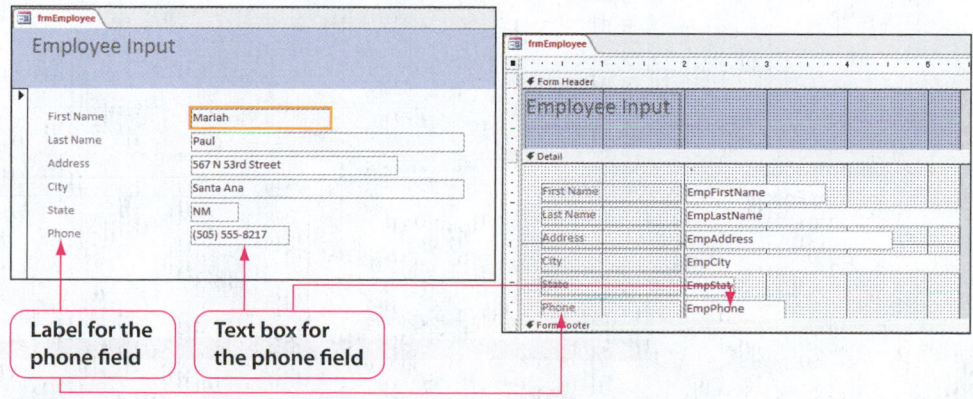

Figure 7 Text box and label controls in Layout view and Design view

For this exercise, the manager of the spa wants the staff to be able to enter and update customer information easily. She thinks it would be much easier to enter data in a form rather than in Datasheet view. You agree with her and offer to help set up the form.

A04.09

To Create a Single-Table Form in Design View

a. Click the **CREATE** tab, and then in the Forms group, click **Form Wizard**. The Form Wizard dialog box opens.

b. Click the **Table/Queries** arrow, and select **Table: tblCustomer**. Click the **All Fields** button `>>` to add all the available fields to the Selected Fields box, and then click **Next**.

c. Verify that **Columnar** is selected as the form layout, and then click **Next**.

d. Under **"What title do you want for your form?"** type frmCustomerInput_initialLastname using your first initial and last name. Verify that the **Open the form to view or enter information** option is selected, and then click **Finish**.

The form opens in Form view so you can immediately start adding or editing records. The form name is also displayed in the Navigation Pane under forms.

e. Switch to **Design** view. Notice the Form Footer at the bottom of the form window. On the DESIGN tab, in the Controls group, click **Label** `Aa`. Point to the Form Footer area, and then when your pointer changes to `⁺A`, drag your pointer to draw a label control about 2.5" wide in the top-left corner of the Form Footer section. In the new label, type **Created by initial Lastname** using your first initial and last name.

SIDE NOTE
Alternative Methods to Expand Footer
You can expand the footer and then add the label or you can add the label and the footer will automatically expand to fit what you add.

> **Troubleshooting**
> If the Field List pane opens, close it.

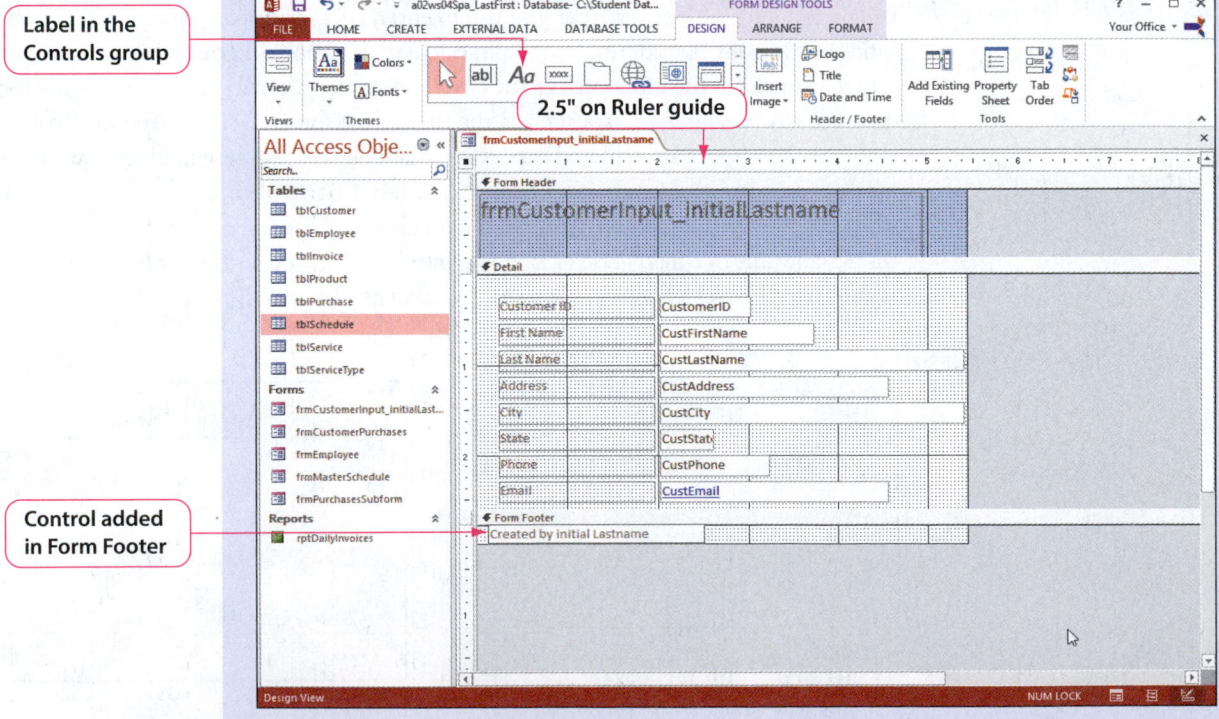

Label in the Controls group

2.5" on Ruler guide

Control added in Form Footer

Figure 8   Form in Design view

f. Switch to **Form** view. Verify that your label has been entered in the bottom-left corner of the form.

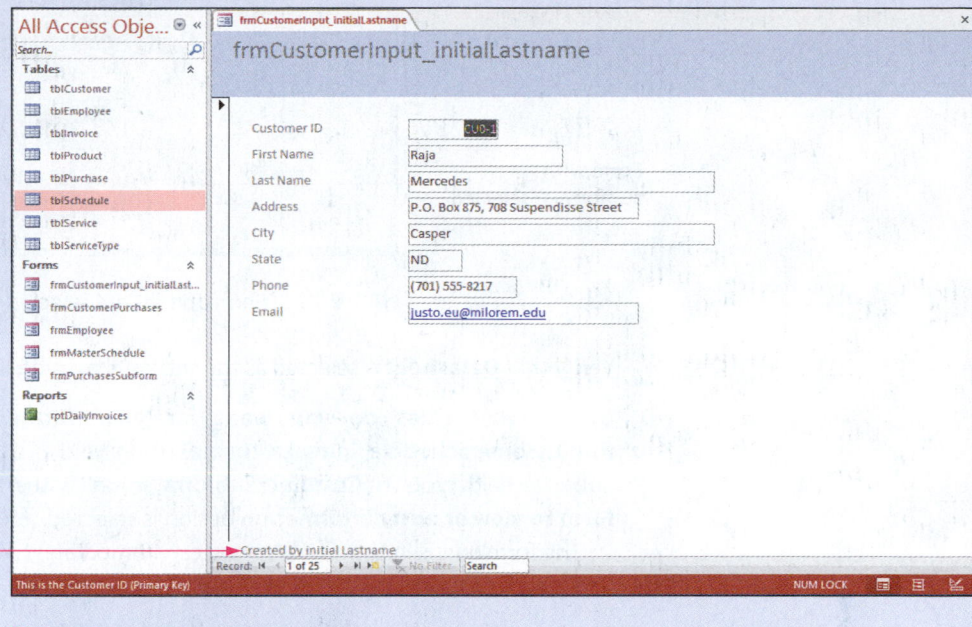

Label added in
Form Footer

Figure 9   Form with footer added

g. **Close** ✕ the form, and then click **Yes** to save the changes.

Creating Subforms (Multiple-Table Forms)

There may be times when you want to create a form using two tables. Before you can use two tables in a form, you must make sure there is a one-to-many relationship between the tables. Access will automatically use the common field between the tables to create the form.

The main form will display the first table one record at a time just like a single-table form. This is the "one" record in the one-to-many relationship. The subform will be displayed as a datasheet below the main form record. This will display the "many" records in the one-to-many relationship.

For this project, you will help the staff create another form that shows each customer in the main form and the customer's scheduled appointments in the subform.

A04.10

 To Create a Subform

a. Click the **CREATE** tab, and then in the Forms group, click **Form Wizard**. The Form Wizard dialog box opens.

b. Click the **Table/Queries** arrow, and then select **Table: tblCustomer**. Click the **All Fields** button ⟩⟩ to add all the available fields to the Selected Fields list.

c. Click the **Tables/Queries** arrow, and then select **Table: tblSchedule**. Click the **All Fields** button ⟩⟩ to add all the available fields to the Selected Fields list, and then click **Next**.

d. Verify that **by tblCustomer** is selected and that **Form with subform(s)** is selected, and then click **Next**.

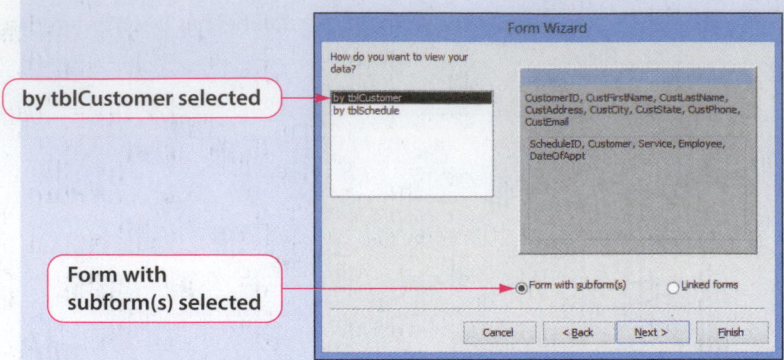

by tblCustomer selected

Form with subform(s) selected

Figure 10   Form options are selected

e. Verify that **Datasheet** is selected as the subform layout, and then click **Next**.

f. Under **What titles do you want for your forms?** in the Form field, type frmCustomerSchedule_initialLastname, using your first initial and last name. In the Subform field, type frmCustomerSubform_initialLastname. Verify that the **Open the form to view or enter information** option is selected, and then click **Finish**.

   The form opens in Form view so you can immediately start adding or editing records. The form and subform names are shown in the Navigation Pane.

g. Switch to **Design** view. Scroll to the bottom of the form to see the Form Footer at the base of the main form. On the DESIGN tab, in the Controls group, click **Label** Aa. When your pointer changes to ^+A, drag your pointer to draw a label control about 2.5" wide in the top-left corner of the Form Footer section. In the new label, type Created by initial Lastname using your initial and last name.

> **Troubleshooting**
>
> If the Field List pane shows and blocks parts of the form you need to see, close the Field List pane.

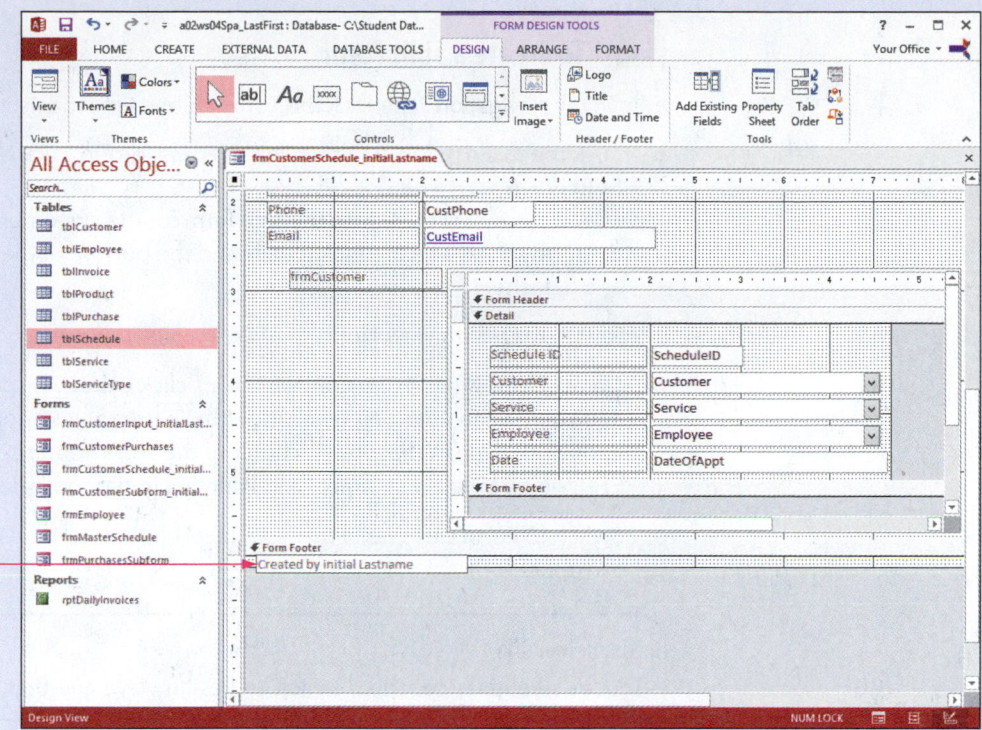

Label added to Form Footer of main form

Figure 11 Add footer to main form

h. Switch to **Form** view. Verify that your label has been entered in the bottom-left corner of the form.

i. **Close** ☒ the form, and then click **Yes** to save the changes.

SS **CONSIDER THIS** | **Include the Subform?**

When two tables are in a one-to-many relationship and you use the Form button to create a form for the table on the "one" side of the relationship, the wizard automatically adds a subform for the table on the "many" side. If you create the form using Form Wizard, you can choose whether to include the subform. When would you want to include the subform? When would you not want to include the subform?

Creating a Split Form

A split form is created from one table and displays each record individually at the top of the window and then again as part of the whole table datasheet in the bottom of the window. This type of form gives you the advantage of seeing each record and the whole table in one place.

For this exercise, the manager would like to see each customer's record individually along with all the records from the customer table. You will show her how to create a split form from the customer table.

A04.11

To Create a Split Form

a. On the Navigation Pane, click **tblCustomer** one time to select the table, but do not open it.

b. Click the **CREATE** tab, and then in the Forms group, click **More Forms**, and then select **Split Form**.

A window will open with the split form for the customer table. Notice that the top of the form shows a record individually and the bottom of the form shows the whole table as a datasheet.

c. Switch to **Design** view. Notice that Design view shows only the top of the split form.

d. On the DESIGN tab, in the Controls group, click **Label** $\boxed{Aa}$, point to the Form Footer area, and then when your pointer changes to $\boxed{^+A}$, drag your pointer to draw a label control about 2.5" wide in the top-left corner of the Form Footer section. In the new label, type **Created by initial Lastname** using your first initial and last name.

e. Switch to **Form** view. Verify that your label has been entered in the bottom-left corner of the upper form.

> **Troubleshooting**
>
> If your label does not show, switch to Design view, and then switch back to Form view.

f. Click **Save** $\boxed{\boxminus}$ on the Quick Access Toolbar, under **Form Name** type **frmCustomerSplit_ initialLastname** using your first initial and last name, and then click **OK**. **Close** $\boxed{\times}$ the form.

Modify a Form's Design

While creating a form using the wizard is quick and efficient, there may be times you will want to change how the form looks or add things to the form after you have created it. Formatting, like colors and fonts, can easily be changed. Controls can also be added to a form to include additional fields or labels with text. Pictures and other objects can also be added to a form to make the form more visually appealing.

Oftentimes, forms are customized to match company or group color themes, or other forms and reports already created by a user. Customizing forms can make them more personal and sometimes easier to use.

Colors, font types, and font sizes are just a few of the formatting changes you can make to an existing form.

Changing the Form Theme

By default, Access uses the Office theme when you create a form using the Form Wizard. Even though there is not a step in the wizard to select a different theme, you can change it once the form has been created. A **theme** is a built-in combination of colors and fonts. By default, a theme will be applied to all objects in a database: forms, reports, tables, and queries. However, you can select to apply a theme to only the object you are working with or to all matching objects. You can also select a theme to be the default theme instead of Office.

Because the form is displayed in Form view, once it is created, the first step is to switch to Layout view to make changes to the form itself. Changing the theme will not only change the colors of the form but also the font type and size and any border colors or object colors added to the form. Once a theme is applied to the form, the colors and fonts can be changed independently of the theme, so you can combine the colors of one theme and a font of another.

For this exercise, the manager of the spa would like to make the customer input form look more like the colors in the spa. The resort has a set of themes that she wants to apply to the selected form.

You will show her how to change the theme and the fonts for the form. The theme will be applied to all objects is the database. The font change will be applied to this form only.

A04.12

To Change the Theme of a Form

a. On the Navigation Pane, double-click **frmCustomerInput_initialLastname** to open the form. Switch to **Layout** view.

b. On the DESIGN tab, in the Themes group, click **Themes** to open the Themes gallery. Click **Browse for Themes**, navigate to where you stored your data files, click **a02ws04Spa**, and then click **Open**. This applies the spa theme to all objects.

c. On the DESIGN tab, in the Themes group, click **Fonts**. Scroll down, right-click the Font theme **Corbel**, and then click **Apply Font Theme to This Object Only**.

d. Double-click the **form title**, select the existing **text**, which by default is the name of the form, and then type **Customer Input**. Press [Enter].

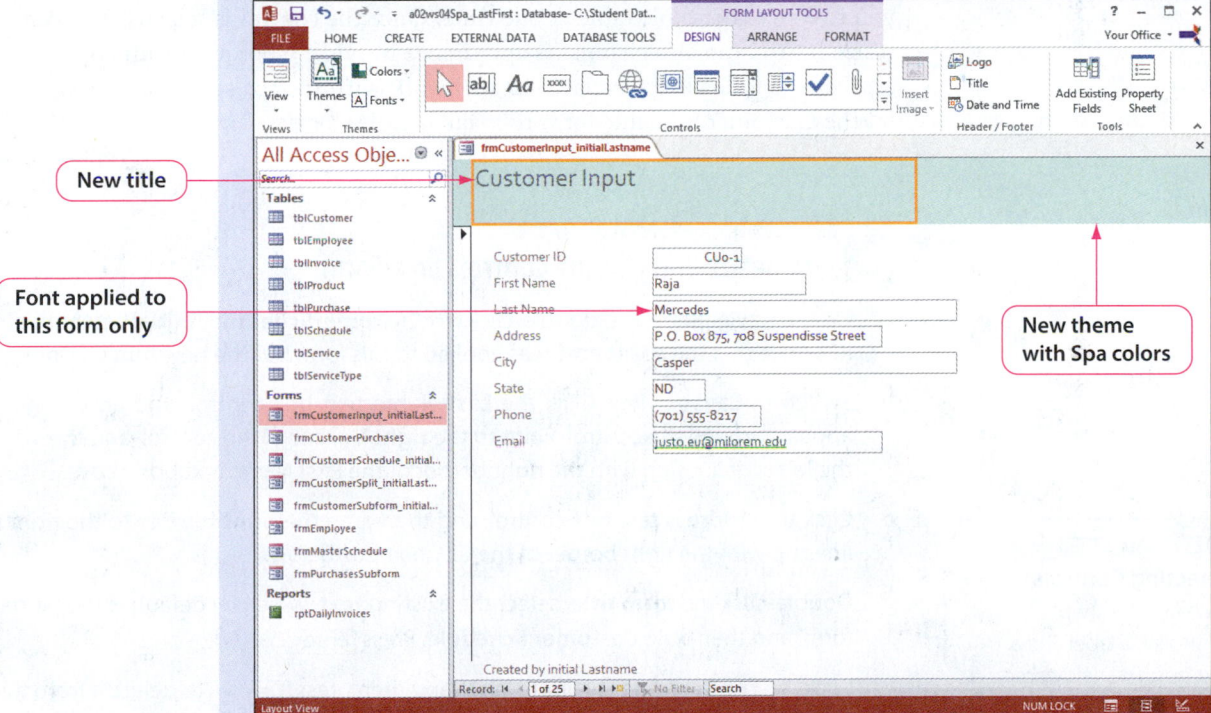

Figure 12 Form with theme, font, and title changed

e. Click **Save** 💾 on the Quick Access Toolbar to save the form. **Close** ✕ the form.

| REAL WORLD ADVICE | Saving Custom Themes |

By default, all themes are saved in the Document Themes folder (C:\Users\username\AppData\ Roaming\Microsoft\Templates\Document Themes). If you save a custom theme in the default folder, it will appear as a custom theme in the Themes gallery. If you save the theme in a different folder, you can select Browse for Themes and look for the saved theme in your Documents folder. You can change where you save the theme, but if another person wants to use that theme for one of their documents, they may not be able to find it if it is saved somewhere other than the default folder. One purpose of saving themes is to have them available for a unified look among various documents, and because you may not be the person creating all the documents, you may want to save the theme somewhere that everyone can find it.

Resizing and Changing Controls

Controls can be resized to make the form more user friendly. When you create a form using the wizard, the order that you choose the fields in the wizard step is the order the fields are added to the form. Once the form is created, you may decide the fields should be in a different order. When you click a control in Layout view, an orange border appears around the control. When you select a subform control, an orange border appears around the control and a layout selector appears in the top-left corner. The **layout selector** allows you to move the whole table at one time. Once the control is selected you can move it or resize it. You can also change its appearance by adding borders or fill color.

For the following exercise, you will work with the spa staff to rearrange the controls on the Customer Schedule form to make it easier for data entry.

A04.13

 To Resize and Change Controls on a Form

a. On the Navigation Pane, double-click **frmCustomerSchedule_initialLastname** to open it. Notice that the spa theme was applied to this form but the new font was not.

b. Switch to **Layout** view. Click the **Last Name** text box control, and an orange border appears around the control. Point to the **right border** of the control, and then drag it to the left so it lines up with the right border of the First Name text box above.

c. Click the **Address** text box control, and then drag the **right border** to the right until it lines up with the right border of the City text box below.

d. Double-click the **form title**, select the existing **text**, which by default is the name of the form, and then type Customer Schedule. Press Enter.

e. Click the **frmCustomer** subform label, and then press Delete to delete it from the form.

f. Use the AutoFit feature on each column of the subform to best fit the data. Use the scroll bar on the Navigation bar of the subform to scroll to the right to see all the fields. Drag the **left border** of the subform to the left so that all fields are visible without scrolling.

g. In the main form, click the **Customer ID** label control, press and hold Shift, and then click the **CustomerID** text box control to select both controls.

SIDE NOTE
Selecting Controls
Each field has two controls—a label and a text box. The field name shows in the label, while the field value shows in the text box.

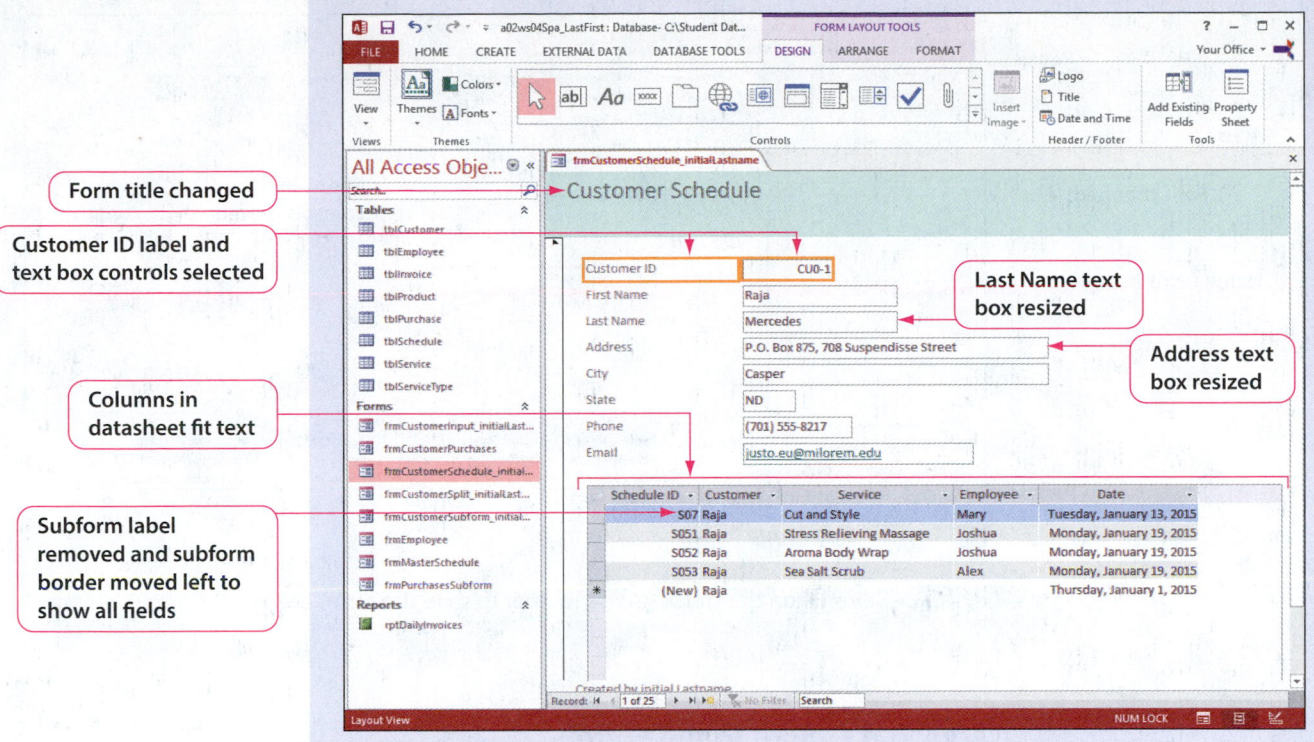

Form title changed

Customer ID label and text box controls selected

Columns in datasheet fit text

Subform label removed and subform border moved left to show all fields

Last Name text box resized

Address text box resized

Figure 13   Select both label and name control to delete

h. Press Delete to delete both controls from the form.

i. Click the **Phone** label, hold down Shift, and then click the **Phone** text box, the **Email** label, and the **Email** text box controls.

j. Point to any of the **selected controls**. When the pointer changes to ⊞, drag all four controls up and to the right until they are right next to the **First Name** and **Last Name** controls.

> **Troubleshooting**
>
> If when you release the pointer, the fields do not line up, repeat Step j, and then adjust the placement.

k. Click the **subform** datasheet to select it. Click the **Layout Selector** ⊞, and then drag it up and to the left so it is just under the State control.

l. Click the **title** of the form to select it. On the **HOME** tab, in the Text Formatting group, click **Bold** B, click the **Font size** arrow 11 ▾, and then select **28**.

m. Click the **First Name** text box control, hold down Shift, and then click the **Last Name** text box control. On the HOME tab, in the Text Formatting group, Click **Bold** B.

SIDE NOTE
Limited Visibility
If you cannot see the whole subform, use the scroll arrow on the right side of the window to scroll down the form.

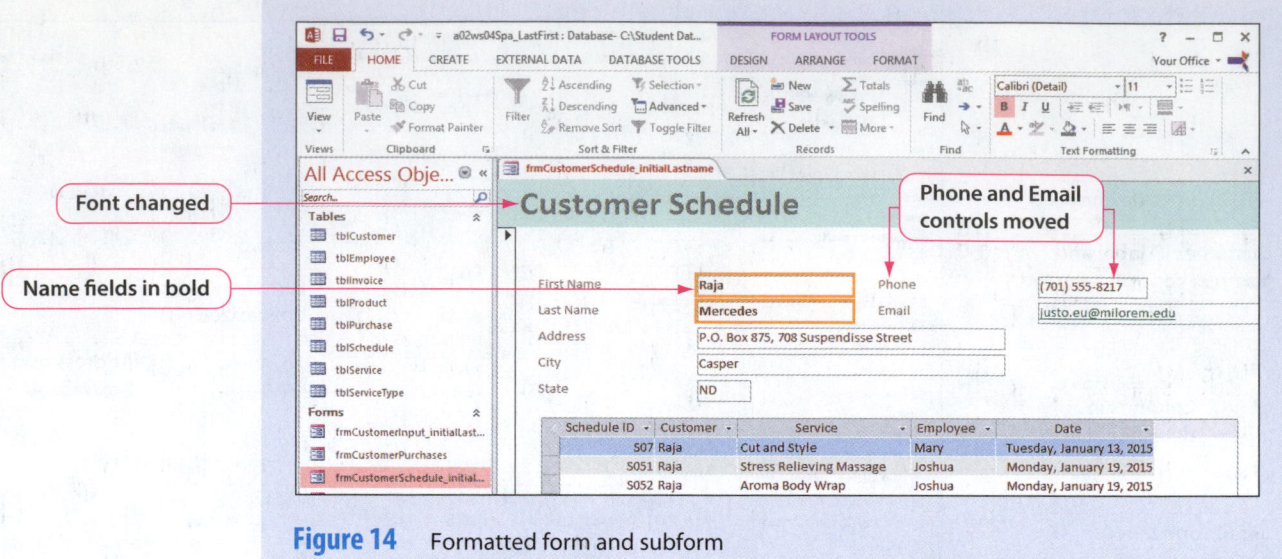

Figure 14   Formatted form and subform

n.   Click **Save** 💾 on the Quick Access Toolbar to save the form.

Adding a Picture to the Form

Pictures can be added to forms to make them more appealing. When a picture is added to a form, then the same picture will appear for every record in the table. A different picture cannot be added for each record. A picture can be inserted in the header, footer, or the Detail area of the form where the record values are shown. For this exercise you will insert the spa's logo in the Detail area of the form to make it more personal for the spa.

A04.14

   To Add a Picture on the Form

a.   Click in the **Detail area** of the form to select it. If a text box or label is selected, then the Insert Image button will not be available to use.

b.   On the DESIGN tab, in the Controls group, click **Insert Image**, and then click **Browse…**.

c.   In the Insert Picture dialog box, navigate to where your student files are located, click **a02ws04Spa,** and then click **OK**. With the image control pointer 🖼, click in the **form detail** to insert the picture. Move your pointer to the **top-left corner** of the picture until it becomes a diagonal resize pointer �. Drag the corner until the picture is small enough to fit under **Email** and above the subform.

d.   Click the **layout selector** ⊞ and move the picture under the **Email** text box. Use the diagonal resize pointer 🢢 to make the picture smaller until the picture fits between the **Email** text box and the subform.

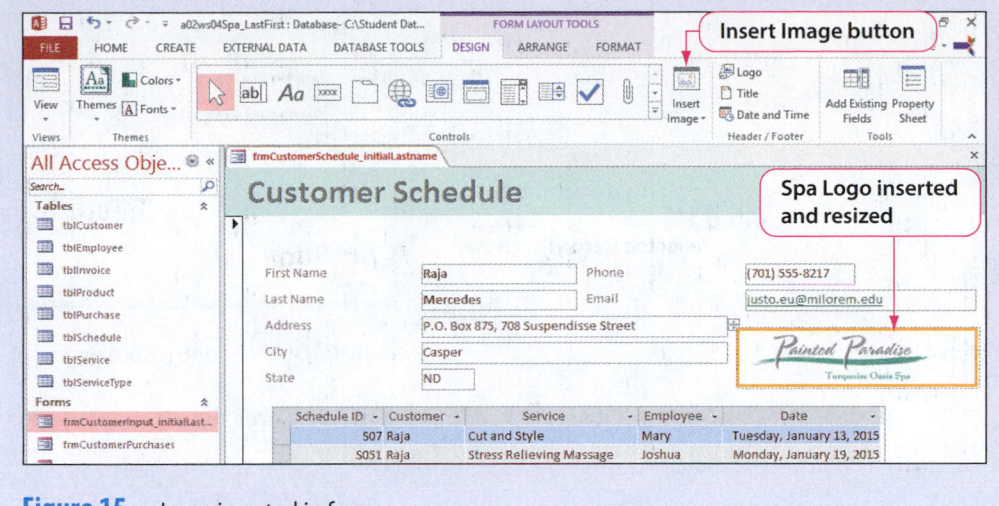

Figure 15 Logo inserted in form

e. **Close** ☒ the form, and then click **Yes** to save the changes.

Printing a Record from a Form

Not only can you see one record at a time using a form, but you can also print one record at a time. Printing a form can be useful if you need only one record's information, or if you want to use a form for other people to manually fill in the information.

For this project, the spa manager would like you to print a record for a particular customer from the customer form. You will show her how to preview the form first, select one record, and then send it to the printer.

A04.15

 To Preview and Print a Record from a Form

a. On the Navigation Pane, double-click **frmCustomerInput_initialLastname** to open it, and then switch to **Layout** view.

b. Click the **Address** text box control, and then drag the **right border** to the right until it is lined up with the Last Name and City text box controls.

c. Click the **FILE** tab, click **Print**, and then click **Print Preview**. Notice all the records will print in Form view.

d. Click **Last Page** ⏭ on the Navigation bar to go to the last record. Notice in the Navigation bar that the number of pages for the printed report will be seven.

e. On the PRINT PREVIEW tab, in the Close Preview group, click **Close Print Preview**.

f. Using the Navigation bar, advance through the customer records to find the record for **Jonah Hogan**.

g. Click the **FILE** tab, click **Print**, and then click **Print**. In the Print dialog box, in the Print Range section, click **Selected Record(s)**. Click **OK** to print the record if requested by your instructor.

   When you view all the records in Print Preview, you cannot choose Selected Record(s) in the Print dialog box. To choose Selected Record(s) you must have one record showing in Form view when you click Print.

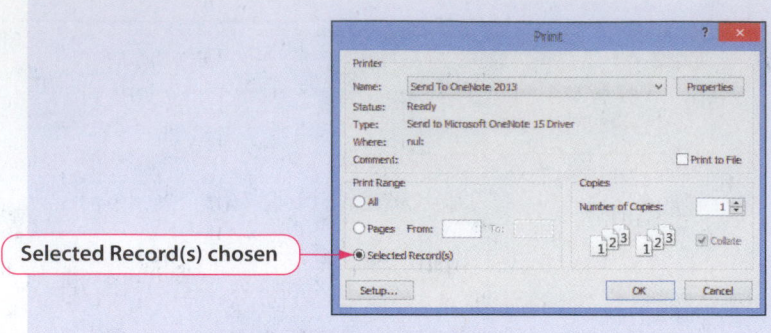

Selected Record(s) chosen

Figure 16   Print one record as a form

h. Close ☒ the form, and then click **Yes** to save the changes.

Creating Customized Reports

While a report and a form may look similar, a form is a method for data entry and a report is a formatted printout of that data. A report can be created from either a table or query. Reports may be based on multiple tables in a one-to-many relationship using a common field to match the records. The "one" record from the first table in the relationship will be shown first—similar to a main form, while the "many" records from the second table will be displayed as detailed records in the **subreport**—similar to a subform. In this section, you will create a report using the report wizard and then make changes to the report in design and layout views.

Create a Report Using the Report Wizard

The Report Wizard will walk you step by step through the process of building your report. You will choose the table or query to base the report on, and choose the fields to include in the report. You will have the option to group the data in your report. A **group** is a collection of records along with introductory and summary information about the records. Grouping allows you to separate related records for the purpose of creating a visual summary of the data. Groups can be created with data from individual tables or from multiple tables.

For example, a report grouped by the primary table containing customer records would show all the selected fields for a customer, and then would list that customer's individual appointments from the secondary table below the customer's record.

Within a report you can also sort using up to four fields in either ascending or descending order. Once a report is created using the wizard, it will open in Print Preview. Print Preview provides a view of the report representing how it will look when it is actually printed and provides you with printing options such as orientation, margins, and size. The current date and page numbers are added, and you can navigate the report in this view using the Navigation bar. To make any changes to the report, you can switch to Layout view.

Creating a Single-Table Report

A report can be created using one table or multiple tables. A single-table report is a report created from one table. Any or all of the fields can be selected, and the report can be created from a table or query.

For this project, the spa manager would like to have a report to help the staff with scheduling. The report will be a list of employee names and phone numbers so the staff can contact each other if necessary.

A04.16

 To Create a Single-Table Report Using Report Wizard

a. Click the **CREATE** tab, and then in the Reports group, click **Report Wizard**.

b. Click the **Tables/Queries** arrow, and then select **tblEmployee**.

c. Double-click **EmpFirstName**, **EmpLastName**, and **EmpPhone** from the Available Fields list. Click **Next**.

d. You will not add any grouping levels to this report, so click **Next**.

e. Click the **1 Sort** arrow, select **EmpLastName**, click the **2 Sort** arrow, select **EmpFirstName**, and then click **Next**.

f. Verify that **Tabular** layout and **Portrait** orientation are selected, as well as **Adjust the field width so all fields fit on a page**. Click **Next**.

g. Under **What title do you want for your report?**, type rptEmployeeList_initialLastname using your first initial and last name, and then click **Finish**.

h. Switch to **Design** view. If necessary, **close** [X] the Field List pane. On the REPORT DESIGN TOOLS DESIGN tab, in the Controls group, click **Label** [Aa], point to the **Report Footer** area, and then when your pointer changes to [⁺A], drag your pointer to draw a label control about 2.5" wide in the top-left corner of the Report Footer section. In the new label, type Created by initial Lastname using your first initial and last name.

> **Troubleshooting**
> If the Label control is not visible, in the Controls group, click the More button to display the gallery, and then click Label.

i. Switch to **Report** view. Verify that your label is fully shown in the bottom-left corner of the report.

j. Switch to **Layout** view. Double-click the **form title**, select the existing text, type Employee List and then press Enter.

In Layout view, you should also check that all the report column headers and data show fully. On this report they do, so there are no further changes necessary.

SIDE NOTE
Field Order
The order you add the fields in the Report Wizard is the order the fields will appear on the report.

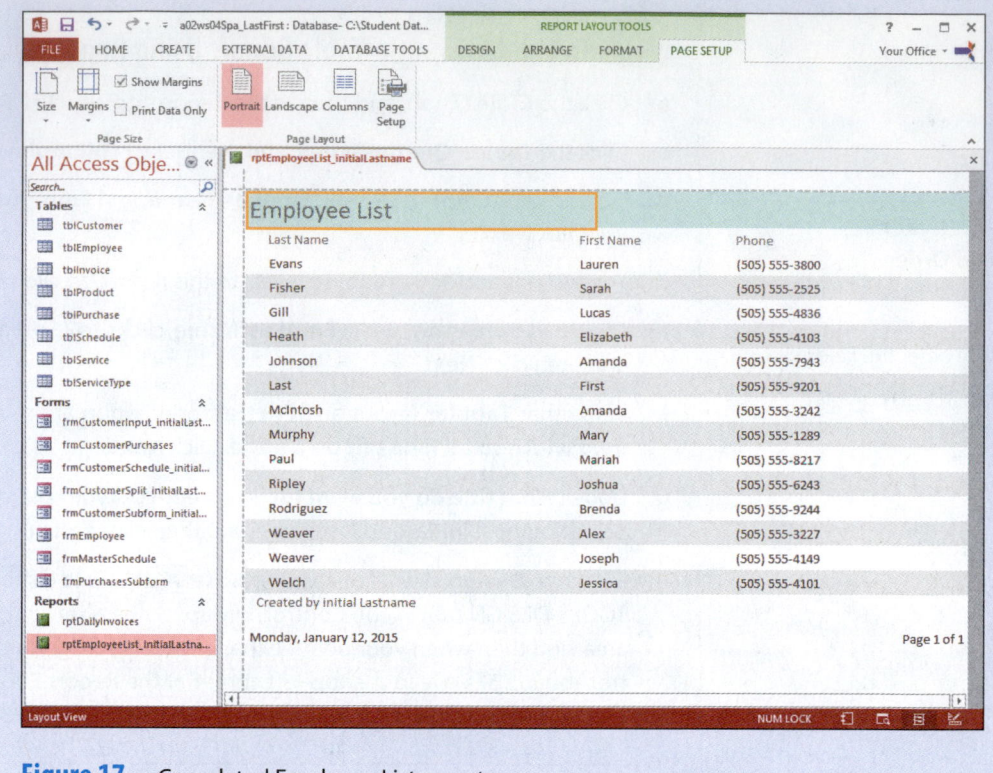

Figure 17 Completed Employee List report

k. **Close** ☒ the report, and then click **Yes** to save the changes.

Creating a Multiple-Table Report

Similar to other objects created using more than one table, a multiple-table report must use tables that have a common field. The first table chosen for the report becomes the primary table, and the next and subsequent tables chosen become the secondary tables.

An employee has a one-to-many relationship with scheduled appointments. Each employee may have more than one appointment, and each appointment is with just one employee. Thus tblEmployee will be the primary table, and tblSchedule will be a secondary table.

In this exercise, the manager would like a report that will show each employee name and their upcoming appointments. This way the staff members can help coordinate their services for a guest who may be seeing more than one staff member in a day.

A04.17

 To Create a Multiple-Table Report Using the Report Wizard

a. Click the **CREATE** tab, and then in the Reports group, click **Report Wizard**.

b. Click the **Tables/Queries** arrow, and then select **Table: tblEmployee**. Double-click **EmpFirstName** and **EmpLastName** in the Available Fields list.

c. Click the **Tables/Queries** arrow, and then select **Table: tblSchedule**. Double-click **Service**, **DateOfAppt**, and **Customer** from the Available Fields list, and then click **Next**.

d. Verify that **by tblEmployee** is highlighted to view the data by Employee, and then click **Next**. Notice that Access defaults to viewing the data by primary table, tblEmployee.

e. Double-click **DateOfAppt** to group by the date. Click **Grouping Options...**, click the **Grouping intervals** arrow, select **Normal**, and then click **OK**.

Access defaults to grouping dates by Month. Normal groups by date value.

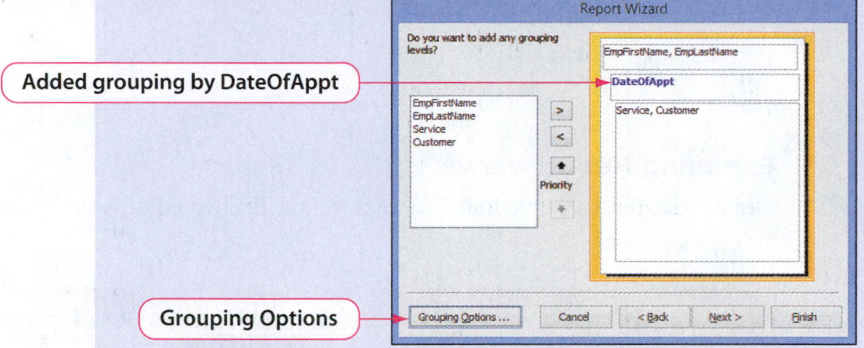

Added grouping by DateOfAppt

Grouping Options

Figure 18   Report Wizard grouping step

f. Click **Next**.

g. Click the **1 Sort** arrow, select **Customer**, and then click **Next**.

h. Verify that **Stepped** is selected under Layout, and then under Orientation, click **Landscape**. Verify that **Adjust the field width so all fields fit on a page** is checked. Click **Next**.

i. Under **What title do you want for your report?**, type **rptEmployeeSchedule_ initialLastname**, using your first initial and last name, and then click **Finish**. The report will open in Print Preview.

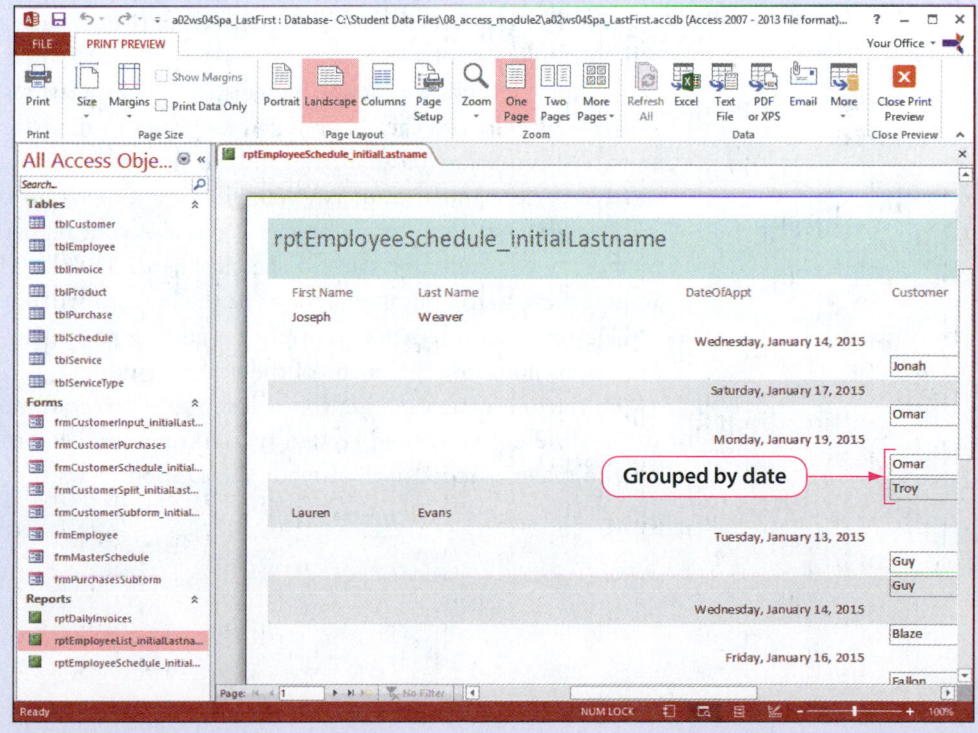

Grouped by date

Figure 19   Report in Print Preview

Notice that the appointments are grouped by date. Your date column may not be wide enough to see the dates, but you will fix that in Layout view. Additionally, notice that in Print Preview view, at the bottom of each page of the report is today's date and the page number.

j. Click **Close Print Preview**.

Exploring Report Views

Recall that reports have four different views. Each type of view has its own features.

QUICK REFERENCE	Different View Options for a Report
View Name	**What the View Is Used For**
Print Preview	Shows what the printed report will look like
Layout view	Allows you to modify the report while seeing the data
Report view	Allows you to filter data or copy parts of the report to the Clipboard
Design view	Allows you to change more details of the report design or add other controls that are only available in Design view

When the Report Wizard is done creating the report, it shows you the report in Print Preview, which is the view that shows you exactly what the report will look like when it is printed. Print Preview adds the current date and page numbers in the page footer at the bottom of each page.

Layout view allows you to change basic design features of the report while the report is displaying data so the changes you make are immediately visible. You can resize controls, add conditional formatting, and change or add titles and other objects to the report in Layout view. In this exercise, you will view a report in Layout view.

Report view provides an interactive view of your report. In Report view, you can filter records or you can copy data to the clipboard. There will be no page breaks shown in Report view so the number of pages at the bottom will show Page 1 of 1.

Design view offers more options for adding and editing controls on a report, as well as options not available in any of the other views.

In the following exercise, you will show the spa staff members what a report looks like in the different views and how to switch from one view to another. You will show them how to make changes in the Layout and Design views.

A04.18

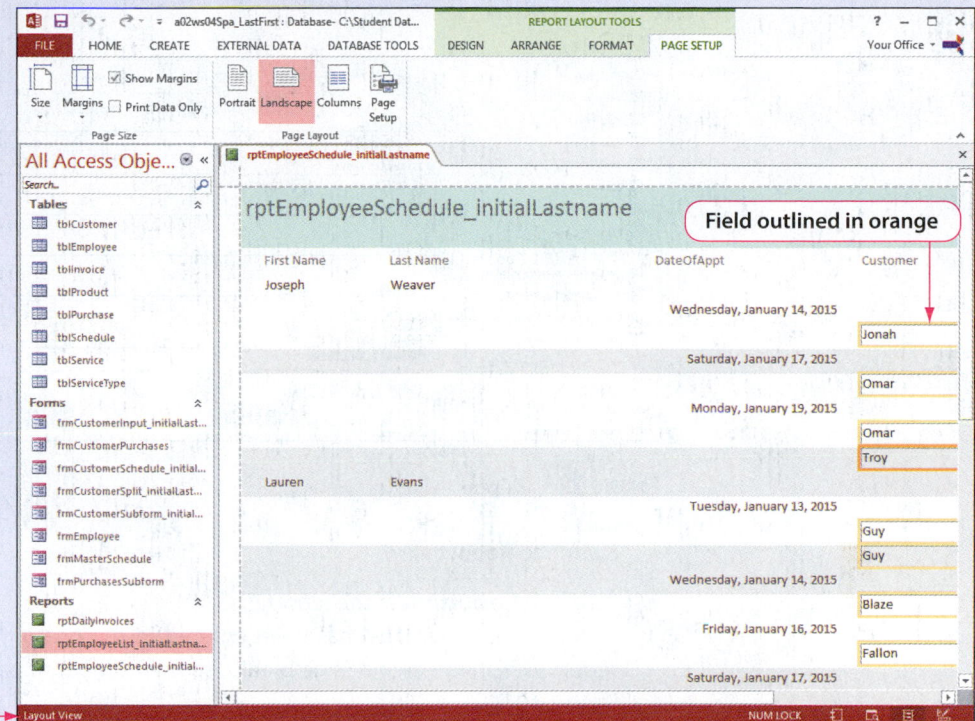

To Explore Report Views

a. Switch to **Layout** view.

Figure 20 Report in Layout view

Notice the orange border around the first Customer field. Customer is the active field. You can make changes such as making a column wider in Layout view.

b. If your dates are not visible, click the **DateOfAppt** column header, press and hold ⇧Shift, and then click the **DateOfAppt** text box. Use your pointer to drag the left border of the column to the left so that the date is fully shown.

c. Scroll to the **bottom right** of the report.

Notice there is the date and page number in the page footer, but the page number shows page 1 of 1. The actual number of pages will not be calculated until you switch to Print Preview.

d. Switch to **Design** view. Data in Design view is not visible, only the controls in each section of the report are.

e. On the DESIGN tab, in the Controls group, click **Label** $\boxed{Aa}$, point to the Report Footer area, and then when your pointer changes to $\boxed{^+A}$, drag your pointer to draw a label control about 2.5" wide in the top-left corner of the Report Footer section. In the new label, type **Created by initial Lastname** using your first initial and last name.

SIDE NOTE
Two Footers

Be sure to put your label in the Report Footer, not the Page Footer.

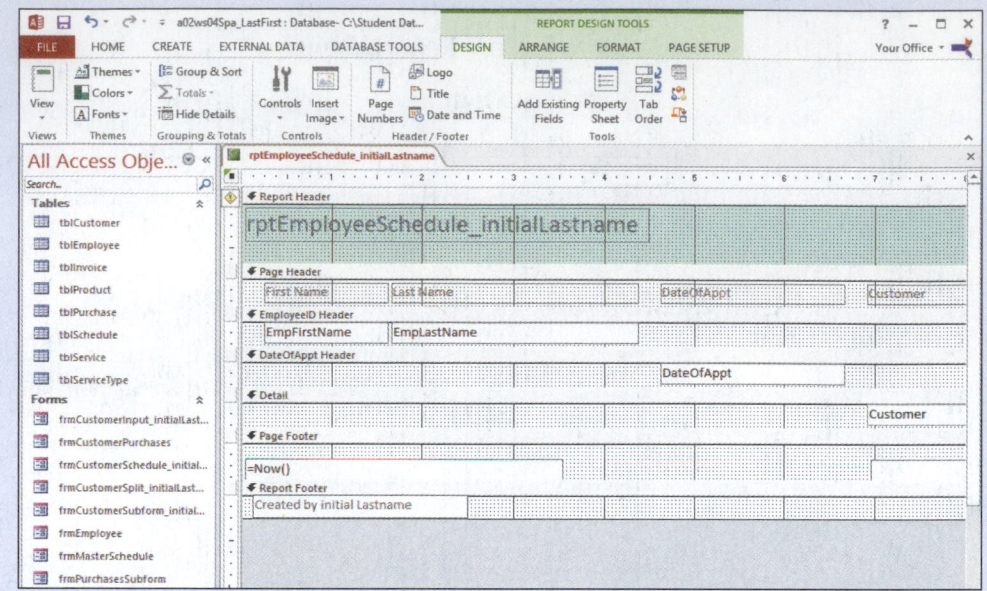

Figure 21   Report in Design view

f. Switch to **Report** view.

g. Scroll to the **bottom** of the report.

Verify that your label has been entered in the bottom-left corner of the report. In report view, there are no page breaks, so the number of pages at the bottom will show Page 1 of 1.

h. **Save** and **close** ☒ your report.

Creating Totals Using the Report Wizard

When you report on numeric data, you have the option to ask Access to calculate sums, averages, minimums, and maximums of the numeric data. The **grand total** calculates the total for all records. **Subtotals** calculate totals for smaller groups of records. In this exercise, you will use the wizard to request these totals. Later, you will add totals to an already created report.

The spa manager asks you to create a report showing the invoices collected each day. You will show her how to provide a daily total as well as a grand total using the Report Wizard.

A04.19

▶ **To Create Report Totals Using the Report Wizard**

a. Click the **CREATE** tab, and then in the Reports group, click **Report Wizard**.

b. Click the **Tables/Queries** arrow, and then select **Table: tblInvoice**. Double-click **InvoiceDate** and **InvoiceTotal** in the Available Fields list. Click **Next**.

c. Double-click **InvoiceDate** to group by the date. Click **Grouping Options…**, click the **Grouping intervals** arrow, and select **Day**.

d. Click **OK**, and then click **Next**.

e. Click the **1 Sort** arrow, and then select **InvoiceDate**.

f. Click **Summary Options...**, and then click the **Sum** check box.

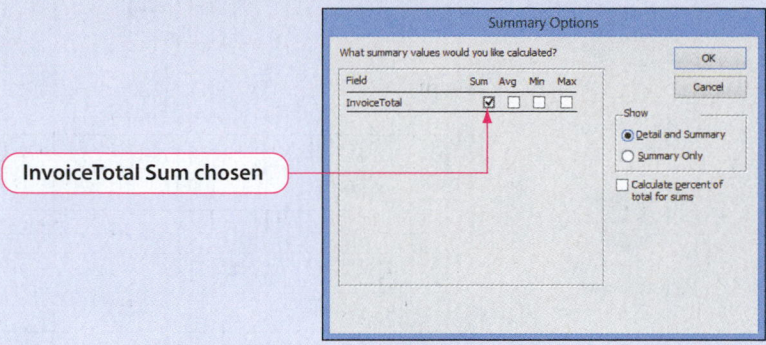

Figure 22 Report Summary Options

g. Click **OK**, and then click **Next**. Verify that **Stepped** and **Portrait** are selected, and then click **Next**.

h. Under **What title do you want for your report?**, type **rptInvoiceTotals_initialLastname**, using your first initial and last name, and then click **Finish**. The report will open in Print Preview. If necessary, scroll down to see the grand total.

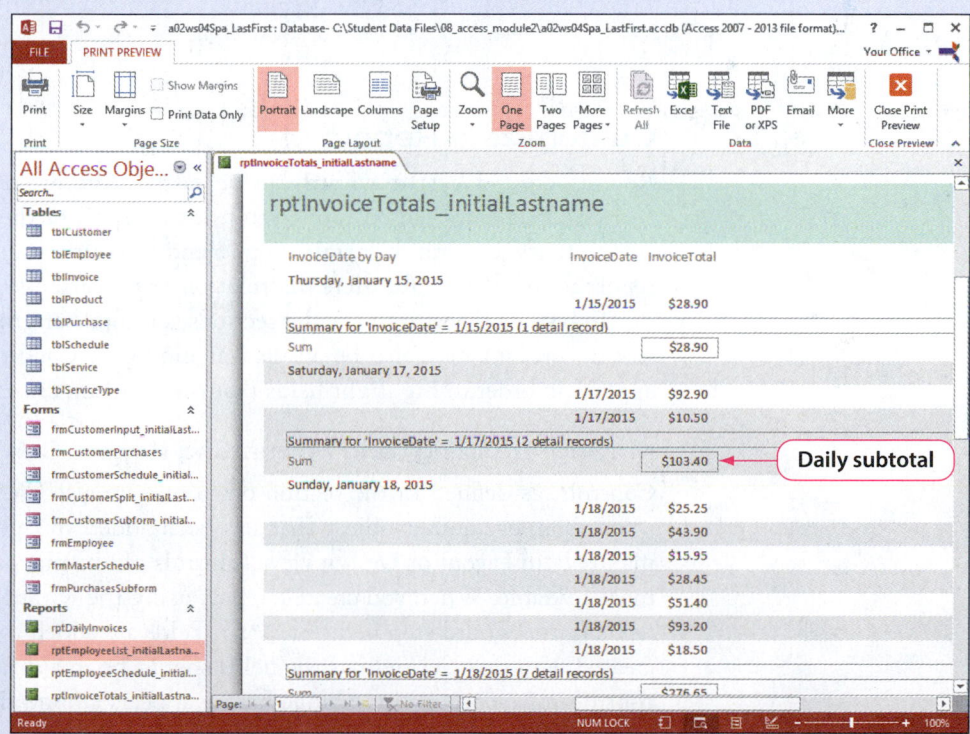

Figure 23 Report with daily subtotals and a grand total

Notice that there is a sum for each day and a grand total of all invoices for all days.

i. Switch to **Design** view. There is a new footer for InvoiceDate where the sum for each day is shown. There is also a Report Footer where the GrandTotal is shown.

j. On the DESIGN tab, in the Controls group, select **Label** Aa, move your pointer to the **Report Footer** just below the existing **Grand Total** label, and then when your pointer changes to ^+A, drag your pointer to draw a label control about 2.5" wide in the Report Footer section. In the new label, type **Created by initial Lastname** using your first initial and last name.

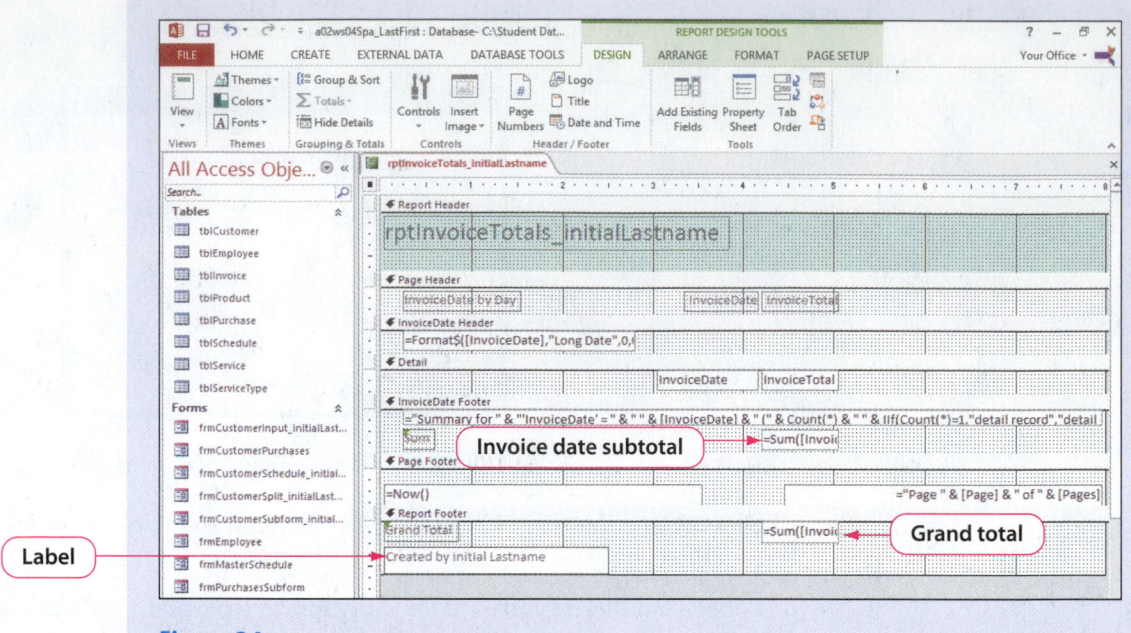

Figure 24 Design view of totals

k. Switch to **Print Preview** to check your label. **Save** and **close** your report.

Customize a Report

Reports created by the wizard can be easily customized after they have been created and saved. Themes can be applied to just the report or the whole database to change the colors, fonts, or both. Controls, bound and unbound, can be added or modified on the report to make room for more information or to rearrange the information already there.

To break a report into smaller sections, subtotals or groups may be added. Additional sorting options may also be applied or modified. Conditional formatting may also be applied in order to highlight fields that meet certain criteria.

Moving, Resizing, and Formatting Report Controls

Controls, as defined in the section on forms, are also used in reports. A control can be a text box, or another object that has been added to the form either by the wizard or manually in Layout or Design view. Controls can be moved or resized to make the report more readable. When you create a report using the wizard, the order that you choose the fields in the wizard step is the order the fields are added to the report. Once the report is created, you may decide that the fields should be in a different order. When you click a control in Layout view, an orange border appears around the control. Once the control is selected you can move it or resize it. You can also change its appearance by adding borders or fill color.

For this exercise, you will change the rptEmployeeSchedule schedule report to make it look more like what the manager expected. You will move the date, service, and customer name fields below the employee name, change the heading, and change the formatting to match the resort theme.

To Move, Resize, and Format a Report Control

a. On the Navigation Pane, right-click **rptEmployeeSchedule_initialLastname**, and then click **Layout View**.

b. Click the **DateOfAppt** text box control to select it, and then drag the field to the left so it is just slightly indented under the employee first name.

c. Click the **First Name** label control—the column header, press and hold ⇧Shift, click the **Last Name** and the **DateofAppt** label controls, and then press ⌦Delete.

d. Click the **Customer** label control, press and hold ⇧Shift, and then click the **Customer** text box, the **Service** label, and the **Service** text box controls. Point to and click any field to drag all the controls to the left, just next to the date field.

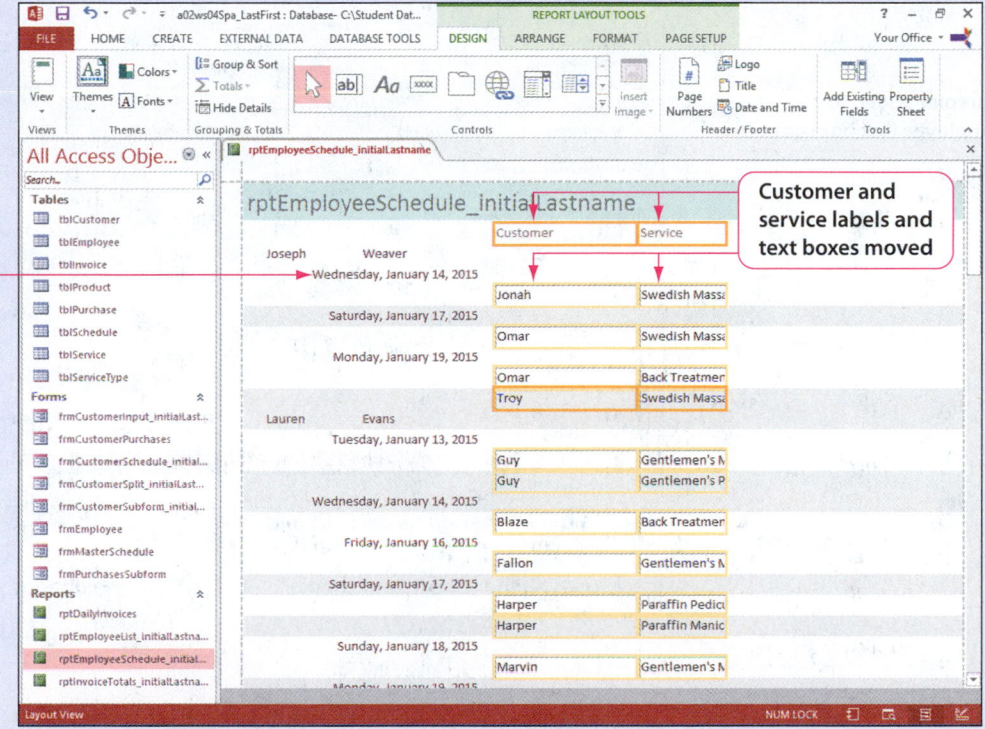

Figure 25 Fields moved

> **Troubleshooting**
> If you drag the controls too far to the left, reselect them, and then drag them back to the right.

e. Click the **Service** text box control. Drag the **right border** of the box to the right to fit all the service description. Scroll down to check **Chakra Body and Balancing Massage** to make sure the description is fully shown. If not, drag the border to make the field wider.

f. Scroll up, click the **Service** label control, and then press ⌦Delete.

g. Click the **Service** text box control, press and hold ⇧Shift, and then click the **Customer** text box control. On the FORMAT tab, in the Control Formatting group, click **Shape Outline**, and then select **Transparent**.

MODULE 2

h. Click the employee's **First Name** text box control, press and hold Shift, and then click the **Last Name** text box control. On the FORMAT tab, in the Control Formatting group, click **Shape Fill**, and then select **Dark Teal Accent 2 Lighter 80%** in the second row of the sixth column under Theme colors. In the Font group, click **Bold** B.

i. Double-click the **title**, select the **text**, type Employee Schedule, and then press Enter.

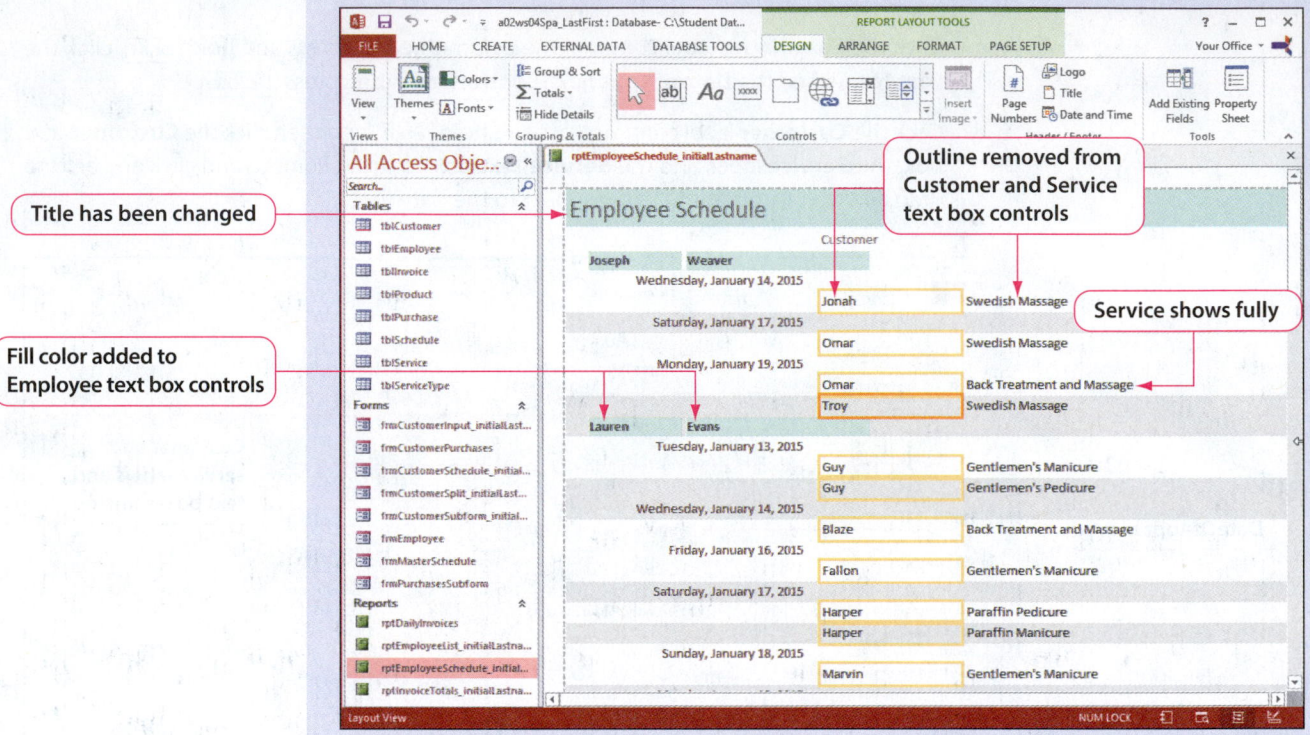

Figure 26 Formatted report in Layout view

j. **Close** X the report, and then click **Yes** to save the changes.

Enhancing a Report with Conditional Formatting

In the previous section, you changed the colors and fonts of fields. You can also change the fonts and colors of fields only when certain conditions are met in the field. This is called **conditional formatting**. If a field value meets the conditions you specify, then the formatting will be applied. This is a useful tool to automatically highlight sales numbers on a report if they meet a certain threshold, or to highlight students' grades when they exceed a certain limit.

To apply conditional formatting, you must select the field value in the field to which you want the formatting applied. You can select a different font color and font effects for the formatting.

For this exercise, the spa manager would like you to create a report and apply conditional formatting to all services currently scheduled that are over $100. These customers usually get some special treatments like complimentary coffee and tea, and the staff would like to be able to easily see which customers will get this service.

A04.21

▶ **To Apply Conditional Formatting to a Report Field**

a. Click the **CREATE** tab, and then in the Reports group, click **Report Wizard**.

b. Click the **Tables/Queries** arrow, and then select **Table: tblSchedule**. Double-click **DateOfAppt**, **Customer**, and **Service** in the Available Fields list. Click the **Tables/Queries** arrow, and then select **Table: tblService**. On the Available Fields list, double-click **Fee**, and then click **Next**.

c. Verify that **by tblSchedule** is highlighted, and then click **Next**. You will not add any grouping to this report, so click **Next**.

d. Click the **1 Sort** arrow, click **DateofAppt**, and then click **Next**. Verify that **Tabular** is selected under Layout and **Portrait** is selected under Orientation. Verify that **Adjust the field width so all fields fit on a page** is checked. Click **Next**.

e. Under **What title do you want for your report?**, type **rptHighFees_initialLastname** using your first initial and last name, and then click **Finish**. The report will open in Print Preview. Switch to **Layout** view. If necessary, **close** the Field List pane.

f. Double-click the **title**, select the **text**, type **High Service Customers**, and then press `Enter`.

g. Click in the **Fee** text box control, and then, on the FORMAT tab, in the Control Formatting group, click **Conditional Formatting**.

h. In the Conditional Formatting Rules Manager dialog box, click **New Rule**. Verify that **Check values in the current record or use an expression** is highlighted. Find the three condition text boxes. The first should display **Field Value Is**. Click in the second condition box, and then select **greater than**. In the third condition text box, type **100**.

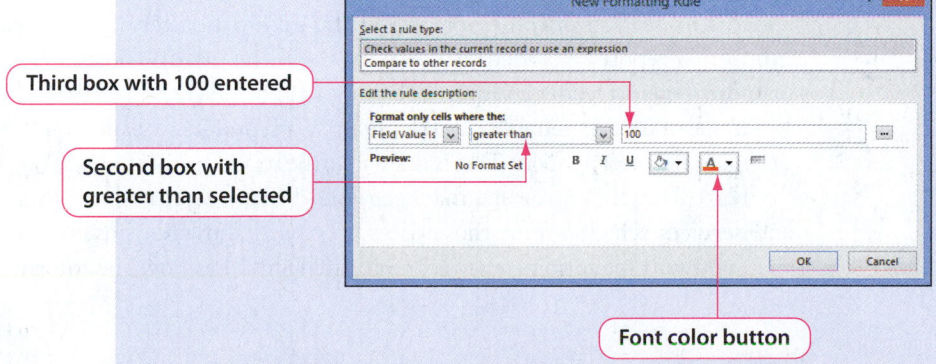

Figure 27   New Formatting Rule dialog box

i. Below the condition text boxes, click **Bold** B, click the **Font color** arrow, and then click **Dark Red**. Click **OK**, verify that your rule states **Value >100**, and then click **OK**.

All values greater than $100 in the Fee field should be highlighted in dark red and bold.

j. Switch to **Design** view. On the REPORT DESIGN TOOLS DESIGN tab, in the Controls group, select **Label** Aa, move your pointer to the **Report Footer**, and then when your pointer changes to ⁺A drag your pointer to draw a label control about 2.5" wide in the top-left corner of the Report Footer section. In the new label, type **Created by initial Lastname** using your first initial and last name.

k. Switch to **Report** view. Verify that your label has been entered in the bottom-left corner of the report.

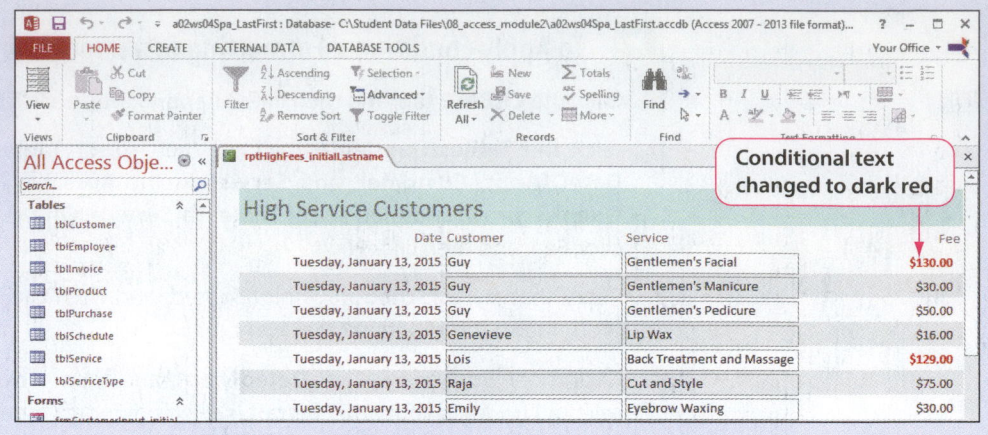

Figure 28 Report with conditional formatting applied

l. **Close** ☒ the report, and then click **Yes** to save the changes.

To delete a conditional formatting rule, click the Format tab in Layout view, click the field that has the conditional formatting applied, in the Control Formatting group, click Conditional Formatting, click the rule you wish to delete, and then click Delete Rule.

Applying Grouping and Sorting

The Report Wizard gives you the opportunity to sort and group records, but sometimes seeing the report changes your mind about what and how to group and sort. You can change the sorting and grouping options from either Layout or Design view. Groups are added to a section of the report called the **group header**. Calculations performed on a group in a report are added to a section called the **group footer**. A report may have one or more Group Headers, Group Footers, both, or neither.

In Layout view, you will use the Group, Sort, and Total pane to select the sort fields and grouping fields for a report. This is done after the report has been created by the Report Wizard.

For this exercise, the spa manager would like a report that shows appointment dates and services scheduled for those dates. You will show her how to create the report, and then you will make some changes to it until she likes how the information is presented.

A04.22

  To Add Group and Sort Fields to a New Report

a. Click the **CREATE** tab, and then in the Reports group, click **Report Wizard**.

b. Click the **Tables/Queries** arrow, and then select **Table: tblSchedule**. Double-click **DateOfAppt**, **Service**, **Customer**, and **Employee** from the Available Fields list. Click **Next**.

c. Click the **One Field Back** button 🔲 ◁ 🔲 to remove the Service grouping level. Click **DateOfAppt**, and then click the **One Field** button 🔲 ▷ 🔲 to add the date as a grouping level. Click **Grouping Options…**, click the **Grouping intervals** arrow, and then click **Normal**. Click **OK**, and then click **Next**.

d. Click the **1 Sort** arrow, select **Service**, and then click **Next**.

e. Verify **Stepped** layout and **Portrait** orientation are selected. Verify that **Adjust the field width so all fields fit on a page** is selected. Click **Next**.

f. Under **What title do you want for your report?**, type rptAppointments_initialLastname using your first initial and last name, and then click **Finish**.

g. Switch to **Design** view. On the DESIGN tab, in the Controls group, select **Label** Aa, move your pointer to the **Report Footer**, and then when your pointer changes to ⁺A drag your pointer to draw a label control about 2.5" wide in the top-left corner of the Report Footer section. In the new label, type Created by initial Lastname using your first initial and last name.

h. Switch to **Layout** view. Verify that your label has been entered in the bottom-left corner of the report.

i. Click the **DateOfAppt** text box control, on the FORMAT tab, in the Font group, click **Align Text Left** ☰. Drag the right border of the DateOfAppt text box to line up with the left border of the Service text box. All the date values should be visible.

j. Click the **Service** text box control, and then drag the left border to the left to make the control wider so all the text can be displayed. Scroll down to the appointments scheduled on January 18, and then confirm that the **Microdermabrasion Treatment (6 sessions)** is showing.

k. Double-click the **title**, select the **text**, and then type Daily Appointments. Press Enter.

l. On the DESIGN tab, in the Grouping & Totals group, click **Group & Sort**, and then notice the Group, Sort, and Total pane that opens at the bottom of the report.

m. Click the line that displays **Sort by Service**, and then click **Delete** ✕ on the far right of the line. This will delete the sort that was added in the Report Wizard.

n. Click **Add a group** in the Group, Sort, and Total pane, and then select **Employee**.

o. Click the **Employee** text box control, and then drag it to the left until it is under the date. Click the **Employee** label control, press and hold Shift, click the **DateOfAppt** label control, and then press Delete.

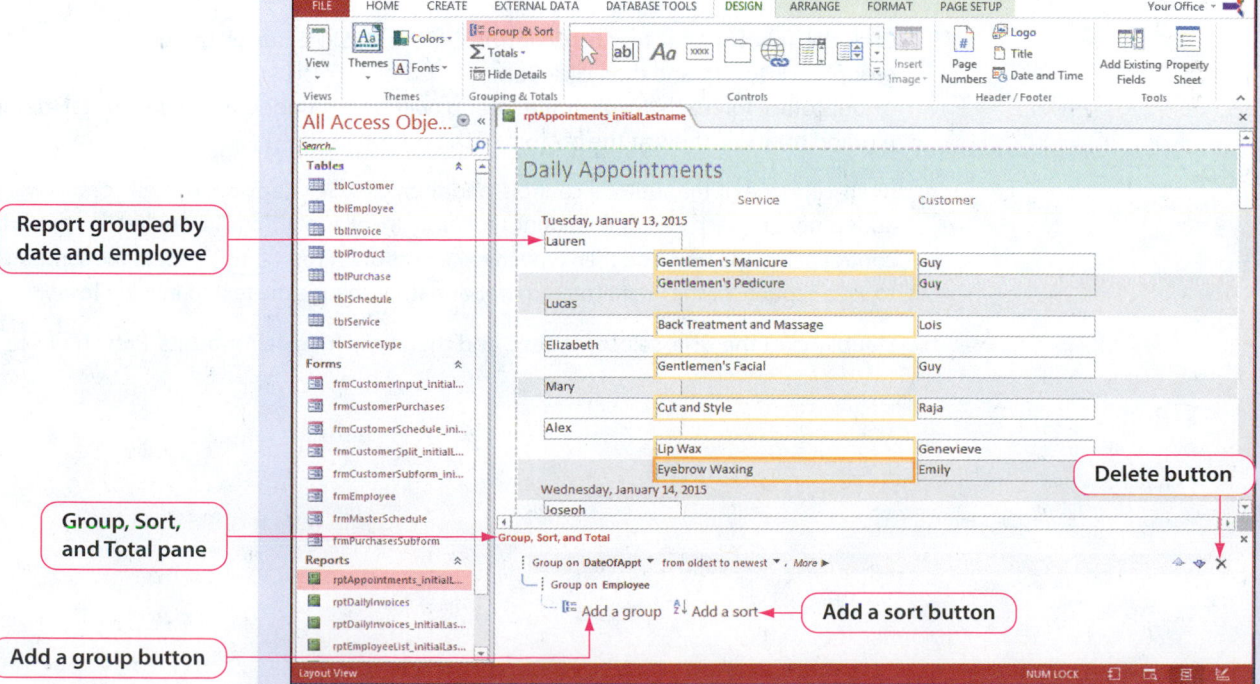

Figure 29 New grouping added to report

p. **Close** ✕ the Group, Sort, and Total pane being careful that you are clicking Close and not the Delete button. **Close** ✕ the report, and then click **Yes** to save the changes.

Adding Subtotals

Earlier, you added subtotals when you created the report using the wizard. However, sometimes seeing the report makes you realize that subtotals would be useful. You can add them in Layout view, using the Group, Sort, and Total pane when you are selecting or modifying groups and sorts for the reports.

For this exercise, the spa manager would like to add subtotals to a report that shows all invoices grouped by date.

A04.23

To Add Subtotals to a Report

a. In the Navigation Pane, right-click rptDailyInvoices, and then select **Copy**. Right-click in the **Navigation Pane**, and then select **Paste**. In the Paste As dialog box, in the **Report Name:** box, type rptDailyInvoices_initialLastname using your first initial and last name. Click **OK**.

b. In the Navigation Pane, double-click **rptDailyInvoices_initialLastname** to open the report. Notice the report shows all invoices by day but has no totals.

c. Switch to **Design** view. On the DESIGN tab, in the Controls group, click **Label** [Aa]. Move your pointer to the **Report Footer**, and then when your pointer changes to [+A] drag your pointer to draw a label control about 2.5" wide in the top-left corner of the Report Footer section. In the new label control, type Created by initial Lastname using your first initial and last name.

d. Switch to **Layout** view. Verify that your label has been entered in the bottom-left corner of the report.

e. Scroll right, click the **Invoice Total** label control, press and hold [Shift], click the **Invoice Total** text box control, and then drag the **right border** to the left so that it is to the right of the dotted line. Drag the **left border** to the right so the field is narrower but the column heading still shows.

f. Click the **InvoiceTotal** text box control. On the DESIGN tab, in the Grouping & Totals group, click **Totals**, and then click **Sum**.

Subtotals for each InvoiceDate group will show under the InvoiceTotal details. A grand total will show at the bottom of the report.

g. Right-click one of the subtotal controls, and then click **Set Caption**. A label control will be added next to each subtotal amount that says "InvoiceTotal Total". Double-click the **label** control, select the **text**, and then type Invoice Subtotal. Press [Enter]. Repeat the same steps to set a caption for the grand total control, and then change the text to Invoice Total.

h. Double-click the **title**, select the **text**, and then type Invoice Amounts. Press [Enter].

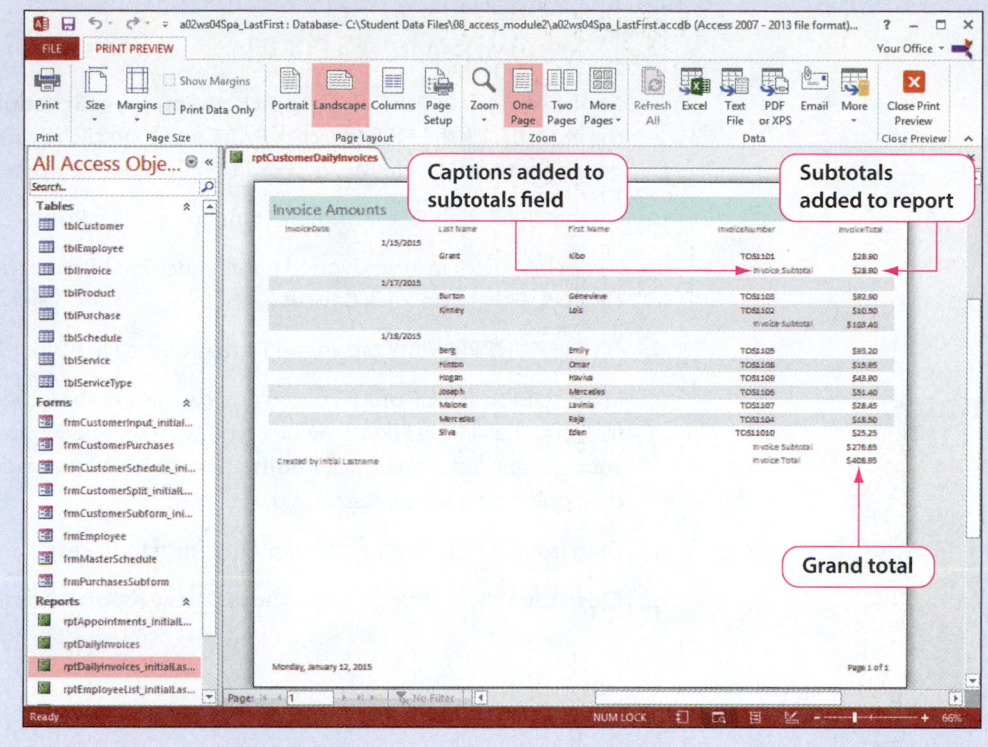

Figure 30 Report with subtotals added

i. **Close** ☒ the report, and then click **Yes** to save the changes.

Save a Report as a PDF File

Reports are formatted printable documents of your data, so the final result of a report will usually be a printout. If not printed, then the report may be shared with other people electronically. When you send a report to someone electronically, they have to have the same program in which the report was created in order to open the report. To avoid this problem, you can save a report as a PDF file, which can be read by Adobe Reader, a free program that you can download from the Internet, or by Word 2013.

To print a report, you use the Print dialog box on the File tab to select your printing options. Before you print, it is always a good idea to view the report in Print Preview to make sure it looks the way you want. Viewing the report in Layout view and Report view does not show you page breaks and other features of the report as it will look when actually printed. In Print Preview, you have many options to make design changes to your report before you send it to the printer. You can change the margins and orientation, and you can select how many pages, if not all, you want to print.

Creating a PDF File

If you need to distribute the report electronically, you also have the option to save the report as an Adobe PDF file. An **Adobe PDF file** is usually smaller than the original document, is easy to send through e-mail, and preserves the original document look and feel so you know exactly what it will look like when the recipient opens it. The correct terminology for saving a report as a PDF file format is to "publish" the report. When you are saving the report as a PDF you will see the option to Publish, not to Save or Print.

For this exercise, you will show the staff how to print and publish a PDF file of the employee schedule so it can easily be e-mailed to the staff each week.

A04.24

 To Save a Report as a PDF File

a. On the Navigation Pane, double-click **rptEmployeeSchedule_initialLastname** to open the report. Click the **FILE** tab, click **Print**, and then click **Print Preview**. Navigate through the pages to make sure the records fit on the pages correctly.

b. On the PRINT PREVIEW tab, in the Print group, click **Print**.

c. If your instructor instructs you to print, under Print Range, verify **All** is selected, and then click **OK**. Otherwise, click **Cancel**.

d. On the PRINT PREVIEW tab, in the **Data** group, click **PDF or XPS**.

e. In the **Publish as PDF or XPS** dialog box, navigate to the location where you are saving your files, and then in the **File name** box type a02ws04SpaEmployeeSchedule_LastFirst using your first and last name. Click **Publish**. The PDF file automatically opens. To close the file, drag down from the top bezel to the bottom.

f. Drag from the left bezel to the right to return to **Access**.

g. **Close** the Export - PDF window. **Close** ☒ the report, and then **close** ☒ Access.

Concept Check

1. What is the difference between Navigation and Edit modes? How can you tell you are in each mode? p. 198–200

2. When you add, change, or delete a record in a form, how does it affect the underlying table? Why? p. 206–207

3. What are controls? What is the difference between a label control and a text box control? Which is bound, and which is unbound? p. 209

4. What is a theme? What is the difference between applying a theme to an entire database and to a single object? p. 214–215

5. What view will you see when the Report Wizard is done creating a report? What is the difference between Report view, Layout view, Design view, and Print Preview when you are creating a report? Which view will show you the most accurate picture of what your printed report will look like? In which views do you see the data? p. 224

6. What is conditional formatting, and when would you use it? p. 230

7. What is a PDF file, and why would you want to save your report as a PDF? p. 235

Key Terms

Adobe PDF file   235
Bound control   209
Calculated control   209
Conditional formatting   230
Control   209
Edit mode   198
Grand total   226

Group   220
Group footer   232
Group header   232
Label control   209
Layout selector   216
Main form   201
Navigation mode   198

Split form   204
Subform   201
Subreport   220
Subtotals   226
Text box control   209
Theme   214
Unbound control   209

Visual Summary

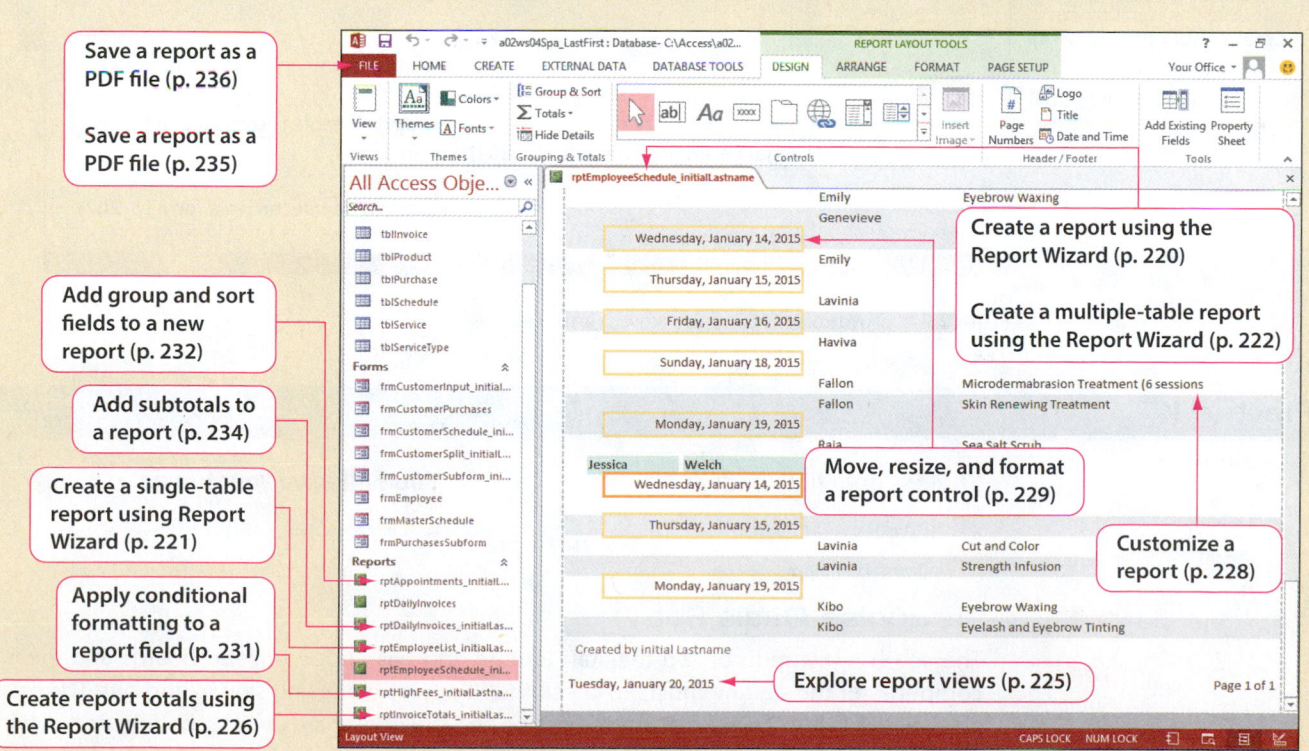

Save a report as a PDF file (p. 236)

Save a report as a PDF file (p. 235)

Add group and sort fields to a new report (p. 232)

Add subtotals to a report (p. 234)

Create a single-table report using Report Wizard (p. 221)

Apply conditional formatting to a report field (p. 231)

Create report totals using the Report Wizard (p. 226)

Create a report using the Report Wizard (p. 220)

Create a multiple-table report using the Report Wizard (p. 222)

Move, resize, and format a report control (p. 229)

Customize a report (p. 228)

Explore report views (p. 225)

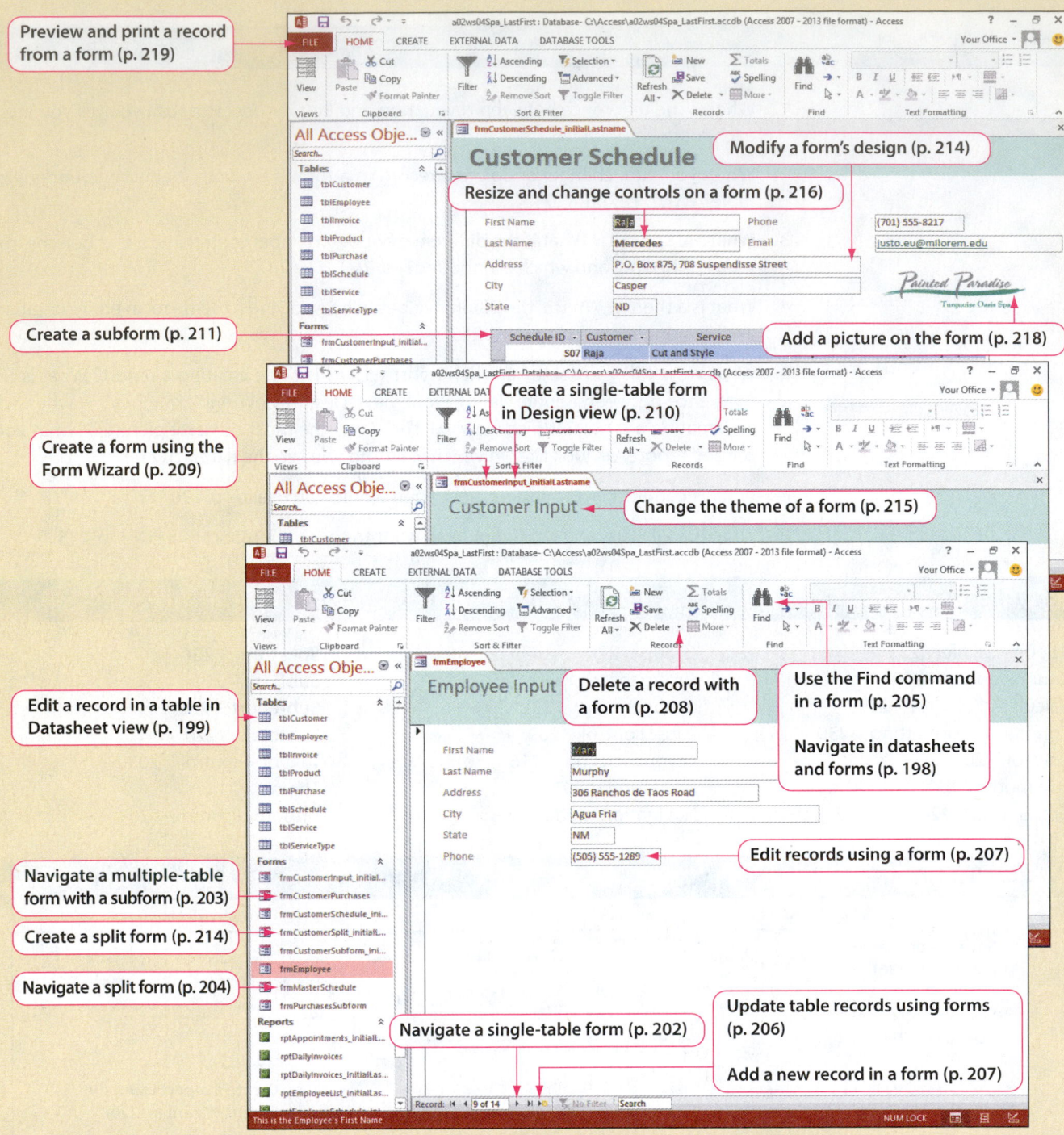

Figure 31 Turquoise Oasis Spa's New Database

Practice 1

Student data file needed:

📄 a02ws04Spa2.accdb

📄 a02ws04Spa.thmx

You will save your file as:

📄 a02ws04Spa2_LastFirst.accdb

Turquoise Oasis Spa

Human Resources

The spa has just redecorated the staff lounge and has added bulletin boards and even a computer for the staff members to check their appointments and sign in and out. The manager would like to create reports to post on the bulletin boards with schedule and service information, as well as make the database as easy to use as possible. You will help create some of the reports as well as forms to make the database easy for data entry and maintenance.

a. Start **Access**, and then open **a02ws04Spa2**.

b. Click the **FILE** tab, click **Save As**. Verify **Save Database As** and **Access Database** are selected. Click **Save As**. In the Save As dialog box, navigate to where you are saving your files and then type a02ws04Spa2_LastFirst, using your first and last name. Click **Save**. If necessary, in the Security Warning, click **Enable Content**.

c. Create a form that will allow employees to edit their personal information as well as their upcoming appointments:

- Click the **CREATE** tab, and then in the Forms group, click **Form Wizard**.
- In the Form Wizard dialog box, click the **Tables/Queries** arrow, and then select **Table: tblEmployee**. Click the **All Fields** button to add all the fields to the Selected Fields list.
- Click the **Tables/Queries** arrow, and then select **Table: tblSchedule**. Double-click **Customer**, **Service**, **Employee**, and **DateOfAppt** to add the fields to the Selected Fields list. Click **Next**.
- Verify that the data will be viewed **by tblEmployee**, and then click **Next**.
- Verify that **Datasheet** is selected as the layout for the subform, and then click **Next**.
- Name the form frmEmployeeSchedule_initialLastname using your first initial and last name, name the subform frmSubform_initialLastname, and then click **Finish**.
- Switch to **Form** view. On the main form Navigation bar, click **New (blank) record**, and then add your first name, last name, address, city, state, and phone number. On the Navigation bar, click **First record** to return to the first record in the table, and then click in the **Last Name** field.
- Click the **HOME** tab, in the Find group, click **Find**. In the **Find What** text box, type Rodriguez and then click **Find Next**. When you find the record for Brenda Rodriguez, click **Cancel**.
- On the HOME tab, in the Records group, click the **Delete** arrow, and then click **Delete Record**. Click **Yes** when prompted to delete the record.
- Switch to **Layout** view. Double-click the **title**, select the **text**, and then type Employee Schedule.
- Click the **Last Name** text box control, and then drag the **right border** of the text box to line up with the right border of the First Name text box.
- Click the **subform label**, and then press $\boxed{\text{Delete}}$ to delete the control. Click the **Subform**, and then using the layout selector, drag it to the left so it is right below the Phone label. Use the AutoFit feature on all the columns to best fit the data.
- Click the **Employee** label in the subform datasheet, and then press $\boxed{\text{Delete}}$ to delete the label. Click the **subform** control, and then drag the **right border** to the right until you can see all the fields in the subform. Click the **Date** heading in the subform datasheet, and then drag it to the left of the Customer field.
- On the DESIGN tab, in the Themes group, click the **Themes** arrow, click **Browse for Themes**, browse to where you stored data files, click **a02ws04Spa**, and then click **Open**.
- Switch to **Design** view, on the DESIGN tab, in the Controls group, select **Label**, move your pointer to the **Report Footer**, and then draw a label control about 2.5" wide in the top-left corner of the Report Footer section. In the new label control, type Created by initial Lastname using your first initial and last name.
- Close the form, and then click **Yes** when prompted to save the changes.

d. Create a report to show a list of customers and their purchases.

- Click the **CREATE** tab, and then in the Reports group, click **Report Wizard**. In the Report Wizard dialog box, click the **Tables/Queries** arrow, and then select **Table: tblCustomer**. Double-click **CustFirstName**, **CustLastName**, **CustState**, and **CustPhone** to add the fields to the Selected Fields list.

- Click the **Tables/Queries** arrow, and then select **Table: tblProduct**. Double-click **ProductDescription** to add the field to the Selected Fields list.
- Click the **Tables/Queries** arrow, and then select **Table: tblPurchase**. Double-click **PurchaseType**, **PurchaseDate**, and **Quantity** to add the fields to the Selected Fields list. Click **Next**.
- Verify that the data will be viewed by **tblCustomer**, and then click **Next**.
- Double-click **ProductDescription** to add it as a grouping level, and then click **Next**.
- Click the **1 Sort** arrow, click **PurchaseDate**, and then click **Next**. Select a **Stepped** layout and **Portrait** orientation, and then click **Next**.
- Name the report rptCustomerPurchases_initialLastname using your first initial and last name, and then click **Finish**.

e. Customize the report's appearance.
- Switch to **Layout** view.
- Click the **Date** text box control, and then drag the **left border** to the left until the date is visible. Move the **Date** text box control to the left until it lines up under the First Name field.
- Click the **ProductDescription** label control, press and hold [Shift], click the **PurchaseDate** label control, click the **PurchaseType** label control, and then press [Delete] to delete the controls.
- Click the **Phone** text box control, and then drag the **right border** so the whole field is visible. Click the **ProductDescription** text box control, and then drag the **right border** to the right until the whole field is visible.
- Double-click the **title**, select the **text**, and then type Customer Purchases.
- **Save** the report.

f. Add totals and subtotals.
- On the DESIGN tab, in the Grouping & Totals group, click **Group & Sort** to open the Group, Sort, and Total pane. Click **Group on ProductDescription**, and then click **Delete** to delete the group.
- In the Group, Sort, and Total pane, click **Add a group**, and then select **PurchaseType**. Click the **PurchaseType** text box control—on the far right of report, and then drag it just below the customer's first name and just above the date.
- In the Group, Sort, and Total pane, click **Add a sort**, and then select **ProductDescription**. Close the Group, Sort, and Total pane.
- Click the **PurchaseType** text box. On the FORMAT tab, in the Control Formatting group, click **Conditional Formatting**, and then click **New Rule**. In the second box, select **equal to**, and then in the third text box type Online. Click **Font color**, and then select **Purple**. Click **OK** twice.
- Click the **PurchaseType** text box control. On the DESIGN tab, in the Grouping & Totals group, click **Totals**, and then select **Count Records**. Click the **PurchaseType** text box control, press and hold [Shift], and then click the **subtotal** text box control. On the FORMAT tab, in the Control Formatting group, click **Shape Outline**, and then select **Transparent**.
- Right-click the **Subtotal** text box control, and then select **Set Caption**. Replace the text in the caption box with Orders.
- Scroll to the bottom of the report. Click the **Grand Total** text box control, and then move it under the product description. Right-click the **Grand Total** text box control, and then click **Set Caption**. Replace the text in the caption box with Total orders.
- Switch to **Design** view. On the DESIGN tab, in the Controls group, select **Label**, move your pointer to the **Report Footer**, and then when your pointer changes drag your pointer to draw a label control about 2.5" wide on the left side of the Report Footer. In the new label control, type Created by initial Lastname using your first initial and last name.

g. Close the report, and then click **Yes** when prompted to save the changes.

h. Close your database. Submit your files as directed by your instructor.

Homework 1

Sales & Marketing

Student data file needed:

 a02ws04Clothing.accdb

You will save your files as:

a02ws04Clothing_LastFirst.accdb

a02ws04RptPriceCategories_LastFirst.pdf

Clothing Sales

Wanda Robinson runs a home business selling designer clothing and has started using an Access database to keep her records. The database has been created and is now able to retain data. Wanda wants to have some forms and reports created to make dealing with the data easier. She has hired you to develop the necessary forms and reports.

a. Start **Access**, and then open the student data file **a02ws04Clothing**. Click the **FILE** tab, and then save the file as an **Access Database** in the location where you store your data files with the name a02ws04Clothing_LastFirst using your first and last name. If necessary, enable the content.

b. Open **tblCustomer** and add a record with CustomerID 16, your last name, first name, address, city, state, and zip code.

c. Create a **split form** to show all the product information from **tblProduct**.

- Save the form as frmProductInfo_initialLastname.
- Apply the theme **Ion** to all objects in the database. Hint: The themes are listed alphabetically.
- Add Created by initial Lastname to the Form Footer. Save and close the form.

d. Use the **Form Wizard** to create a form that will display in the main form the customer's **LastName**, **FirstName**, and display **Product Description**, **Price**, **Size**, and **Color** in the subform. Keep all other default options. Name the form frmCustOrders_initialLastname and the subform frmProductSubform_initialLastname.

- Remove the subform label. Move the subform to line up with the FirstName label control.
- Resize the columns in the subform so all the product information fits. Resize the form to fit the columns.
- Change the title of the form to Customer Orders.
- Add Created by initial Lastname to the main form's Form Footer. Save and close the form.

e. Use the **Report Wizard** to create a report to summarize each customer's purchases. Include **LastName**, **FirstName**, **ProductDescription**, **Price**, and **Quantity**. Hint: this information will come from three different tables. Accept the grouping options, sort by **ProductDescription,** use a format of **Stepped** and **Landscape**, and save the report as rptCustSummary_initialLastname.

- Add the **sum of the quantities** for each customer. Add a caption of Total Products.
- Apply conditional formatting to make any sum of quantities greater than 3 bold and red.
- Add Created by initial Lastname to the Report Footer.
- Change the title of the report to Customer Summary. Save and close the report.

f. Use the **Report Wizard** to create a report that includes all product fields except ProductID. Group products by **category** and then **price**, sort by **ProductDescription** and then **Size**. Use **Summary Options** in the wizard to show the **sum** of **QuantityInStoc**k. Change the setting to **Landscape**. Name the report rptPriceCategories_initialLastname.

- Use the AutoFit feature, and then move the fields as necessary for the best fit.
- Add Created by initial Lastname to the Report Footer.
- Change the title of the report to Products by Category and Price. Save and close the report.
- Create a PDF file from the rptPriceCategories. Save the file as a02ws04RptPriceCategories_LastFirst.

g. Close your database. Submit your files as directed by your instructor.

Student data file needed:

 a02ws04Roadhouse.accdb

You will save your file as:

 a02ws04Roadhouse_LastFirst.accdb

Beverage Database at the Roadhouse Bar and Grill

Production & Operations

You are the bar manager at the Roadhouse Bar and Grill, a local restaurant that specializes in home-cooked meals for breakfast, lunch, and dinner. You have developed a database for managing the inventory of beverage items.

You will expand the database by creating forms and reports to help you manage the database. You have loaded a few sample transactions to help you develop these forms and reports. For each report, choose which fields you need and which sort order makes sense. Choose appropriate titles and attractive formatting for all forms and reports. Add a Created by label to each report and form.

a. Start Access, open the student data file **a02ws04Roadhouse**, and then save it as a02ws04Roadhouse_LastFirst.

b. Open each table and familiarize yourself with the fields. Open the relationships window and note how the tables are related.

c. Create a split form to add a supplier to the database. Name the form frmSupplier_initialLastname. Use your form to change the name of the first supplier to be your full name. Pick an attractive theme, and then apply it to the entire database.

d. Create a form showing suppliers and the beverages they sell. Name the main form frmSupplierBeverage_initialLastname and the subform frmBeverageSubform_initialLastname. Use the form to add Ginger Ale to the canned beverages that you sell.

e. Create a report that shows the supplier, the beverages they sold, and the sales date of the sales. Name it rptSalesBySupplier_initialLastname.

f. Create a report that shows suppliers, the container types, container sizes, serving sizes, and price. Add a subtotal with average prices. Name the report rptAveragePrice_initialLastname.

g. Create a report showing daily sales of beverages, count the number of sales per day of beverages, and then name the report rptDailySales_initialLastname.

h. Create a report with conditional formatting to highlight something that you think is interesting.

i. Create another report that would be useful for your job.

j. Close your database. Submit your files as directed by your instructor. Close your database.

Additional Cases

Additional Workshop Cases are available on the companion website and in the instructor resources.

MODULE CAPSTONE

More Practice 1

Student data files needed:

 a02mpRecipes.accdb

 a02mpIndigo5.jpg

You will save your files as:

 a02mpRecipes_LastFirst.accdb

 a02mpRecipesPDF_LastFirst.pdf

Production &
Operations

Indigo5 Restaurant

Robin Sanchez, the chef of the resort's restaurant, Indigo 5, has started a database to keep track of the recipes and ingredients that the restaurant includes. Right now there are no forms, queries, or reports created for this database, so the information available is very limited. You will help create some queries as well as forms for data entry and reports for the daily management of the food preparation.

a. Start **Access**, and then open **a02mpRecipes**. Click the **FILE** tab, and then save the file as an **Access Database** with the name a02mpRecipes_LastFirst using your last and first name. If necessary, in the Security Warning, click **Enable Content**.

b. Click the **CREATE** tab, and then in the Forms group, click **Form Wizard**. Add all of the fields from **Table: tblRecipes**. From **Table: tblRecipeIngredients**, and then double-click **IngredientID**, **Quantity**, and **Measurement**. View the form **by tblRecipes**, show the subform as a **Datasheet**. Save the form as frmRecipe_initialLastname and the subform as frmRecipeSubform_initialLastname, using your first initial and last name. Switch to **Design** view. On the DESIGN tab, in the Controls group, click **Label**, and then add a label to the form footer that says Created by initial Lastname.

c. Switch to **Layout** view. Click the **DESIGN** tab, in the Themes group, click **Themes**. Click the **Ion Boardroom** theme to apply it to all objects in the database.

d. Change the title of the form to Recipe Input. On the FORMAT tab, in the Font group, change the title font size to **28**, and then apply **Bold**.

e. On the DESIGN tab, in the Themes group, click **Fonts**, and then click **Office Calibri Light** to apply it to all objects.

f. Go to the recipe for **REC006**, **Pueblo Green Chili Stew**. Delete the subform label, and then move the subform to the left under the Instructions label. AutoFit the subform fields **Quantity** and **Measurement** to size them appropriately. Move the **right** border of the subform to the left to fit the subform columns.

g. Click in the form **body**. On the DESIGN tab, in the Controls group, click **Insert Image**, click **Browse**, navigate to your student data files, and then locate **a02mpIndigo5**. Insert the **image** to the right of the Recipe information. Resize the **image** as necessary to fit above the Instructions text box.

h. Switch to **Form** view. Click the **Recipe Name** text box. On the HOME tab, in the Find group, click **Find**, and then in the Find What box, type Pasta Napolitana, and then click **Find Next**. Click **Cancel**. Change the Quantity for the **IngredientID Honey** to 1.

i. Click the **New (blank) record** button on the main form Navigation bar, and then enter the following data into frmRecipe_initialLastname:

Recipe Name	Food Category ID	Subcategory	Prep Time (minutes)	Servings	Instructions
Avocado Salsa	Appetizer	Vegetarian	10	6	Peel and mash avocados. Add cayenne pepper, salt, chopped onion, and chopped tomato. Add lime juice and mix well. Refrigerate for at least 4 hours.

Enter the following data into the subform:

IngredientID	Quantity	Measurement
Avocado	2	whole
Tomato	1	cup
Cayenne pepper	.5	teaspoon
Salt	.5	teaspoon
Onions	1	cup
Lime juice	3	tablespoons

Save and close the form.

j. Click the **CREATE** tab, in the Queries group, click **Query Design**, and then add **tblRecipes**, **tblRecipeIngredients**, and **tblIngredients**. Include **RecipeName**, **Ingredient**, and **Quantity** in the results. In the **Ingredient Criteria**, type cumin or paprika. Sort in **Ascending** order by **Quantity**. Run the query, and then use the AutoFit feature on the query columns. Save your query as qryCuminOrPaprika_initialLastname. Close the query.

k. Create a query to show all ingredients not used in any recipe. Click the **CREATE** tab, and then in the Queries group, click **Query Wizard**, click **Find Unmatched Query Wizard**, and then click **OK**. Click **Table: tblIngredients**, and then click **Next**. Click **tblRecipeIngredients**, and then click **Next**. IngredientID will be the common field between the tables. Click **Next**, and then include all the available fields. Click **Next**. Save the query as qryUnusedIngredients_initialLastname. Click **Finish**. Switch to **Design** view, sort **IngredientID** in **Ascending** order. Save and close the query.

l. Click the **CREATE** tab, in the Queries group, click **Query Design**, and then add **tblRecipes** and **tblFoodCategories**. Include **RecipeName**, **TimeToPrepare**, and **FoodCategory** in the results. Add criteria **< 30** to the **TimetoPrepare** field to find all recipes that take less than 30 minutes to prepare. Add criteria soup or pizza to the **FoodCategory** field. The results should show all recipes that take less than 30 minutes to prepare and are listed with the category of soup or pizza. Sort **TimeToPrepare** in **Ascending** order. **Run** the query. Use AutoFit on each column. Save the query as qryTimeAndCategory_initialLastname and then close the query.

m. Click the **CREATE** tab, in the Queries group, click **Query Design**, and then add **tblRecipes**, **tblRecipeIngredients**, and **tblIngredients**. Include **RecipeName**, **Ingredient**, **Quantity**, **Measurement**, and **RecipeID** from tblRecipeIngredients in the results, in that order. Sort **RecipeID** in **Ascending** order. **Run** the query. Use AutoFit on each column. Save the query as qryRecipeIngredients_initialLastname and then close the query.

n. Click the **CREATE** tab, in the Reports group, click **Report Wizard**, and then from **Table: tblRecipes** add the fields **RecipeName**, **Instructions**, **TimeToPrepare**, and **Servings**. From **Query: qryRecipeIngredients_initialLastname** add the fields **Ingredient**,

Quantity, and **Measurement** in that order. View your report **by tblRecipes**. Group by **RecipeName**. Sort in **Ascending** order by Ingredient. Accept all other default settings, and then name the report rptRecipes_initialLastname.

- Switch to **Layout** view, and then move the **Ingredient**, **Quantity**, and **Measurement** text boxes to the left under the Instructions field. Delete the Ingredient, Quantity, and Measurement labels. Move the **Servings text box** and **label** to the right. Make the **Prep Time (minutes)** and **Servings** labels wider so the text is visible. Double-click the report **title**, and then change it to Recipes.

- Click the **Recipe Name** text field. On the FORMAT tab, in the Font group, click **Bold**. Move the right border for the **Recipe Name** text box to make it wide enough to fit all the text for every record. Scroll down to **Gambas al Ajillo (Shrimp with Garlic)** to make sure the field is wide enough.

- Click the **Quantity** text box, and then move the **left** border to the right to make the field narrower. Click the **Ingredient** text box, and then move the **right** border to the right to make the field completely visible. Scroll down to see **Corn (whole kernel)** to make sure the field is wide enough.

- Click the **Prep Time** text box, and then in the Control Formatting group, click **Conditional Formatting**. Click **New Rule**, select **greater than** in the second box, and then type 15 in the third box. Click **Bold** and change the font color to **Red**, and then click **OK**. Click **OK** again.

- Switch to **Design** view. On the DESIGN tab, in the Controls group, click **Label**, and then add a label saying Created by initial Lastname to the Report Footer.

- Save the report, switch to **Report** view to check your report, and then close the report.

- Right-click **rptRecipes_initialLastname**. Select **Export**, and then select **PDF or XPS**. Navigate to the folder where you are saving your files, type a02mpRecipesPDF_initialLastname, in the **Open after publishing** box, clear the check box, click **Publish**, and then click close.

o. Click the **CREATE** tab, in the Reports group, click **Report Wizard**, and then from **Table:tblRecipeIngredients** add the fields **IngredientID**, **Quantity**, and **Measurement**. From **Table: tblRecipes** add **RecipeName**. Click **Next**, check to make sure you view your data **by tblRecipeIngredients**, click **Next**, and then double-click **RecipeName** to add grouping. Accept all other default options, and then name your report rptIngredientCount_initialLastname.

- Switch to **Design** view. On the DESIGN tab, and then in the Controls group, click **Label**, and then add a label saying Created by initial Lastname to the Report Footer.

- Switch to **Layout** view. On the DESIGN tab, in the Grouping & Totals group, click **Group & Sort**, and then delete the grouping by RecipeName. Click **Add a group**, and then group by **IngredientID**. Move the **IngredientID** text box to the left margin, under the RecipeName label. Click the **IngredientID** text box, and then on the **FORMAT** tab, in the Font group, click **Align Left**. Delete the **RecipeName**, **IngredientID**, **Quantity**, and **Measurement** labels.

- Change the title to Ingredient List. Click the **IngredientID** text box, click **Shape Outline**, and then click **Transparent**. Click **Shape Fill**, and then under Theme Colors, click **Dark Purple, Text 2, Lighter 60%**.

- Click the **Quantity** text box. Click the **DESIGN** tab, in the Grouping & Totals group, click **Totals**, and then click **Sum** to add subtotals. Right-click the **subtotal** text box, select **Set Caption**, and then change the text to Total. Click the **subtotal** text box, and then on the **FORMAT** tab, in the Font group, click **Align Right** to change the alignment. Scroll down to the bottom of the report to find the grand total text box (value 84.5), click the text box and then press **Delete**. Make the **RecipeName** text box wide enough to fit all the text for every record (scroll to find **Gambas al Ajillo (Shrimp with Garlic)** to check the width.

- Close the Group, Sort, and Total pane. Close the report, and then save your changes.

p. Close Access. Submit your file as directed by your instructor.

Homework 1

Student data files needed:

 a02ps1Hotel.accdb

a02ps1Paradise.jpg

a02ps1Paradise.thmx

You will save your files as:

a02ps1Hotel_LastFirst.accdb

a02ps1PdfCharges_LastFirst.pdf

Hotel Reservations

Production & Operations

A database has been started to keep track of the hotel reservations with guest information, reservation information, and additional room charge information. There are no reports, forms, or queries built yet, so the staff feels like the database is not easy to use. You will create reports, forms, and queries to help the staff better manage the data in the database. Complete the following tasks:

a. Start **Access**, and then open the student data file **a02ps1Hotel**. Click the **FILE** tab, and then save the file as an **Access Database** with the name a02ps1Hotel_LastFirst using your last and first name. If necessary, enable the content.

b. Open **tblGuests**, and then add a new record with your last name, first name, address, city, state, zip code, and phone. Close the table.

c. Create a query using **tblReservations** to calculate the average room rate, the minimum room rate, and the maximum room rate for each **DiscountType** of the rooms that are currently reserved. Rename the fields Average Rate, Minimum Rate, and Maximum Rate. Sort the query in **Descending** order by DiscountType. Resize the columns to best fit the data. Save the query as qryDiscountTypeStatistics_initialLastname. Close the query.

d. Use the **Form Wizard** to create a form to enter guest information as well as reservation information. Add all fields from both tables EXCEPT **GuestID** (from either table) and **ReservationID**. The data should be viewed by **Guest information** first, and the subform should be in **Datasheet** layout. Accept all other default options, and then name the form frmGuestReservations_initialLastname and the subform frmGuestSubform_initialLastname.

   • Change the form **title** to Guest Reservations. Make the title font size **28** and **bold**.
   • Apply the theme **a02ps1Paradise** to all objects in your database. Insert and resize the image **a02ps1Paradise** in your form to the right of the guest fields.
   • Resize the **phone number** text field so the entire phone number is fully visible.
   • Delete the subform label. Move the **subform** to the left to line up with the labels for the guest fields. Resize the **column widths** in the subform datasheet, and then resize the object so all columns are visible. If necessary, collapse the navigation pane so you see the entire subform.
   • Add Created by initial Last name to the form footer. Save the form.

e. Find the record for Elaine Foley. Add a new reservation from the information below.

CheckInDate	1/25/2015
Nights Stay	3
# of Guests	2
Crib	No
Handicapped	No
RoomType	Double (1 king bed)
RoomRate	$289
DiscountType	None

Close the form.

f. Create a query to find all guests who do not have matching reservations. Include the fields **GuestLastName**, **GuestFirstName**, **Address**, **City**, **State**, and **ZipCode**. Sort the query by **GuestLastName** and **GuestFirstName** in **Ascending** order. Save the query as qryGuestsWithoutReservations_initialLastname.

- Change the font size of the query results to **14**, change the **Alternate Row Color** to theme color **Red, Accent 4, Lighter 60%**, and use AutoFit on all the columns. Close the query, and then save the changes.

g. Create a query that will calculate the total due for each guest based on the number of nights they have stayed and the room rate for each guest. The results should show the **GuestFirstName**, **GuestLastName**, **NightsStay**, and **RoomRate** in that order. Select only guests who checked in between December 1, 2014 and December 31, 2014 but do not show CheckInDate in your results. Save the query as qryDecemberRoomCharges_initialLastname.

- Name the new field TotalRoomCharge. Use AutoFit on the new column.
- Sort the query in **Ascending** order by **GuestLastName**. Close the query, and then save the changes.

h. Use the **Report Wizard** to create a report to show all room charges incurred for each guest (not including the charge for their room). Add the **GuestFirstName**, **GuestLastName**, **ChargeCategory**, and **ChargeAmount** to the report. View the report by **tblGuests**. Sort by **ChargeAmount** in Ascending order. Accept all other default options, and then save the report as rptRoomCharges_initialLastname.

- Add a subtotal to the **Amount** field, set a caption, and then type Total Charges. Add conditional formatting to the subtotal text box to highlight in **Red** and **Bold** all subtotals that are over $200.
- Add a caption of Grand Total for the grand total.
- Change the title to say Room Charges by Guest.
- Add Created by initial Last name to the report footer. Save and close the report.

i. Save the report as a PDF file and then name it a02ps1PdfCharges_LastFirst.

j. Create a split form from **tblReservations**. Name the form frmReservationSplit_initialLastname. Change the title to Reservations and then bold the title. Add Created by initialLastname to the form footer. Save the form.

k. Close the form, and then exit Access. Submit your file as directed by your instructor.

Problem Solve 2

Homework 2

Student data files needed:

- a02ps2Giftshop.accdb
- a02ps2Giftshop.jpg
- a02ps2Giftshop.thmx

You will save your file as:

- a02ps2Giftshop_LastFirst.accdb

Painted Treasures

Sales & Marketing

The Painted Treasures Gift Shop sells many products for the resort patrons including jewelry, clothing, and spa products. A database has been started to keep track of the customers, purchases, and products. There are no reports, forms, or queries built yet, so the staff feels like the database is not easy to use. You will create reports, forms and queries to help the staff better manage the data in the database. Complete the following tasks:

a. Start **Access**, and open the student data file **a02ps2Giftshop**. Click the **FILE** tab, and then save the file as an **Access Database** with the name a02ps2Giftshop_LastFirst using your last and first name. If necessary, enable the content.

b. Use the **Report Wizard** to create a report showing customers and their purchases. Include **LastName**, **FirstName**, **PurchaseDate**, **Quantity**, **ProductDescription**, **Category**, and **Price**. Accept the default view, and then add no additional grouping. Sort by **Category** and **Product Description**. Save the report as rptCustomerPurchases_initialLastname. Adjust the fields and titles so they are fully visible.

- Add Created by initial Lastname to the report footer.
- Change the report title to Customer Purchases.
- Apply the theme **a02ps2Giftshop** to all objects in the database.

c. Use the Form Wizard to create a form for inputting customers. Select all fields from **tblCustomer**, and then accept all defaults. Name the form frmCustomerInput_initialLastname.

- Add Created by initial Lastname to the form footer.
- Change the form title to Customer Input.
- Click the **label** and **text box** for CustomerID and delete them.
- Adjust the right margin of **LastName** to be as narrow as FirstName. Adjust the right margin of **StreetAddress** to be as narrow as City.
- Change the Shape Fill for **LastName** and **FirstName** to be **Red, Accent 2, Lighter 80%**.
- Insert the image **a02ps2PaintedTreasures** into the form. Resize it, and then move it so the top lines up with **LastName** and it fits in the form.
- Use the form to change the first record to have your last name and first name.

d. Create a query to see which customers made multiple purchases (Hint: This is a Find Duplicates Query). Show all fields available. Save the query as qryMultiplePurchases_initialLastname. Sort in **Ascending** order by CustomerID and PurchaseID.

e. Create a query to see if any customers have made no purchases. Show **LastName**, **FirstName** and **ResortHotelRoom**. Save the query as qryCustomerWithoutPurchase_initialLastname.

f. Create a query to find customers who made purchases but who have no ResortHotelRoom. Show **LastName**, **FirstName**, **PurchaseDate**. Do not show ResortHotelRoom. Sort in **Ascending** order by LastName and FirstName. Adjust the fields so that all fields are fully visible. Save the query as qryNonGuestPurchases_initialLastname.

g. Create a query to show customers who have purchased **Indigo5** or **Spa** category products in January 2015. Show **LastName**, **FirstName**, **PurchaseDate**, and **Category**. Sort in **Ascending** order by LastName and FirstName. Use AutoFit on the fields. Save the query as qrySpaIndigoJanuary_initialLastname.

h. Create a query to calculate the extended amount for each product purchased. Include **PurchaseID**, **PurchaseDate**, **PurchaseLine**, **Quantity**, **ProductDescription**, and **Price**. Save the query as qryExtendedAmount_initialLastname.

- Add a new calculated field to the query to calculate each product's extended amount due based on the quantity and the price. Name the new field ExtendedAmount. Sort in **Ascending** order by PurchaseID. Use AutoFit on all fields. Save the changes, and then close the query.

i. Use the **Report Wizard** to create a report showing a complete purchase. Include all the fields from **qryExtendedAmount_initialLastName**. Group by **PurchaseID**. Sort in **Ascending** order by PurchaseLine. Change orientation to **Landscape**, accept all other default options, and then name the report as rptPurchases_initialLastname.

- Add Created by initial Lastname to the report footer.
- Change the title to Purchase Report.
- Click on **ExtendedAmount**, and then add a sum. Open the Property Sheet pane, and then change the format to **Currency**. Add a caption, and then change it to read

Total Purchase. Repeat for the grand total, and then change the caption to read **Grand Total Purchases**.

- Change the subtotal **Total Purchase** caption and text box to bold with a Shape Fill of **Red, Accent 2, Lighter 80%**.
- Change the grand total **caption** and text box to bold with a Shape Fill of **Red, Accent 2, Lighter 60%**,
- Save and close the report, and then close Access. Submit your file as directed by your instructor.

Perform 1: Perform in Your Life

Student data file needed:

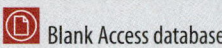 Blank Access database

You will save your file as:

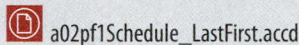 a02pf1Schedule_LastFirst.accdb

Class Schedule

Information
Technology

One way to stay organized during the semester is to keep track of your schedule. You will create a database of all your classes and grades. The database should track the class information, your personal schedule, and the location of the class. To use this for more than one semester, you will keep each of the data in separate tables.

Once the tables are created, you will set up forms to make data entry easier, run queries to get more information, and create reports to help you manage your schedule. For each report, query, or form, make the object attractive and meaningful. You will start by adding data from your current schedule.

a. Start **Access**, and then click the **Blank desktop database**. Save the database as **a02pf1Schedule_LastFirst**.

b. To keep track of class information, design a table that includes fields for at least the class number, class description, credits offered, and professor name. Assign an appropriate primary key, and then save the table as **tblClasses**.

c. Add the class information for your classes from last semester, or fictitious classes, if necessary. Add at least six classes to the table. Use AutoFit on the columns so all text is visible.

d. To keep track of your class locations, design a table that includes fields for the building number, building name, and campus the building is located on. Assign an appropriate primary key, and then save the table as **tblBuilding**.

e. Add the location of the classes you entered in Step c. Include at least three different locations. Use AutoFit on the columns so all text is visible.

f. To keep track of your schedule, design a table that includes fields for the class number, semester, meeting days, meeting time, location, midterm grade (as a number), and Final Grade (as a number). Use AutoFit on the columns so all text is visible. Assign an appropriate primary key, and then save the table as **tblSchedule**.

g. Enter last semester's schedule, or a fictitious one, that includes at least six classes in at least three different locations. The classes and locations should be the ones entered in tblClasses and tblBuildings.

h. Create relationships as appropriate for tblSchedule, tblClasses, and tblBuilding.

i. You would like to be able to enter all your class and schedule information at one time. Create one form that will allow you to enter all the information. Save the form as **frmSchedule_initialLastname**.

j. Use the form to enter a new record for this semester. You should enter all the information except your grade. Add a new theme to the form, change the title to something more meaningful than the form name, add Created by initial Lastname to the form footer. Save and close the form.

k. You would like to see each class individually as well as all the class records at once. Create a form that will show you this view of the data. Change the form title to something meaningful. Save the form as frmClasses_initialLastname.

l. You want to find out what your average midterm grade and average final grade was each semester. Even though grades are only entered for one semester, create a query to perform this calculation.

- Rename the fields to something more meaningful, and then format the fields to show only two decimal places. Sort the query by Semester in **Descending** order. Save the query as qryAverageGrades_initialLastname.

m. You want a schedule of last semester's classes only. Create a query that will show you last semester's classes, the instructor, and where and when it occurred. Save the query as qrySchedule_initialLastname.

n. Create a report that will show you last semester's schedule organized by each day. Sort it in order of class time.

- Make sure all the fields print on one page of the report and that all the fields are visible. Add Created by initial Lastname to the report footer. Save the report as rptSchedule_initialLastname.

o. You want to know how to schedule your weekends. Create a query to see if you have classes after 9 a.m. on Friday. Save the query as qryFridayClasses_initialLastname.

p. You also want to know your average grade for your classes between midterm and final. Create a query to calculate the average grade in each class. Sort the query by an appropriate field. Save the query as qryGrades_initialLastname.

q. You want to print a report to show your parents your grades by class for the semester, including the average grade. Create a report that shows the class number, description, credits, midterm, final, and average grade for each class. Sort by an appropriate field. Resize all labels so all the text is visible. Change the title to something more appropriate. Save the report as rptGrades_initialLastname.

- Add Created by initial Lastname to the report footer. Highlight all average grades over 90. Save and close the report.

r. Close Access. Submit your file as directed by your instructor.

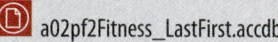

Perform 2: Perform in Your Career

Student data file needed:

Production & Operations

a02pf2Fitness.accdb

You will save your file as:

a02pf2Fitness_LastFirst.accdb

Fitness Center

A new fitness center has opened and is developing a database for keeping track of members. So far the fitness center has two tables for Membership information and Member information, and another table with Roster Information. It has no queries, forms, or reports created, so the center has asked you to help answer some questions with queries, make data entry easier with forms, and print some reports for reference. For each report, query, or form, make the object attractive and meaningful.

a. Start **Access**, and open the student data file **a02pf2Fitness**. Save the database as a02pf2Fitness_LastFirst.

b. Open each table, and then familiarize yourself with the fields. Open the **Relationships** window, and then note how the tables are related.

c. The staff wants to be able to enter all new member and roster information in the database at one time. Create a form that will allow them to enter the member records and the related membership records for a new member. Give the form a meaningful name. Add **Created by initial Lastname** to the report footer. Save the form as **frmMemberInput_initialLastname**.

d. Using frmMemberInput, enter yourself as a member. Use your actual name and address; all other information can be fictitious. Join the club today and have your membership end a year from now.

e. The staff wants to know how old each member is (in whole numbers) as of the date they joined the club. This will help them plan age-appropriate activities. Create a query to calculate the age of each member as of the date they joined the club. (Hint: When you subtract one date from the other, you get a total number of days, not years.) Save the query as **qryMemberAge_initialLastname**.

f. The manager wants to know which membership types are creating the most revenue and are the most popular. Create a query to calculate the total number of each membership type and the total fees collected for each membership type. Format the query so the manager will understand exactly what each field represents. Save the query as **qryMembershipStatistics_initialLastname**.

g. The manager would like to know if any membership types have not been applied for. Find any membership types that are not assigned to a current member. Save the query as **qryMembershipTypesUnused_initialLastname**.

h. The staff likes to celebrate birthdays at the club. Assume the current year is 2014. Everyone born in 1974 will turn 40 this year, and the staff would like a list of all those members along with their actual birthdays so they can quickly see who is celebrating a birthday each day. Save the query as **qry1974Birthdays_initialLastname**.

i. The staff likes to see each member's data as an individual record while still being able to view the whole table of data. Create a form that will allow the staff to view the data this way. Add **Created by initial Lastname** to the form footer. Give the form a meaningful name. Save the form as **frmMemberRecords_initialLastname**.

j. The staff needs a master list of members with their membership information. Create a report that will show the relevant information so the staff knows who is a current member and what kinds of membership each person has. Save the report as **rptExpirationDates_initialLastname**.

- Add **Created by initial Lastname** to the report footer. Change the report title to something meaningful.
- Modify rptExpirationDates_initialLastname so the records are grouped by the month of the expiration date. Highlight the expiration date field with a color so it stands out from the other fields.

k. The staff needs a list of members with the facilities their membership gives them access to. Create a report so the staff can quickly locate a member's name and determine which facilities they are allowed to access. Save the report as **rptFacilities_initialLastname**.

- Add **Created by initial Lastname** to the report footer.
- Change the report theme, change the report title to something other than the name of the report, and save the report.

l. Close Access. Submit your file as directed by your instructor.

Student data file needed:

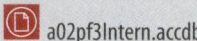 a02pf3Intern.accdb

You will save your files as:

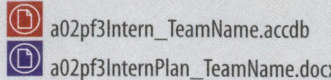 a02pf3Intern_TeamName.accdb

a02pf3InternPlan_TeamName.docx

Internships Coordination

Human
Resources

You take a job with an organization that matches students from Indiana schools to internship opportunities. The database you use keeps track of the companies that offer internships, the potential intern's information, and interview information dates for the interns. You are often called upon to add new records to the table, find information for a company or intern, and provide reports for your staff. Currently there are no reports, forms, or queries, so you will have to build them from the existing data. For all reports, queries, and forms, use meaningful names, and make the objects attractive.

Because databases can only be opened and edited by one person at a time, it is a good idea to plan ahead. You will use a Word document to plan your database and to plan which team member will do what. You will use SkyDrive to store your Word document and Access database.

a. Select one team member to set up the Word document and Access database by completing Steps b–e.

b. Open your browser, navigate to **https://www.skydrive.live.com**, create a new folder, and name it a02pf3Intern_TeamName using the name assigned to your team by your instructor.

c. Start **Access**, and open the student data file **a02pf3Interns**. Save the database as a02pf3Intern_TeamName replacing TeamName with the name assigned to your team by your instructor. If necessary, enable the content.

d. Upload the **a02pf3Intern_TeamName** database to the a02pf3InternshipsFolder_ TeamName folder, and then share the folder with the other members of your team. Make sure that the other team members have permission to edit the contents of the shared folder and that they are required to log in to SkyDrive to access it.

e. Create a new Word document in the assignment folder in SkyDrive, and then name it a02pf3InternPlan_TeamName using the name assigned to your team by your instructor.

f. In the Word document, each team member must list his or her first and last name as well as a summary of their planned contributions. As work is completed on the database, this document should be updated with the specifics of each team member's contributions.

g. Open each table, and then familiarize yourself with the fields. Open the Relationships window, and then note how the tables are related.

h. Create a form to enter data for new interns and their upcoming interviews. Pick a theme to apply to all objects in the database. Save the form as frmInterns and the subform as frmInternSubform.

i. Each team member should add his or her name as a new intern with one interview date and company of your choice.

j. You are scheduling for January and March and need to know which students already have interviews scheduled for those months, as well as the interview date and company the interview is with. Create a query, and then save it as qryJanuaryOrMarch.

k. Indiana University Purdue University Indianapolis (IUPUI) would like to know which of its students have interviews with Del Monte Foods Company or MMI Marketing and when those interviews are scheduled. Create a query, and then save it as qryIUPUI.

l. Your boss wants to know the total number of interns in the database from each university. Create a **query** with descriptive field names, and then sort appropriately to provide this information. Save the query as **qrySchoolCount**.

m. In the past, there have been problems with interns being scheduled more than once with the same company or scheduled for interviews on the same day. You need to find all students who have multiple interviews scheduled to check for conflicts. Create a query, and then save it as **qryMultipleInterviews**.

n. Your boss has asked for a master list of all interns who have interviews scheduled. He would like to be able to look up a student in the report to see when their interview is and who the interview is with. Save the report as **rptInterviewsScheduled**.

o. You need a report that counts and highlights how many interviews are scheduled each month. The report should also show the interview date and intern information. Save the report as **rptInterviewDates**.

p. When a company comes to interview, you need to quickly find who the interview is with. Create a report that will provide a master list of interviews that allows you to quickly see who is interviewing with each company. Save the report as **rptCompanySchedule**.

q. You would like to stay one step ahead of your boss. Create two more queries that may be helpful in analyzing the database information. Name the queries something descriptive so your boss will know what information is provided.

r. Once the assignment is complete, share the **a02pf3InternFolder_TeamName** folder with your instructor. Make sure that your instructor has permission to edit the contents of the folder.

Perform 4: How Others Perform

Student data file needed:

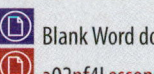 Blank Word document

a02pf4Lessons.accdb

You will save your file as:

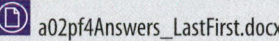 a02pf4Answers_LastFirst.docx

Music Lessons

Production & Operations

You have just taken a new job in a music store, and one of your responsibilities is to manage the music instructors and their students. A database has been created, but as you run the queries you notice they are either missing data or have wrong results. Answer the following questions about each of the objects as completely as possible:

a. Start **Access**, and open the student data file **a02pf4Lessons**.

b. Create a Word document **a02pf4Answers_LastFirst** where you will answer the questions.

c. Open rptListOfTeachers. Why is the image repeated after each record? How could the image have been added to the report so it would not repeat like that?

d. Open qryGuitarPianoAndBeginners. The query is supposed to show all teachers who are teaching piano or guitar and are taking new students. Why are other records in the results? Switch to **Design** view, and then explain how you would correct the query criteria to show the correct results.

e. Open qryLessonTimes. The query is supposed to show the average lesson length for each teacher. Instead, the query shows different lesson times for each teacher. What is wrong with this query, and how can you fix it to show the average lesson length for each teacher?

f. Open rptLessonList. Can you tell what the report is grouped by and sorted by without looking at the Group, Sort, and Total pane? Describe how you would change the grouping to group by Instrument.

g. Open qryInstrumentList. The query was supposed to find all teacher names, student names, and the instrument the student plays. Instead there are over 200 records. What happened, and why did this happen? How can you fix the query so it will provide the information you really want?

h. Open frmStudents. This form was created to see only one student at a time. Why is it showing one student and the whole student table? How was this form created? How would you create the form with only one student record at a time?

i. Submit your file as directed by your instructor.

WORKSHOP 5 | ADVANCED TABLES

Prepare Case

The Red Bluff Golf Club: Modifying Database Tables

Human Resources   Customer Service

The Red Bluff Golf Club generates revenue through its golfers, golfer services, and pro shop sales. The current database tracking this data has erroneous data from a lack of good table design. Barry Cheney, the Golf Club manager, has given you a copy of the database. You have been asked to modify the tables used to track employees and club members. This will make data entry easier and more consistent. To keep the file small while you work with the database, he removed most of the data and left only some sample data. Once Barry accepts your changes, he will load all of the data and implement the new database.

holbox / Shutterstock

REAL WORLD SUCCESS

"Last summer, I interned for a major banking firm in Pittsburgh, Pennsylvania. The departmental database we used to manage clients was built by a former employee who had never used Access before. When I ran queries, all the applicable data never seemed to be displayed even though I knew the data existed in the tables. I took a look at the tables, and I noticed that the fields contained inconsistent data. For example, the state field contained three different abbreviations for the same state. I modified the table structure so the fields would only accept data one way. Once the data was cleansed, my queries were completely accurate. The bank asked me to come back the following summer for another internship!"

- Lyndsai, current information systems management student

Student data files needed for this workshop:

 a03ws05Golf1.accdb

 a03ws05Matrell.jpg

 a03ws05Liu.pdf

 a03ws05Liu.jpg

 a03ws05Condon.jpg

You will save your file as:

 a03ws05Golf1_LastFirst.accdb

Controlling the Way Data Is Entered: Advanced Field Options

By ensuring your data is consistent and accurate, you are enhancing the usability of the data and database. The quality of data that is entered into your database determines the quality of data that is displayed in your query data sets. The **GIGO principle**—Garbage In, Garbage Out—means that inconsistent or inaccurate data leads to inconsistent or inaccurate output. People are not perfect when it comes to data entry. Thus, database designers have to place constraints—rules—on the data to prevent GIGO errors. In this section, you will learn how to help control the way data is entered through the use of advanced field options such as creating input masks, custom formatting, designing validation rules, and requiring data. Additionally, you will learn how to work with field captions and create indexes.

REAL WORLD ADVICE | **Does It Really Matter How Data Is Entered?**

The quality of the information you produce depends on the quality of data entered into your database. For example, you may want to query all customers who live in Ohio. If you did not restrict the number of characters permitted in a State field or create an input mask to assist in data entry, users could enter the 2-character abbreviation or completely spell out the state name. Once you have multiple versions of the state name within the State field, you run the risk of not returning all the customers who reside in Ohio in your query data set. This creates false reporting and ultimately can lead to poor decision making, which is never desirable in the business world.

- Set constraints on as many fields as possible. This will ensure that users are entering data the way you want it to be entered.

- Do not restrict what data can be entered into a field so much that it becomes difficult for users to enter data. You do not want to discourage users from using the database.

- Verify that all restrictions will adequately accept every variant of accurate data. You do not want valid data excluded.

- Remember that garbage in leads to garbage out.

Understand Input Masks

Multiple ways exist to standardize data entry into a database. One of the most common methods includes an input mask. An **input mask** controls the way data is entered. Thus, in most cases, an input mask actually controls the way that data is stored. This minimizes the likelihood that people will omit information or enter the wrong data by mistake. The input mask defines a pattern for how all data will be entered in a field. For example, users entering data will know whether or not to include parentheses around a phone number's area code.

Illustratively, you could create an input mask that ensures all data entered into a Last Name field is an uppercase first letter while the rest remain lowercase, no matter what capitalization the user types. Thus, the data actually is stored as a first capital and the rest in lowercase. You could also format the last name to all uppercase, but the data would still be stored as it was entered and will appear as if it is formatted as all uppercase letters. This technique will ensure that all data on reports and forms will look professional and consistent.

Opening the Starting File

To create input masks, you first need to open the Golf database.

A05.00

 To Save the Golf Database

a. Start **Access**, and then open the student data file **a03ws05Golf1**.

b. Click the **FILE** tab, click **Save As**, and then save the file as an Access database in the location designated by your instructor with the name **a03ws05Golf1_LastFirst** using your actual Last and First name. If necessary, click **Enable Content** in the Security Warning.

Defining Input Masks

You can manually create an input mask and use special characters to require part of the data to be entered, while other parts of the field are optional. For instance, you can require that the area code for a phone number must be entered or that other data such as the additional 4-digits of a zip code is optional. These characters specify the type of data—such as a number or character—needed for each character in the input mask.

QUICK REFERENCE	Common Global Data Variants

Because business is global, customers can be located all over the world. Different countries format data differently.

- Postal codes: Postal codes outside the United States can contain letters and numbers. For example, the postal code for Niagara Falls in Ontario, Canada, is L2G 2A6.

- Phone numbers: International phone numbers have country codes and a different format. For example, the phone number for a hotel near the Eiffel Tower in Paris, France would be +331 45 55 55 55.

- Dates: Most of the world formats a date with the day first, then the month, and then the year. In the United States, the date 05-07-1967 would be read as May 7, 1967. In many countries outside the United States it would be read as July 5, 1967.

- Currency: With businesses competing in a global market, one company could have different locations using their local currency. For example, Alcoa is the world's leading producer of aluminum. In China they would use the Yuan, and in Europe they would use the Euro, just to name a few.

You can also set the Format property for the same field to define how the data is displayed. For example, your input mask can define that a date is entered in a format such as YYYY/MM/DD, but have the date be displayed as DD-MM-YYYY.

CONSIDER THIS | **What Would You Do If You Had International Data?**

Think about what would happen if you had international data along with data from the United States that had to be entered into your table. Consider the common global data variants. How could you change your input masks to allow for these variations? Would you need to create different fields to allow for variations, such as multiple currency fields?

The common input mask characters along with their description are listed below:

- 0—Digit: 0 to 9, data entry is required; plus and minus signs are not permitted
- 9—Digit or space; data entry is not required; plus and minus signs are not permitted
- #—Digit or space; data entry is not required; spaces are displayed as blanks when editing, but blanks are removed when data is saved; plus and minus signs are permitted
- L—Letter: A to Z; data entry is required
- ?—Letter: A to Z; data entry is not required
- A—Letter or digit; data entry is required
- a—Letter or digit; data entry is not required
- &—Any character or a space; entry required
- \—Displays the character that follows as the literal character; for example, \A is displayed as just "A"
- ""—Characters enclosed in quotation marks are displayed as the literal characters; for example, "Cat" is displayed as Cat
- C—Any character or a space; entry optional
- >—Characters display in uppercase
- <—Characters display in lowercase
- !—Causes the input mask to be displayed from left to right, rather than from right to left
- ;—Used to separate the three parts of an input mask setting

A05.01

 To Create a Custom Input Mask

MyITLab®
Workshop 5 Training

a. Open **tblEmployee** in Datasheet view. Add your first and last name in record 1 of the tblEmployee table. **Close** ☒ tblEmployee.

b. Open **tblMember** in **Design** view, click the **State** field, and then in the Format box under Field Properties type **>**.

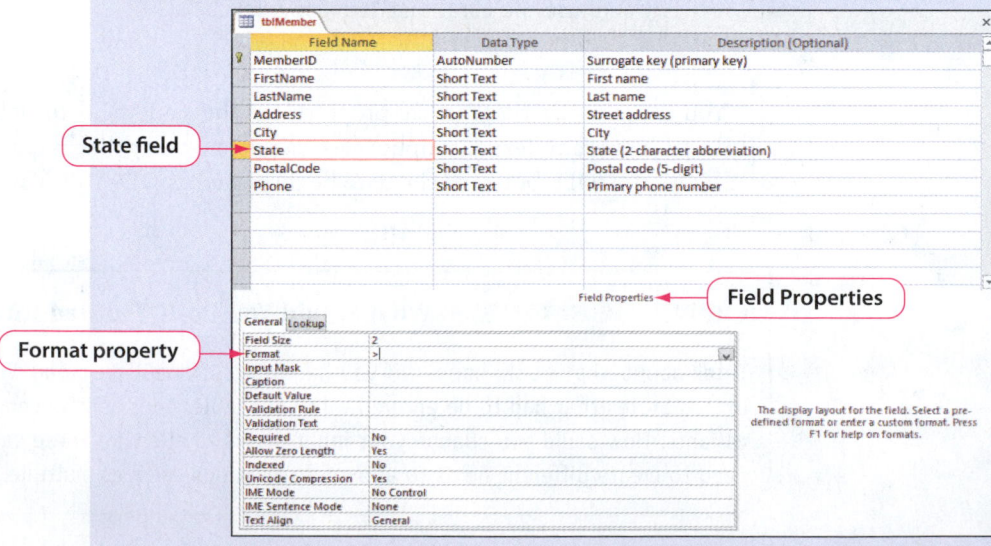

State field

Format property

Field Properties

Figure 1 Design view of the tblMember table

c. Click **Save** 🖫 on the Quick Access Toolbar to save your changes.

d. To see how this formatting works, switch to **Datasheet** view, and then enter the following record, replacing YourName with your own first and last name.

FirstName	LastName	Address	City	State	ZipCode	Phone
YourName	YourName	323 Bigalow Boulevard	Santa Fe	nm (enter as lowercase)	87594	(505) 555-4772

Notice when you enter data as lowercase in the State field, it is displayed as uppercase. However, if you click back into the State field in the record you just entered, the state abbreviation returns to all lowercase. Now you will reformat this field using a custom input mask.

e. Switch to **Design** view.

f. Click the **State** field, under Field Properties click **Input Mask**, and then click **Build** ⋯ to open the Input Mask Wizard. If Access prompts you to save your table first, click **Yes**.

> **Troubleshooting**
> If a Microsoft Access Security Notice appears on your screen, it is safe to click Open. To avoid seeing this message in the future, add your database to the Trust Center.

g. Because there is not an input mask already defined for the State field, you need to create a custom input mask. Begin by clicking **Edit List**.

h. Click **New (blank) record** ▶⁕. To create a custom input mask, enter the following.

Where to enter	What to enter	Why you entered this
Description	**State**	This will be listed in the Input Mask Wizard.
Input Mask	**>LL**	The ">" is to format the field as uppercase. The "L" indicates that a letter must be entered; thus, users must enter two letters into this field.
Placeholder	_ (type an underscore)	This will make it easy to see how much data can be entered into this field.
Sample Data	**NM**	This is the example that will be displayed in the wizard.
Mask Type	**Text/Unbound**	This means that you will type the text in the field.

SIDE NOTE
Changing Input Masks

Custom input masks can be customized by either changing a predefined mask or manually changing the Input Mask property.

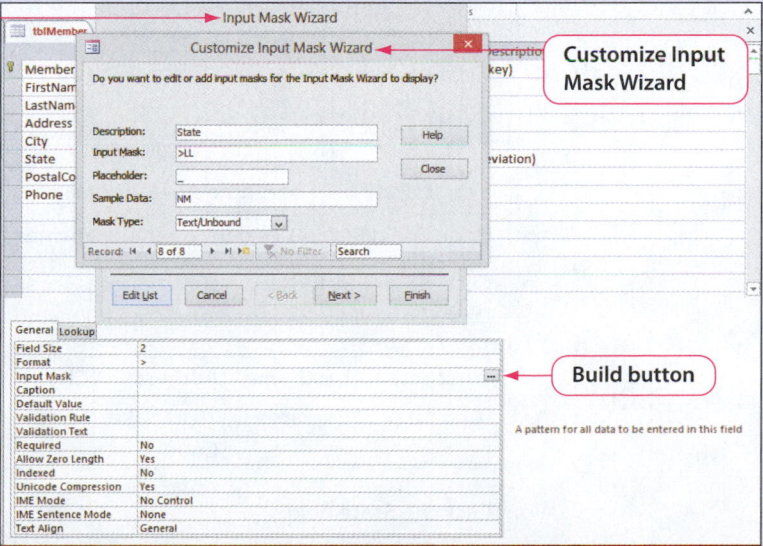

Input Mask Wizard dialog box

Customize Input Mask Wizard

Build button

Figure 2 Customize Input Mask Wizard dialog box

i. Click **Close**. In the Input Mask Wizard dialog box, scroll down the list, if necessary, and then click **State**.

j. Place the insertion point in the **left side** of the Try It box, and then type **nm** in lowercase.

Notice how Access automatically displays it in uppercase and does not allow you to enter more than two letters.

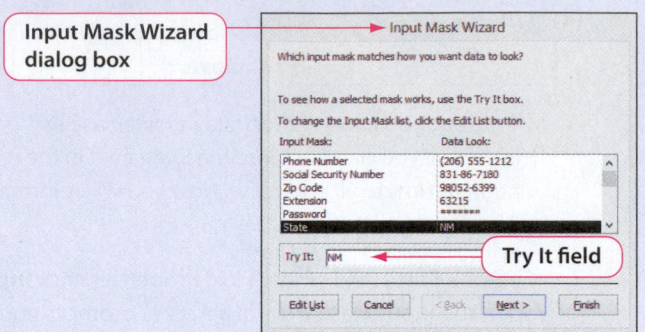

Input Mask Wizard dialog box

Try It field

Figure 3 Input Mask Wizard dialog box

SIDE NOTE
Storing Symbols
When disk space was expensive, symbols were not stored in order to save space and money. Now you can because storage is so inexpensive.

k. Click **Next** two times. Because there are no symbols in the custom input mask you created, it does not matter which option you choose on the screen that asks how you want your data to be stored. Keep the default selection, and then click **Next**.

l. Click **Finish**.

Notice the mask is displayed in the Input Mask field property.

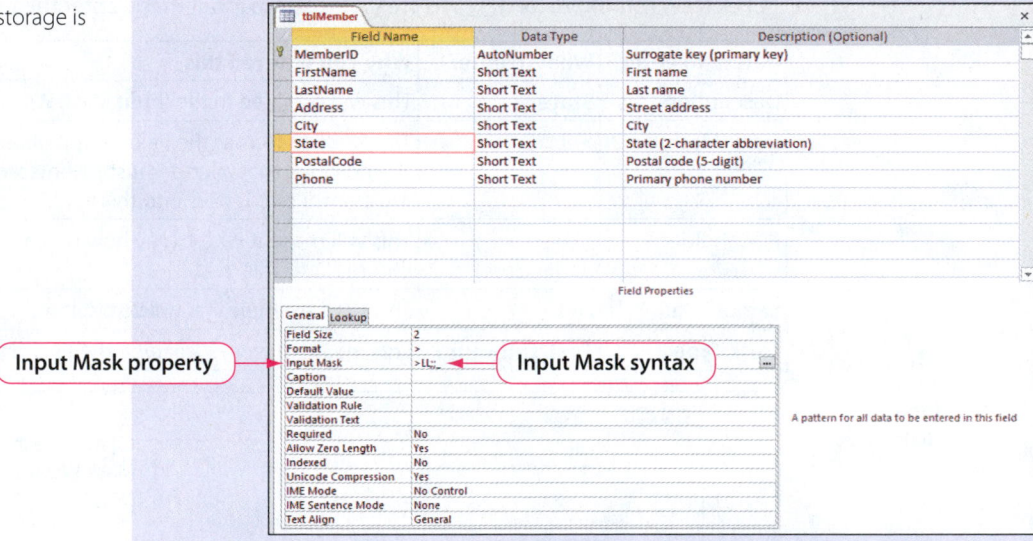

Input Mask property

Input Mask syntax

Figure 4 Design view of the tblMember table with new input mask property

m. Under Field Properties delete > in the **Format** box.

n. Click **Save** 💾 to save your changes. To see how this input mask works, switch to **Datasheet** view, and then enter the following record.

FirstName	LastName	Address	City	State	ZipCode	Phone
Charlie	Edwards	191 Drake Court	Santa Fe	nm (enter as lowercase)	87594	(505) 555-8676

o. Click the **State** field.

Notice that although you entered the state in lowercase, Access changed the storage of the state you entered into uppercase.

QUICK REFERENCE | Useful Custom Input Masks

You can create any number of input masks. Below are some of the more common input masks.

Type of Data	Input Mask	Data Results
Product number	>L0L 0L0	E8M 8C9
License plate number	>AAA\-AAAA	EZN-0987
Book ISBN-13	000-&-&&-&&&&&&-0	978-0-13-256088-7
Phone number with an extension	\(999\) 000\-0000\"x"aaaa	(724) 555-1234x6257
Social Security number	000\-00\-0000	123-45-6789

Table 1   Common input masks and examples

Using the Input Mask Wizard

Microsoft Access also includes several predefined input masks for more common formats such as date, time, Social Security number, password, phone number, and zip code. To apply one of these masks, you can use the **Input Mask Wizard** in the table's Design view. Regardless of the method in which you configure an input mask—manually or via the wizard—you want to select an input mask that is most appropriate for the field. If all the field values contain data with a consistent pattern, you should define an input mask.

A05.02

 To Create an Input Mask Using the Input Mask Wizard

a. Switch tblMember to **Design** view.

b. Click the **Phone** field, under Field Properties click **Input Mask**, and then click **Build** [---] to open the Input Mask Wizard.

c. Select **Phone Number**, and then click **Next**.

   Notice how the input mask characters are already defined for you. You can enter your phone number in the Try It box to see what your users will see when they enter data into the Phone field.

d. Click **Next**.

e. Under How do you want to store the data?, select **With the symbols in the mask**.

f. Click **Finish**.

   Notice the mask is displayed in the Input Mask field property.

g. Click **Save** [icon] to save your changes.

h. To see how this input mask works, switch to **Datasheet** view, and then enter the following record.

FirstName	LastName	Address	City	State	ZipCode	Phone
JoAnn	Pollack	124 6th Street	Spring Hill	NM	87588	(505) 555-2010 (without the symbols)

   Notice how the phone input mask makes it easier to enter and view data. It also saves time because Access enters the symbols for you.

SIDE NOTE
Saving Time Equals
Accurate Data Entry
Input masks make it easier
and save time entering
and viewing data, but they
also help ensure that data
is entered in the same
format.

i. **Close** ✖ tblMember.

j. Open **tblEmployee** in **Design** view.

k. Click the **HireDate** field, and then under Field Properties click the **Input Mask**. Click **Build** ⋯ to open the Input Mask Wizard.

l. Select **Short Date**. You can enter today's date in the Try It box to see what your users will see when they enter data into the HireDate field.

m. Click **Finish**.

n. **Save** 🖫 your changes.

o. To see how this input mask works, switch to **Datasheet** view and enter the following record.

FirstName	LastName	Salary	HireDate	Position
Lilly	Baine	21375	7/05/2015	Golf Caddy

REAL WORLD ADVICE — With or Without the Symbols in the Mask

If you do not store the symbols in the mask, Access will still display them when the field is used on other objects, such as on a form or report. In a Phone Number field, the parentheses and hyphen will not take up storage space. This is a carryover from when storage space was an extreme luxury. Either way, it will look the same to the user. Not storing the symbols saves a little space. If you have hundreds or thousands of customer records in a table and are storing a phone number for each customer, you may decide that you want to save a little space and not store the data with the symbols.

An important item to note is that if you choose not to store the symbols, you will have challenges when working with the data in other programs. For example, if you merge the data into Word or export it into Excel, then symbols will be missing if you did not store them in the mask.

QUICK REFERENCE — Three Parts of an Input Mask

Input masks consist of one mandatory part and two optional parts, separated by semicolons as shown in Figure 5.

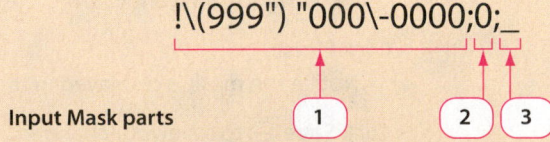

Input Mask parts   ① ② ③

Figure 5 Input mask parts

1. The first part is mandatory and includes the input mask characters, placeholders, and literal data.

2. The second part is optional. This refers to how the input mask characters are stored within the field. A blank or "1" means that input mask characters will not be stored. A "0" means that input mask characters will be stored. Setting the second part to "1" can save database storage space. In certain cases, setting the second part

(Continued)

QUICK REFERENCE **Three Parts of an Input Mask** *(Continued)*

to "1" can also be confusing if the data is ever exported. For example, imagine exporting a list of phone numbers with no parentheses or dashes. A number such as 5555551234 is harder to understand than (555) 555-1234. You should weigh the increase in database size with the potential for confusion.

3. The third part of the input mask is also optional and defines which placeholder symbol appears in the input mask. The default symbol that Access uses is an underscore, but you can choose any character.

Use Custom Formatting

Another common way to control your data is through formatting. A **field format** is like makeup. Makeup may change the way a person looks, but makeup does not change a person's underlying face. The same is true with formatting. Consider an American telephone number. You place parentheses around the area code and a dash between the prefix and last four numbers. The parentheses and dash make the number easier to read, but they do not change the actual number. You can also create your own type of formatting, called **custom formatting**. You can use the Format property to customize the way numbers, dates, times, and text are displayed and printed by using predefined formats or custom formats. If you set a field's Format property in Design view of a table, Microsoft Access uses that format to display data in datasheets, new form controls, and new report controls.

A05.03

To Create a Custom Format Property

a. Switch tblEmployee to **Design** view.

b. Click the **EmployeeID** field, and then under Field Properties click the **Format** property.

c. Customize the Format property of the AutoNumber field because the default AutoNumber property is only displayed as a number. Type "EMP"0.
   The zero will serve as a digit placeholder. You customized the Format property of the AutoNumber field because the default AutoNumber property is only displayed as a number.

SIDE NOTE
Formatting Your Data
Custom formats can be customized by manually changing the Format property where you want the format applied.

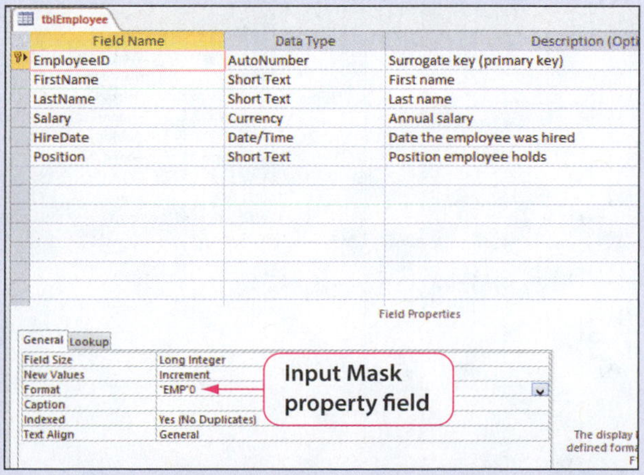

Field Name	Data Type	Description (Opti
EmployeeID	AutoNumber	Surrogate key (primary key)
FirstName	Short Text	First name
LastName	Short Text	Last name
Salary	Currency	Annual salary
HireDate	Date/Time	Date the employee was hired
Position	Short Text	Position employee holds

Field Properties

General	Lookup		
Field Size	Long Integer		
New Values	Increment		
Format	"EMP"0	←	**Input Mask property field**
Caption			
Indexed	Yes (No Duplicates)		
Text Align	General		

The display defined forma

Figure 6 EmployeeID field with custom format property

d. **Save** 🖫 your changes.

e. To see how this format works, switch to **Datasheet** view, and then enter the following record.

FirstName	LastName	Salary	HireDate	Position
Dennis	Matrell	18200	8/12/2015	Golf Caddy

f. Click the **EmployeeID** field of the record you just entered.

Notice that the format did not change the way the data is stored, just its display.

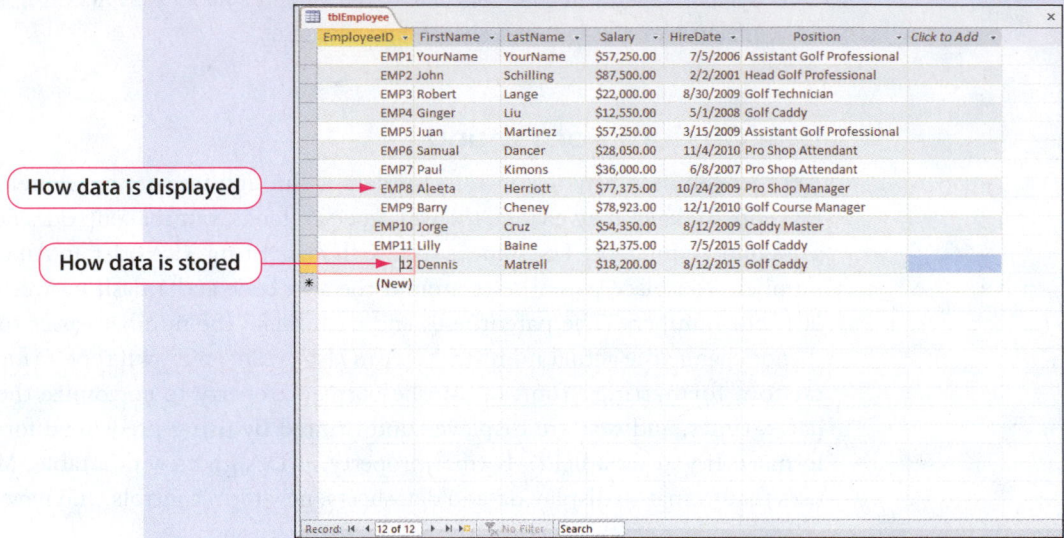

Figure 7 Datasheet view of the tblEmployee table with custom formatting in EmployeeID field

g. Switch to **Design** view.

h. Click the **Position** field, and then under Field Properties click the **Format** property. Type **&&[Green]**. You customized the Format property of the Position field to change the color of the text.

i. **Save** 🖫 your changes.

j. To see how this format works, switch to **Datasheet** view, and then view the data in the Position field.

Notice that the text is now green.

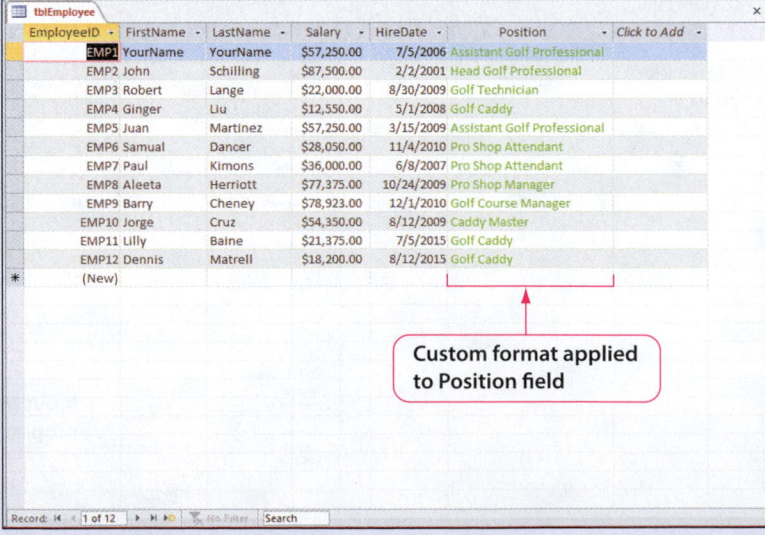

Figure 8 Datasheet view of the tblEmployee table

k. Switch to **Design** view.

l. Click the **HireDate** field, and then under Field Properties click the **Format** property. Select **Medium Date**. You customized the Format property of the HireDate field to format the date.

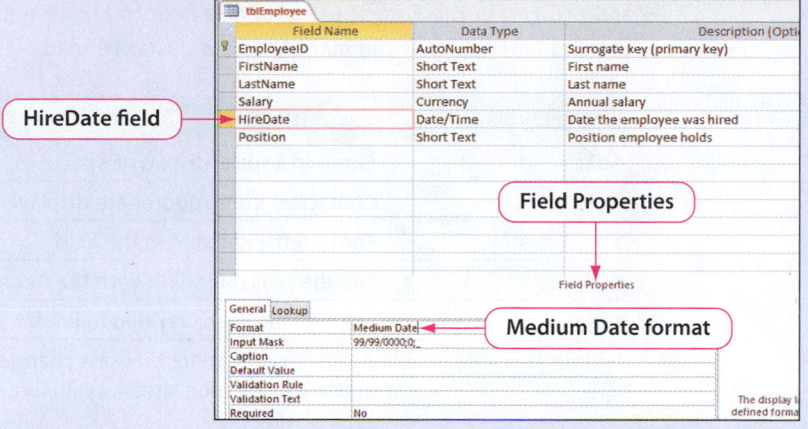

HireDate field

Field Properties

Medium Date format

Figure 9 Design view of the tblEmployee table with Date format

---

Troubleshooting

You may have noticed the Property Update Options button appeared after you changed the HireDate property to Medium Date. If you click the button and choose Update Format everywhere HireDate is used, Access will automatically update all lookup properties everywhere throughout your database where this field is used, including forms, reports, and queries.

---

m. **Save** 💾 your changes.

n. To see how this format works switch to **Datasheet** view, and then enter the following record.

FirstName	LastName	Salary	HireDate	Position
Antonio	Ruweeze	36900	8/24/2015	Pro Shop Attendant

Notice that because of the input mask, you were able to enter the HireDate as a short date. However, because you formatted the field as a Medium Date, it is displayed in the Medium Date format.

SIDE NOTE
The Text Is Still Black
Notice that as you are typing data in the Position field, it remains black. After you leave the field, it will change to green.

REAL WORLD ADVICE   **Can One Property Take Precedence Over Another Property?**

When you define an input mask that is different from the Format property in the same field, the Format property takes precedence when the data is displayed. Some items to note:

1. If you save an input mask, the input mask is ignored when you define a format in the field's Format property.

2. The stored data in the table does not change regardless of how you define the Format property.

3. The Format property only affects how data is displayed, not how it is stored.

You can enter different formatting syntax—placeholders, separators, literal characters, and colors—in the Format property of a field to create a custom format. By combining these characters, you can make the data easier to read.

Character	Description
Space	Entering a space displays a space.
"ABC"	Characters inside quotes are displayed.
!	Forces left alignment in the field.
*	Fills the available space with the next character.
\	Displays the character that follows.
[color]	A color inside square brackets changes the font color. Colors available are black, blue, green, cyan, red, magenta, yellow, and white.

Table 2   Custom format characters

Custom number formats can have one to four sections with semicolons separating each section. Each section also holds the format specification for a different type of number.

Section	Description
First	The format for positive numbers
Second	The format for negative numbers
Third	The format for zero values
Fourth	The format for null values

Table 3   Custom number format properties by section

You can also create custom number formats by using the following symbols:

Symbol	Description
.	Decimal separator
,	Thousand separator
0	Display a digit or 0
#	Display a digit or blank
$	Display a dollar sign
%	Value is multiplied by 100 and a percent sign added
E– or e–	Scientific notation with a minus sign next to negative exponents. This symbol must be used with other symbols such as 0.00E–00 or 0.00E00.
E+ or e+	Scientific notation with a minus sign next to negative exponents and a plus sign next to positive exponents. This symbol must be used with other symbols, as in 0.00E+00.

Table 4   Custom number formats

For example, a custom format for a Date/Time field can contain two sections—one for the date and another for time. Both sections are then separated with a semicolon.

(Continued)

QUICK REFERENCE | **Define Custom Formats Using the Following Characters** *(Continued)*

Thus, you can combine the Short Date format—mm/dd/yyyy—and Medium Time format—hh:mm followed by AM or PM—as shown in Figure 10.

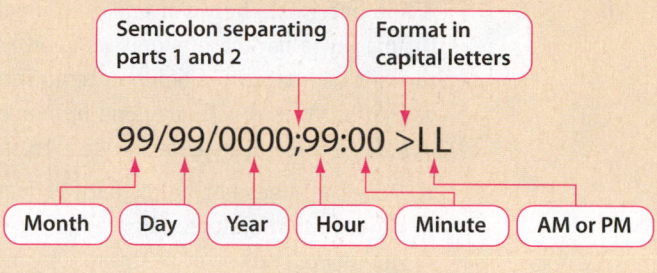

Figure 10   Custom Date/Time field format

Define Data Validation Rules

You can validate data as it is entered to help improve the accuracy and consistency by using data validation rules. **Data validation rules** prevent inaccurate data from being entered and consequentially stored in your database. Validation rules can be set for a specific field or an entire record. For example, a validation rule could be created to ensure that a product price is greater than zero.

When data is entered, Access checks to see whether the data meets the validation rule. If the data is not accepted, Access displays a message—known as **validation text**—designed to help users understand why there is a problem. The **Validation Text property** allows you to specify the error message.

You can create two basic types of validation rules: field validation rules and record validation rules. **Field validation rules** are used to verify the value that is entered in just one field is accurate. If the validation rule is violated, Access prevents the user from leaving the current field until the problem is fixed. For example, you may want to make sure that a product price entered is greater than 0. In the ProductPrice field, you would enter >0 as the Validation Rule property. If you enter 0 in the field, Access would not permit you to move to another field until the problem is corrected.

> **CONSIDER THIS** | **What Would You Recommend?**
>
> What if the resort wants to offer a free item in the inventory? What effect would configuring a validation rule on ProductPrice >0 have? What would you recommend doing in this instance?

A **record validation rule** determines if a record is valid, or meets all criteria, when a record is saved. In other words, you need to compare and validate the values in one field against the values in another field in the same record. For example, suppose your business requires you to ship products within 14 days from when an order was placed. You can define a record validation rule on the ScheduledShippingDate field, ensuring that someone does not schedule a ship date that breaches the company's 14-day rule.

The only difference between establishing a field validation rule and a record validation rule is its structure. In a record validation rule, you would reference field names as opposed to simply entering an expression. If your business follows the above

14-day shipping rule, the Validation Rule property compares the date entered in the OrderDate field against the date entered in the ScheduledShippingDate field. You can enter [ScheduledShippingDate] <= [OrderDate]+14.

REAL WORLD ADVICE	Why Bother with Validation Rules?

A fine line exists between rejecting inaccurate data and accepting all data entered. Ultimately, a database is only as good as the data stored within, so it is important to limit bad data from being entered into a field. However, be careful not to overdo validation rules or you may end up blocking data that is valid, yet unanticipated. The goal is to force users entering data to safeguard the validity of the data.

1. Data that does not follow data validation rules can negatively affect business processes. Therefore, data validation should start with a business process definition and set of business rules within this process.

2. Accuracy is critical when defining data validation rules. Errors in data validation can lead to data corruption or security vulnerability.

3. Periodically evaluate data validation rules. Rather than accepting or rejecting data when entered, consider changing the field properties into an acceptable format.

A05.04

 To Create and Test Validation Rules and Validation Text

a. Switch tblEmployee to **Design** view.

b. Click the **HireDate** field, and then under Field Properties click the **Validation Rule** property. You will notice that the Build button `...` is displayed.

c. Type **[HireDate]>=Date()-14** as the Validation Rule property.

   You created a field validation rule for the HireDate field so employees cannot be entered into the system after 14 days from the hire date as it could cause problems with the payroll department.

d. Enter the following validation text including the punctuation: **This employee began working more than 14 days ago. Please call the Corporate Office at (800) 555-4022.**

SIDE NOTE
Using an Equals Sign
When entering a validation rule, you do not need to begin the expression with an equals (=) sign.

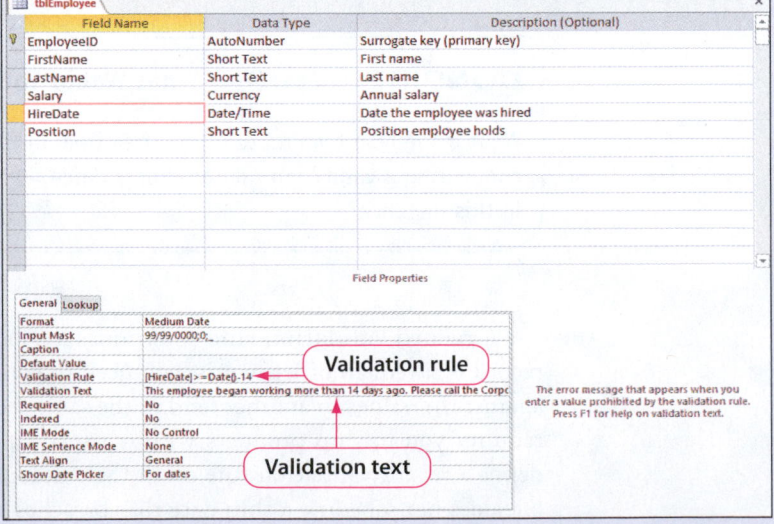

Figure 11 Design view of the tblEmployee table with validation rule and text

Troubleshooting

At times, entering data into field properties can become difficult to see. To enlarge your work area and font, right-click the property you are working on, and then click Zoom.

e.   **Save** 🖫 your changes.

f.   Click **No** when Access prompts you to confirm whether you want to test the existing data against the new rules.

Troubleshooting

You will notice a warning message stating that you have made changes to the table's data integrity rules and that existing data may not meet the new rules. Access wants to confirm whether you want to test the existing data against the new rules. If you know that the data meets the new rules, you can click No. If you are not sure and you want to make certain that all records meet the requirements, click Yes.

g.   To see how the validation rule and validation text work, switch to **Datasheet** view, and then enter the following record.

FirstName	LastName	Salary	HireDate	Position
Dolly	Hunt	23600	Enter a date that is at least 15 days before today's date	Golf Technician

Notice that because you entered a date that was more than 14 days ago, Access keeps you from moving to the next field until you correct the mistake.

h.   Click **OK**, and then change the date to today's date and finish entering the record.

i.   Switch to **Design** view, click the **Salary** field, and then under Field Properties click the **Validation Rule** property.

j.   Create a validation rule for **Salary** so that no salary can exceed $200,000. Enter <=200000 as the Validation Rule property.

k.   Enter the following validation text with the punctuation: The maximum salary an employee can earn is $200,000. Please re-enter this employee's salary.

l.   **Save** 🖫 your changes, and then click **Yes** to make sure that all existing data meets the new validation rule.

m.   To see how the validation rule and validation text work, switch to **Datasheet** view, and then enter the following record.

FirstName	LastName	Salary	HireDate	Position
Allie	Madison	310000	Today's date	Golf Professional

Notice that because you entered a salary that was more than $200,000, Access keeps you from entering the rest of the record until you correct the mistake.

SIDE NOTE
Validation Rules and Numbers

When entering numbers or currency into a validation rule, do not enter symbols like commas or dollar signs.

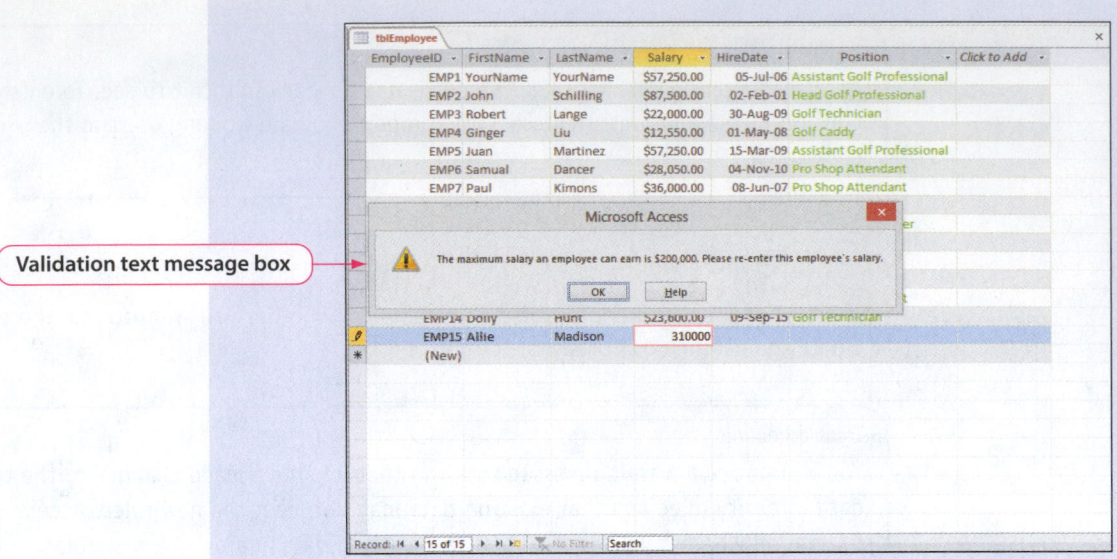

Validation text message box

Figure 12 Datasheet view of the tblEmployee table with validation text displayed

n. Click **OK**, change the salary to 200000, and then finish entering the record.

Work with Captions

When naming fields, you want to use a name that is easy to understand. Although the field name may be the best choice when designing a database, sometimes those names may not be what you want to display on other database objects such as forms, reports, and queries. Or you may be working with a database that someone else created, someone who did not understand the principles of good design.

Instead of having to modify field names, which could require you to modify other objects or settings in your database (e.g., relationships), it would be easier to simply define the **Caption property**. A caption is like an alias. An alias is another name that someone may use to hide their true identity, but their legal name is still what is listed on their birth certificate. A caption does not change the actual field name, just the way users see it—like an alias. Once this property is established, every object you create will display what the caption is instead of the field name. For example, a field named HomePhone would be displayed as "HomePhone" on forms and reports. However, by entering "Home Phone" in the Caption property, objects such as forms, reports, and queries will look more professional. This will also eliminate the need to change "HomePhone" to "Home Phone" on every object you create. This not only makes it easier for users to understand the data within table fields, but also makes it easier for designers to create other objects within the database.

A05.05

 To Create Captions for Existing Fields

a. Switch tblEmployee to **Design** view.

b. Click the **FirstName** field, and then under Field Properties click the **Caption** property. Type First Name in the Caption property.

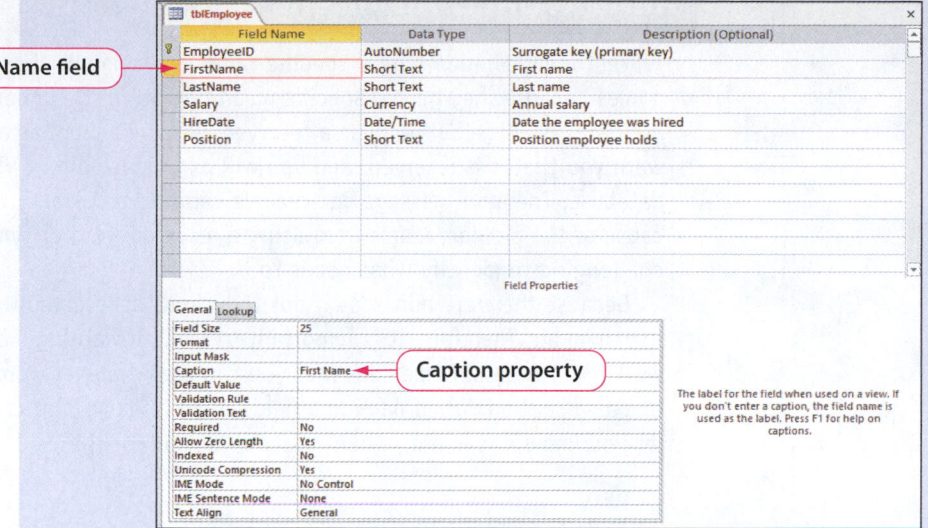

FirstName field

Caption property

The label for the field when used on a view. If you don't enter a caption, the field name is used as the label. Press F1 for help on captions.

Figure 13 Design view of the tblEmployee table with caption entered

c. **Save** 💾 your changes. To see how the Caption property works, switch to **Datasheet** view, and then look at the field heading.

d. Switch to **Design** view, and then enter the following captions for each field.

LastName: **Last Name**
HireDate: **Date of Hire**
Position: **Job Title**

SIDE NOTE
Always Resize Fields
Best practices state that when in Datasheet view, you should always resize the fields so all the data is visible.

e. **Save** 💾 your changes. To see how the table looks after creating your captions, switch to **Datasheet** view, and then view the field headings. Resize your fields if you cannot see the entire caption.

"First Name" caption is displayed

Figure 14 Datasheet view of the tblEmployee table

f. **Close** ✖ tblEmployee.

REAL WORLD ADVICE | Captions Enable You to Use Reserved Words

All relational databases have specific words and symbols that cannot be used as field names because they have a specific meaning within the underlying system files, such as "date" or "time". If you use a reserved word or symbol as a field name, Access will warn you that it is reserved, and you will experience errors when working with the database. The error message you receive will not necessarily communicate that the cause of the problem stems from using a reserved word or symbol. Thus, it can be challenging to identify what needs to be revised.

Because there are hundreds if not thousands of reserved words, it is impractical to list them all. Therefore, it is important to read all warning messages thoroughly when working in Access. Remember that you can use whatever word or symbol you would like as a caption. When naming a field, create a name that is compliant—Access will let you know if it is not—then create a caption for the field as you so choose.

Create Indexes

Many databases contain a large amount of data. Indexes are created and used to increase performance. For example, if you repeatedly search or sort your data on a specific field, you could create an index to speed up the procedure. An **index** in Access is similar to an index in a book. It is a lot easier and faster to find a topic in a book's index than having to search through the book page by page to locate what you need. By creating an index for a field or fields in a table, Access can quickly locate all the records that contain specific values for those fields without having to read through each record in the table.

CONSIDER THIS | What Will Happen in the Future?

Right now, the resort database is small enough that you will not recognize a difference in performance after creating an index. If this database is used for three years, how large do you think this database will get? What would happen in year 3 if you did not create indexes? Would your database run more slowly?

REAL WORLD ADVICE | How Do You Decide What Fields to Index?

- You can index every field if you want to, but it is not a good idea. Indexes can accelerate searches and queries, but they can slow down performance when you add or update data. Performance decreases because the indexes must be updated when data changes.

- You cannot index a field with an OLE Object, Hyperlink, Memo, or Attachment data type.

- Index a field when the data is generally unique and when there are more different entries than duplicate entries.

- Index a field when you plan to frequently search through it or sort it.

- The strategy to indexing efficiently is that an index should improve performance. Do not apply an index for any other reason.

Defining a Single-Field Index

If you create a **single-field index**, Access will not let you enter a new value in the field if that value is already entered in the same field within another record. Access automatically creates an index for primary keys, but you might also want to prevent duplicate values in other fields. For example, you may want to create an index on a field that stores a Universal Product Code (UPC) to ensure that all products have a unique UPC.

MODULE 3

A05.06

 To Create A Single-Field Index

a. Open **tblPosition** in **Design** view.

b. Click the **EmployeePosition** field, and then look at the Indexed property in Field Properties.

> Notice that Access automatically created an index for this field when the table was built.

c. Click the **DESIGN** tab, and then in the Show/Hide group, click **Indexes** to create a single-field index. The Indexes dialog box will open.

d. Enter the following index properties starting at the first blank row in the Indexes dialog box.

SIDE NOTE

Some Indexes Are Automatically Created

For some fields, such as a primary key, Access automatically creates an index for you.

Index Name	Field Name	Sort Order
Position	PositionType	Ascending

Index properties for Position index

Primary	No
Unique	No
Ignore Nulls	No

SIDE NOTE

Create Indexes in Field Properties

You can create a single-field index by changing No to Yes in the Indexed property in Field Properties.

Position single-field index

 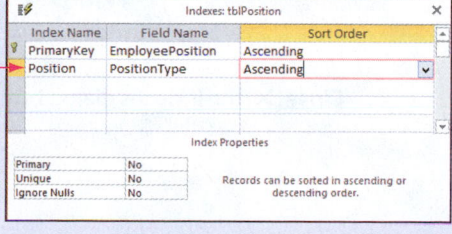

Figure 15 Indexes dialog box with new Index property

e. **Close** ⊠ the Indexes dialog box, and then **Save** 🖫 your changes.

f. **Close** ⊠ to close tblPosition.

SIDE NOTE

Using the Indexes Dialog Box

The Indexes dialog box allows you to easily see all the indexes within the table at the same time.

Defining Multiple-Field Indexes

You can also create an index for a combination of fields with a maximum of 10 fields. For example, if you frequently specify criteria for the Supplier and UPC fields in the same query, database performance would be improved if you create a multiple-field index on both fields.

When you create a **multiple-field index**, you specify the order of the fields. Once you sort a table by defining a multiple-field index, Access sorts the index in the order in which you enter each field into the Indexes dialog box. If there are records with duplicate values in the first field, Access then sorts by the second field defined for the index, and so on.

A05.07

To Define Multiple-Field Indexes

a. Open **tblMember** in **Design** view.

b. Click the **PostalCode** field, and then look at the Indexed property in Field Properties. Notice that Access automatically created an index for this field when the table was built.

c. Click the **DESIGN** tab, and then in the Show/Hide group, click **Indexes** to create a multiple-field index. The Indexes dialog box will open.

d. Enter the following index properties starting at the first blank row in the Indexes dialog box.

Index Name	Field Name	Sort Order
MemberName	LastName	Ascending
	FirstName	Ascending

Index properties for MemberName index

Primary	No
Unique	No
Ignore Nulls	No

SIDE NOTE

Reviewing Your Indexes

By clicking Indexes on the Table Tools Design tab, you can easily view and modify all existing indexes.

SIDE NOTE

Is Something Missing?

At first glance, it appears that something is missing. The index name appears only once in a multiple-field index.

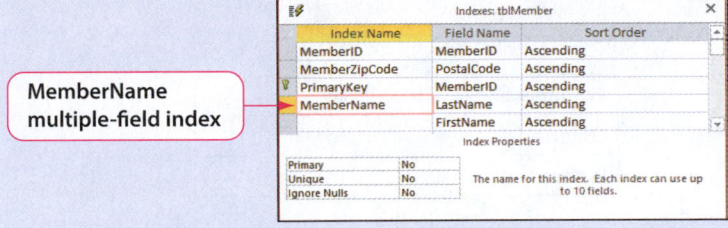

MemberName multiple-field index

Figure 16   Design view of the tblMember table with modified Indexed property

e. **Close** ☒ the Indexes dialog box, and then **Save** 🖫 your changes.

QUICK REFERENCE	Deleting an Index

If you find that an index becomes unnecessary or has a negative impact on performance, it can be deleted. When you delete an index, you only remove the index and not the field or fields on which it was created.

1. In the Indexes dialog box, select the entire row or rows that contain the index you want to delete—make sure that you select the whole row.

2. Press Delete.

3. Click Save on the Quick Access Toolbar.

4. Close the Indexes dialog box.

Use the Required Data Property

Data within Access fields can be required, ensuring that necessary information cannot be omitted from the database, either accidentally or deliberately. For example, in a customer database, a first name, last name, and address might be required, while a phone number may be optional. You can use the **Required property** to specify whether a value is required in a field, ensuring that the field is not left blank, or in database terms, is not **null**. If the Required property is set to Yes, and a user attempts to leave a field blank or removes a value from a required field when trying to save the record, Access will display an error message. The user will need to enter data before moving to the next field.

The Required property applies only to new records, not existing ones. Thus, if that is all that is set, you can cause an existing last name to be blank, even if it is required. To require data in a field, you must set the Required property to Yes and either a length of zero or a validation rule of "is not null". That way, both new and existing records require that field to have data.

REAL WORLD ADVICE	Changing the Required Setting When a Table Contains Data

If you change the Required property to Yes for a field that already contains data, Access allows you to verify whether existing records have values entered in that field. You can require that a value be entered in this field for all new records even if there are existing records without values in the field.

A05.08

 To Set Properties for Required Fields

a. Click the **FirstName** field, and then in Field Properties click the **Required** property.

b. Change the Required property from No to **Yes**.

c. Change the Required property of the LastName, Address, City, State, and PostalCode fields from No to **Yes**.

> **Troubleshooting**
>
> To enforce a relationship between related tables that do not allow null values, set the Required property of the Foreign Key field in the related table to Yes.

d. **Save** 🖫 your changes, and then click **Yes** in the Data Integrity warning dialog box.

CONSIDER THIS | Customer Data Is Important

Data about customers gives companies a way to contact the customers for marketing and customer service purposes. Some customers may not want to give out personal information. Do not restrict the database too much to allow for customers' personal preferences. For example, a customer may have an unlisted phone number. Should this be considered when determining whether data in a field is required? Which fields should never have the Required property set to Yes?

Define Default Values

Default values are one of the easiest ways to help with data entry. A **default value** is a value automatically entered into a field when a new record is created. For example, perhaps the majority of your customers live in a specific city. In a Customer table, you can set the default value for the City field to that specific city, such as Santa Fe. When users add a record to the table, they can either accept this value by just tabbing to the next field or change it by entering the name of a different city.

A05.09

 To Set Additional Properties for Required Fields

a. Click the **City** field, and then in Field Properties click the **Default Value** property.

b. Type **Santa Fe.**

SIDE NOTE
All or Nothing
If you do not enter the quotation marks, Access will enter them for you.

SIDE NOTE
When Typing Quotes, Type Both
If you only enter one, Access will not understand it, and an error will occur. Be sure to enter both or none.

City field

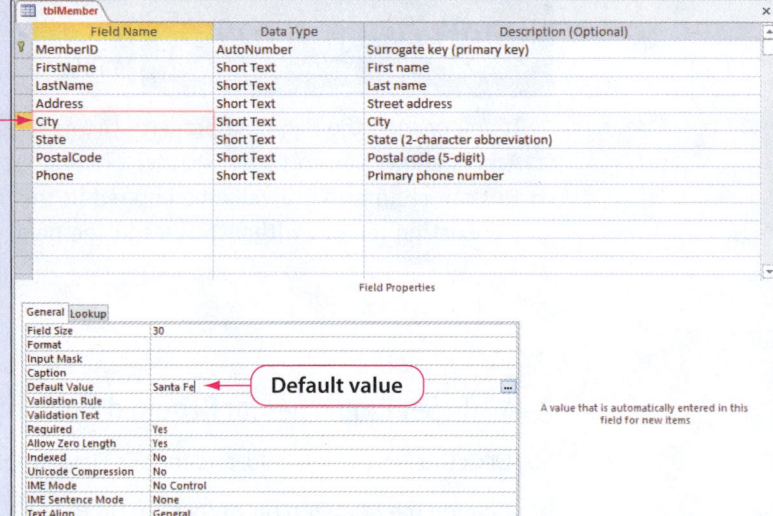

Default value

Figure 17   Design view of the tblMember table with Default value added to the City field

Troubleshooting

Quotation marks are needed around text, also known as string data, to let Access know that it is text. Different data types require specific delimiters or symbols when they become part of an expression—text needs to be enclosed in quotation marks and dates need to be enclosed in number signs. Eliminating the quotes would confuse Access because it would think you entered a number or keyword when you really entered text. Notice that Access automatically places quotes around the **string** if you forget. A string is composed of a set of characters that can also contain spaces, symbols, and numbers. Additionally, if you type in "Santa Fe", Access will automatically recognize it as a string and enter the quotes, unless the word is an operator. For example, if you have a field where the default value contains the word "like", you have to physically type the quotes because "like" is a reserved word.

c. Click the **State** field, click the **Default Value** property, and then change the Default Value to **"NM"**.

d. **Save** 💾 your changes.

SIDE NOTE
When a Default Value Can Be Used
Default values can be used in all fields except AutoNumber or OLE Object data types.

e. To see how the Default Value property works, switch to **Datasheet** view, and then click **New (blank) record** ⏭️.

Notice that the City and State fields are already populated for you.

f. Enter the following records.

FirstName	LastName	Address	City	State	ZipCode	Phone
Karen	Meyer	27 First Avenue	Santa Fe	NM	87594	(505) 555-2787
Harry	Shay	60258 Wildwood Road	Snowflake	AZ	85937	(928) 555-1638

Notice that you saved time entering the first record because the City and State fields were already populated for you. You also were easily able to enter a different city and state when needed.

g. **Close** ❌ tblMember.

SIDE NOTE

What a Default Value Will Not Do

Changing the Default Value property does not affect existing records.

Advanced Data Types

A **data type** defines the type and range of data that may be stored in the field and tells Access how to store and display the data in the field. Advanced data types allow for more efficiency in data entry. It constrains what can be entered into a field, ensuring that typographical mistakes are avoided. By avoiding data entry mistakes, your query results will be accurate. One advanced data type is a lookup field. A **lookup field** is a table field that has values that come either from a table, query, or a value list. In this section, you will learn how to use advanced data types such as Lookup, Calculated, Yes/No, AutoNumber, Attachment, Hyperlink, and OLE Object.

Create Lookup Fields

By creating lookup fields, you can help improve the efficiency of the data entry process. A lookup field can display a user-friendly list that is either linked to another field in a related table or a value list—a list of values that the database designer manually creates. For example, the lookup field can display a company name that is linked to a respective contact identification number in another table, query, or list.

When you create a lookup field that gets data from a table or query—called a source—Access uses the primary key field from the source to determine which value goes with which record. A lookup field replaces what is displayed, which would be the primary key field by default, with something more meaningful, such as an employee name. The value that is stored is called the **bound value**. The value that is displayed is called the display value.

Using the Lookup Wizard

Although a lookup field can be manually defined, the **Lookup Wizard** is the easiest way to create a lookup column. The wizard simplifies the process by automatically populating the appropriate field properties and creating the appropriate table relationships. The Lookup Wizard feature was enhanced in Access 2010 by automatically creating referential integrity settings. At the end of the wizard, you can make a choice to enable referential integrity. The wizard not only creates a relationship, but makes the correct referential integrity settings.

Another feature in Access is the ability to store multiple values in a **multivalued field**. This helps you keep track of multiple related facts about a subject. For example, suppose you have a project management database that helps you manage which employees are assigned to what projects. One employee might be working on several projects, and each project might have more than one employee working on it. This kind of data structure is called a many-to-many relationship. Access makes it easy to keep track of this related data by using a multivalued lookup field. After you create the multivalued field, it appears as a check box list in Datasheet view. The selected people are stored in the multivalued field and are separated by commas when displayed.

REAL WORLD ADVICE | **Enforcing Referential Integrity with Multiple Values**

Access will not allow you to store multiple values in one field if you enforce referential integrity. When Access enforces referential integrity, it is checking to see if related data exists between the primary key and foreign key in two tables. You cannot enter a value in the foreign key field of the related table that does not exist in the primary key field of the primary table. For example, a project cannot be assigned to an employee if that employee does not exist in your database. On the other hand, multiple employees may be assigned to one project. Thus, the foreign key in the Project table—EmployeeID—can have more than one EmployeeID listed and separated by a comma. The combination of the EmployeeIDs will not match any of the EmployeeIDs listed in the Employee table.

When you are building tables, make sure you understand how the data will be used. In many cases, it may be better to create a junction table instead of having a field within a table that allows multiple values to be stored.

CONSIDER THIS | **Multiple Values and Normalization**

Does storing multiple values conform to the principles of normalization? List some examples where using this feature is useful. What are some examples where storing multiple values would be inappropriate?

Using Lookup Field Properties

The purpose of a lookup field is to replace the display of a number such as an ID—or other foreign key value—with something more meaningful, such as a name. For instance, instead of displaying a product item ID number, Access can display a product name. **Lookup field properties** can be viewed in the bottom pane of the table's Design view under Field Properties. When the first property is initially configured, the list of available properties changes to reflect one's choice. Lookup field properties can be set to change the behavior of a lookup column. When the Lookup Wizard is used, many of the lookup field properties are automatically established by the wizard.

Although the wizard establishes the lookup field properties, there are some properties that may need to be modified, based on your own preferences. When the wizard creates the settings of a lookup field, many properties are not established or are configured to the Access default settings. You can set the lookup field properties to change the behavior of the lookup field.

QUICK REFERENCE | Determining Which Setting to Choose

There are three settings that you can select on the last screen in the Lookup Wizard. Choosing the right one depends on how you want to relate your data between the two tables. If you want to create a simple relationship, then you would select No Data Integrity. If you want to make sure that the values in the two tables always match, select the Enable Data Integrity check box, and then click one of the following:

1. Restrict Delete: This option activates referential integrity with no Cascades. Thus if you attempt to delete a record from one table but there is a corresponding record in the other table, the delete operation is not allowed.

2. Cascade Delete: This option activates referential integrity with Cascade Delete. Thus if you delete a record from one table, corresponding records in the other table are also deleted.

A05.10

To Create a Lookup Field

SIDE NOTE

Lookup Fields Have Limitations

The only data types you can create a lookup field for are Text and Number.

a. Open **tblMemberLessons** in **Datasheet** view.
    Notice how only numbers exist in the MemberID and EmployeeID fields. By creating a lookup field, you will be able to display something other than a number—a key from a different table. This will make it easier to see who is scheduling lessons.

b. Switch to **Design** view, and then click the **MemberID** field.

c. Select **Lookup Wizard** from the Data Type list. The Lookup Wizard dialog box will open.

> **Troubleshooting**
>
> If a Microsoft Access Security Notice appears on your screen, it is safe to click Open. To avoid seeing this message in the future, add your database to the Trust Center.

d. Click **I want the lookup field to get the values from another table or query**, and then click **Next**.

> **Troubleshooting**
>
> If a relationship already exists on the field you want to use the Lookup Wizard for, you must open the Relationships window and delete the existing relationship before going through the Lookup Wizard. Access will re-create the relationship automatically upon completion.

SIDE NOTE

Order Is Important

Select the fields in the same order as stated in the book. This specifies how the data will be displayed in the lookup field.

e. Select **tblMember**, and then click **Next**.

f. Select the **MemberID**, **LastName**, and **FirstName** fields to be included in your lookup field. You can move each one to the right side by either double-clicking the field name or clicking once on **One Field** `>`.

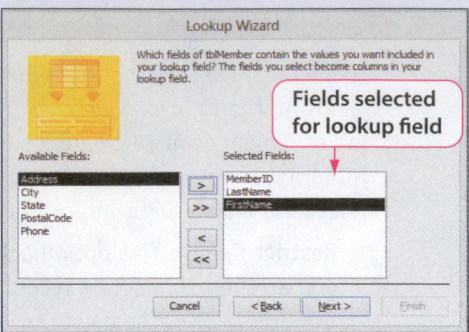

Figure 18 Selecting data in the Lookup Wizard dialog box

SIDE NOTE
Using Descending Order
Ascending order is the default sort order. If you want to sort a field in descending order, click Ascending to change the sort order.

g. Click **Next**, and then sort the following fields in ascending order: LastName, FirstName.

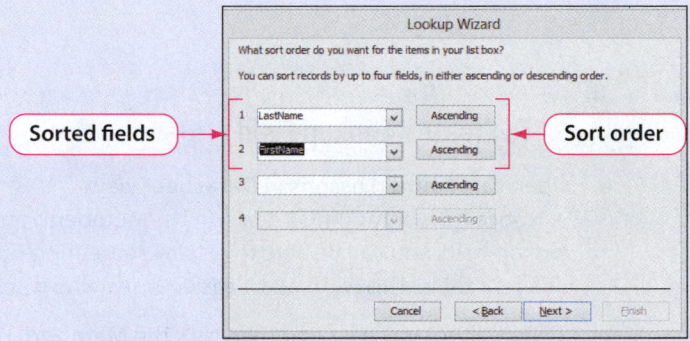

Figure 19 Sorting data in the Lookup Wizard dialog box

h. Click **Next**, and then clear the **Hide key column** check box.

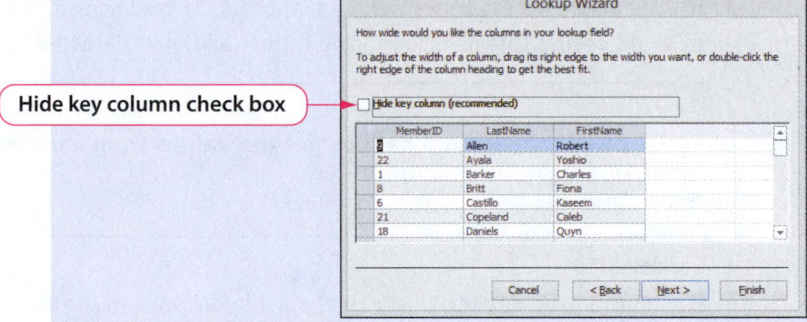

Figure 20 Unhide the Key Column in the Lookup Wizard dialog box

Notice how the key is displayed. If this box is left unchecked, the key column would be displayed in the lookup field. Because the key has no meaning other than helping you relate tables, hide it so that anyone using the lookup column sees only the values that you want them to see and not the values in the primary key field.

SIDE NOTE
Should You Rename the Lookup Field Label?
Because your field is already named, you do not need to rename it.

i. Click **Hide key column**, and then click **Next**.

j. Select **Enable Data Integrity** and **Restrict Delete**.

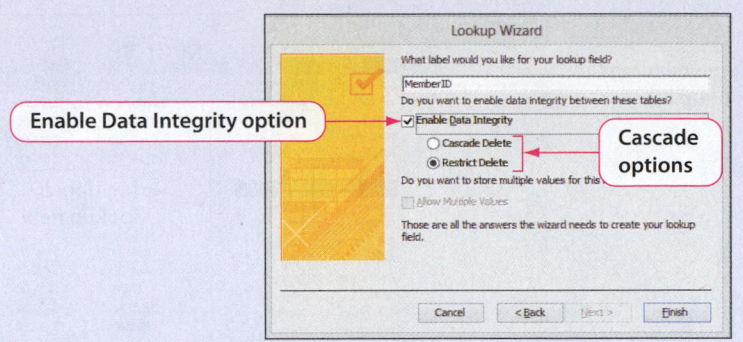

Figure 21 Finalizing the tblMember lookup field

k. Click **Finish**. Click **Yes** when prompted to save the table. Access will automatically create the relationship between tblMemberLessons and tblMember.

l. Switch to **Datasheet** view.

Notice how the lookup field displays the member's last name in the MemberID field. It is now much easier to determine which member has scheduled a lesson.

m. Switch to **Design** view, and then click the **MemberID** field if necessary. Under Field Properties, click the **Lookup** tab.

Notice that the Lookup Wizard configured many of the settings for you.

n. Change the Column Heads property to **Yes**, and then **Save** 💾 your changes.

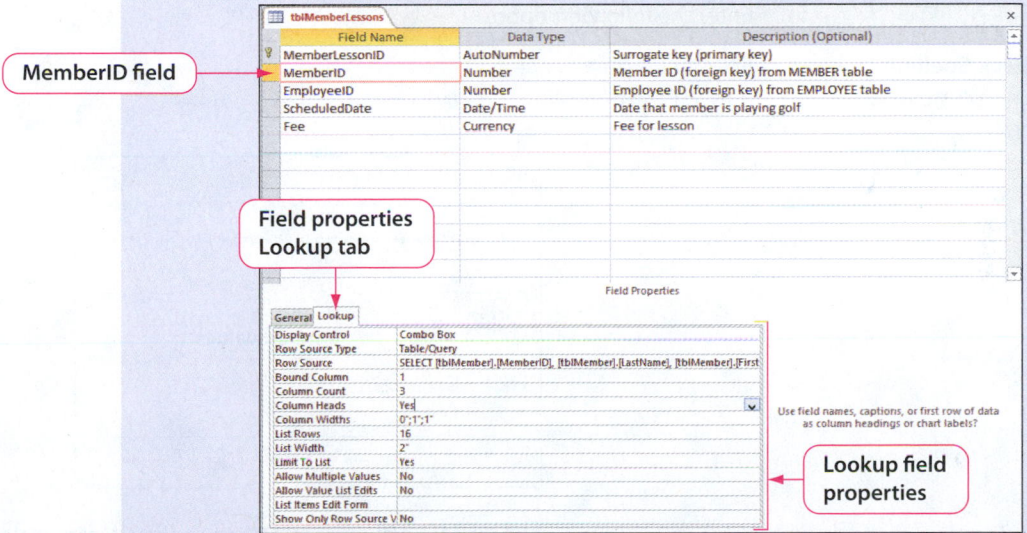

Figure 22 Design view of the tblMemberLessons table

o. Switch to **Datasheet** view, click the **MemberID** field, and then click the **Selection** arrow to expand your lookup field's list.

Notice that there are headings in the columns.

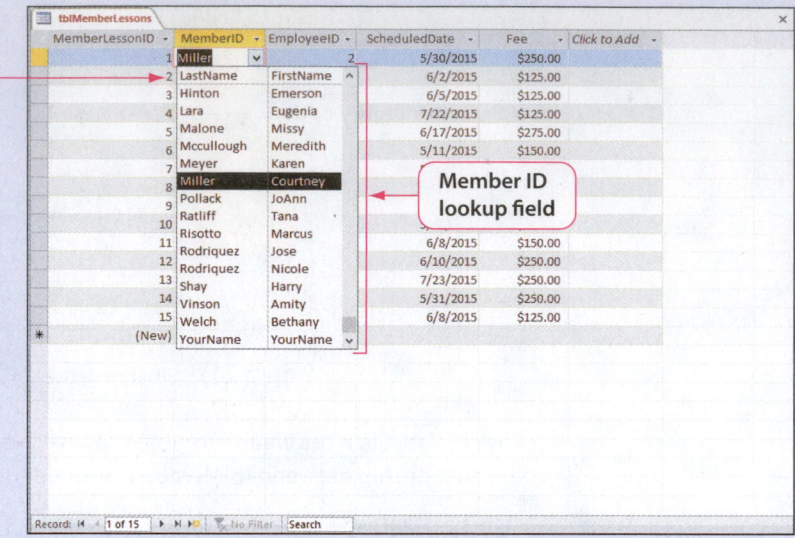

Figure 23 Datasheet view of the tblMemberLessons table

p. **Close** ☒ tblMemberLessons. Open **tblPosition** in **Design** view, and then click the **PositionType** field.

q. Select **Lookup Wizard** from the Data Type list. The Lookup Wizard dialog box opens.

r. Select **I will type in the values that I want**, and then click **Next**.

s. Enter the following options:

Row 1: **Full-time**
Row 2: **Part-time**

SIDE NOTE

Double-Check Spelling

When creating a custom lookup field, always double-check your spelling before moving to the next screen in the wizard.

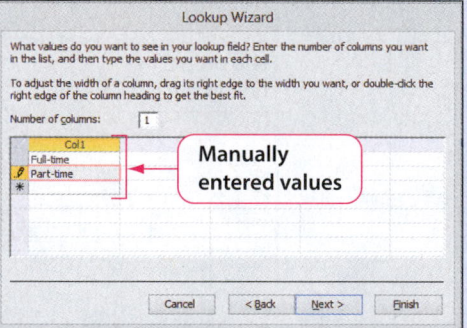

Figure 24 Values entered into Lookup Wizard dialog box

SIDE NOTE

What if I Wanted to Enter "Both"?

If you want to add an option to the list, simply switch to Design view and add the option to your lookup field.

t. Click **Next**. You want to limit the user's selection to the list because there are only part-time and full-time positions at the golf resort. Click **Limit To List**.

u. You do not want to store multiple values in this field because positions entered in this table are categorized as either part-time or full-time. Leave the box next to Allow Multiple Values cleared, and then click **Finish**.

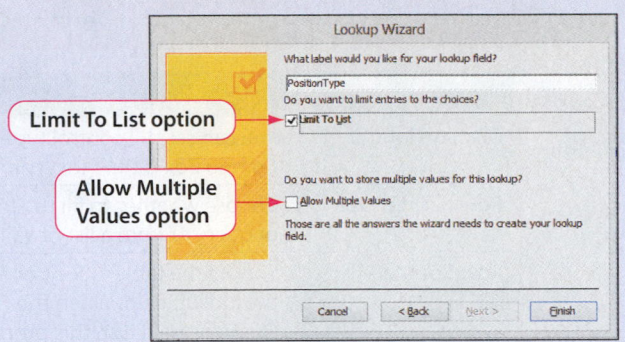

Limit To List option

Allow Multiple Values option

Figure 25 Finalizing the tblPosition lookup field

v. **Save** 💾 your changes. Switch to **Datasheet** view, click the **PositionType** field in the first record, and then type the word Both. Press Enter.

Notice that Access displays a message explaining that you must select an item from the list or enter text that is an item in the list.

w. Click **OK**, and then select **Full-time** from the list.

> **Troubleshooting**
>
> If you had to edit the list, you can also see the Edit List Items button 📝 when you are in Datasheet view and entering a value—the list is showing. However, it is very difficult to see, and it is faint.

x. Enter the following from the list in the PositionType field.

Caddy Master: **Full-time**
Golf Caddy: **Part-time**
Golf Course Manager: **Full-time**
Golf Technician: **Full-time**
Head Golf Professional: **Full-time**
Part-time Golf Professional: **Part-time**
Pro Shop Attendant: **Part-time**
Pro Shop Manager: **Full-time**

> **Troubleshooting**
>
> As you are entering the PositionType data, you may not be able to see the EmployeePosition field. To make it easier to view the EmployeePosition field while entering the PositionType data, highlight the EmployeePosition field, right-click, and then select Freeze Fields from the menu.

y. **Close** ✖ tblPosition.

Property	Description
Display Control	You can set the control type to Text Box, List Box, or Combo Box. Combo Box is the most common choice for a lookup field.
Row Source Type	Choose whether to fill the lookup field with values from another table or query or from a list of values that you enter.
Row Source	Specify the table, query, or list of values that provides the values for the lookup field. When the Row Source Type property is set to Table/Query or Field List, this property should be set to a table or query name. When the Row Source Type property is set to Value List, this property should contain a list of values separated by semicolons.
Bound Column	Specify the column in the row source that supplies the value stored by the lookup field. This value can range from 1 to the number of columns in the row source.
Column Count	Specify the number of columns in the row source that can be displayed in the lookup field. To select which columns to display, you provide a column width in the Column Widths property.
Column Heads	Specify whether to display column headings.
Column Widths	Enter the column width for each column. If you do not want to display a column, such as an ID column, specify 0 for the width.
List Rows	Specify the number of rows that appear when you display the lookup field.
List Width	Specify the width of the control that appears when you display the lookup field.
Limit To List	Choose whether you can enter a value that is not in the list. If you have referential integrity set to Yes, this is irrelevant.
Allow Multiple Values	Indicates whether the lookup field allows multiple values to be selected. You cannot change the value of this property from Yes to No. To remove the option, delete the relationship(s) to the field and rerun the Lookup Wizard.
Allow Value List Edits	Specify whether you can edit the items in a lookup field that is based on a value list. When this property is set to Yes and you right-click a lookup field that is based on a single-column value list, you will see the Edit List Items option. If the lookup field has more than one column, this property is ignored.
List Items Edit Form	Name an existing form to use to edit the list items in a lookup field that is based on a table or query.
Show Only Row Source Values	Show only values that match the current row source when Allow Multiple Values is set to Yes.

Table 5 Lookup field properties

Use the Calculated Data Type

Another Access data type is called a **Calculated data type**. A Calculated data type allows you to display the results of a calculation in a read-only field. The calculation must refer to other fields in the same table and is created in the **Expression Builder**. The Expression Builder is a tool that helps you create formulas and functions.

This feature can be useful for many reasons. For example, in an Invoice table, you could calculate the ExtendedPrice field by multiplying the Quantity and Price fields. In an Inventory table, you could calculate CurrentQuantityOnHand by subtracting the TotalProductsSold from TotalProductsOnHand. In a Customer table, you could join two or more fields—called **concatenate**—such as with FirstName and LastName fields for address labels.

Some database designers say that adding calculated fields in a table violates normalization rules. In some situations, they are right. However, sometimes it is acceptable to break the rules. For example, if you know that you will need the calculation in every object—query, form, and report—based on the table and you know that the expression will not change over time, then use this data type. Additionally, if having the calculation in the table makes your data easier to understand, then this is an acceptable data type to use.

CONSIDER THIS | **Could the Calculated Data Type Cause Challenges?**

The Calculation data type in a table was introduced in Access 2010. Do you think that the use of this data type will affect the speed or size of a database at all? Give examples of when using Calculated data types in a table is and is not appropriate.

REAL WORLD ADVICE | **Using the Expression Builder**

The Expression Builder is a tool you can use to help write expressions, such as calculations in forms, reports, and queries, along with field properties in tables. You can easily retrieve names of fields and controls in your database, as well as built-in functions available when writing expressions. The Expression Builder allows you to build expressions from scratch or select from many prebuilt expressions. Think of the Expression Builder as a way to retrieve and insert fields and functions you might have trouble remembering, such as identifier names for fields, tables, forms, or queries, functions, and arguments.

A05.11

 To Create a Calculated Field

a. Open **tblEmployee** in **Design** view.

b. Create a new field named NameTag, and then select the **Calculated** data type. The Expression Builder dialog box will open as soon as you change the data type to Calculated.

c. Double-click **FirstName** to add it to the Expression box.

d. Type **&**. This is the concatenation symbol that will allow you to combine data from different fields.

e. Type **"** to indicate literal characters, press [Spacebar], and then type **"**.

f. Type **&** again to join the FirstName field to the LastName field.

g. Double-click **LastName** to add it to the Expression box.

SIDE NOTE
The Table Name Is Listed

The Expression Elements box already displays the table you are using.

SIDE NOTE
Square Brackets Around Field Names

Access adds square brackets around field names to denote that the data will come from an existing field.

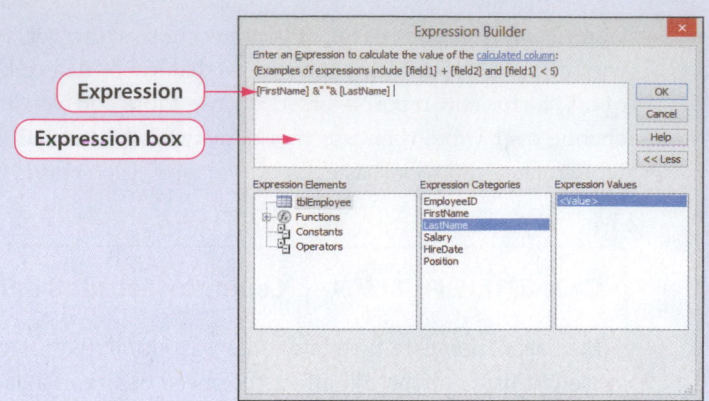

Expression

Expression box

Figure 26 Expression Builder dialog box

h. Click **OK**.

Notice that your expression is displayed in the Expression property under Field Properties.

i. Enter Used for printing name tags into the Description field.

j. **Save** 💾 your changes.

k. To see how the Calculated field property works, switch to **Datasheet** view, resize the NameTag field to see all the data, and then enter the following record:

FirstName	LastName	Salary	HireDate	Position
Ken	Condon	67725	Today's date	Assistant Golf Professional

Notice that Access automatically adds the FirstName and LastName to the NameTag field.

Troubleshooting

A Calculated field is a read-only field and cannot be edited. If you made errors in entering the FirstName or LastName, make the changes you need to make in those fields. Access will automatically update the NameTag field.

Use the Yes/No Data Type

The **Yes/No data type** allows you to set the Format property to either the Yes/No, True/False, or On/Off predefined formats or to a custom format for the Yes/No data type. Access uses a check box as the default display for the Yes/No data type. A **check box** shows whether an option is selected by using a check mark to indicate that the option is selected. Predefined and custom formats apply only to data that is displayed in a box, and therefore they are ignored when a check box control is used.

Access's predefined formats of Yes, True, and On are equivalent just as No, False, and Off are. If you select one predefined format and then enter an equivalent value, the predefined format of the equivalent value will be displayed. For example, if you enter True or On in a Text Box control where the Format property is set to the Yes/No data type, the value is automatically converted to Yes. Regardless of which format is selected, Access stores the values in this field as either a "0" for No, False, and Off or a "–1" for Yes, True, and On. The "0" and "1", or "–1" depending on the system you are using, are a throwback to the earlier days of programming. **Boolean algebra**, which is still used today, uses a "1" or a "0" to represent one of two values—true or false.

Custom formats can also be created with the Yes/No data type. For example, in a Customer table, you may want to have the words "Completed" or "Not Completed" in a field that tracks whether or not a customer has completed a survey sent out by the company. Additionally, you could have the words "Not Completed" displayed in red font, so it is easier to view those customers who have yet to complete the survey.

QUICK REFERENCE	The Three Parts of a Custom Yes/No Data Type

The Yes/No data type can use custom formats containing up to three sections.

1. First section: This section has no effect on the Yes/No data type. However, a semicolon is required and used as a placeholder.

2. Second section: This part contains the text to display in place of Yes, True, or On values.

3. Third section: This part contains the text to display in place of No, False, or Off values.

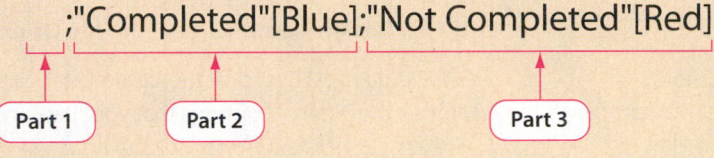

Figure 27   Parts of the custom Yes/No data type

A05.12

    To Create a Yes/No Field

a. Switch tblEmployee to **Design** view.

b. Create a new field called Orientation, and then select the **Yes/No** data type.

c. Type Is new hire orientation complete? into the Description field.

d. **Save** 💾 your changes.

e. To see how the Yes/No field property works, switch to **Datasheet** view, and then check the box for Ken Condon's record, indicating that his orientation has been completed.

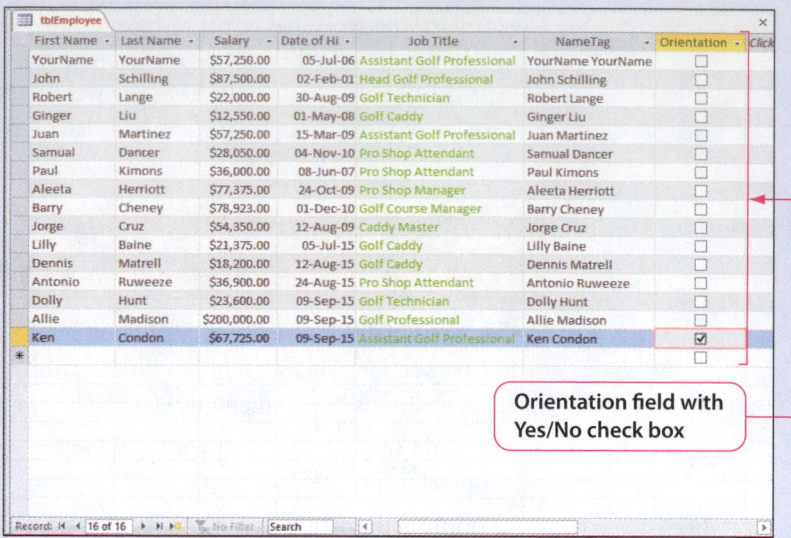

First Name	Last Name	Salary	Date of Hi	Job Title	NameTag	Orientation	Click
YourName	YourName	$57,250.00	05-Jul-06	Assistant Golf Professional	YourName YourName	☐	
John	Schilling	$87,500.00	02-Feb-01	Head Golf Professional	John Schilling	☐	
Robert	Lange	$22,000.00	30-Aug-09	Golf Technician	Robert Lange	☐	
Ginger	Liu	$12,550.00	01-May-08	Golf Caddy	Ginger Liu	☐	
Juan	Martinez	$57,250.00	15-Mar-09	Assistant Golf Professional	Juan Martinez	☐	
Samual	Dancer	$28,050.00	04-Nov-10	Pro Shop Attendant	Samual Dancer	☐	
Paul	Kimons	$36,000.00	08-Jun-07	Pro Shop Attendant	Paul Kimons	☐	
Aleeta	Herriott	$77,375.00	24-Oct-09	Pro Shop Manager	Aleeta Herriott	☐	
Barry	Cheney	$78,923.00	01-Dec-10	Golf Course Manager	Barry Cheney	☐	
Jorge	Cruz	$54,350.00	12-Aug-09	Caddy Master	Jorge Cruz	☐	
Lilly	Baine	$21,375.00	05-Jul-15	Golf Caddy	Lilly Baine	☐	
Dennis	Matrell	$18,200.00	12-Aug-15	Golf Caddy	Dennis Matrell	☐	
Antonio	Ruweeze	$36,900.00	24-Aug-15	Pro Shop Attendant	Antonio Ruweeze	☐	
Dolly	Hunt	$23,600.00	09-Sep-15	Golf Technician	Dolly Hunt	☐	
Allie	Madison	$200,000.00	09-Sep-15	Golf Professional	Allie Madison	☐	
Ken	Condon	$67,725.00	09-Sep-15	Assistant Golf Professional	Ken Condon	☑	

Record: 16 of 16

Orientation field with Yes/No check box

Figure 28   Yes/No field in the tblEmployee table

SIDE NOTE
Using Custom Colors
Custom colors are used to apply a color to all values in a field. You must enclose the color name in brackets.

f. Switch to **Design** view, and then click the **Orientation** field.

g. Under Field Properties, click the **Lookup** tab, and then click the **Display Control** arrow. Notice the different options that you have. Instead of a check box, you can also format a Yes/No field as a text box or combo box.

h. Under Field Properties click the **General** tab.

i. **Save** 💾 your changes, and then switch to **Datasheet** view.

j. Change the following employees' orientation status to "Completed" by clicking the check box in the Orientation field.

John Schilling
Robert Lange
Ginger Liu
Juan Martinez
Samual Dancer
Paul Kimons
Aleeta Herriott
Lilly Baine
Dennis Matrell
Antonio Ruweeze

SIDE NOTE
Check Box or Text Box
Certainly checking a box is easier than typing text. Choose a format based on your customization needs and personal preferences.

k. **Save** 💾 and then **Close** ❌ tblEmployee.

Use AutoNumbers and Determining Preferences for Natural Keys

A primary key uniquely identifies a record in a table. A **surrogate key** is an artificial column added to a table to serve as a primary key that is unique and sequential when records are created. However, these unique, sequential values are meaningless to users from a value standpoint; they are only meaningful in regard to creating relationships between tables.

An ideal surrogate key is short, numeric, and never changes. In Access, a surrogate key is known as the **AutoNumber data type**. The AutoNumber data type stores an integer that Access creates automatically as you add new records. These AutoNumbers can be categorized as increment or random. An **increment AutoNumber** is the most common and is the default setting in Access when selecting the AutoNumber data type. A **random AutoNumber** will generate a random number that is unique to each record within the table. Either type of AutoNumber will serve as a good primary key. AutoNumbers are a great method for ensuring that records are uniquely identified.

Some challenges do exist when working with AutoNumbers, but one in particular causes some stress with users. An AutoNumber of a deleted record will never be used again. For example, if you have a table with 10 records and the primary key is an AutoNumber—meaning that the records are numbered incrementally from 1 through 10—and you delete record number 7, Access will never use 7 again in the AutoNumber field. If this happens to you, do not think you did something wrong. This is simply how relational databases operate. Because of the way that Access does not reuse numbers, they are not designed to count records and they should never be used for that purpose.

CONSIDER THIS | AutoNumbers Are All Around You

A driver's license number can be assigned several ways, but depending on the state, it can be an AutoNumber automatically created for you in the state Driver License Bureau's database. Think of objects in your life that have numbers such as a gym membership, student ID, or debit card. Are the numbers on the items AutoNumbers? Which ones might be? Can you think of any other numbers you encounter throughout the day that may be an AutoNumber?

A05.13

 To Create an AutoNumber Field

a. Click the **CREATE** tab, and then in the Tables group, click **Table Design** to create a new table in Design view. This table will help users track when members have paid their annual dues.

b. Create the following table structure.

Field Name	Data Type	Description	Field Properties
PaymentID	AutoNumber	Surrogate key for each payment (primary key)	Primary Key
PaymentDate	Date/Time	Payment date	Short Date Format
AmountPaid	Currency	Payment amount	
MemberID	Lookup Wizard	This is the member who made the payment.	

c. When the Lookup Wizard opens, click **I want the lookup field to get the values from another table or query**.

d. Click **Next**, and then select **tblMember**.

e. Click **Next**, and then select the following fields to be included in your lookup field: **MemberID**, **LastName**, and **FirstName**.

f. Click **Next**, and then select the following ascending sort order for the data in your lookup field: **LastName**, **FirstName**.

g. Click **Next** two times, and then select **Enable Data Integrity** and **Restrict Delete**.

h. Click **Finish**, and then click **Yes** when Access prompts you to save the table.

i. Save 💾 your table as tblPayment and then click **OK**.

j. In the Description field, type This is the member who made the payment.

k. Save 💾 your changes.

Troubleshooting

Sometimes you may see a warning message that states, "tblPayment has been changed since the last time you opened it, either by another user or because another instance was opened on your own machine." If you know you have not made changes outside the database, click Yes.

---

l. To see how the AutoNumber data type works, switch to **Datasheet** view, and then enter the following records. You may have to scroll down in the list to find the names.

PaymentDate	AmountPaid	MemberID
1/26/2015	1200	Jena Duke
2/23/2015	1500	Marcus Risotto

Notice as you enter the data, Access automatically enters the PaymentID for you.

m. Delete the **record** where the PaymentID is 1. Click **Yes** to confirm the deletion of this record.

n. Enter the following record to see how the AutoNumber data type behaves when a record is deleted.

PaymentDate	AmountPaid	MemberID
3/5/2015	500	JoAnn Pollack

Notice as you enter the data, Access enters a PaymentID of 3.

o. To see how the random AutoNumber data type works, switch to **Design** view.

p. Click the **PaymentID** field, and then under Field Properties select the **New Values** property.

q. Change the Increment property to **Random**. As soon as you do, Access will warn you that once you change this property, you will not be able to change it back.

r. Click **Yes**, and then save your changes.

SIDE NOTE
The Lookup Fields Do Not Display All the Data
Lookup fields that have multiple fields will only display the data that is displayed in the first column.

SIDE NOTE
AutoNumbers Are Used Once
Once a number is used in a table, Access never uses that AutoNumber again, even if a record has been deleted.

s. To see how the random AutoNumber data type works, switch to **Datasheet** view, and then enter the following records.

PaymentDate	AmountPaid	MemberID
4/8/2015	800	Robert Allen
5/25/2015	2250	Fiona Britt

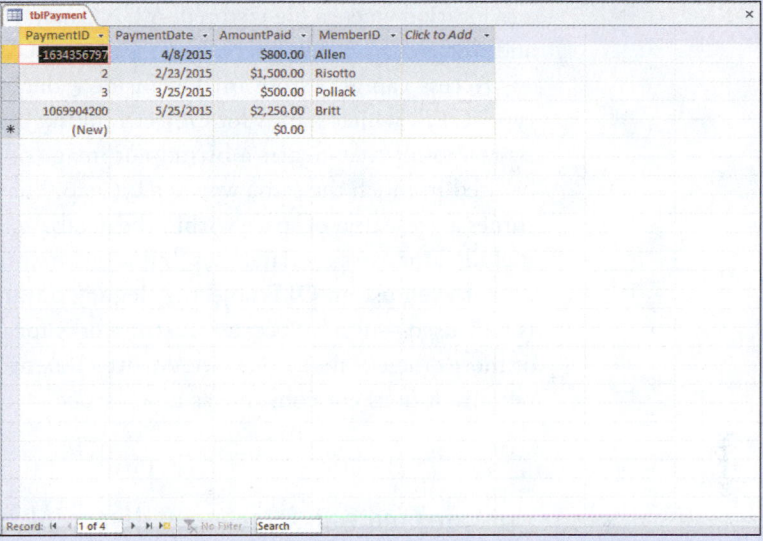

Figure 29   Datasheet view of the tblPayment table with random AutoNumber

> **Troubleshooting**
>
> Because Access creates a random AutoNumber, there is no knowing what number will appear. The number can be positive or negative. Whatever value Access enters and displays is acceptable.

t. **Save** 🖫 your changes. **Close** ✖ tblPayment.

Use the Attachments, Hyperlinks, and OLE Objects Data Types

You can attach images, spreadsheet files, documents, charts, and other types of supported files to the records in your database, much like you attach files to an e-mail message. Access allows you to view and edit the attached files, depending on how the database designer configures the **attachment** field properties. Where you need to use caution is that attachments do increase the size of your database, and developers need to ensure that attachments will not use too much storage space.

You are probably familiar with how all Microsoft applications can change e-mail or website addresses to be formatted as a hyperlink once you finish typing it into an application. In Access, fields that contain e-mail or website addresses should be defined as the Hyperlink data type. A **hyperlink** is an address that specifies a protocol—such as HTTP or FTP—and a location of an object, document, World Wide Web page, or other destination on the Internet, an intranet, or a local computer. An example is **http://www.paintedparadiseresort.com**. If the field is not defined as a hyperlink, Access will store it as plain text. This means that you will not be able to click it to navigate to a particular website or to launch your e-mail application and write an e-mail message.

When you are working with e-mail addresses, Access can add "mailto:" at the beginning of the e-mail address when you prompt Access to do so. The **Mailto command** is a common type of hyperlink that helps generate a link for sending e-mail. Thus by defining that your data is an email address and not a link to a website or document on other destination, users will be able to click the link and write their email.

Because many companies have files that are stored on the company's server so multiple employees have access to them, you can also enter a **universal naming convention (UNC)** path in a hyperlink field. This is a naming convention that provides a link to the machine and location where a file is stored. A UNC name uses the syntax \\server\share\path\filename and works the same way a Uniform Resource Locator (URL) works for a web address.

Access can also store images inside a database field by using the OLE Object data type. **OLE**, which stands for Object Linking and Embedding, is a technology developed by Microsoft that creates a **bitmap** or image of an object. The OLE Object data type can be used in much the same way as a bitmap, but it is less efficient than a bitmap as it consumes a great deal of space within the database. OLE is a legacy data type that needs to be included for existing databases, but attachments are far more functional and efficient and do not even use an OLE object. A **legacy data type** is an old or outdated data type that is still used—usually because it still works for the user—even though newer technology or more efficient methods exist. An attachment is the more efficient of the two data types because it does not consume as much space.

A05.14

 To Create an Attachment, Hyperlink, or OLE Object Field

a. Open **tblEmployee** in **Design** view.

b. Add the following new fields.

Field Name	Data Type	Description
EmailAddress	Hyperlink	Email address
Photo	OLE Object	Golf photo
OrientationSignOff	Attachment	Form verifying orientation completion

c. **Save** 🖫 your changes. To see how the Hyperlink data type works, switch to **Datasheet** view, and then enter the following data. Resize the field so you can see what you are typing.

EmployeeID	NameTag	EmailAddress
EMP4	Ginger Liu	liug@paintedparadise.com
EMP12	Dennis Matrell	matrelld@paintedparadise.com
EMP16	Ken Condon	condonk@paintedparadise.com

Notice that a hyperlink is automatically created once you enter the e-mail addresses.

> **Troubleshooting**
>
> When entering an e-mail address into a Hyperlink field, Access should automatically format it as an e-mail link. You may need to define it as an e-mail address by taking a of extra steps.

d. Right-click **Ken Condon's** e-mail address, click **Hyperlink**, and then select **Edit Hyperlink**. The Edit Hyperlink dialog box opens.

e. Click **E-mail Address** in the Link to section on the left side of the dialog box.
   Notice that the pane changes and allows you to enter Ken Condon's e-mail address.

f. Enter Ken Condon's e-mail address into the **E-mail address** box by either typing it or copying and pasting it from the Text to display box, if necessary.
   Notice that Access adds "mailto:" at the beginning of the e-mail address.

g. Click **OK**. To insert an OLE Object into the Photo field, right-click the **Photo** field in Ginger Liu's record, and then select **Insert Object**. The Microsoft Access dialog box opens.

h. Click **Create from File**.

i. Browse for the following employee photo in your student data files. Insert the following employee photo in the Photo field.

EmployeeID	NameTag	Photo
EMP4	Ginger Liu	a03ws05Liu.jpg

j. Click the **Link** check box, and then click **OK**.
   Notice that once the photo is inserted into the Photo field, the object is displayed as a Package.

> **Troubleshooting**
>
> Sometimes Access can be a little tricky when entering objects like photos or attachments. If you enter one and it will not let you enter any others, click in another field and check to see if Access will let you right-click into the OLE Object field. If that still does not work, close and then reopen the table.

k. Right-click the Photo field in Dennis Matrell's record, and then select **Insert Object**.

l. In the Microsoft Access dialog box click **Create from File**.

m. Browse for the following employee photo in your student data files, and then insert the photo in the Photo field.

EmployeeID	NameTag	Photo
EMP12	Dennis Matrell	a03ws05Matrell.jpg

n. Click the **Link** check box, and then click **OK**.

o. Right-click the **Photo field** in Ken Condon's record, and then select **Insert Object**.

p. In the Microsoft Access dialog box click **Create from File**.

q. Browse for the following employee photo in your student data files. Insert the following employee photo in the Photo field.

EmployeeID	NameTag	Photo
EMP16	Ken Condon	a03ws05Condon.jpg

r. Click the **Link** check box, and then click **OK**.

s. To insert an attachment into the OrientationSignOff field double-click the **Paperclip** button in Ginger Liu's record. The Attachments dialog box opens.

t. Click **Add**, and then browse for **a03ws05Liu.pdf** in your student data files.

SIDE NOTE
Why Can I Not See the Photo?

An OLE Object data type does not display the picture in the table. The Attachment data type for pictures allows a thumbnail to display on forms and reports.

SIDE NOTE
Why Click Link?

Not checking Link will cause Access to embed the image in the database, which takes up more storage space.

SIDE NOTE

Numbers in Parentheses

In the Attachment field, the numbers in the parentheses indicate how many attachments exist in that field.

u. Click **a03ws05Liu.pdf** once, and then click **Open**. The a03ws05Liu.pdf should now be displayed in your Attachments dialog box.

v. Click **OK**. To view the attachment, double-click Ginger Liu's **Attachment** field. The Attachments dialog box opens.

w. Click **a03ws05Liu.pdf**, and then click **Open**. The PDF document will open in another window.

> **Troubleshooting**
>
> If the PDF document did not open, you may not have Adobe Acrobat Reader installed on your computer. You can download this free application at **http://www.adobe.com**.

x. **Close** ☒ the PDF document, and then close the Attachments dialog box by clicking **OK**.

y. **Close** ☒ tblEmployee, and then click **Yes** when prompted to save.

Filtering Data

Filtering is very useful when you want to view and print only selected and required information from your database. Because this is a temporary view of the data, you may want to save the filter as a query if you want to filter the records on the basis of the same criteria again and again. In this section, you will learn how to filter data using Filter by Form, Filter by Selection, and advanced filter options.

Create Filters

Three types of filtering exist. Access provides the ability to filter records containing similar values of data for a specific field. For example, you may want to filter the records that have a "Santa Fe" value in the "City" field. The **Filter by Form** type could be used, which allows you to filter data in a form or datasheet. The Filter by Form method creates a blank table for the selected table. This blank table contains all the fields of the table with a list for each field. Each list contains all the unique values of records for each field. This method allows you to easily select the field value for which you want to filter the table records.

In some cases, the **Filter by Selection** method may not be very helpful as it may require extra steps to find your initial value. This displays only the rows in a table containing a value that matches a selected value in a row by filtering data in Datasheet view. In the above scenario, you may find that the Filter by Form method is better.

Because the Filter by Form or Filter by Selection filters may not give enough options as they are fairly basic, you might want to apply an **advanced filter**, a filter where you write the filter criterion yourself. For example, you may want to find products that contain dates that occurred during the past seven days. After you apply an advanced filter, you can further limit the results to those that have a price of over $100. Using the advanced filters requires writing expressions.

CONSIDER THIS | **Should You Save a Filter?**

A filter is only a temporary display of data. If you want to filter the records on the basis of the same criteria again and again, then it is worthwhile to save the filter. This can be done by selecting Save Object As in Backstage view, selecting Query, and then giving a name to the filter when you save it.

A05.15

To Create a Filter

a. Open **tblMember** in **Datasheet** view.

Notice there are 30 records in tblMember.

b. To filter by selection, click the **City** field of Record 1.

c. On the HOME tab, in the Sort & Filter group, click the **Selection** arrow ▾.

d. Four options are displayed. Select **Equals "Santa Fe"**.

Notice that all 13 members who live in Santa Fe are displayed. Additionally, the Filter button appears at the top of the field where the filter has been applied.

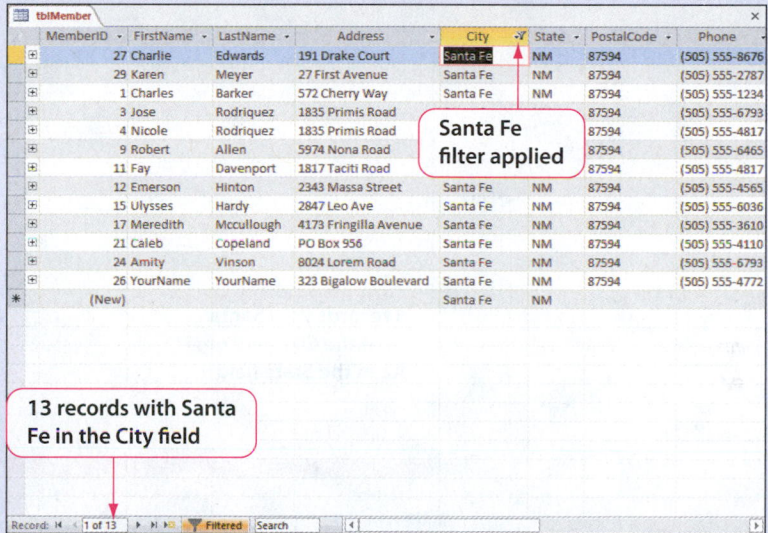

Figure 30   tblMember table with Santa Fe filter applied

e. On the HOME tab, in the Sort & Filter group, click **Toggle Filter**.

Notice that the filter is now removed.

f. Click **Toggle Filter** again, and the filter is reapplied.

g. Click **Toggle Filter** again to remove it.

h. To filter by form, on the HOME tab, in the Sort & Filter group, click **Advanced**, and then click **Filter By Form**.

i. Click in a few of the fields.

Notice that "Santa Fe" remains in the City field and each field has a list and looks much like a form. An Or tab also appears at the bottom of the table.

j. Select **Eagle Nest** from the list in the City field.

k. On the HOME tab, in the Sort & Filter group, click **Toggle Filter**. Three records meet the selected criteria.

l. On the HOME tab, in the Sort & Filter group, click **Advanced**, and then click **Filter By Form**.

m. Leave **Eagle Nest** in the City field. At the bottom of the tblMember: Filter by Form pane, click the **Or** tab.

This will allow you to search for one criterion or another. The Or operator indicates that either of the criteria can be in a record in order to display in the filter results.

n. In the State field select **AZ**, and then click **Toggle Filter**.

Notice that four records meet the filter criteria. The Filter is displayed at the top of the City and State fields, indicating that you have applied a filter to both fields.

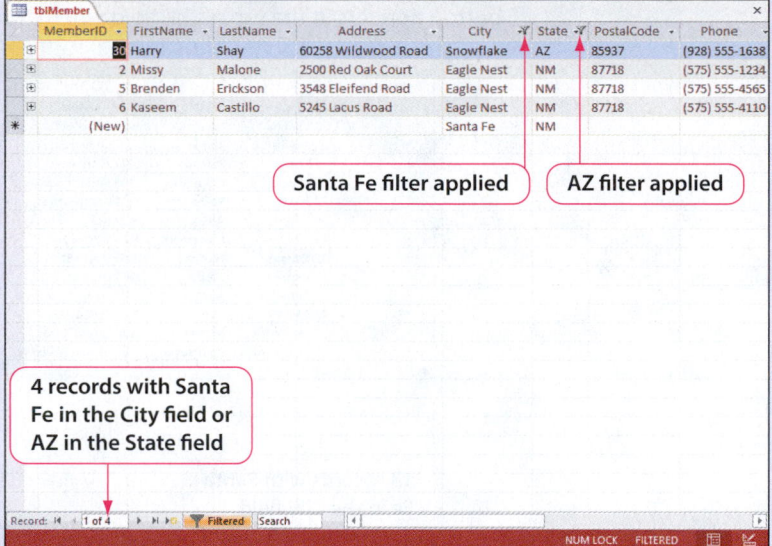

Figure 31   Datasheet view of the tblMember table with Eagle Nest and AZ filter

o. Click **Advanced**, click **Clear All Filters**, and then click **Advanced**.

p. Click the **Advanced Filter/Sort** button. The tblMemberFilter1 pane opens.

q. Select the following fields and enter the following criteria in the tblMemberFilter1 grid.

Field	Field Name	Criteria
1	City	Santa Fe
		Cowles (enter under "or" line below Criteria)

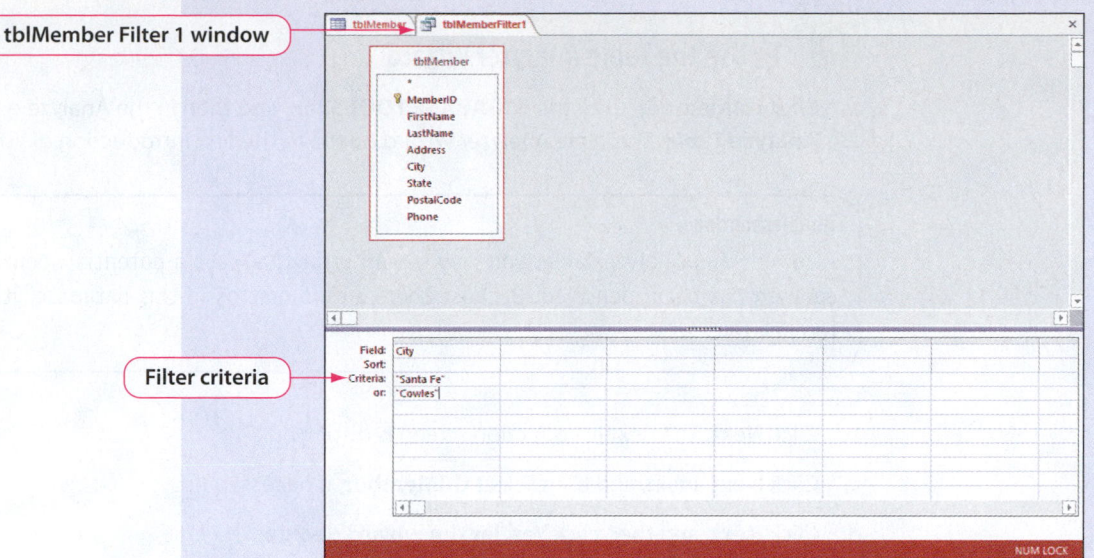

New tblMember Filter 1 window

Filter criteria

Figure 32   Design view of the tblMemberFilter1 query

r.   Click **Toggle Filter**.

Notice the results of the Advanced Filter are now displayed in tblMember.

s.   Click the **FILE** tab. Click **Save As**, click **Save Object As**, and then save your filter with the name qrySantaFeMembers_initialLastname. Under **As**, select **Query** from the list.

t.   Click **OK**.

Notice there is a new object named qrySantaFeMembers_initialLastname. This is the query you just created and saved.

u.   **Close** ☒ qrySantaFeMembers_initialLastname, **Close** ☒ tblMemberFilter1, and then **Close** ☒ tblMember. When Access prompts you to save the changes to tblMember, click **No**.

Using the Table Analyzer Wizard

Many times employees will store data in an Excel spreadsheet because they know how to use Excel, but not Access. Although Excel is a great tool for many tasks, Excel may not allow users to create the sophisticated queries that they need to for decision making. Because of this, there are times that you will want to import a spreadsheet into Access and work with the data. However, Excel spreadsheets often contain repetitive information that is not normalized, making the data impossible to move directly into an efficient Access database. In this section, you will learn how to normalize tables by using the Table Analyzer Wizard.

Normalize a Table

By using the Access **Table Analyzer Wizard**, you can divide the table created from imported data, such as an Excel spreadsheet, into several tables as well as automatically create the relationships needed between them. The Table Analyzer Wizard minimizes the need for data reentry, saving you valuable time and resources. However, the Table Analyzer Wizard is unable to restructure all the imported data properly.

To Use the Table Analyzer Wizard

a. Click **tblMember**. Click the **DATABASE TOOLS** tab, and then in the Analyze group, click **Analyze Table**. The Table Analyzer Wizard opens to the first introduction dialog box.

> **Troubleshooting**
>
> After clicking Analyze Table, you may see an error that says a potential security concern has been identified. Because there are no macros in this database, it is safe to click OK.

b. Click **Next**. The next introduction screen is displayed.

c. Click **Next** again, and then select **tblMember**, if necessary.

d. Click **Next**, and then click **Yes, let the wizard decide**.

e. Click **Next**.

f. Access will create two new tables, noted as Table1 and Table2. Double-click the **current table names**, and then rename them as follows:

   Table1: **tblMemberData**
   Table2: **tblCityState**

g. Click **Next**.
   The primary key in the new tblCityState table will be an AutoNumber, which is an ideal primary key. Access has **Generated Unique ID** as the first field in this table, which implies AutoNumber. You may have to resize the tables to see the whole table and field names.

h. Click **Next**.

i. There are no typographical errors that need to be fixed. Click **Next**. Access will ask if you are sure you want to move on. Click **Yes**.

j. Access asks if you want to create a query that resembles your old table. Because your old table will be saved automatically, you will not need a query with the same data. Click **No, don't create the query**.

k. Click **Finish**. Both tables you just created—tblMemberData and tblCityState—will open.

> **Troubleshooting**
>
> Access sometimes opens the Help window to offer further assistance with analyzing the table. Just close it if it opens.

> **Troubleshooting**
>
> Access sometimes displays an error message that says it cannot tile the tables horizontally. Just close the message if it opens.

l. **Save** 🖫 tblMemberData and tblCityState, and then **Close** ☒ tblMemberData and tblCityState.

m. **Close** ☒ the database.

SIDE NOTE
The Navigation Pane Minimized

After finishing the Table Analyzer Wizard, the Navigation Pane may be closed. Click the Shutter Bar Open/Close button if it does.

SIDE NOTE
tblMember Looks Like a Table

You can check to see what object type tblMember is by switching to Design view.

REAL WORLD ADVICE | **Why Worry About Analyzing Tables?**

When Access creates new tables in the Table Analyzer Wizard, it is looking for a way to minimize storage space in the analyzed table by storing data more efficiently. When a table contains repeating information in one or more fields, such as a city or state, you can use the Table Analyzer Wizard to move the data into related tables. This process is called normalization.

QUICK REFERENCE | **About the Table Analyzer Wizard**

Access takes you through a series of screens when you are working through the wizard:

- Looking at the Problem—This contains an explanation and examples of how duplicate data causes problems in a database.

- Solving the Problem—This contains an explanation and examples of how Access may split the table into multiple tables if there is redundant data in your tables.

- Select Table—Select the table you want to analyze.

- What Fields Go in What Tables Decision—This is where you determine whether you want Access to decide or if you want to select what fields go in what tables.

- Review Grouping—This is where you will either review or edit what Access has created, or where you will create your new tables based on your decision in the previous step.

- Create Primary Keys—Bold fields will indicate what the new primary keys will be. You can either keep them the way they are or edit them.

- Correct Typographical Errors—The wizard gives you the opportunity to fix any errors in your data.

- Create a Query—Access can create a query that resembles your old table. This is a smart idea to have as a backup copy.

Concept Check

1. Explain why it is important to worry about the way data is entered into a database. p. 256

2. What are the similarities and differences between an input mask and custom formatting? p. 263

3. Why are data validation rules helpful in business? p. 267

4. Why are captions also known as aliases? p. 270

5. What is an index? Why would you define an index in a table? p. 272

6. How can the creation of too many constraints or rules, such as requiring data, on a field or fields cause challenges for users? p. 275

7. How do default values assist with data entry? p. 276

8. How do lookup fields help improve the efficiency of the data entry process? p. 277

9. What is the Calculated data type? Explain why some database designers say this is an inappropriate field type. p. 284

10. The Yes/No data type can use custom formats containing up to three sections. Explain the three parts. p. 286

11. Why is the AutoNumber data type ideal to use as a primary key? p. 289

12. What types of documents can you attach to records in your database? Why should you be cautious when using an attachment field property? p. 291

13. Describe the differences between a Filter by Form and a Filter by Selection. p. 294

14. Define the three types of data filters, and give an example of when each may be used. p. 294

15. How does the Table Analyzer Wizard help normalize data within a table? p. 294

Key Terms

Use the Table Analyzer Wizard to normalize a table (p. 297)

Create a lookup field (p. 279)

Configure lookup field properties (p. 277)

Create an AutoNumber field (p. 289)

Create a filter (p. 295)

Create filters to view specific records (p. 294)

Create an input mask using the Input Mask Wizard (p. 261)

Define multiple-field indexes (p. 274)

Create indexes to increase performance (p. 272)

Create a custom input mask (p. 258)

Apply input masks (p. 256)

Set properties for required fields (p. 275)

Apply the Required property (p. 275)

Set additional properties for required fields (p. 276)

Define default values (p. 276)

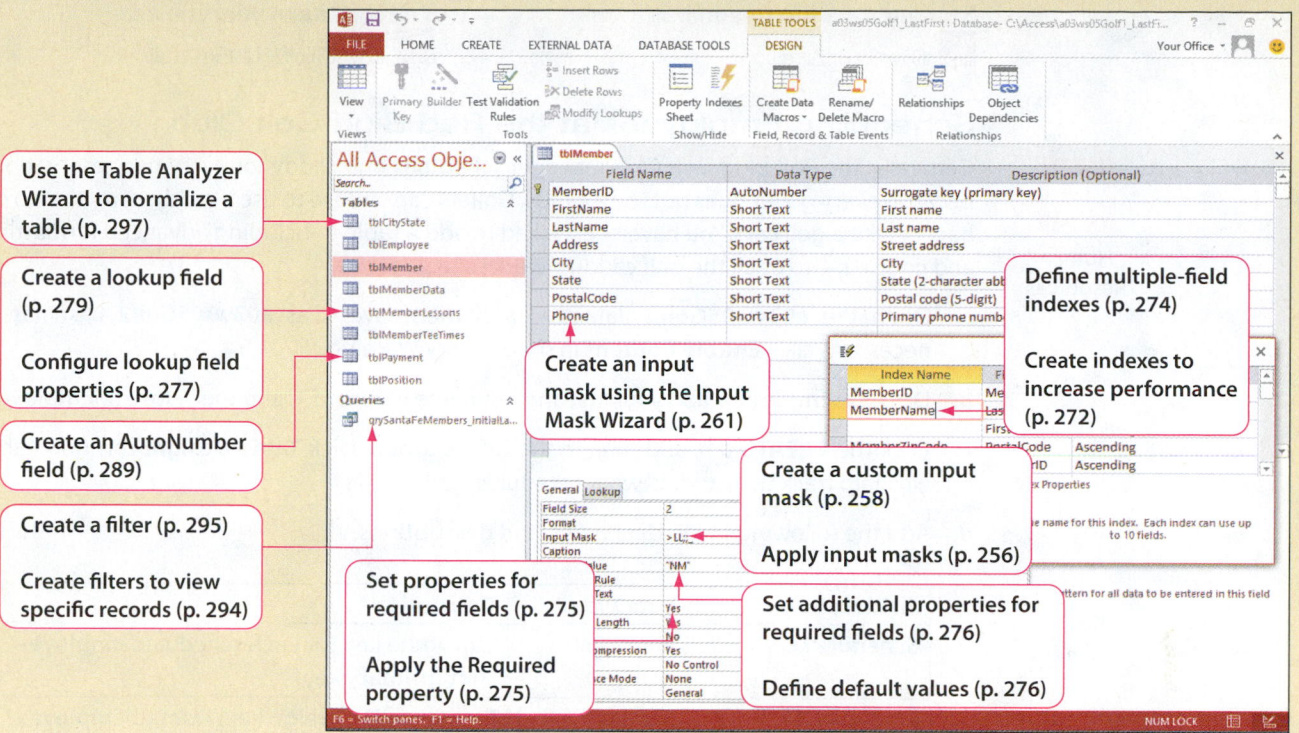

Figure 33   The Red Bluff Golf Club Pro Shop Final tblMember Table

Create a custom format property (p. 263)

Apply custom formatting (p. 263)

Create a single-field index (p. 273)

Create a calculated field (p. 285)

Configure a field using the Lookup Wizard, Calculated, Yes/No, AutoNumber, Attachments, Hyperlinks, and OLE Objects data types (p. 284)

Create a yes/no field (p. 287)

Create an Attachment, Hyperlink, or OLE Object field (p. 292)

Create captions for existing fields (p. 270)

Define caption names using the Caption property (p. 270)

Create and test validation rules and validation text (p. 268)

Create data validation rules (p. 267)

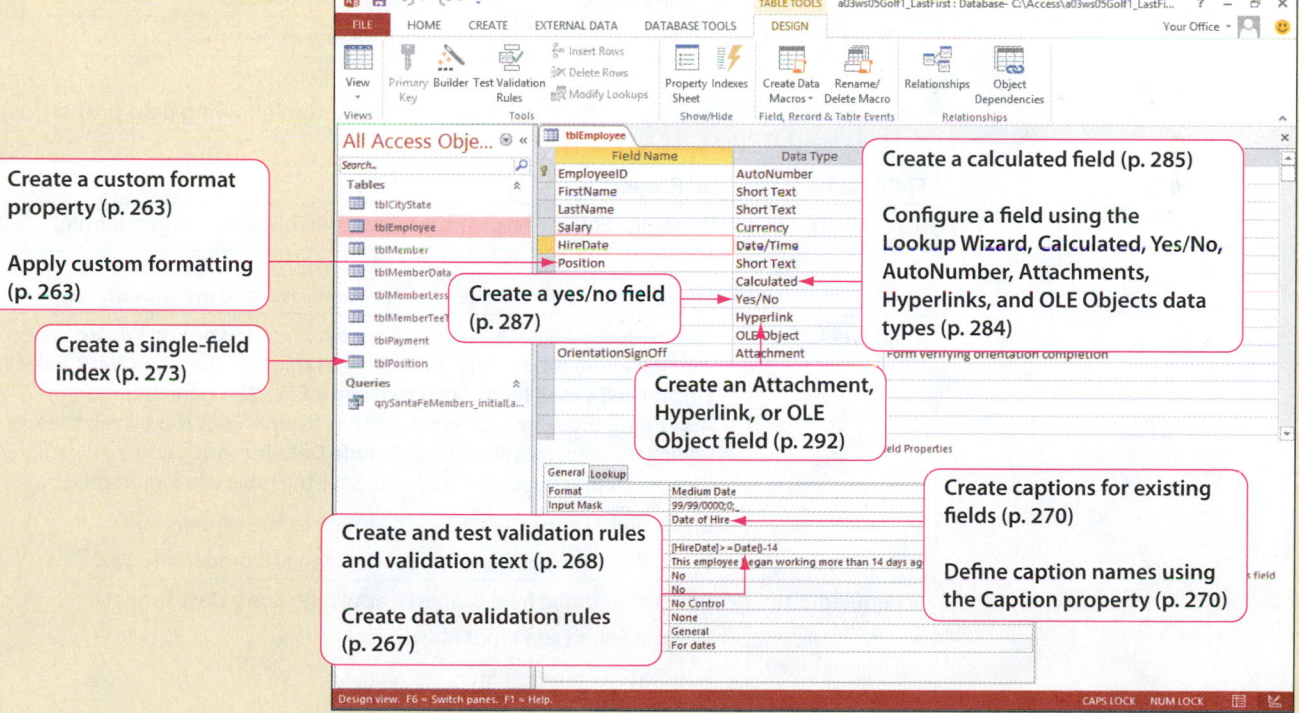

Figure 34   The Red Bluff Golf Club Pro Shop Final tblEmployee Table

Student data file needed:
 a03ws05Golf2.accdb

You will save your file as:
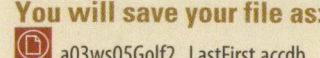 a03ws05Golf2_LastFirst.accdb

Scheduling Employees at the Red Bluff Golf Club

Human
Resources

Generally, the Red Bluff Golf Club manager schedules one caddy for every two reservations because every golfer does not use a caddy. Golfers can choose to use a caddy, carry their own bag, or rent a golf cart. You have been asked to add a table—including advanced formatting and controls—to track the golf caddies' work schedule.

a. Open the **a03ws05Golf2** database, and then save it as **a03ws05Golf2_LastFirst**. If necessary, click **Enable Content** in the Security Warning.

b. Open **tblEmployee**, add your first and last name in record 1, and then close tblEmployee.

c. Click the **CREATE** tab, and then in the Tables group, click **Table Design**. This new table will help track the caddies' work schedules.

d. Add the following fields, data types, and descriptions.

Field Name	Data Type	Description
ScheduleID	AutoNumber	Surrogate key for each scheduled employee shift (primary key)
EmployeeID	Number	EmployeeID (foreign key) from tblEmployee
ScheduledDate	Date/Time	Date employee is scheduled to work
StartTime	Date/Time	Time employee's shift begins
EndTime	Date/Time	Time employee's shift ends
OnTime	Yes/No	Did employee arrive on time

e. Save the table as **tblEmployeeSchedule**, and then create the following field properties.

Field Name	Field Properties
ScheduleID	• Under the Format field property, add the following custom format: **"SID-0"0** • Ensure that the New Values field property is set to **Increment**.
EmployeeID	• Create a lookup field by changing the data type to **Lookup Wizard**. Select your data from the existing tblEmployee table, and then click **Next**. Select **EmployeeID**, **LastName**, and **FirstName**. Click **Next**, and then sort in **Ascending order** by **LastName** and **FirstName**. Click **Next**. Keep the Key Column hidden, click **Next**, click **Enable Data Integrity**, and then click the **Restrict Delete** option. Click **Finish**. Save the table when prompted. • Under **Field Properties**, add **Employee** as the caption. • Under **Field Properties**, change the Required property to **Yes**.
ScheduledDate	• Under the Format field property, apply the **Long Date** format. • Add the Short Date Input Mask. • Add **Date** as the caption. • Change the Required property to **Yes**.
StartTime	• Under the Format field property, add the **Medium Time** format. • Add **Medium Time** as the Input Mask. • Add **Shift Begins** as the caption. • Add **#8:00 AM#** as the Default Value. • Change the Required property to **Yes**.

Field Name	Field Properties
EndTime	• Under **Field Properties**, add the **Medium Time** format. • Add **Medium Time** as the Input Mask. • Add Shift Ends as the caption. • Add #6:00 PM# as the Default Value. • Add the following validation rule: >=[StartTime]. • Add the following validation text: You must enter a time that ends AFTER the scheduled start time.
OnTime	• Under **Field Properties**, add On Time? as the caption.

f. While still in Design view, add a **Calculated field** with the following properties.

Field Name	Data Type	Description
PostedSchedule	Calculated	Calculated field of employee's ScheduledDate, BeginTime, and EndTime

Field Properties
• Enter the following fields into the Expression Builder dialog box, and then separate each one with the appropriate notation as follows: • [ScheduledDate]&", "&[StartTime]&"–"&[EndTime]. Click **OK**. • Under **Field Properties**, add Posted Schedule as the caption.

g. Save your changes, and then switch to **Datasheet** view. Add the following records to test the properties in your new table; and resize your fields as needed to view the data.

Employee	Date	Shift Begins	Shift Ends	On Time
Antonio Ruweeze	7/4/2015	12:00 PM	6:00 PM	Yes
Mary Lou Lovelace	7/8/2015	8:00 AM	6:00 PM	No
Dennis Matrell	7/4/2015	8:00 AM	12:00 PM	Yes
FirstName LastName (using your first and last name)	7/15/2015	8:00 AM	6:00 PM	Yes

h. Switch to **Design** view, and then create a multiple-field index. Click the **TABLE TOOLS DESIGN** tab, and then in the Show/Hide group, click **Indexes**.

i. Enter the following index properties starting at the first blank row in the Indexes dialog box.

Index Name	Field Name	Sort Order
ScheduleTime	StartTime	Ascending
	EndTime	Ascending

Index Properties

Primary	No
Unique	No
Ignore Nulls	No

j. Save your changes, and then close the Indexes dialog box.

k. Close tblEmployeeSchedule, and then close the database.

l. Exit Access, and then submit the file as directed by your instructor.

Production & Operations   Customer Service

Student data file needed:

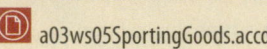 a03ws05SportingGoods.accdb

You will save your file as:

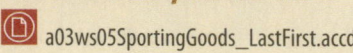 a03ws05SportingGoods_LastFirst.accdb

Managing Inventory at Cem's Sporting Goods

Cem's Sporting Goods has been in business for over a decade. Cem, the owner, has realized the importance of using technology to manage his inventory, and he has created a database to help him do so. Unfortunately, he does not know enough about database design to create tables that help control the way data is entered. Thus, he has only entered a small amount of data. You have been asked to modify the tables to ensure ease of use and functionality so he can begin using the database.

a. Open the **a03ws05SportingGoods** database, and then save it as a03ws05SportingGoods_LastFirst. Enable the content if necessary.

b. Open **tblSupplier**, and then add your first and last name in record 4.

c. Switch to **Design** view, and then make the following modifications to the tblSupplier table.

- SupplierID: Create a custom format so the supplier ID is displayed as ID-001, ID-002, and so on.
- CompanyName: Change the caption to Company Name.
- State: Create a custom format so the state name is displayed in uppercase. Change the field size to only allow 2 characters.
- ZipCode: Create an input mask for ZipCode that appears in the format 15044-1234. Access should store the symbols in the mask and use an underscore as a placeholder. Change the field size to only allow 10 characters. Change the caption to Zip Code.
- Phone: Create an input mask using the Phone Number format. The phone number should appear in the format (555) 555-1234. Access should store the symbols in the mask and use an underscore as a placeholder. Change the field size to only allow 14 characters.
- Fax: Create an input mask using the Phone Number format. The fax number should appear in the format (555) 555-1234. Access should store the symbols in the mask and use an underscore as a placeholder. Change the field size to only allow 14 characters.
- Add a new field named URL. Select **Hyperlink** as the data type, and then enter This is the website home page as the Description.

d. Switch to **Datasheet** view, and then enter the following record to ensure your field settings are correct.

Company Name	Address	City	State	ZipCode	Phone	Fax	URL
Maurice Sporting Goods	1910 Techny Road	Northbrook	il	60065	800-477-3474	847-715-1418	www.maurice.net

e. Close tblSupplier.

f. Make the following modifications to the tblInventory table.

- ItemName: Change the caption to Item.
- Supplier: Create a lookup field that looks up the **CompanyName** in the tblSupplier table. Sort the company names in **Ascending** order. Keep the key column hidden. Enable Data Integrity and Restrict Delete. Make the data in this field required.
- QuantityOnHand: Add a validation rule that requires all data entries to be greater than or equal to zero. Enter the following if a user accidently enters a negative number:

> Values must be greater than or equal to zero. Please reenter the quantity on hand. Make the data in this field required. Change the caption to Qty on Hand.

- Discontinued: Change the field to the **Yes/No** data type.

g. Switch to **Datasheet** view, and then enter the following data in record 1 to ensure your field settings are correct:

InventoryName	Description	Supplier	QuantityOnHand	Discontinued
Basketball	Regulation size	DollarDays International, Inc.	Change to −1 to see if the validation rule works. Change back to 2 once verified.	Yes

h. Filter the data using an advanced filter to display all items that have QtyOnHand greater than or equal to 3. Save the filter as a query named qry3orMore_initialLastname.

i. Make the following modifications to the tblOrder table.

- TransID: Change the data type to **AutoNumber**. Create a custom format so the TransID is displayed as TID-A01, TID-A02, and so on.
- Item: Create a lookup field that looks up the **ItemName** and **Description** in the tblInventory table. Sort the item names in **Ascending** order. Keep the key column hidden. Enable Data Integrity and restrict related records from being deleted. Make the data in this field required.
- TransactionType: Create a lookup field that looks up values that you enter. Enter the following options: Row 1: Check; Row 2: Credit; Row 3: Pay On Delivery. Limit selections to the list, and then do not permit multiple values to be selected. Change the caption to Transaction Type.
- Quantity: Add 1 as the default value.
- OrderDate: Change the caption to Order Date. Format the field as **Medium Date**.
- Create a multiple-field index on the Item, Quantity, and OrderDate fields. Enter OrderDetails as the name. Sort Item, Quantity, and OrderDate in **Ascending** order. Select **No** for the Primary, Unique, and Ignore Nulls properties.

j. Switch to **Datasheet** view, and then enter the following record to ensure your field settings are correct.

Item	Transaction Type	Quantity	Date
Pro Racer Goggles	Check	1	Enter today's date

k. Exit Access, and then submit the file as directed by your instructor.

Perform 1: How Others Perform

Student data files needed:

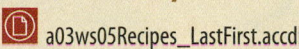 a03ws05Recipes.accdb

a03ws05Recipe.pdf

a03ws05CrabCakes.jpg

You will save your file as:

a03ws05Recipes_LastFirst.accdb

Modifying a Recipe Database

Production & Operations

Your aunt has been the family cook at all family holiday celebrations and events. She built a database so she can easily store her recipes, create shopping lists, and manage her ingredients. Unfortunately, she does not know how to build databases, and this one is not working the way she had hoped. You have been asked to modify the database to ensure ease of use and functionality so she can begin using the database.

a. Open the **a03ws05Recipes** database, and then save it as a03ws05Recipes_LastFirst.

b. Open tblStore, add your first and last name in record 5, and then close tblStore.

c. Open the tblRecipe table in Design view, and make the following changes.
- Add an AutoNumber for the primary key, and create a custom format.
- Add an attachment field that will allow your aunt to insert a printable version of the recipe.
- Add an OLE object field that will allow your aunt to insert a photo of the dish.
- Change the RecipeType field to a lookup field, and then enter the following values: Breakfast, Lunch, Dinner, Dessert, Appetizer, Other. Limit to list, and do not allow multiple values.
- Change the Servings data type to Number.
- Ensure that all captions and field sizes are appropriate, and make changes as necessary.

d. Switch to Datasheet view, and then make the following changes to record 1.
- Change RecipeType to Appetizer.
- Insert a03ws05Recipe.pdf into the PrintFriendly field.
- Insert a03ws05CrabCakes.jpg into the Photo field.

e. Open the tblIngredient table, and then make the following changes:
- Change the Store field to a lookup field that looks up the store name in tblStore. Sort in Ascending order, hide the key column, enable data integrity, restrict related records from being deleted, and do not allow multiple values.
- Create a custom format in the IngredientID field.
- Ensure that all captions and field sizes are appropriate, and make changes as necessary.

f. Create a new table in Design view that will permit your aunt to track what ingredients are used in which recipes.
- Save the table as tblRecipeIngredient.
- Add an AutoNumber for the primary key, and then create a custom format.
- Add a lookup field that looks up the ingredient name in tblIngredient. Sort in Ascending order, hide the key column, enable data integrity, restrict related records from being deleted, and do not allow multiple values.
- Add a lookup field that looks up the recipe name in tblRecipe. Sort in Ascending order, hide the key column, enable data integrity, restrict related records from being deleted, and do not allow multiple values.

g. Normalize the tblIngredient table using the Table Analyzer Wizard. Appropriately name the new tables that are created in the wizard. Do not create the query of the original table.

h. Open the Relationships window, and then ensure that all tables are related and referential integrity is enforced.

i. Consider how the data will be used. Create two queries by using either Filter By Form, Filter By Selection, or Advanced Filter. Save both queries.

j. Submit the file as directed by your instructor.

Additional Cases

Additional Workshop Cases are available on the companion website and in the instructor resources.

WORKSHOP 6 | PATTERN MATCHING AND FUNCTIONS IN QUERIES

Prepare Case

The Red Bluff Golf Club Database

Human Resources

Customer Service

The Red Bluff Golf Club needs useful information in order to run its business efficiently. Barry Cheney, the Golf Club manager, has asked you to create queries to track the golfers who have scheduled tee times and private lessons. Additionally, you need to create queries for decision making, such as scheduling golf pros for private lessons or determining how many golf caddies are needed on a busy day. To keep the file small while you work with the database, Barry removed most of the data and left only some sample data for you to manipulate. Once Barry accepts your changes, he will load all the data and implement the new database.

Kzenon / Shutterstock

REAL WORLD SUCCESS

"I am creating an Access database for my internship. This database will track vendor and supplier data my company will be dealing with for its new company acquisition in Canada. Querying data will be the most critical function of this database—wildcard and parameter queries being the highest on the list. When my supervisor asked our department if anyone knew how to use Access, I was the only one who did! Because of this, I was asked to continue my internship once it officially ended."

- Tina, current information systems management student

Student data file needed for this workshop:

 a03ws06Golf1.accdb

You will save your file as:

 a03ws06Golf1_LastFirst.accdb

Working with Advanced Criteria and Calculations

The most important function of a database is to create useful information for decision making. Queries enable you to retrieve data, filter data, calculate data totals, update data, append data, and delete records in bulk. Becoming proficient in building queries will improve your ability to understand and manage data. Building queries helps turn data into useful information and is critical in creating quality information. Knowing the features of query design allows you to perform advanced analyses quickly.

Once you have quality information, you now have knowledge about your organization, which can help you make decisions about your business. This **knowledge** is defined as applied information once you make the decision. For example, what if you want to reward your high-value customers on their birthdays? You could create a query that shows all customers who have spent more than $500 over the past six months and limit the results to those who were born within the current month. In this section, you will create advanced queries that use wildcard characters in string comparisons, find records with the "most" or "least" values, and create parameter queries. Additionally, you will create queries that use the Concatenate function, as well as Not, In, and other advanced operators.

QUICK REFERENCE	Understanding Expressions

In Access, the term "expression" is synonymous with "formula" in Excel. An expression consists of several possible elements that you can use—alone or in combination—to yield a result. Those elements include:

1. Identifiers—The names of a field, a control on a form or report, or the properties of the fields or controls

2. Operators—Such as [+] or [–] signs

3. Logical operators—Includes And, Or, and Not

4. Functions—A large number of predefined functions within Access including Sum, Count, and Avg—average—just to name a few

5. Constants—Values that do not change, such as strings of text or numbers that are not calculated by an expression.

You can use expressions in a number of ways such as performing calculations, retrieving values of a control on a form or report, supplying criteria to a query, and more.

Wildcard Characters in String Comparisons

Wildcard characters, such as an asterisk (*) or question mark (?), substitute for other symbols or characters when used in the criteria of a query. Many times when creating a query, you will know exactly what you want to find. However, you may want to search for both the singular and plural forms of a word, words that begin with the same root, words that can be spelled in different ways, or words that you are not sure how to spell. For example, you may be searching for a customer who lives in Pittsburgh. Users may have misspelled the city's name when they entered the data. Pittsburgh—with an "h"—is in Pennsylvania. Yet, there is a Pittsburg—without an "h"—in California, Ohio, Kansas, New Hampshire, and Texas. You could use a wildcard—Pittsburg*—and retrieve customers who either live in Pittsburgh or Pittsburg.

Opening the Starting File

To create queries using wildcards, you first need to open the Golf database.

A06.00

To Save the Golf Database

a. Start **Access**, and then open the student data file **a03ws06Golf1**.

b. Click the **FILE** tab, click **Save As**, and save the file as an Access Database in the location designated by your instructor with the name **a03ws06Golf1_LastFirst** using your last and first name. If necessary, click **Enable Content** in the Security Warning.

Using the LIKE Function

You can use the **LIKE function** to find values in a field that match a specific pattern. For a value, you can specify the value within an entire field. For example, you may want to search for a customer with the last name of Smith. This would only return records where the whole last name field is equal to Smith. Thus, someone with the last name of Smithe, Smithers, or Smithfield would not be included in the data set.

A06.01

MyITLab®
Workshop 6 Training

To Use the LIKE Function in a Query

a. Click the **CREATE** tab, and then in the Queries group, click **Query Design**.

b. When the Show Table dialog box opens, click **tblEmployee**, and then click **Add**.

c. **Close** ⊠ the Show Table dialog box.

d. Add the **FirstName**, **LastName**, **Salary**, **HireDate**, and **Position** fields to the query design grid.

e. In the **Criteria** row under Position, type Like "golf caddy".

f. Click the **FILE** tab. Click **Save As**, click **Save Object As**, and then click **Save As**. Save the query as qryLIKE_initialLast using your first initial and last name. Click **OK**.

g. Click the **DESIGN** tab, and then in the Results group, click **Run**.
   Notice that only four employees who match what you typed in the criteria are displayed.

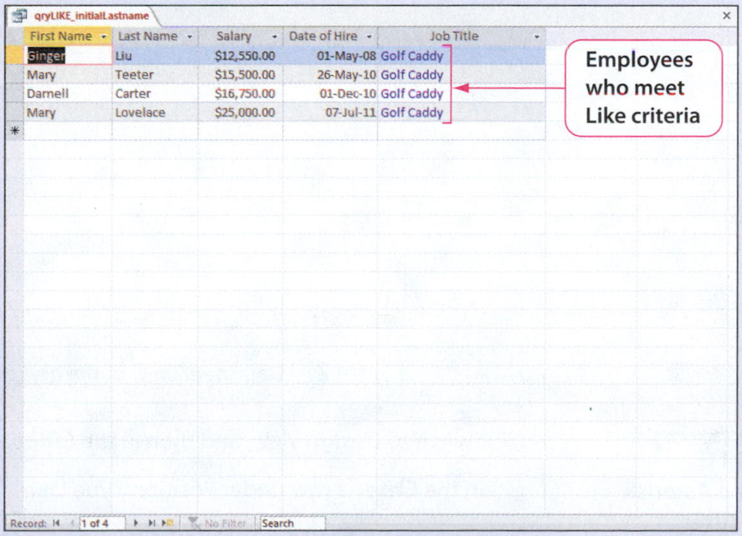

SIDE NOTE
Is LIKE Needed?
Some DBMSs require LIKE in queries. Access has been developed to work with or without it, unless writing a complex expression.

SIDE NOTE
Are Words in the Criteria Row Case Sensitive?
Access has been developed to work regardless of which case you use in the Criteria row.

First Name	Last Name	Salary	Date of Hire	Job Title
Singer	Liu	$12,550.00	01-May-08	Golf Caddy
Mary	Teeter	$15,500.00	26-May-10	Golf Caddy
Darnell	Carter	$16,750.00	01-Dec-10	Golf Caddy
Mary	Lovelace	$25,000.00	07-Jul-11	Golf Caddy

Employees who meet Like criteria

Record: 1 of 4   No Filter   Search

Figure 1   Datasheet view of the qryLIKE query

h. **Close** ⊠ the query.

Working with Wildcard Characters

You can use **wildcard characters** to find a range of values. Many times these are combined with the Like operator to ensure that your query is returning all the data you need. For example, you may want to search for all products that begin with the letters "ch"; that would return products such as cheese, chips, chocolate, and chicken. Or you may want to query a JobTitle field to search for any employees who have a manager position. By using a wildcard, the results of your data set may include senior manager, assistant manager, manager of sales, and manager.

A06.02

To Use Wildcard Characters in String Comparisons

a. Click the **CREATE** tab, and then in the Queries group, click **Query Design**.

b. Click **tblEmployee**, click **Add**, and then **Close** ☒ the Show Table dialog box.

c. Add the **FirstName**, **LastName**, **Salary**, **HireDate**, and **Position** fields to the query design grid.

d. In the Criteria row under **Position**, type *Like "*caddy"*, and then click **Run**.

Notice that four records are returned in the data set that have the word "Caddy" at the end of the field. The asterisk replaced any characters that were before the word "Caddy" in the Position field.

e. Click **Save** 🖫 on the Quick Access Toolbar, and then save your query as *qryCaddy_initialLastname*.

SIDE NOTE

What Will the Asterisk Before "Caddy" Do?

This will return all records that have the word "caddy" at the end of the field.

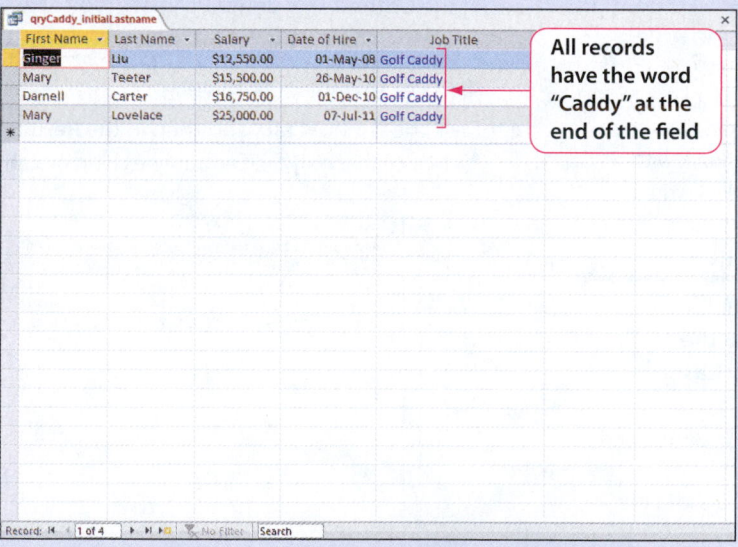

Figure 2 Datasheet view of the qryCaddy query

f. Switch to **Design** view, and then in the Criteria row under **Position**, delete **Like *caddy**.

g. In the **Criteria** row under Position, type *Like "*golf*"*.

h. Click the **FILE** tab. Click **Save As**, click **Save Object As**, and then click **Save As**. **Save** the query as *qryGolf_initialLastname* and then **run** the query.

Notice that all records returned in the data set have the word "Golf" somewhere within the field. The asterisk replaced any characters that were before and/or after the word "Golf" in the Position field.

SIDE NOTE

What Will the Asterisk Before and After Golf Do?

To match specific text anywhere within a string, type an asterisk at the beginning and end of a string of text.

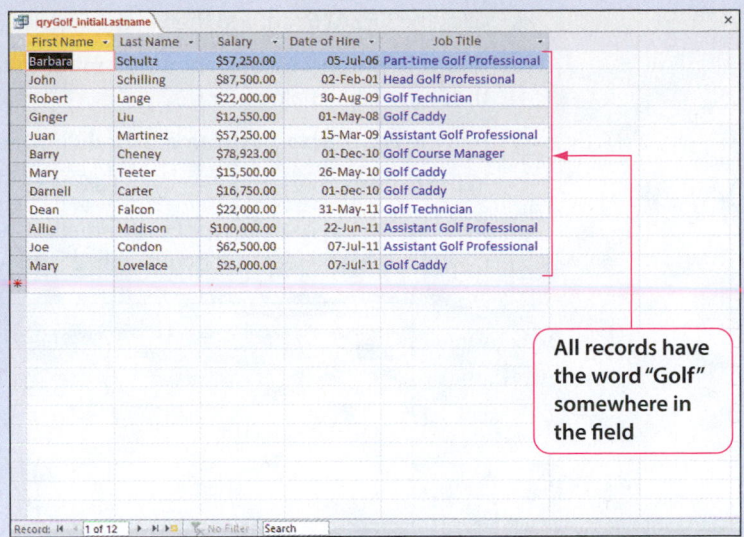

Figure 3 Datasheet view of the qryGolf query

i. **Close** ✗ the query.

j. Click the **CREATE** tab, and then in the Queries group, click **Query Design**.

k. Click **tblMember**, click **Add**, and then **Close** ✗ the Show Table dialog box.

l. Add the **FirstName**, **LastName**, **Address**, **City**, **State**, and **ZipCode** fields to the query design grid.

m. In the **Criteria** row under LastName, type Like "[A-E]*".

n. Sort the LastName field in **Ascending** order.

o. Save your query as **qryMemberAE_initialLastname**, click **OK**, and then click **Run**.
   Notice that all members whose last names begin with "A" through "E" are displayed in ascending order.

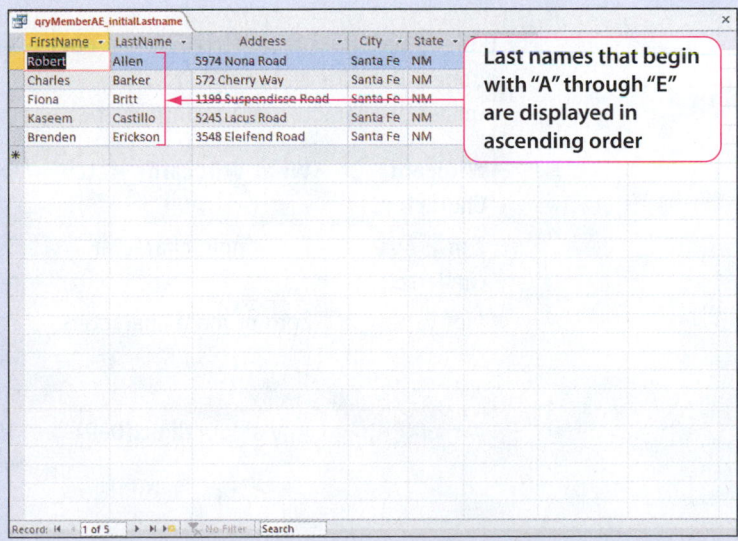

Figure 4 Datasheet view of the qryMemberAE query

p. **Close** ✗ the query.

q. Click the **CREATE** tab, and then in the Queries group, click **Query Design**.

r. Add **tblMemberLessons** and **tblMember** to the query workspace, and then **Close** ☒ the Show Table dialog box.

s. Add the **FirstName**, **LastName**, **ScheduledDate**, and **Fee** fields to the query design grid.

t. In the **Criteria** row under Fee, type Like "2#0".

u. **Save** the query as qryLessonFees_initialLastname, click **OK**, and then click **Run**. Notice that all fees that begin with "2" and end with "0" are displayed.

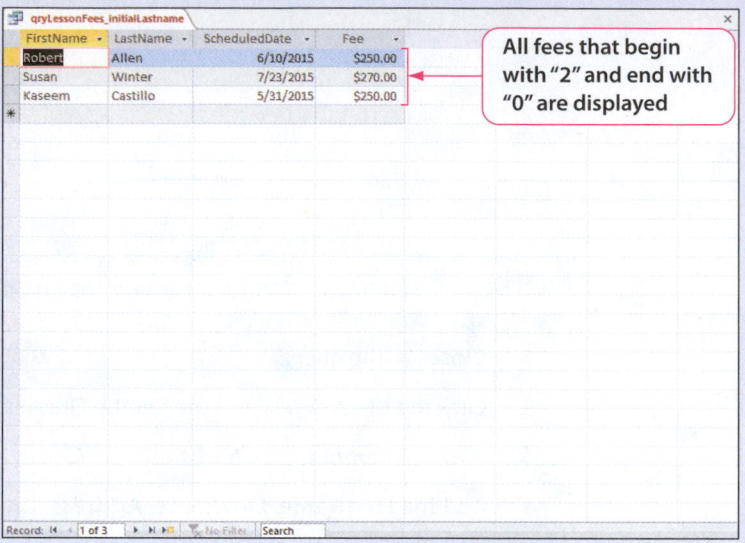

Figure 5   Datasheet view of the qryLessonFees query

v. **Close** ☒ the query.

QUICK REFERENCE	Using Wildcard Characters in Access

Built-in pattern matching provides a handy tool for making string comparisons in queries. Below are the wildcard characters you can use with the Like function and the number of characters they can match.

Wildcard Characters	What Wildcards Match	Example
? or _ (underscore)	Any single character	C?t in the criteria of a Notes field would return cat, cot, and cut.
* or %	Zero or more characters	ch* in the criteria of a FoodName field would return churros, chimichanga, cheese, chips, chives, chicken, and chocolate.
#	Any single digit (0–9)	4#2 in the criteria of an AreaCode field would return 402, 412, 422, 432, and so on. You could use this character for multiple digits such as 4##. This would return 400, 401, 402, 403, 404...499.
[charlist]	Any single character in charlist	[A-D]* in the criteria of a ProductName field would return any products that begin with the letters A, B, C, or D.

(Continued)

QUICK REFERENCE | Using Wildcard Characters in Access (Continued)

Wildcard Characters	What Wildcards Match	Example
[!charlist]	Any single character not in charlist	[!A-D]* in the criteria of a ProductName field would return any products that begin with the letters E through Z, inclusive.
- (hyphen)	Any character within a range	b[a-o]ll in the criteria of a field would return ball, bell, and bill, but not bull.

You can use a group of one or more characters—**charlist**—enclosed in square brackets ([ ]) to match any single character in an expression, and charlist can include almost any characters and digits. Additionally, when you specify a range of characters, the characters must appear in ascending sort order (A–Z or 0–100). [A–Z] is a valid pattern, but [Z–A] is not. Finally, Access is not **case sensitive** in regard to the criteria. You can enter lowercase or uppercase letters in the criteria. Access will return all the applicable data, regardless how it was entered into the table.

CONSIDER THIS | Text Matching and Input Masks

You have a PhoneNumber field with an input mask with symbols stored. Most numbers would look like (555) 555-5555. What criteria would you use to find 7-digit phone numbers such as 555-5555?

REAL WORLD ADVICE | You Do Not Always Have to Type the Word "Like"

Microsoft has made it a little easier for a novice to enter criteria in the query design grid. If you type an asterisk (*) or a question mark (?) and press Tab, Access recognizes the wildcard that you entered. Access will automatically enclose your string in quotes along with entering the word "Like". Thus, as a novice, you can write queries with relative ease.

Find Records with the "Most" or "Least" Values

An occasion may exist where you only want to view a **subset**—a portion or part of a group of records—of your query data set by selecting either a percentage or a fixed number of records. For example, you may want to view the customers who are the bottom 10% of overall customer purchases. You could then target your marketing plan toward them because they may not appear to be as loyal as other customers. Instead of viewing a percentage of your data, you may want to see the top three salespeople within the company. This would help you determine the best salespeople who are eligible for a promotion, raise, or bonus.

Retrieving Top Values

You can use a **Top Values query** when you need to find records that contain the top values in a field. You can use a Top Values query to answer such questions as:

- Which is the most or least expensive product sold at our company?
- Which departments generated the greatest or least sales last year?
- What products are the top 10 most popular?

- Which products are in the top or bottom 5% of sales?
- Which employees' sales are in the top or bottom 10% in the company?

A Top Values query first sorts and then filters your data to return the top values within a field. You can use a Top Values query to search for numeric, currency, and date values.

A06.03

To Create a Top Values Query

a. Click the **CREATE** tab, and then in the Queries group, click **Query Design**.

b. Add **tblMemberLessons** to the query workspace, and then **Close** ☒ the Show Table dialog box.

c. Add the **ScheduledDate** and Fee fields to the query design grid.

d. Click **Run** to view all records.

   Notice there are nine different prices listed in the 15 records displayed.

e. Switch to **Design** view, and then sort Fee in **Descending** order.

f. Click the **DESIGN** tab. In the Query Setup group, click the **Return (Top Values)** arrow, and then select **25%** from the Return (Top Values) list.

SIDE NOTE
Sorting Fields
You must sort data in ascending or descending order in fields containing your top or bottom values before running the query.

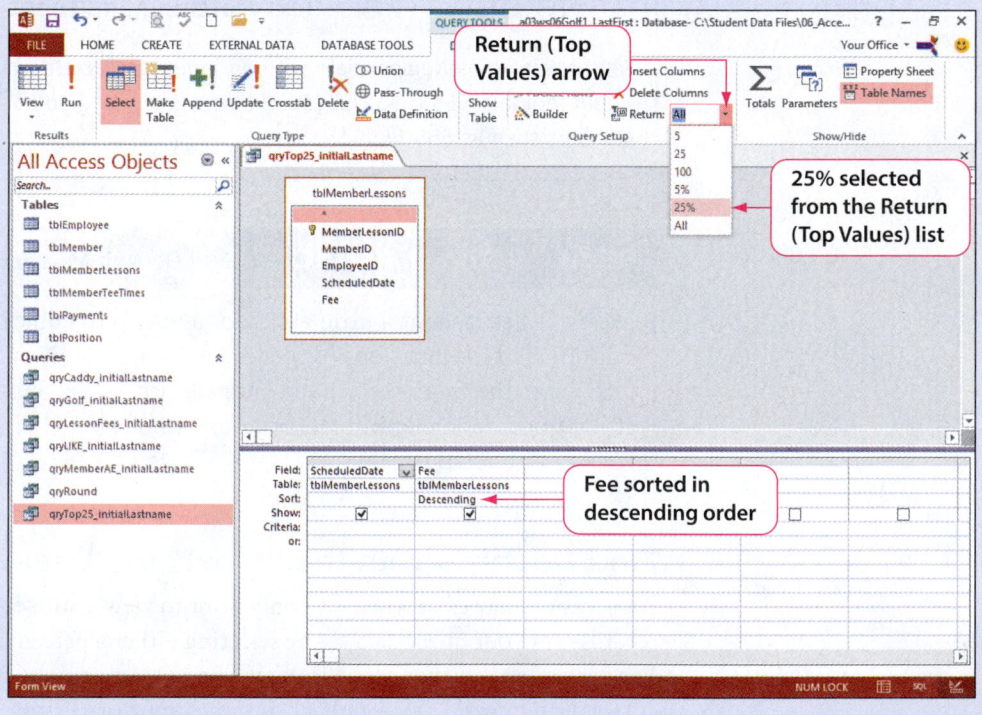

Figure 6 Design view of the Query1 query

g. **Save** the query as **qryTop25_initialLastname**, click **OK**, and then click **Run**.

   Notice that all four records displayed include the top 25% of the fees in your table.

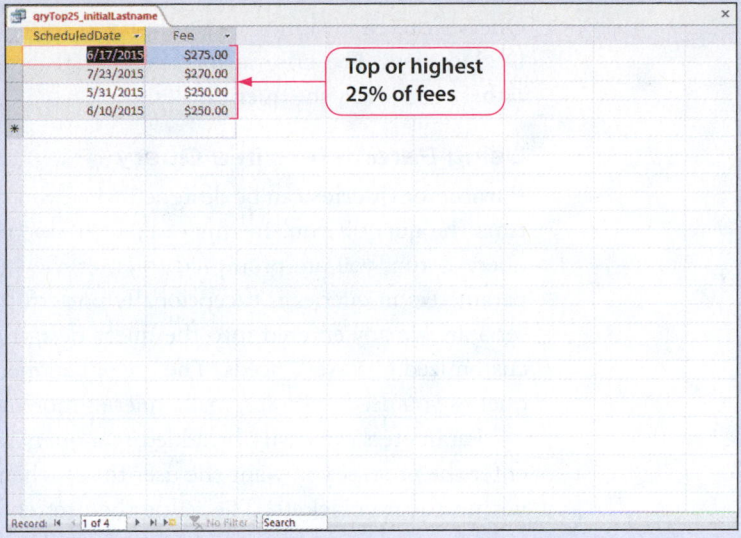

Figure 7 Datasheet view of the qryTop25 query

SIDE NOTE
Using the Return (Top Values) List
You can either enter the number or percentage of records that you want or select an option from the list.

h. Switch to **Design** view, and then change the sort order in the Fee field from Descending to **Ascending**.

i. Delete the **25%** in the Return (Top Values) box, and then type **2**.

> **Troubleshooting**
> After deleting 25% and typing 2, Access may add a "5" after the two. Because 25% is one of the list options, Access is guessing that you want that value. If this occurs, press Delete to remove the "5".

j. Click the **FILE** tab. Click **Save As**, click **Save Object As**, and then click **Save As**.

k. Save the query as **qryBottom2_initialLastname**, click **OK**, and then click **Run**.
Notice that by sorting the field in ascending order, Access now displays the two bottom—or lowest—values.

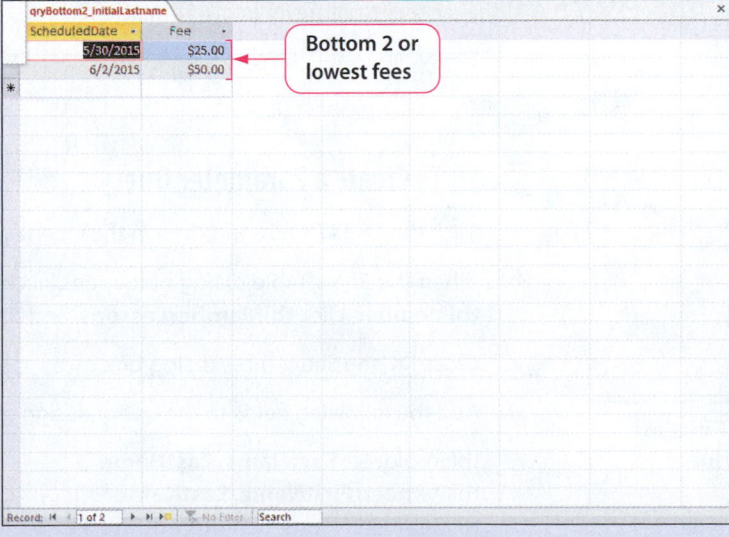

Figure 8 Datasheet view of the qryBottom2 query

l. **Close** X the query.

Make a Parameter Query Ask for Input

Queries can be designed to prompt you for criteria without having to make changes in Design view. The criteria for selecting records are determined when the query is run rather than when the query is designed.

Using Parameters in a Query

Parameter queries can be designed when you need to change the criteria for a search each time the query is run. In this case, a variable parameter can be used. When a parameter query is run, you are prompted to enter the value for each parameter or variable. Using parameters in queries is exceptionally powerful and converts static queries, where the criteria are already entered into the query design grid, to flexible, dynamic queries that are customized to a user's needs. The use of parameters can significantly reduce the number of queries you need to create, make queries more useful, and simplify database maintenance.

Parameters can easily be added to a query. Rather than entering the value of criteria, enter the prompt you want the user to see when the query is run, and enclose the prompt within square brackets. The value the user enters will replace the parameter and create a data set based on what the user enters. For example, the parameter [Enter Zip Code] could be entered in the Criteria row of a Zip Code field. When a user runs the query, the user is prompted to enter a zip code, and the records matching the value entered are retrieved. This type of query can put the user in control of creating queries, even if they have never used Access.

Parameters can be used for any data type within a table, and you can specify what type of data a parameter should accept. Specifying **parameter data types** is particularly important when you have numeric, currency, or date/time data. When you specify a data type that the parameter should accept, users see a more helpful error message if they enter the wrong type of data, such as entering text when currency should be entered.

CONSIDER THIS | **Have You Used Parameter Queries?**

Think about the systems you have previously used. Perhaps you have called the bank to update information—maybe a new address or phone number—and before you can speak with customer service, you have to enter your Social Security number or account number. Can you think of other systems you have used that require you to enter data in order for the system to retrieve your information?

A06.04

 To Create a Parameter Query

a. Click the **CREATE** tab, and then in the Queries group, click **Query Design**.

b. When the Show Table dialog box opens, click **tblEmployee**, and then press Ctrl. Click **tblMember**, click **tblMemberLessons**, and then click **Add**.

c. **Close** ☒ the Show Table dialog box.

d. Add the following fields to the query design grid.

   tblEmployee: **FirstName**, **LastName**
   tblMember: **FirstName**, **LastName**
   tblMemberLessons: **ScheduledDate**, **Fee**

e. In the **Criteria** row of the Employee's LastName field, type [Enter the Employee's Last Name] and then save the query as qryParameter_initialLastname.

SIDE NOTE
Enclose in Square Brackets
Place parameter names inside of square brackets or Access adds quotation marks around text typed in the Criteria row.

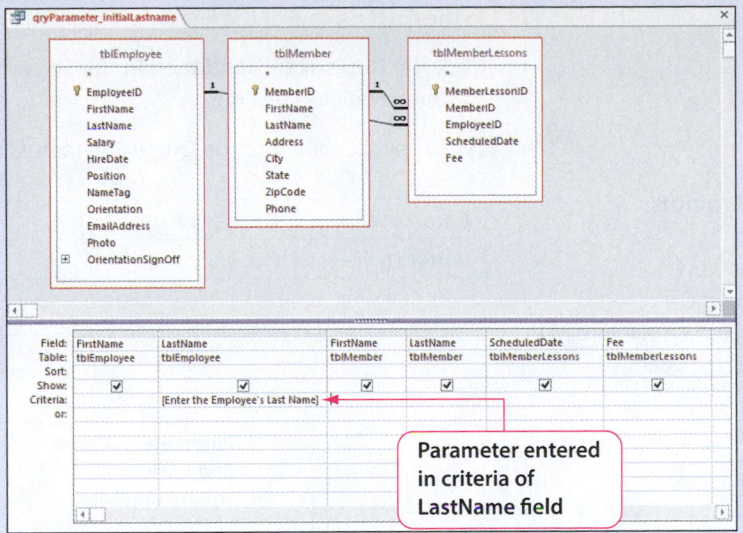

Parameter entered
in criteria of
LastName field

Figure 9   Design view of the qryParameter query

f. Click **Run**. When prompted to enter the employee's last name, type **Schilling** and then click **OK**.

Notice that John Schilling's four scheduled private lessons are easy to retrieve with a parameter query.

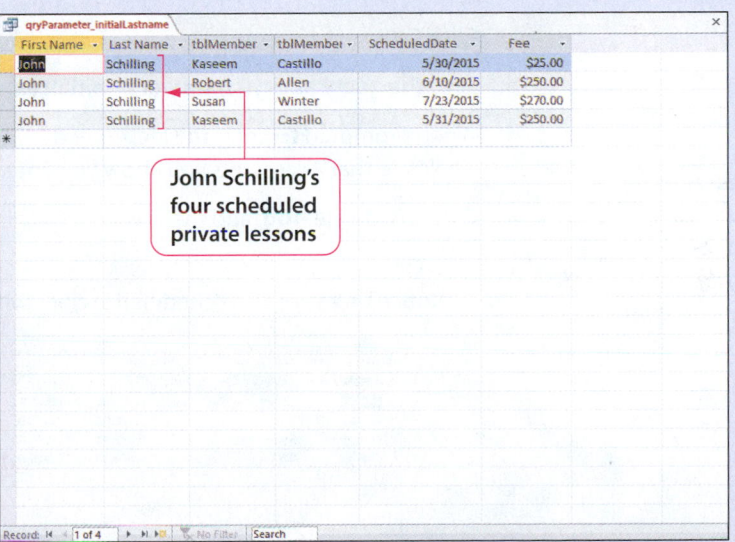

John Schilling's
four scheduled
private lessons

Figure 10   Datasheet view of the qryParameter query

g. **Close** ✕ the query.

h. Click the **CREATE** tab, and then in the Queries group, click **Query Design**.

i. When the Show Table dialog box opens, click **tblMember**, and then press Ctrl. Click **tblMemberLessons**, and then click **Add**.

j. **Close** ✕ the Show Table dialog box.

k. Add the following fields to the query design grid.

tblMember: **FirstName**, **LastName**
tblMemberLessons: **ScheduledDate**, **Fee**

l. In the **Criteria** row of the Fee field, type **[Enter the Fee]**.

m. Click the **DESIGN** tab, and then in the Show/Hide group, click **Parameters**. The Query Parameters dialog box opens.

n. Type the following into the Query Parameters dialog box:

Parameter	Data Type
[Enter the Fee]	Currency

SIDE NOTE
Parameter Prompts Must Match
Make sure that each parameter matches the prompt that you use in the Criteria row of the query design grid.

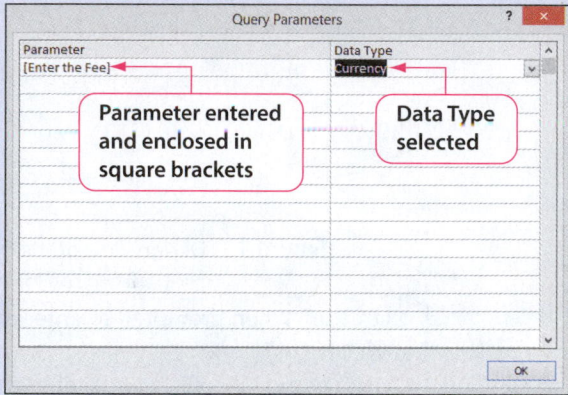

Figure 11   Query Parameters dialog box

o. Click **OK**.

p. Save the query as **qryParameter2_initialLastname**, click **OK**, and then click **Run**.

q. When prompted to enter the fee, enter **dog**, and then click **OK**.
Notice that Access lets you know you entered the wrong type of data.

r. Click **OK**, delete **dog**, and then type **125**.

s. Click **OK**.
Notice there are four scheduled lessons with a fee of $125.

SIDE NOTE
No Error Messages
If a parameter is configured to accept text data, any input is interpreted as text, and no error message is displayed.

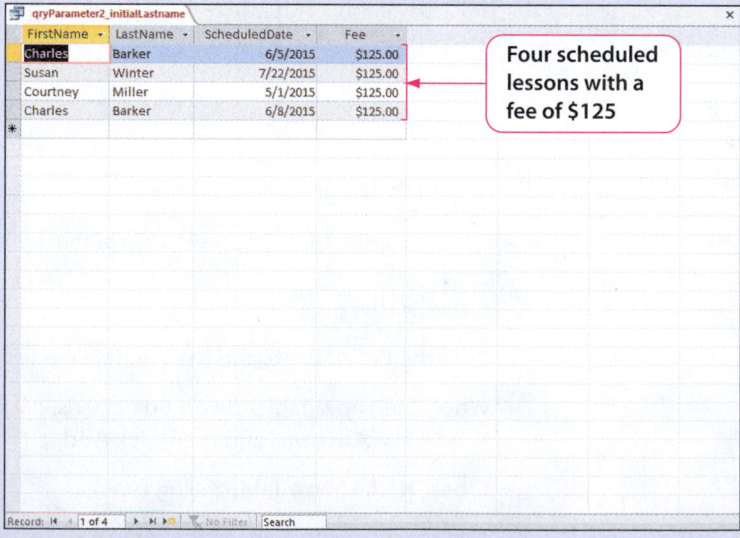

Figure 12   Datasheet view of the qryParameter2 query

t. **Close** ☒ the query.

Concatenate Strings Using the & Operator

You can use the **Concatenate operator** (&) when you want to join two strings together in an expression and create a single field. For example, if you have an Employees table that contains the fields FirstName and LastName, you can use concatenation to create a text string that displays the values of the employee's first name and last name fields separated by a space, creating a full name field in the data set.

A06.05

To Create a Query Using the Concatenate Operator

a. Click the **CREATE** tab, and then in the Queries group, click **Query Design**.

b. When the Show Table dialog box opens, click **tblEmployee** and **tblPosition**, and then click **Add**.

c. **Close** ☒ the Show Table dialog box.

d. Right-click the **first blank field** in the query design grid, and then select **Zoom**. The Zoom dialog box opens and gives you more room to work.

> **Troubleshooting**
>
> After selecting Zoom, you may see an error that says a potential security concern has been identified. Because there are no macros in this database, it is safe to click OK.

e. In the **Zoom** dialog box, type **Employee:[FirstName]&" "&[LastName]**. Be sure to type a space between the quotation marks.

f. Click **OK**.

g. Right-click the **next blank field** in the query design grid, and then select **Zoom**.

h. In the Zoom dialog box, type **Job Title:[PositionType]&" "&[Position]**. Click **OK**.

i. **Save** the query as **qryConcatenate_initialLastname**, click **OK**, and then click **Run**. If necessary, resize your fields to view all the data.

    Notice that Access joined data from multiple fields into one field—Employee and Job Title.

SIDE NOTE
The Zoom Dialog Box
When entering a long expression, you can use the Zoom dialog box to see everything you are typing.

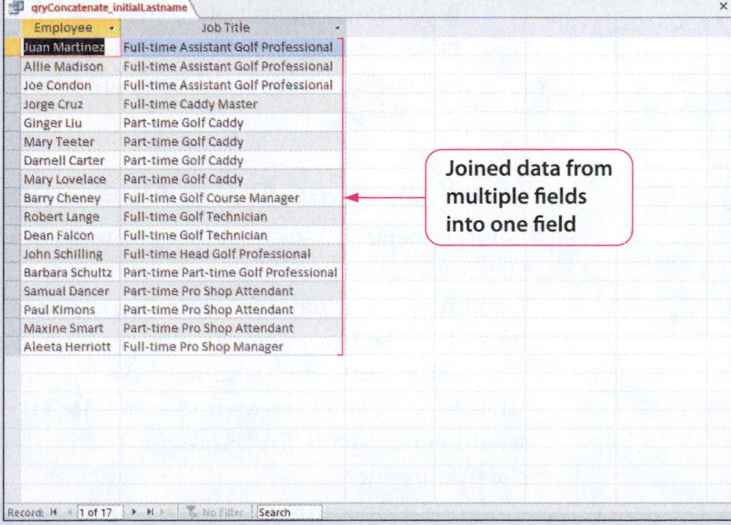

Figure 13   Datasheet view of the qryConcatenate query

Troubleshooting

After clicking OK from within the Zoom dialog box, you may not see the entire expression you just entered in the query design grid. Your field just needs to be resized. It can be resized just like you would resize a column in Excel or a field in an Access table.

j. **Close** ☒ the query.

REAL WORLD ADVICE | Have You Seen Concatenation in Action?

Have you ever logged into a website and there is a welcome message at the top of the web page? For example, "Hi Joe Condon!" As you know from working in Access, storing customers' full names in one field violates the principle of normalization. Developers of the website have used concatenation in the source code of the page. In business, you can use this type of coding on reports, paychecks, and other professional documents.

QUICK REFERENCE | Using the & Operator

At first glance, using the ampersand to concatenate fields can appear complicated. However, if you break it into sections, it can actually be quite simple. Below are some notes to remember about the & operator.

1. You are creating a **virtual field**. This means that the concatenated field imitates its "real" equivalent or equivalents—such as combining FirstName and LastName fields. This concatenated field will not be saved in the table, only in your query. However, you can create this type of field in a table by using the Calculated data type.

2. When writing an expression, including the use of the & operator, everything to the left of the colon is the field name; everything to the right of the colon is the expression.

3. If you are using multiple tables that have the same field name in two or more tables, be sure to preface your field name with the table name, separated by an exclamation point—[tblEmployee]![FirstName].

Use Advanced Query Operators

Logical operators—or Boolean operators—such as Not or In, are used to perform more advanced data analysis. The **Not operator** is used to search for records that do not match specific criteria. For example, if you wanted to search for all customers who live outside of the USA, you would enter Not "USA" as the criterion in the Country field. The Not operator can be combined with other Boolean operators, such as And and Or. Illustratively, you may want to search for all customers outside of North America. You would enter Not "USA" And Not "Canada" And Not "Mexico" in the Criteria row of the Country field.

The **In operator** can be used to return results that contain one of the values in a list. For example, you may want to search for customers who meet certain criteria, such as those who live in specific states. Thus, you would enter In ("Arizona", "Nevada",

"New Mexico") as the criterion in the State field. This would return all customers who live in Arizona, Nevada, or New Mexico. Notice how the customers would only have to meet one of the stated criteria to display in the data set.

The **Between...And operator** verifies whether the value of a field or expression falls within a stated range of numeric values. For example, you may want to view all products with a selling price between $1 and $10. Or you may want to view all customers who live between certain zip codes. By using the And operator in conjunction with the Between operator, you are testing to see if your values are greater than or equal to the lower value—such as $1—and less than or equal to the higher value—such as $10. In the above example, the results would include $1 or $10.

You also can combine the Not and Between...And operators to return records that do not fall within a stated range of numeric values. For example, you may want to view all products with a selling price that are not between $5 and $10. Or you may want to view all customers who do not live between certain zip codes.

Because Access treats values entered into the Between...And operator as actual characters, wildcard characters cannot be used in this operator. For example, if you want to find all clients who were born in the 1960s or 1970s, you cannot use 196* and 197* to find all years that start with 196 and 197. You could write a more advanced expression to allow for wildcard usage, but it would be easier to write your expression as Between 1960 And 1979.

A06.06

 To Create a Query Using the Not, In, And, and Between...And Operators

a. Click the **CREATE** tab, and then in the Queries group, click **Query Design**.

b. Add **tblEmployee** to Design view, and then **Close** ☒ the Show Table dialog box.

c. Add the **FirstName**, **LastName**, and **Salary** fields to the query design grid.

d. In the Criteria row of the Salary field, type **Between 50000 And 75000**, and then save the query as **qryBetween_initialLastname**.

e. Click **Run**.

Notice that the employees listed have a salary that is between $50,000 and $75,000.

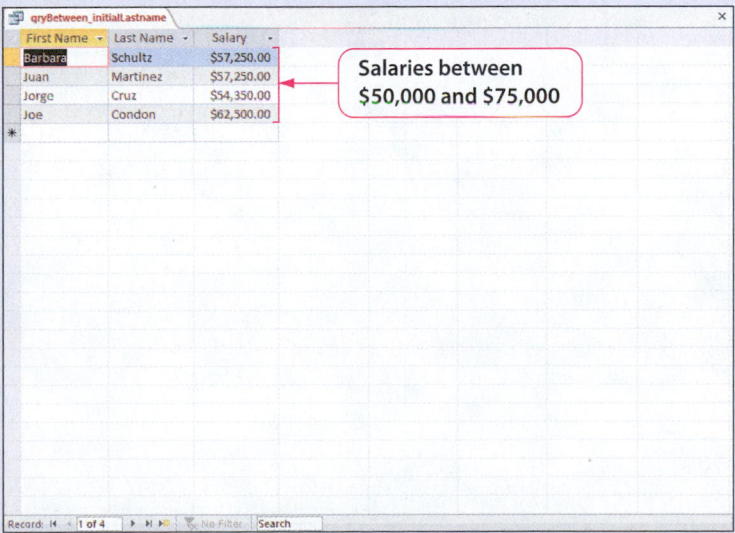

Figure 14   Datasheet view of the qryBetween query

f. Switch to **Design** view, and then modify your expression in the Criteria row of the Salary field. Type Not Between 50000 And 75000.

g. Click the **FILE** tab. Click **Save As**, click **Save Object As**, and then click **Save As**.

h. Save your query as qryNotBetween_initialLastname, click **OK**, and then click **Run**.
Notice that the employees listed have a salary that is not between $50,000 and $75,000.

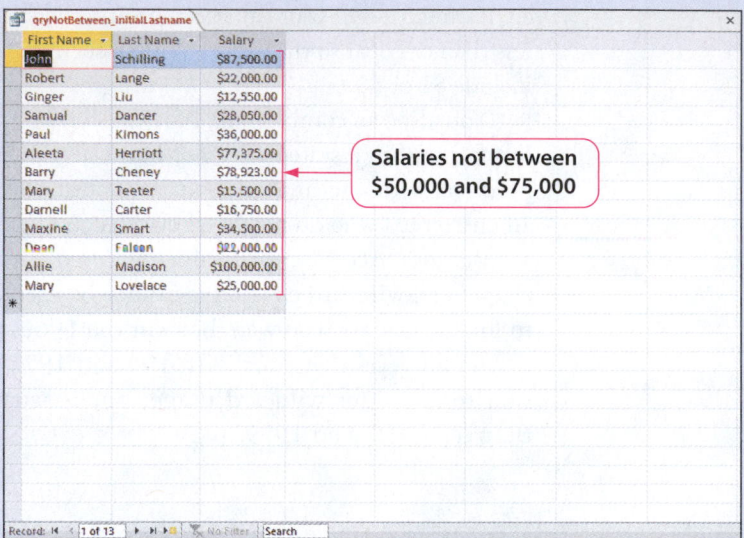

Figure 15 Datasheet view of the qryNotBetween query

i. **Close** ✕ the query.

j. Click the **CREATE** tab, and then in the Queries group, click **Query Design**. Add **tblEmployee** to the query workspace, and then **Close** ✕ the Show Table dialog box.

k. Add the **FirstName**, **LastName**, **Salary**, and **Position** fields to the query design grid.

l. Type In ("Golf Caddy","Caddy Master") into the **Criteria** row of the Position field.

m. **Save** your query as qryIn_initialLastname, click **OK**, and then click **Run**.
Notice that the employees listed hold a position as either a Golf Caddy or Caddy Master.

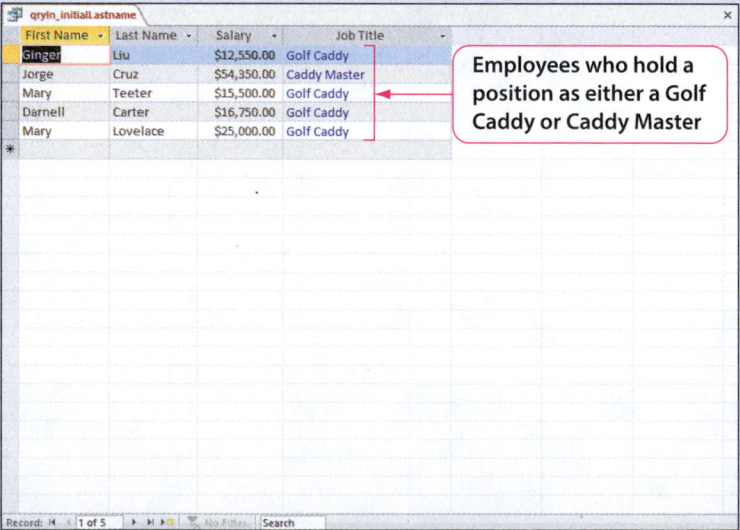

Figure 16 Datasheet view of the qryIn query

n. **Close** ✕ the query.

REAL WORLD ADVICE | **Date Fields Are a Great Place for Using Parameters**

There are many areas—accounting, marketing, sales, and so forth—within an organization that have a tremendous need for reports that fall within a specific date range. Generally, a business operating in the United States will need to file a quarterly tax return to report wages it has paid, tips its employees have reported to their employer, federal income tax withheld, Social Security and Medicare taxes withheld, and its share of Social Security and Medicare taxes. This is mainly to ensure that the business is on track with tax payments and will not have a large amount due at the end of the year. Think about how the Between...And function and a parameter could be combined to print a quarterly report of all the taxes that have been paid. Typically, you could just create a query using the Between...And function and manually enter the dates you need into Design view. However, what happened when the dates change? What if the user does not know how to modify a query? In these cases, it would be best to incorporate a parameter within the Between...And function so the user can simply enter the quarter's start and end date. To do so, you would simply enter **Between [Enter Start Date] And [Enter End Date]** into the Criteria row in Query Design view.

CONSIDER THIS | **Using Advanced Operators Together**

For very advanced data analysis, you can combine two or more advanced operators to help sort through the data. For example, if you wanted to retrieve specific products—coats or boots—that were available in specific colors—black or brown—you could enter the criteria for both of these in one query. You would essentially be asking Access to find "coats or boots" and "black or brown". What examples could you create that would combine multiple advanced operators?

Using Advanced Functions in Queries

Knowing how to write queries in Access by using advanced functions, such as the IIf function, allows you to perform advanced analyses quickly without knowing any type of programming language. In this section, you will create queries using the IIf function, the IsNull function, date functions, and the Round function.

The IIf Function

The IIf function can be used to determine if a specific condition is true or false and then specify an action to be taken depending on the result. The IIf function introduces decision making into a database. Depending on whether or not specified criteria are met, the IIf function returns a different result depending on the outcome of the condition.

Creating Basic IIf Function for Individual Conditions

The **IIf function** in Access, which stands for Immediate If, is similar to the IF function in Excel. The results of this function returns one value if a specified condition is true or another value if it is false. You can use the IIf function anywhere you can use expressions. For example, you may have a database that you use to manage your store's inventory. You can use the IIf function to assist in determining what items need to be reordered. You could write an IIf function that checks to see if your current on-hand values in the Quantity field fall below a certain level. You would enter IIf([Quantity]<=3, "Reorder", "OK"), which returns the string "Reorder" for any values in the Quantity field that are less than or equal to 3, and "OK" if the value is greater than 3, which means you do not need to reorder that specific product.

QUICK REFERENCE	IIf Function Syntax

The IIf function syntax, noted as IIf(expr, truepart, falsepart), has three arguments:

1. expr: Field or expression you want to evaluate. This argument is required.
2. truepart: Value or expression returned if expr is true. This argument is required.
3. falsepart: Value or expression returned if expr is false. This argument is required.

A06.07

To Create a Query Using the IIf Function

a. Click the **CREATE** tab, and then in the Queries group, click **Query Design**. Add **tblEmployee** to the query workspace, and then **Close** [X] the Show Table dialog box.

b. Add the **FirstName**, **LastName**, and **Salary** fields to the query design grid.

c. Right-click the **first blank field** in the query design grid, and then select **Zoom**.

d. In the Zoom dialog box, type
Raise Assessment:IIf([Salary]<=30000,"Give Raise","No Raise") and then click **OK**.

e. Right-click the **next blank field** in the query design grid, and then select **Zoom**.

f. In the Zoom dialog box, type **New Salary:IIf([Salary]<=30000,[Salary]*1.03,[Salary])**. For those employees who earned a salary increase, you want to calculate what the new salary will be if employees receive a 3% raise.

g. Click **OK**, and then click **Run**. If necessary, resize the fields to see the data.
   Notice that the New Salary field is not in Currency format.

h. Switch to **Design** view, and then click the **New Salary** field.

i. Click the **DESIGN** tab, and then in the Show/Hide group, click **Property Sheet**. Format the field as **Currency**, and then close the Property Sheet.

j. **Save** the query as **qryIIf_initialLastname**, click **OK**, and then click **Run**.
   Notice that based on your IIf function, Access determined which employees have earned a raise and calculated the amount of the new salary. If the employee did not earn a raise, the current salary was listed in the New Salary field.

SIDE NOTE

Symbols Are Important

When writing complex expressions, include all symbols. If even one is excluded or incorrect, an error will occur.

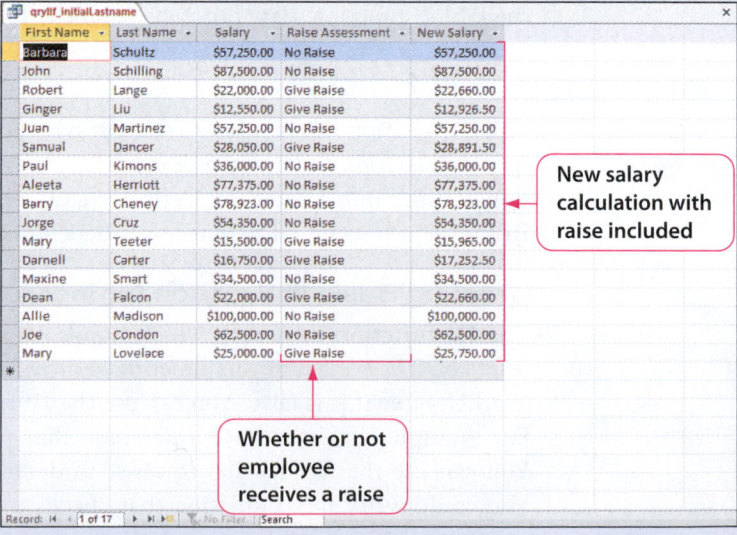

Figure 17 Datasheet view of the qryIIf query

k. **Close** [X] the query.

Creating Nested IIf Functions for Various Conditions

In business, there are many occasions when you need to test for multiple conditions. You saw in the previous section how a basic IIf function allows you to test for one of two conditions. You can also create a **nested IIf function** by placing one IIf function inside another, allowing you to evaluate a series of dependent expressions as shown in Figure 18. A **dependent expression** is an expression that relies on the outcome of another expression.

To continue with the preceding example, you might want to test for several different inventory levels, and then display the appropriate status depending on which value exists. Perhaps you want to see which items are close to having to be reordered, as noted by "Reorder Soon" in the second or nested IIf function. To add this condition to the IIf function from the previous example, you would enter IIf([Quantity]<=3, "Reorder", IIf([Quantity]<=5, "Reorder Soon", "OK")), which returns the string "Reorder" for any values in the Quantity field that are less than or equal to 3, "Reorder Soon" for any values that are either equal to 4 or 5, and "OK" if the value is greater than 5, which means you do not need to reorder that specific product any time soon. Notice how the second IIf function becomes the false condition of the first IIf function.

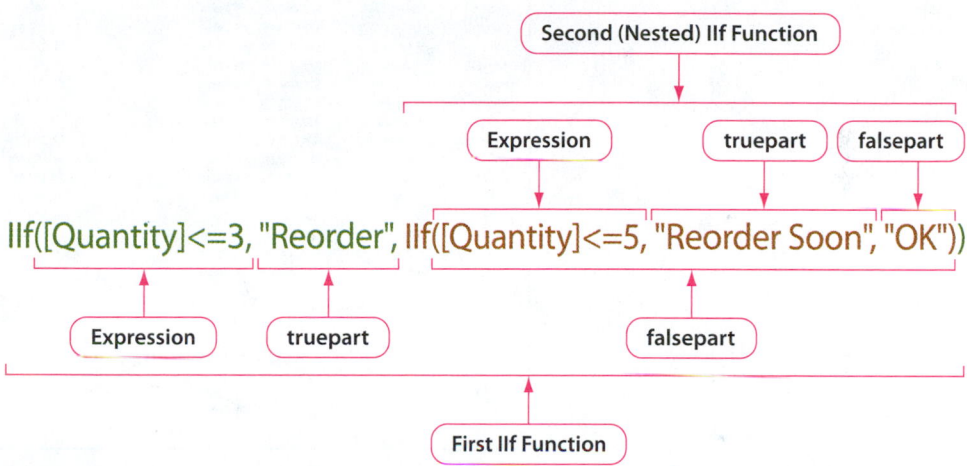

Figure 18 Nested IIf function

A06.08

 To Create a Query Using Nested IIf Functions

a. Click the **CREATE** tab, and then in the Queries group, click **Query Design**. Add **tblEmployee** to the query workspace, and then **Close** ☒ the Show Table dialog box.

b. Add the **FirstName**, **LastName**, and **Salary** fields to the query design grid.

c. Right-click the **first blank field** in the query design grid, and then select **Zoom**.

d. In the Zoom dialog box, type
Raise Assessment:IIf([Salary]<=30000,"7% Raise", IIf ([Salary]<=60000,"4% Raise", "No Raise")) and then click **OK**.

e. Right-click the **next blank field** in the query design grid, and then select **Zoom**.

SIDE NOTE

Count Your Parentheses
There should always be an equal amount of opening and closing parentheses in your expression.

f. In the Zoom dialog box, type **Amount of Raise:IIf([Salary]<=30000,[Salary]* .07,IIf([Salary]<=60000, [Salary]*.04,0))** and then click **OK**. For those employees who received a salary increase, you want to calculate what the amount of the salary increase will be for employees depending on the percentage of the increase. If the employee will not receive a raise, a zero will be displayed.

g. Click the **DESIGN** tab, and then in the Show/Hide group, click **Property Sheet**. Format the field as **Currency**, and then close the Property Sheet.

h. **Save** the query as **qryNestedIIf_initialLastname**, click **OK**, and then click **Run**. If necessary, resize the fields to see the data.

   Notice that the Raise Assessment field has been determined and the Amount of Raise field has been calculated for you.

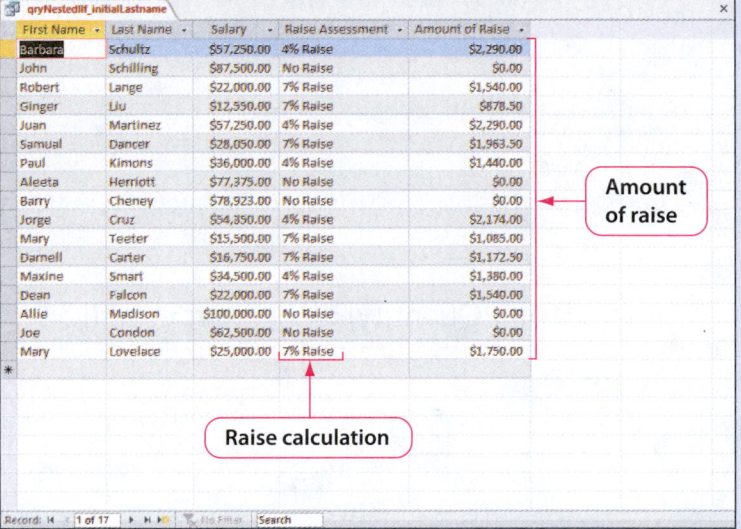

Figure 19   Datasheet view of the qryNestedIIf query

i. **Close** ✕ the query.

The IsNull Function

To understand how to use the **IsNull function**, you need to understand what is meant by "null." First and foremost, null is not zero. Null is used to indicate that a value is unknown, and it is treated differently than other values because it has no value. Instances exist when it is necessary to search for records that contain fields with null values.

Working with Fields That Contain No Valid Data

The IsNull function returns a Boolean value—true or false—that indicates whether or not an expression contains any data. For example, consider a human resources database that you would use to manage current and past employees' data. To create a list of current employees, you could build a query that searches for missing values in the Date Terminated field, showing that the value would be null for all active employees.

Because the IsNull function, written as IsNull(expression) or IsNull([field]), returns a result of either true or false, it is commonly nested or combined with other functions, such as an IIf function. Consider the previous example of using a human resources database to manage current and past employees' data. You could nest the IsNull function inside an IIf function to return values other than true and false, such as Current Employee and Terminated Employee.

It is important to note that using the IsNull function is slightly different than using Is Null and Is Not Null in a query's criteria. When you use Is Null and Is Not Null as field criteria in the query design grid, you are checking to see if a field contains valid data. For example, if you use **Is Null** in the criteria of a Date Terminated field, the data set would include all the employees' names and the empty Date Terminated field. Using the **Is Not Null** criteria would return each employee name and the date in which each employee was terminated.

A06.09

To Create Queries Using Null Criteria and the IsNull Function

a. Click the **CREATE** tab, and then in the Queries group, click **Query Design**. Add **tblEmployee** to the query workspace, and then **Close** ⊠ the Show Table dialog box.

b. Add the **FirstName**, **LastName**, and **Photo** fields to the query design grid.

c. To create a list of the employees who need to have their employee photos taken, type **Is Null** into the **Criteria** row of the Photo field.

d. **Save** the query as **qryPhotoIsNull_initialLastname**, click **OK**, and then click **Run**. Notice that there are 16 employees who need to have their photo taken.

SIDE NOTE
Hide the Photo Field
It is best to uncheck the Show field box after you first run the query to verify it was written correctly.

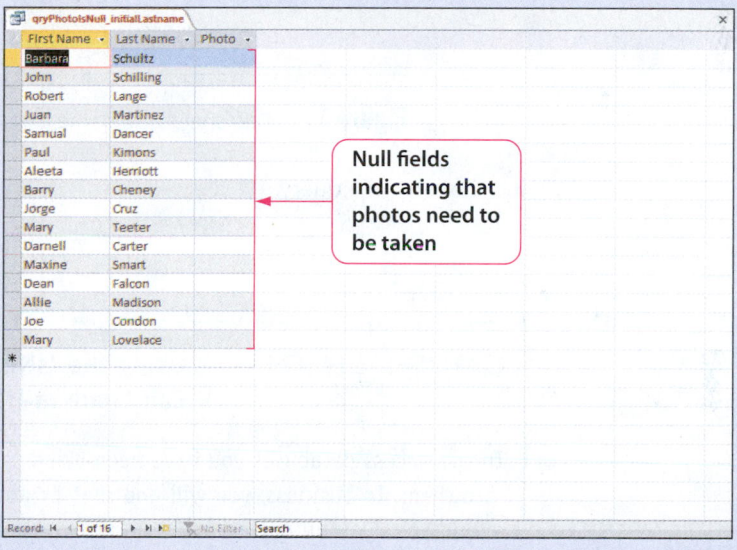

Figure 20 Datasheet view of the qryPhotoIsNull query

e. Switch to **Design** view.

f. To create a list of the employees who have an employee photo, edit the **Criteria** row of the Photo field by typing **Is Not Null**.

g. Click the **FILE** tab. Click **Save As**, click **Save Object As**, and then click **Save As**.

h. Save your query as **qryPhotoIsNotNull_initialLastname**, click **OK**, and then click **Run**. Notice that there is one employee who has an employee photo.

i. **Close** ⊠ the query.

j. Click the **CREATE** tab, and then in the Queries group, click **Query Design**. Add **tblEmployee** to the query workspace, and then **Close** ⊠ the Show Table dialog box.

k. Add the **FirstName** and **LastName** fields to the query design grid.

SIDE NOTE
Editing a Query and Saving the Changes
Remember to use Save Object As. Otherwise, you will overwrite the previously saved query.

l. To create a list of all employees and whether or not they need to have a photo taken, type **PhotoStatus:IIf(IsNull([Photo]),"Needs Photo","Has Photo")** into the first blank field in the query grid.

m. **Save** the query as **qryIsNullFunction_initialLastname**, click **OK**, and then click **Run**.
Notice that all employees are listed along with whether or not a photo needs to be taken.

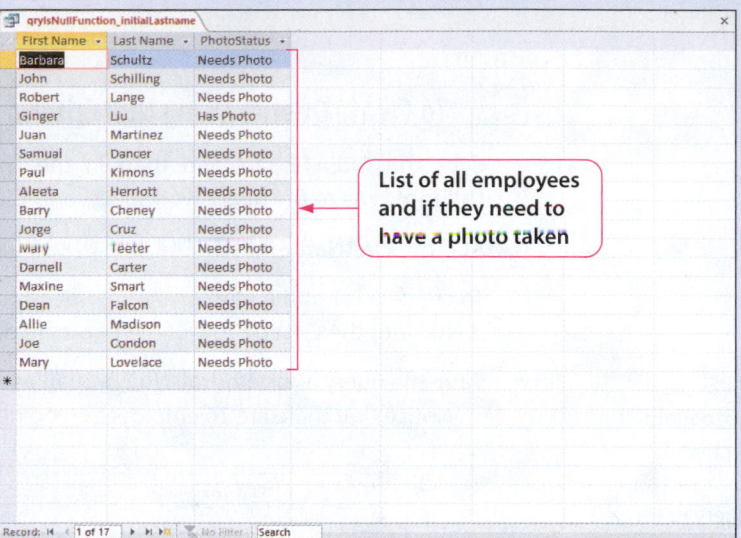

Figure 21   Datasheet view of the qryIsNullFunction query

n. **Close** ☒ the query.

CONSIDER THIS | **Using the IsNull Function and Null Criteria Can Come in Handy**

In the Access databases you have been using, most if not all the fields have data entered into them. In business, you will find that databases can contain many null fields. Think about when you fill out an online form. Not every field is required—meaning that you can leave values empty, or null. Companies make key data required for tasks such as determining their target markets and allow some fields to remain null for customer convenience. Some customers do not want to give all of their information, and companies do not want to deter customers from creating an account or making a purchase. Although a form's fields may be marked as optional, a field still has to exist in the database table to store data when a customer does give the information. Do you always complete an online form, or are there times when you leave fields empty? Are there ever times you do not complete an online form because there are too many required fields? How do you think it affects the company's database?

Date Functions

Access includes a variety of techniques that enable the use of dates and date ranges in the criteria of a query. Date functions are useful when working with the complex logic in a database that contains dates. Two of the more commonly used date functions are the Date and Now functions. Both behave similarly, as they can be used in expressions. Additionally, both retrieve a date and/or time according to your computer's system date and time. The **Date function** returns the current system date. This can be very helpful if you want to track the date that a record was entered into a table and the time of day is not a concern. The **Now function** retrieves the current system date and time. For example, you may want to have a time stamp of when a document was uploaded to a system, such as a student uploading an assignment to a course management system. If an assignment is due at 1:00 PM, the Now function could log the date and time in which the upload occurred. The instructor would then know if the student met the deadline.

The Date and Now functions are more commonly used in a table's field properties. However, if you are using a live database and inserting records with today's date, then these two functions would work very well. In this section, you will build queries using the DateDiff, DateAdd, DateSerial, and DatePart functions.

REAL WORLD ADVICE   **Should You Use the Now or Date Function?**

Avoid mixing the Now and Date functions. If you set the default value of a field to Now, Access will record the time. If you then query that field with the criteria of a date without specifying a time, you might not get the results you expect. For example, if your criteria is >12/28/2013, Access will return any records greater than >12/28/2013 at midnight. Thus, a field placed at 12/28/2013 at 8 AM would be returned in the results. The criteria of >12/28/2013 suggests that you only wanted dates starting on 12/29/2013 at midnight in the results. Generally, use the Now function only when you need time, and make sure you are familiar with the data when writing queries.

Using the DateDiff to Determine a Time Interval

The **DateDiff function** is used to determine the difference between two dates. Generally one date is obtained from a field, and the second date is obtained by using the Date function. Many instances exist in which you could use the DateDiff function. For example, suppose you have a form that you use to automatically refill customer prescriptions. In the Orders table, you have a field named Refill On that contains the earliest date that the prescription can be refilled. You can use the DateDiff function with a text box on the form to display the number of days left before the prescription can be refilled and shipped.

QUICK REFERENCE   **Five Parts of a DateDiff Function**

The DateDiff function syntax, noted as DateDiff(interval, date1, date2, [firstdayofweek], [firstweekofyear]), has five arguments:

1. The first part, interval, is the interval of time—day, month, year, and so on—used to calculate the difference between date1 and date2. This argument is required.

2. The second and third parts, date1 and date2, are the dates you want to use in the calculation. These can include a field name or expression. These arguments are required.

3. The fourth part, firstdayofweek, is a constant that indicates the first day of the week. If not specified, Access assumes that you want to begin on Sunday. This argument is optional.

4. The fifth part, firstweekofyear, is a constant that indicates the first week of the year. If not specified, Access assumes the week in which January 1 occurs. This argument is optional.

A06.10

 To Create a Query Using the DateDiff Function

a. Click the **CREATE** tab, and then in the Queries group, click **Query Design**. Add **tblPayments** to the query workspace, and then **Close** ✖ the Show Table dialog box.

b. Add the **MemberID** and **PaymentDate** fields to the query design grid.

c. Right-click the **first blank field** in the query design grid, and then select **Zoom**.

d. To see how many days it has been since a member paid the club's annual dues, in the Zoom dialog box type **DaysSincePmt: DateDiff("d",Date(),[PaymentDate])** and then click **OK**.

e. **Save** the query as **qryDateDiffDays_initialLastname**, click **OK**, and then click **Run**.
   Notice that you are given how many days ago or in advance a member paid his or her annual dues.

f. Switch to **Design** view.

g. Modify the **DaysSincePmt** expression to see how many months it has been since a member paid the club's annual dues by typing **MonthsSincePmt: DateDiff("m",Date(),[PaymentDate])**.

h. Click **OK**, and then click **Run**.
   Notice that you are given how many months ago or in advance a member paid his or her annual dues.

i. Click the **FILE** tab, click **Save Object As** to save the query as **qryDateDiffMonths_initialLastname** and then close the query.

SIDE NOTE
What Does the Minus Sign Mean?
Negative numbers in your field means that the days have passed. Positive numbers mean that the due date has yet to happen.

Using DateAdd to Subtract a Time Interval

You can use the **DateAdd function** to add or subtract a specific time interval from a date. For example, you can use DateAdd to calculate a date 10 days from today or a time 30 minutes from now. Business professionals work with dates on a regular basis. A human resources manager may want to calculate when a newly hired employee is eligible for benefits, which is generally 90 days after the date of hire. Additionally, the human resources manager may want to calculate the earliest date an employee can retire.

REAL WORLD ADVICE | Using the 1900 Date System

Access uses the 1900 date system to store dates—January 1, 1900 is day 1; January 2, 1900 is day 2; and so forth. When you enter a date into a Date/Time field, Access identifies it as a date and compares it to the calendar to make sure it is an actual date. If you try to enter a date that does not exist—such as September 31—an error message will appear. Access then stores the date as an integer number called the date serial. You do not need to know the date serial number to use a date field in a calculated field; however, you do need to make certain that you enter a valid date.

QUICK REFERENCE | Three Parts of a DateAdd Function

The DateAdd function syntax, noted as DateAdd(interval, number, date), has three arguments, all of which are required:

1. The first part, interval, contains a string expression that represents the interval of time you want to add or subtract.
2. The second part, number, refers to the numeric expression that indicates the number of intervals you want to add. It can be positive to calculate dates in the future, or it can be negative to calculate dates in the past.
3. The third part, date, is the date to which the interval is added.

QUICK REFERENCE | Settings for the Date Interval

Setting	Description
yyyy	Year
q	Quarter
m	Month
y	Day of year
d	Day
w	Weekday
ww	Week
h	Hour
n	Minute
s	Second

REAL WORLD ADVICE | Use Date Interval Settings Carefully

Although date intervals make it easy to calculate dates in Access, it is very important to use the date intervals carefully. For example, DateDiff for the "yyyy" in Access calculates without regard to the day. If you enter the wrong interval, you can get inaccurate results in a query. Be certain you are selecting the appropriate one.

Many times you can test your output using simple math. For example, Date()+10 would result in the same output as using the DateAdd function to add 10 to the current date—DateAdd("d", 10, Date()). Simplify your functions as much as possible. If you can calculate the same result entering a function that is half the length, you decrease the possibility of creating errors while typing in your function.

CONSIDER THIS | Calculating Age with Date Functions

Many companies use an employee's date of birth to calculate such dates as retirement or benefits eligibility. Is the DateDiff function with a year interval appropriate for calculating age? Why or why not?

A06.11

To Create a Query Using the DateAdd Function

a. Click the **CREATE** tab, and then in the Queries group, click **Query Design**. Add **tblMember** and **tblPayments** to the query workspace.

b. Add the following fields to the query design grid.

   tblMember: **FirstName**, **LastName**
   tblPayments: **Amount**, **PaymentDate**

c. Right-click the **first blank field** in the query design grid, and then select **Zoom**.

d. To see when members' next annual membership dues will need to be paid, in the Zoom dialog box, type Next Due Date: DateAdd("y", 365 [PaymentDate]). Click **OK**.

SIDE NOTE
Renaming Fields in a Query
You can choose to use spaces in field names of a query because you are only naming it for display purposes.

e. Save 🖫 the query as **qryDateAdd1_initialLastname**, click **OK**, and then click **Run**.

Notice that all due dates have been created and look the same as the previous year—just the year has changed. However, look at Robert Allen's record. Access does calculate correctly if someone were to pay during a leap year.

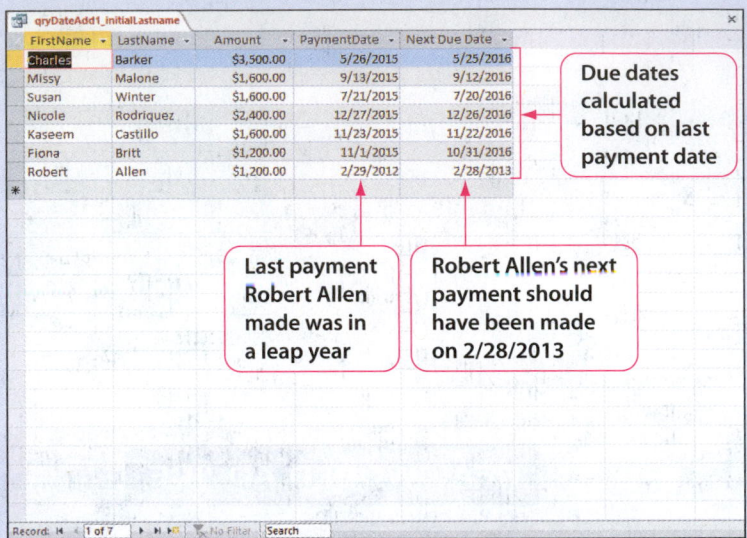

Figure 22 Datasheet view of the qryDateAdd1 query

f. Switch to **Design** view.

g. Modify the **Next Due Date** field to add 52 weeks onto the date that the dues were last paid by typing **Next Due Date: DateAdd("ww", 52 [PaymentDate])**.

h. Click the **FILE** tab. Use **Save Object As** to save the query as **qryDateAdd2_initialLastname**, click **OK**, and then click **Run**.

Notice that Access now calculates 52 weeks from the last payment date. Robert Allen's last payment was on Wednesday, February 29, 2012. His next payment would be exactly 52 weeks from his last payment. Accounting for leap year, the next payment should have been paid on Wednesday, February 27, 2013.

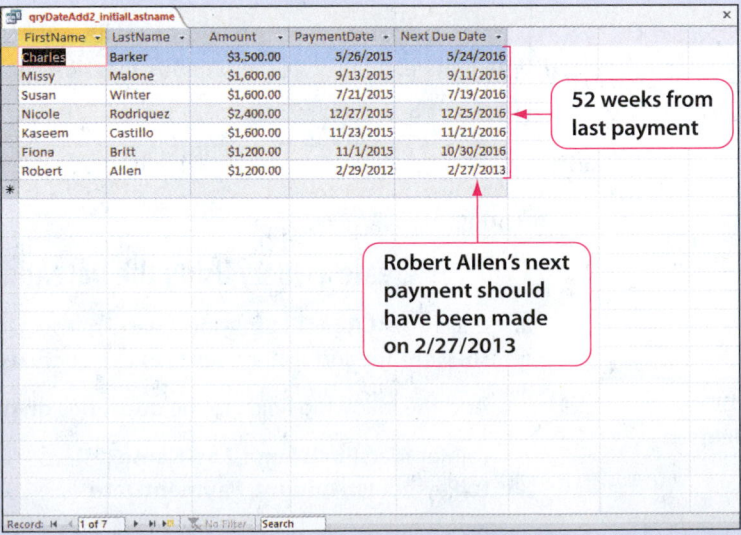

Figure 23 Datasheet view of the qryDateAdd2 query

i. Close ✕ the query.

Using DateSerial to Return a Date (Year, Month, and Day)

To display specific dates, you can use the **DateSerial function**, written as DateSerial(year, month, day) to manipulate the day, month, and year of a date. DateSerial is very flexible because you can manipulate each part individually or together in any combination that meets your needs.

The best way to understand the power of this function is through an example. When the human resources manager wants to prepare paperwork for an employee's retirement, the manager can use the DateSerial function to calculate 90 days prior to the employee's 65th birthday. Naturally, you would take the birthdate and add 65 years. Then take that date and subtract three months. Using the DateSerial function, you can do this in one step. The Employee table includes a field representing Date of Birth called DOB. The function would be written as DateSerial(Year([DOB])+65, Month([DOB])−3, Day([DOB])). Thus, if an employee was born on July 5, 1967, the date returned would be April 5, 2032.

A06.12

To Create a Query Using the DateSerial Function

a. Click the **CREATE** tab, and then in the Queries group, click **Query Design**. Add **tblEmployee** and **tblPosition** to the query workspace, and then **Close** ☒ the Show Table dialog box.

b. Add the following fields to the query design grid.

tblEmployee: **FirstName**, **LastName**, **HireDate**
tblPosition: **PositionType**

c. In the **Criteria** row for the PositionType field, type **"Full-time"** and then clear the **Show** check box.

d. Right-click the **first blank field** in the query design grid, and then select **Zoom**.

e. Each full-time employee is eligible for health benefits after 90 days of employment, which means that the benefits begin on the 91st day of employment. To determine the date when eligibility begins, in the Zoom dialog box, type **Benefits Begin:DateSerial(Year([HireDate]), Month([HireDate]), Day([HireDate])+91)**. Click **OK**.

> **Troubleshooting**
>
> The DateSerial function returns a number that represents a date from January 1, 1900, through December 31, 9999. If the date specified by the three arguments falls outside the acceptable range of dates, an error will occur.

f. Click the **FILE** tab. Use **Save Object As** to save the query as **qryDateSerial_initialLastname**, click **OK**, and then click **Run**.

Notice that Access calculated the date in which all full-time employees are eligible for benefits.

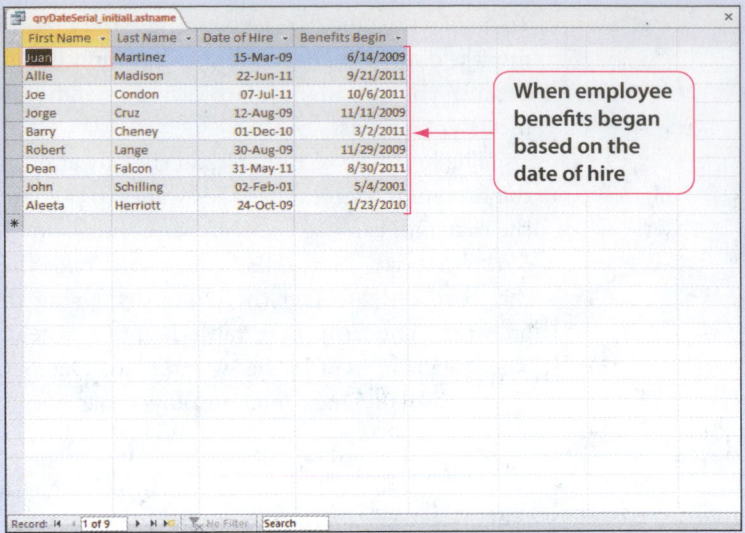

Figure 24 Datasheet view of the qryDateSerial query

> **Troubleshooting**
>
> Be careful where you place the numbers used to calculate. For example, in the above function, the 91 is placed after the parenthesis—Day([HireDate])+91—because the parentheses are enclosing the Day function argument, not the calculation.

g. **Close** ☒ the query.

<table>
<tr><td>QUICK REFERENCE</td><td>Three Parts of a DateSerial Function</td></tr>
</table>

The DateSerial function syntax—noted as DateSerial(year, month, day)—has three arguments, all of which are required:

1. The first part, year, is a number between 1900 and 9999, inclusive, or a numeric expression. A numeric expression is any expression that evaluates to a number. The expression can be any combination of variables, constants, functions, and operators.

2. The second part, month, refers to either an integer or any numeric expression.

3. The third part, day, refers to either an integer or any numeric expression.

Using DatePart to Evaluate a Date

You can use the **DatePart function** to examine a date and return a specific interval of time. For example, you can use DatePart to calculate the day of the week for an order's ship date. As presented in the DateAdd function, an interval is the interval of time that is returned. For example, perhaps you want to compare the number of golfers you had this summer as compared to last summer. Each tee time contains a Scheduled Date. You can use the DatePart function to extract the year from the Scheduled Date in order to group your records in the query.

A06.13

To Create a Query Using the DatePart Function

a. Click the **CREATE** tab, and then in the Queries group, click **Query Design**. Add **tblEmployee** to the query workspace, and then **Close** ☒ the Show Table dialog box.

b. Add the **LastName**, **FirstName**, and **HireDate** fields to the query design grid.

c. Right-click the **first blank field** in the query design grid, and then select **Zoom**.

d. Each employee is eligible for a bonus after five years of service. To determine the year when eligibility begins, in the Zoom dialog box, type
5 Year Anniversary: DatePart("yyyy", ([HireDate]))+5 and then click **OK**.

e. **Save** 🖫 the query as **qryDatePart_initialLastname**, click **OK**, and then click **Run**.
   Notice by looking at the HireDate field that some employees have already earned the five year anniversary bonus.

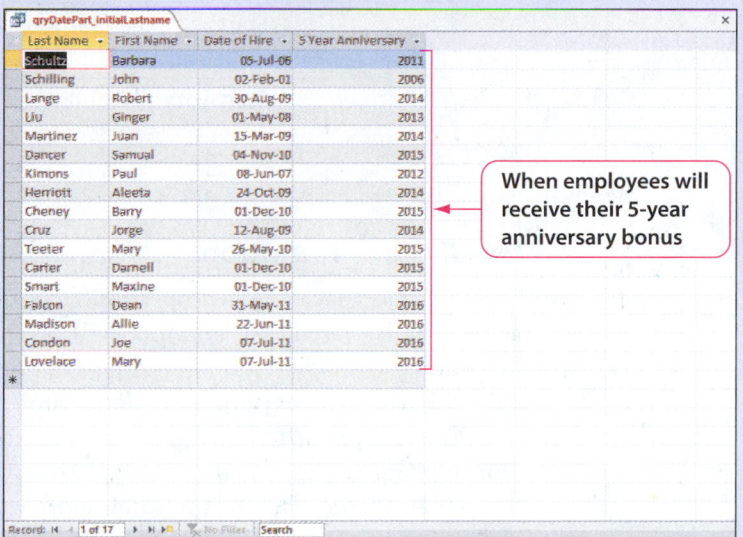

Figure 25 Datasheet view of the qryDatePart query

f. **Close** ☒ the query.

QUICK REFERENCE	Four Parts of a DatePart Function

The DatePart function syntax, noted as DatePart(interval, date, [firstdayofweek], [firstweekofyear]), has four arguments:

1. The first part, interval, contains a string expression that represents the interval of time you want to return. This argument is required.

2. The second part, date, refers to the date you want to evaluate. This argument is required.

3. The third part, firstdayofweek, is a constant that indicates the first day of the week. If not specified, Access assumes that you want to begin on Sunday. This argument is optional.

4. The fourth part, firstweekofyear, is a constant that indicates the first week of the year. If not specified, Access assumes that you want to begin with the week of January 1. This argument is optional.

Setting	Description
1	Sunday (default)
2	Monday
3	Tuesday
4	Wednesday
5	Thursday
6	Friday
7	Saturday

Setting	Description
1	Start with the week in which January 1 occurs (default).
2	Start with the first week that has at least four days into the new year.
3	Start with first full week of the year.

The Round Function

The Decimal Places field property affects only the way the data is displayed, not the way it is stored. The number will appear to be rounded, but when you calculate figures with these numbers, the calculations may be slightly off. If you round the field when calculating your data, your calculation will be correct. The Round function behaves differently than the Format property. For example, you may have a form where employees can enter the time they clock in and clock out of work each day, which then calculates the total hours worked each week. If the fraction portion of the number is below 0.5, then you may want to round the number down, and if the fraction portion is greater than or equal to 0.5, then the fraction should be 0.5. This is a scenario where the Round function is useful, and by using this function, your calculations will be accurate. In this section, you will create a query using the Round function.

Rounding to a Specific Number of Decimal Places

In Access, the **Round function** returns a number rounded to a specific number of decimal places. This is different from formatting a field to a specific number of decimals. When you format a field property as Decimal and set the Decimal Places property to 1, the values displayed will automatically round to the nearest tenth in this case. The key to this formatting option is how the data is displayed; this format does not affect how the data is stored. For example, if you enter 2.64 into this field, it will be displayed as 2.6; however, the data is actually stored as 2.64. The number will appear to be rounded, but when you calculate these numbers, the total may not calculate correctly.

| QUICK REFERENCE | The Precision Argument |

When using the Round function, you can also determine the precision of the rounding. The **precision** argument allows you to determine how many decimal places you want to round your numbers. The syntax would be Round (expression, [precision]). The precision argument is an optional argument. Access will round to 2 decimals—hundredths—if the precision is not entered. Because currency is rounded to 2 decimals, the precision is generally not entered.

| REAL WORLD ADVICE | Could Omitting the Round Function Really Make a Difference? |

An extra half of a penny in your employees' paychecks might not seem like a huge problem, but do the math. If your database is not calculating properly—because a round function is missing—it can cost your company a lot of money. For example, if you have 100 hourly employees, and they were being paid an extra half of a penny per hour, and the average hours worked per employee was 32, it would cost your company $832 annually. However, think about the companies who have thousands or tens of thousands of employees. If you work for a company that has 10,000 employees—such as a large banking firm—this small database error would cost the company nearly $85,000 a year!

A06.14

To Create a Query Using the Round Function

a. Open the **qryRound** query in **Design** view.

b. Right-click the **first blank field** in the query design grid, and then select **Zoom**.

c. The New Salary field has already been calculated. However, the Golf Club wants to pay salaries in whole numbers. To round the New Salary field, in the Zoom dialog box, type Final Salary: Round([New Salary]). Click **OK**.

d. Click the **DESIGN** tab, and then in the Show/Hide group, click **Property Sheet**. Format the Final Salary field as **Currency**. Close the Property Sheet.

e. Click the **FILE** tab. Use **Save Object As** to save your query as qryRound_initialLastname, click **OK**, and then click **Run**.

   Notice by looking at the Final Salary field that the values in the New Salary field are rounded to the nearest dollar.

SIDE NOTE
Calculated Fields in Expressions

Calculated fields can be used in expressions within your query by enclosing the field name in square brackets.

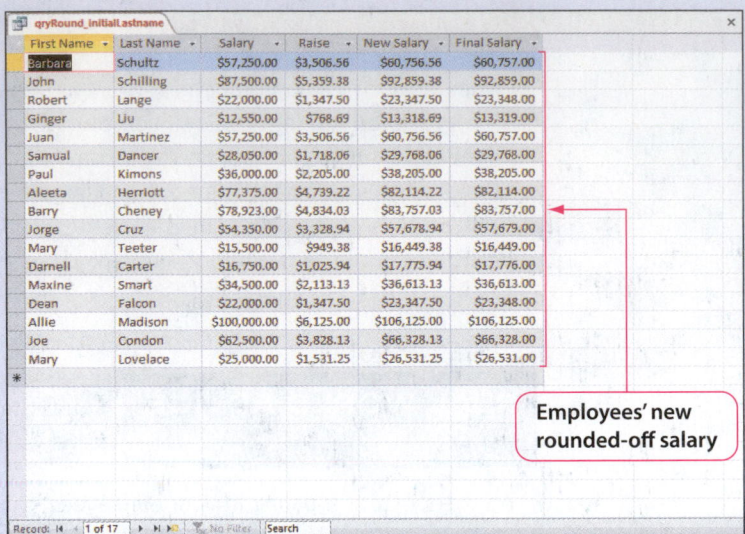

Figure 26 Datasheet view of the qryRound query

f. **Close** ☒ the query, and then **Close** ☒ the database.

CONSIDER THIS | **Databases Can Have Thousands of Records—or More!**

Remember, the database you are using was scaled down by Barry Cheney, the Golf Club manager, and now only contains an extremely small amount of stored data. Think about running queries using advanced criteria and calculations in a database that has hundreds or thousands of records in a table. How could these types of advanced queries save you time? Improve efficiency? Help with decision making?

Concept Check

1. What is the purpose of using wildcards in a query? p. 308

2. What is a Top Values query? Give an example of why you would want to create a subset of your data. p. 313

3. What is the purpose of a parameter query? What happens when a parameter query is executed? p. 316

4. Explain how you would use the Concatenate operator. p. 319

5. What is a logical operator? Give three examples, and state what they do. p. 320

6. Explain the difference between an IIf function and a nested IIf function. Give two examples of when you would use each one. p. 325

7. Explain the term "Null." What would be the result of the IsNull function? p. 326

8. Describe the DateDiff, DateAdd, DateSerial, and DatePart functions, and give an example of each. p. 329–334

9. What is the difference between the Round function and formatting? p. 336

Key Terms

Between…And operator   321
Case sensitive   313
Charlist   313
Concatenate operator   319
Date function   329
DateAdd function   330
DateDiff function   329
DatePart function   334
DateSerial function   333
Dependent expression   325

IIf function   323
In operator   320
Is Not Null   327
Is Null   327
IsNull function   326
Knowledge   308
Like function   309
Nested IIf function   325
Not operator   320
Now function   329

Parameter data types   316
Parameter query   316
Precision   337
Round function   336
Subset   313
Top Values query   313
Virtual field   320
Wildcard characters   310

Create a query using the
DateAdd function (p. 331)

Create a query using the
DateDiff function (p. 330)

Use Date functions (p. 329)

Create a query using the
DatePart function (p. 335)

Create a query using the
DateSerial function (p. 333)

Use wildcard characters
in string comparisons
(p. 308, 310)

Find records with the "most"
or "least" values (p. 313)

Create IIf functions (p. 323)

Use the Round
function (p. 336)

Use the LIKE function
in a query (p. 309)

Create a query
using Nested IIf
functions (p. 325)

Concatenate strings using the & operator (p. 319)

Create a query using the Not, In,
And, and Between…And
operators (p. 321)

Use advanced query operators
(p. 320)

Create parameter queries (p. 316)

Use the IsNull function (p. 326)

Create a top values query (p. 314)

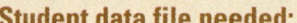

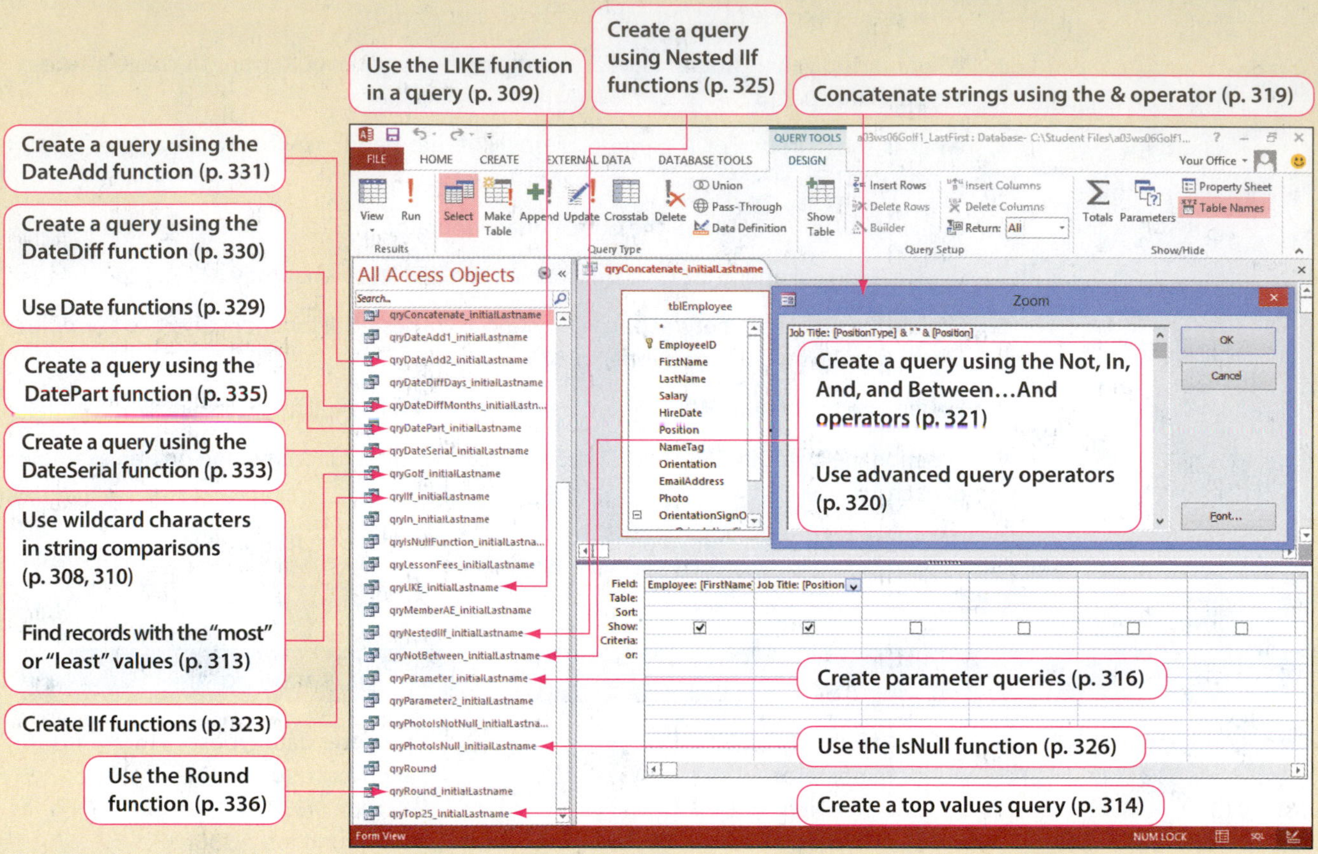

Figure 27   The Red Bluff Golf Final Database

Practice 1

Finance &
Accounting

Student data file needed:

a03ws06Golf2.accdb

You will save your file as:

a03ws06Golf2_LastFirst.accdb

Managing Payroll at the Red Bluff Golf Club Pro Shop

The Red Bluff Golf Club's Pro Shop manager has to manage all employee activities including tracking sales for commissions and hours for payroll. You have been asked to perform advanced queries that will help the Accounts Payable department generate paychecks every two weeks. The queries will mainly focus on part-time employees because their pay varies based on the hours worked. Full-time employees do not have to track their hours worked in the database. However, they still receive a paycheck every two weeks.

a. Start **Access**, open the **a03ws06Golf2** database, and then save it as a03ws06Golf2_LastFirst using your last and first name. If necessary, click **Enable Content** in the Security Warning.

b. Open **tblEmployee**, and then add your information in record **18**. Replace **YourName** in the First Name and Last Name fields with your first and last name. Close tblEmployee.

c. Create a query that calculates full-time employees' payroll for the 2-week period from January 2, 2015, through January 15, 2015.

- Click the **CREATE** tab, and then in the Queries group, click **Query Design**. Add the **tblEmployee**, **tblPayroll**, and **tblPosition** tables to the query workspace. Close the Show Table dialog box.

- Add the following fields to the query design grid.

  tblEmployee: **FullName**, **Salary**
  tblPayroll: **MaritalStatus**, **FTBenefits**, **BenefitsFee**
  tblPosition: **PositionType**

- Nest the Not and Like functions to be sure only full-time employees are shown in the data set. In the **Criteria** row under PositionType, type **Not Like "Part-time"**.

- Calculate each full-time employee's paycheck before taxes. Because they get paid every two weeks and they are salaried employees, you can calculate the gross income by dividing the Salary field by 26—the number of pay periods in a year. Gross income is the amount an employee is paid before any deductions are taken—taxes, benefits, and so forth. Click the **first blank field** in the query design grid, and then type **GrossIncome:[Salary]/26**.

- To format GrossIncome as Currency, right-click the **GrossIncome** field, and then select **Properties** to open the Property Sheet. Click the **General** tab, and then under Format select **Currency**.

- Run the query, save it as **qryFulltimePay_initialLastname** using your first initial and last name, and then switch to **Design** view.

d. Modify the qryFulltimePay_initialLastname query to calculate full-time employees' estimated taxes and net pay for the 2-week period from January 2, 2015 through January 15, 2015.

- Nest the IIf, Like, and Round functions to estimate the taxes that will be deducted from the gross pay. You will name this new field **EstTaxes**. If an employee is single, 30% of his or her gross income goes to taxes. If an employee is married, 25% of his or her gross income goes to taxes. Because this is just an estimate of how much the employee will pay in taxes, you want to use the Round function to work in whole dollars. Click the **next blank field** in the query design grid, and then type **EstTaxes:IIf([MaritalStatus] Like "Single", Round([GrossIncome]*0.3),Round([GrossIncome]*0.25))**. Format this field as **Currency**.

- Create a new calculated field named **NetPay** (GrossIncome minus BenefitsFee and EstTaxes). Click the **next blank field** in the query design grid, and then type **NetPay: [GrossIncome]-[BenefitsFee]-[EstTaxes]**. Format this field as **Currency**.

- Run the query, save it as **qryFullTimeNetPay_initialLastname** using **Save Object As**, and then close the query.

e. Create a query that will help the human resources department keep track of the days off each employee has taken throughout the year.

- Click the **CREATE** tab, and then in the Queries group, click **Query Design**. Add the **tblTimeCard** table to the query workspace. Close the Show Table dialog box.

- Add **EmployeeID**, **TotalHours**, **DateWorked**, and **WorkCode** to the query design grid.

- Use the Between…And function to ensure that you are only displaying records for the year 2015. In the **Criteria** row under DateWorked, type **Between 12/31/2014 And 1/1/2016**.

- In the Criteria row under **WorkCode**, type

  In("Vacation","Sick Day","Comp Day","Training").

- Run the query, save it as **qryOtherHoursTotal_initialLastname** and then close the query.

f. Create a query that shows the employees who have selected benefits, but for whom the human resources department has yet to enter the fee.

- Click the **CREATE** tab, and then in the Queries group, click **Query Design**. Add the **tblPayroll**, **tblEmployee**, and **tblPosition** tables to the query workspace. Close the Show Table dialog box.
- Add **Employee**, **MaritalStatus**, **PTBenefits**, **BenefitsFee**, and **PositionType** to the query design grid.
- In the **Criteria** row under BenefitsFee, type Is Null.
- In the **Criteria** row under PositionType, type Like "Part-time".
- Run the query, save it as qryFees_initialLastname and then close the query.

g. Create a query that will determine how much part-time employees will pay for benefits.

- Click the **CREATE** tab, and then in the Queries group, click **Query Design**. Add the **tblEmployee**, **tblPayroll**, and **tblPosition** tables to the query workspace. Close the Show Table dialog box.
- Add the following fields to the query design grid.
  tblEmployee: **EmployeeID**, **FullName**
  tblPayroll: **MaritalStatus**, **PTBenefits**
  tblPosition: **PositionType**
- In the **Criteria** row under PositionType, type Like "Part-time".
- Because part-time employees pay different fees for their benefits, you want to nest the IIf, IsNull, and Like functions to calculate the total benefits fees for each employee. To do this, you will create a new field named BenefitsFee that determines the employees' fee. Employees can only select one option and are charged accordingly. If an employee has not selected any benefit option, he or she will not need to pay a fee—thus, the fee will be $0. If an employee has selected Dental, the fee is $5. If the employee has selected Vision, the fee is $10. If the employee has selected Medical, the fee is $25. Right-click the **first blank field** in the query design grid, select **Zoom**, and then type BenefitsFee:IIf(IsNull ([PTBenefits]),0,IIf([PTBenefits] Like "Dental",5,IIf([PTBenefits] Like "Vision",10,25))). Click **OK**. Format the field as **Currency**.
- Run the query, save it as qryPTBenefitsFee_initialLastname and then close the query.

h. Close the database, and then exit Access.

i. Submit the file as directed by your instructor.

Problem Solve 1

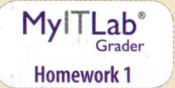

Sales & Marketing

Production & Operations

Student data file needed:

 a03ws06BookCorner.accdb

You will save your file as:

a03ws06BookCorner_LastFirst.accdb

Querying the Book Corner Bookstore Database

The Book Corner is a small, local bookstore that sells to both recreational readers and the local college student population. The manager uses Access to track inventory, customers, and transactions. You have been asked to perform advanced queries that will help the management team make important business decisions. To keep the file small while you work with the database, the store manager removed most of the data and left only some sample data. Once the store manager accepts your changes, she will load all the data and implement the new database.

a. Start **Access**, open the **a03ws06BookCorner** database, and then save it as a03ws06BookCorner_LastFirst. Enable the content if necessary. Open **tblCustomer**, and then add your information in record **25**. Replace **YourName** in the First Name and Last Name fields with your first and last name. Close tblCustomer.

b. Create a query based on the **tblShipments** and **tblTransaction** tables that display the **TransID** and a calculated field entitled DaysToShip that calculates the number of days it took to ship the items from the date purchased using the DateDiff function. Sort the results in **Descending** order by **DaysToShip**. Save the query as qryDaysToShip_initialLastname and then close the query.

c. Create a query that is based on the **tblInventory** table. Display **InventoryID**, **Price**, and a new calculated field called NewPrice. The NewPrice should be 25% more if the book is OutofPrint and 10% more if not. Both values should be rounded to the nearest dollar. Format the NewPrice field as **Currency**. Save the query as qryNewPriceRounded_initialLastname and then close the query.

d. Create a query based on the **tblAuthor** and **tblInventory** tables that contains a calculated concatenated field called Description. The Description field should display the following for all books in the database: Author: **FirstName LastName**; Title: **BookTitle**; Genre: **BookGenre**. Save the query as qryBookDescription_initialLastname and then close the query.

e. Create a query based on the **tblCustomer**, **tblTransaction**, **tblTransactionDetails**, and **tblInventory** tables that will return the top 25% of customers based on a calculated field called Revenue. Display **CustomerID** and **Revenue**. Calculate Revenue by multiplying the price and quantity, format Revenue as **Currency**, and sort the results in **Descending** order. Save the query as qryTop25%Customers_initialLastname and then close the query.

f. Create a query based on the **tblInventory** table to help determine when to order additional copies based on the NumberInStock. Display **InventoryID**, **BookTitle**, and a calculated field called OrderStatus. If there are seven or more copies in stock then display None. If there are between four and six copies in stock then display **Critical**. For those with fewer than four in stock display **Urgent**. Be sure to limit the results to only those books that are not OutofPrint by using Null criteria. Save the query as qryOrderStatus_initialLastname and then close the query.

g. Create a query based on the **tblInventory** table to help determine which books in the fiction and literary genres were written during the 19th century. Display **BookTitle**, **Author**, **YearPublished**, **BookGenre**, and **Condition**. Save the query as qry19thCentury_initialLastname and then close the query.

h. Create a query based on the **tblInventory**, **tblTransaction**, and **tblTransactionDetails** tables to help determine which "Your Office" books have been shipped within a specific 90-day period. Display **CustomerID**, **BookTitle**, **TransactionDate**, and **Qty**. Use a parameter and the Between…And function that allows you to enter a start date and end date when you run the query. Use a wildcard and the Like function to ensure that only books with Your Office in the title are included. Test your query by using 7/1/2015 as your start date and 9/30/2015 as your end date. Save the query as qry90Days_initialLastname and then close the query.

i. Create a query based on the **tblTransaction** table to help determine the date that a purchase should be shipped. Display **TransID**, **CustomerID**, **TransactionDate**, **Shipped**, and a calculated field entitled ShipByDate that calculates the date by which the order should be shipped using the DateAdd function. Orders should be shipped within seven days from the date that the order was placed. Sort the results in **Ascending** order by **ShipByDate**. Save the query as **qryShipByDate_initialLastname**, and then close the query.

j. Close the database, and then exit Access.

k. Submit the file as directed by your instructor.

Perform 1: Perform in Your Life

 Student data file needed:

a03ws06StudentOrg.accdb

 You will save your file as:

a03ws06StudentOrg_initialLastname.accdb

Leading the Business Fraternity

Human Resources

The members of the school's business fraternity elected you as its president. Until now, they have been keeping all membership records manually. Since you took a class that taught you how to organize and manage data in an Access database, you decided to create a database and convert all processes that have traditionally been completed by hand. You already created the tables and are now ready to build your queries.

a. Start **Access**, open the **a03ws06StudentOrg** database, and then save it as **a03ws06StudentOrg_LastFirst**. Open tblMember, and then add your information in the first record.

b. Create a query that concatenates the member's first and last names followed by their major and class standing. Name the concatenated field **Details**. Use commas to separate the full name, major, and class standing. Save your query as **qryMemberDetails_initialLastname**.

c. Create a query that lists all members' names and zip codes. Only display the zip codes that do not begin with either 4 or 7. Sort in Ascending order by zip code, and then save your query as **qryZipCodes_initialLastname**.

d. Create a query that lists all members whose last names begin with letters "D" through "N". Include the members' first and last names, e-mail addresses, and phone numbers. Sort in Ascending order by last name, and then save your query as **qryContactList1_initialLastname**.

e. Create a query that lists all sophomore and junior members whose last names do not begin with letters "D" through "N". Include the members' first and last names, e-mail addresses, phone numbers, and class standing. Sort in Ascending order by last name, and then save your query as **qryContactList2_initialLastname**.

f. Create a query to view all meeting details that fall within a specific 30-day period. Add a parameter that allows you to enter a start and end date. Use 1/28/2015 as the start date and 2/28/2015 as the end date to test your query. Save your query as **qry30Days_initialLastname**.

g. Create a query that determines the members' standing for the Fall 2015 semester based on dues paid. If they have paid less than $5, they are in poor standing; if they have paid less than $15, they are in fair standing; and if they have paid $15 or more, they are in good standing. Save your query as **qryStanding_initialLastname**.

h. Create the following queries using Date functions.

- Using the DateDiff function, calculate how many days have passed between the most recent meeting on 5/2/2015 and the first meeting on 1/18/2014. Make certain the calculation displays only one time. Save your query as **qryDays_initialLastname**.

- Meetings are held every two weeks, and the most recent meeting occurred on 5/2/2015. Using the DateAdd function, calculate the date that the next meeting will be held. Save your query as **qryNextMeeting_initialLastname**.

- Executive board meetings are to be held every 45 days. However, one has not been held since 9/8/2014. Using the DateSerial function, calculate when the next meeting should have been held. Save your query as **qryBoardMeeting_initialLastname**.

- Fundraisers are held every six months, and the most recent one was held on 4/8/2015. Using the DatePart function, calculate the month that the next fundraiser will be held. Save your query as **qryFundraiser_initialLastname**.

i. Submit the file as directed by your instructor.

Additional cases

Additional Workshop Cases are available on the companion website and in the instructor resources.

MODULE CAPSTONE

More Practice 1

Student data file needed: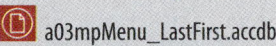

a03mpMenu.accdb

You will save your file as:

a03mpMenu_LastFirst.accdb

Building and Querying the Indigo5 Menu Items Database

Production & Operations

The Painted Paradise Golf Resort and Spa is home to a world-class restaurant with a top chef, Robin Sanchez. The cuisine is balanced and modern. From steaks to pasta to local southwestern meals, this restaurant attracts local patrons in addition to resort guests. Chef Sanchez has been using an Access database to manage menu items. She would like you to modify the tables and then query the data so she can manage her menu much easier.

a. Open the **a03mpMenu** database, and then save it as **a03mpMenu_LastFirst**. In the Security Warning, click **Enable Content** if necessary. Open **tblRecipes**, and then replace **YourName** in the first record using your first and last name. Close tblRecipes.

b. Create a new table that will help track Indigo5's menu items. Click the **CREATE** tab, and then in the Tables group, click **Table Design**.

c. Add the following fields, data types, and descriptions.

Field Name	Data Type	Description
MenuID	AutoNumber	The menu ID automatically assigned to each menu item (primary key)
RecipeID	Number	The recipe ID assigned to each recipe in tblRecipes (foreign key)
Season	Short Text	Season this menu item is served
Meal	Short Text	Time of day this is served
Special	Yes/No	Is this item one of the daily specials?
Price	Currency	The price that guests are charged

d. While still in Design view, modify the field properties as follows.

Field Name	Field Properties
MenuID	• Click the **DESIGN** tab, and then in the Tools group, click **Primary Key**. • Under the **Format** field property, type **"MENU0"0** for the custom format.
RecipeID	• Change the data type to a lookup field by selecting **Lookup Wizard** in the Data Type menu. Select **I want the lookup field to get values from another table or query**, and then click **Next**. Select **tblRecipes**, and then click **Next**. Select **RecipeID** and **RecipeName**, and then click **Next**. Sort in Ascending order by **RecipeName**, and then click **Next**. Keep the key column hidden, and then click **Next**. Enable **Data Integrity**, select **Restrict Delete**, and then click **Finish**. • Under Field Properties, type **Recipe** as the caption. • Change the Required property to **Yes**.

(Continued)

Field Name	Field Properties
Season	• Change the data type to a lookup field by selecting **Lookup Wizard** in the Data Type menu. Select **I will type in the values that I want**, and then click **Next**. Type the following values: Fall, Winter, Spring, Summer, and then click **Next**. Limit the user's selection to what is on the list, allow multiple values, and then click **Finish**.
Meal	• Change the data type to a lookup field by selecting **Lookup Wizard** in the Data Type menu. Select **I will type in the values that I want**, and then click **Next**. Type the following values: Breakfast, Lunch, Dinner, Late Night, Anytime, and then click **Next**. Limit the user's selection to what is on the list, allow multiple values, and then click **Finish**.
Cost	• Format the Result Type as **Decimal**. • Set the precision to 2.

e. Save the table as tblMenu. While still in Design view, add a Calculated field with the following description. When Calculated is selected as the Data Type, the Expression Builder will open. Cost is calculated by multiplying the Price by 40%. Type the following as the Expression: [Price]*.40.

Field Name	Data Type	Description
Cost	Calculated	The cost for the restaurant to prepare this item

f. Save your changes, and then switch to **Datasheet** view. Enter the following records to test the properties in your new table. Resize the fields as needed to view the data.

Recipe	Season	Meal	Special	Price
Avocado Salad	Spring, Summer	Lunch	No	$18.95
Black Beans	Fall, Winter	Lunch	No	$12.95
YourName's Chicken Soup	Fall, Winter	Lunch	No	$6.95
Gambas al Ajillo (Shrimp with Garlic)	Fall, Spring, Summer, Winter	Dinner, Lunch	Yes	$26.95
Pasta Napolitana	Spring, Summer	Dinner	Yes	$18.95
Pueblo Green Chili Stew	Winter	Lunch	No	$14.95
Eggs Benedict	Fall, Spring, Summer, Winter	Breakfast	No	$11.95
Fresh Mozzarella and Basil Pizza	Fall, Spring, Summer, Winter	Dinner, Late Night, Lunch	No	$24.95
Goat Cheese Pizza	Fall, Spring, Summer, Winter	Dinner, Late Night, Lunch	No	$24.95
Reuben Panini	Fall, Spring, Summer, Winter	Dinner, Late Night, Lunch	No	$12.95
Spinach and Mushroom Frittata	Spring, Summer	Breakfast	No	$13.95

g. Close tblMenu. If you are prompted to save your changes, click **Yes**.

h. Click the **DATABASE TOOLS** tab, and then in the Relationships group, click **Relationships**. If necessary, create a one-to-many relationship between **RecipeID** in tblRecipes and **RecipeID** in tblMenu. Enforce referential integrity. Do not cascade update or cascade delete. Save your changes if necessary, and then close the Relationships window.

i. Click the **CREATE** tab, and then in the Queries group, click **Query Design**. Use the query design grid and the data in **tblMenu** to create a query that displays the spring and summer lunch menu using the In operator and Like function. The query results should display **RecipeID**, **Season**, **Meal**, **Special**, and **Price** from tblMenu. In the Criteria row of the Season field, type In("Spring","Summer"). In the Criteria row of the Meal field, type Like "Lunch". Run your query, and then save it as qrySpSuLunch_initialLastname using your first initial and last name. Close the query.

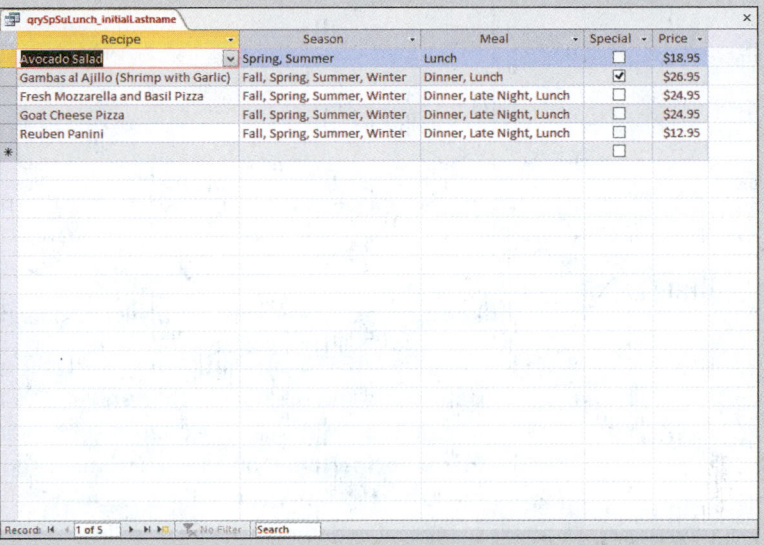

Figure 1 Datasheet view of the qrySpSuLunch query

j. Click the **CREATE** tab, and then in the Queries group, click **Query Design**. Use the query design grid and the data in **tblMenu** to create a Top Values query. The query results should display **RecipeID**, **Season**, **Meal**, **Special**, and **Price**. Sort in **Descending** order by Price. Enter 3 in the Return (Top Values) box to view the three highest priced items. Run your query, and then save it as qryTopValues_initialLastname. Close the query.

k. Click the **CREATE** tab, and then in the Queries group, click **Query Design**. Use the query design grid and the data in **tblMenu** and **tblRecipes** to create a parameter query that allows you to enter two parameters. The query results should display **RecipeID**, **Season**, **Meal**, **Special**, **Price**, **Cost**, **Subcategory**, and **TimeToPrepare**. In the Criteria row of the Season field, type [Enter the season]. In the Criteria row of the Meal field, type [Enter the Meal]. Test your query using Fall for Season and Lunch for Meal. Save your query as qryParameters_initialLastname and then close the query.

l. Click the **CREATE** tab, and then in the Queries group, click **Query Design**. Use the query design grid and the data in **tblMenu** to create a query that uses the Round function. The query results should display **RecipeID**, **Season**, **Meal**, **Special**, **Price**, **Cost**, and a new field named Rounded Cost. Use the Round function to round the data stored in the Cost field with a precision of 1. In the first blank field on the query design grid, type Rounded Cost: Round([Cost],1). Format the field as **Currency**. Run your query, and then save it as qryRound_initialLastname. Close the query.

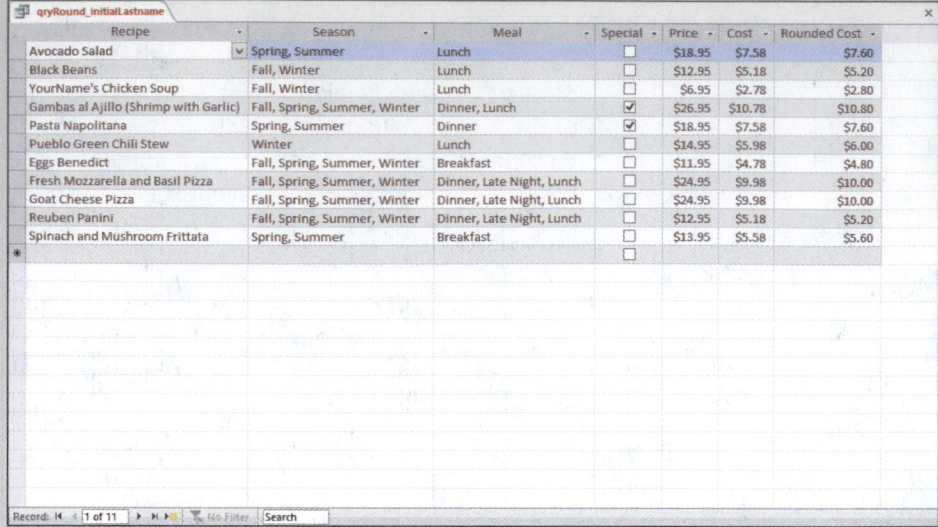

Recipe	Season	Meal	Special	Price	Cost	Rounded Cost
Avocado Salad	Spring, Summer	Lunch	☐	$18.95	$7.58	$7.60
Black Beans	Fall, Winter	Lunch	☐	$12.95	$5.18	$5.20
YourName's Chicken Soup	Fall, Winter	Lunch	☐	$6.95	$2.78	$2.80
Gambas al Ajillo (Shrimp with Garlic)	Fall, Spring, Summer, Winter	Dinner, Lunch	☑	$26.95	$10.78	$10.80
Pasta Napolitana	Spring, Summer	Dinner	☑	$18.95	$7.58	$7.60
Pueblo Green Chili Stew	Winter	Lunch	☐	$14.95	$5.98	$6.00
Eggs Benedict	Fall, Spring, Summer, Winter	Breakfast	☐	$11.95	$4.78	$4.80
Fresh Mozzarella and Basil Pizza	Fall, Spring, Summer, Winter	Dinner, Late Night, Lunch	☐	$24.95	$9.98	$10.00
Goat Cheese Pizza	Fall, Spring, Summer, Winter	Dinner, Late Night, Lunch	☐	$24.95	$9.98	$10.00
Reuben Panini	Fall, Spring, Summer, Winter	Dinner, Late Night, Lunch	☐	$12.95	$5.18	$5.20
Spinach and Mushroom Frittata	Spring, Summer	Breakfast	☐	$13.95	$5.58	$5.60

Figure 2 Datasheet view of the qryRound query

m. Click the **CREATE** tab, and then in the Queries group, click **Query Design**. Use the query design grid and the data in **tblMenu** and **tblRecipes** to create a query that uses the Like function and wildcards. The query results should display **RecipeID**, **Season**, **Meal**, **Special**, **Price**, **RecipeName**, and **Instructions**. Use the Like function and wildcards to view all menu items whose recipe name begins with the letters "A" through "G". In the Criteria row of the RecipeName field type Like "[A-G]*". Sort in **Ascending** order by **RecipeName**. Run your query, and then save it as qryLike1_initialLastname. Close the query.

n. Click the **CREATE** tab, and then in the Queries group, click **Query Design**. Use the query design grid and the data in **tblIngredients** to create a query that uses the Like function and wildcards. The query results should display **Ingredient**. Use the Like function and wildcards to view all ingredients whose name begins with the letters "D" through "P". In the Criteria row of the Ingredient field, type Like "[D-P]*". Sort in **Ascending** order by **Ingredients**. Run your query, and then save it as qryLike2_initialLastname. Close the query.

o. Close the database, and then exit Access.

p. Submit the file as directed by your instructor.

Problem Solve 1

Student data file needed:

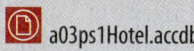 a03ps1Hotel.accdb

You will save your file as:

 a03ps1Hotel_LastFirst.accdb

Working with Tables and Queries in the Hotel Database

Finance & Accounting

The area of Painted Paradise Resort and Spa that generates the most revenue is the hotel. Hotel management must track all aspects of a reservation including the types of packages, such as spa, golf, and special events. If guests register for a package, the Price field must be updated to reflect the package price. If the correct data is not maintained, management will not have accurate data for reporting purposes. This could result in poor decision making and cause the hotel to lose revenue. You have been asked to modify the tables to ensure ease of use and functionality and to create a query that will be used for decision making.

a. Open the **a03ps1Hotel** database, and then save it as a03ps1Hotel_LastFirst. If necessary, enable the content. Open **tblGuests**, and then replace YourName in record 25 with your first and last name.

b. Switch to **Design** view, and then make the following changes.

- In the **State** field, create an input mask to ensure that all data entered in this field is in uppercase format for two characters. Change the field size to only allow 2 characters. Do not specify any of the optional parts for this property.

- In the **ZipCode** field, create an input mask for the ZipCode. The ZipCode should appear in the format 54378-1234. Access should store the symbols in the mask and use the underscore as a placeholder. Change the field size to only allow 10 characters. Change the caption to Zip Code.

- In the **Phone** field, create an input mask using the Phone Number format. The phone number should appear in the format (555) 555-5555. Access should store the symbols in the mask and use the underscore as a placeholder. Change the field size to only allow 14 characters. Close the table.

c. Open tblPackages in **Design** view, and then make the following changes.

- In the **PackageID** field, change the Data Type to **AutoNumber**. Create a custom format that adds PKG0 at the beginning of each number. For example, record 20 should look like PKG020.

- In the **Package** field, change the field size to 40. Set the appropriate properties to make data entry in the Package field required for both new and existing records.

- In the **Description** field, set the appropriate properties to make data entry in the Description field required for both new and existing records.

- In the **Price** field, change the data type to **Currency**. Because all packages offered at the resort are at least $250, you need to ensure that no one enters a lower price. Ensure that any number entered is greater than or equal to 250. Set the appropriate property that if a user enters values less than 250, the resulting error states Packages must be greater than or equal to $250. including the punctuation. Create an index on the field. Close the table.

d. Open tblReservations in **Design** view, and then make the following changes.

- In the **NightsStay** field, set the appropriate property to ensure that any number entered is greater than or equal to 1. Set the appropriate property so that if users enter zero, the resulting error states NightsStay must be 1 or greater. including the punctuation. Set the appropriate property so 1 is the default value.

- In the **NumberOfGuests** field, set the appropriate property to ensure that any number entered is greater than or equal to 1. Set the appropriate property so that if users enter zero, the resulting error states Number of guests must be 1 or greater. including the punctuation. Set the appropriate property so 1 is the default value.

- Create a new field named Package. This should look up data in tblPackages. Display the following fields in your lookup field: **PackageID**, **Package**, **Description**, and **Price**. Sort in **Ascending** order by **Package**. Hide the primary key field. Enable data integrity, and then select **Restrict Delete**. Edit the lookup properties so Column Headings will show. (*Hint*: You do not do this in the wizard.) In the field description type This is the vacation package chosen (if applicable). Close the table.

e. Enter the following data in the **tblPackages** table.

Package	Description	Price
Golf Weekend	Enjoy a two-day package filled with three rounds of golf and one lesson with the golf pro.	1095.00
Spa Special	Enjoy a two-day package filled with pampering.	1295.00
Golf and Spa Special	Enjoy three days filled with pampering and golf.	2275.00

f. Modify the **RoomRate** and **Package** in the following records of the tblReservations table.

ReservationID	RoomRate	Package
R0001	1095.00	Golf Weekend
R0005	1295.00	Spa Special
R0006	2275.00	Golf and Spa Special
R0011	1095.00	Golf Weekend
R0016	2275.00	Golf and Spa Special

g. Create a query using the **tblReservations** table. The query results should display **ReservationID**, **GuestID**, **NumberOfGuests**, **CheckInDate**, **NightsStay**, **RoomType**, **RoomRate**, **DiscountType**, and **Package**. Calculate the nonpackage guests' total room rate in a new field named **TotalCharges** where NumberOfGuests is **2** and RoomType is **Double (1 king bed)**. If a guest has purchased a package, they are not eligible for a discount. Therefore, total charges are already determined and should display the RoomRate field. If the guest is paying a daily rate, multiply the room rate by the number of nights. Subtract any discount from the total. If the guest is an AARP or AAA member, they receive a 15% discount. Format the TotalCharges field as **Currency**. Run your query, save it as **qryDoubleCharges_initialLastname** and then close your query.

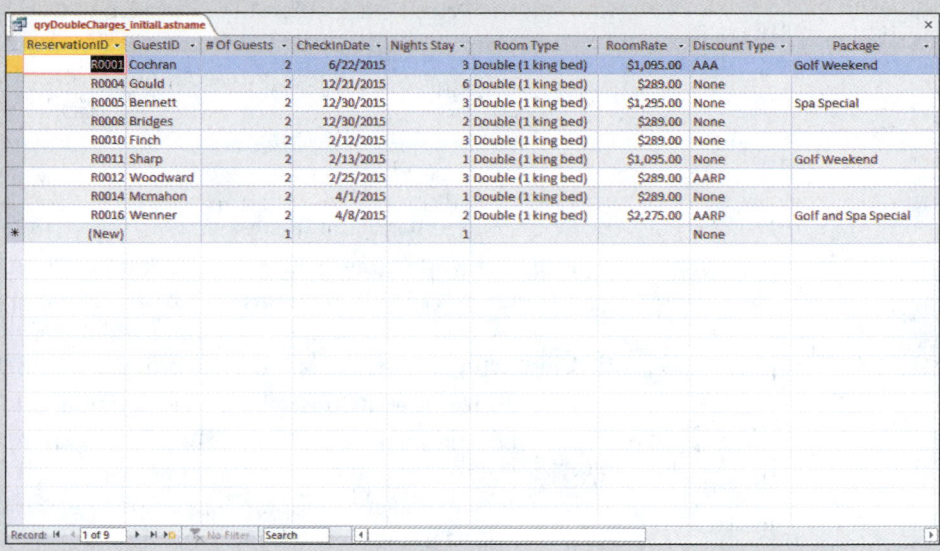

Figure 3 Datasheet view of the qryDoubleCharges query

h. Close the database, and then exit Access.

i. Submit the file as directed by your instructor.

Problem Solve 2

Homework 2

Student data file needed:
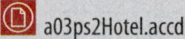 a03ps2Hotel.accdb

You will save your file as:
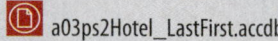 a03ps2Hotel_LastFirst.accdb

Finance &
Accounting

Querying the Hotel Database

The area of Painted Paradise Resort and Spa that generates the most revenue is the hotel. The hotel has rooms that range from nice individual rooms to an exclusive grand villa suite. Hotel management must track all aspects of a reservation including special requests for items such as a crib. The hotel also has to track room charges that guests have made. Room rates vary according to size, season, demand, and discount. The hotel has discounts for typical groups, such as AARP. Additionally, managers need the ability to "comp" a room—give a guest a complimentary room—and charge a rate of $0 for a night or stay. You have been asked to create several queries that will help management with decision making. Additionally, you have been asked to create several queries that will help management with decision making.

a. Open the **a03ps2Hotel** database, and then save it as a03ps2Hotel_LastFirst. If necessary, enable the content. Open **tblGuests**, and then replace **YourName** in record 25 with your first and last name. Close tblGuests.

b. Use the data in **tblGuests** and **tblReservations** to create a parameter query that allows you to look up a reservation by entering a customer's full name. The query results should display **ReservationID**, **CheckInDate**, **NightsStay**, **NumberOfGuests**, and a calculated field named FullName where the **GuestFirstName** and **GuestLastName** fields are concatenated. The first and last names should be separated by a space. The parameter should display Enter a Guest's First and Last Name with a space in between, such as John Smith when you run the query. Sort in **Ascending** order by **CheckInDate**. All reservations that are displayed should not have occurred yet. Run the query, and then enter Susan Wenner to test it. Save the query as qryFindReservation_initialLastname and then close it.

c. Use the data in **tblReservations** and **tblRoomCharges** to create a query that lists all reservations, the guest's room service and restaurant charges, and calculates a mandatory gratuity. The query results should display **ReservationID**, **CheckInDate**, **ChargeCategory**, **ChargeAmount**, and a calculated field named Gratuity. Gratuity should be calculated using the ChargeAmount field and a gratuity of 18%. Using the In operator, include only **Indigo5**, **Terra Cotta Brew**, **Silver Moon Lounge**, and **Room Service** in the ChargeCategory. Format the Gratuity field as **Currency**. Sort in **Ascending** order by **CheckInDate**. Run the query, and then save it as qryCharges_initialLastname. Close the query.

d. Use the data in **tblReservations** to create a query that lists the guests that have future reservations for a double room. The query results should display **GuestID**, **CheckInDate**, **Crib**, **Handicapped**, and **RoomType**. Ensure your query lists all the reservations for both kinds of Double rooms. Sort in **Ascending** order by **CheckInDate**. Run the query, and then save it as qryDoubleRoom_initialLastname. Close the query.

e. Use the data in **tblReservations** and **tblGuests** to create a query that lists the guests who reside in AK, MT, or IA, and who will be paying between $300 and $400 for their room. The query results should display **GuestFirstName**, **GuestLastName**, **Address**, **City**, **State**, **ZipCode**, **CheckInDate**, and **RoomRate**. Sort in **Ascending** order by **CheckInDate**. The front desk employees would like to be able to see which customers will be arriving in two weeks so they can call the guest and confirm the reservation. Create a new field named RSVPCallDate that calculates the date that is 14 days before the scheduled CheckInDate. The RSVPCallDate field should use the CheckInDate field to calculate when the phone call should be made. Run the query, and then save it as qryGuests_initialLastname. Close the query.

f. Use the data in **tblReservations** and **tblGuests** to create a query that calculates the guests' checkout date based on when they check in and how many nights they are staying. The query results should list **GuestFirstName**, **GuestLastName**, **ReservationID**, **CheckInDate**, **NightsStay**, **NumberOfGuests**, and CheckOutDate where CheckOutDate is a new field that calculates each guest's checkout date. Sort in **Ascending** order by **CheckOutDate**. Run the query, and then save it as qryCheckOutDate_initialLastname. Close the query.

g. Use the data in **tblReservations** and **tblGuests** to create a query that determines the discount that qualifying customers will receive. The query results should list **GuestFirstName**, **GuestLastName**, **DiscountType**, and Discount % where Discount % is a new field that displays the percentage that qualifying customers will have deducted from their bill when they check out. If customers have an AAA discount, they will receive

10% off. If customers have an AARP discount, they will receive 15% off. If customers have a Military discount, they will receive 20% off. If they do not receive a discount then leave the field blank. Run the query, and then save it as **qryDiscount_initialLastname**. Close the query.

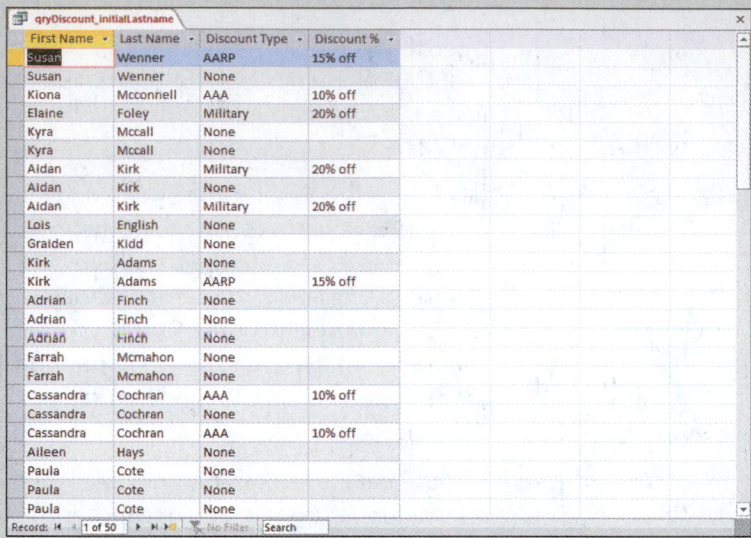

Figure 4 Datasheet view of the qryDiscount query

h. Use the data in tblRoomCharges to create a query that lists the three highest room charges. The query results should list **GuestID**, **ReservationID**, **ChargeCategory**, and **ChargeAmount**. Sort in **Descending** order by **ChargeAmount**. Run the query, and then save it as qryTop3Charges_initialLastname. Close the query.

i. Use the data in **tblReservations** to create a query that lists the number of days that room reservations were made in advance. The query results should display **ReservationID**, **GuestID**, **DateRSVPMade**, **CheckInDate**, and Days In Advance where Days In Advance is a new field that calculates the difference in days between the CheckInDate and DateRSVPMade. Run the query, and then save it as qryAdvanceDays_initialLastname. Close the query.

j. Use the data in **tblReservations** to create a query that lists the number of months that room reservations were made in advance. The query results should display **ReservationID**, **GuestID**, **DateRSVPMade**, **CheckInDate**, and Months In Advance where Months In Advance is a new field that calculates the difference in months between the CheckInDate and DateRSVPMade. Run the query, and then save it as qryAdvanceMonths_initialLastname. Close the query.

k. Close the database, and then exit Access.

l. Submit the file as directed by your instructor.

Perform 1: Perform in Your Life

Student data file needed:

 Blank database

You will save your file as:

 a03pf1JobSearch_LastFirst.accdb

General Business

Creating a Job Search Database

The Job Search database will help you track your internship or job search process, including contacting prospective employers and following up after interviews. Even if you are not currently looking for employment, this database will help keep track of associates you may need to contact in the future. After creating each table, you will need to enter data into each table. Ensure that at least one table has 20 records, including one with your name. If you prefer, you are welcome to make up fictitious reasonable data rather than use real data.

a. Open Access, open a blank database, and then save it as a03pf1JobSearch_LastFirst.

b. To ensure consistency and an ease of understanding the information, create three tables named tblCall, tblCompany, and tblContact.

c. Add fields to each table. Include appropriate data types, such as Lookup, Yes/No, Attachment, Hyperlink, OLE Object, and Calculated.

d. Add appropriate field properties such as Required, Default values, Input Masks, Formats, Captions, Sequential or Random AutoNumbers, Validation rules, and Validation text.

e. Create appropriate indexes in each table.

f. Use the data in your tables to create at least two queries about your job search efforts. Include functions, operators, and expressions.

g. Use the data in your tables to create at least one parameter query.

h. Use the data in your tables to create two queries that include a Date function.

i. Use the Table Analyzer to ensure that your tables are normalized. Modify the database as needed.

j. Close the database, and then exit Access.

k. Submit the file as directed by your instructor.

Perform 2: Perform in Your Career

Student data file needed:

 a03pf2Inventory.accdb

You will save your file as:

 a03pf2Inventory_LastFirst.accdb

Production & Operations

Modifying an Inventory Database

Gaby's Green Groceries, Inc., is a grocery store that specializes in organic and locally produced foods, as well as some unique specialty items. As an inventory manager, you were asked to modify an existing database to make it more functional for completing tasks such as when to reorder items and to track inventory within your company. Consider the marketing and sales departments as you modify your database. The employees in these departments will need to know current inventory levels and when inventory will be replenished so they can better service the company's clientele. You will deliver results of your queries to the marketing and sales departments upon completion. Enter data into each table. Ensure that at least one table has 20 records. If you prefer, you are welcome to make up reasonably fictitious data rather than use real data.

a. Open the a03pf2Inventory database, and then save it as a03pf2Inventory_LastFirst. Add your first and last name to tblSuppliers.

b. To ensure consistency when entering data and ease of understanding the information, modify your tables to include appropriate data types and field properties. Include one calculated field and one Yes/No field.

c. Create appropriate indexes in each table.

d. Create a parameter query using the Between…And operator and the IIf function.

e. Create a query using the Concatenate operator.

f. Create a query using Is Null in the criteria.

g. Create a query that includes an IIf and nested IIf function.

h. Use Date functions in two of your queries.

i. Create a query that uses a wildcard character and the Like function.

j. Create a query using either the Not or In operator.

k. Create a Top Values query.

l. Close the database, and then exit Access.

m. Submit the file as directed by your instructor.

Perform 3: Perform in Your Team

Student data file needed:

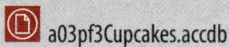 a03pf3Cupcakes.accdb

You will save your files as:

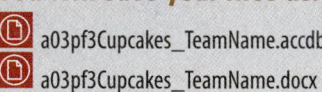 a03pf3Cupcakes_TeamName.accdb
a03pf3Cupcakes_TeamName.docx

Human Resources

Managing Employees at Jellybean's Cupcakes

You are the owner and manager of Jellybean's Cupcakes, a bakery franchise specializing in traditional and trendy cupcakes. The human resources (HR) manager has a difficult time keeping track of training efforts and tracking which training sessions employees have attended. You want to work with your HR manager to ensure that all employees are receiving adequate training. Until one month ago, all data was kept in a notebook. You have entered the paper records into a database. Your HR manager has suggested that you create a shared SkyDrive so you can share the database with your team. After creating the database and running queries, you will distribute the information to each bakery manager via the shared SkyDrive. This will create an environment that will help all managers along with the human resources department track current employees along with training efforts for all the bakeries' employees.

a. Select one team member to set up the document by completing Steps b–d.

b. Open your browser and navigate to either **https://www.skydrive.live.com, https://www.drive.google.com**, or any other instructor assigned location. Be sure all members of the team have an account on the chosen system—such as a Microsoft or Google account.

c. Open **a03pf3Cupcakes**, and then save the file as a03pf3Cupcakes_TeamName replacing TeamName with the name assigned to your team by your instructor.

d. Share the database with the other members of your team. Make sure that each team member has the appropriate permission to edit the database.

e. Hold a team meeting and discuss the requirements of the remaining steps. Make an action and communication plan. Consider which steps can be done independently and which steps require completion of prior steps before starting.

f. Perform the following tasks.

- Open the **a03pf3Cupcakes** database, and then save it as a03pf3Cupcakes_TeamName. Open tblEmployee, add your team name in record 1, and then close tblEmployee.
- Modify the tables using appropriate data types and field properties as you see fit.
- Add the following fields to tblEmployee.

Field Name	Data Type	Description
E-mail	Hyperlink	The employee's e-mail address
Resume	Attachment	The employee's resume
Photo	OLE Object	The employee's photo

- Create appropriate indexes in each table.
- Using filter options, create two filters using Filter by Form. Save both as queries.
- Using filter options, create two filters using Filter by Selection. Save both as queries.
- Using filter options, create one filter using an advanced filter. Save as a query.
- Create a query that displays all employees attending any introductory training session, indicated by 101 in the session name.
- So the HR department can e-mail a reminder to all employees registered for a training session, create a query that calculates the date two weeks prior to when the session will be held.
- So the HR department can plan appropriately for upcoming training sessions, create a parameter query that allows users to find all training sessions that fall between two specific dates.
- To ensure that all your employees are of legal age to work, create a query that calculates each employee's current age. Sort the query in Ascending order by Current Age.
- Create a top values query that uses the query that calculates each employee's current age. Find the top 25% of employee ages.
- Analyze tblEmployee using the Table Analyzer Wizard. Make appropriate changes as you see fit.
- Close the database, and then upload the database to your shared SkyDrive or other cloud technology.
- Create a Word document, and then write a memo to the HR manager explaining that the database you will use to manage your employees has been uploaded. Also let the HR manager know that if she thinks of other queries that need to be created, she can feel free to add them or let you know and you can help her add them. Include your instructor's name in the cc field. Additionally, each team member must list his or her first and last name as well as the specifics of each team member's contributions. Save your memo as a03pf3Cupcakes_TeamName, close the memo, and then upload it to the shared cloud folder if necessary.
- Upon request, invite your instructor to join the shared cloud folder.

g. Submit the files as directed by your instructor.

Perform 4: How Others Perform

Student data file needed:

 a03pf4RealEstate.accdb

You will save your file as:

 a03pf4RealEstate_LastFirst.accdb

General Business

Being an Entrepreneur: Rhubarb Realtors

You are the president of a small real estate agency—Rhubarb Realtors. Your intern created a database for you and your employees to use for tracking properties. At first glance, you notice that it is missing quite a few field properties within the tables that would make the database more functional and easy to use. You also noticed that there are no queries, which would help answer many questions about the properties you have listed. You need to assess the database and apply changes to make it more useful.

a. Open the **a03pf4RealEstate** database, and then save it as a03pf4RealEstate_LastFirst. Open tblAgents, add your first and last name in record 1, and then close tblAgents.

b. Consider each table's structure. Make any changes that you deem necessary to field properties, data types, descriptions, and indexes.

c. Add or delete fields that will enhance the database. Consider data types such as Hyperlink, Attachment, and OLE Object.

d. Consider how the data will be used. Create the following queries that will assist with decision making:

- Create a query that uses the Between…And operand.
- Create a query of all homes built between two specified years that are either a ranch, split level, or 2 story home.
- Create a query that calculates a 7% commission if the house has been sold.
- Create a query that uses the DateAdd function.
- Create a query that uses the DateDiff function.
- Create two queries that use the IIf function.
- Create a query that uses a nested IIf function.
- Create two parameter queries.
- Create a query that uses the Round function.
- Create a Top Values query.

e. Close the database, and then exit Access.

f. Submit the file as directed by your instructor.

WORKSHOP 7 | AGGREGATED CALCULATIONS, SUBQUERYING, AND SQL

Prepare Case

The Turquoise Oasis Spa Database: Querying with Advanced Calculations

Production & Operations

The Turquoise Oasis Spa generates revenue through its spa services, such as facials, mud baths, massages, and so forth. The spa needs useful information in order to run its business efficiently. The spa manager, Meda Rodate, has hired you as an intern and has given you a copy of the database. To keep the file small while you work with the database, she removed most of the data and left only some sample data. Meda has asked you to query the data for decision making,

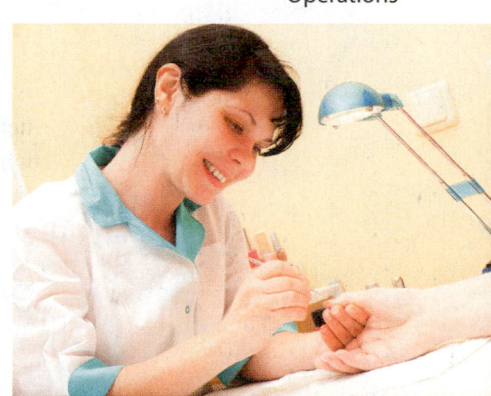

Andrey Armyagov / Shutterstock

such as scheduling employees, booking client services, and managing services. Once Meda accepts your changes, she will load all of the data and implement the new database.

REAL WORLD SUCCESS

"This past summer, I interned for a large hospital in its IT department. I had not had any of my ISM courses yet, but I did have my Microsoft Office course, which taught both Excel and Access. Although I did not have any of my major classes when I interviewed for the position, I had learned SQL and felt comfortable writing SQL queries. Had I not had my Microsoft Office course nor learned Access and how to write SQL queries, I would have never gotten the internship!"

- Lucas, current Information Systems Management student

Student data file needed for this workshop:

 a04ws07Spa1.accdb

You will save your file as:

 a04ws07Spa1_LastFirst.accdb

Understanding the Group By Aggregate Function in Aggregated Calculations

Grouping data in a query can be very informative. By using the **Group By aggregate function**, you can combine records with identical values in a specified field list into a single record. Unless the field data type is Memo or OLE Object data, a field in the Group By field list can refer to any field in a table. When you use tables to record transactions or store regularly occurring numeric data, it is useful to be able to review that data in an aggregate, such as a sum or average. In this section, you will learn how to calculate sales volume and use the Group By clause to summarize duplicate data.

An **aggregated calculation** returns a single value calculated from multiple values in a column. Common aggregate functions include Average, Count, Maximum, Median, Minimum, Mode, and Sum. You may need to create a custom field that includes an aggregate calculation. In this section, you will create queries using the Group By clause and aggregated functions.

The Group By Clause

An aggregate function differs from a calculated field in that when you create a calculated field, you are calculating or summarizing data across a single row at a time. However, when you create an aggregated field, you are calculating or summarizing data across entire groups of rows. The word **aggregate** simply means a summative calculation, such as a total or average, or summarizing data.

Opening the Starting File

To create queries using the Group By clause, you first need to open the Spa database.

A07.00

To Save the Spa Database

a. Start **Access**, and then open **a04ws07Spa1**.

b. Click the **FILE** tab, click **Save As**, and then save the file as an Access Database in the folder or location designated by your instructor with the name **a04ws07Spa1_LastFirst** using your last and first name. If necessary, click **Enable Content** in the security warning.

Summarize Data

Many managers require summarized data in order to make decisions. For example, the spa sells many different products. If a select query is created on the data, it would simply list all the products. However, the Group By clause could group the data by category, such as soap, lotion, and hair care, and calculate the total sales in each category with the Sum aggregate function. By having summary data, you as a manager could learn which category is your best seller. You also could see which category generates the least revenue. This information could assist in making business decisions related to marketing and inventory replenishment.

Not all data within a table can be summed or averaged. Another way that the Group By aggregate function can be used is to take a count, such as a count of orders or a count of customers. For example, the spa manager may want to view how many customers each employee serviced in a given day or week. The Group By aggregate function could group the data by employee and count the customers with the Count aggregate function. Businesses can look at this as sales volume, or the quantity of items sold such as bottles of shampoo or massages given.

REAL WORLD ADVICE | **Making Management Decisions with Grouped Data**

In the world of business, specifically sales, summarized data can help managers make decisions. The data are current, relevant, and concise, and depending on the nature of the organization and goals set forth by the strategic sales plan, the data can help grow their business. Some decisions that the spa manager could make include the following:

- Reorder inventory to ensure proper stocking levels are maintained.
- Advertise items that are not selling as well as others.
- Train employees on selling techniques.
- Place items on sale if the products are generating the lowest revenue.
- Determine whether sales figures are on target to meet sales goals.

CONSIDER THIS | **How Do You Use Grouped Data?**

Have you ever used grouped data? What about when you are calculating your grade point average (GPA) or quality point average (QPA)? Many students not only calculate their overall GPA or QPA, but they also calculate what their GPA or QPA is for their major. Is this considered "grouping" data?

Calculating Sales Volume

Sales volume is the number of items sold or services rendered during normal business hours. This figure is taken over a specific period of time—week, month, year, and so on—and can be expressed in either dollars or percentages.

MyITLab®

Workshop 7 Training

A07.01

To Create a Query Using the Group By Aggregate Function

a. Open **tblCustomer**, and then add your information in record **1**. Replace YourName in the FirstName and LastName fields with your first and last name. **Close** ☒ tblCustomer.

b. Click the **CREATE** tab, and then in the Queries group, click **Query Design**. In the Show Table dialog box, click **tblProduct**, press Ctrl, click **tblPurchase**, and then click **Add**. **Close** ☒ the Show Table dialog box.

c. On the DESIGN tab, in the Show/Hide group, click **Totals**.

d. Add the following fields to the query design grid: **Category**, **Price**, and **Quantity**.

e. Rename the Price field by typing Revenue: in front of the field name **Price**.

f. In the Total row of the query design grid, select the following **Group By** options.

Category: Leave as **Group By**
Revenue Price: Select **Sum**
Quantity: Select **Sum**

Notice that you can modify how you want the data to be displayed by using the SUM aggregate function.

g. Click the **FILE** tab. Click **Save As**, click **Save Object As**, and then click the **Save As** button. Save your query as qryGroupBy1_initialLastname using your first initial and last name.

SIDE NOTE
Group By vs. Sum
Use Group By whenever you can. It is much easier to select an aggregate function from a menu than to write an expression that includes it.

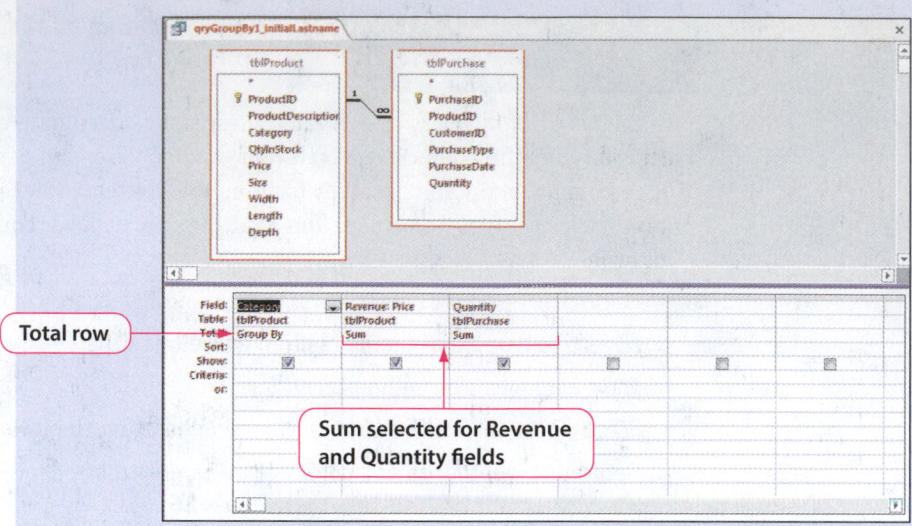

Total row

Sum selected for Revenue
and Quantity fields

Figure 1 Design view of qryGroupBy1 query

SIDE NOTE
Resizing Fields
It is best practice to resize
fields so all the data can
been seen. This is a great
habit to develop.

h. On the DESIGN tab, in the Results group, click **Run**. Resize your fields if you cannot see all
the data or column headings.

Notice that you can see how many products you sold within each category and the
total sales that were generated.

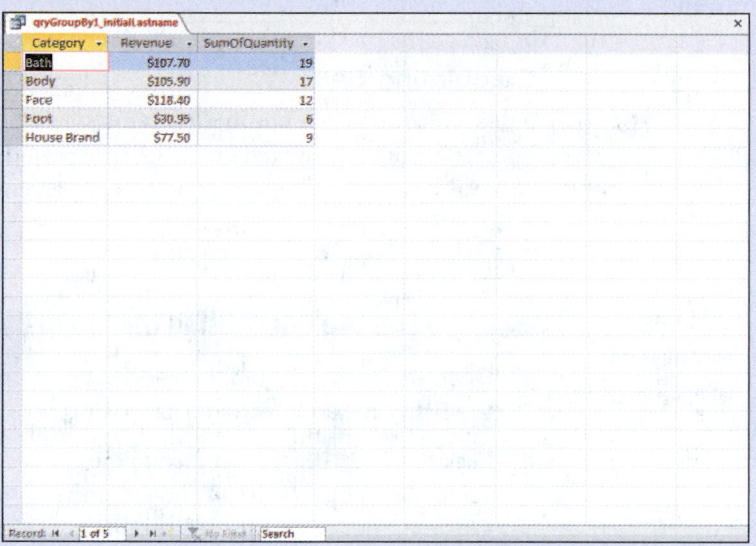

Figure 2 Datasheet view of the qryGroupBy1 query

i. Switch to **Design** view, and then delete the **Quantity** field.

j. Click the **FILE** tab, and then use **Save Object As** to save your query as
qryGroupBy2_initialLastname. Click **OK**.

k. Click the **DESIGN** tab, and then in the Results group, click **Run**.

Because of the relationship between the two tables, none of the fields from
tblPurchase needed to be used in the query. Access still includes calculations for the list
of those products that were purchased.

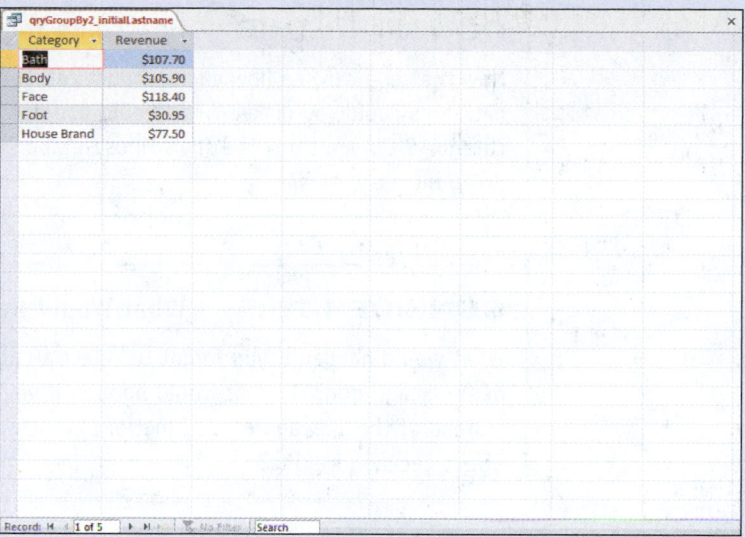

Figure 3 Datasheet view of the qryGroupBy2 query

l. Switch to **Design** view, and then delete the **Revenue: Price** field from the query design grid.

m. Add **ProductID** from the tblPurchase table to the query design grid.

n. In the Total row of the query design grid select the following.

Category: Leave as **Group By**
ProductID: Select **Count**

To see how many times an item was purchased, you can modify how you want the data to be displayed by using the COUNT aggregate function.

o. Click the **FILE** tab, use **Save Object As** to save your query as **qryGroupBy3_initialLastname** and then click **OK**.

p. On the DESIGN tab, in the Results group, click **Run**.

Notice that your output is not the same as when you used the SUM aggregate function to see the quantity of items purchased. The output is actually showing you how many transactions are included for each of the items.

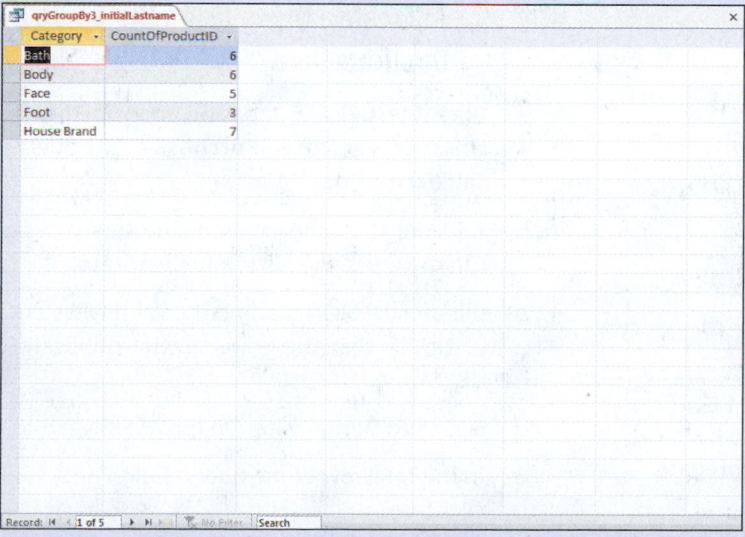

Figure 4 Datasheet view of the qryGroupBy3 query

q. **Close** ☒ the query.

CONSIDER THIS | **How Could You Use the Grouped Data?**

Now that you can see how each product category performed in regard to sales, what decisions could you make? What would you do about the low sales numbers in the Foot category? Do you think the spa's House Brand should be higher in sales? What would you do to increase sales?

CONSIDER THIS | **What Would Happen If You Forgot a Step?**

What would happen if you forgot to select an aggregate function in the Total row of the query design grid? Or what would happen if you selected the Count aggregate function instead of the Sum aggregate function? What would the data look like? How could it affect decision making?

Summarize Duplicate Data

Another way a Group By aggregate function can be used is to summarize multiple records in a table. For example, what if you wanted a list of all customers—along with their mailing information—who have made a purchase during a given period of time? You can simply add a transactions table to the Query Design view and only include the customers who have made a purchase. Additionally, you could exclude people who were added to the Customers table, but never made a purchase—maybe they canceled their appointments. Initially, those who made many purchases will be listed multiple times. However, you can add the Total row to group them and therefore remove duplicates.

Using the Group By Aggregate Function

The column(s) listed in the Group By clause are used to group the dataset. When the query is run, Access performs the grouping first, in order to retrieve the structure used to perform the aggregate expressions.

A07.02

 To Create a Query Using the Group By Aggregate Function to Summarize Duplicate Data

a. Click the **CREATE** tab, and then in the Queries group, click **Query Design**. Add **tblCustomer** and **tblPurchase** to the query workspace, and then **Close** ☒ the Show Table dialog box.

b. Add the following fields to the query design grid: **CustFirstName**, **CustLastName**, **CustAddress**, **CustCity**, and **CustState**.

c. Click the **DESIGN** tab, and then in the Results group, click **Run**.

   Notice that there are several duplicate customer names within the 27 records displaying.

d. Switch to **Design** view. On the DESIGN tab, in the Show/Hide group, click **Totals**.

e. In the Total row of the query design grid, verify all fields are set to **Group By**, and then click **Run**.

   Notice that by adding the Total row to group the records, the duplicates were grouped together and only 12 records are displayed in the dataset.

f. **Save** 💾 the query as **qryGroupBy4_initialLastname**.

SIDE NOTE
Using Group By Without Aggregate Functions
Group By does not have to be used with Sum, Count, and so on to display aggregated—summarized—data.

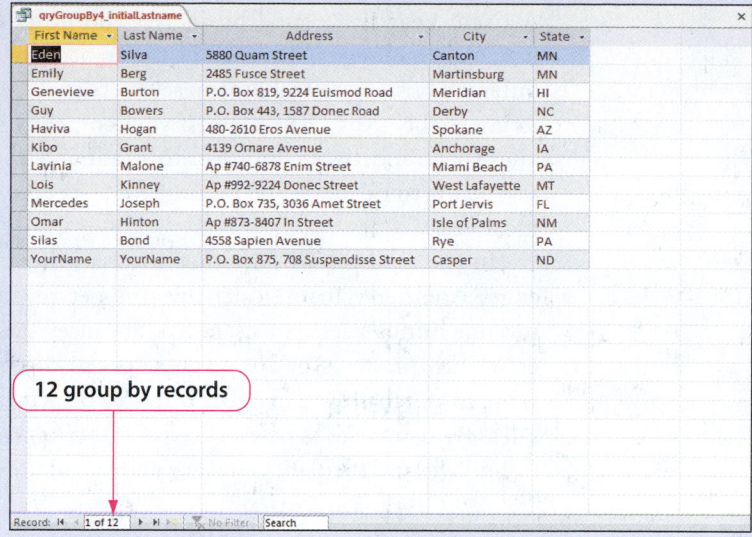

Figure 5 Datasheet view of the qryGroupBy4 query

g. **Close** ✖ the query.

Understanding the Where Aggregate Function in Aggregated Calculations

The **Where aggregate function** allows you to limit the results of your query by specifying criteria that field values must meet without using that field to group the data mathematically. When using a Where aggregate function within your select query, you need to enter query criteria. Access selects the records that meet the condition listed in the query criteria. For example, suppose your customer service representatives need to be able to retrieve customers' e-mail addresses or phone numbers throughout the day, but the representative only knows the customer's last name. You could use a Where aggregate function to limit the results of the query and make it easier for your employees to find the information they need. In this section, you will calculate sales revenue using the Where aggregate function.

<table>
<tr><td>**REAL WORLD ADVICE**</td><td>**When Do You Need to Use the Where Aggregate Function?**</td></tr>
</table>

Determining when you need a Where aggregate function can be difficult at first. Generally, though not in all cases, you want to use a Where aggregate function on a field that is needed to define the criteria, but you do not want the field to display in the query results. If you clear the Show box, then Access will still use the field to group the records. You can also use a Where aggregate function to compare values. You can use other comparison operators, such as greater than (>), less than (<), or equals (=).

Where Aggregate Function

Revenue is one of the most important pieces of information that a company uses to learn more about its financial progress. **Revenue**—or gross sales—is income that a company receives from its normal business activities—the sale of goods and services to customers. Using the Where aggregate function can assist with this calculation. For example, you may want to calculate all sales where the date falls in a specific range, such as a fiscal year. A **fiscal year** is a period businesses and other organizations use for calculating annual financial statements. This can be different from a calendar year and can vary throughout different businesses and organizations because they can choose whatever dates they want to use as the "year." Therefore, if your company uses a fiscal year, you may need to add all sales that are between July 1 of this year and June 30 of the next year. Additionally, you may want to calculate the revenue for a specific department, such as spa services, for the fiscal year.

In the business world, other criteria must be considered to accurately calculate revenue. Another valuable calculation is net revenue. **Net revenue**—or net sales—is the revenue minus sales returns, sales allowances, and sales discounts. For example, if customers return products or are given a special discount—10% off—because a product they want to purchase is damaged, it has to be accounted for and subtracted from your gross sales. By using the Where aggregate function to limit the results, you can make it easier to find the specific data you want and calculate results accurately.

REAL WORLD ADVICE	Setting Up Queries Incorrectly Could Give Zero Results

In these complicated queries, you can actually get zero results if the entire total row is not set correctly. Think about querying departments with revenue over $10,000. If you put the criteria of >=10000 under revenue, but have not specified the sum on the revenue, then you will get zero results—unless one item purchased exceeds $10,000.

Calculating Revenue

The column(s) listed in the Group By clause are used to group the dataset. When the query is run, Access performs the grouping first, in order to retrieve the structure used to perform the aggregate expressions.

A07.03

 To Create Queries That Calculate Revenue

a. Click the **CREATE** tab, and then in the Queries group, click **Query Design**.

b. Add **tblSchedule** and **tblService** to the query workspace, and then **Close** ☒ the Show Table dialog box.

c. Add the following fields to the query design grid: **Service**, **Fee**, and **Type**.

d. Click the **DESIGN** tab, and then in the Show/Hide group, click **Totals**. In the Total row of the query design grid select the following.

Service: Leave as **Group By**
Fee: Select **Sum**
Type: Select **Where**

e. Type the following into the Criteria row of the Type field: Like "*Wax*" and then **Save** 🖫 the query as qryWhere1_initialLastname.

f. Click the **DESIGN** tab, and then in the Results group, click **Run**.
    Notice that Access totaled all wax services performed on clients and grouped the results by each wax service that was given.

SIDE NOTE
Clear the Show Check Box

Access clears the Show check box once "Where" is selected. A dataset cannot display a field that is part of an aggregated function.

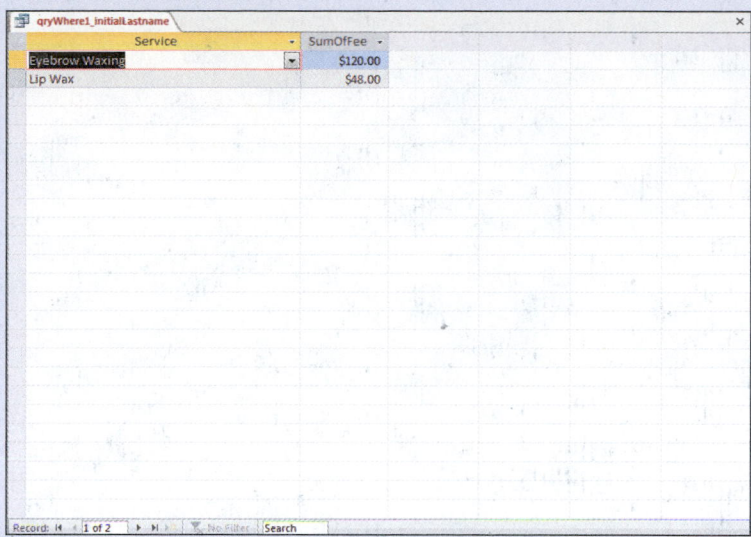

Figure 6 Datasheet view of the qryWhere1 query

g. **Close** ☒ the query.

h. Click the **CREATE** tab, and then in the Queries group, click **Query Design**. Add **tblSchedule** and **tblService** to the query design, and then **Close** ☒ the Show Table dialog box.

i. On the query design grid, right-click the **first blank field**, and then click **Zoom**.

j. In the Zoom dialog box type Net Revenue: Sum([Fee])-(Sum([Fee])*0.38).
   Notice that for some of the spa services given, 38% of the gross revenue needs to be deducted due to sales returns, sales allowances, and sales discounts.

k. Click **OK**. Format the Net Revenue field as **Currency**, and then add the following fields to the query design grid: **Fee** and **Type**.

l. Rename the Fee field by typing Gross Revenue: in front of the field name **Fee**.

m. Click the **DESIGN** tab, and then in the Show/Hide group, click **Totals**.

n. In the Total row of the query design grid select the following.

   Net Revenue: Select **Expression**
   Gross Revenue: Select **Sum**
   Type: Select **Where**

o. In the Criteria row of the Type field, type Like "Body Massage" and then **Save** 🖫 the query as qryWhere2_initialLastname.
   Notice that this allows you to view the net revenue of a specific category.

p. On the DESIGN tab, in the Results group, click **Run**.
   Notice that you now can see the Gross Revenue—the sum of the Fee field—and the Net Revenue for the Body Massage category.

SIDE NOTE

Sales Returns, Sales Allowances, and Sales Discounts

In business, these deductions are tracked individually and totaled at the end of the year or when needed. Once totaled, they are deducted from the gross revenue.

SIDE NOTE

Convert Percent to Decimal

When typing a percentage in an expression, you must convert it to a decimal. If not, an invalid syntax error will occur.

SIDE NOTE

Do You Need the Zero?

When you are typing a percentage as a decimal, you do not need to include the leading zero. This is done to ensure you see the decimal point.

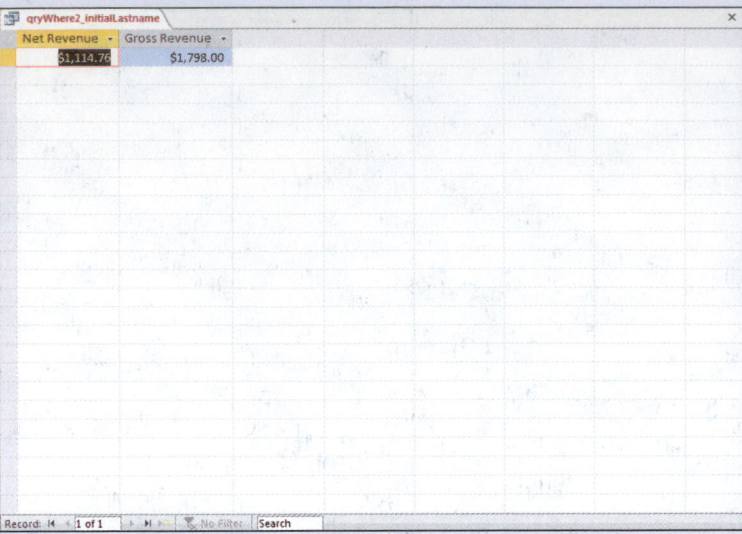

Figure 7 Datasheet view of the qryWhere2 query

q. **Close** [X] the query.

r. Click the **CREATE** tab, and then in the Queries group, click **Query Design**. Add **tblSchedule** and **tblService** to the query workspace.

s. **Close** [X] the Show Table dialog box, right-click the **first blank field** on the query design grid, and then click **Zoom**.

t. In the Zoom dialog box type **Net Revenue:[Fee]*(1-0.16)**.

   Notice that for some spa services that were given, 16% of the gross revenue needs to be deducted due to sales returns, sales allowances, and sales discounts.

SIDE NOTE
Subtract from 1

When you are subtracting a decimal from 1, you are really subtracting the decimal from 100%, or its equivalent in decimal format is 1.00 or 1.

u. Click **OK**, format the Net Revenue field as **Currency**, and then add the following fields to the query design grid: **Fee** and **Type**

v. Rename the Fee field by typing **Gross Revenue:** in front of the field name **Fee**.

w. Click the **DESIGN** tab, and then in the Show/Hide group, click **Totals**. In the Total row of the query design grid select the following.

Net Revenue: Select **Sum**
Gross Revenue: Select **Sum**
Type: Leave as **Group By**

x. You can modify the query to view the net revenue of a specific category. In the Criteria row of the Type field type **Like "Hands & Feet"**.

y. **Save** 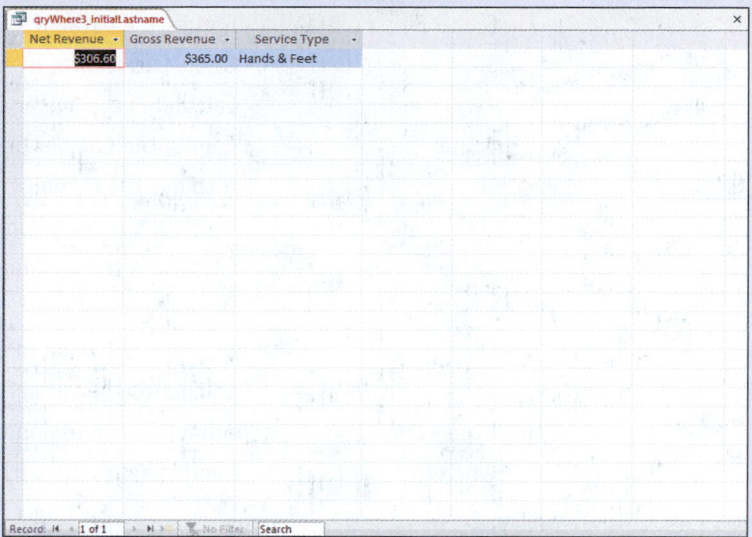 the query as **qryWhere3_initialLastname** and then click **Run**.

   Notice that you now can see the Gross Revenue and the Net Revenue for the Hands & Feet category.

Figure 8 Datasheet view of the qryWhere3 query

z. **Close** ❌ the query.

REAL WORLD ADVICE | **Expressions Can Be Flexible**

Did you think about the calculation you were performing when you typed Sum([Fee])-(Sum([Fee])*0.38)? Think about different calculations that are equally correct. For example, here both Sum([Fee]*(1-.38)) and Sum([Fee]*.62) are mathematically correct. Which of the expressions are more efficient for the computer to calculate? Does it really matter which calculation you use as long as the mathematical result is the same? Would the size of the database play a role in this? What if this were Amazon.com with billions of records?

Function	Use
Group By	Groups the data
Sum	Calculates the total
Avg	Calculates the average
Count	Counts the number of records
Min	Displays the minimum value
Max	Displays the maximum value
StDev	Calculates the standard deviation
First	Displays the value in the first record
Last	Displays the value in the last record
Var	Calculates the variance
Expression	Allows an expression to be entered
Where	Limits the results without grouping the data by the field

Table 1 Functions and uses of aggregate functions

REAL WORLD ADVICE | Calculated Fields and Aggregate Functions

When you combine calculated fields and aggregate functions, pay careful attention to the aggregate function and what data it is aggregating. If you use an aggregate function around a calculated field, Access first calculates each record and then performs the aggregation. For example, if you have a custom field named Average Markup with the formula Average((([RetailPrice]-[WholeSaleCost])/[WholeSaleCost]), Access first calculates the markup for each product and then averages all of the markups.

Business Calculations Using Subquerying

Some managers may want to calculate the sales volume—how much has been sold of a particular item or items. Some of the salon and spa's products were sold to clients who are interested in taking their favorite products home with them. A manager would want to keep track of how many items are sold per day, week, or month. Thus, the need to first take a count of each item is critical to having an accurate calculation.

What is physical volume? **Physical volume** measures how much space is within an object. For example, clients can also phone in orders or place orders online. Thus, the manager would want to pack the products most efficiently and use the smallest shipping box possible to pack and ship the orders as doing so will save on shipping costs.

Because decision making is an important part of a manager's daily routine, some managers may want to calculate the percentages of physical volume, sales volume, or sales revenue to see how the business is performing or to monitor inventory. Once Access provides them with this information, they will be able to make staffing, training, marketing, and inventory decisions. In this section, you will create subqueries that calculate the percentage of sales revenue, the percentage of sales volume, physical volume, and the percentage of physical volume.

Subqueries

Because more sophisticated queries require more advanced manipulation of data, you may need to create a subquery. A **subquery** simply is a select query that is nested inside of another select query. This is used when you want to create a query from previously queried data. For example, when calculating the percentage of sales volume or the percentage of physical volume, a subquery will make the calculation easier.

Creating a Query on a Query

A subquery can easily be created by first building separate queries, using one as the source for the other, and then writing a "master" query that pulls the data from the first two queries together. The quarterly queries act like subqueries. The separate queries run first and the master query runs second. For instance, you may want to write a report showing Painted Paradise Resort & Spa sales for the first quarter, the second quarter, and then both quarters. Because the date ranges are mutually exclusive, they cannot be positioned in the same query.

A07.04

 To Create a Query on a Query

a. Click the **CREATE** tab, and then in the Queries group, click **Query Design**.

b. Add **tblPurchase** and **tblProduct** to the query workspace, and then **Close** ☒ the Show Table dialog box.

c. Add the following fields to the query design grid: **PurchaseType**, **PurchaseDate**, **Quantity**, **ProductDescription**, and **Price**.

d. Click the **DESIGN** tab, and then in the Show/Hide group, click **Totals**. In the Total row of the query design grid select the following.

   PurchaseType: Leave as **Group By**
   PurchaseDate: Leave as **Group By**
   Quantity: Select **Sum**
   ProductDescription: Leave as **Group By**
   Price: Leave as **Group By**

e. **Save** 🖫 the query as qryPurchases_initialLastname. On the DESIGN tab, in the Results group, click **Run**.
   Notice that you now can see the total quantity sold on a given day for each product.

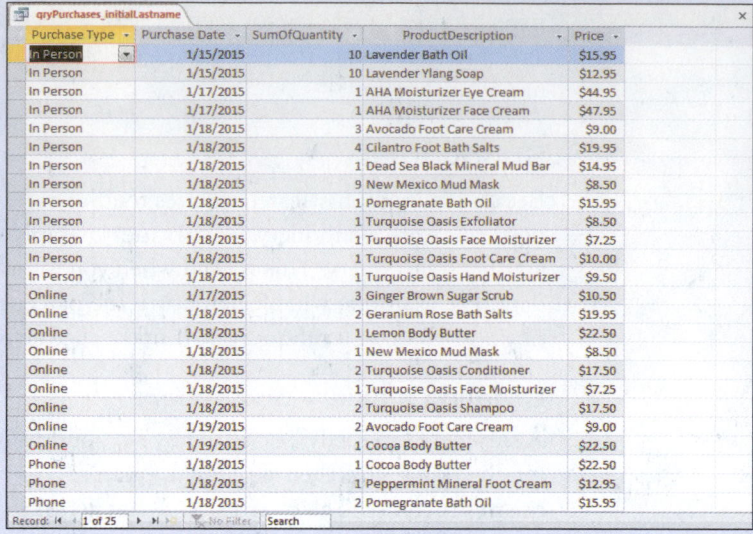

qryPurchases_initialLastname				
Purchase Type ▾	Purchase Date ▾	SumOfQuantity ▾	ProductDescription ▾	Price ▾
In Person	1/15/2015	10	Lavender Bath Oil	$15.95
In Person	1/15/2015	10	Lavender Ylang Soap	$12.95
In Person	1/17/2015	1	AHA Moisturizer Eye Cream	$44.95
In Person	1/17/2015	1	AHA Moisturizer Face Cream	$47.95
In Person	1/18/2015	3	Avocado Foot Care Cream	$9.00
In Person	1/18/2015	4	Cilantro Foot Bath Salts	$19.95
In Person	1/18/2015	1	Dead Sea Black Mineral Mud Bar	$14.95
In Person	1/18/2015	9	New Mexico Mud Mask	$8.50
In Person	1/18/2015	1	Pomegranate Bath Oil	$15.95
In Person	1/18/2015	1	Turquoise Oasis Exfoliator	$8.50
In Person	1/18/2015	1	Turquoise Oasis Face Moisturizer	$7.25
In Person	1/18/2015	1	Turquoise Oasis Foot Care Cream	$10.00
In Person	1/18/2015	1	Turquoise Oasis Hand Moisturizer	$9.50
Online	1/17/2015	3	Ginger Brown Sugar Scrub	$10.50
Online	1/18/2015	2	Geranium Rose Bath Salts	$19.95
Online	1/18/2015	1	Lemon Body Butter	$22.50
Online	1/18/2015	1	New Mexico Mud Mask	$8.50
Online	1/18/2015	2	Turquoise Oasis Conditioner	$17.50
Online	1/18/2015	1	Turquoise Oasis Face Moisturizer	$7.25
Online	1/18/2015	2	Turquoise Oasis Shampoo	$17.50
Online	1/19/2015	2	Avocado Foot Care Cream	$9.00
Online	1/19/2015	1	Cocoa Body Butter	$22.50
Phone	1/18/2015	1	Cocoa Body Butter	$22.50
Phone	1/18/2015	1	Peppermint Mineral Foot Cream	$12.95
Phone	1/18/2015	2	Pomegranate Bath Oil	$15.95

Record: I◀ ◀ 1 of 25 ▶ ▶I ▶* No Filter Search

Figure 9 Datasheet view of the qryPurchases query

f. **Close** ✕ the query.

g. Click the **CREATE** tab, and then in the Queries group, click **Query Design**.

h. In the Show Table dialog box, click the **Queries** tab, and then add **qryPurchases_initialLastname** to the query workspace. **Close** ✕ the Show Table dialog box.

i. Add the following field to the query design grid: **PurchaseDate**.

j. Right-click the **first blank field** on the query design grid, and then click **Zoom**.

k. In the Zoom dialog box type Gross Revenue: Sum([SumOfQuantity]*[Price]). This will calculate the gross revenue for each product. Click **OK**.

l. Click the **DESIGN** tab, and then in the Show/Hide group, click **Totals**. In the Total row of the query design grid select the following.

PurchaseDate: Leave as **Group By**
Gross Revenue: Select **Expression**

m. Format the Gross Revenue field as **Currency**, and then **Save** 🖫 the query as qrySubpurchases_initialLastname.

n. On the DESIGN tab, in the Results group, click **Run**.
   Notice that you now can see the gross revenue for each of the four days.

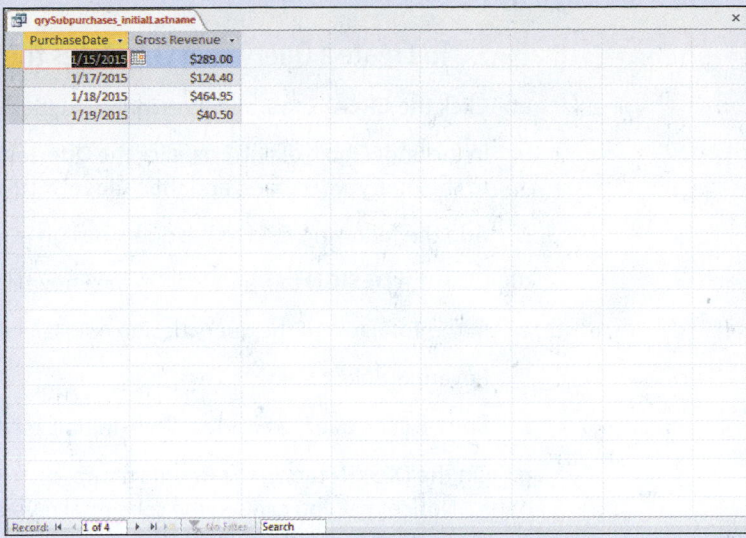

Figure 10 Datasheet view of the qrySubpurchases query

o. **Close** ☒ the query.

Percentage of Sales Revenue

In business, the percentage of sales revenue can be valuable information and can teach a manager a lot about his or her business. The **percentage of sales revenue** compares the portion of the gross revenue to the total gross revenue. As a manager, you may want to forecast or predict what next year's sales will be based on past sales—usually calculated based on the past three years of data. Or you may want to see how each category is performing this year as compared to last year's sales figures. For example, the spa manager may want to see how each product category's sales contributed to the overall sales of the spa. When calculating the percentage of sales revenue, you need to consider the method used to calculate percentage of sales revenue—the number of units sold—as well as the time period over which you plan on measuring the sales.

Calculating the Percentage of Sales Revenue

To calculate the percentage of sales revenue, you first need to calculate the total sales revenue in one query. Then you need to create a query that uses the total sales revenue calculation to calculate the percentage of sales revenue, where the percentage of a whole is the individual item divided by the grand total. For example, if the sales revenue for all spa services given last month was $27,325, the spa manager could create a query that divides the total sales revenue of each service given last month, such as Sea Salt Scrub, by the sales revenue for all spa services given last month. If the sales revenue for Sea Salt Scrubs was $1,768, the query results would illustrate that Sea Salt Scrubs contributed to 6.47% of the total sales revenue.

A07.05

 To Create a Query That Calculates the Percentage of Sales Revenue

a. Click the **CREATE** tab, and then in the Queries group, click **Query Design**.

b. In the Show Table dialog box, click the **Queries** tab, add **qryGroupBy1_initialLastname** to the query workspace, and then **Close** ☒ the Show Table dialog box.

c. Add the following field to the query design grid: **Revenue**

d. Click the **DESIGN** tab, and then in the Show/Hide group, click **Totals**.

e. In the Total row of the query design grid select the following.

   Revenue: Select **Sum**

f. **Save** 🖫 the query as qryTotalRev_initialLastname.

g. On the DESIGN tab, in the Results group, click **Run**.

   Notice that you can see the spa's total revenue—the total dollars generated through the sales of its products. You need to calculate what the total revenue is before you can calculate the percentage of sales revenue.

h. **Close** ☒ the query. Click the **CREATE** tab, and then in the Queries group, click **Query Design**.

i. In the Show Table dialog box, click the **Queries** tab, add **qryGroupBy1_initialLastname** and **qryTotalRev_initialLastname** to the query workspace. **Close** ☒ the Show Table dialog box.

j. Add the following fields to the query design grid: **Category** and **Revenue**

k. In the **first blank field** of the query design grid, open the Zoom dialog box, and then type the expression **Percent to Gross Revenue:[Revenue]/[SumOfRevenue]**.

   This is the equation needed to calculate what percentage of each category's sales contributed to the gross revenue. To calculate this, the category total revenue is divided by the overall gross revenue.

l. Click **OK**, and then format the Percent to Gross Revenue field as **Percent**.

m. **Save** 🖫 the query as qryPctToGrossRev_initialLastname, and then click **Run**.

   Notice that you can see the percentage of sales within each category and how the category revenue contributed to the gross revenue.

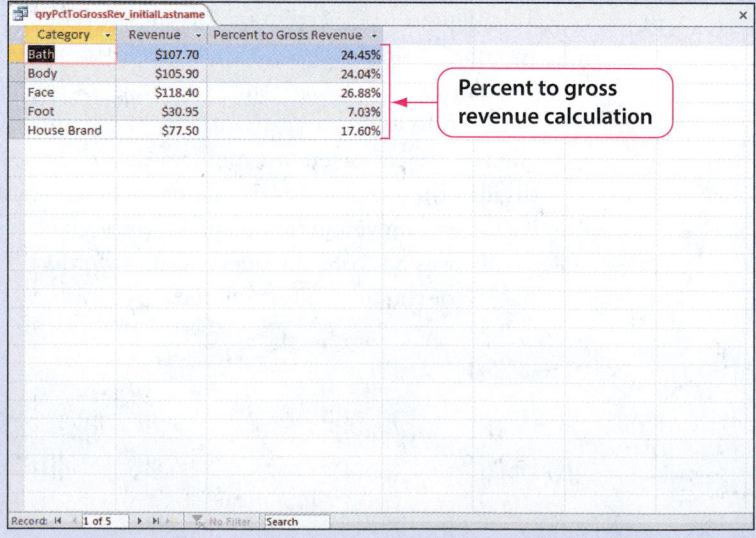

Figure 11   Datasheet view of the qryPctToGrossRev query

n. Click the **HOME** tab, and then in the Records group, click **Totals**.

Not only can you view the percentage of sales volume, you can also format the query output to see the grand totals of each field. Notice that a Total row appeared at the bottom of your datasheet.

o. Click the **Total** row of the Percent to Gross Revenue field, and then select **Sum** from the list.

Notice that you can use this as a way to communicate information better, and it can also help you double-check that your percentage calculations add up to 100%.

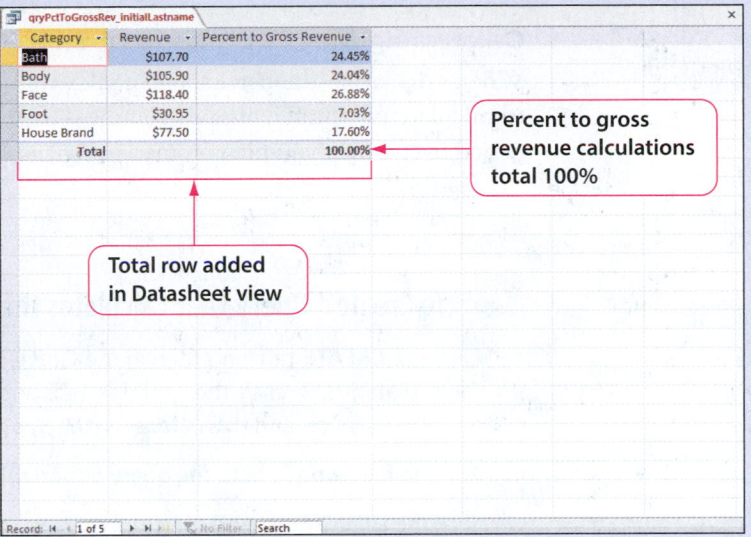

Figure 12 Datasheet view of the qryPctToGrossRev query with totals

p. **Save** 💾 the changes, and then **Close** ✖ the query.

Percentage of Sales Volume

The **percentage of sales volume** can help compare how two or more numbers are related. Consider a pie chart. A pie chart is used to show how certain categories contribute to the pie as a whole and are generally displayed as percentages. As a manager, you may want to forecast or predict how many products you will sell next year based on past sales. Or you may want to see how each category is performing this year as compared to last year's sales volume. For example, the spa manager may want to track how many clients schedule services, and then find out how the total quantity of each service contributed to the overall total quantity of services given. For example, if the spa manager wants to see how many services were given last month, the spa manager could simply create a query that counts each appointment for last month.

To perform this calculation, you need to create a query that counts each service given during a specific period of time. Then you need to create a subquery that displays each service along with a calculation of the total quantity of each service contributed divided by the overall total quantity of services given. For example, if the total spa services given last month were 143, the spa manager could create a query that divides the count of each service given last month, such as Sea Salt Scrub, by the total spa services given last month. If 26 Sea Salt Scrubs were given last month, the query results would illustrate that 18.2% of all services given were Sea Salt Scrubs.

> **CONSIDER THIS** | How Could a Manager Use the Percentage of Sales Volume Data?
>
> Once you can see how services performed relates to the total sales volume, what decisions could you make? What if a service did not sell as well as it did last year? How would that affect marketing? Would you not offer the service anymore? What if you notice that a particular service is more popular than you initially thought? How would that affect staffing?

Calculating the Percentage of Sales Volume

When calculating the percentage of sales volume, you need to consider the method used to calculate percentage of sales volume—the number of units sold—as well as the time period over which you plan on measuring the sales volume.

A07.06

 To Create a Query That Calculates the Percentage of Sales Volume

a. Click the **CREATE** tab, and then in the Queries group, click **Query Design**. In the Show Table dialog box, click the **Queries** tab, add **qryGroupBy1_initialLastname** to the query workspace, and then **Close** ☒ the Show Table dialog box.

b. Add the following field to the query design grid: **SumOfQuantity**

c. Click the **DESIGN** tab, and then in the Show/Hide group, click **Totals**.

d. In the Total row of the query design grid select the following.

   SumOfQuantity: Select **Sum**

e. Rename the **SumOfQuantity** field by typing Total Quantity: in front of the field name **SumOfQuantity**.

f. **Save** 🖫 the query as qryTotalQty_initialLastname. On the DESIGN tab, in the Results group, click **Run**.

   Notice that you calculated the total quantity of items sold. This needs to be done before you can calculate the percentage of sales volume. Notice that there was a total of 63 items sold.

g. **Close** ☒ the query.

h. Click the **CREATE** tab, and then in the Queries group, click **Query Design**.

i. In the Show Table dialog box, click the **Queries** tab, and then add **qryGroupBy1_initialLastname** and **qryTotalQty_initialLastname** to the query workspace. **Close** ☒ the Show Table dialog box.

j. Add the following field to the query design grid: **Category**

k. In the next blank field in the query design grid, in the Zoom dialog box type Percent to Sales Volume: [SumOfQuantity]/[Total Quantity].

   The equation needed to calculate what percentage of each category's sales contributed to the sales volume is the category total sales volume divided by the overall total sales volume.

l. Click **OK**, and then format the Percent to Sales Volume field as **Percent**.

m. **Save** 🖫 the query as **qryPctToSalesVolume_initialLastname** and then click **Run**.

Notice that you can see the percentage of sales volume within each category. Also notice how the category sales volume contributed to the total sales volume.

n. Click the **HOME** tab, and then in the Records group, click **Totals**.

o. Click the **Total** row of the Percent to Sales Volume field, and then select **Sum** from the list.

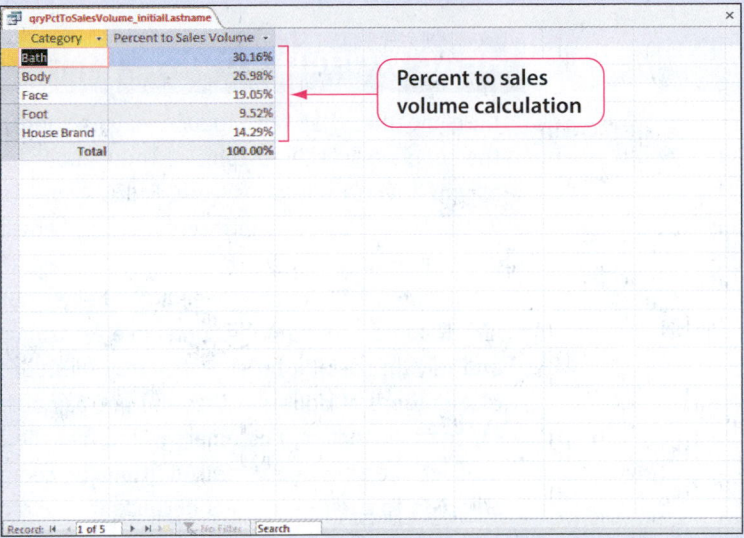

Figure 13 Datasheet view of the qryPctToSalesVolume query with totals

p. **Save** 🖫 the changes, and then **Close** ☒ the query.

REAL WORLD ADVICE **Why Are You Renaming Fields?**

In the previous exercise, you renamed the SumOfQuantity field to Total Quantity. If you had not done that, your calculation would have been [SumOfQuantity]/ [SumOfQuantity]. This would have confused Access as you would have had two fields with the same name. In that case, you would have had to specify the table or query name before the field name like this [qryGroupBy1_initialLastname]![SumOfQuantity]/ [qryTotalQty_initialLastname]![SumOfQuantity]. Renaming one of the fields is easier than having to specify the table or query that each field came from.

CONSIDER THIS **How Could a Manager Use the Grouped Data?**

Now that you can see how each product category performed in regard to gross revenue, what decisions could you make? What if a category did not sell as well as it did last year? What if you displayed the average instead of the sum at the bottom of your query results in Datasheet view? Would this change your decisions?

Physical Volume

Sometimes you might hear a question like "How much can the box hold?" You need to calculate physical volume to determine the answer to this question. For example, many companies sell products online and have to determine the best size of box to use for packing the order. The packaging volume is the difference between the volume of the shipping container and the volume of the object you are shipping. Because some shipping companies can apply surcharges for larger boxes, it is important to use the best size box to keep the overall shipping charge as low as possible. Imagine some of the largest online retailers you know and how much money using the correct box size can generate in terms of cost savings. If you know how to calculate packaging volume, you can calculate the remaining space in the box and then select the appropriate size box for shipping.

REAL WORLD ADVICE | Shipping Merchandise Is Big Business

All companies that sell products have a supply chain that helps move products from the suppliers to the customers. Think about how many UPS or FedEx trucks you pass as you drive to school or work. FedEx averages about 3.4 million packages per day in the United States and internationally, which is equivalent to about 7.2 million pounds of goods in the United States a day, and about 3.6 million pounds overseas. Think about how much money a company would waste if they did not optimize the way they packaged goods. Firms like Amazon.com conduct all their business online and rely on packing orders efficiently in order to maximize their profit. They could lose millions of dollars if they did not pay attention to how they package orders for their customers. Customers would feel the loss as well by having to pay higher product and shipping costs. Additionally, companies would not be able to offer free shipping to their customers because it would cost the company too much money.

Calculating Physical Volume

Consider the Turquoise Oasis Spa. There are times when clients will either place an order via phone or online and then have the order shipped to their home. If you know how much space or volume a product takes up within the box, you can determine what size box to use for the entire shipment. Calculating physical volume can help management manage the spa's shipping supplies.

A07.07

 To Create a Query That Calculates Physical Volume

a. Click the **CREATE** tab, and then in the Queries group, click **Query Design**. Add **tblProduct** to the query workspace, and then **Close** ☒ the Show Table dialog box.

b. Add the following fields to the query design grid: **ProductDescription** and **Size**

c. In the Criteria row of the ProductDescription field type Like "*soap*".

d. In the **first blank field** in the query design grid, in the Zoom dialog box type Volume: [Width]*[Length]*[Depth].

   To calculate the volume that each bar of soap consumes, you need to multiply (length)*(width)*(depth). The result will be in cubic inches.

e. Click **OK**.

f. In the **next blank field** in the query design grid, in the Zoom dialog box type Remaining Pkg Volume:136-[Volume].

   The smallest carton that the spa has to ship items to customers is 136 cubic inches. To calculate the packaging volume that a bar of soap consumes within the smallest box available, subtract the volume of the bar of soap from the volume available within the smallest carton. The result will be in cubic inches.

SIDE NOTE
Why Use Cubic Inches?
In the United States, it is the standard unit for measuring volume. It considers the three sides of a cube, each being 1" long, as a starting point.

SIDE NOTE

What Does Int do?

Because you cannot send a portion of a bar of soap, the Int—Integer—function truncates the decimal and returns only the integer portion of the Total Pkg Volume quotient.

g. Click **OK**.

h. In the **next blank field** in the query design grid, in the Zoom dialog box type **Total Pkg Volume:Int(136/[Volume])**.

Notice that you are now calculating the total bars of soap that can fit into the spa's smallest carton. The result will be in cubic inches.

i. Click **OK**.

j. **Save** 💾 the query as **qryPhysicalVolume_initialLastname**. On the DESIGN tab, in the Results group, click **Run**.

Notice that you can ship up to 22 bars of soap within the smallest available shipping carton.

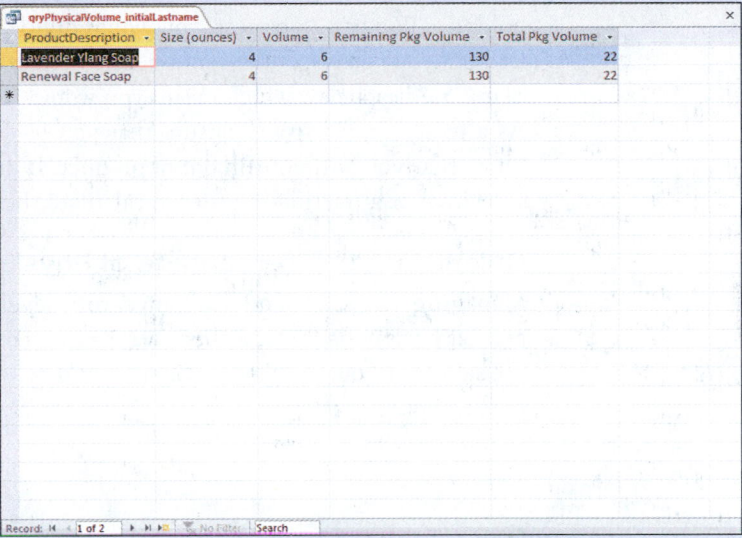

ProductDescription	Size (ounces)	Volume	Remaining Pkg Volume	Total Pkg Volume
Lavender Ylang Soap	4	6	130	22
Renewal Face Soap	4	6	130	22

Figure 14 Datasheet view of the qryPhysicalVolume query

k. **Close** ❌ the query.

REAL WORLD ADVICE | **Things to Note When Calculating Physical Volume**

When calculating volume, consider:

- The basic formula for calculating volume is length*width*depth.

- If the item is not a perfect rectangle, take the average width and length. For example, if the object is 6 inches at its widest point and 2 inches at its narrowest point, use 4 inches for the width.

- If you are wrapping the item in bubble wrap, take your measurements after it is wrapped.

- If you take your measurements in inches, your final calculation will be in cubic inches. If you take them in centimeters, your final calculation will be in cubic centimeters, and so on.

- Finally, consider the overall dimensions of the package. A 6x3x1 bar of soap—18 cubic inches in volume—will not fit in a 3x3x3 box even if it has 50% more volume at 27 cubic inches.

Percentage of Physical Volume

Consider a one-gallon container of shampoo. Some of the salon and spa's products are purchased in pints, quarts, half gallons, or gallons. However, you would not use an entire bottle of shampoo on one client. Thus, the need to first convert these measurements is critical to having an accurate calculation. In a first query, if you use two 1-ounce pumps of shampoo on one client, and you purchased a one-gallon container of shampoo, you would have to calculate how many ounces are in the one-gallon container of shampoo. It does not make a difference if you were to convert the gallons to ounces or ounces to gallons, but it tends to be easier to go from large measures to small measures. The key is to be consistent.

In a second query, you can easily find the daily **percentage of physical volume** used by dividing the amount used per day by the total amount that comes in the gallon container. For example, if you use 54 pumps or ounces of shampoo per day and the container holds 1 gallon or 128 ounces, you would divide 54 by 128, then format it as percentage to find out the percent of the container being used each day. Thus, 42.2% of the container is being used each day, which means you would use 1 gallon of shampoo about every 2 days. As a manager, you could ensure that you have enough inventory for your business and know that you will not run out of product. If needed, you can change the percentage into a decimal or a fraction in order to calculate the percentage of a whole number.

Calculating the Percentage of Physical Volume

Managing the salon and spa's inventory levels is critical for management to do on a regular basis. Imagine if a client was having their hair washed prior to a salon service and the salon runs out of shampoo. This would be unprofessional and send a negative message to the client.

A07.08

 To Create a Subquery That Calculates the Percentage of Physical Volume

a. Click the **CREATE** tab, and then in the Queries group, click **Query Design**. In the Show Table dialog box, click the **Queries** tab, and then add **qryPhysicalVolume_initialLastname** to the query workspace. **Close** ☒ the Show Table dialog box.

b. Add the following fields to the query design grid: **ProductDescription** and **Size**.

c. In the **first blank field** in the query design grid, in the Zoom dialog box type Percent of Physical Volume:[Volume]/136.

   To calculate the percentage of physical volume, you need to divide the volume of the item by the total volume the package can hold. Divide the volume by 136, which is the size of smallest carton that the spa has to ship items to customers—136 cubic inches.

d. Click **OK**, and then format the Percent of Physical Volume field as **Percent**.

e. **Save** 🖫 the query as qryPhysicalVolumePercent_initialLastname. On the DESIGN tab, in the Results group, click **Run**.

   Notice that each bar of soap consumes 4.41% within the smallest shipping carton.

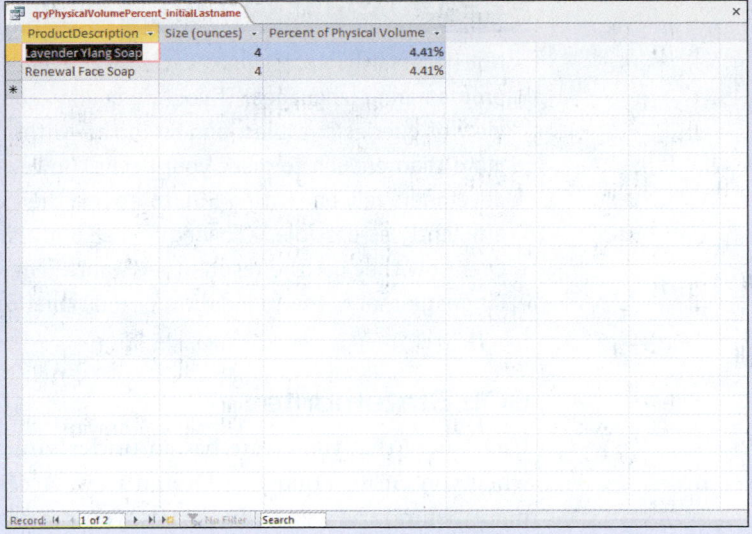

Figure 15 Datasheet view of the qryPhysicalVolumePercent query

f. **Close** ☒ the query.

CONSIDER THIS | **Should the Spa Have Smaller Boxes?**

If a customer ordered two bars of soap and would like to have the items shipped to their home, is the spa's smallest box the best way to do so? If one bar takes up 4.41% of space in the carton, that means two bars takes up 8.82%. Some shipping companies not only charge on the weight of the package, but may also charge on the dimensions of the package. At times companies will pack one shipment in multiple boxes because it is less expensive than packing the entire order in one large box. Do you think the spa should order and ship some products in smaller boxes? Would a padded envelope work better for some orders?

Understanding Structured Query Language

Structured Query Language (SQL)—pronounced SEE-quel—is an internationally recognized standard database language used by many relational databases—although many databases incorporate modified versions of the current standard SQL. The benefit of learning SQL is that once you know it, you can easily adapt to other relational database management systems. In this section, you will learn SELECT statement basics, how to view SQL statements, how to create a basic SQL query, how to use the WHERE and ORDER BY clauses, how to use the HAVING clause with AS and GROUP BY, how to create a union query, how to perform an INNER JOIN and OUTER JOIN, and how to create a SQL subquery.

REAL WORLD ADVICE | **Do You Need to Know SQL?**

Not necessarily. Access makes it easy to create objects without having to know any programming languages. If you are comfortable using the tools—wizards, Design view of queries or tables, and so forth—within Access, then those tools may be more than enough to meet your needs. However, most database administrators and developers rely on writing SQL to ensure their queries meet user requirements as efficiently as possible. Knowing SQL also gives database administrators more control over how they get the results they want. Regardless, you should be familiar with the language that is the foundation of relational databases.

SQL Statements

Each query that you create has an **underlying SQL statement**, which means that even when you create a query in Design view, Access automatically generates the SQL statement behind the scenes. In Access, you can easily change between the Design and SQL views of your query with the click of a mouse. By selecting SQL view instead of Datasheet view, you can view and edit the code as necessary.

The challenge with learning how to write SQL in this manner is that Access does add additional syntax that is not necessarily needed for a SQL query to run properly.

Viewing SQL Statements

Access is a great way to begin learning SQL, and viewing SQL statements is extremely easy to do.

A07.09

 To View a Query in SQL View

a. Click the **CREATE** tab, and then in the Queries group, click **Query Design**. Add **tblCustomer** to the query workspace, and then **Close** ☒ the Show Table dialog box.

b. Add the following fields to the query design grid: **CustFirstName**, **CustLastName**, **CustEmail**, and **CustState**.

c. In the Criteria row of the CustState field, type "MN".

d. **Save** 🖫 the query as qrySQL1_initialLastname. On the DESIGN tab, in the Results group, click **Run**.
   Notice that there are three customers who live in MN.

e. Click the **HOME** tab. In the Views group, click the **View** arrow, and then select **SQL View**.
   Notice that Access created the SQL statement in the background as you created your query in Design view. Access prefaced each field name in the SELECT statement with the table name and added parentheses in the WHERE statement.

SIDE NOTE
Extra Words and Symbols
Remember that many programs use a modified version of SQL. If standard SQL is typed into the SQL view, the query will still run properly.

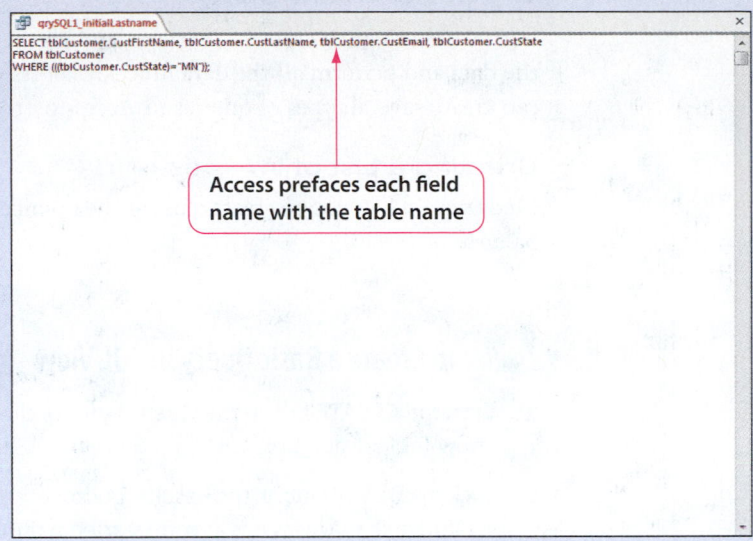

SELECT tblCustomer.CustFirstName, tblCustomer.CustLastName, tblCustomer.CustEmail, tblCustomer.CustState
FROM tblCustomer
WHERE (((tblCustomer.CustState)="MN"));

Access prefaces each field name with the table name

Figure 16   SQL view of the qrySQL1 query

f.   Close ☒ the query.

SELECT Statement Basics

In Access, SQL can be used to query data, just like when you create a select query in the query design grid. As long as you know the basic structure of a SQL SELECT statement, it is fairly easy to create a SQL query. The fundamental framework for a SQL query is the SQL **SELECT statement**. The SELECT statement contains two required clauses—SELECT and FROM—as shown in Table 2. The SELECT clause specifies the columns or fields you want to return in your dataset. The FROM clause specifies the table or tables in which the columns are located. Both of these clauses are required in a SQL SELECT statement.

Clause	Required?	Include	Explanation	Example
SELECT	Yes	Field name(s)	Includes one or more columns from which data are retrieved	SELECT EmpFirstName, EmpLastName
FROM	Yes	Table name(s)	Name of the table(s) from which the columns are located	FROM tblEmployee

Table 2   Basic SELECT statement clauses

For example, the following SELECT statement would list all the employees' first and last names along with their addresses, cities, states, and zip codes, which are all the fields stored in the tblEmployee table. The SELECT statement ends with a semicolon. If you forget to add it, Access will automatically add it for you.

SELECT EmpFirstName, EmpLastName, Address, City, State, ZipCode
FROM tblEmployee;

If you want to retrieve all the information about all employees in tblEmployees, you could use an asterisk (*) as a shortcut for retrieving all of the fields. The results would still be the same as the previous example, however it is much more efficient to write the SQL statement in this manner.

SELECT *
FROM tblEmployee;

Create a Basic SQL Query

SQL is used to interact with your data, and whenever a query is run Access uses SQL to filter the data and perform all the data functions of its Query Design tool. If you know SQL, you can create several types of queries in Access by typing your SQL statement in SQL view.

Creating a List of Invoices

Meda would like you to create a list of the invoices and customers who have an outstanding balance.

A07.10

To Create a Basic Query in SQL View

a. Click the **CREATE** tab. In the Queries group, click **Query Design**, and then **Close** ☒ the Show Table dialog box.

b. Click the **DESIGN** tab. In the Results group, click the **View** arrow, and then select **SQL View**. Notice that Access has already started writing the SELECT clause.

c. Delete **SELECT;**, and then type **SELECT InvoiceNumber, InvoiceDate, AmountDue, CustomerID FROM tblInvoice;**.

d. **Save** 🖫 the query as **qrySQL2_initialLastname**. On the DESIGN tab, in the Results group, click **Run**.

Notice that there are 10 records included in your dataset.

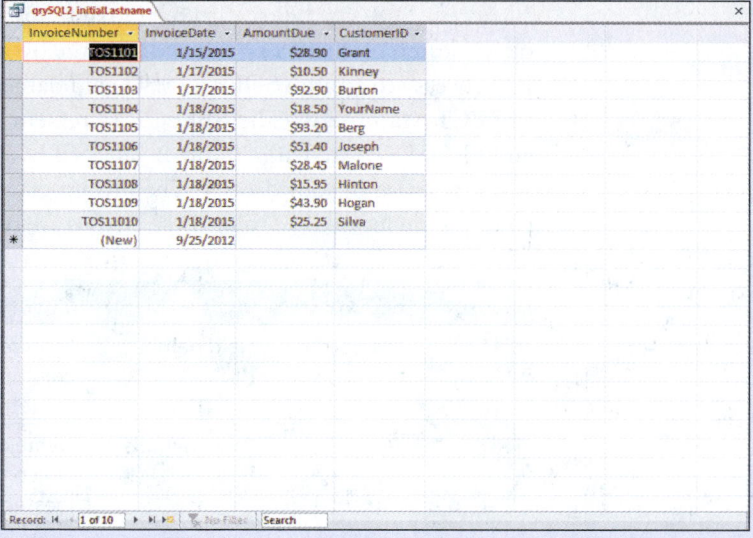

Figure 17 Datasheet view of the qrySQL2 query

Troubleshooting

If a syntax error dialog box appears, check your spelling, and make sure no spaces are in the field or table names.

---

e. **Close** ☒ the query.

f. Click the **CREATE** tab, and then in the Queries group, click **Query Design**. **Close** ☒ the Show Table dialog box.

g. Click the **DESIGN** tab. In the Results group, click the **View** arrow, and then select **SQL View**.

h. Delete **SELECT;**, and then type **SELECT * FROM tblInvoice;**.

SIDE NOTE

Should You Separate Lines?

You can write a SELECT statement all on one line. It is generally written on separate lines to make it easier to read and edit.

SIDE NOTE

Using an Asterisk

The asterisk selects and returns all fields in the table when you run the query.

i. Save the query as **qrySQL3_initialLastname**. On the DESIGN tab, in the Results group, click **Run**.

  Notice that the same 10 records were included in the qrySQL2_initialLastname dataset.

j. Close ☒ the query.

The WHERE Clause

The **WHERE clause**, which is optional in a SELECT statement, narrows the query results by specifying which rows in the table will be returned in the dataset. If the WHERE clause is omitted, all rows will be used. The following SELECT statement

SELECT EmpFirstName, EmpLastName
FROM tblEmployee
WHERE EmpLastName Like "[A-M]*"

lists the results shown in Figure 18. Notice that the results only display the employees' whose last names begin with letters "A" through "M".

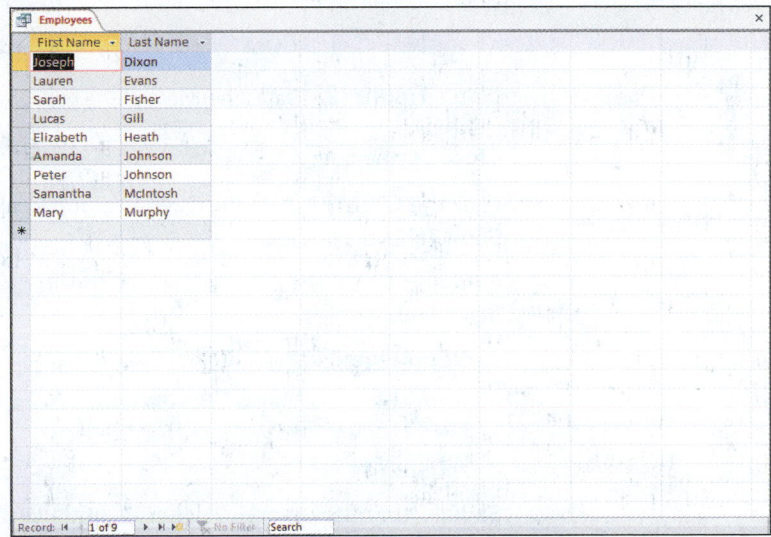

Figure 18 Datasheet view of the Employees query

Using the WHERE Clause

In order to write effective Access queries, you need to master the WHERE clause. The WHERE clause allows you to limit the results of your query based on conditions that you specify.

A07.11

▶ **To Create a Basic Query with the WHERE Clause**

a. Click the **CREATE** tab. In the Queries group, click **Query Design**, and then **Close** ☒ the Show Table dialog box.

b. Click the **DESIGN** tab, and then in the Results group, click the **View** arrow. Select **SQL View**.

c. Delete **SELECT;**, and then type the following.

SELECT *
FROM tblInvoice
WHERE InvoiceDate BETWEEN #1/15/2015# AND #1/17/2015#;

d. Save 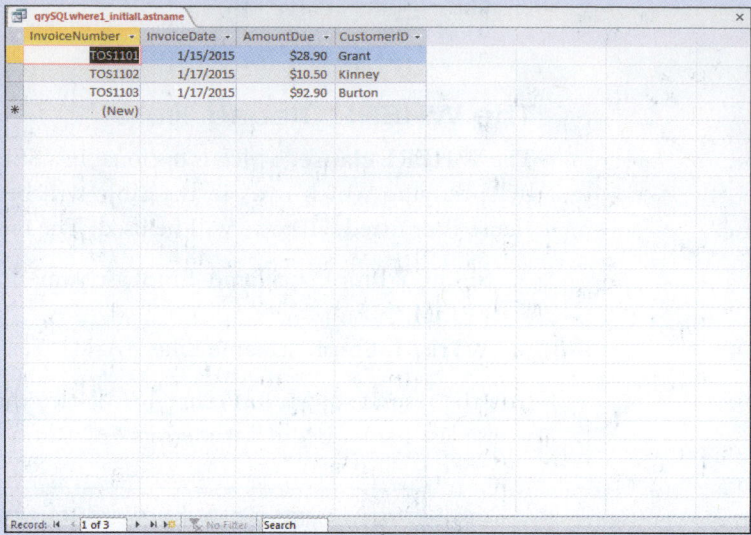 the query as **qrySQLwhere1_initialLastname**. On the DESIGN tab, in the Results group, click **Run**.

> Notice that there are three records included in your dataset.

Figure 19 Datasheet view of the qrySQLwhere1 query

e. **Close** ☒ the query.

f. Click the **CREATE** tab. In the Queries group, click **Query Design**, and then **Close** ☒ the Show Table dialog box.

g. Click the **DESIGN** tab, and then in the Results group, click the **View** arrow. Select **SQL View**.

h. Delete **SELECT;**, and then type the following.

> **SELECT ServiceName, Description, Fee**
> **FROM tblService**
> **WHERE Fee >= 75;**

i. Save the query as **qrySQLwhere2_initialLastname**. On the DESIGN tab, in the Results group, click **Run**.

> Notice that there are 13 services with a fee of $75 or more included in your dataset.

j. **Close** ☒ the query.

k. Click the **CREATE** tab. In the Queries group, click **Query Design**, and then **Close** ☒ the Show Table dialog box.

l. Click the **DESIGN** tab, and then in the Results group, click the **View** arrow. Select **SQL View**.

m. Delete **SELECT;**, and then type the following.

> **SELECT ***
> **FROM tblCustomer**
> **WHERE CustState In ("UT","MN","HI","PA");**

n. Save the query as **qrySQLwhere3_initialLastname**. On the DESIGN tab, in the Results group, click **Run**.

> Notice that there are nine customers who live in either Utah, Minnesota, Hawaii, or Pennsylvania included in your dataset.

o. **Close** ☒ the query.

SIDE NOTE

Using Other Operators

Other operators can be used, such as AND and OR, in place of the IN operator. Thus you could type CustState = "UT" OR CustState = "MN" and so on.

QUICK REFERENCE | Operators Allowed in the WHERE Clause

Operator	Description
=	Equal
<>	Not equal
>	Greater than
<	Less than
>=	Greater than or equal
<=	Less than or equal
BETWEEN...AND	Between an inclusive range
LIKE	Search for a pattern
IN	The exact value you want to return for at least one column
AND	All conditions must be true to return a value
OR	At least one condition must be true to return a value

Table 3   Operators used in the WHERE clause

REAL WORLD ADVICE | Design View vs. SQL View

Everything you have learned how to do in Design view can also be done in SQL view. If you are not sure how to write the SQL statement for a particular query, you can create it in Design view and then switch to SQL view to see how Access generated the code. Even though Access adds some extra words to the SQL statement, it is still correct and will return the proper dataset. Additionally, when you make changes to the query in SQL view, Access modifies Design view to represent the updated SQL statement.

The ORDER BY Clause

The **ORDER BY clause** is used in a SELECT statement to sort results either in ascending or descending order. The ORDER BY clause orders or sorts the result of a query according to the values in one or more specific columns. More than one column can be ordered one within another. It depends on the user's preference or needs that determine whether to order the results in ascending or descending order. The default order is ascending.

Clause	Required?	Include	Explanation	Example
SELECT	Yes	Field name(s)	Includes one or more columns from which data are retrieved	SELECT EmpFirstName, EmpLastName
FROM	Yes	Table name(s)	Name of the table(s) from which the information is retrieved	FROM tblEmployee
WHERE	No	Conditions	Specifies which table rows are used	WHERE EmpLastName Like "[A-M]*"
ORDER BY	No	Field name(s)	Allows you to sort fields in ascending or descending order. The default order is ascending.	ORDER BY EmpLastName, EmpFirstName ASC or DESC

Table 4   SELECT statement clauses with ORDER BY clause

Using the ORDER BY Clause

The ORDER BY clause is optional. However, if you want your data displayed in sorted order, then you must use ORDER BY. The default sorting order in Access is ascending—A-Z—order.

A07.12

To Create a Basic Query with the ORDER BY Clause

a. Click the **CREATE** tab. In the Queries group, click **Query Design**, and then **Close** ☒ the Show Table dialog box.

b. Click the **DESIGN** tab, and then in the Results group, click the **View** arrow. Select **SQL View**.

c. Delete **SELECT;**, and then type the following.

SELECT *
FROM tblSchedule
ORDER BY DateOfAppt;

d. **Save** 🖫 the query as **qrySQLorderby1_initialLastname**. On the DESIGN tab, in the Results group, click **Run**.

Notice that the 53 records included in your dataset are sorted in ascending order by DateOfAppt. You did not need to specify ascending in the SQL statement because ascending is the default sort order.

e. **Close** ☒ the query.

f. Click the **CREATE** tab, and then in the Queries group, click **Query Design**. **Close** ☒ the Show Table dialog box.

g. Click the **DESIGN** tab, and then in the Results group, click the **View** arrow. Select **SQL View**.

h. Delete **SELECT;**, and then type the following.

SELECT Customer, Service, DateOfAppt
FROM tblSchedule
ORDER BY DateOfAppt DESC;

i. **Save** 🖫 the query as **qrySQLorderby2_initialLastname**. On the DESIGN tab, in the Results group, click **Run**.

Notice that the 53 records included in your dataset are sorted in descending order by DateOfAppt. You needed to specify descending in the SQL statement because ascending is the default sort order.

j. **Close** ☒ the query.

k. Click the **CREATE** tab. In the Queries group, click **Query Design**, and then **Close** ☒ the Show Table dialog box.

l. On the DESIGN tab, in the Results group, click the **View** arrow. Select **SQL View**.

m. Delete **SELECT;**, and then type the following.

SELECT ProductDescription, Category, QtyInStock, Price, Size
FROM tblProduct
WHERE Size > 12
ORDER BY Category, Price DESC;

SIDE NOTE

Sorting Data

Ascending order is the default sort order. Thus, you do not need to type ASC at the end of the ORDER BY clause. If you do, the query will still work.

SIDE NOTE

Sorting Both Fields

If you want Category and Price both sorted in descending order, you need to type DESC after both fields, not just Price.

n. **Save** 🖫 the query as **qrySQLorderby3_initialLastname**. On the DESIGN tab, in the Results group, click **Run**.

Notice that the 12 records included in your dataset are sorted in ascending order by Category, and then sorted in descending order by Price. Because you did not specify how the Category would be sorted, it defaulted to ascending order.

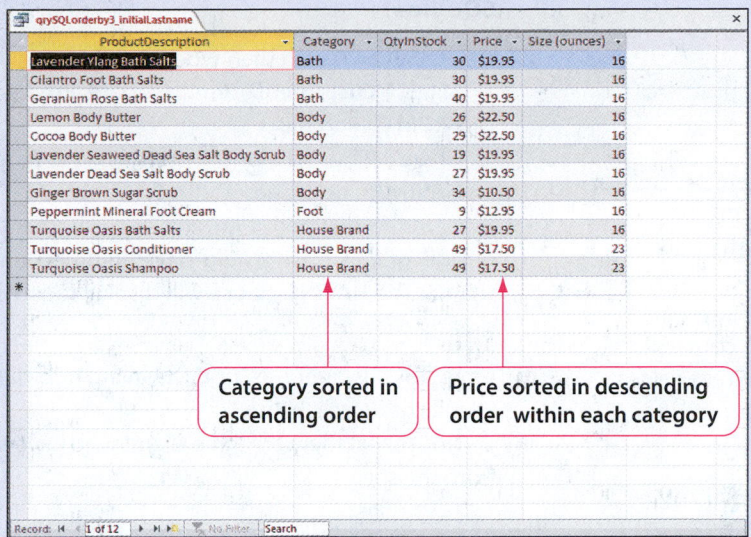

Figure 20 Datasheet view of the qrySQLorderby3 query

o. **Close** ❌ the query.

The HAVING Clause with AS and GROUP BY

If a field includes an aggregate function, you need to use a **HAVING clause**, which specifies the aggregated field criteria and restricts the results based on aggregated values—sum, average, and so forth. The HAVING clause is similar to the WHERE clause. However, the WHERE clause restricts the results based on individual row values. Another way of saying this is that the WHERE clause can eliminate records from the results before the aggregates are calculated. The HAVING clause eliminates entire groups of records from the results based on the aggregated calculations. Because the HAVING clause works on aggregated rows, it always uses an aggregate function as its test. In Access, you cannot use the HAVING clause in the query design grid; thus, you must switch to SQL.

When writing a SQL SELECT statement that includes a HAVING clause, you must also include an AS clause and a GROUP BY statement. When you do not name a field in a query, regardless of whether you are working in SQL view or Design view, Access names it for you with a name such as SumOfQuantity. Thus, the **AS clause** allows you to name or rename a field, which is displayed in the dataset. The **GROUP BY clause** is used in conjunction with the aggregate functions to group the dataset by one or more columns.

Using the HAVING Clause with AS and GROUP BY

The HAVING clause specifies which grouped records are displayed. After the GROUP BY clause combines records, the HAVING clause displays any records grouped by the GROUP BY clause that satisfy the conditions of the HAVING clause.

To Create a Query Using the HAVING, AS, and GROUP BY Clauses

a. Click the **CREATE** tab. In the Queries group, click **Query Design**, and then **Close** ☒ the Show Table dialog box.

b. Click the **DESIGN** tab, and then in the Results group, click the **View** arrow. Select **SQL View**.

c. Delete **SELECT;**, and then type the following.

> SELECT CustomerID, PurchaseDate, ProductID, Sum(Quantity) AS Total
> FROM tblPurchase
> GROUP BY CustomerID, PurchaseDate, ProductID
> HAVING (Sum([Quantity]))>5;

If you had typed a criteria of >5 under the Sum([Quantity]) field in the query design grid, Access would have summed any quantity that is individually greater than 5. The HAVING clause will display records where the sum of the Quantity field is greater than 5.

d. **Save** 🖫 the query as **qrySQLhaving1_initialLastname**. On the DESIGN tab, in the Results group, click **Run**.

Notice that there are three clients who have purchased a total of five or more products from the spa.

SIDE NOTE
Do Not Use the New Field Name
In SQL view, the renamed field in the AS clause is not recognized as a field and cannot be used in a HAVING clause.

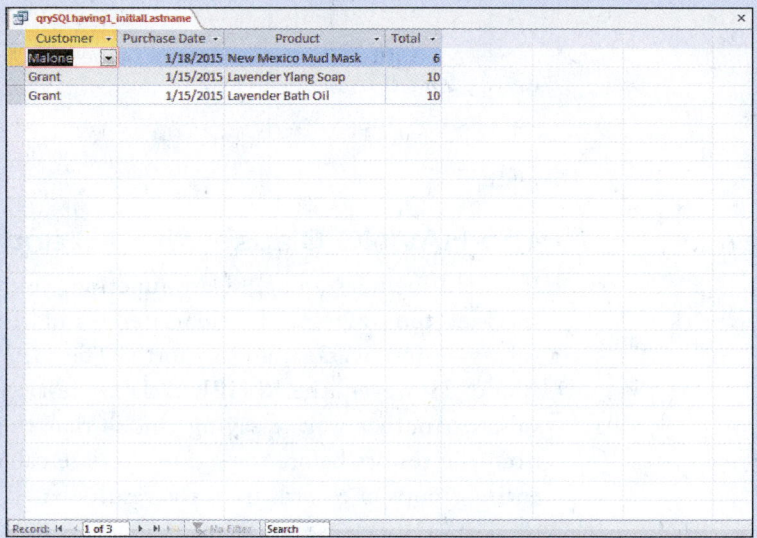

Figure 21 Datasheet view of the qrySQLhaving1 query

e. **Close** ☒ the query.

f. Click the **CREATE** tab. In the Queries group, click **Query Design**, and then **Close** ☒ the Show Table dialog box.

g. Click the **DESIGN** tab, and then in the Results group, click the **View** arrow. Select **SQL View**.

h. Delete **SELECT;**, and then type the following.

> SELECT InvoiceNumber, InvoiceDate, Sum([AmountDue]) AS Total, CustomerID
> FROM tblInvoice
> GROUP BY InvoiceNumber, InvoiceDate, CustomerID
> HAVING Sum([AmountDue])<=25;

SIDE NOTE
Using the Asterisk
Even though you are selecting all the tblInvoice table fields, you cannot use an asterisk in a query that has the GROUP BY clause.

i. **Save** 🖫 the query as **qrySQLhaving2_initialLastname**. On the DESIGN tab, in the Results group, click **Run**.

  Notice that there are three clients who have invoices totaling $25 or less.

j. **Close** ☒ the query.

The INNER JOIN and OUTER JOIN Clauses

A **join** is used to combine the data from two or more tables. The dataset is created based on a field or fields that two tables share—primary and foreign keys. The goal is to extract meaningful data from the dataset. Joins are performed based on a **predicate**, which specifies the condition to use in order to perform a join. A join can be either an inner join or an outer join, depending on how you want the dataset to perform. In this section, you will write inner, outer, right, and full join queries along with union queries in SQL.

Querying with the INNER JOIN Clause

The **INNER JOIN clause** is used to return only the rows that actually match based on the join predicate. An inner join is a join in which the values in the columns being joined are equal—contain a relationship based on a common field. Additionally, compared to using a comparison operator, such as the FROM or WHERE clause, the output of an inner join will include where the two tables intersect or overlap as shown in Figure 22.

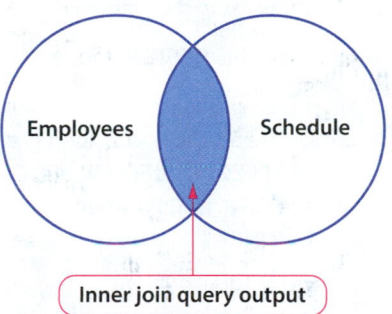

Figure 22 Inner join output lies in the intersection of both circles

The following SELECT statement

SELECT EmpFirstName, EmpLastName, Customer, Service, DateOfAppt
FROM tblEmployee
INNER JOIN tblSchedule ON tblEmployee.EmployeeID = tblSchedule.Employee;

lists the results shown in Figure 23. Notice that the results display all employees that have an appointment scheduled. Additionally, the DateOfAppt field belongs in tblSchedule, which is why the INNER JOIN clause needed to be used. The INNER JOIN is letting Access know that the EmployeeID within tblEmployee—the primary key—is the same data as what is stored in the Employee field within tblSchedule—the foreign key.

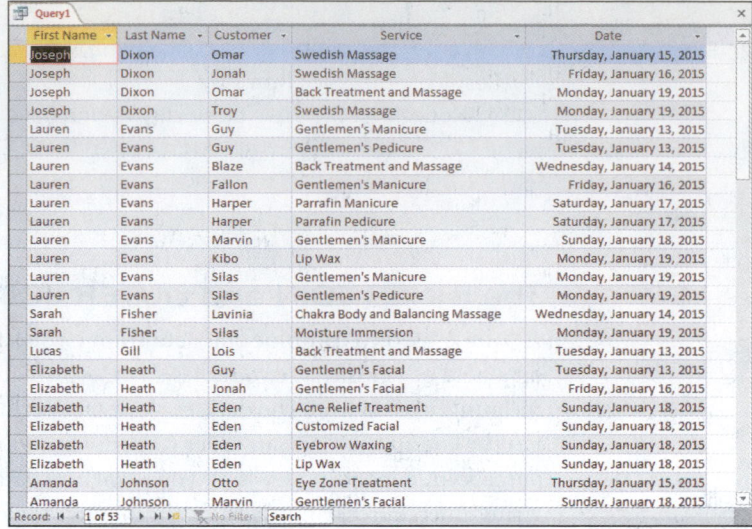

Figure 23 Datasheet view of the Query1 query

A07.14

To Create a Query Using the INNER JOIN Clause

a. Click the **CREATE** tab. In the Queries group, click **Query Design**, and then **Close** ☒ the Show Table dialog box.

b. Click the **DESIGN** tab, and then in the Results group, click the **View** arrow. Select **SQL View**.

c. Delete **SELECT;**, and then type the following.

> SELECT CustFirstName, CustLastName, ProductID, PurchaseType
> FROM tblCustomer
> INNER JOIN tblPurchase ON tblCustomer.CustomerID = tblPurchase.CustomerID;

d. **Save** 🖫 the query as **qrySQLinnerjoin1_initialLastname**. On the DESIGN tab, in the Results group, click **Run**.

  Notice that you created a query that lists the CustFirstName and CustLastName from tblCustomer and ProductID and PurchaseType from tblPurchase. The INNER JOIN clause permitted you to retrieve data from two tables.

e. **Close** ☒ the query.

f. Click the **CREATE** tab. In the Queries group, click **Query Design**, and then **Close** ☒ the Show Table dialog box.

g. Click the **DESIGN** tab, and then in the Results group, click the **View** arrow. Select **SQL View**.

h. Delete **SELECT;**, and then type the following.

> SELECT ServiceName, Customer, Employee, Description, Fee
> FROM tblService
> INNER JOIN tblSchedule ON tblService.ServiceID = tblSchedule.Service;

i. **Save** 🖫 the query as **qrySQLinnerjoin2_initialLastname**. On the DESIGN tab, in the Results group, click **Run**.

  Notice that even though your query lists the ServiceName, Description, and Fee from tblService and Customer and Employee from tblSchedule, you were able to reorder the fields based on how you typed the fields into SQL view.

j. **Close** ☒ the query.

k. Click the **CREATE** tab. In the Queries group, click **Query Design**, and then **Close** ☒ the Show Table dialog box.

l. Click the **DESIGN** tab, and then in the Results group, click the **View** arrow. Select **SQL View**.

m. Delete **SELECT;**, and then type the following.

> SELECT Employee, DateOfAppt, Count(ServiceName) AS TotalServices
> FROM tblService
> INNER JOIN tblSchedule ON tblService.ServiceID = tblSchedule.Service
> GROUP BY Employee, DateOfAppt
> ORDER BY DateOfAppt, Count(ServiceName) DESC;

SIDE NOTE
Different SQL Clauses
You can combine different SQL clauses to create a more focused query.

n. **Save** 💾 the query as **qrySQLinnerjoin3_initialLastname**. On the DESIGN tab, in the Results group, click **Run**.

> Notice that you can see how many appointments each employee has on a given day.

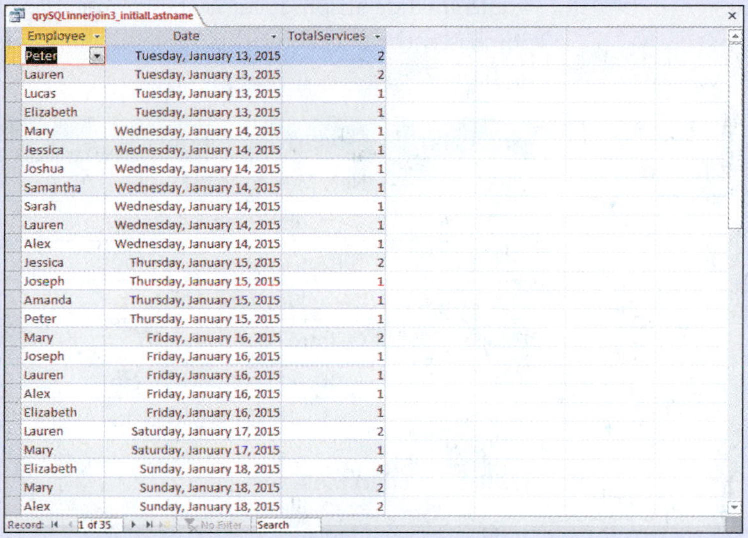

Figure 24 Datasheet view of the qrySQLinnerjoin3 query

o. **Close** ☒ the query.

Querying with the OUTER JOIN Clause

The **OUTER JOIN clause** returns all rows from at least one of the tables within the FROM clause, as long as those rows meet any WHERE or HAVING search conditions. The OUTER JOIN clause is used whenever multiple tables that are accessed through a SQL SELECT statement returns all of the records from one table and only those records from the other table where the joined fields match.

Outer joins are subdivided into left outer joins, right outer joins, and full outer joins, depending on which table's rows are shown in the dataset—left, right, or both. The **LEFT JOIN clause** is used when you want to return all rows in the left table, even if no matching rows exist in the right table. For example, you can create a query that includes all the records from the Product table and related transactions in the Purchase table as shown in Figure 25.

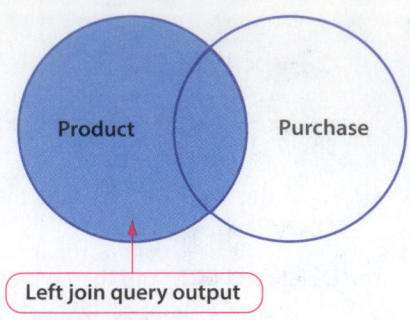

Figure 25 Left join output lies in the intersection of both circles and all the data in the Product table

The dataset of the following SQL query

SELECT ProductDescription, CustomerID, Quantity, Price, PurchaseDate
FROM Product
LEFT JOIN Purchase ON Product.ProductID = Purchase.ProductID;

would include all products as shown in Table 5, regardless of whether or not a customer purchased them as shown in Table 6, along with the matching purchase data as shown in Table 7.

ProductID	ProductDescription	Category	QtyInStock	Price
P001	New Mexico Mud Mask	Face	100	$ 8.50
P002	Turquoise Oasis Exfoliator	House Brand	94	$ 8.50
P003	Turquoise Oasis Face Moisturizer	House Brand	80	$ 7.25
P004	Geranium Rose Bath Salts	Bath	40	$19.95
P005	Cilantro Foot Bath Salts	Bath	30	$19.95
P006	Avocado Foot Care Cream	Foot	104	$ 9.00
P007	Turquoise Oasis Bath Salts	House Brand	27	$19.95

Table 5 Product table

PurchaseID	Product	Customer	Qty	PurchaseDate
PUR1	Cilantro Foot Bath Salts	Grant	2	5/24/2015
PUR2	Turquoise Oasis Exfoliator	Grant	1	5/24/2015
PUR3	Geranium Rose Bath Salts	Jones	1	5/24/2015
PUR4	Geranium Rose Bath Salts	Burton	1	5/25/2015
PUR5	Cilantro Foot Bath Salts	Jones	2	5/26/2015
PUR6	Avocado Foot Care Cream	Berg	1	5/26/2015
PUR7	Turquoise Oasis Bath Salts	Berg	3	5/26/2015

Table 6 Purchase table

ProductDescription	Customer	Qty	Price	PurchaseDate
New Mexico Mud Mask			$ 8.50	
Turquoise Oasis Exfoliator	Grant	1	$ 8.50	5/24/2015
Turquoise Oasis Face Moisturizer			$ 7.25	
Geranium Rose Bath Salts	Jones	1	$19.95	5/24/2015
Geranium Rose Bath Salts	Burton	1	$19.95	5/25/2015
Cilantro Foot Bath Salts	Grant	2	$19.95	5/24/2015
Cilantro Foot Bath Salts	Jones	2	$19.95	5/26/2015
Avocado Foot Care Cream	Berg	1	$ 9.00	5/26/2015
Turquoise Oasis Bath Salts	Berg	3	$19.95	5/26/2015

Table 7 Dataset of left join query

The **RIGHT JOIN clause** is used when you only want to return rows that have matching data in the right table, even if no matching rows exist in the left table. For example, you can create a query that includes all the records from the Purchase table and related transactions in the Product table as shown in Figure 26. In this case, you may have a record of purchases for products that you no longer sell and that have been deleted from the Product table.

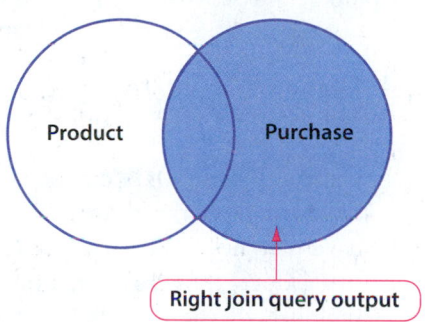

Figure 26 Right join output lies in the intersection of both circles and all the data in the Purchase table

The dataset of the following SQL query

SELECT ProductDescription, Category, CustomerID, Quantity, Price, PurchaseDate FROM Product RIGHT JOIN Purchase ON Product.ProductID = Purchase.ProductID;

would include all purchases, regardless of whether or not the product still exists in the Product table as shown in Tables 8–10.

ProductID	ProductDescription	Category	QtyInStock	Price
P001	New Mexico Mud Mask	Face	100	$ 8.50
P002	Turquoise Oasis Exfoliator	House Brand	94	$ 8.50
P003	Turquoise Oasis Face Moisturizer	House Brand	80	$ 7.25
P006	Avocado Foot Care Cream	Foot	104	$ 9.00
P007	Turquoise Oasis Bath Salts	House Brand	27	$19.95

Table 8 Product table

PurchaseID	Product	Customer	Qty	PurchaseDate
PUR1	Cilantro Foot Bath Salts	Grant	2	5/24/2015
PUR2	Turquoise Oasis Exfoliator	Grant	1	5/24/2015
PUR3	Geranium Rose Bath Salts	Jones	1	5/24/2015
PUR4	Geranium Rose Bath Salts	Burton	1	5/25/2015
PUR5	Cilantro Foot Bath Salts	Jones	2	5/26/2015
PUR6	Avocado Foot Care Cream	Berg	1	5/26/2015
PUR7	Turquoise Oasis Bath Salts	Berg	3	5/26/2015

Table 9   Purchase table

ProductDescription	Category	Customer	Qty	Price	PurchaseDate
Cilantro Foot Bath Salts		Grant	2		5/24/2015
Turquoise Oasis Exfoliator	House Brand	Grant	1	$ 8.50	5/24/2015
Geranium Rose Bath Salts		Jones	1		5/24/2015
Geranium Rose Bath Salts		Burton	1		5/25/2015
Cilantro Foot Bath Salts		Jones	2		5/26/2015
Avocado Foot Care Cream	Foot	Berg	1	$19.95	5/26/2015
Turquoise Oasis Bath Salts	House Brand	Berg	3	$19.95	5/26/2015

Table 10   Dataset of right join query

The **FULL JOIN clause** returns all the rows from the left table—Product, and all the rows from the right table—Purchase. If there are records in Product that do not have matches in Purchase, or if there are records in Purchase that do not have matches in Product, those rows will be listed as well. For example, you can create a query that includes all the records from the Product table and all transactions in the Purchase table as shown in Figure 27.

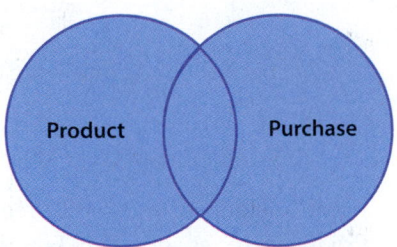

Figure 27   Full join output includes all the data from both circles

Unfortunately, the FULL OUTER JOIN clause is not supported in Microsoft Access. However, you could create a full outer join query by creating a query from two other queries because the rows in a full outer join contain all the rows from a left outer join and a right outer join, with the duplicate rows from both included just once instead of being included twice. This process, however, can be more easily completed with a union query.

A07.15

To Create a Query Using the OUTER JOIN Clauses

a. Click the **CREATE** tab. In the Queries group, click **Query Design**, and then **Close** ☒ the Show Table dialog box.

b. Click the **DESIGN** tab, and then in the Results group, click the **View** arrow. Select **SQL View**.

c. Delete **SELECT;**, and then type the following.

SELECT ServiceName, LengthOfService, Customer, DateOfAppt, Fee
FROM tblService
LEFT JOIN tblSchedule ON tblService.ServiceID = tblSchedule.Service;

d. Save 🖫 the query as **qrySQLouterjoin1_initialLastname**. On the DESIGN tab, in the Results group, click **Run**.

Notice that you created a query that lists all the records from tblService—the left table—even if no customers have scheduled an appointment for a service, and the related records in tblSchedule—the right table. Your query should include 59 records.

e. **Close** ☒ the query.

f. Click the **CREATE** tab. In the Queries group, click **Query Design**, and then **Close** ☒ the Show Table dialog box.

g. Click the **DESIGN** tab, and then in the Results group, click the **View** arrow. Select **SQL View**.

h. Delete **SELECT;**, and then type the following.

SELECT InvoiceNumber, InvoiceDate, CustFirstName, CustLastName
FROM tblCustomer
LEFT JOIN tblInvoice ON tblCustomer.CustomerID = tblInvoice.CustomerID
ORDER BY CustLastName, CustFirstName;

i. Save 🖫 the query as **qrySQLouterjoin2_initialLastname**. On the DESIGN tab, in the Results group, click **Run**.

Notice that you created a query that lists all the records from tblCustomer—the left table—even if the customer did not make a purchase, and the related records in tblInvoice—the right table.

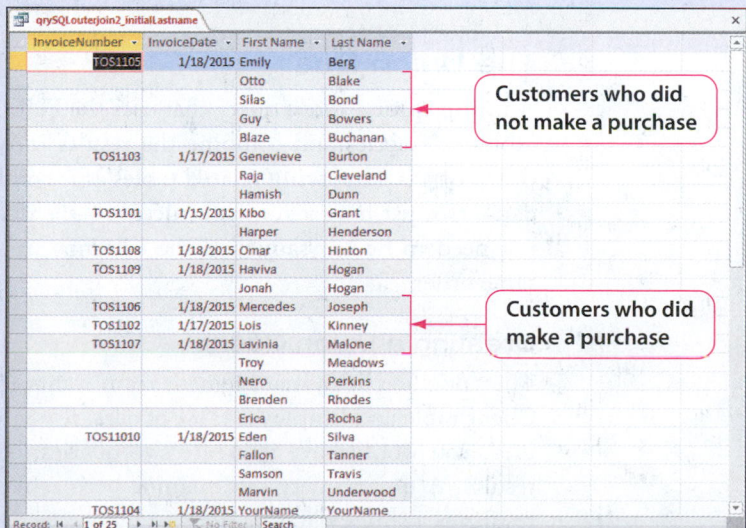

Figure 28 Datasheet view of the qrySQLouterjoin2 query

j. **Close** ☒ the query.

k. Click the **CREATE** tab. In the Queries group, click **Query Design**, and then **Close** ☒ the Show Table dialog box.

l. Click the **DESIGN** tab, and then in the Results group, click the **View** arrow. Select **SQL View**.

m. Delete **SELECT;**, and then type the following.

> SELECT ServiceName, LengthOfService, Customer, DateOfAppt, Fee
> FROM tblService
> RIGHT JOIN tblSchedule ON tblService.ServiceID = tblSchedule.Service;

n. Save 🖫 the query as **qrySQLouterjoin3_initialLastname**. On the DESIGN tab, in the Results group, click **Run**.

Notice that you created a query that lists all the records from tblSchedule—the right table— and the related records in tblService—the left table. Your query should include 53 records.

o. **Close** ☒ the query.

p. Click the **CREATE** tab. In the Queries group, click **Query Design**, and then **Close** ☒ the Show Table dialog box.

q. Click the **DESIGN** tab, and then in the Results group, click the **View** arrow. Select **SQL View**.

r. Delete **SELECT;**, and then type the following.

> SELECT InvoiceNumber, InvoiceDate, CustFirstName, CustLastName
> FROM tblCustomer
> RIGHT JOIN tblInvoice ON tblCustomer.CustomerID = tblInvoice.CustomerID
> ORDER BY CustLastName, CustFirstName;

s. Save 🖫 the query as **qrySQLouterjoin4_initialLastname**. On the DESIGN tab, in the Results group, click **Run**.

Notice that you created a query that lists all the records from tblInvoice—the right table—even if they did not make a purchase, and the related records in tblCustomer— the left table. Your table should include 10 records.

t. **Close** ☒ the query.

The Union Query

A **union query**, like a query that uses the FULL JOIN clause, is used to query unrelated tables or queries and combine the results into a single dataset. This type of query is different from querying related tables as it combines two SQL SELECT statements. The datasets must have a similar structure—the data types must match, but field names do not need to be the same and the columns in each SELECT statement must be in the same order.

Creating a Union Query

The salon and spa's management team wants to create a phone directory from both the Client table and Employee table of data. If you were restricted to using the query design grid, you would have to create two queries, one for each table, and then combine the results. A union query can examine both tables at the same time and then present the results as a single dataset.

A07.16

   To Create a Union Query

a. Click the **CREATE** tab. In the Queries group, click **Query Design**, and then **Close** ☒ the Show Table dialog box.

b. On the DESIGN tab, in the Query Type group, click **Union**. Access will automatically switch to SQL view.

c. Type the following.

> **SELECT CustFirstName, CustLastName, CustPhone**
> **FROM tblCustomer**
> **UNION**
> **SELECT EmpFirstName, EmpLastName, EmpPhone**
> **FROM tblEmployee;**

d. **Save** 💾 the query as **qrySQLUnion1_initialLastname**. On the DESIGN tab, in the Results group, click **Run**.

Notice that you created a phone directory of all employees and customers, which includes a total of 39 records in the dataset. Additionally, notice that the field headings displayed are those from the first SELECT statement.

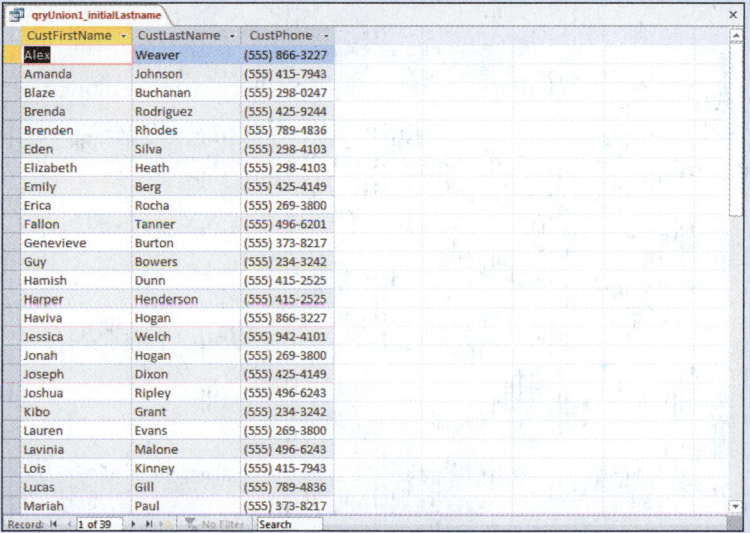

Figure 29   Datasheet view of qrySQLUnion1 query

e. **Close** ☒ the query.

f. Click the **CREATE** tab. In the Queries group, click **Query Design**, and then **Close** ☒ the Show Table dialog box.

g. Click the **DESIGN** tab, and then in the Query Type group, click **Union**. Access will automatically switch to SQL view.

h. Type the following.

> **SELECT CustFirstName AS First, CustLastName AS Last, CustPhone AS Phone**
> **FROM tblCustomer**
> **UNION SELECT EmpFirstName, EmpLastName, EmpPhone**
> **FROM tblEmployee;**

i. **Save** 💾 the query as **qrySQLunion2_initialLastname**. On the DESIGN tab, in the Results group, click **Run**.

Notice that you created the same phone directory of all employees and customers, but now you have more appropriate field names.

j. **Close** ☒ the query.

The SQL Subquery

A SQL subquery is a separate SELECT statement that is nested inside the main SELECT statement. This type of query is an alternate way of returning data from multiple tables and will be performed once for each row of the resulting dataset. A subquery is usually added in the WHERE clause of the SQL SELECT statement. Most of the time, a subquery is used when you know how to search for a value using a SELECT statement but do not know the exact value.

For example, you may want to query your StoreSalesData table to find sales data for a specific district or region. However, if you do not know all the store numbers but know the district or region where the stores are located, you can write a subquery that will retrieve the information you desire as shown in Figure 30.

SELECT SUM(Sales) FROM tblStoreSalesData
WHERE StoreName IN
(SELECT StoreName FROM tblLocations
WHERE Region = "East")

Outer query

Inner query

Figure 30   Structure of a SQL subquery

Creating a SQL Subquery

Perhaps the salon and spa's management team wants to know how frequently a client visits their establishment. Or perhaps management wants to view a list of customers who reside or do not reside in a particular state. A SQL subquery query can display this information.

A07.17

  To Create a SQL Subquery

a. Click the **CREATE** tab. In the Queries group, click **Query Design**, and then **Close** ☒ the Show Table dialog box.

b. Click the **DESIGN** tab, and then in the Results group, click the **View** arrow. Select **SQL View**.

c. Delete **SELECT;**, and then type the following.
   SELECT CustomerID, CustFirstName, CustLastName, CustState, CustEmail
   FROM tblCustomer
   WHERE CustomerID NOT IN (SELECT CustomerID
   FROM tblCustomer
   WHERE CustState = 'MN');

d. **Save** 🖫 the query as **qrySQLsubquery_initialLastname**. On the DESIGN tab, in the Results group, click **Run**.

   Notice that the e-mail list you created for all out-of-state customers includes 22 records in the dataset.

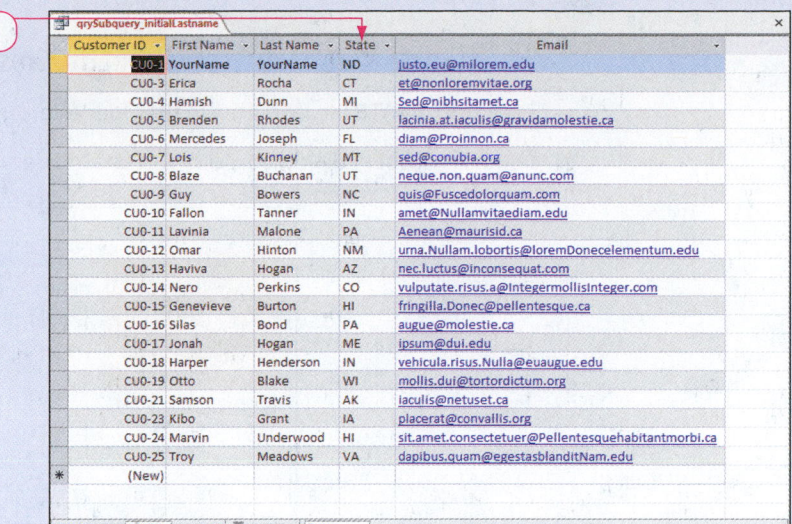

MN customers excluded

Figure 31 Datasheet view of the qrySubquery query

e. **Close** ☒ the query.

Creating a Crosstab Query

A **crosstab query** is different than the aggregate functions that you have been completing thus far because it groups the aggregates by the column and row headings. The added value in decision making is that crosstab queries are useful for summarizing data, calculating statistics, identifying bad data, and looking for trends. Additionally, crosstab queries can be a useful way to present data in a compact and summarized format.

A crosstab query is a special type of query that you use when you want to describe one number in terms of two other numbers. For example, suppose you wanted to know how much money was made from each service at the spa each month. This would require the construction of a crosstab query to display the information. A crosstab query uses aggregate functions and then groups the results by two sets of values—one down the side of the datasheet as rows and the other across the top as columns—and transforms rows of data to columns.

When you create a crosstab query, you specify which fields will be used as the row headings, which field's values will be used as the column headings, and which fields contain values to summarize. Only one field can be used when you specify the column heading and value to summarize. However, up to three fields can be used as row headings. Furthermore, expressions can be used to create row headings, column headings, or values to summarize. In this section, you will create and edit a crosstab query.

Crosstab Query Wizard

As with other wizards in Access, the **Crosstab Query Wizard** is the easiest way to create a crosstab query. While the wizard does help automate the creation process, there are some things that the wizard cannot do for you. Even though the wizard may not be able to create the perfect crosstab query, you can use it to create a basic crosstab query and then modify the query's design within Design view.

Using the Crosstab Query Wizard

Perhaps the salon and spa's management team wants to view each employee along with the total customers and a count of how many appointments each employee has per day. A crosstab query can display this information.

A07.18

To Create a Crosstab Query Using the Crosstab Query Wizard

a. Click the **CREATE** tab, and then in the Queries group, click **Query Wizard**.

b. In the New Query dialog box, click **Crosstab Query Wizard**, and then click **OK**.

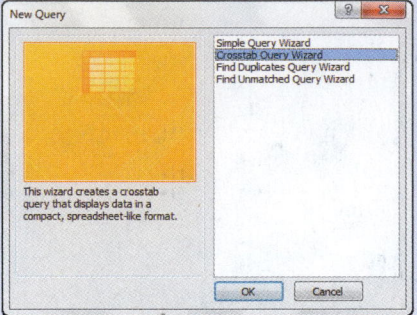

Figure 32 New Query dialog box with Crosstab Query Wizard selected

c. Click **Table: tblSchedule**, and then click **Next**.

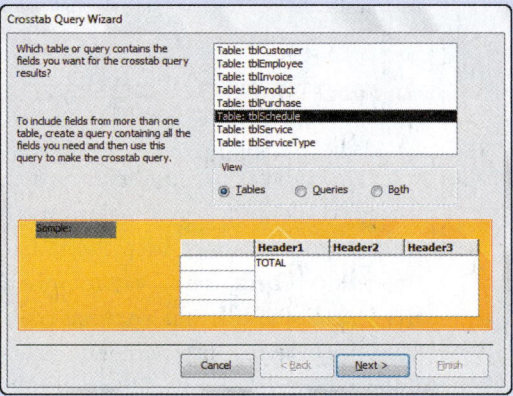

Figure 33 Crosstab Query Wizard with table selection

d. Double-click the **Employee** field, and then click **Next**. The Employee field will be used as the row heading in the crosstab query.

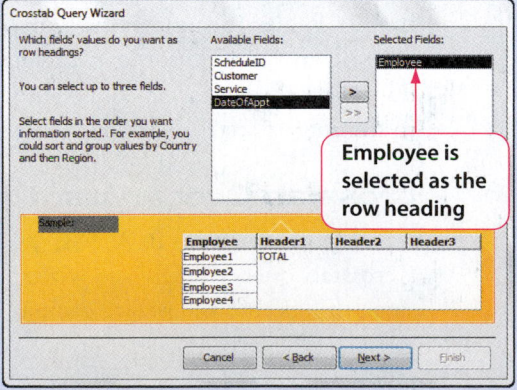

Figure 34 Crosstab Query Wizard with row heading selected

e. Click the **DateOfAppt** field, and then click **Next**. The DateOfAppt field will be used as the column headings in the crosstab query.

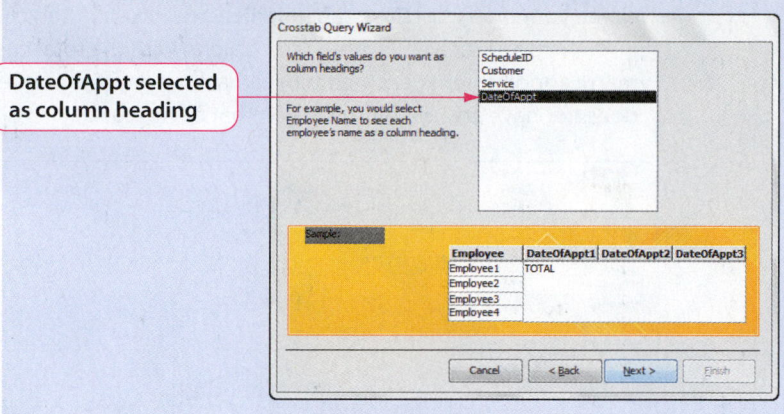

DateOfAppt selected as column heading

Figure 35 Crosstab Query Wizard with column heading selected

f. Click **Date** as the interval, and then click **Next**.

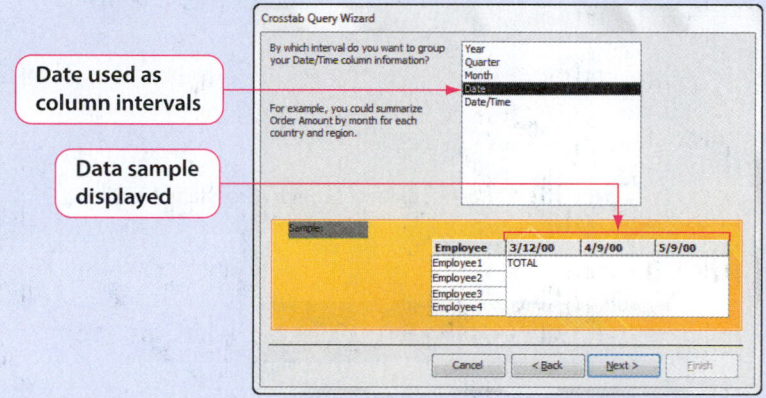

Date used as column intervals

Data sample displayed

Figure 36 Crosstab Query Wizard with interval selected

g. Click **Customer** under Fields, and then click **Count** under Functions to view how many customers each employee has on a given day. Click **Next**.

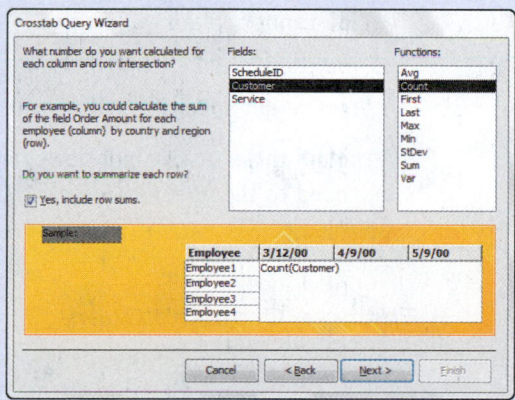

Figure 37 Crosstab Query Wizard with calculation type selected

h. Name your query **qryCrosstab_initialLastname** and then click **Finish**.

Notice that each employee is listed along with the total customers and a count of how many appointments each employee has per day. Empty fields indicate the employee does not have any appointments on that particular day.

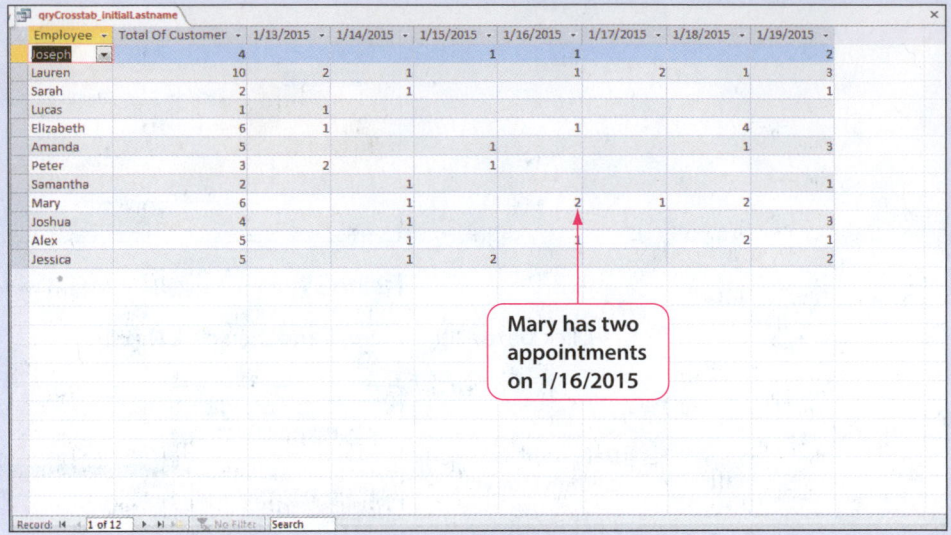

Employee	Total Of Customer	1/13/2015	1/14/2015	1/15/2015	1/16/2015	1/17/2015	1/18/2015	1/19/2015
Joseph	4			1	1			2
Lauren	10	2	1		1	2	1	3
Sarah	2		1					1
Lucas	1	1						
Elizabeth	6	1			1		4	
Amanda	5			1			1	3
Peter	3	2		1				
Samantha	2		1					1
Mary	6		1		2	1	2	
Joshua	4		1					3
Alex	5		1				2	1
Jessica	5		1	2				2

Mary has two appointments on 1/16/2015

Record: 1 of 12 | No Filter | Search

Figure 38   Datasheet view of the qryCrosstab query

REAL WORLD ADVICE | **What the Crosstab Query Wizard Cannot Do**

Although the Crosstab Query Wizard can be very helpful in creating crosstab queries, there are a few things that cannot be completed when progressing through the wizard.

1. The wizard will only let you select fields from one table. If you want to use fields from multiple tables, you need to add the tables in Design view.

2. You cannot create expressions in the wizard.

3. You cannot add a parameter prompt.

4. You cannot specify a list of fixed values to be used as column headings.

Although these tasks cannot be completed within the wizard, any of these tasks can be added to the query design grid by simply going into Design view.

Editing a Crosstab Query

When you work in Design view, you have more control over your query design, which enables features to be added that are not available in the wizard. When you edit a crosstab query in Design view, you use the Total and Crosstab rows in the design grid to specify three criteria:

- Which field value becomes the column heading?
- Which field values become row headings?
- Which field values to calculate?

A07.19

To Edit a Crosstab Query

a. Click the **FILE** tab, use the **Save Object As** option, and then save your query as **qryCrosstabEdit_initialLastname**.

b. Switch to **Design** view, and then resize your fields in the query design grid if you cannot see all the text.

c. In the Criteria row of the Employee field, type **[Enter Employee Number]**. This edits the query so the manager can enter a specific employee number and view how many appointments that employee has scheduled that week.

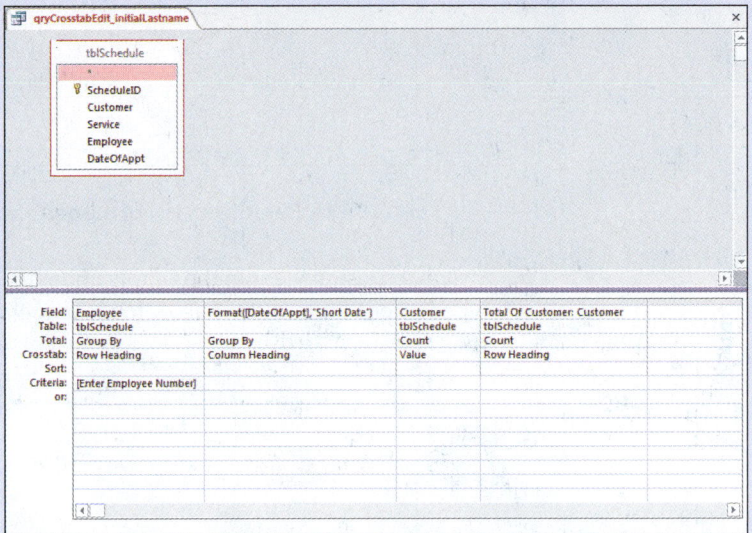

Figure 39 Design view of the qryCrosstabEdit query

d. Click the **DESIGN** tab, and then in the Show/Hide group, click **Parameters**.

e. In the Query Parameters dialog box, in the Parameter column, type the same parameter that you used in the Criteria row: **[Enter Employee Number]**.

f. Press Tab. Click the **Data Type** arrow, select **Integer**, and then click **OK**.

g. On the DESIGN tab, in the Results group, click **Run**. In the Enter Parameter Value dialog box, type **2** and then click **OK**.

Notice how you can only see Joseph's four appointments for the week.

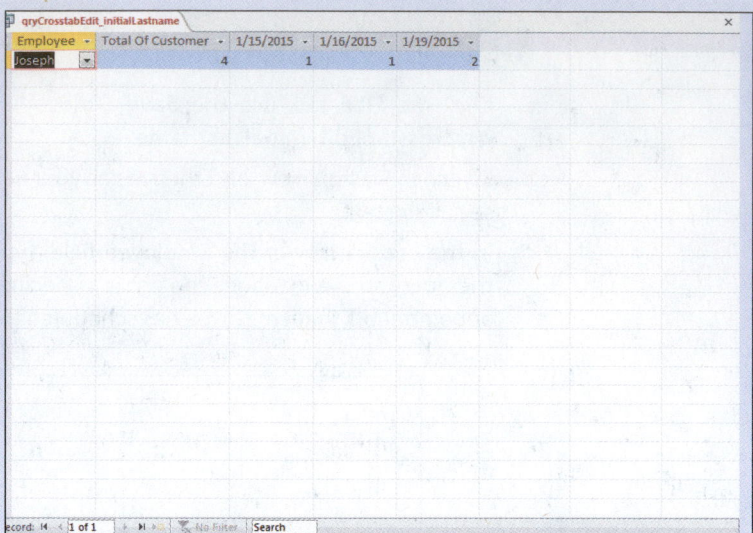

Figure 40 Datasheet view of the qryCrosstabEdit query

h. Switch to **Design** view. In the Or row under the Format([DateOfAppt],"Short Date") field, type **[Enter Date]**. This will allow the manager to enter a specific employee number or a specific date.

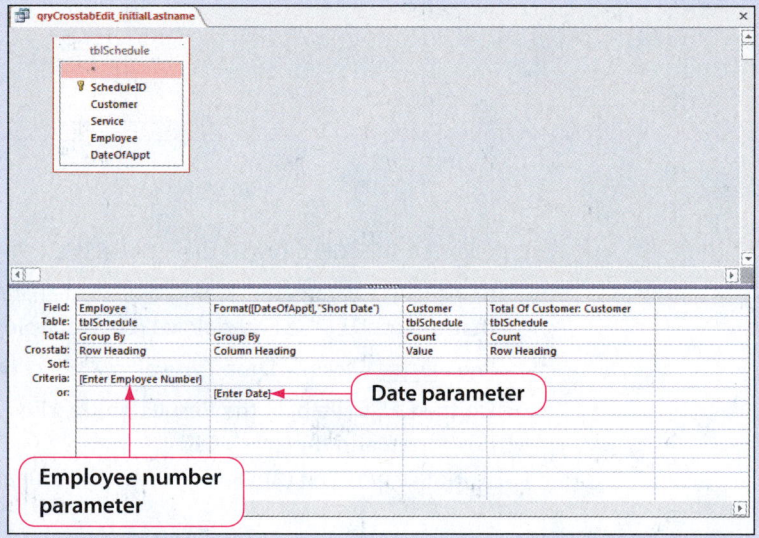

Figure 41 Design view of the qryCrosstabEdit query with second criteria

i. On the DESIGN tab, in the Show/Hide group, click **Parameters**.

j. In the Query Parameters dialog box, in the second row of the Parameter column, type the same parameter that you used in the Criteria row: **[Enter Date]**.

k. Press Tab. Select **Date with Time** in the Data Type column, and then click **OK**.

l. On the DESIGN tab, in the Results group, click **Run**. When the Enter Employee Number Parameter prompt appears, do not enter anything. Click **OK**.

SIDE NOTE
Only a Week of Data Appears
Remember that the spa manager gave you a portion of the data. If you had the full database, you would see every date, which could extend over months or years.

m. When the Enter Date Parameter prompt appears, type **01/18/2015** and then click **OK**.

Notice how you can see all employees who have appointments on 1/18/2015. This happened because you did not enter a specific employee number. Thus, Access displayed every employee number.

> **Troubleshooting**
>
> If you do not use the leading zero in the month, no data will be displayed in your dataset.

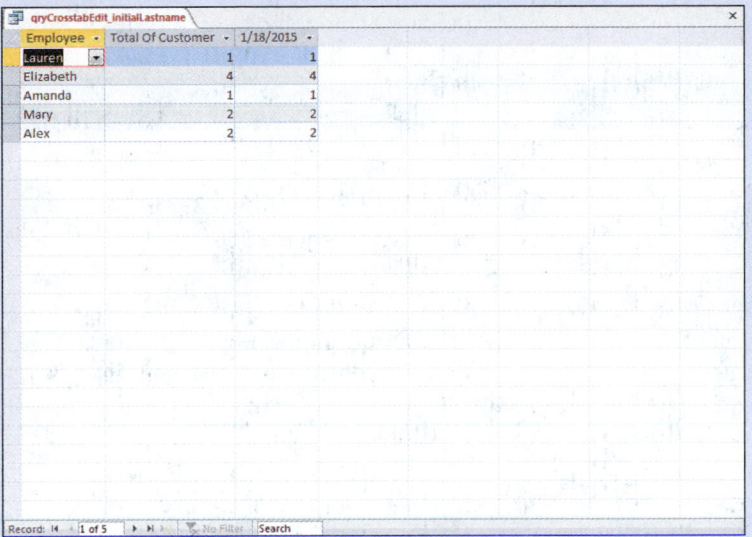

Figure 42 Datasheet view of the qryCrosstabEdit query with second criteria

n. **Close** ☒ the query. If Access prompts you to enter parameters as you are saving your changes, click **OK** twice.

REAL WORLD ADVICE | **When Should You Work in Design View?**

The following are reasons why you will want to work in Design view when creating or editing a crosstab query.

1. You can use fields from multiple tables or queries.
2. You can add a parameter to your query.
3. You can add an expression to your query.
4. You can specify a list of fixed values to be used as column headings.

Concept Check

1. Give two business examples outside of this workshop of when you could use the sales revenue calculation. p. 361

2. Explain how an aggregate function differs from a calculated field. p. 370

3. Give two business examples outside of this workshop of when you could use the volume—either physical or sales—calculation. p. 375

4. What is the difference between using the WHERE clause and the HAVING clause? p. 389

5. When could a crosstab query be more beneficial or helpful to use instead of a SELECT or standard aggregated query? p. 401

Key Terms

Visual Summary

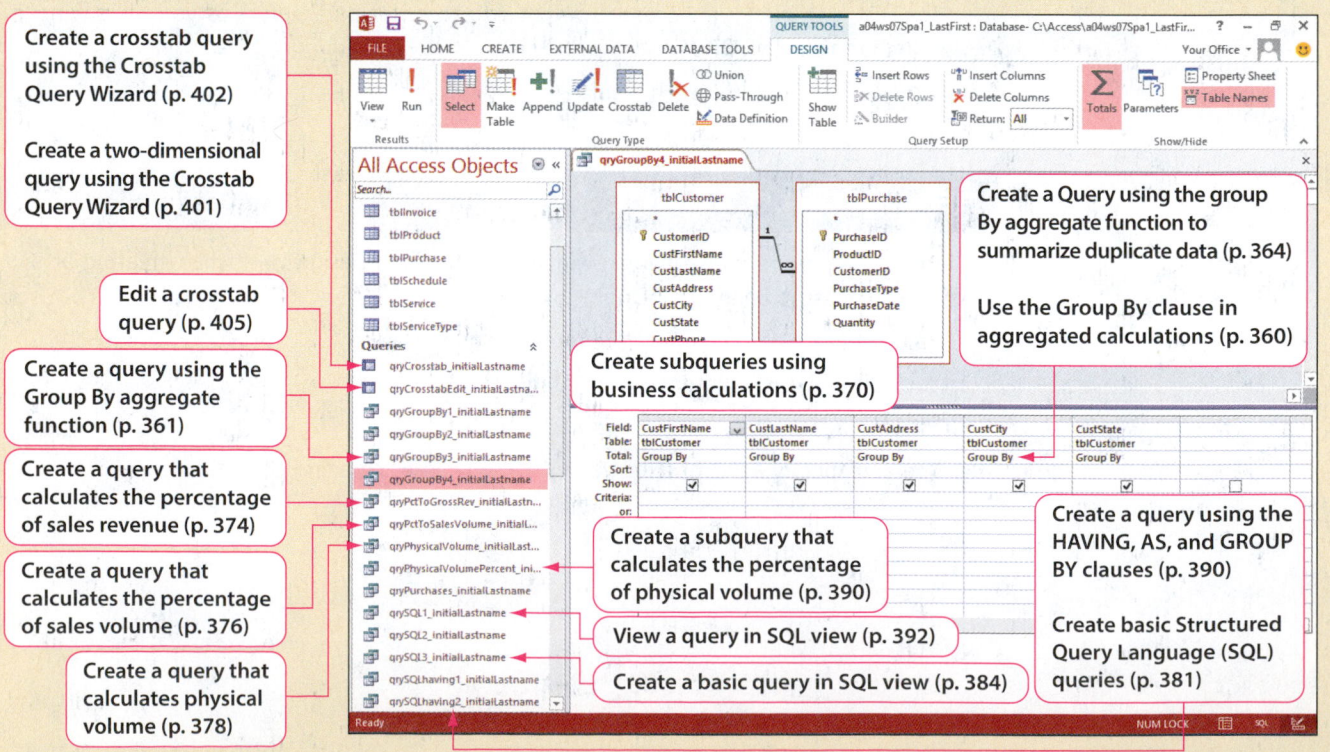

Create a crosstab query using the Crosstab Query Wizard (p. 402)

Create a two-dimensional query using the Crosstab Query Wizard (p. 401)

Edit a crosstab query (p. 405)

Create a query using the Group By aggregate function (p. 361)

Create a query that calculates the percentage of sales revenue (p. 374)

Create a query that calculates the percentage of sales volume (p. 376)

Create a query that calculates physical volume (p. 378)

Create a Query using the group By aggregate function to summarize duplicate data (p. 364)

Use the Group By clause in aggregated calculations (p. 360)

Create subqueries using business calculations (p. 370)

Create a subquery that calculates the percentage of physical volume (p. 390)

View a query in SQL view (p. 392)

Create a basic query in SQL view (p. 384)

Create a query using the HAVING, AS, and GROUP BY clauses (p. 390)

Create basic Structured Query Language (SQL) queries (p. 381)

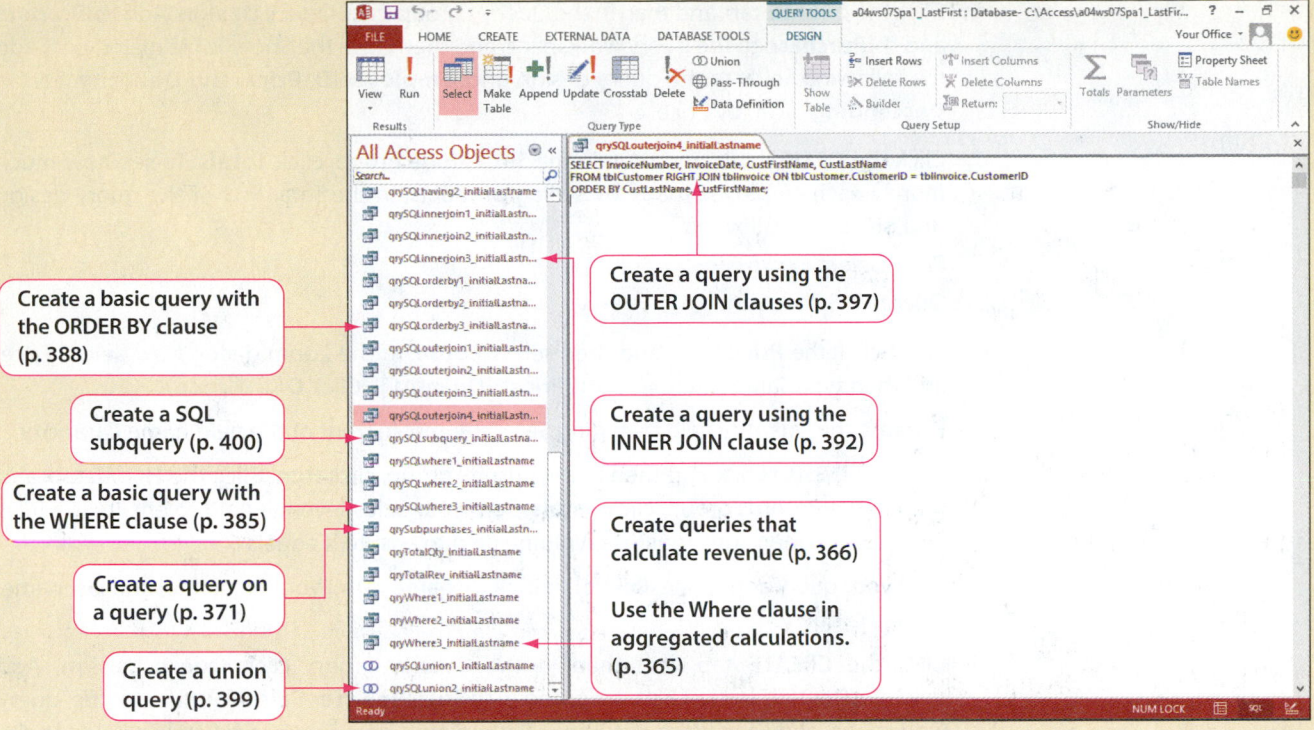

Figure 43 The Turquoise Oasis Spa Final Database

Practice 1

Student data file needed:

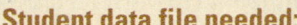 a04ws07Spa2.accdb

You will save your file as:

a04ws07Spa2_LastFirst.accdb

Managing Employee Sales and Inventory at the Turquoise Oasis Spa

Sales & Marketing

Finance & Accounting

The Turquoise Oasis Spa uses Access to track product sales such as shampoo, conditioner, and soaps. You have been asked to query the database to track product sales, the sales revenue, and sales volume that each employee generates in selling products, as well as ensure that products fit into shipping boxes. This way, management can ensure that enough inventory—including boxes for shipping—is in stock based on selling trends.

a. Open the **a04ws07Spa2** database, and then save it as **a04ws07Spa2_LastFirst** using your last and first name. Click **Enable Content** in the security warning if necessary.

b. Open **tblCustomer**, and then add your information in record **1**. Replace YourName in the FirstName and LastName fields with your first and last name. Close tblCustomer.

c. Click the **CREATE** tab, and then in the Queries group, click **Query Design**. Add **tblProduct** and **tblPurchase** to the query workspace, and then close the Show Table dialog box. Add the following fields to the query design grid: **EmployeeID**, **Price**, and **Quantity**. Sort in **Descending** order by Price.

d. Click the **DESIGN** tab, and then in the Show/Hide group, click **Totals**. To see how much money each employee made by selling products, in the Total row of the query design grid, select the following.
Price: Select **Expression**
Quantity: Select **Sum**

e. Right-click the **Price** field, and then select **Zoom**. In the Zoom dialog box, delete Price, and then type SalesRevenue: Sum([Price]*[Quantity]). Click **OK**.

f. Rename the Quantity field by typing SalesVolume: in front of the field name **Quantity**.

g. Click the **DESIGN** tab, and then in the Results group, click **Run**. Click the **HOME** tab, and then in the Records group, click **Totals**. Sum your SalesRevenue field to ensure it equals $918.85, and then sum your SalesVolume field to ensure it equals 63.

h. Save your query as qrySalesRevVol_initialLastname using your first initial and last name. Close the query.

i. Click the **CREATE** tab, and then in the Queries group, click **Query Design**. Add **qrySalesRevVol_initialLastname** and **qryGrossRevenueSalesVolume** to the query workspace, and then close the Show Table dialog box. Add the following fields to the query design grid: **EmployeeID**, **SalesRevenue**, and **SalesVolume**.

j. In the **next blank field** in the query design grid, in the Zoom dialog box type PercentToGrossSalesRevenue:[SalesRevenue]/[GrossSalesRevenue]. Format the PercentToGrossSalesRevenue field as **Percent**. This expression calculates how each employee's sales revenue contributed to the total gross sales revenue.

k. In the **next blank field** in the query design grid, in the Zoom dialog box type PercentToGrossSalesVolume:[SalesVolume]/[GrossSalesVolume]. Format the PercentToGrossSalesVolume field as **Percent**. This expression calculates how each employee's sales volume contributed to the total gross sales volume.

l. Save your query as qryRevenueAnalysis_initialLastname. On the DESIGN tab, in the Results group, click **Run**. Click the **HOME** tab, and then in the Records group, click **Totals**. Average your SalesRevenue and SalesVolume fields. This will determine if employees are selling at, above, or below average. Sum your PercentToGrossSalesRevenue and PercentToGrossSalesVolume fields to ensure they equal 100%.

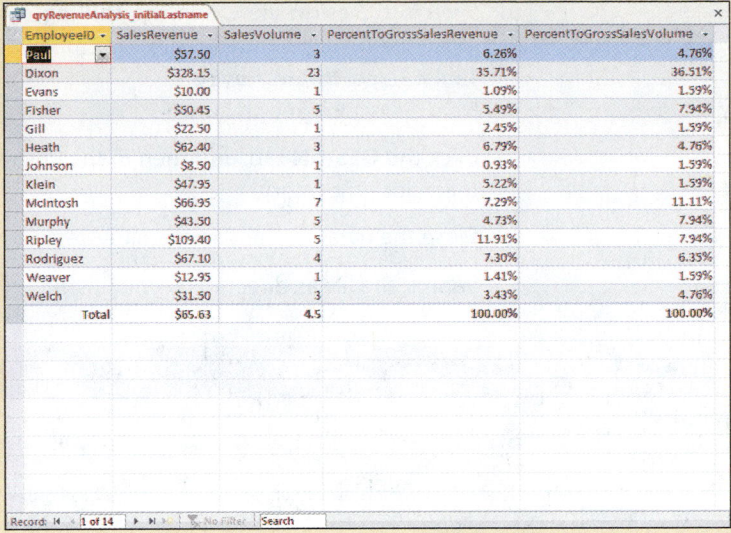

Figure 44 Datasheet view of the qryRevenueAnalysis query

m. Close the query.

n. Click the **CREATE** tab, and then in the Queries group, click **Query Design**. Add **tblProduct** to the query workspace, and then close the Show Table dialog box. Add the following field to the query design grid: **ProductDescription**.

o. Determine the physical volume by calculating width*length*depth. In the **first blank field** in the query design grid, in the Zoom dialog box type **PhysicalVolume:[Width]*[Length]*[Depth]**.

p. The medium-sized carton that the spa has to ship items to customers is 526 cubic inches. You need to calculate the remaining package volume. In the next blank field in the query design grid, in the Zoom dialog box type **RemainingPkgVolume:526-[PhysicalVolume]**.

q. Calculate the total volume by item that can fit into the spa's medium-sized carton. In the **next blank field** in the query design grid, in the Zoom dialog box type **TotalPkgVolume:Int(526/[PhysicalVolume])**.

r. To calculate the percentage of physical volume, use the size of a medium-sized carton that the spa has to ship items to customers—526 cubic inches. In the **next blank field** in the query design grid, in the Zoom dialog box type **PercentOfPhysicalVolume: [PhysicalVolume]/526** and then format the PercentOfPhysicalVolume field as **Percent**.

s. Click the **DESIGN** tab, and then in the Results group, click **Run**. Save your query as **qryVolumePercent_initialLastname** and then close the query.

t. Click the **CREATE** tab, and then in the Queries group, click **Query Wizard** to create a crosstab query. Select **tblPurchase**, and then click **Next**. Double-click the **ProductID** field as the row heading, and then click **Next**. Click the **EmployeeID** field as the column heading, and then click **Next**. Click **Quantity** under Fields, and then click **Sum** under Functions to view the products each employee has sold. Click **Next**. Save your query as **qryCrosstab_initialLastname** and then click **Finish**.

u. Switch to **Design** view, add the **tblEmployee** table to the query workspace, and then make the following changes to the EmployeeID field.
   Table: Select **tblEmployee**
   Field: Select **EmpFirstName**

v. Click the **DESIGN** tab, and then in the Results group, click **Run**. Save your changes, and then close the query.

w Close the database, and then exit Access.

x. Submit the file as directed by your instructor.

Problem Solve 1

Sales & Marketing

Production & Operations

Student data file needed:

a04ws07VegasTours.accdb

You will save your file as:

a04ws07VegasTours_LastFirst.accdb

Vegas Tours Souvenir Shop Database

The Vegas Tours Souvenir Shop is where Las Vegas bus tours start and end, seven days a week. The shop sells a variety of Vegas souvenirs to customers who take the tour and to those who simply want to purchase souvenirs, either in person or online. Managers have been using an Access database to keep track of customers, products, and transactions. You have been given some sample sales data from February 2015. Managers have asked you to create queries that will help them manage their business more efficiently.

a. Open the **a04ws07VegasTours** database. Save it as **a04ws07VegasTours_LastFirst**. Enable the content if necessary.

b. Open **tblCustomer**, and then add your information in record **12**. Replace YourName in the FirstName and LastName fields with your first and last name. Close tblCustomer.

c. Create a query based on **tblPurchase** and **tblPurchaseLine** that displays the **PurchaseDate** from tblPurchase and **ProductID** and **Quantity** from tblPurchaseLine that shows the total of each product sold on a particular date. Group the results by **PurchaseDate**, and then sort the results in **Ascending** order by **PurchaseDate** and **ProductID**. Rename the Quantity field as **TotalSold**. Save the query as **qrySoldByDate_initialLastname**. In Datasheet view, add a total to the bottom of the TotalSold field that displays the total items sold. Save your changes and then close the query.

d. Create a query based on **tblProduct** and **tblPurchaseLine** that displays **Category** from tblProduct and a calculated field named **GrossSales** that shows the gross sales for each category. GrossSales is calculated by multiplying the cost of the item by a markup of 40% times the quantity of items purchased. Group the results by **Category**, sum the **GrossSales**, and then format GrossSales as **Currency**. Save the query as **qryGrossSales_initialLastname** and then close the query.

e. Create a query based on qryGrossSales_initialLastname that displays **GrossSales** and shows the total sales. Group the results by **GrossSales**, and then format GrossSales as **Currency**. Save the query as **qryTotalGrossSales_initialLastname** and then close the query.

f. Create a query based on qryGrossSales_initialLastname and qryTotalGrossSales_initialLastname that displays **Category** and **GrossSales** from qryGrossSales_initialLastname and a calculated field named **PctOfGrossSales** that shows what percentage of each category's sales contributed to the gross revenue. PctOfGrossSales is calculated by dividing GrossSales by the SumOfGrossSales. Format PctOfGrossSales as **Percent**. Save the query as **qryPctOfSales_initialLastname**. In Datasheet view, add a total to the bottom of the GrossSales field that displays the total gross sales, and then add a total to the bottom of the **PctOfGrossSales** field that displays 100 percent. Save your changes, and then close the query.

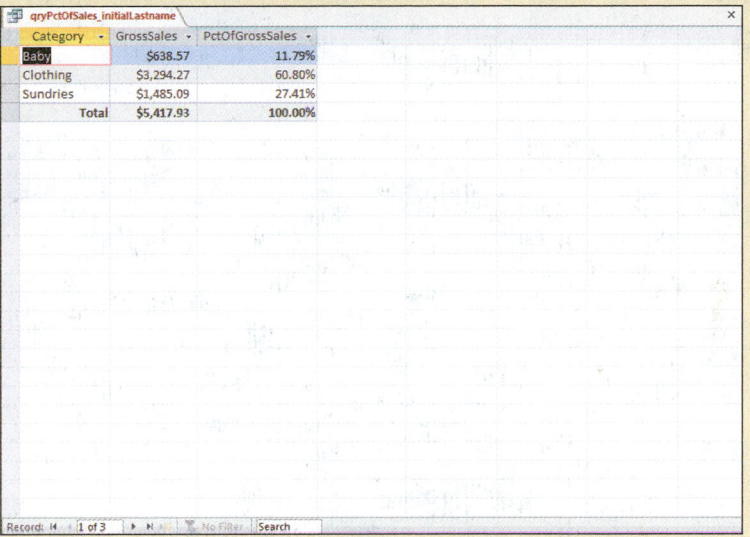

Figure 45   Datasheet view of the qryPctOfSales query

g. Create a query based on qrySoldByDate_initialLastname that displays **TotalSold** and shows the total items sold. Group the results by **TotalSold**. Save the query as **qryTotalItemsSold_initialLastname** and then close the query.

h. Create a query based on qryTotalItemsSold_initialLastname and qryTotalQuantity that displays **Category** and **SumOfQuantity** from qryTotalQuantity and a calculated field named **PctToSalesVolume** that shows the percentage of sales volume within each category. PctToSalesVolume is calculated by dividing SumOfQuantity by the SumOfTotalSold. Format PctToSalesVolume as **Percent**. Save the query as **qryPctToSalesVolume_initialLastname**. In Datasheet view, add a total to the bottom of the **SumOfQuantity** field that displays the total items sold, and then add a total to the bottom of the **PctToSalesVolume** field that displays 100 percent. Save your changes, and then close the query.

i. Create a query based on tblProduct that displays **ProductDescription**, **Category**, a calculated field named Volume that shows the physical volume of each item, and a calculated field named RemainingVolume that determines which items can fit into the smallest shipping box, which has a total volume of 142 cubic inches. Save the query as **qryPhysicalVolume_initialLastname** and then close the query.

j. Create a subquery based on qryPhysicalVolume_initialLastname that displays **ProductDescription**, **Category**, and a calculated field named PctOfPhysicalVolume that calculates the percentage of physical volume for each item. Only display products that are in the Baby category. The smallest shipping box has a total volume of 142 cubic inches. Format PctOfPhysicalVolume as **Percent**. Save your query as **qryPctOfPhysicalVolume_initialLastname** and then close the query.

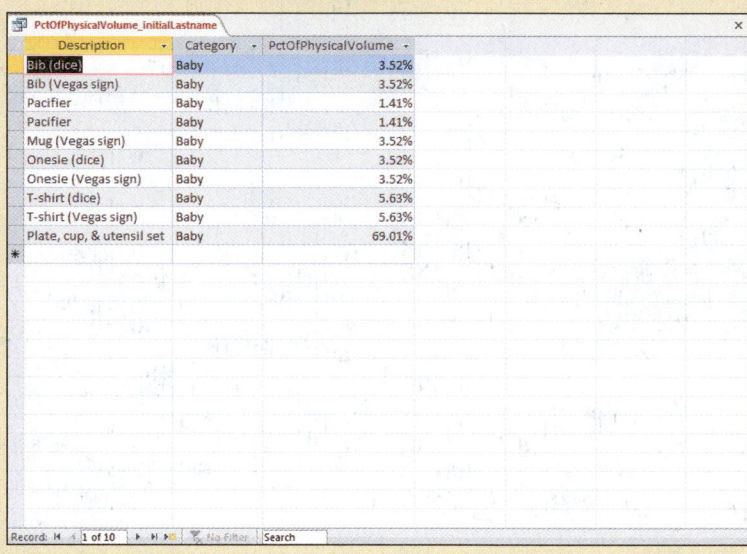

Figure 46   Datasheet view of the qryPctOfPhysicalVolume query

k. Close the database, and then exit Access.

l. Submit the file as directed by your instructor.

Perform 1: Perform in Your Life

Student data file needed:

 a04ws07Electronics.accdb

You will save your file as:

a04ws07Electronics_LastFirst.accdb

Sales & Marketing

Finance & Accounting

Using SQL to Query the Electronics-R-Us Database

Your internship at a local electronics store, Electronics-R-Us, is coming to an end, and management is considering offering you a full-time job. For this position, management is not only looking for someone who is familiar with Access but for someone who is also able to write SQL. You have been asked to create some queries in their sales database using only SQL. Additionally, you will create a crosstab query that will help view quarterly data by employee.

a. Open the **a04ws07Electronics** database, and then save it as a04ws07Electronics_LastFirst.

b. Open tblCustomers, and then add your information in record 1. Replace YourName in the FirstName and LastName fields with your first and last name. Close tblCustomers.

c. Create a SQL query based on tblProducts that will display all the fields of those products in the Computers & Tablets category. Save your query as **qryCategory_initialLastname**.

d. Create a SQL query based on tblCustomers that will display all the fields of those customers who live in states that begin with the letters "F" through "M". Save your query as **qryStates_initialLastname**.

e. Create a SQL query based on tblProducts that will display ProductID, Brand, Description, and Price of the products in which the Brand begins with the letters "A" through "E". Save your query as **qryBrands_initialLastname**.

f. Create a SQL query based on tblTransaction that will display EmployeeID, TransactionDate, and MethodOfPayment of the transactions in which the transaction is between 1/1/2015 and 2/15/2015. Save your query as **qryTransDates_initialLastname**.

g. Create a SQL query based on tblCustomers that will display all the fields of those customers who live in either Pennsylvania or Indiana. Save your query as **qryPAorIN_initialLastname**.

h. Create a SQL query based on tblTransactionDetails that will display the ProductID of those products whose total sales volume has exceeded 140. Name the totaled Quantity field **TotalSalesVolume**, and then group by ProductID. Save your query as **qryHighVolumeProducts_initialLastname**.

i. Create a SQL union query that will display the FirstName, LastName, and Phone for both customers and full-time employees. Name the query **qryPhoneListAll_initialLastname**.

j. Create a SQL subquery that will list the total sales volume for products sold in the first quarter of 2015. Name the totaled Quantity field **Quarter1Volume**. Save the query as **qryQtr1Sales_initialLastname**.

k. Create a SQL subquery that will list the total sales volume for products sold in quarters three and four of 2015. Name the totaled Quantity field **Volume**. Save the query as **qryQtrs3&4Volume_initialLastname**.

l. Create a crosstab query using the Crosstab Query Wizard. Use the tblTransaction table, select EmployeeID as the row heading, select TransactionDate as the column heading, and group the TransactionDate by Quarter. Calculate the total number of transactions for each employee. Modify the crosstab query, and then rename the Total of TransactionID field to **TotalTransactions**. Save the crosstab query as **qryQtrTransactions_initialLastname**.

m. Create a SQL query based on tblProducts and tblTransactionDetails that will display all the fields from tblProducts and the TransactionID and Quantity fields from tblTransactionDetails. Use a join to include all products, regardless if they have been purchased. Sort in ascending order by Brand. Save your query as **qryTransactionDetails_initialLastname**.

n. Create a SQL query based on tblTransaction and tblEmployees that will display all the fields from tblTransaction and the FirstName and LastName fields from tblEmployees. Use a join to include all employees, regardless if they have sold any products. Sort in ascending order by the employee's first name and last name. Save your query as **qryEmpTransaction_initialLastname** and then close the query.

o. Submit the file as directed by your instructor.

Additional
Cases

Additional Workshop Cases are available on the companion website and in the instructor resources.

WORKSHOP 8 | ACTION QUERIES AND ADVANCED RELATIONSHIPS

OBJECTIVES

1. Create a new table using a make table query p. 418

2. Append data to a table p. 423

3. Edit and delete data p. 424

4. Work with update queries p. 425

5. Create, test, and run delete queries p. 430

6. Create inner joins p. 435

7. Create outer joins p. 436

8. Use the Find Unmatched Query Wizard p. 439

Prepare Case

Sales & Marketing

The Turquoise Oasis Spa: Understanding Action Queries

The Turquoise Oasis Spa generates revenue through its spa services and product sales. The spa needs updated information in order to run its business efficiently and make decisions about the business. The Spa Manager, Meda Rodate, and Salon Manager, Irene Kai, have asked you to automate the creation of tables and data updates through the use of action queries. This will make data management easier and more efficient for the managers and spa employees. Additionally, the managers will be able to track marketing campaigns such as viewing the customers who have redeemed coupons and discounts.

Tyler Olson / Shutterstock

REAL WORLD SUCCESS

"After graduation, I obtained a job in the marketing department of a local sports team. I had never imagined that as a marketing major I would need to know Access. My manager had three different databases that she was using to manage our department. Through the use of action queries, I was able to merge all the tables into one database, and cleanse the data to make the database more efficient to use."

\- Beth Ann, recent graduate

Student data files needed for this workshop:

 a04ws08Spa1.accdb   a04ws08Marketing1.accdb

 a04ws08Spa2.accdb   a04ws08Marketing2.accdb

 a04ws08Spa3.accdb

You will save your files as:

a04ws08Spa1_LastFirst.accdb

a04ws08Spa2_LastFirst.accdb

a04ws08Spa3_LastFirst.accdb

a04ws08Marketing1_LastFirst.accdb

a04ws08Marketing2_LastFirst.accdb

Understanding Action Queries

Thus far you have been creating select queries. Select queries are used to display and manipulate data but not change the data. An **action query** is a query that makes changes to records or moves many records from one table to another. Action queries are used to change data in existing tables or make new tables based on a query's dataset. Access offers four different types of action queries:

- A make table query creates a new table based on a query dataset.
- An append query is similar to a make table query, except that a query dataset is appended—added—to an existing table.
- An update query allows the values of one or more fields in a query dataset to be modified.
- A delete query deletes all the records in the underlying table of a query dataset that meet specific criteria.

One important note is that action queries permanently modify the data in tables. Because there is no undo feature for action queries, it is important to be cautious when running any action query. It is a good idea to create a backup of the database in case you need to restore any of the changed data. In this section, you will create and make new table queries, delete queries, update queries, and append queries.

REAL WORLD ADVICE | **Turning Off the Action Query Warning**

When you run an action query, Access will always warn you that you are about to make a change to your data as well as ask you to confirm the change. You can turn the Access warnings off. However, there are dangers to doing so because you will not know for sure if the action query executed. For example, if you are running an update query to update employee salaries by $500, every time you run the query, you will add $500 on to each employee's salary. If you turn off the warning, before you know it, you can increase each employee's salary by $2,500 or more. Of course, employees would not complain, but this can cause tremendous problems for the payroll department and the company's budget. To avoid being prompted when you run such queries, do the following:

1. Click the File tab.
2. Click Options.
3. In the Access Options dialog box, click Client Settings.
4. Under Editing, under Confirm, clear the Action queries check box.

Create a New Table Using a Make Table Query

When you create a database, you store your data in tables—objects that contain records and fields. For example, you can create a customer table to store a list of customers' first and last names, addresses, and telephone numbers, or an inventory table to store information about the products your company sells. Because other database objects—queries, forms, and reports—depend on tables, you should design your database by creating all of its tables first. You have learned that the manual process of creating tables can take some time if you want to create a database that is constructed properly and functions well.

There are times, however, that you will decide to store and track different data than what the database was initially designed to do. Thus, you may use existing data to add a new table that will allow you to make better decisions about your business. The process of creating a new table can be automated through a make table query. For example, your database may have been initially built to track customers and the orders they placed. Now you may also want to track marketing efforts and the number of customers who use coupons that were mailed or e-mailed to them. You would need to create a new table to track which customers redeemed coupons and when they were redeemed.

Opening the Starting Files

To create action queries, you first need to open the Spa and Marketing databases.

A08.00

 To Open the Spa and Marketing Databases

a. Start **Access**, and then open the **a04ws08Spa1** database.

b. Click the **FILE** tab, click **Save As**, and then save the file as an Access database in the folder or location designated by your instructor with the name a04ws08Spa1_LastFirst using your last and first name. If necessary, enable the content.

c. Open the **a04ws08Spa2** database.

d. Click the **FILE** tab, click **Save As**, and then save the file as an Access database in the folder or location designated by your instructor with the name a04ws08Spa2_LastFirst using your last and first name. If necessary, enable the content.

e. Open the **a04ws08Spa3** database.

f. Click the **FILE** tab, click **Save As**, and then save the file as an Access database in the folder or location designated by your instructor with the name a04ws08Spa3_LastFirst using your last and first name. If necessary, enable the content.

g. Open the **a04ws08Marketing1** database.

h. Click the **FILE** tab, click **Save As**, and then save the file as an Access database in the folder or location designated by your instructor with the name a04ws08Marketing1_LastFirst using your last and first name. If necessary, enable the content.

i. Open the **a04ws08Marketing2** database.

j. Click the **FILE** tab, click **Save As**, and then save the file as an Access database in the folder or location designated by your instructor with the name a04ws08Marketing2_LastFirst using your last and first name. If necessary, enable the content.

Creating a Make Table Query

A **make table query** acquires data from one or more tables and then creates a new table from the resulting dataset when you run the query. The new table can be added to the current database that you have open to build the new table. You can create a make table query by first creating a select query and then changing it to a make table query. Your initial select query can include calculated fields and expressions to return the desired data along with allowing you to verify your results before running the query.

You can also create the make table query in one database and then have Access build the table in another database. This allows you to use data in one database—the one in which the make table query resides—and copy that data into a new table within another database. For example, you may decide at some point, perhaps once you have a few years' worth of data, that you want to archive some of the older data into another database.

Archiving data is an important task in business. Managers do not want to delete historical data because it can be used to help manage and develop their businesses. A major use of historical data is for **forecasting**—to predict or estimate future sales trends, budgets, and so forth. Archiving data from the company's **operational database**—the database used to carry out regular operations, such as payroll and inventory management, of an organization—or **transactional database**—the database used to record daily transactions—into another database, one that is used for storing older data, is a concept known as **data warehousing**. A **data warehouse** contains a large amount of different types of data that present a clear picture of your business environment at a specific point in time.

Data warehousing is a technology used to establish business intelligence. **Business intelligence (BI)** helps an organization attain their goals and objectives by giving them a better understanding of past performance as well as information on how the organization is progressing toward its goals. **Business intelligence tools** are a classification of software applications that aide in collecting, storing, analyzing, and providing access to data that helps managers make improved business decisions.

One way BI tools are used is for **data mining**, which helps expose trends, patterns, and relationships within the data that might have otherwise remained undetected. For example, the queries that you have been creating in Access are searching for data that you know exists. You have created queries to find customers who live in specific cities and states as well as queries that help calculate employee raises, just to name a few. With data mining, you are searching, or mining the data within the data warehouse, for unknown trends. The salon manager could mine archived data in the data warehouse to see what two products are most likely to sell together or what two services are most likely to be given to one customer.

Think about how this can help a manager make decisions. What about forecasting? The spa manager could learn a lot about the business and use this information to help increase sales. If the manager knows that two items are most likely to sell together in one transaction, he could ensure he has equal amounts of inventory in stock. He can also train his employees to use a **suggestive sell**—a sales technique used to add more revenue to a sale by suggesting and selling another product to the customer.

Running a Make Table Query

Once your make table query is ready, the table is created once you click the Run button on the Query Tools Design tab as shown in Figure 1. The challenge with clicking Run is that you cannot see what Access is going to do nor can you verify that the data will be displayed how you want it to look. For example, you may be creating a make table query that includes calculated fields and expressions. You probably would want to view the query dataset before actually creating a table. The way around this is to switch from Design view to Datasheet view. This enables you to preview the data that will be added to the new table before actually creating it.

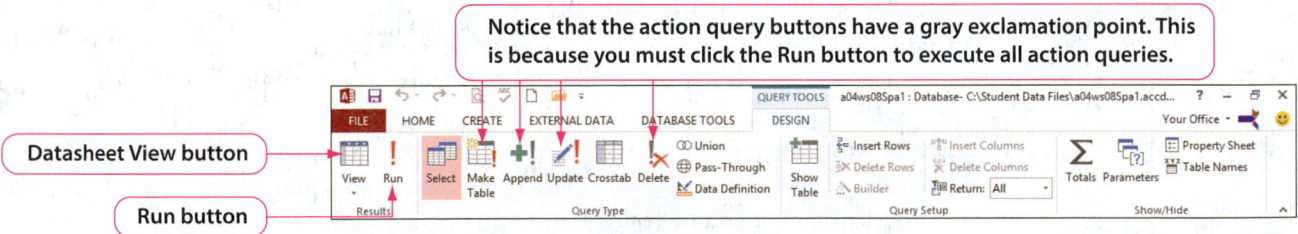

Figure 1 Different action query buttons

REAL WORLD ADVICE | Archiving Data

There are times when you need to copy or archive data, and you will want to make a table from data within your database. For example, you may have a table of past sales data that is used in reports. The sales figures will not change because the transactions have occurred in the past. Continually running a query to retrieve the data can take time, especially if you run a complex query against a large amount of data. Loading the historical data into a separate table and using that table as a data source can reduce time and provide a convenient data archive. Remember, however, that the data in your new table is just a snapshot—an image—of the data at a specific time. It has no relationship or link to other tables in the database.

MyITLab®

Workshop 8 Training

A08.01

▶ To Create and Run a Make Table Query

a. Switch to the **a04ws08Marketing1_LastFirst** database if necessary. Click the **CREATE** tab, and then in the Queries group, click **Query Design**.

b. Add **tblCampaign** and **tblMailing** to the query workspace, and then **Close** ☒ the Show Table dialog box.

c. Add the following fields to the query design grid: **MailingID**, **CustomerID**, and **Redeemed** from the tblMailing table, and **CampaignName**, **CampaignType**, **StartDate**, **EndDate**, **DiscountCode**, **Department**, and **Details** from the tblCampaign table.

d. In the Criteria row of the Department field type "**Turquoise Oasis Spa**". Clear the **Show** check box.

e. Click the **DESIGN** tab. In the Results group, click the **View** arrow, and then click **Datasheet View**.

Notice that you can see the 9 fields and 52 records that will be added to your new table.

f. Switch to **Design** view. On the DESIGN tab, in the Query Type group, click **Make Table** to change the query type to make table query.

g. In the Make Table dialog box, type **tblCampaign** in the Table Name box to name your new table.

h. Click **Another Database**, click **Browse**, navigate to the location where you are saving your files, and then select the **a04ws08Spa1_LastFirst** database. In the Make Table dialog box, click **OK** two times.

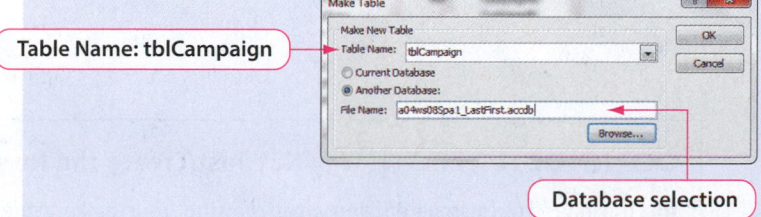

Figure 2 Make Table dialog box

i. Click the **DESIGN** tab, and then in the Results group, click **Run**. Click **Yes** in the Microsoft Access dialog box to confirm that you want to paste 52 rows into a new table. **Save** 🖫 the query as **qryMakeTable_initialLastname** using your first initial and last name. **Close** ☒ the query, and then **Close** ☒ the a04ws08Marketing1_LastFirst database.

SIDE NOTE
Verify the Action
The only way to verify that an action query worked correctly is to look in the table to see if the proper action occurred.

j. Switch to the **a04ws08Spa1_LastFirst** database, and then open the **tblCampaign** table.

Notice that all 52 records were exported from the a04ws08Marketing1_LastFirst database, but all the formatting—such as a check box for the Redeemed field—was not copied.

> **Troubleshooting**
>
> If you do not see the tblCampaign table in the a04ws08Spa1_LastFirst database, close the database and then reopen it.

k. Switch to **Design** view, and then make the following changes to the field properties and descriptions.

Field	Field Properties	Description
MailingID	Change this field to the **primary key** Change the format to **"MID"0**	The Mailing ID (primary key)
CustomerID	Change the caption to **Customer**	The Customer ID (foreign key)
Redeemed	Change the lookup control to a check box	Was the coupon redeemed?
CampaignName	Change the caption to **Campaign Name**	The campaign name
CampaignType	Change the caption to **Campaign Type**	The campaign type
StartDate	Change the caption to **Start Date**	The campaign start date
EndDate	Change the caption to **End Date**	The campaign end date
DiscountCode	Change the caption to **Discount Code**	The POS discount code
Details		The details of the campaign

l. **Save** 💾 the changes, and then **Close** ✖ tblCampaign.

m. Click the **DATABASE TOOLS** tab, and then in the Relationships group, click **Relationships**. Find **tblCampaign** in the Relationships window, and then create a relationship between **CustomerID** in the tblCampaign table and **CustomerID** in the tblCustomer table. Enforce referential integrity.

n. **Close** ✖ the Relationships window, and then click **Yes** in the Microsoft Access dialog box if prompted to save your changes.

SIDE NOTE
Saving Relationships
If you move or resize tables, you will be prompted to save your changes. If you only create the relationship, Access will automatically save that change for you.

> **CONSIDER THIS** | **Why Not Just Create the New Table from Scratch?**
>
> You did have to do some editing after running your make table query, and this is normal. However, you did not have to create the fields, select the field types, and enter the data. Some minor editing took a few minutes. Additionally, you still would have had to create the relationship, whether you built the table from scratch or created it from a make table query. How long would it have taken you if you created it from scratch? What if the table had two or three times as many fields? Could you have created it faster from scratch?

Append Data to a Table

You can use an append query when you need to add new records to an existing table by using data from other sources such as an Excel workbook, a Word document, a text file, or another database. An **append query** selects records from one or more data sources and copies the selected records to an existing table.

Creating an Append Query

Suppose that you have access to another database that contains a table of potential customers. However, you already have a table in your existing database that stores this type of data. Thus, you decide to import the list of potential customers from the other database. To avoid having to import it into a new table and then manually enter the data into your existing table, you can use an append query to copy the records into your existing table. For example, the Painted Paradise Resort and Spa's marketing department regularly updates their database with new marketing campaigns, customers, and redemption status of discounts. If the spa manager wants to ensure he has current data for decision making, he needs to regularly add new records to the table that is storing the marketing data in the spa database. An append query could help the spa's manager easily and regularly add new records to the existing table.

REAL WORLD ADVICE	Benefits of Using an Append Query

- You can append—add—multiple records to a table at one time. If you copy data manually, you usually have to do it multiple times. By using an append query, you eliminate the copy-and-paste process, which can ensure that no mistakes are made and all records are appended.
- You can review the data that will be appended before you run the query. You can view your selection in Datasheet view and modify the data as needed before you append any data. This can be helpful if your query includes criteria or expressions.
- You can use criteria to refine your selection. For example, you might want to only append customers who live within a certain state.
- You can append records when some of the data source fields do not exist in the destination table. For example, suppose that your existing customer table has 11 fields, and the external prospective customers table only has 10 of the 11 fields. You can still use an append query to copy and add the data from the 10 fields that match—and the fields MUST match in order to be able to do this.

Running an Append Query

The data is not appended to your table until you click the Run button on the Design tab. Before you append the records, you can switch to Datasheet view for a preview of the records that will be affected by the action query. If you need to modify your dataset, you can switch back to Design view and make the needed changes. This can be done as many times as needed before actually running the query. It is important to emphasize that you cannot undo an append query. If you make a mistake, you must either restore your database from a backup or correct your error, either manually or by using a delete query. Therefore, you should back up your database or the destination table before running an append query.

A08.02

To Create and Run an Append Query

a. Switch to the **a04ws08Marketing2_LastFirst** database, if necessary. Click the **CREATE** tab, and then in the Queries group, click **Query Design**. The marketing department has added the spring promotions for the Turquoise Oasis Spa, and you need to append the new promotional data to the tblCampaign table in the a04ws08Spa2_LastFirst database.

b. Add **tblCampaign** and **tblMailing** to the query workspace, and then **Close** ☒ the Show Table dialog box.

c. Add the following fields to the query design grid: **MailingID**, **CustomerID**, and **Redeemed** from the tblMailing table, and then add **CampaignName**, **CampaignType**, **StartDate**, **EndDate**, **DiscountCode**, **Department**, and **Details** from the tblCampaign table.

d. In the Criteria row of the Department field type Like "Turquoise Oasis Spa". Clear the **Show** check box of the Department column.

e. In the Criteria row of the StartDate field type #4/1/2015#.

f. On the DESIGN tab, in the Query Type group, click **Append** to change the query type to an append query.

g. When the Append dialog box opens, click the **table name** arrow, select append the data to the **tblCampaign** table, and then click **Another Database**. Click **Browse**, navigate to the location where you are saving your files, and then select the **a04ws08Spa2_LastFirst** database. Click **OK** two times.

h. Click the **DESIGN** tab. In the Results group, click the **View** arrow, and then click **Datasheet View** to preview the data that will be included in your table. You should have 78 records that will be appended automatically to the tblCampaign table in the a04ws08Spa2_LastFirst database.

i. Switch to **Design** view, and then in the Results group, click **Run**. In the Microsoft Access dialog box, click **Yes** to confirm that you want to append 78 rows.

j. **Save** 🖫 the query as qryAppendData_initialLastname and then close the query.

k. Switch to the **a04ws08Spa2_LastFirst** database, and then open the **tblCampaign** table.

   Notice how all 78 records were exported from the a04ws08Marketing2_LastFirst database, along with the formatting, and you now have 130 records in your tblCampaign table.

l. **Close** ☒ the tblCampaign table, switch to the **a04ws08Marketing2_LastFirst** database, and then **Close** ☒ the a04ws08Marketing2_LastFirst database.

SIDE NOTE

To Use or Not Use "Like"

Sometimes Access allows users to enter criteria multiple ways. If you do not include "Like", the query will still return the correct dataset.

SIDE NOTE

Previewing Data

Switching to Datasheet view allows you to preview the records that will be added to the other table before actually running the query.

Edit and Delete Data

Because many databases contain a tremendous amount of data, it would be extremely time consuming to manually update data record by record. For example, many new area codes have been created in the United States over the past few years. It would take too much time to have an employee look through each customer's record and modify the area code as needed. This is when an update query can be helpful. An **update query** can be used to add, change, or delete data in one or more existing records. Update queries are similar to the Find and Replace dialog box, but much more powerful.

You also have the option of using a delete query depending on the type of deletion you need to perform. A **delete query** is used to remove entire records from a table at one time. Delete queries remove all the data in each field, including the primary key. When you need to delete old records from your database, you could search through the table and delete each individual record, which could take some time, or you could use a delete query to delete them all at once. A delete query cannot be used to delete an actual table from the database, but it can be used to delete all of the data from within a table.

Running update and delete queries are different than using the Cascade Update Related Fields and Cascade Delete Related Records properties in the Relationships window. When you set the Cascade Update Related Fields property, Access updates the primary key in all related tables if it changes on the one side of the relationship. When you set the Cascade Delete Related Records property, Access deletes the related records in all related tables if the key field is deleted on the one side of the relationship. If you want to delete data from several related tables, you must enable the Enforce Referential Integrity and Cascade Delete Related Records properties for each relationship. This allows your query to delete data from the tables on the one and many sides of the relationship.

Be careful that you fully understand what Cascade Update and Cascade Delete do before using them. A vast amount of data can be updated or deleted at once and unintentionally if you are not careful. For example, if you delete an employee by accident—because you should never do this—then it would wipe out every transaction the employee was associated with. This is why best practice is to create a backup of your database before making any major changes in the data.

Working with Update Queries

You can use an update query when you have to update or change existing data in multiple records. As a best practice, there are two steps that you must follow to create and run an update query. First, create a select query that identifies the records to update, and then change the query to an update query that upon running will update the records.

A **simple update query** involves updating data in one table, allowing you to specify two values—the value you want to replace and the value to use as a replacement. To create and run an update query, first begin with a select query that identifies the records to be updated. Then change the query to an update query and click Run. The key thing to remember is that although the data types for each table field do not have to match, they must be compatible.

A simple update query can be an easy way to update large amounts of data. For example, perhaps an employee no longer works at the salon, and there are dozens of future appointments that need to be changed to a different employee's name. If the same employee—perhaps the person you hired to fill that employee's position—is now going to handle these appointments, you could create an update query that changes the name of the employee for all future appointments from the employee who left to the new employee.

A08.03

To Create and Run a Simple Update Query

a. Switch to the **a04ws08Spa1_LastFirst** database, if necessary. Click the **CREATE** tab, and then in the Queries group, click **Query Design**. The marketing department has extended the date for all in-house promotions that currently expire on 3/31/2015, and you need to update the data in the tblCampaign table in the a04ws08Spa1_LastFirst database.

b. Add **tblCampaign** to the query workspace, and then **Close** ☒ the Show Table dialog box.

c. Add the following fields to the query design grid: **MailingID**, **CampaignType**, and **EndDate**.

d. In the Criteria row of the CampaignType field type Like "In-house Promotion".

e. In the Criteria row of the EndDate field type Like #3/31/2015#.

f. Click the **DESIGN** tab, and then in the Query Type group, click **Update** to change the query type to an update query. In the Update To property row of the EndDate field, type #6/30/2015# and then **Save** 💾 the query as qryUpdateData_initialLastname.

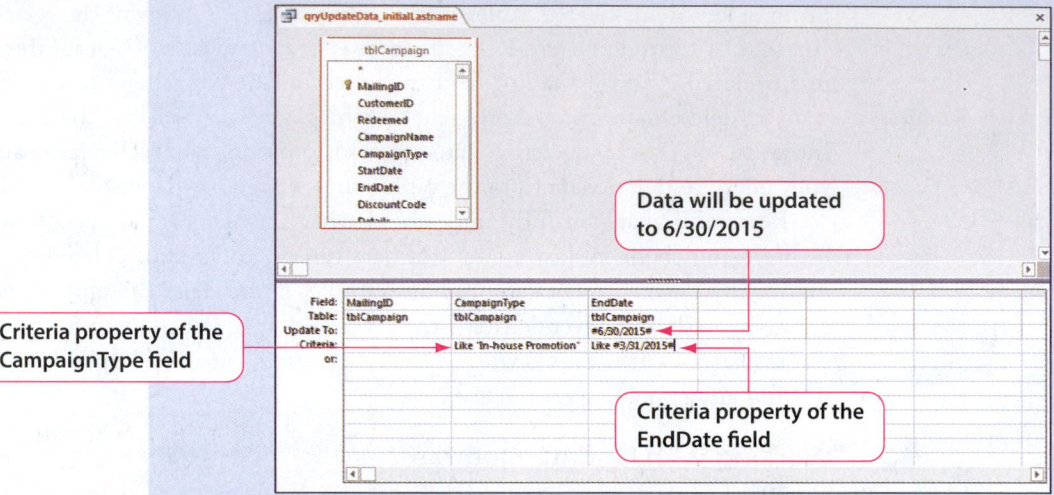

Figure 3   Design view of the qryUpdateData query

SIDE NOTE
What Is Access Showing?

When you preview the data, notice that Access does not show you how the data will look after the update, but shows you which records will be updated.

g. Switch to **Datasheet** view to preview the data that will be included in your update. You should have 52 records that will be updated automatically in your table.

h. Switch to **Design** view, and then in the Results group, click **Run**. Click **Yes** in the Microsoft Access dialog box when Access asks you to confirm that you want to update 52 rows.

i. **Close** ✖ the query.

j. Open the **tblCampaign** table.

   Notice that all In-house Promotions now have an EndDate of 6/30/2015. **Close** ✖ tblCampaign.

k. Click the **CREATE** tab, and then in the Queries group, click **Query Design**. The marketing department has changed the details for all in-house promotions, and you need to update the data in the tblCampaign table. Add **tblCampaign** to the query workspace. **Close** ✖ the Show Table dialog box.

l. Add the following fields to the design grid: **CampaignType** and **Details**.

m. In the Criteria property row of the CampaignType field type "In-house Promotion".

n. Click the **DESIGN** tab, and then in the Query Type group, click **Update** to change the query type to an update query.

o. In the Update To property row of the Details field, type [Details] & " " & "Minimum purchase of $50 is required.". **Save** 💾 the query as qryUpdateDetails_initialLastname.

   You are doing this to modify the specifics of the promotion. The marketing department has informed you that in order for clients to receive this promotion, they have to spend a minimum of $50. To keep the text that is already in the Details field and add the additional information, you can concatenate the existing data with the marketing department's update.

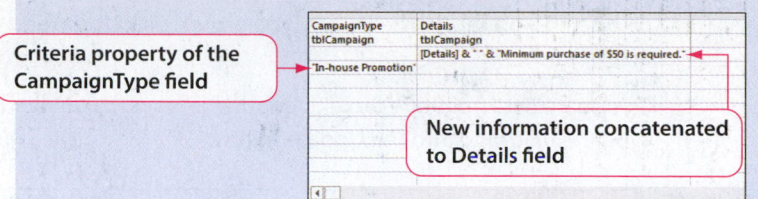

Criteria property of the CampaignType field

New information concatenated to Details field

Figure 4   Design view of the qryUpdateDetails query

SIDE NOTE
Concatenating Data Saves Time
Access did not delete what was in the field prior to the update and simply concatenated what was already in the field with the new data.

p. Switch to **Datasheet** view to preview the data that will be included in your table.
You should have 52 records that will be updated automatically in your table. Notice that Access does not show you how the records will be updated but rather just that 52 records will change.

q. Switch to **Design** view, and then in the Results group, click **Run**. Click **Yes** in the Microsoft Access dialog box when Access asks you to confirm that you want to update 52 rows. **Close** ☒ the query.

r. Open the **tblCampaign** table.
Notice that all In-house Promotions have been adjusted in the Details. For example, some entries are listed as **Receive 10% off. Minimum purchase of $50 is required**.

s. **Close** ☒ the tblCampaign table, and then **Close** ☒ the a04ws08Spa1_LastFirst database.

Creating Complex Update Queries

There are times when you need to update data from one table to another through the use of a **complex update query**. When doing so, the data types for both the source and destination fields must either match or be compatible. Additionally, when you update data from one table to another and use compatible data types instead of matching data types, Access converts the data types of the fields in the destination table. As a result, some of the data in the destination fields may be **truncated**—shortened or trimmed.

A08.04

 To Create and Run a Complex Update Query

a. Switch to the **a04ws08Spa2_LastFirst** database if necessary. Open **tblMktgImport** and **tblCustomer**. The marketing department has updated some of their customer data, and you need to update the tblCustomer table with the new data from the marketing department's database. The table from the marketing department's database has already been imported into your database. Changes in data between the two tables are the addition of data in the Zip Code field and the update of area codes and exchanges. **Close** ☒ tblMktgImport and tblCustomer.

b. Click the **CREATE** tab, and then in the Queries group, click **Query Design**.

c. Add **tblCustomer** and **tblMktgImport** to the query workspace, and then **Close** ☒ the Show Table dialog box.

d. Create a relationship between the CustomerID fields in each table. Drag **CustomerID** in tblCustomer to **CustomerID** in tblMktgImport. Add the following fields to the query design grid: **CustomerID**, **CustCity**, **CustState**, **CustZipCode**, and **CustPhone** from tblCustomer.

e. On the DESIGN tab, in the Query Type group, click **Update** to change the query type to an update query.

f. To update data from one table to another and match the fields between the two tables type the following into the Update To row.

Field	Update To
CustCity	[tblMktgImport]![CustCity]
CustState	[tblMktgImport]![CustState]
CustZipCode	[tblMktgImport]![CustZipCode]
CustPhone	[tblMktgImport]![CustPhone]

Resize the columns in the design grid to see what you have entered.

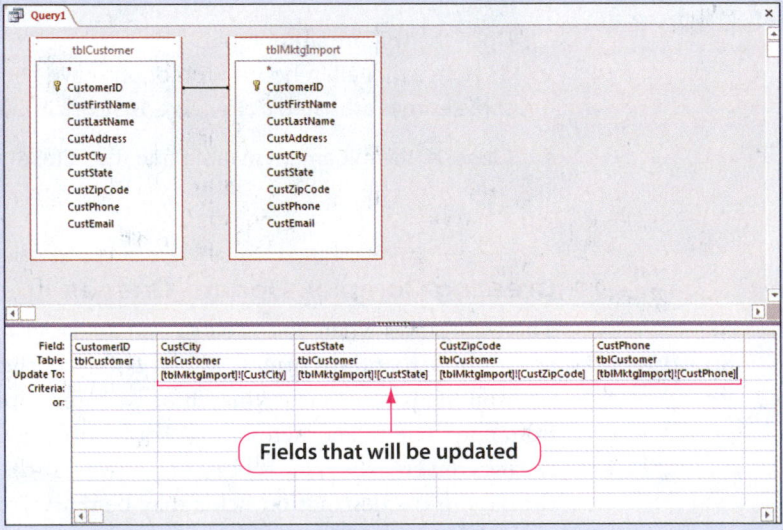

Figure 5 Design view of a complex update query

g. Switch to **Datasheet** view to preview the data that will be included in your update. You should have 25 records that will be updated automatically in your table.

h. Switch to **Design** view, and then in the Results group, click **Run**. Click **Yes** in the Microsoft Access dialog box when Access asks you to confirm that you want to update 25 rows.

i. **Save** 🖫 the query as **qryComplexUpdate_initialLastname** and then **Close** ✕ the query.

j. Open the **tblCustomer** table.
   Notice that all applicable data—area code and zip code—have been updated.

k. **Close** ✕ tblCustomer.

QUICK REFERENCE	Restrictions on Data Type Conversions

The following table outlines the restrictions on how to convert data types and briefly describes any data loss that might occur during conversion.

Convert to	Convert from	Changes or restrictions
Text	Memo	Deletes all except the first 255 characters
	Yes/No	The value –1 converts to Yes. The value 0 converts to No.
	Hyperlink	Truncates links longer than 255 characters
Memo	Yes/No	The value –1 converts to Yes. The value 0 converts to No.
Number	Text	Must consist of numbers, valid currency, and decimal separators. The number of characters in the Text field must fall within the size set for the Number field.
	Memo	Must contain only text and valid currency and decimal separators. The number of characters in the Memo field must fall within the size set for the Number field.
	Number with a different field size or precision	Must not be larger or smaller than what the new field size can store. Changing precision might cause Access to round some values.
	Date/Time	Dates depend on the size of the Number field. To accommodate all possible dates, set the Field Size property of your Number field to Long Integer or greater.
	Currency	Values must not exceed or fall below the size limit set for the field.
	AutoNumber	Values must fall within the size limit set for the field.
	Yes/No	Yes values convert to –1. No values convert to 0.
Date/Time	Text	Must be a recognizable date or date/time combination
	Memo	Must be a recognizable date or date/time combination
	Number	Value must fall between –657,434 and 2,958,465.99998843.
	Currency	Value must fall between –$657,434 and $2,958,465.9999.
	AutoNumber	Value must exceed –657,434 and be less than 2,958,466.
	Yes/No	The value –1 (Yes) converts to December 29, 1899. The value 0 (No) converts to midnight (12:00 AM).
Currency	Text	Must consist of numbers and valid separators
	Memo	Must consist of numbers and valid separators
	Yes/No	The value –1 (Yes) converts to $1. The value 0 (No) converts to $0.
AutoNumber	Text	Not allowed if AutoNumber field serves as primary key
	Memo	Not allowed if AutoNumber field serves as primary key
	Number	Not allowed if AutoNumber field serves as primary key
	Date/Time	Not allowed if AutoNumber field serves as primary key
	Currency	
	Yes/No	

Table 1   Restrictions on data type conversions   *(continued)*

Convert to	Convert from	Changes or restrictions
Yes/No	Text	Must consist only of Yes, No, True, False, On, or Off
	Memo	Must consist only of Yes, No, True, False, On, or Off
	Number	Zero or Null converts to No. All other values convert to Yes.
	Date/Time	Null, or 12:00:00 AM, converts to No. All other values convert to Yes.
	Currency	Zero or Null converts to No. All other values convert to Yes.
	AutoNumber	All values convert to Yes.
Hyperlink	Text	Converts a valid hyperlink in text format to a hyperlink
	Memo	Converts a valid hyperlink in text format to a hyperlink
	Number	Not allowed when a Number field is part of a relationship. If the original value is in the form of a valid Internet Protocol (IP) address (four number triplets separated by a period—nnn.nnn.nnn.nnn) and the numbers happen to coincide with a Web address, the conversion results in a valid link. Otherwise, Access appends "http://" to the beginning of each value, and the resulting links are not valid.
	Date/Time	Access appends "http://" to the beginning of each address, but the resulting links will almost never work.
	Currency	Access appends "http://" to the beginning of each value, but like dates, the resulting links will almost never work.
	AutoNumber	Not allowed when the AutoNumber field is part of a relationship. Access appends "http://" to the beginning of each value, but the resulting links will almost never work.
	Yes/No	Access converts all Yes values to –1 and all No values to 0, and appends "http://" to the beginning of each value. The resulting links do not work.

Table 1 Restrictions on data type conversions *(continued)*

Create, Test, and Run Delete Queries

You can use an update query to delete data in one or more fields in a database. However, to delete entire records, including the primary key value that makes the record unique, you can use a delete query.

Creating Simple Delete Queries

A **simple delete query** is used to remove one or more records from a table. The number of rows deleted is dependent upon the criteria within the Where clause of the delete query. Typically, you use delete queries when you need to remove large amounts of data quickly. If you want to remove a very small number of records, you may want to simply delete them by hand. Undoubtedly, by running a delete query, you reduce and/or eliminate the chance of not deleting—missing—a record if the process is done manually.

A08.05

 To Create and Run a Simple Delete Query

a. In the **a04ws08Spa2_LastFirst** database, click the **CREATE** tab, and then in the Queries group, click **Query Design** to begin creating a query that will help the spa manager. She has decided to discontinue selling soaps because they are not generating enough revenue for the spa.

b. Add **tblProduct** to the query workspace, and then **Close** ⊠ the Show Table dialog box.

c. Add the **ProductDescription** field to the query design grid.

d. In the Criteria property of the ProductDescription field type **Like "*soap*"**.

e. Click the **DESIGN** tab, and then in the Query Type group, click **Delete** to change the query type to a delete query.

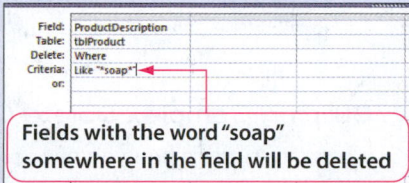

Figure 6 Design view of a delete query

f. Switch to **Datasheet** view to preview the data that will be deleted. You should have two records that will be deleted when you run the delete query.

g. Switch to **Design** view, and then in the Results group, click **Run**. Click **Yes** in the Microsoft Access dialog box when Access asks you to confirm that you want to delete two rows.

> **Troubleshooting**
>
> If you had your table open when you ran your delete query, #Deleted is displayed in the fields or records that were affected by the delete query. The message is displayed until you close and then reopen the table.

h. **Save** 🖫 the query as **qrySimpleDelete_initialLastname** and then **Close** ⊠ the query.

i. Open the **tblProduct** table.

Notice that all applicable records—Lavender Ylang Soap and Renewal Face Soap—have been deleted.

j. **Close** ⊠ tblProduct.

CONSIDER THIS | **What If You Try to Delete Records That Have Related Records?**

What do you think would happen if you tried to run a delete query and the records had related records in another table? Would you still be able to delete the records? Would it change anything if you set your Relationships property to Cascade Delete Related Records?

REAL WORLD ADVICE | **Why Use a Delete Query?**

It is important to ensure that the data in your database is current. Removing unneeded data is a good organizational strategy that all database users should practice. Cleansing outdated or incorrect data creates a database that is easy to use and maintain. Of course, before performing a delete query, you should always back up your database just in case you either make a mistake or think you might want to use the data to be deleted at a later point in time. Data can become unneeded for a few reasons:

- Real-world changes—You may need to delete discontinued products or employees who no longer work at your company.

- Human error—Human error happens. Users could accidently enter duplicate data for a customer or an order. A delete query can make it easier to fix errors.

- Time—At times you may need to archive older data—past employees or last year's sales data—and move it to an archive database or data warehouse.

Building Complex Delete Queries

There are times when you need to delete data in multiple tables. This is a more **complex delete query**. For example, the salon manager may want to remove all coupons that were not redeemed and that have now expired. This will keep the database cleansed. **Data cleansing** is a process where the delete query will remove data that is not useful or needed anymore.

REAL WORLD ADVICE | **Cleansing Data**

In the business world, using incorrect data in business operations can be expensive. Many companies use customer information databases that record data such as contact information, addresses, and preferences. For instance, if customer addresses are inconsistent or incorrect, the company will endure the cost of resending mail or even losing customers. Although cleansing data is critical in order to maintain accurate records, some things need to be considered including:

- Loss of information—Data can be overcleansed to the point that important information is removed from the database. This loss can be particularly pricey if there is a large amount of deleted data.

- Time-consumption—Cleansing data is not an easy or quick process. Once data is cleansed, you would want to avoid recleansing the data in its entirety after some values in data collection change. Thus, the process should only be repeated on values that have changed.

A08.06

 To Create and Run a Complex Delete Query

a. In the **a04ws08Spa2_LastFirst** database, click the **DATABASE TOOLS** tab, and then in the Relationships group, click **Relationships**.

   The marketing department has been notified that two customers want to be removed from the Painted Paradise Resort and Spa's mailing list as they are moving out of the country and will not be customers anymore. You need to delete the records from your database to ensure that the data you have is current and cleansed.

SIDE NOTE
The Relationship Line
You can also double-click the relationship line to open the Edit Relationships dialog box.

SIDE NOTE
Deleting Records on the One Side of a Relationship
To delete records on the one side of the relationship and related records on the many side, enable Referential Integrity and Cascade Delete Related Records.

b. Right-click the **relationship line** between the tblCampaign and tblCustomer tables, and then click **Edit Relationship** to modify the relationship between tblCustomer and tblCampaign. In the Edit Relationships dialog box, click the **Cascade Delete Related Records** check box, and then click **OK**.

c. On the DESIGN tab, in the Relationships group, click **Close**.

d. Click the **CREATE** tab, in the Queries group, click **Query Design**.

e. Add **tblCustomer** to the query workspace, and then **Close** ☒ the Show Table dialog box.

f. Add the following fields to the query design grid: **CustomerID**, **CustFirstName**, and **CustLastName**.

g. Click the **DESIGN** tab, and then in the Query Type group, click **Delete** to change the query type to a delete query.

h. To delete the two customers, in the Criteria property row of the CustLastName field type **"Dunn"**, and then in the Or property row of the CustLastName field, type **"Cleveland"**. **Save** 💾 the query as **qryComplexDelete1_initialLastname**.

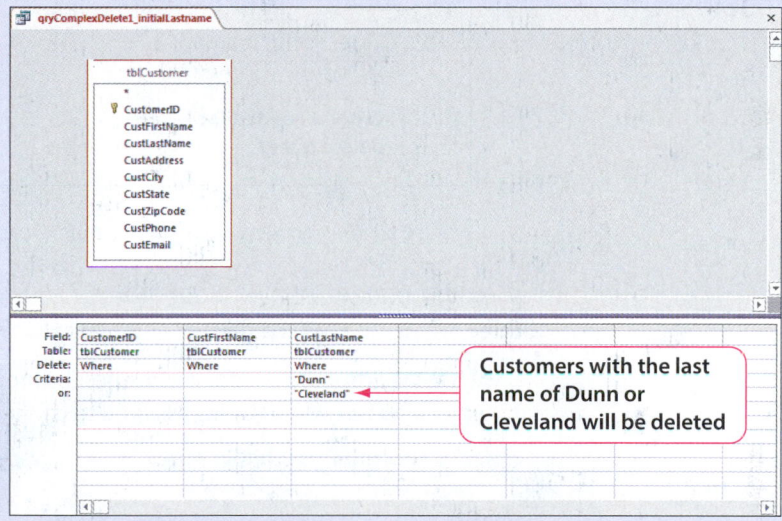

Figure 7 Design view of the qryComplexDelete1 query

i. Switch to **Datasheet** view to preview the data that will be deleted. You should have two records that will be deleted automatically once you run the query.

j. Switch to **Design** view, and then in the Results group, click **Run**. Click **Yes** in the Microsoft Access dialog box when Access asks you to confirm that you want to delete two rows.

k. **Close** ☒ the query.

l. Open the **tblCustomer** table.
Notice that all applicable data—customers with the last name of Dunn and Cleveland—have been deleted.

m. Open the **tblCampaign** table. Notice that all applicable data—customers with the CustomerID of 4 and 22—have been deleted. **Close** ☒ tblCampaign and tblCustomer.

SIDE NOTE
Deleting Records on the Many Side
If you need to remove data only on the many side of the relationship, you can create and run your delete query without having to change the relationship.

n. Click the **CREATE** tab, and then in the Queries group, click **Query Design**.
Management has notified the spa employees and clients that the spa will be closing at 11:00 AM on January 15, 2015, due to some construction work. You need to now delete the appointments that currently have appointments entered at that time.

o. Add **tblSchedule** to the query workspace, and then **Close** ☒ the Show Table dialog box.

Entering Times

You can also type just
>**# 11 AM#** and press
Enter. Access will
automatically enter the
zeros for you.

p. Add the following fields to the query design grid: **DateOfAppt** and **TimeOfAppt**.

q. Click the **DESIGN** tab, and then in the Queries group, click **Delete** to change the query type to a delete query.

r. To delete the three clients scheduled for appointments, in the Criteria property row of the DateOfAppt field, type **#1/15/2015#**, and then type **>#11:00:00 AM#** into the Criteria property row of the TimeOfAppt field. **Save** the query as **qryComplexDelete2_initialLastname**.

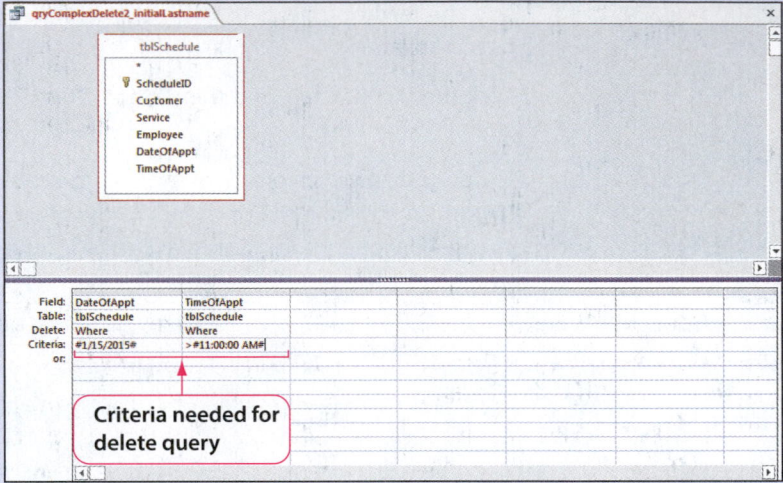

Figure 8 Design view of the qryComplexDelete2 query

s. Switch to **Datasheet** view to preview the data that will be deleted. You should have three records that will be deleted automatically once you run the query.

t. Switch to **Design** view, and then in the Results group, click **Run**. Click **Yes** in the Microsoft Access dialog box when Access asks you to confirm that you want to delete three rows.

u. **Close** ✖ the query, and then **Close** ✖ the a04ws08Spa2_LastFirst database.

QUICK REFERENCE | **Tips When Using a Delete Query**

The reason you deleted records from the tblCustomer table and not the tblCampaign table is because tblCustomer resides on the one side of the relationship. Additionally, you did not have to change any of the other relationships because there were not any related records. In the future, you may need to edit all relationships and ensure the Cascade Delete Related Records property is selected. You first need to decide which records exist on the one side of the relationship and which exist on the many side.

- To delete records on the one side of the relationship and the related records on the many side, enable the Referential Integrity and Cascade Delete Related Records properties.

- To delete records only on the one side of the relationship, first delete the relationship, and then delete the data.

- To remove data only on the many side of the relationship, create and run the delete query without changing the relationship.

Advanced Relationships Using Multiple Tables

When you run a database query to find data in related tables, Access automatically looks for records that have matching values on both sides of the relationship. This is what you will probably do the majority of the time. However, you can control which records will be displayed in the query dataset by using query joins. This enables you to enhance your dataset even further to find the data that you want.

A **query join** is a temporary or virtual relationship between two tables in a query that do not have an established relationship or common field with the same field name and data type. Tables that are joined in a query are only related in that query and nowhere else. The type of join used will indicate which records the query will select or perform an action on. Creating a query join will not establish a permanent relationship between the tables. Permanent relationships can only be created in the Relationships window. In this section, you will create queries that include inner and outer joins as well as create and edit unmatched data queries.

Inner Joins

An **inner join**, the default join type in Access, is a join that selects only those records from both database tables that have matching values. One or more fields can serve as the join fields. Records with values in the joined field that do not appear in both of the database tables will be excluded from the query dataset. For example, consider the spa and how the managers track sales of products to customers. By creating an inner join—a union or marriage of the data—the resulting dataset could include a customer and the products that customer has purchased. However, all products or all customers may not be included in the dataset because some products may not be included on an invoice—maybe the spa just started selling a new product and no one has purchased it yet, or some customers may not have purchased any products because they visit the spa or salon to receive services but not to purchase products.

Creating an Inner Join Query

You can use an inner join in a query to retrieve only the rows that satisfy the join conditions on the tables in the query workspace. In the simplest type of inner join, the join condition is field1 = field2.

A08.07

▶ To Create and Run Inner Join Queries

a. Switch to the **a04ws08Spa3_LastFirst** database.

b. Click the **CREATE** tab, and then in the Queries group, click **Query Design**.

c. Add **tblPurchase** and **tblCustomer** to the query workspace, and then **Close** ☒ the Show Table dialog box.

d. Double-click the **relationship line** between tblPurchase and tblCustomer to open the Join Properties dialog box.

   Notice the default selection—the CustomerID field—is set to only include rows where the joined fields from both tables are equal. This is an inner join. Click **OK** to close the Join Properties dialog box.

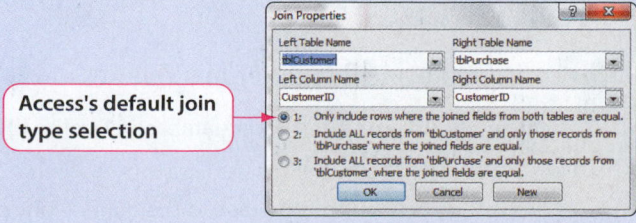

Access's default join type selection

Figure 9 Join Properties dialog box

e. Add the following fields to the query design grid: **CustomerID**, **CustFirstName**, and **CustLastName** from tblCustomer and **ProductID**, **PurchaseDate**, and **Quantity** from tblPurchase.

f. Click the **DESIGN** tab, and then in the Results group, click **Run**.

  Notice that there are 23 customers who have purchased products from the spa. However, if you open tblCustomer there are 46 records. Thus, the query only included the records from both tables that matched on the CustomerID field.

g. Save 💾 the query as qryInnerJoin1_initialLastname and then **Close** ⊠ the query.

h. Click the **CREATE** tab, and then in the Queries group, click **Query Design**.

i. Add **tblCampaign** to the query workspace. Click the **Queries** tab, and then add **qryInnerJoin1_initialLastname** to the query workspace. **Close** ⊠ the Show Table dialog box.

j. Create a relationship between the query and the table. Drag **CustomerID** in the qryInnerJoin1_initialLastname query to **CustomerID** in the tblCampaign table, and then double-click the **relationship line** to open the Join Properties dialog box. Notice that the default selection is set to only include rows where the joined fields from both tables are equal.

k. Click **OK** to close the Join Properties dialog box.

l. Add the following fields to the query design grid: **CustomerID**, **CustFirstName**, **CustLastName**, **ProductID**, **PurchaseDate**, and **Quantity** from qryInnerJoin1_initialLastname, and **CampaignName** and **Redeemed** from tblCampaign.

m. On the DESIGN tab, in the Results group, click **Run**.

  Notice that there are 143 records in the dataset and that some rows appear to be duplicated. Because the join property is set to inner join, Access is listing each purchase multiple times to coincide with each coupon the customers received. Thus, an inner join may not always be the best option for you to view data.

n. Save 💾 the query as qryInnerJoin2_initialLastname and then **Close** ⊠ the query.

Outer Joins

An **outer join** selects all of the records from one database table and only those records in the second table that have matching values in the joined field. One or more fields can serve as the join field. For example, consider again the spa and how the managers track sales of products to customers. An outer join query that includes these two tables could include all customers and only the products that have been purchased. Therefore, you could find out what products are the most popular.

Creating an Outer Join Query

Unlike an inner join, an outer join will give you data even if the common field that you select does not have a value that is the same in both tables.

A08.08

 To Create and Run Outer Join Queries

a. In the **a04ws08 Spa3_LastFirst** database, click the **CREATE** tab, and then in the Queries group, click **Query Design**.

b. Add **tblProduct** and **tblPurchase** to the query workspace, and then **Close** ⊠ the Show Table dialog box.

c. Double-click the **relationship line** between tblProduct and tblPurchase to open the Join Properties dialog box.

   The join is based on the relationship on the ProductID field. Notice that the default selection is set to only include rows where the joined fields from both tables are equal—an inner join.

d. To change this to an outer join, Select **Include ALL records from 'tblProduct' and only those records from 'tblPurchase' where the joined fields are equal**, and then click **OK**.

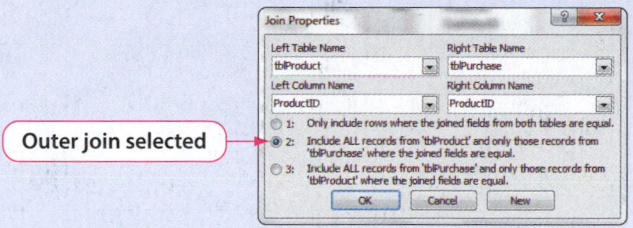

Figure 10 Join Properties dialog box with outer join

> **Troubleshooting**
>
> Be sure to read the options first before automatically selecting option 2. Access randomizes how the relationships are listed in the Join Properties dialog box. On your computer, option 3 may have the join property that you want.

e. Add the following fields to the query design grid: **ProductDescription** from tblProduct and **CustomerID** from tblPurchase.

f. Click the **DESIGN** tab, and then in the Results group, click **Run**.

   Notice that all records from tblProduct appear—even those products in which no customers have purchased. However, the customers who have not purchased any products, such as Buchanan, do not appear. Additionally, products purchased by more than one customer appear multiple times.

g. **Save** 💾 the query as qryOuterJoin1_initialLastname and then **Close** ✖ the query.

h. Click the **CREATE** tab, and then in the Queries group, click **Query Design**.

i. Add **tblProduct** and **tblPurchase** to the query workspace, and then **Close** ✖ the Show Table dialog box.

j. Double-click the **relationship line** between tblProduct and tblPurchase to open the Join Properties dialog box. Select **Include ALL records from 'tblProduct' and only those records from 'tblPurchase' where the joined fields are equal**, and then click **OK**.

k. Add the following fields to the query design grid: **ProductDescription** from tblProduct and **CustomerID** from tblPurchase.

l. Click the **DESIGN** tab, and then in the Show/Hide group, click **Totals**. In the Total row of the CustomerID field, click the **Total row** arrow, and then select **Count**.

m. In the design grid, in the field row of the CustomerID column, click to the left of the **CustomerID** field, type **TotalSold:** to rename the CustomerID field. **Save** 💾 the query as qryOuterJoin2_initialLastname.

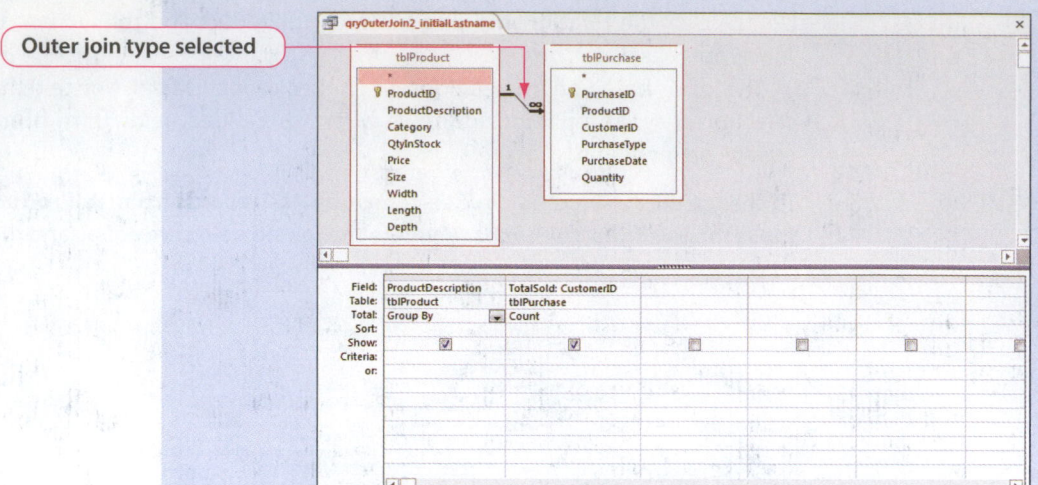

Outer join type selected

Figure 11 Design view of the qryOuterJoin2 query

n. On the DESIGN tab, in the Results group, click **Run**.

Notice there are 33 products returned by the query. This is the same as the number of the products in tblProduct. The TotalSold field reflects the number of purchase transactions for the product. Access automatically places a zero in the fields where there is no record of a customer purchasing this item.

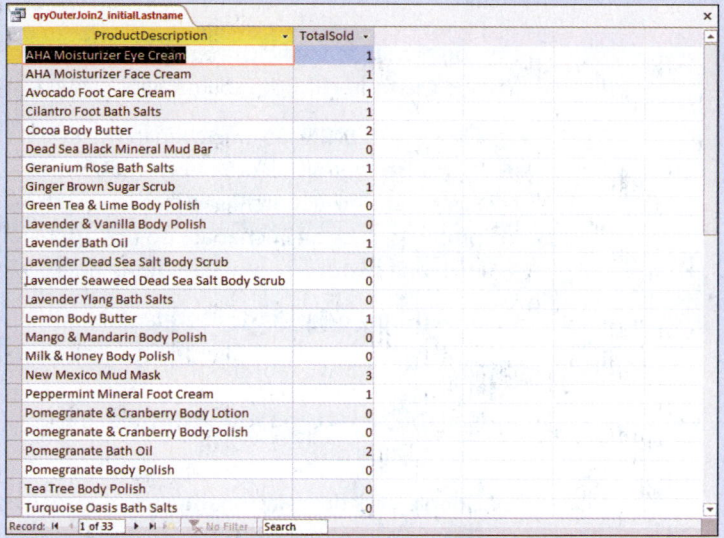

Figure 12 Datasheet view of the qryOuterJoin2 query

o. **Close** ☒ the query.

CONSIDER THIS | **Outer Joins Can Be Extremely Helpful in Managing Your Business**

What would you do if you created an outer join query on your Product and Invoice tables and discovered that you stock products that have never been purchased by a customer? Should you place the products on sale? Develop a better advertising or marketing plan? Discontinue the products?

Use the Find Unmatched Query Wizard

By creating a query using the Find Unmatched Query Wizard, you will be able to edit, analyze, and cleanse data. The **Find Unmatched Query Wizard** finds records in one table that do not have related records in another table. After the wizard constructs your query, you can modify the query's design to add or remove fields or to add a join between the two tables. You can also create your own query to find unmatched records without using the wizard, but at times it is easier to at least begin building such a query by using the wizard.

This type of query can be very helpful in business. What if the spa or salon had a walk-in client—a client who wants to have a service but did not schedule an appointment. The receptionist could find all employees who do not have an appointment scheduled for a specific time to determine who would be able to assist the walk-in client.

Additionally, you can use the Find Unmatched Query Wizard to cleanse data in a table. For example, perhaps the spa manager decided to discontinue a product or stop offering a specific service and probably will not need to use any of the transactional data in the future. The manager could find unmatched records between the Products and Purchases tables to ultimately delete the transactions in which the discontinued items reside. Thus, finding unmatched records may be the first of several steps that you want to take—you may want to then create a delete query to help you delete records that are no longer needed.

Creating a Find Unmatched Data Query

The easiest way to determine the records that are unmatched is by using the Find Unmatched Query Wizard. After the wizard builds your query, you can modify the query's design.

A08.09

▶ To Create Queries Using the Find Unmatched Query Wizard

a. Click the **CREATE** tab, and then in the Queries group, click **Query Wizard** to create a new query that will find which employees do not have any scheduled appointments with clients.

b. In the New Query Wizard dialog box, click **Find Unmatched Query Wizard**, and then click **OK**.

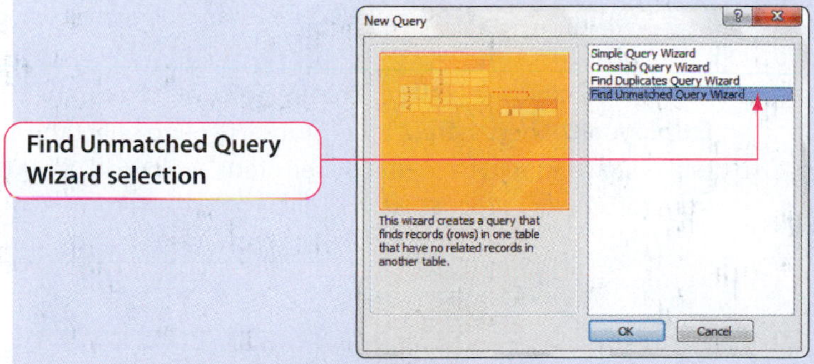

Find Unmatched Query Wizard selection

Figure 13   New Query Wizard dialog box

> **Troubleshooting**
> Access may display a Microsoft Access Security Notice dialog box, warning you that a potential security concern has been identified. The database you are using does not contain unsafe content. Thus, it is safe to click Open.

c. Select **Table: tblEmployee** to select the table that contains the records you want in your query results, and then click **Next**.

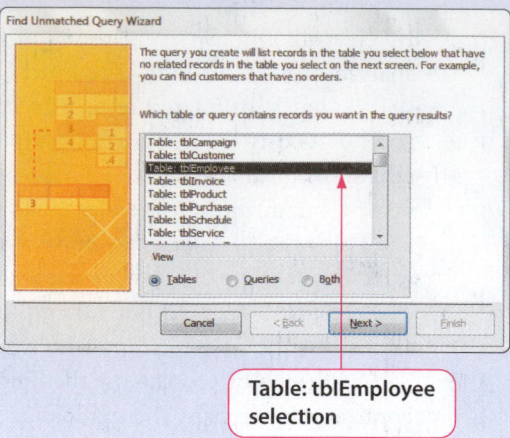

Table: tblEmployee selection

Figure 14 Select tables and/or queries to display in the query

d. Select **Table: tblSchedule** to select the table that contains the related records, and then click **Next**.

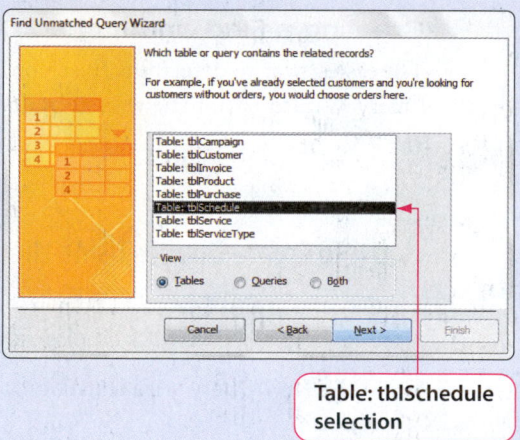

Table: tblSchedule selection

Figure 15 Select tables and/or queries that contain the related records

e. Under tblEmployee select **EmployeeID** if necessary. Under tblSchedule select **EmployeeID** if necessary. Access prompts you to select the common field that is in both tables, and it should have already selected EmployeeID from tblEmployee and Employee from tblSchedule. Click **Next**.

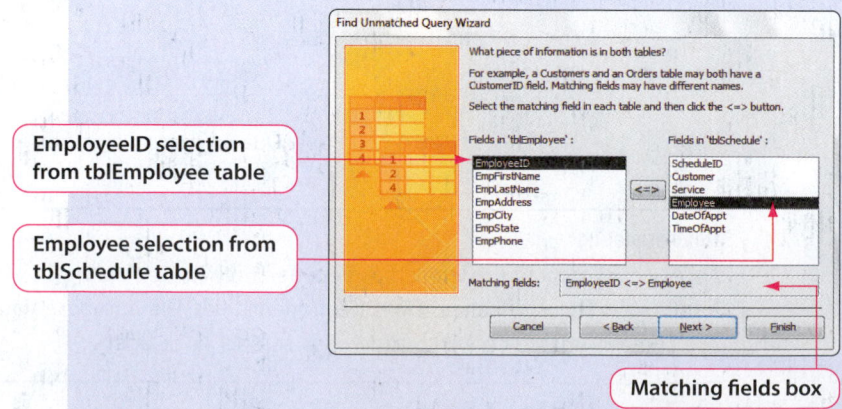

EmployeeID selection from tblEmployee table

Employee selection from tblSchedule table

Matching fields box

Figure 16 Determine the related field between the selected tables

> **Troubleshooting**
> If Access did not automatically select the related fields, click EmployeeID under Fields in 'tblEmployee', click Employee under Fields in 'tblSchedule', and then click the <=> button.

f. In the Find Unmatched query wizard under available fields, click **EmpFirstName**, and then click the **One Field** button `>`. Under available fields select **EmpLastName**, and then click the **One Field** button `>`. Click **Next**.

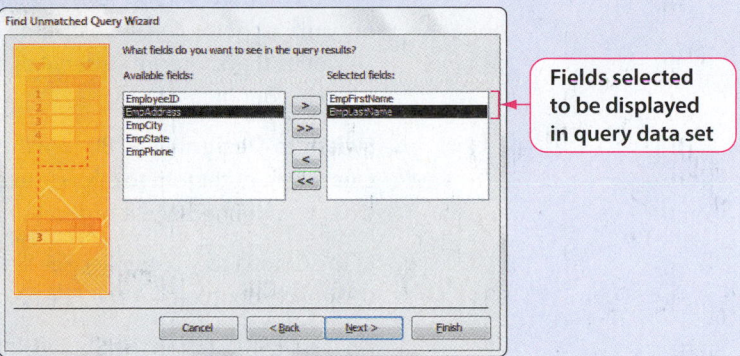

Figure 17   Unmatched fields field selection

g. In the What would you like to name your query? box, replace the existing text with qryUnmatched1_initialLastname and then click **Finish**. Notice that there are two employees that do not have any appointments scheduled at this time.

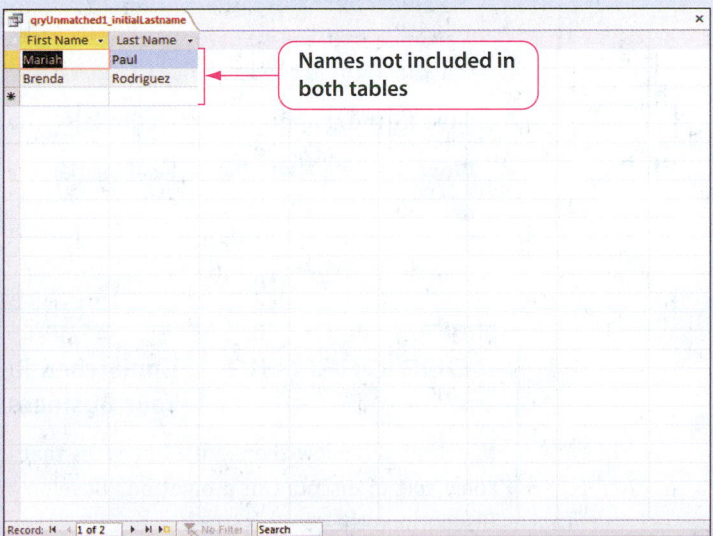

Figure 18   Datasheet view of the qryUnmatched1 query

h. **Close** ⊠ the query.

i. Click the **CREATE** tab, and then in the Queries group, click **Query Wizard** to create a new query that will find which services have not been given to any clients.

j. In the New Query dialog box, click **Find Unmatched Query Wizard**, and then click **OK**.

k. Select **Table: tblService** to select the table that contains the records you want in your query results, and then click **Next**.

l. Select **Table: tblSchedule** to select the table that contains the related records, and then click **Next**.

m. Under tblService, select **ServiceID** if necessary. Under tblSchedule, select **Service** if necessary. Access prompts you to select the piece of information that is in both tables, and it should have already selected ServiceID from tblService and Service from tblSchedule. Click **Next**.

n. In the Find Unmatched Query Wizard, under available fields, click **ServiceName**, and then click the **One Field** button ⟩. Under available fields, select **Description**, and then click the **One Field** button ⟩. Click **Next**.

o. In the What would you like to name your query? box, replace the existing text with **qryUnmatched2_initialLastname** and then click **Finish**.

   Notice that there are six services, four with descriptions and two without descriptions, listed in your dataset.

p. Switch to **Design** view. By looking at the relationship line, you can see that Access created an outer join to allow you to view the results you were interested in seeing—what you defined while progressing through the wizard.

q. In the Criteria row of the Service field, click after **Is**, press ⌷Space⌷, and then type Not. In tblService, double-click the **Fee** field to add it to the query design grid.

r. On the DESIGN tab, in the Show/Hide group, click **Totals**. In the Total row of the Fee field, select **Sum**. In the design grid, in the field row in the Fee column, click to the left of the **Fee** field, and then type GrossRevenue: to rename the Fee field.

s. On the DESIGN tab, in the Results group, click **Run**. Resize the fields to see all the data if necessary.

t. Click the **HOME** tab, and then in the Records group, click **Totals**. In the Total row, click the **arrow** for the GrossRevenue field, and then select **Sum**.

   Notice that the spa would generate additional gross revenue of $5,339 if the spa scheduled these services once in a given day, week, or month.

u. **Save** 🖫 the changes, and then **Close** ☒ the query.

v. **Close** ☒ the a04ws08Spa3_LastFirst database.

CONSIDER THIS | **Unmatched Records Can Help You Manage Your Business**

Now that you know there are 24 services that clients never requested, should you offer some sort of discount or promotion? Develop a better advertising or marketing plan? Discontinue the services?

Concept Check

1. Compare and contrast the four types of action queries. p. 418

2. Give a business example of how you could use each of the four action queries. p. 418

3. What is the difference between a simple action query and a complex action query? p. 427

4. Explain the difference between an inner join and outer join. Why is it important to understand joins when trying to retrieve data for decision making? p. 435

5. How can using the Find Unmatched Query Wizard help you manage your data? p. 439

Key Terms

Action query   418
Append query   423
Business intelligence (BI)   420
Business intelligence tools   420
Complex delete query   432
Complex update query   427
Data cleansing   432
Data mining   420

Data warehouse   420
Data warehousing   420
Delete query   424
Find Unmatched Query Wizard   439
Forecasting   419
Inner join   435
Make table query   419
Operational database   419

Outer join   436
Query join   435
Simple delete query   430
Simple update query   425
Suggestive sell   420
Transactional database   420
Truncated   427
Update query   424

Visual Summary

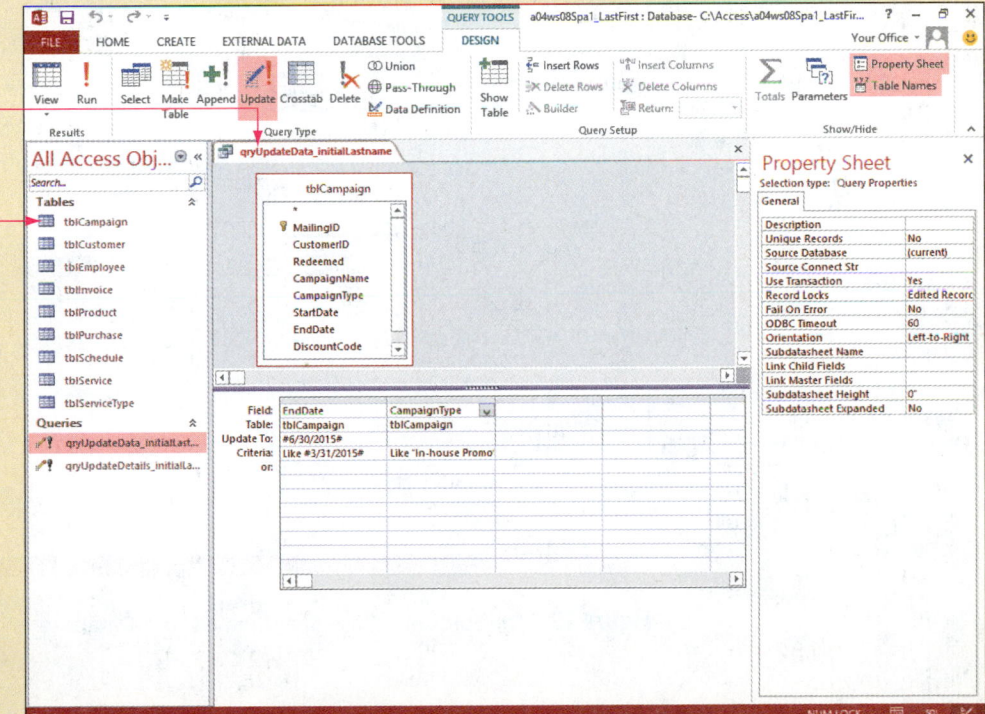

Create and run a simple update query (p. 425)

Work with update queries (p. 425)

Create and run a make table query (p. 421)

Create a new table using a make table query (p. 418)

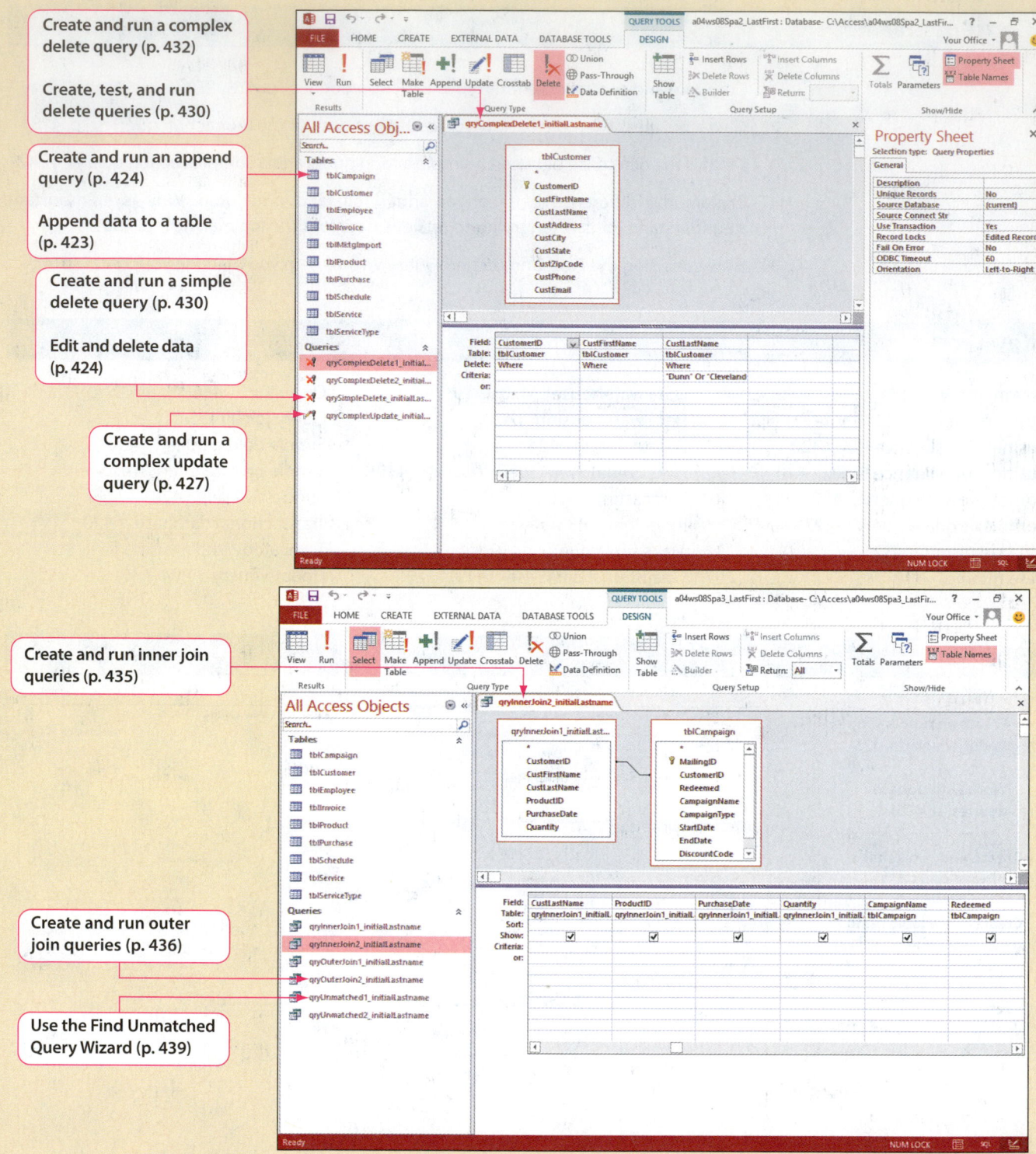

Figure 19 The Turquoise Oasis Spa Updated Final Database

Student data files needed:

 a04ws08Spa4.accdb

 a04ws08HR1.accdb

You will save your files as:

 a04ws08Spa4_LastFirst.accdb

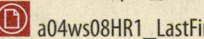 a04ws08HR1_LastFirst.accdb

Managing Employee Training at the Turquoise Oasis Spa

Human Resources

The human resources department at the Painted Paradise Resort and Spa uses Access to track employees' progress such as training efforts and performance evaluations. The spa and salon managers want to keep track of training too, so they can ensure employees are all receiving the training necessary to continue offering clients the best services possible. You have been asked to use action queries to work with data from the human resources database. This way, the salon and spa managers can ensure that employees are being trained and managed both efficiently and effectively. The human resources department has given you a copy of its database to use.

a. Start **Access**. Open the **a04ws08Spa4** database, and then save the database as a04ws08Spa4_LastFirst using your last and first name. Click **Enable Content** in the security warning if necessary. Open **tblEmployee**, add your information in record **1** using your first and last name, and then close tblEmployee.

b. Open the **a04ws08HR1** database, and then save the database as a04ws08HR1_LastFirst using your last and first name. Click **Enable Content** in the security warning if necessary. Open **tblEmployee**, add your information in record **1** using your first and last name and e-mail address, and then close tblEmployee.

c. In the a04ws08HR1_LastFirst database, click the **CREATE** tab, and then in the Queries group, click **Query Design**. Add **tblEmpTrainProg** and **tblTrainingProgram** to the query workspace, and then close the Show Table dialog box.

d. Add the following fields to the design grid: **ProgramID** and **EmployeeID** from tblEmpTrainProg, and **ProgramName**, **ProgramDate**, **ProgramTime**, and **DepartmentID** from tblTrainingProgram.

e. In the Criteria row of the DepartmentID field type Like "Turquoise Oasis*", and then clear the **Show** check box in the DepartmentID field. On the DESIGN tab, in the Results group, click **Run**. You should have seven records that display in your dataset.

f. Switch to **Design** view. On the DESIGN tab, in the Query Type group, click **Make Table**. Name your table tblEmpTrainProg. Click **Another Database**, navigate to where you are saving your student data files, and then click **a04ws08Spa4_LastFirst**. Click **OK** twice.

g. On the DESIGN tab, in the Results group, click **Run**. Click **Yes** to confirm that you want to paste the records into a new table. Save the query as qryMakeTable1_initialLastname using your first initial and last name and then close the query.

h. In the a04ws08HR1_LastFirst database, click the **CREATE** tab, and then in the Queries group, click **Query Design** to create a table. Add **tblEmployee** and **tblEmpDept** to the query workspace, and then close the Show Table dialog box.

i. Add the following fields to the query design: **all fields** from tblEmployee, and **Department** from tblEmpDept.

j. In the Criteria row of the Department field, type Like "Turquoise Oasis*" and then clear the **Show** check box in the Department field. On the DESIGN tab, in the Query Type group, click **Make Table**. Name your table tblEmployee, click **Another Database**, and then navigate to where you are saving your student data files. Click **a04ws08Spa4_LastFirst**, and then click **OK** twice.

Because the structure of tblEmployee has changed—the addition of an e-mail address field—since it was last created in the a04ws08HR1_LastName database, you need to recreate the tblEmployee table.

k. Switch to **Datasheet** view. You should have 22 records displayed in your dataset.

Switch to **Design** view. Click the **DESIGN** tab, and then in the Results group, click **Run**. Access will display a warning that the existing table 'tblEmployee' will be deleted before you run the query. Click **Yes** to confirm. Click **Yes** to confirm that you want to paste 22 records into a new table. Save the query as **qryMakeTable2_initialLastname** and then close the query.

l. Close the a04ws08HR1_LastFirst database, and then switch to the **a04ws08Spa4_LastFirst** database, if necessary.

m. When Access creates a table using an action query, only the basic structure is established. You need to modify the table. Open **tblEmployee** in **Design** view, and then make the following changes to the field properties and descriptions.

Field	Field Properties	Description
EmployeeID	Change this field to the primary key Change the format to **"EMP"0**	The Employee ID (primary key)
FirstName	Change the caption to **First Name**	The employee first name
LastName	Change the caption to **Last Name**	The employee last name
Address		The employee address
City	Change the default value to **Santa Fe**	The employee city
State	Format as all uppercase letters Change the default value to **NM**	The employee state
Phone	Change the input mask to the Phone Number format	The employee phone number
EmailAddy	Format as all lowercase letters Change the caption to **E-mail Address**	The employee e-mail address
JobTitle	Change the caption to **Job Title**	The employee job title

n. Save your changes, and then close tblEmployee.

o. You need to modify the basic table structure that Access created when you ran the make table query. Open **tblEmpTrainProg** in **Design** view, and then make the following changes to the field properties and descriptions.

Field	Field Properties	Description
Create a new AutoNumber field named **EmpTrainProgID**	Change this field to the primary key Change the format to **"ETP"0**	The Employee Training Program ID (primary key)
ProgramID	Change the caption to **Program ID**	The program ID (foreign key)
EmployeeID	Change the caption to **Employee** Change the data type to look up the employee ID in tblEmployee. Be sure to enforce referential integrity and restrict delete.	The employee ID (foreign key)
ProgramName	Change the caption to **Program Name**	The program name
ProgramDate	Change the caption to **Date**	The program date
ProgramTime	Change the caption to **Time**	The program time

p. Save your changes, and then close tblEmpTrainProg.

q. Click the **DATABASE TOOLS** tab, and then in the Relationships group, click **Relationships**. Create a relationship between **EmployeeID** in tblEmployee and **Employee** in tblSchedule. Click **Enforce Referential Integrity**, and then close the Relationships window.

r. Click the **CREATE** tab, and then in the Queries group, click **Query Design**. Add **tblEmployee** to the query workspace, close the Show Table dialog box, and then add the **EmailAddy** field to the query design grid.

s. Click the **DESIGN** tab, and then in the Query Type group, click **Update**. Because EmailAddy is a new field, you need to update the table to enter all employee e-mail addresses to the EmailAddy field. The format of employee e-mail addresses is initialLastname@paintedparadise.com. In the Update To row in the EmailAddy field type Left([FirstName],1)&[LastName]&"@paintedparadise.com".

t. On the DESIGN tab, in the Results group, click **Run**. Click **Yes** to update 22 rows. Save your query as qryUpdateEmail_initialLastname and then close the query.

u. Open **tblEmployee**. Notice that all e-mail addresses have been added to the EmailAddy field and that the e-mail address you entered has been replaced. Close tblEmployee.

v. Click the **CREATE** tab, and then in the Queries group, click **Query Design**. Add **tblEmployee** and **tblEmpTrainProg** to the query workspace, close the Show Table dialog box, and then add the following fields to the query design grid: **FirstName** and **LastName** from tblEmployee and **ProgramName**, **ProgramDate**, and **ProgramTime** from tblEmpTrainProg.

w. To change the relationship to an outer join, double-click the join line to edit the Join Properties. Select **Include ALL records from 'tblEmployee' and only those records from 'tblEmpTrainProg' where the joined fields are equal**, and then click **OK**. On the DESIGN tab, in the Results group, click **Run**. Save the query as qryOuterJoin_initialLastname and then close the query.

x. Close the database, and then exit Access.

y. Submit the files as directed by your instructor.

Problem Solve 1

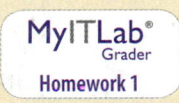

Student data files needed:

04ws08MusicStore.accdb

a04ws08Transactions.accdb

You will save your file as:

a04ws08MusicStore_LastFirst.accdb

Sales &
Marketing

Managing Inventory and Sales at Marshall's Music Store

Marshall's Music Store, located in the trendy area of town, carries many different genres of music. The store has a loyal customer base, which is why they are one of the few successful music stores still in existence today. You have been asked to use queries to manipulate data from both the music store and transaction databases. This way, the owner can ensure that there is enough inventory in stock. He has given you a scaled-down copy of the database to use. Once you create the queries, he will import them into the original database.

a. Open the **a04ws08MusicStore** database. Save it as a04ws08MusicStore_LastFirst. Enable the content if necessary. Open **tblCustomer**, and then add your information in record **1** using your first and last name. Close tblCustomer.

b. Create an outer join query based on tblAlbum and tblPurchaseDetails that displays the **ArtistID**, **AlbumName**, and a field named SalesVolume that calculates the total quantity of all albums sold. Be sure the query lists all albums regardless of whether any have been sold. Save the query as qryAlbumSalesVolume_initialLastname. Close the query.

c. Create a query based on tblEmployee and tblPurchase using the Find Unmatched Query Wizard that lists the **EmployeeID**, **FirstName**, and **LastName** of any employee who has not yet made a sale. Save the query as qryEmployeeNoSales_initialLastname and then close the query.

d. Create a query based on tblCustomer and tblPurchase using the Find Unmatched Query Wizard that lists the **CustomerID**, **FirstName**, **LastName**, **StreetAddress**, **City**, **State**, and **ZipCode** for any customer not living in New Mexico who has never made a purchase. Save the query as qryCustomerNoSales_initialLastname and then close the query.

e. Open the **a04ws08Transactions** database. Enable the content if necessary. Create an append query that appends the data from the **tblPurchase** table in the a04ws08Transactions database to the **tblPurchase** table in the a04ws08MusicStore database. Run the query, and then close it without saving it.

f. Create an append query that appends the data from the **tblPurchaseDetails** table in the a04ws08Transactions database to the **tblPurchaseDetails** table in the a04ws08MusicStore database. Run the query, and then close it without saving it. Close the a04ws08Transactions database.

g. Because the manager just ordered three copies of each album, create an update query to update the number of albums in stock in the tblAlbum table. Save the query as qryUpdateInventory_initialLastname and then close the query.

h. Since Amanda Johnson no longer works at the music store, create a delete query that deletes all transactions entered by employee number 78528 from the tblPurchase table. Update any relationships to the tblPurchase table as needed. Save the query as qryDeleteEmployee_initialLastname and then close the query.

i. Since Jeff Fox moved and is no longer a customer, create a delete query that deletes him from the tblCustomer table and all related tables. Update any relationships to the tblCustomer table as needed. Save the query as qryDeleteCustomer_initialLastname and then close the query.

j. Create an update query to update the selling price of albums in the tblAlbum table. For all albums that currently sell for less than $10, update the selling price to $10.95. Save the query as qryUpdatePrice_initialLastname and then close the query.

k. Close the database, and then exit Access.

l. Submit the file as directed by your instructor.

Perform 1: Perform in Your Career

Student data files needed:

a04ws08Vehicle.accdb

a04ws08CarUpdate.accdb

You will save your file as:

a04ws08Vehicle_LastFirst.accdb

Managing the Vehicle Fleet at Pippy's Pizza

Accounting &
Finance

You are living the entrepreneurial dream of owning your own business and open a pizza shop close to local colleges, businesses, and residential areas. Delivery business contributes to nearly 80 percent of your revenue. Since most of your employees are college students, they do not have cars on campus. Thus, you decided to lease vehicles that can be used for your deliveries. You have created a database that will help you manage the fleet. You want to create some queries that will help you maintain the data within the database. For example, when you purchase a vehicle, the dealership gives the new vehicle's information in a database.

You want to be able to append that data to your vehicle database. Additionally, once a lease has ended and you turn the car back into the dealership, you will need to delete the vehicle and that vehicle's maintenance records.

a. Open the **a04ws08Vehicle** database. Save it as **a04ws08Vehicle_LastFirst**. Open **tblDealer**, and then add your information in record **3**.

b. Create and run the following append queries.
   - Append the data from the tblVehicle table in the a04ws08CarUpdate database to the tblVehicle table in the a04ws08Vehicle_LastFirst database. Close the query without saving it.
   - Append the data from the tblFeatures table in the a04ws08CarUpdate database to the tblFeatures table in the a04ws08Vehicle_LastFirst database. Close the query without saving it.

c. Create, run, and save two update queries.

d. Create, run, and save two delete queries.

e. Create, run, and save two outer join queries.

f. Create, run, and save two inner join queries.

g. Using the Find Unmatched Query wizard, create an unmatched data query. Run and save the query.

h. Submit the file as directed by your instructor.

Additional Cases

Additional Workshop Cases are available on the companion website and in the instructor resources.

MODULE CAPSTONE

More Practice 1

Student data files needed:

 a04mpMenu.accdb

 a04mpArchiveMenu.accdb

You will save your files as:

 a04mpMenu_LastFirst.accdb

a04mpArchiveMenu_LastFirst.accdb

Updating the Indigo5 Menu Items Database

Production & Operations

The Painted Paradise Golf Resort and Spa is home to a world-class restaurant with a top chef, Robin Sanchez. Robin is regularly updating data in her database to make certain she has all the ingredients and recipes needed to offer the high-quality food for which the restaurant is known. You have been asked to manage and cleanse the data in the Indigo5 menu items databases.

a. Start **Access**, and then open **a04mpMenu**. Click the **FILE** tab, and then save the file as an Access database with the name a04mpMenu_LastFirst using your last and first name. Click **Enable Content** if necessary. Open **tblRecipes**, and then add your information in record **1**. Replace YourName in the Recipe Name field with your first and last name. Close tblRecipes.

b. Open the **a04mpArchiveMenu** database, and then save it as a04mpArchiveMenu_LastFirst using your last and first name. Click **Enable Content** if necessary. Open **tblReviews**, and then add your information in record **1**. Replace YourName in the Reviewer field with your first and last name. Close tblReviews.

c. Create the following queries in the a04mpMenu_LastFirst database.

- Click the **CREATE** tab, and then in the Queries group, click **Query Design**. Create an outer join query that lists all records from tblFoodCategories and only those records from tblRecipes where the joined fields are equal. Add **tblFoodCategories** and **tblRecipes** to the query workspace, and then close the Show Table dialog box. Add the following fields to the design grid: **FoodCategory** and **RecipeName**. To change the relationship to an outer join, double-click the join line to edit the Join Properties. Select **Include ALL records from 'tblFoodCategories' and only those records from 'tblRecipes' where the joined fields are equal**, and then click **OK**. On the DESIGN tab, in the Results group, click **Run**. Save your query as qryRecipeCats_initialLastname using your first initial and last name. Close the query.

- Click the **CREATE** tab, and then in the Queries group, click **Query Design**. Create an inner join query that lists all records from tblIngredients and tblRecipes where joined fields are equal. Add **tblIngredients**, **tblRecipeIngredients**, and **tblRecipes** to the query workspace, and then close the Show Table dialog box. Add the following fields to the design grid: **RecipeName** from tblRecipes and **Ingredient** from tblIngredients. On the DESIGN tab, in the Results group, click **Run**. Save your query as qryRecipeIngredients_initialLastname using your first initial and last name. Close the query.

- Click the **CREATE** tab, and then in the Queries group, click **Query Wizard** to create a Find Unmatched data query. In the New Query dialog box, click **Find Unmatched Query Wizard**, and then click **OK**. The query should find all ingredients in tblIngredients that are not listed in tblRecipeIngredients. Under Which table or query contains records you want in the query results? select **tblIngredients**, and then click **Next**. Under Which table or query contains the related records? select **Table: tblRecipeIngredients**, and then click **Next**. Verify that **IngredientID** is selected as the matching field, click <=>, and then click **Next**. Under What fields do you want to see in the query results? select **IngredientID** if necessary, and then click the **One Field** button. Select **Ingredient**, click the **One Field** button, and then click **Next**. Under What would you like to name your query? replace the existing text with qryUnusedIngredients_initialLastname using your first initial and last name. Click **Finish**, and then close the query.

d. Create the following action queries.

- Click the **CREATE** tab, and then in the Queries group, click **Query Design** to create an update query that will update each menu item's price. Add **tblMenu** to the query workspace, and then close the Show Table dialog box. Add the **Price** field to the design grid. On the DESIGN tab, in the Query Type group, click **Update**. Because the restaurant has been awarded a Michelin star—a hallmark of fine dining quality—the chef can justify charging more money for his dishes. In the Update To row of the Price field, type [Price]+5. On the DESIGN tab, in the Results group, click **Run**. In the Microsoft Access dialog box, click **Yes**. Save your query as qryPriceUpdate_initialLastname using your first initial and last name. Close the query.

- Switch to the **a04mpArchiveMenu_LastFirst** database. Click the **CREATE** tab, and then in the Queries group, click **Query Design** to create an append query that will add data from the tblRecipesOld table in a04mpArchiveMenu_LastFirst to tblRecipes in a04mpMenu_LastFirst. Add **tblRecipesOld** to the query workspace, and then close the Show Table dialog box. Add the following fields to the design grid: **RecipeName**, **FoodCategoryID**, **TimeToPrepare**, **Servings**, and **Instructions**. On the DESIGN tab, in the Query Type group, click **Append**. The Append dialog box opens. In the Table Name box, type tblRecipes, select **Another Database**, and then click **Browse**. Navigate to where you are storing your student files, select **a04mpMenu_LastFirst**, and then click **OK** two times. On the DESIGN tab, in the Results group, click **Run**. In the Microsoft Access dialog box, click **Yes**. Save your query as qryRecipes_initialLastname using your first initial and last name. Close the query.

- In the a04mpArchiveMenu_LastFirst database, click the **CREATE** tab, and then in the Queries group, click **Query Design** to create a make table query that copies all records and fields from tblReviews in the a04mpArchiveMenu_LastFirst database into the a04mpMenu_LastFirst database. Add **tblReviews** to the query workspace, and then close the Show Table dialog box. Add the following fields to the design grid: **ReviewID**, **Reviewer**, **ReviewDate**, **Stars**, and **RecipeID**. On the DESIGN tab, in the Query Type group, click **Make Table**. The Make Table dialog box opens. In the Table Name box, type tblRecipes, select **Another Database**, and then click **Browse**. Navigate to where you are storing your student files, select **a04mpMenu_LastFirst**, and then click **OK** two times. On the DESIGN tab, in the Results group, click **Run**. Access will display a warning that the existing table 'tblRecipes' will be deleted before you run the query. Click **Yes** to confirm. In the Microsoft Access dialog box, click **Yes**. Save your query as qryReviewsTable_initialLastname using your first initial and last name. Close the query.

e. Switch to the **a04mpMenu_LastFirst** database, and then make the following changes to the tblReviews field properties, data types, and relationships so you can create your final queries. Right-click **tblReviews**, and then select **Design View**. Make the following changes to the structure of the table.

Field Name	Field Properties
ReviewID	In Format, type "R0"0
Reviewer	In Field Size, delete 50, and then type 35
ReviewDate	In Caption, type Date

(Continued)

Field Name	Field Properties
Stars	In Decimal Places, select **2**
RecipeID	In Caption, type **Recipe**

f. Save your changes and then close the tblReviews table.

g. Click the **DATABASE TOOLS** tab. In the Relationships group, click **Relationships**, and then click **Show Table**. Select **tblReviews**, click **Add**, and then click **Close**. Create a **relationship** between tblRecipes and tblReviews. Drag **RecipeID** in tblRecipes to **RecipeID** in tblReviews. Enforce referential integrity. Select **Cascade Delete Related Records**, and then click **OK**. Double-click the **relationship line** between tblRecipes and tblRecipeIngredients. Select **Cascade Delete Related Records**, and then click **OK**. Double-click the **relationship line** between tblRecipes and tblMenu. Select **Cascade Delete Related Records**, and then click **OK**. Double-click the **relationship line** between tblRecipes and tblFoodCategories. Select **Cascade Delete Related Records**, and then click **OK**. Click **Save**, and then in the Relationships group, click **Close**.

h. Click the **CREATE** tab, and then in the Queries group, click **Query Design** to create a delete query that deletes all pizza recipes from tblRecipes and all items from the related tables. Add **tblRecipes** to the query workspace, and then close the Show Table dialog box. Add the **RecipeName** field to the design grid. In the Criteria row of the RecipeName field, type **Like "*pizza*"**. On the DESIGN tab, in the Results group, click **Run**. In the Microsoft Access dialog box, click **Yes**. Save your query as **qryPizza_initialLastname** using your first initial and last name. Close the query.

i. Click the **CREATE** tab, and then in the Queries group, click **Query Wizard** to create a Find Unmatched data query. In the New Query dialog box, click **Find Unmatched Query Wizard**, and then click **OK**. The query should find all ingredients in tblRecipes that are not listed in tblReviews. Under Which table or query contains records you want in the query results? select **tblRecipes**, and then click **Next**. Under Which table or query contains the related records? select **Table: tblReviews**, and then click **Next**. Verify that **RecipeID** is selected as the matching field, click the **<=>** button, and then click **Next**. Under What fields do you want to see in the query results? select **RecipeID** if necessary, and then click the **One Field** button. Select **RecipeName**, click the **One Field** button, and then click **Next**. Under What would you like to name your query? replace the existing text with **qryNoReviews_initialLastname** using your first initial and last name. Click **Finish**, and then close the query.

j. Close the databases, and then exit Access.

k. Submit the files as directed by your instructor.

Problem Solve 1

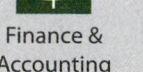
Finance & Accounting

Production & Operations

Student data file needed:	**You will save your file as:**
a04ps1Hotel.accdb	a04ps1Hotel_LastFirst.accdb

Querying and Maintaining the Hotel Database

The hotel area uses an Access database to track all aspects of a reservation including the types of packages, room rates, discounts, and charges to each room. The database is used to analyze revenue and reservations. Additionally, there are times that the database needs to be updated and cleansed to ensure that all data stored within is current and accurate. You have been asked to create useful information through the use of queries and update information through the use of action queries.

a. Open the student data file **a04ps1Hotel**. Save the file with the name a04ps1Hotel_LastFirst using your last and first name. If necessary, enable the content.

b. Open **tblGuests**, and then in record **25**, replace YourName in the Last Name and First Name fields with your last and first name. Close tblGuests.

c. Create a query that lists all discount types from tblReservations and counts how many times each discount type has been redeemed—do not include guests who are not redeeming a discount. The query should include **DiscountType** and **CountOfDiscountType** where CountOfDiscountType is an aggregated field. Rename the CountOfDiscountType field Total Discount. Save the query as qryTotalDiscount_initialLastname. Run the query. In Datasheet view, add a **total** row at the bottom of the data set that totals the number of guests redeeming discounts. Close the query.

d. Create a query that calculates the gross revenue before room charges are added or discounts are subtracted. The query should include a calculated field named GrossRevenue that multiplies **RoomRate** and **NightsStay**. Be sure not to include any reservations for a package as these rates are not for each night's stay. Do not show the Package field in your query results. Save your query as qryRoomRevenue_initialLastname. Run the query, and then close the query.

e. Create a query that calculates the revenue for each customer before room charges are added or discounts are subtracted. The query should include a calculated field named Revenue that multiplies **RoomRate** and **NightsStay**. Be sure not to include any reservations for a package as these rates are not for each night's stay. Do not show the Package field in your query results. Save your query as qryGuestRevenue_initialLastname. Run the query, and then close the query.

f. Create an outer join query that lists all records from tblReservations and tblPackages. Your query should include **ReservationID**, **RoomType**, and **RoomRate** from tblReservations and **Package** from tblPackages. Save your query as qryRoomRatesPkgs_initialLastname. Run the query, and then close the query.

g. Create a query that calculates how each customer contributed to the hotel's gross revenue. Include **GuestID** and **Revenue** from qryGuestRevenue_initialLastname. Type the expression PercentToRevenue:[Revenue]/[GrossRevenue] and then format the PercentToRevenue field as **Percentage** with **1** decimal point. *Hint:* Do not forget to add qryRoomRevenue_initialLastname to your design grid so you can use the GrossRevenue field in your expression. Save your query as qryGuestRevenueAnalysis_initialLastname. Run the query. Sum your **Revenue** and **PercentToRevenue** fields in Datasheet view. Close the query.

h. Create an update query that updates tblRoomCharges for customers who have checked out and paid their bill. This query will update the **ChargeAmount** field to **0** for customers with the last name of **Wenner** and **Woodward**. *Hint:* You will need the GuestID for each guest. Save your query as qryUpdateAmountCharged_initialLastname. Run the query, and then close the query.

i. Create an update query that updates prices in tblPackages. This query will update the **Price** field and increase each package price by $150. Save your query as qryUpdatePrices_initialLastname. Run the query, and then close the query.

j. Create a delete query that will delete all reservations in tblReservations for the year **2014**. *Hint:* You will also need to delete related records. Save your query as qryDelete2014_initialLastname. Run the query, and then close the query.

k. Create a crosstab query that uses the **RoomType** field from tblReservations as the row heading and the **CheckInDate** field from tblReservations as the column heading. Use **Month** as the interval, and then total the **NumberOfGuests** field. Save your query as qryTotalGuestsByMonth_initialLastname. In Datasheet view, add totals at the bottom of your crosstab query, and then sum all fields in your data set. In Design view, rename the **Total Of NumberOfGuests** field Total Guests. Save your changes, and then run the query. Close the query.

l. Use the **Find Unmatched Query Wizard** to find all the guests that did not incur any room charges. Include the **FirstName** and **LastName** fields from the tblGuests table, and then use **tblRoomCharges** as the table that contains related records. Save your query as qryNoCharges_initialLastname. Run the query, and then close the query.

m. Create an **outer join query** that lists all records from tblGuests and tblRoomCharges. Your query should include **FirstName** and **LastName** from tblGuests and **ChargeCategory** and **ChargeAmount** from tblRoomCharges. Save your query as qryGuestRoomChrg_initialLastname. Run the query, and then close the query.

n. Close the database, and then exit Access.

o. Submit the file as directed by your instructor.

Problem Solve 2

Student data file needed:

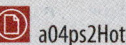 a04ps2Hotel.accdb

You will save your file as:

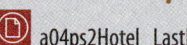 a04ps2Hotel_LastFirst.accdb

Production & Operations

Using SQL to Query the Hotel Database

The main portion of the resort is the hotel. The hotel offers accommodations ranging from individual rooms to a grand villa suite. The hotel area must track all aspects of a reservation including special requests for items such as a crib. The hotel also has to track room charges that guests have made. You have been asked to create useful information through the use of SQL queries.

a. Open the student data file **a04ps2Hotel**. Save the file with the name a04ps2Hotel_LastFirst using your last and first name. If necessary, enable the content.

b. Open **tblGuests**, and then in record **25**, replace YourName in the Last Name and First Name fields with your last and first name. Close tblGuests.

c. Create a SQL query that lists all fields from tblReservations where the number of guests is >=4. Save your query as qrySQLGreaterThan4_initialLastname. Run the query, and then close the query.

d. Create a SQL query that lists all discount types from tblReservations and counts how many times each discount type has been redeemed. The query should include **DiscountType** and **CountOfDiscountType**. *Hint:* CountOfDiscountType is an aggregated field. Rename your CountOfDiscountType field Total Discounts. Save your query as qrySQLTotalDiscount_initialLastname. Run the query, and then close the query.

e. Create a SQL query that calculates the gross revenue before discounts are subtracted on all double rooms. The query should include a calculated field named GrossRevenue that multiplies **RoomRate** and **NightsStay**. Be sure not to include any reservations for a package as these rates are not for each night's stay. Do not show the Package field in your query results. Save your query as qrySQLRoomRevenue_initialLastname. Run the query, and then close the query.

f. Create a SQL query that calculates the revenue for each customer before additional charges, such as room service charges, are added. The query should include **GuestID** from tblReservations and a calculated field named Revenue that multiplies **RoomRate** and **NightsStay**. Be sure not to include any reservations for a package as these rates are not for each night's stay. Do not show the Package field in your query results. Save your query as qrySQLGuestRevenue_initialLastname. Run the query, and then close the query.

g. Create a **union query** that lists the guests' and employees' names, addresses, cities, states, and phone numbers. Sort in **Ascending** order by **GuestFirstName**, **GuestLastName**. Rename **GuestLastName** to LastName and then rename **GuestFirstName** to FirstName. Save your query as qrySQLContactInfo_initialLastname. Run the query, and then close the query.

h. Create a SQL query that lists **GuestID** and **Revenue** from qrySQLGuestRevenue_initialLastname. Use the Between...And operator to view the guests who will be paying between $1500 and $3000. Save your query as qrySQLRevenueBetween_initialLastname. Run the query, and then close the query.

i. Create a SQL subquery that lists all reservations where the guests need a crib. The query should include **GuestID**, **CheckInDate**, **NightsStay**, **RoomRate**, and **Crib** from tblReservations. Save your query as qrySQLSubquery_initialLastname. Run the query, and then close the query.

j. Create a SQL inner join query that lists **EmpFirstName** from tblEmployees and **GuestID**, **CheckInDate**, and **NumberOfGuests** from tblReservations where the employee's first name is **Isabella**. Create an inner join on **EmployeeID**. Save your query as qrySQLInnerJoin_initialLastname. Run the query, and then close the query.

k. Create a SQL outer join query that lists **GuestID** and **NightsStay** from tblReservations and **Package** and **Price** from tblPackages. Create an outer join on **PackageID**. List all records from tblPackages and only those records from tblReservations where the joined fields are equal. Save your query as qrySQLOuterJoin_initialLastname. Run the query, and then close the query.

l. Close the database, and then exit Access.

m. Submit the file as directed by your instructor.

Perform 1: Perform in Your Life

Student data file needed: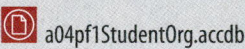

a04pf1StudentOrg.accdb

You will save your file as: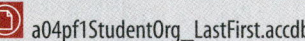

a04pf1StudentOrg_LastFirst.accdb

Managing a Student Organization Database

Finance & Accounting

The Student Organization database will help you track your organization's membership, including companies who attend events. You need to manage the data as it has not been used in the most efficient way possible. You also need to calculate the revenue generated through membership dues.

a. Open the **a04pf1StudentOrg** database. Save the database as a04pf1StudentOrg_LastFirst.

b. Open tblMembers, and then add your information in record 2.

c. To normalize the tblMeetings table, use a make table query to create a table that holds the company names and contacts. Name your table tblCompanies. Modify your table to include appropriate primary and foreign keys, data types, and field properties. Delete the appropriate fields in tblMeetings after creating your new table.

d. Create a union query that lists all members, companies, and the first employer representative.

e. Create a query that calculates the gross revenue from member dues.

f. Create at least one delete query that will help you delete members after they have graduated.

g. Create a subquery that calculates the percentage of revenue for each semester. Add totals to your data set in Datasheet view.

h. Create a query with an outer join that lists all members and the total amount of dues they have paid since they joined the organization. Add data aggregates to the data set in Datasheet view.

i. Create two queries that use the Where function.

j. Create a Group By query that performs an aggregated calculation.

k. Create two queries that use an inner join.

l. Create two queries that perform aggregated calculations.

m. Create a crosstab query that counts the number of students who attended and attended each meeting.

n. Submit the file as directed by your instructor.

Perform 2: Perform in Your Career

Student data file needed:

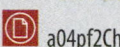 a04pf2Charity.accdb

You will save your file as:

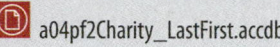 a04pf2Charity_LastFirst.accdb

Querying and Modifying a Charity Database

Finance & Accounting

As a manager for a local nonprofit organization that helps raise money for worthy causes, you were asked to query an existing database to track such things as gross revenue for each campaign. Additionally, you will need to manage the data through the use of action queries. This will ensure that your data is current and cleansed.

a. Open the **a04pf2Charity** database. Save the database as a04pf2Charity_LastFirst.

b. Open tblContributors, and then add your information in record 1.

c. Create a query that calculates gross revenue and percent to gross revenue for all donations based on the campaign. Add data aggregates to the data set when in Datasheet view.

d. Create a query that calculates the volume and percent of volume for all donations based on the campaign. Add data aggregates to the data set when in Datasheet view.

e. Create a crosstab query that uses the ContributorID and CampaignID fields from tblEvents as the row headings and the EventID field as the column heading. Use **Sum** as the interval, and then total the Amount field. Modify the column heading to display the event name as the heading. Change the field name of the TotalOfAmount field to Total. Add totals to sum all fields in Datasheet view.

f. Create a query that calculates the net revenue after administration fees of 15%.

g. Create an outer join query that lists all campaigns and the contributors and donation amount where the joined fields are equal.

h. Create a Find Unmatched query that lists all noncontributors—those who did not donate to any campaign.

i. Use an action query to remove from the mailing list those contributors who have not donated to any campaign.

j. Use an action query to delete The Red Cross campaign from tblCampaigns. Delete all related records.

k. Submit the file as directed by your instructor.

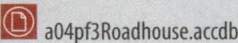 **Student data file needed:**

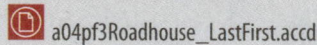 **You will save your file as:**

a04pf3Roadhouse.accdb

a04pf3Roadhouse_LastFirst.accdb

Querying the Beverage Database at the Roadhouse Bar and Grill

Production & Operations

You are the bar manager at the Roadhouse Bar and Grill, a local restaurant that specializes in home-cooked meals for breakfast, lunch, and dinner. The general manager has given you a scaled-down version of the database with one day's worth of transactions. You need to manage the inventory of beverage items to ensure you have enough beverages for each day you are open for business. You decided to create a shared folder in the "cloud" so you can share the database with your management team. All members of the management team will be responsible for updating portions of the database and share the updated database via the shared cloud folder.

Because databases can only be opened and edited by one person at a time, it is a good idea to plan ahead by designing your tables in advance. You will use a Word document to plan which team member will do what. You will use SkyDrive to store your Word document and Access database.

a. Select one team member to set up the Word document and Access database by completing Steps b–e.

b. Open your browser and navigate to **https://www.skydrive.live.com**, create a new folder, and then name it a04pf3RoadhouseFolder_TeamName. Replace TeamName with the name assigned to your team by your instructor.

c. Start Access, and open the student data file **a04pf3Roadhouse**. Save the database as a04pf3Roadhouse_TeamName replacing TeamName with the name assigned to your team by your instructor. If necessary, enable the content. Open **tblSuppliers**, and then add your team information in record **1**.

d. Upload the **a04pf3Roadhouse_TeamName** database to the **a04pf3RoadhouseFolder_TeamName** folder, and then share the folder with the other members of your team. Make sure that the other team members have permission to edit the contents of the shared folder and that they are required to log in to SkyDrive to access it.

e. Create a new Word document in the assignment folder in SkyDrive, and then name it a04pf3Roadhouse_TeamName using the name assigned to your team by your instructor.

f. In the Word document, each team member must list his or her first and last name as well as a summary of their planned contributions. As work is completed on the database, this document should be updated with the specifics of each team member's contributions.

g. In Access, your team members will need to create the following queries.

- Create a query that calculates the percentage of physical volume for milk and orange juice that is used based on the beverage container size.
- Create a query that calculates the number of servings per container. Format the physical volume calculation as an integer.
- Create an inner join query that lists all suppliers and beverages they supply.
- Create a query that calculates the sales volume of how much inventory is used in a typical day. Group your data by the sales date and beverage name. Add data aggregates to sum the sales volume calculation in Datasheet view.
- Create a query that calculates gross revenue by sales date.
- Create a subquery that determines how much inventory you would need to order each week. Format the containers needed calculation as an integer.

- Create a simple query that calculates the net revenue for each beverage. The Roadhouse Bar and Grill makes 66% on each beverage sold. Display beverages that have net revenue of at least $1.25.

- Using the query from the previous step, create a query that calculates the net revenue for each beverage sold.

- Create a union query that lists all suppliers and beverage names. Rename your displaying field as Name.

- Create a query that lists the beverage name and total beverages sold where the totals are between 10 and 20. Rename your total beverages sold field as TotalSold.

h. Once the assignment is complete, share the a04pf3RoadhouseFolder_TeamName folder with your instructor. Make sure that your instructor has permission to edit the contents.

Perform 4: How Others Perform

Student data files needed:

 a04pf4CarRental.accdb

 Blank Word document

You will save your files as:

 a04pf4CarRental_LastFirst.accdb

 a04pf4CarRental_LastFirst.docx

General
Business

Being an Entrepreneur—Cappy's Car Rental

You are the owner of a small rental car company—Cappy's Car Rental. Your intern created a database for you and your employees to use for tracking rentals and assessing monthly performance. At first glance, you notice that it has very few queries, which would help answer many questions about the cars you have rented. You need to evaluate the database, create useful queries, evaluate the existing queries, and cleanse the data, as the intern left a fair amount of older data in the tables.

a. Open the student data file **a04pf4CarRental**. Save the database as a04pf4CarRental_LastFirst.

b. Open tblCustomers, and then add your information in record 1.

c. Open **Word**, create a new blank document, and then save it as a04pf4CarRental_LastFirst. This will be used to answer the questions below.

d. Consider how the data will be used. Create five queries that can be used to assist you and your employees with decision making. In your Word document, explain what question each query would answer, such as calculating sales revenue within a specific date range.

e. Create three action queries. In your Word document, explain what each query would do if you clicked Run, such as updating prices or deleting older data. If you would need to make changes to relationships for the query to run properly, please note that as well.

f. Evaluate and modify the two existing queries to make them easier to read and use. In your Word document, explain what changes you made and why.

g. Submit the files as directed by your instructor.

WORKSHOP 9 | ADVANCED FORM SETTINGS AND FORM TYPES

OBJECTIVES

1. Define bound and unbound forms   p. 462
2. Modify the form property sheet   p. 464
3. Modify the form header   p. 472
4. Modify the form in Design view   p. 474
5. Create specialized forms   p. 493
6. Create a multipage form using tab controls   p. 494

Prepare Case

Enhancing Data Entry at the Red Bluff Golf Club

Customer Service

The Red Bluff Golf Club generates revenues through golfers signing up for tee times and taking golf lessons. You have provided a database to Barry Cheney, the golf club manager, where he can track employees and members. He and his staff have been experimenting with forms with little luck. He would like to have an interface to the database where any of the golf club workers could easily sign members up for lessons and tee times. You will assist Barry and his staff by setting up forms that they can use as the interface.

bikeriderlondon / Shutterstock

REAL WORLD SUCCESS

"My boss was trying to organize a huge reception for out-of-town customers and guests. He had all the data he needed in various tables, but he was trying to manage all the data lookup and data entry from just the tables. I showed him how to create forms, especially forms with tabs, and he was thrilled. It not only reduced the amount of time he had to spend on managing the data, but it turned me into his Access go-to person."

- Rebecca, MBA student and intern

Student data files needed for this workshop:

 a05ws09Golf.accdb

 a05ws09RedBluff.jpg

You will save your file as:

 a05ws09Golf_LastFirst.accdb

Working with Form Properties

A **form** is an object used to enter new records into a table, edit or delete existing records in a table, or display existing records in a table. A form can present a single record at a time rather than displaying all records the way that a table does. This presentation makes it easier for a person using the database to focus on a single record and thus helps prevent data entry errors.

Forms have three views:

- **Form view** shows the data in the form. This is the view you use to enter or change data. You cannot change the form design in this view. This is the view that the golf course employees will use when they are performing their jobs.

- **Layout view** shows a modified form design and the data. Some of the form design such as field lengths and fonts can be changed in this view. The data cannot be changed. This view gives you an easy way to resize fields and check form appearance while you are creating the form.

- **Design view** shows the form design but not the data. Any aspect of the report design can be changed; however, the data cannot be changed. This view is used for creation of the form.

In this section, you will explore the different properties that are available for form fields and controls.

Define Bound and Unbound Forms

A **bound form** is a form that is directly connected to a data source such as a table or query and that can be used to enter, edit, or display data from that data source. When you create a form from a table using a wizard, the form is bound to the table you choose in the wizard setup. The field labels are the captions defined for the fields in the table design. The formatting for the fields and the field lengths are also based upon the field definitions in the table design. All of these can be changed after the form is created. An **unbound form** is not linked directly to a data source. Unbound forms can be used to specify parameters, create buttons to print reports, provide navigation menus, and other similar operations.

Opening the Starting File

You will start working with the golf database that is already created. There are multiple tables that list employees, members, and other data relevant to running the golf course. There are three queries that you will use for calculated controls when creating your forms. There is also a form created with a subform that you will help enhance later in the workshop.

A09.00

 To Open the Golf Database

a. Start **Access**, and then open the student data file **a05ws09Golf**.

b. Click the **FILE** tab, click **Save As**, click **Save Database As**, and then click the **Save As** button. Select the folder where you are saving your files, type **a05ws09Golf_LastFirst** using your last and first name, and then click **Save**. If necessary, click **Enable Content**.

| QUICK REFERENCE | To Save a File with a Different Name |

If you select Save, the file will be saved with the same name in the same location in which it currently exists. However, you can change the file name or save it in another folder by using the Save As command.

1. Click the File tab.
2. Click Save As.
3. Select Save Database As under File Types, and then select Access Database under Save Database As.
4. Click the Save As button, and then type the new file name. If necessary, select a new folder to save it in.
5. Click Save.

Creating a Bound Form

The database used by the golf club contains tables, queries, and forms, but the forms are not fully functional yet. The first form Mr. Cheney would like is a form that can be used to add members one at a time. You will use the Form Wizard to create this form and then make some changes in Layout view.

MyITLab®
Workshop 9 Training

A09.01

▶ To Create a Bound Form

a. Click the **CREATE** tab, and then in the Forms group, click **Form Wizard**.

b. Click the **Tables/Queries** arrow, select **tblMember**, and then click **Select all fields** >> to select all the fields in the table.

c. Click **Next**, make sure that **Columnar** is selected, and then click **Next**.

d. In the form title, type **frmAddMember_initialLastname** using your first initial and last name, verify that **Open the form to view or enter information** is selected, and then click **Finish**.

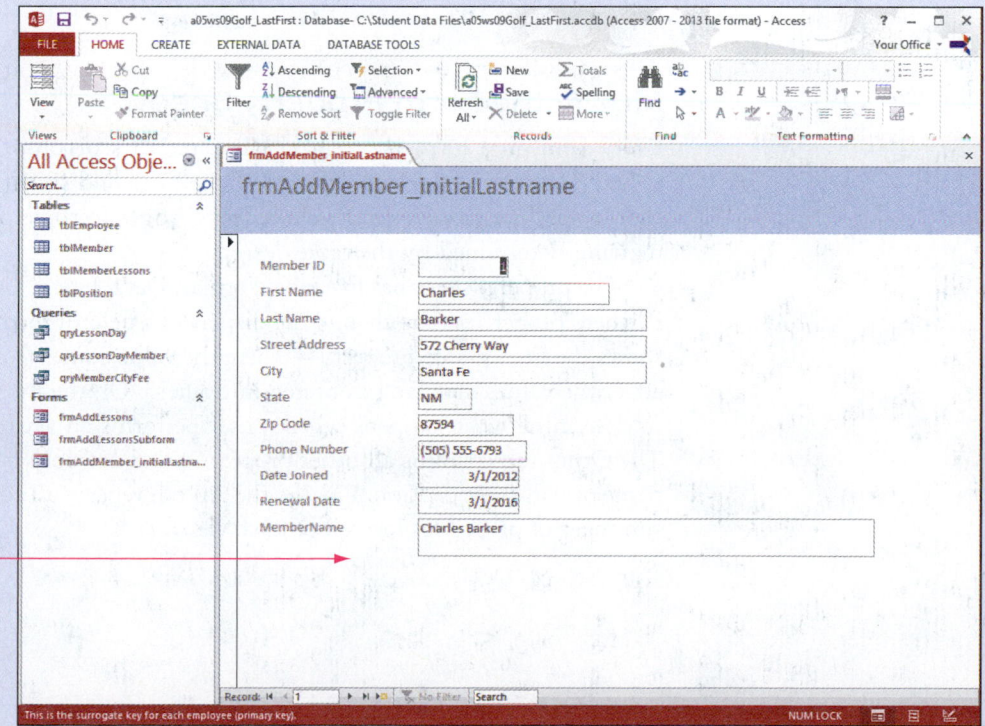

One record shows per page

Figure 1 Form named frmAddMember_initialLastname

Making Changes in Layout View

Recall that Layout view allows a database developer to see a form with data in the fields and make changes to the form layout. Layout view is an ideal view for resizing fields in a form since you can see the data as you are making changes. In frmAddMember, the MemberName field is a calculated field composed of FirstName and LastName, so Access set its length longer than needed. You will change the length of this field in Layout view.

QUICK REFERENCE	Switch to Layout View

You can use the Ribbon, the status bar, or right-click in the Navigation Pane to switch to Layout view for a form.

- To use the Ribbon: On the Home tab, in the Views group, click the View arrow, and then select Layout View.
- To right-click: In the Navigation Pane, right-click the form you want to open and select Layout View.
- To use the status bar: On the status bar, click Layout View.

A09.02

To Change the Size of a Field

a. Switch to **Layout** view.

b. Click the **MemberName field value** in the form detail.

c. Move the pointer to the **right border** of the field until it becomes a double-headed arrow ↔. Move the **border** to the left until it lines up with the address and city fields above.

d. Move the pointer to the **lower border** of the field until it becomes a double-headed arrow ↕. Move the **border** up until the field is a single line. **Save** ⊟ the form.

Modify the Form Property Sheet

Every field on a form has certain characteristics or properties stored in the **property sheet**. There are also characteristics of the form and sections within the forms stored in their respective property sheets. Making changes to these properties will change the formatting determined by the table design.

The property sheet has five tabs: Format, Data, Event, Other, and All. The Format tab is where properties that change the display of a field or form part are listed. The Data tab shows the field source property—where the value comes from—and other properties that affect the values that can be entered into a field. On the Event tab, you can set procedures to determine what happens when a user performs an action such as clicking on a field. The Other tab contains all other properties that are not on one of the other tabs, such as name or datasheet caption. Finally, the All tab repeats all the properties. See Table 1 for a summary of properties located on each tab.

Property Sheet Tab	Properties Included	Examples
Format tab	Properties related to the formatting and design of a field or form	For a field • Decimal places • Width • Font For a form or form part • Background color • Special effects
Data tab	Properties related to the source of a field and how the field data is entered	For a field • Source for the field • Input masks • Validation rules
Event tab	Macro procedures that should be used when a user performs an action	Actions to be taken upon • A click • An update • On double-click
Other tab	Any properties not included elsewhere	For a field • Field name • Caption For a form • Printing information
All tab	All properties	Repeats all properties from the other tabs

Table 1 Property Sheet tab options

The property sheet is opened by selecting a field and then on the Design tab, in the Tools group, clicking Property Sheet. The Data tab shows properties including the field source and the properties that affect the values that can be entered into the selected field, or control. A **control** is an object on a form or report that displays data, performs actions, and lets you view and work with information. A **bound control** is a field that retrieves its data from an underlying table. The properties on the Data tab, as shown in Table 2, are similar to the properties you use when defining a field in a table.

Property	Options
Control Source	The source for the data in a bound control. This may also be a calculated field
Text Format	The format applied to the entered text
Input Mask	Defines input rules for a field
Default Value	Allows you to define a value that will automatically appear in a blank record
Validation Rule	Defines the range of data that will be accepted in a field
Validation Text	The error message that will appear if entered data violates the validation rule
Filter Lookup	Specifies whether values will appear in a bound text box control when using the Filter By Form option
Enabled	Stronger than the Lock property, this determines whether data can be entered or copied using the form
Locked	Determines whether data can be entered into the field using the form

Table 2 Property Sheet Data tab options for bound controls

For an **unbound control**, like a field label, the Data tab has only a Smart Tags property. An unbound control does not have a data source and is often used for labels and other display controls, as there are few properties related to how the control is stored in the database. The properties shown on a tab are context sensitive and show only properties that apply to the selected control.

Changing Default Values for a Field

The **Default Value**, an option on the Data tab in the Property Sheet pane, allows you to define a value that will automatically appear in a new blank record. If a field has a typical value, you can define it here and speed up data entry.

Since most members of the golf club are from Santa Fe, New Mexico, you will enter those values as default values for the City and State. The user will be able to change these values but will not need to enter them for members with this address.

A09.03

 To Change Default Values

a. In the form detail, click the **City field value**.

b. Click the **DESIGN** tab, and in the Tools group, click **Property Sheet**. The Property Sheet pane will open and show the properties for the City text box.

c. In the Property Sheet pane, click the **Data** tab, and then click **Default Value**. Type **Santa Fe**, and then press Tab.

   Access places quotation marks around the value because it is a text value. Adding a default value does change the City field value of existing records to Santa Fe. The default is used only when adding a new blank record.

d. In the form detail, click the **State field value**. In the Property Sheet pane, click **Default Value**, type **NM**, and then press Tab.

SIDE NOTE
Select the Control First
To see the properties of a control, the control on the form must be selected first.

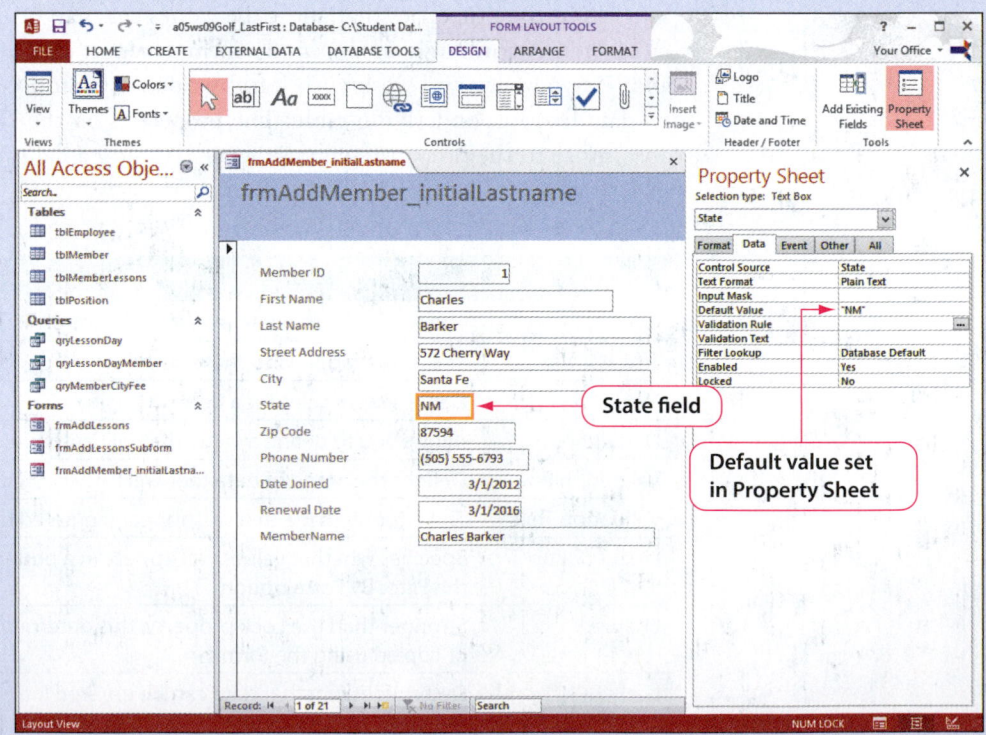

Figure 2 Default Value for State field changed to NM

Using Dates and Calculations as the Default Value

You can also use Date functions and calculations as the default value. The Access function **Current Date** automatically puts the current date—based on your computer's system date—in the field. The function **DateAdd** allows you to add an interval to a date. The advantage of using this function is that it always returns a valid date. The DateAdd function has the following format: DateAdd(interval,number,date). Interval can be a day, month, year, or more as shown in Table 3. Number is how many of the intervals you want to add to the Date shown. You use year rather than 365 days so that Access will automatically take into account the possibility of a leap year.

Argument	Function Wanted	How Indicated
Interval		
	Year	yyyy
	Quarter	q
	Month	m
	Day	d
	Weekday	w
	Day of year	y
	Week	ww
	Hour	h
	Minute	n
	Second	s
Number		
	Add	Positive value
	Subtract	Negative value

Table 3 DateAdd function formatting

There are two date fields in frmAddMember: The first is Date Joined, which refers to the original date that the member joined the golf club. You will set the default value for Date Joined to the current date. To do that, you will use the Access Current Date function.

The second date on the form is Renewal Date, which refers to the date that the membership expires. You will set the Renewal Date default value to be one year after Date Joined by using the DateAdd function. The interval will be yyyy, the number will be 1 for only one interval, and the date will be [DateJoined].

A09.04

▶ To Use Dates as Default Values

a. In the form detail, click the **Date Joined field value**. In the Property Sheet pane, click the **Data** tab, click **Default Value**, and then click **Builder** ┆···┆.

b. Click **Common Expressions** in the Expression Elements list.

c. Double-click **Current Date** in the Expression Categories list, and then click **OK**.

d. In the form detail, click the **Renewal Date field value**. Click **Default Value**, and then click **Builder** ┆···┆. In the Expression Builder dialog box, under **Enter an Expression to define the control property value**, type =DateAdd("yyyy",1,[DateJoined]). Click **OK**. This will create a default value of one year from the date joined entered earlier.

SIDE NOTE
Use Field Names, Not Captions

When creating calculations, you must use the field name and not the field caption so Access knows which field to include in the calculation.

e. Switch to **Form** view. On the Navigation bar, click **New (blank) record** [▶⁎].

Notice that the new blank record has default values of Santa Fe, NM, the current date, and a renewal date one year from the current date entered in the Date Joined field.

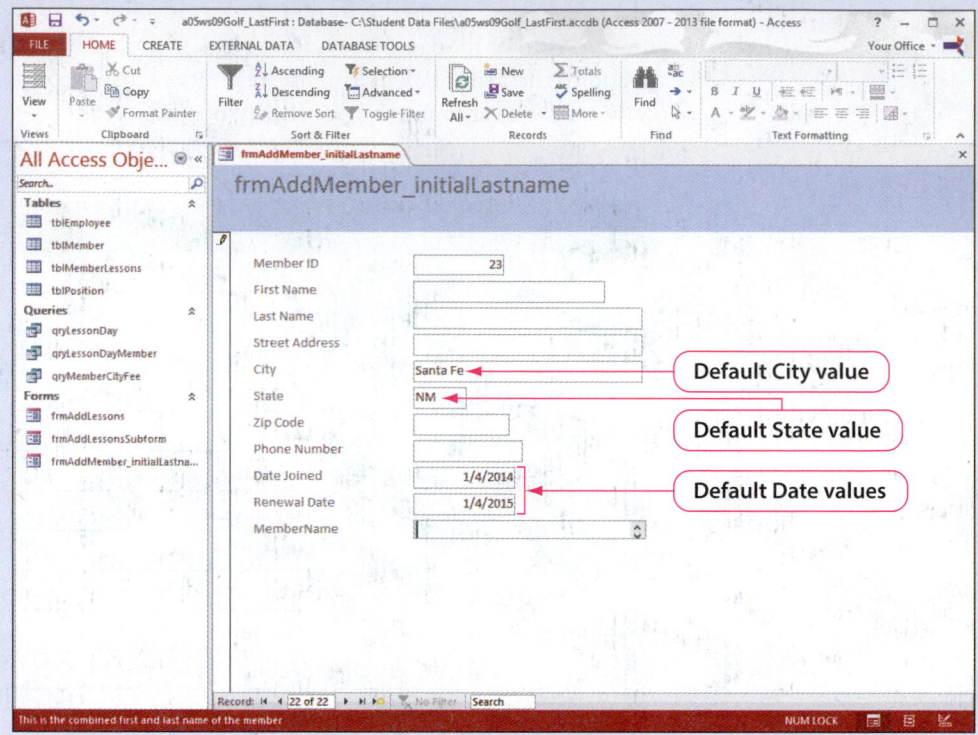

Figure 3 New record with City, State, and Date default values

f. On the Navigation bar, click **First record** [◀] to return to the first record for Charles Barker.

REAL WORLD ADVICE | **Default Date vs. Calculated Date**

Both date fields that were just set to default dates with functions may seem like calculated fields, but they are not! It is important to understand the difference because a calculated date will change and a default date will not. What this means is the Date Joined will always be the current day by default, and the Renewal Date will always be one year later for all new records added in the form.

However, if you change the Date Joined after it has been entered, the Renewal Date will not change—or recalculate—like you might expect. For the Renewal Date to change when the Date Joined is changed, the Source Control, not the Default Value, of the bound field would have to be changed to a calculated field.

SS **CONSIDER THIS** | **Allowing Default Date to Be Changed**

You set the default date to today's date but allowed the date to be changed. You could also have not allowed changes. When would you want to use a default that can be changed, and when would you want to force the value to be a default that cannot be changed? Would it depend on the data being entered, the person doing the data entry, both, or some other variable?

Changing the Background Color of the Form and Properties for Unbound Controls

The properties on the Format tab determine how the control is displayed on a form. The box for each value can be resized or moved—Width, Height, Top, Left. The border can be changed, the font can be changed, and a scroll bar can be added. None of these properties change how the field is stored in the database, but they do make it easier to use the form. You will use the Format tab to change the background color of the form to match the existing form frmAddLessons.

While there are not many properties on the Data tab for an unbound control, there are many properties on the Format tab. This is because labels are displayed on the form, and so the properties related to how a field is displayed are relevant.

You will format the fields that are filled by Access differently than the fields that the user enters. MemberID is an AutoNumber field, and MemberName is calculated, so they will be formatted differently than the other fields. You will change them to have a faded background.

A09.05

 To Change Back Color and Special Effect Properties

a. Switch to **Layout** view, and then click the **background** of the detail section of the form. Access highlights this area by outlining it. It should also say Detail in the Property Sheet pane under Selection type.

b. In the Property Sheet pane, click the **Format** tab, and then click **Back Color**. Click **Builder** ⌞⋯⌟, and then select **White, Background 1, Darker 15%**.

c. In the form detail, click the **MemberID field value**. In the Property Sheet pane, on the Format tab, click the **Special Effect** arrow ⌄, and then select **Sunken**.

d. Click **Back Color**, click **Builder** ⌞⋯⌟, and then select **White, Background 1, Darker 15%**.

e. In the form detail, click the **MemberName field value**, click the **Special Effect** arrow ⌄, and then select **Sunken**.

f. Click **Back Color**, click **Builder** ⌞⋯⌟, and select **White, Background 1, Darker 15%**.

SIDE NOTE
Optional Method to Select Detail Section
You can also select the detail section by clicking the Selection type arrow at the top of the Property Sheet pane and then selecting Detail.

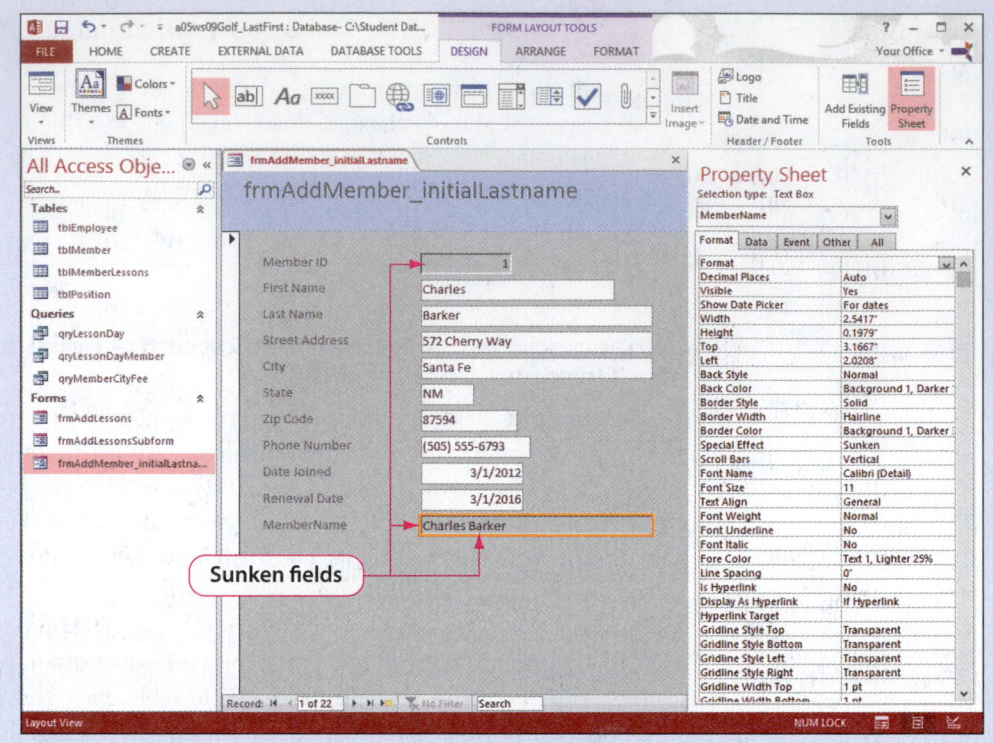

Figure 4 Member ID and MemberName sunken and filled with back color

---

REAL WORLD ADVICE | **Use Formatting Sparingly**

While it is possible to change the formatting for each label and field control, too much formatting can be distracting and make a form harder to use. Instead, use varied formatting only if you have a reason for that variation. Two examples of when you might make this choice: (1) Use a bright color to highlight a single important control; and (2) use one color for protected fields and another color for unprotected fields.

Displaying the Date Picker

The **Date Picker** is a pop-up calendar that allows a user to enter a date by clicking a date in the calendar. By default, the Date Picker will appear next to any date field, unless the date field has an input mask. On frmAddMember, the Date Joined field has an input mask that was set in the table properties of tblMember. You will have to remove the input mask in order for the date picker to be displayed.

A09.06

▶ To Change the Date Format

a. In the form detail, click the **Date Joined field value**. In the Property Sheet pane, click the **Data** tab, select the **Input Mask** value, and then press ⎡Delete⎤ to delete the value.

b. Switch to **Form** view.
   Notice the **Date Picker** 🗓 that appears next to the Date Joined field. This indicates the date picker is available to use for this field.

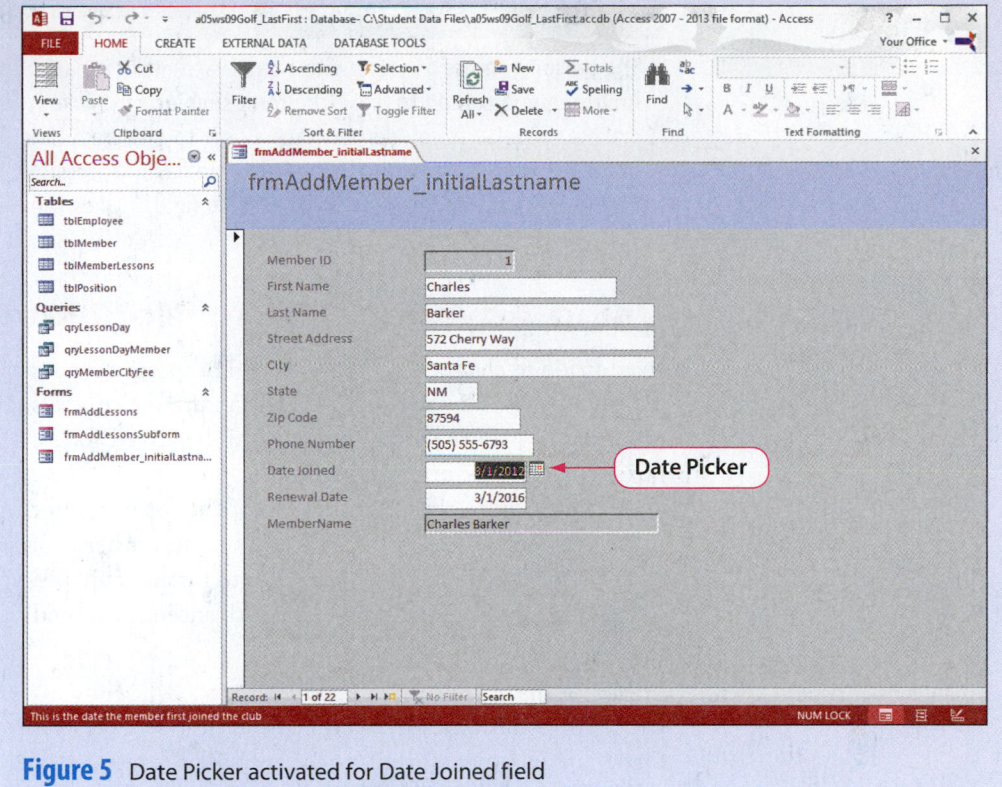

Figure 5 Date Picker activated for Date Joined field

c. **Save** 🖫 the form.

Preventing Fields from Being Updated

The **Locked** property of a form determines whether data can be entered into the field using the form. A value of No means that data can be entered; a value of Yes means that the field is locked and data cannot be entered. The **Enabled** property is stronger than a lock. If the enabled property is No, the data cannot be entered or copied. The default is that bound controls are unlocked and enabled.

When a field is locked, it may confuse the user if ⌷Tab⌷ stops at that field for data entry. To avoid any confusion, locked fields can be skipped when using ⌷Tab⌷.

The frmAddMember form currently allows a user to edit all fields. While Member ID and MemberName are deemphasized, a user could still try to change them. You will lock the fields and also change the form so the fields are skipped when a user tabs from field to field.

A09.07

 To Prevent Fields from Being Updated

a. Switch to **Layout** view, and then in the form detail, click the **Member ID field value**. In the Property Sheet pane, click the **Data** tab, click the **Locked** arrow ⌄, and then select **Yes**.

b. Click the **Other** tab, click the **Tab Stop** arrow ⌄, and then select **No**.

c. In the form detail, click the **MemberName field value**. In the Property Sheet pane, click the **Data** tab, click the **Locked** arrow ⌄, and then select **Yes**.

d. Click the **Other** tab, click the **Tab Stop** arrow ⌄, and then select **No**. **Close** ✗ the Property Sheet pane, and then **Save** 🖫 the form.

REAL WORLD ADVICE	Protect Fields That Should Not Be Changed

The reason you use forms to enter data is to make it easier for users to use the database. Anything you can do to make the form simpler will make it less likely that the user will make a mistake. If you do not want a user to change a field, lock the fields and do not allow the user to tab to it. If the fields are easily accessible, users may try to change them. Removing the ability to change the fields makes the form easier to use.

Using Advanced Form Modification

In addition to changes made to the field properties, you can also add calculated controls to a form, change the tab order, add and rearrange controls, and add subforms, shapes, and other controls to the form. Buttons can be added for easier navigation as well as combo boxes to help look up specific records.

In addition to the detail section of the form, the form also has a header section and footer section. Titles, logos, dates, times, and other controls, both bound and unbound, can be added to the header and footer to further enhance a form. In this section, you will modify an existing form using more advanced form modification techniques.

Modify the Form Header

Every form has a header section. The header section can be used to add a form title, logo, date or time, as well as other unbound controls. The color of the header can also be changed. On frmAddMember, you will make changes to the header including changing the color and title. You also will add a logo, the date, and time to the form.

Editing the Form Header

A **logo** is an unbound control that can be added to the header of a form. It is an embedded picture that includes a blank header box, generally to the right of the picture. The logo can only be placed in the header and will not change as you view different records using the form.

You will add the golf logo to the form header, delete the blank header box, and then change the title of the form to be more meaningful to the form users.

A09.08

 To Edit the Title and Add a Logo

a. In the form header, double-click the title **frmAddMember_initialLastname**. Select the **current text**, and then replace the text with Add a New Member by initialLastname using your first initial and last name. If necessary, resize the title so that it fits on one line.

b. Click the **DESIGN** tab, and then in the Header/Footer group, click **Logo**. Navigate to your student data files, click **a05ws09RedBluff**, and then click **OK** to insert the logo.

c. Click the **blank header** box to the right of the logo you just added, and then press Delete to remove that control from the form.

Troubleshooting

If you delete the title by mistake, click Undo on the Quick Access Toolbar, reselect the blank header box to the right of the logo, and press Delete again. The blank header box will be longer than the title when you select it.

d. Click the **logo** to select it, and then point to the **bottom-right corner** of the logo until your pointer becomes a **diagonal arrow** ⬉. Resize the logo so that the height is the same as the height of the header area and the width about half the width of the title. Move the **logo** to the right of the title, and then **Save** 🖫 the form.

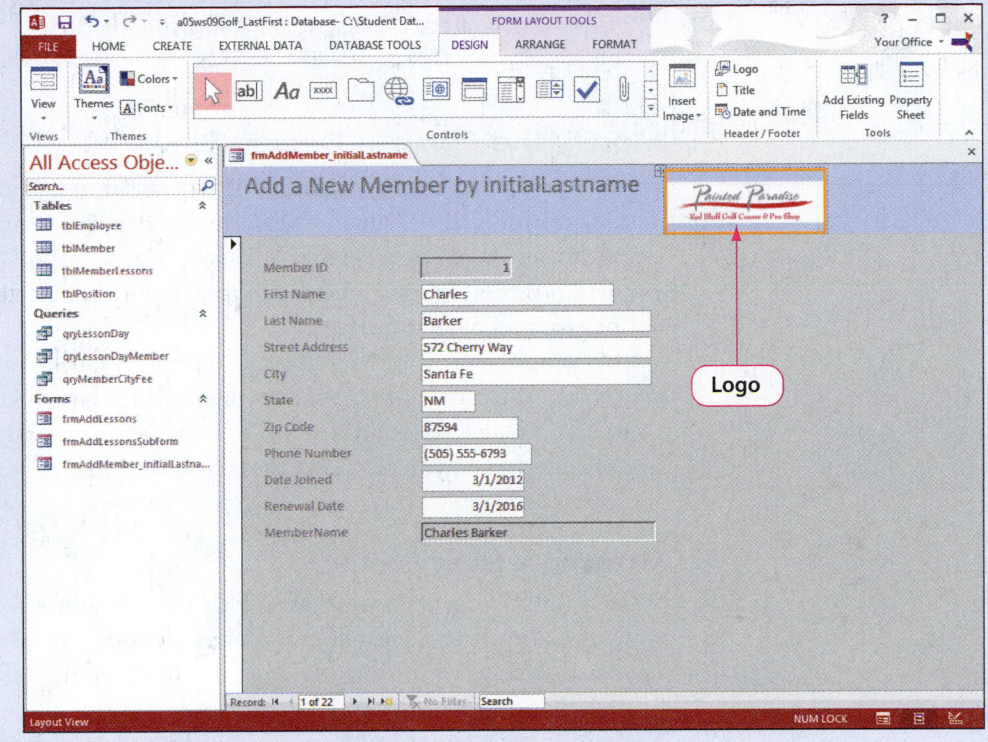

Figure 6 Logo added in form header

Adding the Date and Time and Changing the Background Color

The date and time can also be added to the header, so every time the form is opened, the current date and time will appear. This will also be helpful if the form or record are printed because they will have the current date. You can add the date, the time, or both. Both the date and time have three formatting options to choose from. You will add the date and time and use the default formatting options.

The background color of the header can be changed to match other forms and reports or to make the form unique. You will change the background color of the form header to white to match the existing form frmAddLessons.

A09.09
▶ **To Add the Date and Time and Background Color**

a. Click the **DESIGN** tab, and then in the Header/Footer group, click **Date and Time**.

b. In the Date and Time dialog box, accept the defaults **Include Date** and **Include Time**, and then click **OK**.

c. Click the **form header** to select it. On the DESIGN tab, in the Tools group, click **Property Sheet**. In the Property Sheet pane, click the **Format** tab, click **Back Color**. Click **Builder** , and then select **White, Background 1**. **Save** 🖫 the form.

REAL WORLD ADVICE	Using Date and Time as a Record Keeper

Forms are useful to print out one record at a time. In business, it is helpful to document information, especially when you are giving it to someone else in the organization. If you print a database record using a form, by including the current date and time you will have printed documentation regarding that record, not only when it was printed, but also when it was current.

Modify the Form in Design View

So far, all the modifications to the form have been in Layout view, where you can see the data while you make changes. When more advanced changes need to be made, or you cannot make the desired change in Layout view, Design view is used. In Design view, you will not be able to see the data or make any changes to it, but there are many more options to modify your form.

In Design view, you can add such controls as labels, images, lines, and rectangles to your form. You can edit text boxes without using the property sheet by right-clicking on them and making selections from the shortcut menu. You can move and resize controls independently, and you can resize the different form sections including the header, footer, and detail sections.

Inserting a Form Footer

When a form is created, it is created with a header and a detail section. There is no footer when the form is first created, but footers are useful to add labels and other identifying information about the form.

A footer must be created in Design view, but it can later be modified in Layout view. You will insert a footer and format it to match the rest of the form.

A09.10

▶ To Add a Form Footer

a. Switch to **Design** view. Since a footer has not been inserted yet, you will not see anything below the bottom bar that says Form Footer.

b. Point to the **bottom edge** of the bar that says Form Footer until you see the **pointer** , and then pull the **edge** down to the **1"** mark on the vertical ruler. The footer will be white so you will change it to match the form detail. Click anywhere in the **form footer**.

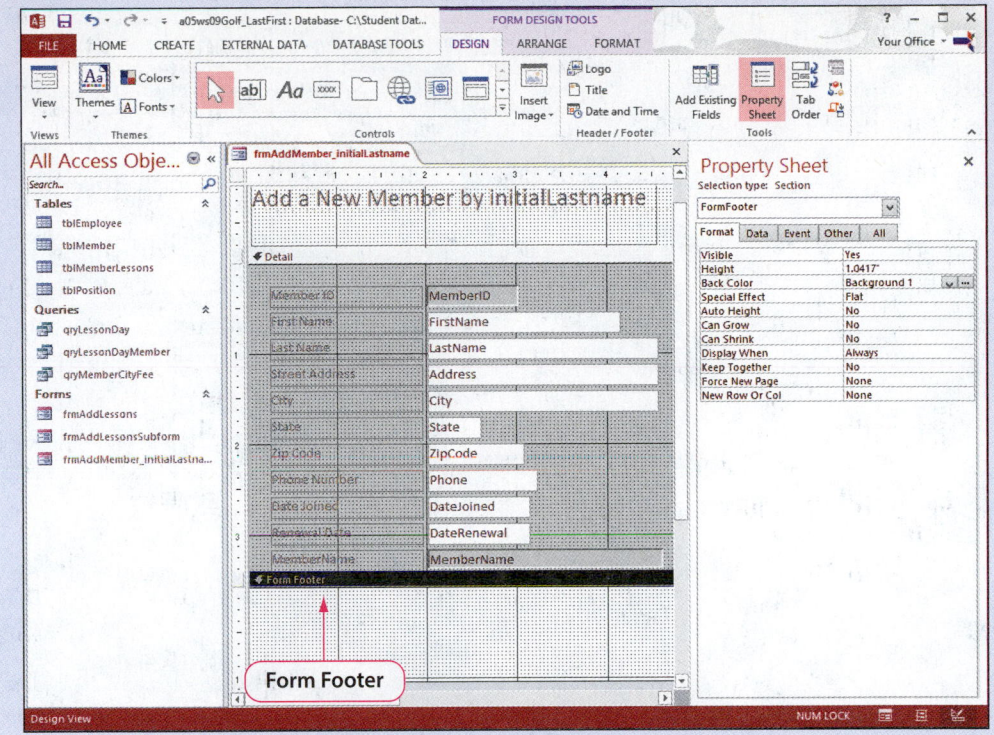

Figure 7 Form Footer on frmAddMember_initialLastname

c. In the Property Sheet pane, on the Format tab, click **Back Color**. Click **Builder** 🔲 and then select **White, Background 1, Darker 15%. Close** ⊠ the Property Sheet pane.

d. Test the form by entering a new record. Switch to **Form** view. On the Navigation bar, click **New (blank) record** 🔳. In the **First Name** field, type your first name, and then in the **Last Name** field, type your last name. In the **Street Address** field, type 1200 Reservoir Street, and then accept the default city and state values. In the **Zip Code** field, type 87593, press Tab, and in the **Phone Number** field, type 5055554882. Accept the default for the **Date Joined**, and accept the default for the **Renewal Date**.

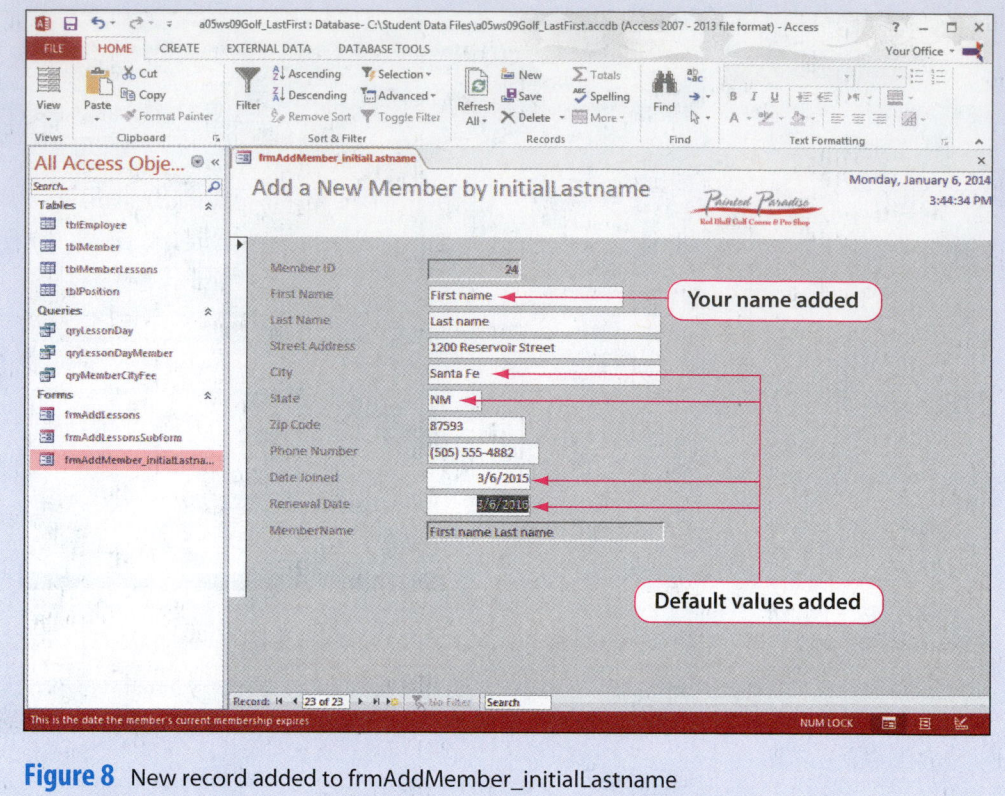

Figure 8 New record added to frmAddMember_initialLastname

e. **Save** 🖫 the form and then **Close** ✖ the form.

Adding and Stacking Fields

Any form can be modified, whether it is created from one table or multiple tables. Often you will decide to add or delete a field after the form is created.

When you add an existing field, Access adds two controls. One is the bound control—a text box—tied to a table field. The second is an unbound control that labels the text box. The two controls are attached to each other. They can be moved as a pair or separately. When a control is selected, Access outlines the control in orange. There are eight boxes or handles on the orange outline. The large grey handle in the top-left corner is called the **move handle**. It is used to move the controls in the form. The smaller orange handles are **sizing handles**. Sizing handles are used to resize the control.

If you use your pointer to move the control, without clicking on the move handle, you will move both controls at the same time. If you click the move handle, you will move just one control. You can use your pointer to move the control a large distance. You can also use the arrow keys on the keyboard to nudge the control a short distance.

The staff used the wizard to create a form with a **subform** from tables tblMember and tblMemberLessons. A subform is created when fields from two or more related tables are used to create a form. The fields from the first table selected become the main form fields, and the fields from the second and subsequent tables become the subform fields. In this case, the staff did not add the Phone field, which needs to be included, so you will add that field to the main form. You will also align the fields by stacking them so they are lined up neatly on the form.

A09.11

To Add a New Field and Align It with an Existing Field

a. Right-click **frmAddLessons** in the Navigation Pane, select **Copy**, and then right-click a blank area of the Navigation Pane. Select **Paste**, name the new form **frmAddLessons_initialLastname** using your first initial and last name and then click **OK**.

b. In the Navigation Pane, double-click **frmAddLessons_initialLastname** to open the form. Note that this form has a main form and a subform. Switch to **Design** view, and then click anywhere in the **background** of the main form.

> **Troubleshooting**
>
> The tab on the open form may still show frmAddLessons—in Form and Layout view—even though you changed the object name when you did the Copy and Paste. You can leave it that way, or you can change the name that shows in the tab in the Property Sheet pane by selecting the Form, clicking the Format tab, selecting Caption and changing it to frmAddLessons_initialLastname.

c. Click the **DESIGN** tab, and then in the Tools group, click **Add Existing Fields**. The Field List pane opens with a list of fields available to add to the form.

SIDE NOTE

Adding Fields

You can also click to select a field in the field list and drag it to the form.

d. In the Field List pane, double-click **Phone** to add it to the form. It may be displayed on top of another field or control, but that is not a problem because you will move it.

e. Move your pointer to the **edge of the orange border** on the Phone text box, but not on one of the handles. When the pointer becomes a **four-headed arrow** ⊞, move the control **below** the Zip Code control. Release the mouse, and you will see that both controls moved at once.

> **Troubleshooting**
>
> If you accidently touched the move handle and moved one of the controls without the other, use Undo ↩ to undo your change.

f. Point to the **top-left corner** of the form background just above the First Name label. Drag diagonally to the right, selecting **all of the controls** except the subform and subform label. Access indicates that all the controls are selected by outlining them in orange.

g. Click the **ARRANGE** tab, and then in the Table group, click **Stacked**.

Access arranges all the member controls in a stacked layout. The stacked layout can be thought of as an invisible table with matching bound and unbound controls for each field in a row. All the unbound controls are in one column; all the bound controls are in the second column.

SIDE NOTE

Arranging Controls

You can also use the Arrange tab to arrange a group of controls automatically on a form.

h. With the controls still selected, on the ARRANGE tab, in the Position group, click **Control Padding**, and then select **Narrow**. This will reduce the amount of vertical space between each control.

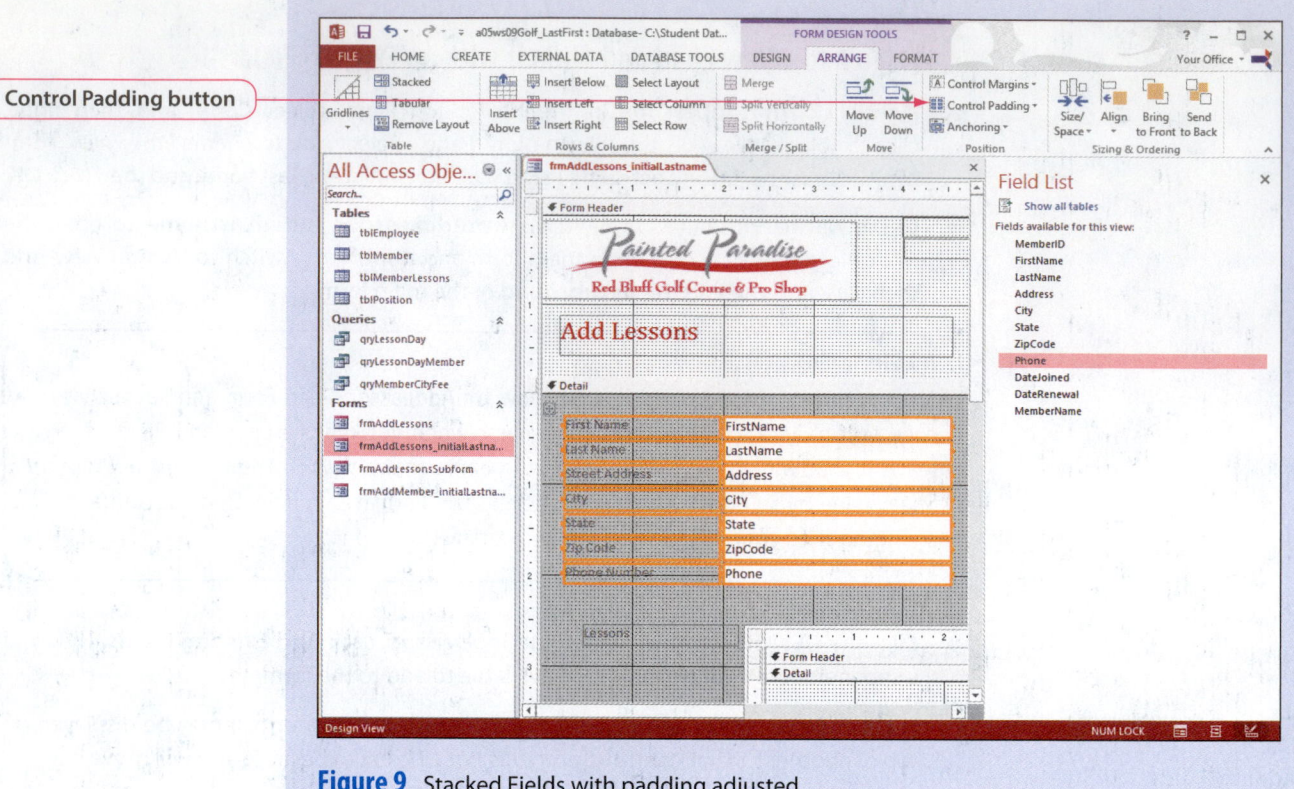

Figure 9 Stacked Fields with padding adjusted

i. **Close** ☒ the Field List pane.

Changing Tab Order

Fields and other controls are placed on a form either in the order they are added in the Form Wizard or in the order they appear in the source table. The **tab order**, or the order you move from one control to another when you press [Tab], is based on the initial location of the control on the form. Moving a control to a new spot on the form does not change the tab order of the control. When you add a new field to the form, unless it is placed after all the other controls, you will have to adjust the tab order. The tab order is changed in the Tab Order dialog box that is accessed from Design view.

You will change the tab order so Phone Number comes after Zip Code when you press [Tab].

A09.12

 To Change Tab Order

a. Click the **DESIGN** tab, and then in the Tools group, click **Tab Order**.

b. In the **Section** pane of the Tab Order dialog box, verify that **Detail** is selected. In the Custom Order list, click the **selection** box ☐ to the left of the Phone field to select the row.

c. Point to the **selection** box ☐ to the left of **Phone**, and then drag the row up to just below **ZipCode**. You will see a thick black line to show where the row will be moved. Click **OK**.

d. Switch to **Form** view, and then test the tab order by tabbing through the fields. When you press [Tab], the fields should be selected in order from top to bottom.

SS **CONSIDER THIS** | **Out of Order Fields**

Forms can be created to match field order in a table, but there are other considerations when planning a form. Can you think of a situation where having the tab move from field to field out of order might be appropriate? Think about the different sources of data you may receive—paper documents, phone calls, online forms—and how you will process that data to input it into the database form.

Adding a COUNT Calculated Field

A **calculated control** is a control that uses an expression as the source of data rather than a field value. A calculated control may be the SUM or COUNT of a field, or any other expression value Access has available in the Expression Builder. Access provides the Expression Builder to help build the calculations, similar to a wizard, so you do not have to know the exact syntax for the expression. A calculated field is an unbound control.

The first function you will add to the form is COUNT to count the number of lessons. You will open the subform in a new window and add the control to the form footer.

A09.13

 To Add a COUNT Function

a. Switch to **Design** view, and then click the **subform** so it is outlined in orange. With your pointer **on the border**, right-click and then select **Subform in New Window**.

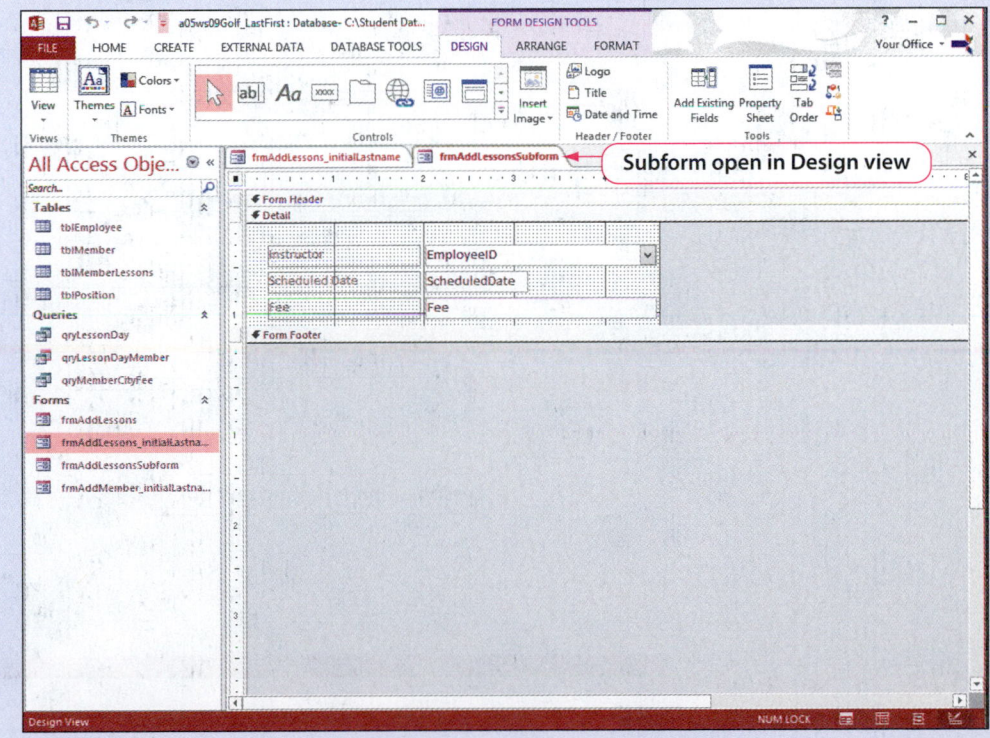

Figure 10 Subform open in new window

b. Point to the Form Footer bar, and then when the **pointer** changes to ⬍, pull down the **bottom edge** of the Form Footer bar to the **1"** mark on the vertical ruler.

c. Click the **DESIGN** tab, and then in the Controls group, click **Text Box** 🔲. Move your pointer to the **footer**, and then click the **1"** vertical grid line in the middle of the footer.

> **Troubleshooting**
>
> If you put your controls too close to the left edge of the footer, the controls will overlap. You can use Undo ↺ and try again. Or, you can use the two Move handles to move each field separately.

SIDE NOTE

Entering Functions

You can type a function directly in the control rather than use the Expression Builder, or type it into the Expression Builder.

d. On the DESIGN tab, In the Tools group, click **Property Sheet** to open the property sheet for the new control.

e. In the Property Sheet pane, click the **Data** tab, and then click **Control Source Builder** 🔘. In the Expression Builder, type **=COUNT(**, in the Expression Categories pane, double-click **ScheduledDate**, and then type **)**. The expression should look like =COUNT([ScheduledDate]). Any extra spaces will be removed once you save the expression. Click **OK**.

f. In the Property Sheet pane, click the **Other** tab, click **Name**, and then replace the text with **LessonCount**.

g. Double-click the new **label** on the form, and then replace the text with **Lesson Count**. **Save** 💾 the subform.

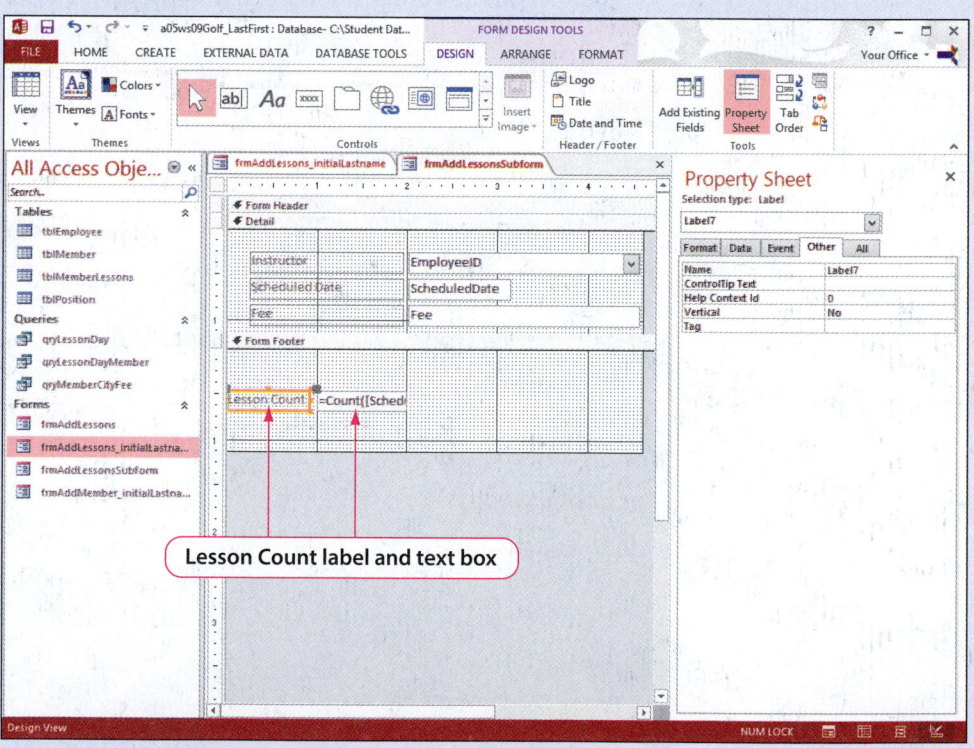

Figure 11 COUNT function added to subform footer

Adding a SUM Calculated Field

The SUM function can also be added to the subform. You will add a calculated control to calculate the total lesson fees in the subform footer.

A09.14

 To Add a SUM Function

a. Click the **DESIGN** tab, and then in the Controls group, click **Text Box** [ab]. Move the pointer to the footer below the Lesson count controls, and then click the **1"** vertical grid line. If necessary, move the Lesson Count control up to make room.

b. With the new text box selected, in the Property Sheet pane, click the **Data** tab, and then click **Control Source Builder** [...].

c. In the Expression Builder box, type **=SUM(**, in the Expression Categories pane, double-click **Fee**, and then type **)**. The expression should look like =SUM([Fee]). Any extra spaces will be removed once you save the expression. Click **OK**.

d. In the Property Sheet pane, click the **Other** tab, click **Name**, and then replace the text with **FeeTotal**. **Close** [X] the Property Sheet pane.

e. Double-click the new **label** in the form footer, and then replace the text with **Fee Total**.

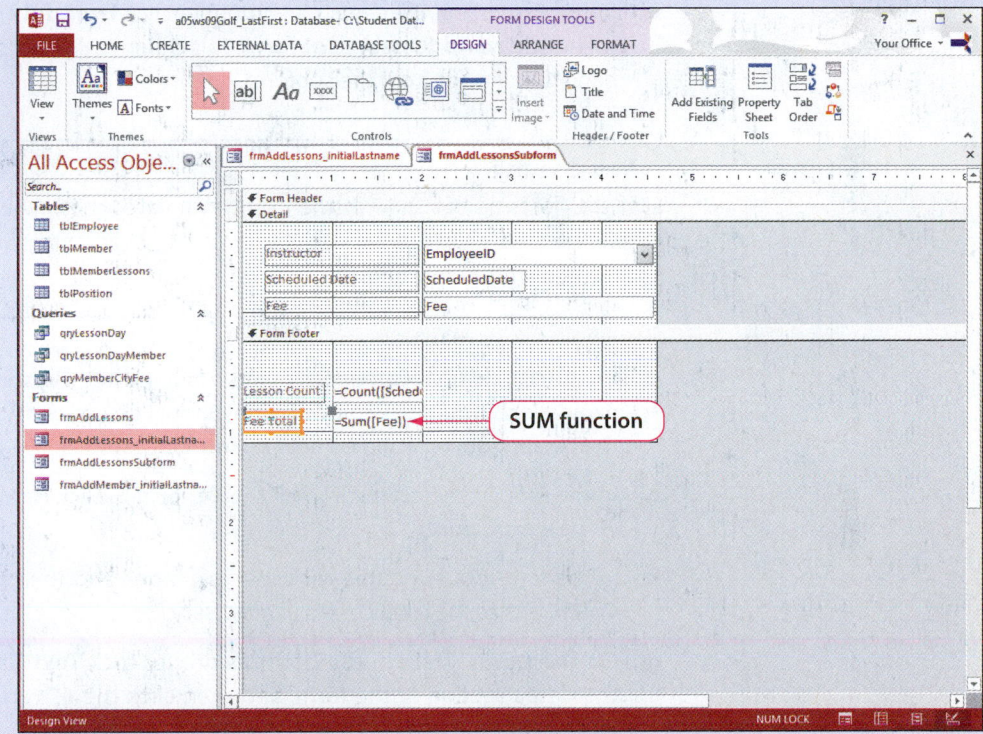

Figure 12 SUM function using the Control Source Builder

f. **Save** [💾] and then **Close** [X] the subform.

> **Troubleshooting**
>
> When you display the main form again, the subform appears blank. Click Form View, and then click Design View and the subform will be populated.

g. On **frmAddLessons_initialLastname**, switch to **Form** view. Note the form footer does not show in the subform when the subform is viewed as part of the main form. **Save** [💾] the form.

Adding Fields from a Subform to the Main Form

On a form with a subform, the footer of the subform is not visible, so any controls that were added to the subform will not be seen in Form view—even though you can see them in Design view. You have calculated the count and sum fields, but you need to show them on the main form. You will create new controls on the main form, and use the fields from the subform as their control source.

A09.15

 To Add Fields from the Subform to the Main Form

a. Switch to **Design** view, click the **DESIGN** tab, and then in the Controls group, click **Text Box** [abl]. Place your pointer in the **detail section** of the form, and then click the **1"** vertical grid line just below Phone Number to place the text box.

b. Open the Property Sheet pane, click the **Data** tab, and then click **Control Source Builder** [...].

c. In the Expression Elements pane, double-click **frmAddLessons_initialLastname**, and then click **frmAddLessonsSubform**. This changes the fields in the Expression Categories pane to the fields from the subform.

> **Troubleshooting**
>
> If the fields do not show in the Expression Categories pane, click Cancel, then switch to Form view and then back to Design view. Click Control Source Builder again and continue with Step c above.

d. In the Expression Categories pane, double-click **LessonCount**. This will build the expression [frmAddLessonsSubform].Form![LessonCount]. This creates a reference to the LessonCount calculated field on frmAddLessonsSubform. Click **OK**.

e. In the Property Sheet pane, click the **Other** tab, click **Name**, and then replace the text with LessonCount.

f. In the form detail, double-click the new **label**, and then replace the text with Lesson Count. Resize the label control if necessary.

g. On the DESIGN tab, in the Controls group, click **Text Box** [abl]. Place the pointer in the detail section of the form, and then click the **4"** vertical grid line to the right of **Lesson Count** to place the text box.

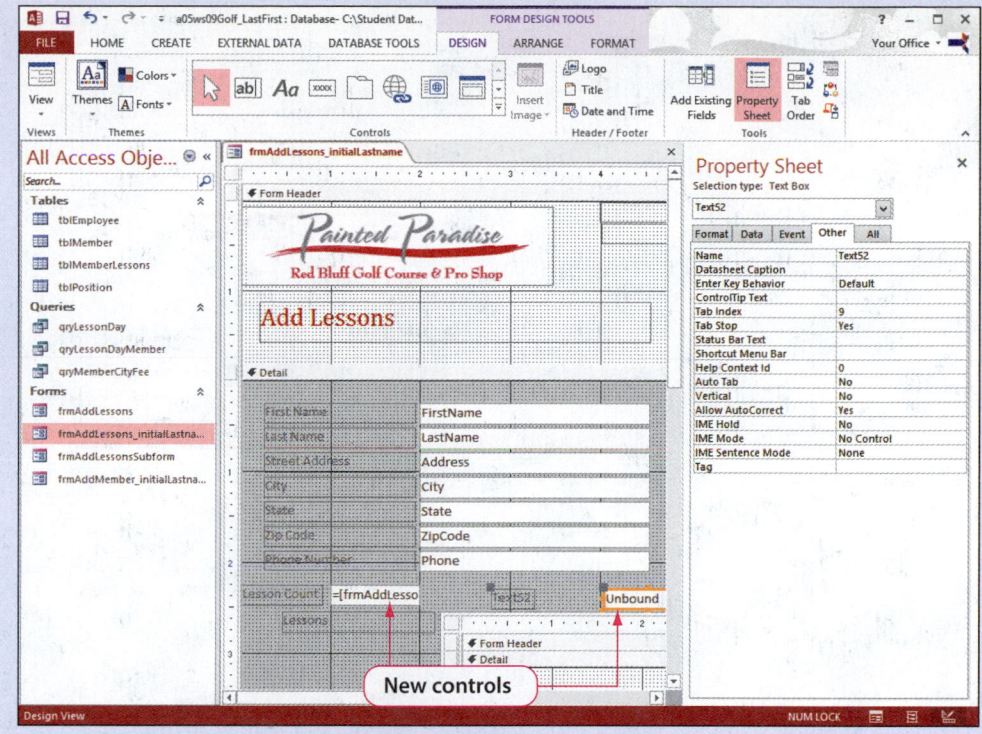

Figure 13 New text boxes added in Design view

h. In the Property Sheet pane, click the **Data** tab, and then click **Control Source Builder** [...].

i. In the Expression Elements pane, double-click **frmAddLessons_initialLastname**, and then click **frmAddLessonsSubform**.

j. In the Expression Categories pane, double-click **FeeTotal**. This will build the expression [frmAddLessonsSubform].Form![FeeTotal]. This creates a reference to the FeeTotal calculated field on frmAddLessonsSubform. Click **OK**.

k. In the Property Sheet pane, click the **Other** tab, click **Name**, and then replace the text with **TotalFees**.

l. Click the **Format** tab, click the **Format** arrow, and then select **Currency**.

m. Double-click the new **label** on the form, and replace the text with **Total Fees**. **Close** [X] the Property Sheet pane, switch to **Form** view to see the new controls, and then **Save** [💾] the form.

SIDE NOTE
Moving Controls
If you need to adjust a control's placement, remember the move handle moves each control individually.

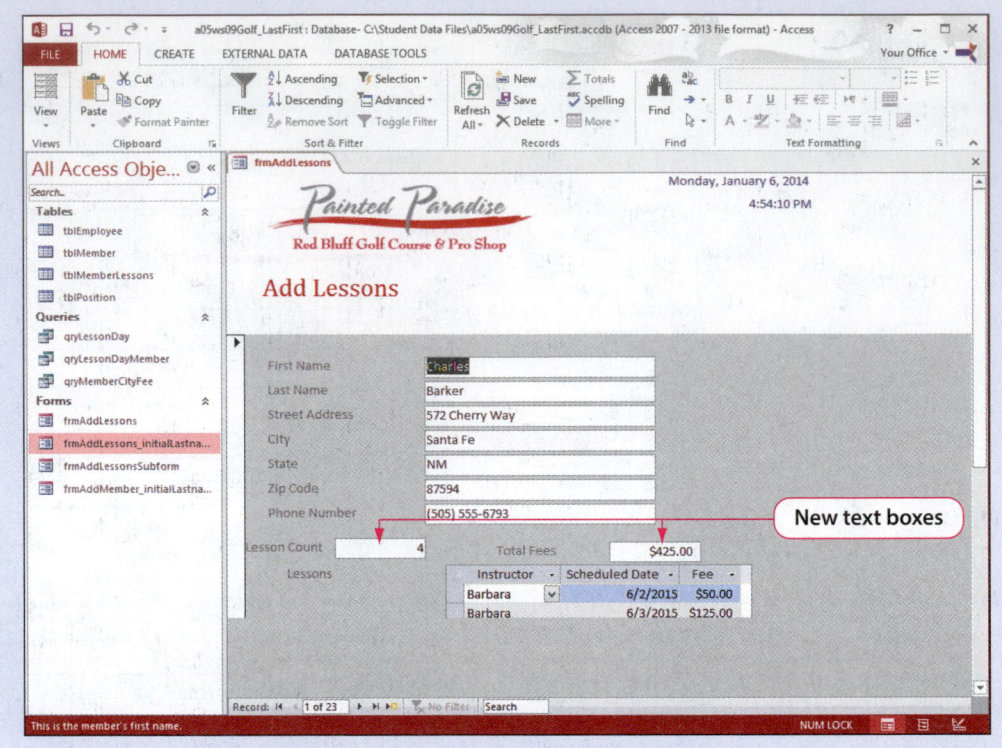

Figure 14 New text boxes in Form view

Adding a Combo Box to Find a Record

A form can be used for looking up information as well as entering information. When a form includes a subform, there are multiple Navigation bars that can be confusing when looking for data. To simplify looking up a member on your form, you will add a combo box to use as a lookup field.

A09.16

   To Add a Combo Box to Look Up a Field Value

a. Switch to **Design** view, and then place the pointer on the **top border** of the Detail section bar. Drag down so that the Form Header section is **2"** high.

b. Click the **DESIGN** tab, and then in the Controls group, click **More** ⊽. Click **Combo Box** 🖽, move the pointer to the **header**, and then click below the **title** and on the **1"** vertical grid line. Access will start the Combo Box Wizard.

> **Troubleshooting**
>
> If the Combo Box Wizard does not open, click More in the Controls group, and then click Use Control Wizards to turn that feature on.

c. Click **Find a record on my form based on the value I selected in my combo box**, and then click **Next**.

d. Double-click **LastName** and **FirstName**, in that order, to add them to the Selected Fields pane, and then click **Next**.

e. Accept the default to **Hide key column**, and then click **Next**.

f. Type **Member Name** as your label, and then click **Finish**.

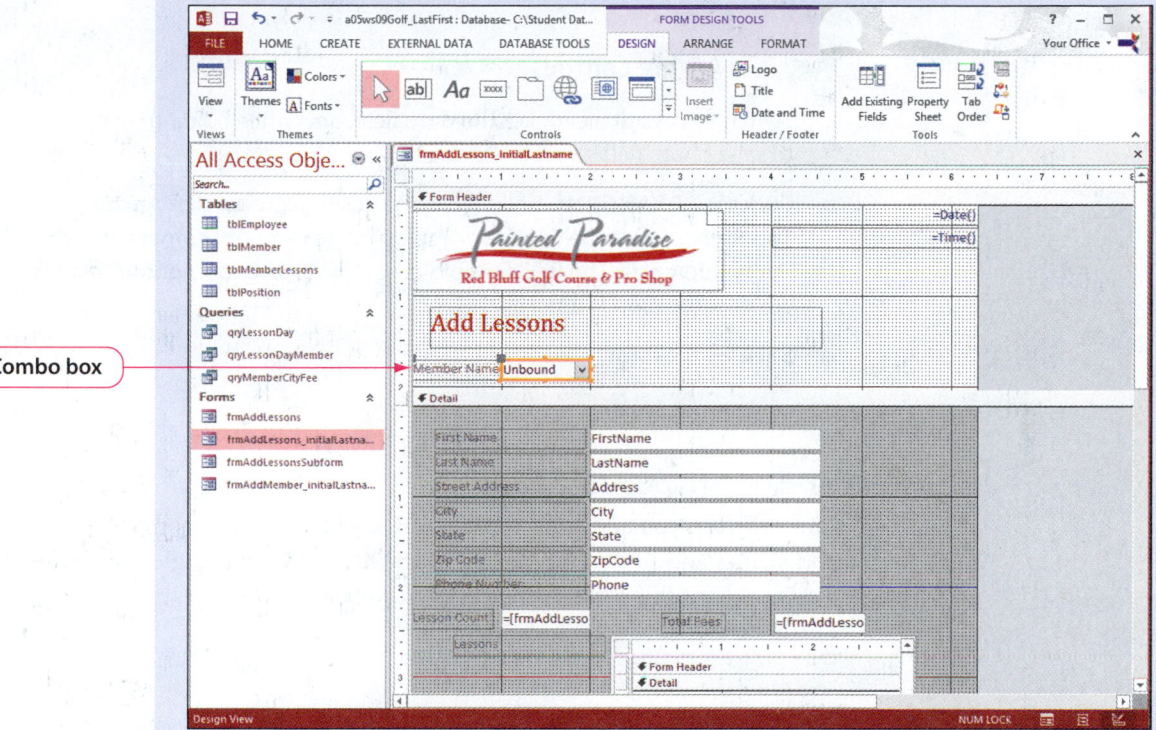

Figure 15 Combo box added to form header

g. If necessary, drag the new **combo** box so all the text in the label is visible. **Save** 💾 the form, and then switch to **Form** view to test the lookup box.

SS CONSIDER THIS | **Lookup Options**

Adding a combo box to look up a field value can be extremely helpful. Can you think of any times where a lookup field may not be appropriate on a form? Think about all the privacy laws that businesses of all types have to follow. How would those privacy laws affect how or if you use lookup options?

Anchoring Controls

Different sized windows may show more or less of your form, just as different sized monitors, or monitors with different resolutions, may show the form a little differently. To preserve the relative position of your controls on a form regardless of the window size, monitor size, or monitor resolution, you can anchor the controls so they are always in the same relative position on the form. You will anchor the date and time controls so they always appear in the top-right corner of the form.

A09.17

To Anchor Controls

a. Switch to **Layout** view, click the **date** field, and while holding Shift, click the **time** field to select both fields.

b. Click the **ARRANGE** tab, and then in the Position group, click **Anchoring**, and then select **Top Right**. If these fields already appear in the top-right corner of the form, try changing the window size. The fields should always be in the top right no matter the size of the window the form is open in.

c. **Save** 🖫 the form.

Adding Shapes to a Form

Not only can you add text controls and calculated controls to the form, but you can also add shapes and lines to the form. You will use the Rectangle tool in Design view to add a rectangle to this form so the Lesson Count and Total Fees fields stand out from the rest of the fields.

A09.18

To Draw a Rectangle in the Form Detail

a. Switch to **Design** view, click the **DESIGN** tab, in the Controls group, click **More** ⊽, and then click **Rectangle** ▢.

b. Place the mouse pointer just above and to the left of the **First Name label**, and then draw the rectangle down and to the right so it encompasses all the stacked fields—First Name label through Phone Number text box.

> **Troubleshooting**
> If the rectangle is not the size you want, you can use the sizing handles to adjust the size and use the move handle to adjust the position.

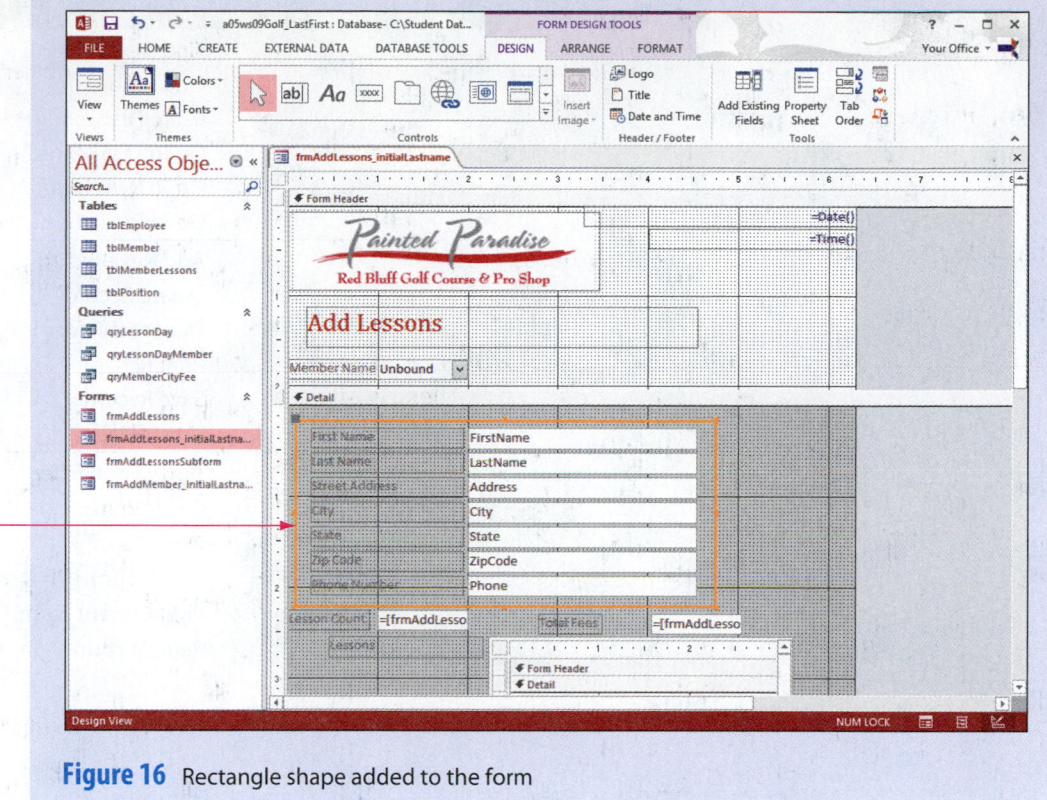

Figure 16 Rectangle shape added to the form

c. Switch to **Form** view to see the rectangle, and then **Save** 🖫 the form.

Adding Navigation Buttons

To make navigating your forms easier, you can add buttons to the form. Buttons are available in several categories and are listed in Table 4. Record Navigation buttons replicate most of the navigation tools available on the Navigation bar. You can create buttons to go to the first, next, last, and previous records. Record Operations buttons allow the user to add, delete, and undo a record. Form Operations buttons open, close, and print forms.

Category	Actions
Record Navigation	Find Next
	Find Record
	Go To First Record
	Go To Last Record
	Go To Next Record
	Go To Previous Record
Record Operations	Add New Record
	Delete Record
	Duplicate Record
	Print Record
	Save Record
	Undo Record
Form Operations	Apply Form Filter
	Close Form
	Open Form
	Print a Form
	Print Current Form
	Refresh Form Data

Table 4   Form Button categories and actions

The Add Lessons form is very easy to use, but it is still navigated using the Navigation bars. In this section, you will add buttons to use for navigation instead.

A09.19

To Add Record Navigation Buttons

a. Switch to **Design** view, click the **DESIGN** tab, and then in the Controls group, click **Button** ⌧.

b. Click the form detail at the **5"** vertical grid line at the **.5"** mark on the vertical ruler—next to the LastName text box. If there is not enough of the form showing, Access will expand the section to fit the button. Access will start the Command Button Wizard.

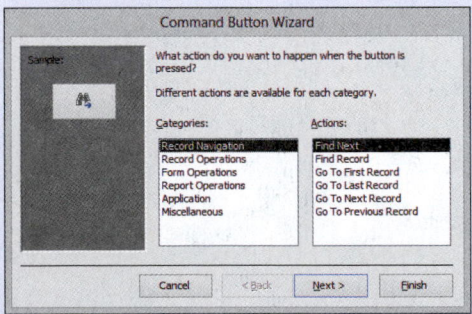

Figure 17   Command Button Wizard

c. In the Categories pane, click **Record Navigation**. In the Actions pane, click **Go To Next Record**, and then click **Next**.

d. Click **Text**, replace the text with Next Member and then click **Next**.

e. Select the button name, replace the **text** with **cmdNextMember** and then click **Finish**.

f. On the DESIGN tab, in the Controls group, click **Button** ⌧. Place your pointer below the **Next Member** button, and then click the **form**.

g. In the Categories pane, click **Record Navigation**. In the Actions pane, click **Go To Previous Record**, and then click **Next**.

h. Click **Text**, replace the text with **Previous Member** and then click **Next**.

i. Select the button name, replace the **text** with **cmdPreviousMember** and then click **Finish**.

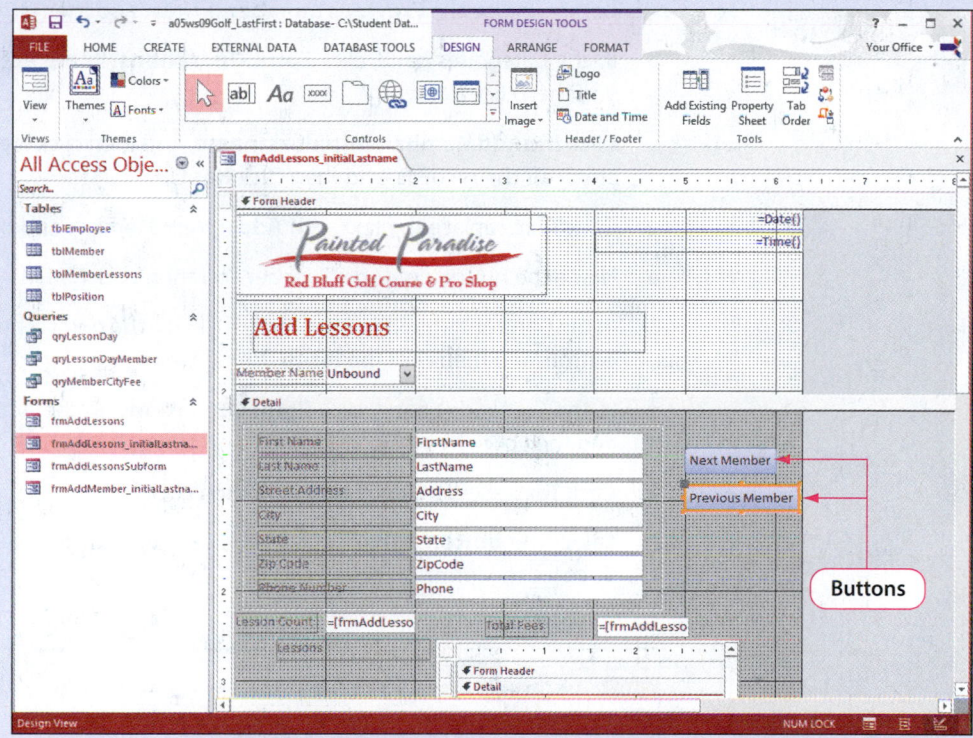

Figure 18 Two new buttons added to the form

REAL WORLD ADVICE **Record vs. Member**

Access suggests text for command buttons that includes the word "Record". In this case, the word "Record" is a technical database term. You know that a record is a row in a table, and that it contains data about a person, place, or thing. However, a user without database training will not know what "Record" means. To make your form user friendly, replace the word "Record" with the name of the person, place, or thing. For example, a record in a member table should be called "Member"; a record in an employee table should be called "Employee".

Adding Form Operations Buttons

In addition to navigation buttons, other types of buttons can also be added to a form. Form Operations buttons provide you with easier ways to work with the form itself. You will add a link to the Add Member form that will allow the user to switch to that form. The other button you will add will close the form.

A09.20
 To Add Form Operations Buttons

a. Click the **DESIGN** tab, and then in the Controls group, click **Button** [xxxx]. Place your pointer below the **Previous Member** button, and then click the **form**.

b. In the Categories pane, click **Form Operations**. In the Actions pane, click **Open Form**, and then click **Next**.

c. Click **frmAddMember_initialLastname**, and then click **Next**. Click **Open the form and show all the records**, and then click **Next**.

d. Click **Text**, replace the text with Add a New Member and then click **Next**.

e. Name the button cmdAddMember and then click **Finish**.

f. In the Controls group, click **Button** [xxxx]. Place the pointer below the **Add a New Member** button, and then click the **form**.

g. In the Categories pane, click **Form Operations**. In the Actions pane, click **Close Form**, and then click **Next**.

h. Click **Text**, accept **Close Form**, and then click **Next**.

i. Select the **button name**, replace the text with cmdCloseForm, and then click **Finish**. Save [💾] the form.

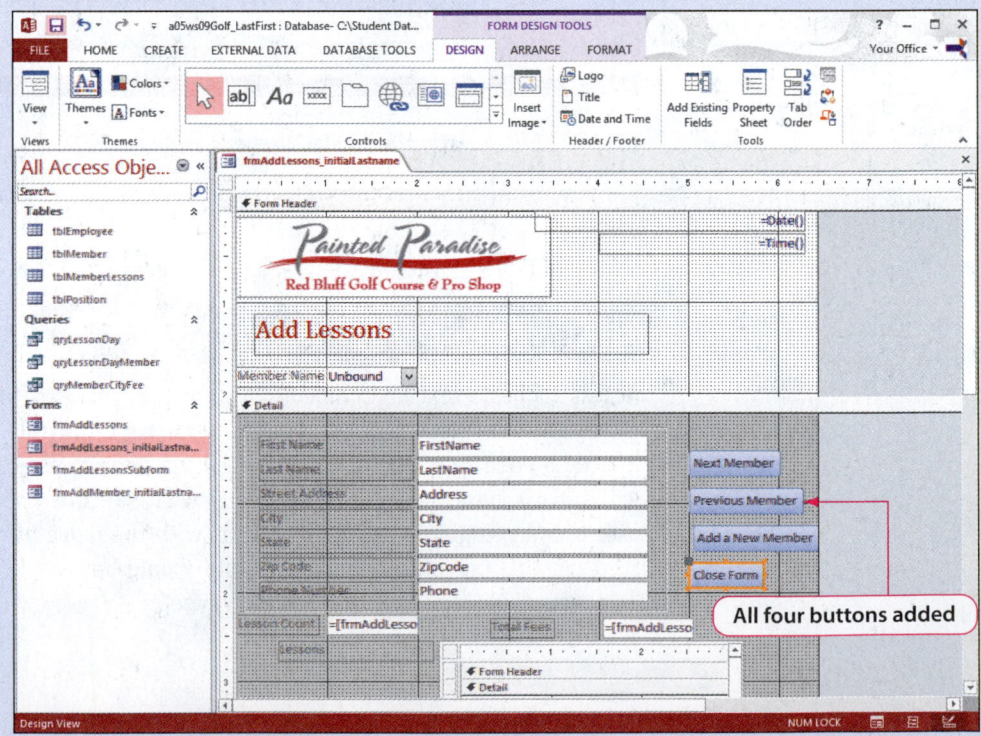

Figure 19 Form with four buttons added

Aligning Controls

You can use the grid to line up controls on a form manually, or you can use the many align tools available. Using the align tools will provide your form with a finished and polished look. Now that you have added all four buttons, you will line them up with one another, make them the same size, and make sure they are spaced evenly on the form.

A09.21

 To Align Buttons

a. Click the **Next Member** button to select it. Then, while holding Shift, click the **Previous Member** button, the **Add a New Member** button, and the **Close Form** button to select all four buttons. Click the **ARRANGE** tab, in the Sizing & Ordering group, click **Align**, and then select **Left**. This will align the buttons by their left edge.

b. In the Sizing & Ordering group, click **Size/Space**, and then select **Equal Vertical**. This will evenly space the buttons vertically, so there is the same amount of space between each button.

c. Click **Size/Space**, and then select **To Widest**. This will make all buttons the same width based on the widest button selected.

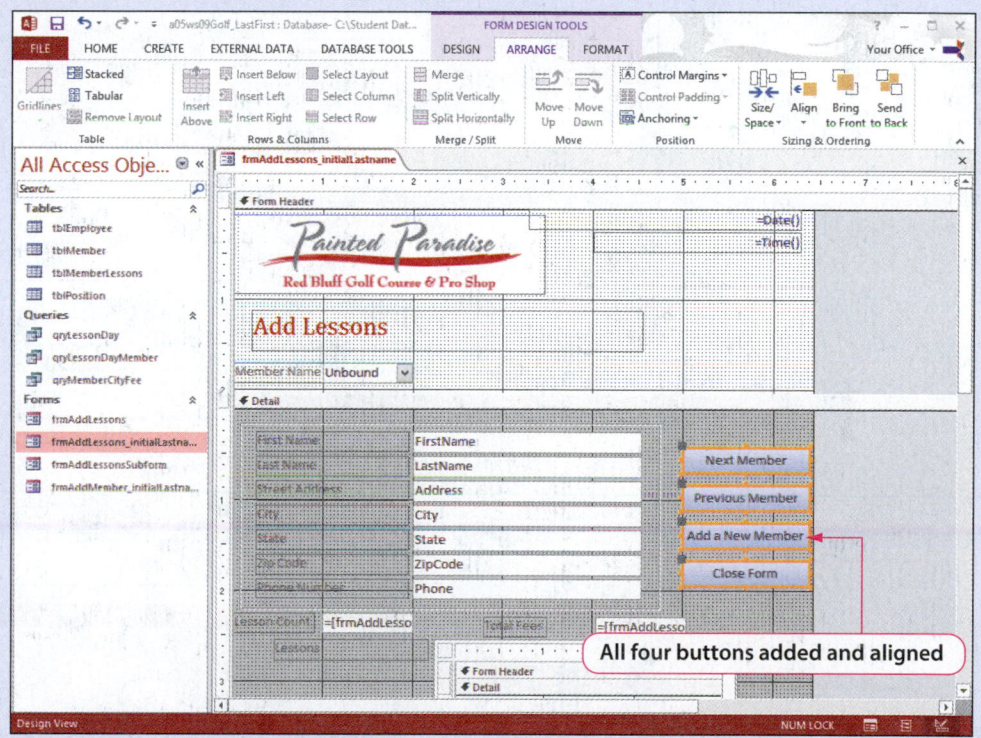

Figure 20 Buttons aligned and resized

d. Save the form.

Turning Off the Navigation Bar

Once you have navigation buttons on a form, the Navigation bars that are the normal part of the forms can be hidden so the user will only navigate the form using the buttons. You will turn off the Navigation bars for both the main form and the subform. You will also turn off the Record Selector on the far left side of the form.

To Turn Off the Navigation Bar

a. Click the **DESIGN** tab, and then in the Tools group, click **Property Sheet** to open the form's property sheet.

b. In the Property Sheet pane, click the **Selection type** arrow at the top of the pane, and then select **Form**. This changes the property sheet to show the properties of the entire form.

c. Click the **Format** tab, click **Navigation Buttons**, click the **Navigation Buttons** arrow, and then select **No**. This removes the navigation buttons from the form.

d. Click **Record Selectors**, click the **Records Selectors** arrow, and then select **No**. This removes the record selectors from the form.

e. In the detail section of the form, click the **Form selector** ☐ on the subform. This changes the property sheet to show the properties of the subform.

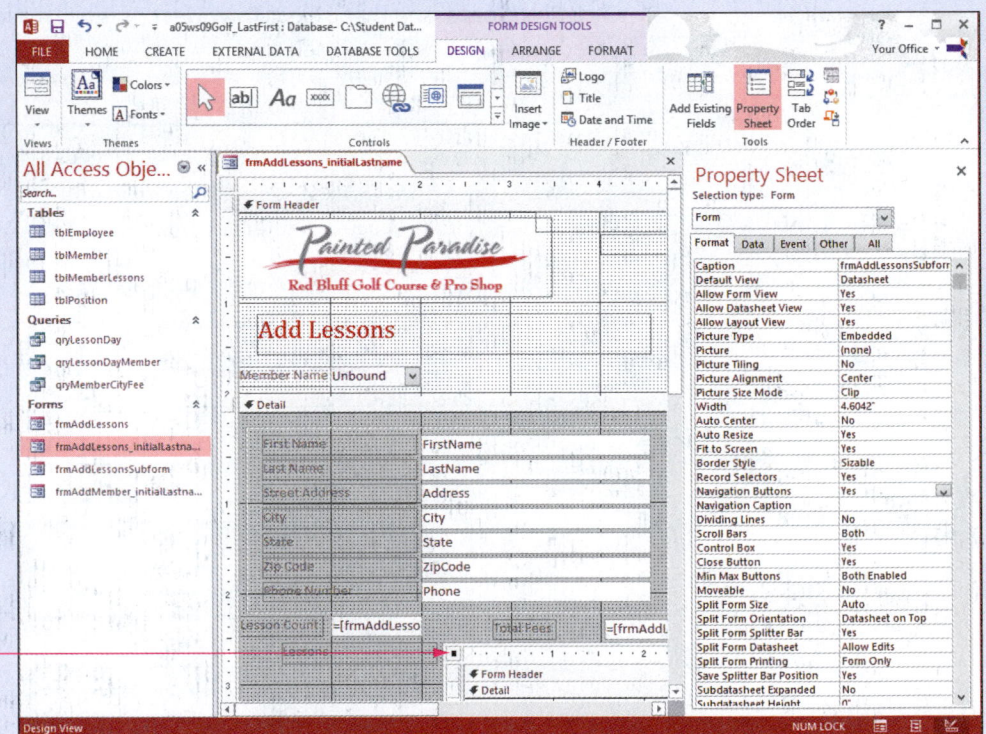

Figure 21 Subform selected in Property Sheet pane

f. In the Property Sheet pane, on the Format tab, click **Navigation Buttons**, click the **Navigation Buttons** arrow, and then select **No**.

g. **Close** ☒ the Property Sheet pane, and then **Save** 🖫 the form. Switch to **Form** view, and then test your buttons. Note if you click **Add New Member** you will open frmAddMember_initialLastname. **Close** ☒ frmAddMember_initialLastname. On **frmAddLessons_initialLastname**, click **Close Form** to close the form. If necessary, click **Yes** to save the objects.

REAL WORLD ADVICE | **Picture vs. Text**

Access allows you to use pictures or text for buttons. Use text unless it is absolutely obvious. For example, does an image of a door mean close or open? "Exit" is not the obvious interpretation. If it is not obvious, use words to label the button. The picture of a printer is universal, and the undo button is well known. The rest may need explanation and are better left as text.

Creating Advanced Forms

Forms do not have to show only one record at a time. Forms can show multiple records at a time in a **multiple-item form**, or continuous form.

Forms can also be multiple pages, each of which is controlled by a tab. This way you can view multiple forms in one window by clicking on different tabs.

In this section, you will create different types of advanced forms to illustrate the different uses for forms in Access.

Create Specialized Forms

On the Create tab, there is a More Forms button that lists different types of forms available to create. Before you choose a form, you should have an object in the Navigation Pane selected. Whatever is selected in the Navigation Pane, whether it is a table or query, will become the source for the form you choose to create.

Creating a Multiple-Item Form

While the multiple-item form looks very similar to a datasheet, it can be customized as a form. The data is arranged in rows and columns, but you can add graphical elements, buttons, and other controls as in other forms. You will create a multiple-items form to list the club's members.

A09.23

 To Create a Multiple-Item Form

a. Click **tblMember** in the Navigation Pane to select the table. Click the **CREATE** tab, in the Forms group, click **More Forms**, and then select **Multiple Items**.

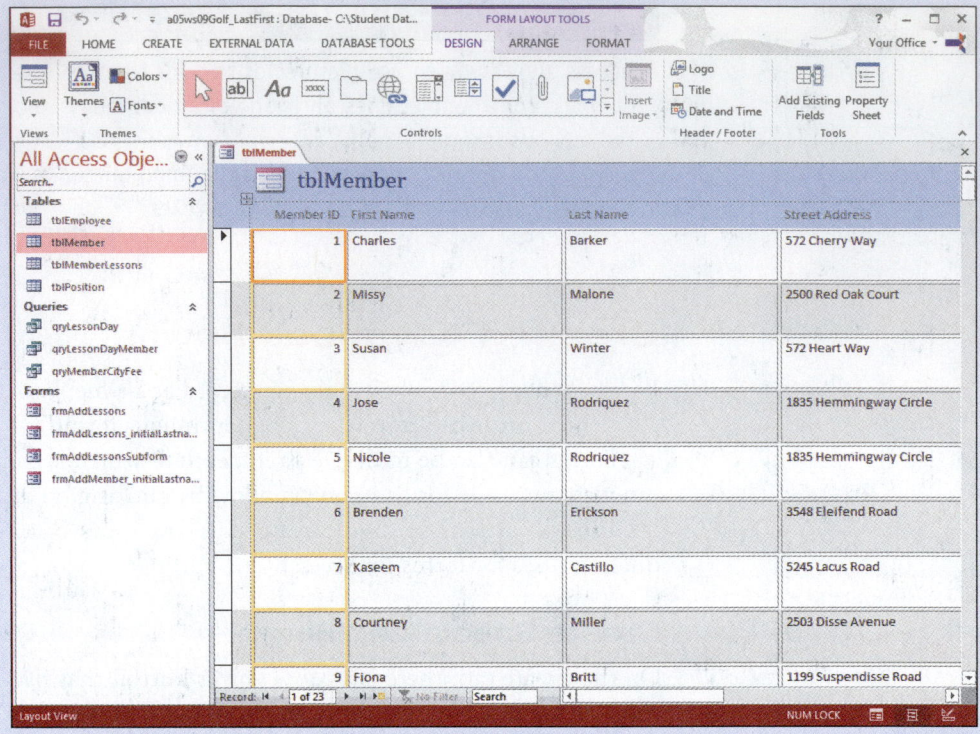

Figure 22 Multiple-items form created

b. Scroll right to find **Date Joined**, and then click the first **Date Joined** field value. Click the **DESIGN** tab, in the Tools group, click **Property Sheet**. In the Property Sheet pane, click the **Data** tab, click **Input Mask**, and then select the **text**. Press Delete to remove the input mask.

c. On the form detail, click the **Renewal Date field value**, and then in the Property Sheet pane, on the Data tab, click **Input Mask**. Select the **text**, and then press Delete to remove the input mask.

d. At the top of the Property Sheet pane, click the **Selection type** arrow, and then select **Form Header**. Click the **Format** tab, and then click **Back Color**. Click **Builder** …, and then select **White, Background 1, Darker 15%**. Close ✕ the Property Sheet pane.

e. Click the form **title**, and then change it to Multiple Members Form. Click the form **icon** to the left of the title, and then press Delete.

f. **Save** 🖫 the form and type frmMultipleMembers_initialLastname. Click **OK** and then **Close** ✕ the form.

Create a Multipage Form Using Tab Controls

A multipage form can be used to show two different forms on one page, or to show groups of fields from multiple tables, and it allows you to switch between them using tabs you create on the form. Multipage forms can be created by using either the Page Break tool or the Tab Control tool. The Page Break tool creates a continuous flow between forms so you can use the Page Up and Page Down keys to move between forms. The **Tab Control** tool creates tabs, with one tab per page, so you switch between pages using the tabs.

Modifying an Existing Form to Add a Tab Control

You will create a modified version of frmAddLessons that has three tabs with all the member information. You will start by creating a copy of frmAddLessons and then modifying that form.

A09.24

To Copy an Existing Form and Add a Tab Control

a. Right-click **frmAddLessons_initialLastname** in the Navigation Pane, and then select **Copy**. Point to a **blank area** in the Navigation Pane, **right-click**, and then select **Paste**. Type **frmMemberPortal_initialLastname** using your initial and last name, and then click **OK**. Double-click **frmMemberPortal_initialLastname** in the Navigation Pane to open the form.

> **Troubleshooting**
>
> The tab on the open form may still show "frmAddLessons_initialLastname"—in Form and Layout view—even though you changed the file name when you copied and pasted. You can leave it that way, or you can change the tab name in the Property Sheet pane by selecting the form, clicking the Format tab, selecting Caption, and then changing it to frmMemberPortal_initialLastname.

b. Switch to **Design** view, right-click the **subform**, and then select **Cut**.

c. Click the **DESIGN** tab, in the Controls group, click **Tab Control** ⬚, and then click the **1"** vertical grid line in the **detail area** below Lesson Count to insert the tab control.

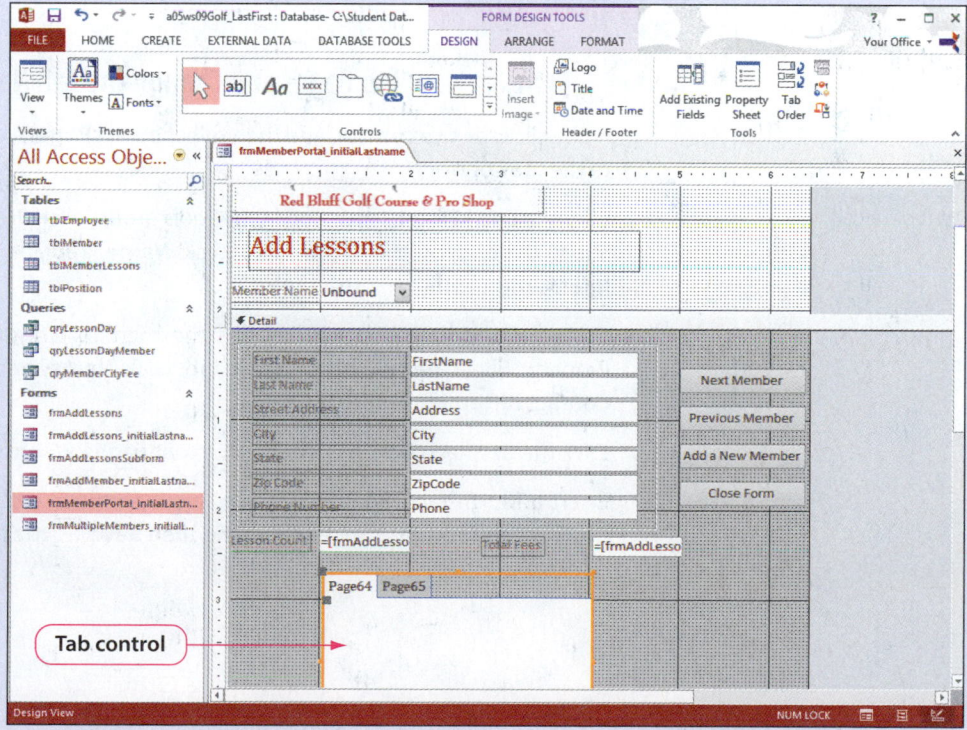

Figure 23 Tab control added to form with two tabs

d. Right-click the **blank area** of the tab control, and then select **Paste**. This will paste the subform on the first tab page. Select the **Lessons** label control, and then press Delete.

e. Click the **First Name** label, click the **selection** box ⊞ at the top-left corner of the stacked controls, and then right-click the **First Name** label. Select **Cut**.

f. Click the **second** tab of the tab control, right-click the **blank** area, and then select **Paste**. This will paste all the stacked controls on the second tab page.

g. Select the rectangle shape in the form detail that was around the stacked controls and press Delete. Move the **Next Member** button so that the top-left corner is on the **.5"** mark on the horizontal ruler and the **.5"** mark on the vertical ruler. Move the **Previous Member**, **Add New Member**, and **Close Form** buttons next to the **Add Member** button so they are in a horizontal line.

h. Press and hold Shift, and then select all four buttons. Click the **ARRANGE** tab, in the Sizing & Ordering group, click **Align**, and then select **Top**.

i. In the Sizing & Ordering group, click **Size/Space**, and then select **Equal Horizontal**. Save 🖫 the form.

Inserting a Tab Page and Changing Tab Captions

By default, the tab control will be inserted with two tabbed pages. You can add more pages as necessary. You will add two more pages to include additional member information and summary details. Every tab is named "Page" with a number. You will change those tab names to something more meaningful.

A09.25

To Insert New Tab Pages and Change the Tab Names

a. Right-click the **tab control**, and then select **Insert Page**. A new blank page will be added to the tab control.

b. Click the **DESIGN** tab, and then in the Tools group, click **Property Sheet**. In the Property Sheet pane, click the **Other** tab, click **Name**, replace the text with Membership Information and then press Tab.

c. Click the **middle** tab page that has the member contact information fields. In the Property Sheet pane, on the Other tab, click **Name**, and then replace the text with Contact Information.

d. Click the **first** tab page, and then name that page Lessons.

e. Insert a fourth tab page, and then name it Summary following Steps a and b above. Close ✕ the Property Sheet pane, and then Save 🖫 the form.

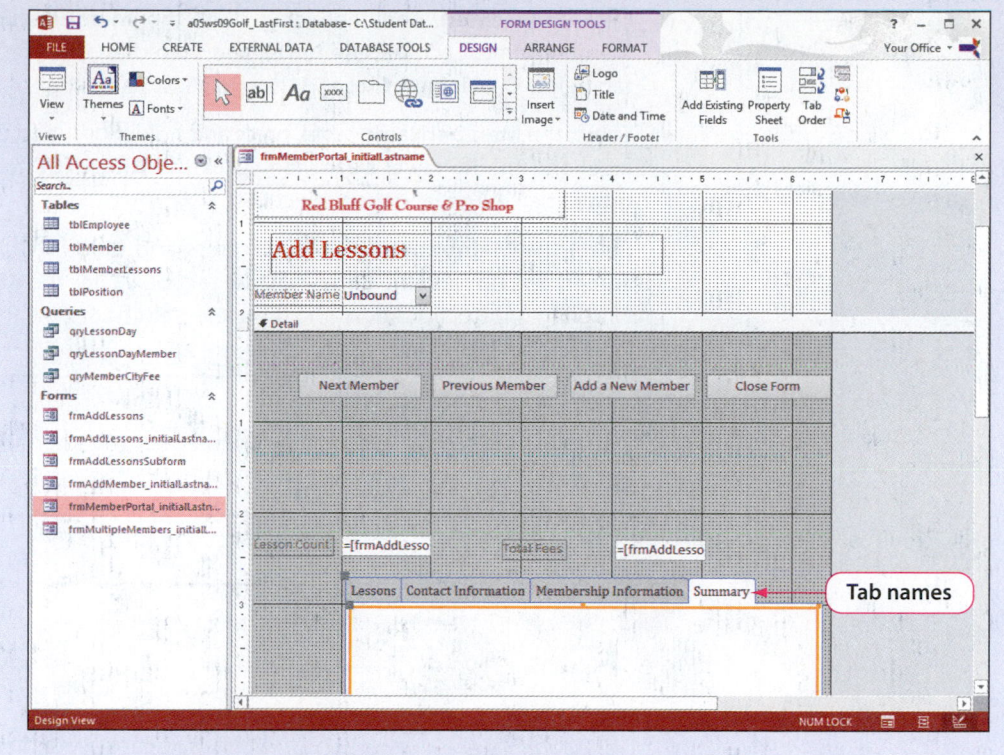

Figure 24 Tabs added to Tab Control and renamed

Inserting Existing Fields in a Tab Page

You can add existing fields and other controls to the tabbed pages. As long as the tables in the database are related in a one-to-many relationship, you can add fields from other tables in the tab control. You will add fields from tblMember that are not already on the form. You will also move the summary controls—Lesson Count and Total Fees—to the Summary tab page.

A09.26

To Insert Existing Fields in a Tab Page

a. On the tab control, click the **Membership Information** tab. Click the **DESIGN** tab, in the Tools group, click **Add Existing Fields**.

b. Click **MemberName**, and then drag it to the top-left corner of the **Membership Information** page.

> **Troubleshooting**
>
> If you cannot see the list of fields from tblMember, click Show all tables at the top of the Field List, and then double-click tblMember to expand the table and see the fields available.

c. Click **DateJoined**, and then drag it to the **Membership Information** tab below MemberName. Click **DateRenewal**, and then drag it to the **Membership Information** tab below DateJoined. **Close** ☒ the Field List pane.

d. Select the **MemberName label**, press and hold Shift, and then select the **Date Joined** label and the **Renewal Date** label. Click the **ARRANGE** tab, in the Sizing & Ordering group, click **Align**, and then select **Left**.

e. Select the **MemberName** text box, press and hold Shift, and then select the **Date Joined** text box and the **Renewal Date** text box. Click the **ARRANGE** tab, in the Sizing & Ordering group, click **Align**, and then select **Right**.

> **Troubleshooting**
>
> If the fields are too far apart, move them closer together and repeat the steps to align them.

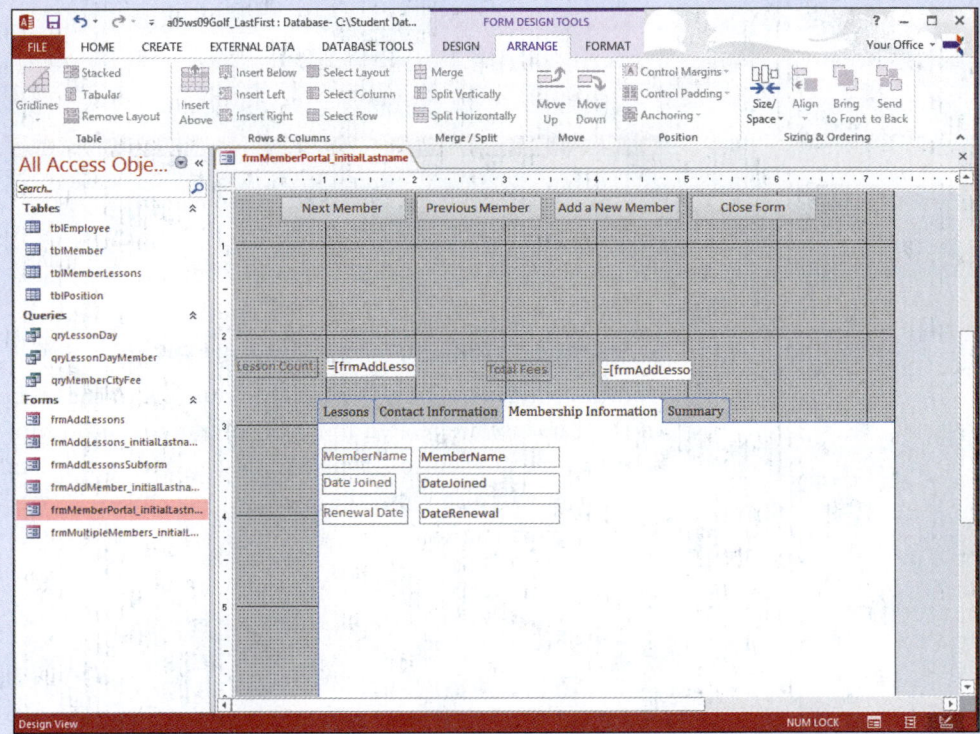

Figure 25 Fields added and aligned on Membership Information tab

f. In the form detail, select the **Lesson Count** label, press and hold Shift, and then select the **Lesson Count** text box, the **Total Fees** label, and the **Total Fees** text box. Right-click the **selected controls**, and then select **Cut**.

g. On the tab control, click the **Summary** tab page to select it. Right-click a **blank area** of the page, and then select **Paste**.

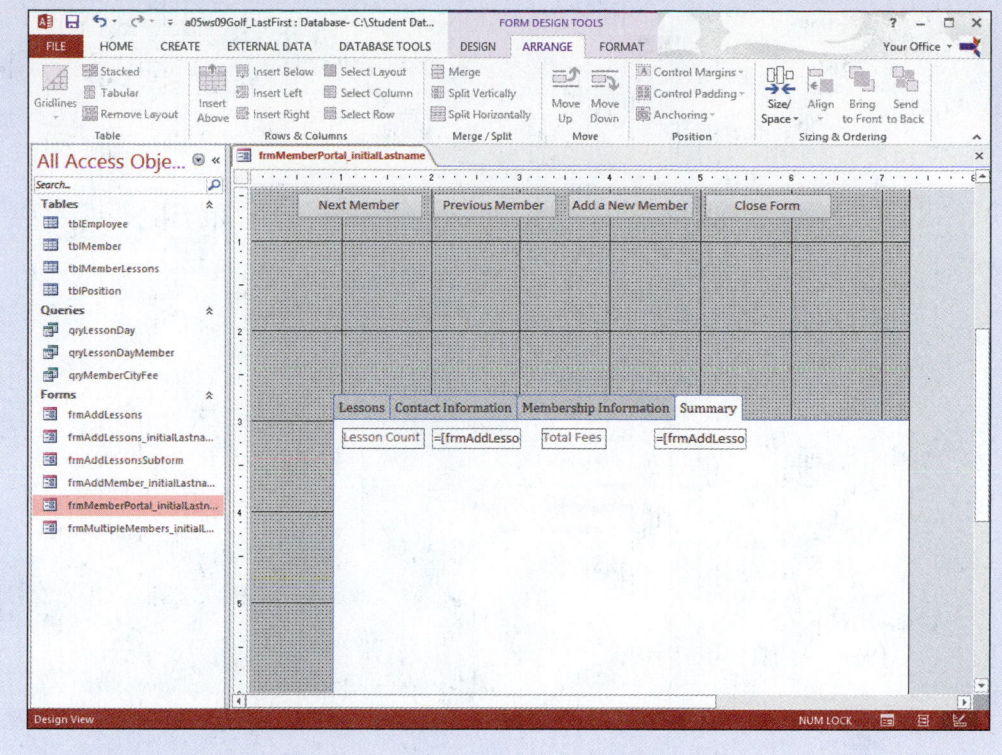

Figure 26 All fields moved from form to tab control pages

Rearranging, Moving, and Resizing the Tab Control

When you have all your pages added to the tab control, and all the controls added to the tabbed pages, you can move the tab control, if necessary, and resize it so all the controls fit well on each page. You will move the tab control to fit just under the navigation buttons on the form, and you will resize the tab control to reduce the amount of blank space on each page. You will also rearrange the pages in the tab control so they are in a different order.

 A09.27

To Rearrange, Move, and Resize the Tab Control

a. Click the **tab control** to select it, point to the **orange border**, and then move the tab control to just below the navigation buttons on the **1"** horizontal grid line and **1"** vertical grid line.

b. Right-click the **tab control**, select **Page Order**, and then click **Summary**. Click **Move Up** three times to move Summary to the top of the list, and then click **OK**.

c. Click the **Summary** tab. Select the **Lesson Count** label, press and hold Shift, select the **Lesson Count** text box, and then move them so the Lesson Count label is in the top-left corner of the page. Select the **Total Fees** label and text box and move them below the Lesson Count controls. Click **Align** to left align the labels and right align the text boxes.

SIDE NOTE

Size of the Tab Control

The tab control is as wide as the widest controls, so if Access prevents you from making a page narrower, it is because another page needs that amount of space.

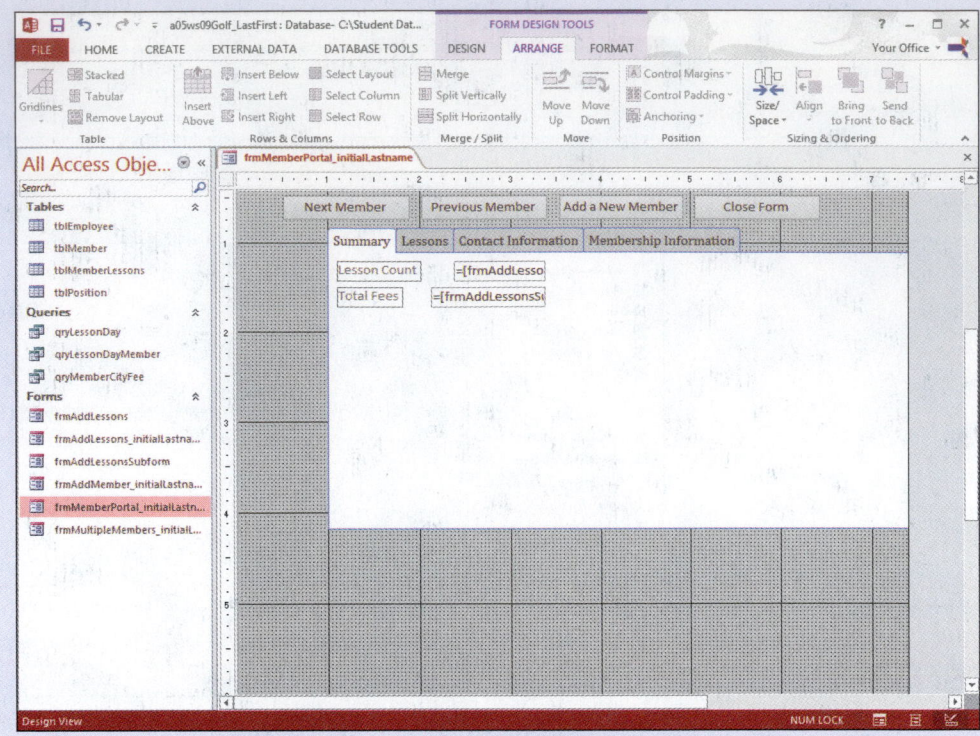

Figure 27 Summary page controls rearranged and aligned

d. Click the **Lessons** tab, click the **subform** to select it, and then if necessary, move it to the top-left corner of the page. Point to the **bottom edge** of the subform, and then drag it up so the **footer** is hidden.

e. Click the **Contact Information** tab. Because these controls were stacked earlier, you can click the **Select** button ⊞ at the top left of the controls to select all the controls at once. Drag the controls so the First Name label is in the top-left corner of the page.

f. Click the **Membership Information** tab, select all **six controls** and then, if necessary, move them so the MemberName is in the top-left corner of the page.

g. Click the **tab control** to select it. The orange box should include the pages and the tabs. Point to the **right sizing handle** of the selection, and then drag the tab control to the left until it will not move anymore. This will resize the tab control to the widest control on any of the pages.

h. Double-click the **title** in the header, and then change it to **Member Portal**.

Troubleshooting

If you cannot click the title because the blank header box from the logo is in the way, click the blank header box and press ⌈Delete⌋ to delete it, and then select the title.

---

i. **Save** 🖫 the form, and then switch to **Form** view to see your form and test your tabs. Select a name from the **Member Name** box in the header of the form to see the detail about that member. **Close** ✖ the form, and then exit Access.

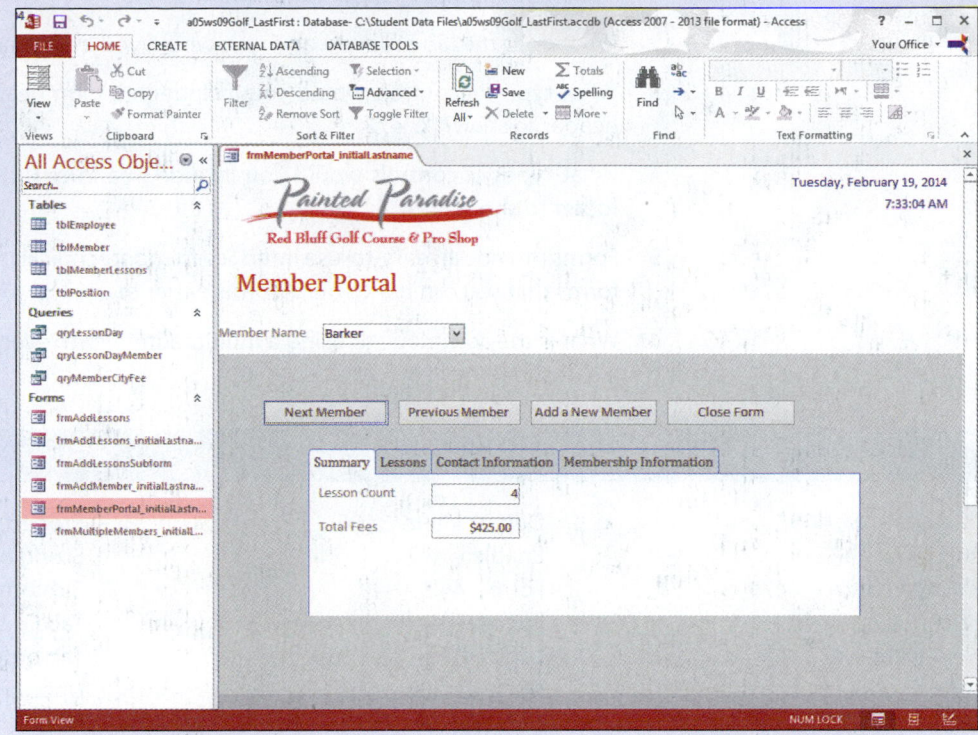

Figure 28 Final Member Portal

Concept Check

1. What is the difference between a bound and an unbound control? Suppose you have a form for entering customers into the table. What would be an example of a bound control on this form? An unbound control? p. 466

2. What does the tab order do, and why would you ever change it? p. 478

3. What types of controls would you include in a form header? How do you get the form header to show? p. 472

4. What types of controls would you include in a form footer? How do you get the form footer to show? p. 474

5. Forms provide an easy-to-use interface for nontechnical users. What are some features of forms that you can use to make forms easier to use? p. 472

6. What is the advantage to using a multiple-item form even though it looks very similar to a datasheet? p. 493

Key Terms

Bound control   465
Bound form   462
Calculated control   479
Control   465
Current Date   467
DateAdd   467
Date Picker   470

Default Value   466
Enabled   471
Form   462
Locked   471
Logo   472
Move handle   476
Multiple-item form   493

Property sheet   464
Sizing handle   476
Subform   476
Tab Control   494
Tab order   478
Unbound control   466
Unbound form   462

Visual Summary

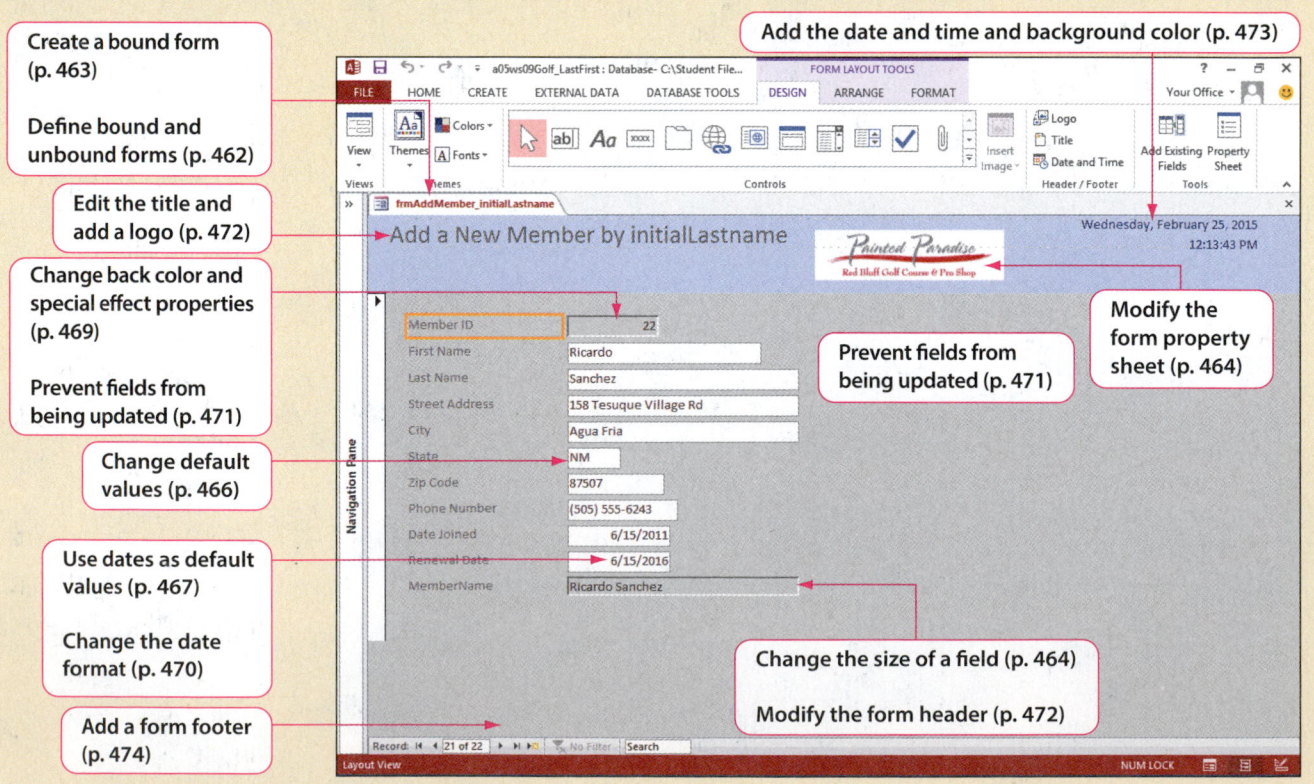

Create a bound form (p. 463)

Define bound and unbound forms (p. 462)

Edit the title and add a logo (p. 472)

Change back color and special effect properties (p. 469)

Prevent fields from being updated (p. 471)

Change default values (p. 466)

Use dates as default values (p. 467)

Change the date format (p. 470)

Add a form footer (p. 474)

Add the date and time and background color (p. 473)

Modify the form property sheet (p. 464)

Prevent fields from being updated (p. 471)

Change the size of a field (p. 464)

Modify the form header (p. 472)

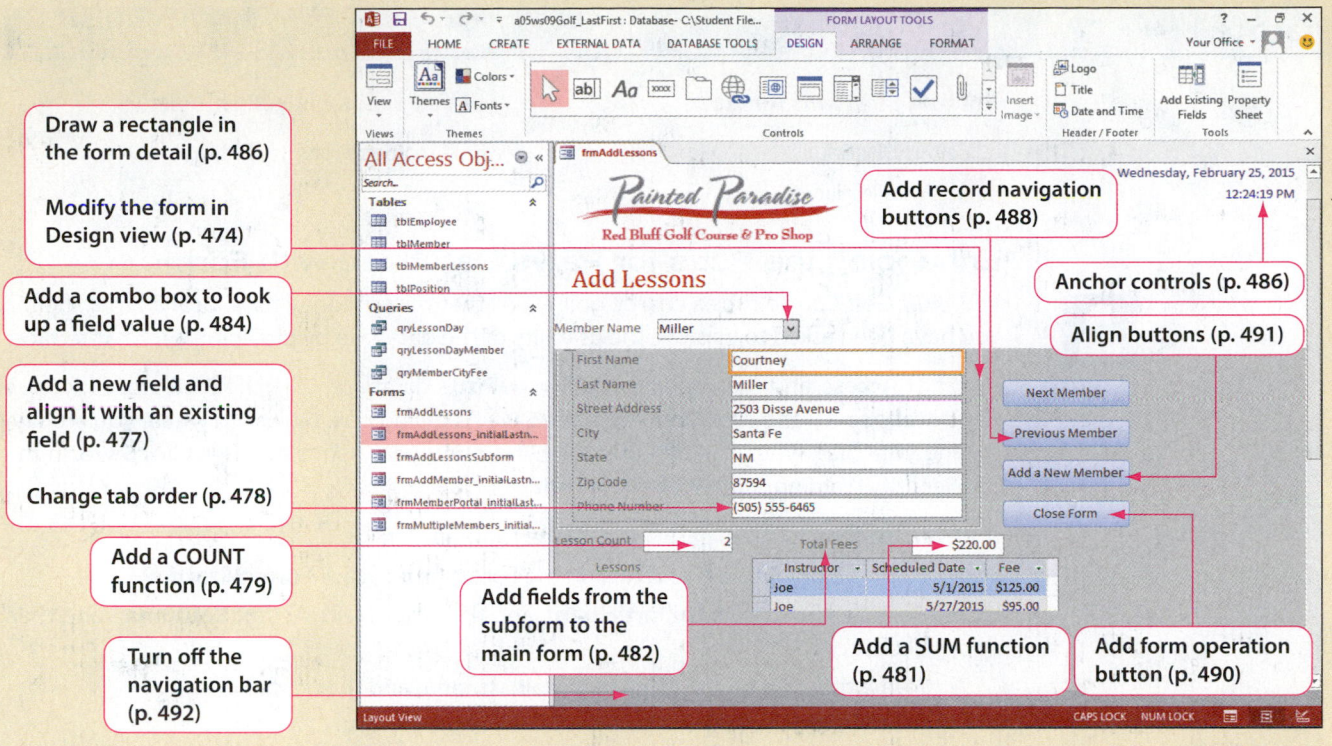

Draw a rectangle in the form detail (p. 486)

Modify the form in Design view (p. 474)

Add a combo box to look up a field value (p. 484)

Add a new field and align it with an existing field (p. 477)

Change tab order (p. 478)

Add a COUNT function (p. 479)

Turn off the navigation bar (p. 492)

Add record navigation buttons (p. 488)

Anchor controls (p. 486)

Align buttons (p. 491)

Add fields from the subform to the main form (p. 482)

Add a SUM function (p. 481)

Add form operation button (p. 490)

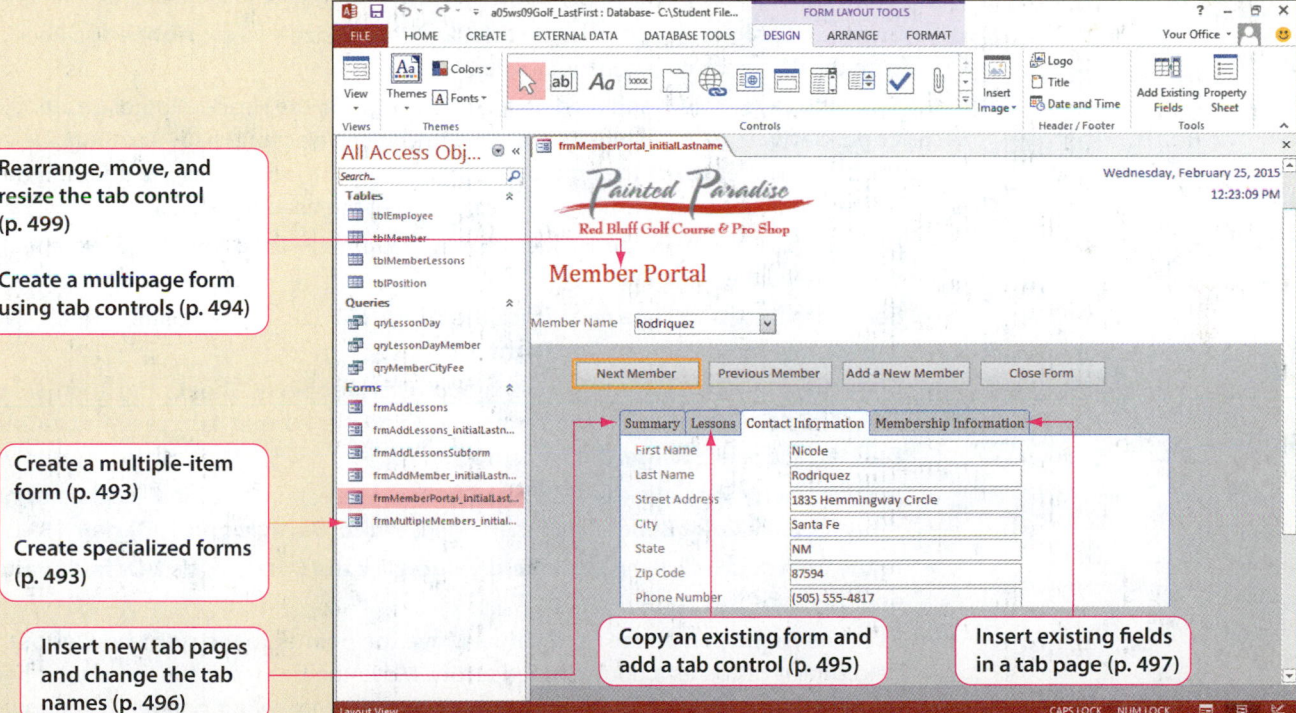

Rearrange, move, and resize the tab control (p. 499)

Create a multipage form using tab controls (p. 494)

Create a multiple-item form (p. 493)

Create specialized forms (p. 493)

Insert new tab pages and change the tab names (p. 496)

Copy an existing form and add a tab control (p. 495)

Insert existing fields in a tab page (p. 497)

Figure 29 Red Bluff Golf Club Final Database

Student data files needed:

 a05ws09Putts.accdb

 a05ws09RedBluff.jpg

You will save your file as:

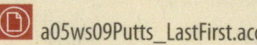 a05ws09Putts_LastFirst.accdb

Enhancing the Putts for Paws Database with Forms

Customer
Service

Red Bluff Golf Course runs a charity golf event that raises money for a local animal shelter. You have been asked to improve the usability of the database by providing a form interface.

a. Start **Access**, and then open the **a05ws09Putts** database. Click the **FILE** tab, click **Save Database As**, and click **Save As**. In the Save As dialog box, browse to where you are saving your files, type a05ws09Putts_LastFirst using your name and then click **Save**. In the Security Warning, click **Enable Content**.

b. Create a form to add a participant to the tournament:

- Click the **CREATE** tab, and then in the Forms group, click **Form Wizard**.
- Select all fields from **tblParticipant**, and then click **Next**. Accept **Columnar**, and then click **Next**.
- Name the form frmParticipant_initialLastname and then click **Finish**.
- Switch to **Layout** view.
- Click the **header**, select the title **frmParticipant_initialLastname**, and then replace the text with Add Participant by initialLastname using your first initial and last name.
- Switch to **Design** view, point to the **title**, and then resize it so the **right edge** lines up with the **4"** mark on the horizontal ruler.
- Switch to **Layout** view, and then on the DESIGN tab, in the Header/Footer group, click **Logo**. Navigate to your student data files, and then select **a05ws09RedBluff**. Delete the blank header box to the right of the logo. Move the logo below the title, and then resize it to fit between the title and the bottom of the header.
- On the DESIGN tab, in the Header/Footer group, click **Date and Time**, accept the defaults, and then click **OK**.
- Select the **Date** and **Time** fields, click the **ARRANGE** tab, in the Position group, click **Anchoring**, and then select **Top Right**.
- Click the **DESIGN** tab, in the Tools group, click **Property Sheet**, and then select **FormHeader** from the Selection type list. Click the **Format** tab, click **Back Color Builder**, and select **White, Background 1**.
- In the Property Sheet pane, select **Detail** from the Selection type list. Click the **Format** tab, click **Back Color Builder**, and then select **White, Background 1, Darker 15%**.
- In the form detail, click the **State field value**, click the **Data** tab, click **Default Value**, and then type NM.
- Click the **ParticipantName field value**. Move the pointer to the **right border** of the field until it becomes a double-sided arrow. Move the border to the left until it lines up with the right border of the StreetAddress field. Move your pointer to the **lower border** of the field until it becomes a double-headed arrow. Move the border up until the field is a single line.
- With ParticipantName still selected, in the Property Sheet pane, on the Data tab, click the **Locked** property, and then select **Yes**. Click the **Other** tab, click **Tab Stop**, and then select **No**.
- With ParticipantName still selected, click the **Format** tab, click **Special Effect**, and then select **Sunken**. Click **Back Color Builder**, and then select **White, Background 1, Darker 15%**.
- Switch to **Form** view, and then change the **name** of the first participant to your name.
- Save and close the form.

c. Modify an existing form to see participant's orders:

- Right-click **frmParticipantOrders** in the Navigation Pane, and select **Copy**. Right-click a blank area in the Navigation Pane, and then select **Paste**. Type frmParticipantOrders_initialLastname using your first initial and last name.

- Switch to **Design view**, and change the title to Participant Orders by initialLastname using your first initial and last name.

- On the DESIGN tab, in the Controls group, click **Combo Box**. Move your pointer to the **header**, and then click in the header to place the **combo box** to the right of the title.

- In the Combo Box Wizard, click **Find a record on my form based on the value I selected in my combo box**, and then click **Next**.

- Double-click **LastName** and **FirstName** in that order, and then click **Next**.

- Accept **Hide key column**, and then click **Next**.

- Type Participant Name, and then click **Finish**.

- If necessary, drag the new **combo box** so the **left edge** of the label lines up with the **3"** mark on the horizontal ruler.

- Save the form.

d. Add a tab control to a form:

- On **frmParticipantOrders_initialLastname**, in **Design** view, delete the **Orders** label and the **Order Details** label.

- Right-click the **Orders** subform, and then select **Cut**.

- Click the **DESIGN** tab, in the Controls group, click **Tab Control**, and then add the control to just below the **FirstName** label. Right-click the **first** tab page, and then select **Paste**.

- Right-click the **Order Details** subform, and then select **Cut**. Click the **second** tab page, right-click, and then select **Paste**.

- Right-click the **tab control** and select **Insert Page**. Select all the **LastName** and **FirstName** controls, right-click, and then select **Cut**. Right-click the **new** tab page, and then select **Paste**.

- On the DESIGN tab, in the Tools group, click **Add Existing Fields**, and then drag **StreetAddress**, **City**, **State**, **ZipCode**, and **ContactPhoneNumber** to add them to the third page of the tab control just below **FirstName**.

- Select all the **controls** on the page. Click the **ARRANGE** tab, in the Table group, click **Stacked**, in the Position group, click **Control Padding**, and then select **Narrow**.

- Click the **first** tab. Click the **DESIGN** tab, and then in the Tools group, click **Property Sheet**. Click the **Other** tab, click **Name**, and then replace the text with Orders. Repeat these steps to name the second tab Order Details and the third tab Participant Information.

- Right-click the **tab** control, click **Page Order**, and then move up **Participant Information** so it is before the **Orders** page.

- Save the form.

e. Add buttons to a form and remove navigation buttons:

- Open **frmParticipantOrders_initialLastname**, and switch to **Design** view. Click the **DESIGN** tab, and then in the Controls group, click **Button**. Move your pointer to the top-left corner of the **Detail** section of the form, and then click to add the button.

- In the Command Button Wizard, click **Record Navigation**, click **Go To Next Record**, and then click **Next**. Click **Text**, replace the text with Next Participant and then click **Next**. Name the button cmdNextParticipant and then click **Finish**.

- In the Controls group, click **Button**. Place your pointer to the right of the Next Participant button, and then click the **form**. Click **Record Navigation**, click **Go To Previous Record**, and then click **Next**. Click **Text**, type Previous Participant and then click **Next**. Name the button cmdPreviousParticipant and then click **Finish**.

- In the Controls group, click **Button**. Place your pointer to the right of the Previous Participant button, and then click the **form**. Click **Form Operations**, click **Open Form**, and then click **Next**. Click **frmParticipant_initialLastname**, and then click **Next**. Click **Open the form and show all the records**, and then click **Next**. Click **Text**, replace the text with Add a New Participant and then click **Next**. Name the button cmdAddParticipant and then click **Finish**.

- In the Controls group, click **Button**. Place your pointer to the right of the **Add a New Participant** button, and then click the **form**. Click **Form Operations**, click **Close Form**, and then click **Next**. Click **Text**, and then click **Next**. Name the button cmdCloseForm and then click **Finish**.

- Select all **four buttons**. Click the **ARRANGE** tab. In the Sizing & Ordering group, click **Align**, and then select **Top**.

- In the Sizing & Ordering group, click **Size/Space**, and then select **To Widest**. Click **Size/Space**, and then select **Equal Horizontal**.

- In the Property Sheet pane, select **Form** for Selection type, click the **Format** tab, click **Navigation Buttons**, and then select **No**.

- Save the form.

f. Use subform calculations in a form:

- On **frmParticipantOrders_initialLastname**, click the **Orders** tab on the tab control, right-click the **Order** subform, and then select **Subform in New Window**.

- Drag the footer down **1"**. Click the **DESIGN** tab, in the Controls group, click **Text Box**, and then click the **1"** vertical grid line in the footer.

- In the Property Sheet pane, click the **Data** tab, and then click **Control Source Builder**.

- In the Expression Builder, type =SUM([AmountPaid]) and then click **OK**.

- In the Property Sheet pane, click the **Other** tab, click **Name**, and then replace the text with TotalPaid. Double-click the **label** in the footer, and then type Total Paid.

- Save and close the subform window.

- Click the **Order Details** tab on the tab control. Open the subform in a new window, drag the **footer** down **1"**, and add a **text box** in the footer with the Control Source =COUNT([Quantity]), the name TotalQuantity, and the label Total Quantity. Save and close the subform, and then save the form.

- Right-click the **tab control**, and then select **Insert Page**. In the Property Sheet pane, click the **Other** tab, click **Name**, and then replace the text with Order Summary.

- On the DESIGN tab, in the Controls group, click **Text Box**, and then click the Order Summary page to add the text box.

- In the Property Sheet pane, click the **Data** tab, and then click **Control Source Builder**. In the Expression Builder, in the Expression Elements pane, double-click **frmParticipantOrders_initialLastname**. Click **frmOrderSubform**. In the Expression Categories pane, double-click **TotalPaid**, and then click **OK**. (*Hint*: If fields are not visible for frmOrderSubform, switch to Form view and then back to Design view.)

- In the Property Sheet pane, click the **Other** tab, click **Name**, and then replace the text with TotalPaid. Click the **Format** tab, click **Format**, and then then select **Currency**. Click the **label** on the Order Summary page, and then replace the text with Total Paid.

- Repeat the steps above to add the **Total Quantity** field from frmOrderLineSubform to the Order Summary page, but do not change the format to Currency. Name the field TotalQuantity and the label Total Quantity.

- Select the **Total Paid** label and the **Total Quantity** label. Click the **ARRANGE** tab, in the Sizing & Ordering group, click **Align**, and then select **Left**. Select the **Total Paid** text box and the **Total Quantity** text box, click **Align**, and then select **Right**. Select all four controls, and then move them to the top-left corner of the page.

- Switch to **Form** view to make sure your fields are all visible on all the tabs.

- Save and close the form.

g. Exit Access. Submit your work to your instructors as directed.

Student data file needed:

 a05ws09AppStore.accdb

You will save your file as:

 a05ws09AppStore_LastFirst.accdb

Phil's Phone App Store Database

Sales & Marketing

An intern has created a database that Phil's Phone App Store can use to sell apps for smartphones. Phil is not happy with how the forms are working and has asked you for help. The form used for looking up information about an app author is not working the way Phil would like it to work. He wants to be able to look up an author name, view information about the author, information about the author's different apps, and see where and when the author's apps were sold. He would also like to see how many apps each author has created and the total royalties each author has earned for all apps they have. You will help Phil by modifying the form so there is a lookup field and multiple tabs with all the information he wants to see.

a. Start **Access**, and then open **a05ws09AppStore**. Save the database as **a05ws09AppStore_LastFirst** using your last and first name, and then click **Enable Content** if necessary.

b. Open **tblCustomer**, change the **CustFirstName** and **CustLastName** in the first record to your actual name, and then close the table.

c. Open **frmAuthor**, switch to **Layout** view, and delete the **FirstName** and **LastName** labels and text boxes. Change the title to App Lookup by initialLastname, using your first initial and last name.

d. Switch to **Design** view, insert a **combo box** in the header below the title to find a record based on the AuthorName field from tblAuthor. Hide the **key column**, and then name the box App Author Lookup.

e. Insert the date and time in the header, accepting the default formatting, and anchor both controls to the top right of the header.

f. Insert a tab control in the top-left corner of the detail section so the top-left corner of the control is at the **1"** vertical grid line and the **.5"** horizontal grid line. Cut **frmAuthorAppSubform**, and then paste it on the first page of the tab control. Delete the subform label, and then move the subform to the top-left corner of the page. Rename the page Author Apps.

g. Cut **frmAuthorPurchaseSubform**, and then paste it on the second page of the tab control. Delete the subform label, and then move the subform to the top-left corner. Rename the page App Purchases.

h. Open the **frmAuthorAppSubform** in a new window, and then add a new field in the footer that will calculate the author's total royalty for all his apps. Name the field TotalRoyalty and then change the label to Total Royalty. Format the field with **Currency** formatting, and then save and close the subform.

i. Open the **frmAuthorPurchaseSubform** in a new window, and then add a new field in the footer that will calculate the total number of apps the author has sold—use the **PurchaseDate** field. Name the field TotalApps and then change the label to Total Apps. Save and close the subform.

j. Switch to **Form** view to view the changes to the subform. Resize the tab control so all fields are visible on both tab pages.

k. Switch back to **Design** view to continue editing the tab control. Insert a **new page** to the tab control, and then call it Author Summary. Insert a new field with the TotalRoyalty calculated field on the page. Name the field TotalRoyalty and then change the label to Total Royalty. Format the field as **Currency**.

l. Insert a **new field** on the Author Summary page that calculates the number of TotalApps. Name the field TotalApps and then change the label to Total Apps. Align the two field labels on the page left and the two text boxes right. Move all four fields to the top-left corner of the page.

m. Lock **frmAuthorAppSubform**, lock **frmAuthorPurchaseSubform**, and lock the fields **Total Royalty** and **Total Apps**.

n. Add a button below the tab control to close the form. Name the button cmdCloseForm and then show the text Close Form on the button. Line the top-left corner of the button up with the **1"** vertical grid line and the **3.5"** horizontal grid line.

o. Add a button to the right of the Close Form button to open frmFindAppSales. Name the button cmdFindAppSales and show the text Find App Sales.

p. Align both buttons by their top **edge**, and then size them to the widest button.

q. Change the background color of the header to **Aqua, Accent 5, Lighter 40%**.

r. Save and close the form. Exit Access. Submit your work as directed by your instructor.

Perform 1: Perform in Your Career

Student data file needed:

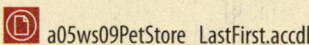 a05ws09PetStore.accdb

You will save your file as:

a05ws09PetStore_LastFirst.accdb

Make a Pet Store Database Friendly

Production & Operations

A pet store owner started creating a database to keep records of animals, breeds, purchases, and customers. Data has been added to the tables, but there are no forms or reports for entering data or looking up data. You have been asked to help create forms to add data to the tables and to look up data that is already in the tables. You will use different kinds of forms for this task.

a. Open **a05ws09PetStore**, and then save the database as a05ws09PetStore_LastFirst, using your last and first name.

b. Open **tblCustomer**, change the **FirstName** and **LastName** in the first record to your actual name, and then close the table.

c. Create a form to add data to tblAnimal. Include all the fields from the table. Change the title to Add Animals by initialLastname, using your first initial and last name, and then save the form as frmAddAnimals_initialLastname.

d. Use the form wizard to create a form with a subform, that is a form using two tables, to show all the animal information and all animal purchase information:

- Save the form as frmPurchases_initialLastname using your first initial and last name and the subform as frmPurchasesSubform_initialLastname using your first initial and last name.

- Change the title to Animal Information by initialLastname, using your first initial and last name.

- Include the date and time in the header, anchored to the top right.

- Lock all the animal information fields in the main form, and then turn off the tab stops.

- Add four buttons: Next Animal, Previous Animal, Add Animal, and Close Form. The Add Animal button should open frmAddAnimals_initialLastname.

- Turn off the Navigation bars for both the form and subform.

- Resize any fields as necessary and make sure all fields are visible on the form and subform. Make the form look professional.

e. Create a form with a tab control that will look up the customer name and show three tabs: Customer, Purchases, and Summary:

- Save the form as **frmCustomer_initialLastname** and the subform **frmCustomerSubform_initialLastname** using your first initial and last name.
- The title of the form should be **Customer Lookup by initialLastname**, using your first initial and last name.
- Add a combo box in the header to look up the customer name.
- Change the header to a different color.
- Add three buttons: **Next Customer**, **Previous Customer**, and **Close Form**.
- The first tab of the tab control should show the customer contact information.
- The second tab of the tab control should show the customer's purchases.
- The third tab of the tab control should show the total number of purchases a customer has made and the total amount the customer has spent.
- Resize any fields as necessary and make sure all fields are visible on the form and subform. Make the form look professional.

f. Create a multiple-item form for tblCustomer. Change the title to **Customer List by initialLastname**, using your first initial and last name, and then delete the form icon from the header. Save the form as **frmCustomerList_initialLastname** using your first initial and last name.

g. Save your forms, and then exit Access. Submit your work as directed by your instructor.15alc389

Additional Cases

Additional Workshop Cases are available on the companion website and in the instructor resources.

WORKSHOP 10 | ADVANCED REPORTS AND MAILING LABELS

OBJECTIVES

1. Use the Summary Options in Report Wizard   p. 513
2. Modify the report in Design view   p. 515
3. Change report properties   p. 520
4. Add and remove fields p. 521
5. Use the Group, Sort, and Total pane   p. 524
6. Add labels and shapes p. 527
7. Modify calculated fields p. 530
8. Create a parameter report   p. 531
9. Use conditional formatting   p. 539
10. Create mailing labels p. 540

Prepare Case

Customer Service

Enhancing Database Reports at the Red Bluff Golf Club

The Red Bluff Golf Club generates revenues through golfers signing up for tee times and taking golf lessons. You have provided a database to Barry Cheney, the golf club manager, where he can track employees and members. Some forms and reports have already been created, but Barry would like to see more to help him manage memberships and lessons. You will assist Barry and his staff by setting up reports that they can use on a regular basis.

Rayjunk / Shutterstock

REAL WORLD SUCCESS

"I never understood why Access was so popular. I could enter data in a table in Excel so much faster and could sort and filter the data to see what I needed. When my first boss asked me for a report based on the data I had in my Excel table, he was not too impressed with what I had printed. After all, it was just rows and columns from Excel. He had someone show me how to import the data into Access and then create a report, and then I understood why Access was so popular! The data was the same, but the report looked so much more professional and was much easier to read. Now I use Access all the time to create reports from my data."

- Lindsay, 2014 graduate

Student data file needed for this workshop:

 a05ws10Golf.accdb

You will save your file as:

 a05ws10Golf_LastFirst.accdb

Creating Customized Reports

An Access **report** provides data in an easy-to-read and professional-looking format suitable for printing. A report is designed to fit well on the printed page, with breaks built in for each page. Column headers automatically repeat on each page, in addition to page numbers. Reports provide ways to report on data by groups, such as by each customer or product. Totals can be calculated for each group, and grand totals can also be shown. The source of data for a report can be a table or query.

QUICK REFERENCE	Query, Form, or Report?

There are three ways to display data from a database: a query, a form, and a report. When would you use each?

- Queries are the most versatile of the three for finding data in your database. They allow complex data selection and data calculation. But the output from a query is tabular and not always suitable for presentation to a client or manager. If you want to share the results of a query in printed form, you often create a report from the query.

- Forms are usually used for data input, and they are best suited for output on the screen. In fact, many types of forms are very difficult to print as they can run for many pages with formatting unsuitable for the printed page, such as no page breaks or page numbers

- Reports are designed for printing. You can use them to provide an easy-to-understand output for a client or manager. You can also create mailing labels and other specialized printable formats.

Reports can be created with the same controls that are available in forms. You can also create mailing label reports or other types of labels.

Reports can be created in four different ways: with the Report tool, with the Report Design tool, with the Blank Report tool, and with the Report Wizard. The **Report tool** creates a report with one mouse click. The report displays all of the fields from the table or query that you select. The **Report Design tool** creates a blank report in Design view to which you can manually add fields or other controls. The **Blank Report tool** creates a blank report in Layout view. You can insert fields or other controls while you see the data. Finally, the **Report Wizard** guides you through creating a report by asking you questions. The report is then created based upon your answers to the questions.

QUICK REFERENCE	Report Views Available

Reports have four views:

- Report view shows how the report will look in a continuous page layout. If a report has multiple pages, this view shows the report as one continuous layout without individual page headers or footers. Reports cannot be changed in this view.

- Print Preview shows how the report will look on the printed page. In this view, you see the page breaks and how they will appear on paper. This view allows you to change the page layout from landscape to portrait view, or to change margins.

- Layout view shows the report and the data. Some of the report design properties, such as column widths and fonts, can be changed in this view. You can add controls in this view. Layout view is ideal for making changes where seeing the data as you make the change would be useful.

- Design view shows the report design but not the data. Any aspect of the report design can be changed in this view.

In this section, you will create a report using the Report Wizard that includes summary fields for subtotals and grand totals. Then you will work with already created reports to modify the existing fields, controls, groups, and totals.

Use the Summary Options in Report Wizard

One of the features of Access reports is the ability to summarize your data. For example, if you have numeric data such as sales quantity, you might want to calculate a grand total of that quantity. When you are creating a report with a wizard, calculations like sums, averages, minimums, and maximums are available as standard summation. In Design view, you can build even more complex formulas and edit existing ones.

Opening the Starting File

The golf course needs a report showing the members to whom the golf course employees give lessons. The report needs to be grouped by the employee who gives the lessons. You will open the database and create this report.

A10.00

 To Open the Golf Database

a. Start **Access**, and then open the student data file **a05ws10Golf**.

b. Click the **FILE** tab, click **Save As**, click **Save Database As**, and then click the **Save As** button. Select the folder where you are saving your files and type a05ws10Golf_LastFirst using your last and first name and click **Save**. If necessary, click **Enable Content**.

Adding Subtotals and Totals

Reports have a grouping feature that allows for records to be presented in sets. One common use of grouping is to use one-to-many relationships in your database and use a record from the one side to group records from the many side. For example, suppose your database has a one-to-many relationship between customers and orders: a customer can place many orders, and an order is placed by one customer. You might report on orders by first showing the customer and then grouping all of the customer's orders together. In the Report Wizard, the one-to-many grouping is the first grouping suggested to you. You can also group other fields together. You could choose to group orders by date placed or by state of shipment. Once you create report groups, you can add summary calculations for each group.

You will create a report for the golf course that groups the member lessons by employee so when you look up an employee, you will see all the lessons he or she has scheduled. The report will also add a subtotal of the fees to be paid to each employee and a grand total of the fees paid to all the employees.

MyITLab®

Workshop 10 Training

A10.01

To Create a Report with Subtotals and Totals Using the Summary Wizard

a. Double-click **tblMember** to open it, navigate to **record 21**, the last record, and then change the **First Name** and **Last Name** to your first name and last name. **Close** ☒ tblMember.

b. Click the **CREATE** tab, and then in the Reports group, click **Report Wizard**. Select the fields for your report in this order: from **tblEmployee**, select **EmployeeLastName** and **EmployeeFirstName**; from **tblMemberLessons**, select **ScheduledDate**; from **tblMember**, select **LastName** and **FirstName**; from **tblMemberLessons**, select **Fee**.

> **Troubleshooting**
>
> If you make a mistake selecting the fields in order above, move them all back to Available Fields and start over again. For the report to work correctly, the fields need to be added in the exact order listed above.

SIDE NOTE
Order Makes a Difference
The order you select the fields in the Report Wizard will determine how the fields are laid out on the report.

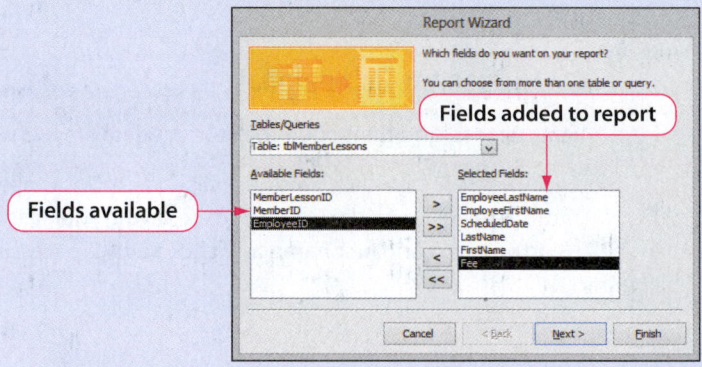

Figure 1   Fields selected in the Report Wizard

c. Click **Next**. Accept the grouping by **tblEmployee**, and then click **Next**. Click **Next** again —you will not select any other grouping—click the first **sort** box arrow, and then select **ScheduledDate**. Click the next **sort** box arrow, select **LastName**, click the third **sort** box arrow, and then select **FirstName**. Make sure all are in **Ascending** order.

d. Click **Summary Options**. Because Fee is the only field with numeric data you selected, Access only gives you the option to calculate summary values for Fee. Click the **Sum** check box, and then click **OK**.

e. Click **Next**, accept the **Stepped** layout, accept **Portrait** orientation, and then click **Next**.

f. In the title box type rptEmployeeLessons_initialLastname, using your first initial and last name, and then click **Finish**.

g. On the PRINT PREVIEW tab, in the Close Preview group, click **Close Print Preview**. Switch to **Layout** view, click the first **Fee** field, point to the **left edge** of the field, and then when the pointer changes to the **horizontal resize pointer** ↔, drag to the left to widen the field.

h. Click the first **Subtotal** field, point to the **left edge** of the field, and then when the pointer changes to the **horizontal resize pointer** ↔, drag to the left to widen the field.

i. Scroll down to the end of the report, select the **Grand Total** field, point to the **left edge** of the field, and then when the pointer changes to the **horizontal resize pointer** ↔, drag to the left to widen the field.

j. Click **Print Preview** 🔍 on the status bar to see how the report will print, and then **Save** 💾 the report.

SIDE NOTE
Fields too narrow
If a field shows ### instead of values, it means the field is not wide enough to display the values. This is corrected by resizing the field.

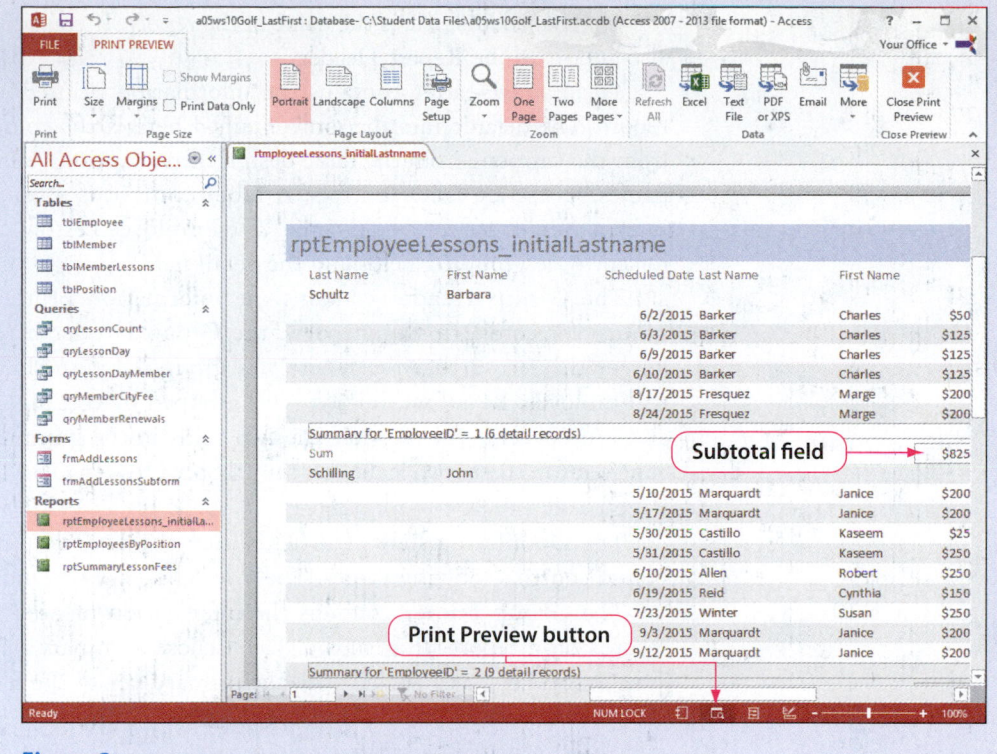

Figure 2 Print Preview of rptEmployeeLessons_initialLastname

Modify the Report in Design View

A report with subtotals and totals has seven areas in Design view as shown in Figure 3.

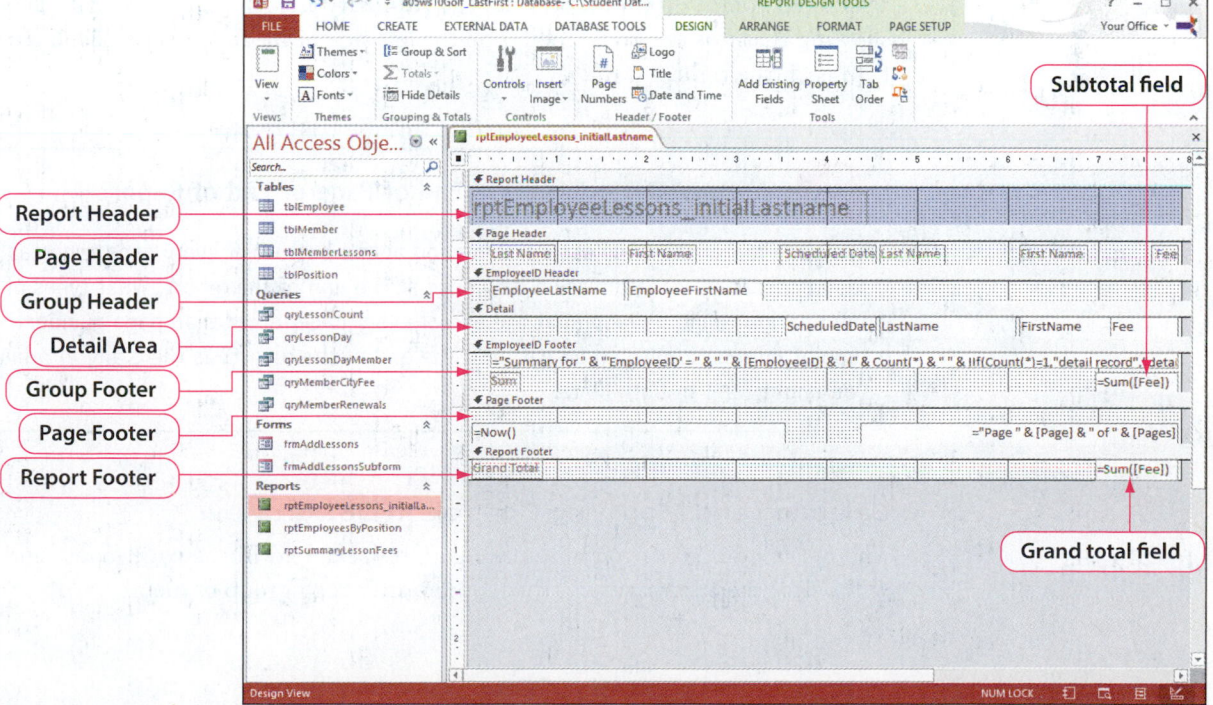

Figure 3 Design view of report with totals and subtotals

The **Report Header** contains the information printed once at the beginning of a report. The default title is the name of the report. If you add a logo or date and time, they also appear in the Report Header

The **Page Header** contains the information printed at the top of every page of a report. The default information contained here is the column headers, which are taken from the captions from the table design. If no captions were defined, the values are field names. These are label controls. A **label control** is a control that contains descriptive information, typically a field name. The Employee Lessons report has the column headers for both the grouping fields and the detail fields.

The **Group Header** contains the information printed at the beginning of every group of records. In Design view, the Group Header bar is labeled with the primary key of the record that the report was grouped by, in this case, the EmployeeID from tblEmployee. Recall when the wizard grouped by tblEmployee, the EmployeeLastName and EmployeeFirstName were the two fields in the grouping header. You see the bound controls for these two fields in the Group Header. The field labels are shown in the Page Header.

The **Detail area** shows the fields from the underlying record source. These are the bound controls showing values. The field labels are shown in the Page Header.

The **Group Footer** contains the information printed at the end of every group of records on a report. It is shown if you chose summary options in the Report Wizard. The Group Footer is labeled with the primary key of the record by which the report was grouped, in this case, the EmployeeID from tblEmployee. The fields shown include a calculated control that shows a count of detailed records, and a calculated control that represents the summary field(s) you chose. The label showing which summary option you picked is on the left side of the footer. The calculated summary field is on the right.

The **Page Footer** shows the information printed at the end of every page of a report. By default, two controls are shown: the current date using the Now function, and a calculated control representing the page number for this page.

The **Report Footer** shows the information printed once at the end of a report. It is shown if you chose summary options in the Report Wizard. The fields shown are the calculated control(s) that represents the summary field(s) you chose. The Label control showing that it is the grand total is on the left side of the footer. The calculated summary field is on the right.

 CONSIDER THIS | **End of Page or End of Report**

The page footer show the same information at the bottom of every page, whereas the report footer shows information only once at the end of the report. What types of information would be helpful at the end of every page, other than page numbers? What type of information would be better at the end of the report? Is there any information you might want in both places?

Selecting and Modifying Controls in Design View

The first modification you will make is to resize a field in the page footer, and then you will delete the Summary field that appears after each group of members.

QUICK REFERENCE | **Design View Areas**

Area	Purpose	Where Displayed	When the Report Wizard Shows It
Report Header	To introduce the report; includes title and often logo	At the beginning of report	By default
Page Header	Includes column headings	At the top of each page	By default
Group Header	To introduce the group; shows values of the grouping variables	At the beginning of each grouping	When your report has grouping
Detail area	Shows the detailed fields	Within groups	By default
Group Footer	To end the group; used to contain subtotals for the group	At the end of each grouping	When your report has grouping and you chose summary options
Page Footer	To end a page; defaults to showing date and page number	At the end of each page	By default
Report Footer	To end the report; can contain grand totals	At the end of report	When you chose summary options

A10.02

To Modify the Headers and Footers in Design View

a. Switch to **Design** view, double-click the title **rptEmployeeLessons_initialLastname**, select the **text**, and then type Employee Lessons by initialLastname, using your first initial and last name.

b. Click the **control** in the EmployeeID footer that begins **="Summary for**, and then press ⌞Delete⌟ to delete the control.

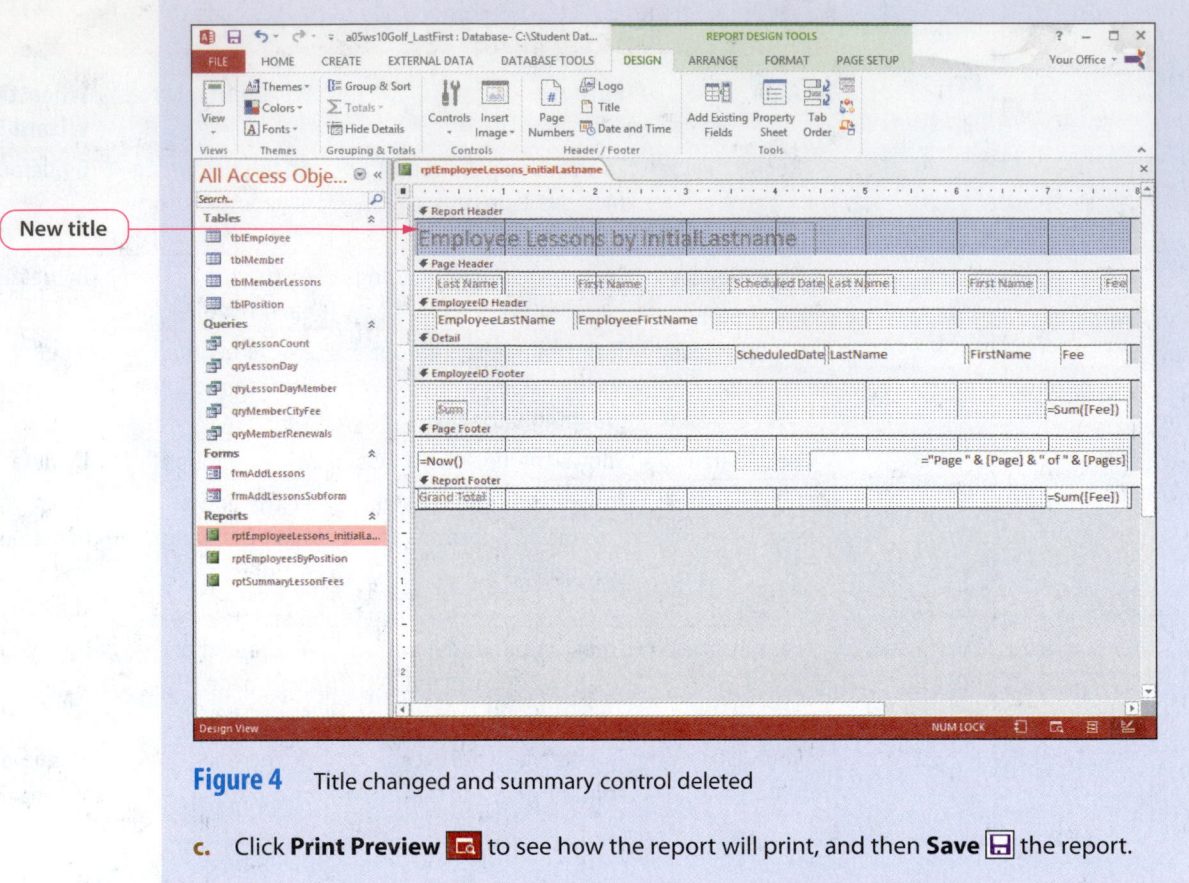

New title

Figure 4   Title changed and summary control deleted

c.   Click **Print Preview** 🔍 to see how the report will print, and then **Save** 💾 the report.

Moving, Resizing, and Aligning Fields in Design View

When a control is selected, in either Layout view or Design view, the control is outlined in orange. There are eight boxes called handles on the outline. The large gray handle in the top-left corner is called the **move handle**. It is used to move the control. The smaller orange handles are **sizing handles**. Sizing handles are used to resize the control. You will resize and align the Subtotal Fees and the Total Fees controls in the EmployeeID footer and in the report footer as well as rename the labels.

When fields are added or moved, you can align them with other fields so the alignment is correct. Controls may be aligned by their top, left, right, or bottom borders, or they may be aligned to the grid.

In Design view, the report grid is made up of vertical lines, as well as rows and columns of dots. By default, the **snap to grid** option for reports is turned on, which means that when you add or move a control in a report, it will automatically align to a point on the grid. If that option is not turned on, then you can manually align a control to the grid so it is lined up exactly with one of the points—dots—on the grid.

You will align the Subtotal and Grand Total labels with their corresponding text boxes after you move them. You will also resize a field in the page footer.

A10.03

To Move, Modify, and Align Labels in a Footer

a. Switch to **Design** view, and then click the **Sum label**. Point to the **label**, and then when the pointer changes to a **four-headed** arrow ⊞, move the label to the right so that the **left edge** lines up with the **5"** mark on the horizontal ruler.

b. Double-click the **Sum label**, and then type Subtotal Fees. Click the **Subtotal Fees** label, press and hold ⇧Shift, and then select the **=Sum([Fee])** text box. Click the **ARRANGE** tab, in the Sizing & Ordering group, click **Align**, and then select **Top**. This will align the label and text box by their top borders.

c. Click the **Grand Total** label in the Report Footer. Point to the **label**, and when the pointer changes to a **four-headed** arrow ⊞ move the label to the right so that the **left edge** lines up with the **5"** mark on the horizontal ruler.

d. Double-click the **Grand Total** label, and then type Total Fees.

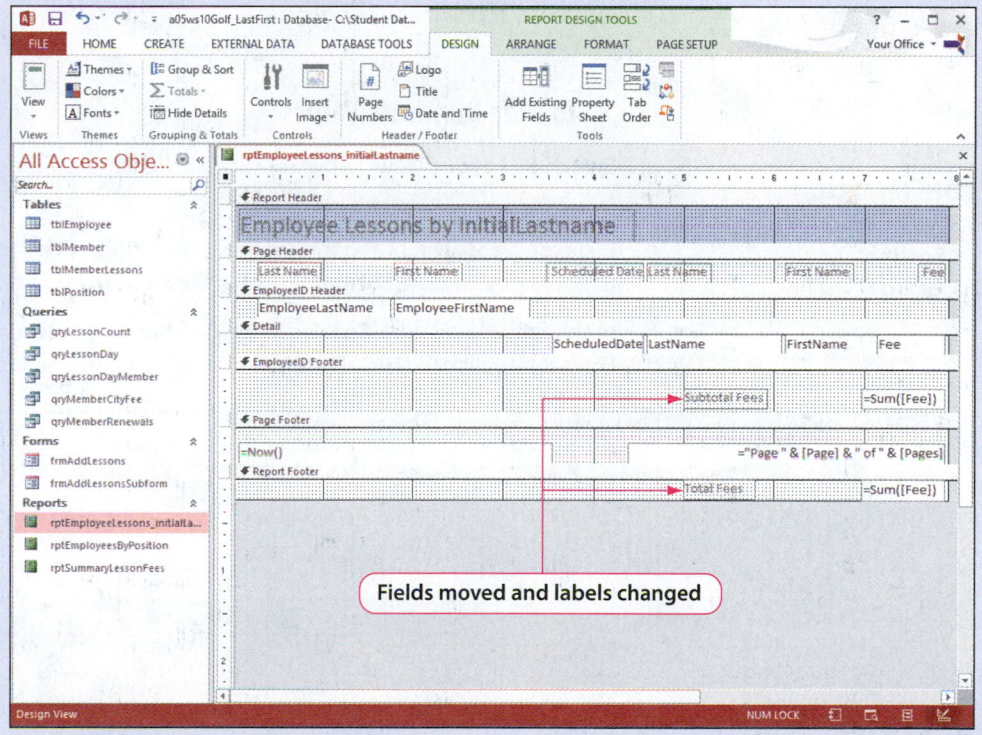

Figure 5   Subtotal and Total fields moved and edited

e. Click **Print Preview** to see how the report will print, and then **Save** the report.

Change Report Properties

Like fields on a form, every field on a report has certain characteristics or properties about the field stored in a **property sheet**. The property sheet is a multitabbed pane that opens and shows all the characteristics that can be changed for whichever part of the form is selected. Different parts of the report will have different properties. For example, the background of the form will have a Back Color property but not a decimal places property like a number field does.

You will change the properties of the report so the duplicate member names, for members with multiple lessons, will be hidden. Since the report is sorted by member last name, all the records for one member will be consecutive, and hiding the duplicates will not hinder reading the report correctly.

Modifying the Hide Duplicates Property

On the Employee Lessons report, lessons are sorted by date and then by the member's name. This means if an employee gives multiple lessons to a member, the member's name is repeated for each lesson. You will hide these duplicate values for Last Name and First Name.

A10.04

▶ To Hide Duplicate Values

SIDE NOTE

To See Grouping and Sorting

Click Group & Sort on the Design tab to open the Group, Sort, & Total pane. This will show how the report is grouped and sorted.

a. Switch to **Layout** view, and then click **Barker** in the first row of the second Last Name column.

b. Click the **DESIGN** tab, and then in the Tools group, click **Property Sheet**. In the Property Sheet pane, click the **Format** tab, click the **Hide Duplicates** arrow, and then select **Yes**.

c. In the form detail, click **Charles** in the first row of the second First Name column. On the Format tab, click the **Hide Duplicates** arrow, and then select **Yes**.

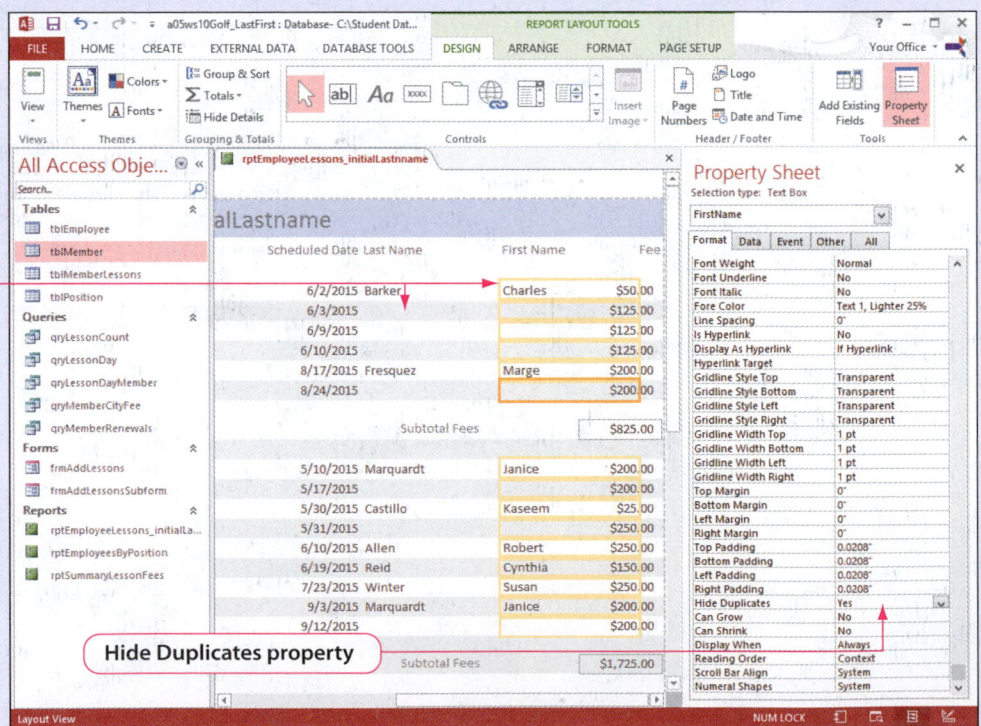

Figure 6   Duplicate field values hidden on report

d. **Close** ☒ the Property Sheet pane, and then click **Report View** to preview the report. **Save** 🖫 and then **Close** ☒ the report.

Add and Remove Fields from a Report

When you create a report using the Report Wizard, you tell the wizard which fields you want, and the wizard formats the report with headers and footers for any grouping you choose. However, you may want to change the fields on existing reports or add or change the grouping. You can add and delete fields in either Layout view or Design view. In the next exercise, you will make these changes in Layout view where you can see how the report will look with the changes.

Removing Fields from a Report

To remove a field from a report, you must remove both the bound control and the label control, or you will end up with data that is not labeled or a label without data. The golf course uses a report named rptEmployeesByPosition, but it pops up a dialog box every time they open it. You determine that the dialog box is opening because Access is looking for a field on the report that does not exist in any of the database tables. You will remove that field since it is not being used.

A10.05

 To Remove a Field from a Report

a. Open **rptEmployeesByPosition** and click **OK** at the Enter Parameter Value prompt. Switch to **Layout** view, click the first **Orientation** check box, and then press Delete to delete the bound control.

b. Right-click the **Orientation** label in the header, and then select **Delete**. This will delete the label control.

c. Click the **FILE** tab, click **Save As**, click **Save Object As**, and then click **Save As**. Type rptEmployeesByPosition_initialLastname, using your first initial and last name.

Adding Fields to a Report

To add a field to a report, you will use the Field List, which will automatically add both the bound control and the label control for the field you choose to add. When you add fields to a report, you may have to change the tab order so that when you press Tab to move from field to field, the fields are selected in a logical order.

You will add a Salary field to the rptEmployeesByPosition_initialLastname report. The report is grouped by position and shows each employee by their hire date. You will also change the tab order so the fields are selected in the correct order.

To Add a Field to a Report

a. Click the **DESIGN** tab, and then in the Tools group, click **Add Existing Fields**. This will open the Field List pane.

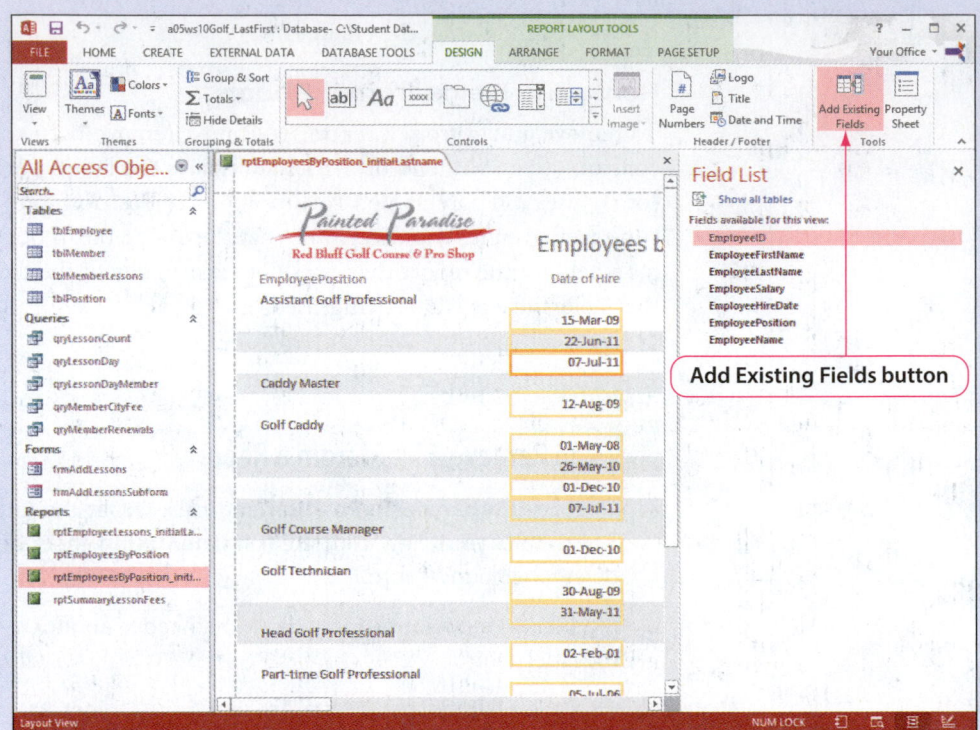

Figure 7   Field List pane open

b. Double-click **EmployeeSalary** in the Field List pane, and the field will be added to the left side of the report overlapping Employee Position. **Close** ✖ the Field List pane.

> **Troubleshooting**
>
> If the EmployeeSalary field is not listed, click **Show all tables** at the top of the Field List pane. This will list additional fields available to use on the report.

c. Click the **layout selector** ⊞ in the top-left corner of the highlighted controls. When the pointer becomes a **four-headed** arrow ⊞, drag the controls to the right of **EmployeePosition** and release the mouse button.

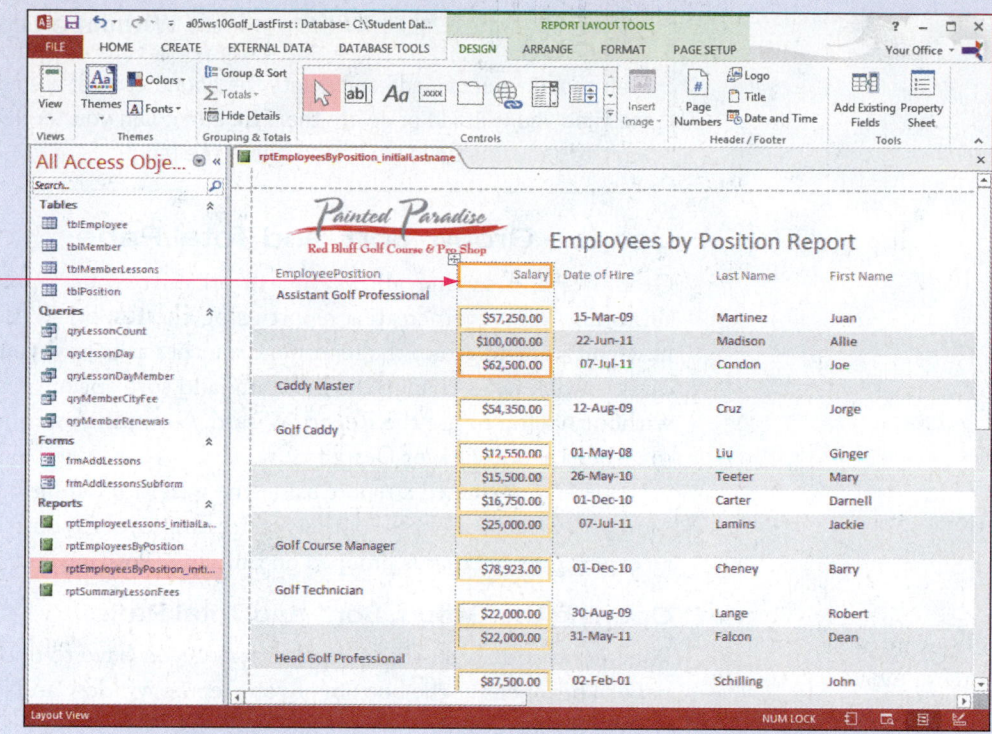

New field added and moved next to EmployeePosition

Figure 8   Salary field added and moved

d. Switch to **Design** view. On the DESIGN tab, in the Tools group, click **Tab Order**. Click the **EmployeeSalary** field to select it, and then using the **selection** box ☐ to the left of the field name, drag the field to the top of the **Custom Order** list.

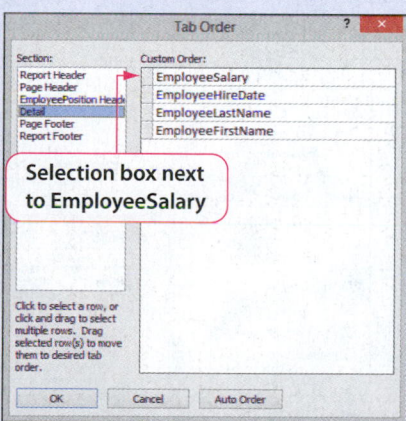

Selection box next to EmployeeSalary

Figure 9   Tab Order dialog box

e. Click **OK**. Click the **Date of Hire** label, press and hold `Shift`, click the **Date of Hire** text box, and then drag the box and label so their **right edges** line up with the **5"** mark on the horizontal ruler.

f. Click the **EmployeeSalary** text box, press and hold `Shift`, click the **EmployeeHireDate** text box, and then click the **EmployeeLastName** text box. Click the **ARRANGE** tab, and in the Sizing & Ordering group, click **Align**, and then select **Top**. Click **Save** 🖫 to save the report.

SS **CONSIDER THIS** | **Field Without a Label?**

Even though you can add and delete the bound control and the label separately, most of the time you will add or delete them together. Can you think of any time when you would want to show the bound control without the label?

Use the Group, Sort, and Total Pane

Grouping and sorting allows you to organize your report as well as add totals and subtotals. When you create a report using the Report Wizard, one of the steps asks you how you want to group the report and another asks how you want to sort the report. You can add, delete, or change the grouping and sort options manually on an existing report without having to use the Report Wizard. Grouping and sorting options can be changed in either Layout view or Design view.

Earlier you created a report using the wizard to add grouping, sorting, and subtotals. Now you will change those options on rptEmployeesByPosition_initialLastname, which is an existing report that is grouped on EmployeePosition and sorted by EmployeeHireDate.

Opening the Group, Sort, and Total Pane

When you add a group or sort to a report, you have to open the Group, Sort, and Total pane. This opens at the bottom of your report window and allows you to add, delete, and change all the group, sort, and total options.

You will change rptEmployeesByPosition_initialLastname so it shows Employee Salary subtotals for each Employee Position and a grand total for all Employee Salaries.

A10.07

▶ To Change Group, Sort, and Total Options on a Report

a. Click the **DESIGN** tab, and in the Grouping & Totals group, click **Group & Sort**.

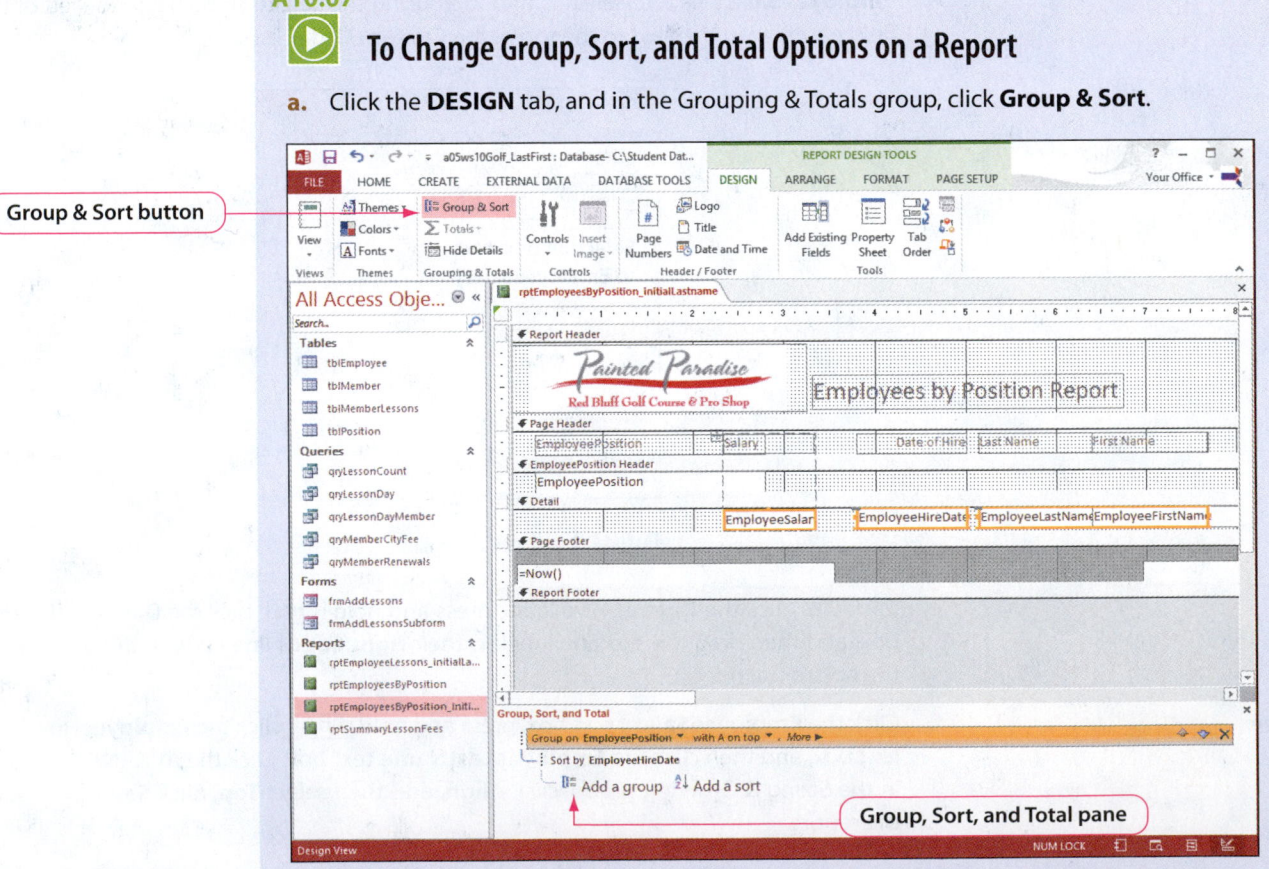

Figure 10 Group, Sort, and Total pane open in Design view

b. On the first row that says Group on EmployeePosition, click **More**. This opens the options for the group of records. Click the arrow next to **with no totals**, click the **Total On** arrow, and then select **EmployeeSalary**. Verify **Sum** is selected in the Type box, and then click both the **Show Grand Total** check box and the **Show subtotal in group footer** check box.

c. Click outside the **Totals** box to close it, and then click **Less** on the Group on EmployeePosition row. You should see a new field called =Sum([EmployeeSalary]) in the EmployeePosition Footer and in the Report Footer. The first calculated field in the EmployeePosition Footer is the subtotal field, and the second calculated field in the Report Footer is the grand total field.

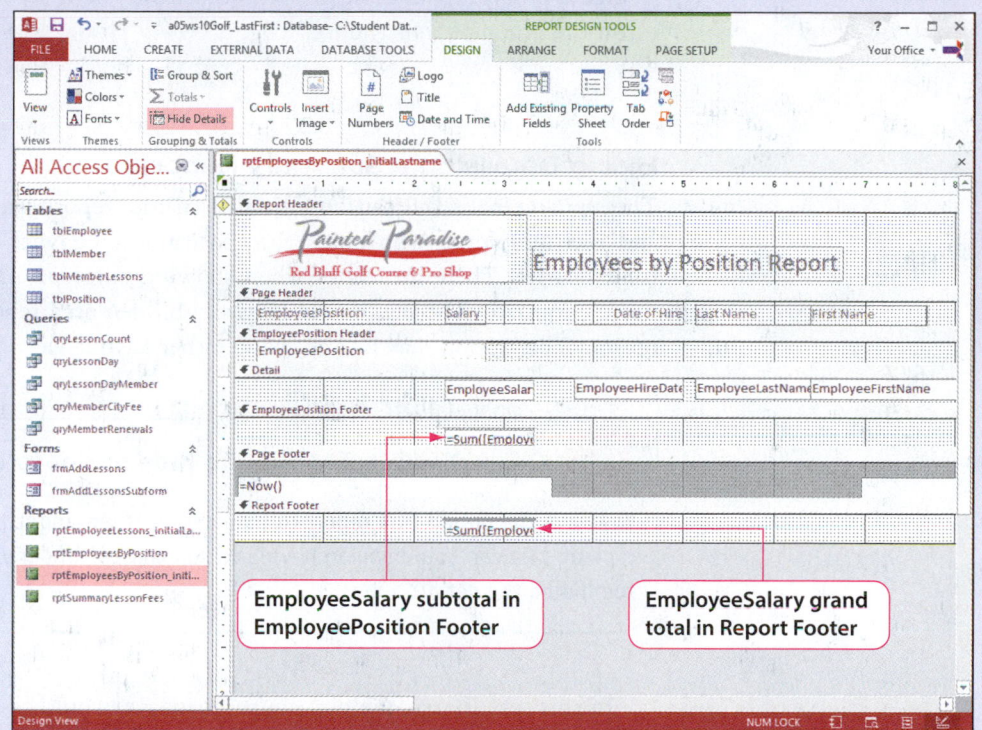

Figure 11 Calculated fields added to the report

d. On the DESIGN tab, in the Grouping & Totals group, click **Group & Sort** to close the Group, Sort, and Total pane, and then **Save** the report.

REAL WORLD ADVICE | Changing Grouping and Sorting

When you change the grouping of a report, the field controls do not move automatically to represent how the data is grouped. This means if the field you have grouped on is in a column on the left side of the report and you change the report to group by a field that is in a column on the right side of the report, those fields will not move when you change the grouping. Sometimes this can lead to a very strange-looking report.

You should be aware that some controls may have to be moved in Design view to adjust for the change in sorting. If this gets too confusing, you can always create a new report using the Report Wizard—it will correctly move fields based on the grouping you choose.

Hiding Details on a Summary Report

The rptEmployeesByPosition_initialLastname report shows the Employee Position and each employee who holds that position along with their individual salaries and total salaries. There are times when showing summary detail is either unnecessary or not appropriate. The details can be easily hidden on a report by using the Hide Details option. This option may be applied in either Layout view or Design view.

 CONSIDER THIS | **To Hide or Not to Hide**

You have the option in a report to hide detail. When might this option be helpful? What type of data can you envision having to summarize? Under what circumstances could you see hiding the detail?

In this case, Barry, the golf course manager, would like a report that shows just the total amount of salaries for each position, without the detail for each employee because the employee information is confidential.

A10.08

 To Hide Detail Lines on a Report

a. Switch to **Layout** view, click the **DESIGN** tab, and then in the Grouping & Totals group, click **Hide Details**. The only rows on the report should now be the Employee Position and the total salaries for each position.

Troubleshooting

If your report does not look like the report in Figure 12, switch to Design view, open the Group, Sort, and Total pane and double-check that the EmployeeSalary subtotal is showing in the group footer and not the group header. If Show subtotal in group header is checked, uncheck it, and then click Show subtotal in group footer.

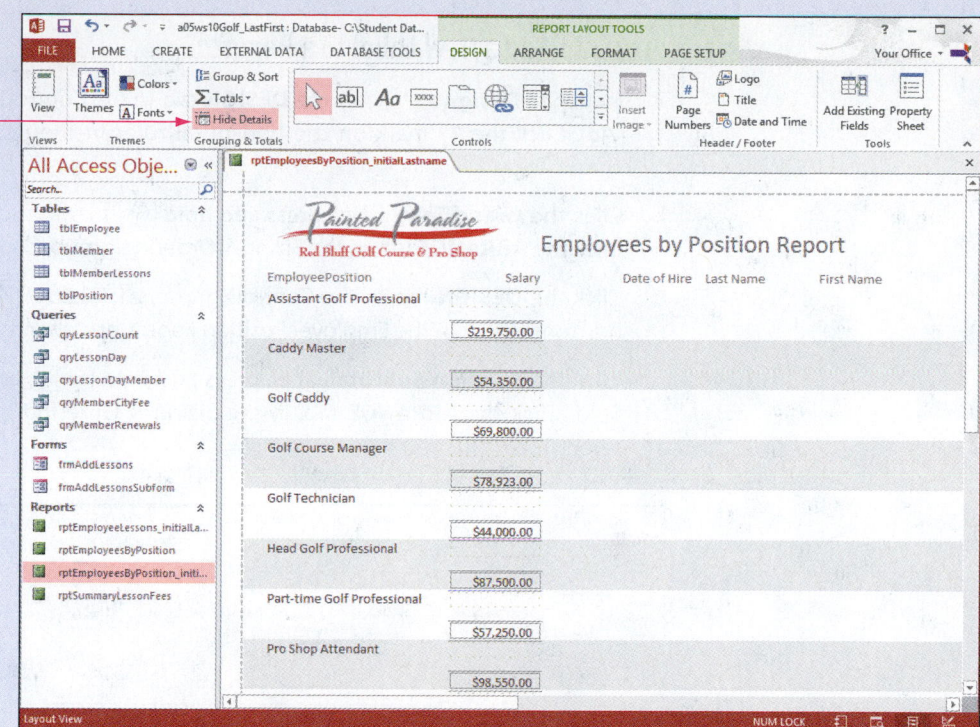

Hide Details button

Figure 12   Report with details hidden

b. On the DESIGN tab, in the Grouping & Totals group, click **Hide Details** again to unhide the details. Now you should see all the employees and their individual salaries, as well as the subtotals of the salaries.

c. Click **Hide Details** again to hide the details, and then **Save** 🖫 the report.

Add Labels and Shapes to a Report

When you create groups and totals, calculated fields are often added to the report without a label. An example of this is the grand total and subtotals of the Employee Salary field that you added in the previous section. You can add labels to go with a calculated field, and then you can add lines and shapes to help bring attention to different parts of a report, like the totals.

Adding Labels to a Report

When Access adds a field to a report without a label, it is good practice to add a label manually so the user of the report knows what he or she is looking at. You will add a label for the subtotal in the EmployeePosition Footer and for the grand total of Employee Salary in the report footer. Because the labels are not actually related to the calculated field, they will be unbound controls.

A10.09

 To Add a New Label to a Report

a. Switch to **Design** view, click the **DESIGN** tab, in the Controls group, and then click **Label** ☐Aa☐. Click the **1"** mark on the horizontal ruler in the Report Footer, and then type **Grand Total**.

b. Click the **Grand Total** label, press and hold ☐Shift☐, and then click the **calculated** field. Click the **ARRANGE** tab, in the Sizing & Ordering group, click **Align**, and then select **Top**.

c. Click the **DESIGN** tab, in the Controls group, click **Label** ☐Aa☐, click the **1"** mark on the horizontal ruler in the EmployeePosition Footer, and then type **Position Subtotal**.

d. Click the **Position Subtotal** label, press and hold ☐Shift☐, and then click the **calculated** field. Click the **ARRANGE** tab, in the Sizing & Ordering group, click **Align**, and then select **Top**.

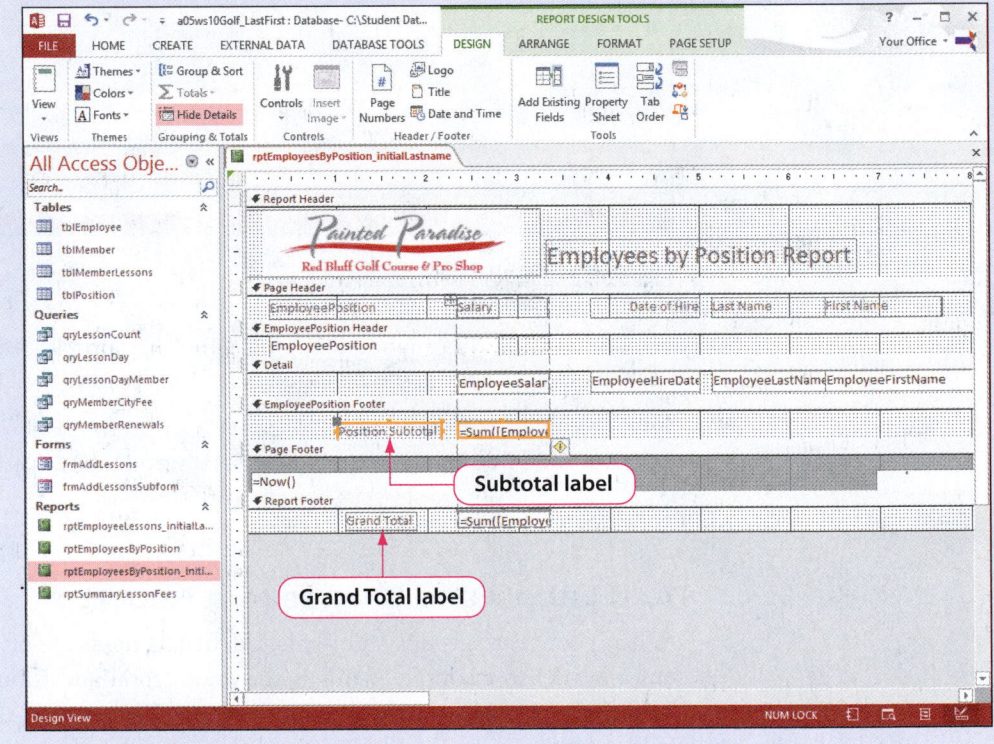

Figure 13   Labels added to report

Adding a Horizontal Line to a Report

You can add a line or other shape to a report in order to highlight different controls. A line is an unbound control that can be moved and resized like any other control on the report. A line also has properties like other controls, although they all have to do with formatting since there is no data connected to the line.

You will draw a line just above the grand total in the Report Footer, so this number stands out as a calculated total on the report. You will then change the line properties so the line has a different color, a different width, and a different border style.

A10.10

To Add a Horizontal Line to a Report

a. Click the **DESIGN** tab, in the Controls group, click **Line**, press and hold Shift, click the **1"** mark on the horizontal ruler in the Report Footer, and then drag the line to the right until you stop at the **4"** mark on the horizontal ruler.

> **Troubleshooting**
>
> If you have trouble keeping the Line control horizontal, you may be trying to drag it before placing the line. First, click to place the Line control in the footer. Once the line appears, you can easily drag it horizontally by holding down Shift.

b. On the DESIGN tab, in the Tools group, click **Property Sheet**. In the Property Sheet pane, click the **Format** tab, click the **Border Style** arrow, and then select **Dash Dot Dot**.

c. Click the **Border Width** arrow, and then select **1pt**.

d. Click **Border Color**, click **Builder**, and then select **Dark Red**, the first color in the bottom row. **Close** the Property Sheet pane, and then click **Report View** to see your changes.

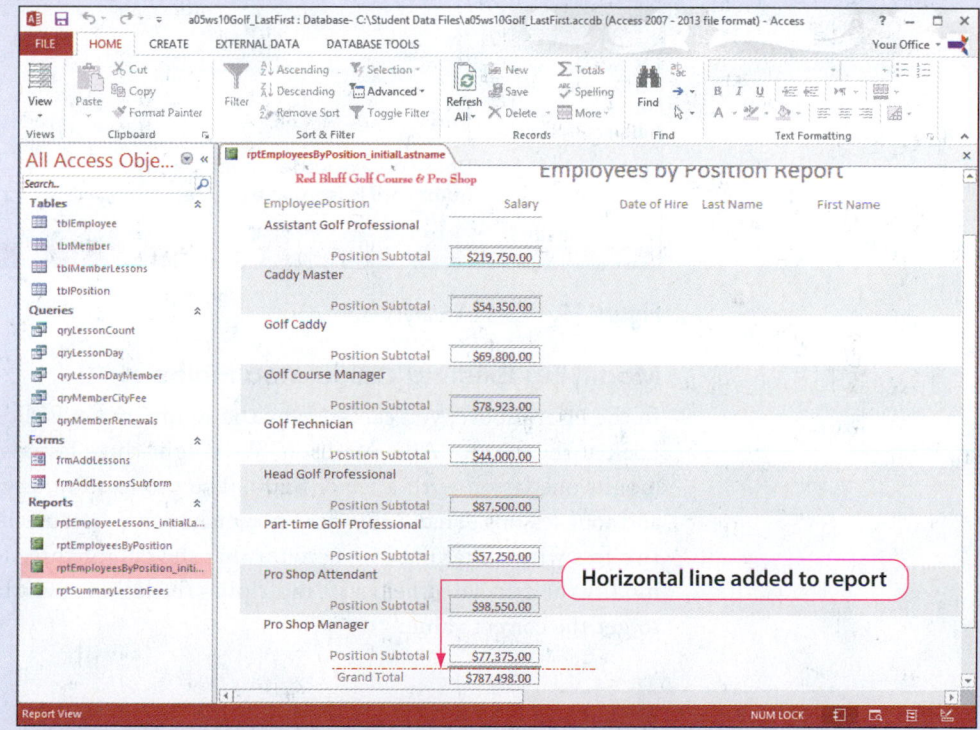

Figure 14 Horizontal line formatted and shown in Report view

e. Click **Save** and then **Close** the report.

Modify Calculated Fields in a Report

The Report Wizard summary functions can be helpful to create simple calculations on a report, but sometimes they do not or cannot complete the calculations the way you want. For example, the rptSummaryLessonFees report shown in Figure 15 was created from a query to show each employee, their fees, and the number of lessons for each fee. When the summary functions of SUM were chosen in the Report Wizard for Fee and LessonCount, it added the totals, but it did not take into account the number of lessons at each different fee amount.

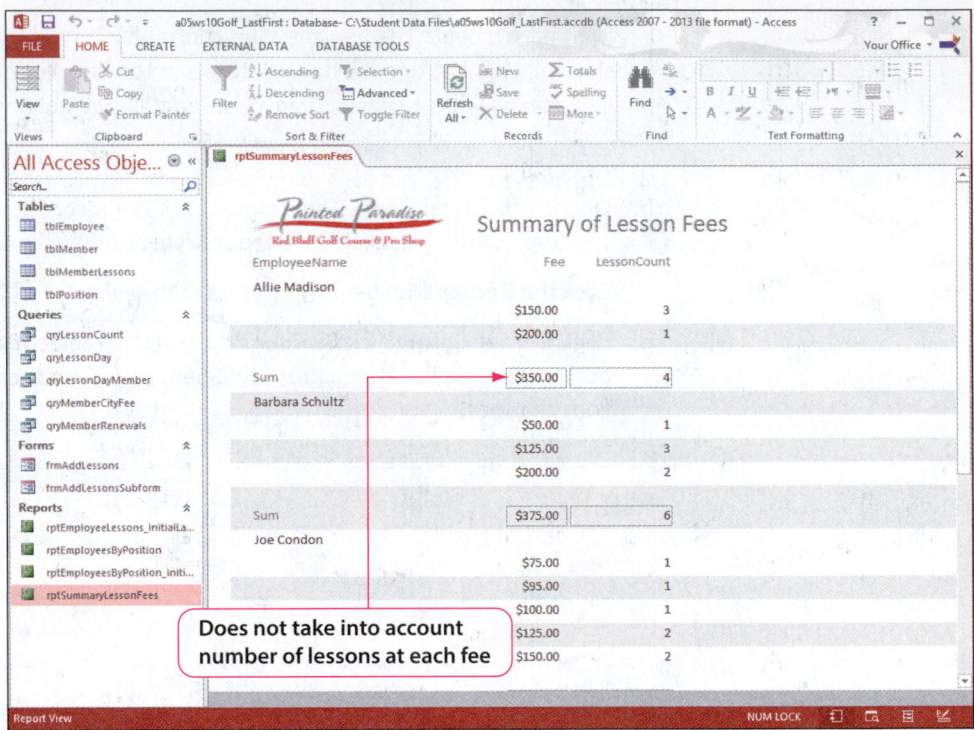

Figure 15   rptSummaryLessonFees

Modifying Existing Calculated Fields

In the figure above, you can see why the summary fields did not give the intended results. Look at the data for Allie Madison. She taught three lessons for a fee of $150.00 each. She taught one lesson with a fee of $200. The group summary shows a total of $350 in fees and four lessons. That $350 does not make sense because it simply is the addition of the two fees without taking into account that she taught three lessons for $150 each. You will modify the calculated field so it multiplies the lesson count by the fee and adds the product to get the correct value.

A10.11

 To Modify a Calculated Control in a Report

a. Open **rptSummaryLessonFees**, click the **FILE** tab, click **Save As**, click **Save Object As**, click **Save As**, and then type **rptSummaryLessonFees_initialLastname** using your first initial and last name.

b. Switch to **Design** view, and then in the EmployeeName Footer, click the calculated control **=Sum([Fee])**. Click the **DESIGN** tab, and then in the Tools group, click **Property Sheet**. In the Property Sheet pane, on the Data tab, click **Control Source Builder** ⋯ . In the Expression Builder, change the formula to **=Sum([Fee]*[LessonCount])** and then click **OK**. This will change the employee subtotals to multiply the lesson count by the related fee and then add the total fees.

c. In the **Report Footer**, click the calculated control **=Sum([Fee])**. In the Property Sheet pane, on the Data tab, click **Control Source Builder** ⋯ , and then in the Expression Builder, change the formula to **=Sum([Fee]*[LessonCount])**. Click **OK**. This will change the grand total. **Close** ✕ the Property Sheet pane. Switch to **Layout** view, and then verify that **Allie Madison** has a subtotal Fee of $650.

> **Troubleshooting**
>
> If you see a prompt that asks you to enter a parameter value, you mistyped the expression for the calculation. Click Cancel and correct the expression.

d. Switch to **Design** view, click the **Sum** label in the EmployeeName Footer, and replace the text with **Employee Summary**.

e. Switch to **Layout** view. Scroll down, click **John Schilling's Employee summary**, and then drag the **left edge** of the box to the left so the dollar sign is shown fully. Click **Grand Total fees**, and then repeat resizing of the field. **Save** 🖫 and then **Close** ✕ the report.

Creating Parameter Reports

Recall that parameter queries are queries where the user enters the criteria, or parameters, when the query is run and the results are based on the parameters entered. A **parameter** is a value that can be changed each time you run the query. These flexible queries can be customized to a user's needs. Reports can then be created from parameter queries to have that same flexibility. In this section you will not only create a parameter report, but you will also create a form for entering the parameters. This will require some modification of the original query, which you will also do.

Create a Parameter Report

A report created from a **parameter query** (a query that uses prompts for criteria) will work just like a parameter query: When you open the report, you will be prompted for values to search for, and only those values will appear on the report. In this section, you will create a report from an existing parameter query. You will create a form for entering the parameters in order to more easily run the report. You will also add conditional formatting to the report to highlight values that meet certain criteria.

Creating a Report from a Parameter Query

The golf course would like a report that shows membership renewals between a specific start and end date. You will make a copy of qryMemberRenewals and create the report from that new query. The query is a parameter query that finds all records with a renewal date between a start date entered and an end date entered.

A10.12

 To Create a Report from a Parameter Query

a. In the Navigation Pane, right-click **qryMemberRenewals**, and then select **Copy**. Right-click a **blank area** in the Navigation Pane, and then select **Paste**. Type **qryMemberRenewals_initialLastname** using your first initial and last name.

b. Click the **CREATE** tab, and then in the Reports group, click **Report Wizard**. Click the **Tables/Queries** arrow, select **qryMemberRenewals_initialLastname**, and then click **add all fields** >> . Click **Next**. Do not add any grouping levels. Click **Next**, click the first **sort** box arrow, select **DateRenewal**, and then click **Next**. Accept the **Tabular** layout, select **Landscape** orientation, and then click **Next**. Name your report **rptMemberRenewals_initialLastname** using your first initial and last name, and then click **Finish**.

c. The first parameter box will open prompting you for a Start Date value. Type **5/1/2016** and then click **OK**.

d. The second parameter box will open prompting you for an End Date value. Type **7/1/2016** and then click **OK**. Your report will open with two records that have a renewal date between the start date you entered and the end date you entered.

e. Click the **PRINT PREVIEW** tab and then, in the Close Preview group, click **Close Print Preview**. Select the report title **rptMembershipRenewals**, and then replace the text with **Membership Renewals by initialLastname**, using your first initial and last name.

f. **Save** 🖫 and then **Close** ✕ the report.

Creating a Form for Entering Parameters

An unbound form can be helpful as an input tool for parameter reports. Rather than opening the report and having parameter windows open one by one, a form can have controls for entering each of the parameters. You will create an unbound form with two controls: one for the start date and one for the end date. These dates will be unbound and will only stay active while the form is open. You will format these controls to be date fields; because it is a good idea to use a default value, you will use the current date for the default in both the start date and end date text boxes.

A10.13

 To Create a Form for Entering Parameters

a. Click the **CREATE** tab, and then in the Forms group, click **Blank Form**.

b. Click the **DESIGN** tab, and then in the Header / Footer group, click **Title** to add a title to the form. Replace the text with **Renewal Date Form by initialLastname**, using your first initial and last name.

c. **Close** ✕ the Field List pane. On the DESIGN tab, in the Controls group, click **Label** *Aa*, move your pointer to the **top-left corner** of the form details area, and then click the **form**. Type **Enter Dates for Renewal Queries and Reports**.

d. Select the label, click the **FORMAT** tab, and in the Font group, click **Font Color** 🅰 ▾, and then select **Red**. Click the **Font Size** arrow, and then select **14**.

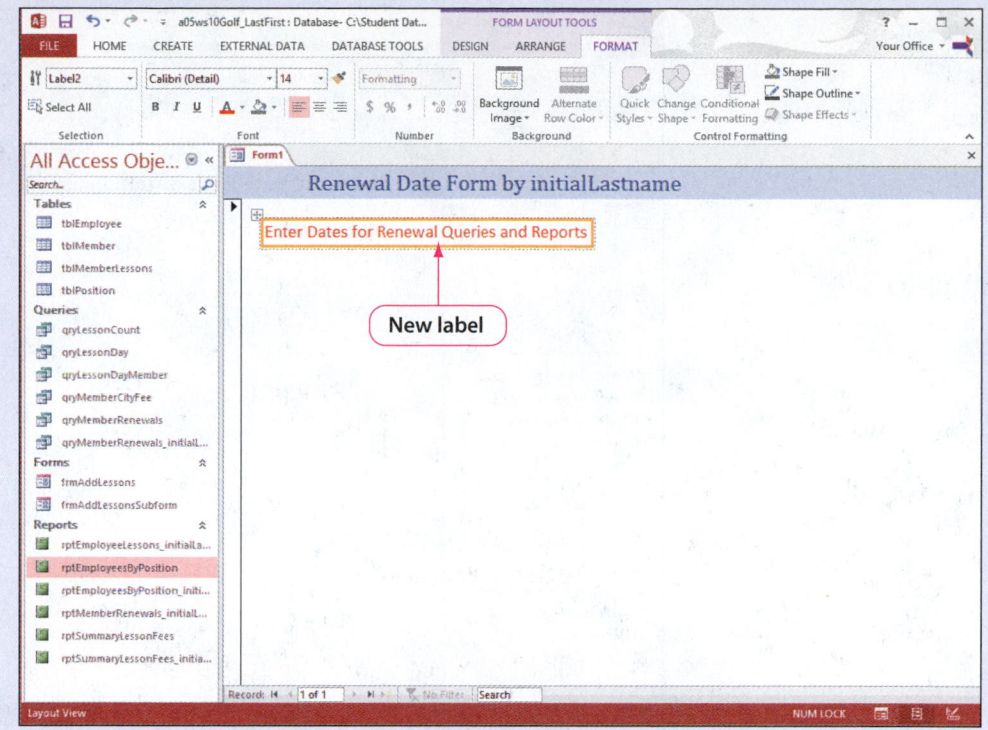

Figure 16 Label added to form

e. Click the **DESIGN** tab, and then in the Controls group, click **Text Box** [abl]. Click the **form** to insert the text box below the **Enter Dates for Renewal Queries and Reports** label. The field will automatically be stacked below the label.

f. Click the new **label**, and then replace the text with Start Date.

g. Click the **text** box, and then on the DESIGN tab, in the Tools group, click **Property Sheet**. In the Property Sheet pane, click the **Format** tab, click the **Format** arrow, and then select **Short Date**.

h. In the Property Sheet pane, click the **Data** tab, click **Default Value**, and then type =Date(). This will make the default value the current date. Click the **Other** tab, click **Name**, and then replace the text with StartDate.

i. On the DESIGN tab, in the Controls group, click **Text Box** [abl]. Click the **form** to insert a text box immediately below **Start Date**. Click the **label**, and then replace the text with End Date.

j. Click the new **text** box, in the Property Sheet pane, click the **Format** tab, click the **Format** arrow, and then select **Short Date**. Click the **Data** tab, click **Default Value**, and then type =Date(). Click the **Other** tab, click **Name**, and then replace the text with EndDate. **Close** [X] the Property Sheet pane.

k. Click the **blank space** above **Start Date**. Click the **ARRANGE** tab, and then in the Rows & Columns group, click **Select Row**. This will select the blank placeholder and the label you entered. In the Merge/Split group, click **Merge**. This merges the two controls in the first row so they line up better with the start date and end date labels.

l. Click the **first date** text box, and then on the ARRANGE tab, in the Merge/Split group, click **Split Horizontally**. Repeat for the **second date** text box. This splits the one long control into two smaller controls to make the data entry field smaller.

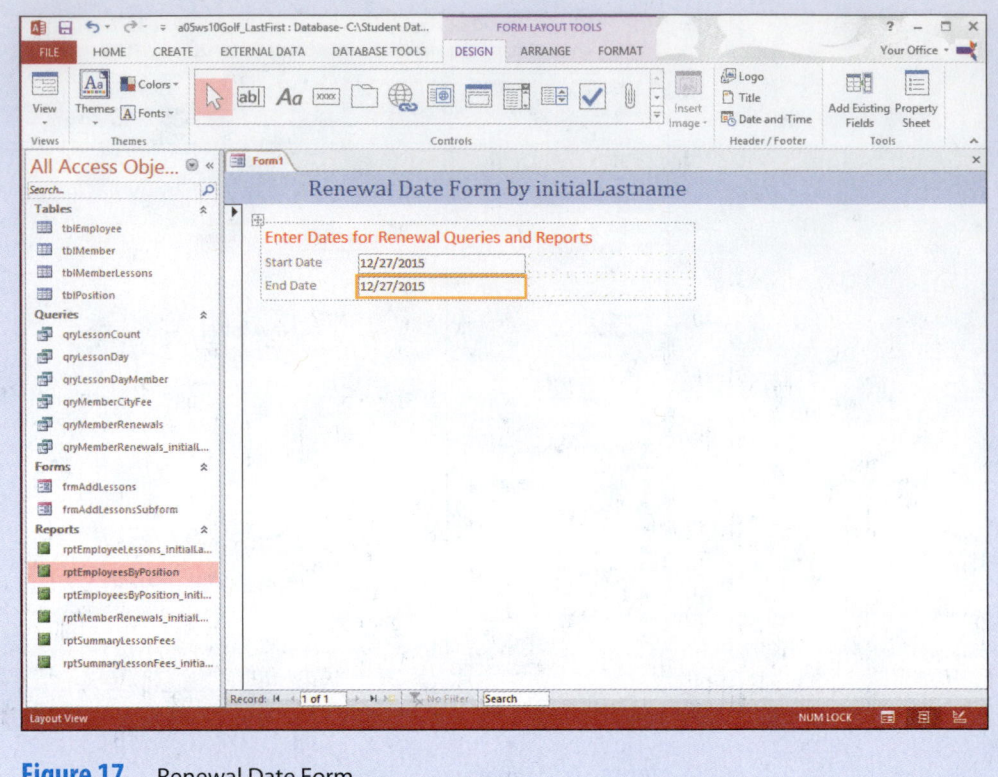

Figure 17 Renewal Date Form

m. **Save**  the form, type **frmMemberRenewals_initialLastname** using your first initial and last name.

Modifying a Query to Use New Form Fields

The form you just created will provide controls to enter the parameter values for the parameter query qryMemberRenewals_initialLastname, on which the report rptMemberRenewals_initialLastname is based. The query was created to accept values from the parameter windows, but since the values will now be entered into a form, the query needs to be updated to get the values from the form. You will change the query so the parameter values point to the values entered in the form and not in the parameter windows like a normal parameter query.

A10.14

▶ To Change Query Criteria to Use Fields from Form

a. In the Navigation Pane, right-click **qryMemberRenewals_initialLastname**, and then select **Design View**.

> **Troubleshooting**
>
> If you double-click the query to open it instead of using the right-click, you will be prompted to enter two parameter values. Click OK through each of the prompts to open the query, and then switch to Design view.

b. Scroll to the right, delete the criteria under **DateRenewal**, and then leave the insertion point in the **Criteria row**. Click the **DESIGN** tab, and then in the Query Setup group, click **Builder**. Type Between in the Expression pane.

c. In the Expression Elements pane, double-click **a05ws10Golf_initialLastname** to expand it. Double-click **Forms**, double-click **All Forms**, and then click **frmMemberRenewals_initialLastname**.

d. In the Expression Categories pane, double-click **StartDate**, type and in the Expression pane above, and then in the Expression Categories pane, double-click **EndDate**. Your expression should read Between Forms![frmMemberRenewals_initialLastname]![StartDate] and Forms![frmMemberRenewals_initialLastname]![EndDate].

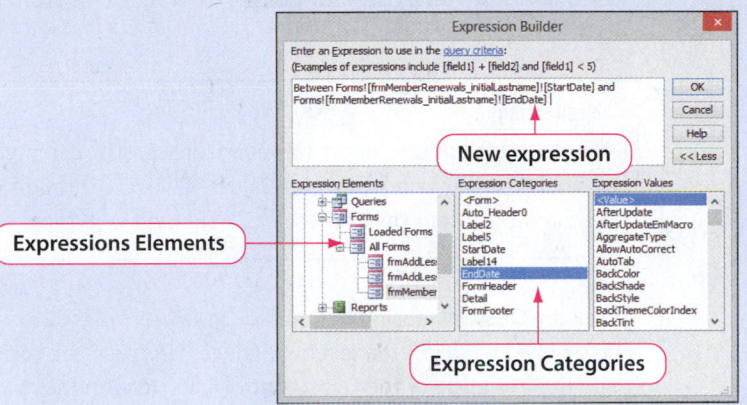

Figure 18   New expression in Expression Builder

e. Click **OK**. Click the **DESIGN** tab, and then in the Results group, click **Run** to run the query. Notice what the prompts now says. Type 5/1/2016 and then click **OK** for the first prompt. Type 7/1/2016 and then click **OK** for the second prompt. You should see the same two records as the last time you ran the query with these parameters. The only thing that changed was the wording of the prompts.

f. **Save** 🔲 and then **Close** ❌ the query.

REAL WORLD ADVICE   **Running the Parameter Report**

Once you change the query to accept the parameters from the form rather than the prompts when you open the report, you will want to use only the form to run the report and the query.

When the query was first created, the prompt was entered as Between [Start Date] and [End Date] so the prompt windows showed the text "Start Date" and "End Date". Now that you are using the form parameters, the prompts will show the name of the form and the name of the field and look something like this: "Forms![frmMemberRenewals_initialLastname]![StartDate]".

If a prompt were to open with this text, the user may not know what to do with it! Therefore, once a form is created and the query points to the form, the report and query should only be run from the form.

Modifying a Report to Use New Form Fields

When reports are built from parameter queries, running the report yields different results depending on the parameter values entered. Because reports are designed to be printed, that means that after time it might not be easy to recall what parameter value was used to run that particular report. You will add the parameter values to the report header so that they can be easily identified.

A10.15

To Add Form Fields to the Parameter Report

a. In the Navigation Pane, right-click **rptMemberRenewals_initialLastname**, and then select **Design View**. Use your pointer to drag the **bottom edge** of the **Report Header** to the **1"** mark on the vertical ruler.

> **Troubleshooting**
>
> If you double-click the report to open it instead of using the right-click, you will be prompted to enter two parameter values. Click OK through each of the prompts to open the report, and then switch to Design view.

b. Click the **DESIGN** tab, in the Controls group, click **Text Box** 🔲 . Click the **Report Header** below the title to insert a text box. If necessary, drag the **control** with the move handle so that the **left edge** of the Label control lines up with the **.5"** mark on the horizontal ruler. Click the **label**, and then replace the text with Start Date.

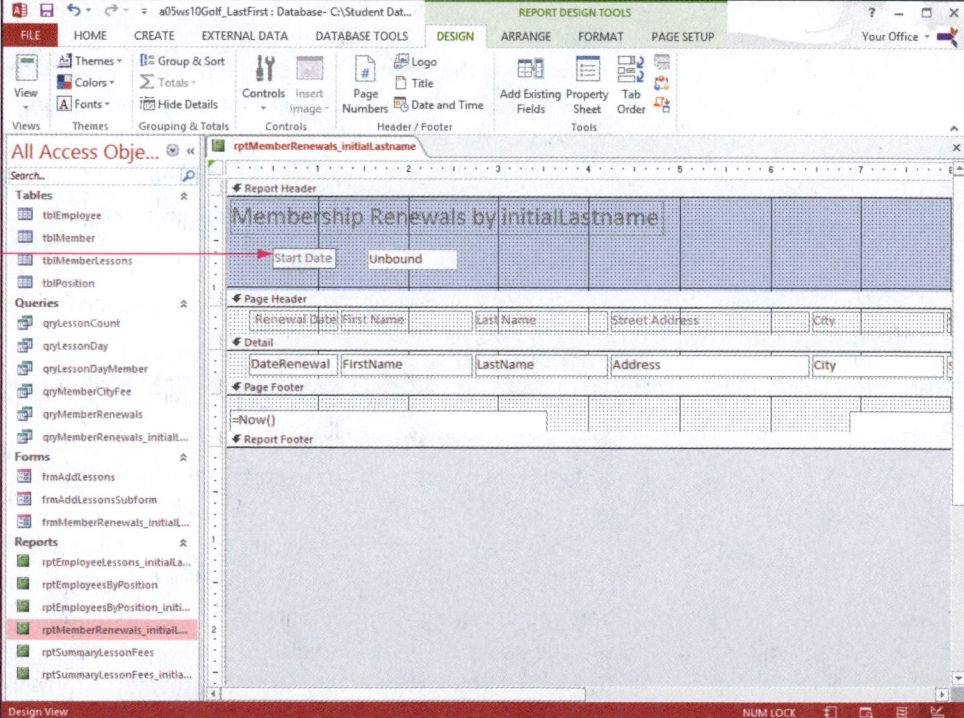

Figure 19 Text box added to report header

c. Click the **text** box, and then on the DESIGN tab, in the Tools group, click **Property Sheet**. In the Property Sheet pane, click the **Format** tab, click the **Format** arrow, and then select **Short Date**.

d. In the Property Sheet pane, click the **Data** tab, and then click **Control Source Builder** [⋯]. In the Expression Elements pane, double-click **a05ws10Golf_initialLastname**, double-click **Forms**, double-click **All Forms**, and then click **frmMemberRenewals_initialLastname**. In the Expression Categories pane, double-click **StartDate**, and then click **OK**.

e. On the DESIGN tab, in the Controls group, click **Text Box** [abl]. Click the **Report Header** to the right of the **Start Date** text box. If necessary, drag the control with the move handle so that the **left edge** of the label control lines up with the **3"** vertical grid line. Click the **label**, and then replace the text with End Date.

f. Click the **text box**, in the Property Sheet pane, on the **Format** tab, click the **Format** arrow [⌄], and then select **Short Date**.

g. Click the **Data** tab, and then click **Control Source Builder** [⋯]. In the Expression Elements pane, double-click **a05ws10Golf_initialLastname**, double-click **Forms**, and then double-click **All Forms**, and then click **frmMemberRenewals_initialLastname**. In the Expression Categories pane, double-click **EndDate**, and then click **OK**. **Close** [✕] the Property Sheet pane.

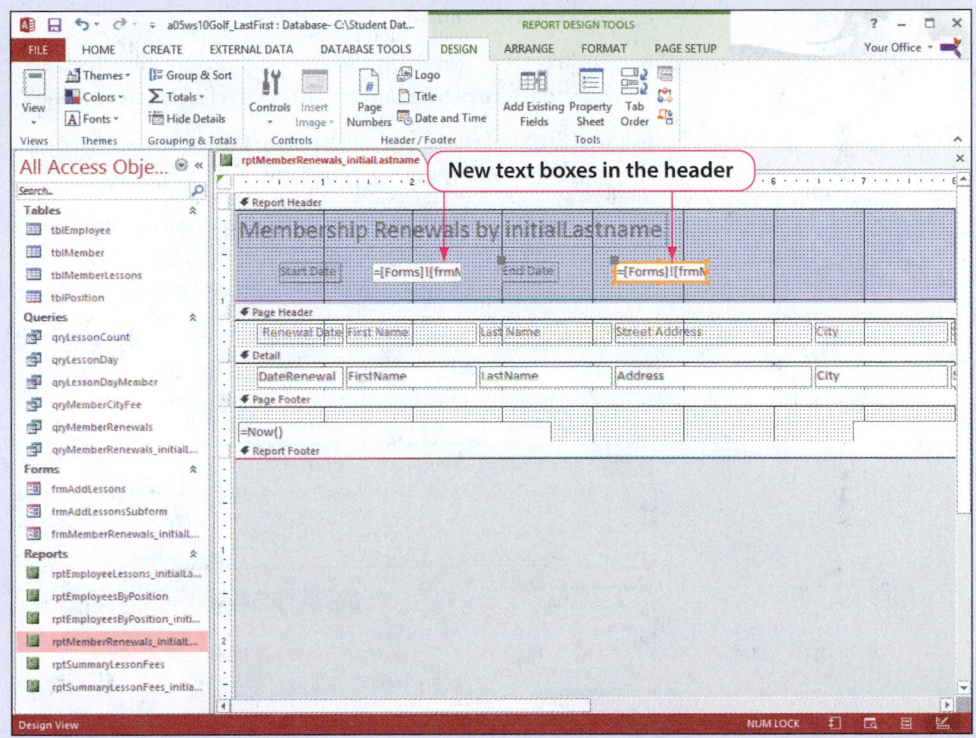

Figure 20   Text boxes added and formatted in report header

h. Click the **Start Date** label, press and hold [Shift], and then click the **Start Date** text box and the **End Date** label and text box. Click the **ARRANGE** tab. In the Sizing & Ordering group, click **Align**, and then select **Top**.

i. **Save** [💾] and then **Close** [✕] the report.

Adding Report Buttons to a Form

To use the form you created to enter parameters and run a report, you need an easy way to run the report from the form. You will add two buttons to the report that will run the parameter query and the parameter report based on the start and end dates entered on the form.

A10.16

To Add Report Buttons to a Form

a. Open **frmMemberRenewals_initialLastname** and then switch to Design view. Drag to expand the **Detail section** of the form to the **2"** mark on the vertical ruler.

b. Click the **DESIGN** tab, and then in the Controls group, click **Button** ⌷ᵪᵪᵪᵪ. Move your pointer below the **End Date** label, and then click the **form**. The Command Button Wizard opens.

c. In the Categories pane, click **Miscellaneous**. In the Actions pane, click **Run Query**, and then click **Next**.

d. Click **qryMemberRenewals_initialLastname**, and then click **Next**. Click **Text**, replace the text with **Run Renewals Query**, and then click **Next**. Name the button **cmdQryRenewals** and then click **Finish**.

e. On the DESIGN tab, in the Controls group, click **Button** ⌷ᵪᵪᵪᵪ. Move your pointer to the right of the existing button, and then click the **form**. The Command Button Wizard opens.

f. In the Categories pane, click **Report Operations**. In the Actions pane, click **Open Report**, and then click **Next**.

g. Click **rptMemberRenewals_initialLastname**, and then click **Next**. Click **Text**, replace the text with **Run Renewals Report**, and then click **Next**. Name the button **cmdRptRenewals** and then click **Finish**. Align the buttons by their top edge.

h. **Save** 🖫 the form and then switch to **Form** view. In **Start Date**, type **5/1/2016**. In **End Date**, type **7/1/2016**. Or, you can use the date picker for each field to pick the dates.

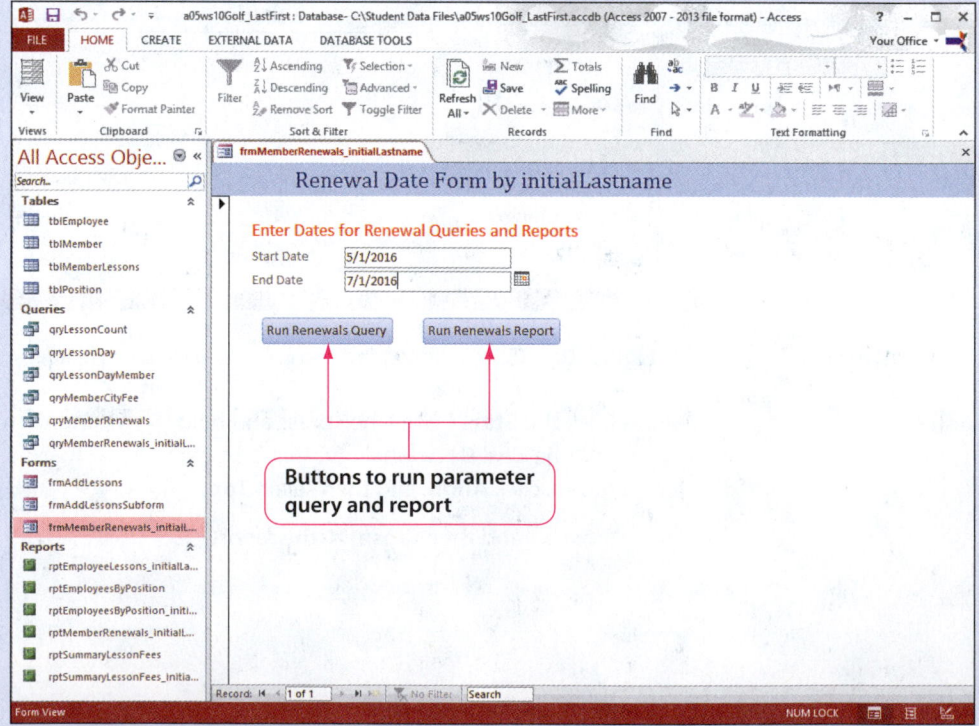

Figure 21   New buttons added to form

i. Click **Run Renewals Query**. The query opens showing the two members who have renewals between the two dates you entered. **Close** ☒ the query, but leave the form open.

j. Click **Run Renewals Report** using the same two dates entered above. The report opens showing the two members who have renewals between the two dates you entered. The dates are also filled in in the header. **Close** ☒ the report. Click **Save** if prompted to save changes.

Use Conditional Formatting in a Report

Conditional formatting formats a control based on one or more comparisons to a set rule. These comparisons can be based on the value of the control or on a calculation that includes other values; for example, to highlight values that are zero or negative. You can also compare the value to the value in other records; for example, you could highlight the value that is highest or lowest.

The Conditional Formatting Rules Manager dialog box is used to set the conditions. You can access the dialog box in Layout or Design view.

Adding Conditional Formatting to a Report

Barry wants a report to see at a glance which memberships have already expired. You will create a simple report with member names and renewal dates and use conditional formatting to highlight the expired memberships with red text.

A10.17

 To Add Conditional Formatting to a Report

a. Click the **CREATE** tab, and then click **Report Wizard**. Click the **Tables/Queries** arrow, select **tblMember**, and then add **DateRenewal**, **DateJoined**, and **MemberName** to the **Selected Fields**. Click **Next**.

b. Do not add any additional grouping, and then click **Next**. Sort in ascending order by **DateRenewal**, and then click **Next**. Accept the **Tabular** layout and **Portrait** orientation, and then click **Next**. Change the title of the report to rptExpiredMemberships_initialLastname using your first initial and last name, and then click **Finish**.

c. On the PRINT PREVIEW tab, in the Close Preview group, click **Close Print Preview**, switch to **Layout** view, and then change the title to Expired Memberships by initialLastname, using your first initial and last name.

d. Click the first **Renewal Date** field value. Click the **FORMAT** tab, and in the Control Formatting group, click **Conditional Formatting** to start the Conditional Formatting Rules Manager.

e. Click **New Rule**, and then accept the selection **Check values in the current record or use an expression**.

Below this you will see four boxes that allow you to create a rule. You need to select a value for at least the first three rule description boxes. The fourth box is only for entering a range of values.

f. Click the second **rule description** arrow that says **between**, and then select **less than or equal to**.

g. Next to the last rule description box, click **Build** ⌐--¬. In the Expression Elements pane, click **Common Expressions**. In the Expression Categories pane, double-click **Current Date**, and then click **OK**.

This tells Access to compare the value in the field with the current date. If the field value is less than or equal to the current date, then the font color—chosen next—will be changed to red.

h. Click **Font color** A, select **Red**, and then click **OK**. Verify that the rule says **Value <= Date()**.

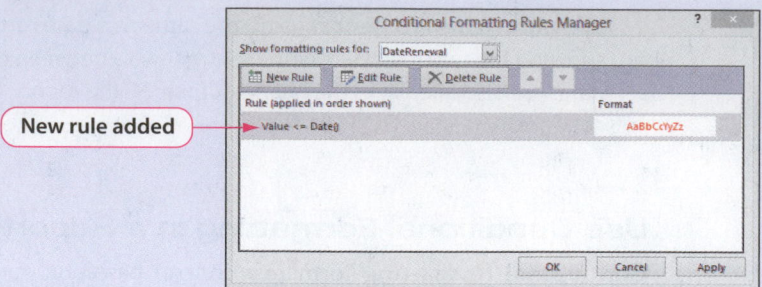

Figure 22 Conditional Formatting Rules Manager

> **Troubleshooting**
> If the rule is not correct, click Edit Rule and change the options. You can also delete the rule and start again by clicking Delete Rule.

i. Click **OK** again. The report should have anywhere from three to six dates highlighted, depending on the current date.

j. **Save** and **Close** the report.

Creating Mailing Labels

Access has a specialized report that can be used for mailing labels, name tags, or other types of labels. Because Access is often used to keep track of customers, employees, or other types of people, this is a common use of Access. You could also export the names and addresses to Word, and then create the mailing labels in Word, but doing it directly in Access saves a step.

Since mailing labels are actually reports, they have the four views that all reports have: Print Preview, Report view, Layout view, and Design view. Because of the mailing label formats, the views look different than those you have seen before. In Print Preview, the labels look the way they will look when you print them. In this section, you will create mailing labels from a query. You will also add buttons to an existing form to request a Print Preview of the labels and to print the labels.

Create Mailing Labels

Access has built-in label formats for many of the leading label makers. The wizard allows you to pick the correct format. You can create labels based on data in tables or queries.

Creating Address Mailing Labels

The golf club needs mailing labels for members whose memberships are expiring soon so the golf club can then mail a renewal letter. You will use qryMemberRenewals_initialLastname as a source for these labels. Because the query will only show results when date parameters have been entered, you will need to enter parameters for the report. If there are no parameters entered and the query is not open when you first create the report, you will get error messages instead of results. To prevent this from happening, you will run the query first. And because the query is based on parameters entered in a form, you will open the form first, enter parameters, run the query, and then create the report.

REAL WORLD ADVICE | Reports Based on Queries

When a report is based on a table with records, you can run the report and there will always be records in the report because there are always records in the table. When you run a report from a query, unless the query has been run first and the query is open, the query will not have any records and neither will the report! Remember, a query does not store any records, so if a report is run on a query with no records, the report will have no records. This should be taken into account when a database is created and given to someone else to use. Instructions should always be provided so the user knows what steps to take to successfully run a query or report. While not discussed in this workshop, a macro can be created to run a query and then a report if necessary.

A10.18

 ### To Create Mailing Labels

a. Open **frmMemberRenewals_initialLastname**, type 1/1/2016 for the start date and 3/1/2016 for the end date. Click **Run Renewals Query**.

b. With both the form and query still open, click the **CREATE** tab, and in the Reports group, click **Labels**. The Label Wizard starts.

 The first task is to match your labels with the standard labels that are part of the wizard. The easiest way to do that is to look at the box or sheet of labels. If you do not have a standard label, you can specify a customized size. The golf club uses Avery C2160 labels, so you will select that type of label.

c. If necessary, click the **Filter by manufacturer** arrow, select **Avery**, select Product number **C2160**, and then click **Next**.

d. Click the **Font name** arrow, select **Times New Roman**, click the **Font size** arrow, and then select **11**. Click the **Font weight** arrow, select **Normal**, and then click **Next**.

e. Double-click **FirstName** to move it to the prototype label. Press [Spacebar], double-click **LastName**, and then press [Enter].

> **Troubleshooting**
>
> The field selection looks like field selection in other wizard dialog boxes, but there are important differences. First, you must format your labels yourself. You will need to type spaces, commas, and line breaks. Second, there is no field back button. If you put the fields in the wrong order, it is sometimes easiest to go back a step in the wizard dialog box and try again.
>
> If you omitted the space, click between the two fields and press [Spacebar].

f. Double-click **Address**, press [Enter], double-click **City**, and then type ,—a comma. Press [Spacebar], double-click **State**, press [Spacebar], and then double-click **ZipCode**.

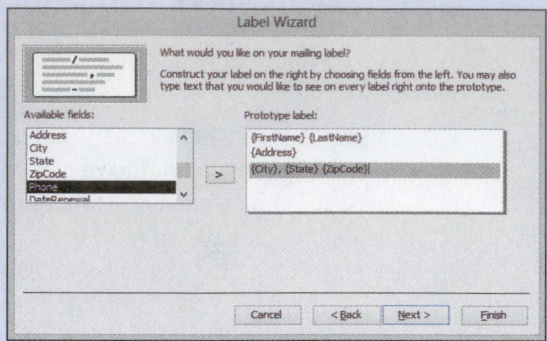

Figure 23   Complete address added in Label Wizard

g. Click **Next**. In the Available fields list, double-click **ZipCode** to add it to **Sort by**, and then click **Next**.

h. Name the report **rptLabels_initialLastname** using your first initial and last name.

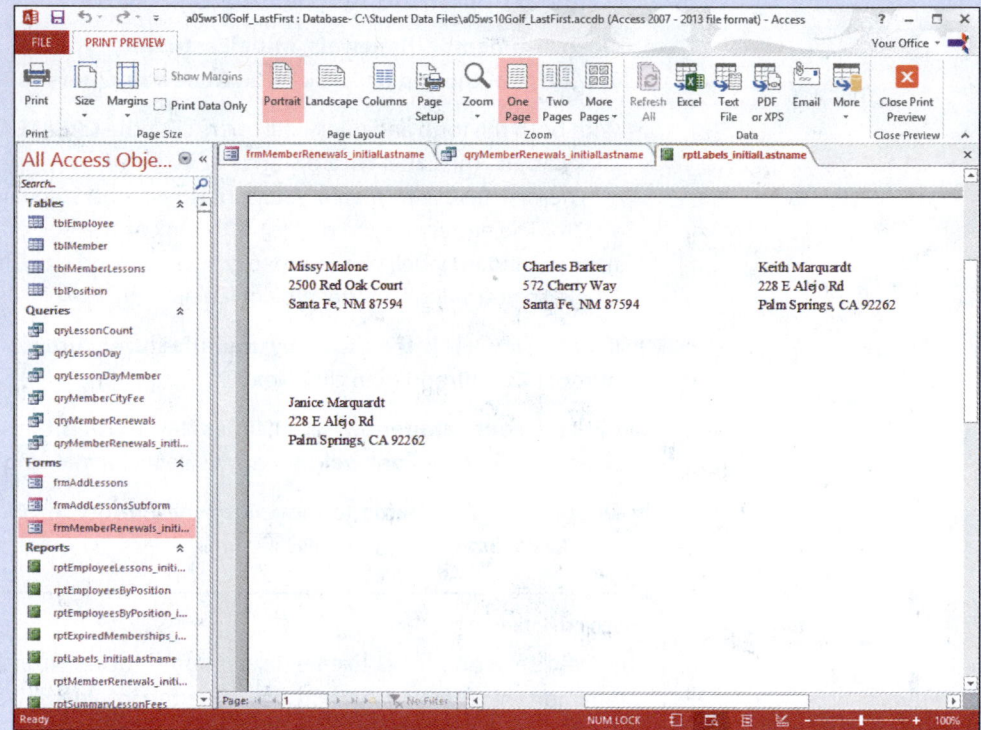

Figure 24   Finished Labels

i. **Save** 💾 and then **Close** ✖ the label report. **Close** ✖ qryMemberRenewals_initialLastname.

> **Troubleshooting**
>
> When you clicked Finish, did the Mailing labels report ask you for parameters? Make sure that frmMemberRenewals_initialLastname is open with parameters entered. If you close the form, Access will not know what dates you want.

Adding Mailing Label Buttons to a Form

To make the mailing labels easier to use, you will add buttons to preview and print the labels to your renewal form.

A10.19

 To Add Mailing Label Buttons to a Form

a. Open **frmMemberRenewals_initialLastname** and then switch to **Design** view. Click the **DESIGN** tab, and in the Controls group, click **Button** ⊠.

b. Move your pointer to below the **Run Renewals Query** button, and then click the form. The Command Button Wizard starts.

c. In the Categories pane, select **Report Operations**. In the Actions pane, select **Preview Report**, and then click **Next**. Select **rptLabels_initialLastname**, and then click **Next**. Click **Text**, replace the text with Preview Mailing Labels, and then click **Next**. Name the button cmdPreviewLabels and then click **Finish**.

d. On the DESIGN tab, in the Controls group, click **Button** ⊠. Move your pointer to the **right** of the Preview Mailing Labels button, and then click the **form**. The Command Button Wizard starts.

e. In the Categories pane, select **Report Operations**. In the Actions pane, click **Print Report**, and then click **Next**. Select **rptLabels_initialLastname**, and then click **Next**. Click **Text**, replace the text with Print Mailing Labels and then click **Next**. Name the button cmdPrintLabels and then click **Finish**.

f. On the DESIGN tab, in the Controls group, click **Button** ⊠. Move your pointer **below** the Preview Mailing Labels button, and then click the **form**. The Command Button Wizard starts.

g. In the Categories pane, select **Form Operations**. In the Actions pane, select **Close Form**, and then click **Next**. Click **Text**, accept **Close Form**, and then click **Next**. Name the button cmdCloseForm and then click **Finish**.

h. Align the buttons to one another:
- Click the **first button**, press and hold ⇧Shift, and then click the other **two buttons** in the first column. Click the **ARRANGE** tab. In the Sizing & Ordering group, click **Align**, and then select **Left**. Click **Size/Space**, and then select **Equal Vertical**.
- Click the **first button** in the first row, press and hold ⇧Shift, and then click the **second button** in the first row. Click **Align**, and then select **Top**.
- Using ⇧Shift, select the **next row of two buttons**. Click **Align**, and then select **Top**.
- Using ⇧Shift, select the **two buttons in the second column**. Click **Align**, and then select **Right**.
- Using ⇧Shift, select **all five buttons**. Click **Size/Space**, and then select **To Widest**.

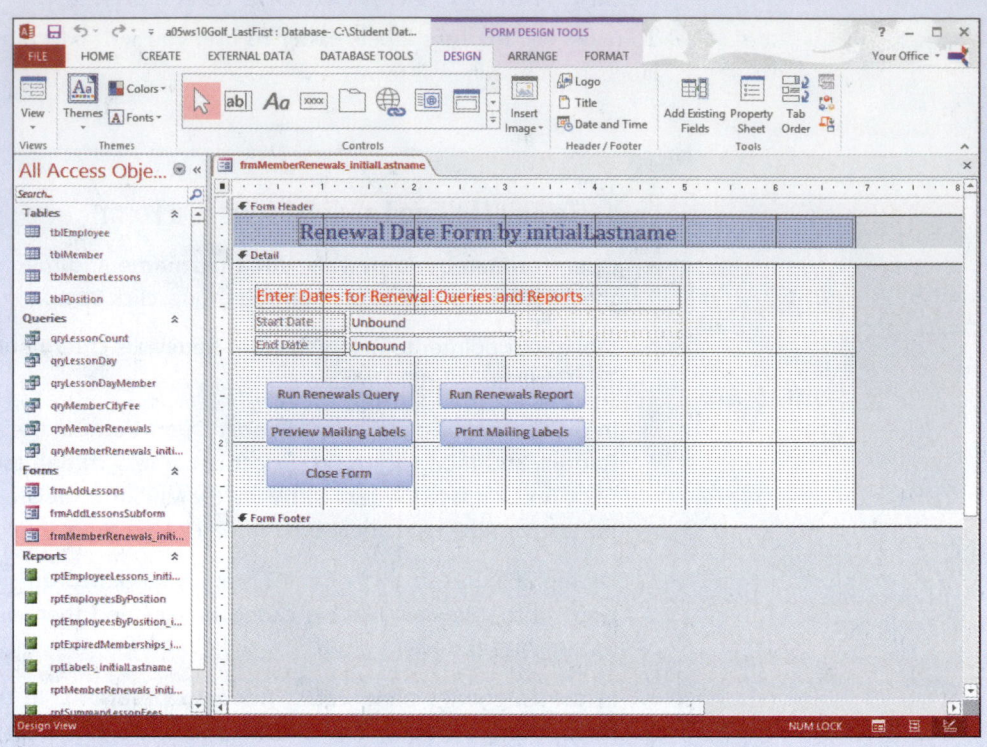

Figure 25 Buttons resized and aligned

i. Click **Save** 🖫 to save the form, and then switch to **Form** view. In **Start Date**, type **1/1/2016**. In **End Date**, type **3/1/2016**. Click the **Preview Mailing Labels** button. The labels report opens showing the members who have renewals between the two dates. **Close** ✕ the report.

j. Click the **Close Form** button, and then exit Access.

REAL WORLD ADVICE | **Preview Before You Print**

When you create a report, it is a good idea to preview it before you print it or send it in PDF form to someone else. Sometimes formatting changes make the report go to two pages when you did not intend it. On mailing labels, it is common for the address to not quite fit into the label or for you to have omitted a space between fields.

Concept Check

1. When you click Summary Options in the Report Wizard, what types of data fields will you see listed? What does it mean if the Summary Options button is not available in the Report Wizard step? p. 513

2. What are the seven different sections of a report in Design view? Will all reports have all seven sections all the time? Why or why not? p. 515-516

3. Where would you go to set the current date to show in a date field automatically? p. 516

4. How do you add a field to an existing report? Are the label and text box added together or separately? How do you delete a field on a report? Are the label and text box deleted together or separately? p. 521

5. What is the difference between grouping and sorting records in a report? p. 524

6. What is the difference between a text box and a label? Give an example of when you would use each. p. 527

7. What does the Builder button in the Control Source property box allow you to do? p. 529-530

8. What is a parameter report? When would a parameter report be more useful than a regular report? p. 531

9. What is conditional formatting, and when would you use it? p. 539

10. What can you use for sources of data for mailing labels? Is there anything special you would do for mailing labels based on parameter queries? p. 540

Key Terms

Blank Report tool   512
Conditional formatting   539
Detail area   516
Group Footer   516
Group Header   516
Label control   516
Move handle   518

Page Footer   516
Page Header   516
Parameter   531
Parameter query   531
Property sheet   520
Report   512
Report Design tool   512

Report Footer   516
Report Header   516
Report tool   512
Report Wizard   512
Sizing handle   518
Snap to grid   518

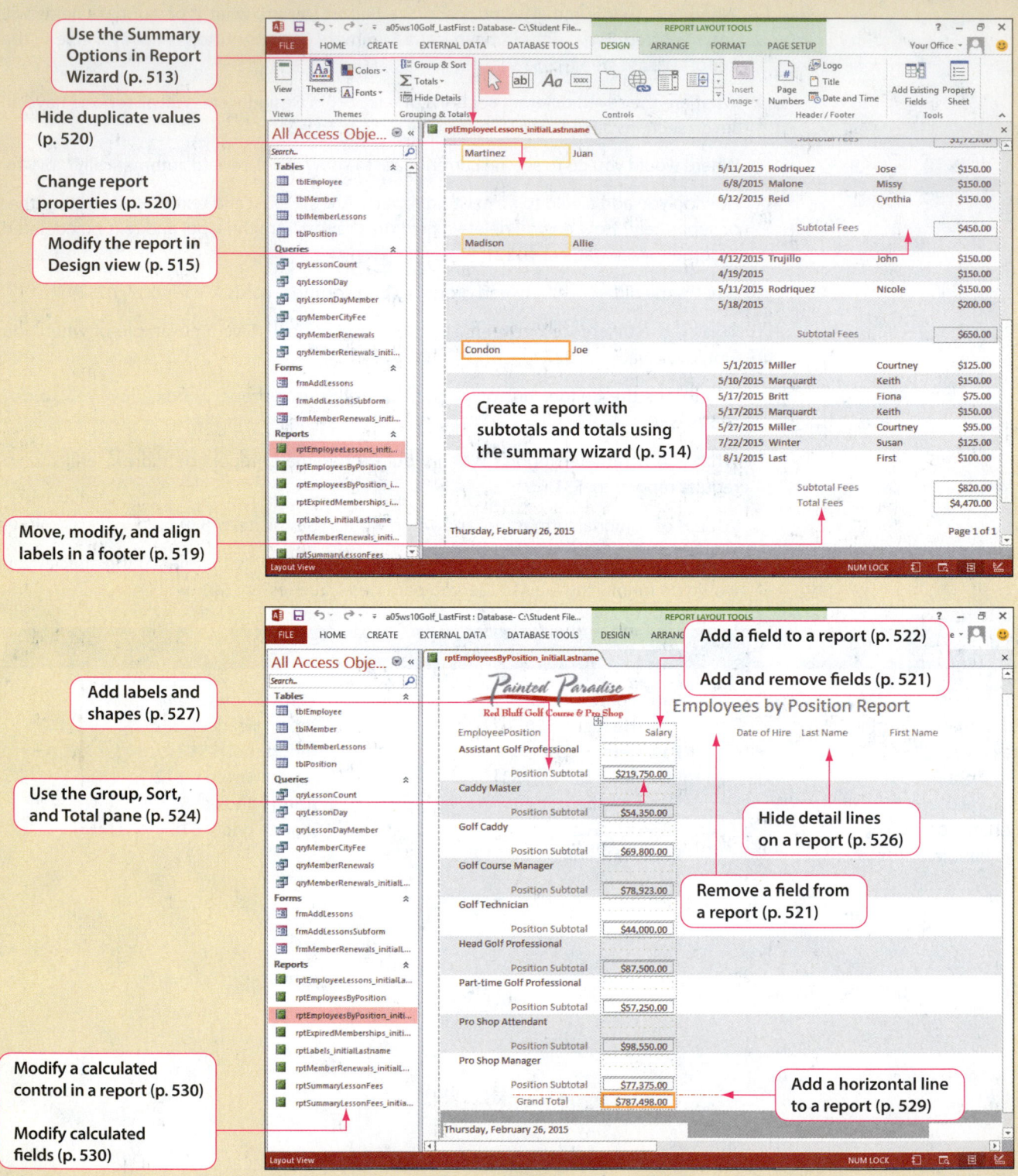

Use the Summary Options in Report Wizard (p. 513)

Hide duplicate values (p. 520)

Change report properties (p. 520)

Modify the report in Design view (p. 515)

Create a report with subtotals and totals using the summary wizard (p. 514)

Move, modify, and align labels in a footer (p. 519)

Add labels and shapes (p. 527)

Add a field to a report (p. 522)

Add and remove fields (p. 521)

Use the Group, Sort, and Total pane (p. 524)

Hide detail lines on a report (p. 526)

Remove a field from a report (p. 521)

Modify a calculated control in a report (p. 530)

Modify calculated fields (p. 530)

Add a horizontal line to a report (p. 529)

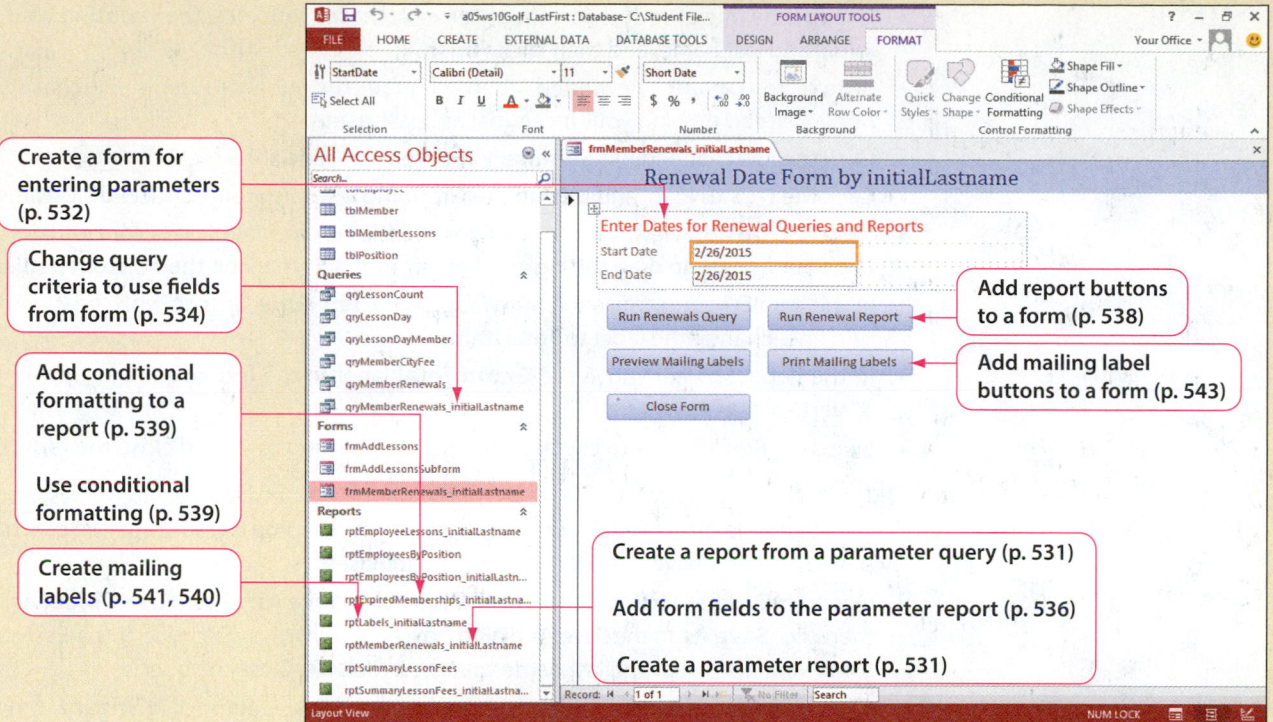

Create a form for entering parameters (p. 532)

Change query criteria to use fields from form (p. 534)

Add conditional formatting to a report (p. 539)

Use conditional formatting (p. 539)

Create mailing labels (p. 541, 540)

Add report buttons to a form (p. 538)

Add mailing label buttons to a form (p. 543)

Create a report from a parameter query (p. 531)

Add form fields to the parameter report (p. 536)

Create a parameter report (p. 531)

Figure 26 Red Bluff Golf Club Final Database

Practice 1

Student data file needed:

 a05ws10Putts.accdb

You will save your file as:

a05ws10Putts_LastFirst.accdb

Putts for Paws

Production & Operations

Red Bluff Golf Course runs a charity golf event that raises money for a local animal shelter. Barry Cheney, the manager of the golf course, has asked you to improve the usability of the database by creating reports. He specifically wants a report to show a summary of items purchased with subtotals and totals and the details hidden. He also wants a way to run an existing query that calculates the total purchase amount—price—by multiplying the quantity of the item by the amount to be charged per item. The query is not set up as a parameter query, so you will add the parameter to come from a form that you will create. You will also add buttons to the form to make it easier to navigate and add the parameter value to the report. Finally, you will create mailing labels for all participants.

a. Start **Access**, open **a05ws10Putts** and then save it as a05ws10Putts_LastFirst, using your last and first name. In the Security Warning, click **Enable Content**.

b. Open **tblParticipant**, change the **FirstName** and **LastName** in the first record to your actual name, and then close the table.

c. The first report you will create will show each item's description, the quantity purchased, and then a subtotal and grand total for each item.

- Click the **CREATE** tab, and then in the Reports group, click **Report Wizard**.
- From tblItem, select **ItemDescription**. From tblOrderLine, select **Quantity**, and then click **Next**.
- Group by **tblItem**, and then click **Next**. Sort by **Quantity** in ascending order, and then click **Summary Options**. Click the **Sum** check box, and then click **OK**. Click **Next**. Accept the **Stepped** layout and **Portrait** orientation, and then click **Next**.

- Change the title of your report to **rptItemsPurchased_initialLastname**, using your first initial and last name, and then click **Finish**.
- Switch to **Layout** view, and then change the title to **Items Purchased by initialLastname**, using your first initial and last name.
- Click the line that begins "**Summary for 'ItemID'**", and then press ⌨Delete.
- Click the **DESIGN** tab, and then in the Grouping & Totals group, click **Hide Details**.
- Switch to **Design** view. In the Page Footer, click the calculated Date control, **=Now( )**. Use your pointer to drag the **right edge** left to the **2"** mark on the horizontal ruler.
- In the ItemID Footer, move the **Sum** label so the **left edge** lines up with the **3"** vertical grid line. Change the label to **Total Items**.
- In the Report Footer, move the **Grand Total** label so the **left edge** lines up with the **3"** vertical grid line.
- Switch to **Report** view to check your report formatting. Save and close the report.

d. You will create a report to show by participant, their order date, item description, quantity, and the price of each item they purchased. Then you will subtotal the purchases by participant and have a grand total for all purchases.

- Open **qryOrdersCalcPrice**, click the **FILE** tab, click **Save As**, select **Save Object As**, and then click **Save As**. In the Save As dialog box, type **qryOrdersCalcPrice_initialLastname**, using your first initial and last name, and then click **OK**. Close the query.
- Click the **CREATE** tab, and then click **Report Wizard**. From **qryOrdersCalcPrice_initialLastname**, select **all fields** except ItemID. Click **Next**.
- Accept grouping by **ParticipantName**, click **Next**, and then sort in ascending order by **OrderDate** and **ItemDescription**.
- Click **Summary Options**, select **Sum** for **Quantity**, **Price**, and **TotalCost**, and then click **OK**.
- Click **Next**, select the **Outline** layout, change to **Landscape** orientation, and then click **Next**.
- Change the title of your report to **rptParticipantPurchases_initialLastname**, using your first initial and last name, and then click **Finish**.
- Switch to **Layout** view, and change the title to **Participant Purchases by initialLastname**, using your first initial and last name.
- Click the line that begins **Summary for 'ParticipantName'**, and then press ⌨Delete.
- Switch to **Design** view. Select the **Total Cost** label, **Total Cost** text box, **Total Cost summary** in the ParticipantName Footer, and the **Total Cost summary** in the Report Footer. Move them all so their left edges lines up with the **7.5"** mark on the horizontal ruler. Then drag the right edges to line up with the **8.5"** mark on the horizontal ruler.
- Select the **Price** label, **Price** text box, **Price summary** in the ParticipantName footer, and the **Price summary** in the Report Footer. Drag the right edges to line up with the left edge of the Total Cost boxes.
- In the ParticipantName footer, change the label from **Sum** to **Participant Total**.
- Select the **TotalCost subtotal** text box and the **TotalCost grand total** text box. Click the **DESIGN** tab. In the Tools group, click **Property Sheet**, and then change the Format of both fields to **Currency**.
- Select the **TotalCost** label, the **TotalCost subtotal** text box, and the **TotalCost grand total** text box. Drag the **right edges** of the controls to the right so the edges line up with the right edge of the **page number** footer control in the Page Footer.
- Switch to **Report** view to check your report formatting. Save and close your report.

e. Now you will create a form to enter the item requested. This value will then be applied to the qryOrdersCalcPrice_initialLastname as a parameter value. Once the data has been found in the query, rptParticipantPurchases_initialLastname can be run with the specific value entered in the form. This will allow the golf course employees to search for purchase information on a particular item.

- Click the **CREATE** tab, and then in the Forms group, click **Blank Form**.
- In the Header/Footer group, click **Title**, and then replace the title with Item Report by initialLastname, using your first initial and last name.
- Close the Field List pane. Click the **Label** control, move your pointer to the **top-left corner** of the form detail, and then click to place the label. Type Enter Item for Queries and Reports.
- Click the **Combo Box** control, and then click the **form** below the label. Select **I want the combo box to get the values from another table or query**, and then click **Next**. Select **Table: tblItem**, and then click **Next**. Double-click **ItemDescription**, and then click **Next**. Sort by **ItemDescription**, and then click **Next**. Adjust the width of the column to fit, and then click **Next**. Accept the name **ItemDescription**, and then click **Finish**.
- Click the **ItemDescription** combo box, and then click **Property Sheet** in the Tools group. In the Property Sheet pane, click the **Other** tab, and click **Name**, and then type ItemDescription.
- Select the **ItemDescription** label, and then double-click the **right edge** to adjust the width.
- Click in the **first row** in the layout, click the **ARRANGE** tab, and then in the Rows & Columns group, click **Select Row**. In the Merge/Split group, click **Merge**.
- Save your form as frmRequestItems_initialLastname using your first initial and last name. Close the property sheet pane and close the form.

f. Now you will modify qryOrdersCalcPrice_initialLastname to use the item description from the form you just created. This will make the query a parameter query.

- Open **qryOrdersCalcPrice_initialLastname**, switch to **Design** view, and then click the **Criteria** row under ItemID. Click the **DESIGN** tab, and then in the Query Setup group, click **Builder**. In the Expression Elements pane, double-click **a05ws10Putts_initialLastname**, double-click **Forms**, double-click **All Forms**, and then click **frmRequestItems_initialLastname**.
- In the Expression Categories pane, double-click **ItemDescription**, and then click **OK**.
- Save and close your query.

g. Next you will modify the report rptParticipantPurchases_initialLastname to put the item description selected in the form in the report header:

- In the Navigation Pane, right-click **rptParticipantPurchases_initialLastname** and then select **Design View**.
- Click the **DESIGN** tab, and then in the Controls group, click **Text Box**. Click to the right of the **report title** in the report header to insert a text box.
- Select the **label**, and then change the text to Item Selected.
- Move and resize the label so the **left edge** lines up with the **5"** vertical grid line, and the **right edge** lines up with the **6"** vertical grid line.
- Select the **text** box, and then in the Property Sheet pane, on the Data tab, click **Control Source Builder**. In the Expression Elements pane, double-click **a05ws10Putts_initialLastname**, double-click **Forms**, double-click **All Forms**, and then click **frmRequestItems_initialLastname**.
- In the Expression Categories pane, double-click **ItemDescription**, and then click **OK**. In the Property Sheet pane, click the **Other** tab, click **Name**, and then type Description.
- Close the Property Sheet pane. Save and close your report.

h. You will add buttons to frmRequestItems_initialLastname to run the query and report:

- Open **frmRequestItems_initialLastname** and switch to **Design** view. Drag the **bottom edge** of the Detail area to the **2.5"** mark on the vertical ruler.
- Click the **DESIGN** tab, and then in the Controls group, click **Button**. Click below the combo box label to start the Command Button Wizard.

- Select **Miscellaneous**, select **Run Query**, and then click **Next**. Select **qryOrdersCalcPrice_initialLastname**, and then click **Next**. Select **Text**, and then type Run Calculate Price Query. Click **Next**. Name the button **cmdQryCalcPrice** and then click **Finish**.
- In the Controls group, click **Button**, and then click below the first button. Select **Report Operations** and **Open Report**, and then click **Next**. Select **rptParticipantPurchases_initialLastname**, and then click **Next**. Select **Text**, type Run Participants Purchases Report and then click **Next**. Name the button **cmdRptRun**, and then click **Finish**.
- Select both buttons, and then click the **ARRANGE** tab. In the Sizing & Ordering group, click **Align**, and then select **Left**. In the Controls group, click **Size/Space**, and then select **To Widest**.
- Drag the **form footer** down until it is on the **.5"** mark on the vertical ruler.
- Switch to **Form** view. Test your form by selecting **Cart sponsor** in the combo box. Click **Run Calculate Price Query**, and you should get four records. Close the query, and then click **Run Participants Purchases Report**. You should see the same four records. Close the report.
- Save and close your form.

i. Create mailing labels for all participants:
- In the Navigation Pane, click **tblParticipant**, click the **CREATE** tab, and then in the Reports group, click **Labels**.
- If necessary, filter by manufacturer **Avery**, select Product Number **C2160**, and then click **Next**.
- Change the font to **Times New Roman**, and then change the font size to **11**. Click **Next**.
- Add **First Name**, press Spacebar, add **Last Name**, and then press Enter.
- Add **StreetAddress**, and then press Enter.
- Add **City**, type ,—a comma—press Spacebar, add **State**, press Spacebar, and then add **ZipCode**. Click **Next**.
- Sort by **LastName** and then **FirstName**. Click **Next**.
- Name your report rptLabels_initialLastname and then click **Finish**.
- Save and close your report.

j. Exit Access and submit your work as directed.

Problem Solve 1

Student data file needed:	**You will save your file as:**
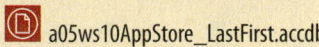 a05ws10AppStore.accdb	a05ws10AppStore_LastFirst.accdb

Phil's Phone App Store Database

Sales & Marketing

An intern has created a database that Phil's Phone App Store can use to sell apps for smartphones. There is a query to look up the count of sales, but Phil would like to be able to enter a range of dates to see all the apps sold over that time period and run a report for that data. He has a query that will find the data but no report. He has asked you to create a report based on his parameter query that will allow him to enter a beginning date and ending date and show purchases made on those days. You will create a form to enter the parameter as well as run the queries and report he wants. You will also modify the report so he will be able to see the parameter values entered. Then you will create mailing labels for all his customers so he can send them a newsletter each quarter.

a. Start **Access**, and then open **a05ws10AppStore**. Save it as **a05ws10AppStore_LastFirst**, using your last and first name. Enable the content if necessary.

b. Create a report from **qryPurchases** that includes all the fields from the query and is grouped by **PurchaseDate**. (*Hint*: To group by specific date and not by month, change Grouping Options in the wizard to **Normal**.) Sort the report by **AppName**, and then include a Summary Option to **Sum** the **AmountCharged** field. Name the report **rptPurchasesByDate_initialLastname**, using your first initial and last name.

c. Type **3/1/2015** for the parameter starting date and **3/31/2015** for the parameter ending date. Modify the report by deleting the **Summary for 'PurchaseDate'** text box. Change the **Sum** label to **Total for Day**, and then move the field so the **right edge** of the label is lined up with the **5"** vertical grid line. Align the **Sum** label and the **Sum** text box to their **bottom borders**.

d. Change the **Grand Total** label to **Total for Period**, and then move the field so the **right edge** of the label is lined up with the **5"** vertical grid line. Change the title of the report to **Purchases by Date**. Change the field properties to **hide duplicates** for AuthorName.

e. Create a blank form named **frmPurchasesByDate_initialLastname**, using your first initial and last name, with a **title Purchases By Date by initialLastname**, using your first initial and last name. Add a **label** that says **Enter Beginning and Ending Dates for Purchase Query and Report**.

f. Add a **text** box for the starting date. Change the label to **Starting Date**. In the Property Sheet pane, name the text box **StartDate** and then format the control as **Short Date**.

g. Add a **text** box for the ending date. Change the label to **Ending Date**. In the Property Sheet pane, name the text box **EndDate** and then format the control as **Short Date**.

h. Merge the **first row** so the text box is lined up with the left side of the stacked controls.

i. Add a **button** to the form to run **qryPurchases**, show the text **Run Purchases Query**, and name the button **cmdPurchasesQry**.

j. Add a second **button** to the form just beside the first button to open **rptPurchasesByDate_initialLastname**, show the text **Run Purchases Report**, and name the button **cmdPurchasesRpt**.

k. Add a third **button** beside the other two to close the form, show the text **Close Form**, and name it **cmdCloseForm**. Resize all three buttons **To Widest**, and then align them by their top edges. Save the form as **frmPurchasesByDate_initialLastname** using your first initial and last name.

l. Modify **qryPurchases** in **Design** view so the query looks for the parameters from the form rather than what is entered when the query is run. (*Hint*: Use the Builder).

m. Modify **rptPurchasesByDate** so the date parameters entered in the form are shown in the header. Change the title to **Purchases By Date by initialLastname**, using your first initial and last name. Change the label of the **StartDate** field to **Starting Date** and then line up the **left edge** with the **2.5"** mark on the horizontal ruler. Format the text box as **Short Date**, and then name it **StartingDate**.

n. Add a second **text** box for the Ending Date, change the label to **Ending Date** and line up the **left edge** with the **7"** vertical grid line. Change the text box so it is formatted as **Short Date** and named **EndingDate**.

o. Select the **title**, **starting date** label and text box, and the **ending date** label and text box. Align all the **controls** to their **bottom edges**.

p. Create **mailing labels** for all customers. Select **Avery** for the manufacturer and **C2160** for the product number. Select **Times New Roman**, font size **11**, and **normal** font weight. Add the **customer first and last name** to the first line, **address** to the second line, and

city, **state**, **and zip** to the last line, with a comma and space between city and state. Sort by **CustLastName**, and then name the report **rptLabels_initialLastname** using your first initial and last name.

q. Save and close all forms, queries, and reports. Exit Access. Submit your work as directed by your instructor.

Perform 1: Perform in Your Career

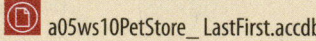

Student data file needed:

 a05ws10PetStore.accdb

You will save your file as:

a05ws10PetStore_ LastFirst.accdb

Pet Store Reporting

Sales & Marketing

A pet store owner started creating a database to keep records of animals, breeds, purchases, and customers. Data has been added to the tables, but there are no forms or reports for entering data or looking up data. There is currently a parameter query that prompts for a range of dates to look up the date of birth for the animals, but there is no report associated with the query. You have been asked to create a parameter report from the parameter query as well as a form for entering beginning and ending dates for the purchase query. The form will include buttons to run the query and report. The report will need to include the date parameters in the header.

Finally, you will create mailing labels for customers who have made purchases so you can send follow-up letters at a later date.

a. Open **a05ws10PetStore**, and then save it as **a05ws10PetStore_LastFirst**, using your last and first name.

b. Create a report from qryAnimalDOB and name it **rptAnimalsByDOB_initialLastname**, using your first initial and last name. The report will count the number of animals born each month as well as:
   • Show all the fields grouped by date of birth by month.
   • Sorted by date of birth.
   • Change the title to **Animals by Month of Birth by initialLastname**, using your first initial and last name.
   • Move or resize the fields as necessary so all the fields and data are visible.
   • Hide duplicate values for the Animal type field.

c. Create a form called **frmAnimalsDOB_initialLastname**, using your first initial and last name, to enter the beginning and ending parameter dates:
   • Add a title to the form and a label so the user knows what the form is for.
   • Add three buttons to the form: one to open qryAnimalDOB, one to open rptAnimalsByDOB_initialLastname, and one to close the form.

d. Modify qryAnimalDOB to use the parameters entered in the form.

e. Modify rptAnimalsByDOB_initialLastname so the date parameters are shown in the header of the report.

f. Create mailing labels for all the customers, and then name the report **rptCustomerLabels_initialLastname** using your first initial and last name.

g. Save and close all forms and reports. Exit Access and submit your work as directed by your instructor.

Additional Cases

Additional Workshop Cases are available on the companion website and in the instructor resources.

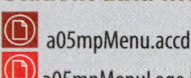

Student data files needed:

a05mpMenu.accdb

a05mpMenuLogo.jpg

You will save your file as:

a05mpMenu_LastFirst.accdb

Indigo5 Restaurant

Production & Operations

Robin Sanchez, the chef of the resort's restaurant, Indigo5, has a database of recipes and ingredients. She uses this to plan menus and create shopping lists. She has asked you to provide forms and reports to make this database easier to use. First you will create a form listing recipes by food category.

Next, you will help her find all recipes that include an ingredient that she has in stock. You will create a query to find those recipes and a report from the query that lists the recipes. You know you want a form to do the lookup for these recipes, so you will start with the form.

She would also like a report on recipes by category that shows the minimum and maximum preparation time for each category.

a. Start **Access**, and open **a05mpMenu**. Save the file as a05mpMenu_LastFirst, using your last and first name. In the Security Warning bar, click **Enable Content**.

b. Create a form for finding details about a specific recipe. You will start by creating a form with a subform. You will add a combo box to find a specific recipe, and then add a tab control to organize the recipe details. You will also remove the navigation bars and replace them with buttons:

- Click the **CREATE** tab, and then in the Forms group, click **Form Wizard**. Add the following fields: from tblRecipes, select **RecipeName**; from tblIngredients, select **Ingredient**; from tblRecipeIngredients, select **Quantity**; and from tblRecipes, select **TimeToPrepare** and **Servings**. Accept the default view and default layout. Name the form frmRecipes_initialLastname and the subform frmRecipesSubform_initialLastname using your first initial and last name.

- Switch to **Design** view, and then change the title of the form to Find Recipes by initialLastname, using your first initial and last name. Drag the **header** down to the **1.5"** mark on the vertical ruler. Resize so the title appears on one line and move the title so the **top edge** lines up with the **1"** mark on the vertical ruler. Insert the logo **a05mpMenuLogo** in the header. Resize the logo so the **bottom edge** is on the **1"** mark on the vertical ruler and the **right edge** is on the **3.5"** mark on the horizontal ruler.

- On the DESIGN tab, click **Date and Time** to add the current date and time to the header, accepting the default formats. Click the **ARRANGE** tab, and then click **Anchoring** to anchor both fields to the top right of the form.

- Click the **DESIGN** tab, and then click **Combo Box** to add a combo box in the form header to the right of the title. In the Combo Box Wizard dialog box, click **Find a record on my form based on the value I selected in my combo box**, double-click **RecipeName**, accept the default to **Hide key column**, and then change the label of the combo box to Recipe Name. Align the combo box and label with the bottom of the title. Resize the combo box text box to fit between the **5"** and **7"** marks on the horizontal ruler.

- Right-click the **frmRecipes subform**, and then select **Cut**. Click the **DESIGN** tab, click **Tab Control**, and then add a tab control to the form just below the **Servings** label. Right-click the **first page** of the tab control, and then select **Paste** to paste the subform.
- Delete the subform label, and then move the subform to the top-left corner of the tab control. In the **Property Sheet** pane, change the name of the page to Ingredients.
- Select and cut the **Prep Time** label, **TimeToPrepare** text box, **Servings** label, and **Servings** text box. Paste these **fields** in the top-left corner of the second tab page, and then change the name of the tab page to Details.
- Right-click the **tab control**, and then select **Insert Page**. Name the new page Directions. On the DESIGN tab, click **Add Existing Fields**, and then drag the field **Instructions** to the third tab page. Delete the **Instructions** label, and then move the text box to the top-left corner of the tab page.
- Move and resize the tab control so the top left corner is at the 1" mark on the vertical ruler and the .5" mark on the horizontal ruler and the bottom right corner is at the 4.5" mark on the vertical ruler and 6.5" mark on the horizontal ruler. Right-click the **tab control**, and then select **Page Order**. Change the order of the tab pages to **Details**, **Ingredients**, and **Directions**.
- In the Property Sheet pane, select **Detail**, click the **FORMAT** tab, and then using the **Build** button, change the back color to **White, Background 1, Darker 15%**. Select the **form header**, and then change the back color to **White, Background 1.**
- Click the value for **RecipeName** in the form Detail. In the Property Sheet, click the **Data** tab, change **Locked** to **Yes**. Click the **Other** tab, change **Tab Stop** to **No**.
- On the DESIGN tab, click **Button** to add a button to the form detail to the right of the tab control. Select **Record Navigation** and **Go To Next Record**. Select **Text**, type Next Recipe, and then name the button cmdNextRecipe. Place a second button on the form below the first. Select **Record Navigation** and **Go To Previous Record**. Select **Text**, type Previous Recipe, and then name the button cmdPreviousRecipe.
- Place a third button below the second button. Select **Form Operations** and **Close Form**. Select **Text**, and then accept **Close Form**. Name the button cmdCloseForm.
- Select all three buttons. Click the **ARRANGE** tab, and then click **Align** to align the buttons **Left**. Click **Size/Space** and select **To Widest**, and then click **Size/Space** and select **Equal Vertical**.
- In the Property Sheet pane, click **Selection type** and select **Form**, click the **Format** tab, and then change the **Navigation Buttons** to **No**. Change **Record Selectors** to **No**.
- View, save, and close the form.

c. Create a form to request recipes by ingredient:
- Click the **CREATE** tab, and then click **Blank Form**. Click the **DESIGN** tab, click **Title** to add a title to the report that says Request Ingredient by initialLastname, using your first initial and last name.
- On the DESIGN tab, in the Controls group, click **Combo Box**, and then insert the combo box in the detail area of the form. Click **I want the combo box to get the values from another table or query**, click **Table: tblIngredients**, double-click **Ingredient**, and then sort by **Ingredient** in ascending order. Adjust the width of the column to fit, and then name your combo box Ingredient.
- Open the **Property Sheet** pane, and then change the name of the text box to Ingredient.
- Click **save**, and then name your form frmRequestIngredient_initialLastname.
- Switch to **Form** view, and then request **Garlic**.
- Leave the form open.

d. Copy and update **qryRecipeIngredient** to find the recipes that include the ingredient picked on the new form:

- Right-click **qryRecipeIngredient** in the Navigation pane, and then select **Copy**. Right-click the Navigation pane, and then select **Paste**. Name the new query qryRecipeIngredient_initialLastname using your first initial and last name.
- Open **qryRecipeIngredient_initialLastname** in **Design** view. Click **Builder** to add criteria to **IngredientID** that selects **Ingredient** from **frmRequestIngredient_initialLastname**.
- Run your query to test it, and then save and close the query.

e. Create a recipe report from **qryRecipeIngredient_initialLastname**.

- Click the **CREATE** tab, click **Report Wizard**, and select the following fields: from qryRecipeIngredient_initialLastname select **RecipeName**, **TimeToPrepare**, **Servings**, and **Instructions**. Group by **TimeToPrepare**, and then sort in ascending order by **RecipeName**. Accept the **Stepped** layout, and then change the orientation to **Landscape**. Name your report rptRecipeReport_initialLastname using your first initial and last name.
- Switch to **Layout** view, change the title of your report to Recipe Prep Time by initialLastname, using your first initial and last name.
- Switch to **Design** view. On the DESIGN tab, click **Text Box**, and then add a text box to the report header to the right of the title. Change the label to Ingredient Selected, and then move the **left edge** of the label so it lines up with the **4"** vertical grid line. Select the **text** box, and then open the Property Sheet pane. On the Data tab, click **Control Source Builder** to point the control source to the **IngredientID** field on **frmRequestIngredient_initialLastname**. Click the **Other** tab, and then name the text box Ingredient.
- Open the report in **Print Preview** to test it, and then save and close the report and form.

f. Add buttons to frmRequestIngredients_initialLastname to open the recipe report and query and to close the form.

- The first button you create should show the text Recipe Report, open **rptRecipeReport_initialLastname**, and have the name cmdOpenReport.
- The second button you create should show the text Recipe Ingredient Query, open **qryRecipeIngredient_initialLastname**, and have the name cmdIngredientQuery.
- The last button you create should close the form, show the text Close Form, and be named cmdCloseForm.
- All buttons should line up under the **Ingredient** label and display all text.
- Save and close the form.

g. Create a report of recipes by category with minimum and maximum preparation times:

- Click the **CREATE** tab, and then click **Report Wizard**. Select the following fields: from tblFoodCategories select **FoodCategory**; and then from tblRecipes, select **RecipeName**, **TimeToPrepare**, and **Servings**.
- Group by **FoodCategory**, sort by **RecipeName**, and in Summary Options, select **Min** and **Max** for **TimeToPrepare**. Accept the default layout, and then change the title of your report to rptTimesToPrepare_initialLastname using your first initial and last name.
- Change the title of your report to Recipe Times to Prepare by initialLastname, using your first initial and last name. Delete the line that starts **Summary for 'Food**.
- Move the Min label and the Max label so their **left edges** are on the **4"** vertical grid line. Change them to read Minimum Prep Time and Maximum Prep Time.
- Switch to **Print Preview** to check your report, and then save and close the report.

h. Close your database and submit your work as directed by your instructor.

Student data files needed:

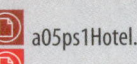 a05ps1Hotel.accdb

a05ps1HotelLogo.jpg

You will save your file as:

a05ps1Hotel_LastFirst.accdb

Creating New Forms for the Hotel Database

Customer
Service

The hotel at Painted Paradise Resort and Spa offers accommodations ranging from individual rooms to a grand villa suite. The hotel must track all aspects of a reservation including special requests for items such as a crib. The hotel also has to track room charges that guests have made. Room rates vary according to size, season, demand, and discount. The hotel has discounts for organizations, such as AARP. The database that is used to track charges needs some forms to make it easier to use; you will provide these.

a. Start **Access**, and then open **a05ps1Hotel**. Save the file as a05ps1Hotel_LastFirst, using your last and first name. In the Security Warning, click **Enable Content**.

b. Open **tblGuests** and change the Last Name and First Name of the first record to your actual first and last name. Close the table.

c. Create a form that includes all fields from tblGuests, uses a **Columnar** layout, and is named frmAddGuest_initial_Lastname using your first initial and last name.

d. Change the title of the form to Add a Guest by initialLastname, using your first initial and last name, and then add the **Date and Time** with default settings to the header. Anchor the date and time to the top right of the form.

e. Change the form detail back color to **White, Background 1, Darker 15%**, and then change the header back color to **White, Background 1**. Move the Detail bar—below the header—down to the **1.5"** mark on the vertical ruler. Resize and move the title so the top edge is lined up with the **1"** mark on the vertical ruler and **1"** mark on the horizontal ruler.

f. Insert the logo **a05ps1HotelLogo** in the form header, and then resize it so the top-left corner is in the top corner of the form and the bottom-right corner lines up with the **4"** mark on the horizontal ruler and the **1"** mark on the vertical ruler.

g. Lock the **GuestID** text box, and then turn off the tab stop. Change the back color to **White, Background 1, Darker 15%,** and then change the special effect to **Sunken**. Save and close the form.

h. Create a form using the **GuestLastName**, **GuestFirstName**, and **Phone** fields from tblGuests and the **CheckInDate**, **NightsStay**, **NumberOfGuests**, **Crib**, **Handicapped**, **RoomRate**, **DiscountType**, and **Room Type** fields from tblReservations. Accept the default view and default layout. Change the title of your form to frmAddReservation_initialLastname and the title of the subform to frmAddReservationSubform_initialLastname, using your first initial and last name.

i. Change the properties of the **Last Name**, **First Name**, and **Phone** fields in the main form so that they are locked and have no tab stop. Add a default value of **1** to **NightsStay**, add a default value of **1** to **NumberOfGuests**, and then add a default value of One King to **Room Type**.

j. Delete the **subform** label. Drag the left edge of the subform to the **.2"** mark on the horizontal ruler, and then line it up with the left edge of the **Phone** label. Drag the right edge of the subform to the **7"** mark on the horizontal ruler.

k. Change the title in the header to Add a Reservation by initialLastname, using your first initial and last name. Insert a **combo** box to the right of the title in the header that finds a record on your form based on the value you select. Select the **GuestLastName** and **GuestFirstName** fields. Change the label of the combo box to Find Guest. Line the left edge of the combo box label up with the **3"** vertical grid line and the top edge with the **.5"** mark on the vertical ruler.

l. Add four buttons to the form to the right of the Last Name and First Name fields. The first button will use the **Go to Next Record** action, show the text Next Guest, and be named cmdNextGuest. The left edge of the button should line up with the **5"** vertical grid line, and the top should line up with the top of the GuestLastName field. The second button will use the **Go to Previous Record** action, show the text Previous Guest, and be named cmdPreviousGuest. The top of the button should line up with the Next Guest button.

The third button should open **frmAddGuest_initialLastname** and show all the records, show the text Add a Guest, and be named cmdAddGuest. The button should be directly below the Next Guest button. The last button should use the **Close the Form** action, show the text Close Form, and be named cmdCloseForm. This button will be directly below the Previous Guest button. Align the buttons in 2 inch by 1 inch square (that is, all four buttons should be between the 5" and 7" vertical grid lines and the 0" and 1" horizontal grid lines.)

m. Remove the Record Selectors and Navigation Buttons from the main form and subform, and then save and close the form.

n. Create a form with a tab control to show all information about a guest and his or her basic reservation information, including room charges. Select the **GuestFirstName**, **GuestLastName**, **Address**, **City**, **State**, **ZipCode**, and **Phone** fields from tblGuests; select the **CheckInDate**, **NightsStay**, **NumberOfGuests**, **RoomRate**, and **Room Type** fields from tblReservations; select the **ChargeCategory** and **ChargeAmount** fields from tblRoomCharges, and then select the **Purchase** field from tblChargeDetails. Accept all default values, change the title of the form to frmGuests_initialLastname, change the title of the first subform to frmGuestsSubform_initialLastname, and then change the title of the second subform to frmGuestsSubform2_initialLastname, all using your first initial and last name.

o. Add a tab control to the bottom of the form detail. Cut and paste all the fields from **tblGuest** to the first page of the tab control. Cut and paste the first subform, to the second page of the tab control. Delete the subform label, and then move the subform to the top-left corner of the page. Drag the right edge of the subform so all the fields are showing.

p. Insert a new page on the tab control, then cut and paste the second subform to the third page of the tab control. Delete the subform label, and then move the subform to the top-left corner of the page. Resize the subform so all the fields are showing. Move and resize the tab control so the top left corner is at the **1"** mark on the horizontal ruler and the **.5"** mark on the vertical ruler.

q. Rename the first page of the tab control Guest Information, the second page Reservation Information, and the third page Room Charges. Reorder the pages so the **Room Charges** page is the second page.

r. Change the title of the form to Guest Details by initialLastname, using your first initial and last name. Insert a combo box to the right of the title in the header that finds a record on your form based on the value you select. Select the **GuestLastName** and **GuestFirstName** fields. Change the label of the combo box to Guest Name. Line the left edge of the combo box label up with the **2.5"** vertical grid line and the top edge with the **.5"** mark on the vertical ruler. Save and close the form.

s. Exit Access and submit your work as directed by your instructor.

Homework 2

Customer
Service

Student data file needed:

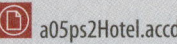 a05ps2Hotel.accdb

You will save your file as:

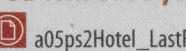 a05ps2Hotel_LastFirst.accdb

Creating New Reports for the Hotel Database

The hotel at Painted Paradise Resort and Spa offers accommodations ranging from individual rooms to a grand villa suite. The hotel area must track all aspects of a reservation including special requests for items, such as a crib. The hotel also has to track room charges that guests have made. Room rates vary according to size, season, demand, and discount. The hotel has discounts for organizations, such as AARP. The database that is used to track charges needs some reports to make it easier to use. You will create various reports for the management and staff to use.

a. Start **Access**, and then open **a05ps2Hotel**. Save the file as a05ps2Hotel_LastFirst using your last and first name. In the Security Warning, click **Enable Content**.

b. Open **tblGuests** and change the Last Name and First Name of the first record to your actual first and last name. Close the table.

c. Create a report grouping room charges by customer and reservation by selecting the **GuestLastName** and **GuestFirstName** fields from tblGuests, the **CheckInDate** field from tblReservations, and the **ChargeCategory** and **ChargeAmount** fields from tblRoomCharges. Accept the default grouping, and then sort in ascending order by **ChargeCategory**. Sum **ChargeAmount**, and then choose the **Outline** layout and **Portrait** orientation. Name your report rptGuestCharges_initialLastname using your first initial and last name.

d. Change the title of your report to Guest Charges by initialLastname, using your first initial and last name. Delete the two **Summary for** controls. Change the **Sum** label in the ReservationID Footer to Total Daily Charges. Change the **Sum** label in the GuestID Footer to Total Guest Charges. Align both **Sum** labels by their right edges. Save and close the report.

e. Create a report of guest room charges by selecting the **CheckInDate** field from tblReservations, the **GuestLastName** and **GuestFirstName** fields from tblGuests, and the **ChargeCategory** and **ChargeAmount** fields from tblRoomCharges. View by **tblRoomCharges**, do not add grouping, and then sort in ascending order by **CheckInDate**, **GuestLastName**, **GuestFirstName**, and **ChargeCategory**. Use a **Tabular** layout with **Landscape** orientation. Name your report rptRoomChargesByDate_initialLastname, using your first initial and last name.

f. Change the title of your report to Room Charges by Date by initialLastname, using your first initial and last name. Use **Group & Sort** to add to the sort details a sort by **CheckInDate** and a **Grand Total Sum** of **ChargeAmount**.

g. Hide duplicates for **CheckInDate**, **LastName**, and **FirstName**. Add the date and time to the header and use all default options. Select the **ChargeAmount** field, the two **Subtotal ChargeAmount** fields, and the **Grand Total ChargeAmount** field and resize them so the right border lines up with the **4.5"** mark on the horizontal ruler. Save and close the report.

h. Create a report from **qryReservationsType** by selecting the **NightsStay**, **DiscountType**, **Room Type**, and **RoomCharge** fields. Group by **DiscountType** and then by **RoomType**. Sort in ascending order by **NightsStay**. Sum **NightsStay** and **RoomCharge**. Show **Summary Only** (*Hint*: It is an option when choosing Summary Options). Accept the default layouts. Name your report rptReservationsByType_initialLastname, using your first initial and last name.

i. Change the title of your report to Reservations Summary by initialLastname, using your first initial and last name. Delete the **Summary for** controls in the Room Type Footer and the DiscountType Footer. Change the **Sum** label in the Room Type Footer to say Room Type Summary and move the label so the left edge lines up with the **3"** mark on the horizontal ruler. Change the **Sum** label in the DiscountType Footer to Discount Type Summary and move the label so the left edge lines up with the **3"** mark on the horizontal ruler. Move the **Grand Total** label in the Report Footer so the **left edge** lines up with the **3"** mark on the horizontal ruler.

j. Change the format of the **RoomCharge** field to **Currency**. Change the format of the **Discount Type Summary** and the **Grand Total for Room Charge** to **Currency**. Save and close the report.

k. Create a blank form with the title Guest Bill.

l. Add a combo box to the detail area, selecting the fields **GuestLastName** and **GuestFirstName** from tblGuests. Sort in ascending order by **GuestLastName** and **GuestFirstName**. Change the combo box label to Guest Name.

m. Change the title to Guest Bill by initialLastname, using your first initial and last name. In the Property Sheet pane, change the name of the combo box to GuestName and then save the form as frmGuestBill_initialLastname, using your first initial and last name. In the combo box, select **Murphy**, and then keep the form open.

n. Modify **qryFindGuestCharges** to use the **GuestName** field from frmGuestBill_initialLastname as criteria for the GuestID field. Save and close the query.

o. Create a report from **qryFindGuestCharges**: Select the **GuestLastName**, **GuestFirstName**, **NightsStay**, **RoomRate**, **RoomCharge**, **ChargeCategory**, and **ChargeAmount** fields from qryFindGuestCharges. Accept the default grouping. Sort in ascending order by **ChargeCategory**, and then sum **ChargeAmount**. Use the **Outline** layout and **Portrait** orientation. Name your report rptGuestBill_initialLastname using your first initial and last name.

p. Change the title of your report to Guest Bill by initialLastname, using your first initial and last name. Delete the **Summary for** controls in the NightsStay Footer and the GuestID Footer. Add a **horizontal line** below the RoomCharge label that begins at the far left edge of the report and ends at the **5"** mark on the horizontal ruler. Draw a second **horizontal line** below the Sum label in the GuestID Footer. Drag the **Page Footer** divider down to the **.5"** mark on the vertical ruler to make room for a line. The line should begin at the left edge of the report and end at the **5"** mark on the horizontal ruler.

q. Using the Group, Sort, and Total pane, change **Group on NightsStay** to not have a footer section, and then click **Yes** to confirm the change. In the Property Sheet pane, change the Grand Total to add the **ChargeAmount** and the **RoomCharge** fields.

r. Resize the **Sum** text field and the **Grand Total** text field so their right edges line up with the **4.5"** mark on the horizontal ruler. In the NightsStay Header, resize the **RoomRate** text box and the **RoomCharge** text box so their right edges line up with the right edge of the **NightsStay** text box. Save and close the report.

s. Add three buttons to **frmGuestBill_initialLastname** to preview and print the guest bill. The first button should preview rptGuestBill, show the text Preview Guest Bill, and be named cmdPreviewGuestBill. The second button should print rptGuestBill_initialLastname, show the text Print Guest Bill, and be named cmdPrintGuestBill. The last button should close the form, show the text Close Form, and be named cmdCloseForm.

t. Resize the first button so the left edge is lined up with the left edge of the Guest Name label and the right edge is lined up with the **2"** vertical grid line. The next two buttons should be lined up below the first in a column. Select all three buttons, align by their left edge and fit to widest. Save and close the form.

u. Close the database, exit Access, and submit your work to your instructor as directed.

Student data file needed: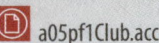

a05pf1Club.accdb

You will save your file as: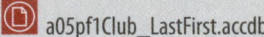

a05pf1Club_LastFirst.accdb

Make Your Club's Database User Friendly

Customer Service

You have developed a database for a club that you belong to. You use it to track the members of the club, events, and member attendance at the events. Make the database user friendly by providing forms and reports.

a. Open **a05pf1Club**, and then save it as **a05pf1Club_LastFirst** using your last and first name.

b. Open **tblMember** and change the Last Name and First Name of the first record to your actual first and last name. Close the table tblMember.

c. Create a form to add records to the tblMember table. Name the form **frmAddMembers_initialLastname**, using your first initial and last name, change the title to **Add a Member by initialLastname**, using your first initial and last name, and add the date and time so it always appears in the top-right corner.

d. Create a new form with a tab control, and then name the form **frmMemberEvents_initialLastname** and the subform **frmMemberEventsSubform_initialLastname**, using your first initial and last name.

- The first tab should have the contact information of the member.
- The second tab should have the related event information, including the name of the events, date of the events, name of the place, event charge, whether they paid, and the amount paid.
- The third tab should have summary information showing the total amount the member has paid for events and the number of events he or she is signed up for.
- Rename each tab with an appropriate name; rename the title; format and resize fields as necessary.
- Add four buttons to frmMemberEvents_initialLastname: **Next Member**, **Previous Member**, **Add a Member**, and **Close Form**. The Add a Member button should open the form to add a new member. The buttons should be the only form of navigation on the form and subform.
- Add a combo box to the header to look up a member's first and last name and show all records related to that member.
- Change the title of the form, and then add the date and time anchored to the top-right corner of the form.

e. Create a parameter report from qryEventDates using starting and ending date parameters for events. Name the report **rptEventAttendance_initialLastname**, using your first initial and last name.

- View the report by **tblEvent**, and then group it by the event date. Sort appropriately. (*Hint*: For best results, use the Outline layout and Landscape orientation.)
- Include a count of the number of members per event on the report.
- Create a blank form to make the date selections. Include buttons to run the query and the report. Name the form **frmEventReporting_initialLastname**, using your first initial and last name.
- Modify the query so it uses the dates from the form.
- Modify the report so the dates entered on the form are also in the report header.
- Add a button to the form to run **qryEventDates**. Add a button to open **rptEventAttendance_initialLastname**.

f. Create a report that shows the member name and the events each member is signed up for. Sort it by the event date, and then sum the event charges for each member. Name the report **rptMemberEvents_initialLastname**, using your first initial and last name. Change the title and labels to something more descriptive. Make sure all the fields are visible.

g. Save and close your database, exit Access, and submit your work to your instructor as directed.

Perform 2: Perform in Your Career

Student data file needed:

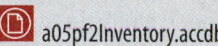 a05pf2Inventory.accdb

You will save your file as:

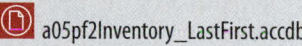 a05pf2Inventory_LastFirst.accdb

Production & Operations

Creating Reports and Forms for Gibby's Great Groceries

As an inventory manager for Gibby's Great Groceries, Inc., you were asked to modify an existing database to make it more functional for completing tasks such as reordering items and tracking inventory within your company.

You have decided to create forms and reports to make the database easier to use.

a. Open **a05pf2Inventory** and save it as **a05pf2Inventory_LastFirst**, using your last and first name.

b. Create a form with a subform for viewing inventory and transaction data. Add a combo box to the form to find an inventory item within the form. Add buttons to navigate and close the form. Name the form **frmInventory_initialLastname** and the subform **frmInventorySubform_initialLastname**, using your first initial and last name for both.

c. Create a report to show all the transactions. Show the details by transaction type and item name. Add subtotals to show how many of each item has been sold for each type of transaction. Hide duplicate values where appropriate. Name the report **rptTransactionSummary_initialLastname**, using your first initial and last name.

d. Create a blank form with a combo box to look up the name of an item. Name the form **frmItemLookup_initialLastname**, using your first initial and last name.

- Create a report from qryItem to show the transactions for that item, and then name the report **rptItemTransactions_initialLastname**, using your first initial and last name.
- Add a subtotal for item quantity and a label to identify the total. Insert a line between the last line item and the subtotal.
- Modify the query so the data comes from the form.
- Add buttons to the form to preview the report, print the report, run the query, and close the form.

e. Create a form with a tab control that shows all item details, transaction details, supplier details, and a summary of how many items have been sold.

- There should be three or four buttons to navigate from one record to another, as well as close the form.
- Name the form **frmItemSummary_initialLastname**, using your first initial and last name. Name the subform **frmItemSubtotal_initialLastname**, using your first initial and last name.

f. Save and close your database. Submit your work to your instructor as directed.

Student data file needed: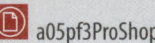

a05pf3ProShop.accdb

You will save your file as: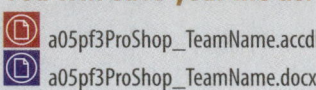

a05pf3ProShop_TeamName.accdb

a05pf3ProShop_TeamName.docx

Production & Operations

Creating Forms and Reports for the Pro Shop

You and your teammates have just taken over a pro shop at the local country club. One of the first things you want to do is analyze the data the shop has been collecting in an Access database. The database consists of four tables and one query: tblCustomers, tblProducts, tblSalesReps, tblTransactions, and qryCustomerTransactions. Unfortunately, that is all the database consists of. You and your teammates need to create forms for looking up data and reports to use to manage the shop. You may choose to use Microsoft's SkyDrive or Google's Google Docs to collaborate on this database. Split your team up as directed by your instructor. Your team will divide up the steps as directed by your instructor. The first person will retrieve the database from the cloud, make their changes to it, and then upload the file for the next person to download, until everyone has made their changes and the database is complete.

a. Select one team member to set up the database by completing steps b-d.

b. Open your browser and navigate to either **https://www.skydrive.live.com**, **https:// www.drive.google.com**, or an other instructor assigned location. Be sure all members of the team have an account on the chosen system - such as a Microsoft or Google account.

c. Open **a05pf3ProShop**, and then save the file as a05pf3ProShop_TeamName using the name assigned to your team by your instructor.

d. Share the database with the other members of your team. Make sure that each team member has the appropriate permission to edit the database.

e. Hold a team meeting and discuss the requirements of the remaining steps. Make an action and communication plan. Consider which steps can be done independently and which steps require completion of prior steps before starting.

f. Create a form that will allow you to enter customer information. Include all the fields. Change the title. Change the default value of Status to Member. Name the form **frmAddCustomer**.

g. Create a form that will show, by Customer name, all their transactions: include date, product, price, and quantity. Name the form frmCustomerTransactions and the subform frmCustomerTransactionsSubform. Change the title, change the date and time in the header, and then anchor it to the top right.

h. Copy **frmCustomerTransactions**, and then paste it as frmCustomerPortal.

- Modify the form to have a combo box in the header to look up the customer name.

- Include a tab control where one tab shows customer transactions and another tab shows two calculated fields: the first tab control determines the total cost of the customer transactions, the second tab control determines the number of transactions, and the third tab control has all the customer detail. Name the tabs appropriately.

- Add buttons to frmCustomerTransactions that will allow the user to navigate to the next customer or previous customer, add a button that will add a customer, and add a button that will close the form.

i. Create a report to show the transactions by month with the transaction date, product type, and quantity sold. Change the title to something more meaningful.

- Include a subtotal of each month's quantities and a grand total.

- Add conditional formatting to show all quantities of five or more in bold and red font.

- Save the report as rptTransactionsByMonth.

j. Copy **rptTransactionsByMonth**, and then save it as rptTransactionSummary.

- Hide the details in rptTransactionSummary so all that the report shows is the month and the total number of items sold each month, with a grand total.
- Delete any unnecessary labels, and then change the title to something meaningful.
- Add a horizontal line between the last subtotal and grand total amount.

k. Create a blank form to enter a start date and end date to look up a range of transactions. Name the form frmTransactionDates.

- Create a report from qryCustomerTransactions to show all transactions by ProductType, including the Transaction Date, Quantity, UnitPrice, and TotalTransaction fields. Name the report rptProductTransactions.
- Format, move, and resize any fields as required.
- Add subtotals for Quantity and TotalTransaction.
- Modify the query so the data comes from the form.
- Add buttons to the form to preview the report, print the report, run the query, and close the form.
- Add the parameter dates to the report header.

l. Upload the final version to the cloud tool you are using, and then direct your instructor to the account. Make sure that your instructor has permission to edit the contents of the shared folder.

m. Create a new Word document in the assignment folder in SkyDrive, and then name it a05pf3ProShop_TeamName using the name assigned to your team by your instructor.

n. In the Word document, each team member must list his or her first and last name, as well as a summary of their contributions. As work is completed in the database, the document should be updated with the specifics of each team member's contributions.

Perform 4: How Others Perform

Student data file needed:

 a05pf4AppStore.accdb

You will save your file as:

 a05pf4AppStore_LastFirst.accdb
a05pf4AppStore_LastFirst.docx

Production & Operations

Phil's Phone App Store Database

An intern has created a database that Phil's Phone App Store can use to sell apps for smartphones. The database is not working well, and Phil has asked you for help.

Authors can write many apps. Each app is sold to many customers. Customers can buy many apps.

a. Open **a05pf4AppStore**, and then save it as a05pf4AppStore_LastFirst using your last and first name. Open Word and create a document called a05pf4AppStore_LastFirst using your first and last name, with the file name in the footer, to answer steps c and e.

b. The form frmAuthorSalesApp is used to show author names and the apps they have written along with the charges and royalties. The form is cluttered and as useful as it could be. What changes would you recommend? You do not have to fix it; just describe the problems and what you would do to fix them.

c. The rptSalesByAuthor shows sales by author. It is based on qryFindApps. Fix it for Phil.

- Fix the report to have subtotals and grand totals.
- Fix the report to be more attractive and easier to read.

d. Phil wants to be able to select sales by apps. The intern created frmFindAppSales to enter the app name and then run qryFindApps. It is not working well.

- Fix either the form or the query or both to make it work.
- Fix the form to make it attractive.

e. The report showing royalties on app sales, rptAppRoyaltiesByAuthor, looks odd to Phil. What is the matter with it? You do not need to fix it; just say what the problems are and what could be done to fix it.

f. Close your Word document, close your database, and then submit your work as directed by your instructor.

WORKSHOP 11 | DEVELOP NAVIGATION FORMS AND THE USER INTERFACE

Prepare Case

Turquoise Oasis Spa Database

General Business   Production & Operations

The Turquoise Oasis Spa has a well-built database with queries, forms, and reports. However, there are a lot of objects, and navigating those objects with the Navigation Pane has become tedious and sometimes confusing. The spa manager, Meda Rodate, has asked you to develop a navigational system and user interface to make the whole database more user-friendly and easier to navigate, especially for someone new to Access. There are already three navigation forms created, but they have to be accessed from the Navigation Pane. You will create a new navigation form for the customer forms and reports, create a navigation form that accesses all the navigation forms already created, and develop an application from the database.

Poznyakov / Shutterstock

REAL WORLD SUCCESS

"The database our company uses was developed without any navigational system. Since then it has grown to include dozens of forms and reports. Finding the right form to enter data into or find information on quickly became a time-consuming task. By utilizing navigation forms, we were able to create a single location within the database that organized our forms and reports in a logical and easy-to-use fashion. The navigation form also allows our employees to decrease the time needed to complete tasks in the database."

- James, alumni

Student data files needed for this workshop:

 a06ws11Spa.accdb

 a06ws11TurquoiseOasis.jpg

You will save your file as:

 a06ws11Spa_LastFirst.accdb

Creating Navigation Forms

A well-designed database includes properly thought-out tables, forms, and reports. An equally important aspect of a well-designed database is how the user will navigate and access objects within the database. Whether the user is a novice or experienced with Access, a well-planned navigation system and **user interface** provides a more streamlined experience. A user interface is part of the computer application or operating system through which the user interacts with a computer or software. A well-designed user interface acts like a menu system—or home page—for users so they do not have to search for objects in the Navigation Pane.

Ideally, a database user should have access to the data through forms and reports. By restricting access to the tables in Datasheet view, the integrity of the data and structure of the data is not at risk. Users should be allowed to enter, edit, and delete data, but not to modify the structure or design of the database. In this section, you will create a navigation system built into a well-designed user interface to allow the user to move seamlessly from object to object to complete the task at hand.

REAL WORLD ADVICE — Where Did the Switchboard Go?

Many Access users are familiar with the Switchboard, a form used for database navigation. The navigation form replaced the Switchboard in Access 2010 with a new, up-to-date Internet-style appearance that can be built directly from the Ribbon.

For those who still want to use the Switchboard, it is available in Access 2013; however, it is not built into the Ribbon as it has been in past versions. The Switchboard Manager can be launched by adding a command to the Quick Access Toolbar, by adding a command to the Ribbon, or by running it automatically in the Immediate window using a VBA command. If your database contains a Switchboard, consider the benefits of building a navigation form in its place.

View a Navigation Form

The **navigation form** provides a familiar Internet-style interface that allows you to access multiple objects in the database from one central location. Similar to websites, the navigation form allows for top-level navigation commands across the top of the page or vertical navigation along the side of the page as well as second-level navigation buttons directly below or along the side of the page. Commands are highlighted when selected, providing you with visual cues as you navigate the form.

REAL WORLD ADVICE — Custom Web Apps

If you want your application to not only look like a website but also exist on a website, Access 2013 can help. A new feature in Access 2013 is the ability to create customized web apps. A customized web app is a web-based application that can be created using Access 2013 templates. A template for custom web apps can be found in the Access Welcome screen. A SharePoint site is required to create a custom web app.

Opening the Starting File

You will use the Turquoise Oasis Spa database to view examples of navigation forms. You will then build additional navigation forms and create a main menu that will, along with the use of command buttons, make a refined user interface.

A11.00

To Open the Spa Database

a. Start **Access**, and then open the student data file **a06ws11Spa**.

b. Click the **FILE** tab, and then save the file as an **Access Database** in the folder or location designated by your instructor with the name **a06ws11Spa_LastFirst** replacing LastFirst with your actual name. If necessary, click **Enable Content**.

Opening and Using a Navigation Form

In this exercise, you will look at three different navigation forms that have already been developed in the database. Each navigation form represents a different area of the spa: employees, products, and services. By viewing each navigation form, you will get an idea of what the format should be for the remaining navigation forms that you will create.

A11.01

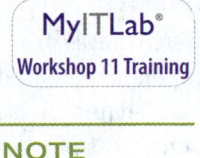

MyITLab®

Workshop 11 Training

To Open and Use a Navigation Form

a. Notice the long list of objects in the Navigation Pane. Double-click **frmEmployeeNavigation** to open the form.

This navigation form provides access to all the forms and reports related to the employees listed in the database. The blue navigation buttons on the left side represent forms, and the green navigation buttons represent reports.

SIDE NOTE

Navigation Form vs. Navigation Pane

The Navigation Pane is a built-in pane that displays database objects. Navigation forms will appear in the Navigation Pane as a form.

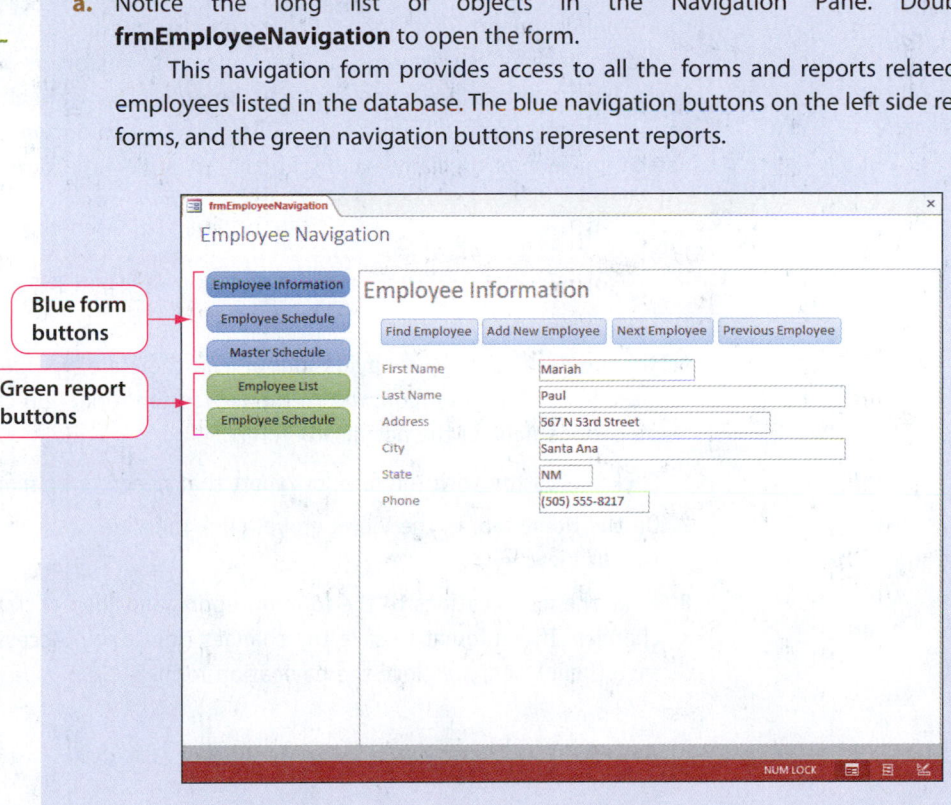

Figure 1 Employee Navigation form

b. Click the blue **Master Schedule** button on the left side of the navigation form to open the Master Schedule form. Click the green **Employee Schedule** button on the left side to open the Employee Schedule report.

Notice how the color and outline change slightly when a button is selected.

c. **Close** ☒ the frmEmployeeNavigation.

d. Double-click **frmProductNavigation** in the Navigation Pane to open the Product Navigation form. Notice the form and reports on the left side are related to the products offered by the spa. Click each one to see the related form or report.

e. Double-click **frmServicesNavigation** in the Navigation Pane to open the Services Navigation form. Notice the forms and report on the left side related to the services offered by the spa. Click each one to see the related form or report.

f. **Close** ☒ the frmServicesNavigation and frmProductNavigation.

SIDE NOTE
Scroll Bars

Scroll bars may or may not appear on your screen depending on the screen resolution and size.

REAL WORLD ADVICE | Color-Coding

Color-coding can be effectively used to distinguish between different tasks or objects on a navigation form. In the previous example, different colors were used to distinguish reports from forms. Colors can also be used to group related tasks or groups of tasks. For example, all tasks related to customers, regardless of which navigation form they are found on, could be one color, while all tasks related to employees could be a different color. This gives you an option to group tasks on one navigation form or on many—and still have them be easy to find.

QUICK REFERENCE | Edit the Navigation Form

As you are developing your navigation form, if there are modifications you need to make in the form or report within the navigation form, you can make those modifications right in the navigation form.

1. Click the button with the form or report that needs to be modified.

2. On the Home tab, in the Views group, click the View arrow, and then select Layout View.

3. Make the modifications to the form or report, and then click Save to save the changes. If you forget to save the changes right away, Access will prompt you to save them when you close the navigation form.

Create a Navigation Form

Access provides six different predefined layouts for navigation forms that are customizable—and they can be redesigned even after they have been created. The predefined layouts use a drag-and-drop method to add new objects to the navigation form. The **navigation control bar** is an area of a navigation form that allows for the addition of new forms, reports, or other database objects. All you do is drag a database object onto the navigation control bar and a new navigation button is added to the form. If you drop the form or report anywhere on the form other than the navigation control bar, the form or report will be added to the form itself rather than as a navigation button. When a button is clicked, the corresponding form or report will be displayed in the **subform control**. A subform control embeds one form into another form.

Using a Predefined Layout to Create a Navigation Form

Of the six predefined layouts to choose from, three provide one level of navigation, either horizontal or vertical, and three provide two levels of navigation, either horizontal or a combination of both horizontal and vertical. In this exercise, you will develop a navigation form for customer navigation that uses a vertical navigation form similar to those you just viewed in the previous exercise.

A11.02

 To Create a New Navigation Form

a. Click the **CREATE** tab, in the Forms group, click **Navigation**, and then click **Vertical Tabs, Left**. A new navigation form will open.

> **Troubleshooting**
>
> You may see the Field List open on the right side of your window. You can close this by clicking the Design tab and then clicking Add Existing Fields in the Tools group, or by clicking the Close button on the Field List.

b. Drag **frmCustomer** from the Navigation Pane to the **[Add New]** button on the navigation form.

c. Drag **frmCustomerInvoices** from the Navigation Pane to the **[Add New]** button on the navigation form.

d. Continue adding **frmCustomerSchedule**, **frmCustomerPurchases**, **rptCustomerList**, and **rptScheduleByCustomer** to the **[Add New]** button on the navigation form.

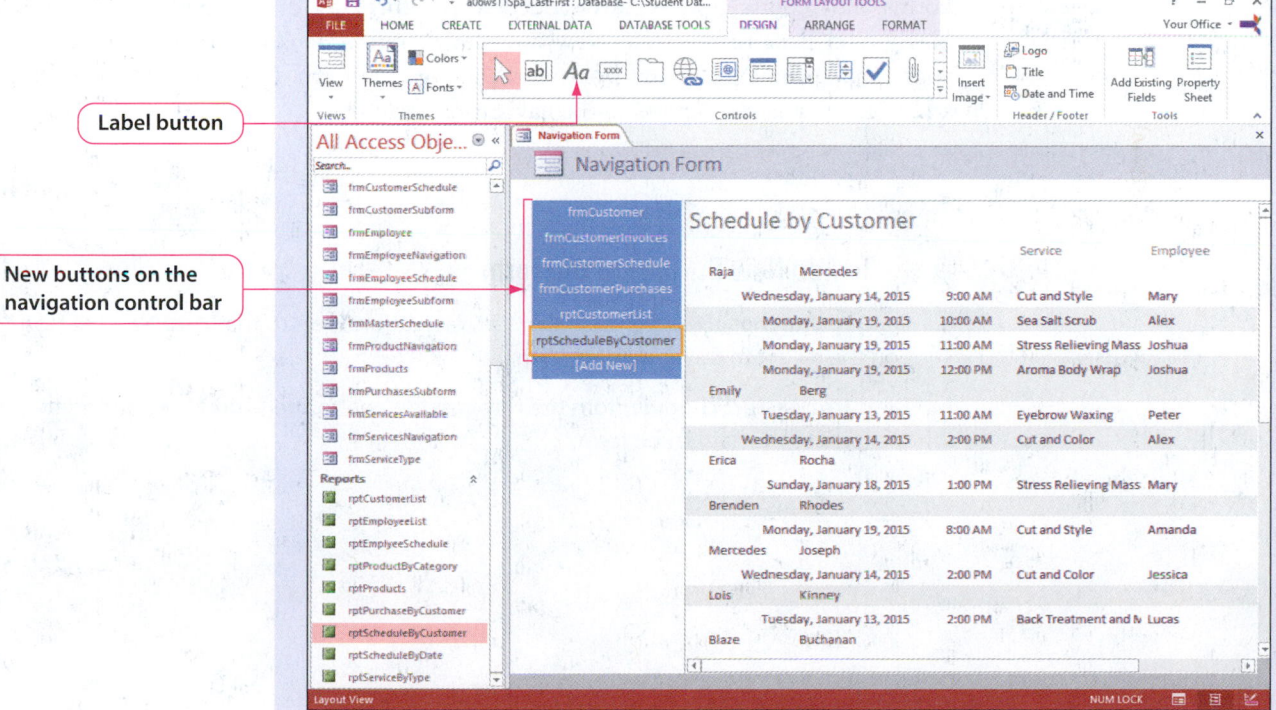

Figure 2 Customer navigation form with six navigation buttons on the left side

e. Click the DESIGN tab, in the Views group, click the **View** arrow, and then click **Design View**. On the DESIGN tab, in the Controls group, click **Label** $\boxed{Aa}$, click to add a label in the **right side** of the form header, and then type your first initial and last name in the label. Resize the labels as needed in the form header so that the text appears on one line.

f. On the DESIGN tab, in the Views group, click the **View** arrow, and then click **Layout View**. Save the form as frmCustomerNavigation_initialLastname using your first initial and last name.

> **Troubleshooting**
>
> When you save forms that are part of other forms, you may see a warning message from Access telling you that the form is being edited by another user. Go ahead and click OK to save the form. Sometimes Access thinks that if the form is opened by you, that you are another user.

Modify a Navigation Form

Once a navigation form has been created, additional forms and reports can be added to the form, deleted from the form, or rearranged on the form.

Once buttons are added to the navigation form, the captions, or text, can be changed or replaced with icons instead of the button caption to further customize the form. Many of the new shapes available in Access 2013 were specifically designed to use with navigation controls like Next, Previous, and Exit.

Adding a Form Button

Forms and reports can be easily added to the form by dragging the object from the Navigation Pane to the [Add New] button; therefore, it is important to be able to see your Navigation Pane as you work on the navigation form. In this exercise, you will add additional forms and reports to the navigation form.

A11.03

 To Add New Buttons to the Form

a. Drag **rptPurchaseByCustomer** from the Navigation Pane to the **[Add New]** button to add the report to the navigation form.

b. Drag **frmMasterSchedule** from the Navigation Pane to the **[Add New]** button to add the form to the navigation form.

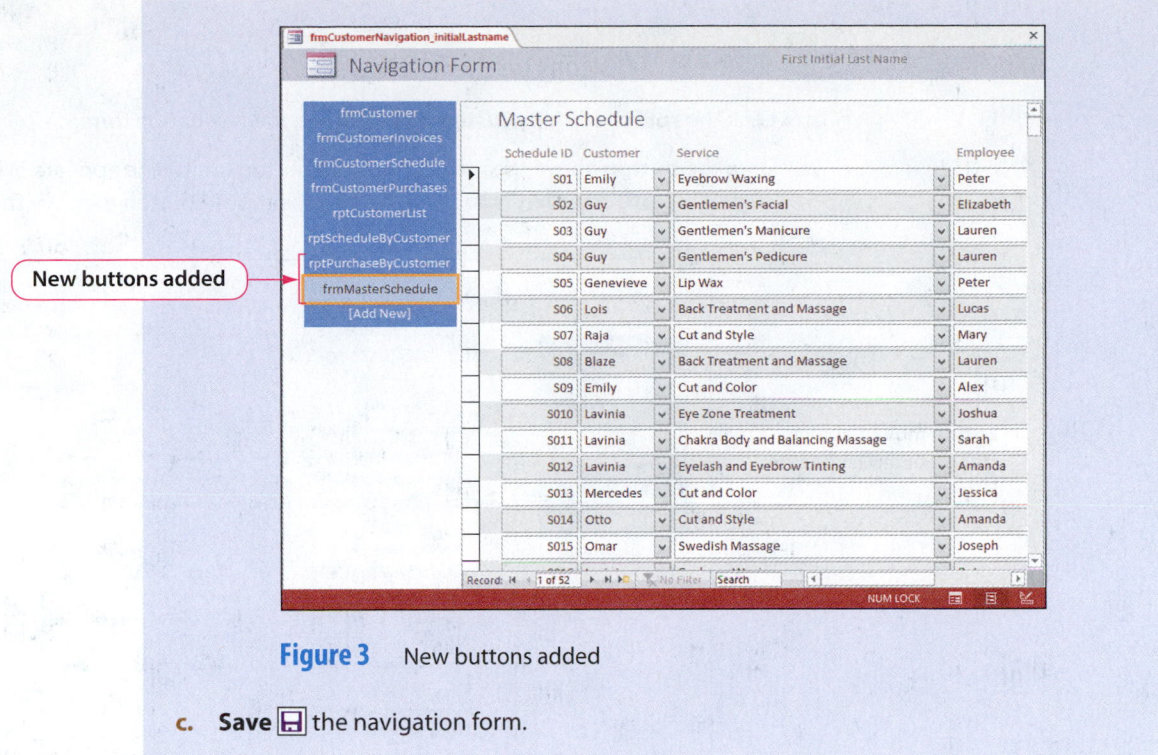

New buttons added

Figure 3 New buttons added

c. **Save** 💾 the navigation form.

Deleting a Form Button

If necessary, forms and reports may be deleted from a navigation form. When a button with a form or report is deleted, only the button is deleted, not the actual form or report. In this exercise, you will delete a button from the navigation form.

A11.04

 **To Delete Buttons from the Form**

a. Click the **frmMasterSchedule** button on the navigation form.

b. Press ⌷Delete⌷ to delete the button from the navigation form.

> **Troubleshooting**
>
> When you delete a button, make sure the button is selected with an orange border around it. If you are in edit mode with the cursor blinking in the text instead of the button selected with the orange border, you will delete the text rather than the button.

c. **Save** 💾 the navigation form.

SIDE NOTE
Alternate Method to Delete
An alternate method to delete the button is to select the button, right-click, and then select Delete from the menu.

Moving a Form Button

Existing buttons can easily be rearranged on their level, or they can be moved from one level of the form to another. In this exercise, you will rearrange the order of the buttons.

A11.05

 To Move Buttons on the Form

a. Click the **rptScheduleByCustomer** button on the navigation form.

b. Drag the **button** above the rptCustomerList button until a line appears. When the line is above the **rptCustomerList** button, release the mouse button to move the button.

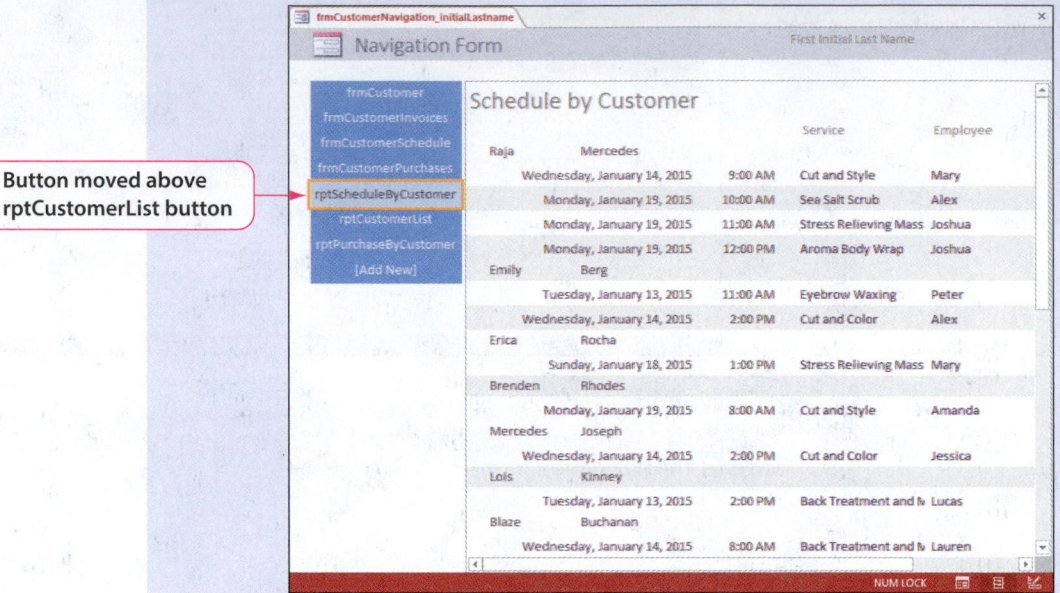

Button moved above rptCustomerList button

Figure 4   Button moved to new position

c. **Save** 🖫 the navigation form.

Modifying the Appearance of a Form Button

Navigation buttons can be modified to customize the form. The button shape and color can be changed. A theme can be added to either the navigation form or to the whole database, including the navigation form. In this exercise, you will add a theme to the database, as well as change the shape and color of the buttons.

A11.06

 To Customize Buttons on the Form

a. Double-click the **Navigation Form title** text, select the **text**, type Customer Navigation and then press Enter. Select the **icon** to the left of the title, and then press Delete.

b. Click the **DESIGN** tab, and then in the Tools group, click **Property Sheet**. Under Selection type, click the **selection** arrow, and then click **FormHeader**. Click the **Format** tab, and then locate **Back Color**. Click the **Builder button**, and then select **White, Background 1**, the first row in the first column under Theme Colors.

c. Click the **frmCustomer** button. Click the **FORMAT** tab, in the Control Formatting group, click **Change Shape**, and then click **Rounded Rectangle**.

d. On the FORMAT tab, in the Control Formatting group, click **Quick Styles**, and then click **Subtle Effect - Blue, Accent 1**—the fourth row of the second column.

SIDE NOTE

Alternate Method to Rename

An alternate method to rename the button is to select the button, double-click, and then type the new name.

e. Click the **frmCustomer** button. In the Property Sheet pane on the right side of the window, select **frmCustomer** in the Caption row, and then type Customer. This should change the text on the button to "Customer".

f. Click the **HOME** tab, and then in the **Clipboard** group, click **Format Painter**. Click the **frmCustomerInvoices** button to change the button format to match the Customers button, and then change the button caption to Invoices.

g. Using the **Format Painter**, change the format of the **frmCustomerSchedule** and **frmCustomerPurchases** buttons to match the Customers button. Change the button names to Appointments and Purchases.

h. Click the button **rptScheduleByCustomer**. Click the **FORMAT** tab, in the Control Formatting group, click **Change Shape**, and then click **Rounded Rectangle**.

i. On the FORMAT tab, in the Control Formatting group, click **Quick Styles**, and then click **Subtle Effect - Green, Accent 6**—the option in the fourth row of the seventh column. Change the button caption to Appointment Report.

j. Using the **Format Painter**, change the format of the **rptCustomerList** and **rptPurchaseByCustomer** buttons to match the Appointment Report button. Change the button names to Customer List and Purchase Report. **Close** the Property Sheet pane.

k. Click the **DESIGN** tab, in the Themes group, click **Themes**, and then click **Integral**. This changes the theme for all the objects in the database, including the navigation form.

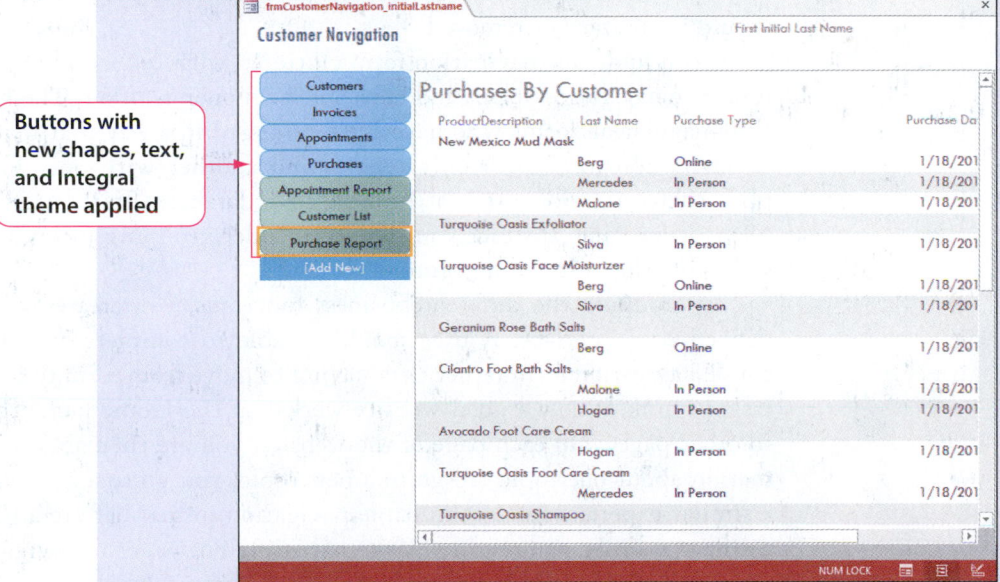

Buttons with new shapes, text, and Integral theme applied

Figure 5 Customer navigation with buttons formatted

m. **Close** the navigation form, and then click **Yes** to save the changes.

Although tab controls and navigation forms look similar, the two objects function very differently. In a tab control, the tabbed windows are hidden behind each other and are all open at the same time. You can picture the layout as pieces of paper laid on top of each other with a tab at the top of each page. As you click a tab, the piece of paper with the selected tab is moved to the top of the pile. In a navigation form, the tabs open a new form or report in the same subform control each time so only one object is open at a time. This is useful when you want to provide a hierarchy of options—navigation tabs and second-level navigation options. Navigation forms provide for better database performance since only one object at a time is open. They also trigger updates and requery the object's data source.

Refining the User Interface

Navigation forms do not display data from a table; therefore, they are an unbound object. Because the user does not have to move from record to record or page to page, some of the form navigation properties can be removed. The navigation buttons and record selectors can be removed because they are not needed. The ability to access a shortcut menu can be disabled, as well as the option to copy data and close the object. Any operations that would distract the user from the purpose of the navigation form should be disabled or removed.

If you find your navigation form cluttered with too many objects, you can create multiple navigation forms and have one form open another. The key to making multiple navigation forms is to have them arranged in a way that makes intuitive sense. A navigation form with only reports and another with only forms may not simplify the navigation process through your database. It is in effect replicating the Navigation Pane. Instead, you should consider grouping forms and reports by topic or by function as seen in Figure 6.

By grouping the different business functions, you create an intuitive and well-defined user interface. A user should be able to complete all related tasks under a single navigation form rather than having to move from form to form to find different tasks. Think of how a good website works: on the Home page, there are links to go to other pages. On each page of the website, you are then able to view related information about one topic. To go to a new topic, you go to a new page. You can create a similar experience using multiple navigation forms that are all linked together. In the Spa example, you might want to have different pages to navigate service, product, employee, and customer tasks as shown in Figure 6.

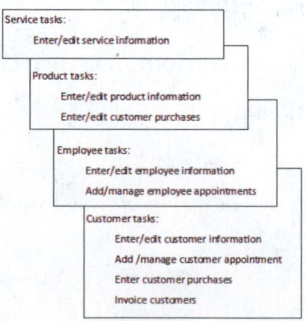

Figure 6 Different task lists

To accomplish this, you can create a main navigation form that has four navigation buttons: Services, Products, Employees, and Customers. Clicking one of the buttons opens another navigation form with additional objects related to the area you clicked.

A well-refined user interface will make sense to any user, even one with no Access experience. The user should be able to look at the navigation form and locate the form or report that he or she needs. In this section, you will create a user interface that includes a navigation form, custom form buttons, and modified start-up options for the database.

CONSIDER THIS | **Websites Compared to Access**

An Access user interface can be set up to look and work just like a web page. Think about websites you enjoy visiting. Other than the content, what makes a web page attractive? Is it how easy things are to find? Is it the consistent color theme? When designing a user interface, think about what makes an interface interesting and easy to use, and replicate this in your user interface.

REAL WORLD ADVICE | **Planning Is Everything**

How do you decide, as the designer, what a good user interface will look like? What makes sense to you may not make sense to the final user, so it is important to understand your end user and the job he or she has to do in order to make the best decisions for the application. The more information you get directly from the user, the better your application will be.

You may consider spending time with users:

- Interviewing them about the tasks they complete with the application
- What changes they would make to improve the application
- What they do not like about the application
- Observe what users do, and take notes to refer to when you are designing the application.

Create a Main Menu

A main menu is essentially a navigation form that provides access to additional navigation forms. In addition to navigation forms, a main menu can also have a command to close the Access application so everything the user needs is in one place. An **application** is a piece of software that is used to perform a task or multiple tasks.

When considering how the main menu will work, you have to look at how the tabs will work. There are two different ways to create a main menu form. You can create a two-level navigation form with top-level tabs and second-level tabs. The top-level tabs can be named to organize groups of tasks. For example, the top-level tabs may be called Customers, Employees, Products, and Services. The second-level tabs could be the forms and reports associated with each task group. For example, the second-level tabs could be forms for customer data entry and reports for customer lists. An example can be seen in Figure 7.

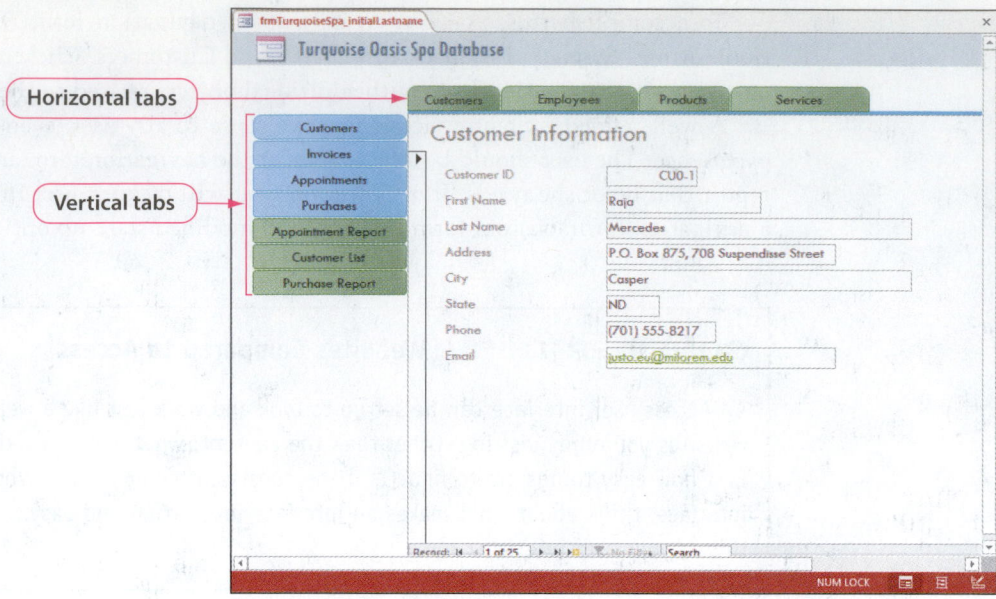

Figure 7 Navigation form created using horizontal and vertical tabs

Another option is to create a navigation form for each group of tasks with only top-level tabs. Each top level points to the related forms and reports. Then, the main menu navigation form has only top-level tabs that open the individual navigation forms for each task group. For example, you can create a customer navigation form, an employee navigation form, and so on. Each top-level tab in the main menu navigation form can open one of the individual navigation forms. As seen in Figure 8, the effect is the same as the method described above, but the look is different.

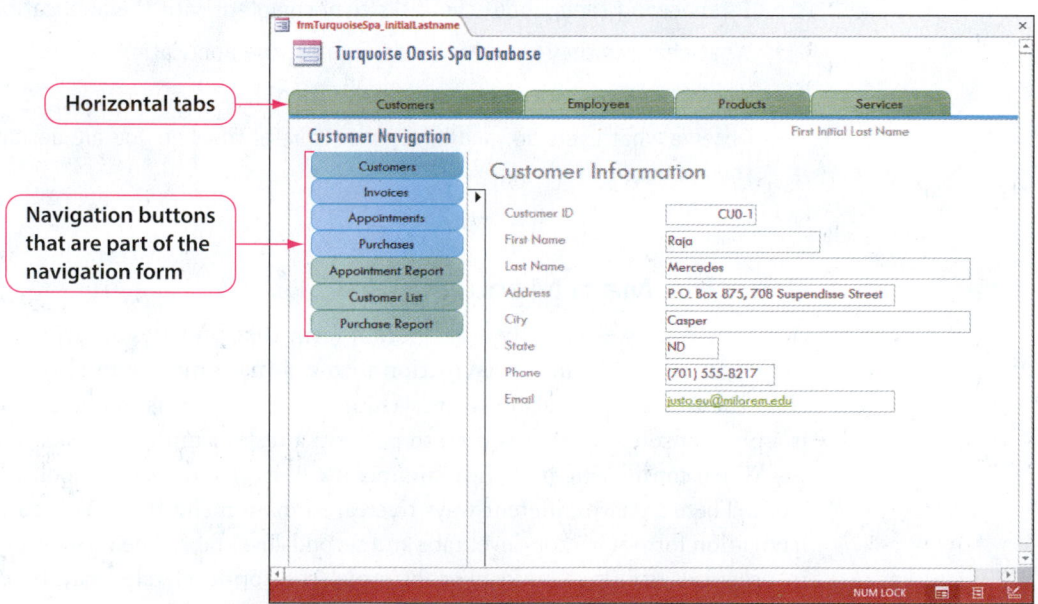

Figure 8 Navigation form created using other navigation forms with only top-level tabs

Creating a Navigation Form for a Main Menu

Because the spa database you are working with has four different navigation forms, in this exercise, you will create a new navigation form to access each of the navigation forms. You will then add command buttons to navigate records and close the database.

A11.07

 To Create a Main Menu Navigation Form

a. Click the **CREATE** tab, in the Forms group, click **Navigation**, and then click **Horizontal Tabs**.

b. Click the **DESIGN** tab, and then in the Tools group, click **Property Sheet**. Under Selection type, click the **selection** arrow, and then click **FormHeader**. On the **Format** tab, locate **Back Color**. Click the **Builder button** ..., and then in the first row in the first column under Theme Colors, select **White, Background 1**.

c. **Close** ✕ the Property Sheet pane.

d. Drag **frmCustomerNavigation_initialLastname** from the Navigation Pane to the **[Add New]** button.

e. One at a time, drag **frmEmployeeNavigation**, **frmProductNavigation**, and **frmServicesNavigation** to the **[Add New]** button.

f. Double-click the **frmCustomerNavigation_initialLastname** tab, select the **text**, type **Customers**, and then press Enter. Repeat for the remaining tabs, and name them **Employees**, **Products**, and **Services**.

g. Click the **Customers** tab on the navigation form. Press and hold Shift, and then click the **Services** tab. Click the **Format** tab, in the **Control Formatting** group, click **Change Shape**, and then click **Round Same Side Corner Rectangle**. On the FORMAT tab, in the Control Formatting group, click **Quick Styles**, and then click **Subtle Effect - Dark Green, Accent 5**—in the fourth row, sixth column.

h. Double-click the **Navigation form** title, select the **text**, and type **Turquoise Oasis Spa Database**.

i. **Save** 💾 the form as **frmTurquoiseSpa_initialLastname** using your first initial and last name.

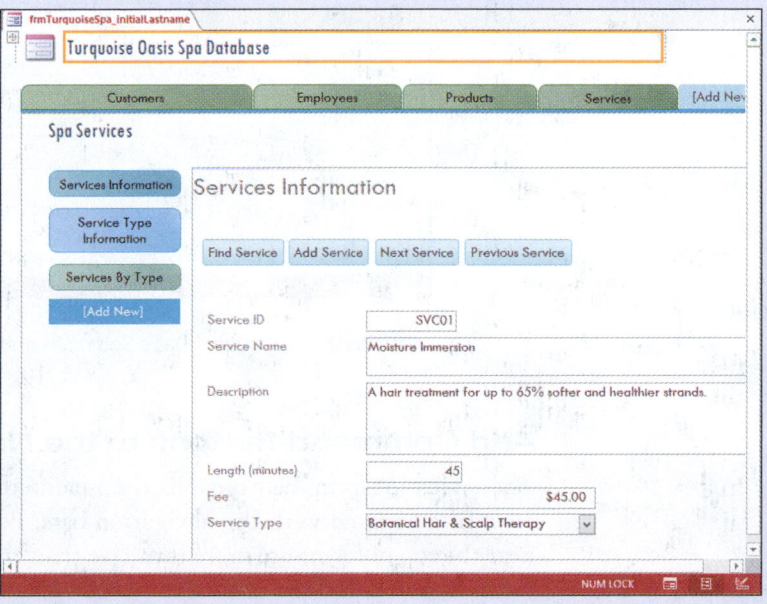

Figure 9 Turquoise Oasis Spa navigation form

Adding an Image to the Main Menu

Meda Rodate would like for you to add the Turquoise Oasis Spa logo to the new main menu. By default, Access adds a form icon to new navigation forms. This icon can be deleted or replaced with a custom image. In this exercise, you will replace the default image with the Turquoise Oasis Spa logo.

A11.08

 To Add the Turquoise Oasis Spa Logo to the Navigation Form

a. On **frmTurquoiseSpa_initialLastname**, click the **icon** to the left of the title, and then click the **DESIGN** tab.

b. In the Controls group, click **Insert Image**. Click **Browse**, and then select the **a06ws11TurquoiseOasis.jpg** image from your student data files. Click **OK** to insert the new image.

c. On the DESIGN tab, click **Property Sheet**. In the Property Sheet pane, click the **Format** tab.

d. Click the **Size Mode** box arrow, and then click **Zoom**.

e. Type **3** for the **Width**, and then type **.8** for the **Height** of the image.

f. **Save** and **Close** the form.

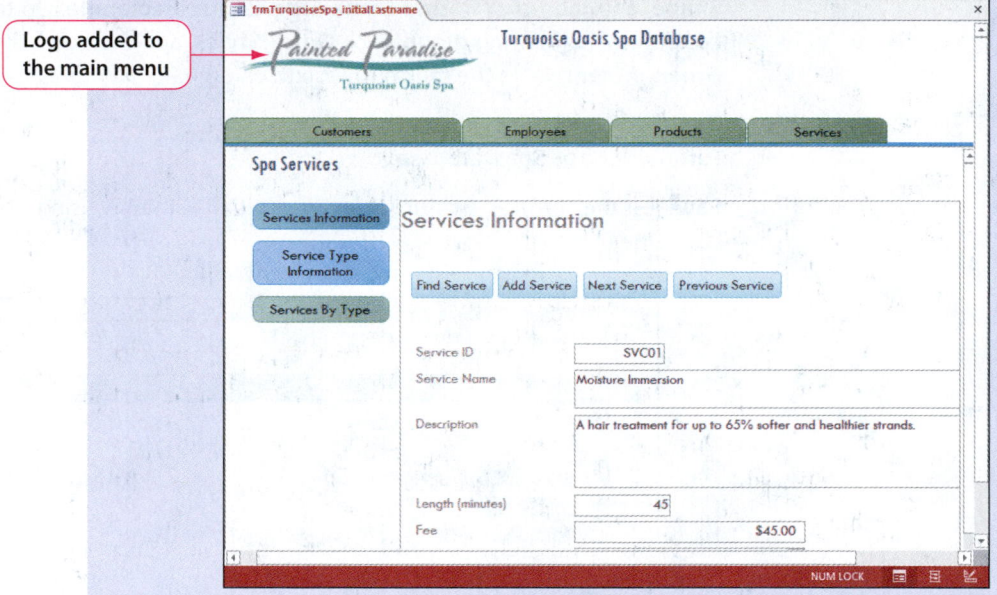

Figure 10   Turquoise Oasis Spa main menu

Add Command Buttons to the Navigation Form

The navigation forms help organize the user interface to the database. But individual records are still navigated with the navigation bars. For users unfamiliar with Access, buttons near the top of forms are more intuitive than the navigational arrows at the bottom of a form. You will add some buttons for navigation and turn off the navigation bar.

Command buttons are available in several categories. Record navigation buttons replicate most of the navigation tools available on the Navigation bar. You can create buttons to go to the first, next, last, and previous records. Record operations buttons allow the user to add, delete, and undo a record. Form operations buttons open, close, and print forms. Command buttons can be added to the navigation form, but they can also be added to forms and reports that are accessed through the navigation form.

QUICK REFERENCE	Form Command Buttons Available

Category	Actions
Record Navigation	Find Next
	Find Record
	Go To First Record
	Go To Last Record
	Go To Next Record
	Go To Previous Record
Record Operations	Add New Record
	Delete Record
	Duplicate Record
	Print Record
	Save Record
	Undo Record
Form Operations	Apply Form Filter
	Close Form
	Open Form
	Print a Form
	Print Current Form
	Refresh Form Data

Creating Navigation Buttons on a Form

If you open the Employee Navigation form, Product Navigation form, or Service Navigation form, you will notice there are buttons on the navigation forms for the user to click to find a record, add a record, or go to the previous and next records. In this exercise, you will add similar buttons to the Customer form as well as an Exit Database button on the main menu navigation form.

A11.09

 To Add Navigation Buttons to a Form

a. Double-click **frmCustomer** on the Navigation Pane to open the form.

b. Click the **HOME** tab, in the Views group, click the **View** arrow, and then click **Design View**.

c. Click the **Customer ID** text box, press and hold Shift, and then click all the **text boxes** and **labels** in the form detail section. Drag all of the controls down to the **.5"** mark on the vertical ruler.

d. Click the **DESIGN** tab, in the Controls group, click **Button** ⌧, and then click in the **top-left corner** of the form detail section to add the button.

e. In the Command Button Wizard, under the Categories list, verify that **Record Navigation** is selected. On the Actions list, click **Find Record**, and then click **Next**.

f. Click **Text**, select the **text**, type Find Customer and then click **Next**.

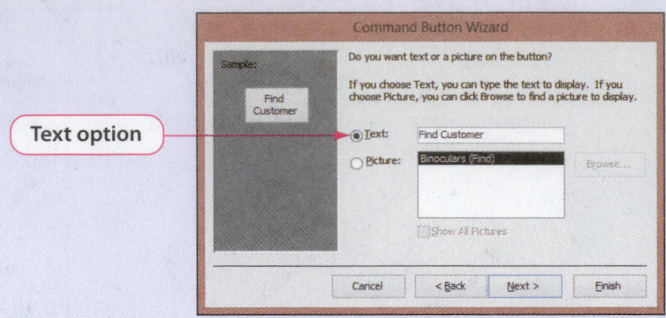

Figure 11 Text selected and changed in Command Button Wizard

g. Name the button **cmdFindCustomer** and then click **Finish**.

h. Click the **DESIGN** tab, in the **Controls** group, click the **Button label** [xxxx], and then click to the **right** of the first button.

i. On the Categories list, click to select **Record Operations**, and then on the Actions list, click to select **Add New Record**. Click **Next**.

j. Click **Text**, select the **text**, type **Add New Customer**, and then click **Next**. Name the button **cmdAddNewCustomer** and then click **Finish**.

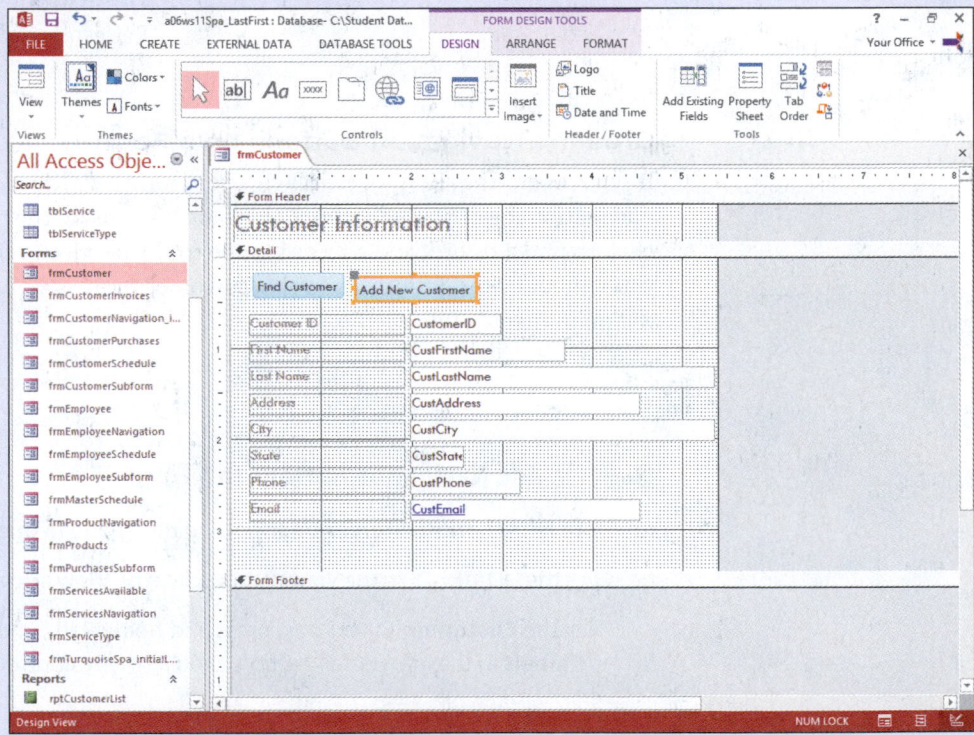

Figure 12 Two buttons added to the form

k. Repeat the above steps to add a button that takes the user to the next customer. Click the **Record Navigation** category and the **Go To Next Record** action; the text should say **Next Customer**, and the button should be named **cmdNextCustomer**.

l. Repeat the above steps to add a button that takes the user to the previous customer. Click the **Record Navigation** category and the **Go To Previous Record** action; the text should say **Previous Customer** and the button should be named **cmdPreviousCustomer**.

m. Click the **first button** to select it. Press and hold ⟨Shift⟩, and then click the remaining **three buttons** to select them. Click the **ARRANGE** tab, in the Sizing & Ordering group, click **Align**, and then click **Top**. In the Sizing & Ordering group, click **Size/Space**, and then click **Equal Horizontal**. This will align the tops of the buttons and space them evenly.

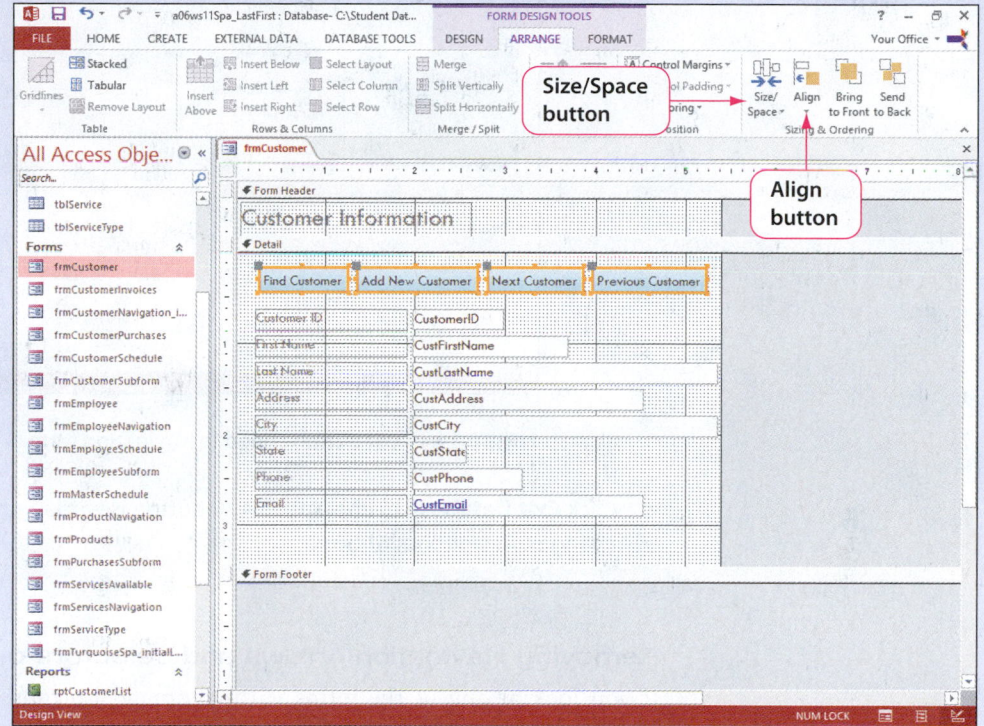

Figure 13   Align and Size/Space buttons in Design view

n. **Close** ☒ the form, and then click **Yes** to save the changes.

o. Double-click **frmTurquoiseSpa_initialLastname** in the Navigation Pane to open the form.

p. Switch to **Design** view, click the **DESIGN** tab, in the Controls group, click the **Button label** [⌧], and then click under the title of the main **form header**. On the Categories list, click **Application**, and then on the Actions list, verify that **Quit Application** is selected. Click **Next**. Click **Text**, select the **text**, type Exit Database and then click **Next**. Name the button cmdExitDatabase and then click **Finish**. Switch to **Form** view.

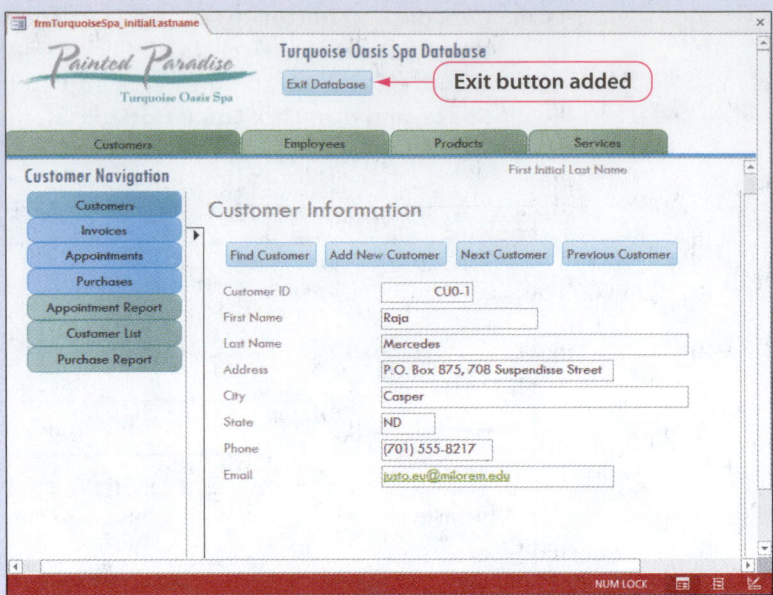

Figure 14 Exit button added to Navigation form

q. Click **Exit Database** to check that your button is working properly. Click **Yes** to save the changes. Access should close.

Removing Navigation Arrows and Selectors on a Form

If you look at any of the forms with command buttons added, the navigation arrows and record selectors have all been removed, which forces the user to use the buttons to manage the records. With the addition of the command buttons, the navigation arrows and record selectors create duplicate functionality. In this exercise, you will remove the record selectors and navigation arrows from the Customer form.

A11.10

 To Remove Navigation Buttons and Selectors from a Form

a. Start **Access**, and then open **a06ws11Spa_LastFirst**. In the Navigation Pane, double-click **frmCustomer** to open the form.

b. Switch to **Layout** view, click the **DESIGN** tab, and then in the Tools group, click **Property Sheet**.

c. Under Selection type, click the **selection** arrow, and then click **Form**.

d. Click the **Format** tab in the Property Sheet pane. Click the **Record Selectors** arrow, and then click **No**. Click the **Navigation Buttons** arrow, and then click **No**.

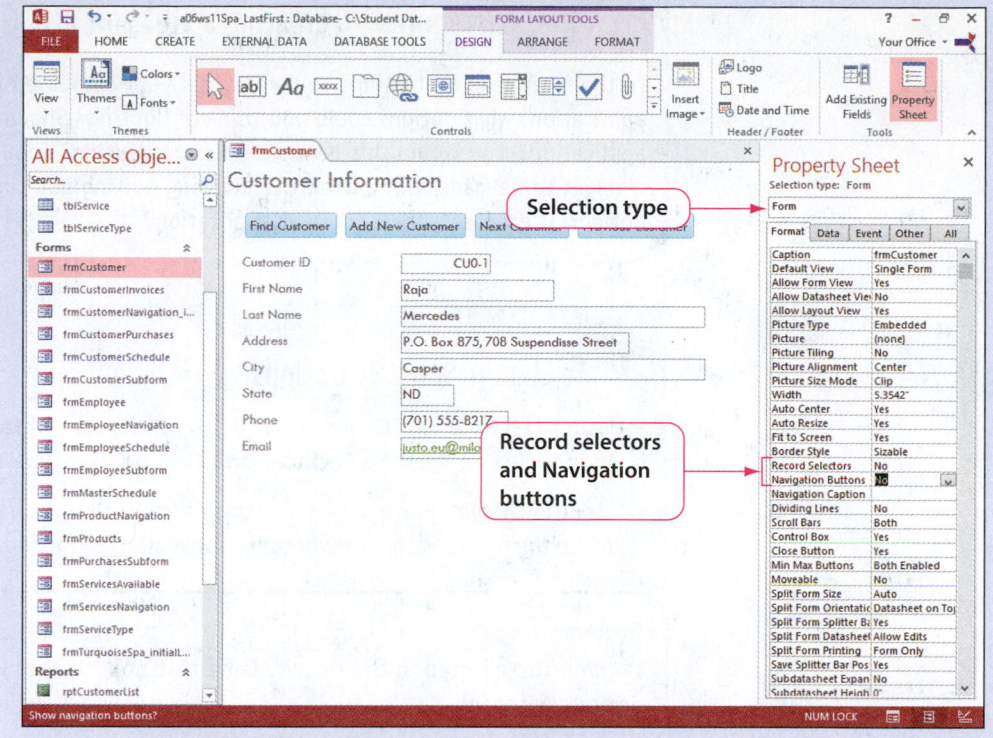

Figure 15 Property Sheet pane open

e. **Close** [X] the Property Sheet pane.

Notice that the record selectors and navigation arrows are hidden.

f. **Close** [X] the form, and then click **Yes** to save the changes.

Set Start-Up Display Options

Once your database is designed, the forms and reports have been created, and a navigation system and user interface is in place, you will have an application for others to use. To make the application as user-friendly as possible, you can name the application and then remove options available to database designers. By doing this, you reduce the chance of changes being made to the data, or the database structure, either intentionally or accidentally by an end user. These options may include removing access to certain application options—the Navigation Pane, the Ribbon, and various toolbar options.

You also will want to show a start-up form when your database opens. The **start-up form** is the form that opens automatically when you open the database. This is generally your navigation form, or the navigation form that will act as your main menu.

Optional commands, such as the command to compact and repair the database when it is closed, may also be set to run automatically so the user does not have to worry about maintenance tasks.

Making Changes to the Start-Up Options

Changing the application title helps to better identify the application and give it an identity separate from the actual database. Selecting a start-up form will determine which form opens when the application is started. Restricting access to the Navigation Pane requires the user to use the user interface you have developed. For this exercise you will change the application title to "Turquoise Oasis Spa" and designate your main menu navigation form as the start-up form.

CONSIDER THIS | Creating a Pleasant Experience

In the interest of protecting the data within your database or creating a more efficient application, what options could you think of limiting? Should you password protect your application? How would this be more or less confusing? Should you only allow certain changes to be made to the data, like allowing editing but not deleting? How would these options affect the usability of your application?

A11.11

 To Change Start-Up Options

a. Click the **FILE** tab, click **Options**, and then click **Current Database**. Under the Application Options section, click the **Application Title**, and then type Turquoise Oasis Spa.

b. Click the **Display Form** arrow, and then click **frmTurquoiseSpa_initialLastname**. This will be the form that opens when the application is opened.

> **Troubleshooting**
>
> If (none) is selected in the Display Form text box, then when your application opens, no form will open.

c. Click the **Compact on Close** check box. This automatically compacts and repairs the database every time it is closed.

A database grows dynamically as data is added or manipulated; however, it does not shrink automatically when data is deleted or the manipulation is complete. Databases may also become fragmented as data is added and deleted. To maintain performance of the database, you should compact and repair the database each time it is closed.

d. Under the Navigation section, clear the **Display Navigation Pane** check box. This hides the Navigation Pane.

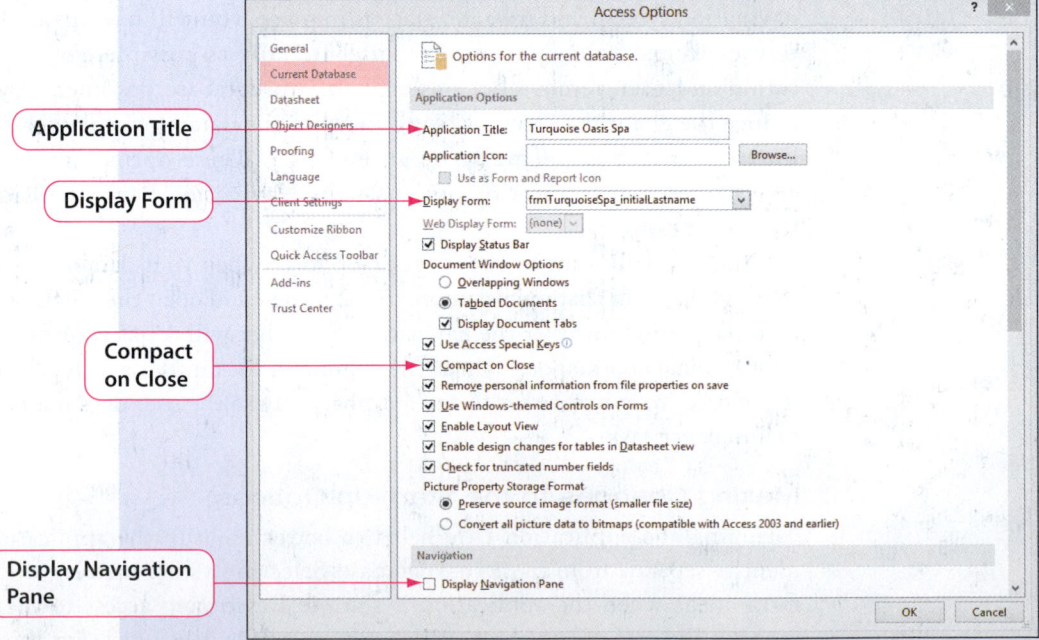

Figure 16 Access Options window

SIDE NOTE

Show Navigation Pane
If the Navigation Pane is hidden, press [F11] to unhide it as long as the option to disable special keys is not selected in the database options.

e. Click **OK** to close the Access Options window.

f. Click **OK** when the message **You must close and reopen the current database for the specified option to take effect** is displayed.

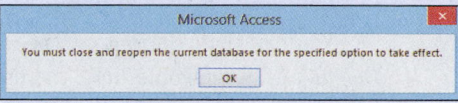

Figure 17 Message displayed after start-up changes have been made

g. **Close** ✕ the database. Start **Access**, and then open **a06ws11Spa_LastFirst**.
When the database reopens, frmTurquoiseSpa_initialLastname should open automatically. Also notice the name of the application, not the database, on the title bar.

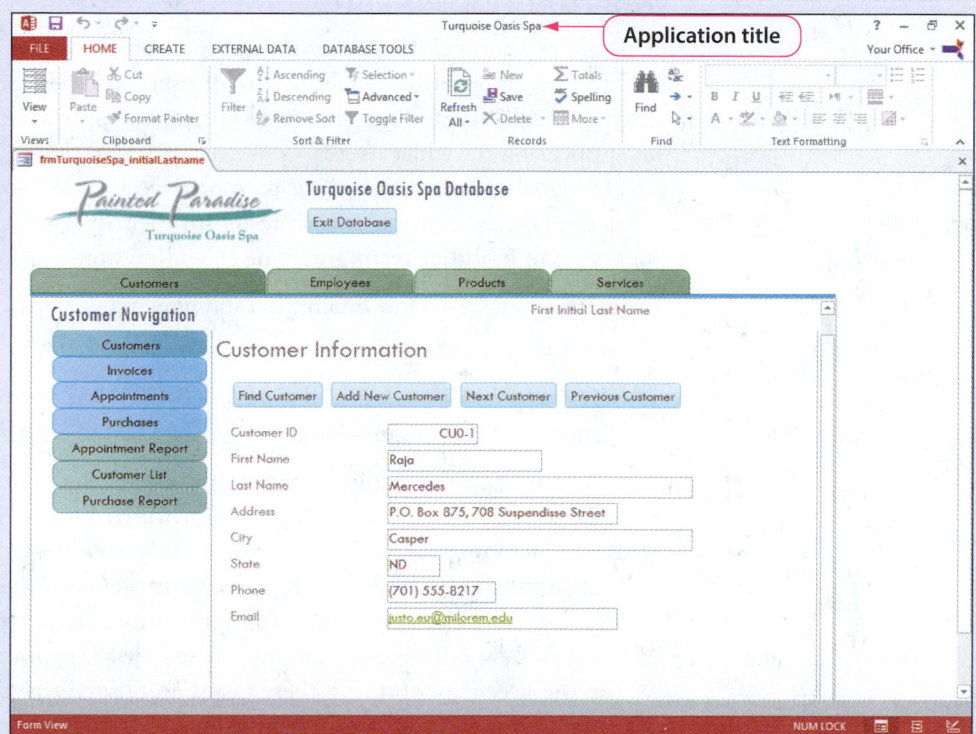

Figure 18 Application opened with start-up settings applied

h. To access the complete database and not just the application, click the **FILE** tab, click **Options**, and then select **Current Database**. Click the **Display Navigation Pane** check box to restore the Navigation Pane. Click **OK** twice. **Close** ✕ and then restart the database.

REAL WORLD ADVICE | **Even More Options**

To create a more fluid user experience, you can hide more options in the start-up form.

- You can also create two different objects—the application for the user and the database for the designer.

- You can limit options on the Ribbon and hide tabs, status bars, and shortcut menus. This would limit the user to only commands and buttons you provide, limiting the accessibility of the data.

By "locking down" the application, you are protecting the data and database structure from accidental or intentional modifications. Many of the options will be presented in Workshop 14.

Test the Application

A good application will be easy to use for all levels of Access users, not just the designer. Before your application is released to all users, the best practice is to undergo usability testing. **Usability testing** consists of testing an application with a user prior to releasing an application for wider use.

The goal of usability testing is to observe people using the application to discover what errors they may make with it and to identify areas that require modification. The four areas of usability testing include the following:

- **Performance**—How much time and how many steps are required to complete a task?
- **Accuracy**—How many mistakes did users make?
- **Recall**—How much did the user remember after a period of nonuse?
- **Emotional response**—How did the user feel about the tasks completed?

Usability testing requires observing a user under controlled circumstances to determine how he or she will use the application for its intended purpose. It has nothing to do with the user's opinion of the application, only how he or she interacts with it.

For successful usability testing, a realistic scenario should be set up where the user is given a list of tasks to perform in the application. In the spa example, this could include entering a new customer, changing an existing appointment, and printing a report. While the user is performing these tasks, an observer is watching and taking notes but not interacting with the user. The user should be allowed to make mistakes that are then noted by the observer. These mistakes will allow the designer to see what modifications may need to be made to the application.

CONSIDER THIS | **Finding a Tester**

All applications should be tested before they are given to the final user. If you are the only person available, you should at least run through the application as if you were a user. Unfortunately, you understand how it should work and may not be able to be objective. What are some options for you to find a tester of your application? Could you ask a co-worker, family member, or a roommate?

Viewing the User Interface as a User

If you cannot test the user interface with an actual person, then you can at least view the user interface as a user rather than the developer. This will give you a better idea of what the user will see and whether modifications are required. For this exercise, you will follow a portion of a previously developed plan to test the user interface as a user rather than the developer.

A11.12

 To Test the User Interface as a User of the Database

a. Make sure the navigation form is open in **Form** view.

b. Using the chart below, begin to test the application as a user. As you complete a task, fill in the Action Taken section and the Comments section. This is what the developer will use to make any modifications to the application if necessary.

Task	Action Taken	Comments
Enter a new customer		
Enter a new customer invoice		
Enter a new product		
Print the product list report		
Exit the database		

Table 2 Task list

c. In addition to the above steps, click each **tab** to launch the form or report. Only one form or report should open at a time, and it should be the one labeled on the tab.

d. Close ☒ the database, and then **Exit** [☒] Access.

1. What elements should a database user have access to? Why should a database user not have access to the entire database? p. 566

2. What is a navigation form? How is it different from the Navigation Pane? p. 567

3. What is the difference between navigation forms and tab controls? When would you use each? p. 574

4. What are some important considerations when constructing a user interface for your database? p. 574

5. What are some benefits of using command buttons on a form? p. 578

6. What is the difference between an Access application and a database? p. 575

7. What is usability testing, and why is it important? p. 586

Key Terms

Application   575
Navigation control bar   568
Navigation form   566

Start-up form   583
Subform control   568

Usability testing   586
User interface   566

Visual Summary

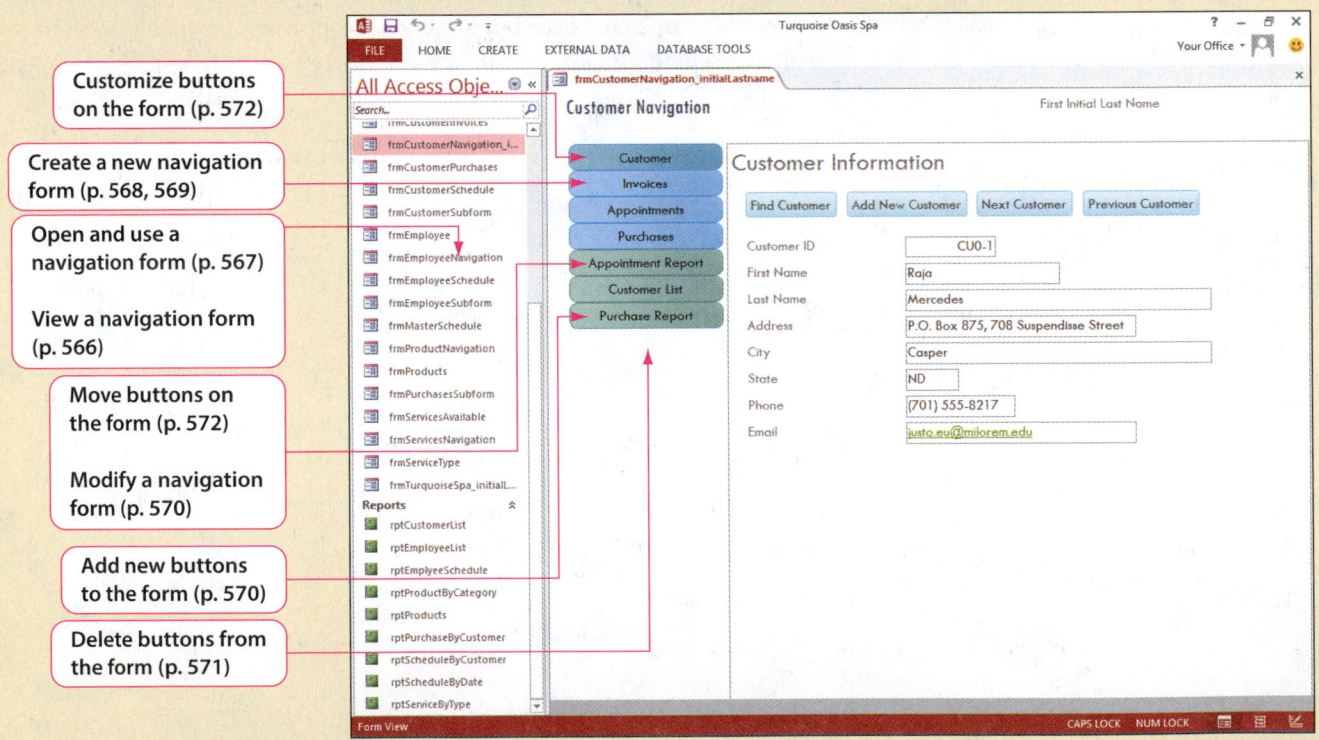

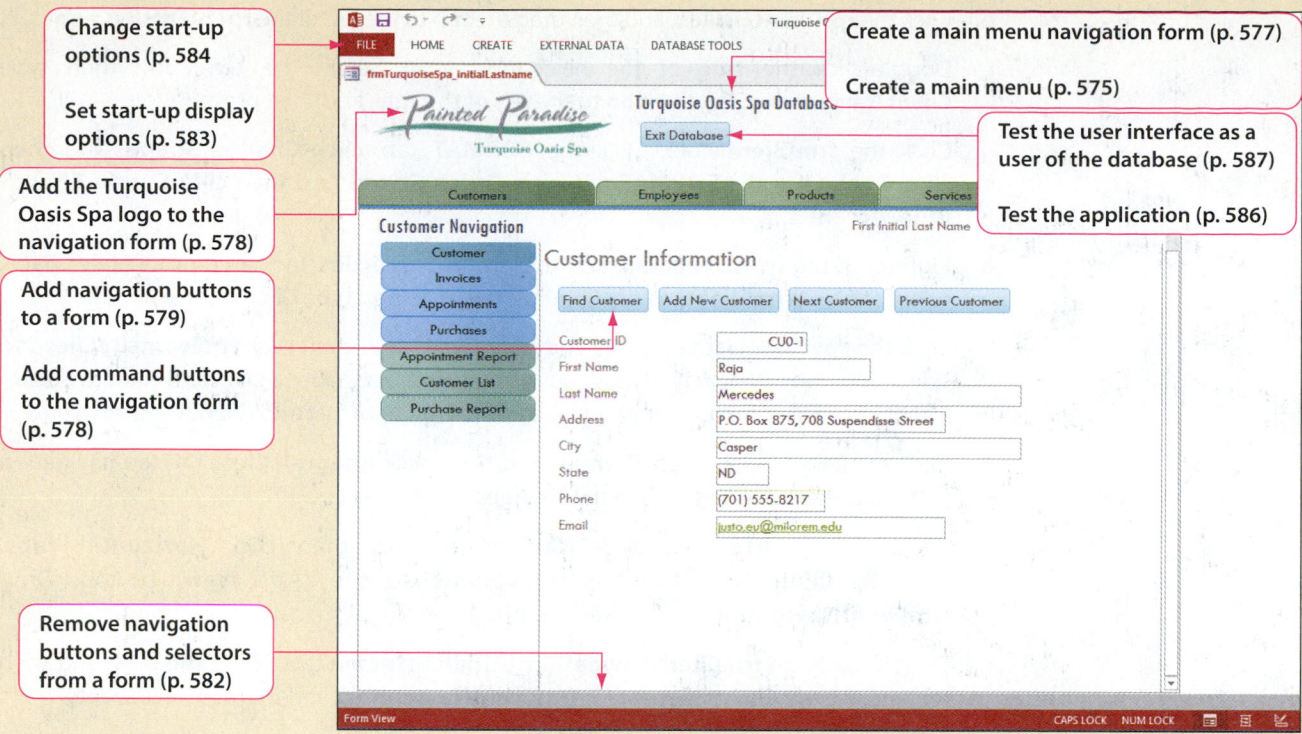

Change start-up options (p. 584

Set start-up display options (p. 583)

Create a main menu navigation form (p. 577)

Create a main menu (p. 575)

Add the Turquoise Oasis Spa logo to the navigation form (p. 578)

Test the user interface as a user of the database (p. 587)

Test the application (p. 586)

Add navigation buttons to a form (p. 579)

Add command buttons to the navigation form (p. 578)

Remove navigation buttons and selectors from a form (p. 582)

Figure 19 Turquoise Oasis Spa Final Database

Practice 1

Student data files needed:

 a06ws11Events.accdb

a06ws11EventPlanning.jpg

You will save your file as:

a06ws11Events_LastFirst.accdb

Event Planning

General Business

You have been asked to create an application for the Event Planning database. The application needs to include a main navigation form built from individual navigation forms. It will also need command buttons on various forms to increase the ease of use of the database. Lastly, the start-up options need to be configured to open the application and the new navigation form.

a. Start **Access**, and then open the student data file **a06ws11Events**. Click the **FILE** tab, and save the file as an **Access Database** in the folder or location designated by your instructor with the name a06ws11Events_LastFirst using your actual Last and First name. If necessary, click **Enable Content**.

b. Click the **CREATE** tab, in the Forms group, click **Navigation**, and then click **Horizontal Tabs**. Drag **frmClients** from the Navigation Pane to the **[Add New]** button on the navigation form. Continue by adding **rptEventsByClient** and **rptClientList** to the **[Add New]** button on the navigation form.

c. Click the **DESIGN** tab, click the **View** arrow, and then click **Design View**. Click the **DESIGN** tab, click **Label**, and then click to add a label in the right side of the **form header**. In the label, type your first initial and last name. Resize the labels as needed in the form header so the text appears on one line.

d. On the DESIGN tab, click the **View** arrow, and then click **Layout View**. Save the form as frmClientNavigation_initialLastname using your first initial and last name.

e. Click the **rptClientList** tab, and then drag the tab to the left of the **rptEventsByClient** tab.

f. Double-click the **title** of the navigation form, select the **text**, and then type Client Navigation. Click the **icon** to the left of the title, and then press ⌷Delete⌷.

g. Click the **frmClients** tab. Click the **FORMAT** tab, click **Change Shape**, and then click **Oval**. Click the **FORMAT** tab, click **Quick Styles**, and then click **Subtle Effect - Blue, Accent 2**.

h. Right-click the **frmClients** tab, and then click **Properties**. In the Property Sheet pane, select the text **frmClients** in the Caption row, and then type Clients.

i. Click the **rptClientList** tab, press and hold ⌷Shift⌷, and then click **rptEventsByClient** to select both tabs. Repeat the steps above to change the shape to **Oval** and color to **Subtle Effect - Blue, Accent 1**. Change the tab names to Client List and Client Events.

j. Click the **DESIGN** tab, click **Themes**, and then click **Integral**. **Close** ⌷X⌷ the navigation form, and then click **Yes** to save the changes.

k. Click the **CREATE** tab, click **Navigation**, and then click **Horizontal Tabs**. Drag **frmClientNavigation_initialLastname** to the **[Add New]** button. Drag **frmEventNavigation** to the **[Add New]** button.

l. Double-click the **frmClientNavigation_initialLastname** tab, select the **text**, and then rename the tab Clients. Repeat for **frmEventNavigation**, and then name it Events.

m. Click the **Clients** tab. Click the **FORMAT** tab, click **Change Shape**, and then click **Snip Single Corner Rectangle**. On the FORMAT tab, click **Quick Styles**, and then click **Intense Effect - Blue, Accent 1**. Repeat for the Events tab.

n. Double-click the **navigation form** title, select the **text**, and then type Events Database.

o. Click the **icon** to the left of the title, and then click the **DESIGN** tab, click **Insert Image**. Click **Browse**, and then select the **a06ws11EventPlanning.jpg** image from the student data files folder. Click **OK** to insert the new image.

p. On the DESIGN tab, click **Property Sheet**. In the Property Sheet pane, click the **Format** tab. Click the **Size Mode** arrow, and then click **Zoom**. Type 3 for the **Width**, and then type .8 for the **Height** of the image.

q. Click the **Selection type** arrow, and then click **FormHeader**. Click the **Back Color** box on the Format tab. Click the **Builder button**, and then select **White, Background 1**, the first row in the first column under Theme Colors.

r. Save the form as frmEventsDatabase_initialLastname and then **Close** ⌷X⌷ the form.

s. In the Navigation Pane, double-click **frmClients** to open the form. Click the **HOME** tab, click the **View** arrow, and then click **Design View**. Click the **ID** text box, press and hold ⌷Shift⌷, and then select all the **text boxes and labels** in the form detail section. Drag the **controls** down to the **.5"** mark on the vertical ruler. Click the **DESIGN** tab, click **Button**, and then click in the **top-left corner** of the form detail section to add the button.

t. On the Categories list, verify **Record Navigation** is selected. On the Actions list click **Find Record**, and then click **Next**. Click **Text**, select the text, type Find Client and then click **Next**. Name the button cmdFindClient and then click **Finish**.

u. Click the **DESIGN** tab, click **Button**, and then click next to the first button. On the Categories list, click **Record Operations**. On the Actions list, click **Add New Record**, and then click **Next**. Click **Text**, select the text, type Add New Client and then click **Next**. Name the button cmdAddNewClient and then click **Finish**.

v. Repeat to add two more buttons, Next Client and Previous Client. Click the **Record Navigation** category and **Go To Next Record** action; the text should say Next Client and the button named cmdNextClient. Click the **Record Navigation** category and **Go To Previous Record** action; the text should say Previous Client and the button should be named cmdPreviousClient.

w. Click the **first button** to select it. Press and hold Shift, and then click to select the remaining **three buttons**. Click the **ARRANGE** tab, click **Align**, and then click **Top**. Click **Size/Space**, and then click **Equal Horizontal**. **Close** ☒ the form, and then click **Yes** to save the changes.

x. In the Navigation Pane, double-click **frmEventsDatabase_initialLastname** to open the form. Switch to **Design** view. Click the **DESIGN** tab, click **Button**, and then click under the text **Events Database** in the **form header**. On the Categories list, click **Application**. On the Actions list, click **Quit Application**. Click **Next**, click **Text**, select the **text**, and then type Exit Database. Click **Next**. Name the button cmdExitDatabase and then click **Finish**. Switch to **Form** view.

y. Click **Exit Database** to check your button. Click **Yes** to save the changes. Open **a06ws11Events_LastFirst**. In the Navigation Pane, double-click **frmClients** to open the form. Switch to **Layout** view, and then click **Property Sheet**. Under Selection type, click the **selection** arrow, and then click **Form**.

z. Click the **Format** tab in the Property Sheet pane. Click the **Record Selectors** arrow, and then click **No**. Click the **Navigation Buttons** arrow, and then click **No**. **Close** ☒ the Property Sheet pane, **Close** ☒ the form, and then click **Yes** to save the changes.

aa. Click the **FILE** tab, click **Options**, and then click **Current Database**. Under the Application Options section, click the **Application Title** text box, and then type Events Database.

bb. Click the **Display Form** arrow, click **frmEventsDatabase_initialLastname**. Click the **Compact on Close** check box. In the Navigation section, click **Display Navigation Pane** to deselect the option. Click **OK** to close the Access Options window, click **OK** again, and then exit Access. Submit your work as directed by your instructor.

Problem Solve 1

Student data file needed:

 a06ws11StudentOrg.accdb

You will save your file as:

a06ws11StudentOrg_LastFirst.accdb

Navigation Forms in the Student Organization Database

Human Resources

Finance & Accounting

The Student Organization database keeps track of members, meetings, and membership dues. The current database consists of many tables and a few forms, queries, and reports. You have been asked to increase the usability of the database by creating navigation forms.

a. Open **a06ws11StudentOrg**, and then save the database as a06ws11StudentOrg_LastFirst. Replace LastFirst with your actual name and then click **Enable Content**.

b. Open the **frmMeetings** form in Layout view, and then apply the **Slice theme** as the database theme.

c.   Add a command button to the **frmMeetings** and **frmMembers** forms that can be used to find a particular record in the form. Place the command button below the existing **Add Meeting** and **Add Member** navigation buttons. Refer to the table below for labels and names:

Form Name	Text Label	Button Name
frmMeetings	Find Meeting	cmdFindMeeting
frmMembers	Find Member	cmdFindMember

d.   Make the following changes to the **frmMeetings**, **frmMembers**, **frmMembersMajors**, and **frmMembersMinors** forms:

- Remove the navigation buttons and record selectors.
- Apply an **Intense Effect - Dark Blue, Accent 1** Quick Style to each of the command buttons.
- Save changes and close the forms.

e.   Create a navigation form with Horizontal Tabs and Vertical Tabs, Left, and then make the following changes:

- Name the first horizontal tab Members and then add the following forms and reports to the vertical navigation controls in this order: **frmMembers**, **frmMembersMajors**, **frmMembersMinors**, **rptMembersByMajor**, **rptTotalDuesBySemester**, and **rptUnpaidDues**.
- Rename each of the vertical tabs Members, Majors, Minors, Members By Major, Membership Dues, and Unpaid Dues.
- Apply the **Moderate Effect, Dark Blue - Accent 1** Quick Style to the vertical tabs containing the forms, and then apply **Subtle Effect, Dark Green - Accent 3** to the vertical tabs containing reports.
- Change the shapes of the vertical tabs containing the forms to **Rounded Rectangle**, and then change the vertical tabs containing the reports to **Snip Single Corner Rectangle**.
- Name the second horizontal tab Meetings and then add the following to the vertical navigation controls: **frmMeetings** and **rptMeetingAttendance**.
- Rename each of the vertical tabs Meetings and Attendance Report.
- Apply the **Moderate Effect, Dark Blue - Accent 1** Quick Style to the vertical tab containing the form, and then apply **Subtle Effect, Dark Green - Accent 3** to the vertical tab containing the report.
- Change the shapes of the vertical tab containing the form to **Rounded Rectangle**, and then change the vertical tab containing the report to **Snip Single Corner Rectangle**.
- Remove the icon from the form header, and then rename the title Student Organization Database.
- Add a command button to the right of the form title in the form header that, when clicked, closes Access. The text label should be Exit Database and the button name should be cmdExitDatabase.

f.   Save the navigation form as frmStudentOrgNavigation_initialLastname using your first name initial and last name.

g.   Make the following modification to the Current Database settings:

- Change the **Application Title** to Student Organization Database.
- Make the database display frmStudentOrgNavigation_initialLastname when opened.
- Compact on close.
- Hide the Navigation Pane.

h.   Save and exit Access.

Student data file needed:

 a06ws11Tablet.accdb

You will save your file as:

 a06ws11Tablet_TeamName.accdb

Renting Tablet Computers

Production & Operations

Your institution has received a grant to test a new version of electronic textbooks. As part of the grant, several tablet computers have been purchased that come preloaded with the new electronic textbooks. These tablets are to be loaned to students to allow them to test the devices and the use of the electronic textbooks. As part of the grant, your team has been asked to enhance the database that tracks each device, the textbooks loaded onto the devices, and who has taken a given device out on loan. You will enhance the database by adding navigation forms, using command buttons for easier record navigation, and performing a usability test.

a. Select one team member to set up the database by completing Steps b–d.

b. Start **Access**, open the database **a06ws11Tablet**, and then name it a06ws11Tablet_TeamName. Replace TeamName with the name assigned to your team by your instructor.

c. Open your browser, and then navigate to **https://www.skydrive.live.com, https://www.drive.google.com**, or any other instructor-assigned storage location. Be sure all members of the team have an account on the chosen system—Microsoft or Google account. Create a new folder, and then name it TeamName_Assignment. Replace TeamName with the name assigned to your team by your instructor.

d. Upload the **a06ws11Tablet_TeamName** database to the **TeamName_Assignment** folder, and then share the folder with the other members of your team. Make sure that the other team members have permission to edit the contents of the shared folder.

e. Create a navigation form to increase the usability of the database:

- Add tabs for the **frmEText**, **frmStudents**, and **frmTablet** forms. Select a shape and style for these tabs. Change the names of the tabs to ETexts, Students, and Tablets.

- Add tabs for the rptBookPairings and rptTabletAssignments reports. Select a shape and style for the tab that differentiates these two tabs from the ones you used for the forms. Change the name of the tabs to Book Pairings and Tablet Assignments.

- Add an image to the navigation form in place of the default image inserted by Access. This could be your school's official logo or an image of your choosing. Change the title of the navigation form to Tablet Assignment Database. Save the form as frmTabletNavigation_TeamName. Replace TeamName with your team name.

- Add a command button to the navigation form that exits the database.

- Change the appropriate setting such that the new navigation form is shown by default and the navigation pane is hidden.

f. Modify the frmEText, frmStudents, and frmTablet forms to make common tasks for the users more intuitive:

- On the frmEText form, add four buttons—one to move to the next EText, one to move to the previous EText, one to find an EText, and one to add an EText.

- On the frmStudents form, add four buttons—one to move to the next student, one to move to the previous student, one to find a student, and one to add a student.

- On the frmTablet form, add four buttons—one to move to the next Tablet, one to move to the previous Tablet, one to find a Tablet, and one to add a Tablet.

- Remove record selectors and navigation buttons from the frmEText, frmStudents, and frmTablet forms.
- Use Tablet Assignments as the title for the database, and then change the appropriate setting such that the database compacts and repairs on close.

g. Perform usability testing on each of the forms individually and on the navigation form either with a team member or a nonclassmate. Use the following table to track your comments.

Task	Action(s) Taken	Comments
Enter a new tablet computer		
Navigate through the tablet computer records		
Enter new student information		
Navigate through the student computer records		
Enter new EText information		
Navigate through the EText computer records		
Pair an EText with a tablet		
Assign a tablet to a new student		
Print the Book Pairings report		
Print the Tablet Assignments report		
Exit the database		

h. Exit Access.

Additional Cases

Additional Workshop Cases are available on the companion website and in the instructor resources.

OBJECTIVES

1. Modify database settings for protection from macro viruses   p. 596

2. Understand the Macro Designer   p. 598

3. Understand how to test and troubleshoot macros   p. 603

4. Improve database design and function by automating manual processes   p. 607

5. Reduce processing time by combining routine tasks   p. 609

6. Create macro groups   p. 613

7. Create macros that run when the database opens   p. 616

8. Increase functionality of forms and reports   p. 620

9. Implement complex business rules with data macros   p. 624

Prepare Case

The Turquoise Oasis Spa Database: Automating Tasks and Increasing Functionality

Sales & Marketing   Production & Operations

Employees of the Turquoise Oasis Spa use the company database to store employee and customer information, record transactions, track inventory, schedule spa services, produce reports, and so on. The spa continues to experience growth, offering new products, services, and catering to more and more clients. It has become apparent that the current database no longer meets the needs of the business. You have been asked to automate some routine

Leonid and Anna Dedukh / Shutterstock

tasks to increase the efficiency of the database and create additional functionality to improve the overall usability of the database.

REAL WORLD SUCCESS

"In my first position after graduation I was asked to work on a database that was used to create 15 different reports. Each week I had to run dozens of queries, print some reports, and export other reports as PDF files. Then I would have to attach the PDF files to e-mails to be sent out. By leveraging macros I was able to automate all of these processes, including automatically attaching PDF versions of reports to e-mails. As a result I was able to turn the time spent previously with the database into more productive ventures."

- Thomas, alumni

Student data files needed for this workshop:

 a06ws12Spa.accdb   a06ws12SpaProducts.xlsx

You will save your files as:

 a06ws12Spa_LastFirst.accdb

 a06ws12rptScheduleByCustomer_LastFirst.pdf

 a06ws12rptLowInventory_LastFirst.xlsx

595

Understanding the Purpose of Macros

A well-designed database application takes, among other things, efficiency and usability into consideration. Macros can help increase both the efficiency and the usability of a database. **Macros** are database objects that provide a method of automating routine database tasks. They can add functionality to reports and forms, as well as the controls that forms and reports contain. **Arguments** are values that provide information concerning the action being carried out by the macro.

There are three different kinds of macros in Microsoft Access: stand-alone, embedded, and data macros. **Stand-alone macros** are separate database objects that are displayed in the Navigation Pane. Stand-alone macros can be executed directly in the Navigation Pane by double-clicking the macro object, clicking Run in Design view, or by attaching the macro to a database object, like a button or text field. **Embedded macros** are stored as part of a database object such as a form or report or any control such as a button. Embedded macros are not displayed in the Navigation Pane and are only executed when the objects they are embedded in trigger events. **Data macros** are stored in Access tables and are triggered by table events. Data macros are typically used to implement business logic into tables and automatically set values in fields. In this section you will learn the purpose of macros as well as how to build, edit, and troubleshoot them.

Modify Database Settings for Protection from Macro Viruses

Turquoise Oasis Spa collects and stores personal information about its clients in the database, such as addresses, phone numbers, and credit card information. Ensuring that this personal information is kept safe and secure is very important to the company. Before explaining how to create macros in the database, it is important to discuss some of the security risks associated with macros and what steps can be taken to mitigate those risks.

A macro is a sequence of commands that run automatically, and as mentioned above, they can increase efficiency and usability of a database. However, the sequence of commands can also be harmful when executed. Harmful macros have been known to add, edit, or remove data from a database—and often spread to other databases or even to the user's computer.

Open the Starting File

The Turquoise Oasis Spa database already contains two stand-alone macros. You will first open the database and review the security warnings provided by Access. You will then change the security settings within Access to allow macros to be enabled with the database.

A12.00

 To Open the Spa Database

a. Start **Access**, and then open the student data file **a06ws12Spa**.

b. Click the **FILE** tab, and save the file as an **Access Database** in the folder or location designated by your instructor with the name **a06ws12Spa_LastFirst** replacing LastFirst with your actual name. If necessary, click **Enable Content**.

SIDE NOTE

Trusted Locations

The Trusted Locations feature does not secure your files from harmful macros. If a file has harmful macros embedded in it, they will be allowed to run if opened from a Trusted Location.

Creating a Trusted Location

To ensure the security of the computers at Painted Paradise all macros have been disabled by default. This means that any macro that exists in a Microsoft Office document will not be allowed to run while the file is open. The Turquoise Oasis Spa database is located in a specific location on the Painted Paradise network. This location can be designated as a Trusted Location. A **Trusted Location** is typically a folder on your hard disk or a network share where trusted files are located. External documents that could potentially contain harmful macros should not be put into a Trusted Location. Such files should be placed in another location until they can be scanned or otherwise verified to be safe. Any file that you put in a Trusted Location can be opened without being checked by the Trust Center security feature.

MyITLab®
Workshop 12 Training

A12.01

 To Add a Trusted Location

a. Click the **FILE** tab, and then click **Options**.

b. Click **Trust Center** on the left, and then click **Trust Center Settings**.

c. Click **Trusted Locations** on the left side of the Trust Center dialog box, and then in the bottom-right corner, click **Add new location**.

d. Click **Browse** to navigate to the directory containing your files, and then click **OK**.

e. Click the **Subfolders of this location are also trusted** check box to ensure that all databases in the directory are trusted.

f. Click **OK** to close the Trusted Location dialog box, click **OK**, and then click **OK** to close the Access Options dialog box.

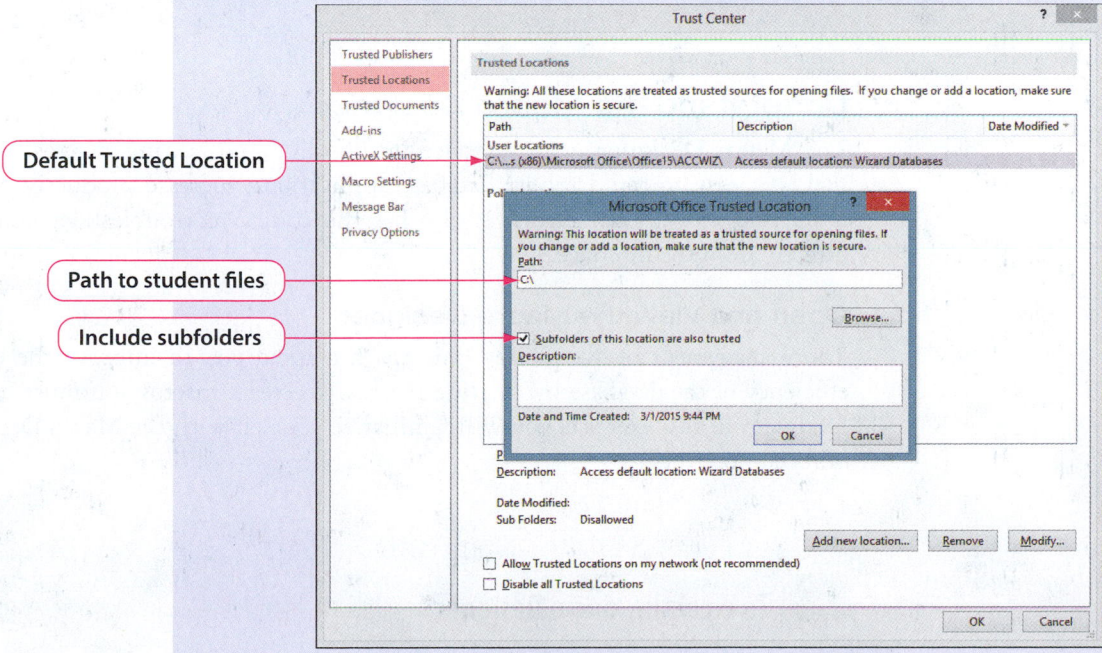

Figure 1 Trusted Location dialog box

QUICK REFERENCE	Macro Settings

Macro settings are part of the Trust Center settings and can be modified based on the needs of the organization. Below are the setting options and their descriptions.

Setting	Description
Disable all macros without notification	All macros and security alerts about macros are disabled.
Disable all macros with notification	This is the default setting. It disables all macros and provides security alerts if there are macros present.
Disable all macros except digitally signed macros	This setting is the same as the Disable all macros with notification option, except digitally signed macros will be enabled by default.
Enable all macros	Allows all macros to run; this setting makes your computer vulnerable to potentially malicious code and is not recommended.

REAL WORLD ADVICE	Selecting the Appropriate Macro Setting

If the database is in a location defined as a Trusted Location, the macros will be ignored by the Trust Center security system. Depending on the nature of the organization, the policy may be to disable all macros. However, the most common settings are Disable all macros with notification and Disable all macros except digitally signed macros. Both of these settings help to mitigate the risk of a macro virus and still allow useful macros to run.

Understand the Macro Designer

The **Macro Designer** is an interface for building and editing macros. This interface makes it easy to build robust database applications, increase productivity of business users, and reduce code errors. It also has the ability to troubleshoot and run macros directly from the interface.

Open and View the Macro Designer

The management of Turquoise Oasis Spa has asked you to improve the usability and efficiency of the database by creating macros. To create macros you must use the Macro Designer. In this exercise, you will familiarize yourself with the Macro Designer and all of its components.

A12.02

 To View the Macro Designer

a. In the Navigation Pane scroll down to the bottom of the Navigation Pane.

b. Right-click **mcrSampleMacro**, and then click **Design View**.

This mcrSampleMacro is a simple macro consisting of two actions. When executed, the macro will perform the OpenReport action, opening the rptEmployeeList report, and then it will send the report to the printer using the RunMenuCommand action.

> **Troubleshooting**
>
> Double-clicking an object in the Navigation Pane normally opens that object. Macros are different however. Double-clicking them in the Navigation Pane will run the macro instead of opening it.

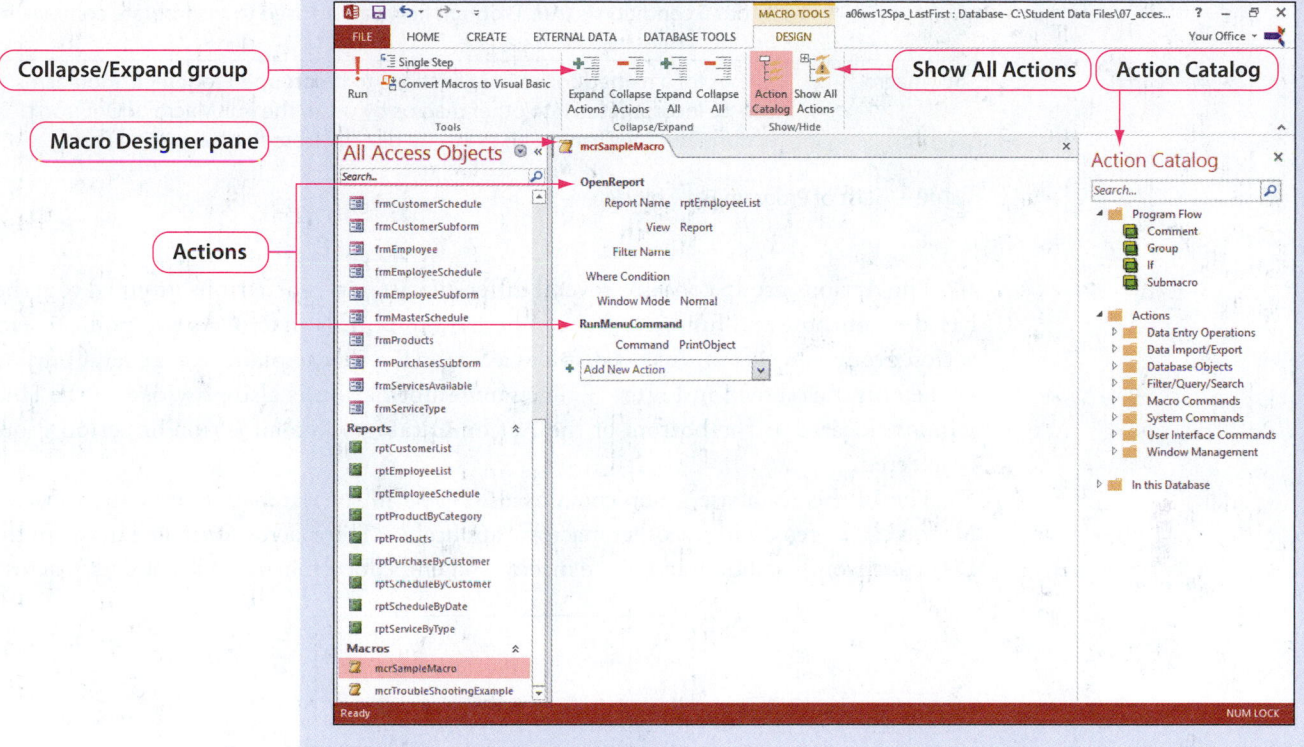

Figure 2   Macro Designer

As shown in Figure 2 the Macro Designer pane consists of all the actions and logic that make up the macro. An **action** is a self-contained instruction that can be combined with other instructions to automate tasks and is considered to be the basic building block of a macro. Actions can be added to the macro by simply selecting one from the Add New Action list or by searching the Action Catalog to the right of the Macro Designer pane. The **Action Catalog** is a searchable set of macro actions that can retrieve actions based on keywords. The Action Catalog consists of three different groups: Program Flow, Actions, and In this Database.

The Program Flow group contains a list of blocks that can control the order in which actions are executed or help structure the macro.

Block Name	Purpose
Comment	A form of internal documentation that can help explain the purpose of the macro.
Group	Allows for actions and program flow to be part of a named group to better organize the view of the macro in the Macro Designer. The group can be collapsed, expanded, and moved together.
If	Implements logic into a macro that will execute actions based on whether or not a condition is true. Program flow can be used to incorporate complex business rules into the database.
Submacro	Allows for a named collection of actions to be grouped together. Submacros can be incorporated into other macros by using the RunMacro or OnError actions, but they cannot be executed directly from the Navigation Pane.

Table 1   List of Program Flow blocks

The Actions group contains several different categories of actions grouped together based on purpose and function that can be used to build a macro. As you point to each action group and action, Access displays a ScreenTip that explains the general purpose of the object as shown in Figure 3. The same information is also provided in the Help window located at the bottom of the Action Catalog when an action or action group is selected.

The In this Database group contains all objects in the database that contain macros. Macros can be reused inside other macros if applicable. The macros contained in the In this Database group include stand-alone macros and embedded macros, but not data macros.

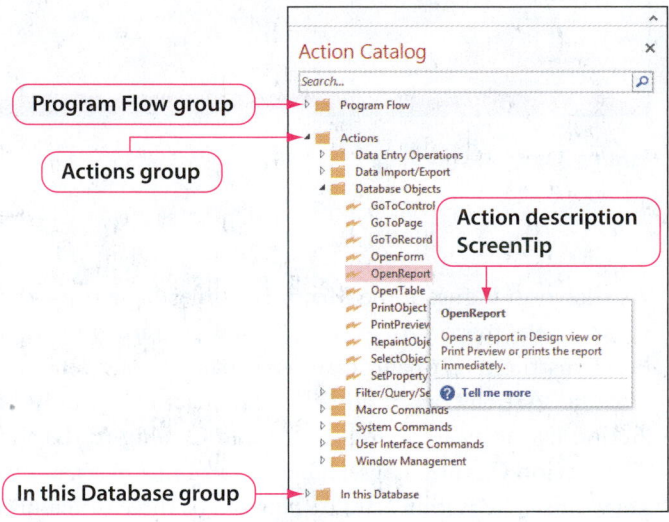

Figure 3   Action Catalog

Editing a Macro

Even a simple macro like mcrSampleMacro can be improved to create a better user experience. In this exercise, you will improve the macro by adding a comment that explains the purpose of the macro and an additional action that displays a message box informing the user that the report is being sent to the printer.

A12.03

 To Edit the Macro

a. In the Action Catalog, under the Program Flow group, drag **Comment** to the top of the Macro Designer pane, above the OpenReport macro action.

> **Troubleshooting**
> If the Action Catalog is not visible on the right, you can toggle between showing or hiding it by clicking the Action Catalog button in the Show/Hide group located on the right of the Design tab.

b. Using your first initial and last name, in the comment field type **Edited by initialLastname. This macro opens the Employee List Report and sends it to the printer.**

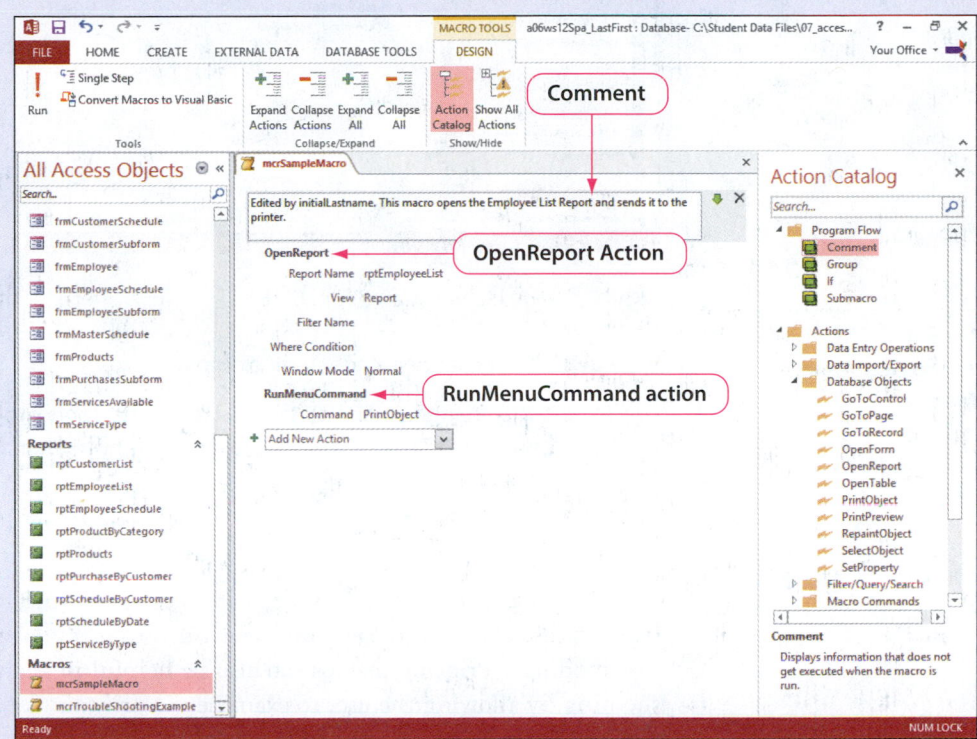

Figure 4 mcrSampleMacro macro

c. On the Add New Action list, click the **arrow**, and then select **MessageBox** from the list of actions.

d. In the Message argument, type **The report is now being sent to the printer**.

e. Click the **Beep** arrow, select **Yes**, click the **Type** arrow, and then select **Information**.

f. In the Title of the message argument, type **Printing Report.**

g. At the far right of the MessageBox, click the **Move up** arrow to move the action above the RunMenuCommand action. This will cause the message box to be displayed before the report is sent to the printer.

SIDE NOTE

Adding Actions to a Macro

Alternatively, you could search for the MessageBox macro in the Action Catalog and either double-click the action or drag it to the macro.

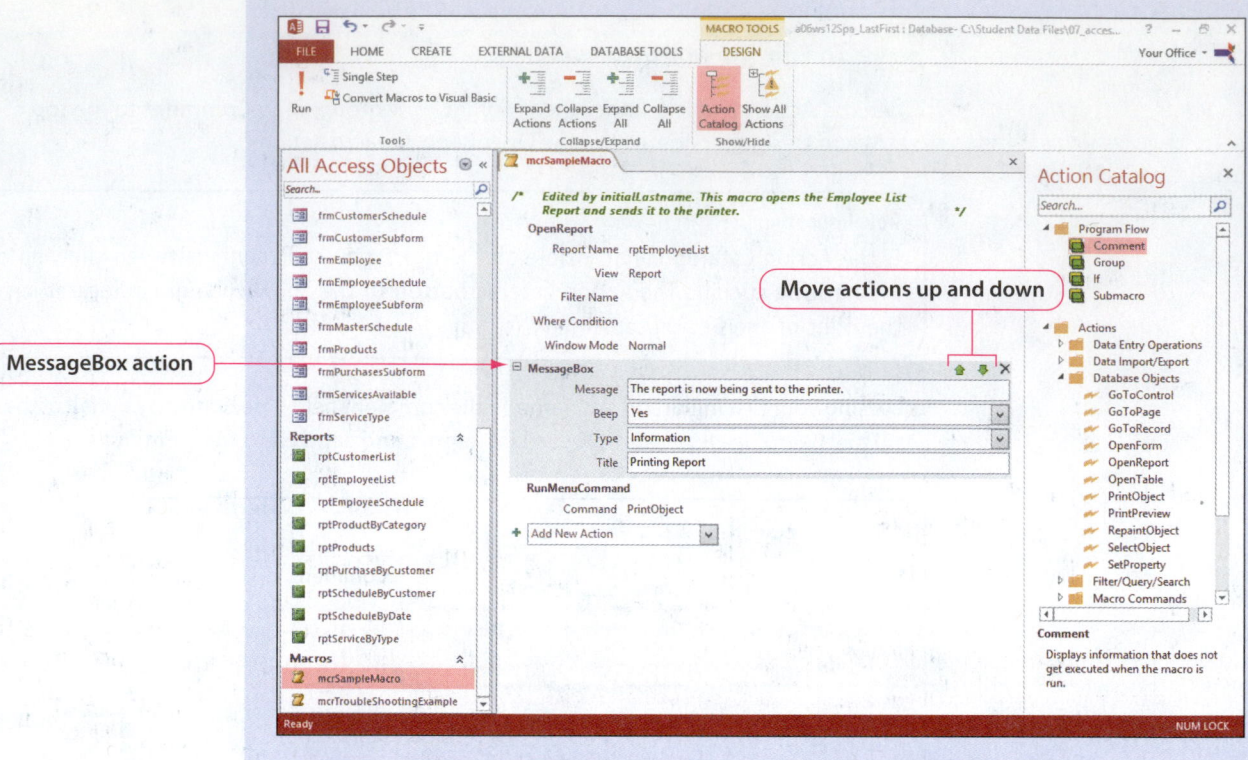

Figure 5   mcrSampleMacro edited

SIDE NOTE
Moving Actions in a Macro

Actions can also be moved around by dragging them to the desired location.

h. **Save** 🔲 the changes made to mcrSampleMacro.

i. To test the changes made to the macro, in the Tools group, click **Run** to execute the macro, and then **Close** ☒ the Employee List report when finished.

Printing a Macro

Management at Turquoise Oasis Spa likes to document any changes made to the databases in case of an audit. You have been asked to print out the mcrSampleMacro that was just modified. Printing macros can also be helpful in analyzing the logic when troubleshooting by allowing the user to examine the printout for errors or inefficiencies.

A12.04

   To Print a Macro

a. If necessary, open the mcrSampleMacro in Design view, click the **FILE** tab, and then click **Print**.

b. Click **Print**, select the options to print the **Properties**, **Actions and Arguments**, and **Permissions by User and Group** in the Print Macro Definition dialog box, and then click **OK**.

SIDE NOTE
Printing Macros

Macros can be printed by clicking the Database Tools tab, clicking Database Documenter, clicking the Macros tab, and then clicking the macro's check box.

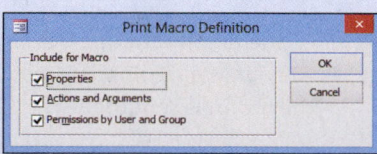

Figure 6   Print Macro Definition dialog box

c. **Close** ☒ the macro.

In addition to the actions and arguments that make up mcrSampleMacro, the printout also includes the database name, directory path, date, and additional information concerning the properties of the macro.

REAL WORLD ADVICE | **Sharing and Backing up Macros**

Both the number and complexity of macros can grow over time as the business grows and needs change. Access allows macros to be copied from the Macro Designer and pasted into a text editor as XML. The XML then can be copied easily from the text editor and pasted directly into the Macro Designer. To copy the macro quickly, with the macro opened in Design view, press ⌈Ctrl⌉ and type A to select all of the macro actions, and then press ⌈Ctrl⌉ and type C to copy the action. Pasting the macro into a text editor allows for easy sharing of the macro. It is also a quick method of creating backups.

Understand How to Test and Troubleshoot Macros

Macros can become very complex with multiple steps and logic built in. It is very important to test macros thoroughly to ensure that they function as intended. It is also important to test macros to ensure that they do not result in errors. These errors can create problems within your database and cause users to have concerns over seeing an unexpected error message.

Figuring out which actions are causing the macro to result in an error can be a tedious task. The **Single Step** feature is located next to the Run button on the Design tab in the Tools group; it allows you to observe the flow of a macro and the results of each action, isolating any action that causes an error or produces unwanted results.

When the Single Step feature is turned on, the macro executes one action at a time and pauses between actions. After each action the Macro Single Step dialog box appears showing the name of the macro, the value of any conditions, the name of the action about to be executed, and the arguments for the action. In addition to this information, the dialog box also provides three choices on what to do next:

• Step executes the action shown in the dialog box.

• Stop All Macros stops all actions in the macro and closes the dialog box.

• Continue resumes normal operation of the macro and exits the single step process.

Single Stepping Through a Macro

An employee of Turquoise Oasis Spa had attempted to create a macro that would open the frmCustomer form, create a new record, and place the pointer in the first name field. However, the macro is not working properly, and you have been asked to troubleshoot and fix the macro. You will be using the Single Step feature to assist you in the process.

A12.05

 To Single Step a Macro

a. In the Navigation Pane, right-click the **mcrTroubleShootingExample** macro, and then click **Design View**.

b. On the **DESIGN** tab, in the Tools group, click **Single Step**, and then click **Run**.

Notice the Macro Single Step dialog box and all of the information displayed. The macro name is at the top along with the action name toward the bottom. Just below the action name are the arguments for the action. This is a MessageBox action that displays a message to the user. To the right is an Error Number of 0. This means there is no error detected with this action.

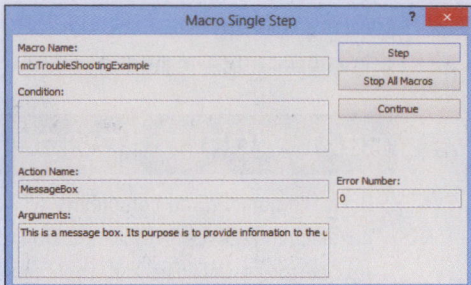

Figure 7   Macro Single Step MessageBox action

SIDE NOTE

Macro Paused with MessageBox Action

The MessageBox action pauses a macro so the message can be displayed. You need to click OK in order for the macro to continue.

c. Click **Step** to execute the MessageBox action, and then click **OK** to close the message box.

d. The next action is the GoToRecord action with an Error Number: 1 that indicates there is an error. Click **Step** to execute this action to get additional information.

e. An information box is displayed with information about the GoToRecord action. The second statement provides some useful information: "The type of object the action applies to isn't currently selected or isn't in the active view."

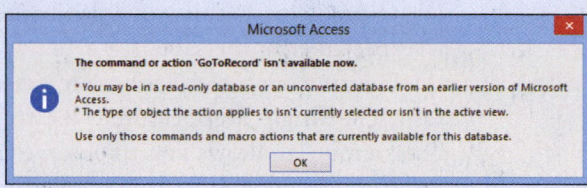

Figure 8   Error message for GoToControl action

f. Click **OK**. The Macro Single Step dialog box now provides only the option to Stop All Macros so that the GoToRecord action error can be addressed. Click **Stop All Macros**.

Notice the order of the actions in the macro. This macro has been designed to go to a specific record and then a specific field in that record before the form is even opened. The error message that was displayed indicates that this is the root cause of the macro failure.

g. Place the pointer over the **OpenForm** action, and then click the **Move up** arrow twice in the OpenForm action to move it so it is above the GoToRecord action and below the MessageBox action.

OpenForm action correct location

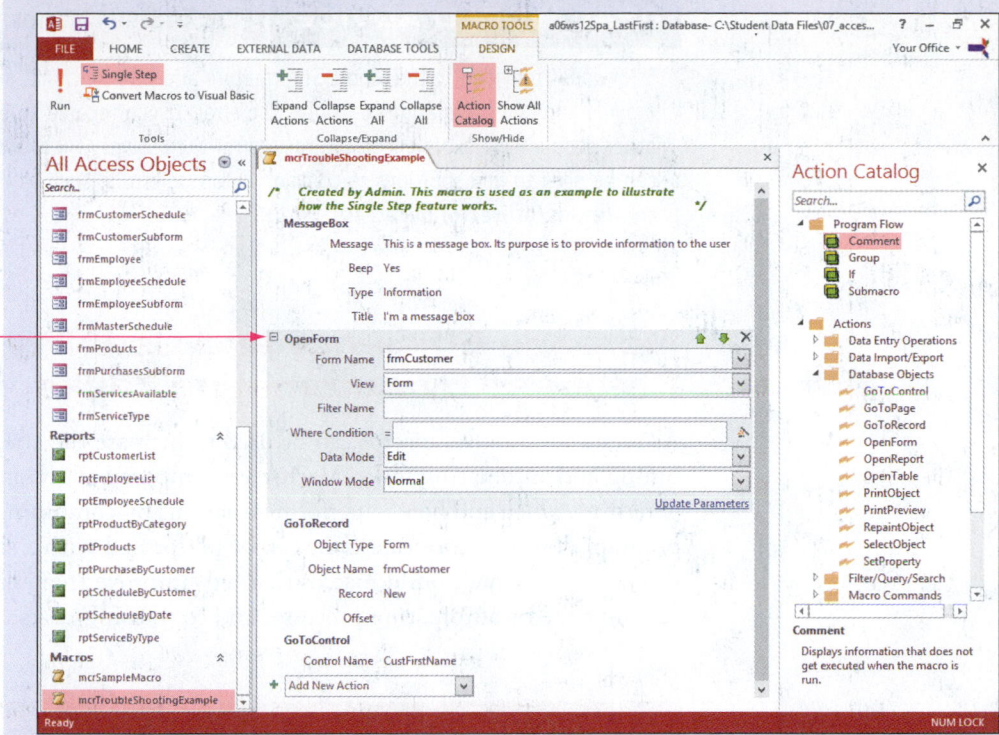

Figure 9 mcrTroubleShootingExample macro corrected

h. **Save** 🖫 the change, and then go through the single step process again to ensure there are no additional errors with the macro.

i. Click the **Single Step** button to turn off the Single Step feature. **Close** ☒ the frmCustomer form, and then **Close** ☒ the macro.

j. Double-click the **mcrTroubleShootingExample** macro in the Navigation Pane to run it and ensure the macro runs as expected. **Close** ☒ the frmCustomer form.

Troubleshooting

If the Single Step feature is on when the macro ends, then it remains on. If you run another macro, it will automatically display the Macro Single Step dialog box again. To turn single stepping off, click Continue in the dialog box, or on the Design tab in the Tools group, click the Single Step button so it is not highlighted.

REAL WORLD ADVICE | **Single Stepping Macros**

If part of your macro is functioning correctly then you can begin single stepping at a specific point in the macro by adding the Single Step macro action at the point where you wish to begin single stepping.

REAL WORLD ADVICE | **Error Codes in Macros**

Error codes provided in the Single Step feature and informational dialog boxes do not always provide enough information to resolve the error. If you receive an error, rest assured that many other people have experienced the same error themselves. There are many forums online that can be used to find solutions to common database errors, such as **http://answers.microsoft.com/en-us/office/forum/access**.

Increase Efficiency and Usability of a Database by Automating Tasks

As mentioned above, macros can be used to increase the efficiency of a database by combining and automating tasks. Macros are composed of actions that often contain logic to determine when and how to perform an action. By combining various macro actions with program flow logic, routine tasks can be performed with a simple click of the mouse. In this section you will build macros that will improve the user experience and reduce processing time by automating processes and combining tasks.

QUICK REFERENCE	Common Macro Actions
Action Name	**Description**
ApplyFilter	Applies a filter to a table, form, or report to restrict or sort the records in the object
AutoExec	An AutoExec macro is a macro that is named AutoExec. It is automatically executed when the database is opened.
Beep	Produces a beep tone through the computer's speakers
CloseWindow	Closes the specified window, or the active window if none is specified
DisplayHourglassPointer	Provides a visual indication that the macro is running
ExportWithFormatting	Outputs the data in the specified database object to one of several possible output formats
FindRecord	Finds the first record, or the next record if the action is used again, that meets a specified criteria
GoToControl	Moves the focus to a specified field or control on the active datasheet or form
MessageBox	Displays a message box containing a warning or informational message
OpenForm	Opens a form in a specified view—Design, Form, or Layout
OpenReport	Opens a report in a specified view—Design, Print Preview, or Report
QuitAccess	Exits Microsoft Access
RunMacro	Runs a macro
SelectObject	Selects a specified object so you can run an action that applies to the object

Improve Database Design and Function by Automating Manual Processes

The management at the Turquoise Oasis Spa frequently requests copies of a report that lists the customers who have scheduled services for a particular date. The current process consists of looking through the report and copying the information for the date requested into a word-processing program before sending it to management.

This process takes too much time and is prone to errors because the information is being copied manually from one location to another. A macro can automate the process and reduce the risk of errors.

Exporting Database Objects Using Macros

In this exercise, you will create a macro that opens the desired report, applies a filter to only show the information for services on a particular date, and exports the report as a PDF-formatted file.

A12.06

 To Create a Macro

a. Click the **CREATE** tab, and then in the Macros & Code group, click **Macro**.

b. In the Action Catalog, under the Program Flow group, double-click **Comment** to add a comment to the macro.

c. Using your first initial and last name, in the Comment box type Created by initialLastname. This macro applies a filter to the customer schedule report and exports the report as a PDF.

> **Troubleshooting**
> By default the Action Catalog and Add New Action combo box only show actions that will execute in nontrusted databases. To see all actions, click Show All Actions in the Show/Hide group on the Design tab.

d. Click the **Add New Action** arrow, and then select **OpenReport** from the list of actions to add the action to the macro.

e. Select **rptScheduleByCustomer** for the Report name, and then select **Report** in the View argument.

f. In the **Where Condition** argument, type the following expression:
[DateOfAppt]= [Enter a date of service, Example (5/2/2015)].
This expression uses the field that stores the appointment date and prompts the user for a date to use as criteria for the filter. The message "Enter a date of service, Example (5/2/2015)" will be displayed in a parameter box when the macro is executed.

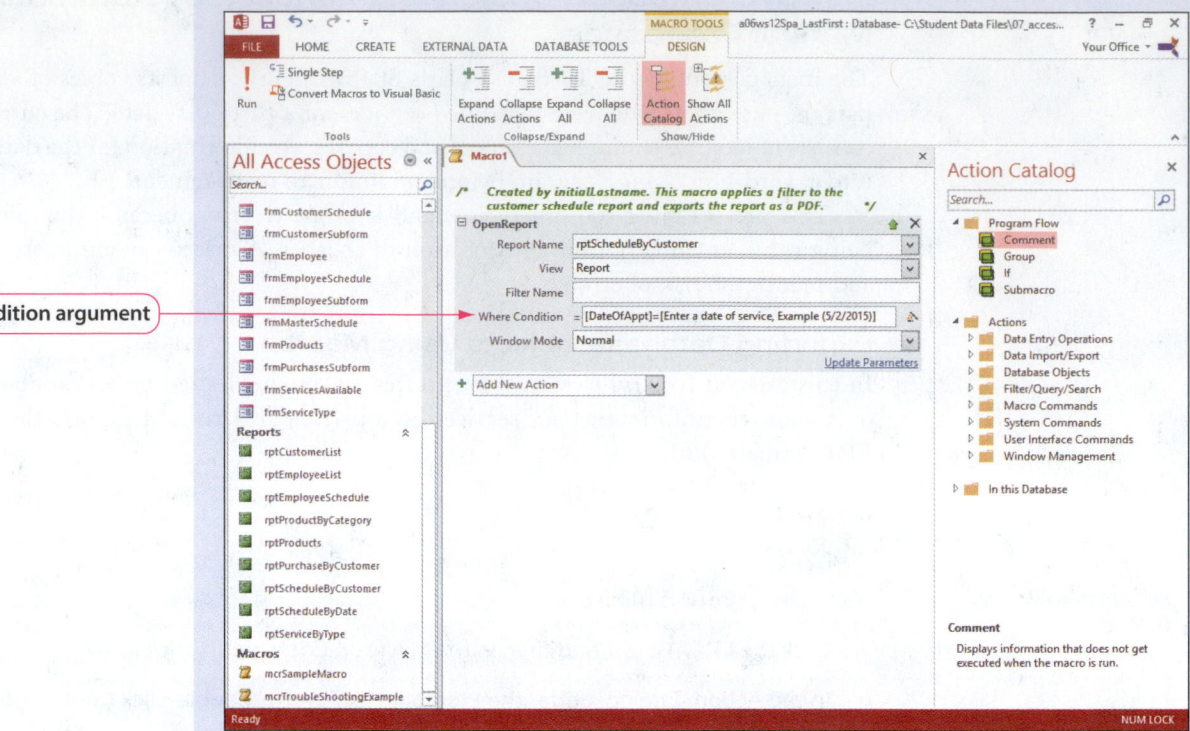

Figure 10   Design view of a macro in progress

SIDE NOTE
Where Condition and Filters

A parameter query could be created to prompt the user for a service date. The query name could then be entered into the Filter Name field.

SIDE NOTE
Output File

A specific file name and location can be entered in the Output File box, such as C:\Reports\ CustomerSchedule.pdf.

g. Click the **Add New Action** arrow, and then select **ExportWithFormatting** from the list of actions to add the action to the macro.

h. Select **Report** for the Object Type, and then select **rptScheduleByCustomer** for the Object Name.

i. Select **PDF Format (*.pdf)** as the Output Format. Leave the Output File argument blank, and keep all other settings the same.

j. **Save** 💾 the macro as **mcrCustomerServicesList**.

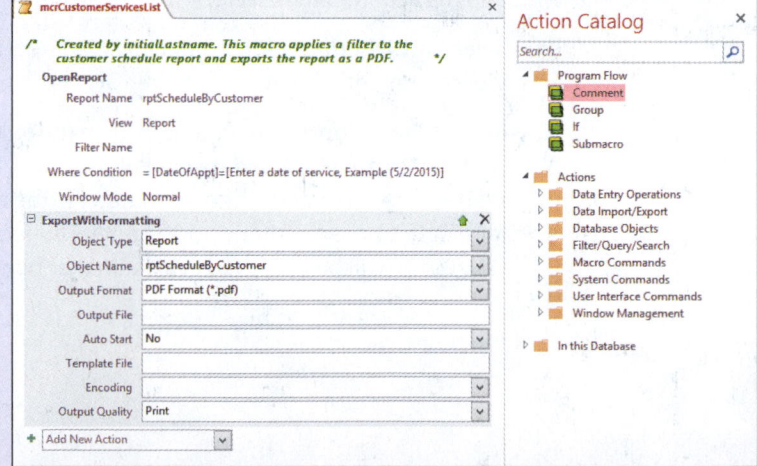

Figure 11   mcrCustomerServicesList macro completed

k. To test the macro, click the **DESIGN** tab, and then in the Tools group, click **Run**. In the Enter Parameter Value dialog box type **1/19/2015** and then click **OK**.

l. **Save** 🖫 the report to your student files as a06ws12rptScheduleByCustomer_LastFirst replacing LastFirst with your last and first names.

m. **Close** ☒ the report, and then **Close** ☒ the macro.

CONSIDER THIS | **Exporting with an Appropriate File Type**

There are several different output file types to consider when exporting database objects using macros. Some of the most commonly used output types are

- XLSX
- PDF
- HTML
- XML

What are some of the things you should take into consideration when deciding which file type to export?

REAL WORLD ADVICE | **Comments Make Macros Easier to Understand and Maintain**

Comments that describe the purpose of a macro or complex program flows are considered best practice but are many times neglected by database programmers. Appropriate comments that provide useful information about the macro and its purpose can be extremely valuable to the organization. They also can save time if a new employee is required to take over the database design and programming.

Reduce Processing Time by Combining Routine Tasks

Turquoise Oasis Spa routinely adds new products to meet the demands of their clients. When new products are acquired the information is sent in a spreadsheet with the product name and other information. This data needs to be entered into the database and is currently done manually by copying and pasting.

Automating an Import-and-Update Process

In this exercise, you will develop a macro that will automate the process of importing new products into the database by executing a query that will convert the product name to proper case and then append the modified records to the products table.

You will be adding several actions to this macro that will import the data from a spreadsheet into a temporary table, and then the data will need to be cleaned by executing an update query. The cleaned data then will be added to the products table by executing an append query. Finally, the data will be removed from the temporary table by executing a delete query.

Macros can be used to automate complex sets of actions. It is important to carefully think through all the actions that a macro will be executing to complete the tasks before beginning work on creating the macro. Taking the time to create a process flow that describes the actions and reasons for those actions can save time and reduce the chance of errors.

Step	Purpose	Specifics
Import new records to a temporary table	To update the list of products	The new product list needs to be modified before importing it into the tblProduct table.
Set warning messages off	To suppress common database warnings	Before action queries are executed, Access issues warnings and prompts that require a user response.
Run the qryUPDATE_ProductDescription query	To clean the data imported	Converts all product names to proper case.
Run qryAPPEND_NewProducts	To append new products to the tblProduct table	Appends newly modified data into the tblProduct table.
Run qryDELETE_TempNewProducts	To delete the contents of the temp table	Prevents excess data from being stored in a temporary table.

Table 2   Process flow table example

A12.07

 To Automate Processes with a Macro

a. Click the **CREATE** tab, and then in the Macros & Code group, click **Macro**.

b. In the Program Flow group under the Action Catalog, drag **Comment** to the macro. Using your initial and last name, in the comment field type Created by initialLastname. This macro automates the process of importing new products into the products table.

c. If necessary, on the DESIGN tab, in the Show/Hide group, click **Show All Actions**.
   By default, Access only shows a subset of possible actions in Add New Action box. By selecting Show All Actions, Access will display all possible actions in the Add New Action list.

d. Click the **Add New Action** arrow, and then select **ImportExportSpreadsheet** from the list of actions to add the action to the macro. If necessary, select **Import** as the Transfer Type and **Excel Workbook** as the Spreadsheet Type.

> **Troubleshooting**
>
> If an action is not available in the Add New Action box, be sure to click Show All Actions. Each time Access is closed the action list is restored to only showing macros that are allowed in databases that have not been trusted regardless of changes made to the Trust Center settings.

e. For the Table Name argument, type tblTempNewProducts.

f. The File Name field must include the complete path to the file being imported. Navigate to the student files using Windows Explorer, click in the **address bar** of Windows Explorer, and then with the path selected press Ctrl + C to copy the path. Press Ctrl + V to paste the path in the File Name field, click at the end of the path, and then type \a06ws12SpaProducts.xlsx into the File Name argument.

g. In the Has Field Names argument, select **Yes**.

h. Click the **Add New Action** arrow, select **SetWarnings** from the list of actions to add it to the macro, click the **Warnings On** argument, and if necessary, select **No**.

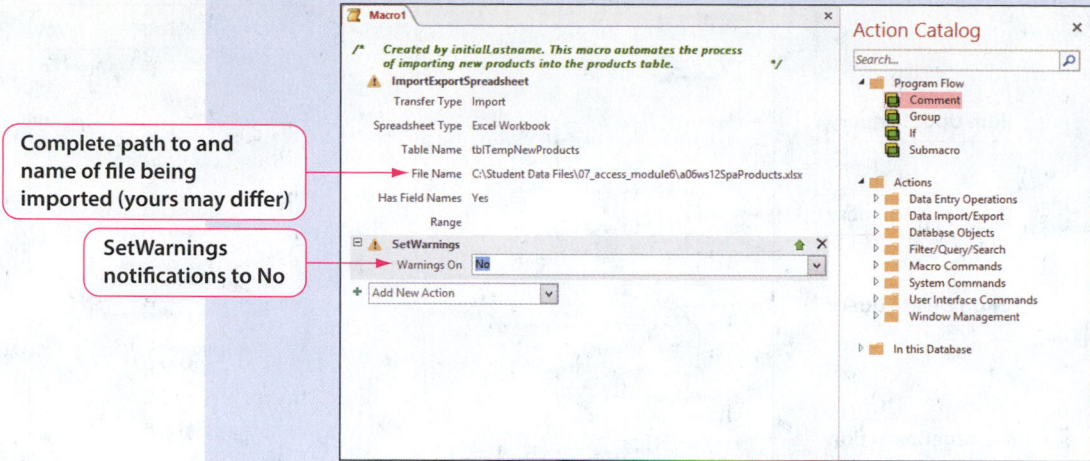

Complete path to and name of file being imported (yours may differ)

SetWarnings notifications to No

Figure 12   Design view of the macro in progress

Figure 12   Design view of the macro in progress

i.   Select **OpenQuery** from the Add New Action list. You will be selecting an action query that will update the new product's names from all capital letters to all proper case so the product names are formatted consistently throughout the table.

j.   Select **qryUPDATE_ProductDescription** for the Query Name argument. If necessary select **Datasheet** for View, and then if necessary select **Edit** for Data Mode.

k.   Add another **OpenQuery** action to this macro. Select **qryAPPEND_NewProducts** for the Query Name, if necessary select **Datasheet** for View, and then if necessary select **Edit** for Data Mode. This action will execute the append query that will add the modified products to the product table.

l.   Add another **OpenQuery** action to this macro. Select **qryDELETE_TempNewProducts** for the Query Name, if necessary select **Datasheet** for View, and then if necessary select **Edit** for Data Mode. This action will execute the delete query that will remove the products from the temp table.

m.   Click the **Add New Action** arrow, select **SetWarnings** from the list of actions to the macro, click the **Warnings On** argument, and if necessary, select **Yes**.

n.   Add the **MessageBox** action to this macro. Type New products have been added to the database. as the Message, and then if necessary select **Yes** for Beep. This will produce a sound from the computer speakers when the message box appears.

o.   Select **Information** for the Message Box Type, and then type New Products Added as the Title.

p.   **Save** 💾 the macro as mcrImportNewProducts.

SIDE NOTE

Bypass Warnings

The SetWarnings action allows the user to bypass all prompts that accompany various actions in a database, such as running an update query.

SIDE NOTE

Message Box

Message boxes are useful to alert the user that an action has been completed, but message boxes could also be used for custom error messages.

SIDE NOTE

Beep

The frequency and duration of the beep depends on the hardware, which varies between computers.

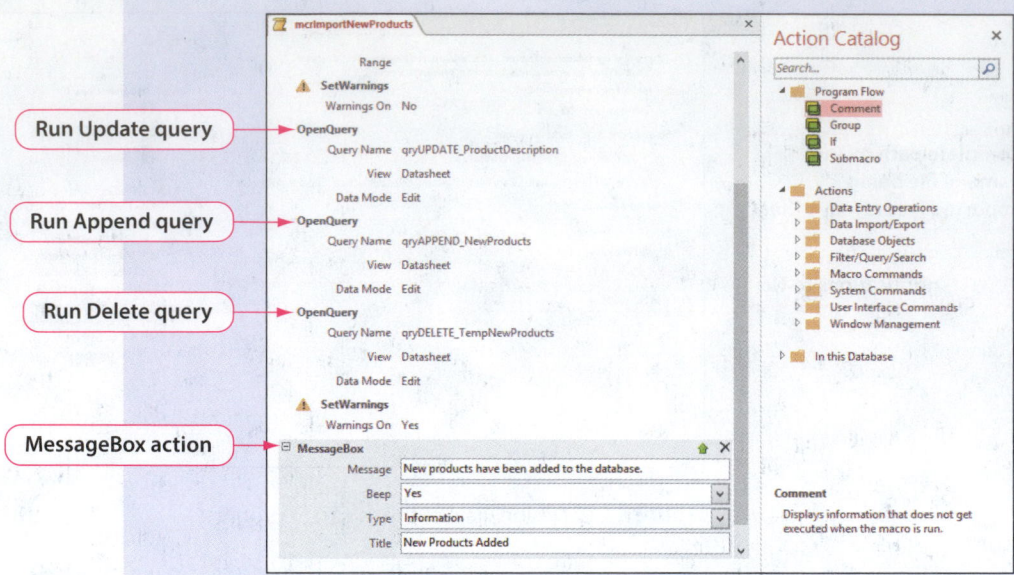

Figure 13 mcrImportNewProducts macro completed

q. **Close** ☒ the macro.

r. Open the **tblProduct** table to view the current list of products. Note that there are 25 records. **Close** ☒ the tblProduct table.

s. To test the macro, double-click **mcrImportNewProducts** in the Navigation Pane.

t. Click **OK** when prompted by the message box, open the **tblProduct** table, and then view the added records. Note that there are now 30 records. **Close** ☒ the tblProduct table.

> **Troubleshooting**
>
> Upon running this macro, if you get an error message stating "The Microsoft Access database engine could not find the object," then you most likely entered the file path incorrectly in the File Name field in the first action. Verify the path and file name are correct.

REAL WORLD ADVICE | **Set Warnings Action**

The SetWarnings action is often used to suppress warning messages when performing various tasks like running update queries and delete queries. This action must be used with caution as some warnings do provide helpful information, and the option to not perform a particular action could cause irreversible damage to the data.

The SetWarnings action does not prevent an error message from displaying if the error forces the macro to stop running. For example, if the file with new products was incorrectly named and placed in the same directory, the macro would fail with the first action.

CONSIDER THIS | Preventing Errors

A properly designed process will prevent users from making errors. What would happen if you tried to import the same file more than once? What role would the primary or composite key play in that process? What if warnings are turned off?

Create Macro Groups

Creating macro groups can make a large number of macros in a database easier to manage and maintain. A **macro group** is two or more macros that are similar in function that are stored under the same macro name. When a macro group is created, only the name appears in the Navigation Pane regardless of how many submacros it contains. For example, a macro group could contain a submacro for every report in a database that exports and or prints each report and only appear once in the Navigation Pane.

Although Access does not require the submacros in a macro group to be similar, it is best practice to create logical groups based on function and purpose when creating them. When a macro group is executed directly in the Navigation Pane or by clicking Run in Design view, only the first submacro is executed. The most common way to run a submacro is to assign it to an event on a form or report.

You can also run submacros by creating an AutoKeys macro. An **AutoKeys macro** is a macro group that assigns keys on the keyboard to execute each submacro. The macro must be named AutoKeys, and each submacro must be named with the key or key combinations on the keyboard that will be used to execute the macros. To name a key-assignment macro, use ^ to indicate Ctrl, + for Shift, and { } around key names that are more than one letter long. You are restricted to numbers, letters, Insert, Delete, and the function keys, used in conjunction with Shift and Ctrl. If the key assignment is a combination that normally does something else, then the submacro key assignment will override the normal function; for example, pressing Ctrl + F, which normally opens the Find and Replace dialog box, would no longer work if you created a new macro with the same key combination.

QUICK REFERENCE	Key Assignments
Key	**Macro Syntax**
Press F5	{F5}
Press Ctrl and type r	^r
Press Shift + F3	+{F3}
Press Insert	{INS}
Press Ctrl + F2	^{F2}
Press Delete	{DEL}

Creating a Macro Group

The Turquoise Oasis Spa database contains several reports that provide information related to employee schedules, inventory, and client services. These reports are often printed and shared with members of management. You have been asked to create a macro group that will automate the steps of opening each report, sending it to the printer, and then closing the report.

A12.08

To Create a Macro Group

a. Click the **CREATE** tab, in the Macros & Code group, click **Macro**.

b. In the Program Flow group under the Action Catalog, add a comment to the macro.

c. In the comment, using your initial and last name, type Created by initialLastname. The following macro group will open specific reports, send them to printer, and then close the reports.

d. In the Program Flow group under the Action Catalog, double-click **Submacro** to add it to the macro, and then in the Submacro name box type PrintEmployeeSchedule to give it a name.

e. In the submacro click the **Add New Action** arrow, and then select **OpenReport**. Select **rptEmployeeSchedule** for the Report Name, if necessary select **Report** for the View argument, and then if necessary select **Normal** for Window Mode.

f. In the submacro click the **Add New Action** arrow, and then select **RunMenuCommand**. Click the **Command** arrow, and then select **PrintObject** for the Command argument.

g. In the submacro click the **Add New Action** arrow, and then select **CloseWindow**. Click the **Object Type** arrow, select **Report**, click the **Object Name** arrow, select **rptEmployeeSchedule**, and then click the **Save** arrow and select **No**. Because you are not editing the report, there are no changes that need to be saved.

SIDE NOTE
Submacro Names
Each submacro in a macro group must have a unique name.

SIDE NOTE
PrintObject
If you add PrintObject to the macro, it will automatically insert the RunMenuCommand action and select PrintObject as the Command.

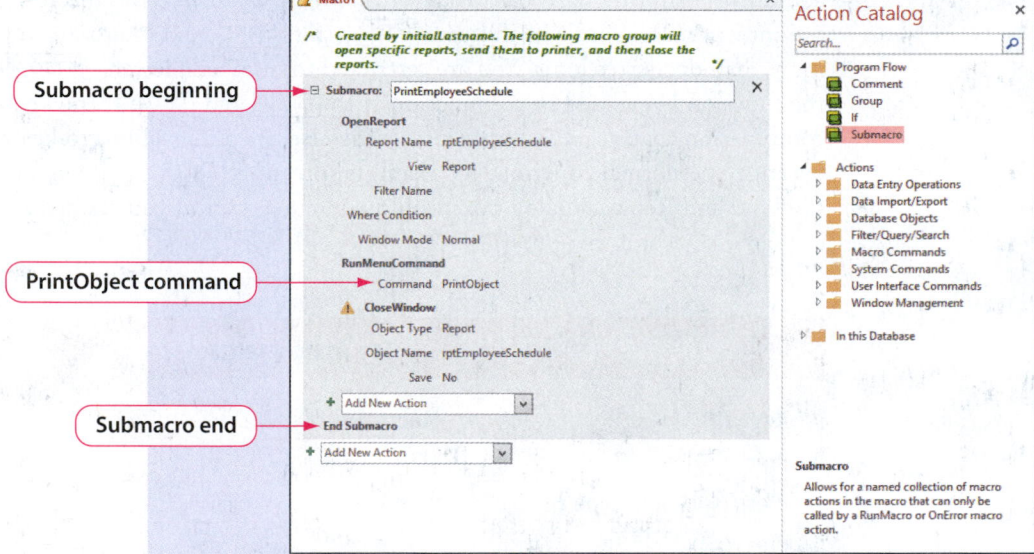

Figure 14   Design view of the macro in progress

h. Repeat Steps e–g to create two more submacros for two additional reports. Create one submacro named PrintProductInventory that opens, prints, and closes the rptProducts report. Create another submacro named PrintCustomerSchedule that opens, prints, and closes the rptScheduleByCustomer report.

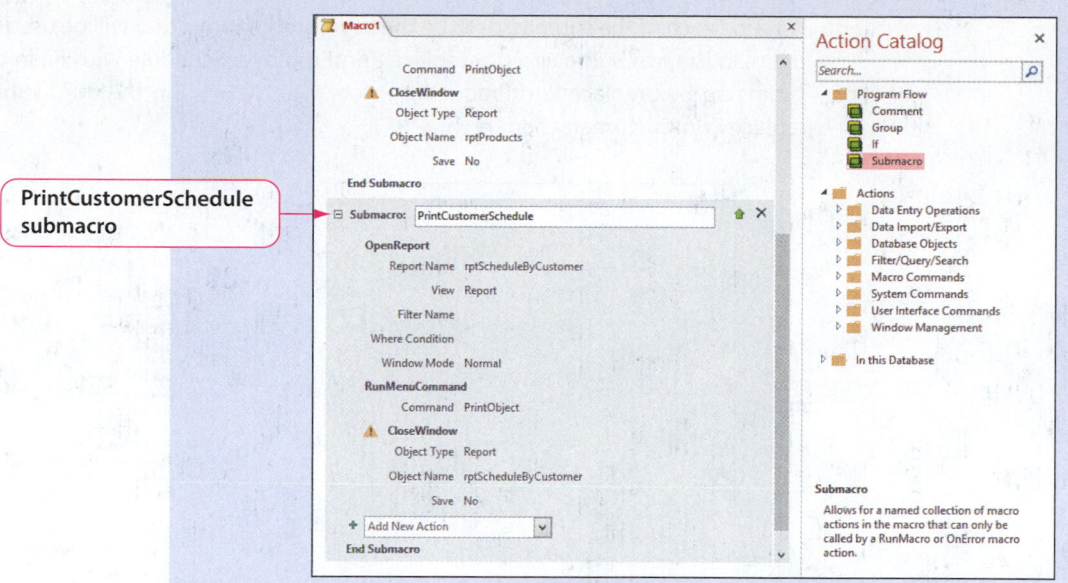

PrintCustomerSchedule submacro

Figure 15   mcrPrintReports macro completed

i.   **Save** 💾 the macro as **mcrPrintReports**, and then **Close** ✖ the macro.

REAL WORLD ADVICE   **Cutting Paper Waste**

Today's businesses rely more and more on information contained in reports to make decisions. However, many businesses are cutting waste by exporting reports and having them sent in an e-mail instead of having them printed directly from a database. You can leverage the use of macros in Access for exporting or email documents to cut back on paper waste.

Creating a Key-Assignment Macro

Because submacros cannot be executed in the Navigation Pane, you have now been asked to make the process easier by assigning keys to each submacro so that the reports can be printed simply by pressing keys on the keyboard.

A12.09

   To Create a Key-Assignment Macro

a.   Right-click the **mcrPrintReports** macro group in the Navigation Pane, select **Copy**, right-click anywhere in the Navigation Pane, and then select **Paste** to create a copy of the macro group.

b.   In the Paste dialog box type **AutoKeys**, and then click **OK**. Now that the macro group is saved as AutoKeys, key combinations can be assigned to each submacro so that they can be executed from the keyboard.

c.   In the Navigation Pane, right-click the **AutoKeys** macro, and then select **Design View**. In the comment at the top of the macro, click at the end of the text, and then type **Each submacro has an assigned set of keys used to execute.**

d. Rename each of the submacros to be the key-combinations that will be used to execute them. In the first submacro box replace PrintEmployeeSchedule with ^i. In the second submacro box replace PrintProductInventory with ^e, and in the third submacro box replace PrintCustomerSchedule with ^{F1}.

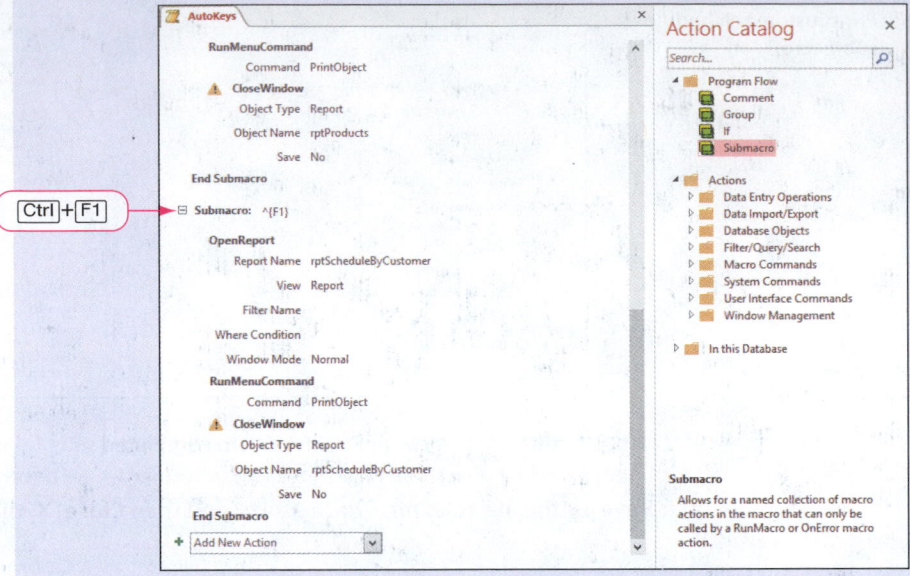

Ctrl + F1

Figure 16   Completed AutoKeys macro

e. **Save** 💾 the changes to the macro group, and then **Close** ✖ the macro.

f. Test out the new key-assigned macro group. Press and hold Ctrl and then press E, I, or F1 to print the employee schedule, inventory, or the customer schedule report.

> **Troubleshooting**
>
> For the AutoKeys macro to run the database, the database may have to be closed and reopened.

REAL WORLD ADVICE | **Maintaining Descriptive Submacro Names**

Submacros can easily be added to other macros by using the RunMacro or OnError actions, or they can be easily assigned to events. For this reason it is important to maintain a copy of the original macro group with descriptive submacro names before adding it to a macro group.

Create Macros That Run When the Database Opens

If you want a set of actions to run every time a database is opened, then you can create an **AutoExec macro**. The name "AutoExec" is reserved for use by a macro that will run automatically before any other macros when a database is opened.

Creating an AutoExec Macro

Every morning, invoice information is entered into the database for any spa service with a remaining balance that has been charged to the customer's hotel room. You have been asked to create an AutoExec macro that will automatically minimize the Navigation

Pane for optimal viewing, open the invoice form, go to a new record, and insert the pointer in the InvoiceDate field.

A12.10

 To Create an AutoExec Macro

a. Click the **CREATE** tab, and then in the Macros & Code group, click **Macro**.

b. In the Action Catalog, double-click **Comment**, and then using your initial and last name, type **Created by initialLastname. This macro will run each time the database is opened. It minimizes the Navigation Pane, opens the Invoice form in a new record, and sets the focus on the Invoice Date field.**

c. Click the **Add New Action** arrow, and then select the **SelectObject** action. Click the **Object Type** arrow, select **Form**, click the **Object Name** arrow, and then select **frmCustomerInvoices**.

d. Click the **In Database Window** arrow, and then select **Yes**.

   By selecting Yes for the In Database Window argument of the SelectObject action, you are selecting the object in the Navigation Pane and making the Navigation Pane the active window.

e. Click the **Add New Action** arrow, and then select the **MinimizeWindow** action.

   The MinimizeWindow action minimizes the active window, which in this case is now the Navigation Pane.

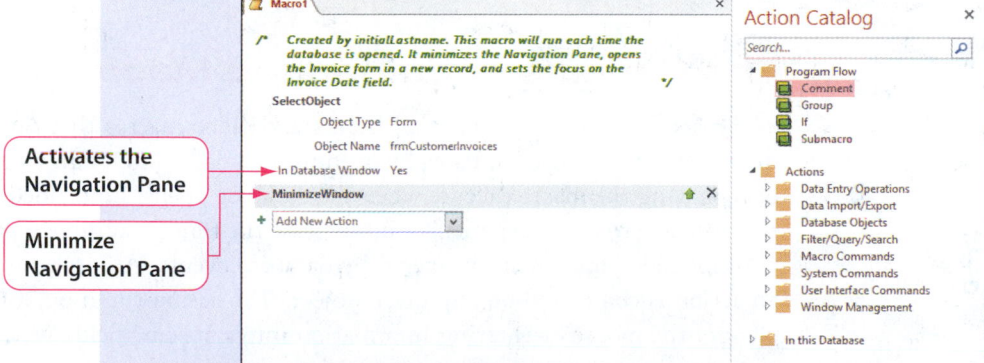

Figure 17 AutoExec macro in progress

f. Click the **Add New Action** arrow, select the **OpenForm** action, click the **Form Name** arrow, and then select **frmCustomerInvoices**.

g. Click the **View** arrow, select **Form**, click the **Data Mode** arrow, and then select **Edit**.
   Selecting Edit for the Data Mode allows data to be entered and/or modified in the form.

h. Click the **Window Mode** arrow, and then select **Normal**.

i. Add the **GoToRecord** action to the macro. Select **Form** as Object Type, select **frmCustomerInvoices** as Object Name, and select **New** for the Record argument in order to go to a new record in the form.

j. Click the **Add New Action** arrow, and then select the **GoToControl** action to the macro. Type **InvoiceDate** as the Control Name.

k. **Save** 🖫 the macro, in the Save As dialog box type **AutoExec**, and then click **OK**.

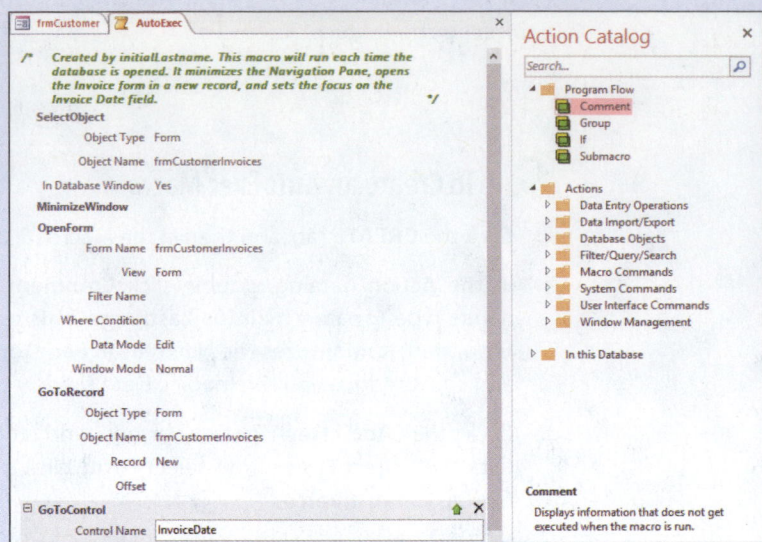

Figure 18 AutoExec macro completed

SIDE NOTE

Bypassing the AutoExec macro

An AutoExec macro can be bypassed by holding down Shift when opening the database.

l. Close ✕ the macro. To test the AutoExec macro, close and reopen the database. Notice the Navigation Pane is minimized, the frmCustomerInvoices form is opened, and the insertion point is in the InvoiceDate field.

m. Close ✕ the customer invoice form.

The Benefits of Embedded Macros

The macros created so far have all been stand-alone macros that can either be executed directly in the Navigation Pane, by opening the macro in Design view and clicking Run, or by having the macro execute when the database opens. Embedded macros can be used to create a better user experience and increase the functionality of a database.

Embedded macros are triggered by database events. A **database event** occurs when an action is completed on any given object. The action could be, for example, a simple click of the mouse or entering information into a specific field. When the specific event occurs the macro executes the actions.

QUICK REFERENCE | Common Events and Descriptions

There are many different events that occur in a database. Below is a table of the common events used to increase the effectiveness of macros and their descriptions.

Event Name	Description
On Click	Event occurs when a user presses and releases the left mouse button over an object
On Open	Event occurs when a form or report is opened
Before Update	Event occurs before an existing record is modified
After Update	Event occurs after an existing record has been modified
On Got Focus	Event occurs when the user presses Tab to focus on an object
On Lost Focus	Event occurs when the user presses Tab to move the focus from one object to another
On Dbl Click	Event occurs when a user presses and releases the left mouse button twice over an object
On Enter	Event occurs when a text-based control is clicked whether it contains text or not
On Exit	Event occurs after using a text-based control and the user presses Tab to move to the next control

Importantly, a simple act of moving from one field in a form to another field triggers several different database events. Knowing the order the events take place is critical in determining which event to associate a macro with. For example, if you have two macros that are to be run in a certain order, you want to make sure that the events they are associated with occur in that order.

QUICK REFERENCE | Order of Common Events for Controls

Events occur in form controls when you move the focus to another control or update and change data in a control.

A control is selected.
1. Enter
2. Got focus

A control is exited.
1. Exit
2. Lost focus

Data in a text box control is changed.
1. Key down
2. Key press
3. Dirty
4. Change
5. Key up

Data in a control is updated and exited.
1. Before update
2. After update
3. Exit
4. Lost Focus

In addition to events associated with controls, such as text boxes and command buttons, there are many events associated with mouse activity. In this section you will build macros that are event driven to create a more interactive user experience with a database.

QUICK REFERENCE	Order of Common Mouse Events

Events occur when a mouse button is pressed while the mouse pointer is on a control on a form.

Click a control.
1. Mouse down
2. Mouse up
3. Click

A control has focus, and the mouse selects another control.
1. Exit
2. Lost focus
3. Enter
4. Got focus
5. Mouse down
6. Mouse up
7. Click

Double-click a control.
1. Mouse down
2. Mouse up
3. Click
4. Double-click
5. Mouse up

Move the mouse pointer over a control.
1. Mouse move (This event is separate from other mouse events.)

Increase Functionality of Forms and Reports

Forms can also be enhanced by embedding macros into the form or form controls to increase the functionality and improve the user experience. By embedding the macro it becomes portable, and if you export the form into another database, any macros embedded will remain with the form object.

Embedding a Macro to Improve User Experience

Users of the Turquoise Oasis Spa database currently enter sales information in the frmCustomerPurchases form. If the patron is a returning customer, there is no easy way to locate the customer's record before adding the transaction information. In this exercise, you will first create a Datasheet form from the tblCustomer table, which is ideal for searching. You will then embed a macro into the Datasheet form that will open the frmCustomerPurchases form for the record selected.

A12.11

To Improve Form Navigation with a Macro

a. Press F11 to open the Navigation Pane. Select the **tblCustomer** table in the Navigation Pane.

b. Click the **CREATE** tab, in the Forms group, click **More Forms**, and then click **Datasheet** in the list.

Notice the Datasheet form is arranged just like a table.

c. **Save** 💾 the datasheet form as frmCustomerList_initialLastname.

d. Click the column heading **Customer ID** to select the Customer ID column.

e. If necessary, on the **DATASHEET** tab, in the Tools group, click **Property Sheet**.

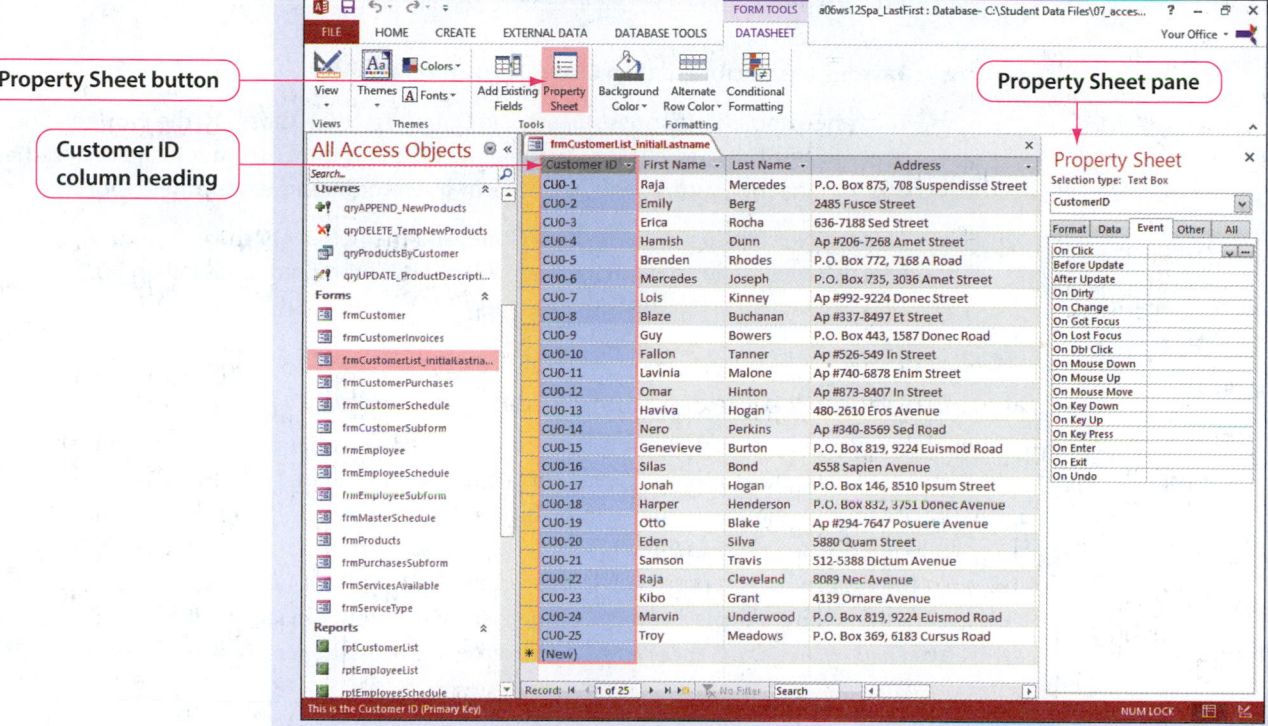

Figure 19 frmCustomerList property sheet

f. Click the **Event** tab in the property sheet, locate the On Click event, and then click the **Expression Builder** ⋯ .

g. Select **Macro Builder**, and then click **OK**.

h. Add a comment to the macro, and then using your initial and last name, type Created by initialLastname. This embedded macro will open the frmCustomerPurchases form for the Customer ID selected in frmCustomerList.

i. Click the **Add New Action** arrow, select the **OpenForm** action, click the **Form Name** arrow, select **frmCustomerPurchases**, click the **View** arrow, and then select **Form**.

j. In the **Where Condition** argument type [CustomerID]=[Forms]![frmCustomerList_initialLastname]![CustomerID].

k. Click the **Data Mode** arrow, select **Edit**, click the **Window Mode** arrow, and then select **Dialog**.

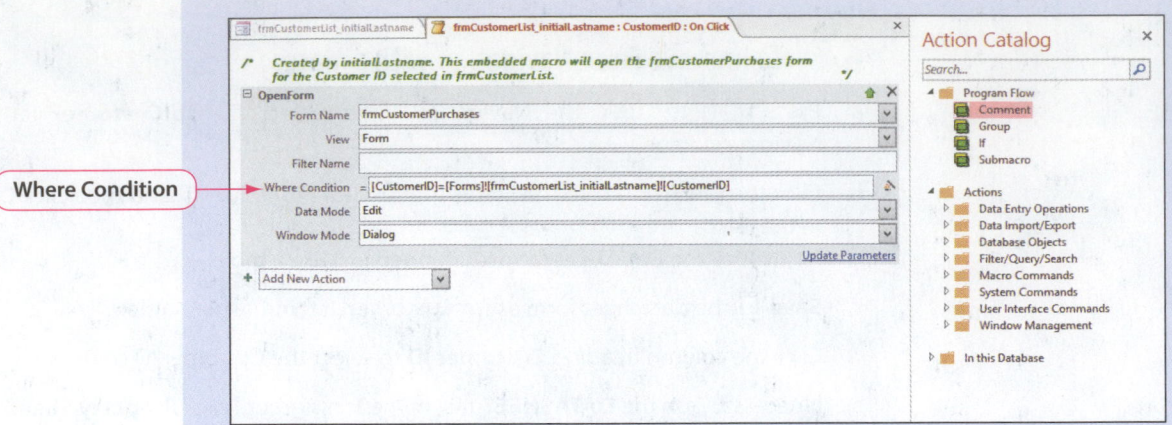

Where Condition

Figure 20 frmCustomerList OnClick macro completed

l. Save the macro, and then **Close** ☒ the Macro Builder.

m. The frmCustomerList form is still open in Datasheet view. **Close** ☒ the Property Sheet pane. To test this macro, click Customer ID **CU0-5** in the Customer ID field, and then observe the frmCustomerPurchases form open to the same customer record.

n. **Close** ☒ the frmCustomerPurchases form, and then **Close** ☒ the frmCustomerList_initialLastname form. Click **Yes** if prompted to save changes.

Embedding a Macro to Increase Functionality

The rptProducts report contains a list of all the product details including the quantity in stock. Management is often asking for the products that are running low so that more can be ordered. Although reports can be filtered by using the Filter feature on the Home tab, it is not a simple process. In this exercise, you will embed a macro that will apply a filter to the rptProducts report that will prompt the user for a number. The report will then only show the products that have fewer than that number in stock. The report will then be attached to an e-mail that can be sent to the appropriate person(s).

A12.12

▶ To Increase Functionality with a Macro

a. Right-click the **rptProducts** report in the Navigation Pane, and then select **Design View**.

b. Click the **DESIGN** tab, in the Controls group, click the **Controls** arrow, and then click the **Button** control.

c. Click to create a button to the right of the Product List report title in the **Report Header**. Position the button in between the **4"** and **5"** markings on the horizontal ruler at the top.

d. Click the **DESIGN** tab, click **Property Sheet**. In the Property Sheet pane click the **Format** tab, and then change the Caption property to Low Inventory.

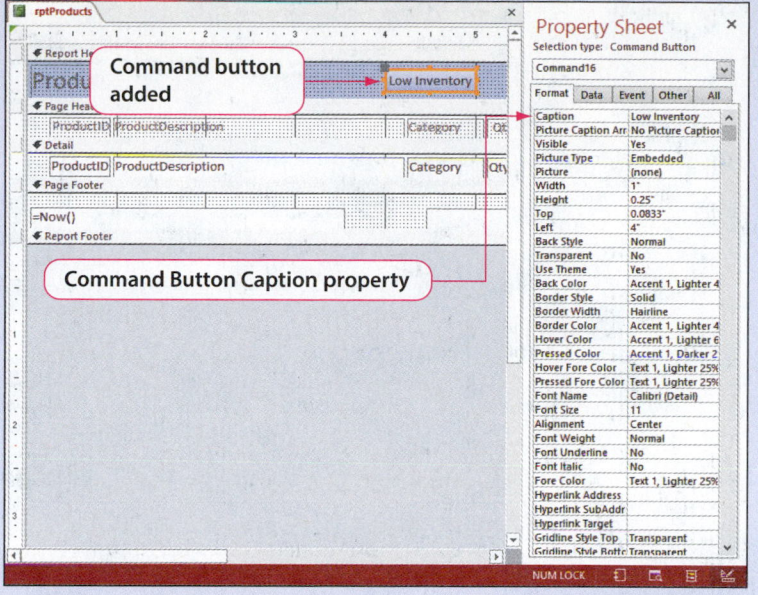

Figure 21   Design view of report with Low Inventory Command button

e. Click the **Event** tab, click in the **On Click** event, and then click the **Expression Builder** ⌶ .

f. Select **Macro Builder**, and then click **OK**.

g. Add a **Comment** to the macro, and then using your initial and last name type Created by initialLastname. This macro will apply a filter to the report, prompting the user for a number. The report will display products with fewer items in stock than the number provided and attach the filtered report to an e-mail.

h. Click the **Add New Action** arrow, and then select **SetFilter**. In the **Where Condition** argument, type [QtyInStock]<[Enter the Maximum Number].

i. Click the **Add New Action** arrow, select the **EMailDatabaseObject** action, click the **Object Type** arrow, select **Report**, click the **Object Name** arrow, and then select **rptProducts**.

j. Click the **Output Format** arrow, and then select **Excel 97 - Excel 2003 Workbook (*.xls)**.

k. Leave the To, Cc, and Bcc arguments blank. You may want to enter your own e-mail address in the To argument for testing purposes.

l. In the **Subject** argument, type Low Inventory Report.

m. Leave the Message Text argument blank.

n. Click the **Edit Message** arrow, and then select **Yes**. This allows the user to review and/or edit the e-mail before sending.

SIDE NOTE

Message Text Character Limit

The Message Text argument has a 255 character limit, just as a Text data type in tables.

The Benefits of Embedded Macros   623

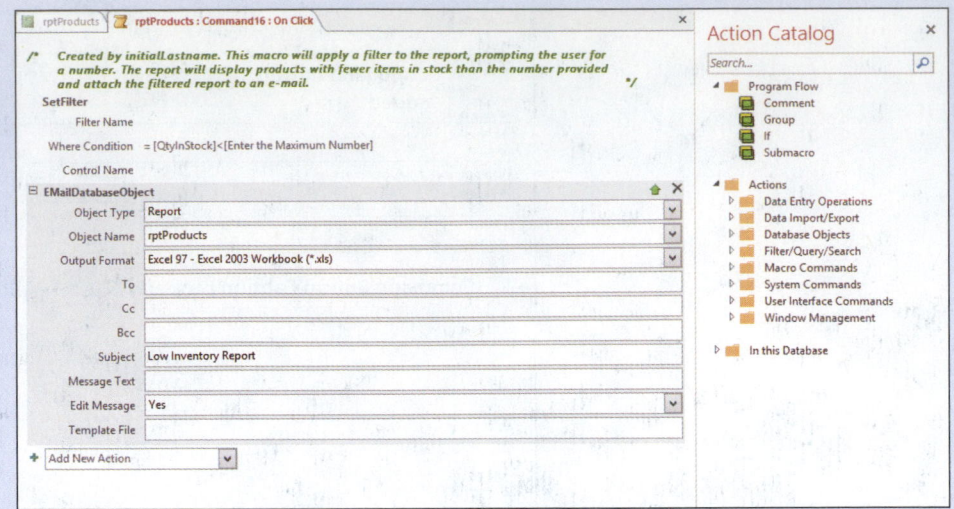

Figure 22   rptProducts Command Button macro completed

o.   **Save** 🖫 the macro, and then **Close** ✖ the Macro Builder.

p.   To test the macro, on the **HOME** tab, in the Views group, click the **View** arrow, and then select **Report View**. Click the **Low Inventory** button. In the **Enter Parameter Value** dialog box, type 25 and then click **OK**.

q.   Once your e-mail client is opened, right-click the **attached report**, and then click **Save As**. Browse to where you are storing your files, and then name the report **a06ws12rptLowInventory_LastFirst**. Replace LastFirst with your actual name and then click **Save**. Close your e-mail window, **Close** ✖ the report, and then click **Yes** to save changes.

> **Troubleshooting**
>
> The EMailDatabaseObject action uses the default e-mail client on the user's computer. This is typically Outlook, Outlook Express, or Thunderbird. The database object being attached to the e-mail is stored in a temporary table that the user must have permissions to access or the object will fail to attach to the e-mail.

Implement Complex Business Rules with Data Macros

Access databases can be enhanced to enforce complex business rules with the use of macros. For example, when a shipment of new products arrives at a warehouse, the items in the shipment must be entered into inventory. A data macro could be constructed that, when a shipment is entered into a database as received, automatically updates the inventory amounts for the products in another table. Remember that data macros are database objects stored in Access tables and are triggered by table events. Data macros are typically used to implement business logic into tables and automatically set values in fields. Since these macros are stored in tables, the logic associated with the macros is automatically applied to any forms or queries that use the tables. This functionality allows for much more complex data validation.

There are five different table events that macros can be associated with: Before Change, Before Delete, After Insert, After Update, and After Delete. The table events can be divided into two categories—"Before" events and "After" events. **Before events** occur before any changes are made to the table data, and **After events** occur after the changes have been successfully made. Before events are very simple and only support a few of the data macro actions, whereas the After events are more robust and support the full range of data macro actions.

Importantly, data macros are limited in what they can do as they only have a limited number of data actions available for use. **Data actions** are a specific, limited set of macro actions that can be used in a data macro. Certain data actions are available for certain table events. For example, data macros associated with Before events cannot prevent a record from being updated or deleted. They can only set a local variable or raise an error if conditions warrant.

QUICK REFERENCE	Table-Level Events
Event	**Description**
After Insert	After a new record has been added to this table
After Update	After any field in a record in this table has been updated
After Delete	After a record in this table has been deleted
Before Delete	When a record in this table is about to be deleted
Before Change	When a record in this table is about to be updated

QUICK REFERENCE	Common Data Actions
Action	**Description**
CancelRecordChange	Cancels the changes made to a record before the changes are committed
DeleteRecord	Deletes a record
ExitForEachRecord	Immediately exits a ForEachRecord data block
OnError	Can specify what should happen if an error occurs in a macro
RunDataMacro	Runs a named data macro
SendEmail	Sends an e-mail message from a default e-mail client
SetField	Assigns a value to a field; has to be used inside a CreateRecord or EditRecord data block
StopMacro	Stops the currently running macro; typically used when a condition makes it necessary to stop the macro

Data macros can incorporate the use of data blocks. **Data blocks** contain an area to add one or more data actions, and it executes all the actions contained as part of its operation. Data blocks are only able to be used with the After events with the exception of the LookupRecord data block, which can also be used with Before events.

Data Block	Description
CreateRecord	Actions within this block are used to create a record.
EditRecord	Actions within this block are used to edit a record.
ForEachRecord	Actions within this block will run on each record returned by the query argument.
LookupRecord	Actions within this block will run with the record selected by the query argument.

Creating a Data Macro

Currently when a customer makes a purchase at the spa the employee must manually adjust the inventory levels to indicate the change in the quantity in stock. You have been asked to automate this process to eliminate errors and increase the accuracy of the product inventory. You will be creating a data macro that will be triggered after a record is created in the tblPurchase table and that will deduct the Quantity ordered from the QtyInStock field in the tblProduct table.

SIDE NOTE

Alternate Method to Creating a Data Macro

While in Design View click the Design tab, in the Field, Record & Table Events group, click Create Data Macros to view a list of all table events.

SIDE NOTE

The Query Argument

SQL SELECT statements, such as SELECT tblProduct. [ProductID],tblProduct. [QtyInStock]FROM tblProduct; can also be used in the Where Condition field.

A12.13

To Create a Data Macro

a. Double-click the **tblPurchase** table in the Navigation Pane to open it in Datasheet view.

b. Click the **TABLE** tab, and then in the **After Events** group, click **After Insert**.

c. In the Program Flow group under the Action Catalog, add a **Comment** to the macro.

d. In the comment, using your initial and last name, type Data macro created by initialLastname. This macro will update the product inventory when a new record is created in the Purchase table.

e. In the Data Blocks group under the Action Catalog, double-click the **LookupRecord** Data Block to add it to the macro.

f. In the Look Up A Record In argument select the **tblProduct** table.

g. In the **Where Condition** argument type [tblProduct].[ProductID]=[tblPurchase].[ProductID]. This statement ensures that the record that will be edited is the record that has the same ProductID as the record being created in the tblPurchase table.

h. In the LookupRecord data block click the **Add New Action** arrow, and then select **EditRecord**.

i. In the EditRecord data block click the **Add New Action** arrow, and then select **SetField**.

j. In the **Name** argument type tblProduct.QtyInStock for the field you want to edit.

k. In the **Value** argument type [tblProduct].[QtyInStock]-[tblPurchase].[Quantity]. This will subtract the number of items being purchased from that item's inventory.

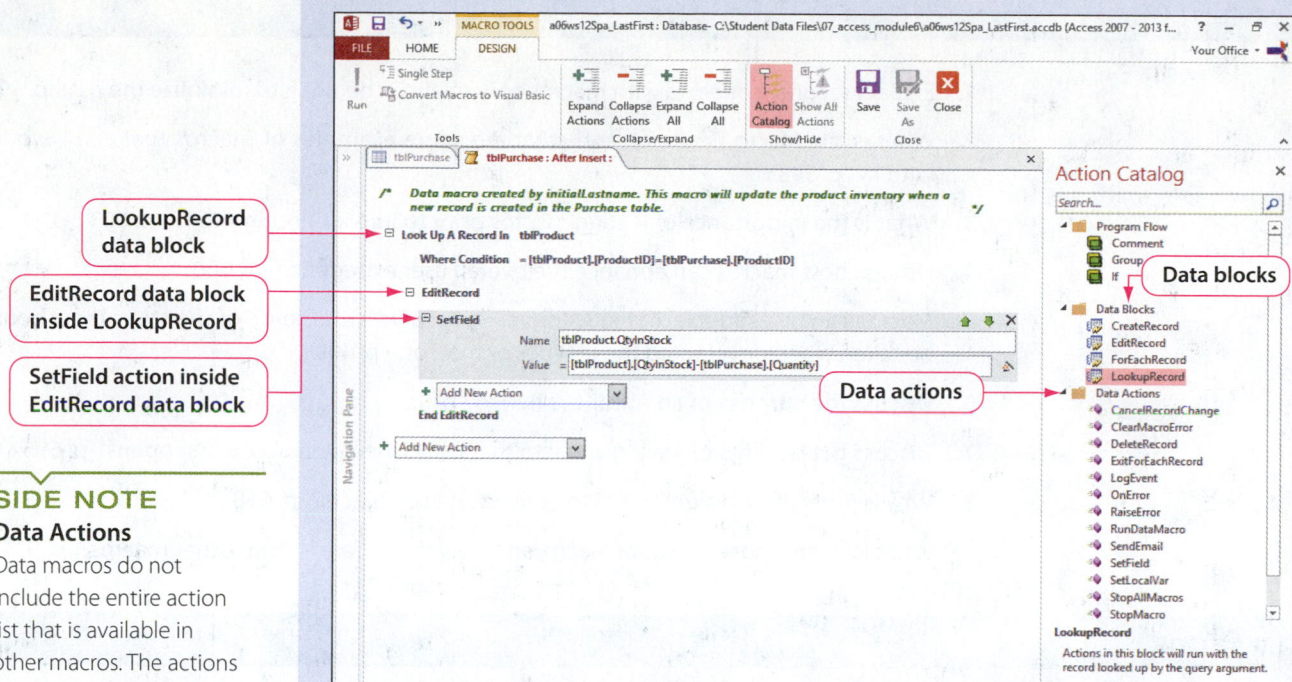

LookupRecord data block

EditRecord data block inside LookupRecord

SetField action inside EditRecord data block

Data blocks

Data actions

Figure 23 tblPurchase after Insert data macro completed

SIDE NOTE
Data Actions

Data macros do not include the entire action list that is available in other macros. The actions available will depend on whether you are using a Before or an After event.

SIDE NOTE
The SetField Action

The SetField action can only be used inside of an EditRecord or CreateRecord data block.

l. **Save** 🖫 the macro, **Close** ☒ the Macro Builder, and then **Close** ☒ the tblPurchase table.

m. Open the **tblProduct** table, take note of the quantity in stock for the New Mexico Mud Mask item, and then **Close** ☒ the tblProduct table.

n. Open the **tblPurchase** table, and on the Navigation bar click **New Record** 📑. Click the **Product** arrow, select **New Mexico Mud Mask**, click the **Customer** arrow, select **Blake**, click the **Purchase Type** arrow, and then select **Online**.

o. In the **Purchase Date** field type **1/16/2015**, and then in the **Quantity** field type **5**.

p. **Close** ☒ the tblPurchase table, and then open the **tblProduct** table to verify that there are now five fewer New Mexico Mud Mask items in stock. **Close** ☒ the tblProduct table.

q. **Close** ☒ Access. Submit your work as directed by your instructor.

CONSIDER THIS | **Product Returns and Cancelled Orders**

Products are often returned and online orders cancelled for various reasons. How could data macros be modified to automate the process of updating the inventory amount if a product is returned?

Concept Check

1. Explain security concerns with macros and what can be done to minimize the risk. p. 596

2. What is the Macro Designer, and what are some examples of macros that can be built with it? p. 598

3. What is the importance of testing macros prior to implementing them? p. 603

4. Discuss how macros can enhance the overall user experience. p. 606

5. Macros can be used to automate complex tasks. Describe some of the steps that should be taken when developing these types of macros. p. 609

6. Discuss the purpose of an AutoKeys macro. p. 613

7. Discuss the benefits of having a macro that runs when a database first opens. p. 616

8. Why is it beneficial to embed macros in database objects? p. 618

9. What is the purpose of a data macro, and how is it different from other macros? p. 624

Key Terms

Action 599
Action Catalog 599
After event 625
Argument 596
AutoExec macro 616
AutoKeys macro 613

Before event 624
Data action 625
Data block 625
Data macro 596
Database event 618
Embedded macro 596

Macro 596
Macro Designer 598
Macro group 613
Single Step 603
Stand-alone macro 596
Trusted Location 597

Visual Summary

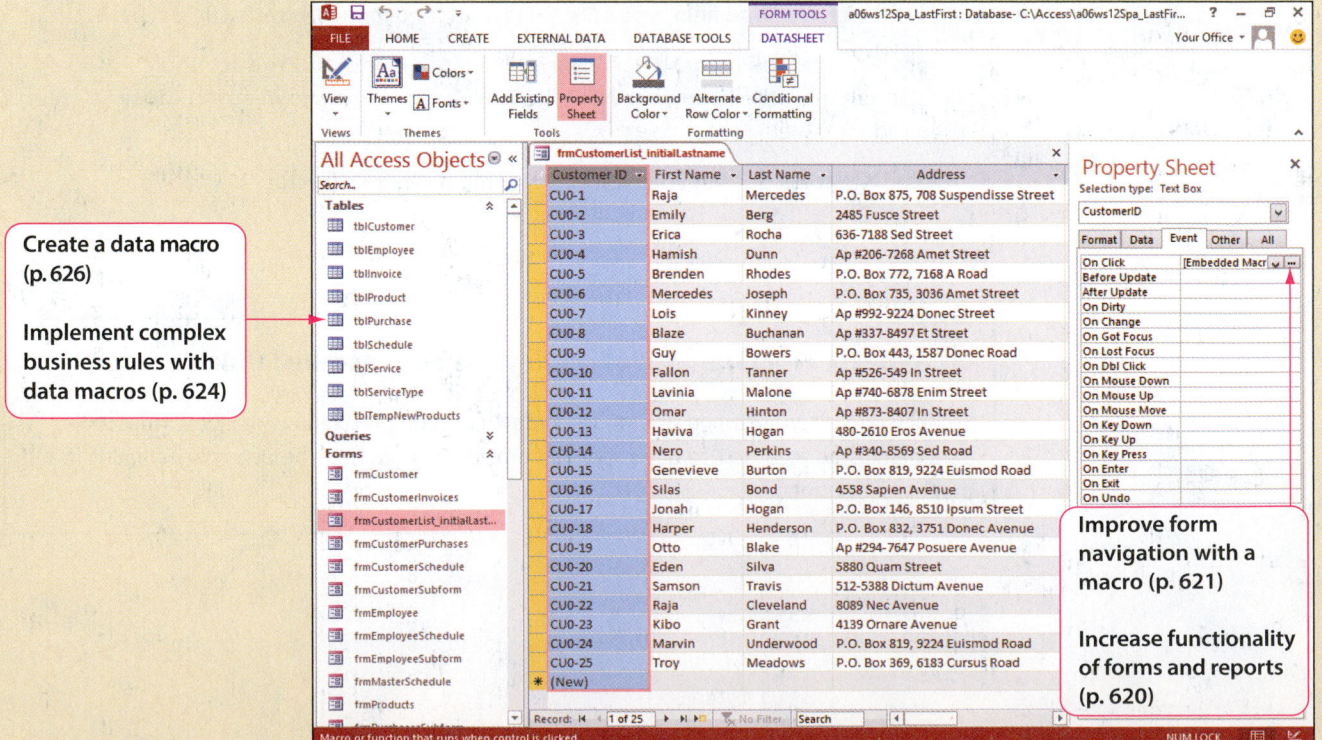

Create a data macro (p. 626)

Implement complex business rules with data macros (p. 624)

Improve form navigation with a macro (p. 621)

Increase functionality of forms and reports (p. 620)

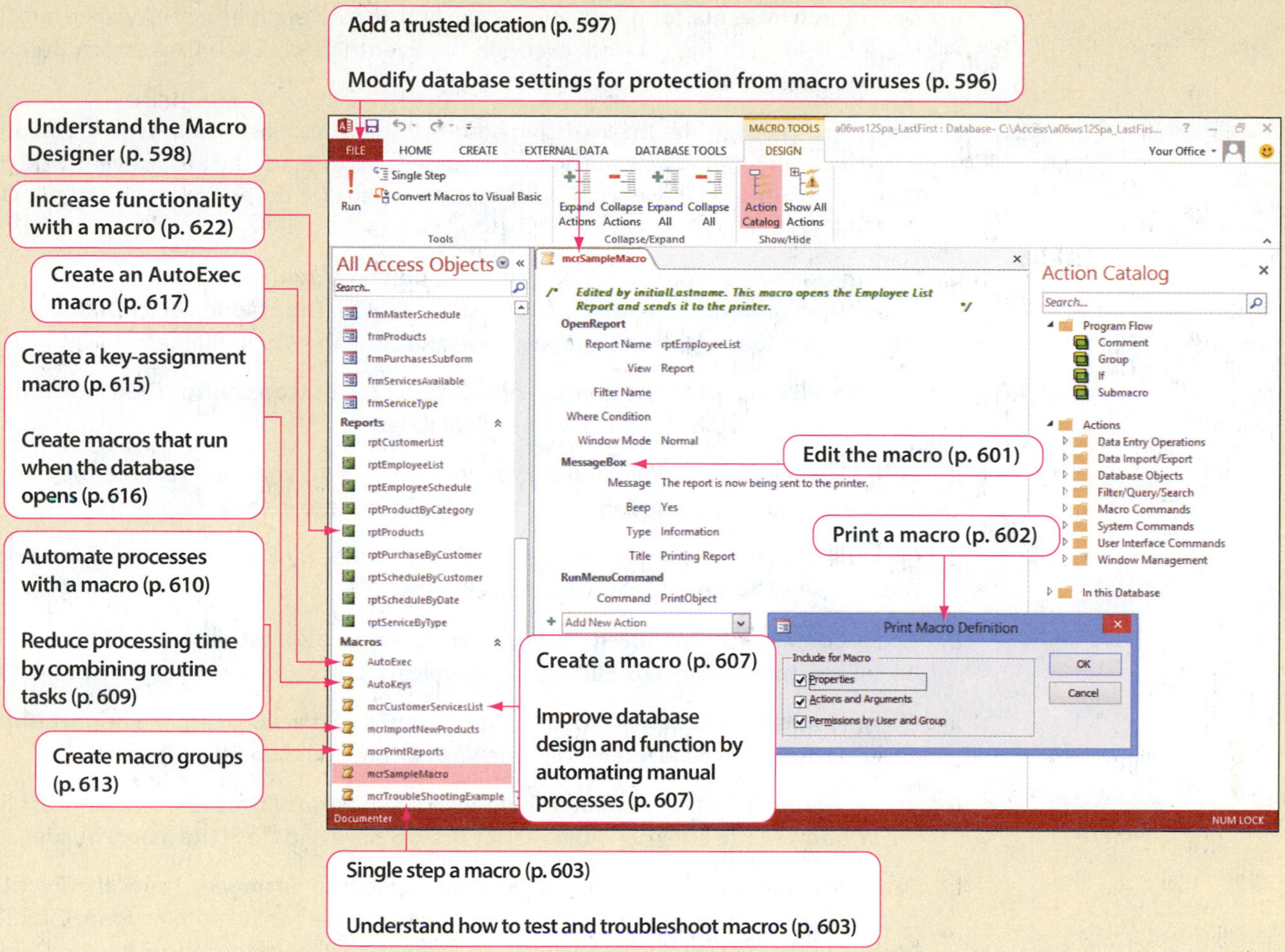

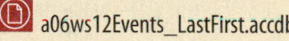

The figure shows callouts around a screenshot:

- Add a trusted location (p. 597)
- Modify database settings for protection from macro viruses (p. 596)
- Understand the Macro Designer (p. 598)
- Increase functionality with a macro (p. 622)
- Create an AutoExec macro (p. 617)
- Create a key-assignment macro (p. 615)
- Create macros that run when the database opens (p. 616)
- Automate processes with a macro (p. 610)
- Reduce processing time by combining routine tasks (p. 609)
- Create macro groups (p. 613)
- Create a macro (p. 607)
- Improve database design and function by automating manual processes (p. 607)
- Edit the macro (p. 601)
- Print a macro (p. 602)
- Single step a macro (p. 603)
- Understand how to test and troubleshoot macros (p. 603)

Figure 24   The Turquoise Spa database with macros

Practice 1

Student data file needed:

a06ws12Events.accdb

You will save your file as:

a06ws12Events_LastFirst.accdb

Production & Operations

Event Planning

The event planning department at the resort has a database containing information about past and upcoming events. The current process of adding event information to the database requires the user to enter information into separate forms, and there is no easy way to calculate and view the estimated costs associated with the event. Additionally, there is a report that contains event information for all the events. Management frequently requests the event information from a specific range of dates. The current process of extracting that information is manual and tedious.

You have been asked to improve the functionality of the Events form and report in the database by embedding macros.

a. Start **Access**, and then open the student data file **a06ws12Events**. Click the **FILE** tab, and save the file as an Access Database in the folder or location designated by your instructor with the name **a06ws12Events_LastFirst** replacing LastFirst with your actual name. If necessary, click **Enable Content**.

b. Open the **frmEvents** form in Design view, and then view the property sheet of the EventID field. Click the On Click event on the **Event** tab, click the **Expression Builder**, click **Macro Builder**, and then click **OK**.

c. Add a **Comment** to the macro. Using your first initial and last name, type Created by initialLastname. This macro will open the event items form for the active event. Add the **OpenForm** action to the macro, select **frmEventItems** for the Form Name, and then for the View argument select **Form**.

d. Type the following expression in the Where Condition argument: [EventID]=[Forms]![frmEvents]![EventID], select **Edit** for Data Mode, select **Dialog** for the Window Mode argument, and then save and close the Macro Builder.

e. Click the **DESIGN** tab, in the Controls group, select the **Button** control. Drag a **rectangle** near the bottom of the form below the Client ID label.

f. Click **Cancel** in the Command Button Wizard dialog box, and then rename the button Invoice by editing the Caption property on the Format tab in the property sheet.

g. Click the **On Click event** on the Event tab of the Property Sheet, click the **Expression Builder**, select **Macro Builder**, and then click **OK**.

h. Add a **Comment** to the macro. Using your first initial and last name, type Created by initialLastname. This macro will open the invoice details report for the active event.

i. Click the **Add New Action** arrow, select the **OpenReport** action, click the **Report Name** arrow, select **rptInvoiceDetails**, click the **View** arrow, and then select **Report**.

j. In the Where Condition argument type [EventID]=[Forms]![frmEvents]![EventID], click the **Window Mode** arrow, and then select **Dialog**. Save and close the macro builder.

k. To test each of these two embedded macros, switch to **Form** view, click the **EventID** field to view the frmEventItems form, and then close the frmEventItems form. Click the **Invoice** button to view the rptInvoiceDetails report, and then close the rptInvoiceDetails report. Save and close the frmEvents form.

l. On the CREATE tab, in the Macros & Code group, click **Macro**.

m. Add a **Comment** to the macro. Using your first initial and last name, type Created by initialLastname. This macro will open a report and filter the contents based on a user-provided date range and then send the report to the printer.

n. Click the **Add New Action** arrow, select the **OpenReport** action, click the **Report Name** arrow, select **rptEventsByDate**, click the **View** arrow, and then select **Report**.

o. In the **Where Condition** argument type [EventDate] Between [Enter first date (mm/dd/yy)] And [Enter second date (mm/dd/yy)]. Click the **Window Mode** arrow, and then select **Normal**.

p. Click the **Add New Action** arrow and select the **PrintObject** action.

q. Click the **Add New Action** arrow and select the **CloseWindow** action, click the **Object Type** arrow and select **Report**, click the **Object Name** arrow and select **rptEventsByDate**, and then click the **Save** arrow and select **No**.

r. Save the macro as mcrPrintEventsByDateRange, and then close the macro.

s. Open **rptEventsByDate** in Design view, and then in the Controls group, select the **Button** control. Create a **button** to the right of the Report title in the **Report Header**. Place the **left edge** of the button on the **3"** mark on the horizontal ruler at the top.

t. If necessary, click **Property Sheet**, and then in the Format tab of the Property Sheet pane replace the text in the Caption box with Events by Date Range. Resize the button so that all text is visible.

u. Click the **Event** tab, and then click the **On Click** event arrow. Select **mcrPrintEventsByDateRange** from the list.

v. Save the changes to the report. Switch to **Report** view, click the **Events by Date Range** button, and then type 01/01/15 for the first date and 03/31/15 for the second date.

w. Cancel or print as directed by your instructor. Close Access. Submit your work as directed by your instructor.

Problem Solve 1

Homework 1

Student data file needed:
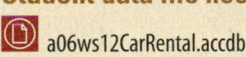 a06ws12CarRental.accdb

You will save your file as:
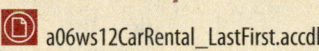 a06ws12CarRental_LastFirst.accdb

Krazy Karl's Rental Cars Database

Production & Operations

Krazy Karl's Rental Cars is a small, locally owned business that specializes in renting cars to college students at discounted rates. The database currently contains tables, queries, forms, and reports used to track customers, cars, and rental contracts. Karl would like to increase the functionality of the database by implementing some macros.

a. Open **a06ws12CarRental** and save the database as **a06ws12CarRental_LastFirst**. Replace LastFirst with your actual name. Enable content if necessary.

b. Create an **AutoExec** macro that will open the **frmContracts** form in edit mode to a new record with the CustomerID textbox control selected.

- Add a comment to the macro. Using your first initial and last name, type Created by initialLastname. This macro will be executed automatically when the database is opened. It opens the frmContracts form to a new record with the CustomerID field selected.

- Add the **OpenForm** action, select **frmContracts** for Form Name, select **Form** for View, select **Edit** for Data Mode, and then select **Normal** for Window Mode.

- Add the **GoToRecord** action, select **Form** for Object Type, select **frmContracts** for Object Name, and then select **New** for Record.

- Add the **GoToControl** action, and then type CustomerID for Control Name.

- Save the macro as AutoExec. Close and test the macro.

c. Create a Before Change data macro to the **tblContracts** table that will calculate the DueDate value based on the RentalDate and NoOfDays.

- Add a comment to the data macro. Using your first initial and last name, type Created by initialLastname. This macro will automatically calculate the DueDate value of any rental based on the RentalDate and the NoOfDays.

- Add the **SetField** action, and then type DueDate for Name and [RentalDate]+[NoOfDays] for Value.

- Save, close, and then test the macro.

d. Create an AutoKeys macro:

- Add a comment to the macro. Type Created by initialLastname as the text for the comment.

- Add **Submacro** from Program Flow.

- Add the **OpenReport** action to the Submacro. Select **rptCustomerContracts** for Report Name, select **Report** for View, type [RentalDate] Between [Enter a start date (MM/DD/YYYY)] And [Enter an end date (MM/DD/YYYY)] for **Where Condition**, and then select **Normal** for Window Mode.

- Add the **RunMenuCommand** action to the Submacro. Select **PrintObject** for Command.

- Add the **CloseWindow** action to the Submacro. Select **Report** for Object Type, select **rptCustomerContracts** for Object Name, and then select **No** for Save.
- Assign the submacro to F6 by naming it {F6}.
- Save and test the macro.

e. Save and exit Access. Submit your work as directed by your instructor.

Perform 1: Perform in Your Career

 Student data file needed:
a06ws12Flash.accdb

 You will save your file as:
a06ws12Flash_LastFirst.accdb

Zippy Flash Drives

Production & Operations

Zippy Flash Drives sells USB flash drives on college campuses. The flash drives are sold in multiple sizes and display a variety of college and sport team logos on them. Zippy Flash Drives has a basic inventory and sales tracking database, and you have been asked to enhance the functionality of the database with macros.

a. Open **a06ws12Flash** and save the database as **a06ws12Flash_LastFirst**. Replace LastFirst with your actual name and Enable Content.

b. Create an After Insert macro on the tblSales table that will update the QuantityInStock field in the tblInventory table when a new sale is made.

c. Create an After Insert macro on the tblOrders table that will update the QuantityInStock field in the tblInventory table when new orders of flash drives are received.

d. Add a command button to the frmSales form that will open the frmCustomers form to a new record so that new customers can be added before a transaction is recorded. Add a comment to the macro containing your first initial and last name that explains the purpose of the macro.

e. Create a macro group that prints the rptInventory and rptEmployeeSales reports. Add a comment to the macro containing your first initial and last name that explains the purpose of the macro group.

f. Assign a key combination to each of the macro groups.

g. Create an AutoExec macro that on startup will minimize the Navigation Pane and open the frmSales form to a new record. Add a comment to the macro containing your first initial and last name that explains the purpose of the macro.

h. Save and exit Access. Submit your work as directed by your instructor.

Additional Cases

Additional Workshop Cases are available on the companion website and in the instructor resources.

MODULE CAPSTONE

Student data file needed:

📄 a06mpMenu.accdb

📄 a06mpIndigo5.jpg

You will save your file as:

📄 a06mpMenu_LastFirst.accdb

Improving Navigation of the Indigo5 Restaurant Database

Production &
Operations

Indigo5 is a five-star restaurant that caters to local patrons in addition to clients of the resort and spa. The Menu database is used to store information regarding ingredients, recipes, and specials. The database consists of several forms used for entering new information as well as a few reports. You will create a navigation system that will give the employees access to the essential forms and reports. You will also implement business logic using a data macro to automatically set the cost of each menu item.

a. Start **Access**, and then open the student data file **a06mpMenu**. Click the **FILE** tab, and then save the file as an **Access Database** with the name **a06mpMenu_LastFirst** using your actual Last and First name. If necessary, enable the content.

b. Right-click the **frmFoodCategories** form, and then click **Design View**. Click the **Food Category ID** text box, press and hold ⇧Shift, and then click all the **text boxes** and **labels** in the form detail. Move them all down about **1"**.

c. Add a **Button** control in the **top-left corner** of the detail section. In the Command Button Wizard, verify **Record Navigation** is selected in the Categories list, click **Go To Previous Record** in the Actions list, and then click **Next**. Click **Text**, and then type **Previous Category** as the button text. Click **Next**, type **cmdPreviousCategory** as the button name, and then click **Finish**.

d. Add two additional command buttons each to the right of the previous. Refer to the table below for the specific values for the Command Button Wizard.

Category	Action	Button Text	Button Name
Record Navigation	Go To Next Record	Next Category	cmdNextCategory
Record Operations	Add New Record	Add Category	cmdAddCategory

e. Select all three buttons, on the ARRANGE tab, in the Sizing & Ordering group, click **Align**, and then click **Top** from the list of options. Click **Space/Size**, and then click **Equal Horizontal** to make all the buttons equally spaced apart.

f. With the buttons still selected, on the FORMAT tab, in the Control Formatting group, click **Quick Styles**, and then click **Moderate Effect - Blue, Accent 1**—the fifth row of the second column.

g. On the DESIGN tab, in the Views group, switch to **Layout** view. On the DESIGN tab, in the Tools group, click **Property Sheet**, under Selection type in the Property Sheet pane, click the **Record Selectors** box, click the **selection** arrow, and then click **Form**. Click the **Format** tab in the Property Sheet pane, click the **Record Selectors** box, click the **Record Selectors** arrow, and then click **No**. Click the **Navigation Buttons** box, click the **Navigation Buttons** arrow, and then click **No**.

h. Referencing the table below, make similar modifications to the **frmIngredients**, **frmRecipes**, and **frmMenu** forms. Place the buttons in a similar position as described above, apply the same Quick Styles format to the navigation buttons, and then set the Record Selectors and Navigation Buttons properties to **No**.

Form Name	Button Text	Button Name
frmIngredients	Previous Ingredient, Next Ingredient, Add Ingredient	cmdPrevIngredient, cmdNextIngredient, cmdAddIngredient
frmRecipes	Previous Recipe, Next Recipe, Add Recipe	cmdPrevRecipe, cmdNextRecipe, cmdAddRecipe
frmMenu	Previous Item, Next Item, Add Item	cmdPrevItem, cmdNextItem, cmdAddItem

i. Save and close all opened forms.

j. Click the **CREATE** tab, in the Forms group, click **Navigation**, and then click **Vertical Tabs, Left**. Save the Navigation form as frmMenuNavigation_initialLastname.

k. Click the **DESIGN** tab, and then in the Tools group, click **Property Sheet**. Under Selection type, click the **selection** arrow, and then click **FormHeader**. On the Format tab, locate **Back Color**. Click the **Builder button**, and then select **White, Background 1**, the first row in the first column under Theme colors.

l. Click the **frmMenu** form in the Navigation Pane, and then drag it to the [**Add New**] vertical tab. Click the **frmRecipes** form, and then drag it to the [**Add New**] vertical tab.

m. Continue adding the **frmFoodCategories** and **frmIngredients** forms and the **rptMenuItems** and **rptRecipeDetails** reports to the [**Add New**] vertical tabs in the Navigation form.

n. Double-click the **frmMenu** tab, select the **text**, and then rename the tab Menu. Double-click the **frmRecipes** tab, select the **text**, and then rename the tab Recipes. Double-click each of the remaining tabs, select the **text**, and then rename the tabs Food Categories, Ingredients, Menu Items, and Recipe Details.

o. Click the **Menu** tab, press and hold [Shift], and then click the **Ingredients** tab. Click the **FORMAT** tab, in the Control Formatting group, click **Change Shape**, and then click **Rounded Rectangle**. Click **Quick Styles**, and then click **Subtle Effect - Blue, Accent 1**—the fourth row of the second column.

p. Click the **Menu Items** tab, press and hold [Shift], and then click the **Recipe Details** tab. Click the **FORMAT** tab, in the Control Formatting group, click **Change Shape**, and then click **Round Single Corner Rectangle**. Click **Quick Styles**, and then click **Light 1 Outline, Colored Fill - Blue, Accent 1**.

q. Click the **icon** to the left of the title, on the DESIGN tab, in the Controls group, click **Insert Image**. Click **Browse**, select the **a06mpIndigo5** image from your student data files folder, and then click **OK** to insert the new image.

r. Click **Property Sheet**, and then, if necessary, in the Property Sheet pane, click the **Format** tab. Click the **Size Mode** box, click the **Size Mode** arrow, and then click **Zoom**. Type 3 for the **Width**, and then type .8 for the **Height** of the image.

s. Double-click the **Navigation form** title, select the **text**, and then type Menu Navigation. Save and close the frmMenuNavigation_initialLastname form.

t. In the Navigation Pane, double-click the **tblMenu** table to open it. On the TABLE tab, in the Before Events group, click **Before Change**. Add a **comment** to the data macro, that reads **Created by initialLastname. This data macro will automatically set the Cost field to be 40% of the amount in the Price field.**

u. Add the **SetField** action to the macro. Type **Cost** in the Name argument, and then type **[Price]*0.4** for the Value argument. This will automatically set the cost of the menu item to be 40% of whatever price is entered. Save and close the data macro.

v. Test the data macro by creating a new record in the tblMenu table using the information below.

MenuID	Recipe ID	Season	Meal	Special	Price	Cost
	Spinach and Mushroom Frittata	Spring, Summer	Breakfast		$8.84	

Notice that once you save the form or change records the Cost field, it is automatically set to $3.54. Changing an existing price will also cause the data macro to update the cost value. Close the table.

w. Click the **FILE** tab, click **Options**, and then click **Current Database**. Under the Application Options section, click the **Application Title** text box, and then type **Indigo5 Database**.

x. Click the **Display Form** arrow, and then click **frmMenuNavigation_initialLastname**. Click the **Compact on Close** check box. In the Navigation section, click **Display Navigation Pane** to deselect the check box.

y. Click **OK** to close the Access Options dialog box, and then click **OK** again.

z. Close the database. Start **Access**, and then open **a06mpMenu_LastFirst**. When the database reopens, the only form to open should be frmMenuNavigation_initialLastname. Also notice that the name of the application is on the title bar.

aa. Close the database, exit Access, and then submit your work as directed by your instructor.

Problem Solve 1

Student data files needed:

 a06ps1Hotel.accdb

 a06ps1Online.xlsx

You will save your file as:

 a06ps1Hotel_LastFirst.accdb

Automating Tasks in the Hotel Database

Customer Service

The hotel provides a variety of room types and amenities to accommodate the needs of its guests. The hotel reservation database is currently used to keep track of hotel reservations including information about guests, reservations, and additional purchases charged to the room from the gift shop, spa, lounge, room service, and so on.

Online and phone reservations are handled by a third party who sends a spreadsheet containing the information that is then entered into this database. You will automate this process using macros. You will also increase the functionality and usability of the database by creating a variety of macros.

a. Start **Access**, and then open the student data file **a06ps1Hotel**. On the FILE tab, save the file as an **Access Database** with the name **a06ps1Hotel_LastFirst** replacing LastFirst with your actual name. If necessary, enable the content.

b. Create a **Before Change** data macro for the **tblReservations** table:

- Using your first initial and last name, add the following comment to the data macro: **Created by initialLastname. This data macro will automatically set the CheckOutDate field based on the CheckInDate and the NightsStay fields.**

- Add the appropriate action to the macro, and then complete the required arguments to implement the business logic described in the above comment.
- Save, close, and then test the macro. In the tblGuests table, add your last name and first name to the appropriate fields. In the tblReservations table, add a new reservation using your name that begins on 5/3/2015 and lasts 3 nights. The checkout date will display 5/6/2015.
- Using your first initial and last name, create a new macro, and then add the following comment: Created by initialLastname. This macro will automate the process of importing guests and reservation info received by a third party.
- You will need to add the **ImportExportSpreadsheet** action to the macro.

  You will first be importing new guest information into the tblGuests table. The guest information to be imported is part of a named range entitled Guests in the a06ps1Online.xlsx workbook included in your student files. The named range does include field names.
- Add a **message box** that displays an informational message stating: New guests have been added to the database. Add a **beep** sound and New Guests Added as the title.
- Add another **ImportExportSpreadsheet** action. You will now be importing the data from the named range Reservations in the same workbook into the tblReservations table. This range also includes field names.
- Add a **message box** that displays an informational message stating: New reservations have been added to the database. Add a **beep** and New Reservations Added as a title.
- Save the macro as mcrImportReservationInfo_initialLastname, test the macros, and then close it.

c. Create an embedded macro in the **On Load** event of the **rptRoomChargesByReservation** report.
- Using your first initial and last name, add the following comment to the macro: Created by initialLastname. This macro will prompt the user for a Reservation ID before displaying the associated charges.
- Add the **SetFilter** action to the macro. The filter should prompt the user to: Please enter a Reservation ID for a list of charges.
- Save, close, and then test the macro.

d. Create a datasheet form based on all the fields in the **tblReservations** table. Save it as frmReservationsList_initialLastname.

e. Create an embedded macro in the **On Click** event of the **ReservationID**.
- Using your first initial and last name, add the following Comment: Created by initialLastname. This macro will display the frmReservationDetails form of the ReservationID clicked.
- Add the appropriate action to open the **frmReservationDetails** form for the same ReservationID that is clicked in this form. Have the form open in Edit mode as a dialog box.
- Save, close, and then test the macro.

f. Create an embedded macro in the **After Insert** event of the **frmGuests** form.
- Using your first initial and last name, add the following comment: Created by initialLastname. This macro will open the frmReservationDetails form after a new guest is entered.
- Add the appropriate action to open the **frmReservationDetails** form where the GuestID fields match. Have the form open in Edit mode as a dialog box.
- Save, close, and test the macro.

g. Close the database, exit Access, and then submit your work as directed by your instructor.

Student data files needed:

 a06ps2Hotel.accdb

a06ps2Logo.jpg

You will save your file as:

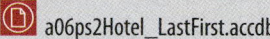 a06ps2Hotel_LastFirst.accdb

Creating a Main Menu Navigation System for the Hotel Database

Customer Service

The hotel database currently consists of several forms, queries, and reports that are all accessed from the Navigation Pane. You will create a comprehensive navigation system that will include a main menu that will include two Navigation forms with information pertaining to guests and reservations.

a. Start **Access**, and then open the student data file **a06ps2Hotel**. Click the **FILE** tab, save the file as an **Access Database** with the name a06ps2Hotel_LastFirst replacing LastFirst with your actual name. If necessary, enable the content.

b. Apply the **Ion** theme to the database.

c. Remove the navigation buttons and record selectors from the **frmGuests**, **frmEmployees**, **frmRoomCharges**, and **frmReservations** forms.

d. Create a Navigation form with vertical tabs on the left and make the following changes:

- Add **frmGuests**, **rptGuestsByLastName**, **rptGuestsByState**, and **rptReservationsByGuest** to the navigation control.

- Rename the buttons to Guests, Guests by Last Name, Guests by State, and Reservations by Guest.

- Change the shapes of the buttons to rounded rectangles.

- Remove the icon in the form header, and then change the title to Guest Navigation.

- Save the Navigation form as frmGuestNavigation_initialLastname.

e. Create a horizontal tabs Navigation form with two levels, and then make the following changes:

- On the top level, name one tab Forms and another tab Reports.

- Add the **frmReservations**, **frmRoomCharges**, and **frmEmployees** forms to the forms navigation control. Rename the tabs Reservations, Room Charges, and Employees.

- Add the **rptReservationsCountByMonth**, **rptCountOfGuestsByMonth**, **rptTotalRoomCountByType**, and **rptTotalRoomChargesByCategory** reports to the Reports navigation control. Rename the tabs Reservations Count by Month, Count of Guests by Month, Total Room Count by Type, and Total Room Charges by Category.

- Change the font color of the second-tier tabs for both Forms and Reports to white.

- Remove the icon in the form header, and then edit the text to be Reservations Navigation.

- Save the Navigation form as frmReservationsNavigation_initialLastname.

f. Create a Navigation form with horizontal tabs for the main menu, and then make the following changes:

- Add **frmGuestNavigation_initialLastname** and **frmReservationsNavigation_initialLastname** to the navigation control.

- Rename the tabs Guest Navigation and Reservations Navigation.

- Change the default logo in the form header using the image file **a06ps2Logo**. Adjust the height and width properties for the image so it is clearly displayed. Change the form header background to **White, Background 1**.

- Change the title in the form header to Main Menu.

- Add a control button to the form header under the title that will close the database when clicked. Type **Exit Database** as the caption, and then type **cmdExitDatabase** as the name.
- Save the Navigation form as **frmMainMenu_initialLastname**.

g. Make the following modifications to the database settings:
- Change the Application title to **Hotel Database**.
- Make the database display the **frmMainMenu_initialLastname** form when opened.
- Make the database compact on close.
- Hide the Navigation Pane when the database opens.

h. Close the database, exit Access, and then submit your work as directed by your instructor.

Perform 1: Perform in Your Life

Student data file needed:
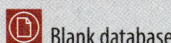 Blank database

You will save your file as:
 a06pf1Music_LastFirst.accdb

Music Collection Database

General Business

As a response to the rise in popularity of digital music libraries, vinyl record sales have begun to regain some lost ground and are increasing in popularity. A music collection database can help you keep track of your growing collection of vinyl records. Create a database that will keep track of artists, albums, and where and when the records were purchased or acquired.

Once the tables are created, you will create some forms to make data entry easier and create various reports. You will then create a Navigation form to provide easy access to these forms and reports.

a. Start **Access**, click **Blank desktop database**, and then save your database in the folder or location designated by your instructor with the name **a06pf1Music_LastFirst**. Click **Create** to create the database.

b. The tables you create should allow you to track at a minimum:
- The names of the musicians/artists
- The album name, artist, genre, and the location and date purchased
- The location name and contact information: e-mail address, website, address, and phone number

c. Create two reports for this database:
- Create one report that lists the albums purchased for each location. Save the report as **rptAlbumsByLocation_initialLastname**.
- Create one report that lists the albums purchased each month. Save the report as **rptAlbumsByMonth_initialLastname**.

d. Create forms for the tables so that information can be entered easily into the tables. You may want to use subforms to combine data entry into multiple tables:
- Add navigation buttons to each form that will allow users to Find, Go To Previous Records, Go To Next Record, and Add New Record.
- Apply a style and shape of your choosing to the navigation buttons.
- Be sure to remove any unnecessary record selectors and navigation buttons from any of the forms.

e. Create a Navigation form with vertical tabs on the left, and then add the forms and reports.
- Rename the tabs appropriately.

- Apply a style and shape of your choosing to the tabs.
- Using your initial and last name, change the title of the Navigation form header to **Initial Last Name's Music Collection**.
- Save the Navigation form as **frmMusicNavigation_initialLastname**.

f. Create an AutoKeys macro that will export each of the reports created as a PDF file to your student files directory.
- Assign the rptAlbumsByLocation_initialLastname report a key combination by pressing Ctrl and typing **a**.
- Assign the rptAlbumsByMonth_initialLastname report a key combination by pressing Ctrl and typing **b**.
- Add a comment to the macro that contains your initial and last name and a brief description of the purpose of the macro.
- Test your AutoKeys macros.

g. Have frmMusicNavigation_initialLastname be displayed when the database opens, hide the Navigation Pane, and give the application a title of **Music Collection**.

h. Close the database, exit Access, and then submit your work as directed by your instructor.

Perform 2: Perform in Your Career

Student data file needed:
 Blank database

You will save your file as:
 a06pf2IndependentFilms_LastFirst.accdb

Independent Films

General Business

Production & Operations

Independent Films is a company that arranges screenings of independent films created by local filmmakers. Independent Films needs a database that can keep track of employees, local filmmakers, venues, scheduled screenings, available films, and a contact list of fans who want to receive e-mail updates on upcoming events. You will create a database with the tables and forms required to track the appropriate information. You will then create several macros to increase the functionality of the database and enhance the user's experience.

a. Start **Access**, click **Blank desktop database**, and then save your database in the folder or location designated by your instructor with the name **a06pf2IndependentFilms_LastFirst**.

b. The tables you create should allow you to track at a minimum:
- Name, address, phone, and e-mail of employees, local filmmakers, fans, and venues that host screenings
- Title, filmmaker, and genre of the films available
- Each screening should include the date, time, venue, film title, and cost of admission.

c. Create two reports:
- One report should list the film titles available for each filmmaker. Save this report as **rptFilmsByFilmmakers_initialLastname**.
- One report should list the screenings occurring each month. Save this report as **rptScreeningsByMonth_initialLastname**.

d. Create forms for each of the tables so that information can be entered easily into each table:
- Add navigation buttons to each form that will allow users to Find Record, Go To Previous Record, Go To Next Record, and Add New Record.
- Apply a style and shape of your choosing to the navigation buttons.

e. Create an AutoExec macro that will minimize the Navigation Pane and display the Screenings form when the database opens and have the insertion point placed in the venue field of a new record. Include a comment to the macro that contains your initial and last name and a brief description of the purpose of the macro.

f. At each screening event, a kiosk is available for guests to sign up for the Independent Films mailing list:

- The information stored in the kiosks is e-mailed as a spreadsheet. Create a macro that will automatically import the information into a temporary table.
- You want to be careful not to automatically import user-generated information into your database as it could create duplicate data.
- You may want to create a sample spreadsheet containing the appropriate information in order to test your macro.
- The macro should display a message box informing the user that the data has successfully been imported into the temporary table.
- Save this macro as **mcrImportFans_initialLastname**. Include a comment to the macro that contains your initial and last name and a brief description of the purpose of the macro.

g. Embed a macro into the On Load event of the rptFilmsByFilmmakers_initialLastname report that will prompt the user for a filmmaker's last name and then display the films for that filmmaker. Include a comment to the macro that contains your initial and last name and a brief description of the purpose of the macro.

h. Embed a macro into the On Click event of a command button on the rptScreeningsByMonth_initialLastname report that will export the report as a PDF to your student file directory. Include a comment to the macro that contains your initial and last name and a brief description of the purpose of the macro.

i. Test your macros, and then exit Access. Submit your work as directed by your instructor.

Perform 3: Perform in Your Team

Student data file needed:

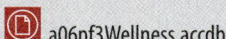 a06pf3Wellness.accdb

You will save your files as:

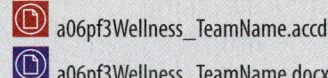 a06pf3Wellness_TeamName.accdb

a06pf3Wellness_TeamName.docx

Employee Wellness Program

Human Resources

Your employer has begun an employee wellness program. To cut health care costs at the company, the human resources department is encouraging all employees to eat healthy foods and exercise more. As part of this initiative, your team has been asked to develop a database that will allow company employees to log basic calories and food intake. The database will also allow for tracking the type and minutes of exercise by each employee. A basic database has been created for your team. You will need to make the following changes to the database.

a. Select one team member to set up the database by completing Steps b–e.

b. Start **Access**, open the database **a06pf3Wellness**, and then name it a06pf3Wellness_TeamName. Replace TeamName with the name assigned to your team by your instructor.

c. Open your browser, and then navigate to **https://www.skydrive.live.com**, **https://www. drive.google.com**, or any other instructor-assigned storage location. Be sure all members of the team have an account on the chosen system—Microsoft or Google account. Create a new folder, and then name it TeamName_Assignment. Replace TeamName with the name assigned to your team by your instructor.

d. Upload the a06pf3Wellness_TeamName database to the TeamName_Assignment folder, and then share the folder with the other members of your team. Make sure that the other team members have permission to edit the contents of the shared folder.

e. Because databases can only be opened and edited by one person at a time, it is a good idea to plan ahead by determining what each team member will be responsible for contributing. Create a new Word document in the assignment folder, and then name it **a06pf3Wellness_TeamName**. Replace TeamName with the name assigned to your team by your instructor.

f. In the Word document, each team member must list his or her first and last name as well as a summary of their planned contributions. As work is completed on the database, this document should be updated with the specifics of each team member's contributions.

g. Insert a Page Footer in the document and include your team number and page number.

h. You will need to complete the following actions in the database.
- Create forms for entering new foods, consumed foods, and exercises into the database.
- Create a Navigation form that organizes the three forms created in the prior step. Change the default title on the Navigation form to your team name. Choose an appropriate picture to replace the default picture on the Navigation form.
- Choose a theme for the database.

i. You will need to complete the following actions to the Navigation form.
- Add the rptCalories and rptExercise reports to the Navigation form.
- Choose a shape and style combination for the buttons representing forms on the Navigation form.
- Choose a different shape and style combination for the buttons representing the reports on the Navigation form.

j. Add navigation buttons to each form that will allow users to Find, Go To Previous Records, Go To Next Record, and Add New Record. Remove any record selectors and navigation buttons from the forms.

k. Create an AutoExec macro that, when the database is opened, will hide the Navigation Pane and open the Navigation form. Add a comment to the macro that contains your team name and a brief description of the purpose of the macro.

l. Create an AutoKeys macro. Choose a key combination that prints the rptExercise report. Choose a second key combination that prints the rptCalories report. Add a comment to the macro that contains your team name and a brief description of the purpose of the macro.

m. Once the assignment is complete, share the TeamName_Assignment folder with your instructor or submit your work as your instructor directs. Make sure that your instructor has permission to edit the contents of the folder.

Perform 4: How Others Perform

Student data file needed:

 a06pf4HipHopFundraising.accdb

You will save your files as:

 a06pf4HipHopFundraising_LastFirst.accdb

 a06pf4HipHop_LastFirst.docx

HipHop Fund-Raising

Sales & Marketing

You have just taken a new job at a local fundraising organization called HipHop Fund-Raising. HipHop Fund-Raising seeks out local hip-hop talent to perform concerts in order to raise funds for various charities. A database has been created to track the various aspects of the organization. As you navigate through the database, you will notice some design flaws in the Navigation forms as well as error messages when attempting to run some of the macros.

You will need to make some changes to this database to increase its usability, and then you'll answer some questions below.

a. Open the **a06pf4HipHopFundraising** database, and then save it as a06pf4HipHopFundraising_LastFirst.

b. Open Word, create a new blank document, and then save it as a06pf4HipHopFundraising_LastFirst. This will be used to answer any questions below.

c. When the database is opened, an error message is displayed. Explain what is causing the error, what can be done to correct it, and then make the appropriate change.

d. There is a data macro associated with the tblDonations table After Insert event that is not working. Explain why it is not working properly, and then make the appropriate changes so that it does.

e. The mcrOpenContributors macro is causing error messages to be displayed when executed. Use the single step process to determine where the macro is failing, and then make appropriate corrections. Explain why the macro was failing and what you did to correct it.

f. The frmHipHopNavigation form needs some work to make it user friendly. List the things you feel are missing from the Navigation form in terms of both content and design. Once you have made your list, implement those changes to improve the design and function of the frmHipHopNavigation Navigation form.

g. Close the database, exit Access, and then submit your work as directed by your instructor.

WORKSHOP 13 | USE VBA IN ACCESS

Prepare Case

The Red Bluff Golf Course & Pro Shop Putts for Paws Charity Database

Finance & Accounting

The Red Bluff Golf Course & Pro Shop sponsors the charity tournament, Putts for Paws, to raise money for the local pet shelter. The scope of the database is limited to tracking the monies being raised for the Putts for Paws event. Participants in the tournament are assigned roles, and any role may donate money to the event. You are adding increased functionality to the database. Some of the functionality that must be added cannot be accomplished with macros and must be accomplished using VBA. This will make tasks such as importing data and data entry more efficient.

Linn Currie / Shutterstock

REAL WORLD SUCCESS

"During an internship at a public accounting firm, I used VBA in Access to create a database that imported data from Excel, allowed for some user manipulation through menus, and printed reports. I also worked with many Access databases in which others had used VBA to transform them into what looked like stand-alone programs. These databases automated much of our work and printed the reports we gave to clients."

- Lauren, recent alumni

Student data files needed for this workshop:

 a07ws13Putts.accdb

 a07ws13List.xlsx

You will save your files as:

 a07ws13Putts_LastFirst.accdb

 a07ws13Putts_LastFirst.accde

Introducing VBA Basics

Microsoft Office contains a powerful programming language called **Visual Basic for Applications**, more commonly known as **VBA**. The tools for using this language are installed by default in most instances. Many people incorrectly perceive that you need to be a programmer in order to use any of it. VBA can allow for a wide variety of enhancements to any Microsoft Office application. In this section, you will use VBA to enhance the functionality of databases.

Understand the Functionality of VBA in Access

VBA is particularly valuable in automating repetitive tasks similar to macros, but it provides you with additional tools. These tools allow you to create more robust and dynamic tasks such as automatically populating a form field or prompting a user to select a file for importing. The code that you will write in this workshop is called a procedure in VBA. Each **procedure** contains a series of statements or instructions that are executed as a unit.

To better understand VBA it is helpful to consider two common approaches to programming. **Object-oriented programming** uses objects—such as a form in Access—to design applications. **Objects** are combinations of data and code that are treated as a single unit. The application can respond to events that occur in relation to the object. **Event-driven programming** uses an event—such as moving to the next record of a form to trigger the execution of code. VBA is triggered by events within a database. The code can then invoke other events or make changes to objects within the application.

In Microsoft Access, this object hierarchy has been replicated in the structure of the application. Access contains a top-level Application object that then contains other objects such as forms or buttons. These objects then have changeable properties such as background colors or the value of a text box. Objects also have **methods** that are actions—such as SaveAs—that control the object's behavior.

VBA in one Microsoft Office application can also be used to interact with other Office applications. Illustratively, VBA can be used to export tables from Access to an Excel spreadsheet or to populate an e-mail message in Outlook with data from an Access form. These are just a couple of the tasks that can be completed with VBA.

Convert an Existing Macro to VBA

Sometimes the best way to learn what VBA can do is to see how Office itself uses VBA. Consider the Putts for Paws charitable event. The event organizers must track participants and the donations made by these participants. The golf course has recently added a web service that allows participants to register for the event online. This system produces an Excel file on a daily basis that lists any new participants who have registered for the event. Given the recent success of the event, the number of participants has increased dramatically, and new participants sign up on a regular basis. You have been asked by Barry Cheney to modify the Putts for Paws database such that it can easily import these new Excel lists.

> **REAL WORLD ADVICE** | **Why Not Use a Saved Import?**
>
> Saved Imports in Access 2013 are extremely useful for automating the repetitive task of importing a file into Access. However, this process only works when the filename and location are always the same. Mobile users or users working with filenames that change on a regular basis can be frustrated with Saved Imports. Any change in the file structure renders the Saved Import useless. VBA can accommodate for changes.

Opening the Starting File

A macro already exists in the database that would import a spreadsheet from the correct folder on the user's computer. The mcrImportParticipants macro imports a list of participants from the file a07ws13List.xlsx into the table tblParticipant. This macro will result in an error if the file is not named exactly as listed previously or if it is in a different location. Currently, the macro is set up to import the a07ws13List.xlsx file from the C:\Temp folder of the user's computer. The macro is embedded in a button on the Imports tab of the frmPuttsMenu navigational form in the Putts database.

A13.00

 To Open the Putts for Paws Database

a. Start **Access**, and then open the student data file **a07ws13Putts**.

b. Click the **FILE** tab, and then save the file as an **Access Database** in your Access Workshop 13 folder with the name a07ws13Putts_LastFirst using your last and first name. If necessary, enable the content.

> **Troubleshooting**
>
> Depending on the configuration of your computer, you may not always be prompted to enable content when you first open a database in Access. Entering the Trust Center and setting the Macro Settings to Disable all macros with notification will display the Security Warning anytime you open a database that contains macros or Visual Basic. Conversely, by establishing a Trusted Location, you have the option of enabling all content in databases that are stored in the specified location.

Converting an Existing Macro to VBA

Because the Macro Builder in Access does not allow for file selection to occur when importing files with the ImportExportSpreadsheet macro action, this process is limited in its functionality. Your task is to convert this macro into VBA and edit the macro to allow the user to select the file to import. Additionally, Barry Cheney wants users to be able to select multiple files for import. He has stated that some participants are still being tracked manually in a different Excel spreadsheet.

A13.01

 To Convert the Macro into VBA

a. Right-click the **mcrImportParticipants** macro in the Navigation Pane, and then click **Design View**.

b. Click the **DESIGN** tab, and then in the Tools group, click **Convert Macros to Visual Basic**.

c. Clear the check box to **Add error handling**, and then leave the check box for **Include macro comments** selected. Error handling and commenting will be discussed later in this workshop, but the conversion process will give a demonstration of this process.

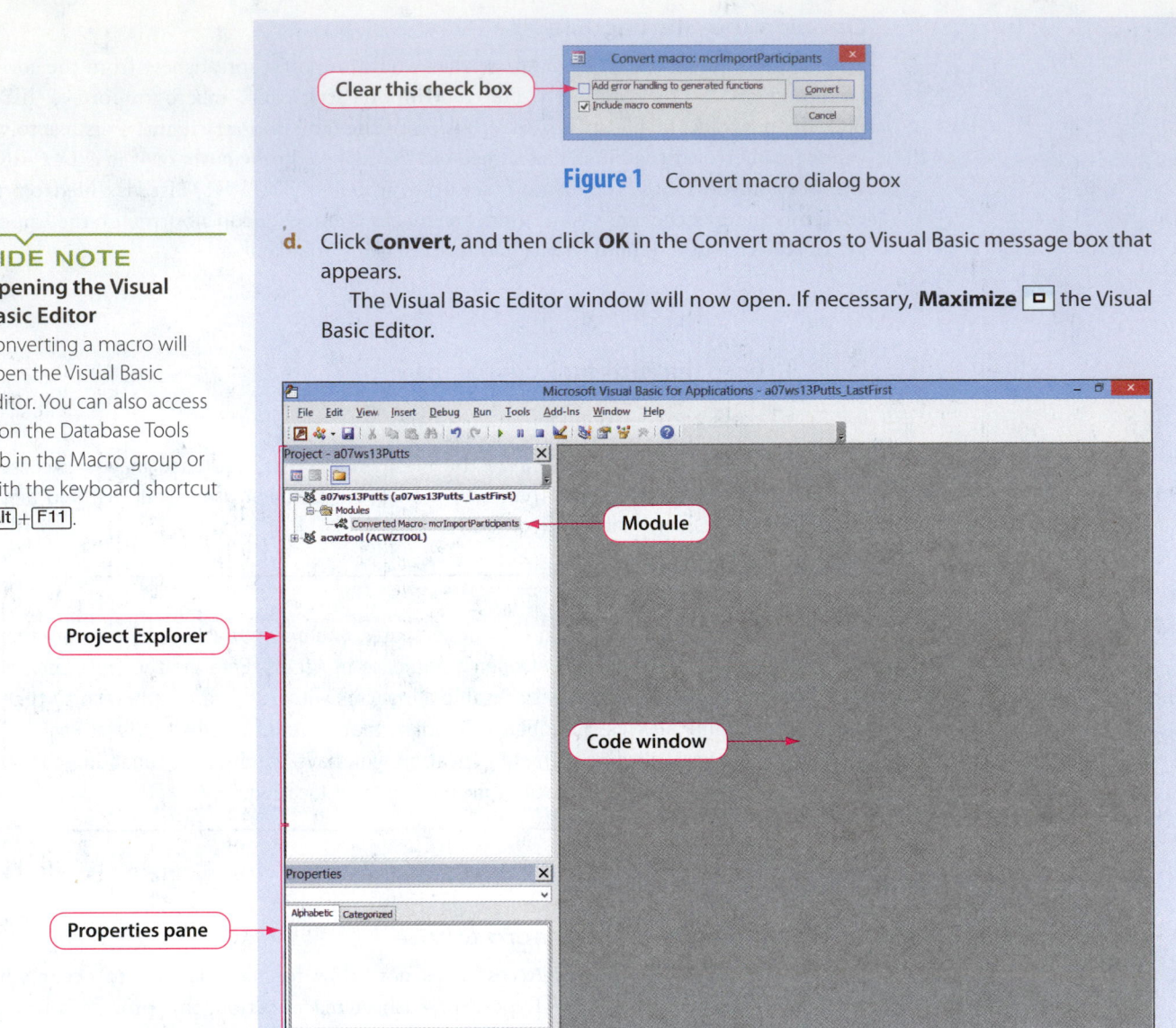

Figure 1 Convert macro dialog box

Clear this check box

d. Click **Convert**, and then click **OK** in the Convert macros to Visual Basic message box that appears.

The Visual Basic Editor window will now open. If necessary, **Maximize** ◻ the Visual Basic Editor.

Module

Project Explorer

Code window

Properties pane

Figure 2 The Visual Basic Editor

SIDE NOTE
Opening the Visual Basic Editor
Converting a macro will open the Visual Basic Editor. You can also access it on the Database Tools tab in the Macro group or with the keyboard shortcut Alt + F11.

Examining the VBA

The **Visual Basic Editor** is the tool built into Microsoft Office that is used for creating and editing VBA. At the top of the screen is the title bar with the name of the database that is currently open and being edited. Directly under the application title are the Menu bar and Standard toolbar that are visible by default. On the left side of the Visual Basic Editor is the Project Explorer. The **Project Explorer** contains a list of the currently open Access Database objects that contain VBA procedures and a list of modules within the current database. VBA in an Access database can be embedded either in a specific Access object—such as a form or a button—or within a module. **Modules** are used to store VBA procedures that can be referenced or called by other procedures or events in the database. This is helpful especially when a single procedure might be used in several different instances in a database. For example, a message box with a common statement could be created as a procedure and then used in other procedures throughout the database.

The larger window on the right of the Visual Basic Editor is the **Code window**. This is where you can edit the text of any procedure.

REAL WORLD ADVICE | **Macros vs. VBA**

Anything that can be done with a macro can be accomplished in VBA. In fact, most macros are created with VBA. So why use VBA if you can use a macro? VBA provides additional functionality that macros do not provide. Once you have experience with VBA it is often faster and more efficient to create a few lines of code than to create macros. In fact, best practice is to try not to switch back and forth between VBA and macros.

A13.02

To Open the Converted Macro in the Code Window

a. Double-click **Converted Macro - mcrImportParticipants** in the Project Explorer window to open the module. If necessary, **Maximize** the Code window.

b. Examine the text of the module displayed currently in the Code window. The Code window contains the individual procedures for the module along with other items discussed later in the workshop.

The contents of the Code window are shown in Figure 3. At the top of the Code window is the Object box. The **Object box** displays the name of the object that contains the procedure such as a form or command button. If the procedure exists within a module, the Object box will display (General). Notice that next to the Object box is the Procedure box. The **Procedure box** is a list that allows you to navigate quickly between the Declarations section and the individual procedures in the open module.

The **Declarations section** contains declarations that apply to all procedures within the module. **Declarations** define user-defined data types, variables, arrays, and constants. By default all Access modules contain the Option Compare statement in the Declarations section. The **Option Compare** statement sets the string comparison method for the module. In a new database, the default statement is Option Compare Database. This sets the string comparison to the database default. The two settings for the Option Compare statement are Text and Binary. The **Option Compare Text** setting results in case-insensitive comparisons. The **Option Compare Binary** setting examines the ASCII values for the characters contained in a string and is therefore case sensitive.

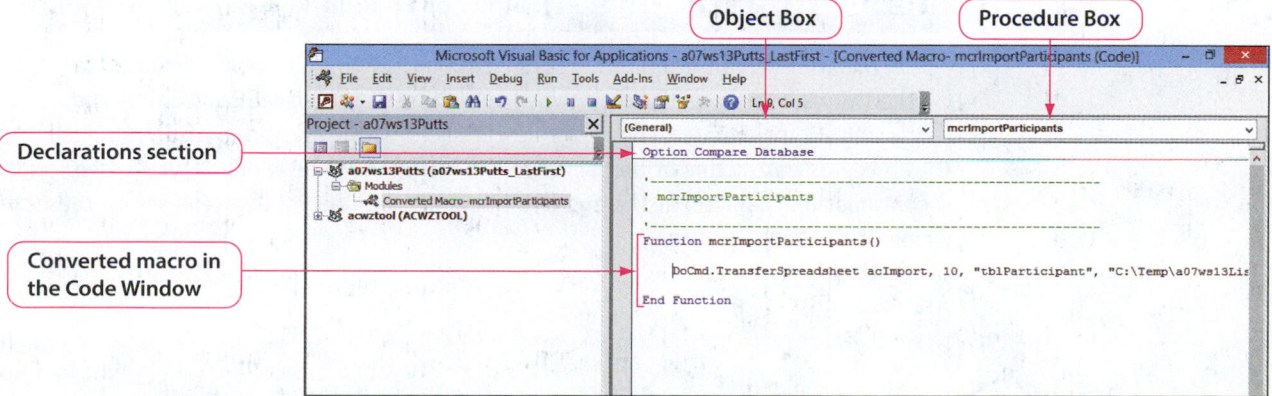

Figure 3 Converted macro in the Visual Basic Editor

CONSIDER THIS | Text vs. Binary

Using the Option Compare Text statement causes Access to evaluate the strings "text" and "Text" as equal in a VBA procedure. Using Option Compare Binary would result in the same two strings being evaluated as not equal in a VBA procedure. The database default is binary. Are there benefits to changing the default setting?

After the Declarations section is the first procedure of the module. Modules can contain multiple procedures. The procedure in this module is the macro that was converted to VBA. In this instance, the procedure is a function. A **function** executes instructions and returns a value to another procedure. Functions are called by other procedures, whereas a **Sub procedure** runs on its own or can be called by another procedure. Sub procedures perform a set of instructions and can pass multiple values to other procedures. Each function you create starts with the statement "Function" followed by the name you give the function. In this case, the name is mcrImportParticipants. The function can contain multiple tasks and must end with the statement "End Function".

Edit and Structure VBA Procedures

In the conversion process, a comment was placed above the function in the newly created module. Comments are strings of text that will not be processed as part of the procedure. Comments will be discussed later in this workshop. Before examining the individual lines of the procedure, look over the format of the text in the Code window. An important aspect of writing VBA is to keep the code legible so that you and others can interpret what is happening. This means using indentation, comments, and line breaks liberally.

You need to take extra steps to keep the code legible and to document what steps you are taking and why. This makes it easier for you and others who work within the database to understand what the procedure is doing while editing it. One of these steps will be using Tab to create indentations in the code.

Also be aware, VBA procedures lack word wrapping in the Code window. Because the Code window does not word wrap like Microsoft Word or other word-processing programs, lengthy strings of code will extend continuously to the right. This creates code that is extremely difficult to read. To break a line of code across two lines, a line continuation character can be used. A **line continuation character** consists of a single space followed by a single underscore character as the last character in a line of code. This tells the Visual Basic Editor that the two lines of code should be treated as one.

REAL WORLD ADVICE | Lines of Code in VBA

The Visual Basic Editor interprets statements of code on a line-by-line basis. In other words, typing part of a statement on a line of the Visual Basic Editor and pressing Enter before the end of the statement will invoke an error. If you need to break a lengthy line of text across two lines of the Code window, type a line continuation character at the end of a line and continue your statements on the next line of the Code window.

The DoCmd Object

The **DoCmd object** allows Access actions to be performed from within VBA. This can include opening a report, telling Access not to show warning messages, or closing an object. Typing DoCmd into the Code window or using the Object Browser will show a list of all methods associated with the DoCmd object. The Object Browser can be opened by clicking on the Standard toolbar in the Visual Basic Editor. The **Object Browser** lists all VBA objects along with the associated methods and properties for each object. Now, you will examine the DoCmd object in more detail.

A13.03

To Examine the DoCmd and Break the Statement

a. Examine the line of code that begins with the DoCmd object.

Notice that this line of code is indented. Indentations indicate that you are taking action within the procedure. Liberal use of white space combined with line indentation creates a more legible procedure.

b. Examine the statement that follows DoCmd.

The TransferSpreadsheet method is used to import an Excel spreadsheet into the database. The properties associated with a method will allow for further control of how the method behaves. In this example, the TransferSpreadsheet method uses several properties to control actions—such as which folder to open by default and whether to import, export, or link to the spreadsheet file.

c. On the line of the Code window that begins with **DoCmd**, click after the **comma** that follows the number **10**. Press [Spacebar], type _ and then press [Enter]. Using a line continuation character will allow you to break a single statement across two lines of code without creating errors in the code.

Underscore allows the Visual Basic Editor to break one statement across two lines

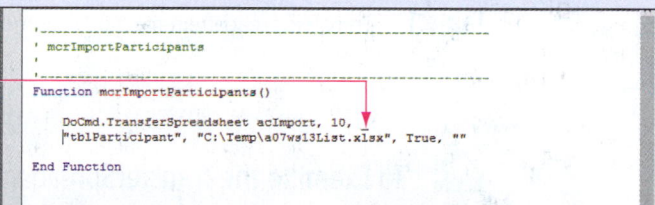

Figure 4 DoCmd object

The TransferSpreadsheet Method

For importing, exporting, and linking tasks, VBA uses the Transfer methods. The particular method used is specific to the object that is the focus of the task. The **TransferSpreadsheet method** allows Access to import, export, or link to spreadsheet files specifically. This object has six arguments. An **argument** is a constant, variable, or expression that is passed to a procedure. Table 1 lists the arguments for the TransferSpreadsheet method.

Argument Name	Description	Example
TransferType	This argument refers to the type of action that is to take place with the object.	acImport, acExport, acLink
SpreadsheetType	This argument refers to the type of spreadsheet that will be imported by the database.	acSpreadsheetTypeExcel12 or the number 10
TableName	This is the name of the Access table that will be used during the process in the Transfer Type argument. This can also be a select query in which the data from the query can be exported. When importing, Access will append records to an existing table. If no table exists, Access will import the records into a new table.	"tblName"
FileName	This is the name of the spreadsheet file to be used during the process selected in the TransferType argument.	"C:\Temp\FileName.xlsx" When a specific file is used, the path and filename must be given in quotation marks.
HasFieldNames	This argument specifies whether the spreadsheet contains field names in the first row of the spreadsheet. If the spreadsheet does contain field names, this argument should be set to Yes. If the spreadsheet does not contain field names, this argument should be set to No. The default is No.	Yes/No and True/False can be used interchangeably here.
Range	This optional argument can be used to define a specific range of cells from the spreadsheet to import. If this argument is left blank, Access will import or link the entire worksheet.	"Data" or "" for blank

Table 1   TransferSpreadsheet method arguments

A13.04

To Examine the TransferSpreadsheet Method

a.   Notice in this TransferSpreadsheet method the Transfer Type is set to **acImport**. This tells Access to import the file.

b.   Notice the Spreadsheet type is set to **10**. This is the numeric equivalent of the default for this argument, Excel Spreadsheet.

c.   Notice the TableName argument is the tblParticipant table and the table name is in quotation marks. This argument requires the name of the table to be a text string.

d.   Notice the FileName argument contains **"C:\Temp\a07ws13List.xlsx"**. This is the path and name of the spreadsheet that will be imported. Here, this value is a fixed path and filename just as it was in the original macro. Using VBA, you will need to change it to make this procedure more flexible.

e.   Notice the HasFieldNames argument is set to **True**. This tells Access the spreadsheet does have the appropriate column headers.

SIDE NOTE
Property Names

When typing an argument, there are often numeric equivalents for the property names. Right-click and select Quick Info after typing an argument to view the numeric equivalent.

> **Troubleshooting**
>
> A HasFieldNames argument set to True requires an exact match. If the column headings in the target Excel spreadsheet do not match the Access field names, an error message will be displayed and the data will not be imported.

f. Notice the Range argument displays "", the equivalent of a blank to indicate the default value. This directs Access to import the entire worksheet.

g. Notice the End Function statement ends the function. When the procedure comes to this statement it will not process any remaining code.

For this macro to work as required by Barry Cheney, it must allow the user to select the correct file or files from a dynamic location on the user's computer. VBA can be used to add this functionality and control how the user interacts with the resulting processes.

The FileDialog Object

To allow users to select one or more files for importing, some new code must be inserted prior to the DoCmd object. The **FileDialog object** can be used to allow the user to select the file or files needed for the import process. The FileDialog object has the following four properties that control how the object is executed in the procedure.

QUICK REFERENCE	FileDialog Object Properties	
Property	**Description**	**Property Name in VBA**
Open	This option allows the user to select one or more files that can be opened in the host application.	msoFileDialogOpen
SaveAs	This option allows the user to select a single file that can then be used to save the current file.	msoFileDialogSaveAs
FilePicker	This option allows the user to select one or more files. The file paths are stored in the SelectedItems method of the FileDialog object.	msoFileDialogFilePicker
FolderPicker	This option allows the user to select a path (folder). The file path text is stored in the SelectedItems method of the FileDialog object.	msoFileDialogFolderPicker

The FileDialog object also has several methods that can be used to customize the behavior of the File Dialog window. In this example, the methods AllowMultiSelect, Title, and SelectedItems will be used. The AllowMultiSelect method lets users select multiple files for import. The Title method allows you to set a customized title for the File Dialog window. The SelectedItems method stores the names of the files that are selected for import.

REAL WORLD ADVICE | The AutoComplete Feature

VBA uses an AutoComplete feature similar to that found in other Microsoft Office applications such as writing field names in query criteria. For example, typing "FileDialog." in the Visual Basic Editor—as seen in Figure 5—will open a list of objects and methods that are found within the FileDialog object. These can be selected with the pointer or by typing enough of the desired item to prompt Access to highlight the item, which you then can complete by pressing Tab.

AutoComplete feature displays methods and properties associated with objects

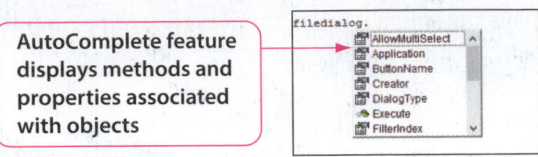

Figure 5 FileDialog object showing the AutoComplete feature

The first step in creating the File Dialog process is to declare a variable as a FileDialog object. Creating and declaring variables will make the procedure more efficient and easier to follow as more statements are added. **Variables** are placeholders that can be set to a hard-coded value or to an object within VBA and then later modified during the execution of the procedure. The different variable data types are listed in Table 2. Because you can customize the names of variables in VBA, you can create variables that are easy to remember and identify. The **Dim statement** begins the process of declaring a variable. This is followed by the name the user wants to define as a variable. This can be any string that does not begin with a number or is not a reserved word in VBA. Following the name of the variable is the As Type portion of the statement.

Name	Description	Example
Byte	An integer from 0 to 255	125
Boolean	Used in true or false variables	True or False
Integer	Numeric data type for whole numbers	125
Long	Numeric data type for large integer numbers	9,000,000,000
Currency	Numeric data type that allows for 4 digits to the right of the decimal and 15 to the left	1234.67
Single	Numeric data type used for numbers that can contain fractions	125.25
Double	Numeric data type used for large numbers that can contain fractions	9,000,000,000.25
Date	Stores date and time data	7/1/2013 8:35:56 AM
String	A variable length of text characters	"Your import is complete"
Object	Used to create a variable that stores a VBA object	FileDialog
Variant	The default data type if none is specified; can store numeric, string, date/time, empty, or null data	125 or "One hundred and twenty-five"

Table 2 Variable types

User-defined types can also be created in VBA modules and assigned to a variable with the Dim statement. In this instance, a variable will be created and set to be equal to the FileDialog object. This allows for easy use of the FileDialog object later in the procedure. Variables do not have to be defined using the Dim statement. Not formally defining variables often leads to errors in your VBA as the result of misspellings of variable names. This is only required if the Option Explicit statement is used in the Declarations section of the module. The **Option Explicit statement** will force any variables in a procedure to be defined using the Dim statement.

CONSIDER THIS | **Using Option Explicit**

VBA can interpret variable names without the use of the Dim statement. By default, defining a variable is not a required action. You could simply type MyVariable = 10, and the procedure would use the value "10" wherever you used the variable "MyVariable". This can lead to problems such as an unnoticed misspelling of a variable name. Additionally, any undefined variables will be of the Variant data type. Because Variant covers such a wide variety of data types, the application must evaluate the data and determine the appropriate data type. This increases the processing time. Using the Option Explicit statement in the Declarations section—the first line of the Code window—forces the definition of any variable names, preventing this type of situation from occurring. What advantages are there to using Option Explicit?

REAL WORLD ADVICE | **What Is the Best Way to Identify the Properties of an Object?**

The properties associated with an object can be referred to by name but also can sometimes be referred to by a defined constant. For example, with the FileDialog object you can choose to use the File Open dialog box by typing msoFileDialogOpen or, more simply, by typing the number 1. Using the defined constant will accomplish the same desired outcome as typing msoFileDialogOpen. The difference is that using the defined constant may be faster to type, but it may not be as intuitive to decipher when reviewing the procedure later on.

A13.05

 To Add the FileDialog Object to the Procedure

a. Place the insertion point on the blank line above the **DoCmd.TransferSpreadsheet** action in the Code window.

b. Press ⌈Enter⌉, and then press ⌈Tab⌉ to indent the code.

c. Type **Dim ParticipantDialog as Object**, and then press ⌈Enter⌉.
   This creates a variable called ParticipantDialog. This variable can be reused throughout the procedure and will be more efficient when setting the object properties later on.

d. Type **Set ParticipantDialog = Application.FileDialog(msoFileDialogOpen)**, and then press ⌈Enter⌉ twice. Before completing this line of code a Microsoft Visual Basic for Applications message box may appear. If it does, click **Yes**, and then see the Troubleshooting tip for further explanation of this message box.

Manually Adding Object Libraries

Plug-in applications and legacy object libraries may need to be added manually. This can be accomplished by clicking the Tools menu and selecting References.

Troubleshooting

Objects in VBA exist in library files. Objects become available in the Code window when these library files are referenced in the Visual Basic Editor. The FileDialog object is not included in the default libraries that are referenced in Access 2013. Access will automatically install a reference for the correct object library when you enter the FileDialog object into the Code window. The message box in Figure 6 is displayed when Access adds the appropriate library for the FileDialog object. If the proper library file did not load, add the Microsoft Office 15.0 Object Library to the list of references.

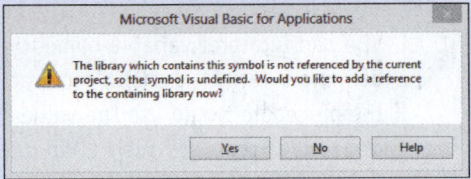

Figure 6   Add a library reference

e.   Examine the Set statement. The Set statement tells the application that the variable, ParticipantDialog, will be used as a FileDialog object.

```
'-----------------------------------------------
' mcrImportParticipants
'-----------------------------------------------
Function mcrImportParticipants()

    Dim ParticipantDialog As Object
    Set ParticipantDialog = Application.FileDialog(msoFileDialogOpen)

    DoCmd.TransferSpreadsheet acImport, 10, _
    "tblParticipant", "C:\Temp\a07ws13List.xlsx", True, ""

End Function
```

Figure 7   FileDialog object added to the procedure

CONSIDER THIS | **Using the Filters Method**

The Filters property of the FileDialog object can prove useful for customizing the File Open dialog box. Using this method, the VBA procedure can reset the filter on the dialog box so that only spreadsheet files are initially viewed. This prevents a user from accidently selecting the incorrect file type. To accomplish this, use the .Filters method. To be safe, start by clearing out any existing filters (.Filters.Clear). Then add the filters you want the user to see. For example, .Filters.Add "Excel Spreadsheet", "*.xlsx" will allow users to select any .xlsx files. Filters.Add "All Files", "*.*" adds an all files option that displays any file in the current folder. Why might it be useful to restrict which files a user can select in a dialog box?

The With Statement

Once a variable has been assigned to serve as a placeholder for the FileDialog object there are several properties that can be set. The **With statement** allows for an efficient way of using several methods or setting multiple properties on a single object. Without it, the developer would be required to type the object's full name for each method used or property set. With statements are simple to use and provide for enormous time savings in coding. To use a With statement type "With ObjectName", where "ObjectName" is the object you want to modify. Inside of a With statement each method used or property to edit is preceded only by a single period. Each With statement must be accompanied by an "End With" statement. While With statements can be nested in order to apply settings to multiple properties within an object, they can only act upon one object at a time.

A13.06

 To Create a With Statement and Set the FileDialog Properties

a. Ensure that the insertion point is on the line above the **DoCmd** object. Type **With ParticipantDialog**, press `Enter`, and then press `Tab`. This inserts an indentation to create a more legible code structure.

b. Type **.Title = "Select New Participant List(s)"**, and then press `Enter`. This sets the title of the dialog box that appears to display "Select New Participant List(s)".

> **Troubleshooting**
>
> Inside the With statement be sure to type a period character before the method or property you are working with. In the prior step, typing "Title" without the period character will result in an error.

c. Type **.AllowMultiSelect = True**, and then press `Enter`.
This allows the user to select multiple files to import. Setting this method to False limits the user to selecting only one file at a time.

d. Press `Backspace` to align the insertion point with the With statement.

e. Press `Enter`.

For the FileDialog object to function properly, the procedure must determine if the user selected any files. Alternatively, the user could end the operation by clicking the Cancel button in the File Dialog window. If this happens, the procedure should end after the Cancel button is clicked. An If statement can be implemented within the With statement to determine the outcome of the user's actions.

REAL WORLD ADVICE | **Capitalization**

While VBA is by default case sensitive, when typing the name of a variable, method, or property, the Visual Basic Editor will automatically capitalize the text for you. For example, in the FileDialog property, .AllowMultiSelect, typing .allowmultiselect will be automatically corrected to the appropriate case.

If Statements in VBA

If statements in VBA work similarly to those found in Access and Excel, though the syntax is slightly different. Each If statement must follow the basic syntax:

If [Condition] Then

[Statement]

Else

[Statement]

End If

REAL WORLD ADVICE | **When to Nest If Statements in VBA**

You can nest If statements to take into account multiple logical tests. In VBA, there is an alternative to nesting If statements. If statements in VBA can use ElseIf before the Else statement in order to continue to consider additional conditions being met. The use of the ElseIf statement would look like this:

IF [Condition1] Then

[Statement]

ElseIf [Condition2] Then

[Statement]

Else

[Statement]

End If

The .Show method of the FileDialog object displays the selected type of dialog box to the user and returns to the procedure a True value if one or more files were selected. If no files were selected .Show returns a False value. For the process being created in the Putts for Paws database, if .Show returns a value of True, the procedure should import the files to the appropriate table. If .Show returns a value of False, a message should be displayed stating that the operation was cancelled and the procedure should be exited.

A13.07

To Create the Import Process

a. Ensure the insertion point is on the line above the **DoCmd** object, and then press [Tab] to indent the current line.

b. Type **If .Show = True then** and then press [Enter].

c. Press [Tab] to create an indentation.

d. Type **Dim ImportFileName as Variant** to define a variable that will hold the names of the files selected by the user. Using the Variant type is required here and will be discussed later.

e. Click **before** the **DoCmd** statement, and highlight the **two lines** of this code. Press [Tab] twice to align this statement with the prior Dim statement.

   This allows the import to run if the .Show property is true. Because the procedure will need to account for multiple files, additional code will be required. This will be revisited in the next step.

f. Click after the last argument of the **DoCmd** statement, press Enter, and then press Backspace. This aligns the pointer with the same column as the If portion of the statement.

g. Type **Else** and then press Enter. This begins the False portion of the If statement.

h. Press Tab, and then type **Msgbox "You cancelled the import"** to create a new message box. This message box will tell the user that the import process has been stopped by clicking Cancel in the File Dialog box.

i. Press Enter, and then press Backspace.

j. Type **End If** and then press Enter.

k. Press Backspace. This aligns the pointer with the same column as the With Statement.

l. Type **End With** and then press Enter.

With statement and the ParticipantDialog object

If statement

End With closes the With statement

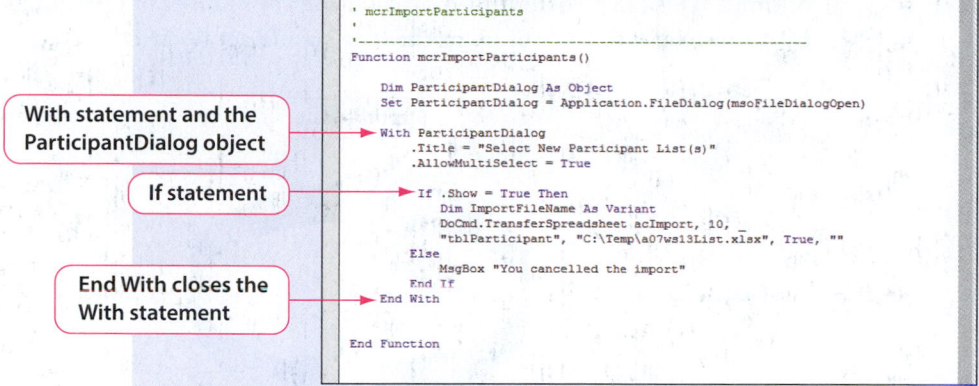

```
'------------------------------------------------------------
' mcrImportParticipants
'------------------------------------------------------------
Function mcrImportParticipants()

    Dim ParticipantDialog As Object
    Set ParticipantDialog = Application.FileDialog(msoFileDialogOpen)

    With ParticipantDialog
        .Title = "Select New Participant List(s)"
        .AllowMultiSelect = True

        If .Show = True Then
            Dim ImportFileName As Variant
            DoCmd.TransferSpreadsheet acImport, 10, _
                "tblParticipant", "C:\Temp\a07ws13List.xlsx", True, ""
        Else
            MsgBox "You cancelled the import"
        End If
    End With

End Function
```

Figure 8 Import procedure

REAL WORLD ADVICE **Message Boxes in VBA**

The Msgbox function is an extremely useful function. In VBA, a message box can display customized text and buttons in addition to the standard OK, Cancel, and Yes/No buttons familiar in Microsoft applications. Similar to the process of commenting code, message boxes provide a convenient method of keeping your users informed about the status of the application that they are using.

The procedure that has been created and edited to this point will function as follows: When the procedure is executed, first it declares the variable ParticipantDialog as an Access object. The procedure then defines the variable as a FileDialog object with a File Open parameter. Next, using a With statement, the title of the File Open dialog box is set, and the object is enabled to accept multiple file selections from the user. Alternatively, Access will display a message box stating that the user cancelled the import if the Cancel button in the dialog box is clicked. To complete the procedure, a loop will be added to the True portion of the If statement to account for situations where the user selects multiple files for importing.

Create and Use Loops in VBA

When the user selects a file to import, the procedure stores the name of the file in the SelectedItems property of the FileDialog object. It then imports that file into the appropriate table. If the user were to select multiple files, each filename would be stored in the same property and imported. The process for importing the appropriate files listed in the .SelectedItems FileDialog property happens on a file-by-file basis. In other words, each file selected will force the procedure to access a new filename and import the file as an individualized action.

This type of repetitive action is often one of the main reasons macros or VBA are used to automate a process in Access. **Loops** are used to execute a series of statements multiple times. Loops are similar to If statements in that they evaluate a condition and act depending on the status of the condition. Loops offer a distinct difference in that they allow the statements contained within the loop to be executed multiple times depending on the constraints of the loop. Figure 9 demonstrates a programmatic loop. The number of times the loop runs can be determined two ways. Loops can run until a condition is determined to be true or false. Loops can also be set to run until they have executed a specific number of times. This can be determined by counting the number of repetitions that have run or by counting the number of items the loop should act upon.

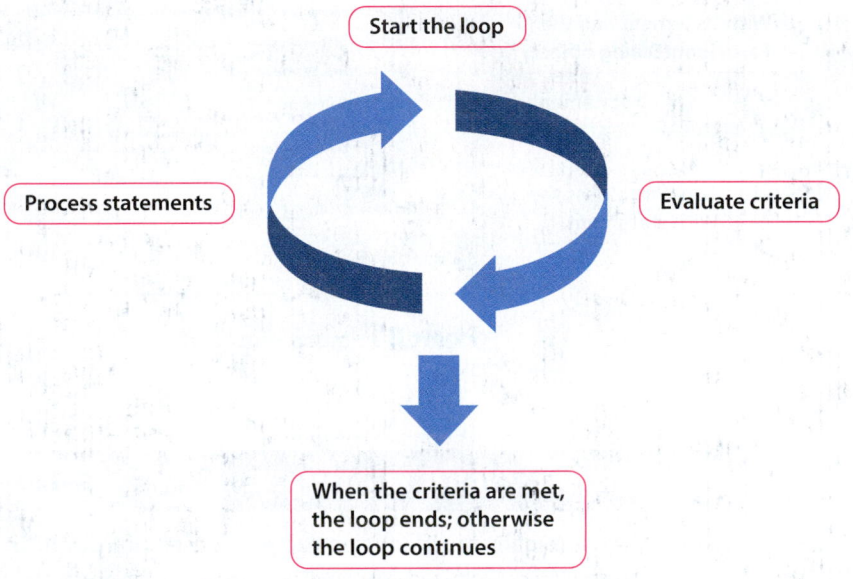

Start the loop

Process statements

Evaluate criteria

When the criteria are met, the loop ends; otherwise the loop continues

Figure 9   A loop

Loops can be conceptually difficult to understand, but they have a simple structure in the actual procedure. In the example of the FileDialog object, the procedure should store a filename for each file selected by the user. The problem with this specific situation is that the number of files may differ from day to day. Monday there might be three files to import while on Tuesday there may only be one. Fortunately, VBA has a statement that handles this very situation.

For Loops

The For Each...In...Next statement executes the nested statements for each item in a defined set of objects. In this example, the For Each...In...Next statement selects the name of each file selected by the user. When there are no more filenames to record, the loop exits. The syntax for a For Each...In...Next statement contains three parts and looks like the following:

For Each [element as data type] In [group]

[Statements]

Next

The element is a variable that refers to the item that requires an action, such as a filename. The group is the object that contains the collection of items over which the statements will be repeated. The statements section contains any actions to be carried out. Once the For Each...In...Next statement has carried out the required actions on all of the available items, the procedure continues with the statement in the procedure after the Next statement.

QUICK REFERENCE	Types of Loops in VBA

1. For Loops
   a. For...Next
   b. For Each...In...Next
2. Do Loops
   a. Do Loop
   b. Do Until...Loop
   c. Do While...Loop

A13.08

To Create the For Each...Next Statement

a. Click at the **end** of the **Dim ImportFileName as Variant** statement, and then press Enter.

b. Press Tab, and then type For Each ImportFileName In .SelectedItems to begin the loop. The loop will continue until there are no additional file names in the .SelectedItems method.

c. Click **before** the **DoCmd** statement, and then highlight the **two lines** of the DoCmd. Press Tab twice to indent the DoCmd statement within the For Each statement.

d. Select the text **"C:\Temp\a07ws13List.xlsx"**, and then press Delete to remove it. Type ImportFileName with no quotation marks.

   This replaces the text in the FileName property of the TransferSpreadsheet statement with the variable you created to hold a file name selected by the user. Because a variable name is used in place of a text string, no quotation marks are needed.

e. Press End, and then press Enter.

   Remember the TransferSpreadsheet method imports the file to the appropriate Access table. In the loop, each time a file is imported the loop starts over again with the next file name that was stored in the .SelectedItems property.

f. Press Backspace, and then type Next to complete the loop.

   This aligns the insertion point with the same column as the For Each statement. The Next portion of the statement exits the loop once all files have been imported.

```
' -----------------------------------------------------------
' mcrImportParticipants
' -----------------------------------------------------------

Function mcrImportParticipants()

    Dim ParticipantDialog As Object
    Set ParticipantDialog = Application.FileDialog(msoFileDialogOpen)

    With ParticipantDialog
        .Title = "Select New Participant List(s)"
        .AllowMultiSelect = True

        If .Show = True Then
            Dim ImportFileName As Variant
            For Each ImportFileName In .SelectedItems
                DoCmd.TransferSpreadsheet acImport, 10, _
                    "tblParticipant", ImportFileName, True, ""
            Next
        Else
            MsgBox "You cancelled the import"
        End If
    End With


End Function
```

The For Each...Next loop

Figure 10   Finished procedure

g. **Close** the Visual Basic Editor. **Close** ☒ the mcrImportParticipants macro.

This completes the For Each...In...Next statement and the procedure as a whole. Now, regardless of how many files are selected by the user for import, each file will be processed separately by Access.

Assigning Procedures to Events in Access

The last step before testing the procedure is to change the assignment of the button on the Imports tab. Because the button was originally set up to run a macro when clicked, you need to change this setting to run the new procedure. To accomplish this you need to call the function that was created by converting the import macro. The **Call statement** will run another Sub procedure or function from within a procedure by transferring to the called routine. Here you will call the mcrImportParticipants procedure when the Import New Participants button is clicked.

A13.09

To Assign the Procedure to the Button

a. In the Navigation Pane, right-click **frmImports**, and then click **Design View**.

b. If necessary, on the DESIGN tab, in the Tools group, click **Property Sheet** to open the Property Sheet pane.

c. In the Design window, click the **Import New Participants** button.

d. If necessary, in the Property Sheet pane, click the **Event** tab. The On Click event lists the macro mcrImportParticipants as the action to take when the button is clicked.

e. Click the **On Click** arrow, and then select **[Event Procedure]**.

f. Click **Builder** ⋯ . This will open the Visual Basic Editor. The Code window will display a new Private Sub statement. This Sub will be run when the command button is clicked. On the blank line of the Sub, press Tab . Type **Call mcrImportParticipants** to call the newly created VBA procedure.

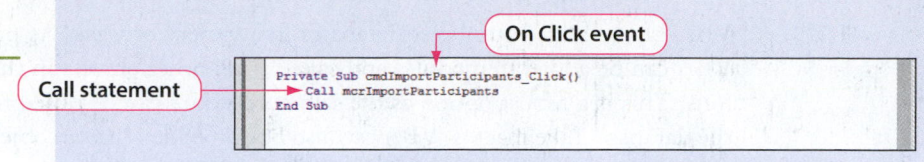

Figure 11   On Click event

SIDE NOTE
Using Call

The Call statement is not required when calling another procedure. Using it will improve the readability of your code.

g. **Close** the Visual Basic Editor. **Save** 🖫 the changes made to the form. **Close** ☒ the form.

Testing a New Procedure

Once code has been completed, it is important to test the process. You have been provided with a file of new participants for the Putts for Paws events. These participants need to be imported into the database. Use your newly created procedure to import these new participants.

CONSIDER THIS | **What Can Happen with an Untested Procedure?**

What type of consequences might occur if an untested procedure runs and contains errors? What about a procedure that imports data into a database? What could happen to the list of Red Bluff's participants?

A13.10

 To Test the Procedure

a. In the Navigation Pane, double-click **frmPuttsMenu** to open the Putts for Paws Database navigation form.

b. Click the **Imports** tab, and then click the **Import New Participants** button.
   You will be presented with a File Open dialog box. Notice that the title of the dialog box is the same as you specified in your procedure.

c. Navigate to the folder where your student data files are stored, click **a07ws13List.xlsx**, and then click **Open**.

d. To verify that the import was successful, click the **Participants** tab, and then click **Last Record** ▶ to view the last record in the tblParticipant table. The last record should now be ParticipantID number 1009.

e. Click the **Imports** tab, and then click the **Import New Participants** button again.

f. Click **Cancel** to stop the import process. You will be presented with a message box stating that you cancelled the import.

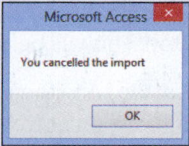

Figure 12   Cancellation message box

g. Click **OK**. Importantly, you must test every action a user might take when developing VBA.

Adding VBA to an Access Database

VBA can be added to Access databases in a variety of ways. As previously demonstrated, VBA can be added to modules and called from other objects in the database, such as buttons. This is a robust option as the same procedure can be called from multiple objects in the database. Like macros, VBA can also be embedded into an object, such as a form. If the object is then copied to another database, the VBA procedure is copied with the object. In this section you will add VBA procedures to a form within the Putts for Paws Database.

REAL WORLD ADVICE | **Creating VBA Procedures from Scratch**

There will not always be a macro to begin with, and often what you will be trying to accomplish with VBA will be more involved than what a macro can be set up to do in Access. Unlike other Microsoft applications, in Access, it is not always the best practice to begin with a recorded macro.

Create VBA Procedures

You have been asked by Barry Cheney to modify the frmParticipant form of the Putts for Paws database. The database has been set up such that each entity that donates can specify a separate billing address from their designated mailing address. This works well when the two addresses are different, but when the addresses are the same the result is a duplicate data entry. To increase the efficiency of the data entry process, you have been asked to provide a method of automation to the form. Barry has requested a button that will copy the billing address fields into the mailing address fields.

Adding a Command Button to a Form

To add the requested functionality, a button must be added to the form that will allow a user to copy the billing address data into the mailing address data with a simple button click.

A13.11

▶ To Add a Button to a Form

a. If necessary, in the Navigation Pane, open the **frmPuttsMenu** form if it is not currently open.

b. On the HOME tab, in the Views group, click the **View** arrow. Click **Layout View**, and then click the **Participants** tab.

c. Click the **DESIGN** tab, and then in the Controls group, click **Button** ⌷.

d. Move the pointer **between** the **BillingZipCode** label and the **MailingStreetAddress** label, and then click to place the Button control.

e. Click **Cancel** in the Command Button Wizard.
   The Command Button Wizard cannot be used to associate a VBA procedure to the button. This will be accomplished in the Property Sheet pane.

f. Press Ctrl, and then click the **empty cell** in the table to the right of the button. Right-click in the cell, point to **Merge/Split** on the shortcut menu, and then click **Merge**.
   The button should act as a separator between the mailing and billing addresses. Merging the button across the table will create a clear break between the two addresses and allow enough room for the button to have a descriptive caption.

---

g. If necessary, click **Property Sheet** to make the Property Sheet pane visible.

h. In the Property Sheet pane, click the **All** tab. In the **Name** field of the property sheet, replace the existing text with **cmdCopyBillingAddress**.

i. In the **Caption** field, replace the existing text with **Mailing and billing addresses are the same**.

j. **Save** 💾 the changes to the form.

REAL WORLD ADVICE   **Renaming Command Buttons**

When a new button is created on a form, Access assigns the button a name, such as Command65. When using the wizard to assign functions to a button, this naming convention may not be an obstacle because you will be able to change the caption on the button as part of the wizard. When creating a button in order to assign Visual Basic code, this can present problems because the name of the button is too vague. Instead, it is helpful to rename the button to describe the event that will take place. This way when you search through your code later, you can quickly find and identify an event button that needs to be modified.

Assigning a Procedure to an Event

The process needed in this example is to copy the data from the billing address fields to the mailing address fields when the button cmdCopyBillingAddress is clicked. Access provides some shortcuts to assign VBA procedures to controls on objects such as forms that you can take advantage of. To quickly copy values from one form object to another you can take advantage of the Me keyword. The **Me keyword** functions like a declared variable that refers to the current object.

A13.12

To Assign a VBA Procedure to the cmdCopyBillingAddress Button

a. In the Views group, click the **View** arrow, and then click **Design View**.

> **Troubleshooting**
> To edit the VBA code of an Access object, the object—such as a form—must be opened in Design view. Opening the object in Layout view, which is often used to create and edit forms, will result in a Microsoft Access error.

SIDE NOTE
Accessing the VBA Code for an Object
Often the most efficient way to access the VBA code related to an event or object is through its property sheet in Design view.

b. If necessary, click the **Participants** tab, and then click the **Mailing and billing addresses are the same** button.

c. In the Property sheet, click the **Event** tab, and then in the field for **On Click**, click **Build** ⋯.

d. In the Choose Builder dialog box, click **Code Builder**, and then click **OK**.
    This opens the Visual Basic Editor. The basic syntax of the procedure in the Code window has been automatically completed. The Option Compare Database statement is in the Declaration section of the Code window. In the Project Explorer, a new Microsoft Access Class object has been created for the form that is being edited.

The object Form_frmParticipant will contain any VBA procedures created to run in response to events occurring on this form.

e. Examine the first line of the procedure.

A Sub statement was automatically created when you chose the Code Builder option. The name of the Sub procedure, cmdCopyBillingAddress_Click(), indicates that the procedure will be run when a user clicks the cmdCopyBillingAddress button. In this procedure, the value property of the individual fields can be used to set one field value equal to that of another field value. In this example, you will use the Me keyword to identify the fields to copy.

Private Sub procedure for the On Click event

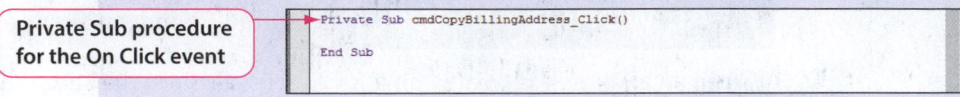

Figure 13   cmdCopyBillingAddress On Click event

f. Click the **blank line** in the Code window under the **Private Sub** statement, and then press Enter.

g. Press Tab.

This will create an indentation for your next statement. The Visual Basic Editor will use this indentation point as a reference for subsequent statements. Pressing Enter after typing a statement will align the pointer with the column in which the previous statement begins.

h. Type **Me.MailingStreetAddress.Value = Me.BillingStreetAddress.Value** and then press Enter.

This uses the Me keyword as the Form object in place of typing Form![frmParticipant] to access the Form objects. The statement in its entirety sets the field value of MailingStreetAddress to that of the BillingStreetAddress value.

i. Type **Me.MailingCity.Value = Me.BillingCity.Value** and then press Enter.

j. Type **Me.MailingState.Value = Me.BillingState.Value** and then press Enter.

k. Type **Me.MailingZipCode.Value = Me.BillingZipCode.Value** and then press Enter.

Me keyword used to refer to the object on the current form

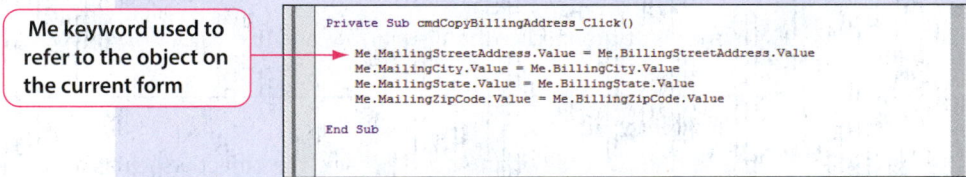

Figure 14   On Click event procedure

l. **Close** the Visual Basic Editor, and then **Save** 🖫 the changes to the form.

SIDE NOTE
Private Sub

A Private Sub is a procedure that is only accessible by other procedures in the module in which it is located.

In this example, the cmdCopyBillingAddress_Click() procedure cannot be used on another form.

m. Click the **HOME** tab, and then in the Views group, click **View** to return to Form view.

n. To test the new procedure on ParticipantID number 1, click the **Participants** tab, and then click the **Mailing and billing addresses are the same** button. Verify that the information in the Billing Address fields was copied to the Mailing Address fields.

REAL WORLD ADVICE   **The Procedure Box and Object Box Shortcuts**

Both the Procedure box and Object box can be used to create event procedures from within the Visual Basic Editor. With the Object box you can select the desired object that the event should be attached to, and the corresponding Private Sub structure will appear in the Code window. Once you are editing a specific object, you can use the Procedure box to select the action that you want a procedure to run in response to an event.

Use Comments to Document VBA Procedures

Adding comments to code in VBA is an excellent way of communicating the intentions of a procedure to other database administrators, and it is a good way of keeping track of your own code. You can add straightforward documentation on what the procedure is doing and what steps to take next. If you are developing more complicated procedures, you might want to leave yourself notes about what still needs to be completed or what statements are not working as expected.

The Edit Toolbar

Adding comments in the Code window begins with typing an apostrophe. The apostrophe character tells the Visual Basic Editor to ignore any text following the apostrophe on a line of the Code window. Comments can take an entire line of the Code window or begin after another statement in the Code window. By default, the Visual Basic Editor also changes the font color of any commented text to green. Commenting only works on a line-by-line basis though. The Visual Basic Editor provides commenting functionality and more on the Edit toolbar.

A13.13

 To Enable the Editing Toolbar

a. If necessary, press $\boxed{Alt}+\boxed{F11}$ to open the Visual Basic Editor.

b. On the Menu bar, click **View**, point to **Toolbars**, and then click **Edit**.
    The Edit toolbar will appear as a floating toolbar. It can be docked by clicking the title bar and dragging it to the top of the Visual Basic Editor window. If no modules are currently open, the buttons on the Edit toolbar will be greyed out.

c. Click the **title bar** of the Edit toolbar, and then drag it to the **right** of the Standard toolbar to dock it at the top of the Visual Basic Editor.

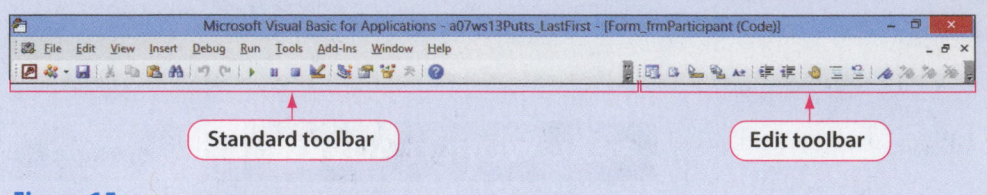

Figure 15   Edit toolbar docked in the Visual Basic Editor

The Edit toolbar has many useful features built into it. The comment block feature can be used to identify large or small strings of text in a procedure as a comment. It also includes buttons for increasing and decreasing indentations and listing the properties and methods of a statement in the Code window. Figure 16 shows the Edit toolbar as it appears in the Visual Basic Editor.

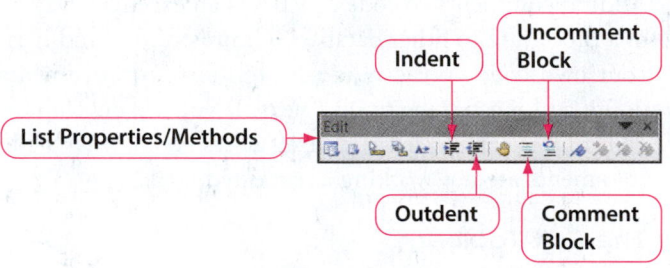

Figure 16   Edit toolbar

Adding Comments to a Procedure

The procedure created to copy the mailing address of the charity participants has no documentation associated with it. It would be helpful for future database administrators to see who wrote the procedure and what the purpose of the procedure was.

A13.14

 To Add a Comment to a Procedure

a. If necessary, in the Project Explorer window, double-click the **Form_frmParticipant** object to open it.

b. Click the **line** under Private Sub in the Code window to place the insertion point.

c. Type **Created by initialLastname** using your first initial and last name. Pressing [Enter] at this point would result in a Visual Basic Compile error because the text above does not contain any VBA statements.

d. On the Edit toolbar, click **Comment Block** [≡].

Notice that an apostrophe now appears in the first character space of the line. The Visual Basic Editor will now ignore this entire line of text when executing the procedure.

e. Press **Enter**, and then type **This procedure will copy the Billing Address information to the Mailing Address fields**. On the Edit toolbar, click **Comment Block** 📄.

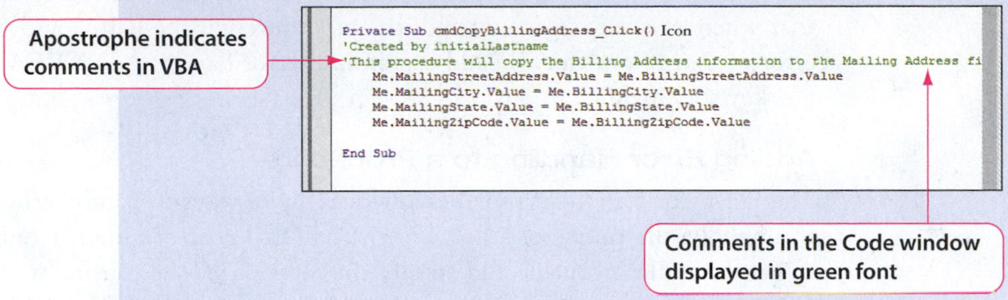

Apostrophe indicates comments in VBA

```
Private Sub cmdCopyBillingAddress_Click() Icon
'Created by initialLastname
'This procedure will copy the Billing Address information to the Mailing Address fi
    Me.MailingStreetAddress.Value = Me.BillingStreetAddress.Value
    Me.MailingCity.Value = Me.BillingCity.Value
    Me.MailingState.Value = Me.BillingState.Value
    Me.MailingZipCode.Value = Me.BillingZipCode.Value

End Sub
```

Comments in the Code window displayed in green font

Figure 17 Comments in a procedure

f. **Close** ☒ the Form_frmParticipant object.

Larger blocks of text can be identified as comments using this technique. Consider the macro that was converted in the "Convert an Existing Macro to VBA" section of this workshop. Several lines of comments were inserted into the procedure when Access converted the macro. This can be accomplished by using the pointer to select each line of text that you want to designate as a comment and clicking Comment Block 📄. Likewise, if you want to remove the apostrophe from a comment, clicking Uncomment Block 📄 will remove the apostrophe from each line that is currently selected.

CONSIDER THIS | **Commenting in VBA Code**

Comments are often overlooked, but they are an important aspect of coding. If you have ever examined a database someone else has created, it can be very difficult to discern a complex series of queries or decipher the relationship of poorly named objects in a database. Likewise, attempting to understand the rationale for an action in a database might be nearly impossible without comments to explain the original developer's intent. Sometimes, years later, even you do not remember your own rationale for the action. Much of the same is true with VBA. What benefits are there to commenting your code? Can you imagine a situation where commenting is unnecessary?

Debug the VBA in a Database and Add Error Handling

Creating a procedure that runs perfectly on the first run or in all situations is virtually impossible. No matter how experienced you might be at writing VBA, a simple typo or misplaced statement can invoke a Visual Basic error. These Visual Basic errors can be confusing to your users and will generally open the Visual Basic Editor in Debugging mode if not handled correctly. While as a developer this might be acceptable, the standard user will be confused by the event and should not be given access to the raw VBA code.

Debugging is the process of identifying and reducing the number of errors that can occur within your code. **Error handling** is the process of anticipating and controlling errors. You want your application to inform the user of a problem, and your application or procedure should exit cleanly. VBA has some error-handling features installed such that when an error is encountered, the procedure will be halted and you will receive an error message. You can also add customized error handling to a VBA procedure using a few key statements.

Adding Error Handling to a Procedure

The On Error statement provides a wide array of ways to handle errors that might arise throughout the course of a procedure. The **On Error statement** can enable or disable an error-handling routine and specify the location of the routine within the procedure. Using the GoTo statement can redirect the procedure to a line label or a specific line number. **Line labels** can be used like bookmarks in a procedure. The combination of On Error statements and line labels provide basic error handling to be built into any VBA procedure. It is important to note that not all errors that occur are negative. For example, when searching for the name of a person in a table, the message you receive that the name cannot be found is the result of an error. The message is simply a controlled response to the error.

Consider the VBA procedure created to import additional participants into the Putts database. If the Excel file being imported does not contain the appropriate column headings, Access will encounter an error and stop the import process. Because the process originates in a VBA procedure, the error will result in the termination of the process, and by default it will open the Visual Basic Editor in Debug mode. To prevent this from occurring, some simple error handling can be added to the procedure to control the outcome of any errors.

After an error occurs, an **Exit statement** can be used to terminate the procedure. The Exit statement works similarly to the End Function statement in that both terminate the function. Using Exit Function is different as additional code can be added after this function is used whereas using End Function will not allow additional code to be added to the procedure.

CONSIDER THIS | **Referring to Specific Lines of Code**

The Visual Basic Editor allows for two ways of referring to a line of code. Line labels are one method. On the Standard toolbar, the Code window tracks the line number and column number of the placement of your pointer. You can use a line number in much the same way you can use a line label to reference a specific place in a procedure. Would there be any differences in referencing with line labels versus line numbers?

A13.15

 To Add Comments and Error Handling to the mcrImportParticipants Procedure

a. If necessary, in the Project Explorer, double-click the **Converted Macro - mcrImportParticipants** module to view it in the Code window. You do not need to close other modules if they are open.

b. Click to place the insertion point on the **line** below the **Function** statement, type **'Created by initialLastname** and then press Enter.

Troubleshooting

Not typing the apostrophe character before the comment will result in an error in the Visual Basic Editor.

c. Type **'This procedure imports new participants into the Putts database** and then press Enter.

d. Type **On Error GoTo ImportParticipants_Err** and press Enter.

Later in this activity you will create a line label named ImportParticipants_Err. If an error occurs during the execution of this procedure, Access will immediately move to the portion of the code that starts on the line that contains the identified line label.

e. Click to place the insertion point above the **End Function** statement. Type **ImportParticipants_Exit:** and then press Enter.

This line label will serve as a bookmark. If no errors occur, the procedure will end on the next line. Be sure to include the colon after the line label.

f. Press Tab, type **Exit Function** and then press Enter.

The Exit Function statement here serves as a stopping point for the procedure. If no error has occurred, the procedure will not execute any statements after the Exit Function statement.

g. Press Enter, and then press Backspace. Next you will insert a bookmark that will be used in the event that an error does occur in the code.

h. Type **ImportParticipants_Err:** and then press Enter.

This is a line label and will serve as a bookmark. If an error occurs, the code will move to this line and continue running the procedure.

i. Press Tab to indent the line, type **Msgbox Error$** and then press Enter.

The Msgbox object will display a message box to the user. The contents of the message box can be a fixed text string or a variable that can be defined elsewhere in the procedure. Here, "Error$" will display the error that Access encountered during the import process in the message box.

In the event of an error, the function will move to this line label and execute the next statement

Exit Function will end the function if no errors occur

Error handling controls what the user sees in the event of a VBA error

```
'----------------------------------------------------------
' mcrImportParticipants
'
'----------------------------------------------------------
Function mcrImportParticipants()
'Created by initialLastname
'This procedure imports new participants into the Putts database
On Error GoTo ImportParticipants_Err

    Dim ParticipantDialog As Object
    Set ParticipantDialog = Application.FileDialog(msoFileDialogOpen)

    With ParticipantDialog
        .Title = "Select New Participant List(s)"
        .AllowMultiSelect = True

        If .Show = True Then
            Dim ImportFileName As Variant
            For Each ImportFileName In .SelectedItems
                DoCmd.TransferSpreadsheet acImport, 10, _
                    "tblParticipant", ImportFileName, True, ""
            Next
        Else
            MsgBox "You cancelled the import"
        End If
    End With

ImportParticipants_Exit:
    Exit Function

ImportParticipants_Err:
    MsgBox Error$

End Function
```

Figure 18 Error handling and comments in the mcrImportParticipants procedure

CONSIDER THIS | On Error Resume Next

The On Error statements can be constructed to respond in a variety of ways when an error occurs in a procedure. The On Error Resume Next statement is used to skip the statement immediately following it in the event of an error. No error message will be displayed when using this statement as it turns off VBA's usual error-handling procedures. In what types of situations might this statement be useful?

QUICK REFERENCE	Printing VBA Code

1. Open the module you want to print.
2. On the File menu, click Print.
3. To select a printer, click Setup.
4. Click OK to print to the selected printer.

Compiling and Securing Your VBA

Before implementing a database that contains VBA, all modules should be checked for potential errors. This will prevent users from encountering unnecessary and confusing errors while using the database. Importantly, you may want to secure your VBA so that it is not altered. Unsecured VBA can be altered either intentionally or unintentionally, but it can be easily secured to prevent this. In this section, you will compile the database to check for errors in the code and then secure the database so that the VBA code cannot be edited.

Compile VBA Modules

Errors in VBA procedures can occur while the code is being written or when the code is executed. A **syntax error** occurs when a completed line of code is entered that the Visual Basic Editor does not recognize. Syntax errors occur within the Visual Basic Editor once the pointer leaves a line of code that the Code window cannot interpret. This type of error is identified immediately and can then be corrected. How can you detect errors that are not caught until the execution of a procedure? Compiling your code before running it is one way of finding errors before the execution of a VBA procedure. When you compile the VBA in your database, Access examines all of the VBA contained in modules or objects for errors. This way you can find the errors in a procedure before users stumble across them.

Compiling VBA Modules to Identify VBA Errors

Access compiles an individual procedure before the procedure is executed. Using the Visual Basic Editor to compile your database forces Access to compile all existing modules, not just the one being executed. This catches any errors in procedures within those modules. For example, declaring a variable more than once in a procedure will result in an error when the procedure is executed. This error is not identified when writing the code; rather, it is identified when the module is compiled. Compiling code before the first execution of a procedure is a simple yet important process.

A13.16

To Compile VBA Procedures

a. On the Menu bar, click **Debug**, and then click **Compile a07ws13Putts**.

If there are no syntax errors with your VBA procedures, Access returns you to the Visual Basic Editor. If an error exists, a compile error occurs and Access indicates what the error is and opens the relevant module to the incorrect line of code. To demonstrate this, you will first create a typical syntax error that the Visual Basic Editor will immediately identify. Then you will create an error that will not be identified until the code is compiled.

b. Click **Insert Module** [icon] to create a new module.

This will create a new module entitled Module1. Notice that the Option Compare Database statement is in the Declarations section by default.

c. Type **Sub TestCompile** and then press Enter twice. When you press Enter, the parentheses are added after the name of the Sub, and the End Sub statement is inserted by default by the Visual Basic Editor on the last line of the procedure.

d. Type **dim** and then press Enter.

This will invoke a Visual Basic compile error. This happens because the Dim statement cannot exist without a variable name.

Statement causing the compile error

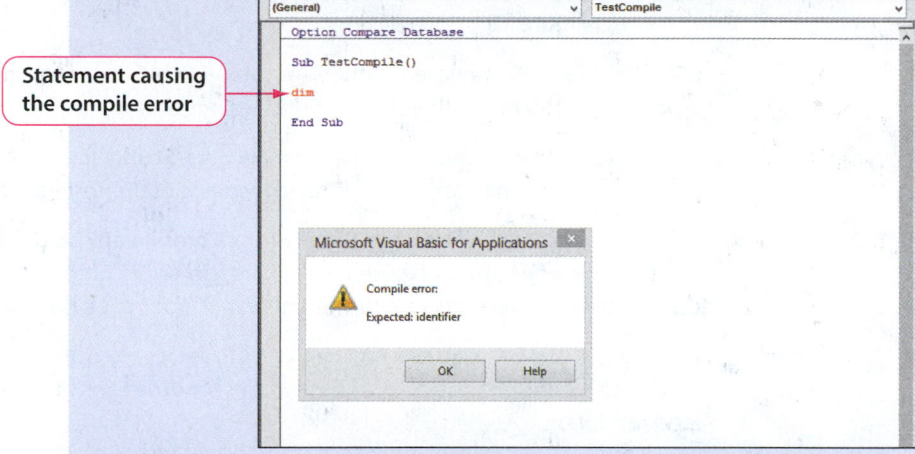

Figure 19 Compile error

> **Troubleshooting**
>
> If a VBA error occurs while Access is running a procedure, you are offered the choice of ending the procedure or entering debugging mode. Choosing to end the procedure halts the execution of any code and returns you to the database. Choosing to enter debugging mode opens the Visual Basic Editor with the incorrect line of code highlighted in yellow. Once you fix the code you need to, click Reset [icon] in the Standard toolbar to return the application to a state where it can again run procedures.

e. Click **OK** in the Compile error message box.

Notice that the Visual Basic Editor has changed the font color of the incorrect line of code to red to indicate the location of the error. Additionally, your pointer is now located in the place where the error was detected.

f. Your insertion point should be located after the **Dim** keyword. Press Spacebar, type **test as string** and then press Enter.

SIDE NOTE

Variant Data Types

Typing Dim Test and pressing Enter does not invoke a compile error because if no data type is specified in the procedure, the Variant data type is used by default.

g. Type **Dim test as String** once more, and then press Enter.

This time no syntax error occurs. The error here, duplicated variable names, will not be detected until the procedure is compiled.

h. On the Menu bar, click **Debug**, and then click **Compile a07ws13Putts**. The duplicate variable names invoke a compile error.

Statement causing the compile error →

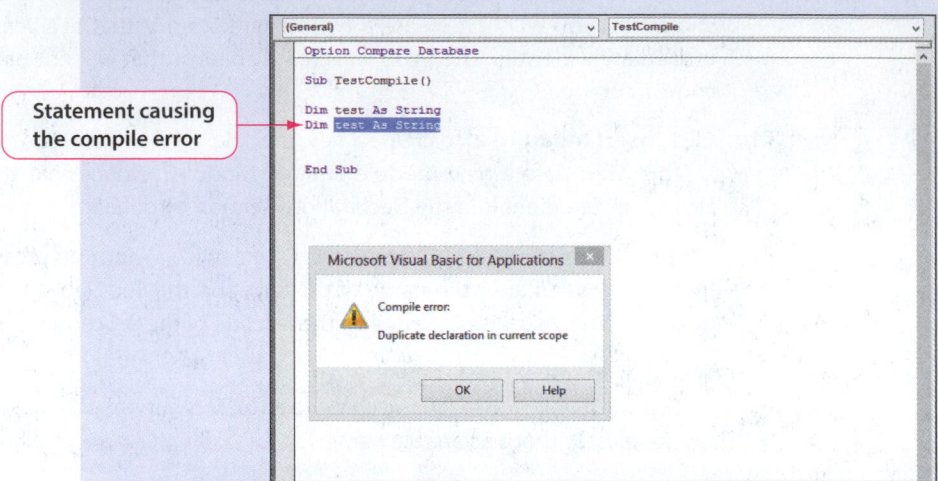

Figure 20 Compile error

i. Click **OK** in the Compile error message box. In this instance, the Visual Basic Editor highlights the incorrect line of code but does not change the font color.

j. Select the second instance of the **Dim test As String** line of code, and then press Backspace. This deletes the duplicated instance of the Test variable declaration.

k. On the Menu bar, click **Debug**, and then click **Compile a07ws13Putts**.

This time when the database is compiled, no errors occur, and you are returned to the Visual Basic Editor without further messages. Your code has successfully compiled!

l. **Close** the Visual Basic Editor. If necessary, **Close** ☒ any open objects in the database and **Save** 🖫 any changes. Accept the name **Module1** for the name of the newly created module.

Secure VBA in a Database

Once the VBA in an Access database has been compiled it is ready to be used within the database environment. Before deploying the database you may want to consider securing the macros and Visual Basic procedures in a database. This is important so that the VBA in a database is not edited by accident, resulting in errors or incorrect execution of VBA procedures.

Working with ACCDE files

The default file format in Access 2013 is the .accdb extension. This format, without additional security measures, allows for full editing of the database by the user. Access provides the .accde format as a method of securing some aspects of the database. In an .accde file, VBA procedures will not be viewable to the user, and any errors that might occur during the execution of a VBA procedure will not result in the Visual Basic Editor being displayed. Additionally, forms and reports can be opened but not edited in .accde versions of a database. Saving a database in .accde format creates a new copy of the database that can then be given to the user.

A13.17
To Create an .accde file

a. Click the **FILE** tab, and then click **Save As**.

b. Under Save Database As, and then under Advanced, click **Make ACCDE**.

c. Click **Save As**.

d. Navigate to the folder where you are saving your files, and then click **Save**.

> **Troubleshooting**
>
> You should have already compiled the database and tested your VBA procedures to make sure there are no errors before creating an .accde file. If Access cannot compile your code, the .accde file will not be created.

> **SIDE NOTE**
> **32-Bit vs. 64-Bit**
> Databases that have been converted to an .accde file cannot be moved between 32-bit and 64-bit versions of Office.

Testing the ACCDE Database

The database will now reopen in its original .accdb format. It is important to remember that converting a database into the .accde format is only one aspect of securing a database for use. In an .accde database, users can still create and modify tables, queries, and macros. If your intention is to implement a fully "locked down" version of the database, there are several more steps to take. These steps are covered in the next workshop. It is important to test the results of saving the database as an .accde file.

A13.18
To Open and Test the .accde File

a. Click the **FILE** tab, and then click **Close** ✕ to close the a07ws13Putts_LastFirst database.

b. Click the **FILE** tab, and then click **Open**.

c. Navigate to the folder where you saved your files for this workshop, and then open **a07ws13Putts_LastFirst.accde**.

> **Troubleshooting**
>
> When .accde databases are created the only difference in the filename may be the last letter of the file extension. Depending on your system settings, you may or may not be able to see the extensions of files on your computer. An alternative way to identify .accde files is to look at the icon for the file. Access databases with the .accdb extension have the 🅰 icon, while .accde databases have a padlock visible on the icon 🅰.

d. If the file is not in a trusted location, you will see a warning message. This message is to alert the user that there are macros and/or VBA code present within the database that could potentially be malicious. If you encounter this message, click **Open**.

Figure 21 Microsoft Access Security Notice

e. In the Navigation Pane, right-click the module **Converted Macro - mcrImportParticipants**. Notice that Design view is greyed out and cannot be selected.

f. Press ⟦Alt⟧+⟦F11⟧ to open the Visual Basic Editor, and then click ⊞ next to the **a07ws13Putts_LastFirst** object to expand the view.

g. Click ⊞ next to the **Modules** objects to expand the view.

h. Double-click the **Converted Macro - mcrImportParticipants** module. You will receive a message stating that the project is not viewable.

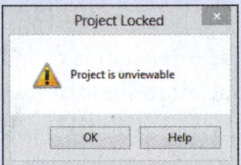

Figure 22 Project Locked dialog box

i. Click **OK**, and then **Close** the Visual Basic Editor.

j. Click the **FILE** tab, and then click **Close** to close the a07ws13Putts_LastFirst.accde database.

k. Click the **FILE** tab, and then click **Open**.

l. Navigate to the folder where you saved your files for this workshop, and then open **a07ws13Putts_LastFirst.accdb**.

REAL WORLD ADVICE   **ACCDB and ACCDE Files**

Once a database is saved as an .accde file it cannot be converted back to the .accdb file format. Therefore, no changes can be made to macros or VBA modules within the database. Instead, any changes would have to be made in the original .accdb file that would then need to be converted. This is critical because any changes that have been made to the database would be lost—or must be made again in the original file. This includes data entered into tables or new Access objects such as tables or queries that have been added to the database.

Password Protecting VBA in a Database

Access provides several methods of securing a database. These security measures can affect many aspects of the database and are extremely useful tools for deploying databases to users. These security features are explored in Workshop 14. The Visual Basic Editor provides a method of securing the VBA in a database without implementing more general security measures. This can allow for full editing of the database by the user without compromising the integrity of the VBA code. Any VBA code in a database can be secured by providing a separate password via the Visual Basic Editor.

A13.19

To Password Protect VBA in a Database

a. Press $\boxed{\text{Alt}}$ + $\boxed{\text{F11}}$ to open the Visual Basic Editor.

b. In the Project Explorer, right-click the **a07ws13Putts_LastFirst** database, and then select **a07ws13Putts Properties**.

c. In the a07ws13Putts - Project Properties dialog box, click the **Protection** tab.

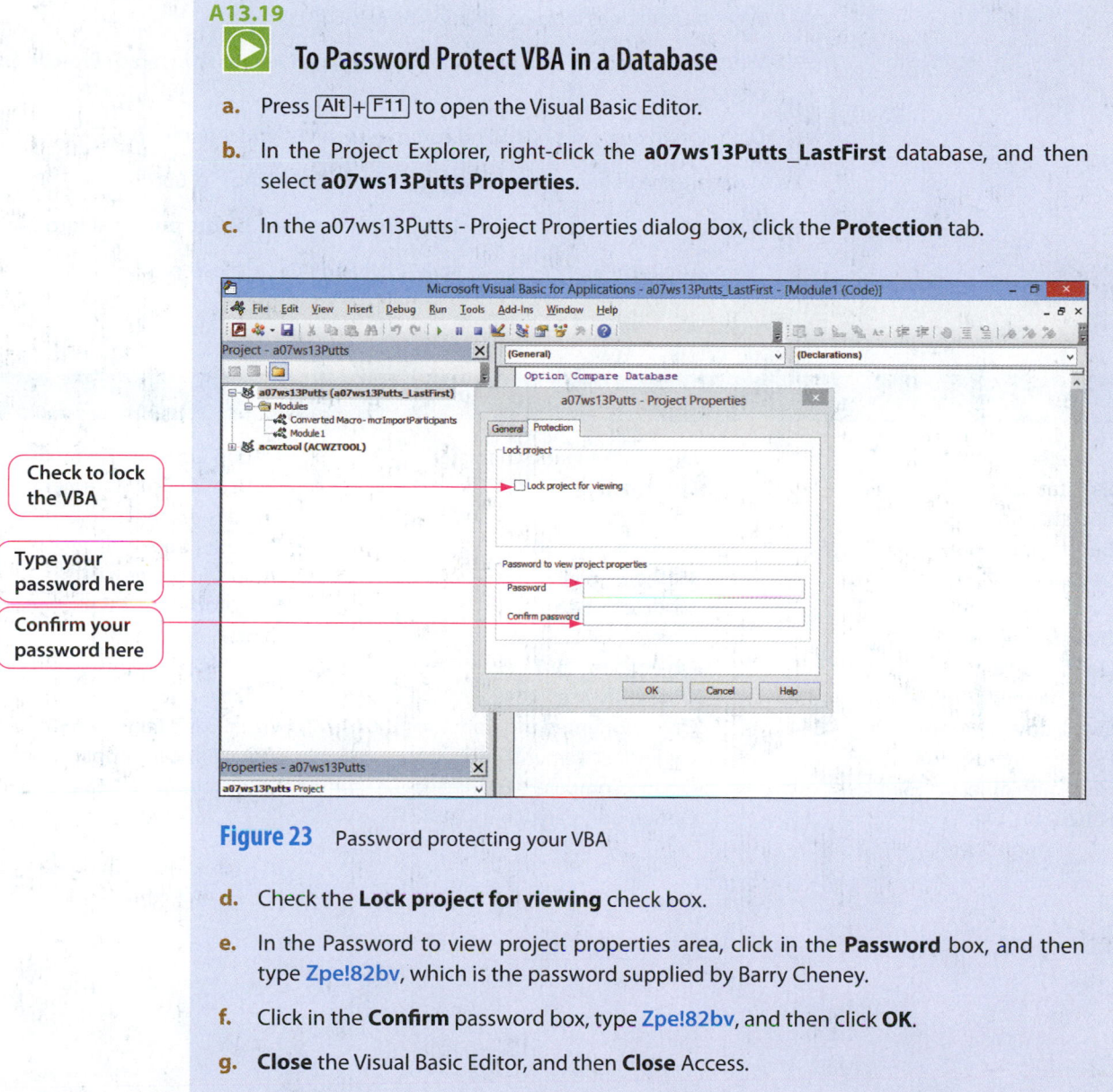

Check to lock the VBA

Type your password here

Confirm your password here

Figure 23 Password protecting your VBA

d. Check the **Lock project for viewing** check box.

e. In the Password to view project properties area, click in the **Password** box, and then type **Zpe!82bv**, which is the password supplied by Barry Cheney.

f. Click in the **Confirm** password box, type **Zpe!82bv**, and then click **OK**.

g. **Close** the Visual Basic Editor, and then **Close** Access.

The a07ws13Putts - Project Properties dialog box will return you to the Visual Basic Editor without a confirmation message that the password was set. The Visual Basic Editor can still be opened by any database user. When a module or object is opened, before any code is displayed, the Visual Basic Editor will prompt you for the VBA password.

Concept Check

1. Discuss the relationship between object-oriented programming and event-driven programming. p. 644

2. Macros and VBA can accomplish many of the same goals. When is it advantageous to use VBA? When would it be advantageous to use macros? p. 644

3. What is the benefit of using indentations and line continuation characters in building a procedure? p. 648

4. What benefit does looping offer in VBA? p. 658

5. What are two locations in Access that VBA procedures can be stored? Provide an example of each. p. 662

6. Discuss two purposes of adding comments to VBA procedures. p. 667

7. What are the benefits of debugging and error handling? p. 668

8. Why is it important to compile the VBA in a database before putting it into use? p. 670

9. What are the differences between ACCDB and ACCDE files? p. 672

Key Terms

Argument   649
Call statement   660
Code window   647
Debugging   668
Declarations   647
Declarations section   647
Dim statement   652
DoCmd object   649
Error handling   668
Event-driven programming   644
Exit statement   668
FileDialog object   651
Function   648

Line continuation character   648
Line labels   668
Loops   658
Me keyword   663
Method   644
Modules   646
Object   644
Object box   647
Object Browser   649
Object-oriented programming   644
On Error statement   668
Option Compare   647
Option Compare Binary   647

Option Compare Text   647
Option Explicit Statement   653
Procedure   644
Procedure box   647
Project Explorer   646
Sub procedure   648
Syntax error   670
TransferSpreadsheet method   649
Variables   652
Visual Basic Editor   646
Visual Basic for Applications   644
With statement   654

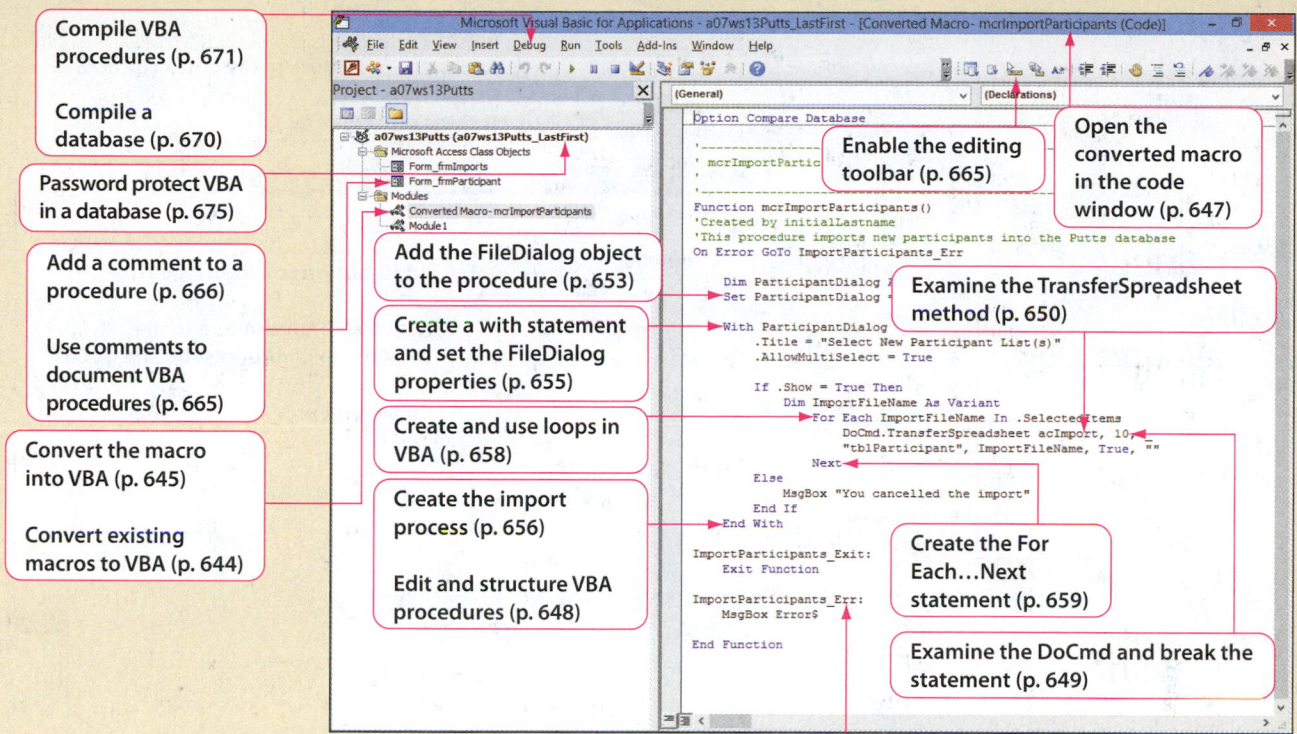

Compile VBA procedures (p. 671)

Compile a database (p. 670)

Password protect VBA in a database (p. 675)

Add a comment to a procedure (p. 666)

Use comments to document VBA procedures (p. 665)

Convert the macro into VBA (p. 645)

Convert existing macros to VBA (p. 644)

Enable the editing toolbar (p. 665)

Open the converted macro in the code window (p. 647)

Add the FileDialog object to the procedure (p. 653)

Examine the TransferSpreadsheet method (p. 650)

Create a with statement and set the FileDialog properties (p. 655)

Create and use loops in VBA (p. 658)

Create the import process (p. 656)

Edit and structure VBA procedures (p. 648)

Create the For Each...Next statement (p. 659)

Examine the DoCmd and break the statement (p. 649)

Add comments and error handling to the mcrImportParticipants procedure (p. 668)

Debug and add error handling to a procedure (p. 667)

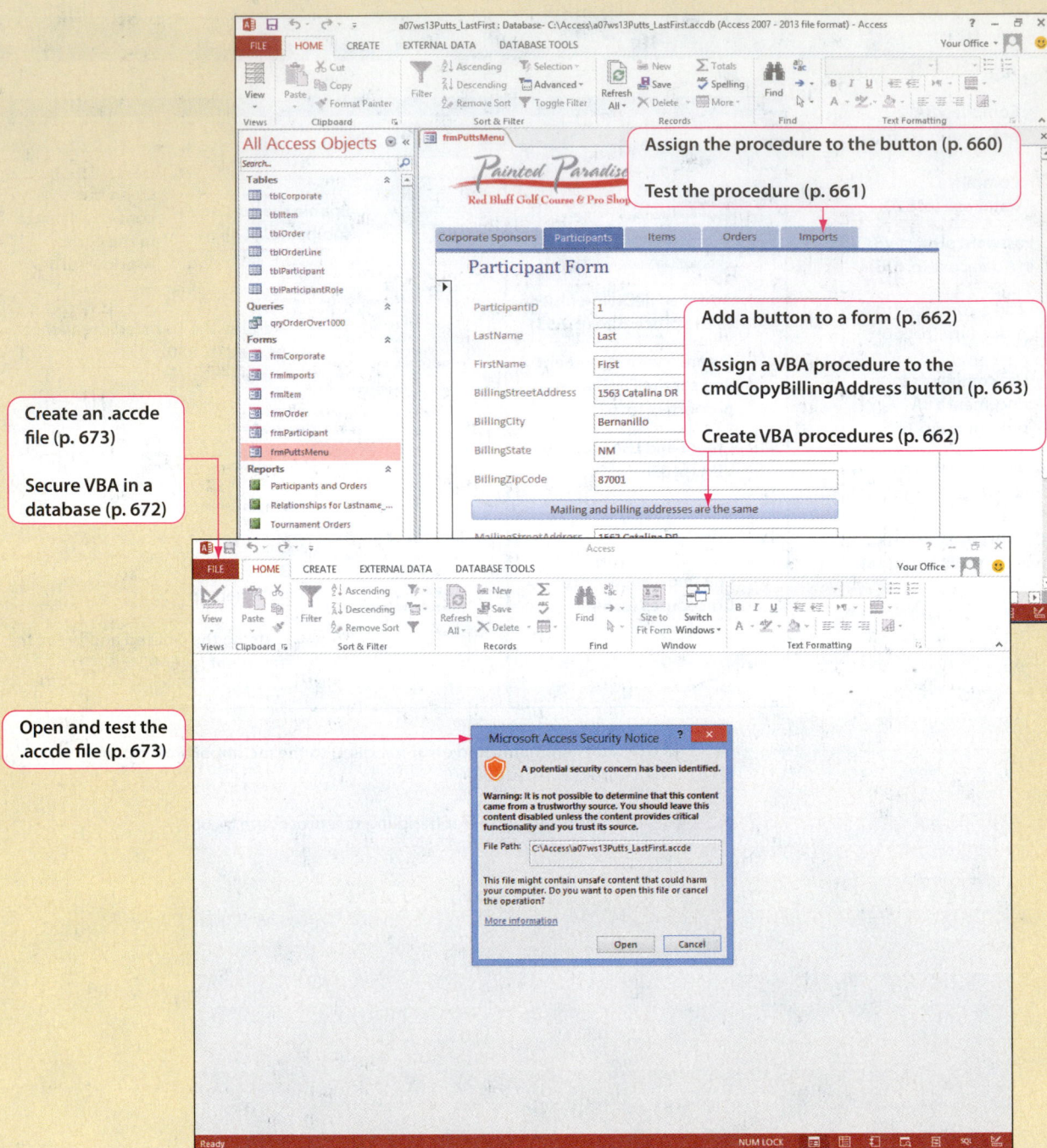

Create an .accde file (p. 673)

Secure VBA in a database (p. 672)

Assign the procedure to the button (p. 660)

Test the procedure (p. 661)

Add a button to a form (p. 662)

Assign a VBA procedure to the cmdCopyBillingAddress button (p. 663)

Create VBA procedures (p. 662)

Open and test the .accde file (p. 673)

Figure 24 VBA Database Final

Student data file needed:

 a07ws13Golf.accdb

You will save your files as:

 a07ws13Golf_LastFirst.accdb

 a07ws13tblMemberLessons_LastFirst.xlsx

Red Bluff Golf Course & Pro Shop

Production & Operations

Having been impressed with your work on databases in the past, Barry Cheney has asked you to build some enhancements into the database that is used to track golf lessons and tee times. The data kept in the tblMemberLessons table will need to be analyzed regularly. Barry would like for this data to be in a Microsoft Excel spreadsheet to facilitate this analysis. He has asked that you create a button on the Members tab of the frmGolfMenu navigational form that will export this file. He would like you to create the export so that the user is prompted to select a folder to export the file into.

a. Start **Access**, and then open the student data file **a07ws13Golf**. Click the **FILE** tab, and save the file as an **Access Database** in the folder or location designated by your instructor with the name **a07ws13Golf_LastFirst** using your last and first name. If necessary, enable the content.

b. In the Navigation Pane, right-click the **frmGolfMenu** form, and then click **Layout View**.

c. Click the **Members** tab. Click the **DESIGN** tab, and then in the Controls group, click **Button**. Place the button in the Members tab form header to the right of the name of the form. If necessary, click **Cancel** on the Command Button Wizard dialog box.

d. Click the **View** arrow, click **Design View**, and then click **Yes** to save changes. If the property sheet is not visible, on the DESIGN tab, in the Tools group, click **Property Sheet**. Click the button just created, and then in the Property Sheet pane, click the **All** tab. In the Name box replace the default name of the button with **cmdExportMemberLessons**.

e. Replace the default text of the button caption with **Export Member Lessons**. Adjust the button's shape to fit the caption text.

f. Click the **Event** tab, and then in the box for the On Click event, click **Builder**. In the Choose Builder dialog box, select **Code Builder**, and then click **OK**.

g. On the line under the **Private Sub** statement, enter the comment **'Export procedure created by initialLastname**, using your first initial and last name. Press Enter.

h. Type **'This procedure exports tblMemberLessons**, press Enter twice, and then press Tab.

i. Define the FileDialog Object.

- To declare a variable that will act as an alias for the Save As dialog box, type **Dim ExportTable as Object** and then press Enter.

- To set the Export variable to be a Save As dialog box, type **Set ExportTable = Application.FileDialog(msoFileDialogSaveAs)** and then press Enter twice.

- To begin a With statement to set the properties of the FileDialog object, type **With ExportTable**, and then press Enter.

- To set the title of the dialog box, press Tab, type **.Title = "Save tblMemberLessons as "**, and then press Enter.

j. Create an If statement and a loop that will determine the filename and folder selected by the user or exit the procedure if no items are selected.

- Type **If .Show = True Then** and then press Enter.
- Press Tab, and then type **Dim Filename As Variant** to declare a variable to store the filename selected by the user. Press Enter.
- Type **For Each Filename in .SelectedItems** to begin the loop, press Enter, and then press Tab.
- Type **.DoCmd.TransferSpreadsheet acExport, acSpreadsheetTypeExcel12xml, "tblMember", Filename, True, ""**, and then press Enter.
- Press Backspace to align the insertion point with the **For Each** statement, type **Next** to complete the loop, and then press Enter. Press Backspace to align the insertion point with the If statement.
- Type **Else**, press Enter, and then press Tab.
- Type **Msgbox "You cancelled the export."** to create a message box telling the user that the export was cancelled. Press Enter, and then press Backspace.
- Type **End If** to end the If statement, press Enter, and then press Backspace.
- Type **End With** and then press Enter.

k. Add comments and error handling to the export procedure.

- Place the insertion point in the **blank line** under the two comment lines. Type **On Error GoTo ExportMemberLessons_Err** to begin the error-handling process, and then press Enter.
- Place the insertion point above the **End Sub** statement. Type **Exit Sub** to create an exit point for situations where the procedure executes as expected, and then press Enter twice.
- Type **ExportMemberLessons_Err:** to add a line label that corresponds with the On Error statement added previously. Press Enter, and then press Tab.
- Type **Msgbox Error$** to return any error message received to a message box.

l. On the Menu bar, click **Debug**, and then click **Compile a07ws13Golf**. If there are no errors in the procedure you created, you will be returned to the Visual Basic Editor. If there are errors, resolve them and compile the database again to confirm that all errors were corrected.

m. Save the newly created Private Sub statement.

n. Password protect the VBA in the database, and then test the new export.

- In the Project Explorer, right-click the **a07ws13Golf** database, click **a07ws13Golf Properties** from the shortcut menu that appears, and then click the **Protection** tab.
- Click the **Lock project for viewing** check box.
- In the Password to view project properties area, click the **Password** box, and then type **423abg70**, which is the password supplied by Barry Cheney.
- Click the **Confirm password** box, retype your password, and then click **OK**.
- Close the Visual Basic Editor.
- On the HOME tab, in the Views group, click the **View** arrow, and then click **Form View**.
- Click **Export Member Lessons** to test the export. In the Save As dialog box, browse to where you are saving your files, and then type **a07ws13tblMemberLessons_LastFirst** to save the exported table.
- Click **Export Member Lessons** again to test the result of cancelling the export. In the Save As dialog box, click **Cancel**, and then click **OK** on the message box that appears.

o. Close the Database. Exit Access. Submit your work as directed by your instructor.

MyITLab®
Grader
Homework 1

Student data files needed:

 a07ws13Electronics.accdb

 a07ws13July.xlsx

 a07ws13August.xlsx

You will save your files as:

 a07ws13Electronics_LastFirst.accdb

 a07ws13Electronics_LastFirst.accde

Customer
Service

Premium Electronics Database

Premium Electronics is a local electronics store that offers discounts on top brand electronics to members of their buyers club. Members sign up online through an outsourced CRM service, and then spreadsheet files are sent on a biweekly basis to be imported into the database. You have been asked to create an import procedure that will allow the user to select multiple files, if necessary, to import into the database. After the importing process is finished, a message box should appear informing the user that the process has been completed. You also have been asked to increase the security of the database to protect the structure and content of the database.

a. Start **Access**, and then open the student data file **a07ws13Electronics**. Click the **FILE** tab, and then save the file as an **Access Database** in the folder or location designated by your instructor with the name **a07ws13Electronics_LastFirst** using your last and first name. If necessary, enable the content.

b. Create a button on the frmImportMembers form towards the top of the Detail section that will initiate the process of importing new members.

- Name the button **cmdImportMembers**.

- Make the button caption read **Import New Members**. If necessary, adjust the size of the button to fit the caption.

c. Assign an event procedure to the On Click event of the button. The import procedure must allow for multiple Excel spreadsheets to be imported into the tblMembers table:

- Insert a comment that states **'Created by initialLastname**. Add another comment on the second line that describes what this procedure will do.

- This procedure needs to include error handling. If an error occurs, display the error to the user, and then exit the procedure.

- In the procedure, construct a process in which a user can import multiple Excel spreadsheets into the tblMembers table. Two Excel spreadsheets of members have been provided to you for importing.

- The file dialog box must have a title of **Import Member File(s)**.

- If the import is cancelled, the following message should be displayed: **The import has been cancelled**.

- Once the files have been imported, a message box should display the following message before exiting: **The file(s) have been imported**.

- Compile the database before exiting the Visual Basic Editor. If an error occurs during the compile process, fix the error, and compile again.

- Test the import process by importing the **a07ws13July** and **a07ws13August** Excel files.

d. Secure the database and VBA from accidental or malicious changes by saving the database in an .accde format as **a07ws13Electronics_LastFirst.accde**.

e. Close the database and exit Access. Submit your work as directed by your instructor.

Student data files needed:

 a07ws13PurrfectPets.accdb

a07ws13Animals.xlsx

a07ws13Breeds.xlsx

You will save your file as:

a07ws13PurrfectPets_LastFirst.accdb

Purrfect Pets Database

Production & Operations

You have been hired as a database administrator for Purrfect Pets Animal Shelter to create a database that will not only help them keep track of their animals but also their customers and adoptions. You have been asked to increase the functionality by creating a VBA procedure that will allow for the importing of multiple files consisting of new breeds and animals acquired by Purrfect Pets. You have also been asked to add the appropriate security measures to prevent unintentional or malicious modifications to the database.

a. Start **Access**, and then open the student data file **a07ws13PurrfectPets**. Click the **FILE** tab, and save the file as an **Access Database** in the folder or location designated by your instructor with the name a07ws13PurrfectPets_LastFirst using your last and first name. If necessary, enable the content.

b. Create a blank form, and then name it frmImportData. Add a title to the form header, and then type Import New Breeds and Animals.

c. Create two command buttons toward the top of the Detail section of the form.

- One button should have the caption Import New Breeds with the name of cmdImportBreeds.

- One button should have the caption Import New Animals with the name of cmdImportAnimals.

d. Create a new procedure for the On Click event of cmdImportBreeds. The procedure should include the following:

- Comments that describe the procedure and who created it.

- Allow for multiple Excel spreadsheets to be imported into the tblBreed table.

- Include error handling where a message containing the error message is displayed to the user and then exit the procedure.

- A message if the import process is canceled

- A message when the import has been completed

- Test the import by importing the Excel spreadsheet **a07ws13Breeds**.

e. Create a new procedure for the On Click event of cmdImportAnimals. The procedure should include the following:

- Comments that describe the procedure and who created it.

- Allow for multiple Excel spreadsheets to be imported into the tblAnimal table.

- Include error handling where a message containing the error message is displayed to the user and then exit the procedure.

- A message if the import process is canceled

- A message when the import has been completed

- Test the import by importing the Excel spreadsheet **a07ws13Animals**.

f. Lock the VBA for viewing, and then protect it with the following password: fw43sW$.

g. Close the database and exit Access. Submit your work as directed by your instructor.

WORKSHOP 14 | IMPLEMENT YOUR DATABASE

Prepare Case

The Red Bluff Golf Course & Pro Shop Putts for Paws Charity Database

Production & Operations

The Red Bluff Golf Course & Pro Shop sponsors the charity tournament, Putts for Paws, to raise money for the local pet shelter. The scope of the database is limited to tracking the monies being raised for the Putts for Paws event. Participants in the tournament are assigned roles, and any role may donate money to the event.

Now that a fully functioning database has been constructed, you have been asked to implement the database.

imageman / Shutterstock

REAL WORLD SUCCESS

"I created a database for a colleague that she later implemented in her business. Later she mentioned that errors had begun to appear when the database was in use. Upon inspection I learned that some of her employees had modified the database incorrectly, resulting in errors. Once the database was fixed I created a front-end database for my colleague's employees and showed her how to modify the startup options to help prevent similar errors in the future."

- Chloe, alumnus

Student data files needed for this workshop:

 a07ws14Putts.accdb

 a07ws14Corporate.xlsx

 a07ws14Icon.ico

You will save your files as:

 a07ws14Putts_LastFirst.accdb

 a07ws14Putts_LastFirst_be.accdb

 a07ws14Putts_LastFirst2003.mdb

Implementing a Database

How do you prepare your database for multiple users? What are the best practices for implementing a database? These are very broad questions with many important ideas to consider. For this workshop the design of the database as well as how data is entered into the database is completed. Now you will consider how the database itself is accessed. Before this can happen, a few questions must be answered: How many people will be using the database? Should the tables for the database be stored in a centralized location? If so, how will the users access those tables? Are there macros or VBA that need to be locked? This workshop will address these concerns and more regarding the implementation of databases.

When securing a database the developer must be careful to ensure that the database is protected adequately. Any database objects that the user will not need access to should be hidden from view or otherwise protected. This way they cannot be deleted or modified—either by accident or maliciously. Often these objects include tables, macros, and Visual Basic code within the database. Securing a database is a detailed process and must be completed carefully. There might be several ways of opening or editing an object in Access. All of these methods must be accounted for when securing a database.

Once the database is secure, it can be implemented or distributed to users. Several implementation methods exist. The appropriate method can vary depending on the number of users and how data is accessed by the database. Some users may have older versions of Access. These users require a copy of the database that is compatible with these previous versions. If a large number of users will be accessing the database, Access provides a helpful utility called the Database Splitter to provide greater access to the database. In this section, you will prepare a database for implementation.

Shared and Exclusive Modes

When a database is opened in Access, by default it is opened with Shared Access. A database is opened with **Shared Access** when multiple users are allowed access to the database at the same time. A database opened with **Exclusive Access** allows only one user at a time the ability to open and edit the database. When establishing security in a database for implementation, Access routinely requires opening the file with Exclusive Access. Exclusive Access also ensures that no other users will be able to open the database while changes are being made. Importantly, some of the changes in this workshop will only take effect once the database or database object has been closed and reopened.

REAL WORLD ADVICE | **Setting the Default Open Mode**

You can set the default open mode to either Shared or Exclusive. This setting is located in the Access Options under Client Settings and Default Open Mode. However, Access only allows for this option as a setting on individual computers. It cannot be set for individual databases. If the default open mode is set to Exclusive, all databases will be opened exclusively. If the open mode is set to Exclusive, no other users will be able to use the database.

Opening the Starting File

You have been asked by Barry Cheney to make modifications to the Putts for Paws database as it will be used by numerous employees in several locations. The file will need to be secured to prevent any of the users from inadvertently modifying the database. The database will also need to be used by multiple users efficiently.

A14.00

 To Open the Putts for Paws Database

a. Start **Access**, and then open the student data file **a07ws14Putts**.

b. Click the **FILE** tab, and save the file as an **Access Database** in the folder or location designated by your instructor with the name **a07ws14Putts_LastFirst** using your last and first name. If necessary, click **Enable Content**.

Opening a Database with Exclusive Access

If you are making changes to a database that is available to multiple users, you may want to ensure that only you have the database open. By opening a database with Exclusive Access you will ensure that no other users can open the database and thus prevent you from being able to make changes.

A14.01

 To Open a Database with Exclusive Access

a. Click the **FILE** tab, and then click **Close**.

b. Click the **FILE** tab, click **Open**, and then browse to the location where you are saving your files.

c. Click to select the student data file **a07ws14Putts_LastFirst**.

d. Click the **Open** arrow, and then select **Open Exclusive**. If necessary, click **Enable Content**.

> **SIDE NOTE**
> **Shared and Exclusive Access**
> Saving a database with a different file name leaves the file in Shared Access mode.

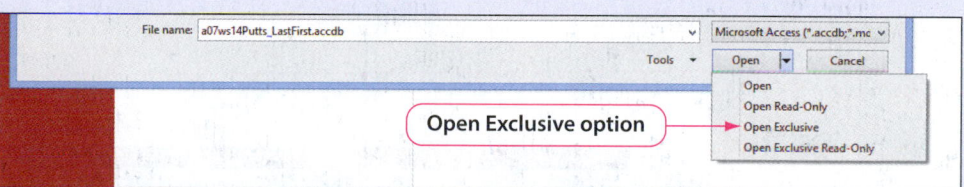

Open Exclusive option

Figure 1 Open Exclusive to provide greater access to the database

Prepare a Database for a Single User

Prior workshops in this text have discussed the importance of carefully choosing the data type for a field in a table, establishing table relationships, and best practices for building queries. These practices are important in database design in part because they can improve database performance. In this section you will prepare a database for a single user.

Using the Performance Analyzer

The **Performance Analyzer** is a tool in Access that analyzes and suggests ways to optimize the performance of a database. The Performance Analyzer can review individual Access objects or the entire database at one time.

After you run the Performance Analyzer, it provides three types of analysis results. Suggestions and recommendations can be performed by Access for you. **Recommendations** are actions that Access believes will improve the performance of your database. **Suggestions** are actions that Access believes will improve your database performance but may have consequences that should be considered first. The Performance Analyzer provides a description of these consequences when you select a specific suggestion.

Ideas are similar to suggestions, but the user must perform these actions. If you decide to pursue an idea from the Performance Analyzer, instructions will be provided by Access to complete the task.

A14.02

To Run the Performance Analyzer

a. Click the **DATABASE TOOLS** tab, and then in the Analyze Group, click **Analyze Performance**.

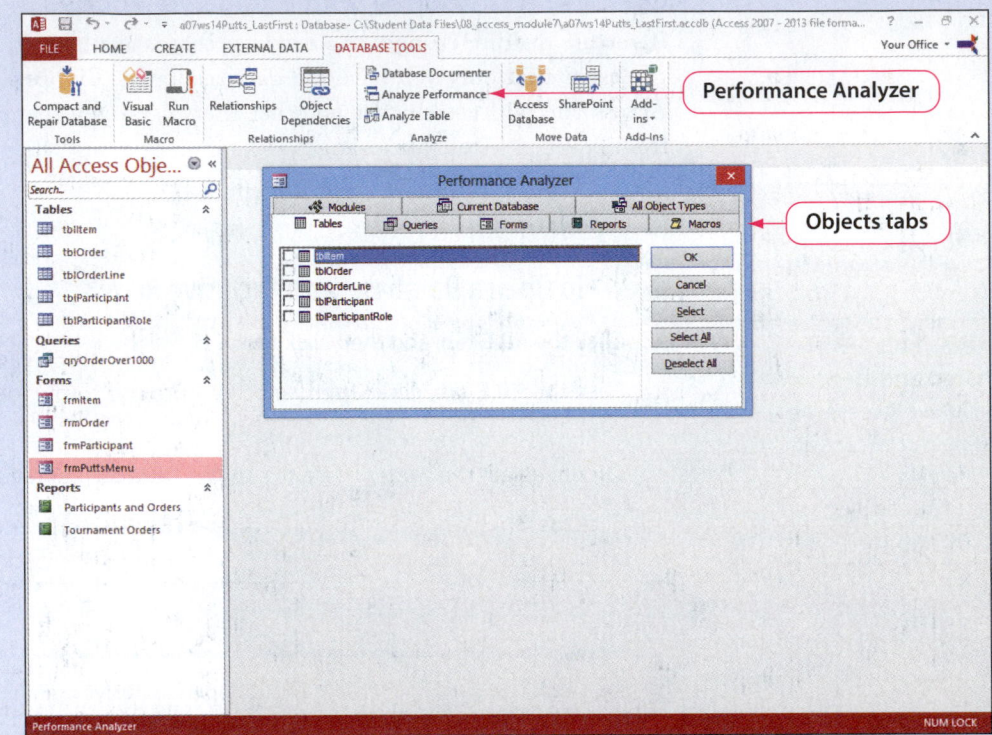

Figure 2 Performance Analyzer

b. In the Performance Analyzer dialog box click the **All Object Types** tab, and then click the **Select All** button. This will check all items, including macros and VBA modules, within the database to be analyzed.

c. Click **OK**.

Any recommendations, suggestions, or ideas will be displayed in the Analysis Results section of the dialog box. A description of the results is provided in the Analysis Notes section of the window. As mentioned previously, some of the optimizations that the Performance Analyzer will make may have consequences that should be carefully considered. For example, consider the first idea presented by the Performance Analyzer. The idea is to save your database in MDE format. This concept will be revisited later in this workshop.

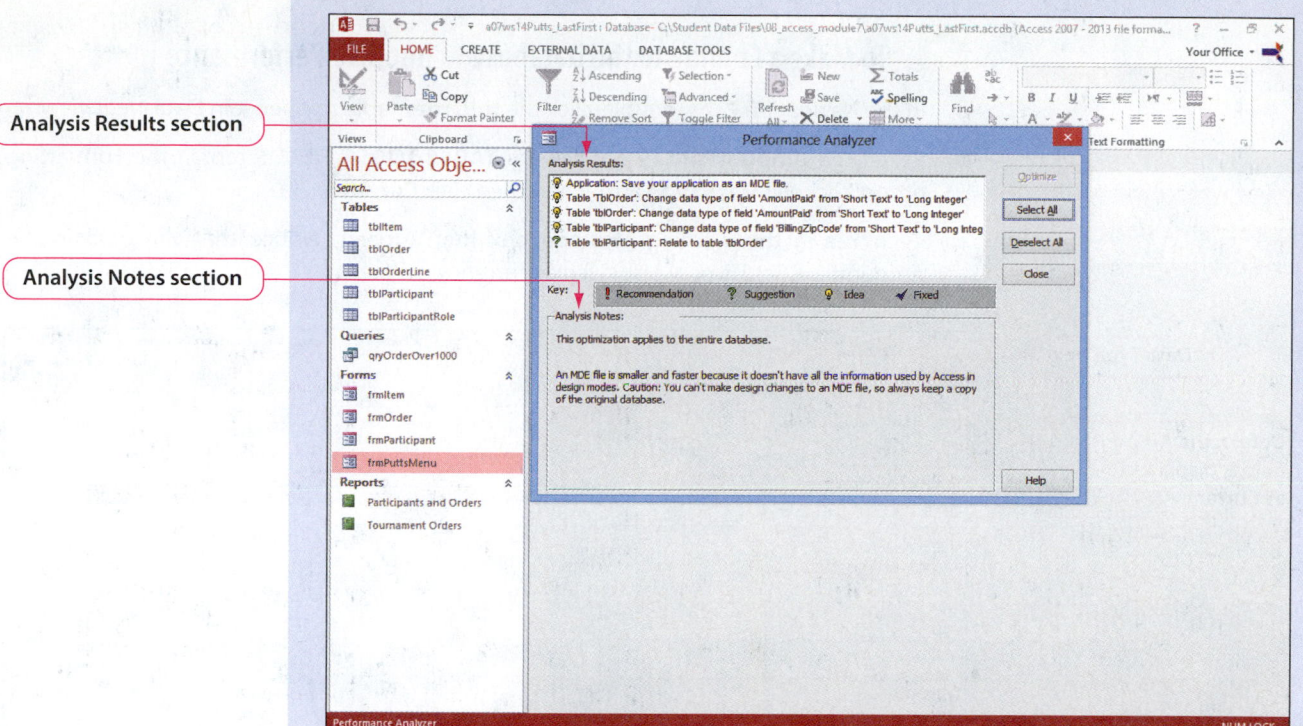

Analysis Results section

Analysis Notes section

Figure 3 Results of the Performance Analyzer

d. Click to select the **fourth idea** presented by the Performance Analyzer.

The idea states that the BillingZipCode field currently has a data type of Short Text and that this should be changed to a Long Integer data type. Access has analyzed the data in the table and determined that all of the data in this field are numeric. This is a correct conclusion as zip codes are numeric in nature. However, if a number will never be used in mathematical calculations—such as zip codes—then the correct data type is Short Text. Zip codes must be stored as text as some zip codes start with a zero. Changing the BillingZipCode field to a number would remove the zero at the front of any existing zip codes and any subsequent data entered into the table. Therefore, you should not take action on this suggestion.

e. Click to select the **second idea** presented by the Performance Analyzer.

This idea is to change the tblOrder field AmountPaid from Short Text to Long Integer. This idea complies with the best practice of a database that storing currency data in a text field can lead to problems with data management. Because this is an idea, you will need to make this change manually.

f. Click **Close** to exit the Performance Analyzer.

Making Changes to a Database to Improve Performance

Data in a database that will be used in mathematical calculations should be stored as an appropriate number field such as Currency or Number. Since the tblOrder table field AmountPaid is stored as Short Text, only a count of text records can be performed on the field. The AmountPaid field cannot be used to provide a sum or average. If you attempt to run the qryOrderOver1000 query you will receive a Microsoft Access error stating there is a data type mismatch in the criteria of the query. This error results because the criteria of the query looks for values greater than 1000 in the AmountPaid field. Since the field is short text, this criteria results in an error.

A14.03

 To Make a Change to the Database to Improve Performance

a. In the Navigation Pane, double-click the **tblOrder** table to open it in Datasheet view.

b. Select the **AmountPaid** field. Click the **TABLE TOOLS FIELDS** tab, in the Formatting group, click the **Data Type** arrow, and then click **Currency**.

c. Click **Yes** in the warning Message box that appears. Notice that the data in the AmountPaid field is now displayed as currency.

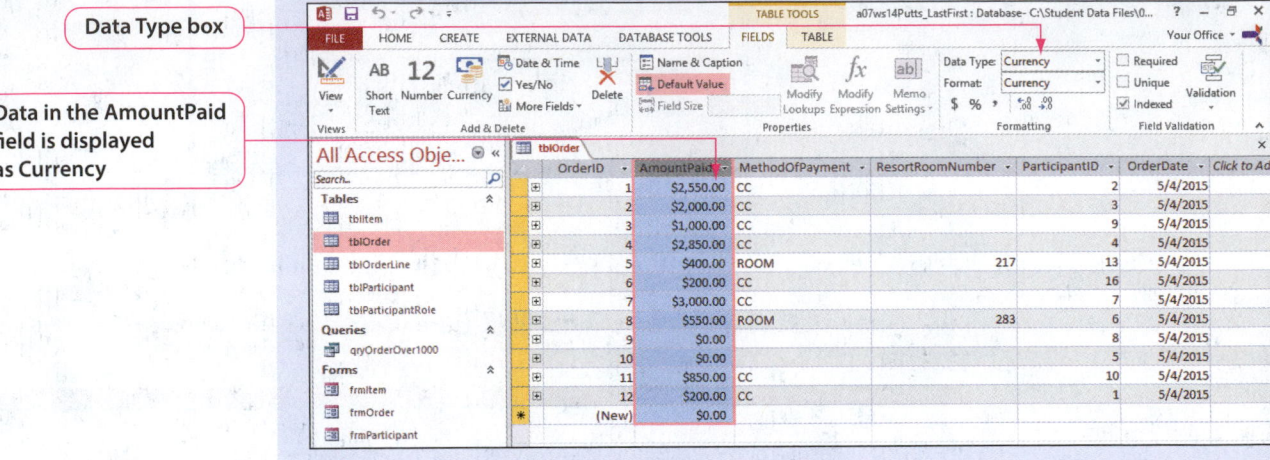

Figure 4 AmountPaid field changed to Currency data type

d. **Save** 💾 your changes, and then **Close** ✖ the tblOrder table.

Making Changes to a Database with the Performance Analyzer

The Performance Analyzer listed several possible optimizations that could improve database performance. These should be reviewed in the event that additional enhancements could be made.

A14.04

 To Make a Change to the Database with the Performance Analyzer

a. Click the **DATABASE TOOLS** tab, and then in the Analyze group, click **Analyze Performance**.

b. In the Performance Analyzer dialog box click the **All Object Types** tab, click **Select All**, and then click **OK**.

Examine the options presented by the Performance Analyzer. Some of the same ideas and suggestions appear, though now the idea to change the AmountPaid data type is no longer present.

c. In the Analysis Results box, click the suggestion that reads **Table 'tblParticipant': Relate to table 'tblOrder'**.

This is a suggestion by the Performance Analyzer to create a relationship between the tblParticipant table and the tblOrder table. This suggestion complies with the best practices of database design as the tblOrder table contains listings of orders participants have made. Because this is a suggestion, the Performance Analyzer can begin this process for you.

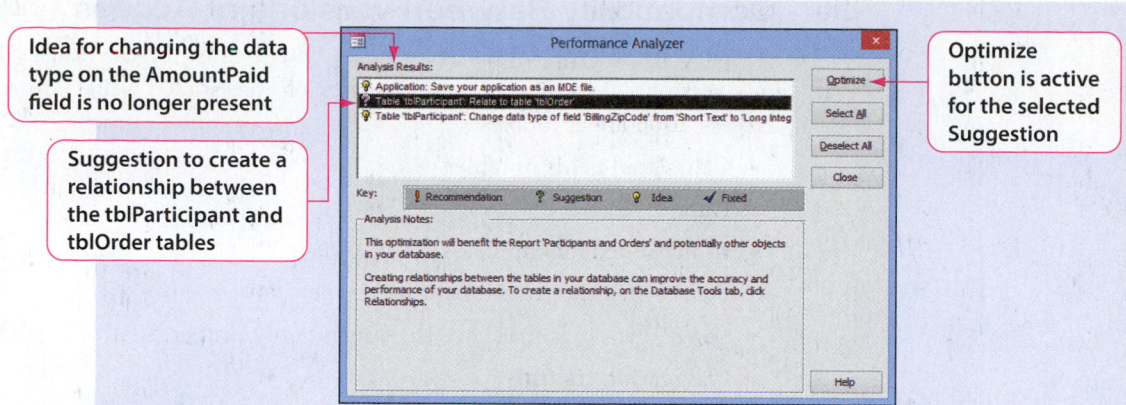

Idea for changing the data type on the AmountPaid field is no longer present

Suggestion to create a relationship between the tblParticipant and tblOrder tables

Optimize button is active for the selected Suggestion

Figure 5 Performance Analyzer after correcting the AmountPaid field

d. Click **Optimize**.

A checkmark will appear next to the suggestion indicating that Access made the change to the database for you. Now you should review the change to ensure that it complies with your database design.

e. Click **Close**. Click the **DATABASE TOOLS** tab, and then in the Relationships group, click **Relationships**.

Examine the relationship created by the Performance Analyzer. Notice that the relationship does not enforce referential integrity.

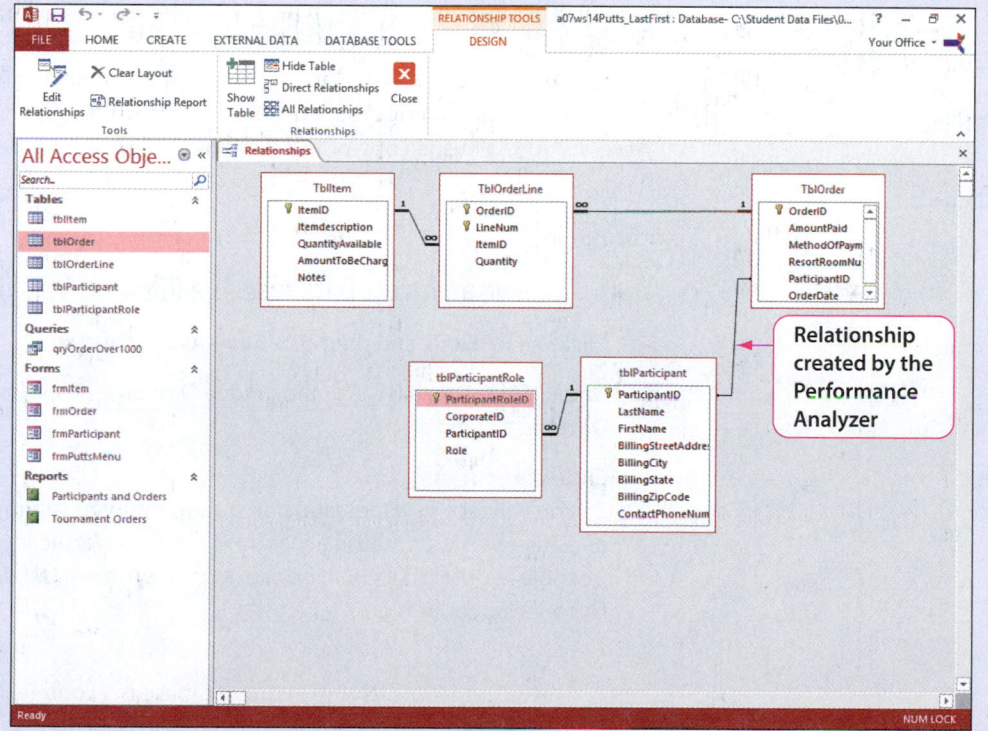

Relationship created by the Performance Analyzer

Figure 6 Relationships in the Putts for Paws database

f. Right-click the **relationship line** between tblParticipant and tblOrder, and then select **Edit Relationship**.

g. Click the **Enforce Referential Integrity** check box, and then click **OK**. This will create a one-to-many relationship between the tblParticipant table and the tblOrder table.

h. On the RELATIONSHIP TOOLS DESIGN tab, in the Relationships group, click **Close**.

Compatibility Between Versions of Access

As with most types of software, each new version of Access has features that previous versions did not. Common features of Access 2013 that are not compatible with Access 2003 are as follows.

- Calculated fields in tables
- Data macros
- Multivalued lookup fields
- Fields with the Attachment data type
- Long Text fields that have the append only property set to Yes
- Navigation controls
- Links to unsupported external files

To convert an .accdb file to the Access 2003 format, these features must first be removed. This includes navigation forms and any links to .xlsx files. The .accdb file type was first implemented in Access 2007, but there are features new even to Access 2013 that will not open or are limited in Access 2007. Some of these features include data macros and calculated fields in tables.

Access 2003 and prior versions use the file type .mdb. While Access 2013 can convert directly to Access versions 2002-2003 or 2000, it cannot directly convert to Access 97 or prior versions. To accomplish this, a database would first need to be converted into a 2002-2003 or 2000 version. The database would then be opened in an earlier version of Access and from there converted to an Access 97 database.

Saving an Access Database as a Previous Version

Barry Cheney has stated that while all new computers in the office are using Access 2013, there are several computers in the Red Bluff Golf Course & Pro Shop still using Access 2003. Thus, a copy of the database should be created in Access 2003 format.

A14.05

 To Save an Access Database as a Previous Version

a. Click the **FILE** tab, and then click **Save As**.

b. Under Save Database As, and under Database Files Types, click **Access 2002-2003 Database (*.mdb)**.

c. Click **Save As**.

   You will receive a message box stating that you cannot save the current database in an earlier version because a feature is not backward-compatible. The message box lists possible features that could be causing the problem but does not identify the issue with this specific conversion.

d. Click **OK**.

   The incompatible feature in this database is a Long Text field in the tblItem table. The Append Only property of this Long Text field is set to Yes.

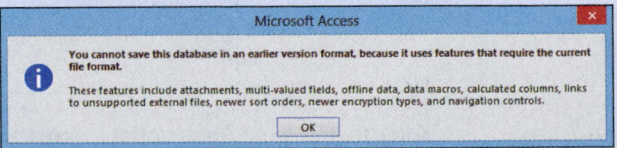

Figure 7   Access conversion error message

SIDE NOTE
Rich Text Long Text Fields

Versions of Access before 2007 will not recognize Rich Text Long Text fields. Instead the text will be displayed with corresponding HTML tags.

e. If necessary, click the **HOME** tab. In the Navigation Pane, right-click the table **tblItem**, and then select **Design View**.

f. Click the **Notes** field. In the Field Properties pane, click the **General** tab. Click the **Append Only** arrow, and then select **No**.

g. Save 💾 the changes to the table. Click **Yes** in the warning message stating that all history in the Notes column will be lost, and then **close** ✖ the table.

h. Click the **FILE** tab, and then click **Save As**.

i. Under Save Database As, under Database Files Types, click **Access 2002-2003 Database (*.mdb)**, and then click **Save As**. Navigate to the location where you are saving your files, name the file a07ws14Putts_LastFirst2003, and then click **Save**.

j. If necessary click **Enable Content**. The database will be converted to an Access 2003 .mdb file type and remain open. Notice that the Navigation Pane view has changed. It now displays only the tables. Click the **Navigation Pane arrow**, and then click **All Access Objects**. All database objects are now visible.

k. Click the **FILE** tab, and then click **Close**.

REAL WORLD ADVICE | **Multiple Versions of Access**

It is not uncommon in large corporations or in companies that are composed of several smaller units for there to be multiple IT systems in place. In some cases, you might find multiple versions of Microsoft Office running in a company. In situations like this, backward compatibility is always a concern. When designing databases carefully consider which versions of Access are in use and which features are not backward compatible.

Prepare a Database for Multiple Users

There are times when you will need to access data that is not contained in the database currently open in Access. While importing can bring this data into the local table structure, this is not always the best option. When data is shared among many databases and is stored in a central location on a computer network, Access provides the ability to link to the data. In this section, you will prepare a database for multiple users.

Linking Tables

A **linked table** provides a link to data stored in another database or application. The data contained in the application becomes available to Access as a table.

Access can link to a table in another Access database, an Excel spreadsheet, or to tables in SQL and Oracle databases. Linking to data is a best practice when the core data is shared among other users or applications or when Access is used as a means of viewing and querying SQL and Oracle database systems. This can reduce data redundancy and provide an efficient way of interacting with the data.

Data for the Putts for Paws corporate partners is currently being stored in the Excel spreadsheet a07ws14Corporate. This data needs to be linked to the Putts for Paws database so it can be used later in the planning of the event.

A14.06

To Link to the Corporate Data Worksheet

a. Click the **FILE** tab, and then click **Open**. Navigate to where you are saving your files, select the **a07ws14Putts** database, and then click **Open**.

b. Click the **EXTERNAL DATA** tab, and then in the Import & Link group, click **Excel**.

Get External Data dialog box

Your file path may be different

Browse button for locating files

Options for storing external data in Access

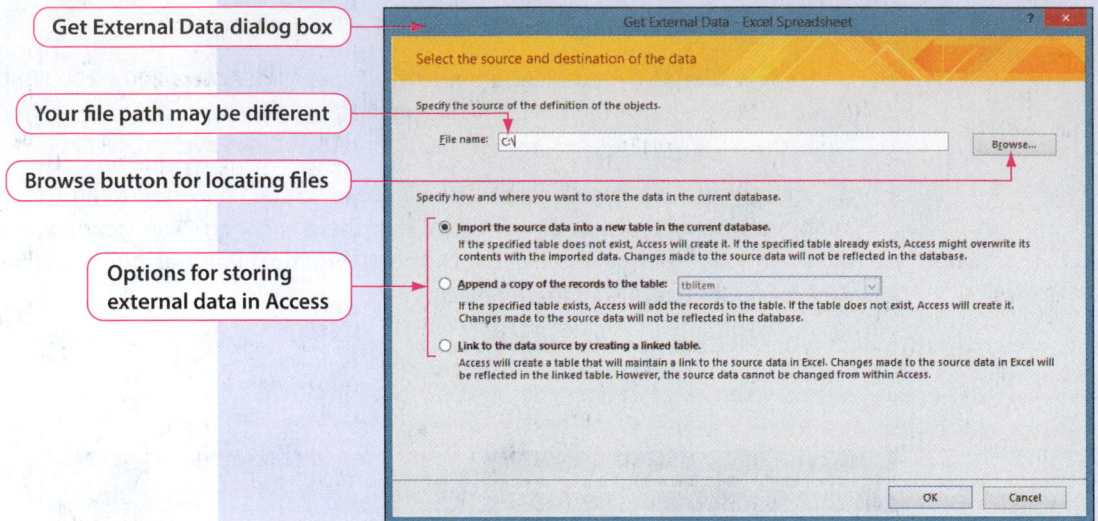

Figure 8   Get External Data dialog box

c. In the Get External Data dialog box, click the **Browse** button, navigate to the place where your student data files are stored, select **a07ws14Corporate** and then click **Open**.

d. Click **Link to the data source by creating a linked table**, and then click **OK**.
The Link Spreadsheet Wizard is now visible. The wizard will display a list of worksheets and named ranges present in the file you selected.

e. Click **Next**.
The wizard will now ask if you want to use the spreadsheet column headings as field names in your table. The column headings in the spreadsheet are appropriate field names in Access.

f. Click the **First Row Contains Column Headings** check box, and then click **Next**.
The wizard has now finished linking the spreadsheet and needs a name for the new table. Access will suggest "Corporate" as the table name.

g. Click in the **Linked Table Name** box, and then **select** the existing text. Type **tblCorporate**, and then click **Finish**.

h. Click **OK** in the message box that appears telling you that the spreadsheet is now linked.
The tblCorporate table now appears in the Navigation Pane. Notice the blue arrow in front of the Microsoft Excel symbol. This indicates that the table is linked. Data can be added, changed, or deleted from a linked table; however, the structure of the table cannot be changed.

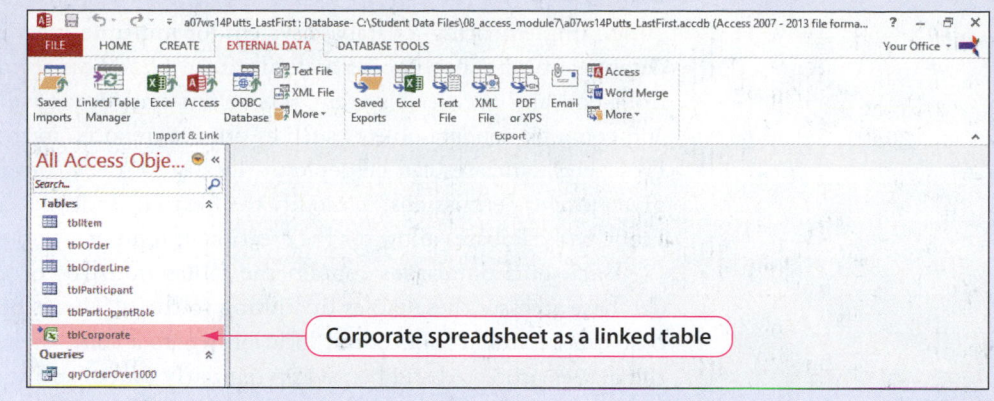

Figure 9 Linked spreadsheet in the Navigation Pane

Viewing Data in a Linked Table

When a linked table is opened, Access refreshes the data contained in the linked object. The a07ws14Corporate spreadsheet currently contains five records in it. Viewing this table in Access will verify this. However, any new data added to the spreadsheet will be visible in Access after opening the table.

A14.07

To Add Data to a Linked Table

a. Start **Excel**, click **Open Other Workbooks**, and browse to your student data files. Locate and select **a07ws14Corporate**, and then click **Open**.

> **Troubleshooting**
>
> If the a07ws14Corporate spreadsheet is opened while the tblCorporate table is open in Access, Excel will notify you that the file is locked for editing. You will have the option to open a read-only copy of the file, be notified when the file is available for full use, or cancel.

b. Click cell A7 of the Corporate worksheet, type **6**, and the press Tab. In cell B7, type your first and last name. Press Ctrl+Enter.

c. **Save** 🖫 your workbook, and then **Close** ✕ Excel.

d. In the Putts for Paws database, in the Navigation Pane, double-click **tblCorporate**. If necessary, adjust the **width** of the Company Name column to view the data. Your name should be displayed as the sixth record in the table.

e. **Close** ✕ the table and if necessary, click **Yes** to accept changes to the layout of the table.

REAL WORLD ADVICE **Linking Access to SharePoint**

Access data can be published outside of the database in many ways. Data can be exported in formats such as PDF and Microsoft Excel spreadsheets. Access objects can also be published to Microsoft SharePoint sites. SharePoint is an online collaboration tool that allows teams to organize and update information online. Access can synchronize forms and reports between the online client and the offline database. You can also make changes to your Access database and update the data online.

Using the Database Splitter

When implementing a database system for multiple users it can be helpful to divide the database objects into two separate database files. This splitting of the database creates a front-end and back-end system. The **front-end database** is deployed directly to users and contains nondata objects such as queries, reports, forms, macros, and VBA modules. Front-end databases can be deployed locally to user's computers. This allows the user, if given proper permissions, to modify the file to include objects for their individualized use. Front-end databases allow for the creation of temporary objects, such as temporary tables.

Back-end databases contain the tables from the original database. The front-end database accesses these tables by linking to them. This is beneficial as the back-end database can be stored in a central location where a company's technical support can ensure the data is protected and backed up regularly. Importantly, the back-end database cannot be on a shared drive with limited file permissions. That is to say, the back-end database must allow the front-end database the ability to add and delete data to its tables.

For database developers, splitting databases is beneficial as changes can be made to the front-end database without having to take the entire database offline. A new form or query can be developed and moved into the front-end system without having to shut down the back-end system.

A14.08

To Split the Database

a. Click the **DATABASE TOOLS** tab, and then in the Move Data group, click **Access Database**. This launches the Database Splitter Wizard.

Database Splitter

Database Splitter Wizard

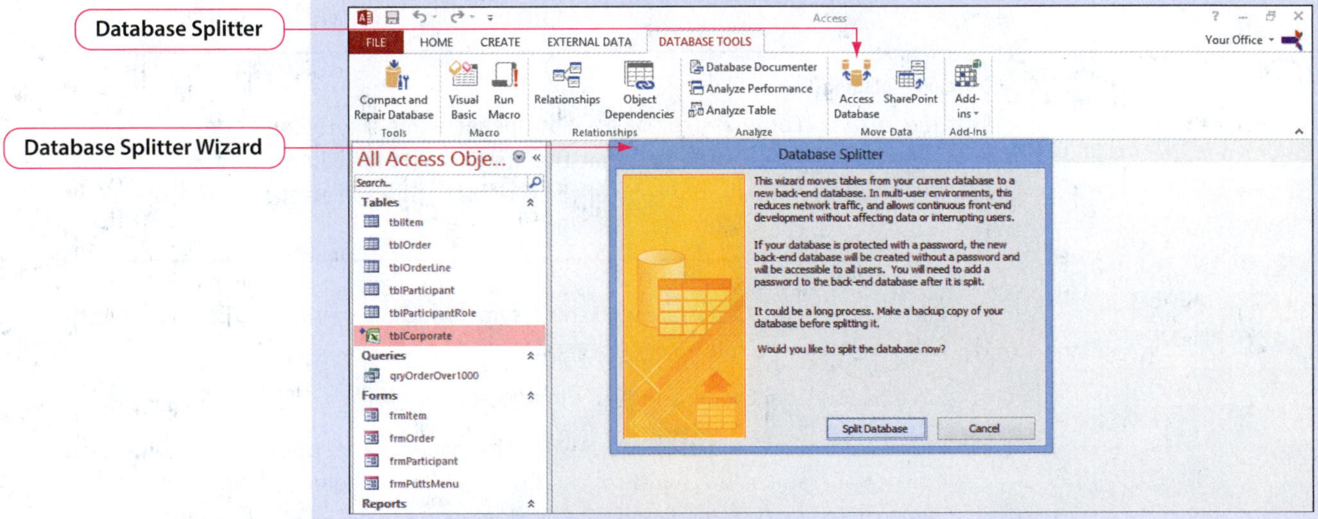

Figure 10   Splitting an Access database

b. Click **Split Database**.
   This will open the Create Back-end Database dialog box. The Database Splitter Wizard will first create the back-end database.

c. Navigate to the location where you store your data files. Notice that the name of the file being created is a07ws14Putts_LastFirst_be. The "be" appended to the end of the file name stands for "back-end". Click **Split**.

d. Click **OK** in the Database Splitter message box stating that the database has been successfully split. The database currently open is now the front-end database.

SIDE NOTE

Linked Tables in Split Databases

If the back-end database is moved, the links in the front-end database must be updated.

e. Examine the Navigation Pane. Notice that all of the tables are now linked. This is indicated with the blue arrow next to the table icon. This front-end database can now be deployed to multiple users.

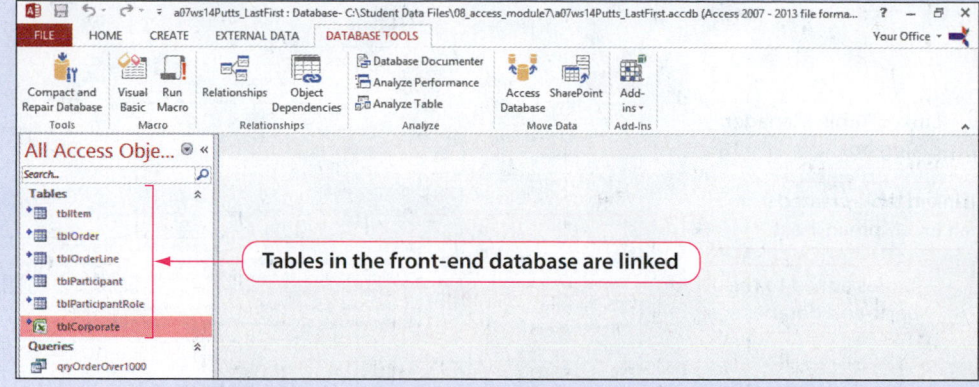

Figure 11   Linked tables in the front-end database

f. In the folder containing the a07ws14Putts_LastFirst database, create a folder called **Putts_be**. Move the **a07ws14Putts_LastFirst_be** database into the Putts_be subfolder.

Using the Linked Table Manager

Access cannot update the data in the database from a linked object if the object has been moved from its original location. Linked tables are dependent on the location of the object, not the database that contains the link. This means that databases containing a linked table can be moved at will with no ill effects. However, the file containing the linked object must remain in the same location in order for the link to function properly.

If a linked object is moved, the Linked Table Manager can be used to refresh the link. The **Linked Table Manager** lists the file location of all linked tables in a database. If the location of a linked object changes, the Linked Table Manager can be used to refresh those links. Attempting to access a linked object that has been moved from its original location will result in an error similar to the one displayed in Figure 12.

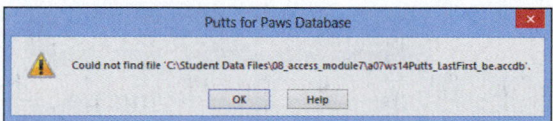

Figure 12   Error message stating a linked object could not be found

Because the back-end database was moved to a different location, the links to the objects contained within it will need to be refreshed.

A14.09

To Use the Linked Table Manager

a. Click the **EXTERNAL DATA** tab, and then in the Import & Link group, click **Linked Table Manager**.

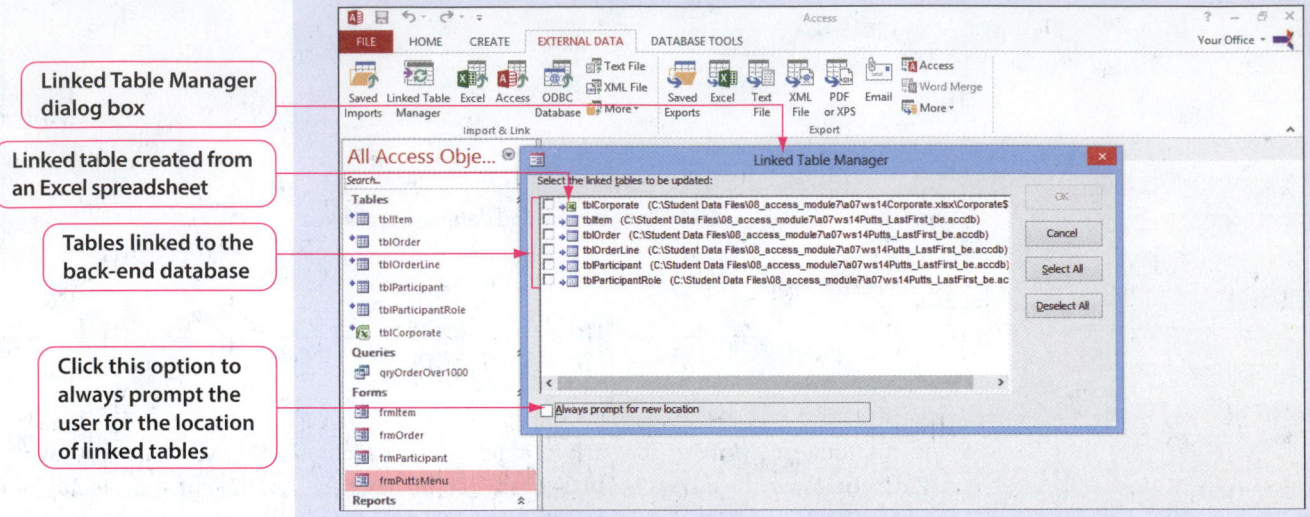

Linked Table Manager dialog box

Linked table created from an Excel spreadsheet

Tables linked to the back-end database

Click this option to always prompt the user for the location of linked tables

Figure 13 Linked Table Manager

SIDE NOTE
The File Path of the Linked Tables

The file paths in Figure 13 might be different in your database. This is dependent upon the configuration of your computer.

b. Click the **tblItem**, **tblOrder**, **tblOrderLine**, **tblParticipant**, and **tblParticipantRole** check boxes, and then click **OK**.

c. In the Select New Location dialog box navigate to the **Putts_be** folder, and then double-click to open it. Select the **a07ws14Putts_LastFirst_be** database, and then click **Open**.

d. Click **OK** in the Linked Table Manager message box stating that all selected linked tables have been successfully refreshed.

e. Click **Close** to close the Linked Table Manager.

f. Click the **FILE** tab, and then click **Close**.

REAL WORLD ADVICE | **Linked Data in Earlier Versions of Access**

If you have an Access 2010 database with links to external data that is not compatible with prior versions of Access, there is a solution. Try importing the data and then deleting the external links. This will provide the database with the ability to convert to a previous version of Access.

Encryption and Passwords

Ultimately to protect a database and its information, passwords and encryption can be implemented. **Encryption** is the process of changing text-based information into a state in which a key is required in order to read the information. An algorithm or cipher is used to process the data from text into an unreadable state. The process of **decryption** will make encrypted information readable again. The information is decrypted using a key. In Access, the key will be a password. In other applications, the key can be a separate file.

CONSIDER THIS | **What Makes a Strong Password?**

Passwords should be created carefully. Common words and phrases in any language should be avoided. The longer and more complex a password, the more secure it will be. How do you build a strong password? What features should a strong password contain?

Encrypting and Setting a Database Password

Barry Cheney has asked that the front-end database file you created be encrypted for added security to the data.

A14.10

To Encrypt and Set a Database Password

a. Click the **FILE** tab, and then click **Open**. Navigate to where you are saving your files, select the **a07ws14Putts_LastFirst** database, click the **Open** arrow, and then click **Open Exclusive**.

Troubleshooting

To encrypt the database it must be opened with Exclusive Access. When Access closes and reopens a database—as it does during the split database operation—the front-end database will be opened with Shared Access.

b. Click the **FILE** tab, and if necessary click **Info**.

c. Click **Encrypt with Password**. In the Set Database Password dialog box, type **917abf70**, retype your password in the Verify box, and then click **OK**.

You will receive a Microsoft Access warning stating the row level locking will be ignored.

Troubleshooting

Row-level locking is used to ensure that when two users are editing a table they cannot edit the same row—record—of data. This is not compatible in an encrypted database. Access will disable this feature and provide the warning message shown in Figure 14.

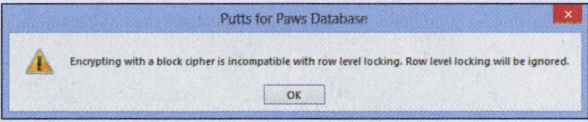

Figure 14 Row-level locking warning message

d. Click **OK**. The database will now prompt the user for a password when it is opened. It is best practice to test opening the database in order to ensure it prompts the user for a password. Click the **FILE** tab, and then click **Close**.

e. Click the **FILE** tab, and then click **Open**. Navigate to where you are saving your files, select the **a07ws14Putts_LastFirst** database, and then click **Open**. In the Password Required dialog box type **917abf70** and then click **OK**.

Setting the User's Experience

Access features several options to assist a database developer in controlling the user's experience in a database. To begin securing a database, there are several key features in Access that should be disabled or modified. This includes controlling the way users navigate in the database, preventing users from editing certain Access objects, controlling what tabs the user will see on the Ribbon, adding a customized icon for the database, and setting a password on the database. To set a password, the database must first be opened with Exclusive Access. In this section, you will control the user interface of an Access database.

Control Startup Options

To ensure the integrity of the database, access to several features must be eliminated. Barry Cheney has asked that users not be able to create new objects in the database or be able to import or export data using the Ribbon. When any of these functions are required, they will be built into the database forms as buttons or other controls. Likewise, any information stored in the database that users will need to access will be included on the navigation form that is displayed when the database is opened.

Preventing a table from being opened directly requires hiding the Navigation Pane. To prevent the creation of new database objects, the Create tab on the Ribbon must be hidden. Importing and exporting data can be prevented by hiding the External Data and Database Tools tabs. Hiding the Database Tools tab will also take one step towards securing any VBA or macros in the database.

Often in Access there are several ways of accomplishing any single task. For example, the Visual Basic Editor can be opened using a button on the Ribbon or by pressing the keyboard shortcut `Alt`+`F11`. To properly secure a database, each of these options must be considered to adequately prevent an object from being accessed. Ultimately, any direct access to the VBA code must be locked down. The `Alt`+`F11` keyboard shortcut is one of the special keys in Access.

Special Keys

Special keys are a set of four keyboard shortcuts that can be disabled when securing a database. A list of special keys is provided in Table 1. To properly secure a database, special keys should be disabled, because special keys allow users access to the Navigation Pane and the Visual Basic Editor even if these items are hidden from view initially in the database. To begin securing the Putts for Paws database, you will hide tabs on the Ribbon, hide the Navigation Pane, and disable special keys.

Key or Key Combination	Description	Why Should This Be Disabled?
`F11`	Shows or hides the Navigation Pane	Prevents users from accessing tables or other objects to protect the integrity of the database
`Ctrl`+`G`	Shows the Immediate Window in the Visual Basic Editor; launches the Visual Basic Editor if it is not already open	Prevents users from accessing or creating Visual Basic code in the database
`Ctrl`+`Break`	Stops Access from retrieving records from a server	This applies when Access is designed to work as the front-end application to a SQL server
`Alt`+`F11`	Opens the Visual Basic Editor	Prevents users from accessing or creating Visual Basic code in the database

Table 1 Table of special keys

Setting Startup Preferences

The first step in securing the database as requested by Barry Cheney is to examine the current database options. Several of the most basic steps to securing a database can be taken in the Access Options dialog box. These options will affect only the database that is currently open.

A14.11

To Set the Startup Preferences on the Putts for Paws Database

a.. Click the **FILE** tab, and then click **Options**. In the navigation options on the left side of the Access Options dialog box, click **Current Database**.

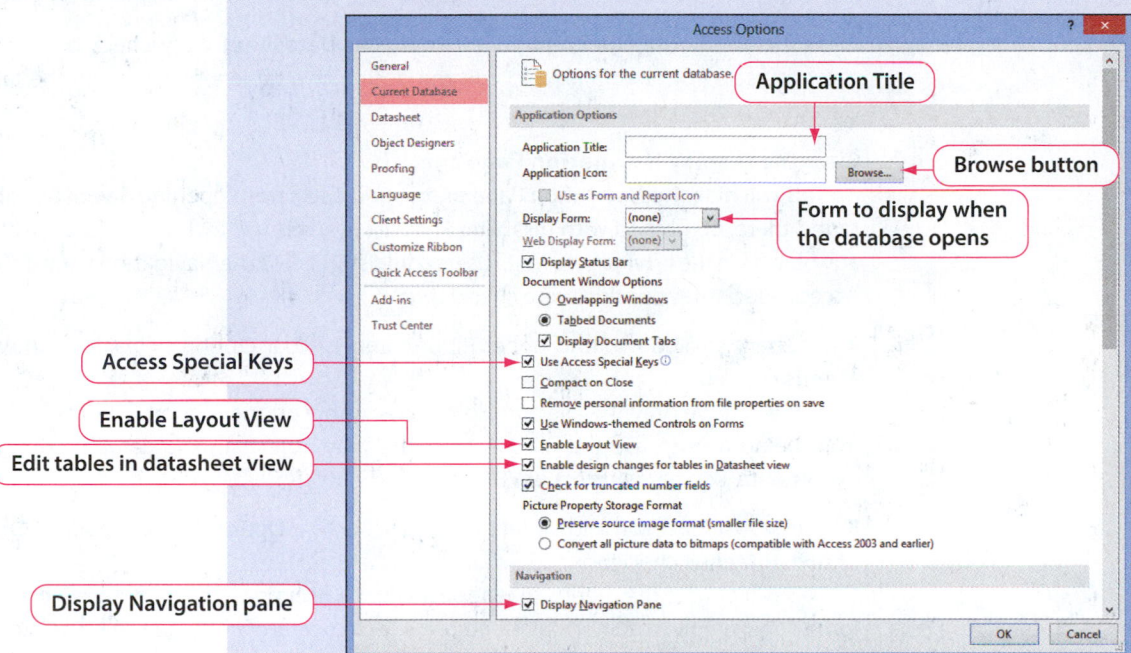

Figure 15 Access Options for the Putts for Paws database

b. In the **Application Title** box, type Putts for Paws Database. This will replace the file name on the title bar in the Access window.

c. To the right of the Application Icon box, click **Browse**. Navigate to where your student data files are stored, select **a07ws14Icon**, and then click **OK**. This will replace the default Access icon in the title bar in the Access window.

> **Troubleshooting**
>
> The location of the file used for the application icon is an absolute reference. If the file is moved once the connection is made the icon will no longer appear in the title bar.

d. Click the **Display Form** arrow, and then select **frmPuttsMenu**. This will automatically open the frmPuttsMenu form when the database is opened.

e. Clear the **Use Access Special Keys** check box. This step disables the four special keys described previously.

f. Clear the **Enable Layout View** check box. By removing the Layout view option from the Views group on the Ribbon, you will prevent users from being able to edit forms and other Access objects.

> **Troubleshooting**
>
> Changes to the options in an Access database might require that a specific Access object that is open when the changes are made be closed and reopened. For example, disabling the Layout view feature will not take effect on an open form. Before the changes take effect, the form must be closed and reopened.

g. Clear the **Enable design changes for tables in Datasheet view** check box. This will prevent users from being able to edit the design of a table while viewing the table in Datasheet view.

h. Clear the **Display Navigation Pane** check box.

This will hide the Navigation Pane preventing users from opening any of the objects found there. Combined with disabling special keys, this will lock users out of accessing any objects in the Navigation Pane. Users could still access the Navigation Pane if the Use Access Special Keys option were checked.

i. If necessary scroll down and under Ribbon and Toolbar Options, clear the **Allow Full Menus** check box.

This will leave only the File and Home tabs visible on the Ribbon. This restricts users from being able to use the Ribbon to create new objects in the database, import or export data, or create macros or VBA.

j. If necessary scroll down and under Ribbon and Toolbar Options, clear the **Allow Default Shortcut Menus** check box.

This will disable the menus that appear when a user right-clicks an Access object. On forms for example, the shortcut menu provides a means of changing to Layout view.

k. Click **OK**. Examine the warning message displayed by Access. Several of the settings you have just enacted will not take effect until the database is closed and reopened. This includes the options to hide the Navigation Pane, Full Menus, Shortcut Menus, and disable design changes for tables in Datasheet view. Click **OK**.

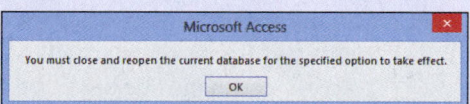

Figure 16 Startup setting warning

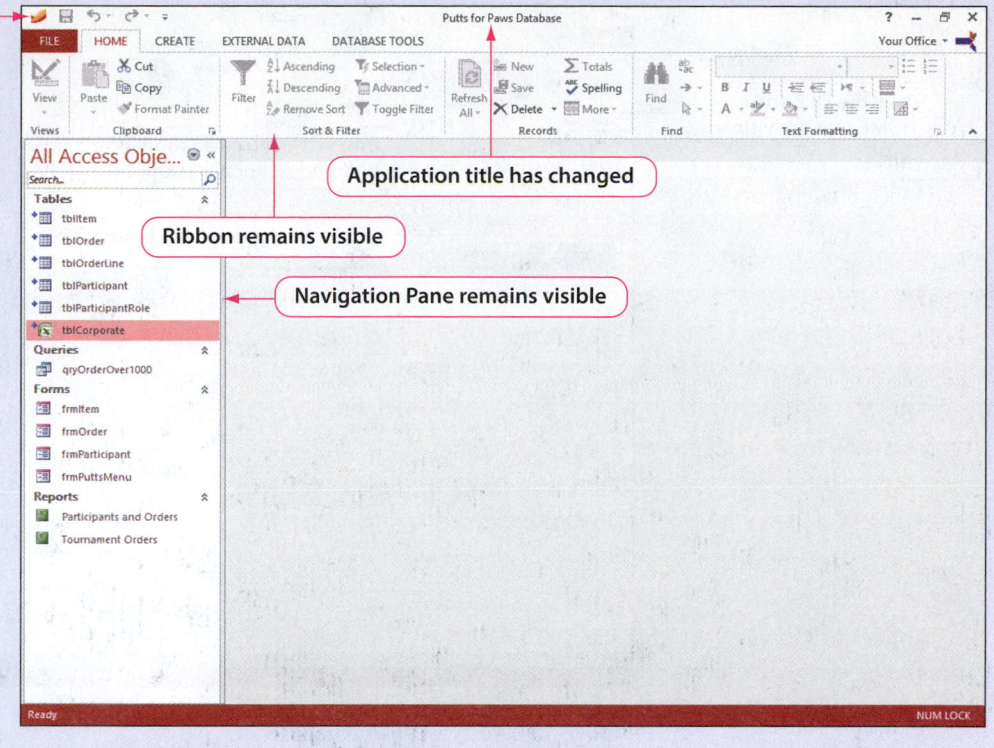

Database icon changed

Application title has changed

Ribbon remains visible

Navigation Pane remains visible

Figure 17 Access options before closing the database

l. Click the **FILE** tab, and then click **Close**.

Testing the Startup Settings

Importantly, you should test any changes made to the user interface of a database. This provides you with a chance to verify that all options are correctly set. It also provides you with a chance to experience the database as other users will.

A14.12

 To Test the Startup Preferences on the Putts for Paws Database

a. To test the changes that have been made to the database, click the **FILE** tab, and then click **Open**.

b. Navigate to where you are saving your files, and then open the **a07ws14Putts_LastFirst** database. Type 917abf70 for the password to open the file when prompted.

c. Notice that only the File and Home tabs on the Ribbon are available. Likewise, the frmPuttsMenu navigation form opened with the database, but the Navigation Pane is not visible.

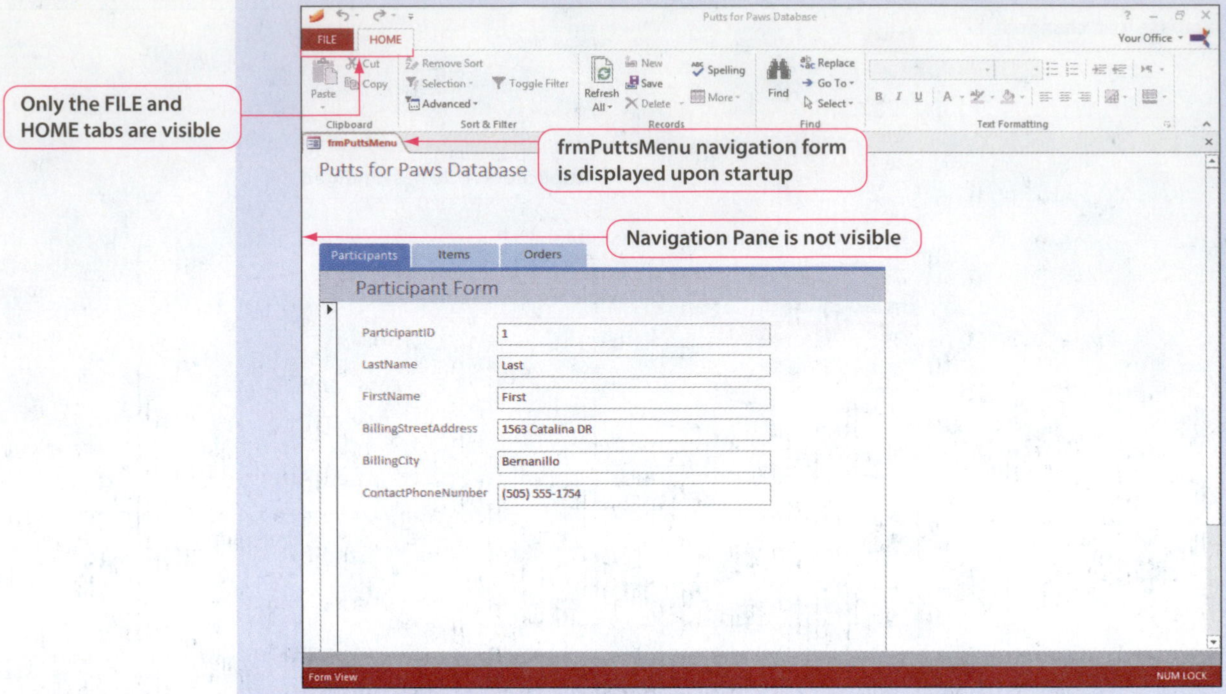

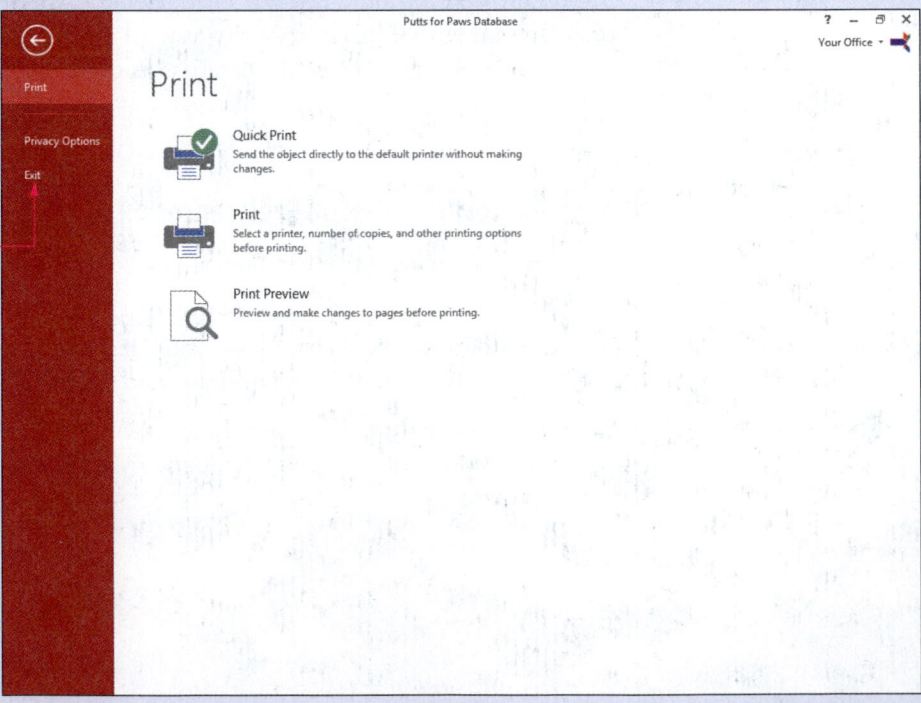

Only the FILE and HOME tabs are visible

frmPuttsMenu navigation form is displayed upon startup

Navigation Pane is not visible

Figure 18 Putts for Paws database

d. Press Alt + F11. Normally this will open the Visual Basic Editor. However, because special keys are disabled, nothing will happen as a result of this key combination.

e. Click the **FILE** tab to examine the changes to this view.

The available options are now limited. Users are allowed to print objects and exit the database. The Privacy Options button will open the Access Options dialog box. Importantly, users can reset the Current Database options from this menu.

SIDE NOTE
Allow Full Menus
To show full menus when Allow Full Menus has been cleared, hold down Shift while opening the database.

Close option eliminated

Figure 19 Putts for Paws database File tab

f. Click **Exit**. Submit your work as directed by your instructor.

Methods of Implementation

Selecting a method of implementing your database—or any information technology solution—is a critical decision. There are several approaches to choose from and many important factors to consider. Cost, time, and the functionality of the new system are three of the most important factors to consider. Importantly, you must choose an approach that fits your business, employees, and technical environment. Your new database will be replacing a legacy system. This might be a paper-based system or a software-based system. **Legacy software** is old technology that is out of date but still in use. Legacy software exists because the basic needs of the business are still met by the software. Often users prefer legacy systems. They are familiar with the system, and any flaws in the system have usually been eliminated. It can be intimidating to learn a new system or business process, and thus implementations can be fraught with the anxiety of the unknown.

You might choose to implement your database all at once. This **cold turkey implementation** approach involves implementing your database in its entirety and replacing the legacy system all at once. This method leaves little room for error. Once the new system is in place, the legacy system is no longer in use. If errors are found with the new system, they must be corrected in the absence of an alternate process. Alternatively, this approach gets users into the new system quickly and limits the need for maintaining more than one active solution.

Other methods involve a more gradual approach. In **piloted implementations**, small groups of a company start using the new database. Gradually, more groups come on board as the system is perfected until the entire organization is using the new system. In **parallel implementations**, the legacy system and new system are used concurrently. In **phased implementations**, a portion of the new system is put into place and perfected before additional pieces of the system are moved into use.

The three strategies discussed above offer a robust way to test a system and correct errors before a new system is put into full use. This provides a backup if the new system needs to be taken out of use and limits the loss of productivity if such an event happens. Conversely, these implementation approaches can take more time to complete and lead to increased costs as two systems must be maintained until the new system completely replaces the legacy system.

1. For what reasons would you want to open an Access database with exclusive rights? p. 684

2. Once the Performance Analyzer has run, what are the differences in the three types of results that it will present? Should these results always be acted upon? p. 685

3. What compatibility issues exist between Access 2003 and Access 2013? What differences are there between Access 2007 and Access 2013? p. 690

4. What types of objects can be used to create linked tables in Access? What are the consequences of poor file management in regard to linked tables? p. 695

5. Define encryption. Describe situations when encrypting a database would be beneficial. p. 696

6. What are the advantages of customizing the startup options of a database? p. 698

7. Discuss the different methods of implementing a new database in an organization. What are the benefits and drawbacks to each method? p. 703

Key Terms

Back-end database 694
Cold turkey implementation 703
Decryption 696
Encryption 696
Exclusive Access 684
Front-end database 694

Ideas 686
Legacy software 703
Linked table 691
Linked Table Manager 695
Parallel implementation 703
Performance Analyzer 685

Phased implementation 703
Piloted implementation 703
Recommendations 685
Shared Access 684
Special keys 698
Suggestions 685

Visual Summary

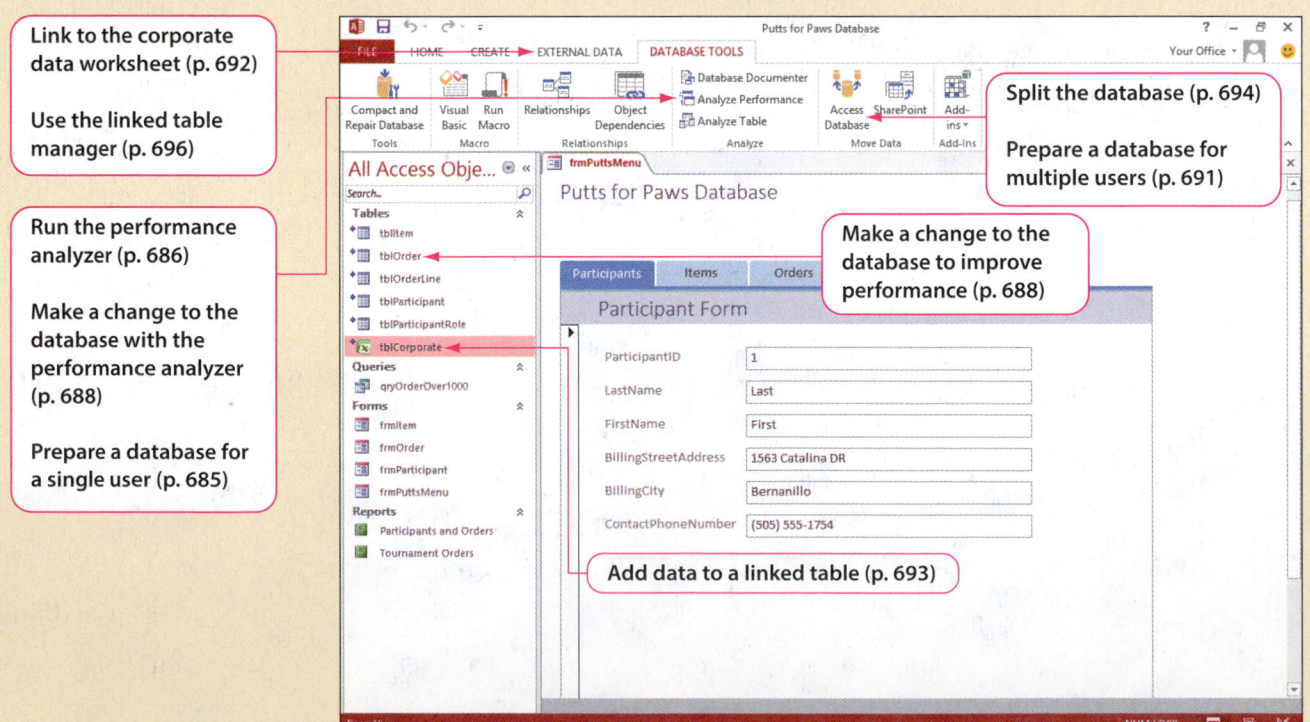

Link to the corporate data worksheet (p. 692)

Use the linked table manager (p. 696)

Run the performance analyzer (p. 686)

Make a change to the database with the performance analyzer (p. 688)

Prepare a database for a single user (p. 685)

Split the database (p. 694)

Prepare a database for multiple users (p. 691)

Make a change to the database to improve performance (p. 688)

Add data to a linked table (p. 693)

Encrypt and set a database password (p. 697)

Understand the differences between versions of Access (p. 690)

Open a database with exclusive access (p. 685)

Save an Access database as a previous version (p. 690)

Encrypt a database with a password (p. 696)

Set the startup preferences on the Putts for Paws database (p. 699)

Modify the startup options in a database (p. 698)

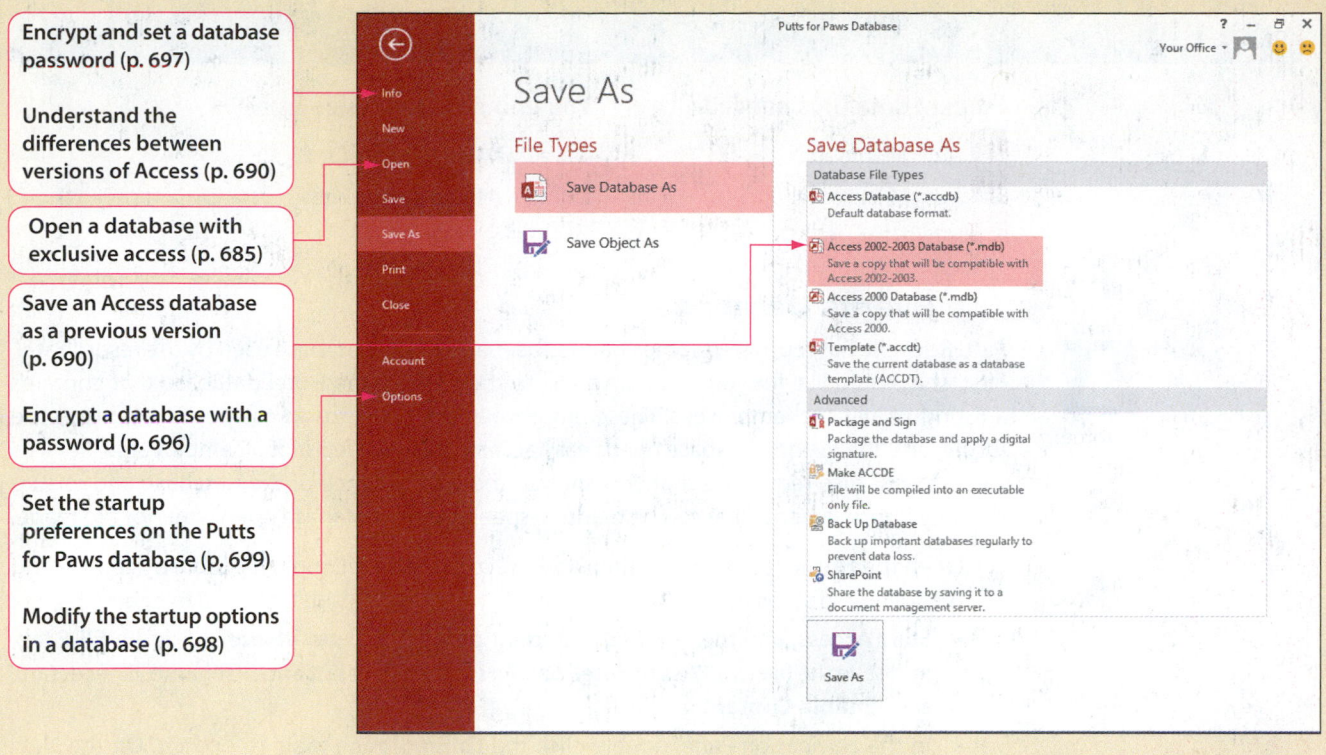

Test the startup preferences on the Putts for Paws database (p. 701)

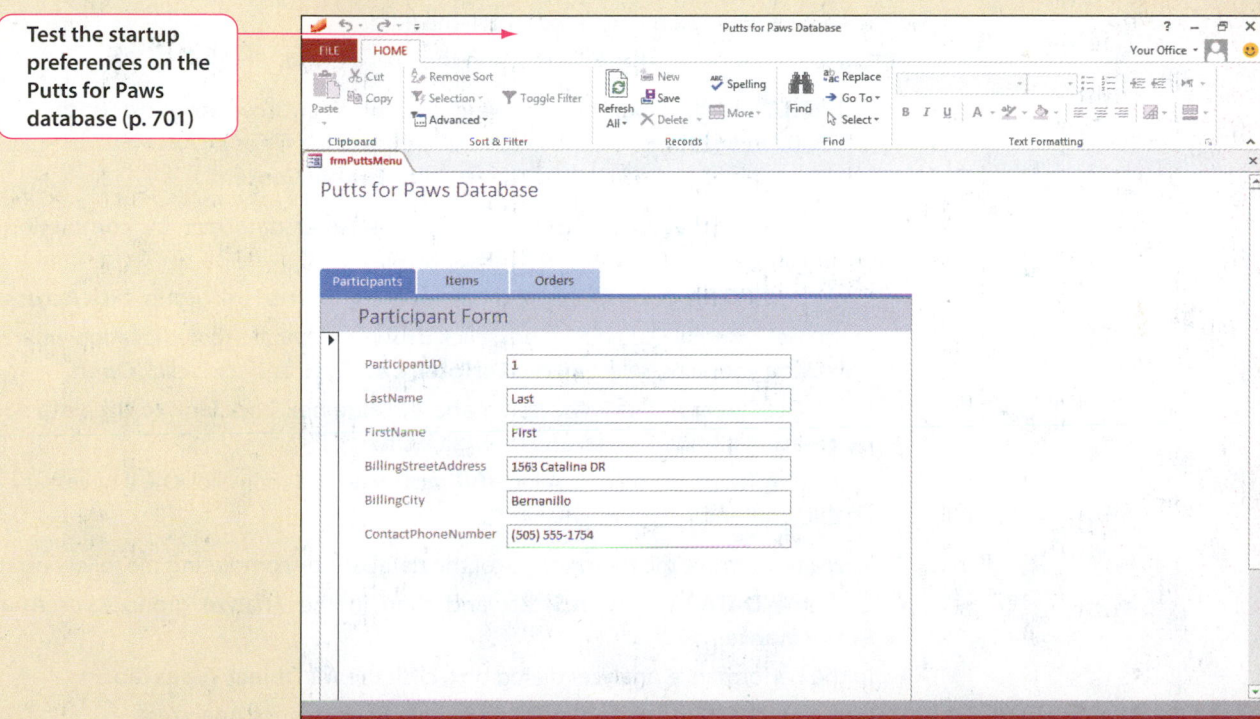

Figure 20 The Red Bluff Golf Course & Pro Shop Putts for Paws Charity Final Database

Student data files needed:

 a07ws14Events.accdb

 a07ws14Hotel.accdb

a07ws14Icon.ico

You will save your files as:

 a07ws14Events_LastFirst.accdb

 a07ws14Hotel_LastFirst.accdb

The Events Database

Customer Service

Patti Rochelle has requested some changes be made to the database used by the resort hotel. First, she would like for you to create a link to the table in the Hotel database that contains a listing of all hotel employees. These employees will be assigned to specific events in the future, and the Events database needs easy access to an active list of all employees.

Patti has also requested that you analyze the performance of the database and ensure that any improvements that can be made to speed up the database's performance are made.

a. Open the **Hotel** database, and then add a record to the tblEmployee table by completing the following steps:

- Start **Access**, and then open the student data file **a07ws14Hotel**. Click the **FILE** tab, and save the file as a07ws14Hotel_LastFirst using your last and first name. If necessary, click **Enable Content**.

- In the Navigation Pane, double-click the **tblEmployee** table to open it. On the New record line, type **6** in the AreaID field. Type your first name in the FirstName field, and then type your last name in the LastName field.

- **Close** the table, click the **FILE** tab, and then click **Close**.

b. Click the **FILE** tab, click **Open**, and double-click **Computer**. Browse to and open the student data file **a07ws14Events**. Click the **FILE** tab, and save the file as a07ws14Events_LastFirst using your last and first name. If necessary, click **Enable Content**.

c. Create a link to the tblEmployee table in the Hotel database by completing the following steps.

- Click the **EXTERNAL DATA** tab, and then in the Import & Link group, click **Access**.

- In the Get External Data dialog box, click **Browse**. Navigate to the location where you are saving your files, select **a07ws14Hotel_LastFirst**, and then click **Open**.

- In the Get External Data – Access Database dialog box, click **Link to the data source by creating a linked table**, and then click **OK**.

- In the Link Tables dialog box, select **tblEmployee**, and then click **OK**. If necessary, click Enable Content.

d. Analyze and improve the performance of the database by completing the following steps:

- Click the **DATABASE TOOLS** tab, and then in the Analyze group, click **Analyze Performance**.

- In the Performance Analyzer dialog box, click the **All Object Types** tab.

- Click **Select All**, and then click **OK** to run the Performance Analyzer.

- Select the suggestion **Table 'tblEvents': Relate to table tblEventItems'**, and then click **Optimize**. This will improve the performance of the qryEventList query.

- Click the idea **Table 'tblMenuChoice': Change data type of field 'CostPerPerson' from Short 'Text' to 'Double'** to examine it. The CostPerPerson field is the price each person would be charged for a meal and should be converted to Currency. Click **Close**.

- In the Navigation Pane, double-click the **tblMenuChoice** table to open it.

- Select the CostPerPerson field, and then click the **TABLE TOOLS FIELDS** tab.

- In the Formatting group, click the **Data Type** arrow, and then select **Currency**. Because currency fields are smaller than text fields, Access will warn you that the potential exists for losing data. This will not be an issue in this table. Click **Yes**.
- **Save** your changes, and **close** the table.

e. To encrypt the database with a password, it will need to be opened with Exclusive Access. Click the **FILE** tab, and then click **Close**.

f. Click the **FILE** tab, click **Open**, and then browse to the folder where you are saving your files. Click to select **a07ws14Events_LastFirst**. Click the **Open** arrow, and then select **Open Exclusive**. If necessary, click **Enable Content**.

g. Encrypt the database with a password and modify the startup options by completing the following steps:
- Click the **FILE** tab, if necessary click **Info**, and then click **Encrypt with Password**.
- In the Password field, type 321efd68, and then in the Verify field type 321efd68. Click **OK**.
- Click **OK** in the message that Access will ignore row-level locking.
- Click the **FILE** tab, and click **Options**. From the navigation options on the left side of the Access Options dialog box, click **Current Database**.
- In the Application Title box type Painted Paradise Resort & Spa.
- To the right of the Application Icon box, click **Browse**, navigate to the student data files, select **a07ws14Icon**, and then click **OK**. Click **OK** again to close the Access Options dialog box.

h. Close the database, and then exit Access. Submit your work as directed by your instructor.

Problem Solve 1

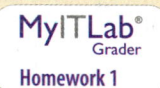

Student data files needed:

 a07ws14StudentOrg.accdb

a07ws14Dues.xlsx

You will save your files as:

a07ws14StudentOrg_LastFirst.accdb

a07ws14StudentOrg_LastFirst_be.accdb

Student Organization Database

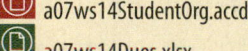

Production & Operations

The Student Organization database is used to keep track of student members and meetings. The member dues for each semester are being tracked in an Excel spreadsheet. You have been asked to incorporate that data into their existing database via a linked table. Because the database stores personal information about students you have also been asked to protect the database from unauthorized access by encrypting it with a password.

a. Start **Access**, and then open the student data file **a07ws14StudentOrg**. Click the **FILE** tab, and then save the file as a07ws14StudentOrg_LastFirst using your last and first name. If necessary, click **Enable Content**.

b. Split the database into front-end and back-end components. Save the back-end file as a07ws14StudentOrg_LastFirst_be.

c. Create a linked table to the **a07ws14Dues** Excel spreadsheet. Use the column headings as field names in the table, and then name the table tblDues.

d. Run the **Performance Analyzer** on all objects in the database. The Performance Analyzer will recommend creating relationships to the tblDues table. Close the Performance Analyzer.

e. Create a relationship from the **tblDues** table to the **tblSemesters** table using the **SemesterID** field. Create a second relationship from the **tblDues** table to the **tblMembers** table using the **MemberID** field. Close the Relationships window.

f. Encrypt the database and protect it from unauthorized access. You will need to close the database and open it with Exclusive Access first. Use s3Ec4!54 as the password for the database.

g. Change navigational options for the front-end database to match the following criteria:
- The application title should display Student Organization Database.
- The **frmStudentOrgNavigation** form should be open when the database starts, and the Navigation Pane should be hidden.
- Special keys, Layout view, and design changes to tables in Datasheet view should be disabled in the database.
- Full menus and default shortcut menus should be disabled in the database.

h. Close the database, and then exit Access. Submit your work as directed by your instructor.

Perform 1: Perform in your Career

Student data files needed:
 a07ws14Pet.accdb
a07ws14Donations.xlsx

You will save your files as:
a07ws14Pet_LastFirst.accdb
a07ws14Pet_LastFirst_be.accdb
a07ws14Pet_LastFirst2003.mdb

Adopt-A-Pet Database

Sales &
Marketing

You have been hired as a database administrator for Adopt-A-Pet, a pet adoption service, to enhance a database that helps keep track of their animals, customers, and adoptions. They have requested that you make the appropriate changes to the database so that it can easily be used by multiple people and that the appropriate security measures be taken to prevent unintentional or malicious modifications to the database.

a. Start **Access**, and then open the student data file **a07ws14Pet**. Click the **FILE** tab, and save the file as a07ws14Pet_LastFirst using your last and first name. If necessary, click **Enable Content**.

b. Add your first and last name to the **tblCustomer** table, and then close the table.

c. Save a copy of the database in **Access 2002-2003 Database (*.mdb)** format. Save the file as a07ws14Pet_LastFirst2003.mdb. Close the database, and then open the **a07ws14Pet_LastFirst** database.

d. Split the database into front-end and back-end systems to make it easier for multiple users to use the database. Name the back-end database a07ws14Pet_LastFirst_be.

e. Create a linked table using the **a07ws14Donations** Excel spreadsheet. Name the table tblDonations.

f. Encrypt the database and protect it from unauthorized access. You will need to close the database and open it with Exclusive Access first. Use td74#nhy as the password for the database.

g. Change navigational options for the front-end database to match the following criteria:
- The application title should display Adopt-A-Pet Database.
- The **frmPetNavigation** form should open when the database starts, and the Navigation Pane should be hidden.
- Special keys, Layout view, and design changes to tables in Datasheet view should be disabled in the database.
- Full menus and default shortcut menus should be disabled in the database.

h. Close the database. Exit Access. Submit your work as directed by your instructor.

MODULE CAPSTONE

More Practice 1

Student data files needed:

 a07mpMenu.accdb

 a07mpSupplier1.xlsx

 a07mpSupplier2.xlsx

You will save your files as:

 a07mpMenu_LastFirst.accdb

 a07mpMenu_LastFirst_be.accdb

 a07mpMenu_LastFirst.accde

Indigo5 Menu Database

Production & Operations

Painted Paradise is home to the world-class restaurant Indigo5. The manager of Indigo5, Alberto Dimas, is looking for ways to leverage technology to make the restaurant more efficient. His discussions with Chef Robin Sanchez have led to the further development of the database that is used to maintain the menus and ingredients used at Indigo5.

Currently the database includes a list of all menus in use and the ingredients used in each recipe. Recent functionality was added to assist Indigo5 in maintaining an inventory of ingredients as well. A macro was added that will update the inventory of ingredients based on the data in a temporary table. After the inventory is updated the temporary table is deleted. You will convert the macro to VBA and create an import procedure that will allow Robin Sanchez to select multiple files from local food distributors to import into the database. After the import takes place, the original macro should then run. After the entire process is finished, a message box should alert the database user that the process has completed. When this process is complete, Alberto has requested that the database be modified to allow multiple users and prevent the creation of new database objects.

a. Start **Access**, and then open the student data file **a07mpMenu**. Click the **FILE** tab, and then save the file as an **Access Database** with the name **a07mpMenu_LastFirst** using your last and first name. If necessary, enable the content.

b. Convert the **mcrUpdateIngredients** macro to VBA, including error handling and comments when converting the macro by completing the following steps:

• In the Navigation Pane, right-click the **mcrUpdateIngredients** macro, and then click **Design View**.

• Click the **DESIGN** tab, and then in the Tools group, click **Convert Macros to Visual Basic**. In the Convert macro: mcrUpdateIngredients dialog box, click **Convert**, and then click **OK**.

• In Project Explorer, double-click **Converted Macro- mcrUpdateIngredients** to open the Code window.

• Insert a comment between the Function statement and the On Error statement. Type **'This procedure updates the ingredients in the database.** and then press Enter.

• Insert another comment under the first one. Type **'This procedure was created by Firstname Lastname.** and replace Firstname Lastname with your actual name.

c. Add an import process to the procedure. The process should allow for multiple Excel spreadsheets to be imported into the tblTempIngredients table:

• To begin a new line of code, click **under** the On Error statement, press Enter, and then press Tab.

• Type **Dim IngredientDialog As Object**, and then press Enter. This declares a variable that will serve as the FileDialog object.

• Type **Set IngredientDialog = Application.FileDialog(msoFileDialogOpen)** to set the variable as the FileDialog object, and then press Enter.

- To use a With statement to handle the IngredientDialog object more efficiently, press Enter, type **With IngredientDialog** and then press Enter.
- Press Tab to indent the next line of code. For the title of the file dialog window, type **.Title = "Import ingredients into the database"** and then press Enter.
- To allow multiple spreadsheets to be imported at the same time, type **.AllowMultiSelect = True** and then press Enter.

d. Use an If statement to determine if any files were selected for import. Use a For Each Next statement to loop through the process of importing each spreadsheet selected by the user. The user should be notified with a message box if no spreadsheets were selected:
- Press Enter, and then type **If .Show = True Then**.
- Press Enter, and then press Tab.
- To declare a variable that will hold the names of the files to be imported, type **Dim ImportFile As Variant** and then press Enter.
- Press Tab, type **For Each ImportFile In .SelectedItems**, press Enter, and then press Tab.
- Type **DoCmd.TransferSpreadsheet acImport, acSpreadsheetTypeExcel12, _** to begin the DoCmd, and then press Enter. The line continuation character will allow the Visual Basic Editor to break the statement across two lines of the code window.
- Type **"tblTempIngredients", ImportFile, True, ""**, press Enter, and then press Backspace.
- Type **Next** to end the For Each Next statement after it has looped through all of the selected files. Press Enter, and then press Backspace twice.
- Type **Else** and then press Enter.
- Press Tab. To create a message box that will inform users that they have cancelled the import procedure, type **MsgBox "You have cancelled the import process."** and then press Enter.
- Press Backspace, type **End If** and then press Enter.
- Press Backspace, type **End With** and then press Enter.

e. After the four DoCmd statements that were created by the macro conversion, create a message box that alerts users that the process is complete.
- Click in the **first blank line** of code after the second DoCmd.SetWarnings statement, and then press Enter.
- Press Tab, and then type **MsgBox "Finished importing new ingredients."**

f. Compile the code to check for any possible errors in the procedure.
- Click **Debug** on the menu bar, and then click **Compile a07mpMenu**.
- If no message appears, your code compiled successfully. If a message appears indicating a problem with your code, fix the problem, and then compile the VBA again.
- Close the Visual Basic Editor, and then close the mcrUpdateIngredients macro.

g. Assign the new procedure to a button on the frmIngredients form:
- In the Navigation Pane, right-click the **frmIngredients** form, and then click **Design View**.
- Select all of the form **labels**, **fields**, and the **subform** in the Detail portion of the form, and then move them down to the **.5" marker**.
- Click the **DESIGN** tab, and then in the Controls group, click **Button**.
- Insert the new command button **above** the IngredientID label and text box. In the Command Button Wizard, click **Cancel**.
- If necessary, click the **DESIGN** tab, and then in the Tools group, click **Property Sheet**.
- In the Property Sheet pane, click the **All** tab, click in the **Name** field, highlight the default name of the command button, and then type **cmdImportNewIngredients**.

- Click in the **Caption** field, highlight the default caption text, and then type **Import New Ingredients**.

- Click the **Event** tab, in the On Click field, click **Build**. In the Choose Builder dialog box, click **Code Builder**, and then click **OK**.

- The Visual Basic Editor will open to a new Private Sub procedure in the Form_frmIngredients object. Click the **blank line** of code after the Private Sub statement.

- Type **Call mcrUpdateIngredients** and then close the Visual Basic Editor.

- Adjust the **width** of the new command button to include the full caption text.

- Save the **frmIngredients** form, and then close it.

h. Split the database to accommodate more users.

- Click the **DATABASE TOOLS** tab, and then in the Move Data group, click **Access Database**.

- Click **Split Database**, navigate to where you are saving your files, and then save the back-end file as **a07mpMenu_LastFirst_be**. Click **Split**, and then click **OK** in the confirmation message that Access split the database.

i. Alberto has also requested that the front-end database only display the FILE and HOME tabs on the Ribbon. The database should have a title, and he would like to prevent users from editing forms by right-clicking them.

- Click the **FILE** tab, click **Options**, and then click **Current Database** in the Navigation Pane.

- In the Application Title box, type **Indigo5 Menu Database**.

- Under Ribbon and Toolbar Options, clear the **Allow Full Menus** check box so that only the HOME and FILE tabs are displayed. If any Add-in applications are installed for Access, the ADD-INS tab will appear.

- Under Ribbon and Toolbar Options, clear the **Allow Default Shortcut Menus** check box. This prevents the shortcut menus from appearing when a user right-clicks a form or report.

- Click **OK**, and then click **OK** in the message box informing you that the changes you have made will not be enabled until the database is closed and reopened.

j. To further secure the database, save a copy of the front-end file as an ACCDE file. This will prevent users from being able to access any VBA or macros in the database.

- Click the **FILE** tab, and then click **Save As**.

- In the Advanced list, click **Make ACCDE**, and then click **Save As**. Navigate to where you are saving your files, and then save the ACCDE file as **a07mpMenu_LastFirst**.

k. Test the finished ACCDE file by importing two files of ingredients into the database.

- Click the **FILE** tab, and then click **Exit**.

- Start **Access**, open the **a07mpMenu_LastFirst.accde** database, and then in the Microsoft Access Security Notice dialog box click **Open**.

- In the Navigation Pane, double-click the **frmIngredients** form to open it.

- Click **Import New Ingredients** to begin the import process. Navigate to where your student data files are located, press and hold Ctrl, and then click **a07mpSupplier1** and **a07mpSupplier2**. Click **Open**.

- Click **OK** in the message box stating that your import has finished.

- Close the **frmIngredients** form, and in the Navigation Pane, double-click the **tblIngredients** table to open it. Examine the ingredient Rice. The value in the InStock field is now 13. Close the tblIngredient table.

l. Close the database, exit Access, and then submit your work as directed by your instructor.

Customer Service

Student data files needed:

 a07ps1Hotel.accdb

 a07ps1Icon.ico

You will save your files as:

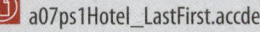 a07ps1Hotel_LastFirst.accdb

a07ps1Hotel_LastFirst_be.accdb

a07ps1Hotel_LastFirst.accde

Preparing the Hotel Database for Multiple Users

The Hotel at Painted Paradise needs to implement the database it uses for reservations for multiple users. There are two tasks to complete before the final project can be implemented. First, create a VBA script that will prompt the receptionist to offer any customer with five or more stays a 10% discount to the spa. This event should take place whenever the focus of the form moves from one record to another.

The entire database cannot be rolled out to different users as the reservations being made in the database must be stored in one location. Additionally, the interface that the receptionists will be using must be secured so they cannot create new database objects or edit existing ones. Secure the database to make sure this cannot happen.

a. Start **Access**, and then open the student data file **a07ps1Hotel**. Click the **FILE** tab, and save the file as an **Access Database** with the name a07ps1Hotel_LastFirst using your last and first name. If necessary, enable the content.

b. Create a new procedure on the frmGuestSummary form that will display a message box if the number of guest stays is five or more:
   - Open the **frmGuestSummary** form, enter Design view for the form, and then display the property sheet.
   - Use the **Code Builder** to create an event procedure for the On Current event that will run when the focus of the form moves from one record to another.
   - In the Visual Basic Editor, at the beginning of the new procedure, add code that presents a message box reading Offer Guest a 10% discount at the Spa. The message box should appear if the value of the NumberOfStays field is 5 or greater.
   - At the beginning of the procedure, insert a comment that includes your first and last name and describes the purpose of the procedure.
   - Close the Visual Basic Editor. Navigate through the records of the database to guest **ID RBH024**. You should be prompted with the message box to offer the guest a 10% discount.

c. Save and close the **frmGuestSummary** form. Split the database into a front-end and back-end system to better accommodate multiple users.
   - Name the back-end database a07ps1Hotel_LastFirst_be.

d. Secure the front-end database. Customize the availability of options in the database to decrease the likelihood that a user might change the database in an unwanted fashion:
   - The database should have the title Hotel Reservations. Use **a07Icon** as the application icon.
   - The form **frmHotelMenu** must show when the database is opened.
   - The hotel does not want the forms in the front-end database to be edited by any of the users. Ensure that users cannot open a database object in Layout or Design view.
   - The Navigation Pane must not be visible when the database opens.
   - Only the FILE and HOME tabs on the Ribbon must be visible when the database opens.
   - Users should not be able to use special keys.
   - Save the front-end database in the ACCDE file format. Save the database as a07ps1Hotel_LastFirst.

e. Close the database, exit Access, and then submit your work as directed by your instructor.

MyITLab®
Grader
Homework 2

Marketing &
Sales

Student data file needed:

 a07ps2Hotel.accdb

 a07ps2Icon.ico

You will save your file as:

a07ps2Hotel_LastFirst.accdb

Membership Status of Hotel Guests

The hotel at Painted Paradise wants to establish a membership system. As a pilot program for this process, they would like to identify potential guests in the Guest Summary form of the database. On the Guest Summary form, the hotel would like for the GuestID field to change format if a guest met a predetermined criteria.

Once this task is completed the VBA in the database should be password protected and locked for viewing. To further secure the database, it should be encrypted with a password.

a. Start **Access**, and then open the student data file **a07ps2Hotel**. Click the **FILE** tab, and save the file as an **Access Database** with the name a07ps2Hotel_LastFirst using your last and first name. If necessary, enable the content.

b. Open the **frmGuestSummary** form in Design view, and then create a new VBA function by completing the following steps:

- In the Property Sheet pane use the Code Builder to create an event that will run when the focus of the form moves from one record to another. Do not add any lines of code to the procedure that is created.

- In the Visual Basic Editor create a new function, and then name it GuestStatus. The function should change the format of the GuestID field if the guest meets specific criteria on either of two fields on the form. The criteria have been outlined as a guest that has four or more stays at the hotel or a guest that has spent at least $1,000.

- If either of these criteria is met, the BackThemeColorIndex property of the GuestID field should be **Accent 3**—a value of 6 in VBA. The BackTint property should be lighter by **25%**—a value of 75 in VBA. The ForeThemeColorIndex property should be **Background 1**—a value of 1 in VBA.

- If the criterion has not been met, the BackThemeColorIndex property should be **Background 1**—a value of 1 in VBA. The BackTint property should be **0**—a value of 100 in VBA. The ForeThemeColorIndex property should be **Text 1**—a value of 0 in VBA. The ForeTint property should be lighter by **25%**—a value of 75 in VBA.

- Insert a comment that describes what this procedure will do.

- Add another comment that includes your first and last name as the author of the procedure.

- The GuestStatus function must also run when the frmGuestSummary form is loaded. Call the **GuestStatus** function from the On Load and On Current events of the frmGuestSummary form.

- Save and close the frmGuestSummary form.

c. Protect the VBA of the database with a password by completing the following steps:

- In the VBA properties of the database, lock the project for viewing.

- Assign a password to the database to keep the VBA from being viewed and edited. Use 959acg71 as the password, and then close the Visual Basic Editor.

d. Secure the user interface of the database by completing the following steps:

- The application title should be Hotel Reservations. Use **a07Icon** as the application icon.

- The form **frmHotelMenu** should be displayed when the database opens.

- Only the FILE and HOME tabs on the Ribbon should be visible.

- The Navigation Pane should not be displayed when the database is opened.

- Users should not be able to edit forms or reports in Layout view or by right-clicking a database object.
- Users should not be able to edit tables in Datasheet view.
- Users should not be able to use special keys in the database.

e. Encrypt the database to protect it from unauthorized access:
- Use **476cha65** as the password.

f. Close the database, exit Access, and then submit your work as directed by your instructor.

Perform 1: Perform in Your Life

Student data file needed:

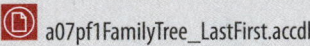 Blank Access database

You will save your file as:

a07pf1FamilyTree_LastFirst.accdb

My Family Tree

General Business

In this project, you will create a family tree within an Access database. The database should be constructed with you as the central focus of the project. In other words, when you enter a family member into the database their relationship status will be relative to you. A database of this nature will include intensive data entry. Build the database with this in mind. Organize the forms in a logical and efficient fashion. You will use VBA to assist you in automating tasks when possible. Family tree information may also be private information. You will take steps to secure your database not only to prevent unintentional editing of database objects but to protect any sensitive information in the database.

a. Start **Access**, and then create a new database. Save the database as **a07pf1FamilyTree_LastFirst**.

b. Create a table that will list the different relationship possibilities. At a minimum this should include items such as mother, father, brother, sister, and so on.

c. Create a table that will hold the personal information for your family members. Create an attachment field that can contain a picture.

d. Create a navigational form that contains two tabbed forms. The first should be a form to enter data into the personal information table. The second should be a form that is not based on a table that can hold command buttons.

e. On the blank form create a command button. This command button will have an import script that will run on the On Click event. Name the command button **cmdImportFamilyData**.

f. As part of this project you could export the personal information table as an Excel spreadsheet. This spreadsheet can serve as a data entry template that you can e-mail to family members. They could complete the form and send it back to you.
- Create an import process that would allow you to select these files and import them into the personal information table. Assume you may be selecting more than one file at a time.
- Compile the code in the database before exiting the Visual Basic Editor.
- In the Visual Basic Editor, lock the project for viewing and provide a password to the VBA properties. Use **853ahe90** for the password.

g. Analyze the performance of your database, and then optimize your database where appropriate.

h. This database will contain private information. Full names and dates of birth are common aspects of a family tree. Encrypt the database with a password using **284enu49** for the password.

i. Close the database, exit Access, and then submit your work as directed by your instructor.

Student data files needed:

 a07pf2Inventory.accdb

 a07pf2Supplier1.xlsx

 a07pf2Supplier2.xlsx

You will save your file as:

 a07pf2Inventory_LastFirst.accdb

a07pf2Inventory_LastFirst_be.accdb

Inventory Management

Production &
Operations

As the inventory manager at a midsize office supply company, it is your duty to keep track of all items in your warehouse and reorder them when necessary. The basic database has been provided for you. Enhance the database with VBA procedures where necessary to improve efficiency. Split the database so that multiple users can access forms and reports in the database while the tables can be centralized.

a. Start **Access**, and then open the student data file **a07pf2Inventory**. Click the **FILE** tab, and save the file as an **Access Database** with the name a07pf2Inventory_LastFirst using your last and first name. If necessary, enable the content.

b. Split the database into a front-end and a back-end system. Name the back-end database a07pf2Inventory_LastFirst_be.

c. In the front-end database, on the frmInventorySummary form is a command button that imports a worksheet into the tblInventoryTransactions table of the database:

- Convert this macro to a VBA procedure that allows for multiple imports.
- Include a comment in the VBA procedure that lists your first name and last name as the author of the procedure.
- Include a comment in the VBA procedure that explains the purpose of the procedure.
- Include error handling in the procedure.
- Provide the title Select Supply spreadsheet(s) to Import for the dialog box that will open for the user.
- Compile the procedure before closing the Visual Basic Editor.
- Change the On Click event of the Import Supplies button to an Event Procedure that calls the mcrImportSupplies procedure.

d. The format of the InStock field of the frmInventorySummary form should change when the stock is below the resupply level:

- Create a function called ReorderAlert on the form that will change the field properties of the InStock field when the quantity is equal to or below the ResupplyLevel field. If this criteria is met, the BackThemeColorIndex property should change to **Accent 2**—a value of 5 in VBA. The ForeThemeColorIndex property should change to **Background 1**—a value of 1 in VBA.
- If the criteria is not met the BackThemeColorIndex property should be **Background 1**—a value of 1 in VBA, and the ForeThemeColorIndex property should be **Text 1**—a value of 0 in VBA.
- The function should run in response to three different events. When the form is loaded, when the record focus changes, and when the InStock field is updated.

e. Run the Performance Analyzer. Make any changes to the ideas suggested by the Performance Analyzer involving adding the Option Explicit statement to the VBA in the database.

f. For the front-end database, secure the navigation of the database:

- The application title should be Inventory Database.
- The form **frmInventorySummary** should be displayed when the database opens.
- Only the FILE and HOME tabs on the Ribbon should be visible.

- The Navigation Pane should not be displayed when the database is opened.
- Users should not be able to edit forms or reports in Layout view or by right-clicking a database object.
- Users should not be able to edit tables in Datasheet view.
- Users should not be able to use special keys in the database.

g. Import the files **a07pf2Supplier1** and **a07pf2Supplier2** into the database. After the import has completed, there should be eight boxes of folders and eight different inventory items in the database.

h. Close the database, exit Access, and then submit your work as directed by your instructor.

Perform 3: Perform in Your Team

Student data files needed:

 a07pf3Scheduling.accdb

a07pf3Scheduling.xlsx

You will save your files as:

a07pf3Scheduling_TeamName.accdb

a07pf3Scheduling_TeamName_be.accdb

Production & Operations

Scheduling at a Medical Facility

You have been hired as the manager of a call center at a regional medical facility. The facility houses a wide range of medical services including general physicians, x-ray services, and a lab service. You have been asked to deploy a database to a small portion of the facility before the database is expanded to additional units.

There are several requirements for the database. The performance of the database must be improved. The database must be prepared for multiple users. All computers running the database will be using Access 2013. However, users should not be able to create new objects in the database or modify existing objects in the database. The information in the database will be private data and must be protected with a password.

a. Select one team member to set up the document by completing Steps b–e.

b. Open your browser and navigate to either https://www.skydrive.live.com, https://www.drive.google.com, or any other instructor assigned location. Be sure all members of the team have an account on the chosen system—a Microsoft or Google account.

c. Create a workbook, and then rename Sheet1 as **Contributors**. List the names of each of the team members on the worksheet, and then add a heading above the name to read **Team Members**. Include a summary of each team member's contributions as well as any additional information required by your instructor.

d. Open the **a07pf3Scheduling** database, and then save it as **a07pf3Scheduling_TeamName** using the name assigned to your team by your instructor.

e. Share the database with the other members of your team. Make sure that each team member has the appropriate permission to edit the database.

f. Create an import process that will allow a user to import a clinician's availability from a Microsoft Excel spreadsheet:
- The command button cmdImportAppointments has been created on the frmSchedulingMenu form. Assign a function to this button that will run in response to the On Click event.
- For the import process, assume that multiple spreadsheets could be imported at the same time.
- The procedure should import Excel spreadsheets to the tblAppointments table. The clinic physicians will have an Excel template to fill out so that the fields in the spreadsheet match that of the database.

- Add comments to the procedure to explain what the procedure is doing.
- Add a comment to the procedure listing your team name as the author of the procedure.
- Add error handling to the procedure. The error handling should show the user the error encountered and then exit the function.
- Provide a title to the dialog box that will be presented to the user.
- If the import is cancelled, a message box should alert the user that they have cancelled the import.
- Compile the database before closing the Visual Basic Editor.

g. Split the database into a front-end and a back-end system. Name the back-end database a07pf3Scheduling_TeamName_be.

h. Secure the front-end database by encrypting it with a password:
- Close the database and open it with Exclusive Access. Use the password 727ebc67.

i. Secure the user interface of the front-end system:
- The application title should be Scheduling Database.
- The frmSchedulingMenu form menu should be displayed when the database is opened.
- Prevent users from using special keys.
- Only the FILE and HOME tabs should be visible on the Ribbon.
- Prevent users from editing tables in Datasheet view.
- Prevent users from editing forms and reports in Layout view or by right-clicking a database object.
- The Navigation Pane should not be visible when the database is opened.

j. Test the import process. Click the **Import Clinician Appointments** button to import the **a07pf3Scheduling** Excel file.

k. Close the database, exit Access, and then submit your work as directed by your instructor.

Perform 4: How Others Perform

Student data file needed:

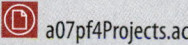 a07pf4Projects.accdb

You will save your files as:

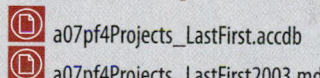 a07pf4Projects_LastFirst.accdb
a07pf4Projects_LastFirst2003.mdb

Project Management Database

Production &
Operations

You are the project manager at a midsize technology company. As your company has grown, the task of tracking projects has become overwhelming with the current paper-based process. The company decided to build an Access database that will better track projects.

You have been asked to review the database and fix any errors or improve any inefficiencies that can be found. Additionally, some users will be using Access 2003 to view the database. Create a copy of the database in 2003 format.

a. Start **Access**, and then open the student data file **a07pf4Projects**. Click the **FILE** tab, and save the file as an **Access Database** with the name a07pf4Projects_LastFirst using your last and first name. If necessary, enable the content.

b. Open the **frmProjectSummary** form. Examine the Project Start Date field. The BackThemeColorIndex property of this field is supposed to change under two conditions. First, when the number of days from the project start date to the date last updated is greater than 30 and the project status is "development." Second, when the number of days from the project start date to the date last updated is greater than 60 days and the project status is "implementation." If neither of these conditions are met or if the project status is completed, the BackThemeColorIndex property of the Project Start date field should be **Background 1**—a value of 1 in VBA.

c. Examine Project ID number 1:

- The correct format is presented when the form is first opened. Change from Project ID 1 to 2, then back to 1. Why does the format stay the same when records are changed? There are two reasons for why this problem is occurring. You will need to correct both before proceeding.

- Update the status of Project ID 3 to "Complete" by clicking **Completed** from the Project Status list. Save the form. This should remove the formatting from the Project Start Date field. Why did the format remain?

- Examine Project ID 1. Could a better choice of background and font colors be used to highlight the data? Change the colors used to provide a more legible result.

- Add comments to the procedure that explain the process.

d. Analyze the performance of the database. Make any changes categorized as suggestions or ideas.

e. Save the database in **Access 2003** format. This will fail initially. Examine the tables, and resolve any issues that might prevent this from happening. Save the database in Access 2003 format as a07pf4Projects_LastFirst2003.

f. Close the database, exit Access, and then submit your work as directed by your instructor.

NORMALIZE A DATABASE FOR EFFECTIVE DESIGN

OBJECTIVES

1. Identify insertion, deletion, and update anomalies in data   p. 720

2. Modify a table to satisfy the first normal form   p. 722

3. Modify a table to satisfy the second normal form   p. 725

4. Modify a table to satisfy the third normal form   p. 728

5. Join tables together in relationships with referential integrity enforced   p. 731

6. Understand entity relationship diagrams   p. 733

Prepare Case

The Terra Cotta Brew Coffee Shop Designing a Normalized Database

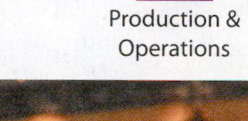

Production & Operations

Aidan Matthews, the chief technology officer, wants all of the resort to be electronic. The Terra Cotta Brew coffee shop was one of the last areas of the resort still not tracking data electronically. The prior intern for the resort started an Excel spreadsheet to track the sales. When the employees started to use it, they found it to be cumbersome. Further, it requires too much time to enter data. Aidan gave you a copy of the Excel spreadsheet with four transactions in it. He asked you to analyze the data, import it into a database, and fix it.

allensima / Shutterstock

REAL WORLD SUCCESS

At my internship at a local concert venue my boss asked me to perform some data entry in an Access database. There was a tremendous amount of redundancy in the tables. I showed her how to reorganize the tables and use relationships between tables to improve the efficiency of the database. Not only did I save myself a lot of time and data entry, but I also secured another internship for next summer.

- Sarah, marketing intern

Student data files needed for this workshop:

 a00AppendixTerraCotta.accdb   a00AppendixImport.xlsx

a00AppendixTerraCotta.xlsx

You will save your file as:

 a00AppendixTerraCotta_LastFirst.accdb

Normalizing a Database

Designing the table structure for a database is not an easy task. Some of the best relational database designers start a design and then after working with it for a while, throw it in the trash and start over. A poor relational database designer tends to structure a database like an Excel spreadsheet, which results in redundancy, inefficiencies, and anomalies. Similar to a well-written paper, one set of business requirements can lead to several different yet equally good database designs. **Normalization** is the process of minimizing the duplication of information in a relational database through effective database design. In addition to minimizing duplication, normalization also prevents anomalies, avoids the need for redesigning as the database is expanded, and provides a better structure for querying. The goal of normalization is that every field in a relation—a table—is directly dependent on every part of the key for the relation. While normalization is not the only component to a well-designed database, it is an important start.

In this appendix, you will learn how to implement the normalization process. Before starting, you should understand the basics of a database including the following terms: attribute, cardinality, composite key, entity, foreign key, join, junction table, many-to-many relationship, natural primary key, numeric key, one-to-many relationship, one-to-one relationship, primary key, record, and table. These concepts can be found in earlier workshops and the glossary.

The process of normalization holds each table to a progressive series of criteria known as **normal forms (NF)**. There are several levels of normal forms. Each level represents the table's vulnerability to redundancy, anomalies, and inaccuracies. The **highest normal form (HNF)** is the level that a table satisfies along with all levels below. Thus, if a table has an HNF of 2NF, then the table complies with the first and second normal form. If a table reaches the 3NF level, then the table is considered normalized. If a database is stated to be 3NF, this means that all tables in the database meet the criteria for the first three normal forms. Higher levels than 3NF do exist; however, discussion of the higher levels is beyond the scope of this workshop.

Types of Anomalies

One goal of normalization is to minimize anomalies. **Anomalies** are unmatched or missing data that is caused by limitations in database design. Anomalies can be categorized into three types—insert, delete, and update. An **insertion anomaly** forces you to enter data about two different entities when you have data on only one entity. A **deletion anomaly** forces you to delete two different pieces of data when you only wanted to delete one piece of data, resulting in information loss. An **update anomaly** forces you to change data in multiple records, such as when you need to change the name of a product and you must change multiple rows to make the update. Update anomalies can be difficult to detect.

Identifying Anomalies

Examples of each type of anomaly exist in the Excel spreadsheet containing transactions for the coffee shop. Identifying the anomalies in the spreadsheet will better prepare you for converting the data into an Access tables.

A00.00

 To Identify Anomalies

a. Start **Excel**. Click the **FILE** tab, click **Open**, and then double-click **Computer** to browse to your student data files. Open the **a00AppendixTerraCotta** workbook.

b. Examine the data in cells **A2:N9** representing four different items ordered:

Field Name	Description
ID	An automatically generated number to represent each order
Date	Date the order was placed
EmployID	Employee ID who took the order
EmpFirst	Employee first name who took the order
EmpLast	Employee last name who took the order
Address	Employee address who took the order
City	Employee city who took the order
State	Employee state who took the order
Zip	Employee zip code who took the order
ProductName	This is the name of the product ordered. Notice that additional products are dropped down to the next row in Excel.
RetailPrice	This is the normal price of the product.
PricePaid	This is the RetailPrice of the product. This may be different than the typical retail price if the product was at a discounted rate.
Qty	This is the quantity ordered.
Subtotal	This is the RetailPrice multiplied by the Qty.

Table 1   Data in the spreadsheet tracking orders

c.   Examine the ProductName data in column **J2:J9**.

Terra Cotta brew just added a new product, a breakfast soufflé. This new product cannot be added until it is sold for the first time. This is an insertion anomaly.

d.   Examine the data in cells **J7:L7**.

This purchase of orange juice sold by Suzanne Kay was erroneous and needs to be deleted. Notice that this is the only entry for orange juice. Thus, if this order is deleted, the information that orange juice is $2.00 will be lost. This is a deletion anomaly.

e.   Examine the data in cells **E2:E9**.

James Kilroy just got married to Jessica McAfee. He decided to change his name to a hyphenated McAfee-Kilroy. Because James has sold more than one order, his information would need to be updated in multiple places—once for every order placed. This is an update anomaly.

SIDE NOTE
Preventing Update Anomalies

You may think a field is highly unlikely to change. However, if it is remotely possible, you must account for that in the database design to avoid an update anomaly.

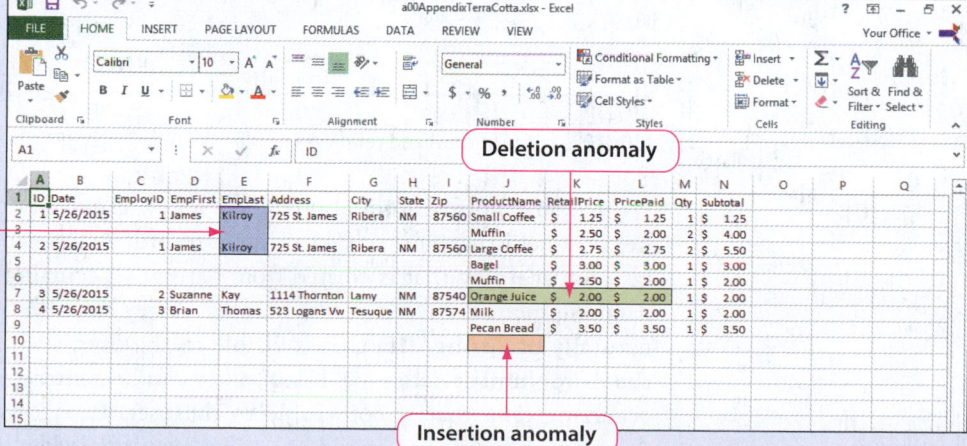

Figure 1   Insertion, deletion, and update anomalies

f. Examine the data and identify other insertion, deletion, and update anomalies.

What if this data set had 2,000 orders? It would be difficult to query, prone to typos causing inconsistent data, and inefficient at storing data.

g. Notice that many of the Excel rows are blank and that each order could span several rows.

This format is not conducive to converting into Access tables and breaks the first normal form. Aidan Matthews—the chief technology officer—knew this and already converted the data into a better starting point in another file.

h. Click **Close** ⊠.

The First Normal Form

The **first normal form** (1NF) dictates that the table must not have repeating groups of values in a single column—atomicity—and that it must have a key. Also, in 1NF, each nonkey field needs some sort of dependency on the key. A record is considered **atomic** when none of the values are repeating or concatenated for a single column. In Figure 2, each order has a repeating group for ProductName, PricePaid, Qty, and ItemTotal. In other words, each order may have several different products that were purchased. Thus, each row in the spreadsheet is not atomic. Rather, each database record equivalent—also known as a **tuple**—may be in more than one row due to this repeating group. Thus, the field of ProductName—also known as an attribute—can have multiple values. If the values are repeated in the rows that are currently blank, each row will become atomic and each row will represent one database record or tuple. This may seem like you are adding in redundancy rather than decreasing it. This redundancy will be taken care of as you progress through the normal forms.

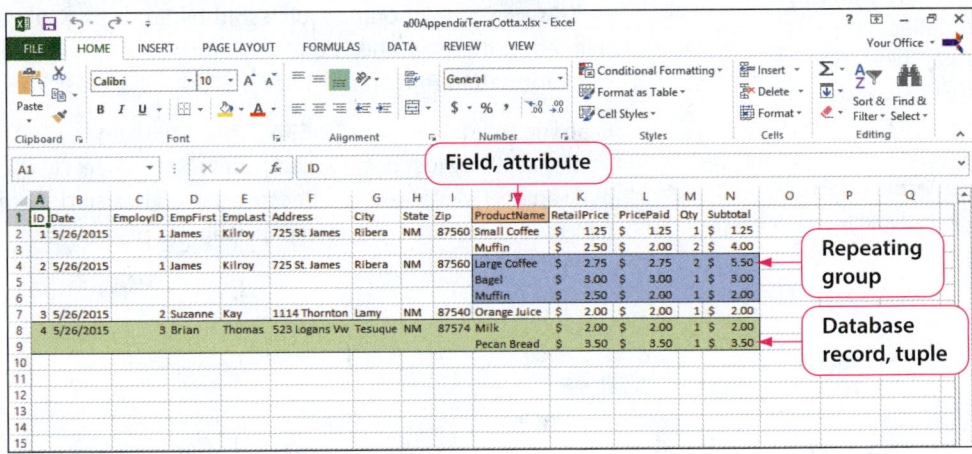

Figure 2   Unnormalized relation—table

The first normal form also requires a key. Figure 2 does not have a key. A **primary key** is a field that uniquely identifies a record. A key can be one of three kinds. It may be a **natural key** that is created from naturally occurring data generated outside of this database such as driver's license number. A key can also be an **artificial key** that is nonnaturally occurring data that is visible to the user, such as sequential numbering from the AutoNumber data type. Lastly, a key can be a **surrogate key**, which is nonnaturally occurring data that is not visible to the user. In Access, an ID field created with an AutoNumber data type could be used as a surrogate key.

Each table may have several **candidate keys** that could be used as the primary key. Candidate keys that are not used for the primary key are **alternate keys**. Sometimes, more than one field is needed to uniquely identify a record. When multiple fields are used to identify a record, it is a **composite key**—sometimes referred to as a **concatenated key**.

| REAL WORLD ADVICE | Why Would You Use a Surrogate Key? |

Using a surrogate key has its pros and cons. If the key never has a foreign key, you do not need a surrogate key. The advantage with a surrogate is that it can help prevent some cascading changes from primary to foreign key errors. However, a surrogate key can increase the file size and require more joins. Many database designers debate the need for surrogate keys. However, if you have a primary key with a foreign key that may need to be changed frequently or more than normal, a surrogate key should be considered.

In Figure 3, what are the potential candidate keys? Each row had the values copied down to create an atomic table. However, it still does not have a key specified. Each row represents a product purchased in an order. The ID field represents an order. So, by itself, it cannot be a key. There is also a ProductName field. Each product name is unique, but it may be purchased on multiple occasions. However, when considered together, the product name and order ID fields in combination are unique. Thus, in this example, the key is a composite key with ID—representing the order—and ProductName—representing the product ordered.

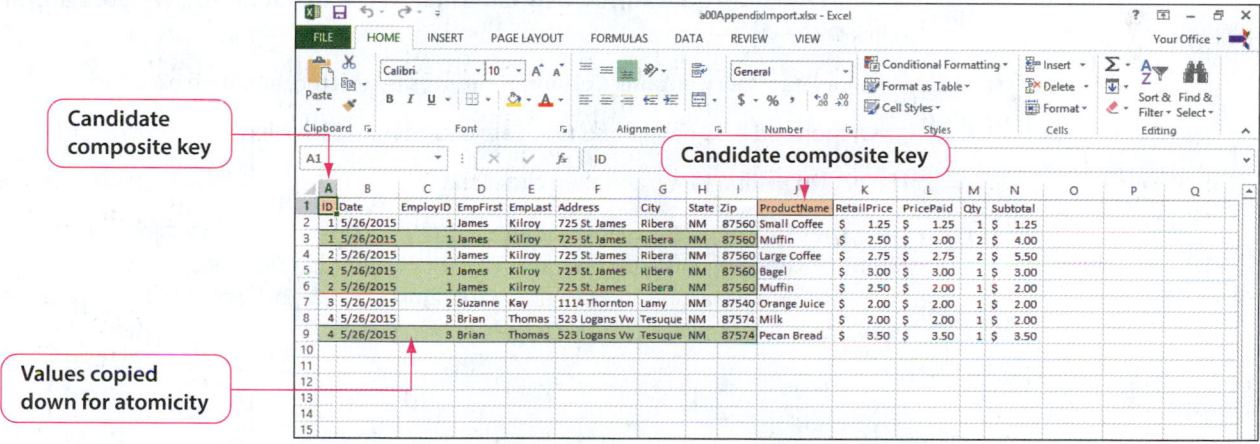

Figure 3 1NF relation—table—with a composite key

| CONSIDER THIS | Appropriate Keys |

In this example, product name is unique to each product. However, is it the best key to use? Could two products ever have the same product name? What if you separated the size from the product name—with "small" and "coffee" in different fields? Would a surrogate key be better?

Satisfying Atomicity

Once this data is imported into Access and the composite key is designated, it will satisfy 1NF. However, it is still subject to the insertion, deletion, and update anomalies. Because further modification as you progress through the normal forms is required, in the next exercise, you will import the data into an Access table, but you will not actually designate the key.

A00.01

To Satisfy Atomicity for the First Normal Form

a. Start **Excel**. Click the **FILE** tab, click **Open**, browse to your student data files, and then open **a00AppendixImport**.

   Notice the changes to this file compared to the spreadsheet prepared by the intern. As seen in Figure 3, Aidan Matthews copied down the Date, EmpFirst, EmpLast, Address, City, State, and Zip fields, temporarily creating more redundancy. Each order is really represented in several rows—for example, the first order is in rows 2–3. Even though this is two rows in the spreadsheet, in the database it represents one database record. Further, each column represents a database field. By copying the values to each row, each row becomes atomic and a separate database record.

b. Click **Close** ❌.

c. Start **Access**, and then open the student data file **a00AppendixTerraCotta**.

d. Click the **FILE** tab, and then save the file as an **Access Database** in the folder or location designated by your instructor with the name a00AppendixTerraCotta_LastFirst using your last and first name. If necessary, click **Enable Content**.

e. Click the **EXTERNAL DATA** tab, and then in the Import & Link group, click **Excel**.

f. Click **Browse**, locate and select **a00AppendixImport**, and then click **Open**. Ensure **Import the source data into a new table in the current database** is selected, and then click **OK**.

g. Ensure **First Row Contains Column Headings** is selected, and then click **Next**.

h. The imported field names and types are acceptable. Click **Next**.

i. Select **No primary key**, and then click **Next**.

j. In the Import to Table name box, replace the existing text with tblItemsOrdered_initialLastname. Click **Finish**, and then click **Close**.

   You now have a table in 1NF named tblItemsOrdered. This table has a composite key, which you will specify later in this workshop.

REAL WORLD ADVICE | **Does the Address Field Violate Atomicity?**

While the address field represents only one address, it is really a concatenated value of street number and street name. In that sense, the address field actually has multiple values in it and is not atomic even though it is not a repeating group—because it is just a single address. You could have separate fields for street number and street name to satisfy 1NF. For many businesses, a single field for address is sufficient. You want to look at the business requirements when creating your tables and keep the future in mind. If you would never want to query how many employees live on the same street, separating the values is not necessary. However, if you were building a database for the postal office, you would want to separate the values into two fields.

The Second Normal Form

The **second normal form (2NF)** requires that the table has no fields with partial dependencies on a composite or concatenated key and satisfies 1NF. A **dependency** exists when a field relates to a key. For example, the order date is dependent on the order ID. While several orders can be placed on the same day, one order cannot be placed on more than one date. Thus, order date is dependent on the key of order ID. Further, a **determinant** is a field that determines the value of another field. For example, the order ID determines the order date. An order can be placed on one specific date. Thus, if you know the key order ID, you should be able to determine the order date. A **partial dependency** exists when the field depends on one part of a composite or concatenated key. In other words, the field is determined by only one piece of a multifield key. A **transitive dependency** exists when a field depends on another field in the table, which then depends on a candidate key. A depends on B and B depends on C, thus A implies C. If C is a candidate key and B is not a candidate key, this is a transitive dependency. For 2NF, transitive dependency is acceptable, but partial dependency is not.

Ask yourself whether each field could still be there if one part of the key was removed. For example, can employee first name remain if the product name was not part of the composite key? The answer is yes. If you answer yes for even one field, the table is not in 2NF. Thus, employee first name is not dependent on the product that was purchased—ProductName—and so this is a partial dependency. To get a table to satisfy 2NF, you break the table up into several tables. Dependencies are frequently shown in a **functional dependency diagram** as shown in Figure 4.

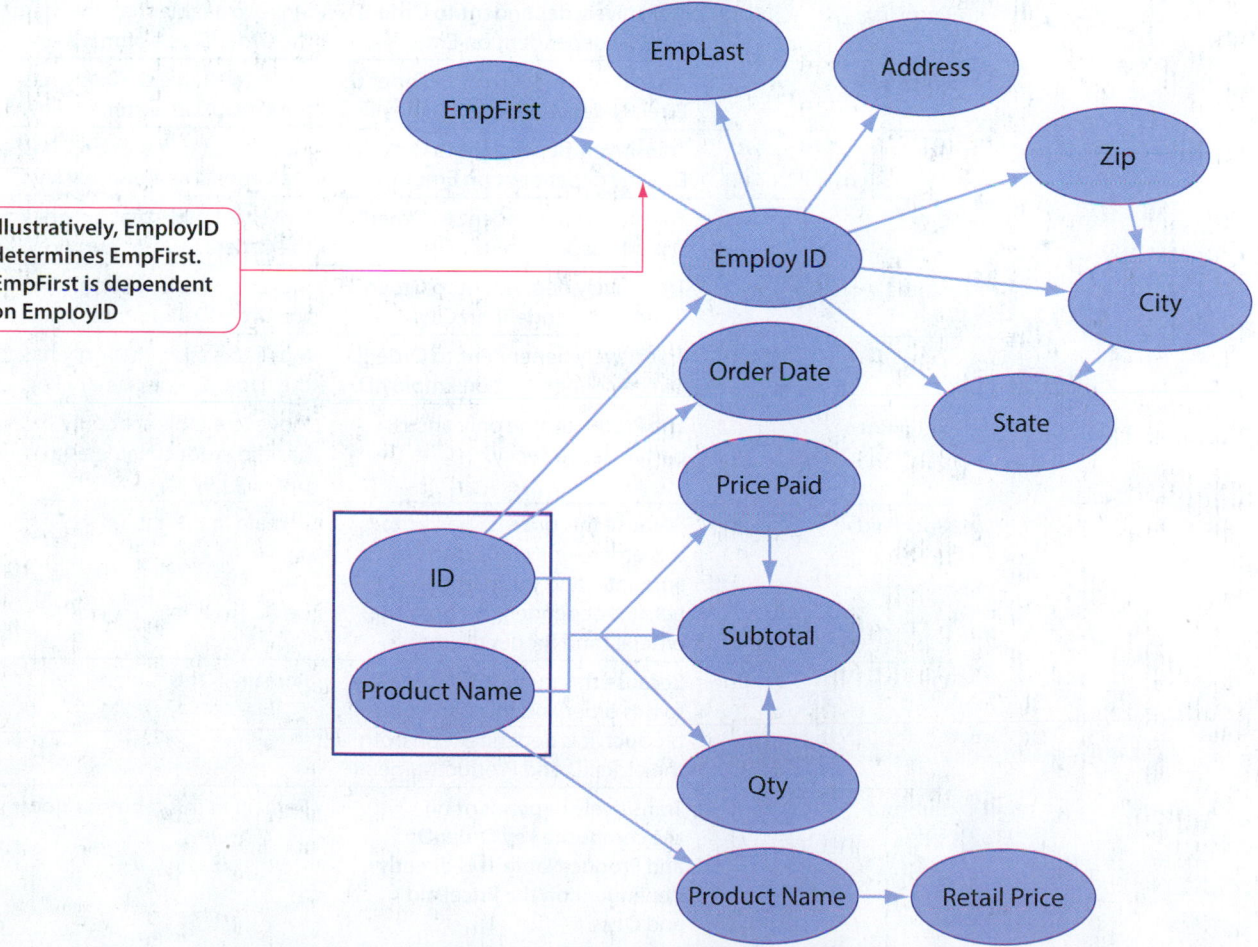

Illustratively, EmployID determines EmpFirst. EmpFirst is dependent on EmployID

Figure 4   Functional dependency diagram of tblItemsOrdered

Removing Dependencies

To construct a database based on the provided data that satisfies the 2NF, the tblItemsOrdered table will need to be split into multiple tables. This will involve making duplicate copies of the original table and removing dependent data from them.

A00.02

 To Remove Partial Dependencies to Satisfy the Second Normal Form

a. In the Navigation Pane, right-click the **tblItemsOrdered** table, and then click **Design View**.

b. Change the **Field Name ID** to **OrderID** to be more easily identified.

c. Click **Save** 🖫, and then on the FILE tab, in the Views group, click **View** to change to Datasheet view.

d. Examine each nonkey field for partial dependencies:

Field Name	Dependent to Which Key Field: OrderID, ProductName, or Concatenated OrderID and ProductName?	Action Needed to Conform to 2NL
Date	The OrderID only and is a partial dependency.	Move to a table that only has the OrderID as a primary key.
EmployID	The OrderID only and is a partial dependency.	Move to a table that only has the OrderID as a primary key.
EmpFirst	Transitively dependent to OrderID. Directly dependent on EmployID.	Move to a table that only has the OrderID as a primary key.
EmpLast	Transitively dependent to OrderID. Directly dependent on EmployID.	Move to a table that only has the OrderID as a primary key.
Address	Transitively dependent to OrderID. Directly dependent on EmployID.	Move to a table that only has the OrderID as a primary key.
City	Transitively dependent to OrderID. Directly dependent on Zip.	Move to a table that only has the OrderID as a primary key.
State	Transitively dependent to OrderID. Directly dependent on City.	Move to a table that only has the OrderID as a primary key.
Zip	Transitively dependent to OrderID. Directly dependent on EmployID.	Move to a table that only has the OrderID as a primary key.
RetailPrice	The ProductName only and is a partial dependency.	Move to a table that only has the ProductName as a primary key.
PricePaid	Because this price is specific to this order—may be a discounted amount—and this particular product, it is dependent on both the order ID and ProductName.	Remain in this table.
Qty	Because this quantity is specific to this order and this particular product, it is dependent on both the order ID and ProductName.	Remain in this table.
Subtotal	Transitively dependent on the composite key OrderID and ProductName. It is directly dependent on the PricePaid and Qty.	Remain in this table, for now.

Table 2 Table evaluating partial dependency

e. Click the **FILE** tab, click **Save As**, and then double-click **Save Object As**.

f. In the Save As dialog box, in the Save 'tblItemOrdered' to box, type **tblInventory_initialLastname**. Click **OK**.

> **Troubleshooting**
> If Access responds with an error message stating that there is no primary key defined, click No. You will add a key later.

g. Click the **HOME** tab, and then in the Views group, click **View**.

h. Delete all fields except ProductName and RetailPrice. For each field you need to delete, right-click the **field's name**, and then select **Delete Rows**. When prompted, click **Yes** to confirm that you want to delete the field. Access responds with an error message when you delete some of the fields. The error message states that deleting a field requires Microsoft Access to delete one or more indexes. This deletion is acceptable. Click **Yes** when prompted with this error.

i. Click **Save**. Click the **TABLE TOOLS DESIGN** tab, and then in the Views group, click **View**. To delete the record for the second occurrence of the product named **Muffin**, click the **record selector** for the row, and then press Delete. Click **Yes** to confirm deletion.

j. On the HOME tab, in the Views group, click **View**. In the Field Name column, click the **ProductName** field, click the **TABLE TOOLS DESIGN** tab, and then in the Tools group, click **Primary Key** to designate ProductName as a natural primary key.

You have separated the ProductName portion of the original concatenated or composite key into its own table.

> **Troubleshooting**
> If you get an error that prevents you from adding the primary key, check carefully that you deleted the second occurrence of the product named "Muffin".

k. **Save** and **Close** the tblInventory table.

l. In the Navigation Pane, double-click **tblItemsOrdered** to open it in Datasheet view. Click the **FILE** tab, click **Save As**, and then double-click **Save Object As**.

m. In the Save As dialog box, in the Save 'tblItemsOrdered' to box, type **tblOrders** and then click **OK**.

> **Troubleshooting**
> If Access responds with an error message stating that there is no primary key defined, click No. You will add a key later.

n. Click the **HOME** tab, and then in the Views group, click **View**.

o. Delete RetailPrice because that field is now in the tblInventory table. If prompted, click **Yes** to confirm the deletion.

p. Delete ProductName, PricePaid, Qty, and Subtotal. These fields will remain in the original tblItemsOrdered table. If prompted, click **Yes** to confirm deletion, and then click **Yes** again for the index message.

Access responds with an error message. This says that deleting a field requires Microsoft Access to delete one or more indexes. This deletion is acceptable.

q. Click **Save** 🖫. Click the **TABLE TOOLS DESIGN** tab, and then in the Views group, click **View**.

r. Delete the record for the second occurrence of the OrderIDs 1 and 4. Delete the record for the second and third occurrence of the OrderID 2.

s. On the HOME tab, in the Views group, click **View**, and then click the **OrderID** field. Click the **TABLE TOOLS DESIGN** tab, in the Tools group, click **Primary Key** to designate OrderID as an artificial primary key.

t. **Save** 🖫 and **Close** ☒ tblOrders.

u. In the Navigation Pane, right-click **tblItemsOrdered**, and then click **Design View**.

v. Delete all fields except OrderID, ProductName, PricePaid, Qty, and Subtotal. If prompted, click **Yes** to confirm deletion, and then click **Yes** again if necessary for index error messages.

w. Select both **OrderID** and **ProductName**. Click the **TABLE TOOLS DESIGN** tab, in the Tools group, click **Primary Key** to designate OrderID and ProductName as the concatenated or composite key.

   You have separated the ProductName portion of the original concatenated or composite key into its own table named tblInventory. You also have moved the field—RetailPrice—that was dependent on only that portion of the ProductName into the new table tblInventory.

   The tblItemsOrdered and tblInventory tables now satisfy at least 2NF in a practical sense. In the strictest sense, tblOrders is not even 1NL as Address is a multivalued field—street number and street name. Also, tblOrders and tblItemsOrdered still suffer from insertion, deletion, and update anomalies.

x. **Save** 🖫 and **Close** ☒ tblItemsOrdered.

The Third Normal Form

The **third normal form (3NF)** requires that the table has to be free of transitive dependencies and that the table satisfies both 1NF and 2NF. Remember, a transitive dependency exists when a field depends on another field in the table and that field depends on a candidate key. A depends on B and B depends on C, thus A implies C. If C is a candidate key and B is not a candidate key, this is a transitive dependency. When multiple overlapping candidate keys exist, you also should satisfy an additional criterion. Known as the **Boyce–Codd normal form (BCNF, 3.5NF)**, this additional criteria requires that all determinants are candidate keys and that the table satisfies 1NF, 2NF, and 3NF. By normalizing to BCNF, you are eliminating all functional dependencies.

Ask yourself, if I update this field, does another field in the table also need to be updated? If the answer is yes, then you have a transitive dependency. For example, think about a zip code. If you needed to change the zip code, then you may also have to change the city and state. In its strictest sense, 3NF would have a table of cities and zip codes, a table of cities and states, and the original table would only require you to enter the zip code. However, this level of normalization will create more joins, increase complexity, and potentially decrease the speed of the database system. Thus, the business requirements must be taken into consideration.

Satisfying the Third Normal Form

Other times, you clearly want to normalize to 3NF. Think about the employee last name in the orders table. The employee's last name is a nonkey field. Is the OrderID a determinant for the employee's last name? No. Instead, EmployID determines the employee's last name. Therefore, employee's last name is dependent on something other than the OrderID and needs to be moved into its own table.

A00.03

▶ **To Satisfy the Third Normal Form**

a. In the Navigation Pane, double-click the table **tblOrders** to open it in Datasheet view.

b. Examine each nonkey field for transitive dependencies:

Field Name	What Field Is This Field Dependent On and Is It a Candidate Key?	Action Needed to Conform to 3NL
Date	OrderID—a candidate key	Remain in this table.
EmployID	OrderID—a candidate key	Remain in this table.
EmpFirst	EmployID—a noncandidate key	Move to a table with EmployID as the primary key.
EmpLast	EmployID—a noncandidate key	Move to a table with EmployID as the primary key.
Address	EmployID—a noncandidate key	Move to a table with EmployID as the primary key.
City	State—a noncandidate key	Move to a table with EmployID as the primary key.
State	City—a noncandidate key	Move to a table with EmployID as the primary key.
Zip	EmployID—a noncandidate key	Move to a table with EmployID as the primary key.

Table 3 Table evaluating 3NL for tblOrders

c. Click the **FILE** tab, click **Save As**, and then double-click **Save Object As**.

d. In the Save As dialog box, in the Save 'tblOrders' to box, type **tblEmployees_initialLastname** and then click **OK**.

e. Click the **HOME** tab, and then in the Views group, click **View**.

f. Delete the **OrderID** and **Date** fields. If prompted, click **Yes** to confirm deletion. Click **Yes** again as needed. Access responds with an error message. This says that deleting the field requires Access to delete the primary key. Click **Yes** to confirm. You will reset the primary key later.

g. Click **Save** 💾. On the HOME tab, in the Views group, click **View**.

h. Delete the record for the second occurrence of the EmployID 1, and then click **Yes** to confirm deletion.

i. Add a record to the tblEmployees with the following values:
- EmployID—**4**
- EmpFirst—**Your First Name**
- EmpLast—**Your Last Name**
- Address—**123 Elm Street**
- City—**Lamy**
- State—**NM**
- Zip—**87540**

j. On the HOME tab, in the Views group, click **View**. Click the **EmployID** field, and then on the TABLE TOOLS DESIGN tab, in the Tools group, click **Primary Key** to designate EmployID as an artificial primary key.

k. **Save** 🖫 and **Close** ✖ the tblEmployees table.

l. In the Navigation Pane, right-click the **tblOrders** table, and then click **Design View**.

m. Delete all the fields except OrderID, Date, and EmployID. If prompted, click **Yes** to confirm deletion.

n. **Save** 🖫 and **Close** ✖ the tblOrders table.

o. In the Navigation Pane, double-click the **tblItemsOrdered** table to open it in Datasheet view.

p. Examine each nonkey field for transitive dependencies:

Field Name	What Field Is This Field Dependent On and Is It a Candidate Key?	Action Needed to Conform to 3NL
PricePaid	The Order ID and ProductName, a candidate key	Remain in this table.
Qty	The Order ID and ProductName, a candidate key	Remain in this table.
Subtotal	PricePaid and Qty, both noncandidate keys; further, subtotal is a value that can easily be calculated in queries.	Delete this field.

Table 4 Table evaluating 3NL for nonkey fields in tblItemsOrdered

q. On the HOME tab, in the Views group, click **View**. Delete the Subtotal field. If prompted, click **Yes** to confirm deletion.

r. **Save** 🖫 and **Close** ✖ the tblItemsOrdered table.

The tblItemsOrdered, tblInventory, and tblOrders tables are all in 3NF. The table tblEmployee is not even 1NF because of the transitive dependencies of State and City and the multivalued column of Address. For a database to be considered normalized, all tables need to be in 3NF. However, most expert database designers consider leaving the state and city in the Employees table and placing the Street Number and Name in the same column as an acceptable variation from normalization.

QUICK REFERENCE	Normal Forms

Normal Form Level	Description
First normal form (1NF)	The table must not have repeating groups of values in a single column—atomicity—and it must have a key.
Second normal form (2NF)	The table has no fields with partial dependencies on a composite or concatenated key and satisfies 1NF.
Third normal form (3NF)	The table has to be free of transitive dependencies and satisfy all lower levels of NF.
Boyce–Codd normal form (BCNF, 3.5NF)	All determinants are candidate keys and satisfy all lower levels of NF.

Table 5 Table of normal forms

Join Tables Together in Relationships with Referential Integrity

Once the tables are set, the database needs relationships to join the data from various tables. A **one-to-many relationship (1:M or 1:N)** is a relationship between two tables where one record in the first table corresponds to many records in the second table. One-to-many is called the cardinality of the relationship. **Cardinality** indicates the number of instances of one entity that relates to one instance of another entity. For example, each employee can only be in the employees table exactly one time. However, an employee can be in the orders table many times—once for each sale. These two tables are related by a one-to-many relationship using the EmployID key.

A **many-to-many relationship (M:N)** is a relationship between tables in which one record in one table has many matching records in a second table, and one record in the related table has many matching records in the first table. For example, a product can be in many different orders. Also, each order can have many products in inventory. Because these two tables do not have a common field, in Access this kind of many-to-many relationship must have an additional table in between these two. This intermediate table is referred to by several synonymous terms: "intersection," "junction," or "link table."

A **one-to-one relationship (1:1)** is a relationship between tables where a record in one table has only one matching record in the second table. In a small business, a department might be managed by no more than one manager, and each manager manages no more than one department. That relationship in the business is a one-to-one relationship.

Access allows you to add some **integrity constraints**—or rules—to your database to help ensure the data's validity. The entity integrity constraint requires all primary keys have a value—not be null. **Referential integrity** in relationships requires that only values that have a corresponding value in the primary table can be entered for a foreign key. **Cascade update** will update a foreign key automatically when the primary key changes. For example, if you change an employee's ID, cascade update will change every instance in the orders table. **Cascade delete** will delete every record with the foreign key if the record with the value is deleted from the primary table. For example, if you deleted an employee—which is not good practice—it would delete every order that the employee processed. Lastly, **domain integrity constraints** are rules that are specific for each field. For example, setting the data type of currency for price will require that the data entered is numeric.

Joining Tables with Relationships

Setting all the constraints for this database is beyond the scope of this workshop, but doing so is an important next step in database creation. Some relationships can be created in order to ensure the database operates efficiently.

A00.04

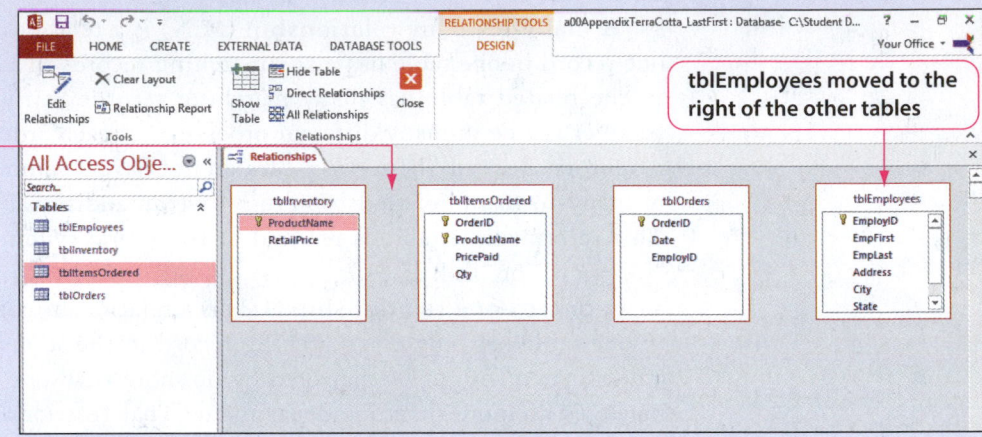

▶ To Join Tables with Relationships

a. Click the **DATABASE TOOLS** tab, and then in the Relationships group, click **Relationships**.

b. In the Show Table dialog box, tblEmployees should already be selected. Press and hold [Shift], click **tblOrder** to select all four tables in the list, and then click **Add**.

c. Click **Close** to close the Show Table dialog box. Drag the **tables** in the Relationships window so there is some space between the tables to form the relationships. Move the **tblEmployees** table to the right of the other tables, after tblOrders.

SIDE NOTE
Adding Tables
You can also use the [Ctrl] key to select multiple tables at once (that are not in contiguous order) to add to the relationships window.

Tables added to the Relationships window with space to create relationships

tblEmployees moved to the right of the other tables

Figure 5   Tables added to the Relationships window

SIDE NOTE
Order of Tables
The order or arrangement of the tables in the relationship view does not matter. The relationships between fields are the important part!

d. Drag the primary key **EmployID** from tblEmployees to **EmployID** in tblOrders.

e. Access displays the Edit Relationships dialog box. Click **Enforce Referential Integrity** to select it, and then click **Create**.

> **Troubleshooting**
> If you get the error, "Microsoft Access cannot create this relationship and enforce referential integrity," double-check that your data is all correct and that you did not delete a record by accident.

f. Drag the primary key **OrderID** from tblOrders to **OrderID** in tblItemsOrdered.

g. Access displays the Edit Relationships dialog box. Click **Enforce Referential Integrity** to select it, and then click **Create**.

SIDE NOTE
Creating Relationships
Alternatively, you could drag from EmployID in tblOrders to EmployID in tblEmployees.

h. Drag the primary key **ProductName** from tblItemsOrdered to **ProductName** in tblInventory.

i. Access displays the Edit Relationships dialog box. Click **Enforce Referential Integrity** to select it, and then click **Create**.

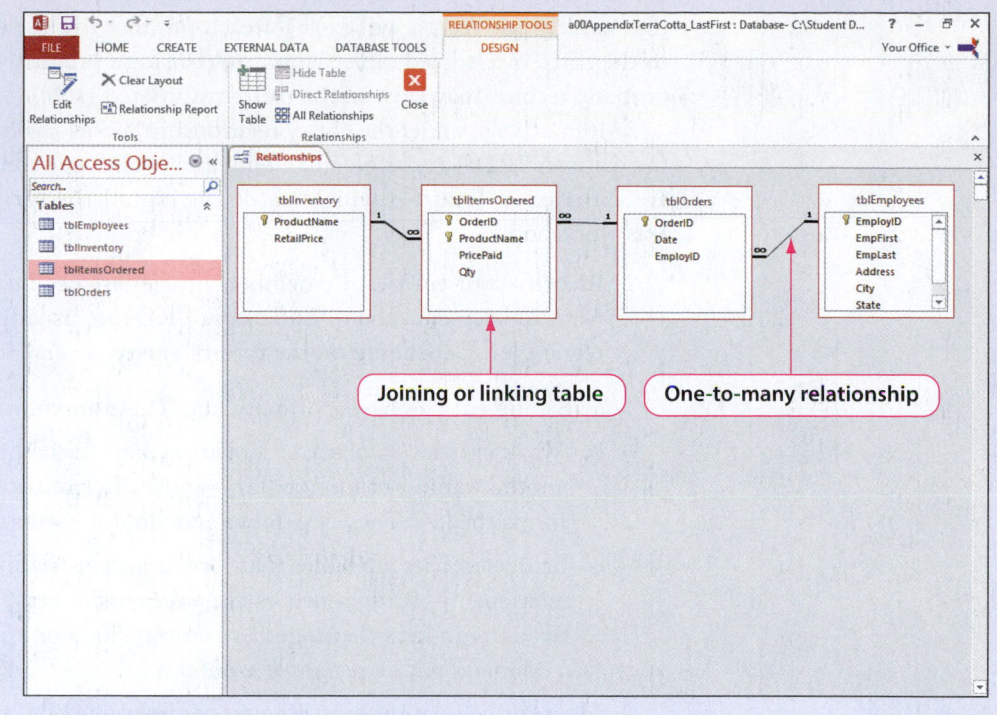

Figure 6 Final Relationships window

j. **Save** 🖫 and **Close** ⊠ the Relationships window. Close Access. Submit your work as directed by your instructor.

Understanding an Entity Relationship Diagram

Many ways of visually expressing the database structure exist. Best practice is to use one of these methods both when designing the database and documenting the database. An **entity relationship diagram (ERD)** is a common way to visually express the tables and relationships in your database. An ERD does not tell you anything about data flow—it is a fixed view of the database structure.

There are variations in how designers represent ERDs. For example, some designers may prefer the crow's feet approach. The crow's feet approach will list the tables in a database as rectangles with lines and symbols representing the types of relationships between them. An example of a crow's feet diagram displaying a one-to-many relationship is shown in Figure 7.

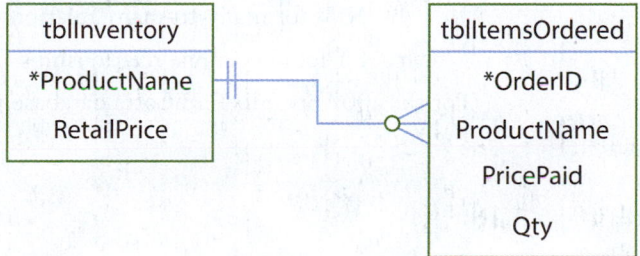

Figure 7 Crow's feet diagram

Here the tblInventory table is related to the tblItemsOrdered table by the ProductName field. The asterisk next to the field name designates the primary key field in each table. The line between the tables represents the relationship between the two ProductName fields. The lines intersecting the relationship next to the tblInventory table symbolizes that exactly one record will exist for each product in the table. The circle and lines next to the tblItemsOrdered table symbolize that for a product in the tblInventory table zero or many records may exist in the tblItemsOrdered table.

Alternatively, under the entity relationship model the following basic shapes are used to create an ERD—rectangle, diamond, and oval. Some common variations in the shapes are included in Figure 8. However, discussing all the variations is beyond the scope of this workshop.

1. Identify your entities. Remember, entities are people, places, or items that you want to keep data about. Entities in ERDs are usually nouns and are drawn in rectangles. Depending on the type of entity, several variations exist:

   a. Strong entities have a primary key. These are drawn in a normal rectangle.

   b. Weak entities do not have a primary key. Rather, they have a primary key from another table—or foreign key—and a discriminator value in the table that forms the key. These are drawn in a double rectangle.

   c. Bridge entities are tables that form a join or linking table for a many-to-many relationship. Bridge entities use a composite key. A composite key consists of two foreign keys that together combine for a unique value. These are drawn in a diamond with a rectangle around it.

2. Identify the relationships. Remember, relationships are associations between tables based on common fields. Relationships in ERDs are usually verbs and are drawn in diamonds.

3. Identify the attributes. Remember, attributes are information about the entity, or the data. Consider the business requirements of the system. Ask yourself, what fields are needed in queries? What common fields and keys are needed for the relationships? You may find a new entity and need to revise your ERD in this step. Attributes in ERDs are generally drawn inside an oval. Depending on the type of attribute, several variations exist.

   a. Key attributes are underlined.

   b. A second inside circle is used for multivalued attributes, like an address that contains both street number and street name.

   c. Derived values are represented with a dashed oval line. For example, city is derived from zip, which is not a candidate key.

4. Determine the cardinality of the relationships. This may require you to add a join or linking table. Cardinality in ERDs is listed depending on the type of relationship.

   a. 1:N or 1:M for one-to-many relationships

   b. N:M for many-to-many relationships

   c. 1:1 for one-to-one relationships

For the a00AppendixTerraCotta database, an entity relationship diagram would look like Figure 8.

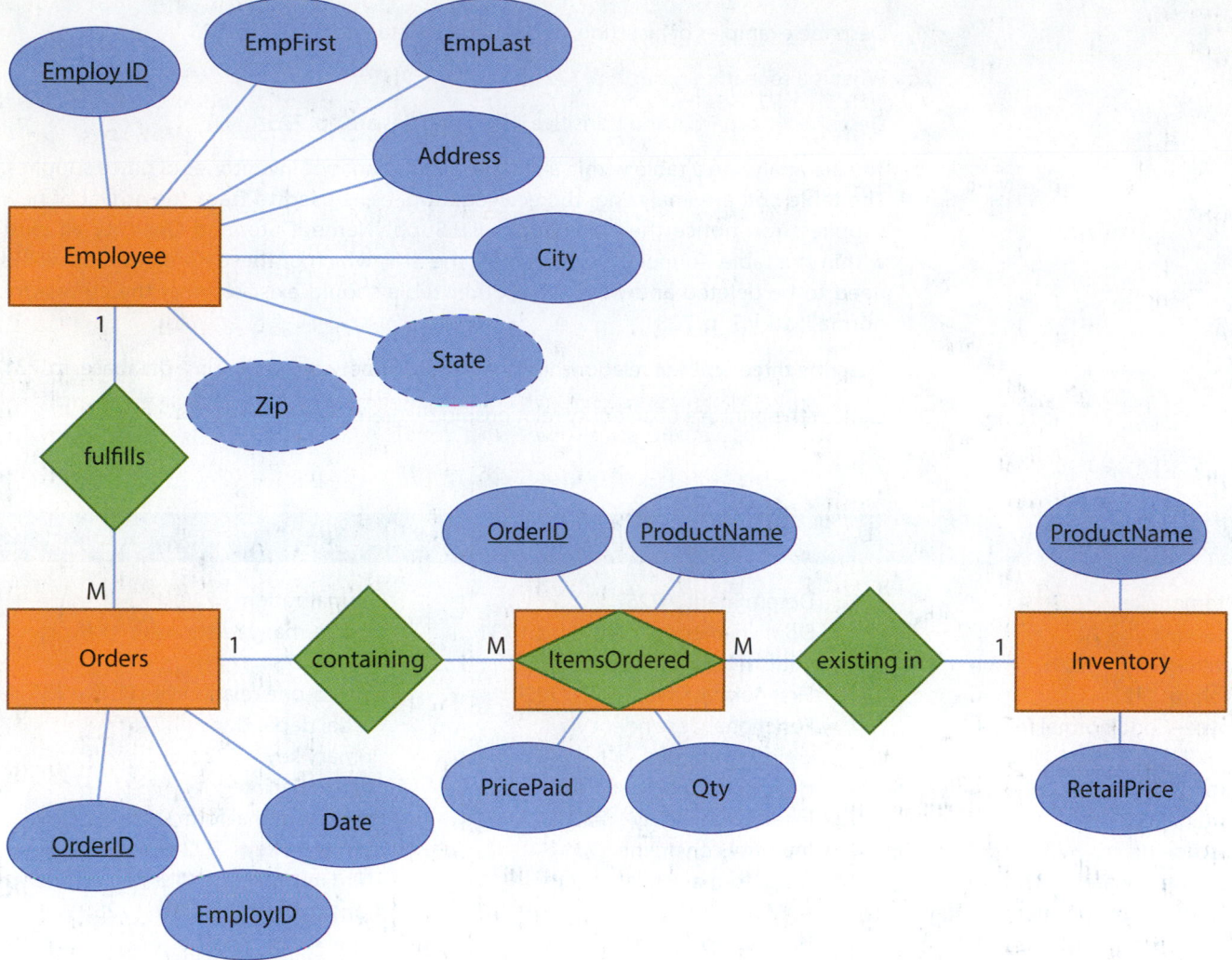

Figure 8   Entity relationship diagram

Concept Check

1. Describe examples of insertion, update, and delete anomalies. p. 720

2. What is a repeating group? p. 722

3. Describe what partial and transitive dependencies are. p. 725

4. You are analyzing a table within a database that manages inventories of office supplies. The table you are analyzing, tblReceivedSupplies, is used to track the arrival of new supplies. You notice the fields SupplyID, SupplyName, Date, and Quantity all exist within the table. To meet the criteria for the 3NF, which of these nonkey fields would need to be deleted and why? What other table should exist to meet the criteria for normalization? p. 728

5. Describe three types of relationships that can exist between tables in a database. p. 731

6. Explain the purpose of an entity relationship diagram. p. 733

Key Terms

Visual Summary

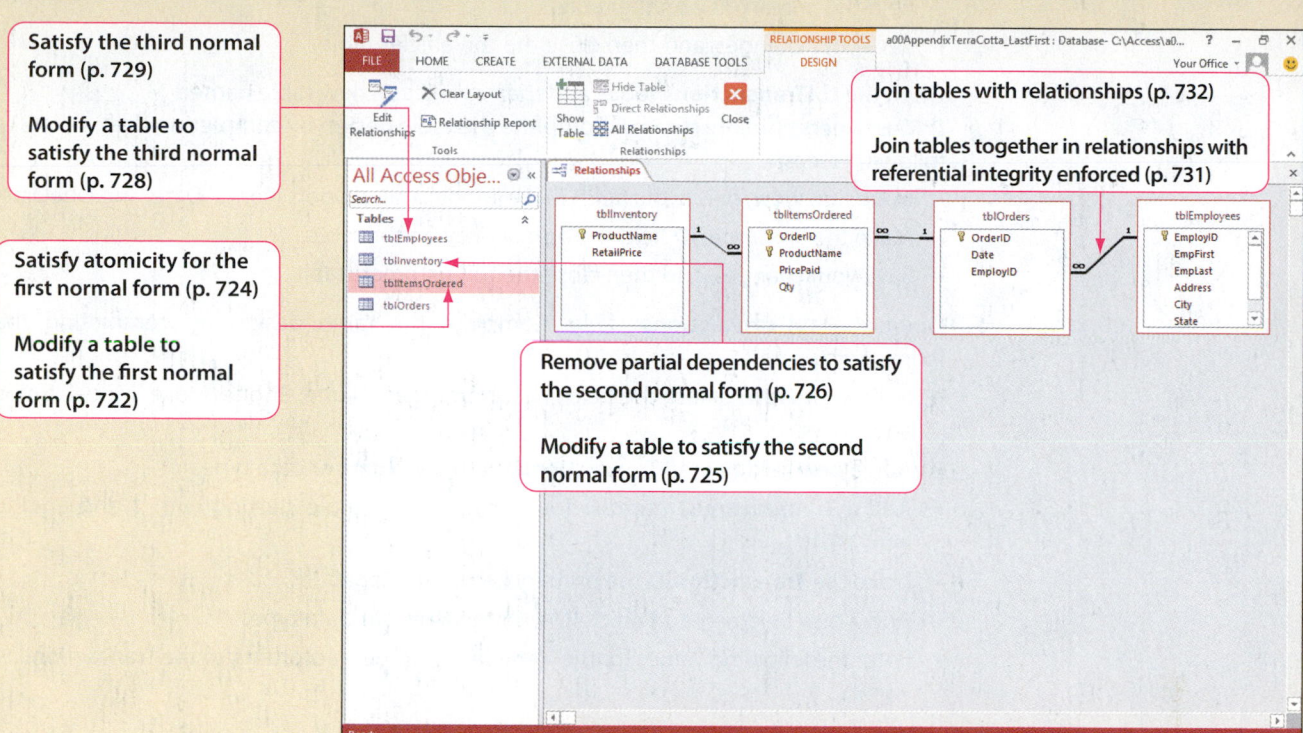

Satisfy the third normal form (p. 729)

Modify a table to satisfy the third normal form (p. 728)

Satisfy atomicity for the first normal form (p. 724)

Modify a table to satisfy the first normal form (p. 722)

Join tables with relationships (p. 732)

Join tables together in relationships with referential integrity enforced (p. 731)

Remove partial dependencies to satisfy the second normal form (p. 726)

Modify a table to satisfy the second normal form (p. 725)

Figure 9 Normalizing a Database Final

Problem Solve 1

Student data files needed:

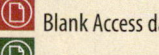 Blank Access database

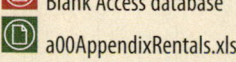 a00AppendixRentals.xlsx

You will save your file as:

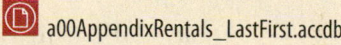 a00AppendixRentals_LastFirst.accdb

Normalize Data for Karl's Car Rentals

Production & Operations

Karl runs a car rental business and has hired you to help make his business paperless. As part of the process, he would like to create an Access database to manage the business customers, inventory of cars, and rental transactions. Each customer should be stored in the database one time. Each customer can have multiple rentals. Each rental should only include one vehicle.

a. Start **Access**, and then create a new blank database. Save the database as **a00AppendixRentals_LastFirst**.

b. Import the **a00AppendixRentals** spreadsheet into the a00AppendixRentals database as a new table. Do not identify a primary key. Name the table **tblTransactions_initialLastname**.

c. Open the **tblTransactions** table, and then save it as a new table named **tblVehicles_initialLastname**. Complete the table design by completing the following steps:

  • In **Design view**, delete the fields CustomerID, First Name, Last Name, Phone, Rental Date, and DueDate.

  • In **Datasheet view**, delete the second entry in the table for the Chevrolet, Sedan, Gray, 2 door.

- Save changes to the table, and then add a new field named VehicleID with the **Number** data type. Enter values for each vehicle starting with 1 and ending with 9. Make this field the primary key on the table.
- Save your changes, and then close the tblVehicles table.

d. Open the **tblTransactions** table, and then save it as a new table named tblCustomers_initialLastname. Complete the table design by completing the following steps:

- In **Design view**, delete the fields Make, Model, Color, Doors, Rental Date, and DueDate.
- Make the **CustomerID** field the primary key on the table.
- Save your changes, and then close the tblCustomers table.

e. Open the **tblTransactions** table. Complete the table design by completing the following steps:

- In **Design view**, delete the fields First Name, Last Name, Phone, Make, Model, Color, and Doors.
- Add a new field named TransactionID with the **Number** data type.
- Add a **TransactionID** number for all rows in the table starting with 1 and ending with 10.
- Make the **TransactionID** the primary key on the table.
- Add a new field named VehicleID with the **Number** data type.
- Enter the following values for the **VehicleID** numbers according to the TransactionIDs:
    1. 1
    2. 6
    3. 8
    4. 4
    5. 7
    6. 3
    7. 9
    8. 2
    9. 5
    10. 8
- Save and close the table.

f. If necessary, delete Table1.

g. In the Relationships window, show all three tables. Create **relationships** between the tables based on the appropriate fields, and then enforce referential integrity. Save your changes, and then close the relationships window.

h. Close and exit Access. Submit your work as directed by your instructor.

Perform 1: Perform in Your Career

Student data file needed:

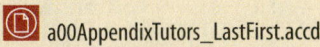 a00AppendixTutors.xlsx

You will save your file as:

a00AppendixTutors_LastFirst.accdb

Normalize Appointments for Business Tutors

Production & Operations

A local company runs a tutoring service for local business students. Each tutor has only one topic that he or she tutors. Each tutor may have several appointments. Each appointment may have one or more students at the appointment. Only one tutor may be assigned to an appointment. The price per hour varies based on topic and number of students at the appointment. However, the price per student is the same for all students in the same appointment. Currently, the appointments are tracked in Excel. At the urging of the Access tutor, your manager has asked you to convert this spreadsheet into a normalized database.

a. Start **Access**, and then create a new blank database. Save the database as **a00AppendixTutors_LastFirst**.

b. Populate the database with the data from **a00AppendixTutors.xlsx**.

c. Normalize the database. Note in the field descriptions in Design view whether each field is a candidate key—and what kind—or nonkey. If a candidate key is not the determinant of a nonkey field, place a short explanation why in the description. Also, note any other derivations from HNF of BCNF.

d. Add your name as one of the tutors, and then use fictitious data for all other data in the record containing your name.

e. Add appropriate keys and relationships.

f. Create an entity relationship diagram for your database. Ask your instructor whether to use Word, PowerPoint, paper, or some other program to create the diagram.

g. Close and exit Access. Submit your work as directed by your instructor.

Perform 2: How Others Perform

Student data file needed:

 a00AppendixSashasLaughHouse.accdb

You will save your file as:

 a00AppendixSashasLaughHouse_LastFirst.accdb

Sasha's Laugh House

Production & Operations

An intern has created a database that Sasha's Laugh House—a local comedy club—uses to schedule acts. The database is not normalized. Each act can perform many shows. Each show has several acts. Each act charges a single act fee, and all tickets to a single show are the same price. Each show has only one employee responsible for booking the acts. Sasha noticed that data errors started to occur and asked you to evaluate and fix the database.

a. Open **a00AppendixSashasLaughHouse**, review the database, and save it as **a00AppendixSashasLaughHouse_LastFirst**.

b. Change the second employee—EmployID 2—to be your name in the tblEmployee table.

c. Normalize the database. Note in the field descriptions in Design view whether each field is a candidate key—and what kind—or nonkey. If a candidate key is not the determinant of a nonkey field, place a short explanation why in the description. Also, note any other derivations from HNF of BCNF.

d. Add at least two additional fields you think Sasha might find helpful. Add a description in Design view explaining why you added the field. Leave the data for the field blank.

e. Ensure you have specified all keys and added relationships.

f. In the Navigation Pane, right-click each table, and then select Table Properties. In the Description for each table, specify the HNF for the table before changes and after your changes.

g. Close and exit Access. Submit your work as directed by your instructor.

EFFICIENT INTERACTION WITH A TOUCH SCREEN

OBJECTIVES

1. Understand variations in tablets   p. 742

2. Understand methods for interacting with a tablet PC   p. 744

3. Use flick, touch, and bezel gestures   p. 748

4. Use Office 2013, and other, touch features   p. 753, 754

Prepare Case

Painted Paradise Resort and Spa Works with Touch Features

IT

Information Technology

In his position as the CIO of Painted Paradise Resort and Spa, Aidan Matthews travels frequently. Traditionally, Aidan would take four devices with him—a laptop to work on Microsoft Office files, a Kindle to read, a Google tablet to watch videos, and an iPhone to make phone calls. He recently acquired a Windows 8 tablet PC and Windows 8 phone with Office 2013. This will allow him to only carry two devices and still complete all the same tasks. Aidan has asked you to teach him the most efficient ways to interact with his new Windows 8 tablet PC, a Surface Pro.

NAN / Fotolia

REAL WORLD SUCCESS

"As a business analyst for a large technology consulting company, I travel four days a week. Most of my colleagues carry four or more devices while traveling. I only carry my Windows 8 tablet PC and phone. I can do everything my colleagues can and more—with less hassle in the security line and more room in my luggage! My colleagues and clients have been quite impressed with the efficiency of the touch and pen integration."

- Dana, recent graduate

Interacting with a Windows 8 Tablet PC

Microsoft Windows 8 is the latest version of the Windows operating system. The **operating system** is system software, which controls and coordinates computer hardware operations so other programs can run efficiently. The operating system acts as an intermediary between **application software**—programs that help you perform specific tasks, such as word processing—and the computer hardware.

Like previous versions of Windows, Windows 8 uses a **graphical user interface (GUI)**, an interface that uses icons, which are small pictures representing commands, programs, and documents. However, Windows 8 introduces a number of new features that will leave even an experienced user in need of some retraining.

Windows 8 has moved away from the Start button and moved towards a touch-screen interface. Windows 8 also supports gesture recognition, which allows you to control the computer with gestures instead of mouse clicks, if you have a touch-screen device. Gestures allow you to perform actions like zooming and switching programs by performing certain movements. In this section, you will learn about the various ways to efficiently interact in the Windows 8 environment.

Understand Variations in Tablets

People use different devices for different purposes. You may use your tablet for information consumption and entertainment. Likewise, you may prefer your desktop computer to write a paper. These preferences account for the vast market diversity in devices. You may even know someone who regularly uses five or more devices. The capabilities of these devices can be quite divergent and cause consumer confusion. Further, some consumers—particularly cost-conscious consumers—seek to minimize the number of devices.

There are many types of tablet computers in terms of hardware, software, and size. Further, the types are constantly changing as new versions come out. Some of the most popular currently available devices are the Microsoft Surface, Apple iPad, and the Android tablet computer. Each device runs a different operating system and has different features and capabilities. Which tablet is the best for you depends on many questions.

- How much are you willing to spend?
- Do you need to use it for business production?
- Do you need to connect to specific hardware such as a camera or microphone?
- Do you want a high-quality display?
- How does the device feel when you hold it?
- Do you find the device easy to use?
- Do you need it to connect to a cellular network?

One major discriminator when answering these questions is the operating system it runs. Table 1 describes the capabilities of the various operating systems and the devices they are found on. Since technology is constantly changing, you should research any potential changes to the table that follows.

Operating System	Software It Runs	Types of Devices	Hardware Manufacturers	Office Capabilities
Mac OS X	Runs software written for the Mac OS X operating system	Laptops and desktops	Apple only	Mac Office versions such as Office 2011 and PC versions via dual boot or parallels
Windows 8	Runs software written for Windows 7 and above. Also, runs apps from the Windows store	Laptops, desktops, and some newer Intel chip-based tablets	Various: Microsoft, Lenovo, Dell, ASUS, and others	Full Office 2013
Windows 8 RT	Runs apps from the Windows store only	ARM chip-based tablets	Various: Microsoft, Lenovo, Dell, ASUS, and others	Office 2013 RT: Visually, the same as the full Office 2013 but lacks some sophisticated Office features
Android	Runs apps from the Google Play Store only	Smartphones and tablets	Various: Google, Samsung, ASUS, HTC, LG, and others	Some limited native capability to work with Office files
iOS	Runs apps from the iTunes Store only	iPads and iPhones	Apple only	Very limited ability to work with Office files. Some capability with purchased third-party apps
Windows Phone	Runs apps from the Windows store only, including Office 2013 for Windows Phone	Smartphones	Various: Nokia, HTC, Samsung, and others	Office 2013 for Windows Phone: Visually different than the full Office 2013 but similar functionality to Office 2013 RT
Blackberry	Runs apps from BlackBerry App World only	Smartphones and tablets	Blackberry only	Very limited ability to work with Office files. Some capability with purchased third-party apps

Table 1 Operating system capabilities

Tablets can run one of two kinds of chips: an Intel-based or ARM-based chip. An **Advanced RISC Machine chip (ARM chip)** is designed for low-energy embedded systems, such as in an iPad. An **Intel chip** is a series of microprocessors made by the manufacturer Intel, for example the chip used in most traditional laptops or desktops.

In October 2012, Microsoft released the Surface tablet. This tablet comes in two versions, the Surface and Surface Pro—as seen in Figure 1. The Surface RT runs on an ARM chip device and contains substantively similar functionality for Word, PowerPoint, Excel, and OneNote as the Windows version of Office 2013. Visually, Windows RT even looks the same as the full Office 2013 for Windows. However, applications that run on Windows Phone and RT do not support some of the more sophisticated Office features or back-end Visual Basic programming.

The Surface Pro tablet runs Windows 8 Pro and is built with a more traditional Intel chip hardware that lets it perform like a traditional PC. Tablets capable of performing like a traditional PC are typically referred to as a **tablet PC**.

Aidan Matthews purchased a Surface Pro tablet PC because he can use it for personal, business, and mobile tasks. Thus, you need to learn about the touch interface for the full Windows 8 specifically—the same touch interface for any PC with any kind of touch screen.

Figure 1 Microsoft Surface

Understand Methods for Interacting with a Tablet PC

Users can interact with the tablet PC via several built-in ways: speech, keyboard, trackpad, digitizer pen, or touch screen. Windows 8 is smart enough to detect the method of input you are using and adapts the menus and options accordingly. To maximize your efficiency, you need to understand when to use which method of input.

Inputting Text with Speech Recognition

Speech recognition in Windows 8 is better than any prior version of Windows. Typically, whether speech recognition is desirable or efficient is highly dependent on voice, accent, and personal preference. Windows 8 has a built-in speech recognition app. By default, the app is not pinned to the Start screen. However, you can easily find it by doing a search as shown in Figure 2. While the Surface Pro includes a microphone, most users prefer and have better accuracy with a headset or desktop microphone—purchased separately.

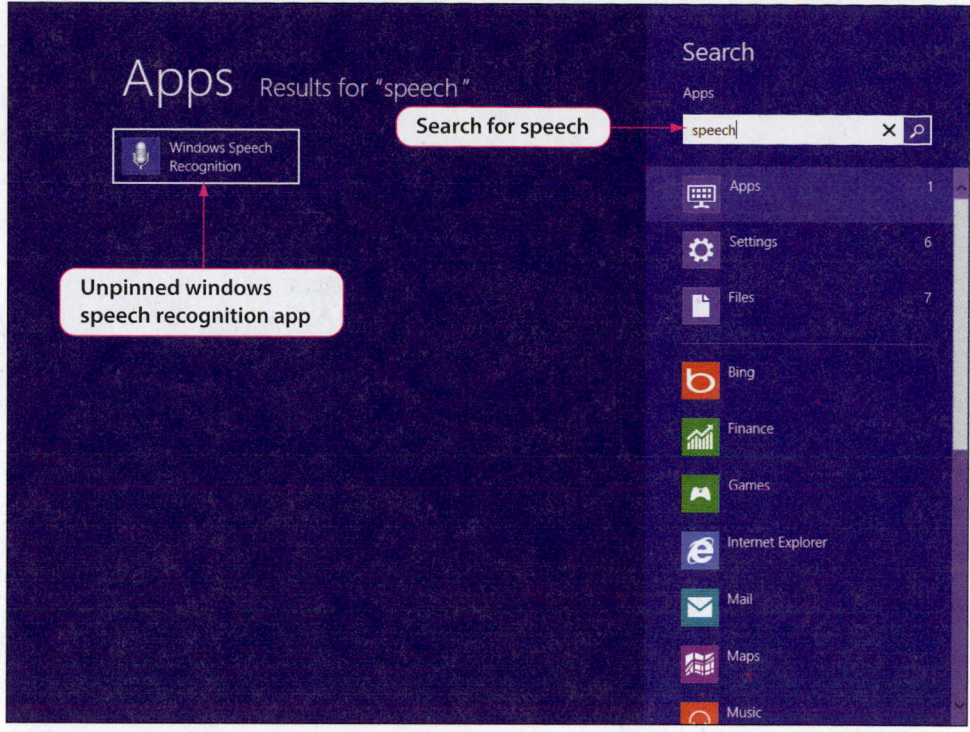

Figure 2   Search for speech recognition app

Using the Keyboard and Trackpad

The Surface comes with two types of covers: the touch cover and type cover as seen in Figure 3. The type cover provides a depression keyboard similar to traditional keyboards. Both keyboards have the same functionality except that only the type cover has the traditional F1–F12 keys. Thus, personal preference is the most important determinant on which is best. Even though Windows 8 has a touch keyboard, most users still find an actual keyboard preferable when needing more than a few words entered.

Figure 3   Microsoft Surface covers

The covers come with a built-in **trackpad**—a pad that works like a traditional mouse but uses touch. Trackpads are typically found on laptops and tablet PCs. Many users find a trackpad awkward when needing to drag. Thus, a user that drags a lot may want to consider purchasing a USB wireless mouse.

The touch interface can replace the need for a mouse in many situations. In fact, keyboard shortcuts can also cut down dramatically on the need for a mouse. Thus, keyboard shortcuts improve efficiency in Windows 8 more than any prior version of Windows.

REAL WORLD ADVICE | **Using Keyboard Shortcuts and KeyTips**

Keyboard shortcuts are extremely useful because they allow you to keep your hands on the keyboard instead of reaching for the mouse to make Ribbon selections. This can dramatically increase your efficiency and save you time.

Pressing the Alt key will display KeyTips—or keyboard shortcuts—for items on the Ribbon and Quick Access Toolbar. After displaying the KeyTips, you can press the letter or number corresponding to Ribbon items to request the action from the keyboard. Pressing Alt again will remove the KeyTips.

Many keyboard shortcuts are universal to all Windows programs. Keyboard shortcuts usually involve two or more keys, in which case you hold down the first key listed, and press the second key once.

QUICK REFERENCE | **Common Keyboard Shortcuts**

Press Ctrl and type C	Copy the selected item
Press Ctrl and type V	Paste a copied item
Press Ctrl and type A	Select all the items in a document or window
Press Ctrl and type B	Bold selected text
Press Ctrl and type Z	Undo an action
Press Ctrl + Home	Move to the top of the document
Press Ctrl + End	Move to the end of the document
Press F1	Microsoft Help
Press Ctrl and type S	Save a file

Using the Digitizer Pen

The Surface Pro tablet PC also comes with a **digitizer pen**—a device that allows you to write on a touch screen like a pen does on paper as shown in Figure 4. Windows 8 can recognize whether you use a mouse, finger, or digitizer pen. Apps may react differently based on your input method.

Figure 4   Surface digitizer pen

If you use the pen in Word, the Pens contextual Ribbon tab automatically appears for drawing options: Highlighter, Eraser, or Selection as seen in Figure 5. Word accepts only drawing input from the pen and cannot recognize handwritten text. Thus, best practice is to use the pen in Word to replace a mouse or to draw a picture.

If you want to take handwritten notes—for example in a meeting—best practice is to use OneNote. OneNote has excellent handwriting-to-text conversion capabilities using the Ink to Text button as shown in Figure 6. Thus, you gain efficiency by using the pen in situations where handwriting is most natural.

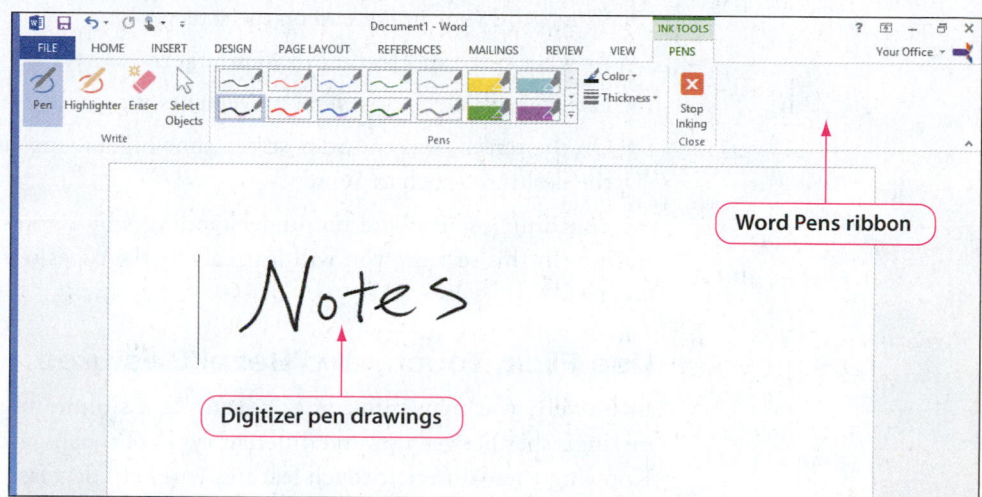

Figure 5 Pens Ribbon in Word

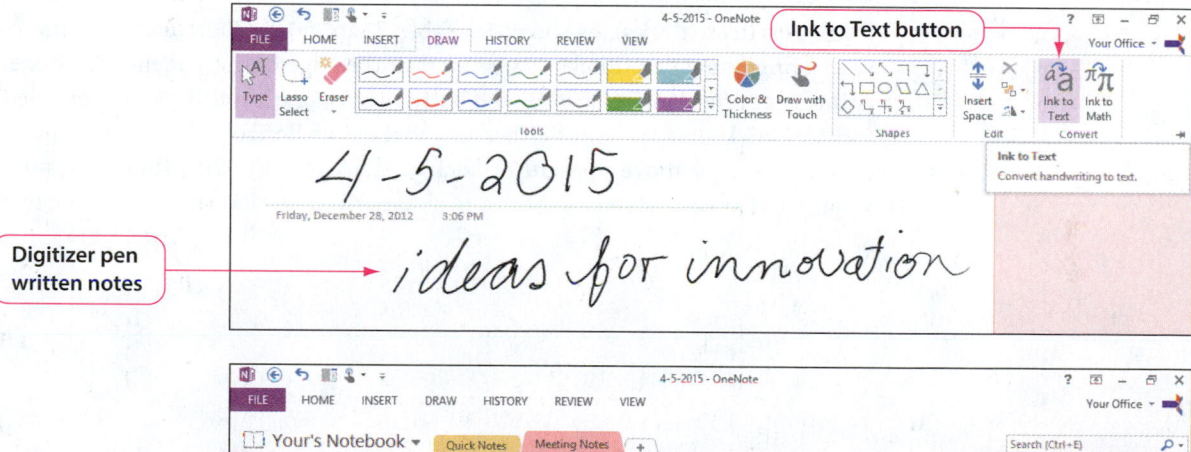

Figure 6 Handwriting in OneNote

Understanding When the Touch Interface Is Effective

Windows 8 and Office 2013 have fully integrated the touch environment. If you have a touch screen, you can manipulate Windows, Office, and other apps by just touching the screen. Fingers are larger than a mouse point. Thus, the app must be designed to be easy to use with a simple touch. One of Microsoft's main goals with the latest release of Windows and Office was to make it easier to use with touch. Touch increases efficiency and productivity when used while mobile, to replace traditional mouse movements, and to use apps specifically designed for touch.

Using the Touch-Screen Interface

One of the key features that sets Windows 8 apart from previous versions is the built-in touch-screen recognition. A **gesture** is a movement of the user's finger, fingers, or pen on a touch screen resulting in a particular action. Many gestures are available, and several factors determine the result.

- Are you using one or two fingers?
- Where did your finger start on the screen?
- Where did your finger end on the screen?
- At what speed did you move your finger?
- Did you make one or several movements together?
- On the screen, was the Start screen showing, an app running, or an app that runs on the desktop—such as Word?

Touching a screen and not understanding why the resulting action occurred is frustrating. In this section, you will learn about the types of touch and other touch-friendly features.

Use Flick, Touch, and Bezel Gestures

Intuitively, you may think of a "touch" as a simple finger tap. However, Windows 8 distinguishes between several different types of touch gestures—flicks, touch, and bezel. Knowing these different touch features will help decrease frustration, increase efficiency, and increase productivity.

Using Flick Gestures

Flick gestures (flicks), as shown in Table 2, are quick short gestures that can be made with a finger or a pen. Flicks cannot start at the edge of the screen—the **bezel**. There are two types of flicks, navigational and editing. **Navigational flicks** are enabled by default and are quick short gestures either in a vertical or horizontal direction that either scroll up and down or move forward or backward a page. **Editing flicks** are not enabled by default and are quick short gestures in a diagonal direction that either delete, copy, paste, or undo.

Flick Gesture	Result Action	Image
Up	Scroll up	
Down	Scroll down	
Right	Turn page to the right	
Left	Turn page to the left	
Diagonally to upper left	Delete	
Diagonally to upper right	Copy	
Diagonally to lower left	Undo	
Diagonally to lower right	Paste	

Table 2 Flick gestures

You can adjust settings, modify sensitivity, enable editing flicks, turn flicks off, and practice flicks from the Pen and Touch dialog box. To modify these settings, search Windows settings for flicks as seen in Figures 7 and 8 shown here. In the same dialog box, you can also change settings and customize the pen and other touch actions.

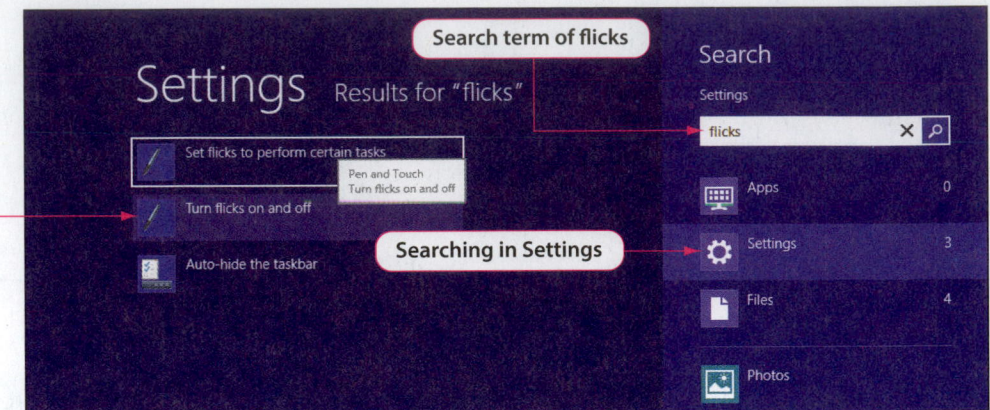

Figure 7   Search settings for flicks

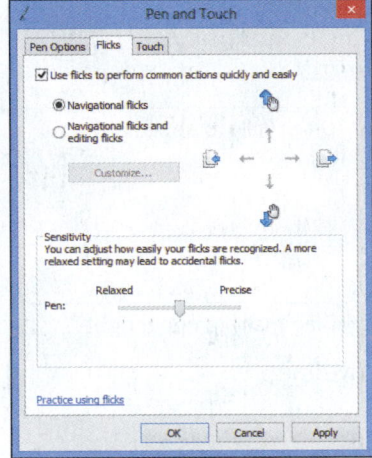

Figure 8   Pen and Tools dialog box

Using Touch Gestures

Touch gestures are gestures made with a finger. Generally, these gestures cannot be completed with a pen—except pen actions set by default for tap, double-tap, and tap and hold. Touches can bring up additional menus and mimic traditional mouse actions such as double-clicking. Table 3 shows the available touch gestures.

Touch Gesture	Result Action	Image
Tap	Same action as a single mouse click	
Double-tap	Same action as a double-click on a mouse	
Tap and hold	Same action as a right-click on a mouse	
Slide	Pans or scrolls	
Pinch and stretch	Zoom in or out	
Rotate	Rotates the item that is selected	
Tap and swipe in the opposite direction as any scroll bars, not starting at a bezel	Selects the item and brings up additional menus	

Table 3 Touch gestures

Using Bezel Gestures

A **bezel gesture** is a gesture that starts and/or ends at the edge of the screen, as shown in Table 4. For example, a left bezel starts with your finger on the left edge—middle of the screen is the easiest—and swipes to the center of the screen. Some tablet cases can make these gestures difficult. These gestures are easiest when they start completely off screen.

Bezel Gesture	Result Action	Image
Left bezel	Switches to the last app that was used	
Right bezel	Opens the charms menu	
Top bezel	Brings up additional menus dependent on the currently open app. On the Start screen, it brings up menu to go to all apps. In Internet Explorer, it brings up a menu of all tabs.	
Bottom bezel	Brings up additional menus dependent on the currently open app; usually, a menu similar to the options given from a right-click on a mouse	
Left bezel and then back to left bezel again	Brings up a menu of all open apps	
Slow left bezel*	When multiple apps are open, snaps the current app to a docked position to view more than one app at the same time on the same screen	
Top bezel ending at the bottom bezel	Shows the app window shrinking and then closes the app when the bottom bezel is reached	
From title bar of a program window to the left or right bezel*	Snaps app to left or right portion of the screen docking it to view multiple apps on the same screen	

*Must have a screen resolution of at least 1366 * 768 to snap.

Table 4 Bezel gestures

Use Office 2013 Touch Gestures

Gestures can be combined or have different effects within different apps, including Office 2013. For example, the Mini toolbar is particularly helpful with the touch interface. When Office recognizes that you are using touch instead of a mouse or digitizer pen, it creates Mini toolbars that are larger and designed to work with fingers easier. To get the Mini toolbar in Excel, a combination of several gestures are needed.

1. Tap a cell.
2. Use the touch handles to select the desired cells.
3. Tap again anywhere but on the handle.

Figure 9 is an example of a touch Mini toolbar in Excel when using touch input.

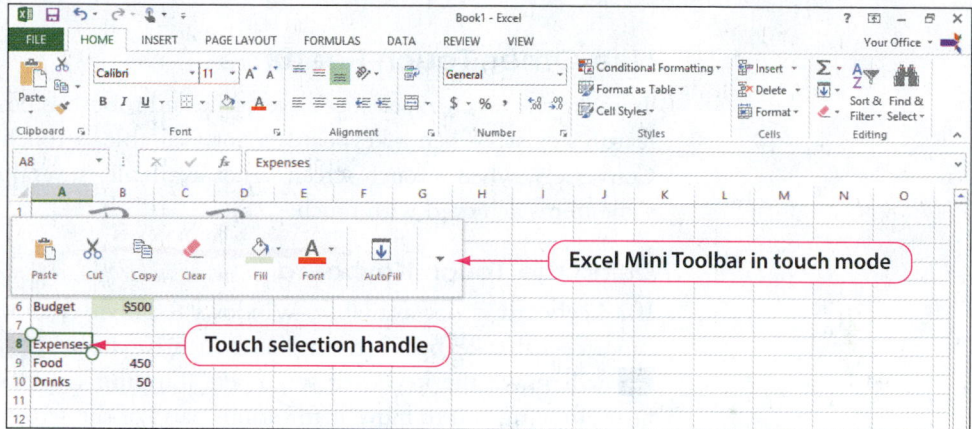

Figure 9   Excel Mini toolbar when using touch input

If you need to use Office by touch for an extended period of time, you can also use touch mode. **Touch mode** switches Office into a version that makes a touch screen easy to use, as shown in Table 5. Click the Touch Mode button on the Quick Access Toolbar, and the Ribbon spreads its icons further apart for easier access to fingers. When you toggle this display mode, the on-screen controls space out a bit from each other to make them more accessible to users via touch. Figure 10 displays the normal Word 2013 Ribbon. Figure 11 displays the Ribbon in touch mode.

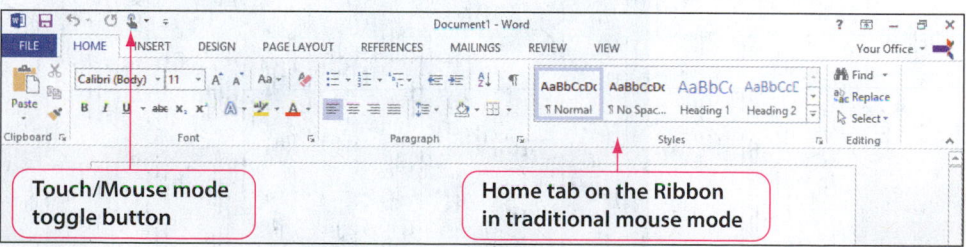

Figure 10   Normal Ribbon

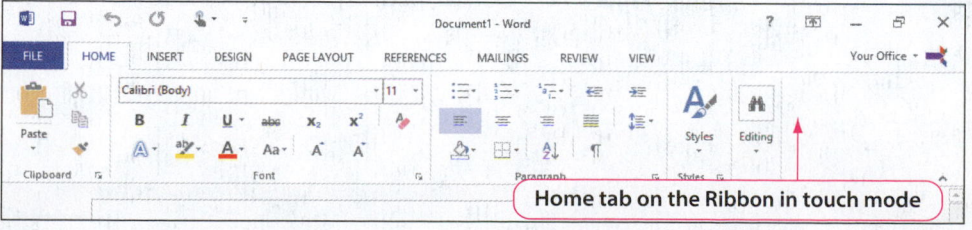

Figure 11   Touch mode Ribbon

To	Gestures Steps
Place the cursor insertion point	Tap the location for the cursor.
Select and format text	Tap the text, drag the selection handle to the desired selection, and tap the selection to show and use the Mini toolbar.
Edit an Excel cell	Double-tap.
Change PowerPoint slides in Normal view	A quick vertical flick
Customize the Quick Access Toolbar	Tab and hold any button on the Quick Access Toolbar.

Table 5 Common Office 2013 gestures

Use Other Touch Features

To make the touch experience as versatile and robust as possible, a few last touch-friendly features exist. When a keyboard is not available, a touch-screen keyboard can be used. Conversely, when a touch screen is not available, several options exist for accessing the same items achieved with touch.

Using the Touch Keyboard

If a keyboard is not available, Windows 8 provides an on-screen touch keyboard. You can access this keyboard by tapping Touch Keyboard [⌨] in the taskbar. Tapping Dock [▭] will make the keyboard stay open. Tapping Undock [▭] will make the keyboard float allowing you to move it to various parts of the screen. Tapping Keyboard Mode [⌨] allows you to switch between a full, thumbs, or pen handwriting mode as seen in Figures 12, 13, and 14.

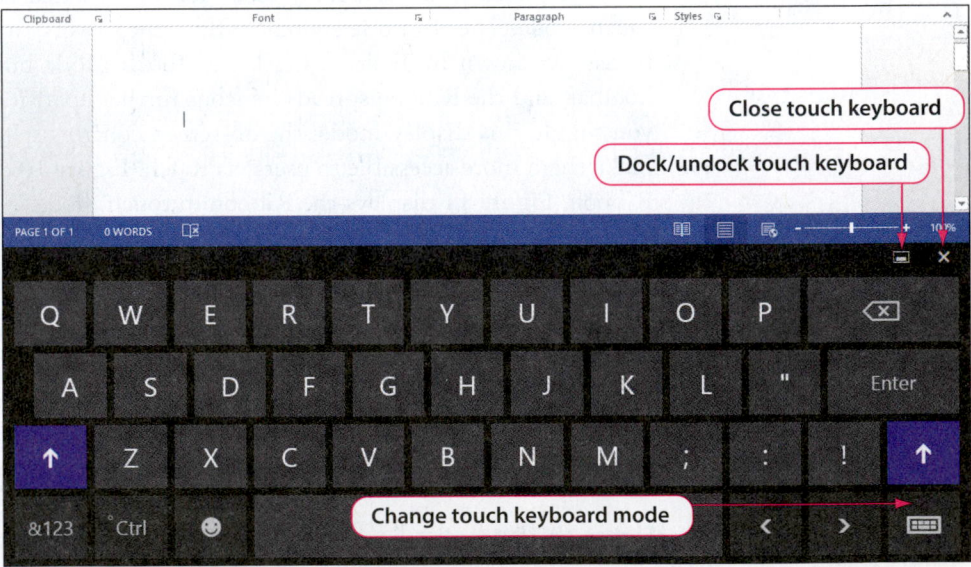

Figure 12 Docked touch keyboard in full mode

Figure 13   Docked touch keyboard in thumbs mode

Figure 14   Docked touch keyboard in pen handwriting mode

Using Alternatives to a Touch Screen

If a touch screen is not available, you have three choices. You can use a traditional mouse and point it in particular places to access the Start screen and charms menu as shown in Table 6. You can use gestures on your trackpad or Windows 8 mouse. Not all gestures work on the trackpad and may be slightly different than on a touch screen. However, device makers can add custom gestures accessible via the trackpad only. You should consult your touchpad or Windows 8 mouse manufacturer for specifics. Lastly, you can use keyboard shortcuts to access the most common bezel gestures as shown in Table 7.

Result Action	Mouse Equivalent
Start screen	Point mouse to edge of lower-left corner.
Charms menu	Point mouse to edge of lower-right or upper-right corner.

Table 6   Mouse alternatives for Windows 8

Result Action	Touch Gesture	Keyboard Shortcut
Charms menu	Right bezel	Press Windows and type C
Additional menus, similar to the right-click menus, when additional options exist	Bottom bezel	Press Windows and type Z
Switch between open apps	Left bezel swipe and then back to bezel	Press Windows + Tab or press Alt + Tab
Shrinks and then closes program	Top bezel to bottom bezel	Alt + F4

Table 7   Keyboard shortcut alternatives for bezel gestures

Concept Check

1. What is the difference between a tablet and a tablet PC? Provide an example of each. p. 743

2. What is a digitizer pen, and when is it the most effective to use? p. 746

3. What is the difference between a flick, touch, and bezel gesture? Provide an example of each. p. 748–752

4. Does touch differ at all inside of Office 2013? Explain. How could you use a tablet PC without a keyboard? How could you use a tablet PC without a touch screen? p. 755

Key Terms

Advanced RISC Machine chip
  (ARM chip)   743
Application software   742
Bezel   748
Bezel gesture   752
Digitizer pen   746

Editing flicks   748
Flick gestures (flicks)   748
Gesture   748
Graphical user interface (GUI)   742
Intel chip   743
Navigational flicks   748

Operating system   742
Tablet PC   743
Touch gestures   751
Touch mode   753
Trackpad   746

Glossary

A

Action—A self-contained instruction that can be combined with others to automate tasks and is considered to be the basic building block of macros.

Action Catalog—A searchable set of macro actions that can retrieve actions based on keywords.

Action query—A query that makes changes to records or moves many records from one table to another. Action queries are used to change the data in existing tables or make new tables based on a query's data set.

Adobe PDF file—A file format that is easy to send through e-mail and preserves the original document look and feel so it opens the same way every time for the recipient.

Advanced filter—This hides records that do not match the criteria that you chose and can have several criteria in multiple fields, combined with sorting.

Advanced RISC Machine Chip (ARM chip)—This microprocessor chip is designed for low-energy embedded systems and used in devices such as an iPad.

After events—Events that occur after the changes have been successfully made to the table data.

Aggregate—A summative calculation, such as a total or average.

Aggregate function—Calculations that perform arithmetic operations, such as averages and totals, on records displayed in a table or query.

Aggregated calculation—A calculation that returns a single value, calculated from multiple values in a column. Common aggregate functions include Average, Count, Maximum, Median, Minimum, Mode, and Sum.

Alternate key—A candidate key that is not used for the primary key.

Anomalies—Unmatched or missing data that is caused by limitations in database design.

Append query—A query that selects records from one or more data sources and copies the selected records to an existing table.

Append row—The first blank row at the end of the table.

Application—A piece of software that is used to perform a task or multiple tasks.

Application software—Programs that help you perform specific tasks, such as word processing.

Application Start screen—The first screen seen when an existing program file is not open but when the program is launched. In the screen you can select a blank document, workbook, presentation, database, or one of many application specific templates.

Apps for Office—These third-party applications run in the side pane to provide extra features like web search, dictionary, maps, and so on.

Argument—Value that provides information concerning the action being carried out by the macro.

Artificial key—A key composed of nonnaturally occurring data that is also visible to the user, such as sequential numbering from the AutoNumber data type.

AS clause—When used in a SQL SELECT statement, the AS clause allows you to name or rename a field, which will be displayed in the dataset.

Atomic—A record where none of the values are repeating or concatenated for a single column.

Attachment—A data type that stores images, spreadsheet files, documents, charts, and other types of supported files to the records in your database, much like you attach files to an e-mail message.

Attribute—Information about an entity.

AutoExec macro—A macro that has been given the name of AutoExec. When a database is opened, Access will check for a macro with that name and run that macro before any others.

AutoFit—A method to change the column width of the data to match the widest data entered in that field

AutoKeys macro—A macro group that assigns keys on the keyboard to execute each submacro. The macro must be named AutoKeys, and each submacro must be named with the key or key combinations on the keyboard that will be used to execute the macros.

AutoNumber data type—A data type that stores an integer that is generated automatically for each new record.

AutoRecovery—A feature that attempts to recover any changes made since the prior save to a document if something goes wrong—for example, automatically saving a backup version at specified time intervals.

B

Back-end database—Contains the tables to which front-end databases link to.

Backstage view—Provides access to the file-level features, such as saving a file, creating a new file, opening an existing file, printing a file, and closing a file, as well as program options.

Backup database—An extra copy of a database created in case the database is lost. Access appends the current date to the file name.

Before events—Events that occur before any changes are made to the table data.

Between…And operator—An operator that verifies whether the value of a field or expression falls within a stated range of numeric values and is combined with the And or Or operators. For example, to find data that falls between two dates, you would type Between 2/3/2013 And 8/6/2013.

Bezel—The edge of the screen.

Bezel gesture—A gesture that starts and/or ends at the edge of the screen. For example, a left bezel gesture starts with your finger on the left edge and swipes horizontally towards the center of the screen.

Bezel swipe gesture—A touch gesture that starts on the physical touch insensitive frame that surrounds the display. The user swipes a finger from a part of the display edge into the display.

Bitmap—An image of an object.

Blank Report tool—An Access tool with which you can create a blank report in Layout view.

Boolean algebra—Still used today, a 0 and 1 are used to represent one of two values—true or false. The 0 and 1—or −1 depending on the system you are using—are a throwback to the earlier days of programming.

Bootcamp—Mac software that allows the user to decide which operating system to launch on Intel chip-based Macs.

Bound control—A control on a report or form whose data source is a field in the table.

Bound form—A form that is directly connected to a data source such as a table or query and that can be used to enter, edit, or display data from that data source.

Bound value—A value that is stored in a lookup field.

Boyce–Codd normal form (BCNF, 3.5NF)—Additional criteria that are useful when multiple overlapping candidate keys exist. Requires that all determinants are candidate keys and that the table satisfies 1NF, 2NF, and 3NF. By normalizing to BCNF, you are eliminating all functional dependencies.

Business intelligence (BI)—Helps an organization attain their goals and objectives by giving them a better understanding of past performance as well as information on how the organization is progressing toward its goals.

Business intelligence tools—A classification of software applications that aid in collecting, storing, analyzing, and providing access to data that helps managers make improved business decisions.

C

Calculated control—A control whose source of data is an expression rather than a field.

Calculated data type—A Calculated data type allows you to display the results of a calculation in a read-only field.

Call statement—Runs another Sub procedure or function from within a procedure by transferring to the called routine.

Candidate key—Fields that could be used as the primary key.

Caption property—The text that is displayed for the field name when the field name appears in queries, forms, or reports.

Cardinality—The number of instances of one entity that relates to one instance of another entity. Cardinality is expressed as one-to-many, many-to-many, or one-to-one.

Cascade delete—Deletes every record with the foreign key if the value is deleted from the primary table.

Cascade update—Updates a foreign key automatically when the primary key changes.

Case sensitive—Query results will return all matching data, regardless of how the data is stored, when a user enters lowercase or uppercase letters in the criteria property.

Charlist—A group of one or more characters.

Charms—A specific and consistent set of buttons in every application: Search, Share, Connect, Settings, and Start.

Check box—A control that shows whether an option is selected by using a check mark to indicate when the option is selected.

Close—The ability to close an Office file without exiting the associated program.

Cloud computing—Computing resources—either hardware or software—being used by another computer over a network.

Code window—The larger window on the right of the Visual Basic Editor where code is entered.

Cold turkey implementation—The process of implementing a new system in its entirety and replacing a legacy system all at once.

Compacting—An Access feature that rearranges objects in your database to use space more efficiently.

Comparison operator—An operator used in a query to compare the value in a database to the criteria value entered in the query.

Complex delete query—A query used to delete data between multiple tables.

Complex update query—A query used to update data between multiple tables.

Composite key—A primary key composed of two fields.

Composite or concatenated key—A key where multiple fields are used to identify a record.

Concatenate operator—This is a function that helps join data from multiple fields to create a single text string of data. This is done by using an ampersand (&) to create a single field by combining data in multiple fields. For example, to concatenate first and last name fields, you would type FullName:[FirstName]& " "&[LastName], where FullName would become the name of the concatenated field.

Conditional formatting—Allows the specification of rules that apply formatting to cells, appointments, contacts, or tasks as determined by the rule outcome.

Contextual tab—A Ribbon tab that contains commands related to selected objects so you can manipulate, edit, and format the objects. This Ribbon tab does not appear unless the object is selected.

Contextual tools—Tools that only appear when needed for specific tasks.

Control—An object on a form or report that displays data, performs actions, and lets you view and work with information.

Crosstab query—A special type of query used when you want to describe one field in terms of two or more other fields in the table.

Crosstab Query Wizard—This wizard helps create a basic crosstab query. For a more advanced query, changes would need to be made in the query's Design view after finishing the wizard.

Current Date—A function that automatically puts the current date in a field based on your computer's system date.

Custom formatting—This is used to customize the way numbers, dates, times, and text are displayed and printed.

D

Data—Facts about people, events, things, or ideas.

Data actions—A specific, limited set of macro actions that can be used in a data macro.

Data blocks—An area in a data macro to add one or more data actions. The data block executes all the actions contained as part of its operation.

Data cleansing—A process of removing data that is not useful or needed anymore.

Data macro—Database objects stored in Access tables that are triggered by table events. Data macros are typically used to implement business logic into tables and automatically set values in fields.

Data mining—The act of using BI tools is called data mining, which helps expose trends, patterns, and relationships within the data that might have otherwise remained undetected.

Data type—The characteristic that defines the kind of data that can be entered into a field, such as numbers, text, or dates. The data type tells Access how to store and display the field.

Data validation rule—A rule that prevents inaccurate data from being entered and consequentially stored in a database. Validation rules can be set for a specific field or an entire table.

Data warehouse—Data warehouses contain large amounts and different types of data that present a clear picture of business environments at specific points in time.

Data warehousing—When older data is exported from transactional and operational databases into a "storage" database, called a data warehouse.

Database—A collection of data.

Database event—An event that occurs when an action is completed on any given object. The action could be, for example, a simple click of the mouse or entering into a specific field.

Database management system (DBMS)—Database management software that can be used to organize, store, manipulate, and report on your data.

Datasheet view—A view of an Access object that shows the data.

Date function—This function returns the current system date.

Date Picker—A pop-up calendar that allows a user to enter a date by clicking the date in the calendar.

DateAdd function—This function can be used to add or subtract a specific time interval from a date. For example, Date()+10 would result in the same output as using the DateAdd function to add 10 to the current date—DateAdd("d", 10, Date()).

DateDiff function—This function is used to determine the difference between two dates. For example, to see how many days it has been since a member paid the club's annual dues, you could type DaysSincePmt: DateDiff("d",Date(),[PaymentDate]).

DatePart function—This function can be used to examine a date and return a specific interval of time. For example, if each employee is eligible for a bonus after five years of service, you can determine the year when eligibility begins by typing 5 Year Anniversary:DatePart("yyyy", ([HireDate]))+5.

DateSerial function—This function, written as DateSerial(year, month, day), can be used to manipulate the day, month, and year of a date. For example, if each full-time employee is eligible for health benefits after 90 days of employment, which means that the benefits begin on the 91st day of employment you could determine the date when eligibility begins by typing Benefits Begin:DateSerial(Year ([HireDate]),Month([HireDate]), Day([HireDate])+91).

Debugging—The process of identifying and reducing the number of errors that can occur within programming code.

Declarations—Define user-defined data types, variables, arrays, and constants.

Declarations section—Declarations that apply to all procedures within the module.

Decryption—The process of making encrypted information readable again using a key.

Default value—A value that is automatically entered into a field when a new record is created.

Delete query—A query that is used to remove entire records from a table at one time. Delete queries remove all the data in each field, including the primary key.

Deletion anomaly—Forces you to delete two different pieces of data when you only wanted to delete one piece of data, resulting in information loss.

Delimiter—A character used in a text file to separate the fields; it can be a paragraph mark, a tab, a comma, or another character.

Dependency—Exists when a field relates to a key.

Dependent expression—This is an expression that relies on the outcome of another expression.

Design view—A view of an Access object that shows the detailed structure of a table, query, form, or report.

Detail area—The section of a report that displays the records from the underlying table or query.

Determinant—A field that determines the value of another field.

Dialog box—A window that provides more options or settings beyond those provided on the Ribbon.

Dialog box launcher—An icon on the Ribbon that opens a corresponding dialog box or task pane.

Digitizer pen—A device that allows you to write on a touch screen like a pen does on paper.

Dim statement—The beginning of the process of declaring a variable.

DoCmd object—Allows Access actions to be performed from within VBA.

Document—Depending on the application, a document can be a letter, memo, report, brochure, resume, or flyer.

Domain integrity constraint—Database rules that are specific for each field.

E

Edit mode—A mode that allows you to edit or change the contents of a field or change the name of a file or folder.

Editing flicks—These are quick short gestures in a diagonal direction that either delete, copy, paste, or undo, and are not enabled by default.

Embedded macro—A macro stored as part of a database object like a form or report or any control such as a button or text box. An embedded macro is triggered by database events.

Enabled—A property option that allows a field to have the value changed or copied. By default, all fields are enabled.

Encryption—The process of changing text-based information into a state in which a key is required in order to read the information.

Entity—Person, place, item, or event about which you want to keep data.

Entity relationship diagram (ERD)—A common way to visually express the tables and relationships in your database. An ERD does not tell you anything about data flow; it is a fixed view of the database structure.

Error handling—The process of anticipating and controlling errors.

Event-driven programming—Uses an event—such as moving to the next record of a form to trigger the execution of code.

Exclusive Access—Allows for only one user to open and edit a database at a time.

Exit—The ability to close all of the program's files and close the program itself.

Expression Builder—A tool that helps you create formulas and functions.

F

Field—A specific piece of information that is stored in every record and when formatted appears as a column in a database table.

Field format—These are used to customize the way numbers, dates, times, and text are displayed and printed by using predefined formats or custom formats.

Field size—The maximum length of a data field or a range of values.

Field validation rule—Verifies the value entered in a field. If the validation rule is violated, Access prevents the user from leaving the current field until the problem is fixed.

File extension—A suffix that helps Windows understand what kind of information is in a file and what program should open it.

FileDialog object—Can be used to allow the user to select the file(s) needed for the import process.

Filter—A condition applied temporarily to a table or query to show a subset of the records.

Filter by Form—Allows you to filter data in a form or spreadsheet by creating a blank table for the selected table.

Filter by Selection—Selecting a value in a record and filtering the records that contain only the values that match what has been selected.

Filtering—Allows you to view and print only the desired and required information from a database.

Find command—A command used to find records in a database with a specific value.

Find Duplicates Query Wizard—Finds duplicate records in a table or a query.

Find Unmatched Query Wizard—Finds records in one table that do not have related records in another table.

First normal form (1NF)—Dictates that the table must not have repeating groups of values in a single column—atomicity—and that it must have a key. Also, in 1NF each nonkey field needs some sort of dependency on the primary key.

Fiscal year—A period businesses and other organizations use for calculating annual financial statements. This can be different from a calendar year and can vary throughout different businesses and organizations because they can choose whatever dates they want to use as the "year."

Flick gestures (flicks)—Quick short gestures that can be made with a finger or a digitizer pen.

Forecasting—When historical data is used to predict or estimate future sales trends, to develop budgets, and so forth.

Foreign key—A field in a table that stores the value of the primary key of a related table for the purpose of creating a relationship.

Form—An object that allows you to enter or view your table data.

Form view—Data view of a form.

Format—Specifies how data is displayed.

Front-end database—A database that is deployed directly to users and contains nondata objects such as queries, reports, forms, macros, and VBA modules.

FULL JOIN clause—Used when you want to return all the rows from the left table and all the rows from the right table in a SQL query.

Function—In programming it executes instructions and returns a value to another procedure.

Functional dependency diagram—A visual representation of dependencies in a table.

G

Gallery—A set of menu options that appear when you click the arrow next to a button which, in some cases, may be referred to as a More arrow.

Gesture—Movement of the user's finger, fingers, or digitizer pen on a touch screen resulting in a particular action.

GIGO principle—Stands for Garbage In, Garbage Out. It means that inconsistent or inaccurate data leads to an inconsistent or inaccurate output.

Grand total—Controls added to a report to perform calculations on all records.

Graphical user interface (GUI)—An interface that uses icons.

Graphics—Pictures, online pictures, SmartArt, shapes, and charts.

Group—A collection of records along with some introductory and summary information about the records.

GROUP BY aggregate function—A function that can help combine records with identical values in a specified field list into a single record.

Group Footer—Information printed at the end of every group of records; used to display summary information for the group.

Group Header—Information printed at the beginning of every new group of records, for example, the group name.

Group, Sort, and Total pane—A pane that is displayed at the bottom of the screen in which you can control how information is sorted and grouped in a report.

H

HAVING clause—If a field includes an aggregate function, a HAVING clause specifies the aggregated field criteria and restricts the results based on aggregated values.

Help—Microsoft help is a window opened via the Help button or the F1 key.

Highest normal form (HNF)—The level of normal form that a table satisfies along with all levels below.

Hyperlink—An address that specifies a protocol (such as HTTP or FTP) and a location of an object, document, World Wide Web page, or other destination on the Internet, an intranet, or local computer, for example, http://www.paintedparadiseresort.com.

I

Ideas—Actions that Access believes will improve your database performance but may have consequences that should be considered first, and must be performed by the user.

IIf function—This function, which stands for Immediate If, is similar to the IF function in Excel. The results of this function returns one value if a specified condition is true or another value if it is false. For example, for employees who received a salary increase, you can calculate what the new salary will be if employees receive a 3% raise by typing New Salary:IIf([Salary]<=30000,[Salary]*1.03, [Salary]).

Importing—The process of copying data from another file, such as a Word file or Excel workbook, into a separate file, such as an Access database.

In operator—This operator can be used to return results that contain one of the values in a list of values. For example, you may want to search for customers who meet certain criteria, such as those who live in specific states. Thus, you would type In("Arizona", "Nevada", "New Mexico") as the criterion in the State field.

Index—This stores the location of records based on the field that you choose.

Information—Data that has been manipulated and processed to make it meaningful.

Information management program—Provides the ability to print schedules, task lists, phone directories, and other documents.

Inner join—The default join type in Access, an inner join selects only those records from both database tables that have matching values.

INNER JOIN clause—Used to return only the rows that actually match based on the join predicate.

Input mask—A way to control how data is entered by creating a typing guide. In most cases, an input mask controls the way that data is stored.

Input Mask Wizard—Provides input masks for most common formatting needs and helps automate the process of establishing an input mask.

Insertion anomaly—Forces you to enter data about two different entities when you may have only data on one entity.

Integrity constraint—A rule your database conforms to in order to help ensure the data's validity.

Intel chip—A series of microprocessors made by the manufacturer Intel and used in devices such as a tablet PC, laptop, or desktop.

Is Not Null—By entering this into a field's criteria in the Design view of a query, the results will include records that contain valid data. For example, to create a list of the employees who have not had an employee photo taken, you could type Is Not Null in the Criteria property of the Photo field.

Is Null—By entering this into a field's criteria in the Design view of a query, the results will include records that do not contain valid data.

IsNull function—This function is used to indicate that a value is unknown and it is treated differently than other values because it has no value. For example, to create a list of the employees who have had an employee photo taken, you could type Is Null in the Criteria property of the Photo field.

J

Join—Used to combine the data from two or more tables.

Join lines—The lines connecting tables in the Relationship windows.

Junction table—A table that breaks down a many-to-many relationship into two one-to-many relationships.

K

Key tip—A form of keyboard shortcut. Pressing (Alt) will display key tips (or keyboard shortcuts) for items on the Ribbon and Quick Access Toolbar.

Keyboard shortcut—Keyboard equivalents for software commands that allow you to keep your hands on the keyboard instead of reaching for the mouse to make Ribbon selections.

Knowledge—This is applied information once you make the decision.

L

Label—An unbound control. It may be the name of a field or other text you manually enter.

Label control—A control on a form or report that contains descriptive information, typically a field name.

Layout selector—A tool that allows you to move a whole table at one time.

Layout view—A view that shows data and allows limited changes to a form or report design.

LEFT JOIN clause—Used when you only want to return rows that have matching data in the left table, even if no matching rows exist in the right table in a SQL query.

Legacy data type—An old or outdated data type that is still used—usually because it still works for the user—even though newer technology or more efficient methods exist.

Legacy software—Old technology that is out of date but still in use.

Like function—A function that helps find values in a field that match a specified pattern. For example, you could find all employees who have the job title of caddy by typing Like "caddy" in the Criteria property under Position.

Line continuation character—The single space character followed by an underscore character as the last line of code that allows a VBA statement to span multiple lines in the Code window.

Line labels—Are used like bookmarks in VBA procedures.

Linked table—A link within Access to a table stored in another database or application.

Linked Table Manager—Lists the file location of all linked tables in a database.

Live Preview—Shows the results that would occur in your file if you were to click that particular option.

Locked—A property option that determines whether the value in a field can be entered using a form.

Logical operator—An operator used in a query used to combine two or more criteria.

Logo—An unbound control that can be added to the header of a form.

Lookup field—A table field that has values that come either from a table, query, or a value list.

Lookup field properties—Can be set to change the behavior of a lookup column.

Lookup Wizard—This automatically populates the appropriate field properties and creates the appropriate table relationships.

Loops—Programming code used to execute a series of statements multiple times.

M

Macro Designer—An editor for creating macros that makes it easier to build robust database applications, increase productivity of business users, and reduce code errors.

Macro group—Two or more submacros that are usually similar in function, placed inside the same macro file.

Macro—Database objects that provide a method of automating routine database tasks and that can add functionality to reports and forms, as well as the controls that forms and reports contain.

Mailto command—A common type of hyperlink that helps generate a link for sending e-mail.

Main form—The primary, or first table, selected when creating a form.

Make table query—A query that acquires data from one or more tables, and then automatically loads the resulting data set into a new table once you run the query.

Many-to-many relationship (M:N)—A relationship between tables in which one record in one table has many matching records in a second table, and one record in the related table has many matching records in the first table.

Maximize—The button is located in the top-right corner of the tile bar. This option offers the largest workspace.

Me keyword—Functions in a similar fashion as a declared variable in the current object.

Method—An action—for example SaveAs—that controls an object's behavior.

Mini toolbar—A menu that appears after text is selected and contains buttons for the most commonly used formatting commands, such as font, font size, font color, center alignment, indents, bold, italic, and underline.

Minimize—Used to reduce a window to a taskbar button.

Module—Stores VBA procedures that can be referenced or called by other procedures or events in the database.

Most Recently Used list—A list maintained by Office of your most recently modified files: documents, spreadsheets, databases, and presentations.

Move handle—The spot in the top-left corner of an object that, when selected, allows the object to be moved.

Multiple-item form—A form that looks similar to a datasheet but that can be customized as a form.

Multiple-field index—This stores the location of records based on the fields that you choose.

Multiplier effect—When Access joins two tables without a common field, each record in the first table is matched with each record in the second table.

Multivalued field—A field that helps keep track of multiple related facts about a subject.

N

Natural key—A key that is created from naturally occurring data generated outside of the database, such as a driver's license number.

Natural primary key—A primary key has a logical relationship or meaning in the data.

Navigation bar—Provides a way to move through records in table, query, table, report, and form objects.

Navigation control bar—The area of the navigation form where you drag a form or report to create a navigation button.

Navigation form—Provides a familiar Internet-style interface that allows you to access multiple objects in the database from one central location.

Navigation mode—Allows you to move from record to record or field to field using keystrokes and the Navigation bar.

Navigation Pane—The window in Access that shows all the objects in the database.

Navigational flicks—Quick short gestures either in a vertical or horizontal direction that either scroll up and down or move forward or backward a page and are enabled by default.

Nested IIf function—This function nests IIf functions, or places one inside another, allowing a series of dependent expressions to be evaluated. For example, if you wanted to determine how much of a raise each employee received, you can type Raise Assessment:IIf([Salary]<=30000,"7% Raise",IIf([Salary]<=60000,"4% Raise","No Raise")).

Net revenue—The revenue minus sales returns, sales allowances, and sales discounts. Also known as net sales.

Normal form (NF)—A progressive series of criteria with several levels, each representing the table's vulnerability to redundancy, anomalies, and inaccuracies.

Normalization—The process of minimizing the duplication of information in a relational database through effective table design.

Not operator—This function is used to search for records that do not match specific criteria and can be combined with other operators. For example, you may want to search for all customers outside of North America. You would enter Not "USA" And Not "Canada" And Not "Mexico" in the Criteria property of the Country field.

Now function—A function that retrieves the current system date and time.

Null—A term used to indicate that a field is blank.

Number data type—A data type that can store only numeric data. The data field will be used in calculations.

Numeric key—A primary key with a number data type. AutoNumber is often used for numeric keys.

O

Object—A table, form, query, or report.

Object box—Displays the name of the object that contains the procedure such as a form or command button.

Object Browser—Lists all VBA objects along with the associated methods and properties for each object.

Object-oriented programming—A method of programming that uses objects to design applications.

Office 365—A cloud-based version of Office offered on a subscription basis.

Office Backstage—Provides access to the file-level features, such as saving a file, creating a new file, opening an existing file, printing a file, and closing a file, as well as program options and account settings.

OLE—OLE, which stands for Object Linking and Embedding, is a technology developed by Microsoft that creates a bitmap or image of an object. OLE objects allow you to store images inside a database field.

On Error statement—Enables or disables an error-handling routine and specifies the location of the routine within the procedure.

One-to-many relationship (1:M or 1:N)—A relationship between two tables where one record in the first table corresponds to many records in the second table.

One-to-one relationship (1:1)—A relationship between tables where a record in one table has only one matching record in the second table.

Operating system—System software that controls and coordinates computer hardware operations so other programs can run efficiently.

Operational database—The database used to carry out regular operations, such as payroll and inventory management, of an organization.

Option Compare—Sets the string comparison method for the module.

Option Compare Binary—Setting for the Option Compare that compares the ASCII values for the characters contained in a string and is therefore case sensitive.

Option Compare Text—Setting for the Option Compare that results in case-insensitive comparisons.

Option Explicit Statement—Requires that all variable names be defined using a Dim statement.

ORDER BY clause—Used in a SELECT statement to sort results either in ascending or descending order.

Orphan—A orphan is a foreign key in one table that does not relate to a primary key in another table.

Outer join—A join that selects *all* of the records from one database table and only those records in the second table that have matching values in the joined field. One or more fields can serve as a join field.

OUTER JOIN clause—Used when you want return all rows from at least one of the tables within the FROM clause, as long as those rows meet any WHERE or HAVING search conditions in a SQL query.

P

Page Footer—Information printed at the end of every page in a report; often used to display page numbers.

Page Header—Information printed at the top of every page of a report.

Parallel implementation—An implementation method where the legacy system and the new system are used simultaneously.

Parameter—A value that can be changed each time you run the query.

Parameter data types—When this is defined, users see a more helpful error message if they enter the wrong type of data, such as entering text when currency should be entered.

Parameter query—This type of query can be designed when search criteria is unknown. When a parameter query is run, the user is prompted to enter the value for each parameter.

Partial dependency—When a field only depends on one part of a composite or concatenated key. In other words, the field is determined by only one piece of a multifield key.

Percentage of physical volume—This calculation can compare how much an object holds as compared to how much space is being used.

Percentage of sales revenue—This calculation can compare a portion of the gross revenue to the total gross revenue.

Percentage of sales volume—Compares how two numbers are related, such as this year's sales over last year's sales. Consider the method used to calculate sales volume as well as the time period over which you plan on measuring the sales volume.

Performance Analyzer—A tool within Access that analyzes a database and makes suggestions on how to optimize the performance of a database.

Phased implementation—An implementation method where a portion of the new system is put into place and perfected before additional pieces of the system are moved into use.

Physical volume—Measures how much space an object can hold.

Piloted implementation—An implementation method that starts with small groups of users and gradually incorporates more users over time.

Portable Document Format (PDF)—A type of document that ensures the document will look the same on someone else's computer.

Precision—This allows you to determine how many decimal places you want to round your numbers to when using the Round function.

Predicate—Specifies the condition to use in order to perform an inner or outer join.

Primary key—The field that uniquely identifies a record in a table.

Primary sort field—The first field chosen in a multiple field sort.

Print Preview—A view of a report or other object that shows how it will appear if printed.

Procedure—A series of statements or instructions that are executed as a unit.

Procedure box—A list that allows you to navigate quickly between the Declarations section and the individual procedures in the open module.

Project Explorer—A list of the currently open Access database objects that contain VBA procedures and a list of modules within the current database.

Property sheet—A collection of options, or characteristics, available for each control on a form or report.

Protected view—The file contents can be seen and read, but you are not able to edit, save, or print the contents until you enable editing. By default, Office will open files from e-mail or a web browser in this view.

Q

Query—An object that retrieves specific data from one or more database objects—either tables or other queries—and then, in a single datasheet, displays only the data you specify.

Query by example—A type of query where a sample of the data is set up as criteria.

Query design grid—Selected fields in a query. Shown at the bottom of a query's Design view.

Query join—A temporary or virtual relationship between two tables in a query that do not have an established relationship or common field with the same field name and data type.

Query results—A recordset that provides an answer to a question posed in a query.

Query workspace—Displays the source for data in the query. Shown at the top of a query's Design view.

Quick Access Toolbar—Located in the top-left corner of the Office window, it can be customized to offer commonly used buttons.

R

Random AutoNumber—This will generate a random number that is unique to each record within the table.

Read Mode—A view of the document that hides the writing tools and menus to leave more room for the pages themselves. This is optimized for touch screens.

Recommendations—Actions that Access believes will improve the performance of your database.

Record—All of data pertaining to one person, place, thing, event, or idea; a row in a database table.

Record selector—The small box at the left of a record in Datasheet and Form view that is used to select an entire record.

Record validation rule—Determines if a record is valid, or meets all criteria, when a record is saved. In other words, you need to compare and validate the values in one field against the values in another field in the same record.

Recordset—A run-time table.

Redundancy—Data that is repeated in more than one place in the database—an indicator of poor design.

Referential integrity—Requires that only values that have a corresponding value in the primary table can be entered for a foreign key.

Relational database—Three-dimensional database software—because it is able to connect data in separate tables to form a relationship when common fields exist—that can offer reassembled information from multiple tables.

Relationship—An association between two tables based on a common field.

Replace command—A command used to automatically replace values in a table or query.

Report—An object that summarizes the fields and records from a table or query in an easy-to-read format suitable for printing.

Report Design tool—An Access tool with which you can create a blank report in Design view.

Report Footer—Information printed once at the end of a report; used to print report totals or other summary information for the entire report.

Report Header—Information printed once at the beginning of a report; used for logos, titles, and dates.

Report tool—The Access tool that creates a report with one mouse click, which displays all of the fields from the record source that you select.

Report view—A view that allows you to see what the printed report will look like in a continuous page layout.

Report Wizard—An Access feature that guides you through creating a report by asking you questions.

Required property—The Required property can be used to specify whether a value is required in a field, ensuring that the field is not left blank.

Restore down—Allows you to arrange and view several windows so they all can be viewed at the same time.

Revenue—Income that a company receives from its normal business activities, from the sale of goods and services to customers. Also known as gross sales.

Ribbon—Where you will find most of the commands for the application. The Ribbon differs from program to program, but each program has two tabs in common, the File tab and the Home tab.

Ribbon display options—Three options—Auto-Hide Ribbon, Display Tabs, and Display Tabs and Command—that are located next to the Help button in the top-right corner.

RIGHT JOIN clause—Used when you only want to return rows that have matching data in the right table, even if no matching rows exist in the left table in an SQL queryRoaming settings—A group of settings that offer easy remotely synced user-specific data that affects the Office experience.

Round function—This function returns a number rounded to a specific number of decimal places.

Run time—When an object is created at the time of request.

S

Sales volume—The number of items sold or services rendered during normal business hours. These figures would be taken over a specific period of time and can be expressed in either dollars or percent.

ScreenTip—Provides a name or other information about the object to which you are pointing.

Second normal form (2NF)—Requires that the table has no fields with partial dependencies on a composite or concatenated key and satisfies 1NF.

Secondary sort field—The second and subsequent fields chosen in a multiple field sort.

SELECT statement—The fundamental framework for a SQL query is the SQL SELECT statement.

Sequential AutoNumber—The most common and default setting in Access when selecting the AutoNumber data type.

Shared Access—Allows for multiple users to access a database at the same time.

Shortcut menu—A group or list of context-sensitive commands related to a selection that appears when you right-click.

Simple delete query—A query that is used to remove one or more records from a table or another query. The number of rows deleted is dependent upon the criteria within the Where clause of the delete query.

Simple update query—A query that involves updating data in one table, allowing you to specify two values—the value you want to replace and the value to use as a replacement.

Single Step—A feature that allows you to observe the flow of a macro and the results of each action, and isolate any action that causes an error or produces unwanted results.

Single-field index—An index set on an individual field, such as a primary key.

Sizing handles—The small boxes around a selected control that allow you to resize the control.

SkyDrive—An online cloud computing technology that offers a certain amount of collaborative storage space free that is integrated with Office 2013.

Sort field—A field used to determine the order of the records in a table.

Sorting—The process of rearranging records into a specific order.

Special keys—A set of four keyboard shortcuts in Access that can be disabled in a secured database.

Special operator—An operator used to compare text values in a query.

Split form—A form created from one table with a Form view and a Datasheet view in the same window.

Stand-alone macro—Separate database objects that Access displays in the Navigation Pane. Stand-alone macros can be executed directly in the Navigation Pane by double-clicking the macro object, clicking Run in Design view, or embedding the macro inside a database object, like a button or text field.

Start-up form—A form that opens automatically when you open a database.

String—A set of characters that can also contain spaces, symbols, and numbers.

Structured Query Language—An internationally recognized standard database language that is used by every relational database—although many databases incorporate modified versions of the current standard SQL.

Sub procedure—A set of programming instructions that can run on its own or can be called by another procedure.

Subform—A subform is created when fields from two or more related tables are used to create a form. The fields from the first table become the main form fields, and the fields from the second and subsequent tables become the subform fields.

Subform control—The area of a form that embeds another form.

Subquery—A select query that is nested inside another select query.

Subreport—The report section created for the secondary table records when creating a report from two or more tables.

Subset—This is a portion or part of a query dataset.

Subtotals—Controls added to a report to perform calculations on a group of records.

Suggestions—Actions that Access believes will improve your database performance but may have consequences that should be considered first.

Suggestive sell—A sales technique used to add more revenue to a sale by suggesting to the customer that he or she purchase another product.

Surrogate key—An artificial column added to a table to serve as a primary key that is unique and sequential when records are created. In Access, the AutoNumber data type is used as a surrogate key.

Syntax error—Occurs when a completed line of code is entered that the Visual Basic Editor does not recognize.

T

Tab order—The order fields on a tab are accessed using the Tab key.

Table—The database object that stores data organized in an arrangement of columns and rows, and which is the foundation of an Access database.

Table Analyzer Wizard—This is designed to read a large table of data and convert it into an efficient database by looking for repetitive information in the table and determining which information might be better served by the use of a lookup field.

Tablet PC—Tablets that perform like a traditional PC.

Task pane—A smaller window pane that often appears to the side of the program window that offers options or helps you to navigate through completing a task or feature.

Template—A database shell providing tables, forms, queries, and reports.

Text box—A bound control that represents the actual value of a field or a drawing object that can contain text.

Text data type—A data type that can store either text or numeric characters.

Text filter—Filters that allow you to create a custom filter to match all or part of the text in a field that you specify.

Theme—A set of design elements that enables you to create professional, color-coordinated documents.

Third normal form (3NF)—Requires that the table has to be free of transitive dependencies and that the table satisfies both 1NF and 2NF.

Thumbnail—A small picture of the open application file.

Toggle button—A type of button that one click turns the feature on and a second click turns the feature off.

Top Values query—This query is used to find records that contain the top or bottom values in a field.

Total row—A temporary row that can be added to the end of a datasheet that allows for statistical calculations of field values.

Touch gestures—Gestures made on a touch screen with a finger. Generally, these gestures cannot be completed with a pen—except pen actions set by default for tap, double-tap, and tap and hold.

Touch mode—Office switches into a version that makes a touch screen easy to use.

Trackpad—A pad that works like a traditional mouse but uses touch. A trackpad is typically found on a laptop or a tablet PC.

Transactional database—The database used to record daily transactions.

TransferSpreadsheet method—Allows for Access to import, export, or link to spreadsheet files specifically.

Transitive dependency—Exists when a field depends on another field in the table which then depends on a candidate key: A depends on B and B depends on C, thus A implies C. If C is a candidate key and B is not a candidate key, this is a transitive dependency.

Truncated—When data is shortened or trimmed because of a change in the database, such as reducing the Field Size property.

Trusted Location—A folder on your hard disk or a network share. Any file that you put in a Trusted Location can be opened without being checked by the Trust Center security feature.

Tuple—A database record equivalent.

U

Unbound control—A control that does not have a data source and is often used for labels and other display controls.

Unbound form—A form that is not linked directly to a data source and used to specify parameters, create buttons to print reports, provide navigation menus, and other similar operations.

Underlying SQL statement—Even when you create a query in the QBE grid, Access automatically generates the SQL statement in the background.

Union query—Used to query unrelated tables or queries and combine the results into a single dataset.

Universal naming convention (UNC)—A naming convention for files that provides a link to the machine and location where the file is stored. A UNC name uses the syntax \\server\share\path\filename and works the same way in which a Uniform Resource Locator (URL) works.

Update anomaly—Forces you to change data in multiple records.

Update query—Can be used to add, change, or delete data in one or more existing records. Update queries are similar to the Find and Replace dialog box, but much more powerful.

Usability testing—Testing an application on a user before the application goes live.

USB drive—A small and portable storage device—popular for moving files back and forth between a lab, office, or home computer.

User interface—Part of a computer application or operating system through which a user interacts with a computer or software.

V

Validation text—A message designed to helps users understand why there is a problem.

Validation Text property—The Validation Text property allows you to specify the error message that helps users understand why there is a problem.

Variables—Placeholders that can be set to a hard-coded value or to an object within VBA and then later modified during the execution of the procedure.

View—One of several perspectives of an object.

Virtual field—This means that the concatenated field initiates its "real" equivalent or equivalents—such as combining FirstName and LastName fields.

Visual Basic Editor—The tool built into Microsoft Office that is used for creating and editing VBA.

Visual Basic for Applications—A powerful programming language used within Microsoft Office Applications. Also known as VBA.

W

WHERE aggregate function—Allows you to limit the results of your query by specifying criteria that field values must meet without using that field to group the data.

Wildcard character—Characters, such as an asterisk (*) or question mark (?), substitute for other characters when used in a selection.

Windows Phone—A version of Windows that runs on phone devices that has some of the same functionality as full Windows 8 but not all.

Windows Run Time—A version of Windows that runs on devices with an ARM chip that has many of the same functionality as full Windows 8 but not all.

Windows Start screen—The main interface to launch applications; it replaces the Windows 7 Start button.

With statement—A statement that allows for an efficient way of using several methods or setting multiple properties on a single object.

Wizard—A step-by-step guide to completing a task.

Workbook—An Excel file that contains one or more worksheets.

Y

Yes/No data type—The Yes/No data type allows you to set the Format property to either Yes/No, True/False, or On/Off predefined formats or to a custom format for the Yes/No data type.

Index